History of Art

The Western Tradition

REVISED SIXTH EDITION

VOLUME II

History of Art

The Western Tradition

REVISED SIXTH EDITION

VOLUME II

H. W. Janson

Anthony F. Janson

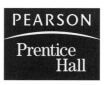

PEARSON

Prentice
Hall

UPPER SADDLE RIVER, NEW JERSEY 07458

Library of Congress Cataloging-in-Publication Data

Janson, H. W. (Horst Woldemar), (date)
     History of art / H. W. Janson and Anthony F. Janson.–Rev. 6th ed.
     p. cm.
     Includes bibliographical references and index.
     ISBN 0-13-182623-9 (hardcover)—ISBN 0-13-182895-9 (trade)—ISBN 0-13-182622-0 (v. 1)—ISBN 0-13-192621-7 (v. 2)
          1. Art–History. I. Janson, Anthony F. II. Title.

N5300 .J3 2003
    709–dc21   2003000760

COVER: Sarah Siddons, detail of fig. 20-14, Thomas Gainsborough. *Mrs. Siddons.* 1785. Oil on canvas. The National Gallery, London
Reproduced by courtesy of the Trustees

This book was set in 11.15/13.25 Granjon. It was printed and bound in Italy by Mondadori Printing S.P.A.
The cover was printed in Italy by Mondadori Printing S.P.A.

NOTE ON THE PICTURE CAPTIONS: Each illustration is placed as close as possible to its first discussion in the text.
Measurements are given throughout, except for objects that are inherently large: architecture, architectural sculpture, interiors,
and wall paintings. Height precedes width. A probable measuring error of more than one percent is indicated by "approx."

Titles of works are those designated by the institutions owning the works, where applicable, or by custom.
Dates are based on documentary evidence, unless preceded by "c."

The birth, death, and ruling dates of individuals, when contained within parentheses, are abbreviated throughout
the text as follows: b. = born; d. = died; r. = ruled; fl. = flourished.

©2004 by Pearson Education
Upper Saddle River, NJ 07458

Printed in Italy
10 9 8 7 6 5 4 3 2 1

ISBN 0-13-192621-7

Pearson Education Ltd., London
Pearson Education Australia Pty, Limited, Sydney
Pearson Education Singapore, Pts. Ltd.
Pearson Education North Asia Ltd., Hong Kong
Pearson Education de Mexico, S.A. de C.V.
Pearson Education—Tokyo, Japan
Pearson Education Malaysia, Pte. Ltd.
Pearson Education, Upper Saddle River, New Jersey

Contents

[ALL SIDEBARS ARE IN SMALL ITALICS]

Preface and Acknowledgments to the First Edition

The title of this book has a dual meaning: it refers both to the events that *make* the history of art and to the scholarly discipline that deals with these events. Perhaps it is just as well that the record and its interpretation are thus designated by the same term. For the two cannot be separated, try as we may. There are no "plain facts" in the history of art—or in the history of anything else for that matter, only degrees of plausibility. Every statement, no matter how fully documented, is subject to doubt and remains a "fact" only so long as nobody questions it. To doubt what has been taken for granted, and to find a more plausible interpretation of the evidence, is every scholar's task. Nevertheless, there is always a large body of "facts" in any field of study; they are the sleeping dogs whose very inertness makes them landmarks on the scholarly terrain. Fortunately, only a minority of them can be aroused at the same time, otherwise we should lose our bearings; yet all are kept under surveillance to see which ones might be stirred into wakefulness and locomotion. It is these "facts" that fascinate the scholar. I believe they will also interest the general reader. In a survey such as this, the sleeping dogs are indispensable, but I have tried to emphasize that their condition is temporary and to give the reader a fairly close look at some of the wakeful ones.

I am under no illusion that my account is adequate in every respect. The history of art is too vast a field for anyone to encompass all of it with equal competence. If the shortcomings of my book remain within tolerable limits, this is due to the many friends and colleagues who have permitted me to tax their kindness with inquiries, requests for favors, or discussions of doubtful points. I am particularly indebted to Bernard Bothmer, Richard Ettinghausen, M. S. İpşiroğlu, Richard Krautheimer, Max Loehr, Wolfgang Lotz, Alexander Marshack, and Meyer Schapiro, who reviewed various aspects of the book and generously helped in securing photographic material. I must also record my gratitude to the American Academy in Rome, which made it possible for me, as art historian in residence during the spring of 1960, to write the chapters on ancient art under ideal conditions, and to the Academy's indefatigable librarian, Nina Langobardi. Irene Gordon, Celia Butler, and Patricia Egan have improved the book in countless ways. Patricia Egan also deserves the chief credit for the reading list. I should like, finally, to acknowledge the admirable skill and patience of Philip Grushkin, who is responsible for the design and layout of the volume; my thanks go to him and to Adrienne Onderdonk, his assistant.

H. W. J.
1962

Preface and Acknowledgments to the Revised Sixth Edition

This edition marks the fortieth anniversary of Janson's *History of Art.* That is remarkable in itself. No less notable is that until now there have been only two authors: H. W. Janson, who wrote much of the book at the American Academy in Rome, and myself, who took over the revisions upon his death in 1982. Actually, I have been associated with Janson's *History of Art* since 1961, when, still in my teens, I proofread much of the original edition over the summer in the Amsterdam office of Harry N. Abrams, Inc. Without that experience, I probably would not have become an art historian. My "apprenticeship" consisted of revising my parents' *Story of Painting for Young People* and *A Basic History of Art* under my father's nominal supervision. Yet, somehow I never really expected to take on the full *History of Art,* and merely assumed it would be turned over to some famous scholar. Least of all was I prepared to take on the responsibility for it so soon after my father's unexpected death in 1982.

Those who have known the book over the years will recognize my increasing contribution, which is now roughly equal to my father's. The original character of the book has inevitably changed in the process—whether for better or worse I leave to the reader to judge. One thing has not changed: Janson's *History of Art* continues to be based on a humanist vision. It makes no claim to have adopted newer theories and approaches to the subject, which I consider perfectly legitimate in their own way. (See "Approaches to Art History" in the Introduction.) The book is still based on the experience of looking at works of art in person and, through thoughtful seeing, understanding what they have to say.

Although there have been only two authors, there have now been nearly a dozen different editors who have put red pencil to manuscript over the years. Thus my main objective in this edition was to restore the integrity of voice and style, which had become noticeably frayed by the Sixth Edition, and to give it the directness that characterizes the writing of both authors. I have also made innumerable small factual corrections throughout the book, which specialists will recognize. Toward that end, I engaged Dr. Mary Ellen Soles, who has given me much good advice in the past, to review Part One for errors and provide suggestions that proved extremely helpful. For the same reasons, I also asked modernist Joe Jacobs to contribute entries on Jeff Koons and Andreas Gursky and to suggest other choices, such as Alison Saar.

A new feature of this edition is the Primer of Art History by Julia Moore, which provides a handy starting point for understanding the field and its basic concepts, as well as the fundamentals of visual analysis, which had been treated at the end of previous Introductions. Another new feature is extended captions featuring commentaries by a number of the great art historians of the past, as well as some from the present. Although it was not possible to accommodate as many of the founders of the discipline as I would have liked, the intent is to honor the giants on whose shoulders we still stand, whether we admit it or not. Having known quite a few of them personally, it is a privilege for me to quote some of their finest insights.

The most significant change in content is Chapter Fourteen, "The Late Renaissance." Its previous title, "Mannerism and Other Trends," was cumbersome as well as misleading. I have chosen to look at the period from the other end of the telescope, so that it now takes the religious art seriously and ties it to the Catholic Reform movement, whose early history I have traced in some detail because it is so little known to most readers. I would like to express my gratitude to my colleague James McGivern for guiding me to the latest literature on the theology of the period, which over the past few years has revolutionized our understanding of the Counter Reformation, as the movement is also known, and to David Lyle Jeffrey of Baylor University, for reading the chapter to ensure its accuracy. I have also rearranged Early Renaissance art according to genres instead of chronological sequence, which many readers found confusing. Finally, I have followed the reinterpretation of Etruscan funerary art initiated in recent years by German and English art historians, which gives new meaning to this fascinating subject.

I have undertaken the task of adding the historical setting systematically to the text wherever it is relevant, rather than solely for its own sake—lest it float irrelevantly like fat on top of chicken soup (as Gustav Mahler's music was once aptly described) without mixing with the art itself. Most of this background is to be found in Parts One and Two, although a large amount of the historical framework has also been supplied for several chapters in Part Three. Because I was a history major as an undergraduate, it is the one thing I have always felt this book needed most, along with a proper representation of women and minority artists, which I have added over the years. My approach to history emphasizes people and events that have affected art history , rather than social history. While admirable in itself, social history too often ignores the work of art by focusing exclusively on context, while adding more background material than most readers and students can assimilate. As in previous editions, the history of music and theater is treated in separate "boxes" within chapters for those who share my enthusiasm for these art forms. Several of them have been updated, especially those on twentieth-century music owing to my "discovery" of the work of a number of composers, particularly Shostakovich's chamber music.

I want to correct a serious but unintentional omission from the preface to the Sixth Edition. My former student Gregory Plow wrote an independent study paper under me on Raphael's Stanza della Segnatura frescoes, which led me to rethink their meaning. While we reached somewhat different conclusions, his help was invaluable, not only in digging up research that was sometimes hard to find, but also in bouncing ideas off each other. This experience was wonderfully stimulating and rewarding for both of us, and represents the finest ideal of teaching, which was first established by Plato at the grove of Akademia outside Athens.

There is a larger debt as well. Plow and his closest friend, David Myers, who wrote an equally splendid honor's thesis under me on Thomas Cole's "The Cross of the World," inspired me to rethink the meaning of Christianity and its contribution to the art and culture of the past, which gave rise to the sweeping changes in the chapter on the Late Renaissance and elsewhere in this edition A great deal of religious art in the West is badly misunderstood because many art historians, it is safe to say, are nonbelievers. They include Christianity as part of iconography and history without accepting it or comprehending it in spiritual terms, especially in the terms it was understood by the faithful as it evolved over time and space. Good students learn from good teachers. Fortunately, the reverse is true, too: Good teachers learn from good students. It is thus with great pleasure that I can at last properly acknowledge the contribution of two of my best pupils.

This edition marks the passing of an era in several important respects. La Martinière Groupe, which purchased Harry N. Abrams, Inc., from the Los Angeles Times-Mirror Corporation several years ago, recently sold the textbook division to Prentice Hall, Inc., which has distributed this and other Abrams books to the college market from the beginning of the association between the two firms in 1962, which was brought about by the publication of Janson's *History of Art.* Then in June

2002, Paul Gottlieb, Abrams' long-time publisher, who built the company into what it became and was its very heart and soul, died unexpectedly. He was a reassuring presence as long as he was still associated, however distantly, with Abrams. He passed away shortly after accepting the opportunity to lead the photography publisher Aperture. Paul was more than my publisher. He was a friend and ally to whom I could turn for advice on the most sensitive professional and personal matters. When the occasional differences of opinion arose, we simply agreed to disagree, even after the most heated exchange. All of us who knew him well feel a gaping hole that stubbornly refuses to close.

I want to express my gratitude to the many people of who have worked so hard on this book. Above all I want to acknowledge Julia Moore, Director of the Textbook Division at Abrams for more than ten years, who has been an important muse and intellectual collaborator for me. She understands what makes Janson unique and has maintained that standard against the odds. In this edition, Julia was assisted in-house by a most gifted editorial assistant, Julia Chmaj, who I am sure will one day make her own mark as an art historian, and who handled even the most difficult chores calmly and ably; and by freelance copy editor Margaret Oppenheimer. Beth Tondreau of Beth Tondreau Design was the art director of this beautiful edition and directed its production, which maintains the high quality of the past. I also want to thank Barbara Lyons, now retired, who for many editions went out of her way to procure some extremely rare photographs. Equally resourceful and dogged in pursuing images was Laurie Platt Winfrey of Carousel Research, which was responsible for assembling the illustrations and reproduction rights. My sincere appreciation goes to the many others at Prentice Hall and Abrams, who are too numerous to include here but who are listed in the masthead, for their invaluable contributions to the success of this edition, which I believe is the best one yet.

A. F. J.
January 2003

This edition is dedicated to Helen, who has launched my ship a thousand times.

Primer of Art History

The Introduction to this book, which begins on page 20, has been written by H. W. Janson and Anthony F. Janson over a period of more than 40 years. Although presented as a deceptively simple narrative, the Introduction is actually a gathering of eloquent linked essays, some of which explore questions that are among the most meaningful we could be asked: What is art? What is essential to the creation of art? What makes a visual artist different from other people? Why does an artist make art? Does it matter whether anyone besides the artist sees and experiences the things an artist creates? Is your opinion as good as the next person's? These questions have many possible responses and, wisely, the Jansons ask us to try to answer them for ourselves, with as much authenticity as we can summon.

This brief Primer of Art History, by contrast, does not ask profound questions. Its two purposes are quite plain. One is to introduce you to the field of art history as a humanistic discipline. The other is to provide you with a set of basic tools to take with you on your journey with art from prehistory to the present.

The oldest surviving expressions of human culture are prehistoric. Almost 90,000 years ago, human beings began fashioning and decorating beads—evidence of symbolic thinking—and they had been shaping specialized tools far longer. Recent genetic studies suggest that spoken languages probably developed more than 50,000 years ago. Then, about 30,000 years ago, our ancestors began painting subtly expressive images of animals on the walls of caves in southern Europe. Thus the tangible evidence we have of our distant ancestors' lives and values is their handiwork and their art. When you study art history, from the very beginning you are engaging with real objects of human experience. As the Jansons' Introduction says so eloquently, however, art objects are not ordinary, forced-by-necessity creations, but are things made to satisfy uniquely human aspirations and longings.

The Field

Art history is a relatively new field of study compared, for example, to literature and philosophy. In the United States, art history began to flourish as a scholarly discipline and a college and university curriculum only in the twentieth century, and mostly after World War II. (Technology affected art history's late start, because until the advent of photography and of printing technologies that could reproduce images cheaply enough to circulate widely, it was rare for one person to see, remember, and compare a great number of physical objects—to say nothing of publishing illustrated books and articles about art.) Art appreciation, which is taught at colleges and universities and is an important component of museum education programs, invariably includes some art history in the process of exposing and sensitizing us to visual culture. Likewise, art history's more rigorous and systematic study of art across time inevitably ignites a lifelong appreciation of the objects of study.

ART HISTORIANS. Men and women who devote their lives to the study of art are called art historians. Most art historians have advanced degrees, and most are passionate and articulate about art and ideas. This edition of *History of Art* draws attention to these qualities in 24 extended captions that capture the rigor, passion, and curiosity of some of this century's most distinguished art historians.

What, besides teaching, do art historians do? Some research and write, thus contributing to art history's body of knowledge or disseminating what is known to a wider audience. Others are museum professionals: curators, administrators, archivists, and conservators. Fewer independent experts advise museums and collectors about acquisitions. Some gallery owners and staff are art historians, and so are a number of publishing professionals, especially editors. What they all share is a pervading sense of excitement about the object of their attention, art.

APPROACHES. Like all fields of inquiry, art history has undergone some fundamental changes. For a long time, art history was confined to the so-called fine arts of painting, sculpture, and architecture. Drawing and the graphic arts—works printed on paper—were also included. Stained glass and decorated (illuminated) manuscripts were regarded as painting, and so qualified as fine art. Photography was admitted to the field of study a few decades ago. More recently, art historians have expanded the definition of art to include works in many mediums (*mediums,* not *media,* is the art historian's preferred plural; medium is the material the artist uses to make the artwork). Today textiles and other fiber arts, metalworking and silver- and goldsmithery, ceramics, glass, beadwork, and mixed mediums are in art history's realm. Modern and contemporary art, especially, has forced open the borders by constantly questioning and expanding the range. Happenings (one-time performed creations staged by artists in the 1950s), earth art, video art, performance art, installations, computer art, and almost anything selected by an artist and declared to be art are now generally acknowledged to be forms of art-making.

Not all art historians approach the subject the same way. Some concentrate on *connoisseurship:* the way art looks. They note and savor visual elements—such as line, color, shape, mass—and the materials and techniques the artist used to create a work of art, then analyze how these were brought together to achieve a certain appearance and have a certain effect. The visual elements are referred to as *formal elements,* and the term *formalism* denotes art history that emphasizes the art object per se, comparatively independent of historical and other non-artistic influences. A formalist looks first and foremost to other artworks to find the answers to why something looks the way it does and what the artist meant by it.

Clearly allied to formalism is *iconography,* the description of images and the study of their meanings, which includes decoding visual symbols (see below, "Symbols"). *Iconology,* which is related to iconography, is the science of images' meanings synthesized with insights from many other fields, such as psychology, sociology, and economics; this process greatly expands the context of any work's creation—and thus possibility for larger interpretation of its meaning. Iconography and iconology were for many years a mainstream tradition of art history. Only recently have they shared the stage with newer schools that view art history from the vantage points of gender, nationality, politics, social criticism, and the humanistic disciples. The most important of these are discussed at the end of the Introduction.

Art historians who take into consideration what was happening at the time and place of an artwork's creation to explain why a work looks the way it does are practicing *contextualism* and are known as *contextualist* art historians. They explore questions such as: What do we know about the artist? Who had political and economic power at the time? Who paid for artworks, and what were the motives of these people, called patrons? What ideas were circulating in educated circles at the time? Today, most art history, including Janson's *History of Art,* is a fusion of formalism and contextualism.

Where Will You Find Art?

The answer is, "Almost everywhere." We can experience it firsthand or secondhand. Museums are obvious places for face-to-face encounters with the real thing. However, art sheltered in museums is separated from the original context of its creation, whether dug from the site of a long-buried civilization, taken from a church or palace, or even removed from the living room wall of a wealthy collector One of the pleasures of studying art history is that it equips us to re-create the contexts, which we bring to bear on art wherever we find art: painted on the inside walls of caves, built as architectural sites all over the world, carved into rock, laid into floors, woven into special garments, erected in parks and malls, installed in corporate offices and private dwellings, and now, winking at us from computer screens.

When we look at reproductions of art, as we do in illustrated books, journals, magazines, posters, and notecards, in the darkened classroom, and on CDs, dedicated websites, and the Internet, we trade quantity for quality. Only real objects can tell us size and scale, true color and texture, and can reveal aesthetic attributes too subtle to capture except by direct experience. Still, most of us begin our relationship with art through the medium of reproductions, invariably accompanied by words.

The Specialized Vocabulary of Art

The fundamental quality of art is visual and/or spatial. We need to "read" art and architecture in their terms. To do so, however, it is almost essential to master and use the vocabulary and grammar that have been devised to help convert the visual experience into the common currency of language. We need to accept the premise that words are symbolic translations of the visual experience, which is a powerful and direct transaction between eye and mind. Much of the great power of images lies in that fact.

The better we understand the specialized vocabulary, grammar, and syntax of art history, the more we benefit from the work of people who spend their lives looking at and making sense of art. Art historians and critics are, after all, attempting to bring order and meaning to this vast—and specialized—form of human expression.

BASIC TERMINOLOGY. Both two-dimensional art (paintings and works of graphic art, for example) and three-dimensional sculpture rely on descriptors such as *representational, realistic, abstract,* and *nonobjective* to broadly categorize an artist's visual approach to a subject. **Representational art** has subject matter that is recognizable from the natural world. **Realistic art** shows a high degree of imitation, or verisimilitude, of the actual object or subject. **Abstract art** simplifies and alters the appearance of actual forms (they can still be recognizable) for various purposes, often to suggest an essence or universality. **Nonobjective art** deals with forms that lack any reference to the natural world. Also referred to as **nonrepresentational** or **nonfigurative,** it relies solely on the interplay of formal visual elements. Much modern art is nonobjective.

FORMAL ELEMENTS. What are the formal elements? They include *line, shape, mass,* and *color,* as well as texture and composition. **Line** can be drawn to define outlines, edges, and contours of forms and delineating shapes. Line imparts direction and movement, even when it is not a continuous mark. Implied lines, which our eyes seek out and our brains mentally connect, can be pictorially as effective as an actual, continuous line.

Shape is a two-dimensional form, an area on a flat plane. **Form** is three-dimensional, occupying a volume of space. Sculpture that is freestanding is **mass.** So is architecture. But you experience architecture by moving around, into, and through it, not merely around it, as you have to do with sculpture.

Texture and color, which are activated by light, are the two other most important formal elements. Texture can refer to the actual surface quality of a work of art or architecture or to the surface that the artist has imitated.

Full understanding of color lies in the realm of physics. **Color** is the effect on our brains of light of differing wavelengths reflected off objects. The source light is usually white light, which is a combination of all colors. Objects absorb particular parts of white light, while reflecting others, so that they give the optical impression of having a particular color. It is helpful to understand the meaning of three color-related terms when you are reading about art. They are *hue, value,* and *intensity.* **Hue** refers to the essential color. The visible colors of a rainbow are the so-called spectral hues of red, orange, yellow, green, blue-violet and violet. In the case of a rainbow, when the white light of the sun passes through drops of water in the air, the raindrops become like crystal prisms that separate wavelengths of light into the spectral hues.

Value refers to the degree of lightness or darkness of a color. Two additional terms are sometimes used when describing value. One is **tint,** a color lighter than the hue's normal value, and the other is **shade,** a color darker than normal. Thus, apple green is a tint of pure green, and forest green is a shade. Finally, there is the term **intensity** (also called *saturation* or *chroma*). Intensity is the degree of a hue's purity. The closer a color is to the original rainbow-spectrum hue, the higher its intensity and the brighter its appearance.

THE ILLUSION OF SPACE. Artists working in two-dimensional arts are challenged with representing the real world of three-dimensionality on a flat plane. The flat surface, termed the **picture plane,** is the field on which the artist builds the illusion of space and three-dimensionality. **Picture space** is a term for what is created in that illusion. Artists have devised many pictorial strategies for suggesting space and objects in space, among them:

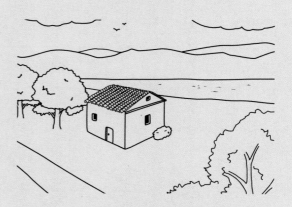

The *picture plane* is the actual, physical surface on which the artist works. It may be a wall, a wood panel, canvas, shield, box lid or whatever surface is chosen. The *picture space* is the apparent depth—the pocket of space that seems to exist behind the picture plane—created by the use of perspective.

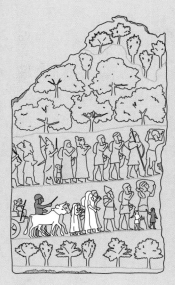

In *vertical perspective*, objects in the lower zone or zones are to be understood as closer to the viewer than objects in the upper zone or zones. *Overlapping* is another way of indicating relative position of objects in space; it relies on our experience that forms partly obscured behind other forms are further distant from us. In this loose rendering of an Akkadian tablet, we see both vertically arranged and overlapping forms. Notice that although all feet are on the same ground-line, the upper parts of some of the animals and people overlap. Both these methods of suggesting depth and distance prevailed until the fifteenth century.

vertical stacking of forms, the **overlapping** of forms, and the illusion of distance by gradation of color from intense to pale, often bluish hues (**atmospheric** or **aerial perspective**).

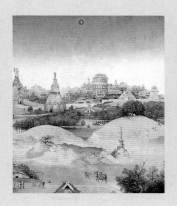

Atmospheric, or *aerial, perspective* relies on re-creating in color the appearance of distance: colors that pale as the distance deepens or are bluish or hazy. This detail is from a sixteenth-century altarpiece painted by a northern European artist. (Hieronymus Bosch. Detail from the central panel of *The Adoration of the Magi* triptych. c. 1510. Oil on panel. The Prado, Madrid)

Since the Italian Renaissance in the fifteenth century, the Western tradition has settled on **scientific,** or **linear, perspective** as the most satisfactory method. It is based on two observations. One is that forms look smaller the farther away they are, and the other is that parallel lines (such as railroad tracks) appear to converge and vanish at the point in the distance where sky meets earth. Scientific perspective assumes the artist's (and viewer's) fixed position and one or more **vanishing points** on a **horizon line.**

ONE-POINT PERSPECTIVE

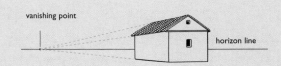

One-point perspective has all planes and angles receding along imaginary lines to a single point on a real or imaginary *horizon line,* the so-called *vanishing point.*

TWO-POINT PERSPECTIVE

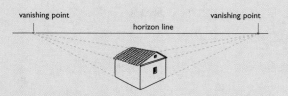

In *two-point perspective,* planes are angled to two different points on the horizon line.

Another way artists suggest three-dimensionality is with the depiction of **light.** It is, after all, light that allows us to perceive forms. In the dark, form is invisible. By manipulating the range from light to dark, called the *value scale,* artists can define forms by suggesting shadow, and they can tell us where the light source is.

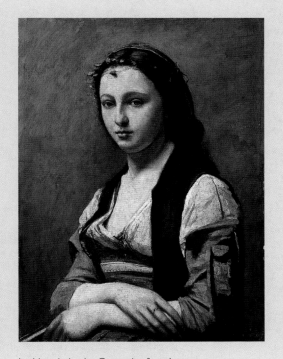

In this painting by Corot, the figure's appearance of three-dimensionality is created chiefly by the manipulation of light and shadow. The cast shadows indicate the direction of the light source. (Jean-Baptiste-Camille Corot. *The Woman with the Pearl.* c. 1858–68. Oil on canvas. Musée du Louvre, Paris)

COMPOSITION. The way an artist puts the formal elements together is called **composition.** Whether it be a painting, a sculpture, or even a work of architecture, composition is distinctive from artist to artist and from culture to culture. Composition is one of the most closely studied attributes of an artwork, especially in formalist art history, because composition is one of the most revealing dimensions of style in a work of art.

STYLE. The word *style* used in art history is different from other, more general uses for the word. With art, it describes the combination of distinguishing characteristics that imprint a work of art as the creation of a certain artist, or time, or place. As the Jansons say so eloquently in their Introduction, "To art historians the study of styles is of central importance. It not only enables them to find out, by means of careful analysis and comparison, when, where, and often by whom a given work was produced, but it also leads them to understand the artist's intention as expressed through the style of the work."

SUBJECT MATTER. What else reveals the artist's intention? **Subject matter**—so to speak, the topic of an artwork—is an obvious clue to intention. Although the choice is always significant in itself, subject matter is neutral. But the way the artist handles the subject is infinitely variable and is not neutral. Subject matter does not need to be pictorially recognizable. An artist intending to create an expression of grief, for example, has many choices, from making a realistic portrayal of a person grieving the death of a loved one, to a totally nonobjective, subjective evocation of the emotional state of grief. The subject matter will be the same. The appearance, or form, will be utterly different.

SYMBOLS. For as long as people have been making images, they have been devising and using pictorial **symbols** to represent abstract ideas or abstract dimensions of real objects. The earliest written languages employ pictographic symbols to stand for objects and ideas; Egyptian hieroglyphics are examples of this. The evangelists of New Testament theology are often represented by symbols: an angel or human being for Matthew, a lion for Mark, a steer for Luke, and an eagle for John. At this level, these images can be either symbols for the individual evangelists or, when shown in connection with a picture of an evangelist, an **attribute,** or visual identifier of the figure in the picture. Symbols constitute a language of their own, and iconography, one of art history's most fascinating sub-disciplines, is devoted to exploring their meaning.

SYMBOLS OF THE EVANGELISTS

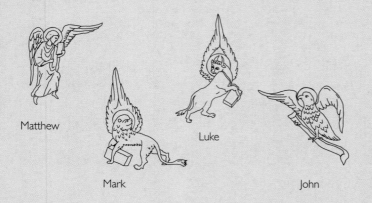

Matthew

Mark

Luke

John

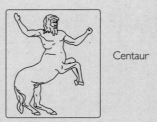

Centaur

The centaur—the part human/part horse creature of ancient Greek mythology—is symbolic in a different way. One of its references is to the dual nature of man: the wild and irrational alongside the rationally self-controlled. Another is to the body/mind duality and conflict so prevalent in Western thinking.

FORM AND CONTENT. Symbols are form. Their meaning is an aspect of content. **Form** is what we see in a work of art, what is visible. It is indisputable. What we interpret from the form is called **content**—the message or meaning of the work. The content of the realistic and the nonrepresentational images of grief mentioned above will vary for every single viewer, not just because the forms are different but because every person brings a different set of experiences, emotional makeup, cultural conditioning, and kinds of knowledge to his or her experience.

Content is nourished by whatever knowledge we can bring to our encounters with works of art, including knowing the times and places of their creation, having an understanding of style, and possessing an informed notion of what the artist intended to say. But it is also fed by life itself. It is safe to say that the more you know about life, the more you know about art, because you bring broader and richer experience to your encounters.

Museum Labels and Illustration Captions

Museums as places where the general public can go to see and learn more about art are a relatively recent invention. As permanent as they seem today, museums as we know them did not exist before the eighteenth century. The same is true of privately owned galleries, which sell works of art. Art museums are as large as The Metropolitan Museum of Art in New York City or Musée du Louvre (the Louvre) in Paris and as small as a one- or two-room exhibition space associated with a college or university to house a small or specialized collection.

What almost all museums have in common is a strong educational component, including a lot of explanatory written material: illustrated catalogues and labels and informative interpretations (wall texts) that appear in proximity to artworks. In addition, most museums have websites (see pages 1003–07, Art and Architecture Websites, for many museum website addresses).

Museum labels and **illustration captions** in a book such as this one use specialized conventions:

1 Name of artist. Usually given first name first, the artist's name is followed by nationality and life dates. From the information in this label, we learn that although Duchamp was born in France, the Philadelphia Museum of Art refers to him as American. (In fact, he did spend many decades of his long life in the U.S.)

2 Name of work. The Philadelphia Museum of Art is among a slowly growing number of institutions to place the title of the work before the name of the artist.

The title a museum gives to a work in its possession is considered authoritative and should be used. When titles are changed, it is usually because research has revealed important reasons to rename a work.

3 Date of work. The date of creation usually follows the name of the work.

4 Material. The medium is oil paint on canvas. Technique will be given when it is relevant. An example would be "cast bronze."

5 Dimensions. Size is sometimes given and sometimes omitted in museum labels. Dimensions in a caption are given height before width before depth, often in both imperial (inches/feet) and metric (centimeters/meters) measure. Size is deceiving in reproductions. Measurements are less critical to have when one is standing in front of the original.

6 Donor or collection information. While not essential information to identifying the work of art, the names of the donors who gave the work to the institution—or donated funds used to purchase it—are part of the work's history. Museums want to credit the generosity of donors, who are vital to the health of the institution.

7 Accession number. Invariably the last item of information on a museum label, the accession number is a unique identifying code. Usually, it includes the year the work came into the collection, in this case, 1950.

8 Copyright information. More and more, as copyright of artworks is claimed by institutions, heirs of artists, and image providers, copyright information appears in illustration captions. This copyright line indicates that Succession Marcel Duchamp holds copyright of this image and is represented by Artist Rights Society, New York (ARS, NY).

Some museums provide additional information and interpretation in the form of **wall text**. When an installation has a lot of written information on the walls, it almost begins to replicate the experience of reading an art book. In that case, the challenge to us is how to balance our attention between the artwork and the information about it.

JULIA MOORE
January 2003

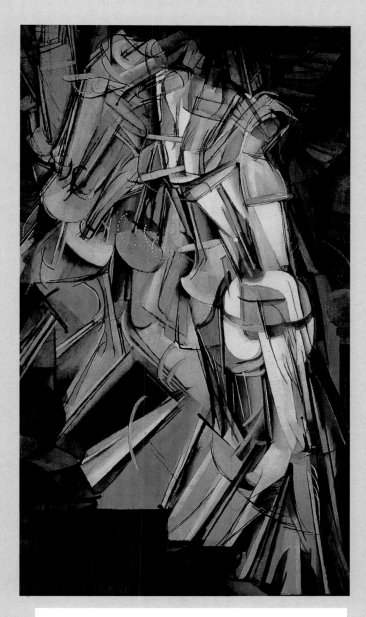

2   *Nude Descending a Staircase (No. 2)*

1   Marcel Duchamp, American, born France, 1887–1968

3   1912

4   Oil on canvas

5   58 x 35" (147.3 x 89 cm).

6   The Louise and Walter Arensberg Collection, 1950

7   950-134-59

8   [in an illustration caption]
© Succession Marcel Duchamp, 2001, ARS, NY

Introduction

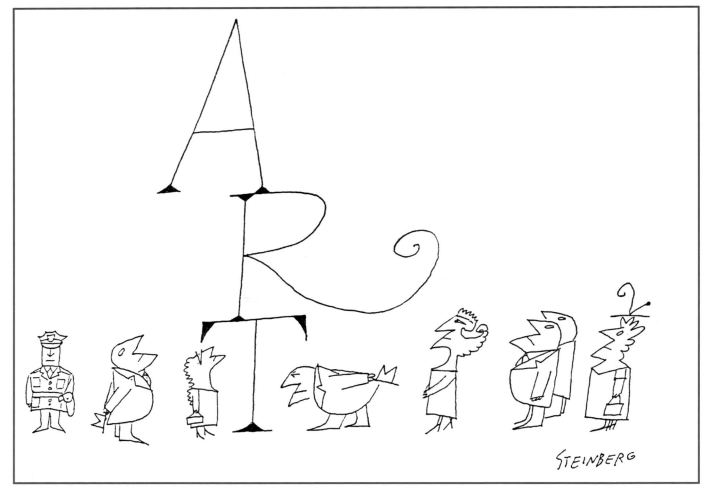

ART AND THE ARTIST

What is art? Few questions have given rise to so many different answers. The problem, as we see in the above cartoon, is that art is an object and a word. Both vary widely in different times and places and in different cultures. In the past hundred years they have changed so much that all the old definitions and even the categories of art are obsolete. The reason is not hard to find: more change occurred in the twentieth century than in any other period in history. The modern era has been both exhilarating and disturbing. It opened up new horizons that greatly expanded life's possibilities, but at the same time it challenged our most cherished beliefs. Art as we know it is a direct outgrowth of the industrialized world, with its advanced technology, global economy, large middle-class yet highly fragmented society, and democratic institutions. Under such unique conditions it is impossible to come up with a universally valid definition of art. We must therefore leave this task to philosophers and aestheticians.

Nevertheless, there is still a good deal that can be said. Looking again at our cartoon, we see that art is not just any kind of object. It is an aesthetic object. Art is meant to be looked at and appreciated for its own sake. Its special qualities set art apart, so that it is often placed away from everyday life—in museums, caves, or churches—though much of it was made to be lived with. What does aesthetic mean? It is defined as "that which concerns the beautiful." Of course, not all art is beautiful to each person's eyes, but it is still art. No matter how unsatisfactory, the term will have to do for lack of a better one.

Aesthetics is a branch of philosophy that has occupied thinkers from Plato to the present day. Like all philosophical matters, it is subject to debate. During the last hundred years, aesthetics has also become a field of psychology, which has come to equally little agreement. Why is this so? On the one hand, people the world over make many of the same basic judgments. Our brains and nervous systems are the same because, according to recent theory, every human being is descended from one woman who lived in Africa a quarter-million years ago. On the other hand, taste is a product of culture, which is so varied that it is impossible to judge art by any one set of standards. It seems, therefore, that we cannot establish absolute standards for judging art. Instead, we must view works of art in the context of the culture in which they were created, whether past or present. How indeed could it be otherwise, so long as art is still being created all around us, opening our eyes almost daily to new experiences and forcing us to adjust our thinking?

Imagination

We all dream. That is imagination at work. To imagine means to make an image—a picture—in our minds. Human beings are not the only creatures who have imagination. Animals also dream. However, humans are the only creatures who can tell one another about imagination in words, pictures, or music. No other animal has ever been observed to draw a recognizable image spontaneously in the wild. In fact, their only images have been produced under carefully controlled laboratory conditions that tell us more about the experimenter than they do about art. There can be little doubt, though, that humans have the ability to create art. By the age of five every normal child has drawn a moon pie-face. This ability is one of our most distinctive features.

Imagination is a mysterious gift. It can be viewed as the link between the conscious and the subconscious, where most of our brain activity takes place. It is the glue that holds our personality, intellect, and spirituality together. Because it responds to all three, it acts in ways that are determined by the mind. Imagination is important, as it allows us to conceive of all kinds of possibilities in the future and to understand the past in a way that has real survival value. It therefore is an essential part of our makeup. In contrast, the ability to make art must have been acquired relatively recently in the course of human evolution. Human beings have been walking the earth for nearly 4.5 million years, although our own species (homo sapiens) is much younger than that. By comparison, the oldest known prehistoric art was made only about 35,000 years ago, but it was undoubtedly the culmination of a long process of development that we cannot trace because the record of the earliest art is lost.

Who were the first artists? In all likelihood, they were shamans. Like the legendary Greek poet Orpheus, who sang his words while playing the lyre, they were believed to have divine powers of inspiration and to be able to enter the underworld of the subconscious in a deathlike trance—but unlike ordinary mortals, they could then return to the realm of the living. With this unique ability to penetrate the unknown and express it through art, the artist-shaman gained control over the forces hidden in human beings and nature. Even today artists are magicians whose work can mystify and move us—an embarrassing fact to civilized people, who do not like to give up their veneer of rational control.

Creativity

The making of a work of art is much like the story of Creation told in the Bible. However, this divine ability was not fully realized until Michelangelo described the creative experience as "liberating the figure from the marble that imprisons it." Perhaps that is why the concept of creativity was once reserved for God, as only he could give material form to an idea. In human terms, the metaphor of birth comes closer to the truth than the notion of a transfer or projection of an image from the artist's mind. The making of a work of art is both joyous and painful, full of surprises, and in no sense mechanical. Moreover, artists themselves tend to look upon their creations as living things. This magical aspect of art was given charming expression by the Roman poet Ovid in his *Metamorphoses*. He tells the story of Pygmalion, who carved such a beautiful statue of the nymph Galatea that he fell in love with it and prayed to Venus, the goddess of love, to bring it to life. Fortunately for him, his wish was granted. (The tale is familiar to us as the basis for the musical *My Fair Lady*.) We can readily understand the tale when it comes to realistic sculpture. But would the artist feel the same way today, when abstract art is the norm? Strange though it may seem, the answer is Yes, as the cartoon on this page suggests. The reason is that a work represents the artist's highest aspirations and deepest understanding, no matter what form it takes.

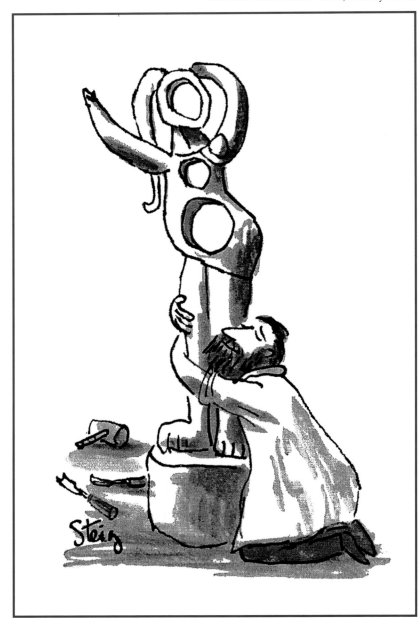

The creation of a work of art has little in common with what we usually mean by making. It is a strange and risky business in which the makers never quite know what they are making until they have actually made it. To put it another way, making art is like a game of hide-and-seek in which the seekers are not sure what they are looking for until they have found it. In some cases, it is the bold "finding" that impresses us most; in others, it is the strenuous "seeking." For the non-artist, it is hard to believe that this uncertainty, this need to take a chance, is the essence of the artist's work. Whereas artisans generally attempt what they know to be possible, artists are driven to attempt the impossible—or at least the improbable or seemingly unimaginable. What defines art, then, is not any difference in materials or techniques from the applied arts. Rather, art is defined by the artist's willingness to take risks in the quest for bold, new ideas.

What sets great artists apart from others is not simply the desire to seek but the mysterious ability to find. This talent is often called a "gift," implying that it is a sort of present from some higher power. It is also described as "genius," a term that originally meant that a higher power—a kind of "good demon"—inhabits and acts through the artist. When creativity is at its height, artists speak of being inspired by the muses that were believed to govern the liberal arts in antiquity. And when the well runs dry, they feel as if the muse has abandoned them.

Inspiration is sometimes experienced as a sudden leap of the imagination, but only rarely does a new idea emerge full-blown like the Greek goddess Athena from the head of Zeus, her father. Instead, it is usually preceded by a long period in which all the hard work is done without finding the solution to the problem. At the critical point, the imagination makes connections between seemingly unrelated parts. Ordinarily, artists work with materials that have little or no shape of their own. The creative process then consists of a long series of smaller leaps of the imagination and the artist's attempts to give them form by shaping the material.

One of the attributes that distinguishes great artists is their great mastery of technique, which enables them to give their ideas full expression in visible form. Their superior ability is recognized by other artists, who admire their work and seek to emulate it. This is not to say that facility alone is all that is needed. Far from it! The academic painters and sculptors of the nineteenth century were among the most proficient artists in history—as well as the dullest. Clearly, the making of a work of art should not be confused with manual skill or craftsmanship. Some works of art may demand a great deal of technical skill; others do not. And even the most painstaking piece of craft does not deserve to be called a work of art unless it involves a leap of the imagination.

Nor should talent be confused with aptitude. Aptitude is what the artisan needs. It means a better-than-average knack for doing something. An aptitude is fairly constant and specific. It can be measured with some success by means of tests that permit us to predict future performance. Creative talent, on the other hand, is utterly unpredictable. It can be spotted only on the basis of past performance. Even past performance is not enough to ensure that a given artist will continue to produce on the same level. Some artists reach a creative peak early in their careers and then "go dry," while others, after a slow start, may do astonishingly original work in middle age or even later.

Originality and Tradition

Originality is what distinguishes art from craft. It is the yardstick of artistic greatness or importance. Unfortunately, it is also very hard to define. The usual synonyms—uniqueness, novelty, freshness—do not help us very much. Unless a work is a copy, the problem comes not in deciding whether it is original but in saying exactly how original it is. In addition, every work of art has its own place in tradition. Without tradition—the word means "that which has been handed down to us"—no originality would be possible. Tradition provides the platform from which artists make their leap of the imagination. The place where they land becomes the point of departure for further leaps. Tradition also serves as the meeting ground of art and craft. What the art student or apprentice learns are skills and techniques: ways of drawing, painting, carving, designing—established ways of seeing.

For us, too, tradition is essential. Whether we are aware of it or not, tradition is the framework within which we form our opinions of works of art and assess their originality. This is especially true of masterpieces, the standards by which we measure other works of art. A masterpiece is a work that can bear close scrutiny and withstand the test of time. Such judgments are always subject to revision, however. In fact, tastes have varied greatly over time. Works that were once thought of as cornerstones of tradition have been discarded, while others that were ignored or even despised are now seen as important. Thus the "canon," or core body, of Western art is not static and unchanging but is constantly shifting. Although it is fashionable to attack the idea of a canon, some works really are better than others, whether we wish to acknowledge it or not.

Meaning and Style

Why do people create art? Surely one reason is the urge to adorn themselves and decorate the world around them. Both are part of a larger desire, not merely to remake the world in their image but to recast themselves and their environment in ideal form. Art is, however, much more than decoration. Like science and religion, it fulfills the urge of human beings to understand themselves and the universe. This function makes art especially important and worthy of our attention. Art allows us to communicate our understanding in ways that cannot be expressed otherwise. In art, as in language, people invent symbols that convey complex thoughts in new ways. We must think of art not in terms of prose but of poetry, which is free to rearrange words and syntax in order to convey new, often multiple, meanings and moods. A work of art likewise suggests much more than it states. And as with poetry, the value of art lies equally in what it says and how it says it. But what is art trying to say? Artists often provide no clear explanation, since the work itself is the statement. If they could say what they mean in words, they would be writers instead.

Nevertheless, art is full of meaning, even if its content is slender or obscure at times. What do we mean by content? The word refers not only to a work's subject and literal meaning (its iconography) but to its appearance as well, for the visual elements are themselves filled with significance. Hence the content of art is inseparable from its formal qualities, that is, its style. For that reason, understanding a work of art begins with a sensitive appreciation of its surface. (In fact, art can be enjoyed for its purely visual appeal.) The word *style* is derived from stilus, the writing tool of the ancient Romans. Originally, it referred to distinctive ways of writing—the shape of the letters as well as the choice of words. Today it refers to the distinctive way in which a thing is done. In the visual arts, style means the specific way in which the forms that make up any given work of art are chosen and fitted together. To art historians the study of styles is of great importance. Not only does it enable them to find out, through careful analysis and comparison, when, where, and by whom something was produced, it also leads them to understand the artist's intention as expressed in the way it looks. This intention depends on both the artist's personality and the context of time and place. Thus art historians often speak of "period styles."

Art, like language, requires that we learn the style and outlook of a country, period, and artist if it is to be understood properly. Style need only be appropriate to the intent of the work. This idea is not always easy to accept. Westerners are used to a tradition of naturalism, in which art imitates nature as closely as possible. But accurate reproduction of visual phenomena, called illusionism, is just one means of expressing an artist's understanding of reality. Truth, it seems, is indeed relative. It is a matter not simply of what our eyes tell us but also of the concepts through which our perceptions are filtered. An image is a separate and self-contained reality that has its own ends and responds to its own rules as determined by the artist's creativity. Even the most convincing illusion is the product of the artist's imagination and understanding, so that we must always ask why this subject was chosen and expressed in this way rather than in some other way.

Self-Expression and Audience

The birth of a work of art is a very private experience, so much so that many artists can work only when they are alone and refuse to show their unfinished works to anyone. Yet for the birth to be successful, the work must be shared with the public. Artists do not create art just to satisfy themselves. They want their work validated by others. In fact, the creative process is not completed until the work has found an audience. In the end, works of art exist in order to be liked rather than to be debated. This paradox can be resolved once we understand what artists mean by "public." They are concerned not with the public at large but with their particular public, their audience. What matters to them is quality rather than wide approval. This audience is a limited and specialized one. Its members may be other artists as well as patrons, friends, critics, and interested viewers. What they all have in common is an informed love of works of art—an attitude that is at once discriminating and enthusiastic which lends particular weight to their judgments. They are, in a word, experts, people whose authority rests on experience and knowledge (see the cartoon on this page).

Tastes

The road to expertise in art is open to anyone who wants to take it. All that is required is an open mind and a capacity to absorb new expe-

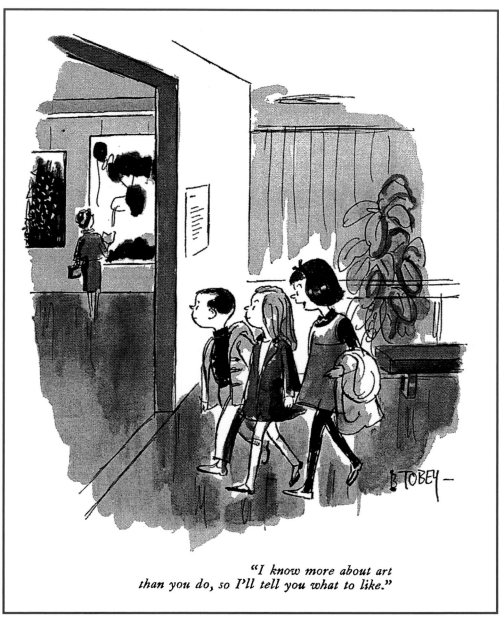

"I know more about art than you do, so I'll tell you what to like."

riences. The biggest roadblock is the old saying, "I don't know much about art, but I know what I like." When they say, "I know what I like," people really mean, "I like what I know [and I am uncomfortable with whatever is unfamiliar]." Such likes are not products of personal choice; they are imposed by habit and culture. Art is part of the fabric of our daily life; we see it all the time, even if only in the form of magazine covers, advertising posters, war memorials, television, and the buildings where we live, work, and worship. Much of this art, to be sure, is pretty shoddy, representing the common denominator of popular taste. Still, it is art of a sort, and since it is the only art most people experience, it molds their ideas about art in general. When faced with unfamiliar art, they often ask, "Why is that art?" when what they really mean is, "Why is that good art?" Deciding what is art and rating a work of art are two separate problems. Even if there were a tried-and-true way of distinguishing art from non-art, it would not necessarily help in measuring quality. Even so, people tend to combine these two problems into one.

But isn't the average person's opinion just as valid as an expert's? This notion has strong appeal in a democratic society. Let's see if it holds up to closer scrutiny. Take any subject in which you have some expertise. It might be sports, cars, carpentry, fashion, pop music. If I happen to be ignorant in the same area, is my judgment really as good as yours? Of course not! The expert always has the edge. As you also know from your own experience, having expertise in a subject greatly increases your enjoyment. The same is true of art. As their understanding grows, most people find themselves liking many more things than they had thought possible. They gradually acquire the courage of their own convictions, until they are able to say, with some justice, that they know what they like.

LOOKING AT ART

How we experience art has changed greatly over the course of history. To view art, most people go to museums. Museums, however, are a relatively recent invention. Although the Akropolis in Athens included a pinakotheke, or painting gallery, the idea of a museum ("home of the muses") where the public can go for inspiration arose only in the early nineteenth century. Before then, most people could see art only in churches. Except in seventeenth-century Holland, only wealthy collectors, most often members of the aristocracy, could afford to own art. Today museums have become temples where anyone can worship at the altar of art. Of course, most works of art were not created for such a setting. The art in museums is not the only kind worth looking at. On the contrary, it should provide the point of departure for exploring other forms of art.

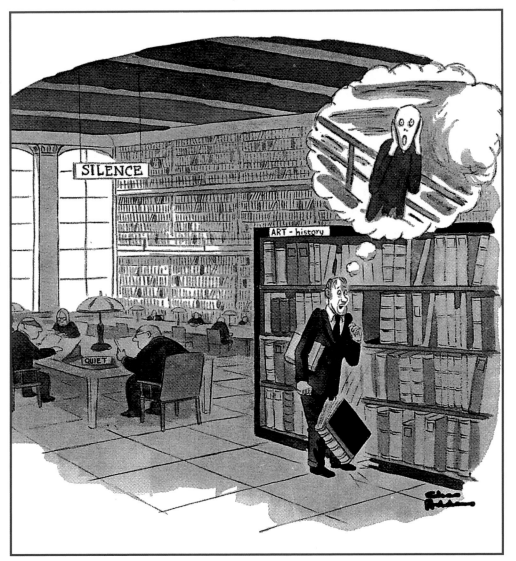

Books like this one can serve as a guide to art, but no text or reproduction can substitute for viewing original works, even in an era when the written word has higher status than artists and their works. To those who love art, few pursuits are more pleasurable. A major benefit is being able to understand cartoons about art, since their humor is not obvious to everyone. Finding the cartoon on this page amusing requires knowing the painting entitled *The Scream* by Edvard Munch (see fig. 23-21). Learning to look at art is not an easy task, however, for art has become commonplace. We live in a sea of images that convey the culture and learning of modern civilization. Fueled by the mass media, this "visual background noise" has become so much a part of our daily lives that we take it for granted. In the process, we have become desensitized to art as well. Anyone can buy cheap paintings and reproductions to decorate a room, where they often hang unnoticed, perhaps deservedly so. It is small wonder that we look at the art in museums with equal casualness. We pass quickly from one object to another, sampling them like dishes in a cafeteria line. We may pause briefly before a famous masterpiece that we have been told we are supposed to admire. But we are likely to ignore the equally beautiful and important works around it (see the cartoon on page 27). We will have seen the art but not really looked at it.

Looking at great art is not an easy task, for art rarely reveals its secrets at first glance. While the experience of a work can be electrifying, we sometimes do not realize its impact until it has had time to filter through our imagination. It even happens that something which at first repelled or confused us emerges many years later as one of the most important artistic events of our lives. If we are going to get the most out of art, we will have to learn how to look and think for ourselves in an intelligent way, which is perhaps the hardest task of all. After all, we will not always have someone at our side to help us. In the end, the confrontation of viewer and art remains as solitary an act as making it.

Art represents the play between artists' imaginations and their surroundings. It also provides a personal record of life as it has been experienced by people at very different times and places. Because so much goes into art, it makes many of the same demands on us that it did on the person who created it. For that reason, we must be able to respond to a work on many levels. To understand it therefore requires a knowledge of both art history and life. The two go hand in hand. The more one knows about one, the more one can appreciate the other.

What people get out of art varies greatly from person to person. We each have different talents. Just as some people have a special ability in athletics or a knack for fixing things, others have a bent for spirituality or philosophy, or they may possess a historical imagination or a playful mind. Moreover, we each have different backgrounds and experiences. Thus we bring different skills to bear on looking at art, just as artists do in making it. Variety is indeed the spice of life. The world would be a dull place if everyone had the same views and backgrounds. Fortunately, there is room for almost limitless diversity. At the same time, there are broad common denominators, including culture and tradition, that bind us together just as much as human nature itself does.

APPROACHES TO ART HISTORY

The art historical approach of this book is often labeled *formalistic* insofar as it is concerned with the evolution of style. Thus it is akin to connoisseurship, although this should not be taken to mean the visual analysis of aesthetic qualities. It also draws on *iconography,* that is, the meaning of a work of art, and what art historian Erwin Panofsky called *iconology,* its cultural context. This book takes a classical approach to art history as defined by three generations of mainly German-born scholars—including H. W. Janson, a student of Panofsky. It is well suited to introducing beginners to art history by providing the framework for how to look at and respond to art in museums and galleries—something both authors have greatly enjoyed throughout their lives. In nearly every case, the works illustrated here (or very similar ones) have been seen by one or both authors to be certain that they are indeed worthy of inclusion. In some cases we have changed our minds, especially when it comes to recent art that has not had the benefit of time to gain the historical perspective needed for a full appraisal.

Readers should be aware that there are other approaches. The oldest is Marxism, which views art in terms of the social and political conditions determined by the prevailing economic system. Marxist analysis has been especially useful in treating art since the Industrial Revolution, which created the conditions that were analyzed by Karl Marx in the mid-nineteenth century. It remains to be seen what will become of Marxist art history in the wake of the collapse of Communism in Russia and Eastern Europe.

Psychology, too, has added many insights into the meaning works of art have for their creators, particularly when that meaning is hidden even from the artists themselves. The more extreme attempts to psychoanalyze Leonardo and Michelangelo, for instance, have caused some scholars to distrust this method. But some works, such as Fuseli's *The Nightmare* (whose meaning was analyzed by H. W. Janson in a pioneering article), cannot be understood without it (see fig. 21-43).

Three newer approaches—feminism, multiculturalism, and deconstruction—are perhaps the most radical of all. Feminism reexamines art history from the point of view of gender. Because this approach is embedded in current gender politics, there is a risk that a major shift in social outlook might call some of feminism's conclusions into question. In principle, however, feminist theory can be applied to all of art history. It certainly forces us to reconsider what is "good" art. After all, when this book first appeared, not a single woman artist was included—nor was one to be found in any other art history survey. Today such omissions seem nothing short of unthinkable.

Feminism is related to the larger shift toward multiculturalism, which addresses the gap in our understanding of the art of nontraditional and non-Western cultures. Why should we not include artists who express very different sensibilities from that of the European and American mainstream? Indeed, there is no reason whatsoever not to. However, this book is limited to Western art for both practical and philosophical reasons. I have chosen instead to focus on the contribution of African-American art. In the process, however, I have taken a stand about what art is most important that not all readers will agree with, since it favors universalism over ethnocentrism. In part, this reflects my own views on the stereotyping ethnocentrism fosters on both sides of the racial fence. In my opinion, such an approach is doomed as a cultural dead end, although I cannot deny that art with a racial "edge" has a legitimate place. Feminism and multiculturalism have both attacked the "canon" of masterpieces in this and similar books as embodying male chauvinism and colonialist attitudes. Readers should judge the issue for themselves. I would only point out that one must walk before one can run.

Because they are so central to postmodern thought, semiotics and deconstruction are briefly summarized toward the end of the book. I am sympathetic to semiotics, which I first became interested in more than 20 years ago, although I find Noam Chomsky's theory of linguistics more satisfying. Deconstruction has likewise made art historians consider meaning in new ways that have breathed fresh life into the field. Nevertheless, I know from classroom experience that it is nearly impossible for beginning art history students to understand semiotics. Deconstruction is even more taxing. What began as a feud between two schools of French semiologists has spread to art history, where it pits older, mostly German-trained scholars against a younger generation. And perhaps that is the point. People are constantly reinventing art history in their image. But if art history reflects our times, the reader may wonder how it can have any claim to objectivity and, hence, validity. In fact, people's understanding of history has always changed with the times. How could it be otherwise? It seems almost necessary for each generation to reinvent history so that we may understand both the past and the present. Yet the danger is that ideology, regardless of its noble intent, will undermine the search for truth, no matter how relative truth may be. Such a thing happened during the 1930s, when scholarship was made to serve the political ends of dictatorships—which led Panofsky and Janson to leave Germany.

Neither author of *History of Art* is an ideologue. Both are (in the case of my father, were) humanists who believe that the study of humane letters is enjoyable and enriching. Such a view requires that scholarly discourse be temperate, although it is rarely dispassionate. I would encourage the reader to examine all forms of art history with an open mind. One cannot view something as rich and complex as art from a single perspective any more than it is possible to see a diamond from a single vantage point. Each approach can add to our understanding. To be sure, a plea for tolerance may seem outdated at a time when art history, like all fields, has become so contentious. In this regard, scholarship reflects the rapid political change, social unrest, ideological dogmatism, and religious fanaticism that characterize postindustrial society and the new world order that is emerging in its wake. Let all ideas meet the test of the marketplace of ideas,

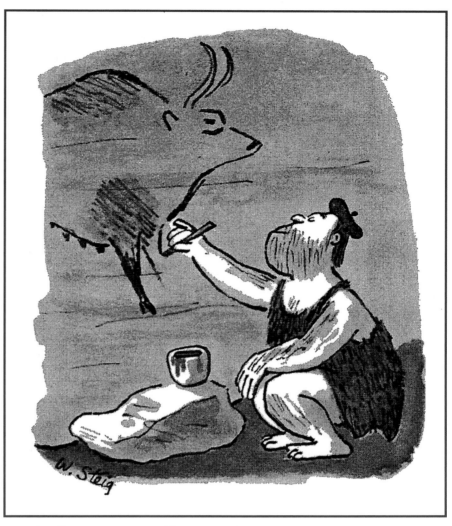

where they can be discussed openly and fairly. Let us also allow everyone to tend his own intellectual garden in peace. Some may have a larger plot than others, but even the biggest of them is rather small in the scheme of things, as H. W. Janson, among the most famous art historians of his time, came to understand.

Both authors have given a great deal of thought to this book, which is written in the authoritative tones that intellectuals habitually adopt as their public voice. It is difficult, of course, to resist the temptation to pontificate—to hand down the "canon" as if it were immutable. Yet, if the truth be told, the experience of surveying such a broad field as art history provides a lesson in humility. One becomes only too aware of the painful omissions and how little one knows about any given subject in this age of increasing specialization. If it requires the egotism of the gods to undertake such a project in the first place, in the end one sees it clearly for what it is: an act of hubris. It also requires a faith in the power of reason to produce such a synthesis, something that is in short supply these days.

Prologue

The term **Gothic** was first coined for certain architecture of the twelfth century, and it is in architecture that the characteristics of the style are most easily recognized. The origin of our concept of Gothic art also suggests the way the new style actually grew. It began with architecture, and for a century—from about 1150 to 1250, during the Age of the Great Cathedrals—architecture retained its dominant role. Thereafter we find a gradual shift of emphasis from architecture to painting or, better perhaps, from architectural to pictorial qualities.

Overlying this broad pattern was another one: international diffusion as against regional independence. Starting as a local development in the Île-de-France, Gothic art radiated from there to the rest of France and to all of Europe. As the new style gradually lost its imported flavor, regional variety began to reassert itself. Toward the middle of the fourteenth century, we notice a growing tendency for these regional achievements to influence each other until, about 1400, a surprisingly homogeneous "International Gothic" style prevailed almost everywhere. Shortly thereafter, this unity broke apart. Italy, with Florence in the lead, created a radically new art, that of the Early Renaissance, while north of the Alps, Flanders assumed an equally commanding position in the development of Late Gothic painting and sculpture. A century later, finally, the Italian Renaissance became the basis of another international style.

ARCHITECTURE

ST.-DENIS AND ABBOT SUGER. We can pinpoint the origin of no previous style as exactly as that of Gothic. It was born between 1137 and 1144 in the rebuilding by Abbot Suger of the royal Abbey Church of St.-Denis just outside the city of Paris. Suger, as chief adviser to Louis VI, championed the French monarchy not only in practical politics but also in "spiritual politics." By investing the royal office with religious significance and glorifying it as the strong right arm of justice, he sought to rally the nation behind the king. The abbey enjoyed a dual prestige that made it ideally suitable for Suger's purpose. It was the shrine of St.-Denis, the Apostle of France and special protector of the realm, as well as the chief memorial of the Carolingian dynasty. Suger wanted to make the abbey the spiritual center of France, a pilgrimage church to outshine the splendor of all the others, the focal point of religious as well as patriotic emotion. But in order to become the visible embodiment of such a goal, the old edifice had to be enlarged and rebuilt.

The great abbot himself has described the entire campaign in eloquent detail. Suger's account of the rebuilding of his church insistently stresses both the emphasis on strict geometric planning and the quest for luminosity as the highest values achieved in the new structure. "Harmony" (that is, the perfect relationship among parts in terms of mathematical proportions or ratios) is the source of all beauty, since it exemplifies the laws according to which divine reason has constructed the universe. The "miraculous" light that floods the choir through the "most sacred" windows becomes the Light Divine, a mystic revelation of the spirit of God. For Suger, the material realm was the stepping-stone for spiritual contemplation. Thus the actual experience of dark, jewel-like light that disembodies the material world lies at the heart of Suger's mystical intent, which was to be transported to "some strange region of the universe which neither exists entirely in the slime of earth nor entirely in the purity of Heaven."

Suger's views shaped his mental image of the kind of structure he wanted, we may assume, and determined his choice of a master as the chief architect. This great artist must have been singularly responsive to the abbot's ideas and instructions. For the master who built the choir of St.-Denis under Suger's supervision, the technical problems of vaulting must have been inextricably bound up with considerations of form (that is, of beauty, harmony, fitness, and so forth). But in order to know what constituted beauty, harmony, and fitness, the medieval architect needed the guidance of Suger. Together, they created the Gothic style. The success of the choir design at St.-Denis is proved not only by its inherent qualities but also by its extraordinary impact. Every visitor to St.-Denis, it seems, was overwhelmed by Suger's achievement, and within a few decades the new style had spread far beyond the confines of the Île-de-France.

NOTRE-DAME, PARIS. We know more about what Suger desired to achieve than we do about the final result, for most of St.-Denis is sadly mutilated today. Notre-Dame ("Our Lady," the Virgin Mary) at Paris, begun in 1163, reflects the salient features of St.-Denis more directly than does any other church. The most monumental aspect of the exterior of Notre-Dame is the west facade (fig. P-1). Except for its sculpture, which suffered heavily

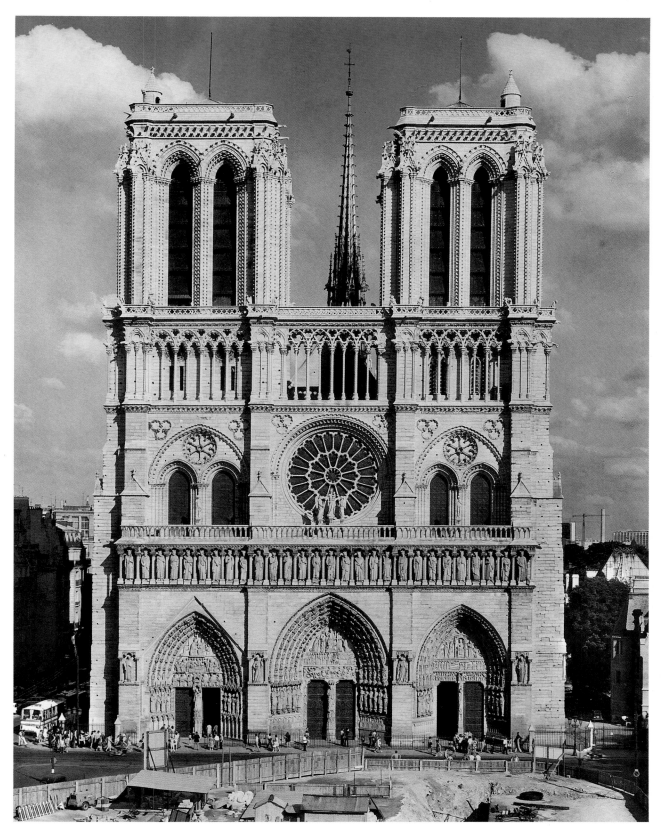

P-1. West facade of Notre-Dame, Paris. 1163–c. 1250

during the French Revolution and is for the most part restored, it retains its original appearance. The style is instantly recognizable. Although its elements derive from Romanesque architecture, all the details have been integrated into a wonderfully balanced and coherent whole. The meaning of Suger's emphasis on harmony, geometric order, and proportion here becomes strikingly evident. This formal discipline also embraces the sculpture, which has been assigned a precisely defined role within the architectural framework. At the same time, lacelike arcades, huge portals, and windows dissolve the continuity of the wall surfaces, the total effect approximating that of an openwork screen.

The interior (fig. P-2) seems graceful, almost weightless, since the windows have been enlarged to the point that they are no longer openings cut into a wall. They now fill the entire wall area,

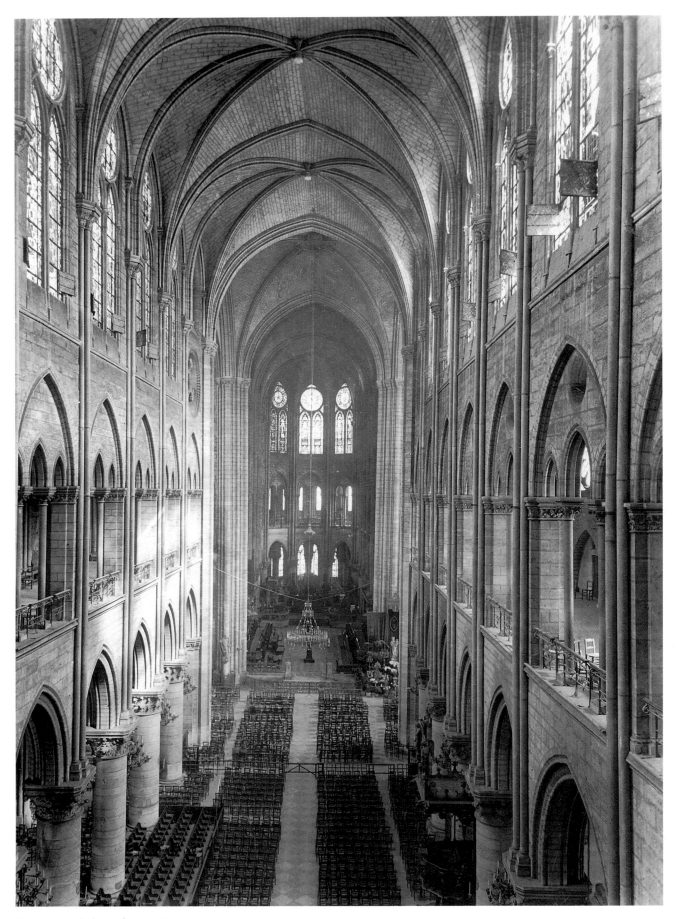

P-2. Nave and choir of Notre-Dame, Paris

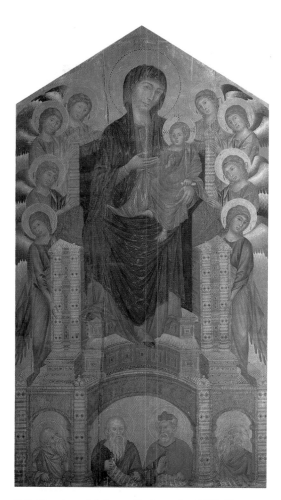

P-3. Cimabue. *Madonna Enthroned*. c. 1280–90.
Tempera on panel, 12'7½" x 7'4"
(3.9 x 2.2 m). Galleria degli Uffizi, Florence

PAINTING

Italy

At the end of the thirteenth century, Italian painting produced an explosion of creative energy that had far-reaching impact upon the future. What were the conditions that made this possible? Medieval Italy, although strongly influenced by Northern art from Carolingian times on, had always maintained close contacts with Byzantine civilization. A new wave of Byzantine elements overwhelmed the lingering Romanesque elements in Italian painting. It is ironic that this neo-Byzantine (or "Greek manner," as the Italians called it) made its appearance soon after the conquest of Constantinople by the armies of the Fourth Crusade in 1204. Be that as it may, the Greek manner prevailed almost until the end of the thirteenth century, so that Italian painters were able to absorb the Byzantine tradition far more thoroughly than ever before. Eventually, toward 1300, Gothic influence spilled over into Italian painting as well, and it was the interaction of this element with the neo-Byzantine that produced the revolutionary pictorial style of which Giotto was the greatest exponent.

CIMABUE. Among the painters of the Greek manner, the Florentine master Cimabue (c. 1250–after 1300), who may have been Giotto's teacher, enjoyed special fame. His huge altar panel, *Madonna Enthroned* (fig. P-3), rivals the finest Byzantine icons (compare fig. P-4) or mosaics. What distinguishes it from icons is

so that they themselves become translucent walls. Missing, however, are the original stained-glass windows, which endowed light with the poetic and symbolic values—the "miraculous light"—so highly praised by Abbot Suger. The ethereal light served to dissolve the physical solidity of the church and hence the distinction between the temporal and the divine realms. The intensely mystical experience it created lies at the heart of Gothic spirituality. Ribbed groin-vaulting based on the pointed arch is employed throughout. The outward pressure of the vaults is contained by heavy buttresses jutting from the walls so that they are visible only from the outside. Above the aisles, these become flying buttresses—a characteristic feature of Gothic architecture—arched bridges that reach upward to the critical spots between the clerestory windows where the outward thrust of the nave vault is concentrated. The lightness and slenderness of the forms help further to create the weightless effect that we associate with Gothic interiors. Gothic, too, is the verticality of the interior space. This depends less on the actual proportions of the nave than on the constant accenting of the verticals and on the soaring ease with which the sense of height is attained.

P-4. *Madonna Enthroned*. Late 13th century.
Tempera on panel, 32⅛ x 19⅜" (81.9 x 49.3 cm).
National Gallery of Art, Washington, D.C.

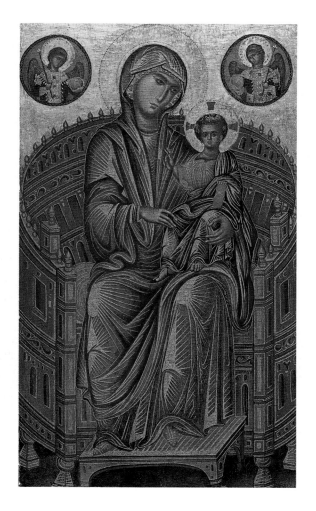

mainly a greater severity of design and expression, which befits its huge size. Panels on such a monumental scale had never been attempted in the East. Equally un-Byzantine is the picture's gabled shape and the way the throne of inlaid wood seems to echo it.

DUCCIO. A quarter of a century after Cimabue painted his *Madonna Enthroned,* Duccio of Siena (c. 1255–before 1319) painted the main altar of Siena Cathedral (fig. P-5), which was honored by being called the *Maestà* (majesty) to identify the Virgin's role here as the Queen of Heaven surrounded by her celestial court of saints and angels. At first glance, the picture may seem much like Cimabue's, since both follow the same basic scheme. Yet the differences are important. They reflect not only two different personalities and contrasting local tastes—the gentleness of Duccio is

characteristic of Siena—but also the rapid evolution of style. In Duccio's hands, the Greek manner has become unfrozen. The rigid, angular draperies have given way to an undulating softness. The abstract shading-in-reverse with lines of gold is reduced to a minimum. The bodies, faces, and hands are beginning to swell with a subtle three-dimensional life. Clearly, the heritage of Hellenistic-Roman illusionism that had always been part of the Byzantine tradition, however dormant or submerged, is asserting itself once more. But there is also a half-hidden Gothic element here. We sense it in the fluidity of the drapery folds, the appealing naturalness of the Infant Christ, and the tender glances by which the figures communicate with each other. The chief source of this Gothic influence must have been Giovanni Pisano, who was in Siena from 1285 to 1295 as the sculptor–architect in charge of the cathedral facade.

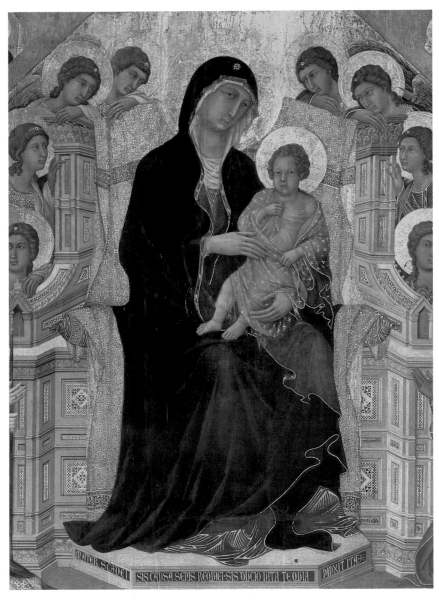

P-5. Duccio. *Madonna Enthroned,* detail from the center of the *Maestà Altar.* 1308–11. Tempera on panel, height 6'10½" (2.1 m). Museo dell'Opera del Duomo, Siena, Italy

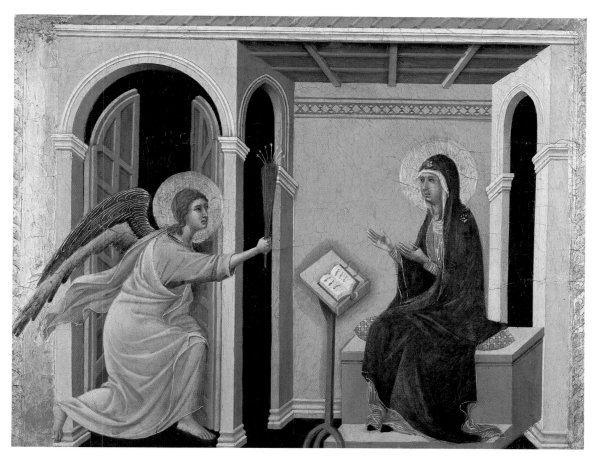

P-6. Duccio. *Annunciation of the Death of the Virgin,* from the *Maestà Altar*

Apart from the *Madonna,* the *Maestà* includes many small compartments with scenes from the lives of Christ and the Virgin. In these panels, the most mature works of Duccio's career, the cross-fertilization of Gothic and Byzantine elements has given rise to a development of fundamental importance: a new kind of picture space. The *Annunciation of the Death of the Virgin* (fig. P-6) shows us something we have never seen before in the history of painting: two figures enclosed by an architectural interior. Ancient painters and their Byzantine successors were quite unable to achieve this. Their architectural settings always stay behind the figures, so that their indoor scenes tend to look as if they were taking place in an open-air theater, on a stage without a roof. Duccio's figures, in contrast, inhabit a space that is created and defined by the architecture, as if the artist had carved a niche into his panel. This spatial framework derives from the architectural "housing" of Gothic sculpture. Northern Gothic painters, too, had tried to reproduce these architectural settings, but they could do so only by flattening them out completely. The Italian painters of Duccio's generation, on the other hand, trained as they were in the Greek manner, had acquired enough of the devices of Hellenistic-Roman illusionism to let them render such a framework without draining it of its three-dimensional qualities.

GIOTTO. Turning from Duccio to Giotto (1267?–1336/7), we meet an artist of far bolder and more dramatic temper. Ten to 15 years younger, Giotto was less close to the Greek manner from the start, despite his probable apprenticeship under Cimabue. As a Florentine, he fell heir to Cimabue's sense of monumental scale, which made him by instinct a wall painter rather than a panel painter. Of his surviving murals, those in the Arena Chapel in Padua, done in 1305–6, are the best preserved as well as the most characteristic. A single glance at Giotto's *Lamentation* (fig. P-7) will convince us that we are faced with a truly revolutionary development. It is a work of intense dramatic power. The tragic mood is brought home to us by the formal rhythm of the design as much as by the gestures and expressions of the participants. The very low center of gravity and the hunched, bending figures communicate the somber quality of the scene and arouse our compassion even before we have grasped the specific meaning of the event depicted. With extraordinary boldness, Giotto sets off the frozen grief of the human mourners against the frantic movement of the weeping angels among the clouds, as if the figures on the ground were restrained by their collective duty to maintain the stability of the composition while the angels, small and weightless as birds, do not share this burden. The impact of the drama is heightened by the

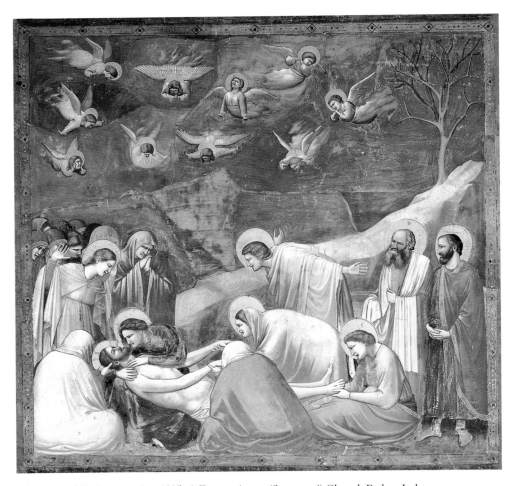

P-7. Giotto. *The Lamentation.* 1305–6. Fresco. Arena (Scrovegni) Chapel, Padua, Italy

severely simple setting. The descending slope of the hill acts as a unifying element and at the same time directs our glance toward the heads of Christ and the Virgin, which are the focal point of the scene.

Giotto presents it in such a way that the beholder's eye level falls within the lower half of the picture. Thus we can imagine ourselves standing on the same ground plane as these painted figures, even though we see them from well below. Giotto also endows his forms with a three-dimensional reality so forceful that the figures seem as solid and tangible as sculpture in the round. Yet his aim was not simply to transplant Gothic statuary into painting. By creating a radically new kind of picture space, he had also sharpened his awareness of the picture surface. His large, simple forms, the strong grouping of his figures, and the limited depth of his "stage"—all these factors help endow his scenes with an inner coherence that we have never found before.

To Giotto's contemporaries, the tactile quality of his art must have seemed a near-miracle. It was this quality that made them praise him as equal, or even superior, to the greatest of the ancient painters, because his forms looked so lifelike that they could be mistaken for reality itself. Equally significant are the stories linking Giotto with the claim that painting is above sculpture. This was not an idle boast, as it turned out, for Giotto does indeed mark the start of what might be called "the era of painting" in Western art.

The art of Giotto is so daringly original that its sources are far more difficult to trace than those of Duccio's style. Apart from his Florentine background as represented by the Greek manner of Cimabue, the young Giotto seems to have been familiar with the work of neo-Byzantine masters of Rome. There he must have become acquainted with Early Christian and ancient Roman mural decoration. Classical sculpture likewise left an impression on him. More fundamental than any of these, however, was the influence of the Pisanos—Nicola and especially Giovanni. They were the chief intermediaries through whom Giotto first came in contact with the world of Northern Gothic art. And these artists remain the most important of all the elements that entered into Giotto's style. Without the knowledge, direct or indirect, of Northern works such as the *Death of the Virgin* from Strasbourg Cathedral (see fig. P-18), Giotto could never have achieved the emotional impact of his *Lamentation.*

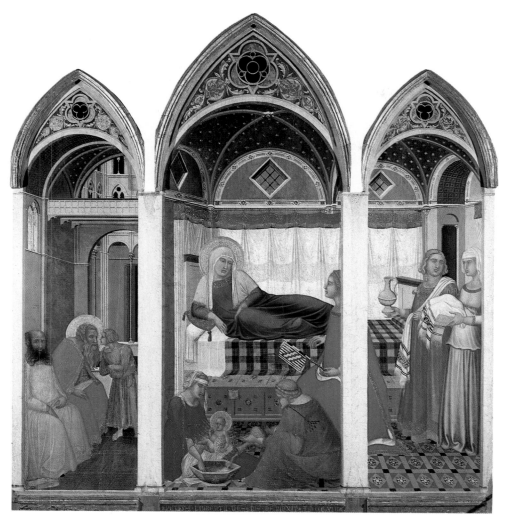

P-8. Pietro Lorenzetti. *Birth of the Virgin*. 1342. Tempera on panel, 6'1 1/2" x 5'11 1/2" (1.9 x 1.8 m). Museo dell'Opera del Duomo, Siena

THE LORENZETTI BROTHERS. There are few artists in the entire history of art who equal the stature of Giotto as a radical innovator. His very greatness, moreover, tended to dwarf the next generation of Florentine painters, which produced followers rather than new leaders. Their contemporaries in Siena were more fortunate in this respect, since Duccio never had the same overpowering impact. As a consequence, it was they, not the Florentines, who took the next decisive step in the development of Italian Gothic painting. The new closeness to everyday life depicted in the work of the brothers Pietro and Ambrogio Lorenzetti (both died 1348?) is coupled with Giotto's monumentality and Duccio's keen interest in problems of space. The boldest spatial experiment is Pietro's triptych of 1342, the *Birth of the Virgin* (fig. P-8), where the painted architecture has been correlated with the real architecture of the frame in such a way that the two are seen as a single system. Moreover, the vaulted chamber where the birth takes place occupies two panels. It continues unbroken behind the column that divides the center from the right wing. The left wing represents an anteroom that leads to a large and only partially glimpsed architectural space suggesting the interior of a Gothic

church. What Pietro Lorenzetti achieved here is the outcome of a development that began three decades earlier in the work of Duccio (compare fig. P-6): the conquest of pictorial space. Only now, however, does the painting surface assume the quality of a transparent window through which—not on which—we perceive the same kind of space we know from daily experience. Duccio's work alone is not sufficient to explain Pietro's astonishing breakthrough. It became possible, rather, through a combination of the architectural picture space of Duccio and the sculptural picture space of Giotto.

The same procedure enabled Ambrogio Lorenzetti to unfold a comprehensive view of the entire town before our eyes in his frescoes of 1338–40 in the Siena city hall (fig. P-9). His mural forms part of an elaborate allegorical program depicting the contrast of good and bad government. The artist, in order to show the life of a well-ordered city-state, had to fill the streets and houses with teeming activity. The bustling crowd gives the architectural vista its striking reality by introducing the human scale. On the right, outside the city walls, the Good Government fresco provides a view of the Sienese countryside fringed by distant mountains. It

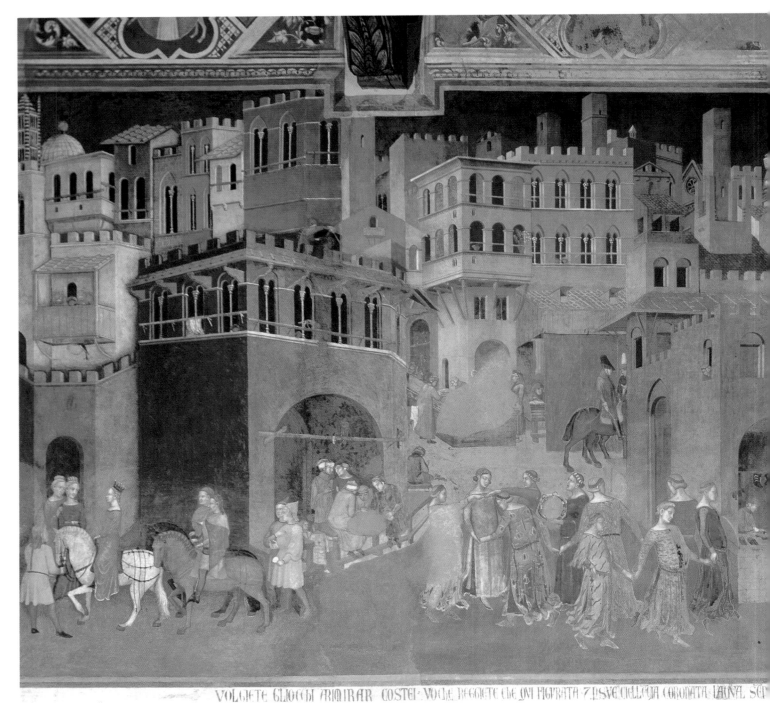

P-9. Ambrogio Lorenzetti. *Good Government in the City.* 1338–40. Fresco, width of entire wall 46' (14 m). Palazzo Pubblico, Siena

is a true landscape—the first since ancient Roman times—full of sweeping depth yet with an ingrained orderliness, which lends it a domesticated air. Here the presence of people is not accidental. They have taken full possession of nature, terracing the hillsides with vineyards and patterning the valleys with the geometry of fields and pastures.

THE BLACK DEATH. The first four decades of the fourteenth century in Florence and Siena had been a period of political sta-

bility and economic expansion as well as of great artistic achievement. In the 1340s both cities suffered a series of catastrophes whose echoes were to be felt for many years. Banks and merchants went bankrupt by the score, internal upheavals shook the government, there were repeated crop failures, and in 1348 the epidemic of bubonic plague—the Black Death—that spread throughout Europe wiped out more than half their urban population. The popular reaction to these calamitous events was mixed. Many people regarded them as signs of divine wrath, warnings to a sinful

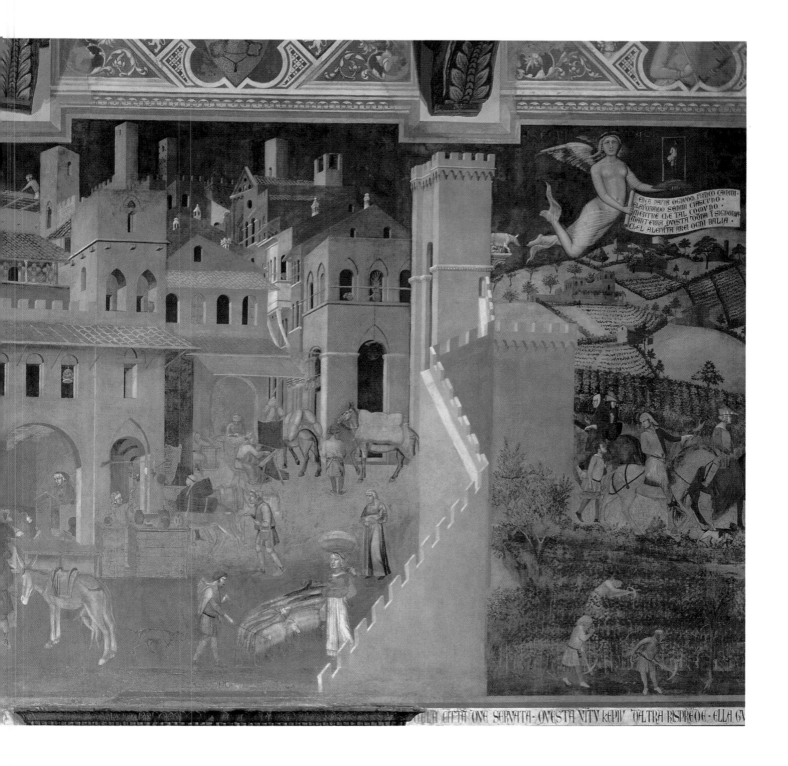

humanity to forsake the pleasures of this earth; in such people the Black Death engendered a mood of otherworldly exaltation. To others, such as the merry company in Boccaccio's *Decameron,* the fear of sudden death merely intensified the desire to enjoy life while there was yet time. These conflicting attitudes are reflected in the pictorial theme of the Triumph of Death.

TRAINI. The most impressive version of this subject is an enormous fresco, attributed to the Pisan master Francesco Traini (documented c. 1321–1363), in the Camposanto, the cemetery building next to Pisa Cathedral. In a particularly dramatic detail (fig. P-10), the elegantly costumed men and women on horseback have suddenly come upon three decaying corpses in open coffins. Even the animals are terrified by the sight and smell of rotting flesh. Only the hermit, having renounced all earthly pleasures, calmly points out the lesson of the scene. But will the living accept the lesson, or will they, like the characters of Boccaccio, turn away from the shocking spectacle more determined than ever to pursue

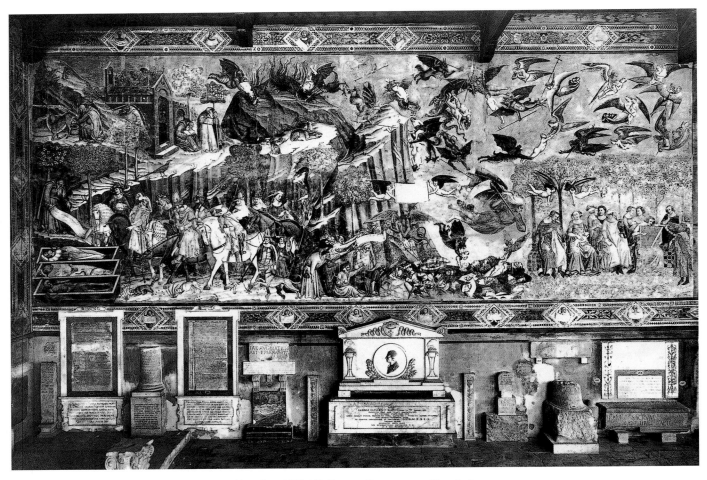

P-10. Francesco Traini. *The Triumph of Death* (detail). c. 1325–50. Fresco. Camposanto, Pisa, Italy

their own hedonistic ways? The artist's own sympathies seem curiously divided. His style, far from being otherworldly, recalls the realism of Ambrogio Lorenzetti, although the forms are harsher and more expressive.

Northern Gothic Painting

We are now in a position to turn to Gothic painting north of the Alps. What happened there during the latter half of the fourteenth century was determined in large measure by the influence of the great Italians, which was sometimes transmitted by Italian artists working on Northern soil. A major gateway of Italian influence was the city of Prague, which in 1347 became the residence of Emperor Charles IV and rapidly developed into an international cultural center second only to Paris. The *Death of the Virgin* (fig. P-11), made by an unknown Bohemian painter about 1360, again brings to mind the achievements of the great Sienese masters, although these were known to our artist only at second or third hand. The carefully articulated architectural interior betrays its descent from such works as Pietro Lorenzetti's

Birth of the Virgin (see fig. P-8) but lacks the spaciousness of its Italian models. Italian, too, is the vigorous modeling of the heads and the overlapping of the figures, which reinforce the three-dimensional quality of the design but raise the awkward question of what to do with the halos (a problem faced by Italian artists as well). Still, the Bohemian master's picture is not just an echo of Italian painting. The gestures and facial expressions convey an intensity of emotion that represents the finest heritage of Northern Gothic art. In this respect, our panel is far more akin to the *Death of the Virgin* at Strasbourg Cathedral (see fig. P-18) than to any Italian work.

The International Style

BROEDERLAM. Toward the year 1400, the merging of Northern and Italian traditions gave rise to a single dominant style throughout western Europe. This International Style was not confined to painting, but painters clearly played the main role in its development. Among the most important was Melchior Broederlam (fl. c. 1387–1409), a Fleming who worked for the court of the

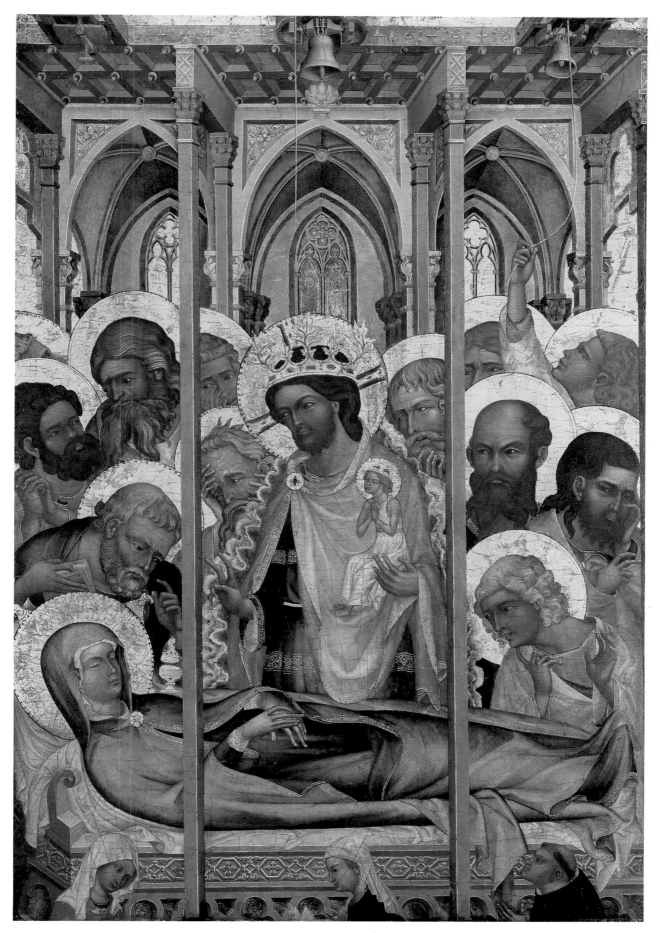

P-11. Bohemian Master. *Death of the Virgin*. 1350–60. Tempera on panel, 39⅜ x 28" (100 x 71 cm). Museum of Fine Arts, Boston

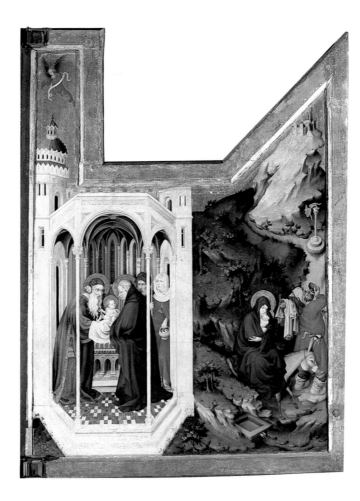

P-12. Melchior Broederlam. *Presentation in the Temple and Flight into Egypt.* 1394–99. Tempera on panel, 65¾ x 49¼" (167 x 125 cm). Musée de la Ville, Dijon, France

duke of Burgundy in Dijon. His shutter for an altar shrine (fig. P-12), done between 1394 and 1399, is really two pictures within one frame. The temple of the Presentation and the landscape of the *Flight into Egypt* stand abruptly side by side, even though the artist has tried to suggest that the scene extends around the building.

Compared to paintings by Pietro and Ambrogio Lorenzetti, Broederlam's picture space still strikes us as naive in many ways. The architecture looks like a doll's house, and the details of the landscape are quite out of scale with the figures. Yet the panel conveys a strong feeling of depth. The reason for this is the subtlety of the modeling. The softly rounded shapes and the dark, velvety shadows create a sense of light and air that more than makes up for any shortcomings of scale or perspective. Our panel also exemplifies a chief characteristic of the International Style: its "realism of particulars." We find it in the carefully rendered foliage and flowers, in the delightful donkey (obviously drawn from life), and in the rustic figure of St. Joseph, who looks and behaves like a simple peasant and thus helps to emphasize the delicate, aristocratic beauty of the Virgin. This painstaking concentration on detail gives Broederlam's work the flavor of an enlarged miniature rather than of a large-scale painting, even though the panels are more than five feet tall.

THE LIMBOURG BROTHERS. Book illumination remained the leading form of painting in northern Europe at the time of the International Style, despite the growing importance of panel painting. Thus the International Style reached its most advanced phase in the luxurious book of hours known as *Les Très Riches Heures du Duc de Berry,* produced for the brother of the king of France, a man of far from admirable character but the most lavish art patron of his day. The artists were Pol de Limbourg and his two brothers, a group of Flemings who, like Broederlam, had settled in France. They must have visited Italy as well, for their work includes numerous motifs and whole compositions borrowed from the great masters of Tuscany.

The most remarkable pages of *Les Très Riches Heures* are those of the calendar, with their elaborate depiction of the life of humanity and nature throughout the months of the year. Such cycles, originally consisting of 12 single figures each performing an appropriate seasonal activity, had long been an established tradition in medieval art. The Limbourg brothers, however, integrated all these elements into a series of panoramas of human life in nature. Thus the February miniature (fig. P-13), the earliest snowy landscape in the history of Western art, gives an enchantingly lyrical account of village life in the dead of winter. We see the sheep huddled together in their fold, birds hungrily scratching in the barnyard, and a maid blowing on her frostbitten hands as she hurries to join her companions in the warm cottage. (The front wall has been omitted for our benefit.) In the middle distance is a villager cutting trees for firewood and another driving his laden donkey toward the houses among the hills. Here the promise of the Broederlam panels has been fulfilled, as it were: landscape, architectural interiors, and exteriors are harmoniously united in deep, atmospheric space. Even such intangible things as the frozen breath of the maid, the smoke curling from the chimney, and the clouds in the sky have become paintable.

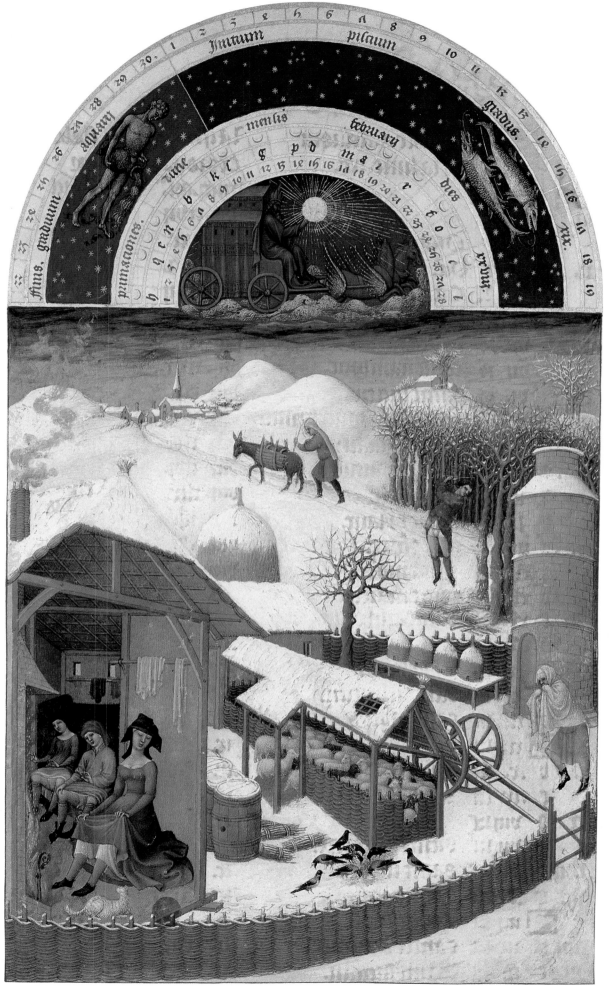

P-13. The Limbourg Brothers. February, from *Les Très Riches Heures du Duc de Berry*. 1413–16. Musée Condé, Chantilly, France

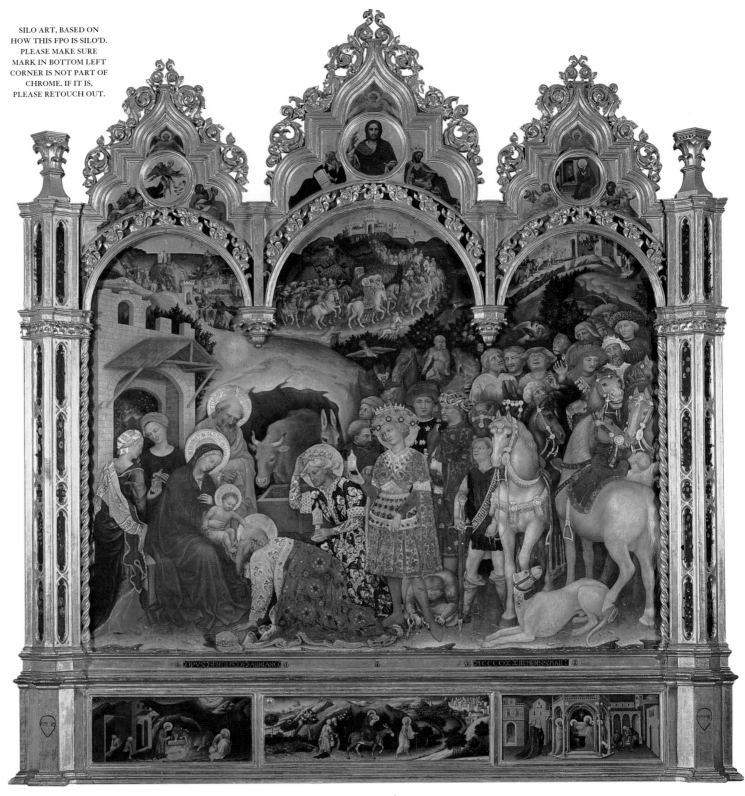

P-14. Gentile da Fabriano. *The Adoration of the Magi*. 1423. Oil on panel, 9'10⅛" x 9'3" (3 x 2.8 m). Galleria degli Uffizi, Florence

GENTILE DA FABRIANO. During the later fourteenth century, it was in northern Italy, particularly hospitable to artistic influences from across the Alps, that the International Style found its greatest Italian representative in Gentile da Fabriano (c. 1370–1427). He worked mainly in Venice before moving to Florence, where he painted his masterpiece, *The Adoration of the Magi* (fig. P-14). In his altarpiece, the costumes are as colorful, the draperies as ample and softly rounded as in Northern painting. The Holy Family, on the left, almost seems in danger of being overwhelmed by the festive pageant pouring down upon it from the hills in the distance. The foreground includes more than a dozen marvelously well-observed animals, not only the familiar ones but leopards, camels, and monkeys. (Such creatures were eagerly collected by the princes of the period, many of whom kept private zoos.) The Oriental background of the Magi is further emphasized by the Mongolian facial cast of some of their companions. It is not these exotic touches, however, that mark our picture as the work of an Italian master but something else, a greater sense of weight, of physical substance, than we could hope to find among the Northern representatives of the International Style. Despite his love of fine detail, Gentile is obviously a painter used to working on a monumental scale, rather than a manuscript illuminator at heart.

SCULPTURE

THE PIETÀ. Gothic sculpture reflects a desire to endow the traditional themes of Christian art with an ever greater emotional appeal. Toward the end of the thirteenth century, this tendency gave rise to a new kind of religious imagery designed to serve private devotion. It is often referred to by the German term *Andachtsbild* (contemplation image), since Germany played a leading part in its development. The most characteristic and widespread type of *Andachtsbild* was the Pietà (an Italian word derived from the Latin *pietas,* the root word for both *pity* and *piety*): a representation of the Virgin grieving over the dead Christ. No such scene occurs in the scriptural account of the Passion. The Pietà conflates two iconic types: the Madonna and Child and the Crucifixion, which were often paired as objects of veneration once they became familiar to Europeans following the conquest of Constantinople in 1204. Exactly where or when this imagery was invented we do not know, but it represents one of the Seven Sorrows of the Virgin, a tragic counterpart to the familiar motif of the Madonna and Child, which depicts one of her Seven Joys.

The Pietà reproduced here (fig. P-15) is carved of wood, with a vividly painted surface to enhance its impact. Like most such groups, this large cult statue was meant to be placed on an altar. The style, like the subject itself, responds to the emotional fervor of lay religiosity, which emphasized a personal relationship with the deity as part of the tide of mysticism that swept the fourteenth century. Realism here has become purely a vehicle of expression to enhance its impact. The agonized faces convey unbearable pain and grief. The blood-encrusted wounds of Christ are enlarged and elaborated to an almost grotesque degree. The bodies and limbs have become puppetlike in their thinness and rigidity. The purpose of the work, clearly, is to arouse so overwhelming a sense of horror and pity that the faithful will share completely in Christ's suffering and identify their own feelings with those of the grief-stricken Mother of God. The ultimate goal of this emotional bond is a spiritual transformation that comprehends the central mystery of God in human form through compassion (which means "to suffer with"). The lean, "deflated" quality of form is the characteristic period flavor of Northern European art from the late thirteenth to the mid-fourteenth centuries. Only after 1350 do we again find an interest in weight and volume, coupled with a renewed impulse to explore tangible reality.

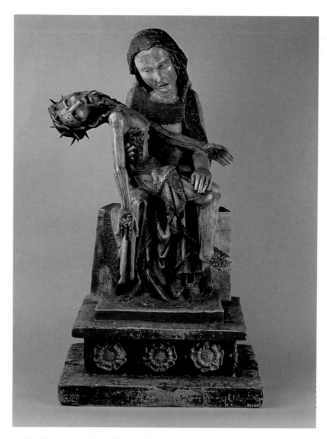

P-15. *Roettgen Pietà.* Early 14th century. Wood, height 34½" (87.5 cm). Rheinisches Landesmuseum, Bonn, Germany

SLUTER. The climax of this new trend came around 1400, during the period of the International Style. Its greatest exponent was Claus Sluter, a sculptor of Netherlandish origin working for the duke of Burgundy at Dijon. Much of his work belongs to a category that, for lack of a better term, we must label church furniture (tombs, pulpits, and the like), which combine large-scale sculpture with a small-scale architectural setting. The most impressive of these is *The Moses Well* at the Chartreuse de Champmol (fig. P-16), which also housed Broederlam's altar wings. The majestic Moses epitomizes Sluter's statues. Soft, lavishly draped garments envelop the heavyset body like an ample shell, and the swelling forms seem to reach out into the surrounding space, determined to capture as much of it as possible. (Note the outward curve of the scroll, which reads, "The children of Israel do not listen to me.") The effect must have been heightened greatly by polychromy, which has unfortunately disappeared. At first glance, Moses seems a startling premonition of the Renaissance. (Compare Michelangelo's treatment of the same subject in fig. 13-13.) Only upon closer inspection do we realize that in his vocabulary Sluter remains firmly allied to the Gothic.

In the Isaiah, facing left in our illustration, what strikes us is the precise and masterful realism of every detail, from the minutiae of the costume to the texture of the wrinkled skin. The head, unlike that of Moses, has all the individuality of a portrait. Nor is this impression deceiving, for the sculptural development that culminated in Claus Sluter produced, from about 1350 on, the

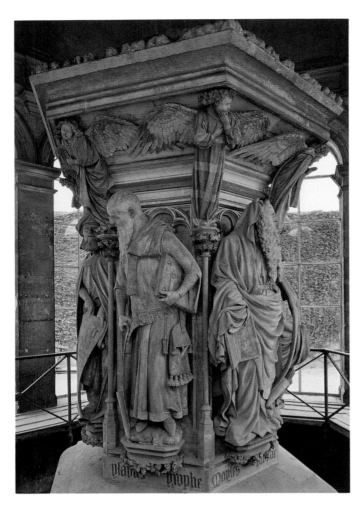

P-16. Claus Sluter. *The Moses Well.* 1395–1406. Stone, height of figures approx. 6' (1.8 m). Chartreuse de Champmol, Dijon

first genuine portraits since late antiquity. This attachment to the tangible and specific distinguishes his realism from that of the thirteenth century.

NICOLA AND GIOVANNI PISANO. Italian architects and sculptors followed a very different course from that of the painters. Untouched by the Greek manner, they were assimilating the Gothic style. The founder of Italian Gothic sculpture was Nicola Pisano (c. 1220/5 or before–1284?), who came to Tuscany from southern Italy around 1250. His work has been well defined as that of "the greatest—and in a sense the last—of medieval classicists." The narrative scenes, such as the *Nativity* (fig. P-17), on the marble pulpit he completed in 1260 for the Baptistery of Pisa Cathedral, tell us that he must have been thoroughly familiar with Roman sarcophagi. The relief is treated as a shallow box filled almost to the bursting point with solid, convex shapes. This dense crowding of figures has no counterpart in Northern Gothic sculpture. On the other hand, it shares a striking Gothic quality of human feeling with the *Death of the Virgin* (fig. P-18) at Strasbourg Cathedral. The draperies, the facial types, and the movements and gestures in the Strasbourg relief have a classical flavor. The pathos also has classical roots, but what marks it as Gothic is the tender-

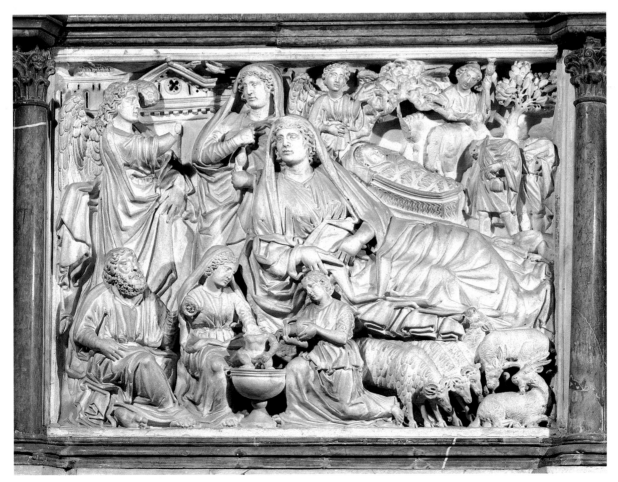

P-17. Nicola Pisano. *Nativity,* detail of pulpit. 1259–60. Marble. Baptistery, Pisa

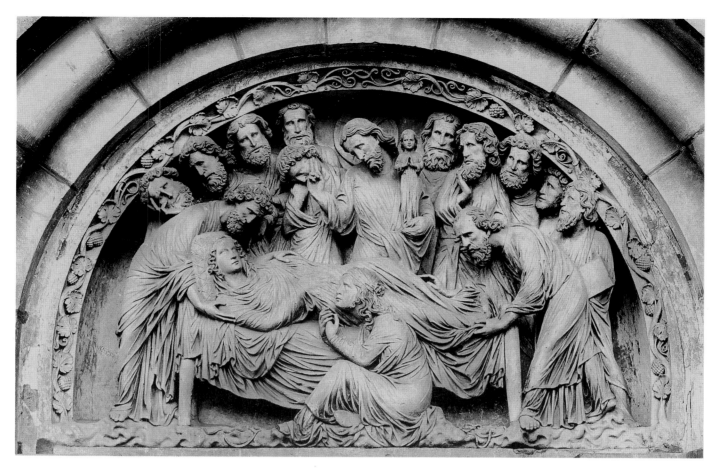

P-18. *Death of the Virgin,* tympanum of the south transept portal, Strasbourg Cathedral, France. c. 1220

ness that pervades the entire scene. We sense a bond of shared emotion among the figures and in their ability to communicate by glance and gesture with moving eloquence.

Some 50 years later, Nicola's son Giovanni (1245/50–after 1314), who was an equally gifted sculptor, carved a marble pulpit for Pisa Cathedral that also includes a *Nativity* (fig. P-19). Both panels have a good many things in common, as we might well expect. Yet Giovanni's slender, swaying figures, with their smoothly flowing draperies, recall neither classical antiquity nor the *Visitation* group at Reims. Instead, they reflect the elegant style of the royal court at Paris, which had become the standard Gothic formula during the later thirteenth century. And with this change there came about a new treatment of relief: to Giovanni Pisano, space is as important as plastic form. The figures are no longer tightly packed together. They are now spaced far enough apart to let us see the landscape setting that contains them, and each figure has been allotted its own pocket of space. If Nicola's *Nativity* strikes us as essentially an agglomeration of bulging, rounded masses, Giovanni's appears to be composed mainly of cavities and shadows. Here Giovanni Pisano is following the trend toward disembodiment found north of the Alps around 1300.

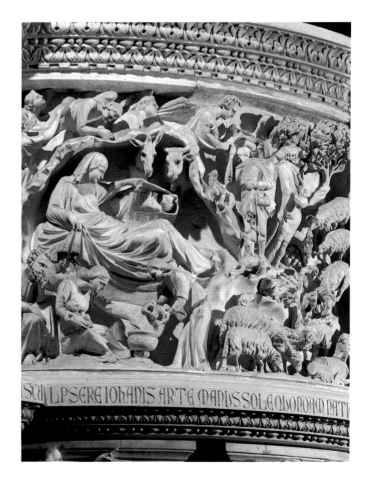

P-19. Giovanni Pisano. *Nativity,* detail of pulpit. 1302–10. Marble. Pisa Cathedral

	1200–1225	1225–1250	1250–1275
HISTORY AND POLITICS	**1202–4** Fourth Crusade sets out for Palestine in Venetian ships. Diverted to Christian Constantinople, crusaders sack the city; entire enterprise excommunicated by the pope; 1208–74, numerous other crusades shift possession of lands in the Middle East from one of the Western powers to another and confront the Muslims, who nevertheless hold Jerusalem from 1244 until 1917 **1206–23** Mongol ruler Genghis Khan crosses Asia and Russia, threatening Europe **1215** Magna Carta, a pact between the English monarch and the feudal barons, signed by King John. The document, limiting the absolute powers of the monarchy, is the genesis of a new constitution that places the law over the will of the king, contains new legal, religious, and taxation rights for the individual, including the right to a trial and other reforms, and establishes a parliament	**Louis IX, king of France (St. Louis, ruled 1226–70),** leads Seventh and Eighth Crusades	**1254–73** Period of strife in Germany, with contested claims to the throne of the Holy Roman Empire, confirms fractured nature of individual German states and signals the end of the empire as a political power **By 1263** Papal grant to trade awarded to Teutonic Knights, originally a crusading order of chivalry. The order grows powerful in the absence of any strong monarch and controls much of Prussia, northern Germany, and parts of Lithuania and Poland. Founds numerous independent cities as a mercantile corporation; these later form part of the Hanseatic League of free trading cities of northern Europe **1271–95** The trader Marco Polo travels from Venice to the court of Kublai Khan. His journeys through India, China, Burma, and Persia open the first diplomatic relations between European and Asian nations
RELIGION	**1215** Fourth Lateran Council of bishops, in Rome, establishes major Catholic doctrines: transubstantiation, practice of confession, and worship of relics **1223** St. Francis of Assisi founds Franciscan monastic order, emphasizing poverty	**COURTLY LIFE AND THE INTERNATIONAL STYLE** Intricate miniature illuminations, small personal diptychs, and precious, jeweled objects epitomize one aesthetic thread of the fourteenth century. The small scale and great elegance of these works reflect the rise, particularly in France, of a class of wealthy nobles whose refined taste and habit of traveling required art to be both beautiful and portable. Illuminated books of hours containing daily prayers, calendars, and parts of the Gospels were fashionable items that advertised the owner's wealth, piety, good taste, and connoisseurship. Contemporary with this graceful, decorative style was a parallel new style in literature—secular, romantic, and written in contemporary language, rather than the educated Latin of previous generations; the troubadour poets in Provençal, the *Roman de la Rose* in French, and much of Dante's and Petrarch's poetry in Italian are examples. Poems and paintings alike celebrate the sensual pleasures of the material world.	

Interior, Chartres
Cathedral, c. 1194–1220

Notre-Dame, Paris,
1163–c. 1250

	1200–1225	1225–1250	1250–1275
MUSIC, LITERATURE, AND PHILOSOPHY	**1200** Foundation of the University of Paris (called the Sorbonne after 1257); 1209, University of Valencia; 1242, University of Salamanca; these become centers for interchange between Arabs and Christians	**St. Thomas Aquinas (1225–74),** Italian Scholastic philosopher. His *Summa Theologica,* a founding text of Catholic teaching, examines the relationship between faith and intellect, religion and society	**Vincent of Beauvais (died 1264),** French encyclopedist **Dante Alighieri (1265–1321),** author of *The Divine Comedy,* in Tuscan vernacular. The poem is immensely influential for the development of the Italian language **1266–83** *The Golden Legend,* a collection of apocryphal religious stories by the Italian prelate Jacopo da Voragine (c. 1228–98)
SCIENCE, TECHNOLOGY, AND EXPLORATION	**1200s** Use of coal gains over wood fuel; mining begins in Liège, France. Advances in seafaring: sternpost rudder and compass in use in Europe; spinning wheel and gunpowder introduced	**Roger Bacon (died 1292),** English scientist who utilized observation and experiment in studying natural forces	

1289 John of Montecorvino establishes a permanent Christian mission in China

1290 Jews expelled from England; 1306, from France

1295 King Edward I of England institutes the Model Parliament, first bicameral English parliament

1302 First known convocation of French estates-general, parliamentary assembly of the crown, clergy, and commons, to support Philip IV the Fair in his struggle with Pope Boniface VIII over questions of papal authority

1305 Fearing political anarchy and desperate conditions in Rome, Pope Clement V establishes Avignon as the primary residence of the papacy; beginning of the so-called Babylonian Captivity (to 1376)

1310–13 Holy Roman Emperor Henry VII invades Italy to reestablish imperial rule

1325 Foundation of the city of Tenochtitlán by the Aztecs

1338 Hundred Years' War between England and France begins (until 1453)

1347–50 Black Death in Europe. Bubonic plague kills an estimated one-third of population

EUROPE AND THE EAST The relationship of Christian European cultures to non-Christian nations had been alternately cordial and combative since the Muslim conquest of the Mideast and Spain in the eighth century. Arab scholarship and technology were commonly exchanged with those of Europe through trade and travel, and the Crusades did much to increase knowledge of Arab culture in the West, but the regions farther to the East were little known. European contacts with Asia underwent a transformation in the late thirteenth century, after the Venetian trader Marco Polo, traveling to the courts of the Mongol emperor Kublai Kahn, China, India, and Persia, brought back the first accurate account of these places. As understanding of Asia grew, trade routes and trading colonies were established, as well as Christian missions. Lured by the prospect of great profit from trade in silk, exotic spices, and gold, as well as by adventure, merchants began to venture to these previously hostile nations in great numbers. Much of the zeal for the later Crusades has been attributed not only to religious fervor but to the opportunity to open trade routes and mercantile contacts with Eastern countries. The effect on European culture was dramatic. The city of Venice became a thriving center for trade from the East, as did the Spanish coastal cities; these cities became not only mercantile but cultural centers for the exchange of arts and ideas. The influence of Asian taste can be seen in such images as the English heraldic lion, which is thought to derive from a Chinese dragon figure, no doubt woven in a precious silk textile.

JEAN PUCELLE
Illuminated pages from the
Hours of Jeanne d'Evreux,
Paris, 1325–28

c. 1297 Publication of Marco Polo's *Book of Various Experiences.* These enormously popular tales of travels in the Far East fostered a general interest in foreign lands

c. 1300 The *Roman de la Rose,* satire on society written in vernacular French

William of Ockham (c. 1300–49), English Nominalist philosopher, stresses mystical experience over rational understanding

Petrarch (1304–74), Italian humanist scholar and poet

Giovanni Boccaccio (1313–75), Italian author of *The Decameron,* a collection of tales

1325–27 Ibn Batutah (1304–c. 1368), Arab traveler and scholar, visits North Africa, the Mideast, and Persia; 1334, reaches India and later, 1342, China; his memoirs contain commentary on political and social customs

Franco Sacchetti (1332?–1400), Italian poet and author of *Three Hundred Stories*

Geoffrey Chaucer (1340–1400), English diplomat and author of *The Canterbury Tales*

Late 1200s Arabic numerals introduced in Europe

c. 1286 Spectacles invented

Early 1300s Earliest cast iron in Europe; gunpowder first used for launching projectiles

1335–45 Artillery first used on ships

1340 Francesco Pegolotti writes *The Merchant's Handbook,* an Italian manual for traders

1346 Longbow replaces crossbow: at the Battle of Crécy the English use it to defeat the French, including cavalry; greater participation of foot soldiers in warfare follows

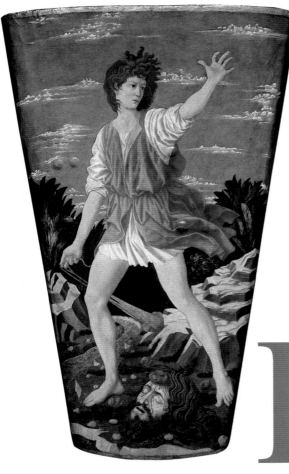

I N DISCUSSING THE TRANSITION FROM CLASSICAL ANTIQUITY TO THE MIDDLE AGES, WE WERE ABLE TO POINT TO TWO GREAT CRISES—THE FALL OF THE ROMAN EMPIRE AND THE RISE OF ISLAM—marking the separation between the two eras. No comparable event sets off the Middle Ages from the Renaissance. The fifteenth and sixteenth centuries, to be sure, witnessed far-reaching developments: the fall of Constantinople and the Turkish conquest of southeastern Europe; the journeys of exploration that led to the founding of overseas empires in the New World, in Africa and Asia, and with it the rivalry of Spain and England as the leading colonial powers; and the deep spiritual crises of the Reformation and Counter Reformation. But none of these events, however great their effects, can be said to have produced the new era. By the time they happened, the Renaissance was well under way. Even if we disregard the minority of scholars who deny the existence of the Renaissance altogether, we are left with an extraordinary range of views on the period. Perhaps the only essential point on which most experts agree is that the Renaissance had begun when people realized they were no longer living in the Middle Ages.

This statement is not as simple-minded as it sounds. It highlights the undeniable fact that the Renaissance was the first period in history to be aware of its own existence and to coin a label for itself. Medieval people did not think they belonged to an age separate from classical antiquity. To them the past was divided simply by B.C. and A.D., that is, before and after the birth of Christ. The two eras were

PART THREE

The Renaissance through the Rococo

further distinguished as the time "under the Law" (the Ten Commandments and Covenant of the Ark in the Old Testament) and the time "of Grace" (the New Dispensation of Christ and the redemption of original sin through his sacrifice). From their point of view, then, history was made in Heaven rather than on earth. The Renaissance, in contrast, divided the past not according to the divine plan of salvation, but on the basis of human achievements. It saw classical antiquity as the era when civilization had reached the peak of its creative powers—an era brought to a sudden end by the barbarian invasions that destroyed the Roman empire. During the thousand-year interval of "darkness" that followed, little was accomplished, but now, at last, this "time in-between" or "Middle Age" had been superseded by a revival of all those arts and sciences that flourished in classical antiquity. The present, the "New Age," could thus be fittingly labeled a "rebirth": *rinascita* in Italian (from the Latin *renascere,* to be reborn), *renaissance* in French and, by adoption, in English.

The origin of this revolutionary view of history can be traced back to the 1330s in the writings of the Italian poet Francesco Petrarca (1304–1374), the most learned person of the day and the first of the great individuals who made the Renaissance. Petrarch, as we call him, thought of the new era mainly as a "revival of the classics," limited to the restoration of Latin and Greek to their former purity and the return to the original texts of ancient authors. During the next two centuries, this concept of the rebirth of antiquity grew to embrace almost the entire range of cultural endeavor, including the visual arts. The arts, in fact, came to play a particularly important part in shaping the Renaissance, for reasons that we shall explore later.

That the new view of history (to which we owe our concepts of the Renaissance, the Middle Ages, and classical antiquity) should have had its start in the mind of one man is itself a telling comment on the new era, although the idea was soon taken up by many others. Individualism—a new self-awareness and self-assurance—enabled Petrarch to proclaim, against all established authority, his own conviction that the "age of faith" was actually an era of darkness, while the "benighted pagans" of antiquity really represented the most enlightened stage of history. Such readiness to question traditional beliefs and practices was to become profoundly characteristic of the Renaissance as a whole. Humanism, to Petrarch, meant a belief in the importance of what we still call the humanities or humane letters (rather than divine letters, or the study of Scripture). It included the pursuit of learning for its own sake in languages, literature, history, and philosophy, in a secular rather than a religious framework.

We must not assume, however, that Petrarch and his successors wanted to revive classical antiquity lock, stock, and barrel. By accepting the concept of "a thousand years of darkness" between themselves and the ancients, they acknowledged (unlike the medieval classicists) that the Graeco-Roman world was irretrievably dead. Its glories could be revived only in the mind, by nostalgic and admiring contemplation across the barrier of the "dark ages," by rediscovering the full greatness of ancient achievements in thought and art, and by endeavoring to compete with these achievements on an ideal plane.

Thus the aim of the Renaissance was not to duplicate the works of antiquity but to equal and, if possible, to surpass them. In practice, this meant that the authority granted to the ancient models was far from unlimited. Writers strove to express themselves with the eloquence and precision of Cicero, but not necessarily in Latin. Architects continued to build the churches demanded by Christian ritual, but they did not duplicate pagan temples. Rather, their churches were designed *all'antica,* "in the manner of the ancients," using an architectural vocabulary based on the study of classical buildings. The humanists, however great their enthusiasm for classical philosophy, did not become neo-pagans but went to great lengths trying to reconcile the heritage of the ancient thinkers with Christianity.

The people of the Renaissance found themselves in the position of the legendary sorcerer's apprentice, who set out to imitate his master's achievements and in the process released far greater energies than he had bargained for. But since their master was dead, rather than merely absent, they had to cope with these unfamiliar powers as best they could, until they became masters in their own right. This process of forced growth was filled with crises and tensions. The Renaissance must have been an uncomfortable but intensely exciting time to live in. Yet these very tensions, it seems, called forth an outpouring of unprecedented creative energy. It is a fundamental paradox that the desire to return to the classics, based on a rejection of the Middle Ages, brought about not the rebirth of antiquity but the birth of modern civilization.

As we narrow our focus from the Renaissance as a whole to the Renaissance in the fine arts, we are faced with some questions that are still under debate. When did Renaissance art begin? Did it, like Gothic art, originate in a specific center or in several places at the same time? Should we think of it as a unified style or as an attitude that might be embodied in different styles? "Renaissance-consciousness," we know, was an Italian idea, and there can be no doubt that Italy was the leader in the development of Renaissance art, at least until the early sixteenth century. This fact does not necessarily mean, however, that the Renaissance was confined to the South.

So far as architecture and sculpture are concerned, modern scholarship agrees with the traditional view, first expressed more than 500 years ago, that the Renaissance began soon after 1400 in Florence. For painting, however, an even older tradition claims that the new era began with Giotto, who, as Boccaccio wrote about 1350, "restored to light this art which had been buried for many centuries." (The same idea was repeated forcefully almost a hundred years later by the sculptor Lorenzo Ghiberti.) We cannot disregard such testimony. Yet if we accept it at face value, we must assume that the Renaissance in painting dawned about 1300, a full generation before Petrarch.

Giotto himself certainly did not reject the past as an age of darkness. After all, the two chief sources of his own style were the Byzantine tradition and the influence of the Northern Gothic. The artistic revolution he created from these elements does not inherently place him in a new era, since revolutionary changes had occurred in medieval art before. Nor is it fair to credit this revolution to him alone, and to disregard Cimabue, Duccio, and the other great masters to whom he was linked. Petrarch was well aware of the achievements of all these artists—he wrote admiringly of both Giotto and Simone Martini—but he never claimed that they had restored to light what had been buried during the centuries of darkness. And, in fact, such a thing was inherently impossible, because neither could have known more than a few remains of classical painting, which did not fully emerge until the excavation of Pompeii and Herculanaeum in the eighteenth century.

How, then, do we account for Boccaccio's statement about Giotto? Boccaccio (1313–1375), an ardent disciple of Petrarch, was chiefly concerned with advancing humanism in literature. In his defense of the status of poetry, he found it useful to draw analogies with painting. Had not the ancients themselves proclaimed that the two arts were alike, in Horace's famous saying that poetry is like painting (ut pictura poesis)? Boccaccio thus cast Giotto in the role of "the Petrarch of painting" in order to take advantage of his already legendary fame. Boccaccio's view of Giotto as a Renaissance artist is, then, a bit of intellectual strategy, rather than a trustworthy reflection of Giotto's own attitude. Nevertheless, what he has to say interests us because Boccacio was the first to apply Petrarch's concept of "revival after the dark ages" to one of the visual arts, even though he did so somewhat prematurely.

Boccaccio's way of describing Giotto's achievement is also noteworthy. It was he who claimed that Giotto depicted every aspect of nature so truthfully that people often mistook his paintings for reality itself. Here he implies that the revival of antiquity means for painters an uncompromising realism. This, as we shall see, was to become a constant theme in Renaissance thought. It justified the imitation of nature as part of the great movement "back to the classics" and tended to minimize the possible conflict between these two aims. There was some justification for this attitude. After all, Classical Greek art was itself based on a synthesis of naturalism and ideal proportions. Yet Gothic art, too, had relied on realism, albeit of a different kind—a realism of particulars. In fact, realism itself is highly relative, for there have been many forms of realism throughout the history of art.

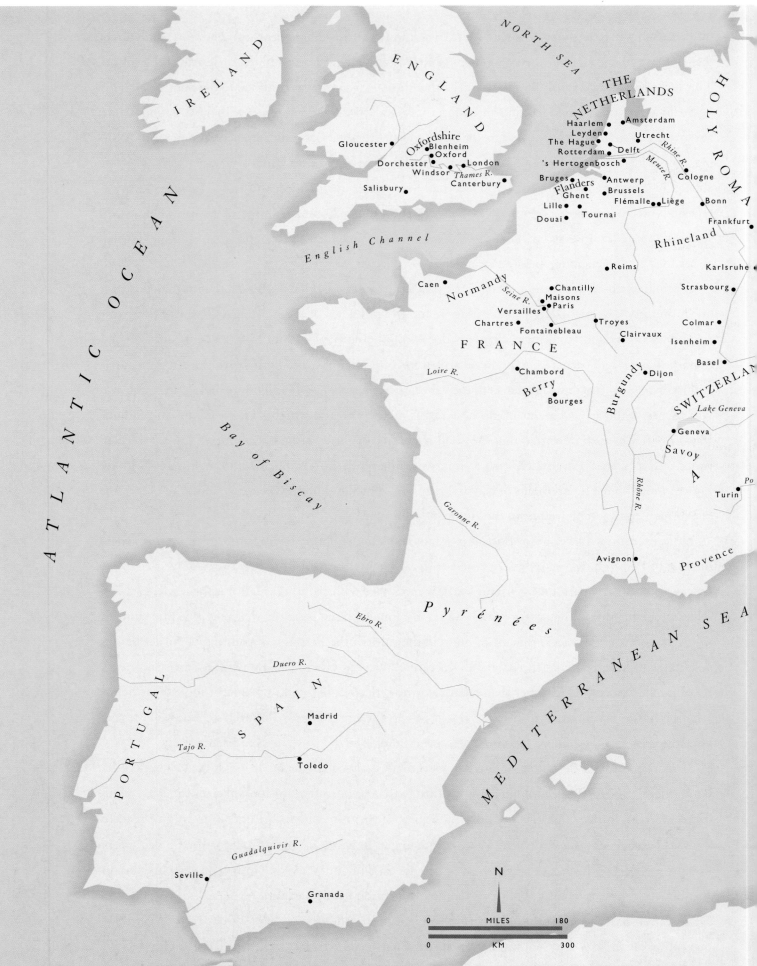

EUROPE IN THE RENAISSANCE AND BAROQUE ERAS

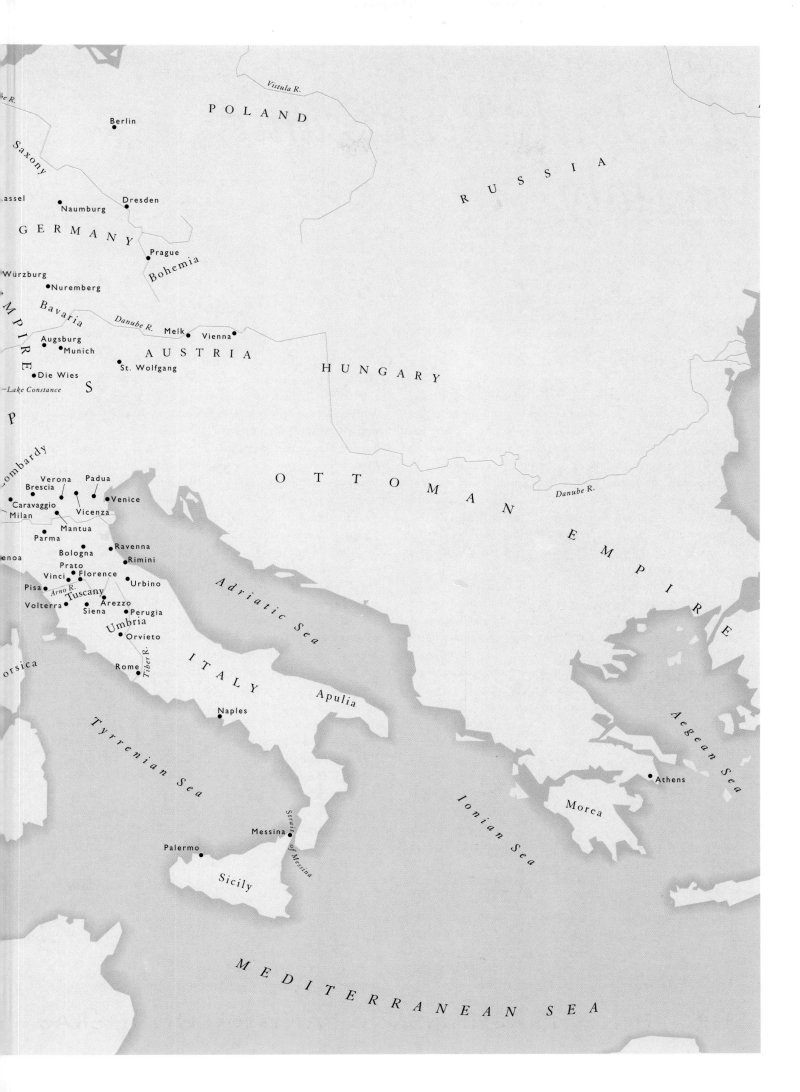

CHAPTER TWELVE

The Early Renaissance in Italy

There are a number of reasons that help to explain why the Early Renaissance was born in Florence at the beginning of the fifteenth century, rather than in some other place or at some other time. Around 1400 Florence's independence was threatened by Gian Galeazzo Visconti (1351–1402), the powerful duke of Milan, who was trying to bring all of Italy under his rule. He already controlled the Lombard plain and most of the Central Italian city-states. Florence was the only major obstacle to his ambition. Just when Florence was on the point of being overwhelmed by the duke's forces, it was saved by his sudden death in 1402; under his son, Giovanni Maria Visconti (1388–1412), Lombardy lost much of its power until his assassination a decade later.

The city put up a vigorous defense on three fronts: military, diplomatic, and intellectual. Of these, the intellectual was by no means the least important. The duke was admired by some as a new **Caesar,** bringing peace and order to the country. In opposition, Florence proclaimed itself the champion of freedom against unchecked tyranny. This propaganda war was waged by humanists on both sides, but the Florentines gave by far the better account of themselves. Their writings, such as *Praise of the City of Florence* (1402–3) by Leonardo Bruni (see fig. 12-12), give new focus to Petrarch's ideal of a rebirth of the classics. Speaking as a citizen of a free republic, Bruni asks why, among all the states of Italy, Florence alone had been able to defy the superior power of Milan. He finds the answer in her institutions, her cultural achievements, her geographical situation, the spirit of her people, and her descent from the city-states of ancient Etruria. Florence, he concludes, has taken on the same role of political and intellectual leadership as Athens had during the Persian Wars.

The patriotic pride, the call to greatness that can be seen in this image of Florence as the "new Athens" must have aroused a deep response throughout the city. Just when they were on the point of being overwhelmed by the Milanese forces, the Florentines began an ambitious campaign to finish the great artistic works begun a century before at the time of Giotto. After the competition of 1401–2 for the bronze doors of the Baptistery of S. Giovanni (see fig. 11-65), another major program was initiated to continue the sculptural decoration of Florence Cathedral and other churches.

At the same time, debate resumed over how to build the dome of the Cathedral, the largest and most difficult project of all. The artistic campaign, which lasted more than 30 years, gradually petered out after the completion of the dome in 1436. It was comparable in total cost to rebuilding the Akropolis in Athens. The huge investment was not a guarantee of artistic quality, but it provided an excellent opportunity for the emergence of creative talent and a new style worthy of the "new Athens."

From the start the visual arts were viewed as central to the rebirth of the Florentine spirit. Throughout most of antiquity and the Middle Ages, they had been classed with the crafts, or "mechanical arts." It cannot be by chance that the first statement claiming a place for them among the liberal arts occurs about 1400 in the writings of the Florentine chronicler Filippo Villani, a position solidified by Alberti's treatise on painting (see page 423). A century later this idea was acknowledged throughout most of the Western world. What does it imply?

The liberal arts were defined by a tradition going back to Plato. They consisted of the intellectual disciplines necessary for a "gentleman's" education: mathematics (including musical theory), dialectics, grammar, rhetoric, and philosophy. The fine arts were initially excluded because they were "handiwork"— and lacked a theoretical basis. During the early fourth century B.C., however, they were included in the liberal arts (see page 150). When Renaissance artists gained admission to the select group of humanists, they were viewed as people of ideas rather than mere manipulators of materials. Works of art came to be viewed more and more as the visible records of creative minds. This meant that art need not—indeed, should not—be judged only by the standards of craftsmanship. Soon anything that bore the imprint of a great master was eagerly collected: drawings, sketches, fragments, and unfinished pieces as well as finished works.

The outlook of artists changed as well. Now in the company of scholars and poets, they themselves often became learned and literary. They might write poems, autobiographies, or theoretical treatises. Another outgrowth of this new social status was that their personalities tended to develop in either of two contrasting ways. One was the person of the world, self-controlled, at ease in aristocratic society. The other was the solitary genius, secretive, subject to fits of melancholy, and likely to be in conflict with patrons. It is remarkable how quickly this modern view of art and artists took root in the Florence of the Early Renaissance. However, it was not accepted immediately everywhere, nor did it apply equally to all artists. England, for example, was slow to grant artists special status, and women in general were denied the training and opportunities available to men.

In addition to humanism and historical forces, individual genius played a decisive role in the birth of Renaissance art. It began with three men of exceptional ability—Filippo Brunelleschi, Donatello, and Masaccio. It is hardly a coincidence that they knew one another. Moreover, they all faced the same task: to reconcile classical form with Christian content. Yet each approached this problem in a unique way. Thanks to them, Florentine art held leadership of the movement during the first half of the fifteenth century, which we now think of as the heroic age of the Early Renaissance. To trace its beginnings, we must discuss sculpture first because the sculptors had earlier and more plentiful opportunities to meet the challenge of the "new Athens."

Sculpture

LORENZO GHIBERTI. The artistic campaign began in Florence with the competition for the Baptistery doors, and for some time it consisted mainly of sculptural projects. Ghiberti's trial relief (fig. 11-65) does not differ greatly from the International Gothic; nor do the doors themselves, even though it took another 20 years to complete them. Only in the torso of Isaac can Ghiberti's admiration for ancient art be linked with the classicism of the Florentine humanists. Similar examples can be found in other Florentine sculpture around 1400, but they are isolated and small in scale, and merely recapture what Nicola Pisano had done a century before (see fig. 11-59).

NANNI DI BANCO. A decade later this medieval classicism was surpassed by a younger artist, Nanni di Banco (c. 1384–1421). The four saints, called the *Quattro Coronati* (fig. 12-1), which he made about 1410–14 for one of the niches on the exterior of the church of Or San Michele, must be compared not with the work of Nicola Pisano but with the Reims *Visitation* (see fig. 11-46). They represent four Christian sculptors who were executed for not carving the statue of a pagan god ordered by the Roman emperor Diocletian, a story that was later merged with one of four martyrs who refused to worship in the god's temple. The figures in both groups are about lifesize, yet Nanni's give the impression of being a good deal larger than those at Reims. Their monumental quality was beyond the range of medieval sculpture, even though Nanni depended less directly on ancient models. Only the heads of the second and third of the *Coronati* directly recall Roman sculpture—specifically, portraits of the third century A.D. (see fig. 7-42). Nanni clearly was impressed by their realism and their agonized expressions. His ability to preserve these qualities indicates a new attitude toward ancient art, one that unites classical form and content instead of separating them as medieval classicists had done.

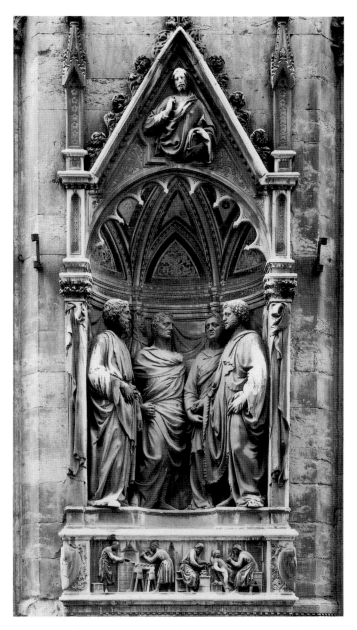

12-1. Nanni di Banco. *Four Saints (Quattro Coronati)*. c. 1410–14. Marble, about lifesize. Or San Michele, Florence

DONATELLO. Early Renaissance art reestablished an attitude toward the human body similar to classical antiquity's. Donatello, the greatest sculptor of his time, played a particularly important role in forming this new approach. Among the founders of the new style, he alone lived well past the middle of the century. (He was born in 1386, several years after Nanni and outlived him by 45 years.) Together with Nanni, Donatello spent his early career working on commissions for Florence Cathedral and Or San Michele after completing his apprenticeship under Ghiberti. They often faced the same artistic problems and strongly influenced each other, although their personalities had little in common.

Their different approaches can be seen by comparing Nanni's *Quattro Coronati* with Donatello's *St. Mark* (fig. 12-2, page 410). Both are located in Gothic niches, but Nanni's figures, like Antelami's *King David* (see fig. 10-30), cannot be divorced from the architectural setting. The figure of *St. Mark*, however, would lose none of its authority if it were removed from the niche. Perfectly

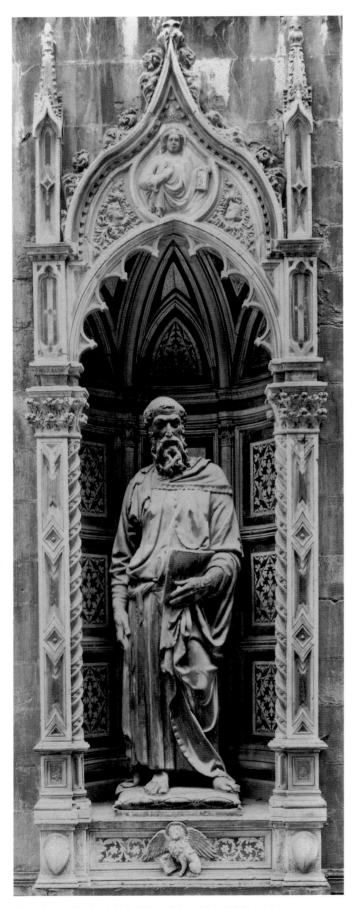

12-2. Donatello. *St. Mark.* 1411–13. Marble, 7'9" (2.4 m).
Or San Michele, Florence

balanced, it could stand by itself, like the statues of antiquity. Donatello has recaptured the full meaning of the classical contrapposto, the central achievement of Classical sculpture. He treats the human body as an articulated structure, capable of movement, and its drapery as a separate element that is based on the shapes underneath rather than on patterns imposed from outside. Unlike the *Coronati, St. Mark* is not at all classical in appearance: ancient features are not quoted as they are in Nanni's figures. Perhaps *classic* is a better word for him.

A few years later, about 1415–17, Donatello carved another statue for Or San Michele, the famous *St. George* (fig. 12-3). The niche is shallower than that of the *St. Mark,* so that the warrior saint actually protrudes from it slightly. Although dressed in armor, his body and limbs are not rigid. His stance, with the weight placed on the forward leg, conveys his readiness for combat. (The right hand originally held a lance or sword.) The controlled energy of his body is reflected in his eyes, which seem to scan the horizon for the enemy. *St. George* is portrayed as the Christian soldier in his Early Renaissance version, spiritually akin to the *St. Theodore* at Chartres (see fig. 11-44), but now he is also the proud defender of the "new Athens."

Below *St. George*'s niche is a relief panel showing the hero's best-known exploit, the slaying of a dragon. (The maiden on the right is the princess whom he had come to free.) Here Donatello devised a new kind of relief that is shallow (called *schiacciato,* "flattened-out") yet creates an illusion of infinite depth. This result had been achieved to some degree in Greek and Roman reliefs, as well as by Ghiberti (compare with figs. 5-60, 7-31–7-38, and 11-65). In all these cases, however, the actual carved depth is roughly proportional to the apparent depth of the space represented. The forms in the front plane are in very high relief, while more distant ones become progressively lower, as if immersed in the background. Donatello takes an entirely different approach. Behind the figures the landscape consists of delicate surface modulations that catch light from varying angles. Every tiny ripple has a descriptive power that is much greater than its real depth. The sculptor's chisel, like a painter's brush, becomes a tool for creating shades of light and dark. Yet Donatello cannot have borrowed his landscape from any painting, for no painter at the time had achieved so unified and atmospheric a view of nature. In creating pictorial effects, sculptors remained far in advance of most painters until well past mid-century.

Further evidence of Donatello's genius can be seen in the statues he made for the campanile of Florence Cathedral. When the campanile was built between 1334 and 1357, a row of tall Gothic niches was designed for statues. (They are barely visible above the rooftops in fig. 11-35.) In 1416 half of these niches were still empty, but in the next twenty years Donatello filled five of them. The most impressive statue in his series (fig. 12-4, page 412) is of an unidentified prophet who has been nicknamed *Zuccone* ("pumpkin-head"). Made a dozen years after the *St. Mark,* it is strikingly realistic, far more so than any ancient statue or its nearest rivals, the prophets on Sluter's *Moses Well* (see fig. 11-56). But what kind of realism have we here?

This is not the standard image of a prophet—a bearded old man in Oriental-looking costume, holding a large scroll (compare

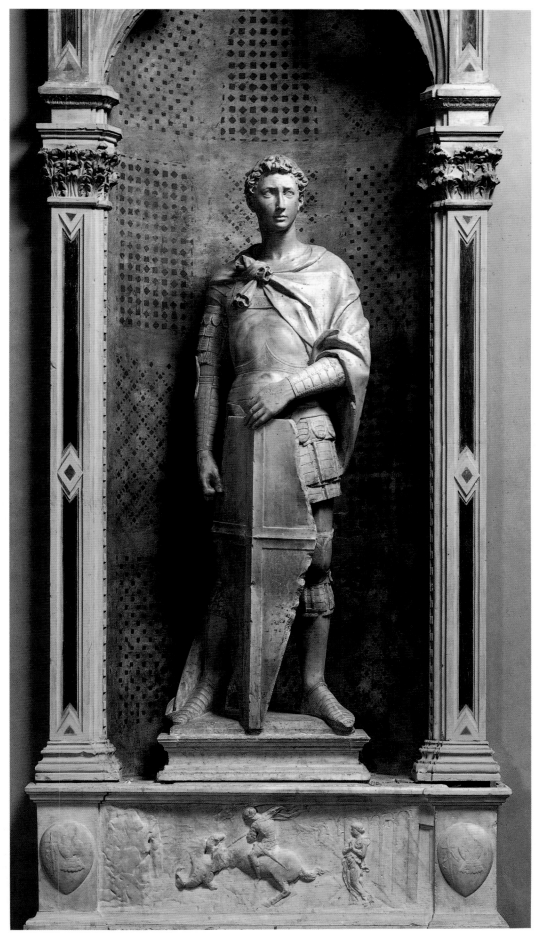

12-3. Donatello. *St. George Tabernacle,* from Or San Michele, Florence. c. 1415–17.
Marble, height of statue 6'10" (2.1 m). Museo Nazionale del Bargello, Florence

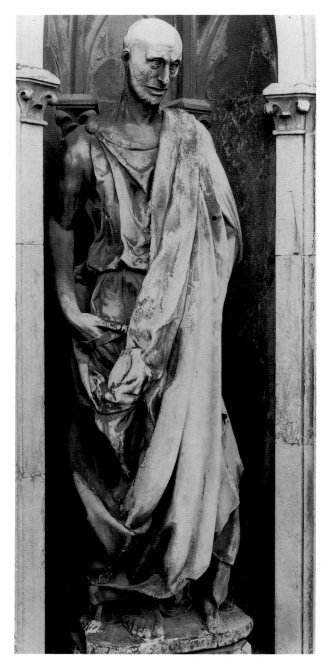

12-4. Donatello. *Prophet (Zuccone),* on the campanile of Florence Cathedral. 1423–25. Marble, height 6'5" (2 m). Original now in the Museo dell'Opera del Duomo, Florence

fig. 11-56). Rather, Donatello invented an entirely new type. Why did he not simply reinterpret the conventional image from a realistic point of view, as Sluter had done? Donatello obviously felt that the old type would not suit his purposes. But how did he conceive the new one? Surely not by observing the people around him. More likely, he imagined the personalities of the prophets from what he had read about them in the Old Testament. He saw them as divinely inspired orators speaking to the multitudes. In turn he was reminded of the Roman orators he had seen in ancient sculpture. Hence the classical costume of the *Zuccone,* whose mantle falls from one shoulder like those of the patricians in figures 7-26 and 7-32. Hence, too, the prophet's head is ugly yet noble, like those of Roman portraits of the third century A.D. (compare fig. 7-43). To shape these elements required an almost visible struggle.

Donatello himself seems to have regarded it as an especially important achievement: the *Zuccone* is the first of his surviving works that bears his signature. He is said to have sworn "by the Zuccone" and to have shouted at the statue while working on it, "Speak, speak, or the plague take you!"

Donatello had learned the technique of bronze sculpture as a youth by working under Ghiberti on the first Baptistery doors. By the 1420s, he began to rival his former teacher in that medium. *The Feast of Herod* (fig. 12-5), which he made about 1425 for the baptismal font of S. Giovanni (the Baptistery of Siena Cathedral), has the same exquisite surface finish as Ghiberti's panels (see fig. 11-65) but is much more expressive. By classical or medieval standards, the main scene is poorly composed. The focus of the drama—the executioner presenting the head of St. John to Herod—is far to the left, while the dancing Salome and most of the spectators are massed on the right and the center is empty. Yet we see at once why Donatello created this gaping hole. Far more than the witnesses' gestures and expressions, it conveys the impact of the shocking sight. Moreover, the centrifugal movement of the figures helps persuade us that the picture space does not end within the panel but continues in every direction. The frame thus becomes a window through which we see a segment of an unlimited reality. The arched openings within the panel frame additional segments of the same reality, luring us farther into the palace.

This architecture, with its round arches, its fluted columns and pilasters, is not Gothic at all. It reflects the new style launched by Filippo Brunelleschi (discussed below). More important, *The Feast of Herod* may be the earliest surviving example of a picture space using Brunelleschi's scientific perspective (see box page 423). This perspective assumes an ideal vantage point at the center of the panel. In the Baptistery, however, one must crouch low to see it correctly, as the basin to which the relief is attached is only a few feet high. Furthermore, the building could not be built the way the artist has portrayed it. Why, then, did Donatello use scientific perspective? It was a convenient way to organize the image, which

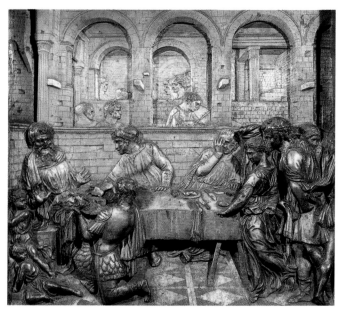

12-5. Donatello. *The Feast of Herod.* c. 1425. Gilt bronze, 23½" (59.7 cm) square. Baptismal font, Siena Cathedral

shows the action as a continuous narrative. (Note that the Baptist's severed head is seen twice.)

Donatello's bronze *David* (fig. 12-6) is the first freestanding lifesize nude statue, as well as the first large bronze sculpture, since antiquity. It was made possible by advances in armor making and the rediscovery of the lost wax **(cire perdu)** method of casting. In the Middle Ages it would have been condemned as an idol, and even in Donatello's day people must have felt uneasy about it, because for many years it remained the only work of its kind. The David was surely meant for an open space. It probably stood on top of a column in the garden of Cosimo de' Medici, the most powerful person in Florence, where the figure would have been visible from every side.

The key to the meaning of the statue is the helmet of Goliath, with its visor and wings. It was derived from depictions of the Roman wind god Zephyr, an evil figure who killed the young boy Hyacinth. We may assume that the helmet is a reference to the dukes of Milan, who had threatened Florence about 1400, since the new duke, Filippo Maria Visconti (1392–1447), was warring against it once more in the mid-1420s. The statue thus is a patriotic monument identifying David—weak but favored by the Lord— with Florence, and Goliath with Milan. David's nudity may be a reference to the classical origin of Florence; his wreathed hat, the opposite of Goliath's helmet, probably represents peace versus war.

Donatello chose to model an adolescent boy, not a full-grown youth like the athletes of Greece, so that he lacks their swelling muscles. Nor is the torso sharply defined like Classical sculpture (compare figs. 5-43 and 5-44). Rather, it is softly sensuous, like the cult statues of the Roman youth Antinous (compare fig. 7-47, right). *David* resembles ancient sculpture mainly in its contrapposto. If he has a classical appearance, the reason lies in the expression, not anatomy. The lowered gaze signifies humility, which triumphs over the sinful pride of Goliath. It was inspired by Classical examples, which equate the lowered gaze with modesty and virtue (compare fig. 5-43). As in ancient statues, however, the body speaks to us more eloquently than the face, which by Donatello's standards strangely lacks individuality.

In 1443 Donatello was invited to Padua to produce his largest freestanding work in bronze: the *Equestrian Monument of Gattamelata*. This statue, which honors the recently deceased commander of the Venetian armies (fig. 12-7) is still in its original position on a tall pedestal near the church dedicated to St. Anthony of Padua. We may compare it with the mounted *Marcus Aurelius* in Rome and the *Can Grande* in Verona (see figs. 7-40 and 11-63). Like the *Marcus Aurelius*, the *Gattamelata* is impressive in scale and shares a sense of balance and dignity. The horse, a heavy-set animal fit to carry a man in full armor, is so large that the rider must dominate it by authority rather than by force. The link with the *Can Grande,* although less obvious, is equally significant. Both statues were made to stand next to a church facade, and both are memorials to military figures. But the *Gattamelata* is not part of a tomb. It was designed solely to commemorate a great soldier. Nor is it the self-glorifying statue of a ruler; it is a monument authorized by the Republic of Venice. Donatello therefore has united the ideal with the real. The armor combines modern construction with classical detail; the head is a portrait, yet displays a truly Roman nobility of character.

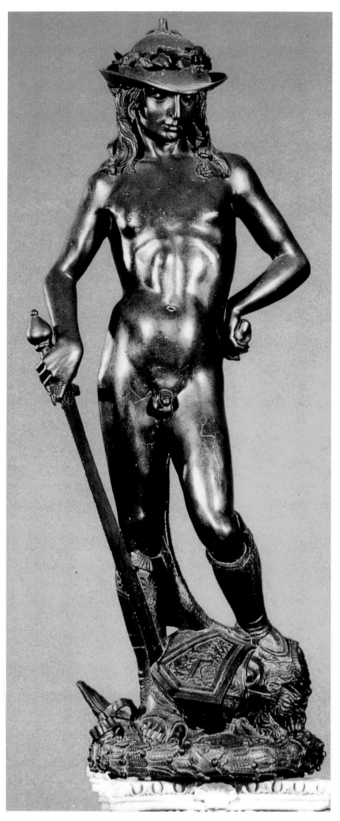

12-6. Donatello. *David*. c. 1425–30. Bronze, height 62¼" (158 cm). Museo Nazionale del Bargello, Florence

After a decade in Padua, Donatello returned to Florence. He must have felt like a stranger. The political and spiritual climate had changed, and so had the taste of artists and public (see page 409). His later sculpture (1453 to 1466) stands apart from the main trend. Its expressiveness surpasses anything Donatello had achieved before.

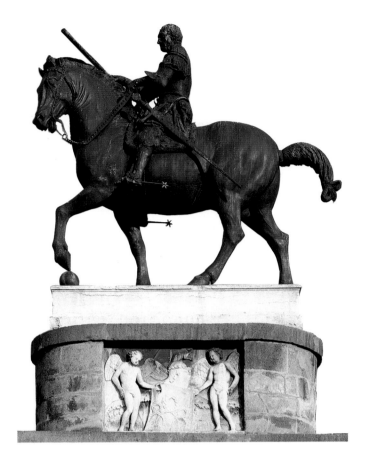

The extreme individualism of these works confirms his reputation as the earliest "solitary genius" among the artists of the new age.

In contrast to the *David,* the *Mary Magdalen* (fig. 12-8) of some twenty years later seems so far removed from Renaissance ideals that at first we are tempted to compare it with Gothic devotional images like the Bonn *Pietà* (see fig. 11-54). Both give the viewer an almost physical shock. But when we look back at the *Zuccone* (see fig. 12-4), we realize that it is not so very different. *Mary Magdalen* conveys deep and utterly personal religious feeling. Her ravaged features and wasted body make her the embodiment of penitence, so that we share her anguish and longing for redemption.

GHIBERTI. Donatello's only serious rival was his former teacher, Lorenzo Ghiberti. After the great success of his first doors for the Florence Baptistery, Ghiberti was commissioned to do a second pair of bronze doors for the Baptistery in Florence (fig. 12-9), which are so beautiful that they were soon called the Gates

(LEFT) 12-7. Donatello. *Equestrian Monument of Gattamelata.* 1445–50. Bronze, approx. 11 x 13' (3.35 x 3.96 m). Piazza del Santo, Padua

(RIGHT) 12-8. *Mary Magdalen.* c. 1455. Wood, partially gilded, height 6'2" (1.88 m). Museo dell'Opera del Duomo, Florence.

Only Donatello himself could have created a work of such shocking impact; the Magdalen has been both praised and damned—sometimes, paradoxically, in the same breath—but never treated with indifference. . . .[The Magdalen's] harsh grandeur, so different from anything created in Florence during Donatello's absence, must have jolted both artists and public like a thunderclap: one could hardly imagine a more dramatic way for our master to reassert his artistic authority in his native city. . . . Yet this popularity was due only in part to the greatness of the Magdalen as a work of art. The overpowering religious fervor expressed in the statue would have met a less ready response had it not coincided with a broader devotional trend which can be felt in Florence from the 1450's on. . . . Its climax was to come forty years later, under Savonarola. Donatello's Magdalen is strangely prophetic of the mood of that cataclysmic fin de siècle.

— H. W. Janson. *The Sculpture of Donatello.* 2 Vols. Princeton: Princeton University Press, 1979, p. 191. Originally published in 1963.

H. W. JANSON (1913–1982) became the most famous American art historian because of his popular books, *History of Art* (1962), *History of Art for Young People* (written with Samuel Cauman, 1971), and *The Story of Painting for Young People* (1952), which he wrote with his wife, art historian Dora Jane Janson (1916–2002). The fame of the Janson name tends to overshadow H. W. Janson's reputation as a distinguished scholar. Like other art historians educated in Europe in the first half of the twentieth century, he wrote on an enormous range of topics that unite the intellect and imagination with masterly methodology and a playful use of the English language that was unique to him. His two-volume work on Donatello, from which this excerpt is drawn, exemplifies his lively scholarship.

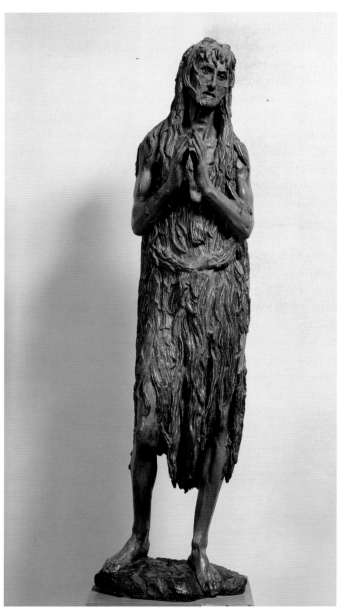

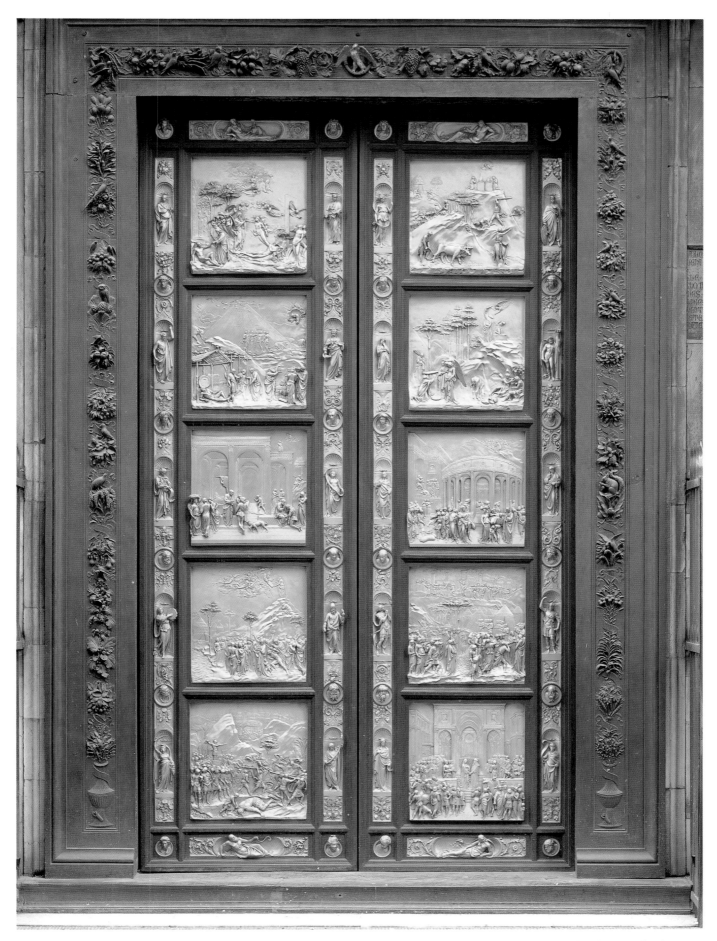

12-9. Lorenzo Ghiberti. *"Gates of Paradise,"* east doors of the Baptistery of S. Giovanni, Florence. c. 1435. Gilt bronze, height 15' (4.57 m)

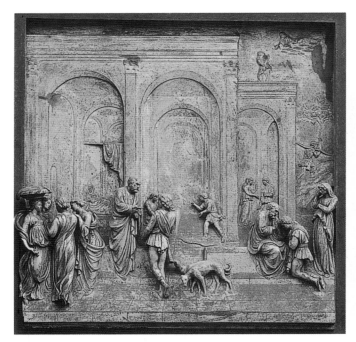

12-10. Lorenzo Ghiberti. *The Story of Jacob and Esau,*
panel of the *"Gates of Paradise."* c. 1435.
Gilt bronze, 31 ¼" (79.5 cm) square.

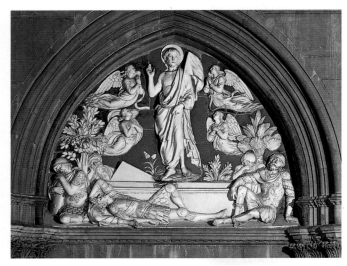

12-11. Luca della Robbia. *The Resurrection.* 1442–45.
Glazed terra-cotta, 5'3" x 7'3 ½" (1.6 x 2.22 m).
Museo Nazionale del Bargello, Florence

of Paradise. Each contains ten large panels in simple square frames, which create a larger field than the 28 small panels in quatrefoil frames of the earlier doors. The program was probably by the humanist Ambrogio Traverasi (1386–1439), but with the input of Leonardo Bruni (see page 408). The style reveals the in-fluence of Donatello and other pioneers of the Early Renaissance style. The only remnants of the Gothic style are seen in the graceful classicism of the figures, which reminds us of the International Style.

The *"Gates of Paradise"* show the pictorialism found in many Renaissance reliefs. The hint of depth we saw in *The Sacrifice of Isaac* (see fig. 11-65) has grown in *The Story of Jacob and Esau* (fig. 12-10) into a complete setting that goes back as far as the eye can reach. We can imagine the figures leaving the scene. They are not necessary to the deep space of this relief, even though it was planned with them in mind. Ghiberti's spacious hall is a fine example of Early Renaissance architectural design. Like Donatello, Ghiberti uses Brunelleschi's scientific perspective (see box page 423) and presents his story in continuous narrative. Because *The Story of Jacob and Esau* is about a decade later than *The Feast of Herod,* its perspective is more assured and the scene as a whole more consistent, as if all seven episodes were taking place at once.

LUCA DELLA ROBBIA. Aside from Ghiberti, the only important sculptor in Florence after Donatello left for Padua in 1443 was Luca della Robbia (1400–1482), who had come to prominence in the 1430s. Unfortunately, Luca lacked a capacity for growth, despite his great gifts. So far as we know, he never did a freestanding statue, and a singers' pulpit he made for Florence cathedral remained his greatest achievement. Instead, he devoted himself to sculpture in terra-cotta, a cheaper and less demanding

medium than marble. He covered this material with enamel-like glazes to mask its surface and protect it from the weather. Despite their limitations, his finest works in this technique, which include *The Resurrection* in figure 12-11, have considerable dignity and charm. The white glaze creates the effect of marble against the deep blue background of the lunette. Other colors were confined almost entirely to the decorative framework of the reliefs. This restraint, however, lasted only while he was in charge of his workshop. Later, the quality of the modeling declined and the simple harmony of white and blue often gave way to more vivid hues. At the end of the century, the della Robbia shop had become a factory, turning out scores of small Madonna panels and garish altarpieces for village churches.

BERNARDO ROSSELLINO. As Luca limited himself to terra-cotta, there was a shortage of marble sculptors in Florence during the 1440s. By the time Donatello returned from Padua in 1453, this gap had been filled by a group of men, most still in their twenties, from the hill towns north and east of Florence that had long supplied the city with stonemasons and carvers. Taking advantage of the unusual opportunities open to them, the most gifted of them developed into artists of considerable importance. The oldest of these, Bernardo Rossellino (1409–1464), came to Florence about 1436 and worked mainly at the cathedral under Filippo Brunelleschi (see pages 421–422). Not until 1444 did he receive his first major commission: the Tomb of Leonardo Bruni (fig. 12-12). This great humanist and statesman had played a vital part in the city's affairs since the beginning of the century (see page 408). When he died in 1444, he received a grand funeral "in the manner of the ancients." His monument was probably ordered by the city government. Since Bruni had been born in Arezzo, his

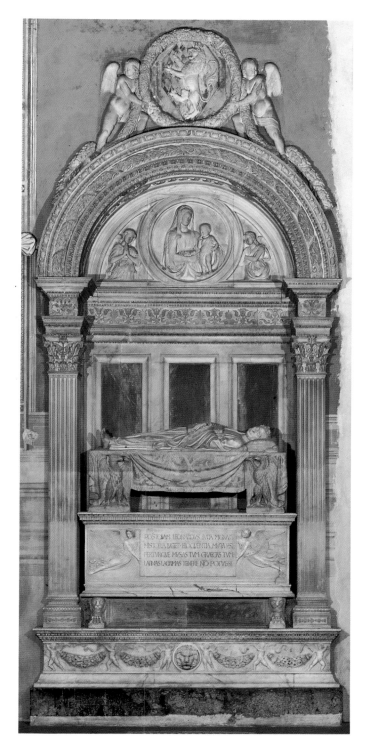

12-12. Bernardo Rossellino. Tomb of Leonardo Bruni. c. 1445–50. Marble, height 20' (6.1 m to top of arch). Sta. Croce, Florence

the sarcophagus, two winged genii hold an inscription that is very different from those on medieval tombs. Instead of recording Bruni's name, rank, age, and date of death, it refers only to his achievements: "At Leonardo's passing, history grieves, eloquence is mute, and it is said that the Muses, Greek and Latin alike, cannot hold back their tears." The religious aspect of the tomb is confined to the lunette, where the Madonna is adored by angels.

The monument may be viewed as an attempt to reconcile two contrasting attitudes toward death: the retrospective, commemorative outlook of the ancients (see page 153) and the Christian concern with afterlife and salvation. Bernardo's design, adapted from the Tomb of Guglielmo de Braye by Arnolfo di Cambio (fig. 11-64), is well suited to this task. It balances architecture and sculpture within a compact framework. The two pilasters supporting a round arch resting on a strongly accented architrave recall the work of Alberti, who used this motif often. It is derived from the doorway to the Pantheon (fig. 7-15), which accounts for its use in church portals such as that of S. Andrea in Mantua (see fig. 12-32). While Bernardo may have used it for aesthetic reasons, he may also have meant it to symbolize the gateway between one life and the next. Perhaps he even wanted us to associate the motif with the Pantheon, the "temple of the immortals" for both pagans and Christians. Originally dedicated to the planetary Roman gods, it had been rededicated to all the martyrs when it became a church. (In the High Renaissance it was to house the tombs of another breed of immortals: famous artists such as Raphael.)

All the tombs, tabernacles, and Madonna reliefs produced in Florence between 1450 and 1480 owe much to the Bruni monument. Nevertheless, its style is not easy to define. Broadly speaking, it reflects the classicism of Ghiberti and Luca della Robbia. Despite his early impact on Bernardo, there are few echoes of Donatello, who was in Padua until shortly before the Bruni project. By the same token, we do not have a clear idea of Bernardo's style, since there are so few works by his hand. Other than the Bruni tomb, the handful of works show that he had great difficulty overcoming his provincial origins. He surely employed assistants here, as he did for later commissions. During the late 1440s, his workshop was the only training ground for young marble sculptors, such as his younger brother Antonio (1417–1470) and others of the same generation. Their share in Bernardo's sculptural projects is hard to pin down, because their personalities were not yet distinct. Nonetheless, the sculpture they did when they set out on their own has much in common with Bernardo's.

DESIDERIO DA SETTIGNANO. Of the many sculptors who passed through the Rossellino shop, the most gifted was Desiderio da Settignano (1429/30–1464), who came from a family of stonemasons. But it was the influence of Donatello, to whom he was probably apprenticed in the early 1440s, that proved decisive. Indeed, his *St. John the Baptist* (fig. 12-13, page 418) was long thought to have been done by Donatello. Although Desiderio is remembered for his beautiful Madonnas and enchanting children, no other sculptor of the day was so attuned to the ascetic side of Donatello's later sculpture. Desiderio's *Baptist* was clearly inspired by Donatello's *Mary Magdalen* (see fig. 12-8). The differences are equally important, however, for Desiderio has magnified

native town also wished to honor him and may have helped Bernardo get the commission.

Although Bruni's is not the earliest Renaissance tomb, it is the first to express the spirit of the new era. The references to antiquity contain many echoes of Bruni's funeral: the deceased lies on a bier supported by Roman eagles, his head wreathed in laurel and his right hand resting on a book (presumably his own *History of Florence* rather than a prayer book). The monument is a fitting tribute to the man who, more than any other, had helped establish the historical perspective of the Florentine Early Renaissance. On

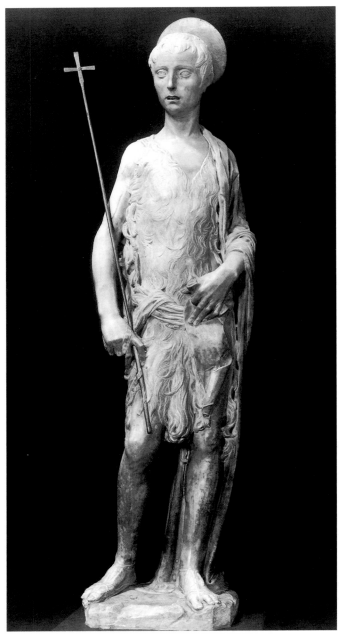

12-13. Desiderio da Settignano. *St. John the Baptist*. c. 1455–60. Marble, height 63" (160 cm). Museo Nazionale del Bargello, Florence

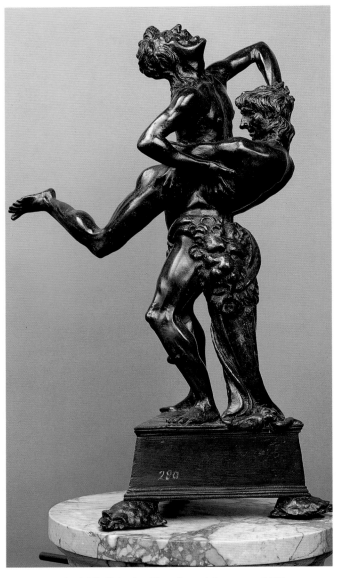

12-14. Antonio del Pollaiuolo. *Hercules and Antaeus*. c. 1475. Bronze, height with base 18" (45.8 cm). Museo Nazionale del Bargello, Florence

the figure's expressiveness by turning it inward. The young St. John has a disturbing, haunted look, as if torn by a spiritual experience of almost unbearable intensity. The effect is heightened by the subtlety of the carving, so refined that it is small wonder the statue passed as Donatello's.

ANTONIO DEL POLLAIUOLO. By 1450 the great civic art campaign had come to an end in Florence, and sculptors had to depend mainly on private commissions. This loss of patronage put them at a serious disadvantage because of the high cost of making their work. Since there were few commissions for monuments, they created pieces of moderate size and price, such as bronze statuettes. The collecting of sculpture, common in ancient times, had

stopped during the Middle Ages. The taste of kings, feudal lords, and the wealthy ran to gems, jewelry, goldsmith's work, illuminated manuscripts, and precious fabrics. The demand for sculpture resumed in fifteenth-century Italy as part of the revival of antiquity. Humanists and artists first collected ancient sculpture, especially small bronzes (such as fig. 5-80), of which there were many. Before long, artists began to cater to the demand by creating portrait busts and small bronzes "in the manner of the ancients."

A splendid work of this kind is *Hercules and Antaeus* (fig. 12-14) by Antonio del Pollaiuolo (1431–1498). Pollaiuolo's style was very different from that of the marble carvers discussed above. He was trained as a goldsmith and metalworker, probably in the Ghiberti workshop, but was deeply impressed by the late styles of

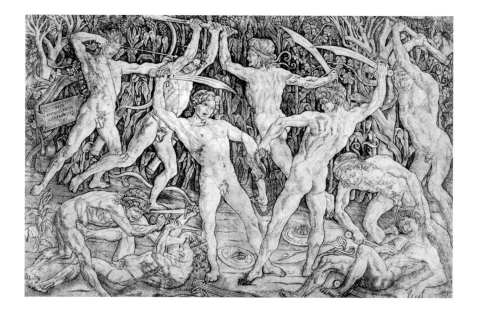

12-15. Antonio del Pollaiuolo. *Battle of the Ten Naked Men.* c. 1465–70. Engraving, 15⅛" x 23¼" (38.3 x 59 cm). The Metropolitan Museum of Art, New York

JOSEPH PULITZER BEQUEST, 1917

Donatello and Andrea del Castagno, as well as by ancient art. From these sources, he developed the distinctive style that appears in our statuette. To create a freestanding group of two struggling figures, even on a small scale, was a daring idea. There is no precedent for this design among earlier statuary groups, ancient or Renaissance. Even bolder is the centrifugal force of the composition. Limbs seem to move outward in every direction. We see the full complexity of their movements only when we view the statuette from all sides. Despite its violent action, the group is in perfect balance. To stress the central axis, Pollaiuolo in effect grafted the upper part of Antaeus onto the lower part of Hercules as he lifts him in a stranglehold. Pollaiuolo was a painter and engraver as well as a bronze sculptor, and we know that about 1465 he did a closely related picture of Hercules and Antaeus for the Medici, who also owned the statuette. (The picture has been lost but the design is preserved in a smaller copy.) Here, for the first time, a sculptural group has been given the pictorial quality seen in reliefs since the early years of the Renaissance.

Few of Pollaiuolo's paintings have survived, and only one engraving (see page 532), the *Battle of the Ten Naked Men* (fig. 12-15). This print, however, is of great importance, since it is Pollaiuolo's most elaborate design. Its subject, undoubtedly a classical one, is not known for certain, but that matters little. The main purpose of the engraving obviously was to display the artist's mastery of the nude body in action. About 1465–70, when the print must have been produced, this was still a novel problem, and Pollaiuolo did more to solve it than any other artist. An interest in movement, coupled with slender proportions and an emphasis on outline rather than on modeling, could be seen in Castagno's *David* (see fig. 12-51). Pollaiuolo also drew upon the action poses he found in certain types of Greek vases (compare fig. 5-64). But he realized that a full understanding of movement demands a detailed knowledge of anatomy, down to the last muscle and sinew. And in fact these naked men look as if their skin had been stripped off to reveal the play of muscles underneath. So to a lesser extent do the two figures of Pollaiuolo's statuette.

Artists may have begun to study dissected cadavers as early as 1425, and the practice was almost certainly established during the 1450s by Andrea Mantegna (see page 448), among others. But this print is the clearest evidence we have of a custom that was to be followed by artists through the High Renaissance and after. Equally novel are the facial expressions, which are as strained as the bodily movements. We have already seen contorted features in the work of Donatello (see fig. 12-8), but the anguish it conveys is internal. It does not arise from or accompany the physical action of Pollaiuolo's struggling nudes.

ANDREA DEL VERROCCHIO. Although Pollaiuolo did two large bronze tombs for St. Peter's in Rome during the late years of his career, he never had a chance to create a large-scale freestanding statue. For such works we must turn to Andrea del Verrocchio (1435–1488), the greatest sculptor of his day and the only one to share some of Donatello's range and ambition. A modeler as well as a carver—we have works of his in marble, terra-cotta, silver, and bronze—he combined elements from Rossellino and Pollaiuolo into a unique style. He was also a respected painter and the teacher of Leonardo da Vinci.

Like *Hercules and Antaeus* by Pollaiuolo, Verrocchio's *The Doubting of Thomas* (fig. 12-16) is closely related to a painting: a *Baptism of Christ,* painted with the assistance of the young Leonardo. The result is a pictorialism unique in monumental sculpture of the Early Renaissance. In contrast to the *Quattro Coronati* of Nanni di Banco (see fig. 12-1), the subject is a narrative. Also, Verrocchio's group does not quite fit its niche on Or San Michele, for it replaced a figure by Donatello that had been moved. Hence the statues have no backs so that they can fit in the shallow space, which acts as a foil rather than as a container.

Although the biblical text is inscribed on the drapery, the drama is conveyed by the eloquent poses and bold exchange of gestures between Christ and Thomas. It is heightened by the active drapery, with its deep folds, which echo the contrasting states of mind. *The Doubting of Thomas* is of great importance in the history

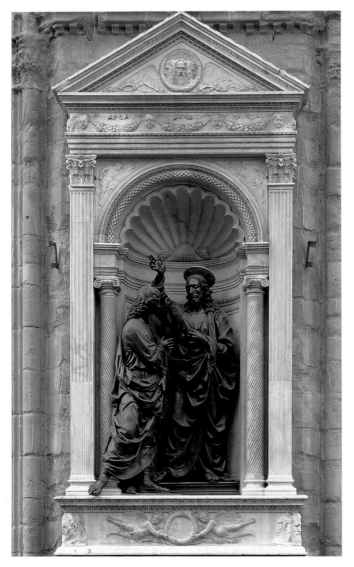

12-16. Andrea del Verrocchio. *The Doubting of Thomas.* 1465–83. Bronze, lifesize. Or San Michele, Florence

of sculpture. The work was admired for its great beauty, especially the head of Christ, which was to inspire Michelangelo. For Leonardo it served as a model of figures whose actions express the passions of the mind. Later it stimulated the sculpture of Bernini (compare fig. 17-29).

By coincidence, the crowning achievement of Verrocchio's career, as of Donatello's, was a bronze equestrian statue: the monument of a Venetian army commander, Bartolommeo Colleoni (fig. 12-17). Colleoni had asked for such a statue in his will, in which he left a large fortune to the Republic of Venice. He obviously knew the Gattamelata statue and wanted the same honor for himself. Verrocchio, too, must have viewed Donatello's work as the model for his statue, yet he did not simply imitate it. Although perhaps less subtle, his version is no less impressive. The horse, graceful and spirited rather than robust and placid, conveys the same sense of anatomy-in-action that we saw in the nudes of Pollaiuolo. Its thin hide reveals every vein, muscle, and sinew, in contrast to the rigid surfaces of the armored figure bestriding it. Since the horse is also smaller in relation to the rider

than Gattamelata's, Colleoni looms in the saddle as the very image of forceful dominance. Legs straight, one shoulder thrust forward, he surveys the scene before him with the same concentration we saw in Donatello's *St. George* (see fig. 12-3), but his lip is curled in contempt.

Neither *Gattamelata* nor *Colleoni* is a portrait in the specific sense of the term. Both idealize the personality that each artist associated with leadership in war. If *Gattamelata* conveys steadfast purpose and nobility, *Colleoni* radiates an almost frightening sense of power. As an image of self-assurance, it recalls the *Can Grande* (see fig. 11-63) rather than Donatello's statue. Perhaps Verrocchio visited the tomb of the Can Grande (who was well remembered in Florence as the patron of Dante) and decided to translate its arrogance into the style of his own day. In any case, Colleoni got a great deal more than he had asked for in his will.

JACOPO DELLA QUERCIA. The development of Early Renaissance sculpture was very much a Florentine endeavor. Outside Florence, the only major sculptor before the end of the fifteenth century was Jacopo della Quercia of Siena (c. 1374–1438). Like Ghiberti, he changed his style from Gothic to Early Renaissance in mid-career, mainly through contact with Donatello. Had

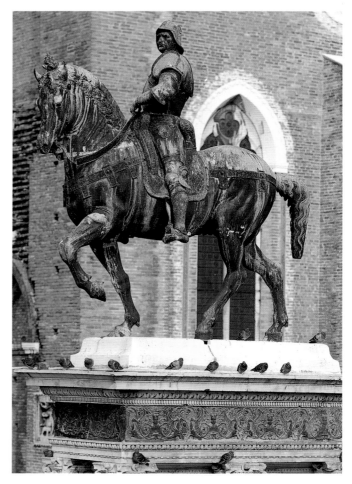

12-17. Andrea del Verrocchio. *Equestrian Monument of Colleoni.* c. 1483–88. Bronze, height 13' (3.9 m). Campo SS. Giovanni e Paolo, Venice

he grown up in Florence, he might have been one of the leaders of the new movement, but his highly individual art remained outside the main trend. It had no effect on Florentine art until the very end of the century, when the young Michelangelo fell under its spell.

Michelangelo's admiration was aroused by the scenes from Genesis framing the main entrance of the church of S. Petronio in Bologna. Among them was *The Creation of Adam* (fig. 12-18). The relief modeling of these panels is conservative—Jacopo had little interest in pictorial depth. Adam slowly rising from the ground, like a statue brought to life, recaptures the heroic beauty of a Classical athlete. Here the nude body expresses the dignity and power of the individual as it did in classical antiquity. As he faces the Lord, Jacopo's Adam conveys a hint of the conflict that will lead to Original Sin. He will surely fall, but in a spirit of pride rather than as a mere victim of evil.

It is useful to compare Jacopo's *The Creation of Adam* with the work that probably inspired it. The Adam in Paradise from an Early Christian ivory diptych (fig. 12-19) represents a classicizing trend that arose around 400 A.D. (compare fig. 8-22) as a final attempt to preserve the Greek ideal of physical beauty in a Christian context. Adam appears as the Perfect Man to whom God has granted "dominion . . . over every living thing," but the classic form has become a formula. Not until the fifteenth century was the beauty of the unclothed body rediscovered. Jacopo's Adam is clearly nude, in the full classical sense.

Jacopo's style, so unlike Florentine sculpture, was to have a profound effect on Michelangelo, whose admiration for the Bolognese relief is reflected in his own Creation of Adam (compare fig. 13-18).

Architecture

FILIPPO BRUNELLESCHI. Donatello did not create the Early Renaissance style in sculpture all by himself. The new architecture, in contrast, owed its existence to one person, Filippo Brunelleschi (1377–1446), who was arguably the central figure in Early Renaissance art. Ten years older than Donatello, he, too, had begun his career as a sculptor. After losing the competition for the first Baptistery doors, he certainly went to Rome with Donatello. There he studied ancient structures and seems to have been the first person to take exact measurements of them. His discovery of scientific perspective (see box page 423) may well have grown out of his search for an accurate way of recording their appearance. We do not know what else he did during this period, but between 1417 and 1419 he again competed with Ghiberti, this time for the job of building the Florence Cathedral dome (see figs. 11-35 and 11-36). The dome had been designed half a century earlier, so only details could be changed, but its vast size posed a difficult problem of construction. Brunelleschi's proposals so impressed the authorities that this time he won—thanks in part to a model he built with the help of Donatello and Nanni di Banco. Thus the dome may be viewed as the first work of post-medieval architecture, as an engineering feat if not for style.

Brunelleschi's main achievement was to build the dome in two separate shells. The traditional practice had been to construct a base across the span of the dome out of giant wood spokes radiating from a hub, but no trees were long enough for the task. He used a skeletal system inspired by the coffered dome of the Pantheon (see fig. 7-12). The two are ingeniously linked so as to

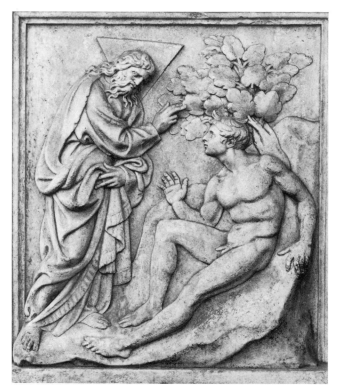

12-18. Jacopo della Quercia. *The Creation of Adam.* c. 1430. Marble, 34½ x 27½" (87.7 x 69.8 cm). Main portal, S. Petronio, Bologna

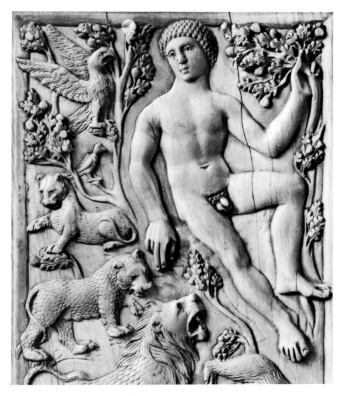

12-19. *Adam in Paradise,* detail of an ivory diptych. c. 400 A.D. Museo Nazionale del Bargello, Florence

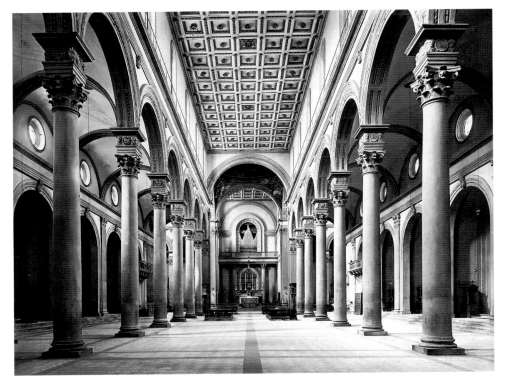

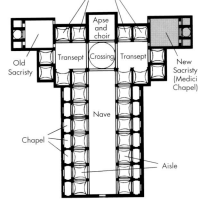

12-20. Filippo Brunelleschi. S. Lorenzo, Florence. 1421–69

12-21. Plan of S. Lorenzo. Gray area indicates Michelangelo's later addition

reinforce each other, rather than to form a solid mass. Because the weight of the structure was lightened, Brunelleschi could also dispense with the massive and costly wooden trusswork required by the older method of construction. And instead of having building materials carried up on ramps to the required level, he designed hoisting machines. Although Brunelleschi was neither a man of letters nor a scientist, his entire scheme reflects a bold, analytical mind that was willing to discard conventional solutions if better ones could be devised. This approach is very different from the methods of the Gothic stonemason-architects.

In 1419, while he was working out the final plans for the dome, Brunelleschi received his first opportunity to create buildings entirely of his own design. It came from the head of the Medici family, one of the leading merchant-bankers of Florence, who commissioned him to add a **sacristy** to the Romanesque church of S. Lorenzo. His plans for this sacristy (which was to serve also as a burial chapel for the Medici) were so successful that he was asked to develop a new design for the entire church. The construction, begun in 1425, proceeded in fits and starts. It was interrupted by renewed war with Milan, so that the nave, which probably dates from the mid-1430s, was not completed until 1469, more than 20 years after the architect's death. (The exterior remains unfinished to this day.) Nevertheless, the building in its present form is essentially what Brunelleschi had envisioned about 1420 and represents the first full statement of his architectural aims (figs. 12-20 and 12-21).

At first glance, the plan may not seem very novel. It recalls Cistercian Gothic churches (see fig. 11-31), while the unvaulted nave and transept link it to Sta. Croce (see fig. 11-33). What distinguishes it is a new emphasis on symmetry and regularity. The entire design consists of square units. Four large squares form

the choir, the crossing, and the arms of the transept. Four more are combined into the nave. Other squares, one-fourth the size of the large ones, make up the aisles and the chapels attached to the transept. (The oblong chapels outside the nave aisles were not part of the original design but were added sometime after 1470.)

As we study the plan, we see that Brunelleschi must have decided to make the floor area of the choir equal to four of the small square units. The nave and transept thus would be twice as wide as the aisles or chapels. Thus Brunelleschi conceived S. Lorenzo as a grouping of "space blocks," the larger ones being simple multiples of a standard unit. (He was not concerned with the thickness of the walls between these compartments, so that the transept arms are slightly longer than they are wide, and the length of the nave is not four but four and one-half times its width.) Once we understand this, we realize how revolutionary he was. His clearly defined space compartments were a radical change from the Gothic architect's way of thinking. The difference is one of consistency. Although they may approach it now and then, Gothic churches such as Notre-Dame in Paris (fig. 11-4) never show systematic proportions throughout, despite Abbot Suger's emphasis on harmonious ratios and the uniform bays required by groin and ribbed vaulting.

In the interior, static order has replaced the flowing spatial movement of Gothic church interiors. S. Lorenzo does not sweep us off our feet. It does not even draw us forward after we have entered; we are content to remain near the door. From there our view seems to take in the entire structure, almost as if we were looking at a demonstration of scientific perspective (compare fig. 12-10). The effect recalls the "old-fashioned" Tuscan Romanesque, such as Pisa Cathedral (see fig. 10-18), as well as Early Christian basilicas (compare fig. 8-11). These monuments, to Brunelleschi, exemplified the church architecture of classical antiquity. They inspired his use of round arches and columns, rather than piers, in the nave arcade. Yet these earlier buildings lack the lightness and clarity of S. Lorenzo. Their columns are larger and more closely spaced, so that they tend to screen off the aisles from the nave. Only the arcade of the Florentine Baptistery is as graceful in its proportions as S. Lorenzo's, but it is a blind arcade, without any supporting function (see fig. 10-19). Since the Baptistery was thought to have once been a classical temple, it was an appropriate source of inspiration for Brunelleschi.

Clearly, then, Brunelleschi did not revive the architectural forms of the ancients out of mere enthusiasm. The very quality that attracted him to them—their inflexibility—must have seemed their chief drawback from the medieval point of view. Unlike a medieval column, a classical column is strictly defined; its details and proportions can be varied only within narrow limits. The classical round arch, unlike any other arch (horseshoe, pointed, and so forth), has only one possible shape, a semicircle. The classical architrave, profiles, and ornaments are all subject to similarly strict rules. This is not to say that classical forms are completely rigid. If they were, they could not have endured to the fourth century A.D. But the discipline of the Greek orders, which can be felt even in the most original Roman buildings, demands regularity and discourages arbitrary departures from the norm.

Without such "standardized" forms, Brunelleschi would have been unable to define his space blocks so clearly. With remarkable logic, he emphasizes the edges of the units without disrupting their rhythmic sequence. To take one noteworthy example, consider the vaulting of the aisles. The transverse arches rest on pilasters attached to the outer wall (corresponding to the columns of the nave arcade), but between arch and pilaster there is a continuous architrave linking all the bays. We would expect these bays to be covered by unribbed groin vaults. Instead, we find a vault that is, in effect, a radically simplified dome on pendentives. (Its radius equals half the diagonal of the square compartment.) Obviously adapted from Byzantine architecture, it had already been used in two earlier projects by Brunelleschi: first in the porch of the Ospidale degli Innocenti (Foundlings Hospital; c. 1419), then in modified form for the dome of the Old Sacristy. By avoiding the ribs and even the groins, Brunelleschi has created a one-piece vault, strikingly clear and regular, in which each bay is a distinct unit.

At this point we may ask: If the new architecture consists of separate elements added together, be they spaces, columns, or vaults, how do they relate to each other? What makes the interior of S. Lorenzo seem so fully integrated? There is indeed a principle that accounts for the balanced nature of the design. For Brunelleschi, the secret of good architecture was to give the "right" proportions—that is, proportional ratios expressed in simple whole numbers—to all the major measurements of a building. The ancients had possessed this secret, he believed, and he tried to discover it when he measured their monuments. What he found, and exactly how he applied it, we do not know for sure. He may have been the first to discover what would be stated a few decades later in Leone Battista Alberti's *Treatise on Architecture:* the mathematical ratios that determine musical harmony must also govern architecture, for they recur throughout the universe and thus are divine in origin. (See also box page 525.)

Similar ideas, derived from the theories of the Greek philosopher Pythagoras, had been current during the Middle Ages, but they had never before been expressed so directly and simply. When Gothic architects "borrowed" the ratios of musical theory, they did so far less consistently. But even Brunelleschi's faith in harmonious proportions did not tell him how to allot these ratios to the parts of any given building. It left him many alternatives, and his choice was necessarily subjective. We may say, in fact, that the main reason S. Lorenzo strikes us as the product of a great mind is the individual sense of proportion that can be found in every detail.

In the revival of classical forms, Renaissance architecture found a standard vocabulary. And the theory of harmonious

SCIENTIFIC PERSPECTIVE

Although it is not certain, Brunelleschi probably invented linear, or scientific, perspective. The system is a geometric procedure for projecting space onto a plane, analogous to the way the lens of a camera projects a perspective image on film. Its central feature is the vanishing point, a single point toward which any set of parallel lines will seem to converge. If these lines are perpendicular to the picture plane, their vanishing point will be on the horizon, corresponding exactly to the position of the beholder's eye. Brunelleschi's discovery in itself was scientific rather than artistic, but it immediately became highly important to Early Renaissance artists. Unlike the intuitive perspective practices of the past, scientific perspective was objective, precise, and rational. In fact, it soon became an argument for upgrading the fine arts to liberal arts.

While empirical methods could also yield strikingly lifelike results, scientific perspective made it possible to represent three-dimensional space on a flat surface in such a way that all the distances remained measurable. This meant, in turn, that by reversing the procedure the plan could be derived from the perspective picture of a building. On the other hand, the scientific implications of the new perspective demanded that it be consistently applied, a requirement that artists could not always live up to, for practical as well as aesthetic reasons. Since the method presupposes that the beholder's eye occupies a fixed point in space, a perspective picture automatically tells us where we must stand to see it properly. Thus the artist who knows in advance that his work will be seen from above or below, rather than at ordinary eye level, can make his perspective construction correspond to these conditions. If, however, these are so abnormal that he must foreshorten his entire design to an extreme degree, he may disregard them and assume instead an ideal beholder, normally located. In 1435, Brunelleschi's discovery was described in *De Pictura,* the first Renaissance treatise on painting, by Leone Battista Alberti, who later became an important architect in his own right (see pages 412–14; Primary Sources, no. 40, page 644).

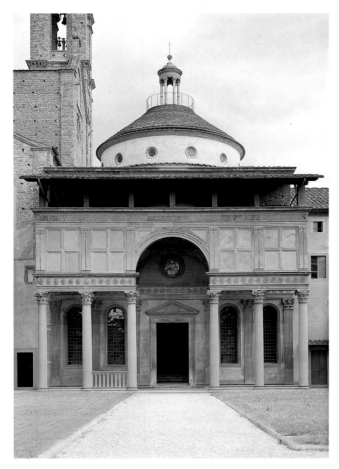

12-22. Filippo Brunelleschi and others.
Pazzi Chapel, Sta. Croce, Florence. Begun 1430–33

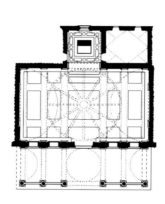

12-23. Plan of the Pazzi Chapel

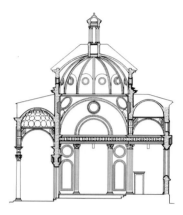

12-24. Longitudinal section of
the Pazzi Chapel

proportions gave it a syntax that had been mostly absent in medieval architecture. To take our linguistic analogy further, we may draw a parallel between the "unclassical" flexibility of medieval architecture, expressed in numerous regional styles, and the equally "unclassical" attitude toward language that prevailed at the time, as found in its barbarized Latin and regional vernaculars, the ancestors of today's Western languages. The revival of Latin and Greek in the Renaissance did not stunt these languages. On the contrary, it made them much more stable, precise, and articulate, so that before long Latin lost its dominant position as the language of intellectual discourse. It is not by chance that we can read Renaissance literature in Italian, French, English, or German without much trouble, while texts of a century or two earlier can often be understood only by scholars. Similarly, the revival of classical forms and proportions enabled Brunelleschi to transform the architectural "vernacular" of his region into a stable, precise, and coherent system. We may say that he did for architecture what Petrarch had accomplished for Italian: he placed it on a firm footing and applied the lessons of classical antiquity for modern Christian ends. The principles of his buildings, with their humanist basis, soon spread to the rest of Italy and later to all of Northern Europe.

Of the five surviving structures by Brunelleschi, not one escaped later alteration. Such is the case with the Pazzi Chapel (fig. 12-22). Begun about 1430, it is a considerably more developed outgrowth of the Old Sacristy at S. Lorenzo some eleven years earlier. Brunelleschi could not have planned either the portico or

the facade in their present form. They date from many years later and are perhaps the work of his follower Giuliano da Maiano (1432–1490). The porch screens the front from the rest of the structure. The plan (fig. 12-23) shows us that this porch has two barrel vaults, which in turn help support a small dome, an arrangement that echoes the interior. By screening the front from the rest of the structure, however, the porch disrupts the facade and prevents light from entering the four windows over the niches that flank the portal. If Brunelleschi intended a portico at all, it almost surely consisted of three identical pendentive domes and arches, with a plain architrave and simple roofline.

Inside the chapel, we find two barrel vaults on either side of a dome on pendentives, which was completed in 1461. A second dome on pendentives, half the diameter of the first, is above the square space housing the altar (figs. 12-24 and 12-25). The interior surfaces are very much as in S. Lorenzo, but their effect is richer and more festive. Here we also find some sculpture. On the four pendentives of the central dome are large roundels with terracotta reliefs of the evangelists that are sometimes considered to have been designed by Brunelleschi himself. On the walls are 12 smaller reliefs of the apostles, which Vasari is probably right in giving to Lucca della Robbia and his shop (compare fig. 12-11). Despite their obvious program, these reliefs are not essential to the design of the chapel. Brunelleschi provided the frames, but he may not have intended them to be filled with sculpture, even though Donatello had provided similar reliefs for the roundels in the Old

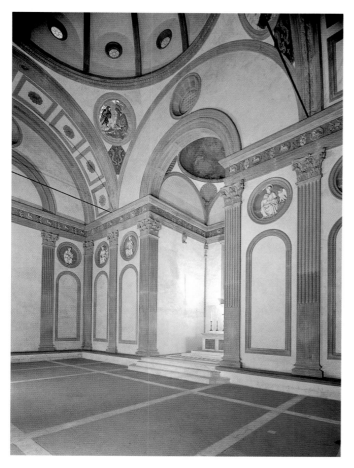

12-25. Interior of the Pazzi Chapel

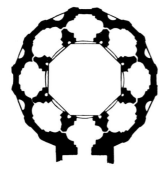

12-26. Filippo Brunelleschi. Plan of Sta. Maria degli Angeli, Florence. 1434–37

details in the plan. It is nevertheless clear that Brunelleschi has recaptured the ancient Roman principle of the "sculptured" wall. The dome was to rest on eight heavy piers that belong to the same mass of masonry from which the eight chapels have been "excavated." Both the wall and the space are charged with energy, and the plan reveals the precarious balance created by their pressures and counterpressures. In concept, Sta. Maria degli Angeli went so far beyond Brunelleschi's previous work that it must have bewildered his contemporaries. It had, in fact, no echoes until the end of the century, in the architecture of Leonardo da Vinci and the young Donato Bramante (see pages 458–460). While he continued to oversee these and other projects, Brunelleschi was employed after 1445 mainly at the cathedral, to which he contributed the very Roman-looking semicircular structures (called exedras) over the niches on either side of the transept arms (see fig. 11-35). These, too, did not bear fruit until Bramante's work.

MICHELOZZO. Brunelleschi's growing classicism ought to have ideally suited his old patron, Cosimo de' Medici, who had been compared favorably by humanists to the great patrons of Greece and Rome. Since the 1420s the Medici family had gained such power that they were in practice, if not by law, the rulers of Florence. But the Medici rejected Brunelleschi's design for their huge new palace. Instead the commission was awarded to the younger architect Michelozzo di Bartolomeo (1396–1472), who had first established his reputation as a sculptor after working with both Ghiberti and Donatello. His design (fig. 12-27) recalls

Sacristy. Instead, they may very well have been planned "blind," like the recessed panels below them. In any case, the strong link between architecture and sculpture (never as strong in Italy as in Northern Europe during the Middle Ages) had been broken. Brunelleschi's conception of architecture as the visual counterpart of musical harmonies did not permit sculpture to play a more prominent role than we see here.

In the mid-1430s, when the Cathedral dome was nearing completion, Brunelleschi's career entered a new phase in the church of Sta. Maria degli Angeli (fig. 12-26). The domed, central-plan church—the first of the Renaissance—was inspired by the round and polygonal structures of Roman and Early Christian times. In many respects it perfects ideas explored in the Pazzi Chapel and the Old Sacristy. Because of financial problems, however, the church was not completed above the ground floor. We therefore cannot be sure of the design of the upper part, or even of some

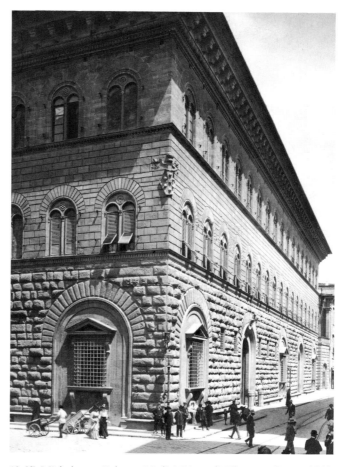

12-27. Michelozzo. Palazzo Medici-Riccardi, Florence. Begun 1444

the fortresslike Florentine palaces of old, and it was precisely this conservatism that appealed to the Medici. (The windows on the ground floor were added by Michelangelo in 1516–17 and extended by the Riccardi family in the seventeenth century.) However, the type has been transformed (compare fig. 11-39). The three stories form a graded sequence, each complete in itself. The lowest is built of rough-hewn, "rusticated" masonry with indented joints, like the Palazzo Vecchio; the second has smooth-surfaced blocks also with indented joints; and the third has an unbroken surface. On top of the structure rests, like a lid, a strongly projecting cornice like those of Roman temples. The change in style reflects a change in purpose: unlike Gothic palaces, which functioned partly as businesses and warehouses, the Palazzo Medici-Riccardi served mainly as a residence, although banking was conducted on the ground floor. Thus the large courtyard that dominates the interior is ceremonial rather than commercial. Being private, not public, it is entirely Brunelleschian in appearance.

LEONE BATTISTA ALBERTI. After the death of Brunelleschi in 1446, Leone Battista Alberti (1404–1472) emerged as the foremost architect in Italy. Like Brunelleschi's, his career had been long delayed, although for very different reasons. Highly educated in mathematics, classical literature, and philosophy, he was both a priest and a person of the world. Although the son of a wealthy Florentine merchant, he was born and raised in Genoa. After receiving his degree in canon law at the University of Bologna in 1428, he entered the papal court in Rome and spent the rest of his career in the Church. Alberti was a gifted writer on a wide range of subjects. He wrote an essay on moral philosophy ("On the Family," begun 1432) and one on geography (c. 1435), which lays out rules for surveying and mapping that were widely used during the rest of the Renaissance.

Until he was 40 Alberti seems to have been interested in the fine arts only as a scholar and theorist. Following a visit to Florence as part of the papal court in 1434, he became close to the leading artists of his day. As a result, he authored the first Renaissance treatises on sculpture (written c. 1433, published in 1464) and painting (written and published in 1435). *On Painting* (which is dedicated to Brunelleschi and refers to "our dear friend" Donatello) includes the first systematic treatment of linear perspective. [See Primary Sources, no. 40, page 644.] During a stay at the court of Ferrara in 1438, he was asked to restore Vitruvius' treatise on architecture, then known in various manuscripts. Upon his return to Rome five years later, he began a systematic study of the monuments of ancient Rome that led to the *Ten Books on Architecture* (finished 1452, published 1485)—the first book of its kind since Vitruvius', on which it is modeled. [See Primary Sources, no. 41, page 644.]

Alberti began to practice architecture as an amateur but soon became a professional of outstanding ability. The design for the Palazzo Rucellai (fig. 12-28), his first important project, may be Alberti's critique of the slightly earlier Medici Palace by Michelozzo (see fig. 12-27). He was responsible only for the exterior; the rest was probably the work of the sculptor Bernardo Rosellino. Again we see three stories topped by a heavy cornice, but the treatment is more strictly classical, especially on the ground floor, which con-

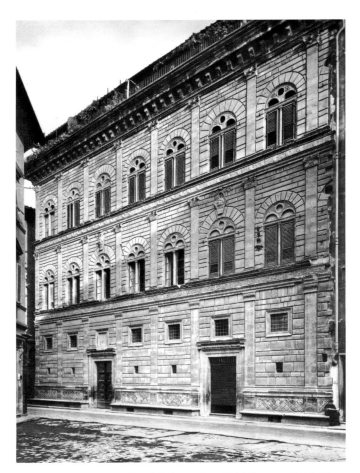

12-28. Leone Battista Alberti. Palazzo Rucellai, Florence. 1446–51

trasts sharply with the rustication of the Medici facade. It consists of three orders of pilasters, separated by wide architraves, in imitation of the Colosseum (see fig. 7-11). Yet the pilasters are so flat that they remain part of the wall, and the facade seems to be one surface on which the artist projects a linear diagram of the Colosseum exterior. Here Alberti was trying to resolve what became a fundamental issue of Renaissance architecture: how to apply a classical system to the exterior of a nonclassical structure. Whether Brunelleschi ever dealt with this problem is hard to say. Only his exterior for the Pazzi Chapel survives (see fig. 12-22), but it is too heavily altered to permit general conclusions. Be that as it may, Alberti's solution emphasizes the wall surface by reducing the classical system to a network of incised lines in order to impose a sense of unity.

For his first church exterior, Alberti tried a very different approach. Around 1450 Sigismondo Malatesta, lord of Rimini, commissioned him to turn the Gothic church of S. Francesco into a "temple of fame" and a burial site for himself, his wife, and members of his court. Alberti encased the older building in a Renaissance shell. The sides consist of deeply recessed arched niches containing stone sarcophagi (fig. 12-29). The facade has three similar niches: the large one framing the central portal and the other two (now filled in) intended to hold the sarcophagi of Sigismondo and his wife.

This scheme was based on the Arch of Constantine (fig. 7-46) and the similar Arch of Augustus in Rimini itself, as were the columns flanking the niches. Unlike the pilasters of the Palazzo

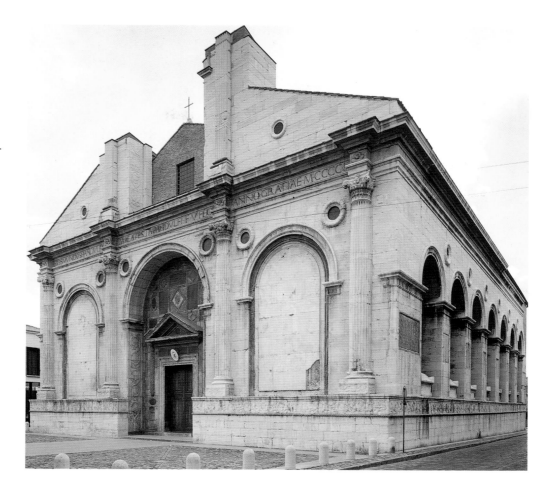

12-29. Leone Battista Alberti.
S. Francesco, Rimini.
Facade designed 1450

Rucellai, these columns are not part of the wall. They project so strongly that we see them as separate from the wall, even though they are partly embedded in it. Moreover, they are set on separate blocks, rather than on the platform supporting the walls. They would have nothing to support if the entablature did not project above each capital. As a result, the vertical rather than the horizontal divisions of the facade are emphasized. We expect each column to support an important element of the upper story. Yet Alberti planned only an arched niche (which remains incomplete) above the portal, with a window and framed by pilasters. Thus the second story does not fulfill the promise of the first. However, the church was never finished as designed, and the great dome intended to crown it was never built. Its appearance is known from a commemorative medal issued in 1450, the year the church was begun (fig. 12-30).

Like most of Alberti's work, S. Francesco was a remodeling project, as was his next undertaking: the facade of Sta. Maria Novella in Florence, begun in around 1456 (fig. 12-31), the parish church of the Rucellai. The exterior of this Dominican church, built largely between 1278 and 1350, had been left unfinished above the row of polychromed Gothic niches, with their Gothic portals. Like those on S. Francesco, these niches were intended as tombs for family members. (They were extended by walls on either side.) Because of its associations with the antique (see pages 285–86), polychromy enabled Alberti to use a surprisingly classical vocabulary that nevertheless seems entirely harmonious with

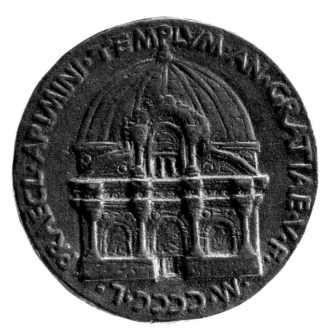

12-30. S. Francesco, Rimini medal of 1450 by Matteo dei Pasti. Bronze, diameter 1⁹⁄₁₆" (4.0 cm). The British Museum, London

the Gothic lower tier. The result brings to mind not only Florence Cathedral (fig. 11-35) but also the Baptistery of S. Giovanni (fig. 10-19) and the Romanesque Florentine church S. Miniato, especially in its emphatic arcades.

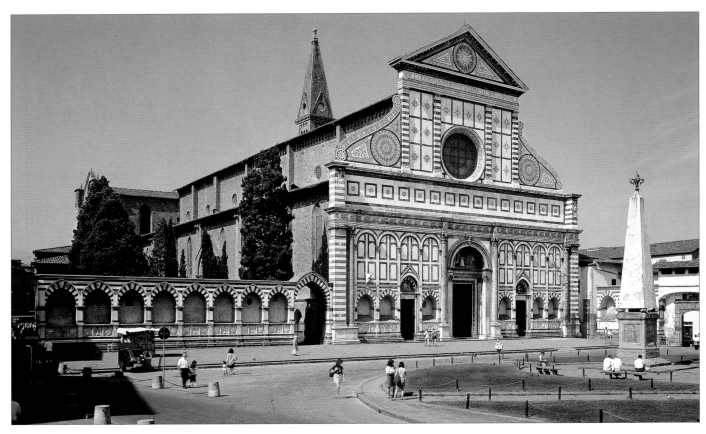

12-31. Leone Battista Alberti. S. Maria Novella, Florence. 1456–1470

Other than the doorways and giant oculus, which were fixed, Alberti's facade bears only a general relation to the rest of the church, which was famous for the refined proportions of the nave. By refusing to be bound by the original structure, the architect conceived the main masses as a complex system of squares. For example, the height equals the width; the walls flanking the extraordinarily classical main portal are squared; and the miniature "temple" atop the tall frieze, so reminiscent of one on S. Miniato, likewise fits within a square. The real stroke of genius is Alberti's use of graceful scrolls to bridge the gap between the temple and the tall frieze. This simple device, which was to prove extremely influential (compare fig. 14-31), is so clear, so elegant that we wonder why no one had thought of it before. It also helps to disguise the loose fit of the facade with the main body of the church by hiding the clerestory. Here again the architect was thinking in terms of squares, for the height of these scrolls equals the width.

Alberti's ultimate goal was to superimpose a classical temple front on the traditional basilican church facade. (For the medieval approach to this task, see the facade of Pisa Cathedral in fig. 10-17.) However, the classical system of S. Francesco retains too much of its ancient Roman character to fit the basilican shape, while Sta. Maria Novella remains too Romanesque in flavor, despite its abundant classical details. Only toward the end of his career did Alberti achieve this seemingly impossible feat: in the majestic facade of S. Andrea at Mantua (fig. 12-32), his last work, designed in 1470 for Lodovico Gonzaga, Duke of Mantua. He superimposed the triumphal-arch motif, now with a huge recessed center niche, in place of a colonnade upon a classical temple front (compare fig. 7-2). As on the exterior of the Palazzo Rucellai, he

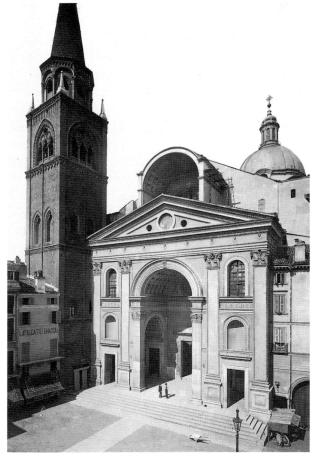

12-32. Leone Battista Alberti. S. Andrea, Mantua. Designed 1470

used flat pilasters that stress the primacy of the wall surface. Here, however, they are clearly set off from their surroundings. There are two sizes. The smaller pilasters support the arch over the huge central niche. The larger ones are linked with the unbroken architrave and the strongly outlined pediment. They form what is known as a **colossal order** (meaning that it is more than one story high). Extending across all three stories of the facade, it balances the horizontal and vertical elements of the design.

So intent was Alberti on creating a unified facade that he inscribed the entire design within a square, even though it is much lower than the nave of the church. (The effect of the west wall protruding above the pediment is more disturbing in photographs than at street level, where it can hardly be seen.) While the facade is distinct from the main body of the structure, it offers a "preview" of the interior, where the same colossal order, the same proportions, and the same triumphal-arch motif reappear on the walls of the nave (fig. 12-33).

Compared with Brunelleschi's S. Lorenzo (fig. 12-21), the plan (fig. 12-34) is extraordinarily compact. Had the church been completed as planned, the difference would be even stronger. Alberti's design had no transept, dome, or choir, all of which were added in the mid-eighteenth century; there was only a nave ending in an apse. Following the example of the Basilica of Constantine (see figs. 7-16–7-18), the aisles are replaced by alternating large and small vaulted chapels. There is no clerestory. The colossal pilasters and the arches of the large chapels support a coffered barrel vault of impressive size. (The nave is as wide as the facade.) Here Alberti has drawn upon his memories of the massive vaulted halls in ancient Roman baths and basilicas, but he interprets these models freely. No longer is their authority absolute. Instead, they serve as a storehouse of motifs to be used at will. Liberated from having to quote his sources literally, Alberti was able to create a structure that can truly be called a "Christian temple."

CENTRAL-PLAN CHURCHES. Because it occupies the site of an older basilican church (note the Gothic campanile next to the facade), S. Andrea does not conform to the ideal shape of sacred buildings as defined in Alberti's *Treatise on Architecture*. There Alberti explains that their plan should be either circular or derived from the circle (square, hexagon, octagon, and so forth). The reason is that the circle is the perfect, as well as the most natural, figure and therefore a direct image of divine reason. This claim rests, of course, on Alberti's faith in the God-given validity of mathematical proportions (discussed on page 423). He took to heart Virtuvius' belief that architecture must employ the same principles of symmetry and proportion as a "well-shaped man." (In support of this rule, Vitruvius pointed out that a man with arms and legs outstretched fits into a circle or square—an image later visualized by Leonardo da Vinci in a famous drawing.) How could Alberti reconcile his belief in the central plan with historical evidence? After all, the standard form of both ancient temples and Christian basilicas was longitudinal (see fig. 7-3). But, he reasoned, the basilican plan became traditional only because the early Christians worshiped in private Roman basilicas. Since pagan basilicas were associated with the dispensing of justice, which originates from God, he granted that their shape has some relationship to

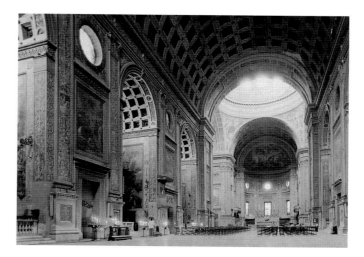

12-33. Leone Battista Alberti. Interior of S. Andrea

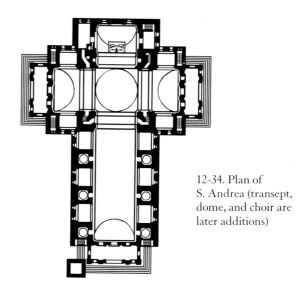

12-34. Plan of S. Andrea (transept, dome, and choir are later additions)

sacred architecture. However, since they cannot rival the sublime beauty of the temple, their purpose is human rather than divine.

In favoring the central plan, Alberti relied instead on the Pantheon (see figs. 7-12–7-15), the round temple at Tivoli (see figs. 7-4 and 7-5), and domed mausoleums, which he mistook for temples. Moreover, he asked, had not the early Christians themselves acknowledged the sacred nature of these structures by converting them to their own use? Here he could point to such buildings as Sta. Costanza (see figs. 8-7–8-9), the Pantheon itself (which had been used as a church ever since the early Middle Ages), and the Baptistery in Florence (then thought to be a former temple of Mars).

Alberti's ideal church must have such a harmonious design that it would be a revelation of God and would arouse pious contemplation in the worshiper. It should stand alone, above its surroundings. Light should enter through openings placed high, for only the sky should be seen through them. The fact that such a structure was not well suited to Catholic ritual meant little to Alberti. A church, he believed, must embody "divine proportion," which could be attained only by the central plan.

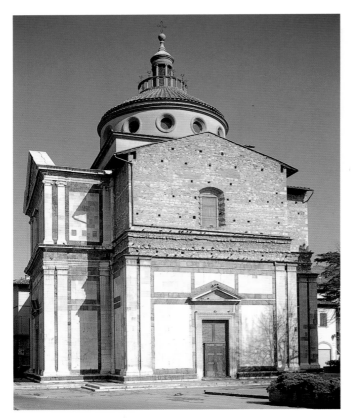

12-35. Giuliano da Sangallo. Sta. Maria delle Carceri, Prato. Begun 1485

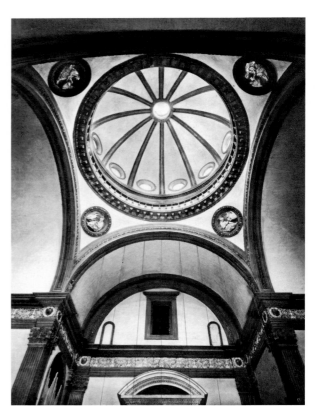

12-37. Interior of Sta. Maria delle Carceri

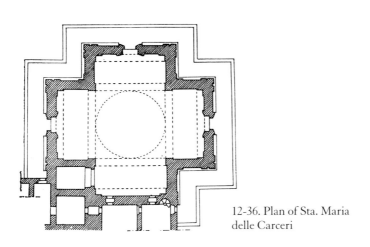

12-36. Plan of Sta. Maria delle Carceri

When Alberti first set forth these ideas in his treatise, about 1450, he could have cited only Brunelleschi's unfinished Sta. Maria degli Angeli as a modern example of a central-plan church (see fig. 12-26). In 1460 he undertook a church in the shape of a Greek cross for the Duke of Mantua, but the result was unsatisfactory and the building likewise was never completed. Toward the end of the century, after his treatise became widely known, the central-plan church gained wide acceptance. Between 1500 and 1525 it reigned supreme in High Renaissance architecture.

GIULIANO DA SANGALLO. It is no coincidence that Sta. Maria delle Carceri in Prato (see figs. 12-35–12-37) was begun in 1485, the date of the first printed edition of Alberti's treatise. Its architect, Giuliano da Sangallo (c. 1443–1516), must have been an admirer of Brunelleschi. Many features of the interior and the plan recall the Pazzi Chapel (see figs. 12-23 and 12-25). The basic shape of his structure, however, conforms to Alberti's ideal. Except for the dome, the entire church would fit neatly inside a cube: its height (up to the drum) equals its length and width. By cutting into the corners of this cube, Giuliano has formed a Greek cross, a plan he preferred for its symbolic value. The dome on pendentives is supported by the barrel-vaulted arms (compare fig. 8-31). Yet the dark ring of the drum does not quite touch the arches, so that the dome seems to hover weightlessly, like the domes of Byzantine churches (compare figs. 8-43 and 8-45). There can be no doubt that Giuliano was influenced by Byzantine architecture. Moreover, he clearly wanted his dome to accord with the age-old tradition of the Dome of Heaven. The single round opening in the center and the 12 on the perimeter clearly refer to Christ and the apostles. Brunelleschi had anticipated this design in the Pazzi Chapel, but Giuliano's dome, which crowns a perfectly symmetrical structure, conveys its symbolism far more strikingly.

Painting

MASACCIO. Early Renaissance painting did not appear until the mid-1420s, a decade later than Donatello's *St. Mark* and some six years after Brunelleschi's first designs for S. Lorenzo. The new style was launched by a young genius named Masaccio (Tommaso di Giovanni di Simone Guidi, 1401–1428), who was only 21 years old at the time and who died just six years later. The fact that the Early Renaissance was already well established in sculpture and architecture made Masaccio's task easier but his achievement was nonetheless remarkable.

Masaccio's first mature work is a fresco of 1425 in Sta. Maria Novella (fig. 12-38) depicting the Holy Trinity in the company of the Virgin, St. John the Evangelist, and two donors who kneel on either side. The lowest section, linked with a tomb below, shows a skeleton lying on a sarcophagus. The inscription (in Italian) reads, "What you are, I once was; what I am, you will become." With its large scale, severe composition and sculptural volume, the style brings to mind the art of Giotto and his school (compare figs. 11-79 and 11-86). For Masaccio, however, Giotto was only a starting point. In Giotto's work, body and drapery form a single unit. In contrast, Masaccio's figures, like Donatello's, are "clothed nudes," whose drapery falls like real fabric. The Christ still follows the example set by Duccio's *Maestà* altarpiece, but the nearly sculptural treatment recalls an early *Crucifixion* by Brunelleschi that translates the same model into solid form. Like Donatello and Brunelleschi, Masaccio had a thorough knowledge of anatomy not seen since Roman art. It is tempting to think that they may have initiated the modern practice of dissecting cadavers to study the inner workings of the human body.

The up-to-date setting reveals the artist's understanding of Brunelleschi's new architecture and of scientific perspective. For the first time in history, we are given all the data needed to measure the depth of this painted interior, to draw its plan, and to duplicate the structure in three dimensions. It is, in short, the earliest example of a *rational* space in painting. This barrel-vaulted chamber is not a shallow niche, but a deep space in which the figures could move freely. As in Ghiberti's relief panel *The Story of Jacob and Esau* (see fig. 12-10), the picture space is independent of the figures. They inhabit the space, but they do not create it. Take away the architecture and you take away the figures' space. We could go even further and say that scientific perspective depends on this particular kind of architecture, so different from the Gothic.

First we note that all the lines perpendicular to the picture plane converge toward a point below the foot of the Cross, on the platform that supports the kneeling donors. To see the fresco correctly, we must face this point, which is at normal eye level, somewhat more than five feet above the floor of the church. The figures within the chamber are five feet tall, slightly less than life-size, while the donors, who are closer to us, are fully lifesize. The framework therefore is "lifesize," too, since it is directly behind the donors. The distance between the pilasters equals the span of the barrel vault, seven feet. The circumference of the arc over this span is 11 feet. That arc is subdivided by eight square coffers that are one foot wide and nine ridges four inches wide. If we apply these measurements to the length of the barrel vault (it has seven coffers, the nearest being hidden behind the entrance arch), we find that the vaulted area is nine feet deep.

We can now draw a complete floor and ceiling plan (fig. 12-39). However, the position of God the Father is puzzling at first. His arms support the Cross, close to the front plane, while his feet rest on a ledge attached to a wall. How far back is this

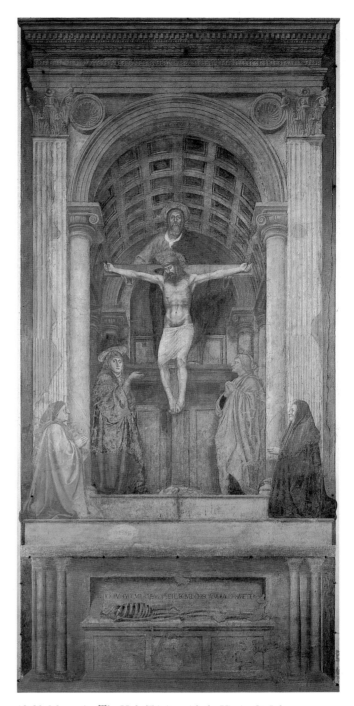

12-38. Masaccio. *The Holy Trinity with the Virgin, St. John, and Two Donors*. 1425. Fresco. Sta. Maria Novella, Florence

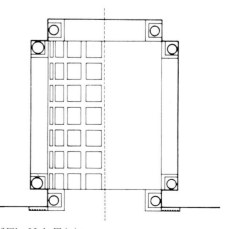

12-39. Plan of *The Holy Trinity*

structure? Masaccio must have intended to locate the ledge directly behind the Cross, as we can tell by the strong shadow that St. John casts on the wall below. What, then, is God standing on? Most likely it is the tomb of Christ, which is placed at a right angle to the wall and measures five and a half feet high by four feet wide and six or seven feet deep.

We realize, then, that *The Holy Trinity* is a restatement of the promise of eternal life in the Bardi chapel frescoes by Maso di Banco and Taddeo Gaddi (see fig. 11-88). But instead of combining painting with an actual tomb, Masaccio has created an illusion that is far more convincing, even though the niche is treated as a separate realm that the viewer, like the two donors, cannot enter. The rational pictorial space plays a key role in other ways. For Masaccio, as for Brunelleschi, it must have been a symbol of the universe ruled by divine reason. This attitude further explains the subdued atmosphere, the calm gesture of the Virgin as she points to the Crucifixion, and the solemn grandeur of God the Father as he holds it effortlessly. The fervent hope of salvation portrayed in the Bardi chapel (note the prayerful poses of the deceased) is presented here as a conviction based on reason as well as faith. Such, indeed, was the purpose of Renaissance humanism, in which the artist now assumed a position comparable to that of a philosopher.

The largest group of Masaccio's works to come down to us are frescoes in the Brancacci Chapel in Sta. Maria del Carmine, Florence (figs. 12-40 and 12-41), which are devoted to the life of St. Peter. The most famous of them is *The Tribute Money,* located in the upper tier (fig. 12-42). It depicts the story in the Gospel of Matthew (17:24–27) as a continuous narrative. In the center, Christ instructs Peter to catch a fish, whose mouth will contain the tribute money for the tax collector. On the far left, in the distance, Peter takes the coin from the fish's mouth, and on the right he gives it to the tax collector. Since the lower edge of the fresco is almost 14 feet above the floor of the chapel, the artist could not assume an ideal vantage point. Instead, we must imagine that we are looking directly at the central vanishing point, which is behind the head of Christ. Oddly enough, this feat is so easy that we take note of it only if we stop to analyze it. But then, any pictorial illusion is an imaginary experience. No matter how eager we are to believe in a picture, we never mistake it for reality, just as we never confuse a statue with a living thing. If we could see *The Tribute Money* from the top of a ladder, the illusion of reality would not improve very much, because it does not depend mainly on scientific perspective, although it is present in the building and continues in the mountains that merge almost imperceptibly with the architecture. Masaccio controls the flow of light, which comes from the right, where the window of the chapel is located. He also uses atmospheric perspective in the subtle tones of the landscape. The effect recalls the setting a decade earlier in Donatello's small relief of St. George (compare fig. 12-3).

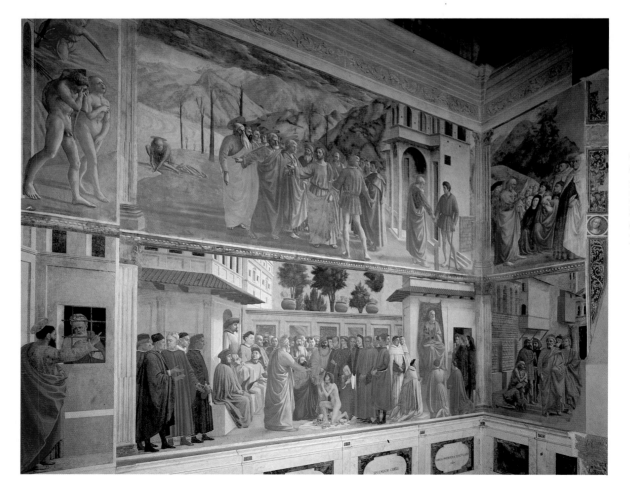

12-40. Left wall of Brancacci Chapel, with frescoes by Masaccio. Sta. Maria del Carmine, Florence

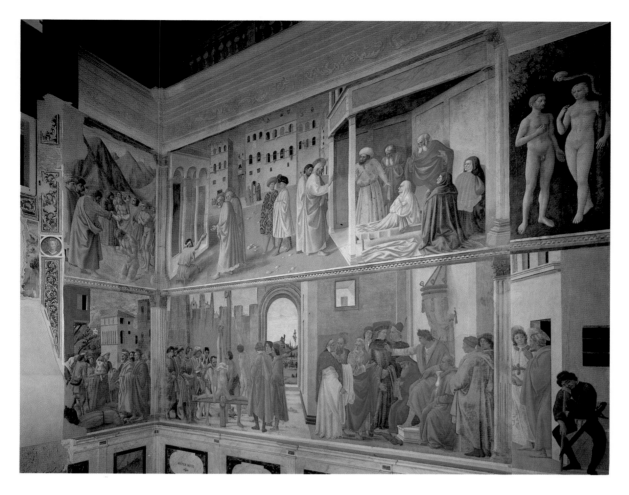

12-41.
Right wall of
Brancacci
Chapel, with
frescoes by
Masolino and
Filippino
Lippi.

(BELOW)
12-42.
Masaccio.
*The Tribute
Money.* c. 1427.
Fresco.
Brancacci
Chapel

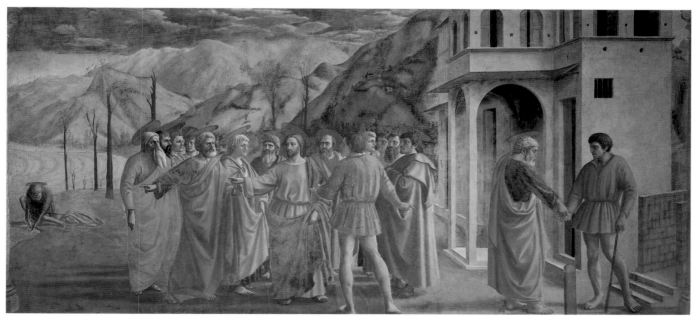

The figures in *The Tribute Money,* even more than those in the *Trinity* fresco, show Masaccio's ability to merge the weight and volume of Giotto's figures with the new functional view of body and drapery. All stand in balanced contrapposto. Fine vertical lines scratched in the plaster establish the axis of each figure from the head to the heel of the engaged leg. In accord with this dignified approach, the figures seem rather static. The narrative is conveyed by intense glances and a few strong gestures, rather than by physical movement. But in *The Expulsion from Paradise* just to the left (fig. 12-43, page 434), Masaccio proves that he can show the human body in motion. The tall, narrow format leaves little room for a spatial setting. The gate of paradise is barely indicated, and in the background are a few shadowy, barren slopes. Yet the soft, atmospheric modeling and especially the boldly foreshortened angel

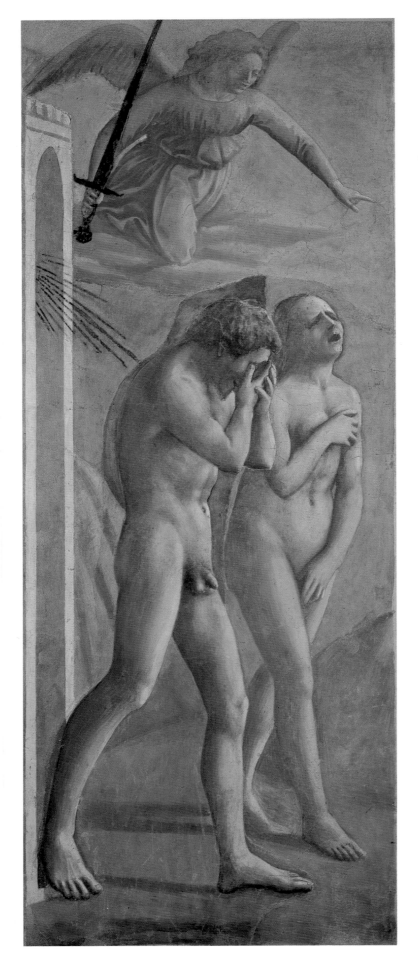

12-43. Masaccio. *The Expulsion from Paradise.* c. 1427. Fresco. Brancacci Chapel

(compare Ghiberti's, fig. 11-65) convey a sense of unlimited space. Masaccio's grief-stricken Adam and Eve, although hardly dependent on ancient models, are striking representations of the beauty and power of the nude human form. Their closest kin are to be found in Jacopo della Quercia's treatment of the same subject in his reliefs for Bologna (compare fig. 12-18).

It seems hard to believe that Gentile da Fabriano had completed *The Adoration of the Magi* only a few years before (see fig. 11-98). Masaccio's style abandons the lyrical grace of the International Gothic. Yet he shared the work on the Brancacci Chapel with a much older artist, Masolino (documented 1423–died 1440), who had been strongly influenced by Gentile. The two nevertheless worked well together and even collaborated on some of the frescoes. (The head of Christ in *The Tribute Money* is by Masolino, for instance.) However, Masolino continued to use the International Style. Thus the figures in the upper tier of the right wall (see fig. 12-41) are simply larger versions of those in Pietro Lorenzetti's *Birth of the Virgin* (see fig. 11-82). The setting, too, remains Gothic in character, despite the scientific perspective (compare fig. 11-84). Masolino constructs a theatrical space that remains separate from his figures, whereas Masaccio's are closely tied to their surroundings, despite their independence.

Nowhere is the contrast between the two artists' styles more striking than in *The Temptation* by Masolino (visible in the upper right of fig. 12-41). This work forms an enchanting companion to the anguish in Masaccio's *Expulsion from Paradise*. Despite their contrapposto, the figures of Adam and Eve are no more classical than Adam in figure 12-19. In fact, they may be derived from a similar source, for Masolino was unable to treat the nude in convincing organic terms. In comparing these works, we see that Masaccio, like Donatello, captured the substance of antiquity without simply relying on its forms. Masaccio left for Rome before he could finish the Brancacci Chapel; Masolino's work, too, was interrupted for several years. The fresco cycle was finally completed near the end of the century by Filippino Lippi (1457/8–1504), who was responsible for the lower tier to either side.

While he preferred murals, Masaccio was skilled in panel painting. The many panels of his large altarpiece, or polyptych, made in 1426 for the Carmelite church in Pisa are now dispersed among various collections. The center panel (fig. 12-44) is a more fully developed restatement of his earliest known work. The *Madonna Enthroned* is of the monumental Florentine type introduced by Cimabue and reshaped by Giotto (see figs. 11-72 and 11-80). The usual elements, including the gold ground, are present: a large, high-backed throne with angels on each side (here only two). Despite these traditional elements, the painting is revolutionary in several respects. The kneeling angels in Giotto's *Madonna* have become lute players seated on the lowest step of the throne. The Christ Child no longer blesses us but eats a bunch of grapes, a symbol of the **Passion** (the suffering of Jesus in his last days). (The grapes refer to wine, which represents the Savior's blood in the sacrament of the **Eucharist**.) Above all, the powerful proportions of the figures make them much more concrete and impressive than even Giotto's, although they are hardly beautiful by the standards of the International Style. This is nevertheless the

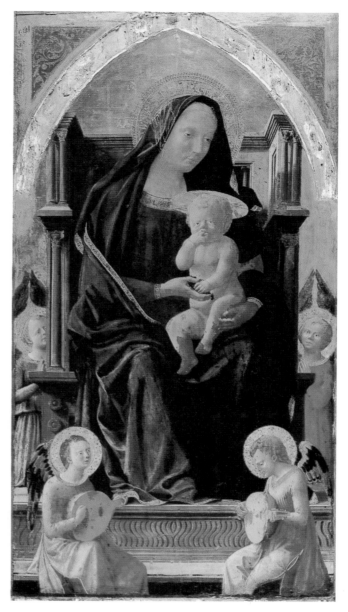

12-44. Masaccio. *Madonna Enthroned*. 1426. Oil on panel, 56 x 29" (142 x 73.6 cm). The National Gallery, London

most convincingly human Christ child we have yet seen. In this regard, Masaccio set a new standard that was soon taken up by other artists such as Fra Filippo Lippi (see fig. 12-52).

In light of the *Trinity* fresco, it is no surprise that Masaccio replaces Giotto's ornate but frail Gothic throne with a solid and plain stone seat in the style of Brunelleschi, or that he makes expert use of perspective. (Note especially the two lutes.) We are less prepared for the delicate yet precise rendering of the light on the surfaces. Within the picture, sunlight enters from the left, like the glow of the setting sun. (We can determine its exact angle from the shadows on the throne.) Hence there are no harsh contrasts between light and shade. The use of half-shadows results in a rich scale of transitional hues. The light retains its descriptive function while imposing a common tonality and mood on the picture.

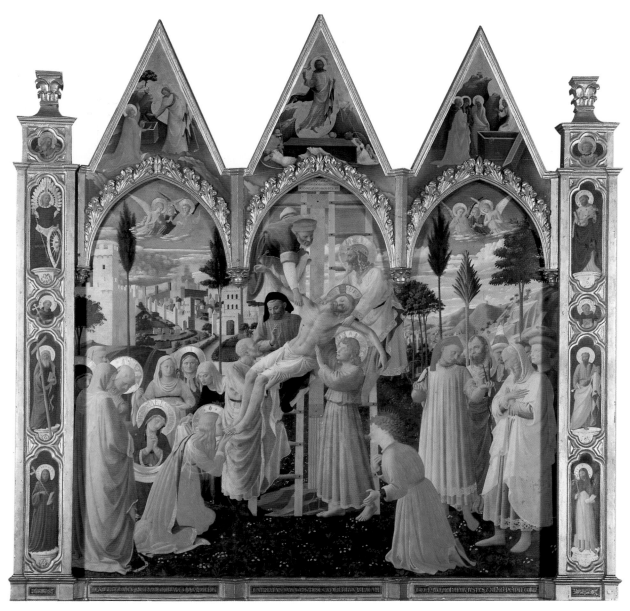

12-45. Fra Angelico. *Deposition*. Probably early 1440s. Oil on panel, 9'1¼" x 9'4¼" (275 x 285 cm). Museo di S. Marco, Florence

TEMPERA AND OIL TECHNIQUES. These refinements were made possible by oil painting. The basic medium of medieval panel painting had been **tempera,** in which the finely ground pigments were mixed ("tempered") with diluted egg yolk. It produced a thin, tough, quick-drying coat that was well suited to the medieval taste for high-keyed flat color surfaces. However, in tempera the different tones on the panel could not be blended smoothly, and the continuous progression of values necessary for three-dimensional effects was difficult to achieve. Also, dark shades tended to look muddy. These were major drawbacks that were overcome by replacing the diluted egg yolk with oil. Medieval artists knew about oil, but they used it only for special purposes, such as coating stone surfaces or painting on metal. Its artistic potential was discovered around the 1420s by the Master of Flémalle and his contemporaries in the North (see page 514). Oil, a viscous, slow-drying medium, can produce a variety of effects, from thin, translucent films (called **glazes**) to a thick layer of creamy, heavy-bodied paint (called **impasto**).

The tones can also yield a continuous scale of hues, including rich velvety dark shades previously unknown. **Oil painting** offers another unique advantage over egg tempera, **encaustic,** and **fresco**: it allows artists the unprecedented ability to change their minds almost at will. Without oil, the conquest of visible reality would have been much more limited. The new medium spread quickly to Italy, where it became the foundation of modern painting. Although pigments continued to be mixed with tempera for some time, oil has been the painter's basic medium ever since.

FRA ANGELICO. Masaccio's early death left a gap that was not soon filled. For more than a decade, the leading painter in Florence was the conservative Fra Angelico (c. 1400–1455), a friar who rose to a high position within his order. ("Fra" means "brother.") We sense his reverential attitude in the large *Deposition* (fig. 12-45), which was probably done for the same chapel as Gentile da Fabriano's *Adoration of the Magi* (see fig. 11-98). Fra Angelico took over the commission from Gentile's contemporary, Lorenzo Monaco. Lorenzo was responsible for the paintings in the sides of the frame and in the triangular pinnacles, but he died before he could complete the altar. The *Deposition* may date anywhere from about 1435 to the early 1440s, for Fra Angelico, like Ghiberti, developed slowly, and his mature style underwent very little change.

This painting is an object of devotion. Fra Angelico retains Masaccio's dignity, directness, and spatial order. Thus his dead Christ is the true heir of the monumental figure in the *Trinity* (fig. 12-38). Yet Fra Angelico's art is something of a paradox. It combines Gothic piety (compare fig. 11-88) with Renaissance grandeur in an atmosphere of calm contemplation. The setting spreads behind the figures like a tapestry. The landscape, with the town in the distance, harks back to the *Allegory of Good Government* by Ambrogio Lorenzetti (see figs. 11-84 and 11-85). The artist also shows his awareness of the achievements of Northerners such as the Limbourg brothers (compare fig. 11-94): he evokes a brilliant sunlit day with striking success. Yet the scene does not seem at all Gothic. It has the same natural light that produces softly modeled forms in Masaccio's *Madonna Enthroned* (fig. 12-44). This light fills the landscape with a sense of wonderment at God's creation, an effect that is wholly Renaissance in spirit. We shall meet it again in the work of Giovanni Bellini (see fig. 12-62), which it anticipates in another respect: the beautiful but uninhabited city in the distance is surely the Heavenly Jerusalem. At the same time, the bright, enamel-like hues, although holdovers from the International Style, look forward to the colorism of Domenico Veneziano.

DOMENICO VENEZIANO. In 1439 a gifted painter from Venice, Domenico Veneziano, settled in Florence. We can only guess at his age, training, and previous work. (He was probably born about 1410 and died in 1461.) He must, however, have been in sympathy with the spirit of Early Renaissance art, for he quickly became an important artist in his new home. His *Madonna and Child with Saints* (fig. 12-46) is one of the earliest examples of a new kind of altar panel, called a *sacra conversazione* ("sacred conversation"), that was invented around 1440 by Fra Angelico and became popular from the mid-fifteenth century on. An enthroned Madonna and Child is framed by architecture and surrounded by saints and sometimes angels, who may converse with her, one another, or the viewer. (The saints are, from left to right, Francis, John the Baptist, Zenobius, the patron saint of Florence, and Lucy, an early Christian martyr who holds a dish containing her eyes.)

We can readily understand the appeal of the sacra conversazione. The architecture is clear and convincing, yet the space it defines is an ideal one elevated above the everyday world. The figures, while echoing the formality of their setting, are linked with each other by a fully human awareness. We are admitted to their presence, but they do not invite us to join them. Like spectators in a theater, we are not allowed "on stage."

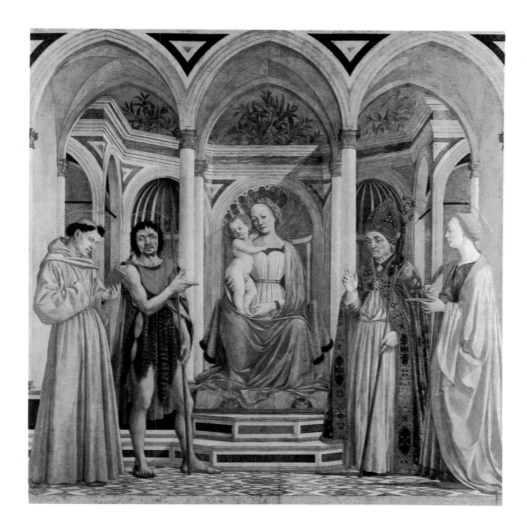

12-46. Domenico Veneziano.
Madonna and Child with Saints.
c. 1455. Oil on panel,
6'10" x 7' (2.08 x 2.13 m).
Galleria degli Uffizi, Florence

The basic elements of our panel were already present in Masaccio's *Holy Trinity* fresco. Domenico must have studied it carefully, for his St. John looks at us while pointing toward the Madonna, repeating the glance and gesture of Masaccio's Virgin. Domenico's perspective setting is worthy of Masaccio's, although the slender proportions and colored inlays of his architecture are more decorative. His figures, too, are balanced and dignified like Masaccio's but less monumental. The slim, sinewy bodies of the male saints, with their highly individualized, expressive faces, show Donatello's influence (see fig. 12-4).

Unlike Masaccio, Domenico treats color as an integral part of his work, and the sacra conversazione is as noteworthy for its palette as for its composition. The blond tonality—its harmony of pink, light green, and white set off by spots of red, blue, and yellow—reconciles the brightness of Gothic panel painting with natural light and perspective space. Like Fra Angelico's, this sacra conversazione takes place outdoors but is set in a kind of loggia (a covered open-air arcade) with sunlight streaming in from the right, as we can tell from the cast shadow behind the Madonna. The surfaces reflect the light so strongly that even the shadowed areas glow with color. While Masaccio had achieved a similar effect in his *Madonna,* here the technique has been applied to a more complex set of forms and combined with Domenico's exquisite color sense. The influence of his distinctive tonality can be seen throughout Florentine painting during the second half of the century.

PIERO DELLA FRANCESCA. When Domenico settled in Florence, he had with him a young assistant from southeastern Tuscany named Piero della Francesca (c. 1420–1492), who became his most important disciple and one of the great artists of the Early Renaissance. Surprisingly, however, Piero left Florence after a few years, never to return. The Florentines seem to have viewed his work as provincial and old-fashioned, and from their point of view they were right. Piero's style, even more than Domenico's, reflected the aims of Masaccio. Piero retained his allegiance to the founder of Italian Renaissance painting throughout his long career, even while Florentine taste developed in a different direction in the years after 1450.

Piero's most impressive work is the fresco cycle in the choir of S. Francesco in Arezzo, painted from about 1452 to 1459 (fig. 12-47). Its many scenes depict the legend of the True Cross (the story of the Cross used for Christ's crucifixion). The section in figure 12-48 shows the empress Helena, mother of Constantine the Great, discovering the True Cross and the crosses of the two thieves who died beside Jesus. (All three had been hidden by enemies of the Faith.) On the left, they are being lifted out of the ground; on the right, the True Cross is identified by its power to bring a dead youth back to life.

Piero's link with Domenico is seen in his colors. The tonality of this fresco, although inherently less luminous than in Domenico's panel, is similarly blond and evokes morning sunlight in much the same way. Since the light enters at a low angle almost in front of the picture, it defines every shape and lends drama to the scene. But Piero's figures have an austere grandeur that recalls Masaccio, or even Giotto, more than Domenico. These men and women seem to belong to a lost heroic race, beautiful and strong—and

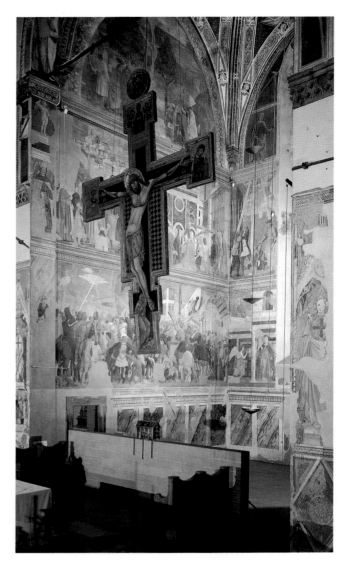

12-47. View into main chapel, with frescoes by Piero della Francesca. S. Francesco, Arezzo

silent. Their inner life is conveyed by glances and gestures, not by facial expressions. They have a gravity that brings to mind Greek sculpture of the Severe style (see fig. 5-51).

How did Piero arrive at these images? They were born of his passion for perspective. More than any other artist of his day, Piero believed in scientific perspective as the basis of painting. In a mathematical treatise that was the first of its kind, he showed how it applied to stereometric (scientifically measured) bodies and architectural shapes, as well as to the human form. This geometric outlook can be seen in all of his work. When he drew a head, an arm, or a piece of drapery, he treated them as variations on spheres, cylinders, cones, cubes, and pyramids. Medieval artists, in contrast, built natural forms on geometric scaffolds (see fig. 11-68). Thus he endowed the visible world with unprecedented clarity and permanence.

PAOLO UCCELLO. In mid-fifteenth-century Florence only one painter shared, and may have helped inspire, Piero's passion for perspective: Paolo Uccello (1397–1475). His *Battle of San Romano* (fig. 12-49) may have influenced the battle scenes in Piero's frescoes at Arezzo (see fig. 12-47). Uccello's design also stresses stereometric shapes. The ground is a gridlike design that is covered with discarded weapons and pieces of armor. They

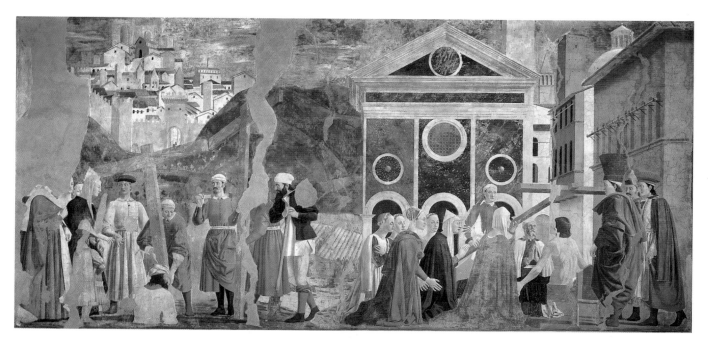

12-48. Piero della Francesca. *The Discovery and Proving of the True Cross.* c. 1455. Fresco. S. Francesco, Arezzo

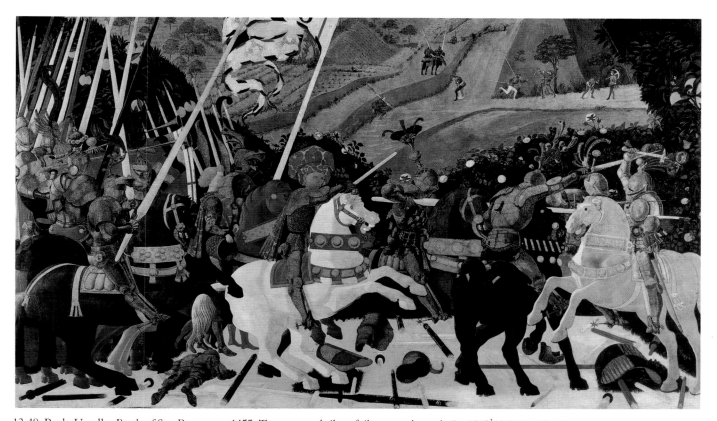

12-49. Paolo Uccello. *Battle of San Romano.* c. 1455. Tempera and silver foil on wood panel, 6' x 10'5¾" (1.8 x 3.2 m). The National Gallery, London

form a display of perspective studies that is neatly arranged to include a fallen soldier. The landscape, too, has been subjected to stereometric abstraction. The panel nevertheless lacks the order and clarity of Piero della Francesca's work. In the hands of Uccello, perspective produces strangely disturbing effects. What unites his picture is not its spatial structure but its surface pattern, which is reinforced by spots of brilliant color and lavish use of gold.

Uccello had been trained in the Gothic International Style. It was only in the 1430s that he was converted to the Early Renaissance outlook by the new science of perspective. He superimposed this technique on his earlier style like a strait-jacket. The result is a fascinating but unstable mixture. As we study this panel, we realize that surface and space are more at war than the mounted soldiers, who get entangled with each other in all sorts of implausible ways.

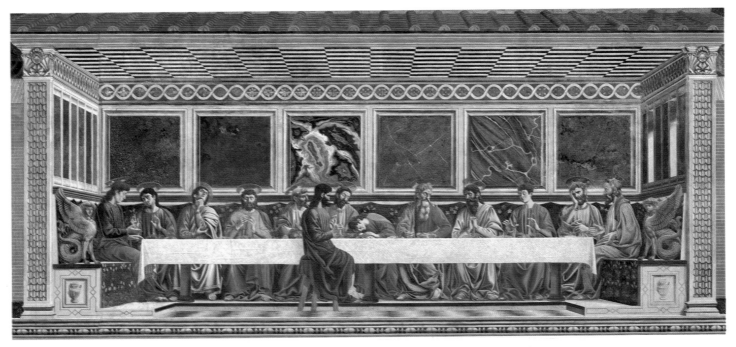

12-50. Andrea del Castagno. *The Last Supper.* c. 1445–50. Fresco. S. Apollonia, Florence

ANDREA DEL CASTAGNO. The third dimension held no difficulties for Andrea del Castagno (c. 1423–1457), the most gifted Florentine painter of his day. Less subtle but more forceful than Domenico Veneziano, Castagno recaptures some of Masaccio's monumentality in his *Last Supper* (fig. 12-50). In this fresco, one of a set he painted in the refectory (dining hall) of the convent of S. Apollonia, the event is set in a richly paneled alcove that is designed as an extension of the real space. As in medieval representations of the subject, Judas sits alone on the near side of the table. The symmetry of the architecture, emphasized by the colorful inlays, imposes a similar order among the figures and threatens to imprison them. There is little communication among the apostles—only a glance here, a gesture there—so that a brooding silence hovers over the scene.

Castagno, too, must have felt confined by a scheme imposed on him by the demands of both tradition and perspective. He used a daring device to break the symmetry and focus the drama of the scene. Five of the six marble panels on the wall behind the table are filled with subdued colored marble, but above the heads of St. Peter, Judas, and Christ its veining is so garish and explosive that a bolt of lightning seems to descend on Judas' head.

Shortly before his death, Castagno painted the *David* on a leather shield that was used only for display (fig. 12-51). Its owner probably wanted to suggest an analogy between himself and the biblical hero, since David is here defiant as well as victorious. This dynamic linear style is far removed from Masaccio's. Solid volume and statuesque immobility have given way to graceful movement, conveyed by the pose and the windblown hair and drapery. The modeling of the figure has been minimized. The forms are now defined mainly by outlines, so that the *David* seems in relief rather than in the round.

FRA FILIPPO LIPPI. This dynamic linear style owed much to Fra Filippo Lippi (c. 1406–1469). Unlike Fra Angelico, his

slightly older contemporary, he did not take his vows seriously, even though his subjects are entirely religious. Over the course of his long career, he absorbed the full range of Italian art—from Giotto and the great Sienese painters through Masaccio (with whom he had close contact early on), Domenico Veneziano, Piero della Francesca, and even the Venetian Andrea Mantegna (see pages 447–48). But he was also decisively influenced by Early Renaissance sculpture and Flemish art, which he must have seen during his visit to northeastern Italy in the mid-1430s. Thus Fra Filippo is at once the most representative and the most individual of Florentine painters in the middle decades of the fifteenth century.

Madonna and Child with the Birth of the Virgin (fig. 12-52) shows Lippi's mature style at its best. The circular shape (called a "tondo") was reserved for private devotional images. This large, handsome panel was probably commissioned by the Florentine banker Lionardo Bartolini to celebrate the birth of a member of his family. Saint Anne, Mary's mother, was the patron saint of childbirth. The Madonna and infant Jesus are presented as the ideal mother and child. The group reminds us of Masaccio's *Madonna* (fig. 12-44) in several ways, but Fra Filippo's artistic temperament was clearly very different. He replaces Masaccio's monumentality and severity with a new intimacy. The youthful Mary has a slender elegance and gentle sweetness that come from Domenico Veneziano (compare fig. 12-46). The stagelike composition is surprisingly cluttered and the perspective undisciplined. (There are several vanishing points.) Here Fra Filippo reduces the divine to the mundane, in keeping with the painting's purpose. In the background to the left is a domestic interior showing the Virgin's birth—note the bed of St. Anne. Such a wealth of realistic detail can have come only from Late Gothic realism (compare fig. 15-8). To the right is the meeting of Saint Anne and her husband, Saint Joachim, at the Golden Gate of Jerusalem after the angel of the Lord had appeared to them separately and promised them a child in answer to their prayers. For that reason, the elderly, barren couple was

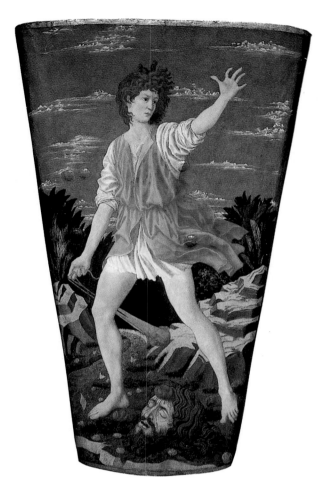

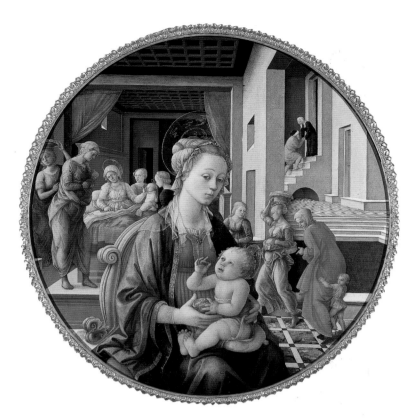

12-52. Fra Filippo Lippi. *Madonna and Child with the Birth of the Virgin* (The Bartolini Tondo). 1452–53. Oil on panel, diameter 53" (134.6 cm). Palazzo Pitti, Florence

12-51. Andrea del Castagno. *David*. c. 1450–57. Tempera on leather on wood, height 45½" (115.8 cm). National Gallery of Art, Washington, D.C. Widener Collection

considered a model of conjugal love and steadfast faith. In contrast to all other depictions of this legend, the event is presented as if it were taking place before the entrance to a private house.

Finally, we note the painter's interest in movement. We see it in the attendants and the drapery. The curly edge of the Virgin's headdress and the curved folds of her mantle streaming to the left, which accentuate her turn to the right, show an emphasis on a graceful decorative quality that has become an end in itself. Such effects are also found in the reliefs of Donatello and Ghiberti: compare *The Feast of Herod* (see fig. 12-5) and *The Story of Jacob and Esau* (see fig. 12-10), which incorporate similarly complex spaces as part of continuous narrative. It is not surprising that these two sculptors had such a strong effect on Florentine painting following Masaccio's death. Age, experience, and prestige gave them an authority unmatched by any painter active at the time. Their influence, and that of the Flemish masters, on Fra Filippo's outlook was of great importance, since he played a vital role in setting the course of Florentine painting during the second half of the century.

SANDRO BOTTICELLI. The climax of the trend established by Lippi's *Birth of the Virgin* and Castagno's *David* came during the final quarter of the century in the art of Sandro Botticelli (1444/5–1510). He was trained by Fra Filippo and influenced by Pollaiuolo. Botticelli soon became the favorite painter of the Medici circle—the group of nobles, scholars, and poets surrounding Lorenzo the Magnificent, the head of the Medici family and, for all practical purposes, the real ruler of the city.

Botticelli painted *The Birth of Venus* (fig. 12-53), his most famous picture, for the young prince Lorenzo de' Medici. (It once hung in Lorenzo's summer villa.) The picture's kinship with Pollaiuolo's *Battle of the Ten Naked Men* (see fig. 12-15) is unmistakable. The shallow modeling and emphasis on outline produce an effect of low relief rather than of solid, three-dimensional shapes. Both works show little concern with deep space. The grove on the right-hand side of the Venus forms a screen much like the ornamental thicket behind the naked men. But the differences are just as striking. Botticelli obviously does not share Pollaiuolo's passion for anatomy. His bodies are drained of all weight, so that they seem to float even when they touch the ground. The picture seems to deny the basic values of the founders of Early Renaissance art, yet it does not look medieval. The bodies, however ethereal, remain voluptuous. They are genuine nudes, with full freedom of movement. (See the discussion on pages 413 and 419.)

Botticelli's *Venus* is derived from a variant of the *Knidian Aphrodite* by Praxiteles (see fig. 5-69). The subject itself was inspired by the Homeric *Hymn to Aphrodite,* which begins: "I shall sing of beautiful Aphrodite . . . who is obeyed by the flowery sea-girt land of Cyprus, whither soft Zephyr and the breeze wafted her in soft foam over the waves. Gently the golden-filleted Horae received her, and clad her in divine garments." Yet no single literary source accounts for the pictorial conception. It owes something as well to

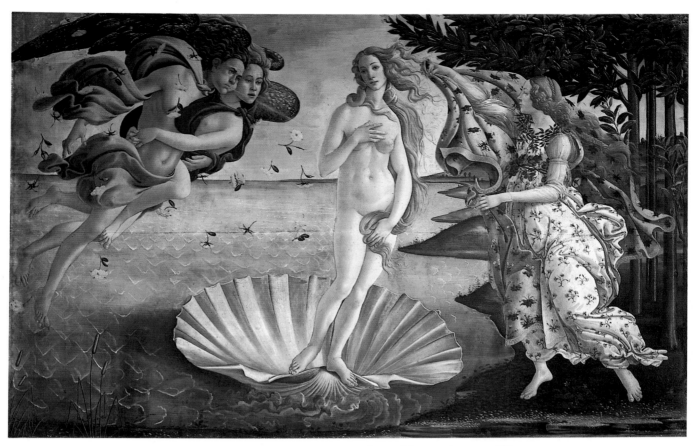

12-53. Sandro Botticelli. *The Birth of Venus*. c. 1480. Tempera on canvas, 5'8⅞" x 9'1⅞" (1.8 x 2.8 m). Galleria degli Uffizi, Florence

Ovid and the humanist poet Angelo Poliziano, who was, like Botticelli, a member of the Medici circle and may well have advised him on the painting, as he undoubtedly did on others. (See Early Italian Renaissance Music and Theater box page 444.)

NEO-PLATONISM. *The Birth of Venus* is clearly meant to be serious, even solemn. How could it be justified in Christian terms without both the artist and his patron being accused of neo-paganism? To answer this question we must consider the meaning of the picture as well as the use of classical subjects in Early Renaissance art. During the Middle Ages, classical form had become divorced from classical subject matter. Artists could draw upon ancient poses, gestures, expressions, and types only by changing the identity of their sources. Philosophers became apostles, Orpheus turned into Adam, Herakles was now Samson. When medieval artists wanted to represent the pagan gods, they based their pictures on literary descriptions rather than images. This was the situation, by and large, until the mid-fifteenth century. Only with Pollaiuolo and Mantegna in northern Italy does classical form begin to rejoin classical content. Pollaiuolo's lost paintings of the Labors of Hercules, of about 1465, mark the earliest case, as far as we know, of large-scale subjects from classical mythology depicted in a style inspired by ancient monuments.

In the Middle Ages, classical myths had sometimes been interpreted as allegories of Christian ideas, however remote the similarities might be. Europa carried off by the bull, for instance, was said to signify the soul redeemed by Christ. But such weak analogies were a poor excuse for reinvesting the pagan gods with their ancient beauty and power. To fuse the Christian faith with ancient mythology, rather than merely relate them, required a stronger argument. This justification was provided by the Neo-Platonic philosophers. The best known of them was Marsilio Ficino (1433–1499), who enjoyed great prestige during the late fifteenth century and after. Ficino, who was also a priest, based his thinking as much on the mysticism of Plotinos (see pages 199–200) as on the works of Plato. He believed that the life of the universe, including human existence, was linked to God by a spiritual circuit continuously ascending and descending. For that reason, all revelation, whether from the Bible, Plato, or classical myths, was one. He also proclaimed that beauty, love, and beatitude were united, since they are phases of this same circuit. Thus Neo-Platonists could speak of both the "celestial Venus" (the nude Venus born of the sea, as in our picture) and the Virgin Mary as sources of "divine love" (meaning the recognition of divine beauty).

The celestial Venus, according to Ficino, dwells purely in the sphere of Mind. Her twin, the ordinary Venus, gives rise to human love. Of her Ficino wrote to the Medici prince: "Venus . . . is a nymph of excellent comeliness, born of heaven and more than others beloved by God all highest. Her soul and mind are Love and Charity, her eyes Dignity and Magnanimity, the hands Liberality and Magnificence, the feet Comeliness and Modesty. The whole, then, is Temperance and Honesty, Charm and Splendor. Oh, what exquisite beauty! . . . a nymph of such nobility has been wholly given into your hands! If you were to unite with her in wedlock and claim her as yours she would make all your years sweet." In both form and content, this passage follows medieval odes to the Virgin.

Once we know that Botticelli's picture has this quasi-religious meaning, it seems less surprising that the wind god Zephyr and the breeze goddess Aura on the left look so much like angels. It also makes sense that the Hora personifying Spring on the right, who welcomes Venus ashore, recalls the relationship of St. John to the Savior in the Baptism of Christ (compare fig. 10-31). As baptism is a "rebirth in God," so the birth of Venus evokes the hope for "rebirth," from which the Renaissance takes its name. Thanks to the fluidity of Neo-Platonic thought, the number of possible associations in our painting is endless. All of them, however, like the celestial Venus herself, "dwell in the sphere of Mind," and Botticelli's Venus would hardly be a fit vessel for them if she were less ethereal. Thus rather than being merely decorative, the highly stylized treatment of the surface is what elevates the picture to allegory.

A similar meaning can be assigned to *Primavera* (fig. 12-54). Although it also once hung in Lorenzo's country home, the large canvas was probably painted originally for Lorenzo di Pierfrancesco, a cousin who grew up in the household of Lorenzo the Magnificent upon the death of his own father. Since it hung in the antechamber to Lorenzo di Pierfrancesco's bedroom along with two other mythological pictures devoted to the theme of love, the group may well have been commissioned for the young man's wedding. *Primavera* was inspired by Poliziano's lighthearted poem about the birth of love in spring. Other elements cannot be explained by this source alone. They must have been derived from Ovid and the Roman poet Lucretius. We see Venus in her sacred grove, with Eros flying overhead. Her companions the Three Graces and Hermes are on the left, and on the right is Zephyr grasping for the nymph Chloris, whom he later transforms into Flora, the goddess of flowers. That the painting has a hidden meaning is suggested once more by the decorative treatment of the surface and the strange appearance of the groups, which seem frozen despite their graceful rhythms.

According to one recent interpretation, *Primavera* can be understood on several levels based on Ficino's writings. It is first of all a metaphor of Platonic love between two friends: Mercury points the way to divine love in the guise of Venus, which is born of the Three Graces, symbolizing beauty. In contrast is physical love, represented by Flora, who was often thought of in lascivious terms during the Renaissance. On another level, the painting signifies the immortality of the soul through death and rebirth. This meaning arose by analogy of the Rape of Chloris to the Rape of Persephone, the subject of a poem by the Roman author Claudian that was popular among humanists at the time. Thus Venus becomes Demeter/Ceres of the Eleusian mysteries, with Mercury as the god of the dead. Eros is the vehicle of divine revelation, while the Three Graces stand for the soul. Finally, *Primavera* denotes the Last Judgment, in which Venus takes on the role of Mary the Divine Intercessor, Mercury becomes St. Michael, and Eros is the Holy Spirit. The Three Graces are seen as the Saved, as well as the three virtues Faith, Hope, and Love. Zephyr depicts Satan snatching up the Damned, personified by Chloris. Flora, content with earthly pleasures, remains as unaware of her fate as the fashionable couples in Traini's *Triumph of Death* (see fig. 11-86). Even if we do not agree with every detail of this controversial reading, it accords well with Ficino's lofty Neo-Platonism. It also provides the most satisfactory explanation to

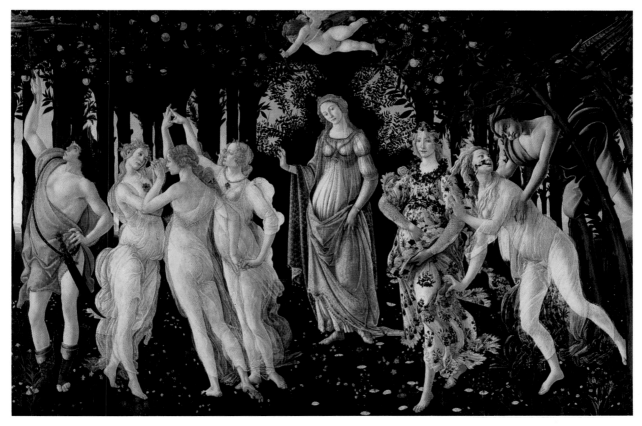

12-54. Sandro Botticelli. *Primavera.* c. 1482. Tempera on canvas. 6'8" x 10'4" (2.03 x 3.15 m). Galleria degli Uffizi, Florence

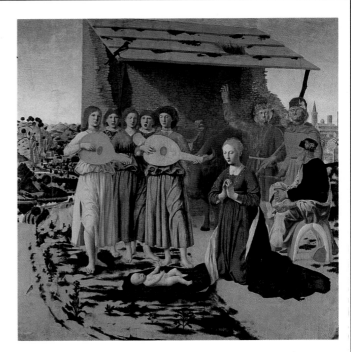
date of Botticelli's complex work by linking its content with that of *The Birth of Venus.*

Neo-Platonic philosophy and its expression in art were obviously too complex to become popular outside the small, highly educated Medici circle. In 1494, the suspicions of ordinary people were aroused by the friar Girolamo Savonarola, who attacked the "cult of paganism." He is usually portrayed unsympathetically as a book-burning firebrand whose sermons gained him a huge following. Yet he was an ardent reformer and began a vigorous campaign against corruption not only within the Church but also in the city of Florence, which he briefly ruled after the Medici were expelled. Because of the many enemies he made in the city's ruling circle, Savonarola was unjustly burned at the stake as a heretic in 1498 at the urging of the corrupt Pope Alexander VI.

Botticelli himself may have been a follower of Savonarola. It is said that he burned a number of his "pagan" pictures. In his last works he returned to traditional religious themes, but with no major change in style. He seems to have given up painting after 1500, even though Savonarola's prediction that the world would be destroyed in that year was not fulfilled.

DOMENICO GHIRLANDAIO. The fresco cycles of Domenico Ghirlandaio (1449–1494), a contemporary of Botticelli, contain so many portraits that they almost serve as family chronicles of the wealthy patricians who sponsored them. Among his most touching individual portraits is the panel *An Old Man and His Grandson* (fig. 12-55). The attention to surface texture and facial detail emphasizes the old man's nose, which has been disfigured by rosacea. Ghirlandaio has shown the tender relationship between the little boy and his grandfather with unique understanding. Psychologically, our panel plainly bespeaks its Italian origin.

The painting is nevertheless indebted to Northern art in several ways. It has a realism that can have come only through acquaintance with Netherlandish art, which, as we have seen, was widely admired in Italy. The faces are described in loving detail, which helps to convey the affection between the child and the old man. The addition of a landscape view through the window to break up the picture plane is also a Northern idea. But the most important contribution was the three-quarter view of the human face, which had been used in Flanders ever since Robert Campin introduced it in the donor portraits of the *Mérode Altarpiece* (fig. 15-1). Italian artists since the middle years of the fifteenth century had favored the rigid profile view adopted from Roman coins, which always showed emperors from the side. The pose was favored through association with the rulers of the classical past. But both Botticelli and Ghirlandaio began to adopt the three-quarter view in their portraits around 1480, and the practice soon became widespread.

PIETRO PERUGINO. Rome, long neglected during the papal exile in Avignon (see page 371), once more became a major artistic center in the later fifteenth century. As the papacy regained power on Italian soil, the popes began to beautify both the Vatican and the city. They believed that the monuments of Christian Rome must outshine those of the pagan past. The most ambitious pictorial project of those years was the decoration of the walls of the recently completed Sistine Chapel for Pope Sixtus IV (see fig. 13-17). Begun around 1481–82, this large cycle consists of events from the life of Moses (left wall) and Christ (right wall), representing the old and new covenants (see box page 266). The artists include most of the important painters of central Italy, among them Botticelli and Ghirlandaio. If the Sistine murals do not, on the whole, present their best work, it is because these mostly young artists had little experience in monumental fresco painting, for which there had been few opportunities since mid-century.

There is, however, one notable exception: *The Delivery of the Keys* (fig. 12-56) by Pietro Perugino (c. 1450–1523) is this artist's finest achievement. Born near Perugia in Umbria (the region

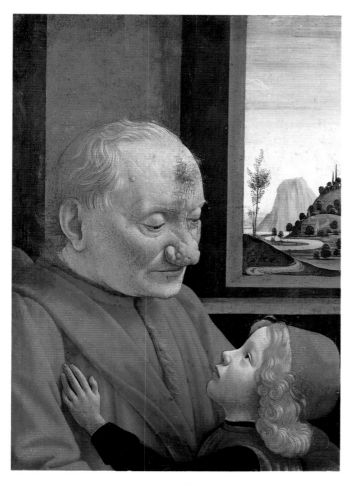

12-55. Domenico Ghirlandaio. *An Old Man and His Grandson.* c. 1480. Tempera and oil on wood panel, 24⅛ x 18" (61.2 x 45.5 cm). Musée du Louvre, Paris

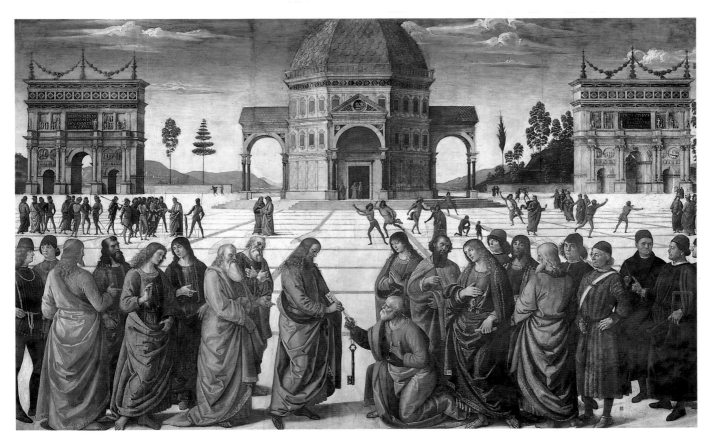

12-56. Pietro Perugino. *The Delivery of the Keys.* 1482. Fresco. Sistine Chapel, the Vatican, Rome

southeast of Tuscany), Perugino maintained close ties with Florence. Early in his career he was strongly influenced by Verrocchio, as can be seen in the statuesque balance and solidity of his figures (compare fig. 12-16). The symmetrical design conveys the importance of the subject. The authority of St. Peter as the first pope, as well as of all those who followed him, rests on his having received the keys to the Kingdom of Heaven from Christ himself, in the same way that the Christian church in the background is built on the rock that is Peter. A number of Perugino's contemporaries, with highly individualized features, witness the solemn event.

Equally striking is the vast expanse of the background. To the left, in the middle distance, is the moment when Jesus says, "Render to Caesar what is Caesar's"; to the right, the stoning of Christ. The inscriptions on the two Roman triumphal arches (modeled on the Arch of Constantine; see fig. 7-46) favorably compare Sixtus IV to Solomon, who built the Temple of Jerusalem where the Covenant of the Ark was later housed. The pair of arches flank a domed structure representing the ideal church of Alberti's *Treatise on Architecture*. Also Albertian is the mathematically exact perspective, which lends the view its spatial clarity. [See Primary Sources, no. 40, page 644.] (In order to simplify the scheme, however, the squares are far larger than those recommended by Alberti for such a piazza.)

This scene, so rational and lucid in its construction, nevertheless achieves a stunning visionary effect. Despite its novel spacial qualities, Perugino's fresco in many respects continues the tradition of Piero della Francesca, who spent much of his later life working for Umbrian clients, notably the duke of Urbino. Also from Urbino was a pupil Perugino received shortly before 1500 whose fame would soon outshine his own: Raphael.

LUCA SIGNORELLI. The Sistine frescoes were completed by Luca Signorelli (1445/50–1523). Signorelli's background was similar to Perugino's, but his personality was more dramatic. Of provincial Tuscan origin, he had been a student of Piero della Francesca before coming to Florence in the 1470s. Like Perugino, he was impressed by Verrocchio, but he also admired the energy, expressiveness, and anatomic precision of Pollaiuolo's nudes. Signorelli combined these influences with Piero's solidity of form and mastery of perspective foreshortening to achieve an epic style that later had a lasting impact on Michelangelo. He reached the climax of his career just before 1500 with a cycle of frescoes on the walls of the S. Brizio Chapel in Orvieto Cathedral.

The commission from Pope Alexander VI was an important one: it was a reward for Orvieto's faithfulness to the Vatican. The cycle, whose subject is the end of the world, conforms to the typology established by St. Augustine. But it is also rooted in St. Thomas Aquinas and Dante, as well as fifteenth-century Dominican theologians, especially St. Vincent Ferrer. The 1490s were a time of great hardship for Orvieto. It suffered from the plague, political unrest, economic decline, and fear of the Turks. (The Turks had crushed the Christian forces at Lepanto, Greece, in 1499—a defeat that was to be avenged in a second, more famous battle at the same site in 1571.) This turmoil is reflected in *The Rule of the Antichrist* (fig. 12-57), which is flanked by *The End of the World* and *The Coronation of the Elect*. The false Christ represents the chaos caused by political leaders and the "infidel" forces of Islam. As Satan's chief ally, he rules the world before being defeated by St. Michael (seen in the upper left-hand corner). He appears before the third Temple of Solomon, the center of his evil realm, which is shown in a skewed view that contrasts strikingly with the rational calm of Perugino's *The Delivery of the Keys* (see fig. 12-56).

The most dynamic of the Orvieto frescoes is *The Damned Cast into Hell* (fig. 12-58). What most strikes us is not the harsh style, which befits the tumultuous scene. Nor is it Signorelli's use of the nude body as an expressive instrument, even though he goes far beyond earlier painters in this respect. Rather it is the sense of tragedy that commands our attention. Signorelli's Hell, the exact opposite of Giotto's (compare fig. 11-78), is bathed in daylight; there are no monsters or machines of torture. The damned keep their dignity and the devils are less demonic. Even in Hell, it seems, the Renaissance faith in humanity does not lose its force.

VENICE AND PADUA. In northern Italy, the International Style in painting and sculpture lingered until mid-century, and architecture long retained a strongly Gothic flavor. As a result, there were hardly any major achievements in these fields.

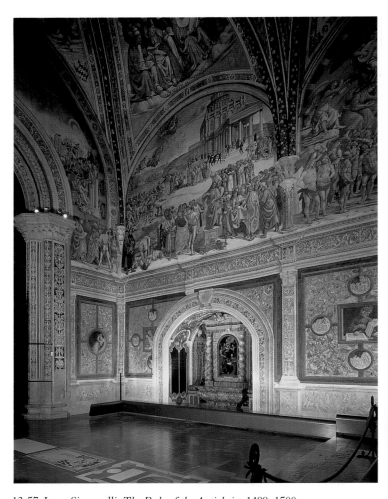

12-57. Luca Signorelli. *The Rule of the Antichrist*. 1499–1500. Fresco. S. Brizio Chapel, Orvieto Cathedral

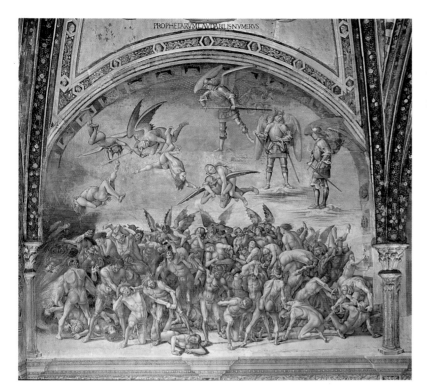

12-58. Luca Signorelli.
The Damned Cast into Hell.
1499–1500. Fresco.
S. Brizio Chapel

Between 1450 and 1500, however, a great painting tradition was born in Venice and its territories that was to flourish for the next three centuries. The Republic of Venice, although an oligarchy with strong political and trading ties to the east, had many connections with Florence. Hence it is not surprising that Venice, rather than Milan, became the center of Early Renaissance art in northern Italy.

ANDREA MANTEGNA. Florentine masters had been carrying the new style to Venice and nearby Padua since the 1420s. Fra Filippo Lippi, Uccello, and Castagno had worked there. Still more important was Donatello's ten-year stay. Their presence, however, had little effect until shortly before 1450. At that time, Andrea Mantegna (1431–1506) emerged as an independent master. He was trained by a minor Paduan painter, but his early career was shaped by his impressions of Florentine works and, we may assume, contact with Donatello. Next to Masaccio, Mantegna was the most important painter of the Early Renaissance. He, too, was a young genius, able to carry out commissions of his own by age 17. In the next decade he reached artistic maturity, and over the next half-century (he died at the age of 75) he broadened the range of his art, without abandoning the style he had developed in the 1450s.

The greatest achievement of Mantegna's early career, the frescoes in the Church of the Eremitani in Padua, was almost entirely destroyed by an accidental bomb explosion in 1944. *St. James Led to His Execution* (fig. 12-59) is the most dramatic scene of the cycle because of its daring "worm's-eye view" perspective, which is based on the viewer's actual eye level. (The central vanishing point is below the bottom of the picture, somewhat to the right of center.) As a result, the setting looms large, as in Masaccio's *Trinity* fresco (see fig. 12-38). Its main feature is a huge triumphal arch, which, although not a copy of any known Roman monument, looks so authentic that it might as well be.

Here Mantegna's devotion to the remains of antiquity shows his close ties to the humanists at the University of Padua, who were as dedicated to ancient literature as he was to ancient monuments. No Florentine painter or sculptor of the time could have transmitted such an attitude to him. The same desire for authenticity

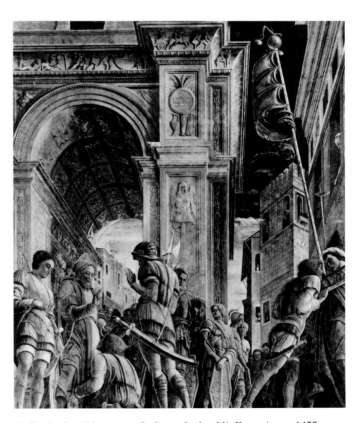

12-59. Andrea Mantegna. *St. James Led to His Execution.* c. 1455. Fresco. Ovetari Chapel, Church of the Eremitani, Padua. Destroyed 1944

can be seen in the costumes of the Roman soldiers (compare fig. 7-37). It even extends to the use of "wet" drapery patterns, a Classical Greek invention that was adopted by the Romans (see fig. 7-32). But the tense figures, lean and firm, and especially their interaction, are derived from Donatello. Mantegna's subject hardly requires such a dramatic treatment. The saint, on the way to his execution, blesses a paralytic and commands him to walk. Through their glances and gestures, the bystanders express how deeply the miracle has stirred them. The crowd generates an emotional tension that erupts in violence on the far right, where the spiral curl of the banner echoes the turbulence below.

By rare good luck, a sketch for this fresco has survived (fig. 12-60). It is the earliest known drawing that allows us to compare the preliminary and final versions of a design. (None of the drawings by earlier masters is related to a surviving picture in the same way.) This sketch differs from sinopie (full-scale drawings on the wall; see fig. 11-87) in its tentative quality. The composition has not yet taken full shape. The image is "unfinished" in both the conception and the quick, shorthand style. For example, here the perspective is closer to normal, indicating that the artist worked out the exact scheme directly on the wall. The drawing also offers proof of what we suspected in Masaccio: that Early Renaissance artists envisioned their compositions in terms of nude figures. The group on the right is still in that first stage; in the others, the outlines of the body show beneath the costume. But the drawing is also a work of art in its own right. The very quickness of its "handwriting" gives it an immediacy and force that are lost in the fresco.

St. Sebastian (fig. 12-61), painted only a few years after the Paduan frescoes, shows that Mantegna was much concerned with light and color. In the foreground we find classical ruins (along with the artist's signature in Greek). But in the distance we see an atmospheric landscape and a deep blue sky dotted with soft white clouds. The scene is bathed in warm late-afternoon sunlight, which creates a melancholy mood and makes the pathos of the dying saint even more poignant. The background shows the influence, direct or indirect, of the Van Eycks (compare fig. 15-2, left). Some works of the great Flemish masters had reached Florence as well as Venice between 1430 and 1450. They created the interest in light-filled landscapes that became such an important part of Venetian painting.

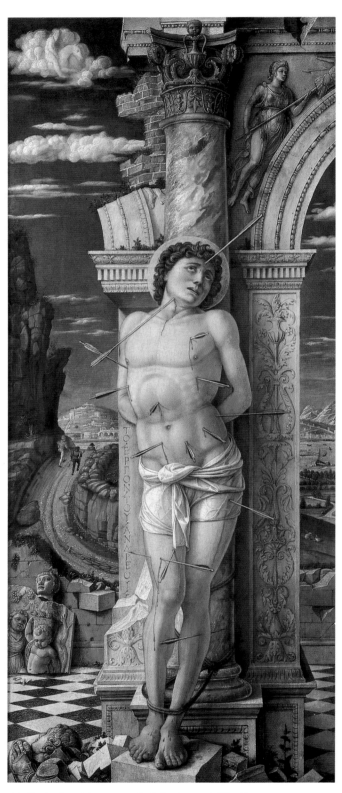

12-61. Andrea Mantegna. *St. Sebastian.* c. 1455–60. Tempera on panel, 26¾ x 11⅞" (68 x 30.6 cm). Kunsthistorisches Museum, Vienna

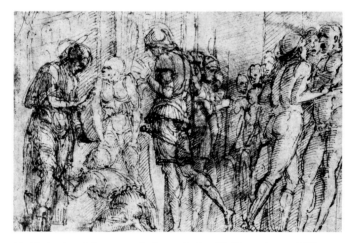

12-60. Andrea Mantegna. *St. James Led to His Execution.* c. 1455. Pen drawing, 6⅛ x 9¼" (15.7 x 23.5 cm). Collection G. M. Gathorne-Hardy, Donnington Priory, Newbury, Berkshire, England

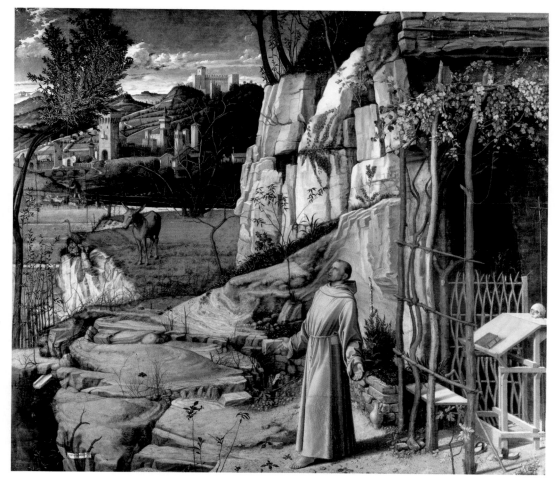

12-62. Giovanni Bellini. *St. Francis in Ecstasy.* c. 1485. Oil and tempera on panel, 49 x 55⅞" (124 x 141.7 cm). The Frick Collection, New York

GIOVANNI BELLINI. In the painting of Giovanni Bellini (c. 1431–1516), Mantegna's brother-in-law, we can trace the further impact of the Flemish tradition in the south. Bellini was slow to mature. His finest pictures, such as *St. Francis in Ecstasy* (fig. 12-62), date from the last decades of the century or even later. The subject is unique. The scene is treated as the equivalent of Moses and the burning bush in the book of Exodus. In that story, when the patriarch of the Jews came to the mountain of God, an angel appeared to him in a flame of fire out of a bush which was not consumed and from which the Lord commanded him to remove his shoes, because he was on holy ground (see also page 58). It was then that God promised to deliver the Hebrews from the hands of the Egyptians and into the land of milk and honey.

The saint has left his wooden pattens behind and looks up ecstatically to the sky. The painting is often thought to show Francis receiving the stigmata (the wounds of Christ) on the Feast of the Holy Cross in 1224, when a crucified seraph appeared to him on Mount Alverna. However, the marks on his hands and feet are barely visible and have clearly healed. Instead, the scene most likely "illustrates" the Hymn of the Sun, which Francis composed the next year, after his annual fast at a hermitage near his hometown of Assisi. During that time he could not bear the sight of light and was plagued by mice. The monk finally emerged from his cell after the Lord assured him that he would enter the Kingdom of Heaven.

For Francis, "Brother Sun, who gives the day . . . and . . . is beautiful and radiant with great splendor," was a symbol of the Lord. What he sees, however, is not the sun itself, which is obscured by a cloud, but God revealed as the light divine. This miraculous light is so intense that it illuminates the entire scene. Even the lone tree at the left, a counterpart to the burning bush, bends in response to it, as if moved by an unseen powerful force.

In the background is a magnificent expanse of Italian countryside. Yet this is no ordinary landscape. It represents the Heavenly Jerusalem, inspired by the Revelation of St. John the Divine. The city remains empty until Judgment Day, when it will receive the souls of the blessed. It lies across the river, separated from the everyday world by the bridge to the left. Behind looms Mount Zion, where the Lord dwells. How, then, shall we enter the gate to paradise, shown as a large tower? For Francis, the road to salvation lay in the ascetic life, symbolized by the cave, which also links him to St. Jerome, the first great hermit saint. The donkey stands for St. Francis himself, who referred to his body as Brother Ass, which must be disciplined. The other animals—the heron, bittern, and rabbit—are, like monks, solitary creatures in Christian lore.

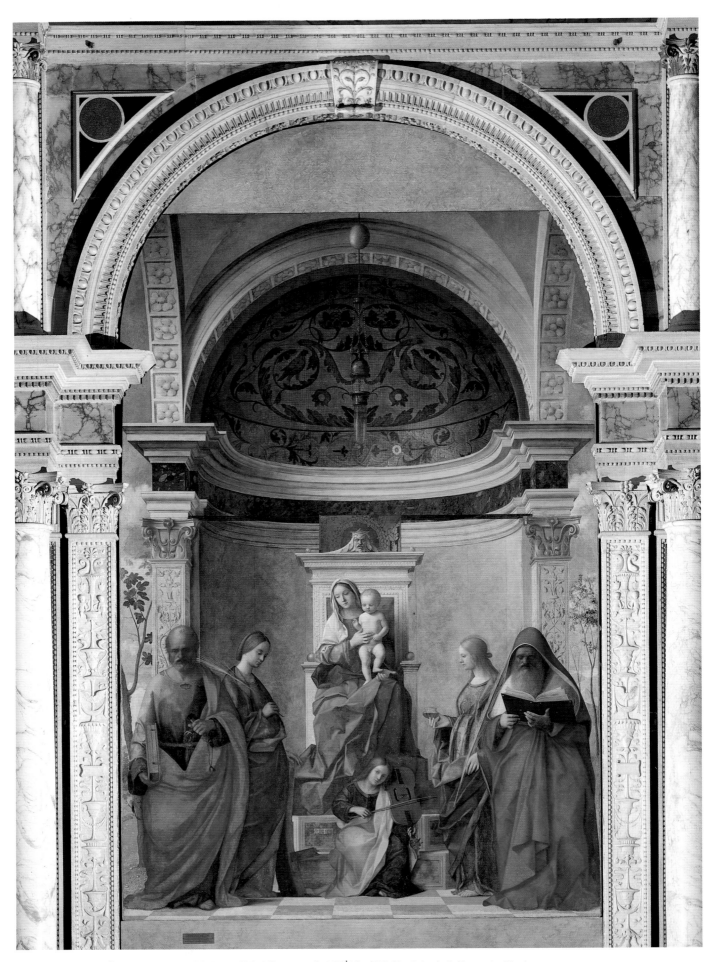

12-63. Giovanni Bellini. *Madonna and Saints*. 1505. Oil on panel, 16'5⅛" x 7'9" (5 x 2.4 m). S. Zaccaria, Venice

This symbolism does not by itself explain the picture. More important is the treatment of the landscape. St. Francis is so small compared to the setting that he seems almost incidental. Yet his mystic rapture before the beauty of the visible world guides our own response to the view that is spread out before us, which is ample and intimate at the same time. St. Francis believed that the Lord had created nature for the benefit of humanity. Bellini clearly shares his reverence for the Lord's handiwork, as expressed in the Hymn of the Sun:

Be praised, my Lord, with all Your creatures,
Above all Brother Sun,
Who gives the day and by whom You shed light on us.
And he is beautiful and radiant with great splendor.
Of Thee, Most High, he is a symbol.

Bellini's contours are less brittle than Mantegna's. The colors are softer and the light more glowing. He also shares the concern of the great Flemings for every detail and its symbolism. Unlike the Northerners, however, he can define the viewer's relationship to the landscape. The rock formations of the foreground are clear and firm, like architecture rendered by the rules of scientific perspective.

As the foremost artist of Venice, Bellini produced a number of altarpieces of the sacra conversazione type. The last one and the most monumental of all is the *Madonna and Saints* in S. Zaccaria (fig. 12-63), done in 1505. (When the painting was fitted with its present frame a decade later, it was cut at the sides, and a piece, since removed, was added at the top.) Compared to Domenico's sacra conversazione of 50 years earlier (see fig. 12-46), the setting is simpler but even more impressive. We stand in the nave of a church looking toward the enthroned Madonna and Child in the apse, which fills most of the panel. The rest of the figures appear, however, under the vaulted canopy of the crossing, which is partly visible. The structure is obviously not a real church, for its sides are open and the scene is flooded with sunlight. (Domenico also placed his figures in a semi-outdoor setting.) The Madonna's high-backed throne and the music-making angel on its lowest step are derived (no doubt through many intermediaries) from Masaccio's *Madonna Enthroned* of 1426 (see fig. 12-44).

What distinguishes this altar from earlier Florentine examples is not only the spaciousness of the design but its calm, meditative mood. Instead of "conversation," we sense the figures' deep communion, which makes gestures unnecessary. We shall encounter this quality again in Venetian painting. Here it is enhanced by the way the artist has bathed the scene in a delicate haze. There are no harsh contrasts. Light and shadow blend in almost imperceptible gradations, and colors glow with a new richness. In this magical moment, Bellini unites Florentine grandeur with Venetian intimacy.

CHAPTER THIRTEEN

The High Renaissance in Italy

It used to be taken for granted that the High Renaissance followed the Early Renaissance as inevitably as night follows day. The great masters of the sixteenth century—Leonardo, Bramante, Michelangelo, Raphael, Giorgione, Titian—were thought to have shared the ideals of their predecessors, but to have expressed them so completely that their names became synonyms for perfection. They represented the climax, the classic phase, of Renaissance art, just as Pheidias had brought the art of ancient Greece to its highest point. This view could also explain why these two classic phases, although 2,000 years apart, were so short. If art is assumed to develop along the pattern of a ballistic curve, its highest point cannot last more than a moment. Art historians have come to realize the drawbacks of this scheme. When we apply it literally, the High Renaissance becomes so brief that we wonder whether it happened at all. Moreover, it hardly helps our understanding of the Early Renaissance if we regard it as a "not-yet-perfect High Renaissance," any more than an Archaic Greek statue can be satisfactorily viewed from a Classical standpoint. Nor is it very useful to insist that the post-Classical phase, whether Hellenistic or Late Renaissance, must be one of decline. The image of the ballistic curve has now been abandoned. As a result, we have gained a less assured, but also less arbitrary, estimate of what, for lack of another term, we still call the High Renaissance.

In some basic respects, the High Renaissance was indeed the fulfillment of the Early Renaissance. In others, however, it was a major departure. Certainly the tendency to view artists as geniuses, rather than simply as artisans, was never stronger than during the first half of the sixteenth century. Plato's concept of genius—the spirit that enters poets and causes them to compose in a "divine frenzy"—had been broadened by Marsilio Ficino and his fellow Neo-Platonists to include architects, sculptors, and painters. For Giorgio Vasari, geniuses were set apart by "grace," in the sense of both divine grace (a gift from God) and gracefulness (which reflected it). To him, this concept had moral and spiritual significance, inspired in part by Dante's *Inferno*. Building further on Petrarch's scheme of history (see page 404), he saw the High Renaissance as superior even to antiquity, because it belonged to the era of Christian grace, which had not been revealed to the pagans (see box page 266). Thus in his *Lives of the Painters* (1550–68), Vasari praises the "gracious," virtu-ous personalities of Michelangelo, Leonardo, and Raphael, as a way of accounting for their talent. Grace also served to justify his treatment of Michelangelo as the greatest artist of all time. This view remains with us to this day, although Michelangelo's character was far from admirable in some respects. [See Primary Sources, no. 43, pages 645–47] Finally, Vasari's descriptions accord with the ideal defined in Baldassare Castiglione's *The Courtier* (1528), to which Vasari himself aspired as architect and courtier to Cosimo I de' Medici (see discussion pages 506–07; fig. 14-23).

What set these artists apart was the inspiration guiding their efforts, which was worthy of being called "divine," "immortal," and "creative." (Before 1500, *creating,* as distinct from *making,* was the privilege of God alone.) To Vasari, the painters and sculptors of the Early Renaissance, like those of the Late Gothic, had learned only to imitate nature. The geniuses of the High Renaissance, in contrast, had conquered nature by ennobling or transcending it. In actual fact, the High Renaissance remained thoroughly grounded in nature. Its achievement lay in the creation of a new classicism.

Faith in the divine origin of inspiration led artists to rely on subjective standards of truth and beauty. Whereas the Early Renaissance felt bound by what were believed to be universal rules, such as the numerical ratios of musical harmony and the laws of linear perspective, the High Renaissance was less concerned with rational order than with visual and expressive effectiveness. It evolved a new drama and a new rhetoric to engage the emotions of the beholder, whether sanctioned or not by classical precedent. Indeed, the works of the great masters of the High Renaissance soon became classics in their own right, equal in authority to the most famous monuments of antiquity. At the same time, this cult of the genius had a profound effect on the artists themselves. It spurred them and their patrons to ambitious goals. Since these projects often went beyond what was humanly possible, they were apt to be limited by external as well as internal difficulties. Artists were often left with a sense of having been defeated by malevolent fate.

If the creations of genius are unique by definition, they cannot be successfully imitated by lesser artists, however worthy they are of emulation. Thus, unlike the founders of the Early Renaissance, the leading artists of the High Renaissance did not set the pace for a broadly based period style. Indeed, the High Renaissance produced surprisingly few minor artists. It died with the six great masters who created it, or even before. Only Michelangelo and Titian lived beyond 1520.

Conditions after that date were less favorable to the High Renaissance style than those of the first two decades of the sixteenth century. Yet the High Renaissance might well have ended soon anyway. The harmonious grandeur of the High Renaissance was an inherently unstable balance of conflicting elements, as was Pheidian classicism. Only these components, not the balance itself, could be transmitted to others. But despite its limited and precarious nature, the period had a tremendous impact upon later art. For most of the next 300 years, the early sixteenth century loomed so large that the achievements of earlier artists seemed to belong to a forgotten era. Even when the art of the fourteenth and fifteenth centuries was finally rediscovered, people still saw the High Renaissance as the turning point and referred to all painters before Raphael as "the Primitives."

Leonardo da Vinci

One reason the High Renaissance deserves to be called a period is the fact that most of its key monuments were produced between 1495 and 1520, despite the great differences in age of the artists who created them. Bramante, the oldest, was born in 1444, Michelangelo in 1475, Raphael in 1483, and Titian about 1488–90. Yet the distinction of being the earliest High Renaissance master belongs to Leonardo da Vinci (1452–1519). Born in the little Tuscan town of Vinci, Leonardo was trained in Florence by Verrocchio. Conditions there must not have suited him, however. At the age of 30 he went to work for the duke of Milan as a highly paid military engineer, and only secondarily as an architect, sculptor, and painter.

ADORATION OF THE MAGI. When he left Florence, Leonardo left behind, unfinished, the most ambitious work he had then begun, a large *Adoration of the Magi* (fig. 13-1), for which he had made several preliminary studies. The design of the ruins shows a geometric order and exact perspective that recall Florentine painting in the wake of Masaccio rather than the style prevailing about 1480, which is reflected solely in the gracefulness of the Madonna and Child. Yet this structure is so peculiar as to heighten the contrast with the landscape. Without the trees to anchor it, the composition would consist of two separate parts. The background cannot be explained in rational terms. What are we to make of the figures on the stairs of the wrecked building, or the combat of horsemen to either side?

The foreground is no less visionary. The main figures are contained in a triangle surrounded by the sweeping arc of onlookers. The assembly is as spellbinding as it is strange. The scene is framed to the left by a philosopher lost in thought and on the right by a young soldier looking outside the picture to something that has caught his attention. They undoubtedly represent ideal types—but what do they signify? The contemplative and active lives surely, youth and old age as well, perhaps moral and physical beauty, as one critic has suggested. Within these contrasts lies a duality of mind

and body that Leonardo sought to resolve in his mature work. Thus the image already contains the seeds of his later paintings.

The most striking, and indeed revolutionary, aspect of the panel is the way it is executed, although Leonardo did not even complete the underpainting. The forms seem to materialize softly and gradually, never quite detaching themselves from the dusky atmosphere. Leonardo, unlike Pollaiuolo or Botticelli, thinks not in terms of outlines but of three-dimensional bodies made visible in varying degrees by the angle of light. In the shadows, these shapes remain incomplete; their contours are only implied. This method of modeling is called *chiaroscuro,* the Italian word for "light and dark." Forms no longer stand abruptly side by side. Instead they share in a new pictorial unity, for the barriers between them have been partially broken down. There is a comparable emotional continuity as well. The gestures and faces of the crowd convey with touching eloquence the reality of the miracle they have come to behold. We will recognize the influence of both Verrocchio and Pollaiuolo in the expressiveness of these figures. Leonardo may also have been impressed by the breathless shepherds in *The Portinari Altarpiece,* by the Flemish artist Hugo van der Goes, which had recently been brought to Florence (see fig. 15-12).

THE VIRGIN OF THE ROCKS. Soon after arriving in Milan, Leonardo painted *The Virgin of the Rocks* (fig. 13-2). This altar panel suggests what the *Adoration* might have looked like had it been completed. The figures emerge from the semidarkness of the grotto, enveloped in a moist atmosphere that delicately veils their forms. This fine haze, called **sfumato,** is more pronounced than similar effects in Flemish and Venetian painting. It lends an unusual warmth and intimacy to the scene. It also creates a remote, dreamlike quality, and makes the picture seem a poetic vision rather than an image of reality. In his notebooks Leonardo had much to say about the relation between art and literature. Called the *paragone,* it was rooted in Horace's statement that poetry is like painting (*ut pictura poesis*), which the High Renaissance reinterpreted to mean that painting ought to conform to poetry. [See Primary Sources, no. 42, page 645.] The subject—the infant St. John adoring the Christ Child in the presence of the Virgin and an angel—is entirely new in art. The story of their meeting is one of the many legends that arose to satisfy curiosity about the "hidden" early life of Jesus, which is hardly mentioned in the Bible. (According to a similar legend, St. John, about whom equally little is known, spent his childhood in the wilderness; hence he is shown wearing a hair shirt.)

Leonardo was the first to depict this scene, but the treatment is mysterious in many ways. The secluded setting, the pool in front, and the carefully rendered plant life hint at levels of meaning that are hard to define. How are we to interpret the relationships among the four figures, expressed in their gestures? Protective, pointing, blessing, they convey with infinite tenderness the wonderment of St. John's recognition of Christ as the Savior. The gap between these hands and St. John makes the exchange all the more telling. Although present in *The Doubting of Thomas* by Leonardo's teacher, Verrocchio (see fig. 12-16), the elegant gestures and refined features are the first example of that High Renaissance "grace" signifying a spiritual state of being.

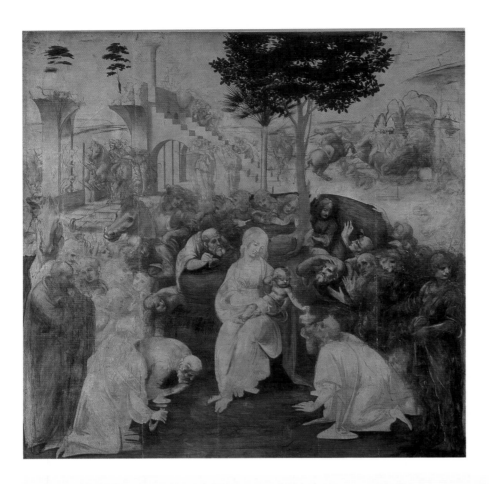

13-1. Leonardo da Vinci. *Adoration of the Magi.* 1481–82.
Monochrome on panel, 8' x 8'1" (2.43 x 2.46 m).
Galleria degli Uffizi, Florence

The final composition has been made the subject of much ingenious analysis, some of it more exhaustive than the unfinished state of the picture will allow. But I may point out how the simple parallelism of the earlier composition has been entirely superseded. Instead, the main lines form a triangle backed by an arc. The right side of the triangle is a relatively straight line from the kneeling King's foot to St. Joseph, and is echoed in the background by the line of the staircases. The left side rises in a series of curves, which are repeated in the arcades of the ruin, and supported by the leading gestures and glances. Round this triangle, an arc of shadowy figures flows like the Stream of Ocean Ptolemaic Geography. To stabilize this restless pattern Leonardo has placed four verticals, the two trees near the centre of the triangle, the two upright figures at its bases.

Even this bare, geometrical analysis of the composition gives a hint of its dramatic meaning. The symbolical homage of wisdom and science to a new faith is firmly expressed by the main figures; but pressing round them, like ghosts from the magical paganism of Apuleius, are those evasive creatures which writers on Leonardo are content to call angels. In the background, agitation of spirit inhabits the half-ruined construction of the intelligence. There remain the two figures at the sides, which seem to stand outside the scene, like leaders of a Greek chorus. To the left is the philosopher . . . morally and materially he has the grandeur of one of Masaccio's apostles. Opposite the Masaccio is a Giorgione: for no other name will fit the deeply romantic figure of a youth in armour on the right. He looks out of the picture with complete indifference. . . .the student of Leonardo may feel that in these two figures

of youth and age, moral and physical beauty, active and passive intelligence, he has indeed represented his own spirit, symbolizing his dual nature as he does in those familiar expressions of his unconscious mind, the contrasted profiles.

—Kenneth Clark. *Leonardo Da Vinci.*
Revised and with an Introduction by Martin Kemp.
New York: Penguin Books, 1993, pp. 76, 78.
Originally published in 1939 by Cambridge University Press.

A protégé of Bernard Berenson (see page 484), **SIR KENNETH CLARK** (1902–1983) began his illustrious career by being appointed director of The National Gallery, London, at the remarkably young age of 30. Thereafter he was involved in numerous ventures and held a professorship at St. Andrew's. Sir Kenneth was made a life peer in 1969, the year he achieved international renown for his television series *Civilization;* he was, in fact, a spellbinding presence in person and on television. At the same time, he was a genuinely great art historian. His book on Leonardo, although superseded in some respects by later scholarship, is still inspiring because of Sir Kenneth's eloquence, range of knowledge, and lucid understanding.

THE LAST SUPPER. Despite their originality, the *Adoration* and the *Virgin of the Rocks* do not yet differ clearly in conception from Early Renaissance art. *The Last Supper,* of a dozen years later, is the first full statement of the ideals of High Renaissance painting (fig. 13-3). Unfortunately the famous mural began to deteriorate a few years after its completion. The artist, dissatisfied with the limitations of the traditional fresco technique, experimented with an oil-tempera medium in plaster that did not adhere well to the wall. We thus need some effort to imagine its original splendor, even though the painting was recently restored. Yet what remains is more than adequate to account for its tremendous impact. Viewing the composition as a whole, we are struck at once by its balanced stability. Only afterward do we realize that Leonardo achieved this balance by the reconciliation of competing, even conflicting, aims that no previous artist had attempted.

A comparison with Castagno's *Last Supper* (see fig. 12-50), painted half a century before, is particularly revealing here. In both murals the spatial setting seems like an annex to the real interior of the refectory (dining hall). But unlike Leonardo's, Castagno's architecture has an oppressive effect on the figures. The reason for this becomes clear when we realize that this space has been conceived independently. It was there before the figures entered and would suit another group of diners equally well. By

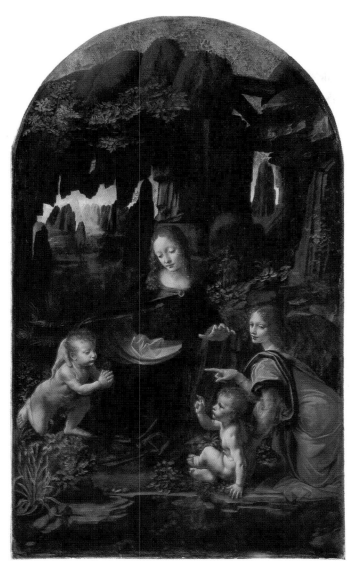

(LEFT) 13-2. Leonardo da Vinci. *The Virgin of the Rocks.* c. 1485.
Oil on panel transferred to canvas, 6'6" x 4' (1.9 x 1.2 m).
Musée du Louvre, Paris

(BELOW) 13-3. Leonardo da Vinci. *The Last Supper.* c. 1495–98.
Tempera wall mural, 15'2" x 28'10" (4.6 x 8.8 m).
Sta. Maria delle Grazie, Milan

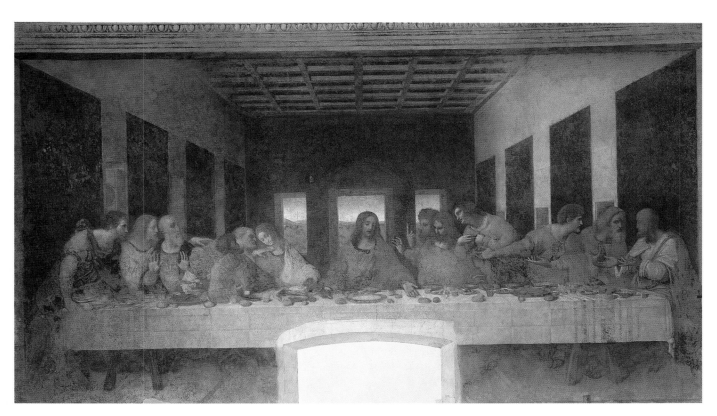

contrast, Leonardo began by composing the figures first, as we know from preliminary drawings. The architecture had merely a supporting role from the start. Hence the pictorial space is the very opposite of Castagno's rational picture space, even though it, too, uses scientific perspective.

Leonardo's perspective is an ideal one. The painting, high up on the wall, assumes a vantage point some 15 feet above the floor and 30 feet back. This position is clearly impossible, yet we accept it as readily as in Piero della Francesco's *The Discovery and Proving of the True Cross* (fig. 12-48). The central vanishing point, which determines our view of the setting, is located behind the head of Jesus in the exact middle of the fresco and thus becomes charged with symbolic significance. Equally plain is the symbolic function of the opening behind Christ: it acts as the architectural equivalent of a halo. The three windows in turn stand for the Trinity. We thus tend to see the perspective framework of the scene almost entirely in relation to the figures, rather than as something preexisting. We can easily test how vital this relationship is by covering the upper third of the picture. The composition then takes on the character of a frieze. The grouping of the apostles is less clear, and the calm triangular shape of Jesus becomes passive, instead of acting as a physical and spiritual force. At the same time, the perspective system helps to "lock" the composition in place. It thus gives the scene an eternal quality without making it look static.

The Savior has presumably just spoken the fateful words, "One of you shall betray me." The disciples are asking, "Lord, is it I?" We see nothing that contradicts this interpretation. But to view the scene as just one moment in a psychological drama does not do justice to Leonardo's aims, which went well beyond a literal rendering of the biblical narrative. The artist crowded the disciples together on the far side of the table, in a space too small for so many people. He clearly wanted to condense his subject, both physically (by the compact, monumental grouping of the figures) and spiritually (by presenting many levels of meaning at one time). Thus Christ's gesture is one of submission to the divine will, and of offering. It is a hint at his main act at the Last Supper, the institution of the Eucharist, in which bread and wine become his body and blood through transubstantiation.

The apostles do not simply react to these words. Each reveals his own personality, his own relationship to Christ. (Note that Judas is no longer segregated from the rest; his defiant profile sets him apart well enough.) Leonardo has carefully calculated each pose and expression so that the drama unfolds across the picture plane. The figures exemplify what the artist wrote in one of his notebooks, that the highest and most difficult aim of painting is to depict "the intention of man's soul" through gestures and movements of the limbs. As we can tell from the complete lack of anecdotal interest in *The Last Supper,* this statement must be interpreted as referring not to momentary emotional states but to the inner life as a whole. Here we realize that Leonardo has recaptured the central achievement of Classical art, for he shared the same goal as Polygnotos (see page 150). He thus set the stage for the other artists of the High Renaissance in creating a new classicism that rivaled, and even surpassed, antiquity.

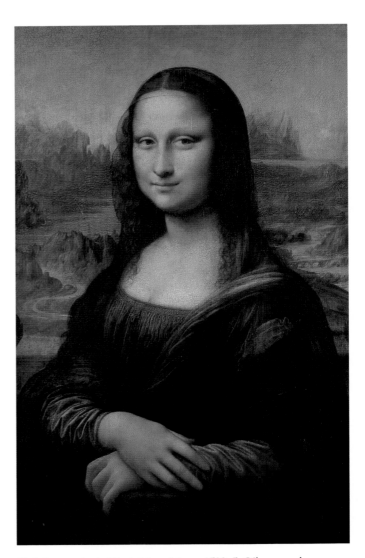

13-4. Leonardo da Vinci. *Mona Lisa.* c. 1503–5. Oil on panel, 30¼ x 21" (77 x 53.5 cm). Musée du Louvre, Paris

MONA LISA. In 1499, the duchy of Milan fell to the French as part of their growing rivalry with the Spanish (see page 430), and Leonardo returned to Florence after brief trips to Mantua and Venice. He must have found the cultural climate very different from what he remembered. The Medici had been expelled, and until their return, the city was briefly a republic again. For a while, Leonardo seems to have been active mainly as an engineer and surveyor. Then in 1503 the city commissioned him to do a mural of some famous event from the history of Florence for the council chamber of the Palazzo Vecchio. He chose the Battle of Anghiari, but in 1506 he abandoned the commission and returned to Milan at the request of the French. The painting is known only through various copies of the cartoon (including one by Peter Paul Rubens) which survived for more than a century.

While working on the mural, Leonardo also painted the *Mona Lisa* (fig. 13-4). Here the sfumato of *The Virgin of the Rocks* is perfected, so that it seemed miraculous to the artist's contemporaries. The forms are built from layers of glazes so thin that the panel appears to glow with a gentle light from within, despite the

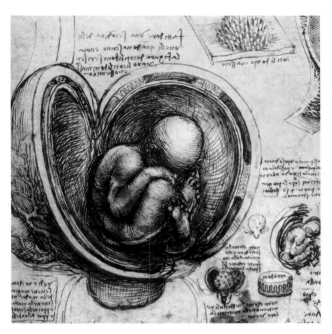

13-5. Leonardo da Vinci. *Embryo in the Womb.* c. 1510.
Detail of pen drawing, 11⅞ x 8⅜" (30.4 x 21.5 cm).
Windsor Castle, Royal Library

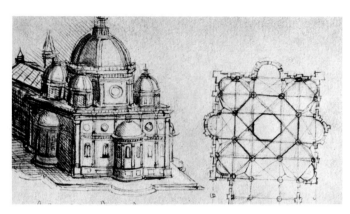

13-6. Leonardo da Vinci. *Project for a Church* (Ms. B). c. 1490.
Pen drawing, 9⅛ x 6¾" (23 x 17 cm).
Bibliothèque de l'Arsenal, Paris

dirty varnish that obscures the painting. But the fame of the *Mona Lisa* comes not just from this subtle technique. Even more intriguing is the sitter's personality. Why, among all the smiling faces ever painted, has this one been singled out as mysterious? Perhaps the reason is that, as a portrait, the picture does not fit our expectations. The features are too individual for Leonardo to have simply depicted an ideal type, yet they are so idealized that they blur the sitter's character. Once again the artist has brought two opposites into harmonious balance. The smile also may be read in two ways: as the echo of a momentary mood and as a timeless, symbolic expression akin to the Archaic smile of the Greeks (see figs. 5-15 and 5-16).

The *Mona Lisa* seemingly embodies a maternal tenderness that was the essence of womanhood to Leonardo. Even the landscape, made up mainly of rocks and water, suggests elemental generative forces of nature, which fascinated the artist. Who was the sitter for this, the most famous portrait in the world? Her true identity, said by Vasari to be wife of Francesco del Giocondo, long remained a mystery. We now know that she was the wife of a Florentine merchant born in 1479 and dead before 1556. This was not the only painting of the Mona Lisa: Leonardo also painted a nude version, now lost, that once belonged to the king of France.

DRAWINGS. In his later years, Leonardo devoted himself more and more to his scientific interests. Art and science, we recall, were first united in Brunelleschi's discovery of systematic perspective. Leonardo's work is the climax of this trend. He believed the world to be intelligible through mathematics, which formed the basis for his investigations. Thus the artist must know not only the rules of perspective but all the laws of nature. To him the eye was the perfect means of gaining such knowledge. The extraordinary range of his inquiries can be seen in the hundreds of drawings and notes that he hoped to turn into an encyclopedic set of treatises. How original he was as a scientist is still a matter of debate, but in one field there is no doubt of his importance: he created modern scientific illustration, an essential tool for anatomists and biologists. A drawing such as the *Embryo in the Womb* (fig. 13-5) combines his own vivid observation with the analytic clarity of a diagram—or, to paraphrase Leonardo's own words, sight and insight.

Contemporary sources show that Leonardo was esteemed as an architect. He seems, however, to have been less concerned with actual building than with problems of structure and design. For the most part, the many architectural projects in his drawings were intended to remain on paper. Yet these sketches, especially those of his Milanese period, have great historical importance. In them we can trace the transition from the Early to the High Renaissance in architecture.

The domed central-plan churches of the type shown in figure 13-6 hold particular interest for us. The plan recalls Brunelleschi's Sta. Maria degli Angeli (see fig. 12-26), but the relationship of the spatial units is more complex, while the exterior, with its cluster of domes, is more monumental than any Early Renaissance structure. In conception, this design stands halfway between the dome of Florence Cathedral and the most ambitious structure of the sixteenth century, the new basilica of St. Peter's in Rome (compare figs. 11-35, 13-9, and 13-10). It is evidence, too, of Leonardo's close contact with the architect Donato Bramante (1444–1514).

Bramante

Bramante arrived in Milan around 1479, several years before Leonardo. A native of Urbino, he began his career as a fresco painter under the influence of Piero della Francesca and Andrea Mantegna. Thus he was already skilled at rendering architectural settings in correct perspective (compare figs. 12-48 and 12-59). His earliest work as a professional architect was the rebuilding of Sta. Maria presso San Satiro, which takes Brunelleschi and Alberti as its main points of departure. However, his east end for the Gothic church of Sta. Maria della Grazie, begun in 1492 for the Duke of Milan, has a complexity and grandeur that suggest the influence of Leonardo's drawings. Since Leonardo was not a practicing architect but a military engineer, it is likely that he benefited in turn from Bramante, as well as from other architects who were active in Milan.

THE TEMPIETTO. After Milan fell to French forces in 1499, Bramante went to Rome, where he made a study of ancient buildings that was to transform him as an architect. Thus it was in Rome, during the last 15 years of his life, that he created High Renaissance architecture. The new style is shown fully formed in the Tempietto at S. Pietro in Montorio (fig. 13-7), commissioned by King Ferdinand and Queen Isabella of Spain and designed soon after 1500. This round chapel is a martyrium, for it marks the site of St. Peter's crucifixion. If the original plan had been carried out, the Tempietto would have appeared less isolated from its environment than it does today. It was intended to be surrounded by a circular, colonnaded courtyard set within a "molded" exterior space, a conception as bold and novel as the design of the chapel itself (fig. 13-8).

The nickname "little temple" is well deserved. The three-step platform and the severe Doric order of the colonnade recall classical temple architecture more directly than does any fifteenth-century building, and with good reason: it relies on the recently excavated Roman Temple of Hercules Victor. Moreover, it incorporates sixteen ancient Roman columns that form the module on which the entire design is based. For example, the distance between them is four times their diameter, and they are placed two diameters from the wall. This insistent logic follows the rules of temple design established by Vitruvius. Equally striking is Bramante's use of the "sculptured wall" in the Tempietto itself and the courtyard, as shown in the plan. Not since Brunelleschi's Sta. Maria degli Angeli have we seen such deeply recessed niches "excavated" from masses of masonry. These cavities are counterbalanced by the convex shape of the dome and by strongly projecting moldings and cornices. As a result, the Tempietto has a monumentality that belies its modest size.

The building, including the sculptural decoration in the metopes and frieze around the base, is a brilliant example of papal propaganda. The Tempietto proclaims Christ and the Christian popes (considered the successors of St. Peter, who received his authority directly from the Lord, see fig. 12-56) as the direct heirs of ancient Rome. In this way the Spaniard Pope Alexander VI asserted his claim to supremacy in both the spiritual and temporal realms. He was supported by the Spanish monarchy, then the most powerful in all of Europe.

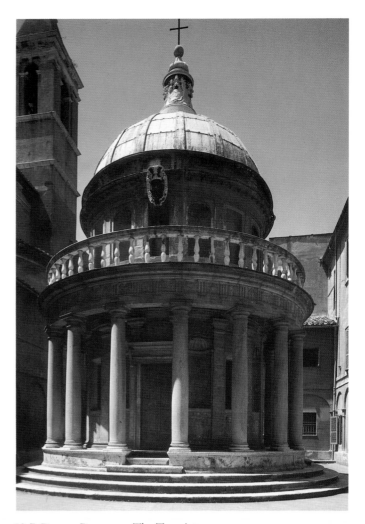

13-7. Donato Bramante. The Tempietto, S. Pietro in Montorio, Rome. 1502–11

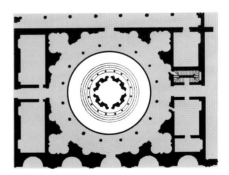

13-8. Plan of the Tempietto (after Serlio, in *Regole generali di Architettura*). Gray tint indicates unbuilt sections

ST. PETER'S, ROME. The Tempietto is the earliest of the great achievements that made Rome the center of Italian art during the first quarter of the sixteenth century. Most of them belong to the decade 1503–13, the papacy of Julius II. These projects testify to his personal ambition, but they were also essential to his goal of restoring papal authority over Christendom. Julius II decided to replace the old basilica of St. Peter's, which was in poor condition, with a church so magnificent that it would overshadow all the monuments of imperial Rome. The task was given to Bramante, who had quickly established himself as the foremost architect in the city. His original design of 1506 is known only from a plan (fig. 13-9) and from the medal commemorating the start of the building campaign (fig. 13-10), which shows the exterior in rather general terms. They are enough, however, to bear out Bramante's reported aim: "I shall place the Pantheon on top of the Basilica of Constantine."

The goal thus was to surpass the two most famous structures of Roman antiquity by a Christian building of unprecedented grandeur. Nothing less would have satisfied the ambitious Julius II, who also wanted to unite all Italy under his command and thus gain a temporal power that matched his spiritual authority. Bramante's design is indeed magnificent. A huge round dome, similar to the Tempietto's, crowns the crossing of the barrel-vaulted arms of a Greek cross, with four lesser domes and tall corner towers at the intersections. This plan fulfills all the demands laid down by Alberti for sacred architecture (see pages 412–14), yet it is strikingly different from anything envisioned by him (compare

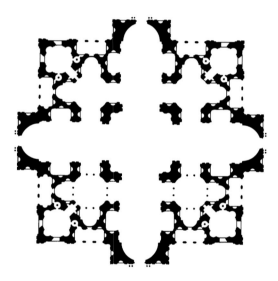

13-9. Donato Bramante. Original plan for St. Peter's, Rome. 1506 (after Geymuller)

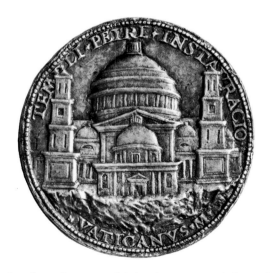

13-10. Caradosso. Bronze medal showing Bramante's design for St. Peter's. 1506. The British Museum, London

fig. 12-32). Based entirely on the circle and the square, it is so symmetrical that we cannot tell which apse was to hold the high altar. Bramante envisioned four identical facades dominated by severely classical forms: domes, half-domes, colonnades, and pediments.

Inside the church, however, the sculptured wall reigns supreme. The plan shows no continuous surfaces, only great, oddly shaped islands of masonry that have been well described by one critic as giant pieces of toast half-eaten by a voracious space. The actual size of these islands can be visualized only if we compare the measurements of Bramante's church with those of earlier buildings. S. Lorenzo in Florence, for instance, has a length of 268 feet, less than half that of the new St. Peter's (550 feet). Bramante's reference to the Pantheon and the Basilica of Constantine thus was no idle boast. His plan dwarfs these monuments, as well as every Early Renaissance church. (Each arm of the Greek cross has about the same dimensions as the Basilica of Constantine.) How did Bramante propose to build such an enormous structure? Cut stone and brick, the materials favored by medieval architects, would not do, for technical and economic reasons. Only concrete, as used by the Romans but largely forgotten during the Middle Ages, was strong and cheap enough (see page 177). By reviving this ancient technique, Bramante opened a new era in the history of architecture. Concrete permitted far more flexible designs than the building methods used by medieval masons. However, its possibilities were not exploited fully for some time. The construction of St. Peter's progressed so slowly that in 1514, when Bramante died, only the four crossing piers had been built. For the next three decades the project was carried on by architects trained under Bramante, who altered his design in a number of ways. A new and decisive phase in the history of St. Peter's began in 1546, when Michelangelo took charge. The present appearance of the church is largely shaped by his ideas (see fig. 13-27). But this must be considered in the context of Michelangelo's career as a whole.

Michelangelo

Nowhere is the concept of genius as divine inspiration—a superhuman power granted to a few individuals and acting through them—embodied more fully than in the life and work of Michelangelo (Michelangelo di Lodovico Buonarroti Simoni, 1475–1564). It was not only his admirers who viewed him in this light. He himself, steeped in Neo-Platonist thought (see pages 442–44), accepted the idea of his genius as a living reality, although it seemed to him at times a curse rather than a blessing. What brings continuity to Michelangelo's long and stormy career is the sovereign power of his personality, his faith in the subjective rightness of everything he created. Conventions, standards, and traditions might be observed by lesser artists, but for him there was no higher authority than the dictates of his genius.

Unlike Leonardo, for whom painting was the noblest of the arts because it embraced every visible aspect of the world, Michelangelo was a sculptor to the core. More specifically, he was a carver of marble statues. Art, for him, was not a science but "the making of men," analogous (however imperfectly) to divine creation. Hence the limitations of sculpture, which Leonardo condemned as mechanical, unimaginative, and dirty, were virtues in Michelangelo's

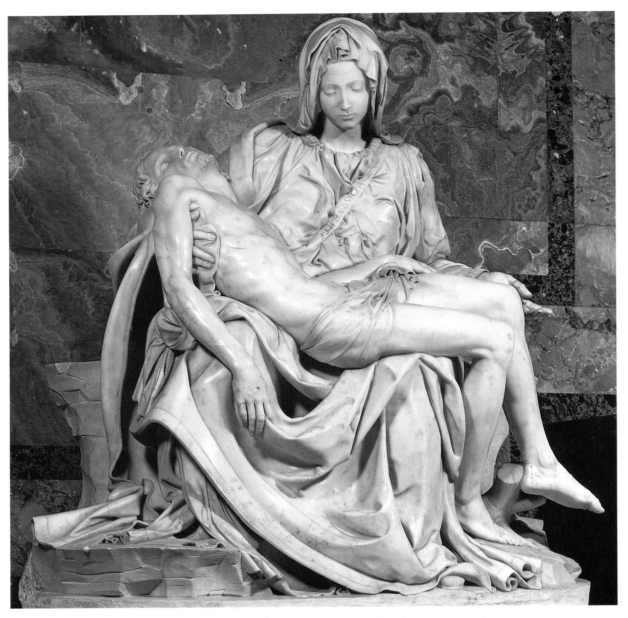

13-11. Michelangelo. *Pietà*. c. 1500. Marble, height 68½" (173.9 cm). St. Peter's, Rome

eyes. Only the "liberation" of real, three-dimensional bodies from recalcitrant matter could satisfy his creative urge. Painting, for him, must imitate the roundness of sculptured forms. Architecture, too, ought to share the organic qualities of the human figure.

Michelangelo's faith in the human image as the supreme vehicle of expression gave him a sense of kinship with classical sculpture closer than that of any Renaissance artist. Among Italian masters he admired Giotto, Masaccio, Donatello, and Della Quercia more than the painters and sculptors he knew as a youth in Florence. Of his training little is known. He was apprenticed to Ghirlandaio and carefully studied Masaccio's frescoes in the Brancacci Chapel (see figs. 12-40, 12-41, and 12-42). Soon he was taken under the wing of Lorenzo de' Medici, which enabled him to study the antique statues in the garden of one of the family's houses. The collection was overseen by Bertoldo di Giovanni (c. 1420–1491), a pupil of Donatello, who presumably taught him the rudiments of sculpture. From the beginning, however, Michelangelo was a carver rather than a modeler.

The young artist's mind was decisively shaped by the cultural climate of Florence during the 1480s and 1490s, even though the troubled times led him to flee the city for Rome in 1496. Both the Neo-Platonism of Marsilio Ficino and the religious reforms of Savonarola affected him profoundly. These conflicting influences reinforced the tensions in Michelangelo's personality, his violent changes of mood, his sense of being at odds with himself and with the world. Just as he conceived his statues as human bodies released from their marble prisons, so he saw the body as the earthly prison of the soul—noble perhaps, but a prison nonetheless. This dualism of body and spirit endows his figures with extraordinary pathos. Although outwardly calm, they seem stirred by an overwhelming psychic energy that finds no release in physical action.

PIETÀ. We sense none of these struggles in the *Pietà* commissioned in 1497 by a French cardinal for his tomb chapel in St. Peter's (fig. 13-11). The subject, of Northern origin (see pages 353–54), is rare, though not unknown, in Italy before this time. Michelangelo probably knew it from a German example that is documented as being in Florence during his youth. One of the Seven Sorrows of the Virgin, the pietà owed its sudden popularity at the end of the fifteenth century to the growing veneration of Mary. Seated on Golgotha, Michelangelo's beautiful and youthful Madonna stands for the Church and serves as the gateway to Heaven. This Lamentation lacks the pathos of the German *Andachtsbild* (compare fig. 11-54). We are meant to contemplate the central mystery of Christian faith—Christ as God in human form who sacrificed himself to redeem original sin—with the same serenity as Mary herself. In spiritual as well as aesthetic terms, the statue still belongs to the fifteenth century. It is indebted to Jacopo della Quercia for the figure of the Virgin and to Andrea Verrocchio for the nobility of the faces and the ornamental treatment of the drapery. The cloak flowing like a river over the Madonna enables Michelangelo to resolve her physically and visually awkward relationship with her dead son. This problem seems to have been of little interest to the German Gothic artist, who instead used it to heighten the expressiveness of the figures. Michelangelo succeeded in his ambition to carve "the most beautiful work of marble in Rome, one that no living artist could better." To Vasari it "was a revelation of all the potentialities and force of the art of sculpture."

DAVID. The unique qualities of Michelangelo's art do not emerge fully until his *David* (fig. 13-12), the earliest monumental statue of the High Renaissance. Commissioned in 1501 as the symbol of the Florentine republic, the huge figure was designed to be placed high above the ground, on one of the buttresses of Florence Cathedral. However, a committee of civic leaders and artists decided instead to put it in front of the Palazzo Vecchio (see fig. 11-39), the fortresslike palace of the Medici near the center of town.

We can well understand the decision. By omitting the head of Goliath, Michelangelo transforms his *David* from a victorious hero into the champion of a just cause. To Michelangelo, he embodied Fortitude—as did the "Herakles" on Nicola Pisano's pulpit (see fig. 11-59), which the *David* resembles in colossal form. Here, however, the figure has a civic as well as a moral significance. Vibrant with pent-up energy, he faces the world like Donatello's *St. George* (see fig. 12-3), although his nudity links him to the older master's bronze *David* as well (see fig. 12-6). The style of the sculpture proclaims an ideal very different from the wiry slenderness of Donatello's youth. Michelangelo had just spent several years in Rome, where he had been deeply impressed with the emotion-charged, muscular bodies of Hellenistic sculpture. Their heroic scale, their superhuman beauty and power, and the swelling volume of their forms became part of Michelangelo's own style and, through him, of Renaissance art in general.

Whereas his earlier work could sometimes be taken for ancient statues, in the *David* Michelangelo competes with antiquity on equal terms and replaces its authority with his own. This resolute individualism is partly indebted to Leonardo da Vinci, who had recently returned to Florence. (As with all of Michelangelo's great peers, the two soon became bitter rivals.) So is the expressive attitude of the figure, which conveys the "intention of man's soul." In

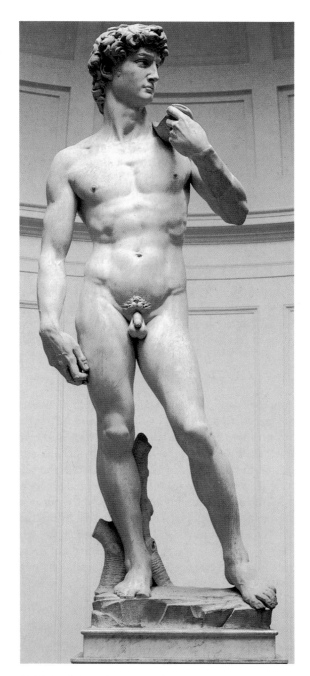

13-12. Michelangelo. *David.* 1501–4.
Marble, height 13'5" (4.08 m).
Galleria dell'Accademia, Florence

Hellenistic works (compare fig. 5-76) the body "acts out" the spirit's agony, while the *David,* at once calm and tense, shows the action-in-repose that is so characteristic of Michelangelo.

THE TOMB OF JULIUS II. This feature is seen again in the *Moses* (fig. 13-13) and the two *"Slaves"* (figs. 13-14 and 13-15, page 462) about ten years later. They were part of the ambitious sculptural program for the Tomb of Julius II, which would have been Michelangelo's greatest achievement if he had been able to carry it out as originally planned. The *Moses,* meant to be seen from below, has the awesome force called *terribilità*—a concept similar to the

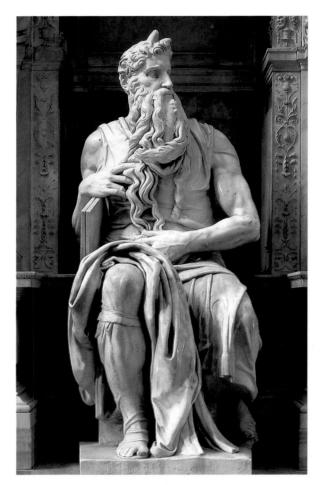

13-13. Michelangelo. *Moses.* c. 1513–15.
Marble, height 7'8½" (2.35 m).
S. Pietro in Vincoli, Rome

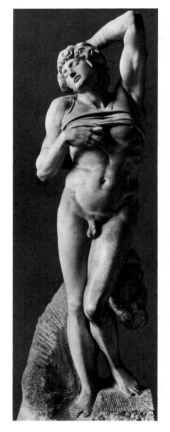

13-14. Michelangelo.
"The Dying Slave." 1513–16.
Marble, height 7'6" (2.28 m).
Musée du Louvre, Paris

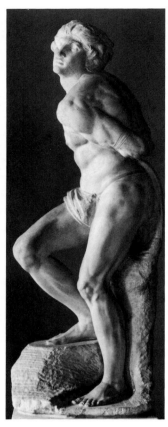

13-15. Michelangelo.
"The Rebellious Slave." 1513–16.
Marble, height 7' (2.13 m).
Musée du Louvre, Paris

sublime. His pose, both watchful and meditative, suggests a man capable of wise leadership as well as towering wrath. We must not interpret the statue as showing a specific action or moment in time, though it is clear that Moses has just received the Ten Commandments. The position of the hands denotes awe in the presence of the Lord. The horns, a traditional attribute based on a mistranslation of the Hebrew word for light in the Vulgate (Latin Bible) that is also seen in Sluter's *Moses Well* (see fig. 11-56), signify the divine favor bestowed on Moses, whose face shone after he came down from Mount Sinai (Exodus 34). Whatever symbolic meaning the sculpture may have had was soon lost as Michelangelo reworked the plan of the tomb. (Originally *Moses* was to have been paired with a Saint Paul, who also "saw the light" of the Lord.)

The *"Slaves"* are more difficult to interpret. They seem to have belonged to a series representing the arts, now shackled by the death of their greatest patron. Later they came to signify the territories conquered by Julius II. In any event, Michelangelo has treated the two figures as a contrasting pair. *"TheDying Slave"* (fig. 13-14) yields to his bonds, while *"The Rebellious Slave"* (fig. 13-15) struggles to free himself. In them we may see the influence of *The Laocoön Group* (see fig. 5-78), whose unearthing Michelangelo witnessed in 1506. Perhaps their meaning mattered less to him than their expressive content, which evokes the Neo-Platonic

image of the body as the earthly prison of the soul. They represent the spiritual state of humanity, with all its conflicts, as reflected in one of the artist's own verses:

He cannot act who by himself is bound
And of himself no one is freely loosed.

The unfinished *Awakening Prisoner* (fig. 13-16), from a later plan for the tomb, provides invaluable insights into Michelangelo's artistic personality and working methods. For him the making of a work of art was both joyous and painful, full of surprises, and not mechanical in any way. It appears that he started the process of carving a statue by trying to visualize a figure in the block as it came to him from the quarry. (At times he may even have done so while picking out his material on the spot.) At first Michelangelo did not see the figure any more clearly than one can see an unborn child inside the womb. He may have believed that he could see "signs of life" within the marble—a knee or an elbow pressing against the surface. To get a firmer grip on this dimly felt image, he made numerous drawings, and sometimes small models in wax or clay, before he dared to assault the "marble prison" itself. For that, he knew, was the final contest between himself and his material. We know that he drew the main view on the front of the

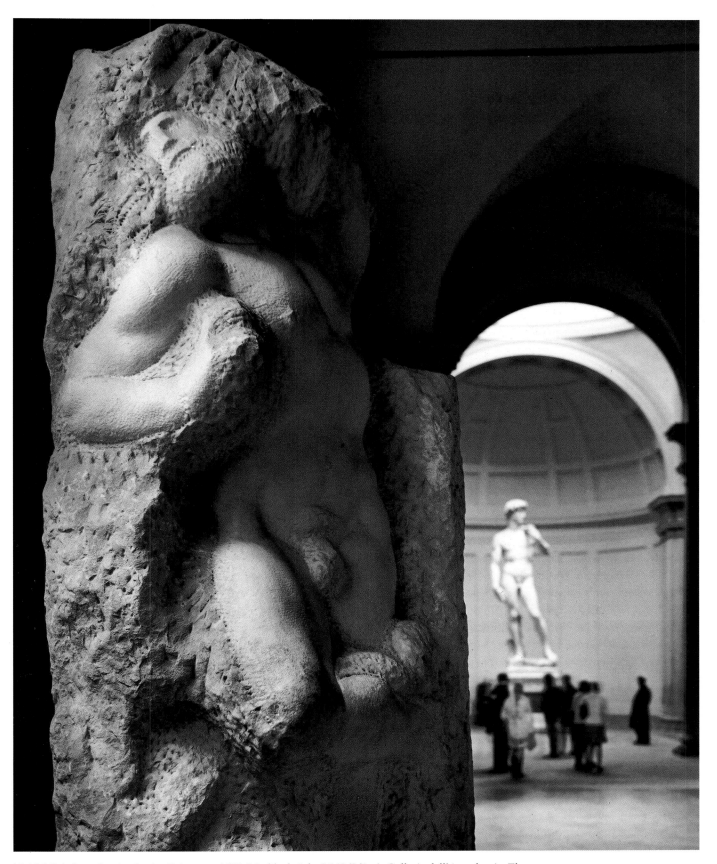

13-16. Michelangelo. *Awakening Prisoner.* c. 1525. Marble, height 8'11" (2.7 m). Galleria dell'Accademia, Florence

block. Once he started carving, every stroke of the chisel would commit him more and more to a specific conception of the figure hidden in the block. The marble would permit him to free the figure only if his guess about its shape was correct. Through a flow of impulses back and forth between the mind and the partly shaped material, the artist gradually defined more and more of the image, until at last all of it had been given visible form. Sometimes he did not guess well enough. The stone refused to give up some essential part of its prisoner, and he left the work unfinished. Michelangelo himself came to appreciate the expressive qualities of incomplete works. Although he abandoned *Awakening Prisoner* for other reasons, every gesture seems to record the struggle for liberation and embody his inspiration even more faithfully than the *"Slaves."*

THE SISTINE CEILING. Julius II interrupted Michelangelo's work on the tomb at an early stage. He decided to enlarge St. Peter's—at first, it seems, to house his tomb, an idea that was soon abandoned. When the project was turned over to Bramante (see pages 458–59), Michelangelo left Rome in anger. Two years later, the pope half-forced, half-coaxed him to return to paint frescoes on the ceiling of the Sistine Chapel in the Vatican (fig. 13-17). Driven by his desire to resume work on the tomb, Michelangelo finished the ceiling in only four years, between 1508 and 1512. [See Primary Sources, no. 43, pages 645–47.] He produced a work of truly epochal importance. The ceiling is a huge organism with hundreds of figures distributed rhythmically within the painted architectural framework.

THEATER AND MUSIC DURING THE HIGH RENAISSANCE

Although the term applies specifically to art, the High Renaissance was intimately connected to literature, theater, and music. Indeed, these arts created the cultural climate that made the High Renaissance possible in the first place. The early sixteenth century ushered in the first great age of Italian literature since the time of Dante and Petrarch some 200 years earlier. It centered on the poet Ludovico Ariosto (1474–1533), whose masterpiece, *Orlando Furioso* (1532), used the story of the crusader knight Roland to glorify his patron, the d'Este family of Ferrara. As early as 1508, Ariosto had written the first comedy along classical lines in Italian: *The Chest,* which initiated the genre known as *commedia erudita* (learned or serious comedy). Even Niccolò Machiavelli (1469–1527), who is best known for his manual of power and courtly life, *The Prince* (published posthumously in 1532), wrote a comedy, *The Mandrake.* The first vernacular tragedy, *Sofonisba* (1515) by Giangiorgio Trissino (1478–1550), was written in the Greek style to combat the influence of Seneca, thus setting off a debate that was effectively won by partisans of Latin drama in 1541, when *Orbecche* by Giambattista Cinthio (1504–1573) became the first Italian tragedy actually to be produced.

The High Renaissance counterpart to Ariosto in music was the Fleming Josquin Des Prés (c. 1440–1521), who became the most celebrated composer of his time. Artistically he belonged to the same generation as Leonardo da Vinci, though he was even older. Despite his notorious artistic temperament, he was employed at one time or another by all the leading courts in Italy and France and enjoyed the patronage of no fewer than three popes. (He was present at the Vatican when Perugino and Botticelli were decorating the walls of the Sistine Chapel.) Josquin was regarded with much the same awe as Michelangelo came to be by his peers. The first true musical genius we know of, Josquin was a virtuoso equally at ease in secular and religious music. His work represented the perfect marriage of Flemish composition and Italian humanism, which, inspired by Greek accounts, sought unity between text and music. He thus found his ideal outlet in the song *(chanson)* and the motet (from the French term *mot* for "word"), which made an entire realm of human action and feeling that lay outside the scope of the traditional Mass available to

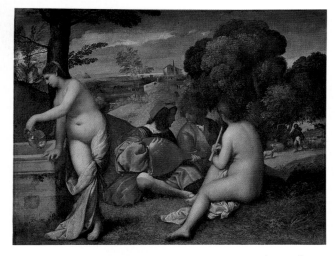

Titian. *Pastoral Concert.* c. 1509–10. Oil on canvas, 43¼ x 54⅜" (105 x 136.5 cm). Musée du Louvre, Paris

him. He cultivated a smooth, homogeneous style that has aptly been compared to the art of Raphael as the embodiment of the classical ideal in its calm, balanced perfection. He was also important for beginning to lead music away from the system of modes used throughout the Middle Ages and Early Renaissance.

Josquin became famous throughout Europe, thanks not only to his travels but also to the invention of music publication using movable type by the Venetian Ottaviano Petrucci (1466–1539) in 1498, a development that proved as revolutionary as printing had been for books and printmaking. Petrucci enjoyed such success that during the 1520s and 1530s France, Germany, and the Netherlands emerged as rival centers of music publishing. The diffusion of music and ideas in print helped to elevate composers in humanist circles. Like artists, they now became "learned" and joined in debates over matters of theory with other intellectuals. Their status was further enhanced by the appearance of the first primers, which taught amateurs how to play instruments and set off a new wave of enthusiasm for music.

It is a sign of the growing importance of music that courts competed eagerly for the leading composers and musicians, who commanded high salaries. Moreover, the ideal prince or courtier was expected to cultivate some musical ability in addition to his other talents. That consummate courtier Leonardo da Vinci was himself an accomplished musician, as were Giorgione and Titian.

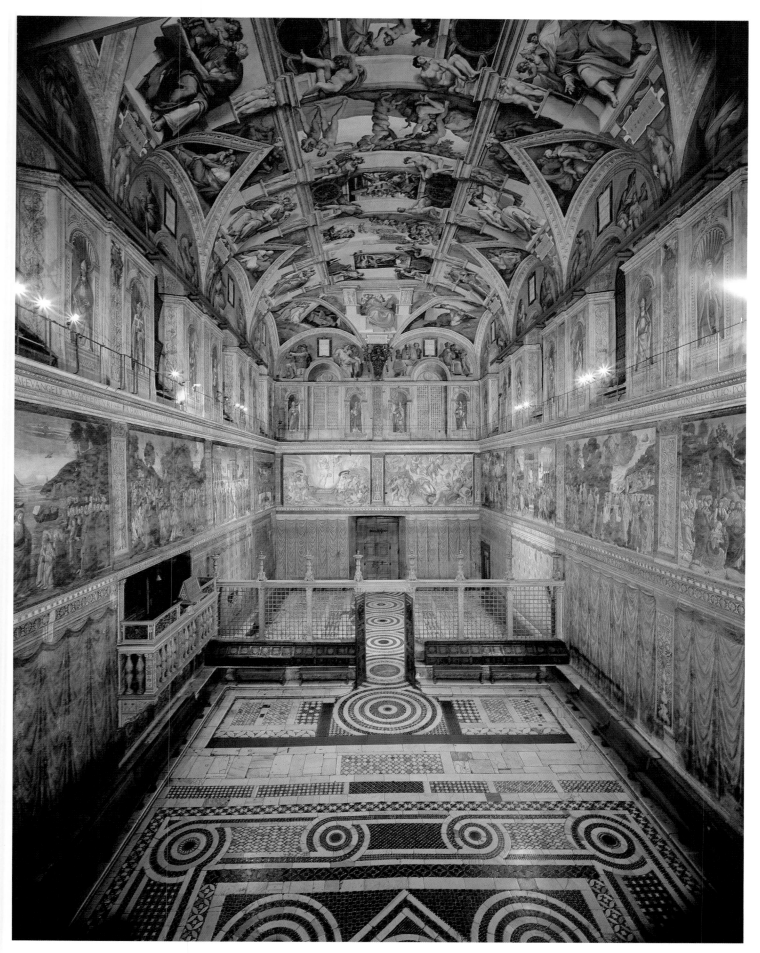

13-17. Interior of the Sistine Chapel showing Michelangelo's ceiling fresco. The Vatican, Rome

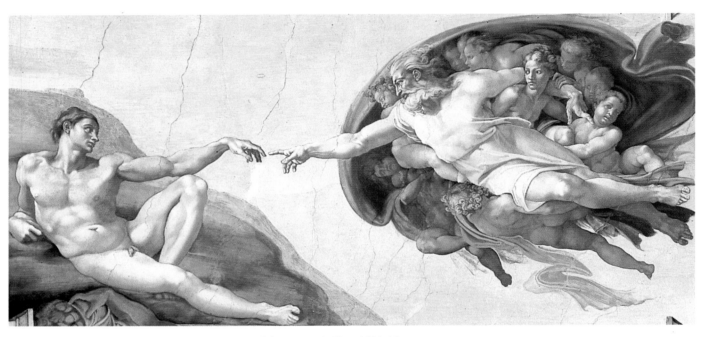

13-18. Michelangelo. *The Creation of Adam,* portion of the Sistine Ceiling. 1508–12.

In the central area, subdivided by five pairs of girders, are nine scenes based on the Old Testament Book of Genesis, from the Creation of the World (at the far end of the chapel) to the Drunkenness of Noah. The theological scheme of these and other subjects and the prophets, sibyls, nude youths, medallions, and the scenes in the **spandrels** that accompany them, has not been fully explained. We know, however, that they link early history and the coming of Jesus. What greater theme could Michelangelo wish than the creation, destruction, and salvation of humanity? It is unclear how much responsibility he had for the program, but the subject fits his cast of mind so perfectly that his own desires cannot have conflicted strongly with his theological advisor's.

A detailed survey of the ceiling would fill a book, and we shall have to be content with two of the four major scenes in the center portion. Of these, *The Creation of Adam* (fig. 13-18) must have stirred Michelangelo's imagination most deeply. It shows not the physical molding of Adam's body but the passage of the divine spark—the soul—and thus achieves a dramatic relationship unri-

valed by any other artist. Della Quercia had approached it in his relief panel (see fig. 12-18), which Michelangelo admired. But Michelangelo's design has a dynamism that contrasts the earthbound Adam, who has been likened to an awakening river-god (compare fig. 13-34), with the figure of God rushing through the sky. This relationship takes on even more meaning when we realize that Adam strains not only toward his Creator but also toward Eve, whom he sees, yet unborn, in the shelter of the Lord's left arm. The image is the perfect expression of Michelangelo's view of his own artistic creativity.

Michelangelo was long regarded as a poor colorist, but the recent cleaning of the frescoes revealed this view to be unjust. *The Fall of Man* and *The Expulsion from the Garden of Eden* (fig. 13-19) show the bold, intense hues that characterize the whole ceiling. The range of his palette is astonishing. Contrary to what had been thought, the heroic figures are nothing like painted sculpture. Full of life, they act out their epic roles in illusionistic "windows" that puncture the architectural setting. Michelangelo does not simply

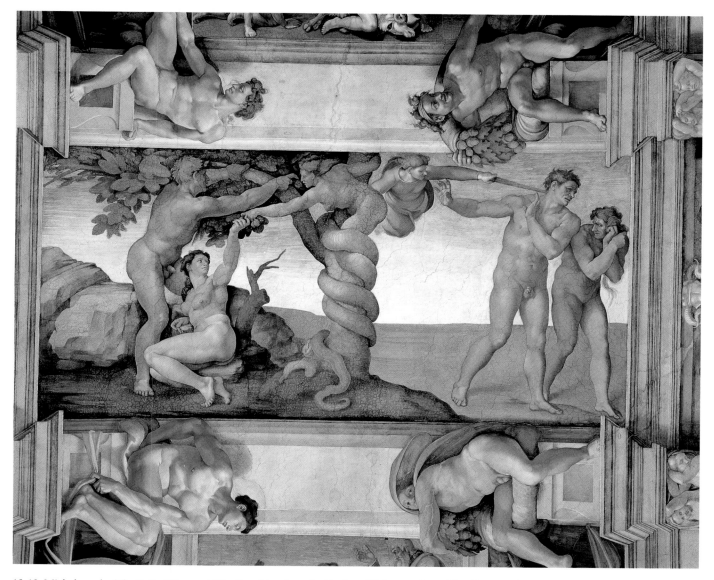

13-19. Michelangelo. *The Fall of Man* and *The Expulsion from the Garden of Eden,* portion of the Sistine ceiling. 1508–12.

color the areas within the contours. Rather, he builds up his forms from broad and vigorous brushstrokes in the tradition of Giotto and Masaccio. Indeed, *The Expulsion* is particularly close to Masaccio's (see fig. 12-43) in its intense drama. *The Fall,* in contrast, has an elegance that surely expresses not only beauty but a spiritual state of grace as well.

The nude youths that accompany the main sections of the ceiling play an important role in Michelangelo's design. These wonderfully animated figures, which are found at regular intervals, form a kind of chain linking the Genesis scenes. Yet their significance remains uncertain. Do they represent the world of pagan antiquity? Are they angels or images of human souls? They seem to be ideal beings, but ones who have not yet attained a state of grace and thus yearn for salvation. Whatever the answer, they clearly belong to the same category as the *"Slaves"* from the Tomb of Julius II, to which they are closely related visually and conceptually. Once again the symbolic meaning is overpowered by the expressiveness Michelangelo has poured into these figures.

THE LAST JUDGMENT. When Michelangelo returned to the Sistine Chapel in 1534, more than 20 years after completing the ceiling, the Western world was undergoing the spiritual and political crisis of the Reformation and Catholic Reform (see page 534). Michelangelo's religious beliefs had changed as well. We see the new mood with shocking directness as we turn from the radiant vitality of the ceiling fresco to the somber vision of *The Last Judgment* (fig. 13-20, page 468), which illustrates Matthew 24:29–31.

How unlike the well-ordered, majestic treatment of Giotto (compare fig. 11-78), whose conception of Hell in the lower right-hand corner is still closely related to that on the west tympanum at Autun (see fig. 10-24). Michelangelo must have looked partly to Luca Signorelli's frescoes for Orvieto Cathedral (fig. 12-58). In the Sistine Chapel, however, the agony has become essentially spiritual, as expressed through violent physical contortions within the turbulent atmosphere. The Blessed and Damned alike huddle together in tight clumps, pleading for mercy before a wrathful God. The only trace of classicism is the Apollo-like figure of the

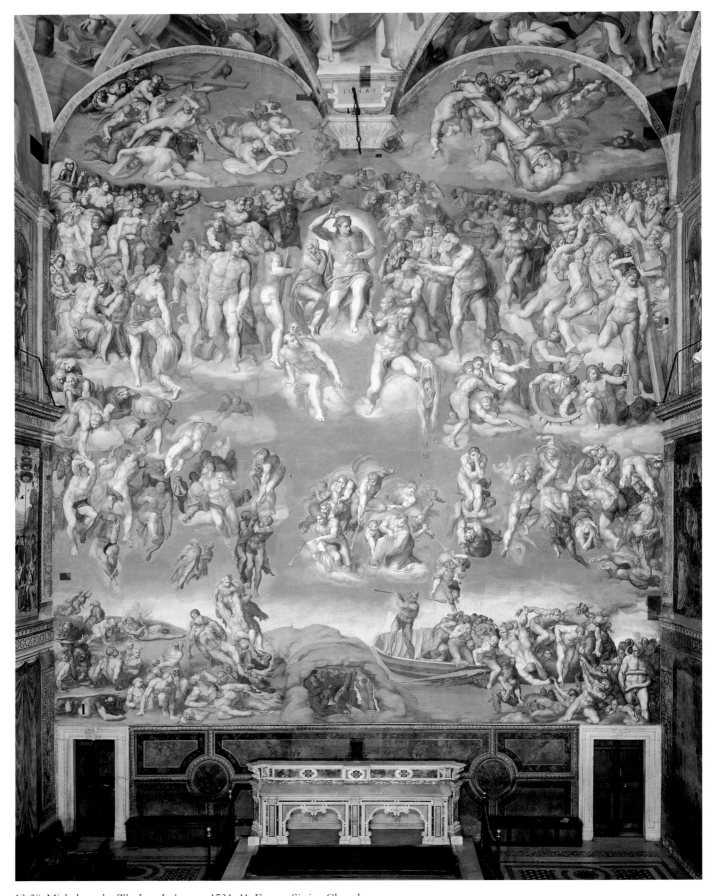

13-20. Michelangelo. *The Last Judgment.* 1534–41. Fresco. Sistine Chapel

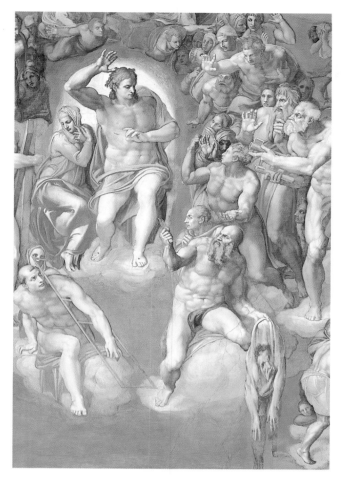

13-21. Michelangelo. *The Last Judgment* (detail, with self-portrait)

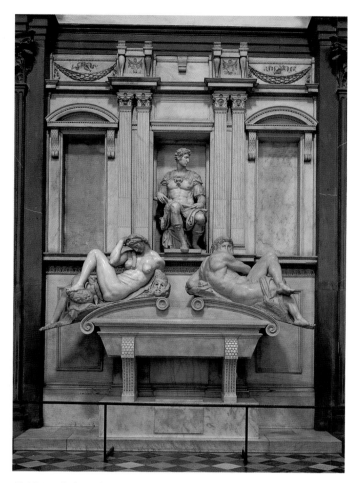

13-22. Michelangelo. Tomb of Giuliano de' Medici. 1524–34. Marble, height of central figure 71" (180.5 cm). New Sacristy, S. Lorenzo, Florence

Lord. Straddling a cloud just below him is the apostle Bartholomew (fig. 13-21), holding a human skin to represent his martyrdom by flaying. The face on that skin, however, is not the saint's but Michelangelo's own. In this grim self-portrait, so well hidden that it was recognized only in modern times, the artist has left his personal confession of guilt and unworthiness.

THE MEDICI CHAPEL. The time between the Sistine Ceiling and *The Last Judgment* coincides with the papacies of Leo X (1513–21) and Clement VII (1523–34). Both were members of the Medici family and preferred to employ Michelangelo in Florence. His activities centered on the Medici church of S. Lorenzo. A century after Brunelleschi's design for the sacristy (see page 422), Leo X decided to build a matching structure, the New Sacristy. It was to house the tombs of Lorenzo the Magnificent, Lorenzo's brother Giuliano, and two younger members of the family, also named Lorenzo and Giuliano. Michelangelo worked on the project for 14 years and managed to complete the architecture and two of the tombs, those for the lesser Lorenzo and Giuliano (fig. 13-22); these tombs are nearly mirror-images of each other. The New Sacristy was thus conceived as an architectural-sculptural ensemble. It is the only one of the artist's works in which the statues remain in the setting intended for them, although their exact placement is problematic. Michelangelo's plans for the Medici tombs underwent many changes while the work was under way. Other figures and reliefs were designed but never executed. The present state of the Medici tombs can hardly be the final solution, but the process was halted when the artist left permanently for Rome in 1534.

The tomb of Giuliano remains an imposing visual unit, although the niche is too narrow and shallow to accommodate the seated figure easily. The triangle of statues is held in place by a network of verticals and horizontals whose slender, sharp-edged forms heighten the roundness and weight of the sculpture. The design still shows some kinship with such Early Renaissance tombs as Leonardo Bruni's (see fig. 12-12), but the differences are more important. There is no inscription, and the effigy has been replaced by two allegorical figures—*Day* on the right and *Night* on the left. What is the meaning of this group? Some lines penned on one of Michelangelo's drawings suggest an answer: "Day and Night speak, and say: We with our swift course have brought the Duke Giuliano to death . . . It is only just that the Duke takes revenge [for] he has taken the light from us; and with his closed eyes has locked ours shut, which no longer shine on earth."

Giuliano, the ideal image of the prince, is in classical military garb and bears no resemblance to the deceased Medici. ("A

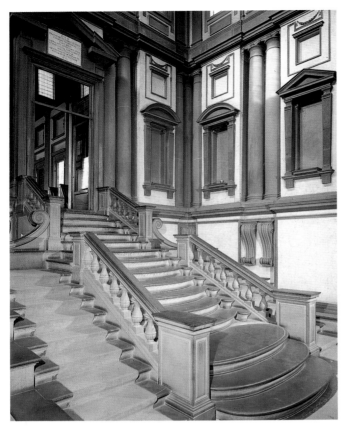

13-23. Michelangelo. Vestibule of the Laurentian Library, Florence. Begun 1524; stairway designed 1558–59

the columns support piers, which in turn support the roof beams—this feature flies in the face of convention. In the classical post-and-lintel system the columns (or pilasters) and entablature must project from the wall in order to stress their separate identities. The system could be reduced to a linear pattern (as in the Palazzo Rucellai; fig. 12-28), but no one before Michelangelo had dared to defy it by incorporating columns into the wall.

The purpose of these innovations is expressive rather than functional. The walls push inward between the columns to make the vestibule a kind of "compression chamber" where the viewer feels an almost physical stress. Our discomfort is heightened by the blank stare of the empty niches and by the nightmarish stairway, whose solution came to Michelangelo in a dream many years later. The steps, built from his design by Bartolommeo Ammanati (see page 507), flow downward and outward so relentlessly that we wonder if we dare brave the current to ascend them.

THE CAMPIDOGLIO. During the last 30 years of Michelangelo's life, his main pursuit was architecture. In 1537–39, he received the most ambitious commission of his career: to reshape the Campidoglio, the top of Rome's Capitoline Hill, into a piazza and frame it with a monumental architectural ensemble worthy of the site, which once had been the symbolic center of ancient Rome. At last he could plan on a grand scale, and he took full advantage of the opportunity. Although not completed until long after his death, the project was carried out essentially as he had designed it. The Campidoglio remains the most imposing civic center ever built, and it has served as a model for countless others. Pope Paul III transferred the equestrian monument of Marcus Aurelius (see fig. 7-40) to the Campidoglio, and Michelangelo designed its base. The statue became the focal point of his entire scheme, placed at the top of a gently rising oval mound that serves to integrate the space.

Three sides of the piazza are defined by palace facades. After climbing the flight of steps on the fourth side, visitors find themselves in a huge "outdoor room." The effect cannot be seen in photographs. Even the best view, an engraving based on Michelangelo's design (fig. 13-24), conveys it imperfectly. The print shows the symmetry of the scheme and the sense of

thousand years from now, nobody will know what he looked like," Michelangelo is said to have remarked.) Originally the base of each tomb was to have included a pair of river-gods. The reclining figures, themselves derived from ancient river-gods (compare fig. 13-35), contrast in mood like the *"Slaves."* They embody action-in-repose more dramatically than any other works by Michelangelo. In the brooding menace of *Day,* whose face was left deliberately unfinished, and in the disturbed slumber of *Night,* the dualism of body and soul is expressed with unforgettable grandeur.

THE LAURENTIAN LIBRARY. The Tomb of Giuliano de' Medici is squeezed uncomfortably into an architectural framework that takes considerable liberties with classicism. The New Sacristy inspired Vasari to write that "all artists are under a great and permanent obligation to Michelangelo, seeing that he broke the bonds and chains that had previously confined them to the creation of traditional forms." However, his full powers as a creator of new architectural forms are displayed for the first time in the vestibule (fig. 13-23) to the Laurentian Library, adjoining S. Lorenzo. This library was built at the same time as the New Sacristy to house, for the public, the huge collection of books and manuscripts belonging to the Medici family.

According to the standards of the 1520s as defined by the classical ideal of Bramante, everything in the vestibule is wrong. The pediment above the door is broken. The pilasters of the niches taper downward, and the columns belong to no recognizable order. The scroll brackets sustain nothing. Most paradoxical of all are the recessed columns. Although logical in structural terms—

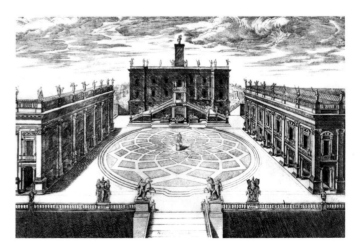

13-24. Michelangelo. The Campidoglio
(engraving by Étienne Dupérac, 1569)

progression along the main axis toward the Senators' Palace. However, it distorts the shape of the piazza, which is not a rectangle but a trapezoid (fig. 13-25). This peculiarity was dictated by the site. The Senators' Palace and the Conservators' Palace on the right were older buildings that had to be preserved behind new exteriors, but they were placed at an angle of 80 instead of 90 degrees. Michelangelo turned this problem into an asset. By adding the "New Palace" on the left, which complements the Conservators' Palace in style and placement, he makes the Senators' Palace look larger than it is, so that it dramatically dominates the piazza.

The whole conception has the effect of a stage set. All three buildings are long but relatively narrow, like a show front with little behind it. However, these are not shallow screens but three-dimensional structures (fig. 13-26). The "New Palace" and its twin, the Conservators' Palace, combine voids and solids, horizontals and verticals in a way not found in any piece of architecture since Roman antiquity (compare fig. 7-23). They also share a striking feature: an open portico which links the piazza and facades, just as a courtyard is related to the arcades of a cloister.

The columns and beams of the porticoes are contained in a colossal order of pilasters that supports a heavy cornice topped by a balustrade. We have seen these elements before (see figs. 12-15, 12-38, and 13-7), but it was Michelangelo who made full use of them. For the Senators' Palace he used the colossal order and balustrade above a tall base, which emphasizes the massiveness of the building. The single entrance at the top of the double-ramped stairway (see fig. 13-24) seems to gather all the spatial forces set in motion by the oval mound and the flanking structures. It thus provides a dramatic climax to the piazza.

ST. PETER'S. Michelangelo used the colossal order again on the exterior of St. Peter's (fig. 13-27). He took over the design of the church in 1546 upon the death of the previous architect, Antonio da Sangallo the Younger (the nephew of his friend Giuliano da Sangallo but a rival nonetheless), whose work he completely recast. The system of the Conservators' Palace could be adapted to the jagged contour of the plan, but with windows instead of open loggias and an attic instead of the balustrade. Unlike Bramante's many-layered elevation (fig. 13-10), Michelangelo's uses a colossal order of pilasters to emphasize the compact body of the structure, thus setting off the dome more dramatically. We have encountered the colossal order before, on the facade of Alberti's S. Andrea (see fig. 12-32), but it was Michelangelo who welded it into a fully coherent system. The same desire for compactness and

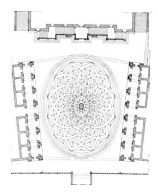

13-25. Plan of the Campidoglio, Rome

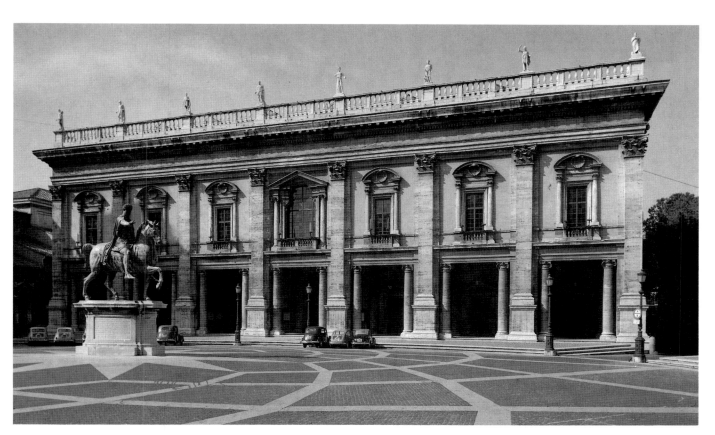

13-26. Michelangelo. Palazzo dei Conservatori, Campidoglio, Rome. Designed c. 1545

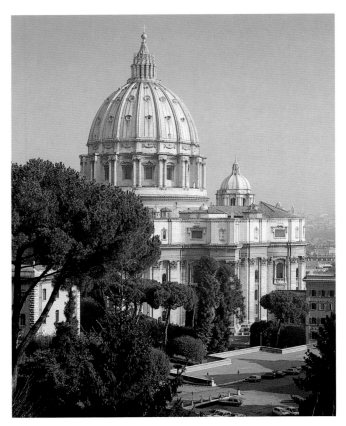

13-27. Michelangelo. St. Peter's, Rome, seen from the west. 1546–64 (dome completed by Giacomo della Porta, 1590)

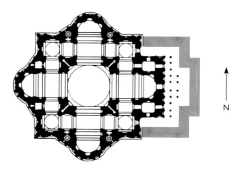

13-28. Michelangelo. Plan for St. Peter's

organic unity led him to simplify the interior (fig. 13-28). He brought the complex spatial sequences of Bramante's plan (see fig. 13-9) into one cross-and-square. He further defined its main axis by modifying the eastern apse and adding a portico to it; this part of his design was never carried out (see page 571). The dome, however, reflects Michelangelo's ideas in every important respect, although it was largely built after his death and has a steeper pitch.

Bramante had planned his dome as a stepped hemisphere above a narrow drum, which would have seemed to press down on the church. Michelangelo's, in contrast, has a powerful thrust that draws energy upward from the main body of the structure. Michelangelo borrowed not only the double-shell construction but also the Gothic profile from the Florence Cathedral dome (see fig. 11-35), yet the effect is very different. The smooth planes of Brunelleschi's dome give no hint of the internal stresses.

Michelangelo, however, gives sculptured shape to these forces and relates them to the rest of the building. The impetus of the paired colossal pilasters is taken up by the double columns of the high drum and the strongly projecting buttresses accented by double columns. It continues in the ribs and the raised curve of the cupola, then culminates in the tall lantern. The logic of this design is so persuasive that almost all domes built between 1600 and 1900 were influenced by it.

Michelangelo's magnificent assurance in handling the Campidoglio and St. Peter's seems to belie his portrayal of himself as a limp skin in *The Last Judgment.* It is indeed difficult to reconcile these contrasting sides of his personality. Perhaps toward the end of his life he found greater fulfillment in architecture than in shaping human bodies, for we have no finished sculpture from his hand after 1545, when he at last completed the Tomb of Julius II. He devoted much of his final two decades to poetry and drawings of a religious and Neo-Platonic sort that are highly personal in content. The statues undertaken for his own purposes, including a *Pietà* intended for his tomb that he mutilated and partly reworked, show him groping for new forms, as if his earlier work had become meaningless to him.

Raphael

If Michelangelo represents the solitary genius, Raphael of Urbino (Raffaello Sanzio, 1483–1520) belongs to the opposite type: the artist as a man of the world. As a result, the two were natural antagonists. The contrast between them was as clear to their contemporaries as it is to us. Although each had his defenders, they enjoyed equal fame. Thanks to Vasari, Michelangelo's chief supporter, as well as to the authors of historical novels and fictionalized biographies, Michelangelo still fascinates people. Today Raphael is usually discussed only by historians of art, although his life, too, was the subject of a fanciful account. The younger artist's career seems too much a success story, his work too marked by effortless grace, to match the tragic heroism of Michelangelo. Raphael also seems to have been less of an innovator than Leonardo, Bramante, and Michelangelo, whose achievements were basic to his. Nevertheless, he is the central painter of the High Renaissance. Our conception of the entire style rests more on his work than on any other artist's. During his relatively brief career he created the largest body of pictorial work outside of Titian's, one that is notable for its variety and power.

Raphael had a unique genius for synthesis that enabled him to merge the qualities of Leonardo and Michelangelo. Yet he was far more original than this statement suggests. His art is lyrical and dramatic, pictorially rich and sculpturally solid. These qualities are already present in the Madonnas he painted in Florence (1504–8) after his apprenticeship with Perugino. The meditative calm of *La Belle Jardinière* (fig. 13-29) still reflects the style of his teacher (compare fig. 12-56). However, the forms are ampler and enveloped in sfumato. The Virgin, grave and tender, makes us think of the *Mona Lisa,* but without her mystery. The idealization of form already shows the grace and perfection that are the hallmarks of Raphael's style. The enigmatic gestures in *The Virgin of the Rocks* (see fig. 13-2) are replaced by a gentle, rhythmic interplay. In place of the intricate grouping, we find a stable pyramid whose severity is relieved by Mary's billowing cape. Most striking is the beautiful landscape which, unlike any by Leonardo, is carefully observed. The human forms, too, have a firmness that further demonstrates Raphael's devotion to nature.

THE STANZA DELLA SEGNATURA. One of the reasons *La Belle Jardinière* looks different from *The Virgin of the Rocks,* to which it is otherwise so clearly indebted, is Michelangelo's influence, which is seen in the figural composition. Its full force can be felt only in Raphael's Roman works, however. In 1508, at the time Michelangelo began to paint the Sistine ceiling, Julius II summoned Raphael from Florence at the suggestion of Bramante, who also came from Urbino. At first Raphael mined ideas he had developed under his teacher Perugino, but Rome utterly transformed him as an artist, just as it had Bramante, and he underwent an astonishing growth. The results can be seen in the Stanza della Segnatura (Room of the Seal, fig. 13-30), the first in a series of rooms he was called on to decorate at the Vatican Palace, that show an almost endless fertility in creating daring narrative compositions. The stanza housed Julius II's personal library; only later did the tribunal of the seal *(segnatura),* presided over by Pope Paul III, meet there to dispense canon and civil law.

Raphael's cycle of frescoes on its walls and ceiling refers to the four domains of learning: theology, philosophy, law, and the arts. The program is derived in part from the Franciscan St. Bonaventure, who sought to reconcile reason and faith. It has roots as well in St. Thomas Aquinas, the Dominican chiefly responsible for reviving Aristotelian philosophy, who was influenced by Franciscan thought (see box pages 299–300). (Pope Julius II himself was a Franciscan, but there was also a major Dominican presence at the Vatican.) More generally, the Stanza represents a summation of High Renaissance humanism, for it attempts to unify all under-

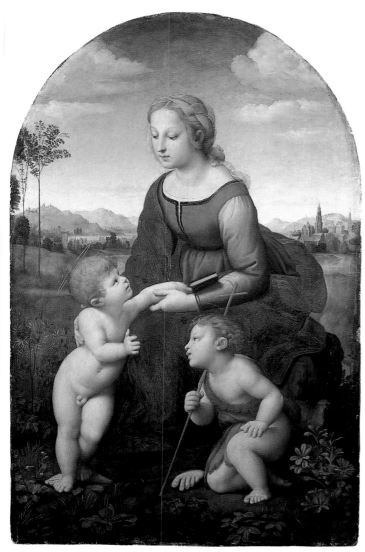

13-29. Raphael. *La Belle Jardinière.* 1507. Oil on panel, 48 x 31½" (122 x 80 cm). Musée du Louvre, Paris

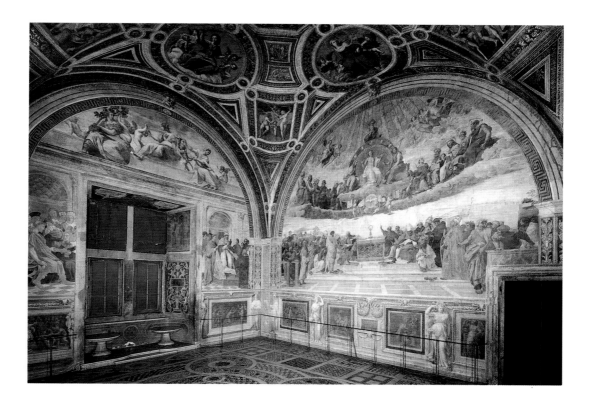

13-30. Stanza della Segnatura, with frescoes by Raphael. 1508–11. Vatican Palace, Rome

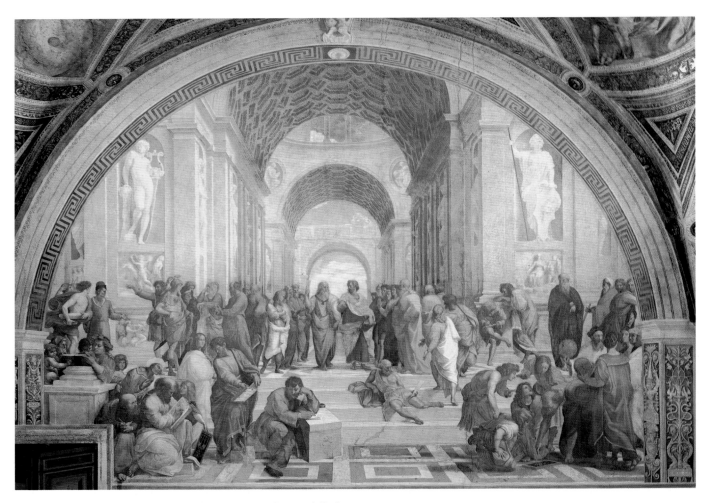

13-31. Raphael. *The School of Athens.* 1510–11. Fresco. Stanza della Segnatura

standing into one grand scheme. Raphael probably had a team of scholars and theologians as advisors, yet the design is his alone.

To the right in figure 13-30 is *La Disputa,* or *Disputation over the Sacrament.* This was the first mural to be painted and theologically the most important. Jesus sits enthroned in heaven between the Virgin and St. John the Baptist. God the Father is behind him, with saints and prophets to either side, and the Holy Spirit hovering over the Eucharist below. Around the altar are church doctors, popes, artists, poets, and other personages, many of them unidentified. The title *La Disputa,* assigned in the seventeenth century, is misleading. The participants are not so much discussing as bearing witness to the Eucharist and its central place in the Catholic faith. The architectural space of the earthly realm is still treated in the geometric perspective of Perugino's *Delivery of the Keys* (see fig. 12-56), while the landscape makes subtle use of atmospheric perspective to emphasize the Host as the Light of the World. But it is the visionary space of the heavens that gives the mural a majesty in keeping with the sacred subject. The idea seems to have been inspired by the passage in Hebrews 12:1, "we also are encompassed about with so great a cloud of witnesses. . . ." It further embodies Bonaventure's quote from Ecclesiasticus (the apocryphal book Sirach), "In the highest heavens did I dwell, my throne on a pillar of cloud," as well as his definition of god, cited from Alan of Lille, "as an intelligible sphere whose center is everywhere and whose circumference is nowhere." Interestingly, the

ratios of the circles are the musical intervals established by Pythagoras (see box page 139).

In the lunette over the door to the left are personifications of *The Three Legal Virtues*—Fortitude, Prudence, and Temperance. Beneath are *The Granting of Civil Law* (left) and *The Granting of Canon Law* (right), which attest to Julius II's activist view of the church militant. The opposite doorway depicts *Parnassus,* the sacred mountain of Apollo. The Muses appear in the company of the great poets from antiquity to the artist's own time. Humanists had regarded artistic inspiration as a means of revelation since the time of Dante and Petrarch. The painting reflects the papal court's dream of a Golden Age under Julius II, in which the Vatican Hill would become the new Parnassus. The message of the Stanza della Segnatura is that the philosophy of antiquity, along with knowledge and the arts, are forms of revelation that emanate from God. They lead to religious truth but are subordinate to it, just as civic law is subordinate to canon law. They are united by one of the most potent Christian concepts: *Logos* (the Word), which arises from the One and thus is absolute.

Of all the frescoes in the Stanza della Segnatura, *The School of Athens* (fig. 13-31), facing *La Disputa,* has long been acknowledged as Raphael's masterpiece and the perfect embodiment of the classical spirit of the High Renaissance. Its subject is "the Athenian school of thought": a group of famous Greek philosophers gathered around Plato and Aristotle, each in a characteristic pose or activity. Raphael must have already looked at the Sistine ceiling, then nearing completion. He owes to Michelangelo the expressive energy, the physical power, and dramatic grouping of his figures. Yet Raphael has not simply borrowed Michelangelo's gestures and poses. He has absorbed them into his own style and thus given them a different meaning. [See Primary Sources, no. 42, page 645.]

Body and spirit, action and emotion, are now balanced harmoniously, and all members of this great assembly play their roles with magnificent, purposeful clarity. The total conception of *The School of Athens* suggests the spirit of Leonardo's *The Last Supper* (see fig. 13-3) rather than the Sistine ceiling. Raphael makes each philosopher reveal "the intention of his soul." He further distinguishes the relations among individuals and groups, and links them in a formal rhythm. (The artist worked out the poses in a series of drawings, many from life.) Also in the spirit of Leonardo is the symmetrical design, as well as the interdependence of the figures and their architectural setting. But Raphael's building plays a greater role in the composition than the hall of *The Last Supper.* With its lofty dome, barrel vault, and colossal statuary, it is classical in spirit, yet Christian in meaning. Inspired by Bramante, who, as Vasari informs us, helped Raphael with the architecture, it seems like an advance view of the new St. Peter's. It bears a striking resemblance to drawings by the Northerner Maerten van Heemskerk in 1532–35 recording the great church under construction, from which it differs mainly in the decorative details. (Raphael developed into a skilled architect in his own right and succeeded Bramante at St. Peter's.) The dimensions and overall ground plan of the structure can be determined with considerable accuracy. This geometric precision, along with the spatial grandeur of the work as a whole, brings to a climax the tradition begun by Masaccio (see fig. 12-38). It was transmitted to Raphael by Perugino, who had inherited it from Piero della Francesca. What is new is the active role played by the architecture in creating narrative space. This innovation was of fundamental importance and had a profound impact on the course of painting far beyond the sixteenth century.

The School of Athens has a complex program that reflects the most learned humanism of the day. We can give only the briefest account here. The building is in the shape of a simplified Greek cross to suggest the harmony of pagan philosophy and Christian theology. There are two huge niche sculptures. To the left is Apollo with a lyre, who reappears as the central figure in the mural *Parnassus.* To the right is Athena in her Roman guise as Minerva, goddess of wisdom and patron deity of the arts, who, in the words of the poet Dante, hastens the arrival of Apollo. The identity of most of the figures is not certain, but we can be sure that many incorporate portraits of Raphael's friends and patrons. At center stage (fig. 13-32) Plato (whose face resembles Leonardo's) is holding his book of cosmology and numerology, *Timaeus,* which provided the basis for much of the Neo-Platonism that came to pervade Christianity. It presents a universe ruled by Divine Intelligence *(Nous)* instilled by the Demiurge, the giver of Forms, who takes over the chaos left by the Creator-God. Of particular importance is his theory of an ascending ladder of forms, which he called the Great Chain of Being. To Plato's proper left (the "sinister," or inferior side) his pupil Aristotle grasps a volume of his *Ethics,* which, like his science, is grounded in what is knowable in the material world.

Although he studied with Plato, Aristotle rejected his teacher's belief in Absolute Good arising from Forms as the Ideas of God. Instead, he took a pragmatic approach based as much on psychology as philosophy. The tomes explain why one is pointing rhetorically to the heavens (the same gesture is found in *La Disputa*), the other to the earth. Thus stand reconciled the two most important Greek philosophers, whose approaches, although seemingly opposite, were deemed complementary by many Renaissance humanists. From the spatial construction of the two murals, it is clear that Raphael shows *The School of Athens* leading quite literally to *La Disputa:* if it were extended, the heavenly circle of saints and Old Testament figures in *La Disputa* would locate the ideal vantage point about 26 feet across the room, a little in front of *The School of Athens.*

To Plato's right (his "good" side) is his mentor, Socrates, in a purple robe, who was already viewed as a precursor of Jesus because he died for his beliefs (see fig. 21-2). He is addressing a group of disciples that includes the warrior Alkibiades. Standing before the steps are figures representing mathematics and physics (the lower branches of philosophy that are the gateway to higher knowledge). Raphael borrowed the features of Bramante for the head of Euclid, seen drawing or measuring two overlapping triangles with a pair of compasses in the foreground to the lower right. The diagram must be a reference to the star of King David, who occupies an analogous position on the second level of *La Disputa.* These triangles, in turn, form the plan for the arrangement of the figures in the fresco.

On the other side is the bearded Pythagoras, for whom all things were numbers. He has his sets of numbers and harmonic ratios arranged on a pair of inverted tables that each achieve a total of the divine number ten. They refer in turn to the two tablets with the Ten Commandments held by Moses, who is found directly opposite in *La Disputa.* However, this is also the format of an inverted canonical table, thus giving a Christian meaning to a

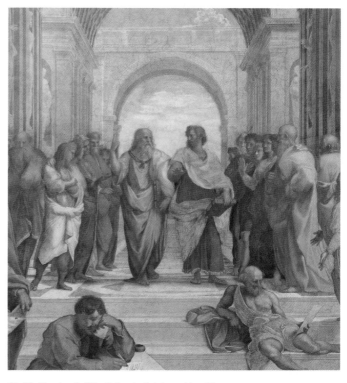

13-32. Raphael. *The School of Athens* (detail)

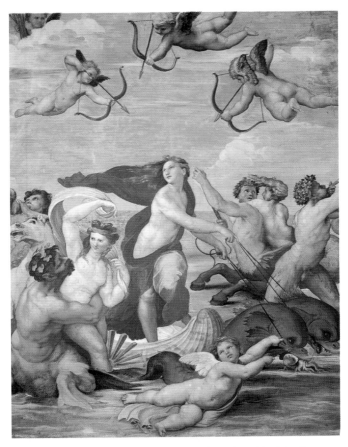

13-33. Raphael. *Galatea*. 1513. Fresco, 9'8⅛" x 7'4" (3 x 2.2 m). Villa Farnesina, Rome

pagan concept. In addition to positing the One (a counterpart to God in Neo-Platonic thought), Pythagoras believed in a rational universe based on harmonious proportions, the foundation for much of Greek philosophy.

This conviction was shared by the geographer, astronomer, and mathematician Ptolemy, seen from behind holding a terrestrial globe to the right of Euclid. He is shown crowned because he bore the same name as the Greek kings who ruled Egypt for 250 years after it was conquered by Alexander the Great (see page 69). (He is wrongly considered to be the astrologer Zoroaster by Vasari and by the seventeenth-century writer Pietro Bellori, who identified the relief above as Virtue seated beneath the Zodiac.) Ptolemy is linked to the scientist Aristotle and is paired in turn with a man holding a celestial globe. Modern scholars often identify the latter as Zoroaster, but more likely he is the Greek astronomer Hipparchus, whose catalog of the stars was the foundation of Ptolemy's astronomy. Next to them are two artists, perhaps Apelles and Protagoras. Vasari states that the man wearing a black hat is a self-portrait of Raphael. The other has generally been assumed to be Il Sodoma, the painter displaced by Raphael in the Stanza della Segnatura, but more likely he is Raphael's teacher, Perugino.

Despite their rivalry, Raphael added Michelangelo at the last minute as Heraclitus writing on the steps. Heraclitus, the first to posit *Logos* (later equated with Christ; see Primary Sources, no. 18, pages 385–86), was often paired with Diogenes the Cynic, shown lying at the feet of Plato and Aristotle, according to Vasari. Attempts to name other great philosophers who must have been

included, such as the hedonist Epicurus and the Stoic Zeno, who were always paired, have proved too speculative to be of any real value, or are simply wrong. The inclusion of so many artists among, as well as in the guise of, famous philosophers is testimony to their recently acquired—and hard-won—status as members of the learned community.

GALATEA. Raphael rarely set so splendid a stage again. To create pictorial space, he relied increasingly on the movement of human figures rather than perspective vistas. In the *Galatea* of 1513 (fig. 13-33), the subject is again classical: The beautiful nymph Galatea, vainly pursued by the giant Polyphemus, belongs to Greek mythology. Like the verse by Angelo Poliziano that inspired it, the painting celebrates the lighthearted, sensuous aspect of antiquity, in contrast to the idealism of *The School of Athens*. While the latter presents an ideal view of the antique past, *Galatea* captures its pagan spirit as if it were a living force. The composition recalls Botticelli's *The Birth of Venus* (see fig. 12-53), a picture Raphael had known in Florence, which shares a debt to Poliziano (see page 441). Yet the very resemblance emphasizes their profound differences. Raphael's figures take on their dynamic spiral movement from the vigorous contrapposto of Galatea. In Botticelli's picture, the movement is not generated by the figures but imposed on them by the decorative, linear design, so that it remains on the surface of the canvas.

THE JUDGMENT OF PARIS. Raphael's statuesque, full-bodied figures suggest his careful study of ancient Roman sculpture, such as the so-called Altar of Domitius Ahenobarbus (c. 30 B.C., Staatliche Aktinensammlungen, Munich). (He was later appointed superintendent of antiquities for all of Rome.) An even more direct example of his use of antique sources is his design for the engraving *The Judgment of Paris* by Marcantonio Raimondi (figs. 13-34 and 13-35). It is based on a Roman sarcophagus panel then in the collection of Cardonal della Valle. (Later the panel was hung on a wall overlooking the garden of the Villa Medici in Pincio.)

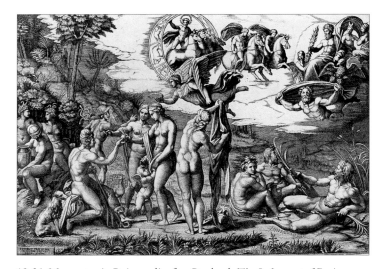

13-34. Marcantonio Raimondi, after Raphael. *The Judgment of Paris*. c. 1520. Engraving. The Metropolitan Museum of Art, New York

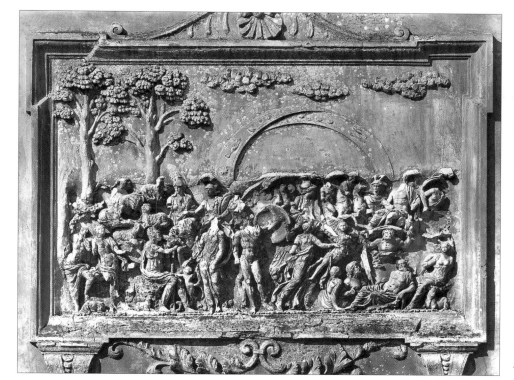

13-35. *The Judgment of Paris.*
Roman sarcophagus. 3rd century A.D.
Villa Medici, Rome
GIVEN ANONYMOUSLY

(BELOW) 13-36. Raphael. *Pope Leo X
with Giulio de' Medici and
Luigi de' Rossi.* c. 1518. Oil on panel,
60⅝ x 46⅞" (154 x 119 cm).
Galleria degli Uffizi, Florence

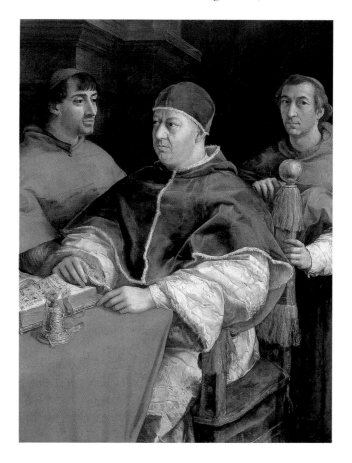

In both compositions we see the Judgment of Paris to the left, and to the right Mars accompanying Venus to Olympia, where they are greeted by Zeus holding his thunderbolt. While Raphael has taken obvious liberties with the scene, rarely did he quote as directly as here. His main departure is to clarify the subject matter of the antique panel by separating the different activities into distinct pictorial pockets, instead of having them all take place on the same ground plane. Like Michelangelo, Raphael competes with Antiquity, but on equal terms, rather than as follower or imitator, by "improving" on the sarcophagus instead of literally copying it. What is equally remarkable is that Marcantonio did not reverse the direction of Raphael's drawings, as is normally the case, but painstakingly copied it in reverse, a very difficult task, so that the engraving would look as close to the original as possible when printed. Even the size is identical. The same technique was used in three other drawings designed by Raphael specifically as prints for Marcantonio (as against sheets he had lying around his studio, which sometimes were also made available to the engraver). In each, the artist dictated the network of the engraver's lines precisely, so that there is a nearly ideal balance of light and dark for the sake of pictorial clarity.

PORTRAITS. In his portraits Raphael combined the realism of fifteenth-century portraits (such as fig. 12-55) with the human ideal of the High Renaissance, which in the *Mona Lisa* nearly overpowers the sitter's individuality. It is a tribute to his genius that he did not flatter his subjects or impose conventions on them. Surely Pope Leo X (fig. 13-36) looks no more handsome here than he did in reality. The heavy-jowled features of this hedonistic pope have been recorded in detail, yet he has a commanding presence. His aura of power and dignity emanates more from his inner being than from his office. Raphael, we feel, has not falsified the sitter's personality but ennobled and focused it, as if he had observed Leo X in his finest hour. The contrast with the two cardinals, who lack this balanced strength, enhances his regal character. Even the pictorial treatment has this effect. Leo X has been set off from his companions and his presence heightened by intensified light, color, and texture.

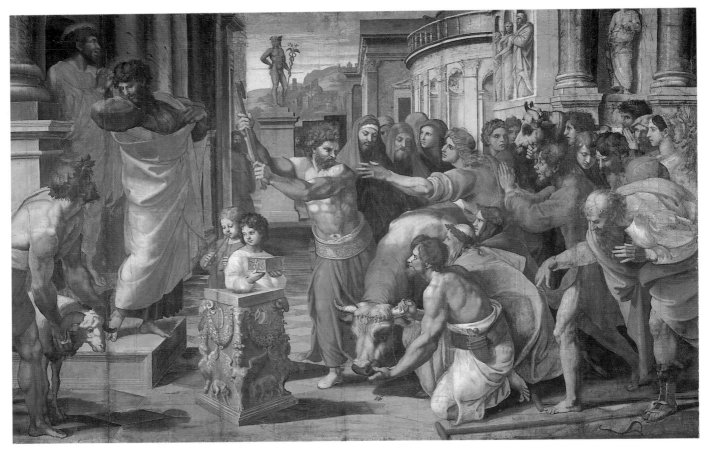

13-37. Raphael. *The Sacrifice at Lystra*. 1514–15. Tempera on paper, 11'5¾" x 17'8½" (3.5 x 5.4 m). Victoria & Albert Museum, London

LATER WORKS. When Leo X sent Michelangelo to Florence in 1516 to work on the Medici Chapel (see page 469), Raphael assumed undisputed leadership of art in Rome. Now he was flooded with commissions, and of necessity depended increasingly on his growing workshop. As a result, few of Raphael's later works, other than the portraits, are entirely by his own hand. His reliance on assistants, as well as the intervention of later restorers, has obscured his achievement. The final phase of his brief career is nevertheless unusually rich and complex.

Raphael raised narrative painting to a new plane in his tapestry cartoons for the Sistine Chapel. The commission placed him in direct competition with Michelangelo, and the series was consequently designed and executed entirely by his own hand. Each cartoon is marked by a creative tension between grandiose rhetoric and high theater that pushes classicism to its limits and sometimes beyond. At times these forces coexist in an uneasy truce, but in *The Sacrifice at Lystra* (fig. 13-37) they are held in a state of dynamic equilibrium that is masterful. The painting greatly expands the pictorial and expressive range of Raphael's art. The scene, taken from Acts 14, shows Paul urging a crowd not to sacrifice animals in his honor after he had healed a cripple (to the far right in our illustration) and was mistaken for Mercury (seen as the statue of the god at upper center in the background). The architectural setting, reconstructed from the antique with the passion of an archaeologist, is disposed across the picture plane, partly in imitation of Roman reliefs (compare fig. 7-37). Besides framing the action, the buildings play an important expressive role by echoing the agitation of the surging crowd and the dignified strength of the saint and his companion, Barnabas.

Raphael has left a telling gap that not only highlights the figure of Mercury but also heightens the contrast between the two groups. The drama differs from anything by Leonardo and Michelangelo thanks to Raphael's unique power of concentration. In this work the artist has exhausted the possibilities of classicism. What steps he might have taken next we shall never know, as his life was cut short at the turning point of the High Renaissance. Yet it is significant that some of the leading Mannerists of the next generation emerged from his workshop and took his style as their point of departure.

Giorgione

The difference between Early and High Renaissance art, so clear in Florence and Rome, is far less sharp in Venice. Giorgione (Giorgione da Castelfranco, 1478–1510), the first Venetian painter to belong to the new era, left the orbit of Giovanni Bellini only during the final years of his short career.

THE TEMPEST. Among his few mature works, *The Tempest* (fig. 13-38) is both the most unusual and the most enigmatic. There have been many attempts to explain this image. The most persuasive one is that the painting depicts Adam and Eve after the Fall. Their fate as decreed by God, whose voice is represented by the lightning bolt, is that man shall till the ground from which he was taken, and that woman shall bring forth children in sorrow.

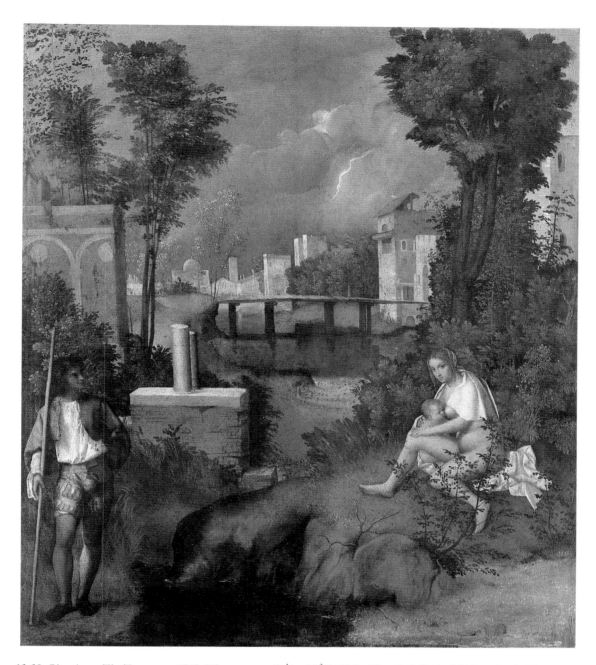

13-38. Giorgione. *The Tempest.* c. 1505. Oil on canvas, 31 ¼ x 28 ¾" (79.5 x 73 cm). Galleria dell'Accademia, Venice

Adam, dressed in Venetian costume, is seen resting from his labors. Eve, whose draped nudity signifies shame and carnal knowledge, suckles Cain, her firstborn son. In the distance is a bridge over the river surrounding the city of the earthly paradise, from which they have been expelled. Barely visible near the rock at river's edge is a snake, signifying the Temptation. The broken columns stand for death, the ultimate punishment of Original Sin.

The Tempest was probably commissioned by the merchant Gabriele Vendramin, one of Venice's greatest patrons of the arts, who owned the picture when it was first recorded in 1530. It certainly reflects the taste for humanist allegories in Venetian painting, whose subjects are often obscured, as here, by static poses and alien settings. The symbolism does not tell us the whole story of *The Tempest,* however. It is the landscape, rather than Giorgione's figures, that interprets the scene for us. Belonging themselves to nature, Adam and Eve are passive victims of the thunderstorm

that seems about to engulf them. The contrast to Bellini's *St. Francis in Ecstasy* (see fig. 12-62) is striking. Bellini's landscape is meant to be seen through the eyes of the saint, as a piece of God's creation. Despite its biblical subject, the mood in *The Tempest* is subtly, pervasively pagan. The scene is like an enchanted idyll, a dream of pastoral beauty soon to be swept away. In the past, only poets had captured this air of nostalgic reverie. Now it entered the repertory of the artist. Indeed, the painting is very similar in mood to *Arcadia* by Jacopo Sannazaro, a poem about unrequited love that was popular in Giorgione's day. Thus *The Tempest* initiates what was to become an important new tradition in art.

Titian

Giorgione died before he could fully explore the sensuous, lyrical world he had created in *The Tempest.* This task was taken up by

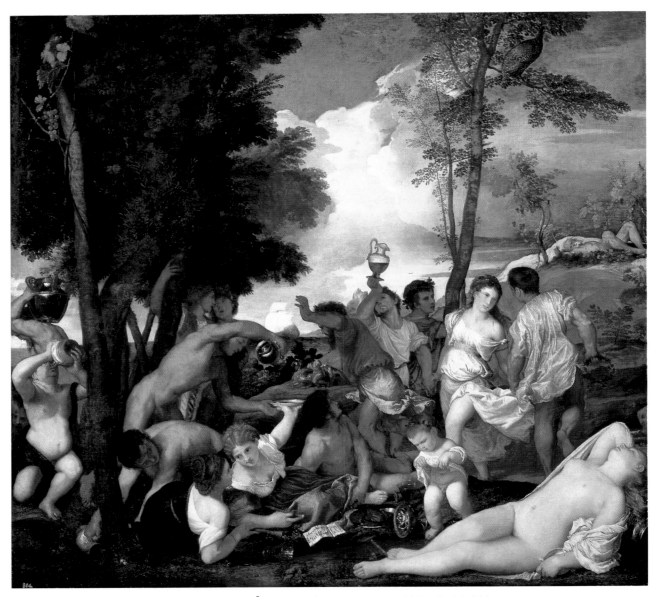

13-39. Titian. *Bacchanal*. c. 1518. Oil on canvas, 5'8⅝" x 6'4" (1.7 x 1.9 m). Museo del Prado, Madrid

Titian (Tiziano Vecellio, 1488/90–1576), who was influenced first by Bellini and then by Giorgione. An artist of incomparable ability, Titian repainted a number of their works. He was to dominate Venetian painting for the next half-century. [See Primary Sources, no. 43, pages 645–47.]

BACCHANAL. Titian's *Bacchanal* (fig. 13-39) is the last of three frankly pagan subjects commissioned around 1518 by Alfonso d'Este, the duke of Urbino, for the Camerino d'Alabastro. This and the similar *Offering to Venus* (Prado, Madrid) were inspired by the Roman author Philostratus' description of two such paintings in a villa outside Naples, and it is likely that the duke himself defined the program. The landscape, rich in contrasts of cool and warm tones, has all the poetry of Giorgione, but the figures are of another breed. Active and muscular, they move with a joyous freedom that recalls Raphael's *Galatea* (see fig. 13-33). By this time, many of Michelangelo's and Raphael's compositions had been engraved (see fig. 13-34), and from these reproductions Titian became familiar with the Roman High Renaissance. A number of

the figures in his *Bacchanal* also reflect the influence of classical art. Titian's approach to antiquity, however, is very different from Raphael's. He visualizes the realm of classical myths as part of the natural world, inhabited not by animated statues but by beings of flesh and blood. The figures of the *Bacchanal* are idealized just enough to persuade us that they belong to a long-lost Golden Age. They invite us to share their blissful state in a way that makes the *Galatea* seem cold and remote by comparison.

THE PESARO MADONNA. This festive quality reappears in many of Titian's religious paintings. *Madonna with Members of the Pesaro Family* (fig. 13-40) is a variant of the sacra conversazione, but he has thoroughly transformed it. For the first time we feel that the participants are actually sharing in a dialogue. The Holy Family is no longer timeless and remote, as in Domenico Veneziano's altar (compare fig. 12-46). The Infant Jesus is as natural as the child in the *Bacchanal*, while the Virgin and St. Peter turn to the donor, Jacopo Pesaro, seen kneeling in devotion at the left. On the other side are the donor's brothers and sons with Saints Francis and Anthony.

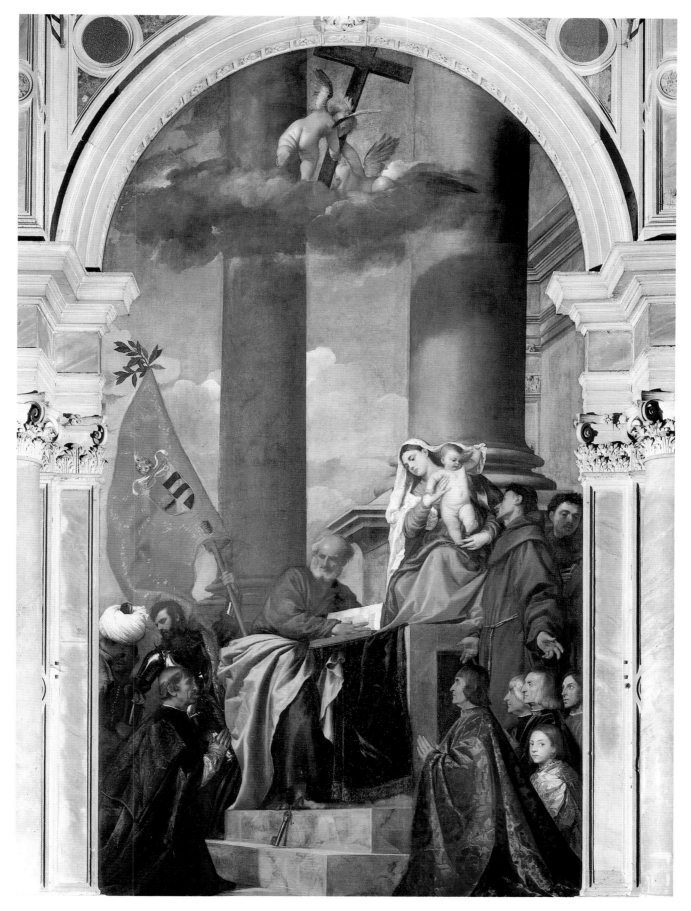

13-40. Titian. *Madonna with Members of the Pesaro Family*. 1526. Oil on canvas, 16' x 8'10" (4.9 x 2.7 m).
Sta. Maria del Gloriosa dei Frari, Venice

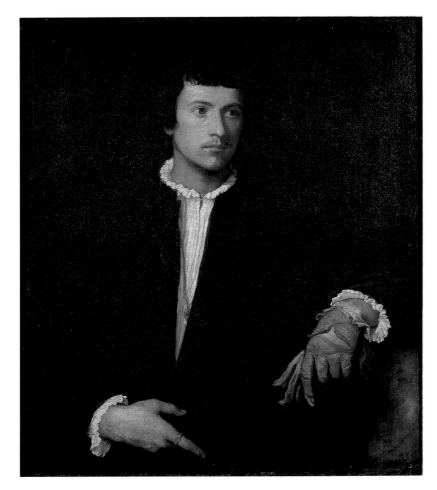

13-41. Titian. *Man with the Glove*. c. 1520.
Oil on canvas, 39½ x 35" (100.3 x 89 cm).
Musée du Louvre, Paris

Much of the picture's effectiveness is due to the composition, which replaces the familiar frontal view with an oblique one that is far more active. The Virgin is enthroned in a barrel-vaulted hall that is open on either side. The setting is a High Renaissance counterpart of the architectural framework in Bellini's *Madonna and Saints* in S. Zaccaria (see fig. 12-63). The elevated columns, which are the key to the setting, represent the gateway to Heaven, traditionally identified with Mary herself. They are furthermore a symbol of both eternal life and the Immaculate Conception (the belief that Mary conceived without Original Sin). Because the view is diagonal, open sky and clouds fill most of the background. Except for the kneeling donors, every figure is in motion. The officer with the flag bearing the coats of arms of Pesaro and of Pope Alexander VI seems almost to lead a charge up the steps. He is probably St. Maurice, namesake of the battle at Santa Mauro where the the papal fleet commanded by Pesaro, bishop of Paphos, and the Venetian navy under his cousin Benedetto Pesaro, defeated the Turks in 1502—note the turbaned figure beside him. St. Peter, identified by the key to the church near his foot that was presented to him by Christ (compare fig. 12-56), represents the Catholic church victorious over Islam and, as Pesaro's patron saint, acts as his intercessor with the Madonna. The design remains harmoniously self-contained, despite the strong drama. Brilliant sunlight makes every color and texture sparkle, in keeping with the joyous spirit of the altar. The only hint of tragedy is

the Cross of the Passion held by the two little angels. Hidden by clouds from the participants in the sacra conversazione but not from us, it adds a note of poignancy to the scene.

PORTRAITS. After Raphael's death, Titian became the most sought-after portraitist of the age. His immense gifts, evident in the donors' portraits in the *Pesaro Madonna,* are even more striking in the *Man with the Glove* (fig. 13-41). The dreamy intimacy of this portrait, with its soft outline and deep shadows, still reflects the style of Giorgione. Lost in thought, the young man seems unaware of us. This slight melancholy in his features has all the poetic appeal of *The Tempest.* The breadth and power of form, however, go far beyond Giorgione's. In Titian's hands, the possibilities of the oil technique—rich, creamy highlights, deep dark tones that are transparent and delicately modulated—now are fully realized, and the separate brushstrokes, hardly visible before, become increasingly free.

We can trace Titian's development as a portraitist by turning to the group portrait *Pope Paul III and His Grandsons* (fig. 13-42), painted a quarter-century later. The composition is derived from Raphael's *Pope Leo X* (see fig. 13-36). The quick, slashing strokes here give the entire canvas the spontaneity of a sketch. (In fact, some parts are unfinished.) In this freer technique, Titian's uncanny grasp of human character also comes out. The tiny figure of the pope, shriveled with age, dominates his tall grandsons with awesome authority.

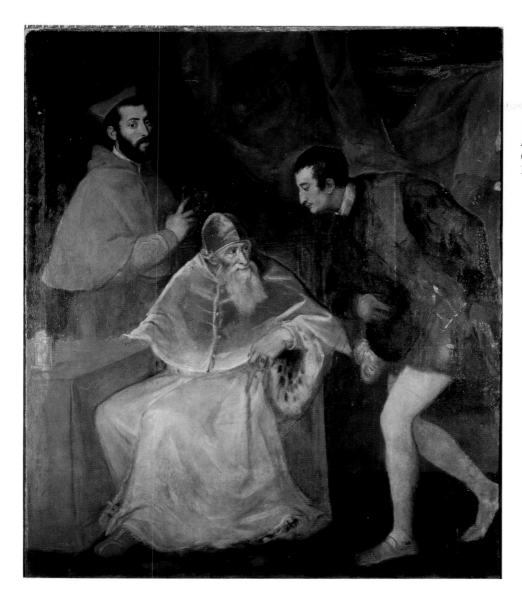

13-42. Titian. *Pope Paul III and His Grandsons.* 1546. Oil on canvas, 6'10" x 5'8" (2.1 x 1.7 m). Museo di Capodimonte, Naples

DANAË. The portrait of Paul II was painted in the middle of Titian's career during a long stay in Rome. *Danaë* (fig. 13-43, page 484), which dates from the same time, is a masterful display of the painterly use of sonorous color. (The story, taken from Ovid's *Metamorphoses,* shows Jupiter in the guise of a gold shower seducing the young woman, who had been locked in a tower by her father to keep away all suitors.) By varying the consistency of his pigments, the artist was able to capture the texture of Danaë's flesh with uncanny accuracy, while distinguishing it clearly from bed sheets and covers. To convey these tactile qualities, Titian built up his surface in thin, transparent glazes. The interaction between these layers produces unrivaled richness and complexity of color; yet the medium is so filmy that it becomes nearly as translucent as the cloud trailing off into the sky.

The figure shows the impact of Michelangelo's *Night* on the Tomb of Giuliano de' Medici (see fig. 13-22), which Titian probably knew from an engraving. After seeing the canvas in the artist's studio, Michelangelo is said to have praised Titian's coloring and style but criticized his design. [See Primary Sources, no. 42, page 645.] We can readily understand Michelangelo's discomfort, for

Titian has rephrased his sculpture in utterly sensual terms. Michelangelo, we know, made detailed drawings for his figures. Titian, too, was a fine draftsman and was influenced by Michelangelo. But although he presumably worked out the essential features of his compositions in preliminary drawings, none has survived. Nor, it seems, did he transfer the design onto the canvas. Instead, he worked directly on the surface and made adjustments as he went along.

Ever since Michelangelo and Titian, the merits of line versus color—*of disegno* and *colore*—have been the subject of intense debate. The role of color rests mainly on its sensuous and emotional appeal, in contrast to the more intellectual quality of line. Titian thus stands at the head of the coloristic tradition that descends through Rubens, Delacroix, and Van Gogh to the Expressionists of the twentieth century.

LATE WORKS. A change of pictorial technique is no mere surface phenomenon. It always indicates a change in the aim of the artist. This correspondence of form and technique that we have already seen in *Danaë* is even clearer in *Christ Crowned with*

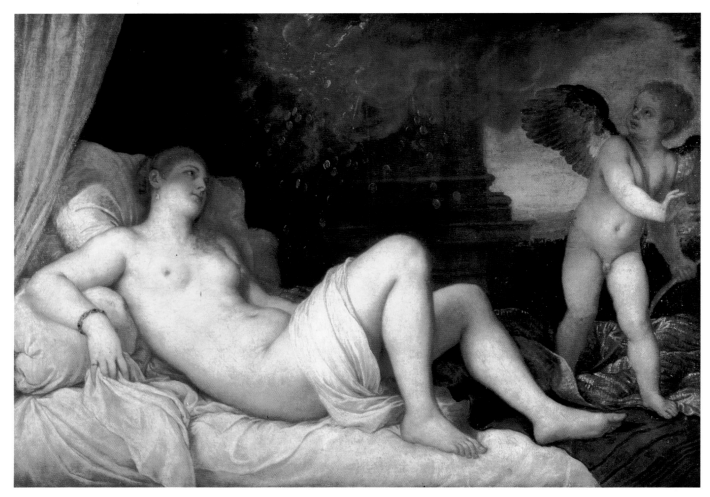

13-43. Titian. *Danaë.* c. 1544–46. Oil on canvas, 47¼ x 67¾" (120 x 172 cm). Museo e Gallerie Nazionale di Capodimonte, Naples

(OPPOSITE) 13-44. Titian. *Christ Crowned with Thorns.* c. 1570.
Oil on canvas, 9'2" x 6' (2.8 x 1.8 m). Alte Pinakothek, Munich.

Titian did not paint man as if he were as free from care and as fitted to his environment as a lark on an April morning. Rather did he represent man as acting on his environment and suffering from his reactions. He made the faces and figures show clearly what life had done to them. The great "Ecce Homo" and the "Crowning with Thorns" [fig. 13-42] are imbued with this feeling no less than the equestrian portrait of Charles the Fifth. . . .In the "Crowning with Thorns" we have the same god-like being almost brutalized by pain and suffering. . . .

Yet Titian became neither soured nor a pessimist. Many of his late portraits are even more energetic than those of his early maturity. He shows himself a wise man of the world. . . .Titian, then, was ever ready to change with the times, and on the whole the change was towards a firmer grasp of reality, necessitating yet another advance in the painter's mastery of his craft. Titian's real greatness consists in the fact that he was as able to produce an impression of greater reality as he was ready to appreciate the need of a firmer hold on life. . . .The difference between the old Titian, author of these works, and the young Titian, painter of the "Assumption" and of the "Bacchus and Ariadne," is the difference between the Shakespeare of the Midsummer Night's Dream *and the Shakespeare of the* Tempest. *Titian and Shakespeare begin and end so much*

in the same way by no mere accident. They were both products of the Renaissance, they underwent similar changes, and each was the highest and completest expression of his own age. . . .I have dwelt so long on Titian, because, historically considered, he is the only painter who expressed nearly all of the Renaissance that could find expression in painting.

—Bernard Berenson. *The Italian Painters of the Renaissance.*
New York: Ursus Press, 1998, pp. 22–23.
Originally published in 1952 by Phaidon Press Inc.

BERNARD BERENSON (1865–1959) was for many decades the most famous name of all in art history, in large part because of successful self-promotion and his association with high-profile patrons of the arts. Born in Lithuania and educated at Harvard, where his classmates included William James and George Santayana, Berenson believed that through connoisseurship one could learn more about art and artists than by any other means or methodology. He had a lifelong, passionate love of Italian art, and his observation-based attributions of thousands of Italian paintings are the core of his great seven-volume *Italian Pictures of the Renaissance* (1932 and 1957). This rumination on Titian's painting in old age is typically appreciative and insightful.

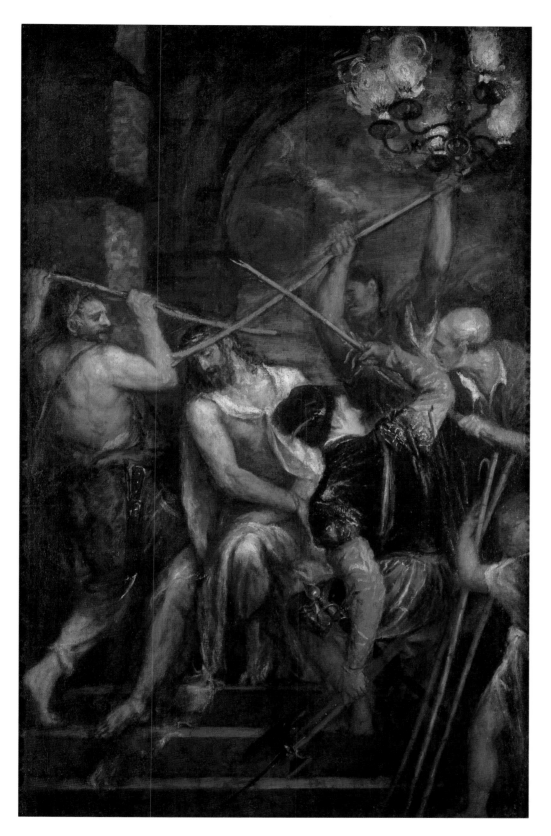

Thorns (fig. 13-44), the most awesome work of Titian's old age. To what does this canvas owe its power? Surely not only to its large scale or dramatic composition, although these are contributing factors. (The painting is a variant of one the artist had made a quarter-century earlier that is less successful.) The answer lies in Titian's technique. The shapes emerging from the semidarkness now consist wholly of light and color. Despite the heavy impasto, the shimmering surfaces have lost every trace of material solidity and seem translucent, as if aglow from within. The violent action has been miraculously suspended. What lingers in our minds is the mood of serenity arising from deep religious feeling rather than the drama. As a result, we contemplate not Jesus' physical suffering but its purpose: the redemption and salvation of humanity. In this respect the painting is the very opposite of a German *Andachtsbild* (compare fig. 11-54). In its ethereality, *Christ Crowned with Thorns* reflects a widespread visionary tendency that was shared by other Venetian artists of the late sixteenth century. We shall meet it again in the work of Tintoretto and El Greco.

CHAPTER FOURTEEN

The Late Renaissance in Italy

Art historians have yet to agree on a name for the 80 years separating the High Renaissance from the Baroque. We have run into this difficulty before, in dealing with the problem of Late Classical versus Hellenistic art. Any label implies that the period has only a single style. This interval, however, was a time of crisis that gave rise to a number of competing tendencies rather than a main ideal. In fact, there is no clear dividing line between them, and we often find several trends in the work of a single artist, which adds to the complexity of the age. Since there was no single style in the years 1520 to 1600, why should this span be thought of as a period at all? What was its relation to the two eras that it separates? The term *Late Renaissance,* which used to be common, is controversial. It implies a period of decline from the peak attained by the High Renaissance and a transition to the great next phase, the Baroque, that followed. Yet we have no truly satisfactory alternative. Until one is found, we have chosen to retain "the Late Renaissance" as a matter of convenience, but with the understanding that it is the rich diversity that gives this epoch its peculiar flavor. We look in vain for an underlying unity, be it historical, social, cultural, or religious. The one common denominator we find is a tidal wave of change on all fronts that reshaped Europe.

The great voyages of discovery that took place during the High Renaissance—Columbus's landing in the New World in 1492, Amerigo Vespucci's exploration of South America seven years later, and Magellan's voyage around the world beginning in 1519—had far-reaching consequences. The most immediate effect was the rise of the great European colonial powers, which vied with each other for commercial supremacy around the world. The Spanish, then the Portuguese, quickly established themselves in the Americas: Mexico was conquered by Hernán Cortés in 1519–21, Peru by Francisco Pizarro during the next decade. By 1585 Sir Walter Raleigh had founded the first English settlement in North America, and the French soon followed with outposts of their own. An unexpected effect was the explosion of knowledge as explorers brought back a host of natural and artistic wonders never before seen in Europe. Avid collectors formed *Kunst- und Wunderkammern* (literally, art and wonder rooms) to display exotic treasures from every corner of the earth.

As Europeans struggled to absorb the new discoveries into old categories of thought, the science inherited from ancient Greece and Rome was largely discarded by 1650 in favor of the new body of learning.

After 1500 the European order was reshaped by new rulers of extraordinary ambition; it is mirrored in the new imagery of court portraiture. Chief among them were Charles V of Spain, Francis I of France, and Henry VIII of England. Charles and Francis spent their reigns in nearly constant warfare against each other. At first the Spanish monarch had the edge. He even took Francis captive in 1525 at the Battle of Pavia and held him prisoner for several years. Eventually, however, Charles abdicated his throne in favor of his son, Philip II, when he was unable to gain a decisive victory over the French king. Yet the French advantage proved short-lived, and Spain emerged as the leading power in Europe after the Treaty of Cateau-Cambrésis in 1559.

Much of the conflict was played out in Italy, where Spain established itself as a force by taking over Naples and Sicily, while France laid claim to Milan. Spanish forces sacked Rome in 1527 and then took Florence in 1530, when they also imprisoned the Medicean pope Clement VII (ruled 1523–34) in Rome. The conflict inevitably came to involve the papacy, which formed the Holy League from leading Italian cities to protect its assets and those of the powerful families that occupied the Throne of St. Peter for most of the first half of the century: the Medicis from Florence and the Farneses of Rome. The struggle for power between France and Spain engaged much of the rest of Europe in constantly shifting alliances on both sides. They vied for the support of the princes and dukes of Germany, England, and Scotland, and even the Turks, who became allies of the French for a while. As a result, no side gained the upper hand for long, and treaties were made and broken in rapid succession.

The Reformation and Counter Reformation ultimately became embroiled in the political upheavals and social unrest that gripped Europe after 1520. Yet religion played a relatively small and inconsistent part in this larger arena before 1560, despite intense sectarian wars at the local level. Catholics and Protestants regularly entered into unions based on self-interest, economic necessity, and the need to maintain a balance of power between France and Spain. Although they were sometimes passionate in their beliefs, rulers usually allied themselves with the Reformation and Counter Reformation for dynastic reasons. Thus Henry VIII of England established the Church of England in 1534 so that he could divorce his queen in the hope of producing a male heir. Later Philip II of Spain embraced the Catholic cause to advance Hapsburg ambitions and cloaked his motives in the mantle of a crusade for the true faith.

THE COUNTER REFORMATION. The Reformation, which began in Germany in 1517 (see above), eventually led the Catholic church to launch a reform movement of its own, known today as the Counter Reformation. In reality, it had begun more than a half-century before the Council of Trent in 1545, which marks its official onset. In fact, the Church had been in an almost constant state of reform since the middle of the thirteenth century. The roots of Catholic reform were complex, but several main causes can be defined. It was a reform not simply of the Church doctrinally or institutionally but also spiritually. By the end of the fifteenth century there was a growing urge among Christians throughout Europe for a more meaningful relationship with God. Much of it sprang from the rediscovery of the *Confessions* and other writings of St. Augustine of Hippo. In Italy this renewed emphasis on personal faith and good works was embodied in the exemplary life of St. Francis of Assisi, himself an ardent reader of St. Augustine.

The Franciscan Egidio de Viterbo, a contemporary of Martin Luther, was one of the earliest and staunchest advocates of reform in Italy. Moreover, the Franciscans initiated a reform of their own by establishing the austere Capuchin order in 1529. This was but one of many orders that were founded before 1540. Even earlier, the Oratories of Divine Love had been established in Genoa in 1497 by the nobleman Ettore Vernazza and in Rome by his followers 20 years later. Their members included Gaetano da Thiene, founder of the Theatine order in 1524, and Gian Pietro Carafa, its first superior, who later reigned as the ultra-orthodox Pope Paul IV. Da Thiene and Carafa had already served as advisors to Pope Adrian VI during his brief reign in 1522–23. After the Sack of Rome in 1527, Carafa and the Theatines, who were a small but elite group, sought refuge in Venice, where they began to confront the problems facing the Church. As a result, the growing reform movement was spearheaded by north Italians: Gasparo Contarini, the cardinal of Venice; Gregorio Cortese, abbott of the Benedictine monastery San Giorgio Maggiore in Venice; and Gian Matteo Giberti, the bishop of Verona. Brescia, too, was an important religious center. Girolamo Savonarola began his preaching in that city; it was home to the famous Augustinian mystic Laura Mignani; and Bartolomeo Stella founded a branch of the Oratory of Divine Wisdom there during the mid-1520s. Geography helped make northern Italy open to Reformation ideas: Venice had close trading relations with Germany, as did Brescia, while Milan had commercial ties to Switzerland just across the Alps, along with several other major cities in northern Italy. The Tyrol was heavily German in both its language and culture. Soon after 1520 Reformation ideas began to spread rapidly throughout Italy, including Tuscany.

In Florence, Lucca, and other Tuscan cities, the origin of reform can be traced back to Savonarola (see page 444). His memory was kept alive by his many followers, including the Medicis themselves, whose taste for luxury he had condemned and whom he drove from power, and his reputation was restored by Pope Julius II, a bitter enemy of Pope Alexander VI, who had tried Savonarola for heresy. The papacy was rightly seen as the root of many of the Church's ills. Indeed, it was slow to respond to the challenges posed by Protestantism and the rising Catholic rebellion against abuses, such as the sale of indulgences. The ignorant, all-too-wordly clergy was an even deeper problem, as were the bishops, many of whom did not reside in their sees. The Fifth Lateran Council, convened by Pope Julius II in 1511 and his successor Leo X (see fig. 13-36) in 1513–14, had little effect; neither did the decrees of Leo in 1514 and Clement VII in 1525. Pope Paul III (see fig. 13-42), who had been elected in 1534 on the promise of convening a council to discuss the Church's problems, called Contarini to Rome as his advisor a year later, and also encouraged the founding of the Society of Jesus by the Spaniard Ignatius of Loyola. However, he summoned the Council of Trent only after a decade on the throne of St. Peter. (Trent itself was a hotbed of Lutheran sentiments.) Predictably, the Council, which met at various times for nearly 20 years, reinforced the primary position of the papacy and reasserted traditional dogma as it had been defined over the long history of the Church. Yet it was also in the forefront of genuine reform. After the inaugural meeting of the Council of Trent, held in 1545–47, the reform movement was spearheaded by the Jesuit order, representing the Church militant. However, the internal reforms were carried out mainly by Pope Paul IV after he ascended the throne of St. Peter in 1555, and by St. Carlo Borromeo, who initiated the model of reform five years later as bishop of Milan, where the Reformation had made considerable inroads.

Central to both the Reformation and Counter Reformation was humanism. Humanistic scholarship insisted on a correct understanding of the original Greek and Hebrew sources of the Bible, and of the writings of the early Church Fathers. The efforts of the humanists, such as Gasparo Contarini, the cardinal of Venice, and Pietro Bembo at the University of Padua, resonated with those seeking a more authentic spirituality unburdened by later doctrine. In Spain the principal representative of humanism was Francisco Ximénes de Cisneros, who initiated the reform movement there after becoming the archbishop of Toledo in 1495. He also established Alcalá as a leading center of learning, and it was there that the first comprehensive edition of the Bible was published in its original languages, with correct translations. The same period witnessed the sudden rise around 1500 of mysticism in Spain in the works of Gómez García and García de Cisneros. Mysticism and reform soon became allied. This tendency was to culminate in Juan Valdez, who was driven by the Spanish Inquisition to Naples, where he died in 1541, and St. Theresa of Ávila (see page 558), who was a vigorous reformer of the Carmelite order.

PAINTING

Mannerism in Florence and Rome

Among the trends in art in the wake of the High Renaissance, Mannerism is the most significant, as well as the most problematic. The original meaning of the term was narrow and derogatory. It referred to a group of mid-sixteenth-century painters in Rome and Florence whose "artificial" style (maniera) was derived from certain aspects of the work of Raphael and Michelangelo. This phase has since been recognized as part of a wider movement that had begun around 1520. Keyed to a sophisticated taste, early Mannerism had appealed to a small circle of aristocratic patrons such as Cosimo I, the grand duke of Tuscany, and Francis I, the king of France. The style soon became international as a number of events—including the plague of 1522, the Sack of Rome by Spanish forces under Charles V in 1527, and the conquest of Florence three years later—drove many artists abroad, where most of the style's next phase developed. Charles V also overthrew the brief Republic of Florence (1527–30) and restored the Medici to power under Cosimo I (1519–74). As titular ruler, he was named Duke of Florence in 1537 and then Duke of Tuscany in 1569 by Pope Pius V, after defeating Siena in the war of 1552–55.

This new phase, High Mannerism, was the assertion of a purely aesthetic ideal. Through formulaic abstraction, it became a style of utmost refinement that emphasized grace, variety, and virtuoso display at the expense of content, clarity, and unity. This taste for affected elegance and bizarre conceits appealed to a small but sophisticated audience. In a larger sense, however, Mannerism signaled a fundamental shift in Italian culture. In part it resulted from the High Renaissance quest for originality as a projection of the individual's character, which had given artists license to explore their imaginations freely. While this investigation of new modes was ultimately beneficial, the Mannerist style itself came to be regarded by many as decadent, and no wonder: given such subjective freedom, it produced extreme personalities who today seem the most "modern" of all sixteenth-century painters.

The formalism of High Mannerist art was part of a wider movement that placed inner vision, however private or fantastic, above the twin standards of nature and the ancients. Hence the definition of Mannerism has sometimes been expanded to include the later style of Michelangelo, who would acknowledge no artistic authority higher than his own genius. Mannerism is often viewed as a reaction against the ideal created by the High Renaissance as well. Except for a brief early phase, however, Mannerism did not consciously reject the tradition from which it stemmed. The subjectivity inherent in its aesthetic was unclassical, but it was not deliberately anticlassical, save for its most extreme forms. Even more important than Mannerism's anticlassicism is its insistent antinaturalism.

The relation of Mannerism to religious trends was equally ambiguous. Although a deep reverence is found in many works by the first generation of painters, the extreme worldliness of the second generation was inherently opposed to both the Reformation, with its stern morality, and the Counter Reformation, which demanded strict adherence to doctrine. After mid-century there was nonetheless a "Counter Mannerist" trend, centering on Bronzino and Vasari (see below), which adapted the vocabulary of Mannerism for Counter Reformation ends. The result was an arid style geared solely to supporting the Church and its dogma. These "official" Counter Reformation images were given a convincing physical presence to convey their theological messages as clearly as possible.

The Counter Reformation had a well-founded concern over the proliferation of images that were unsupported by the Bible or traditional doctrine. Worse still were images that might be deemed disrespectful or even sacrilegious. However, commentators were not always in agreement about what was permissible. As the Catholic church sought to define itself against the Protestant Reformation, religious imagery nevertheless became increasingly standardized. Much of the reason can be found in the Inquisition, a medieval institution that was revived in Italy in 1542 after a lapse of several hundred years and established separately in Spain in 1478 to enforce religious orthodoxy. Yet these visual sermons also reflect a sincere response to the Catholic reform. Indeed, the sculptor and architect Bartolomeo Ammanati (see pages 506–07) renounced the nude statues he had produced early in his career. At the same time, the subjective freedom of Mannerism came to be valued for its visionary power as part of a larger shift in religious sentiment toward mysticism, especially in northern Italy.

ROSSO FIORENTINO. The first signs of discord in the High Renaissance appear shortly before 1520 in Florence. Art had been left in the hands of a younger generation that could refine but not further develop the styles of the great masters who had spent their early careers there. Chief among these was Andrea del Sarto (1486–1530), a pupil of Piero di Cosimo (1461/62–1521). Early in his career, Andrea visited Rome during the formative years of the High Renaissance, as well as Venice, then worked for a while at the court of Francis I in France. Yet his was an arrested style based largely on the young Raphael, to which he added a Venetian sense of color. Its chief qualities were an inward quality and, occasionally, a visionary space inspired by the cartoon for *The Adoration of the Magi* (fig. 13-1) by Leonardo, from whom he derived his use of sfumato. Having absorbed the lessons of the leading artists for the most part at one remove, the first generation of Mannerists was free to apply High Renaissance formulas to a new style divorced from its previous content. While this early phase of Mannerism may be a reflection of the growing turmoil in Italy, its highly personal spirituality is almost certainly the legacy of Savonarola, who placed great emphasis on the power of visions.

The first full expression of the new attitude is *The Descent from the Cross* (fig. 14-1) painted by Rosso Fiorentino (1495–1540), the most eccentric of the first-generation Mannerists. It was commissioned in 1521 by the Company of the Cross of the Day, a confraternity of flagellants, in the Tuscan city of Volterra. Although it looks back in part to Early Renaissance art, nothing has prepared us for the shocking impact of the spidery forms spread out against the dark sky. The figures are agitated yet rigid, as if frozen by a sudden icy blast. Even the draperies have brittle, sharp-edged planes. The acid colors and the light, brilliant but unreal, reinforce the nightmarish effect of the scene. Here is clearly a full-scale

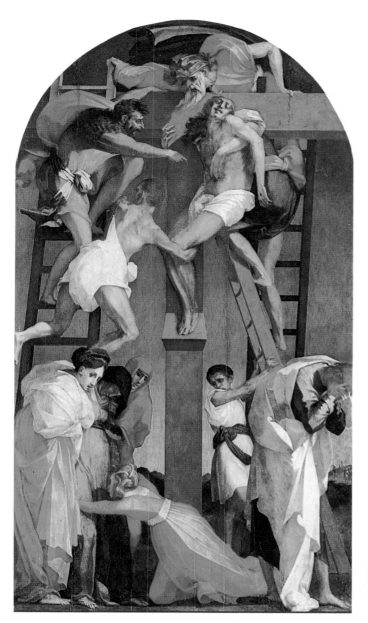

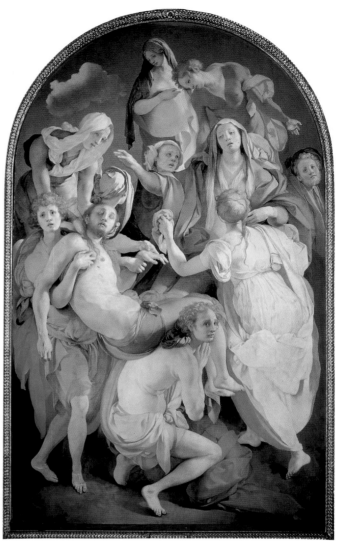

14-1. Rosso Fiorentino. *The Descent from the Cross*. 1521.
Oil on panel, 11' x 6'5½" (3.4 x 2 m).
Pinacoteca Communale, Volterra

14-2. Jacopo da Pontormo. *The Deposition*. c. 1526–28.
Oil on panel, 10'3" x 6'4" (3.1 x 1.9 m).
Sta. Felicita, Florence

revolt against the classical balance of High Renaissance art—a profoundly disquieting, willful, visionary style that indicates a deep inner anxiety. Amid the violent activity the limp, astonishingly serene figure of Christ appears to hover almost effortlessly. We are, then, meant to experience the painting on two levels: as something akin to an *Andachtsbild,* with its intense emotion, and as an object of devotion, like an icon. As such, it accords with Savonarola's urging of continuous, "inflamed" contemplation of the meaning of the crucified Christ and his role in the salvation of humanity. Thus this Descent from the Cross was especially appropriate to the religious order that commissioned it.

JACOPO DA PONTORMO. Jacopo da Pontormo (1494–1556/7), a friend of Rosso's, had an equally strange temperament. Introspective, headstrong, and shy, he worked only when and for whom he pleased. He would shut himself up in his quarters

for weeks on end, and refuse to see even his closest friends. His *Deposition* (fig. 14-2) is a reflection of his character. The painting contrasts sharply with Rosso's *Descent from the Cross* but is no less disturbing. Unlike Rosso's elongated forms, Pontormo's have a nearly classical beauty and sculptural solidity inspired by Michelangelo, who in turn admired his art. Yet the figures are confined to a stage so claustrophobic as to cause acute discomfort in the viewer. The very implausibility of the image, however, makes it convincing in spiritual terms. Indeed, this visionary quality is essential to its meaning, which is conveyed by formal means alone.

We have entered a world of innermost contemplation in which every pictorial element responds to a purely subjective impulse. Everything is subordinate to the play of graceful rhythms created by the tightly interlocking forms. These patterns unify the surface and give the work a poignancy unlike any we have seen. Although they seem to act together, the mourners are lost in a grief

MUSIC AND THEATER OF THE LATE RENAISSANCE

The music and theater of Italy between 1530 and 1600 reflect the same rich variety found in art. The most characteristic musical form after about 1530 was the madrigal, which was an outgrowth of French and Italian popular songs. It was similar to the motet in that all the voices were equally important, but it was livelier and more expressive. The madrigal was also closely connected to the resurgence of Italian poetry in the work of Ludovico Ariosto (see box page 464) and Torquato Tasso (1544–1595), Ariosto's successor as court poet to the ruling d'Este family of Ferrara. Like Ariosto, Tasso treated the Crusades in *Jerusalem Delivered* (1575), which remained the most popular poem of its kind through the seventeenth century. Although at first the best composers of madrigals were Flemish, after 1575 Italians dominated the form. Foremost among them was Carlo Gesualdo (c. 1560–1613), an aristocrat whose music was as bold and flamboyant as his personality. His madrigals, like those of Luca Marenzio (1553–1599), are full of complex verbal and musical conceits that make them counterparts to the paintings of the Late Renaissance.

The church dignitaries at the Council of Trent (1545–63), which spearheaded the Counter Reformation in the Catholic church, objected to the growing use of secular melodies in sacred music, as well as to elaborate polyphony that obscured the words of the liturgy. In response, Giovanni Palestrina (c. 1525–1594) based his masses on traditional Gregorian chants. In many respects, however, his works are the successors of Josquin Des Prés' in their seamless texture and the perfect balance of melodic and harmonic values—that is, the beauty both of the principal melody and the other notes that accompany it, known as harmony. Palestrina, who held all the important musical posts in Rome during his lifetime, had special authority because of the backing of the papacy, and his style became "classic": it was held up as a model for imitation into the twentieth century.

Venice, unlike Rome, was ruled by secular authorities, so that Venetian music differed greatly from that composed for the pope. The vast spaces of St. Mark's Church—which was the palace chapel of the Doges—encouraged the colorful music of Palestrina's contemporary, Andrea Gabrieli (1510–1586), who had studied under the Fleming Adrian Willaert (c. 1490–1562), and his nephew and pupil Giovanni Gabrieli (1557–1612). The compositions of the Gabrielis emphasized sensuous effects of sound over coun-

terpoint (different melodic lines moving independently, or "counter" to each other). Giovanni was also the first composer to specify which instruments should play which parts, to include dynamic markings in his music as indications of loudness and softness, and to make use of harmonies that sound "modern" to our ears, although Palestrina had effectively abandoned the modes except insofar as they were an inescapable part of church music. Much of Giovanni's music was purely instrumental. Instrument-only music in the late sixteenth century began to achieve its independence from vocal music by adapting popular dance tunes, often treated as a theme with variations. Such dances had been performed for centuries, although they were rarely written down. This development coincided with the creation of new families of instruments, such as viols and recorders, whose ranges—soprano, contralto, tenor, and bass—approximated those of human voices. These instruments lent Late Renaissance music a wonderfully diverse and distinctive sound.

The principal theatrical performances in sixteenth-century Italy were public spectacles paid for by the aristocracy. They were an outgrowth of comic interludes *(intermezzi),* which were performed between the acts of dramas and featured such sensational scenery, costumes, music, dance, and special effects that they soon became more important than the plays themselves. The most splendid spectacles were produced in Florence to glorify the Medici family in allegorical terms: *Masque of the Genealogy of the Gods* (1566), with sets and costumes designed by Giorgio Vasari, and *The Battle of the Argonauts,* mounted in 1608 on the Arno River. These displays spurred the development of more elaborate and sophisticated scenery design at the Medici court under Bernardo Buontalenti (1536–1608) and his pupil

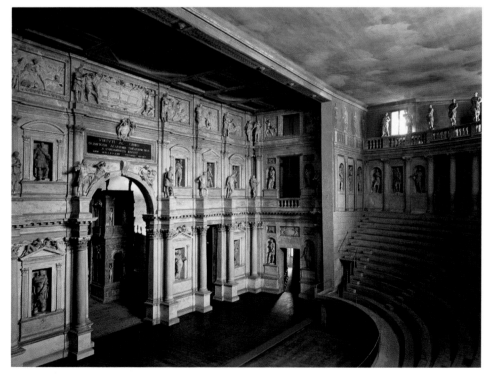

Andrea Palladio and Vincenzo Scamozzi. *Stage of the Teatro Olimpico, Vicenza.* c. 1585 (executed by Scamozzi)

Giulio Parigi (c. 1570–1635), as well as in Ferrara, Mantua, Urbino, Milan, Parma, and Rome. Scenography initially relied on the accounts of Roman theater in the architectural treatise of Vitruvius, which was published in 1486, the same year that the humanist antiquarian Pomponius Laetus (1424–1498) began to produce ancient plays at the Roman Academy. Even more important was the influence of Leon Battista Alberti's linear perspective (see Primary Sources, no. 40, page 644). Sebastiano Serlio (1475–1554) published an architectural treatise in 1545, which included a number of stage designs that made use of Alberti's perspective system to visualize Vitruvius' descriptions of Roman theaters. Serlio's designs proved so influential throughout Europe that they were often used to illustrate later editions of Vitruvius.

The occasional nature of dramatic presentations meant that few permanent theaters were built during the sixteenth century. The first court theater was erected by Buontalenti for the Medici in Florence. More important was the first public theater, built in 1565 in Venice, which immediately established its leadership in theater writing and production. Twenty years later the architect Andrea Palladio (see pages 508–509) designed a theater for the Olympic Academy in Vicenza, which opened with a performance of Sophocles' *Oedipus Rex*. Although the theater was soon abandoned, its construction is a measure of sixteenth-century interest in serious classical theater. The most popular form of theater was pastoral plays. These shared a common story line, in which a sophisticated young man or woman—in Torquato Tasso's *Aminta* (1573) this was actually the god Cupid—is forced by circumstance to spend some time among simple rural folk. The healthy manner of living and innocent goodness of the country people teach an important moral lesson and send the protagonist back to normal life refreshed in spirit.

After 1550, Renaissance theories of drama centered on Horace's *Art of Poetry* and Aristotle's *Poetics,* which had been published in a Latin translation in 1498. Drawing on these sources, Julius Caesar Scaliger (1484–1558) and Lodovico Castelvetro (1505?–1571) insisted that both tragedy and comedy be presented in five acts and that they obey the "unities" of time, space, and action sanctioned as inviolable rules by classical precedent: the events portrayed had to take place in roughly the same time as it took to present them (or at least within one day); in a space approximately the size of the actual stage; and with the story line revolving around a single incident or problem. The new body of theory also promoted the concept of verisimilitude, incorporating realism, morality, and universality (typical, normative traits). These ideas in turn led to an insistence on decorum: strict adherence to what was considered appropriate to the age, sex, temperament, and social status of each character. Drama was further divided into tragedy and comedy along class lines. Tragedy involved the actions of noble, that is, aristocratic, characters while comedy was devoted to the buffooneries of the lower classes. However, the few plays written according to these rules met with a mixed reception in sixteenth-century Italy.

too personal to share with one another—or us. In this hushed atmosphere, anguish is transformed into a lyrical expression of exquisite sensitivity. The entire scene is as haunted as Pontormo's self-portrait just to the right of the swooning Madonna. The artist, moodily gazing into space, seems to shrink from the outer world, as if scarred by the trauma of some half-remembered experience, and into one of his own invention.

PARMIGIANINO. The first phase of Mannerism was soon replaced by one less openly anticlassical, less charged with subjective emotion, but equally far removed from the seemingly confident, stable world of the High Renaissance. The *Self-Portrait* (fig. 14-3) done as a demonstration piece by Parmigianino (Girolamo Francesco Maria Mazzuoli, 1503–1540) suggests no psychological turmoil. The artist's appearance is bland and well groomed. The features, painted with Raphael's smooth perfection, are veiled by a delicate Leonardesque sfumato. The distortions, too, are objective, not arbitrary, for the picture records what Parmigianino saw as he gazed at his reflection in a convex mirror. Earlier painters who used the mirror as an aid to observation had filtered out such distortions, except when the mirror image was contrasted with a direct view of the same scene (see fig. 15-9). But Parmigianino substitutes his painting for the mirror itself, even using a specially prepared convex panel. Why was he so fascinated by his self-image? With his hand nearly touching the mirror, he becomes a counterpart of Narcissus (see page 173). The painting suggests an interest in magic as well. In the Renaissance the convex mirror was valued for its visionary effects, which seemed to reveal the future, as well as hidden aspects of the past and present. This interest may help to explain why, according to Vasari, the artist was obsessed with alchemy as he neared the end of his brief career, and became "a bearded, long-haired, neglected, and almost savage or wild man."

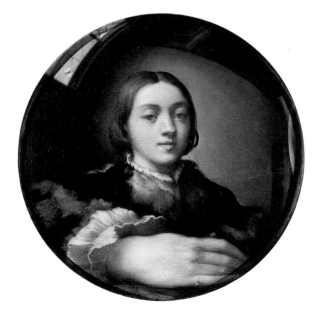

14-3. Parmigianino. *Self-Portrait.* 1524.
Oil on panel, diameter 9⅝" (24.7 cm).
Kunsthistorisches Museum, Vienna

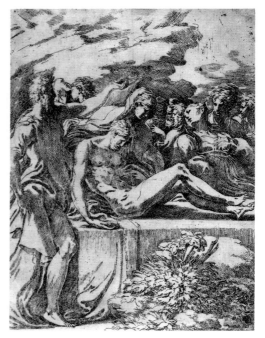

14-5. Parmigianino. *The Entombment.*
c. 1535. Etching printed in brown ink,
12¼ x 9⅜" (31.3 x 23.8 cm).
Los Angeles County Museum of Art

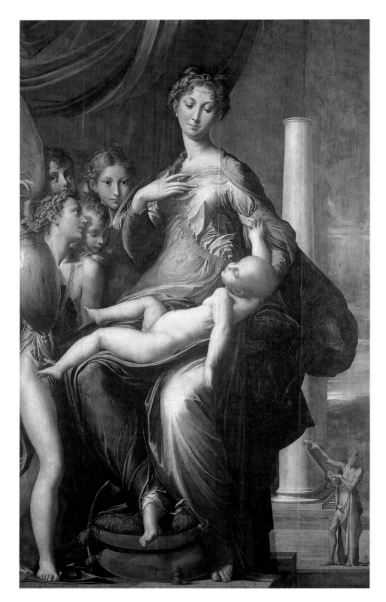

14-4. Parmigianino. *The Madonna with the Long Neck.* c. 1535.
Oil on panel, 7'1" x 4'4" (2.2 x 1.3 m). Galleria degli Uffizi, Florence

Parmigianino's strange imagination is evident in his most famous work, *The Madonna with the Long Neck* (fig. 14-4), which was painted after he had returned to his native Parma from a stay of several years in Rome. He had been deeply impressed with the rhythmic grace of Raphael's art, but here he has transformed the older artist's figures into a remarkable new breed. The limbs, elongated and ivory-smooth, move with effortless languor, and embody an ideal of beauty as remote from nature as any Byzantine figure. The pose of the Christ Child balanced precariously on the Madonna's lap echoes that of a *Pietà* (compare fig. 11-54), which shows that he is already aware of his mission to redeem original sin through his death. Although sometimes also found in Byzantine icons, this unusual device evidently is Parmigianino's own invention and helps to explain the setting, which is not as arbitrary as it may seem. The gigantic column is a symbol often associated with the Madonna as the gateway to heaven and eternal life, as well as the Immaculate Conception (see page 482). It may also refer to the

flagellation of Jesus during the Passion, thus reminding us of his sacrifice, which the tiny figure of a prophet foretells on his scroll. The column serves to disrupt our perception of the pictorial space, which is strangely disjointed. Parmigianino seems determined to prevent us from judging anything in this picture by the standards of ordinary experience. Here we approach the "artificial" style for which the term Mannerism was coined. *The Madonna with the Long Neck* is a vision of unearthly perfection, with a cold elegance that is no less compelling than the violence in Rosso's *Descent.*

Parmigianino is important as a printmaker as well as a painter. He was the first artist to explore the possibilities of etching seriously. Although the technique was introduced in the North shortly after 1510 (see page 532), it took the Italian Mannerists to appreciate the new medium. We can see why in Parmigianino's *The Entombment* (fig. 14-5). The print looks very much like the artist's ink drawings, in its sketchlike immediacy, which conveys the agitation of the scene. Indeed, etching was ideally suited to the artist's individual style and nervous temperament—traits prized above all others by the Mannerists.

AGNOLO BRONZINO. High Mannerism is identified with the second generation of artists surrounding Agnolo Bronzino and Giorgio Vasari. They transformed the styles of Rosso, Pontormo, and Parmigianino into one of cool perfection that filtered out the intensely individual outlooks of those artists. As a result, the High Mannerists produced few masterpieces. In their best works, however, formal beauty becomes the aesthetic counterpart to obscure, even perverse thought.

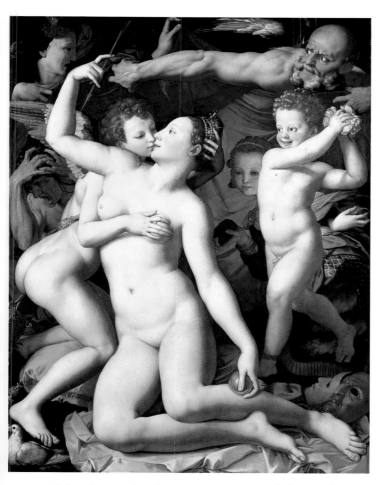

14-6. Agnolo Bronzino. *Allegory of Venus*. c. 1546. Oil on panel, 57½ x 45⅝" (146.1 x 116.2 cm). The National Gallery, London

14-7) by Giorgio Vasari (1511–1574) owe more to Raphael. The debt is surprising, as Vasari esteemed Michelangelo above all others (see page 452). The painting, one of his last works, is a play on Raphael's *Galatea* (see fig. 13-33). It is part of Vasari's decorative scheme devoted to the four elements for the study of Francesco I de' Medici of Florence. (The program was devised by the humanist Vincenzo Borghini.) The artist has chosen to represent water with the story of coral, which according to legend was formed by the blood of the monster slain by Perseus when he rescued Andromeda. The subject provided an excuse to show voluptuous nudes, but here the story has become an enchanting fantasy, in contrast to the lewdness typical of Mannerist imagery. In keeping with this playful treatment, the Nereids, lighthearted versions of Raphael's mythological creatures, frolic with bits of coral they have discovered in the sea. Vasari's painting became a classic in its own right. It spawned a host of imitations by minor artists in the waning years of Mannerism, and was revived by the Romantics.

PORTRAITS. The Mannerists also produced splendid portraits in the same highly cultivated style. A superb example is Bronzino's painting of his main patron, Eleanora of Toledo (fig. 14-8, page 494), the wife of Cosimo I de' Medici. The sitter here appears as a member of an exalted social class, not as an individual personality. It is, in fact, a highly idealized portrayal of Eleanora, who wore her blond hair (which has been darkened to conform to Italian norms) close to the head and whose strong jaw had a distinct cleft that the artist has ignored. She was nevertheless

Nowhere is this better seen than in the *Allegory of Venus* (fig. 14-6) by Agnolo Bronzino (1503–1572), Pontormo's favorite pupil. It was painted as a gift to Francis I of France from Cosimo I de' Medici. The central motif of Cupid embracing Venus was suggested by a lost *Triumph of Love* by Michelangelo that Pontormo and Bronzino are both known to have copied. As with so much else in High Mannerism, however, the source has been corrupted in content and treatment. Father Time tears back the curtain from Fraud in the upper left-hand corner to reveal Venus and Cupid in an incestuous embrace, much to the delight of Folly, who is armed with roses, and to the dismay of Jealousy, who tears her hair, as Pleasure, half-woman and half-snake, offers a honeycomb. The moral is that folly blinds one to the jealousy and fraud of sensual love, which time reveals. The unmasking of this fraud revels in the lustfulness that it pretends to condemn. The painting is thus a debasement of the high-minded humanism in Botticelli's *Birth of Venus* (see fig. 12-53). With its extreme stylization, Bronzino's elegance proclaims a refined erotic ideal that reduces passion to a genteel exchange of serpentine gestures, so characteristic of High Mannerism, between figures as polished as marble.

GIORGIO VASARI. Bronzino's figures are indebted to Michelangelo in their sculptural quality (compare the Venus to *Night* in fig. 13-22). Those in *Perseus and Andromeda* (fig.

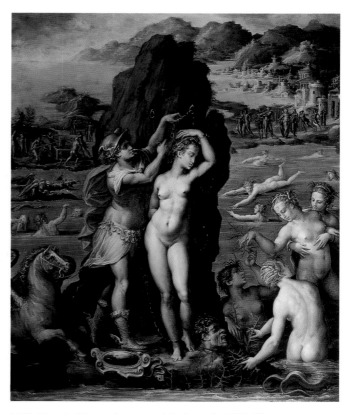

14-7. Giorgio Vasari. *Perseus and Andromeda*. 1570–72. Oil on slate, 45½ x 34" (115.6 x 86.4 cm). Studiolo, Palazzo Vecchio, Florence

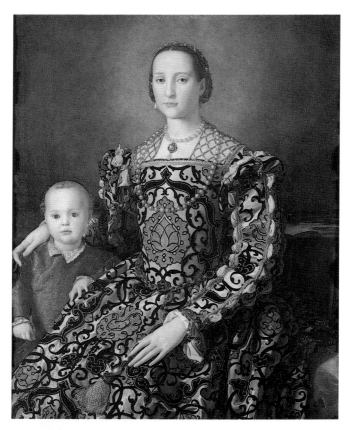

gianino's *Madonna* (compare the hands) than to ordinary flesh and blood. Bronzino's painting, which developed from a type first defined by Pontormo, thus elevates the sitter to a deity. No wonder it quickly became the ideal of court portraiture throughout Europe. (Compare the portrait of Queen Elizabeth I in box page 547.)

North Italian Realism

Although Mannerism spread to other cities, as a style it did not become dominant outside Florence and Rome. Elsewhere it competed with other tendencies. In Venice and the towns along the northern edge of the Lombard plain under its sway, such as Brescia and Verona, there were a number of artists who worked in styles based on Titian's, but with a stronger interest in everyday reality. After 1560, however, Mannerism became thoroughly absorbed into north Italian realism.

GIROLAMO SAVOLDO. One of the earliest of these north Italian realists was Girolamo Savoldo (c. 1480–1550) from Brescia, near Venice. His *St. Matthew and the Angel* (fig. 14-9) must have been painted around the same time as Parmigianino's *Madonna with the Long Neck.* The *St. Matthew* represents a new approach to religious painting. Never before have we seen the sacred brought down to earth with such tangible immediacy. The style shows the influence of Titian, who would not, however, have placed the evangelist in such a domestic setting. The scene in the background shows the saint's environment to be lowly indeed and makes the presence of the angel doubly miraculous. This tendency to visualize sacred events among ramshackle buildings and simple people had been characteristic of Gothic painting, especially in the North, and Savoldo must have acquired it from that source.

The religious content, too, may have originated across the Alps. Even the poorest, the artist seems to say, may experience revelation directly, reflecting that hunger for personal religious experience which swept Europe. The picture reminds us that the Bible and natural reason were the twin pillars of authority to Martin Luther.

14-8. Agnolo Bronzino. *Eleanora of Toledo and Her Son Giovanni de' Medici.* c. 1550. Oil on panel, 45¼ x 37¾" (115 x 96 cm). Galleria degli Uffizi, Florence

considered a great beauty, much as her husband, Cosimo, duke of Florence, was admired for his virile good looks and courage. The portrait acts as proof that she has fulfilled her main dynastic duty to provide Cosimo with an heir: Giovanni, born in 1543, two years after their first son, Francesco. (She bore 11 children before her death from tuberculosis in 1562 at about the age of 43.) Eleanora represents a new breed, more divine than human. Frozen behind the barrier of her ornate costume, she seems more akin to Parmi-

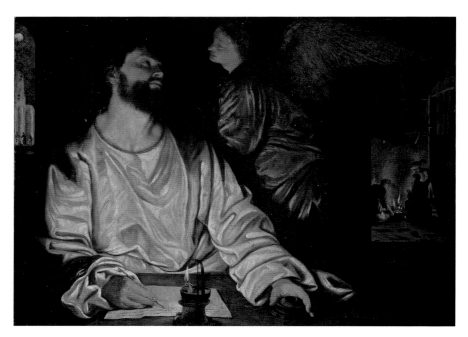

14-9. Girolamo Savoldo.
St. Matthew and the Angel. c. 1535.
Oil on canvas, 36¾ x 49" (93.3 x 124.5 cm).
The Metropolitan Museum of Art,
New York

MARQUAND FUND, 1912

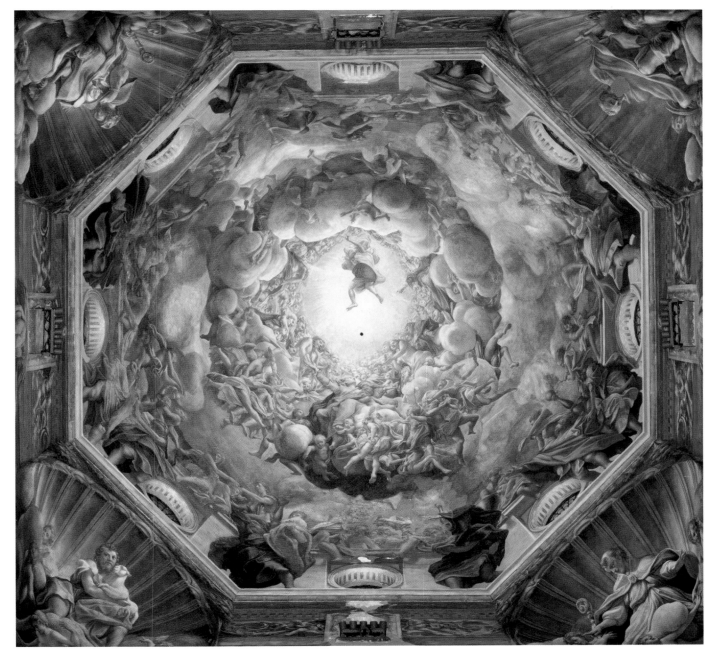

14-10. Correggio. *The Assumption of the Virgin*. Dome, Parma Cathedral, Parma, Italy. c. 1525. Fresco, diameter of base of dome 35'10" x 37'11" (10.93 x 11.56 m)

Luther also argued that there was no need for the clergy, saints, or angels to act as intercessors on behalf of the faithful, but here the angel plays an essential role by dictating the gospel as the word of God to the unlettered apostle. The nocturnal lighting recalls such International Style pictures as the *Nativity* by Gentile da Fabriano (see fig. 11-98). But instead of divine radiance, Savoldo uses an ordinary oil lamp for his magic and intimate effect, so filled with sacred overtones, however disguised.

Savoldo labored in obscurity in his hometown. Around 1600, however, at the dawn of the Baroque, his direct realism became an important source for the revolutionary style of Caravaggio, another North Italian who carried these ideas to Rome, where they were to influence artists throughout Europe. Moreover, his style became the basis for that of Rembrandt's main teacher, Pieter Lastman (1583–1633).

CORREGGIO. Correggio (Antonio Allegri da Correggio, 1489/94–1534), an extraordinarily gifted north Italian painter, spent most of his brief career in Parma, which lies to the west along the Lombard plain. As a result, he absorbed a wide range of influences: first Leonardo and the Venetians, then Michelangelo and Raphael. However, their ideal of classical balance did not attract him for long. Correggio's work applies north Italian realism with the imaginative freedom of the Mannerists. (Surprisingly, we do not find any hint of his fellow townsman Parmigianino in his style.) His largest work, the fresco of *The Assumption of the Virgin* in the dome of Parma Cathedral (fig. 14-10), is a masterpiece of illusionistic perspective. In transporting us into the heavens, it is the very opposite of Savoldo's painting. Correggio here initiates an entirely new kind of visionary representation in which heaven and earth are joined visually and

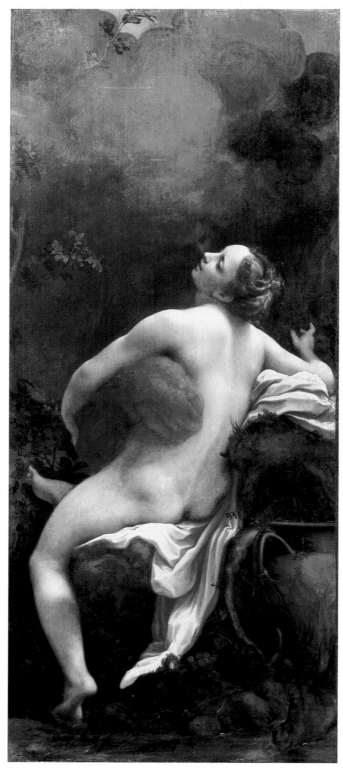

14-11. Correggio. *Jupiter and Io.* c. 1532. Oil on canvas,
64½ x 27¾" (163.8 x 70.5 cm). Kunsthistorisches Museum, Vienna

spiritually. While not the first to execute an illusionistic dome painting—that honor belongs to Mantegna, from whom he got the idea—he was the first to apply it to a religious subject. Also new are the figures themselves. They move with such exhilarating ease that the force of gravity seems not to exist for them, and they frankly delight in their weightless condition. These are healthy, energetic beings of flesh and blood, reflecting the influence of Titian, not the disembodied spirits so often found in earlier art.

There was little difference between spiritual and physical rapture for Correggio, who thereby established an important precedent for Baroque artists such as Gianlorenzo Bernini (see pages 577–79). We can see this relationship by comparing *The Assumption of the Virgin* with his *Jupiter and Io* (fig. 14-11), part of a series depicting the loves of the classical gods. The nymph Io, swooning in the embrace of a cloudlike Jupiter, is the direct kin of the jubilant angels in the fresco. The use of sfumato, combined with a Venetian sense of color and texture, produces frank sensuality that far exceeds Titian's in his *Bacchanal* (see fig. 13-39).

Correggio had no immediate successors, nor did he have any lasting influence on the art of his century, but toward 1580 his work began to be appreciated by Federico Barrocci (1528?–1612) and Annibale Carracci (see pages 533–35). Like Savoldo's, it embodies so many features which later characterized the Baroque that his style has been labeled Proto-Baroque; such a term, however, hardly does justice to Correggio's highly individual qualities. For the next century and a half he was admired as the equal of Raphael and Michelangelo, while the Mannerists, so important before, were largely forgotten.

JACOPO BASSANO. In the work of Jacopo da Ponte (c. 1510–1592), called Bassano after the town 30 miles northwest of Venice where he passed most of his career, North Italian realism is blended with elements taken from a rich array of sources to convey essentially the same spiritual attitude as Savoldo's. Bassano inevitably fell under the influence of Titian, but just as important to the formation of his style were prints by Germans such as Albrecht Dürer, who had twice visited Venice (see page 538), and by the Mannerists, notably Parmigianino. In *The Adoration of the Shepherds* (fig. 14-12), Bassano's most characteristic subject, the landscape will remind us of the setting in Titian's *Bacchanal* (fig. 13-39). The figures, however, show the impact of Parmigianino. Their interlocking rhythms, the gentle grace of the Madonna, the gesture of the Infant Christ, the seemingly arbitrary column, all can be found in *The Madonna with the Long Neck* (fig. 14-4). The pose of the shepherd doffing his hat, too, has its source in Parmigianino's etching *The Entombment* (fig. 14-5). The high-pitched color is Mannerist as well.

The role of Northern art seems less clear until we realize that the tender relationship between the Virgin and Child has an intimacy that can have come only from German prints (compare fig. 15-24), not Italian painting. The humble setting shows that he must also have known a similar engraving by Martin Schongauer (see fig. 15-23). And the mountains in the distance find their nearest counterpart in the watercolor *Italian Mountains* (see fig. 16-5) that Dürer sketched on his way back from Venice, rather than any

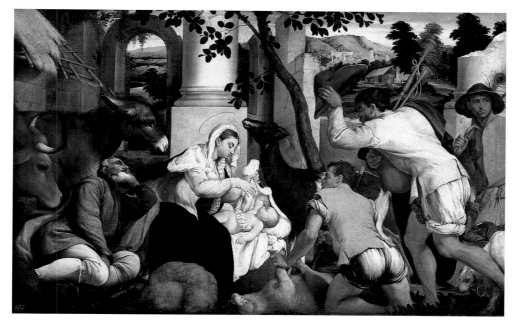

14-12. Jacopo Bassano. *The Adoration of the Shepherds*. 1542–47. Oil on canvas,
4'7" x 7'2¼" (1.39 x 2.19 m). The Royal Collection

work by an Italian. Unlike Dürer's, Jacopo's landscape is a "portrait" showing Mount Grappa near Bassano.

The Adoration of the Shepherds is more than a synthesis of diverse influences, however. What is novel in all this is the pastoral quality of the scene. The artist includes peasants of the sort he must have met around his native town. Andrea Mantegna and the Fleming Hugo van der Goes had been among the few to show such simple people (see fig. 15-12). Yet for Bassano they were an essential feature of his work. Beyond their picturesque quality, which appealed strongly to collectors, they express some of the main tenets of the Counter Reformation, especially in northern Italy, with its strong German ties. The painting reminds us that Christ was of humble origin and that he preached his message of love and salvation to all humanity, including the poor and the outcast. Bassano's Madonna of Humility (a type first made popular in the North) is distinguished from the awestruck shepherds only by the column, symbol of Mary as the Queen of Heaven (compare fig. 13-38).

Venice

PAOLO VERONESE. In the work of Paolo Veronese (Paolo Caliari, 1528–1588), who was born and trained in Verona, north Italian realism takes on the splendor of a pageant. In *Christ in the House of Levi* (fig. 14-13), Veronese avoids all reference to the supernatural. His symmetrical composition harks back to paintings by Leonardo and Raphael, while the festive mood of the scene reflects examples by Titian of the 1520s, so that at first glance the picture looks like a High Renaissance work born 50 years too late. Missing, however, is the ideal conception of humanity that underlies the High Renaissance. Veronese paints a sumptuous banquet, a true feast for the eyes, but not "the intention of man's soul."

We are not even sure which event from the life of Jesus he originally meant to depict. He gave the painting its present title only after he had been summoned by the religious tribunal of the Inquisition on the charge of filling his picture with "buffoons, drunkards, Germans, dwarfs, and similar vulgarities" unsuited to its sacred character. The account of this trial shows that the tribunal thought the painting represented the Last Supper, but Veronese's testimony never made clear whether it was the Last Supper or the Supper in the House of Simon. To him this distinction made little difference. In the end, he settled on a convenient third title, *Christ in the House of Levi,* which permitted him to leave the offending incidents in place. He argued that they were no more objectionable than the nudity of Jesus and the Heavenly Host in Michelangelo's *Last Judgment.* Nevertheless, the tribunal failed to see the analogy, on the grounds that "in the Last Judgment it was not necessary to paint garments, and there is nothing in those figures that is not spiritual."

The Inquisition, of course, considered only the impropriety of Veronese's art, not its lack of spiritual depth. His refusal to admit the justice of the charge, his insistence on his right to include directly observed details, however "improper," and his indifference to the subject of the picture spring from an attitude so extroverted that it was not widely accepted until the nineteenth century. The painter's domain, Veronese seems to say, is the entire visible world, and here he acknowledges no authority other than his senses. Although tame by Mannerist standards, the presentation is supremely theatrical, from the vast, stagelike space to the lavish costumes, which hardly differ from those in

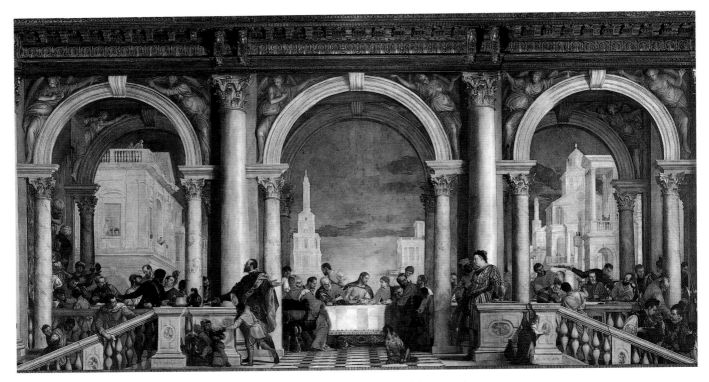

14-13. Paolo Veronese. *Christ in the House of Levi.* 1573. Oil on canvas, 18'2" x 42' (5.5 x 12.8 m). Galleria dell'Accademia, Venice

Venetian productions of the day. And just as it goes against the religious outlook of the day, the painting also violates the concept of decorum in contemporary dramatic theory (see box pages 490–91).

JACOPO TINTORETTO. Veronese and Jacopo Tintoretto (1518–1594) both found favor with the public. They certainly looked at each other's work, but the differences in their styles are readily apparent. Tintoretto reportedly wanted "to paint like Titian and to design like Michelangelo," but his relationship to those two masters, although real enough, was as peculiar as Parmigianino's was to Raphael. Tintoretto fully assimilated the influence of Mannerism into his personal style in order to heighten the visionary effects found in Titian's late work (see fig. 13-44).

Christ Before Pilate (fig. 14-14), one of his many huge canvases for the Scuola di San Rocco, the home of the Confraternity of St. Roch, provides a striking contrast with Titian's *Christ Crowned with Thorns* (see fig. 13-44). The bold brushwork, the glowing colors, and the sudden lights and shadows show what Tintoretto owed to the older artist. Indeed, the composition recalls the *Madonna with Members of the Pesaro Family* (see fig. 13-40). Yet the total effect is unmistakably Mannerist. The feverish emotionalism of the flickering, unreal light, and the ghostly Christ, pencil-slim and motionless among the agitated Michelangelesque figures, remind us of Rosso's *Descent*. There is, too, the suggestion of Raphael's influence—absorbed (like Michelangelo's) at second hand through prints and copies. His impact can be seen not only in individual figures, such as the seated scribe, but also in the strangely claustrophobic space (compare fig. 13-37). The composition also owes something to Albrecht Dürer's two Passion cycles. The debt is significant, for the painting, like the rest of Tintoretto's for the Scuo-

la, is clearly reformist in its religious sentiment, which enjoyed a revival in the 1560s and 1570s, although the Confraternity of St. Roch itself was one of the richest and most powerful in the city.

The presentation is highly theatrical. The fantastic setting with its deep space is very close to stage scenery of the times, notably the designs published by Sebastiano Serlio (see box pages 490–91). The figures twist and turn in exaggerated poses to heighten the action, as the crowd strains to see and hear what is going on. Occupying center stage in the midst of all this drama is Jesus, who faces Pilate with surprising calm. His stoic dignity emphasizes the Passion as the necessary fulfillment of his mission on earth to redeem humanity's sins through his sacrifice. His silence recalls the account in the Gospel of Matthew: "And when he was accused by the chief priests and elders, he answered nothing." Pilate washes "his hands before the multitude, saying, I am innocent of the blood of this just person." The turbaned figure in the foreground is Herod, with whom Pilate became reconciled; the seated man in the white robe is the prophet Isaiah, who foretold the Passion in Chapter 53:

> "He was despised and rejected of men; a man of sorrows, and acquainted with grief . . . the Lord hath laid on him the iniquity of us all. He was oppressed and he was afflicted, yet he opened not his mouth; he is brought as a lamb to the slaughter, so he openeth not his mouth."

Tintoretto's final major work, *The Last Supper* (14-15, page 500), is also his most spectacular. It seems to deny in every possible way the classic values of Leonardo's version (see fig. 13-3), painted almost exactly a century before, which still underlie Veronese's picture.

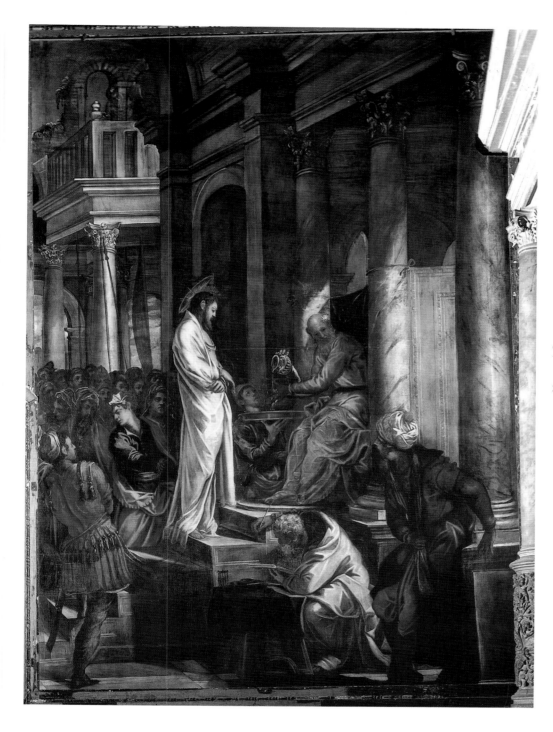

14-14. Jacopo Tintoretto. *Christ Before Pilate.* 1566–67. Wall painting, approx. 18'1" x 13'3½" (5.5 x 4.1 m). Scuola di San Rocco, Venice

Christ, to be sure, is at the center of the composition, but his small figure in the middle distance is distinguished mainly by the brilliant halo. Tintoretto barely hints at the human drama of Judas' betrayal, so important to Leonardo. Judas can be seen isolated on the near side of the table across from Christ, but his role is so insignificant that he could almost be mistaken for an attendant. The table is now placed at a sharp angle to the picture plane in exaggerated perspective. This arrangement was designed to relate the scene to the space of the chancel of the Benedictine monastery church S. Giorgio Maggiore in Venice, for which it was commissioned. It was seen on the wall by the friars as they knelt at the altar rail to receive Communion, so that it receded less sharply than when viewed head on.

In keeping with Italian Realism, Tintoretto has gone to great lengths to give the event an everyday setting, cluttering the scene with attendants, containers of food and drink, and domestic animals. There are also celestial attendants who converge upon Christ just as he offers his body and blood, in the form of bread and wine, to the disciples. The smoke from the blazing oil lamp miraculously turns into clouds of angels, blurring the distinction between the natural and the supernatural and turning the scene into a magnificently orchestrated vision. The artist's main concern has been to make visible the miracle of the Eucharist—the transubstantiation of earthly into divine food—in both real and symbolic terms. The central importance of this institution to Catholic doctrine was forcefully reasserted during the Counter Reformation. The painting was especially appropriate for its location in S. Giorgio Maggiore, which played such a prominent role in the reform movement.

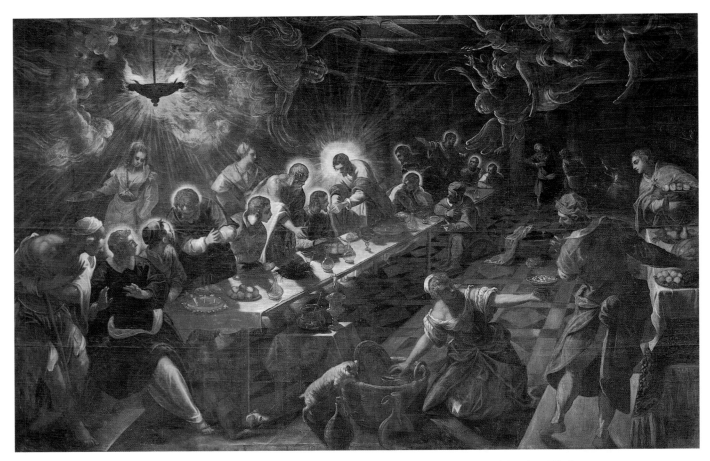

14-15. Jacopo Tintoretto. *The Last Supper.* 1592–94. Oil on canvas, 12' x 18'8" (3.7 x 5.7 m). S. Giorgio Maggiore, Venice

Spain

EL GRECO. If we can call Tintoretto a Mannerist only with some hesitation, there can be no such doubt about Domenikos Theotocopoulos (1541–1614), called El Greco, even though his work, too, falls outside the mainstream of that tradition. He came from Crete, which was then under Venetian rule. There he must have been trained by an artist still working in the Byzantine tradition. Soon after 1560 he arrived in Venice and quickly absorbed the lessons of Titian, Tintoretto, and other artists. A decade later, in Rome, he came to know the art of Raphael, Michelangelo, and the Central Italian Mannerists. In 1576/77 El Greco went to Spain and settled in Toledo for the rest of his life. He became a member of the leading intellectual circles of the city, then a major center of learning, as well as the seat of Catholic reform in Spain. Although it provides the context of his work, Counter Reformation theology does not account for the exalted emotionalism that informs his painting. The spiritual tenor of El Greco's mature work was primarily a response to mysticism, which was especially intense in Spain. Contemporary Spanish painting, however, was too provincial to affect him. His style had already been formed before he arrived in Toledo.

The largest and most splendid of El Greco's major commissions, and the only one for a public chapel, is *The Burial of Count Orgaz* (figs. 14-16 and 14-17) in the church of Sto. Tomé. The pro-gram, which was given at the time of the commission, emphasizes the traditional role of good works in salvation and of the saints as intercessors with Heaven. This huge canvas honors a medieval benefactor so pious that St. Stephen and St. Augustine miraculously appeared at his funeral and lowered the body into its grave. The burial took place in 1323, but El Greco presents it as a contemporary event and even portrays many of the local nobility and clergy among the attendants. The dazzling display of color and texture in the armor and vestments could hardly have been surpassed by Titian himself. Above, the count's soul (a small, cloud-like figure like the angels in Tintoretto's *Last Supper*) is carried to Heaven by an angel. The celestial assembly in the upper half of the picture is painted very differently from the group in the lower half: every form—clouds, limbs, draperies—takes part in the sweeping, flamelike movement toward the figure of Christ. The painting is close in its unearthly spirit and style to Rosso's *Descent from the Cross* (fig. 14-1). Here, even more than in Tintoretto's art, the entire range of Mannerism fuses into a single ecstatic vision.

The full meaning of the work, however, becomes clear only when we see it in its original setting (fig. 14-17). Like a huge window, it fills one entire wall of its chapel. The bottom of the canvas is six feet above the floor, and as the chapel is only about 18 feet deep, we must look sharply upward to see the upper half of the picture. The violent foreshortening is calculated to achieve an

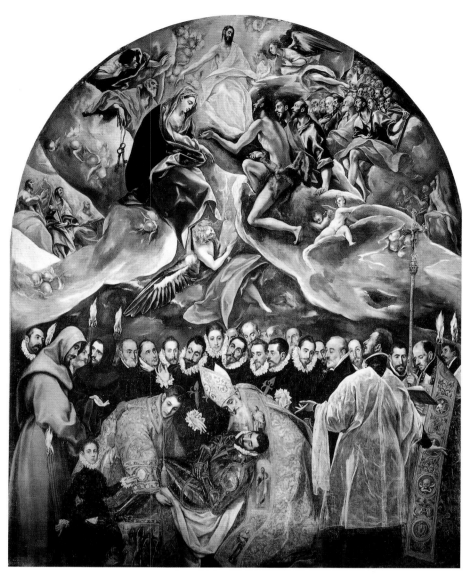

14-16. El Greco.
The Burial of Count Orgaz. 1586.
Oil on canvas, 16' x 11'10" (4.9 x 3.6 m).
Sto. Tomé, Toledo, Spain

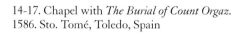

14-17. Chapel with *The Burial of Count Orgaz.*
1586. Sto. Tomé, Toledo, Spain

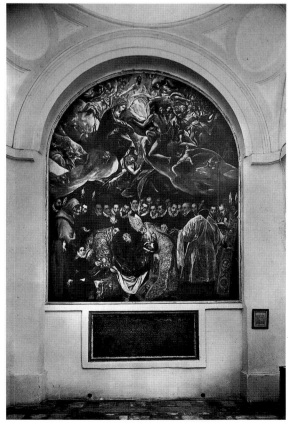

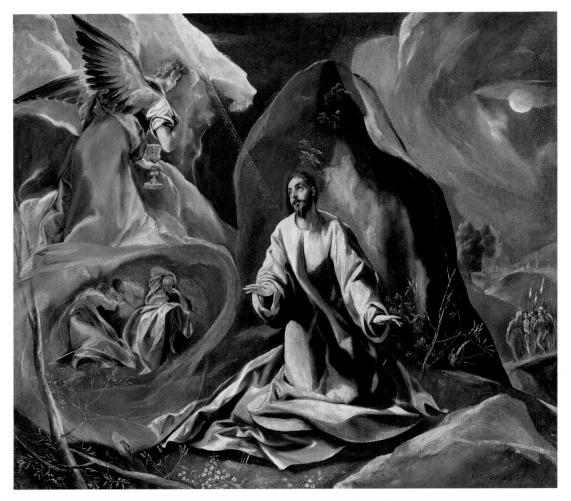

14-18. El Greco. *The Agony in the Garden*. 1597–1600. Oil on canvas, 40¼ x 44¾" (102.2 x 113.6 cm).
The Toledo Museum of Art, Toledo, Ohio

illusion of boundless space above, while the figures in the lower foreground appear as on a stage. (Their feet are cut off by the molding just below the picture.) The large stone plaque set into the wall also belongs to the ensemble. It represents the front of the sarcophagus into which the two saints lower the body of the count and thus explains the action in the picture. The viewer, then, perceives three levels of reality. The first is the grave itself, supposedly set into the wall at eye level and closed by an actual stone slab; the second is the reenactment of the miraculous burial; and the third is the vision of celestial glory witnessed by some of the participants. El Greco's task here was similar to Masaccio's in his *Trinity* mural (see fig. 12-38). But whereas Masaccio constructed the illusion of reality through a rational pictorial space that appears continuous with ours, El Greco summons an apparition that remains separate from its architectural surroundings.

El Greco has created a spiritual counterpart to his imagination. Every passage is alive with his peculiar religiosity, which is felt as a nervous exaltation occurring as the dreamlike vision is conjured up. This kind of mysticism is very similar in character to parts of the Spiritual Exercises of Ignatius of Loyola, the founder of the Jesuits, although his teachings are based on a long tradition that achieved new popularity after 1490. St. Ignatius sought to make visions so real that they would seem to appear before the very eyes of the faithful. Such mysticism could be achieved only through strenuous devotion. That effort is mirrored in the intensity of El Greco's work, which fully retains a feeling of intense spiritual struggle.

El Greco never forgot his Byzantine background. (Until the very end of his career, he signed his pictures in Greek.) *The Agony in the Garden* (fig. 14-18) builds on the Byzantine example seen in figure 8-52. However, it uses an irrational space to help conjure up a mystical vision representing a spiritual, rather than visual, reality. Jesus, isolated against a large rock that echoes his shape, is comforted by the angel bearing a golden cup, symbol of the Passion. The angel appears to kneel on a mysterious oval cloud, which envelops the sleeping disciples. In the distance to the right we see Judas and the soldiers coming to arrest the Lord. The composition is balanced by two giant clouds on either side. The entire landscape resounds with Jesus' agitation, represented by the sweep of supernatural forces. The elongated forms, eerie moonlight, and expressive colors help us to identify with his suffering.

SCULPTURE

Italian sculptors of the later sixteenth century failed to match the achievements of the painters. Perhaps Michelangelo's overpowering personality discouraged new talent in this field, but there was also a lack of major commissions outside of portraiture, as we can tell from the considerable number of small bronzes that were made during this period. In any case, the most interesting sculpture of this period was produced outside of Italy. After the death of Michelangelo in 1564 even the leading sculptor in Florence was a Northerner.

Mannerism

BENVENUTO CELLINI. The early phase of Mannerism, seen in the style of Rosso, has almost no sculptural counterpart, except for the stucco framework he created for the Gallery of Francis I at Fontainebleau (1531–40). However, the second, elegant stage appears in countless sculptures in Italy and abroad. The best-known representative of the style is Benvenuto Cellini (1500–1571), a Florentine goldsmith and sculptor who owes much of his fame to his colorful autobiography. The gold saltcellar (fig. 14-19) made for Francis I of France while Cellini was working at the French royal chateau of Fontainebleau, is his only important work in precious metal to survive. The piece displays the virtues and limitations of his art. The main function of this lavish object is clearly as a conversation piece. Because salt comes from the sea and pepper from the land, the boat-shaped salt container is protected by Neptune. The pepper, in a tiny triumphal arch, is watched over by a personification of Earth who, in another context, might be the god's consort Amphitrite. On the base are figures representing the four seasons and the four parts of the day.

The saltcellar reflects the cosmic significance of the Medici tombs (compare fig. 13-22). But on this miniature scale Cellini's program turns into playful fancy on the same order as Vasari's *Perseus and Andromeda* (see fig. 14-7). Cellini wants to impress us with his ingenuity and skill. Earth, he wrote, is "fashioned like a woman with all the beauty of form, the grace and charm, of which my art was capable." The allegorical significance of the design is simply a pretext for this display of virtuosity. For instance, when he tells us that Neptune and Earth each have a bent and a straight leg to signify mountains and plains, form is completely divorced from content. Despite his admiration for Michelangelo, Cellini creates elegant figures that are as elongated, smooth, and languid as Parmigianino's (see fig. 14-4).

FRANCESCO PRIMATICCIO. Parmigianino also influenced Francesco Primaticcio (1504–1570), who arrived at Fontainebleau in early 1532 after working under Raphael's chief assistant, Giulio Romano, in Mantua (see fig. 14-22). Almost nothing survives of the rooms Primaticcio decorated for the king and queen before 1540, when he was sent by Francis I to Rome to acquire works of art. Upon his return a year later, he replaced Rosso, who had died in the meantime, as the chief designer at the royal château. The influence of Parmigianino is clearly seen for the first time in his most important surviving work, the decorations for the Room of the Duchesse d'Étampes (fig. 14-20). Primaticcio follows Rosso's general scheme in the Gallery of Francis I of embedding paintings in a luxuriously sculptured stucco framework, which nearly swallows them. However, the figures are subtly elongated and show an ease that contrasts sharply with Rosso's often tense poses and complex compositions. The section shown in here caters to the same aristocratic taste that admired the saltcellar of Cellini, who was Primaticcio's

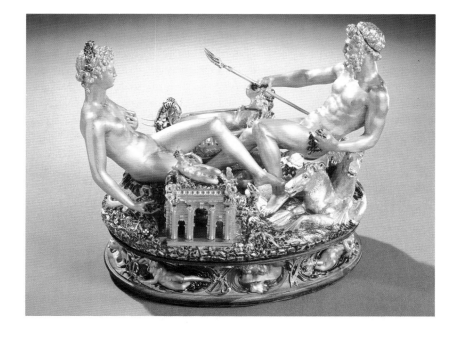

14-19. Benvenuto Cellini. *Saltcellar of Francis I.*
1539–43. Gold with enamel, 10¼ x 13⅛"
(26 x 33.3 cm). Kunsthistorisches Museum, Vienna

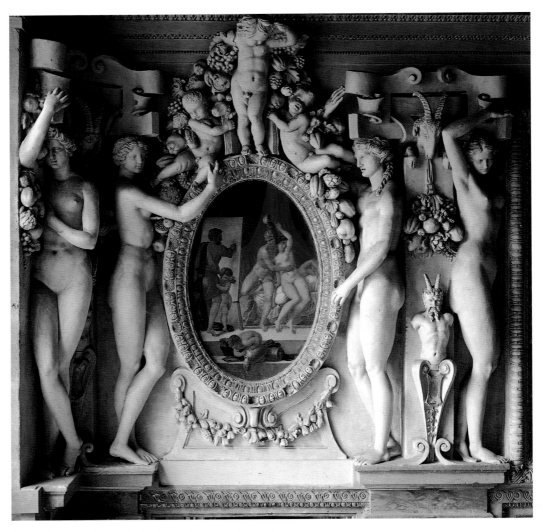

14-20. Francesco Primaticcio. *Stucco Figures*. c. 1541–45.
Gallery of Francis I, designed for the Room of the Duchesse d'Étampes, Château of Fontainebleau, France

rival at the court of Francis I in 1540–45. The four maidens have no specific allegorical significance, although their role recalls the nudes of the Sistine ceiling. They seem to perform a task for which they are equally ill-fitted: to reinforce the piers that sustain the ceiling. These willowy caryatids epitomize the studied nonchalance of second-phase Mannerism.

The paintings, executed by assistants from Primaticcio's designs and later heavily restored, are devoted to Alexander the Great. The scene in figure 14-20 shows Apelles painting the abduction of Campaspe by Alexander, who gave his favorite concubine to the artist when he fell in love with her. Such a heady mixture of violence and eroticism appealed greatly to the Mannerists. Yet the story was interpreted as a gesture of uncommon respect and nobility by the Roman historian Pliny, which justi-

fied the subject. The picture also draws a parallel between Alexander and Francis I, and between Campaspe and the duchesse, the king's mistress, who had taken Primaticcio under her wing. The Duchesse d'Étampes (Anne de Piseleu, 1508–c.1580) supported the Duc d'Orleans against the dauphin, the future Henry II, and plotted with Charles V against him. She was banished when Henry II took power in 1547 upon the death of Francis I and died in obscurity.

GIOVANNI BOLOGNA. Rosso, Primaticcio, Cellini, and the other Italians employed by Francis I at Fontainebleau made Mannerism the dominant style in sixteenth-century France. Their influence went far beyond the royal court. It reached Jean de Bologne (1529–1608), a gifted young sculptor from Douai in northern

France, who went to Italy about 1555 for further training. He stayed and, under the Italianized name of Giovanni Bologna, became the most important sculptor in Florence during the last third of the century. His over-lifesize marble group, *The Abduction of the Sabine Woman* (fig. 14-21), was especially admired, and still has its place of honor near the Palazzo Vecchio.

The subject, drawn from the legends of ancient Rome, seems an odd choice for statuary. According to the story, the city's founders, an adventurous band of men from across the sea, tried in vain to find wives among their neighbors, the Sabines. Finally, they resorted to a trick. Having invited the entire Sabine tribe into Rome for a festival, they attacked them, took the women away by force, and thus ensured the future of their race. Actually, the artist designed the group with no specific subject in mind.

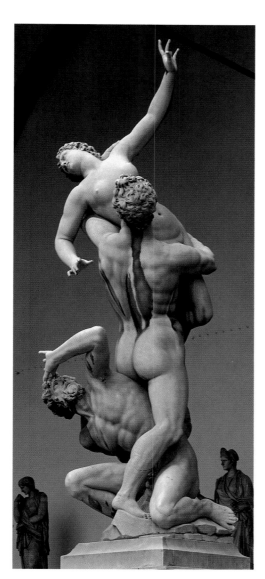

14-21. Giovanni Bologna.
The Abduction of the Sabine Woman.
Completed 1583. Marble, height 13'6" (4.1 m).
Loggia dei Lanzi, Florence

It was meant to demonstrate his ability while he was a student at the Academy of Design, founded by Vasari in 1562 under the patronage of Cosimo I de' Medici. He chose what seemed to him the most difficult feat: three contrasting figures united in a single action. When asked to identify the figures, the artist proposed Andromeda, but another member of the Academy, Raffaello Borhini, suggested *The Abduction of the Sabine Woman* as the most suitable title.

Here, then, is another artist who is noncommittal about subject matter, although his motive was different from Veronese's. Like Cellini, Bologna wished to display his virtuosity. His task was to carve in marble, on a massive scale, a sculptural composition that was to be seen from all sides. This had previously been attempted only in bronze and on a much smaller scale (see fig. 12-14). He has solved this formal problem brilliantly, but at the cost of removing his group from the world of human experience. These figures, spiraling upward as if confined inside a tall, narrow cylinder, perform their well-rehearsed exercise with ease. But, like much Hellenistic sculpture (compare fig. 5-76), they lack emotional meaning. We admire their discipline but find no trace of genuine pathos.

ARCHITECTURE

Mannerism

The term *Mannerism* was first coined to describe painting. We have had no difficulty in applying it to sculpture. But can it be usefully extended to architecture as well? And if so, what qualities must we look for? These questions have proved difficult to answer. The reasons are all the more puzzling, because the important Mannerist architects were leading painters and sculptors. Yet today only a few buildings are generally considered Mannerist.

GIULIO ROMANO. The main example is the Palazzo del Te in Mantua by Giulio Romano (c. 1499–1566), Raphael's chief assistant. The courtyard facade (fig. 14-22) features unusually squat proportions and coarse **rustication.** The massive keystones of the windows have been "squeezed" up by the force of the triangular lintels. The effect is an absurd impossibility. There are no true arches except over the central doorway, which is surmounted by a pediment in violation of classical canon. Even more bizarre is how the triglyph midway between each pair of columns "slips" downward in defiance of all logic and accepted practice, thereby creating the sense that the frieze might collapse before our eyes.

The reliance on eccentric gestures that depart from Renaissance norms does not in itself define Mannerism as an architectural period style. What, then, are the qualities we must look for? Above all, form is divorced from content for the sake of surface effect. The emphasis instead is on picturesque devices, especially encrusted decoration, with the occasional distortion of form and novel, even illogical rearrangement of space. Thus Mannerist architecture lacks a consistent integration of elements.

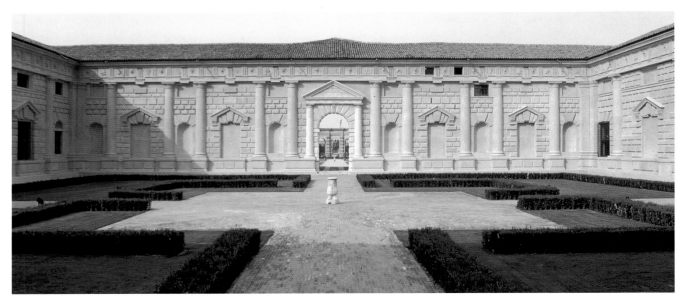

14-22. Giulio Romano. Courtyard of the Palazzo del Te, Mantua. 1527–34

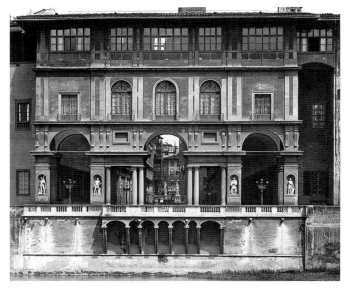

14-23. Giorgio Vasari. Loggia of the Palazzo degli Uffizi, Florence (view from the Arno River). Begun 1560

GIORGIO VASARI. We see many of these features in the Palazzo degli Uffizi in Florence designed by Giorgio Vasari, whom we have already met as a painter and biographer. Situated behind the Palazzo Vecchio (fig. 11-39), which Cosimo I de' Medici occupied as his personal residence in 1540, it consists of two long wings (intended for offices, as the name Uffizi suggests) that face each other across a narrow court and are linked at one end by a loggia, or **testata** (fig. 14-23). (It was originally conceived as a huge square but this plan was deemed too grandiose by Cosimo.) Begun in 1560, it brought together the widely dispersed Florentine ministries and was widely seen as symbolizing Cosimo's consolidation of power. As such, it represented a new kind of building.

The facade of the courtyard is insistently Michelangelesque in its vocabulary but more orthodox in its composition. So, too, in a different way, is that of the river facade. The main archway with two smaller and lower openings separated by columns is technically called a serliano, after the architect Serlio (see box pages 490–91), who probably derived it from Bramante, though it was actually used most by Palladio (see below). The upper story, called a belvedere, is where Pope Pius V crowned Cosimo Duke of Tuscany in 1569. However, the source of the "tired" scroll brackets and the odd combination of column and wall is the vestibule of the Laurentian Library. We will recall Vasari's praise for Michelangelo's unorthodox use of classical forms (see page 470).

Does this mean that the Laurentian Library itself is Mannerist? The case can be argued both ways. On the one hand, Michelangelo's design subverts High Renaissance classicism as willfully as does Rosso's *Descent from the Cross* (see fig. 14-1). On the other hand, in the Laurentian Library these devices serve an expressive purpose that responds to the imperative of Michelangelo's genius, whereas in Vasari's design they are empty gestures. Whichever side one takes (they are not mutually exclusive), the differences in the results are plain enough. The Uffizi loggia lacks the sculptural power of its model. Instead, it forms a seemingly weightless screen that could just as well serve as a theater set, where the statues in their niches make their appearance as if on stage. What is tense in Michelangelo's design becomes merely ambiguous. Vasari's architectural members seem as devoid of energy as the human figures in his *Perseus and Andromeda* (see fig. 14-7), and their relationships as deliberately "artificial."

BARTOLOMMEO AMMANATI. The same is true of the courtyard of the Palazzo Pitti (fig. 14-24) by the sculptor Bar-

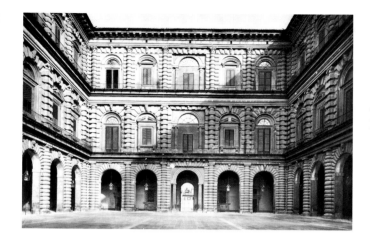

14-24. Bartolommeo Ammanati. Courtyard of the Palazzo Pitti, Florence. 1558–70

14-25. Jacopo Sansovino. Mint (left) and Library of St. Mark's, Venice. Begun c. 1535/7

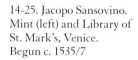

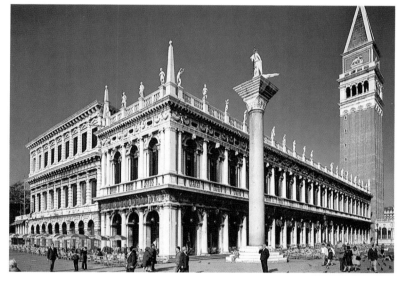

tolommeo Ammanati (1511–1592), who collaborated with both Vasari and Michelangelo (see page 470). (He probably had a hand in helping to design the interior spaces of the Uffizi and contributed the famous Neptune fountain to its courtyard.) Here the three-story scheme of superimposed orders, derived from the Colosseum, has been overlaid with an extravagant pattern of rustication that "imprisons" the columns and reduces them to a passive role, despite the display of muscularity. These welts disguise rather than enhance the massiveness of the masonry, and the corrugated texture makes us think of the fancies of a pastry cook.

Ammanati had worked under Jacopo Sansovino in Venice (Vasari knew him as well), and the Palazzo Pitti stands in the same relation to Sansovino's Mint (see fig. 14-25, left) as Vasari's Palazzo degli Uffizi does to Michelangelo's Laurentian Library. Likewise, the Uffizi's long arcades are indebted to Sansovino's Library of St. Mark's.

JACOPO SANSOVINO. We have not discussed the architecture of Venice since the Ca' d'Oro (see fig. 11-40), for it remained outside the mainstream of the Renaissance. Its essential characteristics were defined by Jacopo Sansovino (1486–1570), a Florentine sculptor from the circle of Raphael. He was called to Venice after the Sack of Rome in 1527 and established himself as the chief architect of the city. Not surprisingly, his buildings are sculptural in treatment. His masterpiece is the Library of St. Mark's (fig. 14-25, right), which forms part of a major reworking of the Piazzetta along the Grand Canal. The sculptural decoration is so luxurious that the building looks like a huge wedding cake. The street-level arcade consists of the Roman Doric order, inspired by the Colosseum (see fig. 7-11), while the upper story shows an elaborate treatment of the Ionic order (including triple engaged columns) surmounted by a garlanded entablature. The structure is capped off by a balustrade, with lifesize statues over every column cluster and obelisks at each corner. The extravagant

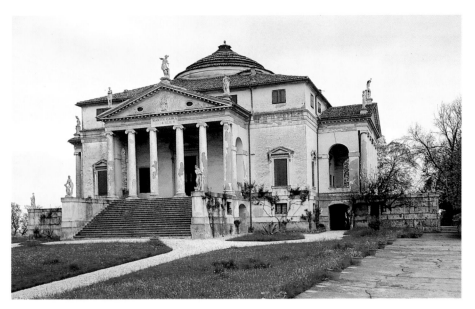

14-26. Andrea Palladio. Villa Rotonda, Vicenza. c. 1567–70

ornamentation, which set a new standard for lavish architecture, creates an effect of ponderous opulence that proclaims the Venetian republic as a new Rome. Sansovino's style was so authoritative that it enjoyed classic status and was followed in Venice for the remainder of the century. Nevertheless, it abandoned the logic of the High Renaissance.

Stranger still is the Mint to the left of the Library. Once again the facade has been penetrated wherever possible, but the results are even more massive. Though of equal height, the rusticated arcade seems barely able to sustain the weight of the upper two stories. (The top story was added belatedly around 1560.) The unique corkscrew columns and heavy cornices seem on the verge of Mannerism, but a glance at Ammanati's Pitti courtyard (see fig. 14-24) reveals the differences. Art historians have yet to find a term to describe Sansovino's grandiose style, but it might be called the architecture of conspicuous consumption, which is what made it so appealing to the nineteenth century, with its love of ornate revival styles (see Chapter 21).

Classicism

ANDREA PALLADIO. Most later sixteenth-century architecture can hardly be called Mannerist at all. Andrea Palladio (1518–1580), next to Michelangelo the most important architect of the century, belongs to the tradition of the humanist and theoretician Leone Battista Alberti (see page 426). Although Palladio's career centered on his native Vicenza, a town near Venice, his buildings and theoretical writings brought him international renown. Palladio believed that architecture must be governed by reason and by certain rules that were exemplified by the buildings

of the ancients. He thus shared Alberti's basic outlook and faith in the cosmic significance of numerical ratios (see page 429). The two differed in how they related theory and practice, however. With Alberti, this relationship had been flexible, whereas Palladio believed quite literally in practicing what he preached. This view stemmed in part from the fact that he began his career as a stonemason and sculptor before entering the humanist circles of Count Giangiorgio Trissino of Vicenza at the age of 30. As a result, his treatise *The Four Books of Architecture* (1570) is more practical than Alberti's, which helps to explain its huge success, while his buildings are linked more directly with his theories. It has even been said that Palladio designed only what was, in his view, sanctioned by ancient precedent. Indeed, the usual term for both Palladio's work and theoretical attitude is *classicistic*. This term denotes a conscious striving for classic qualities, although the results are not necessarily classical in style.

Much of Palladio's architecture consists of town houses and country villas. The Villa Rotonda (fig. 14-26), one of Palladio's finest buildings, perfectly illustrates the meaning of his classicism. This country residence, built near Vicenza for Paolo Almerico, consists of a square block surmounted by a dome, with identical porches in the shape of temple fronts on all four sides. Alberti had defined the ideal church as a symmetrical, centralized design of this sort (see page 429). Palladio adapted the same principles for the ideal country house. As he tells us in the second book on architecture, his design takes advantage of the pleasing views offered in every direction by the site.

How could Palladio justify such a secular context for the solemn motif of the temple front? Like Alberti, he interpreted the historical evidence selectively. He was convinced, on the basis

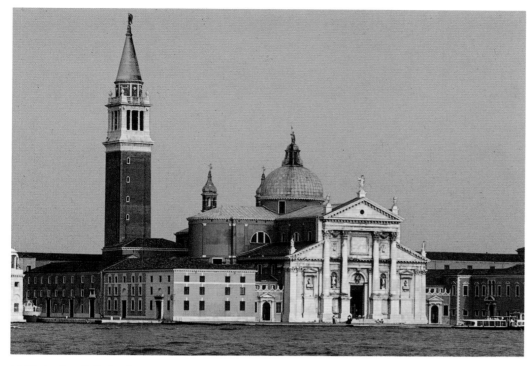

14-27. Andrea Palladio. S. Giorgio Maggiore, Venice. Designed 1565

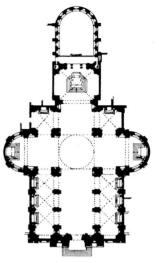

14-28. Plan of S. Giorgio Maggiore

of Vitruvius and Pliny, that Roman private houses had porticoes like these. (Excavations have since proved him wrong; see page 186.) But Palladio's use of the temple front here is not mere antiquarianism. He regarded this feature as both legitimate and essential for decorum—namely, appropriateness, beauty, harmony, and utility—befitting the houses of "great men." This concept, embedded in the social outlook of the later sixteenth century, was similar to that introduced in theater by Julius Caesar Scaliger and Castelvetro (see box pages 490–91). Beautifully correlated with the walls behind and the surrounding vistas, the porches of the Villa Rotonda give the structure an air of serene dignity and festive grace that is enhanced by Lorenzo Vicentino's sculptures.

Religious Architecture

ANDREA PALLADIO. At S. Giorgio Maggiore in Venice (fig. 14-27), designed shortly before the Villa Rotonda, Palladio confronted the greatest challenge faced by Italian architects: how to impose a temple front on a basilica. He undoubtedly knew Alberti's solution at S. Andrea in Mantua (see fig. 12-32), but this design, although logical and compact, did not fit the cross section of a basilica, and was too unusual to provide a guideline for later architects. While acknowledging that round temples are ideal because they are uniform, Palladio chose a basilican plan as the only one appropriate for Christian worship, because it echoes the cross of the Savior. But being a thoroughgoing classicist, he added a flattened-out temple porch to the entrance on the grounds that "Temples ought to have ample porticos, and with larger columns than other buildings require; and it is proper that

they should be great and magnificent . . . and built with large and beautiful proportions. They must be made of the most excellent and the most precious material, that the divinity may be honored as much as possible . . . and so disposed in each of their parts that those who enter there may be astonished and remain in a kind of ecstasy in admiring their grace and beauty." Palladio superimposed a tall, narrow temple front on another low, wide one to reflect the different heights of nave and aisles. The interlocking design is held together by the four gigantic columns, a device he had already used on several villas; in effect, they function as a variant of Alberti's colossal order. Theoretically, it was a perfect solution. No matter how ingenious, however, he found it difficult in practice to integrate the two systems into a harmonious whole. This conflict makes parts of the design seem ambiguous. The plan (fig. 14-28), too, suggests a duality, which in this case reflects the church's twofold purpose of serving a Benedictine monastery and a lay congregation. The main body of the church is strongly centralized—the transept is as long as the nave—but the longitudinal axis reasserts itself in the separate compartments for the main altar and the large choir beyond, where the monks worshiped.

GIACOMO VIGNOLA AND GIACOMO DELLA PORTA. The most widely accepted solution to the problem of how to fit a classical facade onto a basilican church was provided by Giacomo della Porta (c. 1540–1602) at Il Gesù (Jesus) in Rome (see fig. 14-31). Since it was the mother church of the Jesuits, its design must have been closely supervised so as to conform to the aims of the militant order (see page 486). We may therefore view it as the architectural embodiment of the spirit of the Counter Reformation. Indeed, the

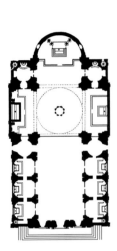

14-29. Giacomo Vignola.
Plan of Il Gesù, Rome. 1568

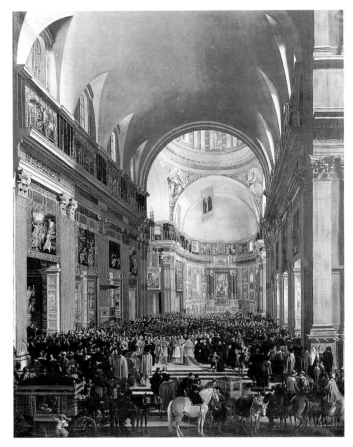

14-30. Andrea Sacchi and Jan Miel. *Urban VIII Visiting Il Gesù.*
1639–41. Oil on canvas. Galleria Nazionale d'Arte Antica, Rome

planning of the structure began in 1550, only five years after the Council of Trent was first convened (see page 486). Michelangelo himself once promised a design, but apparently never furnished it. The present plan by Giacomo Vignola (1507–1573), a former assistant of Michelangelo, was adopted in 1568 (fig. 14-29).

Il Gesù contrasts in almost every possible way with Palladio's S. Giorgio. It is a compact basilica dominated by its mighty nave. The aisles have been replaced by chapels, thus assembling the congregation in one large, hall-like space directly in view of the altar. The attention of the audience is strongly directed toward altar and pulpit, as our view of the interior shows (fig. 14-30). (The painting depicts how the church would look from the street if the center part of the facade were removed. For the later, High Baroque decoration of the nave vault, see fig. 17-12.) We also see

here a feature that the ground plan cannot show: the dramatic contrast between the dim nave and the amply lighted eastern part of the church, thanks to the large windows in the drum of the dome. Light has been consciously exploited for its expressive possibilities—a novel device, theatrical in the best sense of the term—to give Il Gesù a stronger emotional focus than we have yet found in a church interior.

The facade by Giacomo della Porta (fig. 14-31) is as bold as the plan and no less theatrical, although it has earlier sources. The paired pilasters and broken architrave on the lower story are clearly derived from the colossal order on the exterior of St. Peter's (compare fig. 13-27), and small wonder: Della Porta had completed Michelangelo's dome and was still using his architectural vocabulary. In the upper story the same pattern recurs on a some-

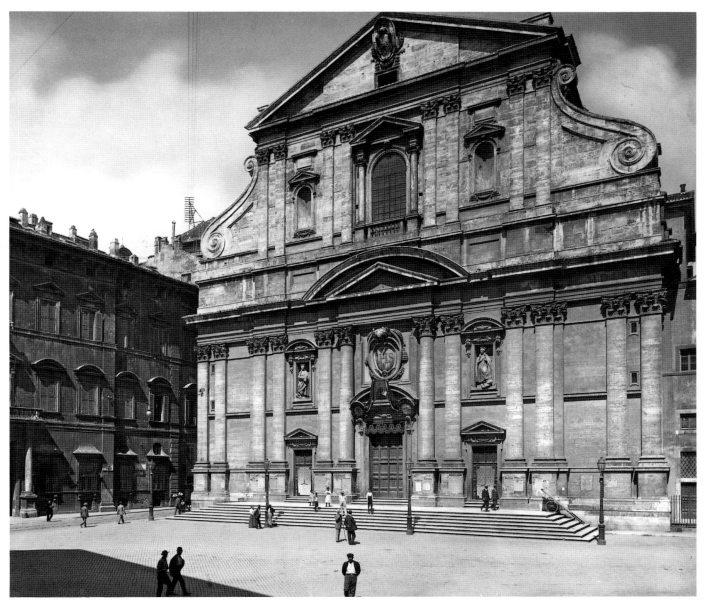

14-31. Giacomo della Porta. Facade of Il Gesù, Rome. c. 1575–84

what smaller scale, with four instead of six pairs of supports. The difference in width is bridged by two scroll-shaped buttresses, which hide the roof line. This device, taken from the facade of S. Maria Novella in Florence by Alberti (fig. 12-31), forms a graceful transition to the large pediment crowning the facade, which retains the classic proportions of Renaissance architecture. (The height equals the width.)

What is fundamentally new here is the integration of all the parts into a single whole. Della Porta, freed from classicistic scruples by his allegiance to Michelangelo, gave the same vertical rhythm to both stories of the facade. This rhythm is obeyed by all the horizontal members. (Note the broken entablature.) In turn, the horizontal divisions determine the size of the vertical members; hence no colossal order. Equally important is the sculptural

treatment of the facade, also inspired by Michelangelo, which places greater emphasis on the main portal. Its double frame—two pediments resting on coupled pilasters and columns—projects beyond the rest of the facade and gives strong focus to the entire design. Not since Gothic architecture has the entrance to a church received such a dramatic concentration of features. The total effect is remarkably theatrical, in the best sense of the term.

What are we to call the style of Il Gesù? Obviously, it has little in common with Palladio. The label Mannerist will not serve us either. As we shall see, the design of Il Gesù became basic to Baroque architecture. As with the paintings of Savoldo and Correggio, we may call it Proto-Baroque, which suggests both its great importance for the future and its special place in relation to the past.

CHAPTER FIFTEEN

"Late Gothic" Painting, Sculpture, and the Graphic Arts

Many scholars treat fifteenth-century Northern painting as the counterpart of the Early Renaissance in Italy, and with good reason. It had an impact that went far beyond its own region. In Italy Flemish artists were admired as much as the leading Italian artists. To Italian eyes, their work was clearly post-medieval. Its intense realism had a marked influence on Early Renaissance painting. The Italians, as we have already noted, associated the exact imitation of nature in painting with a "return to the classics." Should we, then, think of the Renaissance as a unified style? Or should we view it as an attitude that was embodied in several styles? "Renaissance consciousness," we know, was an Italian idea. There can be no doubt that Italy played the leading role in the development of Renaissance art, at least until the early sixteenth century. This fact does not necessarily mean, however, that the Renaissance was confined to the South. When Boccaccio praised Giotto's imitation of nature, he could not know how many aspects of reality Giotto and his contemporaries had failed to investigate. These, we recall, were further explored by the painters of the International Style, however tentatively. To go beyond Gothic realism required a second revolution, which began in Italy and in the Netherlands about 1420. We must think of two events linked by a common aim—the conquest of the visible world—yet sharply divided in almost every other way.

The Italian, or Southern, revolution was more systematic. In the long run, it was also more fundamental, since it included architecture and sculpture as well as painting. There are still many unanswered questions about the Northern revolution and its relation to the Renaissance as a whole. We do not yet know why the new style emerged in Flanders around 1420, in contrast to the Early Renaissance, which started in Florence under very specific circumstances. Italian Renaissance art, moreover, made very little impression north of the Alps during the fifteenth century. Not until the final decades did humanism begin to play an important role in Northern thought, which it then changed decisively. Nor do

we find an interest in the art of classical antiquity before that time. Rather, the artistic and cultural environment of Northern painters clearly remained rooted in the Gothic tradition.

We have, in fact, no satisfactory name for Northern fifteenth-century art as a whole. Whatever we choose to call the style, we shall find that it has some justification. For the sake of convenience, we shall use the label "Late Gothic." The term hardly does justice to the special character of the new Flemish painting. No matter how cumbersome, it suggests the continuity with the world-view of the late Middle Ages. Netherlandish art, unlike the Italian Renaissance, did not entirely reject the International Style. Instead, Northern painters took it as their point of departure, so that the break with the past was less abrupt than in the South. Despite its great importance, their work may be seen as the final phase of Gothic painting. The term *Late Gothic* also reminds us that fifteenth-century architecture and sculpture outside Italy was an outgrowth of the Gothic.

Netherlandish Painting

ROBERT CAMPIN. The first phase of the painting revolution in Flanders begins with the work of an artist formerly known as the Master of Flémalle (after the fragments of a large altar from Flémalle), who was undoubtedly Robert Campin, the foremost painter of Tournai. We can trace his working life in documents from 1406 to his death in 1444 (he was born about 1378), although his career declined after his conviction in 1428 for adultery, a serious criminal offense at that time. His masterpiece is the *Mérode Altarpiece (*fig. 15-1), which he must have painted soon after 1425. It clearly falls in the same tradition as the Franco-Flemish pictures of the International Style (see fig. 11-92). Yet it also provides a new and very different pictorial experience.

Here, for the first time, we have the sense of actually looking through the surface of the panel into a world that has all the

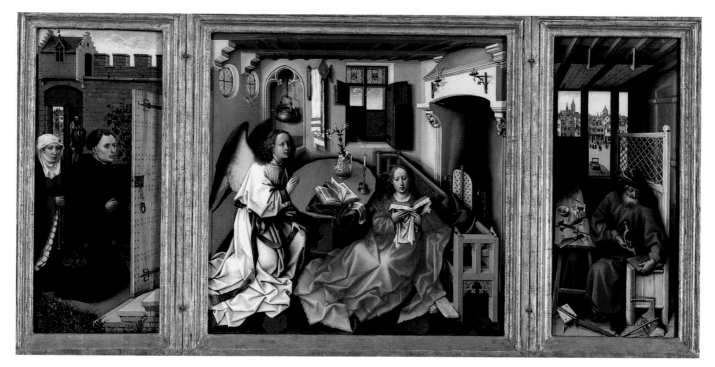

15-1. Robert Campin (Master of Flémalle). *Mérode Altarpiece.* c. 1425–30. Oil on panel, center 25 ³⁄₁₆ x 24 ⁷⁄₈" (64.3 x 62.9 cm); each wing approx. 25 ³⁄₈ x 10 ⁷⁄₈" (64.5 x 27.4 cm). The Metropolitan Museum of Art, New York, The Cloisters Collection, 1956

essential features of everyday reality: unlimited depth, stability, continuity, and completeness. The painters of the International Style, even at their most daring, had never aimed at such consistency, and their commitment to reality was far from absolute. Their pictures have the enchanting quality of fairy tales. The scale and relationship of things can be shifted at will, and fact and fancy mingle without conflict. Campin, in contrast, has tried to tell the truth, the whole truth, and nothing but the truth. To be sure, he does not yet do it with total ease. His objects, overly foreshortened, tend to jostle each other in space. But he defines every last detail of every object to make it as concrete as possible: its shape and size; its color, material, and hardness; its surface texture and way of responding to light. The artist even distinguishes between the diffused light, which creates soft shadows and delicate gradations of brightness, and the direct light entering through the two round windows, which produces the pair of sharply defined shadows in the upper part of the center panel and the twin reflections on the brass vessel and candlestick.

The *Mérode Altarpiece* transports us from the aristocratic world of the International Style to the household of a Flemish burgher. Campin was no court painter but a townsperson who catered to the tastes of well-to-do fellow citizens such as the two donors piously kneeling outside the Virgin's chamber. This is the earliest Annunciation in panel painting that takes place in a fully equipped domestic interior. It is also the first to honor Joseph, the humble carpenter, by showing him at work next door.

This bold departure from tradition forced our artist to face a problem no one had dealt with before. He needed to transfer supernatural events from symbolic settings to an everyday environment

without making them look either trivial or out of place. He met this challenge by the method known as **disguised symbolism**, which means that almost any detail in the picture, however casual, may carry a symbolic message. We saw its beginnings during the International Style in the *Annunciation* by Melchior Broederlam (see fig. 11-91), but his symbolism seems simple compared with the many hidden meanings in the *Mérode Altarpiece.*

The flowers, for example, are associated with the Virgin. In the left wing the roses denote her charity and the violets her humility, while in the center panel the lilies symbolize her chastity. The shiny water basin and the towel on its rack are not just household equipment. They are further attributes of Mary as the "vessel most clean" and the "well of living waters." Perhaps the most intriguing symbol of this sort is the candle next to the vase of lilies. It has been extinguished only moments before, as we can tell from the glowing wick and the curl of smoke. But why had it been lit in broad daylight, and what made the flame go out? Has the divine radiance of the Lord's presence overcome the material light? Or did the flame of the candle itself represent the divine light, now extinguished to show that God has become human, that in Jesus "the Word was made flesh"?

Clearly, the entire range of medieval symbolism not only survives in our picture but has been greatly expanded. It is nevertheless so completely tied to the world of everyday appearances that we often wonder whether a given detail has a symbolic meaning. Scholars long wondered, for instance, about the boxlike object on Joseph's workbench and a similar one on the ledge outside the open window. Finally they were identified as mousetraps that convey a specific theological message. According to St. Augustine,

God had to appear on earth in human form so as to fool Satan: "The Cross of the Lord was the devil's mousetrap."

Since it takes much scholarly ingenuity to explain this sort of iconography, we tend to think of the *Mérode Altarpiece* and similar pictures as puzzles. We can still enjoy them without knowing all their symbolism. But what about the patrons for whom these works were painted? Did they understand the meaning of every detail? They would have had no trouble with well-established symbols in our picture, such as the flowers, and they probably knew the significance of the water basin. The message of the extinguished candle and the mousetrap could not have been common knowledge even among the well-educated, however.

These two symbols—and we can hardly doubt that they are symbols—appear for the first time in the *Mérode Altarpiece*. They must be unusual, too. St. Joseph with the mousetrap has been found in only one other picture, and the freshly extinguished candle occurs nowhere else, as far as we know. It seems that Campin introduced them into Northern painting, yet hardly any artists adopted them despite his great influence. If the candle and the mousetrap were difficult to understand even in the fifteenth century, why are they in the picture at all? Was Campin told to put them in by his exceptionally educated patron? This would be possible if it were the only case of its kind; since, however, there are many instances of equally subtle or obscure symbolism in "Late Gothic" painting, it seems more likely that the initiative came from the artists, rather than from their patrons.

Campin either was a man of unusual learning, or he had contact with theologians or scholars who could supply him with the references that suggested the symbolic meanings of such things as the extinguished candle and the mousetrap. In other words, the artist did not simply continue the symbolic tradition of medieval art within the framework of the new realistic style. He enlarged and enriched it by his own efforts. To him, even more than Broederlam (see pages 378), realism and symbolism were interrelated. We might say that Campin needed a growing symbolic repertory because it encouraged him to explore features of the visible world that had not been depicted before, such as a candle just after it has been blown out or the interior of a carpenter's shop, which provided the setting for the mousetraps. For him to justify painting everyday reality, he had to sanctify it with spiritual significance.

This reverence for the physical world as a mirror of divine truths helps us to understand why the smallest details are rendered with the same attention as the sacred figures in the Mérode panels. The disguised symbolism of Campin and later painters was not simply grafted onto the new realistic style. It was ingrained in the creative process. Their Italian contemporaries must have sensed this, for they praised both the realism and the piety of the Flemish masters.

Campin's distinctive tonality makes the Mérode *Annunciation* stand out from earlier panel paintings. The jewel-like quality of the older works, with their brilliant hues and lavish use of gold, have given way to a color scheme that is far less decorative but much more flexible and refined. The muted tonality shows a new subtlety and wider range, the brighter colors a greater richness and depth, while the scale of intermediate shades is smoother. These effects are essential to the realistic style of Campin. They were made possible by the use of oil (see discussion page 436). Although oil was not unfamiliar to medieval artists, it was Campin and his contemporaries who discovered its artistic possibilities. Thus, from the technical point of view, too, they deserve to be called the founders of modern painting.

JAN AND HUBERT VAN EYCK. The full possibilities of oil were not discovered all at once, nor by any one artist. The greatest contribution was made by Jan van Eyck, who was long thought to have invented oil painting. [See Primary Sources, no. 47, pages 648–49.] We know a good deal about Jan's life and career. A somewhat younger and much more famous artist than Campin, he was born about 1390 near Liège, he worked in Holland from 1422 to 1424, in Lille from 1425 to 1429, and thereafter in Bruges, where he died in 1441. Both a townsperson and a court painter, he was highly esteemed by Duke Philip the Good of Burgundy, who occasionally sent him on diplomatic errands. After 1432 we can follow Jan's career through a number of signed and dated pictures. His older brother Hubert remains a shadowy figure, however. We know only that he died in 1426, as the inscription on the frame of the *Ghent Altarpiece* tells us.

There are a number of "Eyckian" works, clearly older than the *Ghent Altarpiece,* that may have been painted by either or both of the two brothers. The most fascinating is a pair of panels showing the *Crucifixion* and the *Last Judgment* (fig. 15-2). Their date must be between 1420 and 1425. These paintings have much in common with the *Mérode Altarpiece*. They show the same total devotion to the visible world, unlimited depth, and angular drapery folds, which are less graceful but far more realistic than the unbroken loops of the International Style. At the same time, the individual forms seem less tangible and "sculptural" than Campin's. The sweeping sense of space is the result not so much of foreshortening as of subtle changes of light and color. If we look closely at the *Crucifixion* panel, we see a gradual decrease in the intensity of local colors, and in the contrast of light and dark, from the foreground figures to the far-off city of Jerusalem and the snow-capped peaks beyond. Everything tends toward a uniform bluish-gray, so that the farthest mountain range merges imperceptibly with the color of the sky.

This optical phenomenon is known as **atmospheric perspective**. The Van Eycks were the first to use it systematically, although the Boucicaut Master and the Limbourg brothers were aware of it (see fig. 11-93). The atmosphere is never wholly transparent. Even on the clearest day, the air between us and what we are looking at acts as a hazy screen that interferes with our ability to see distant shapes clearly. As we approach the limit of visibility, it swallows them completely. Atmospheric perspective is more essential to our perception of deep space than scientific perspective, which records the decrease in the apparent size of objects as their distance from the viewer increases. It is effective not only in distant vistas. In the *Crucifixion* panel, even the foreground seems to be enveloped in a delicate haze that softens contours, shadows, and

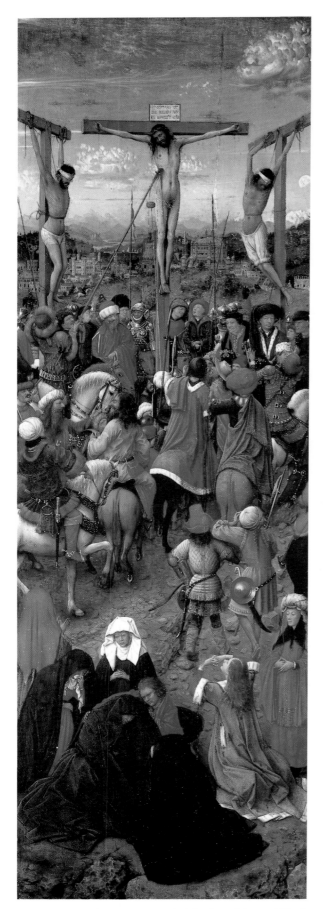
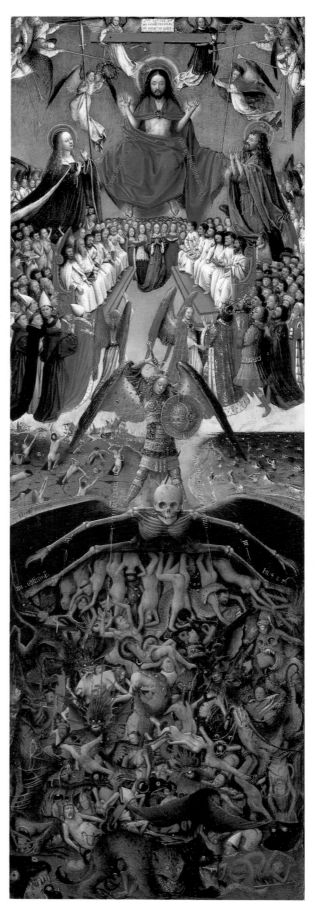

15-2. Hubert and/or Jan van Eyck. *The Crucifixion and The Last Judgment.* c. 1420–25. Tempera and oil on canvas, transferred from panel; each panel 22¼ x 7¾" (56.5 x 19.4 cm). The Metropolitan Museum of Art, New York

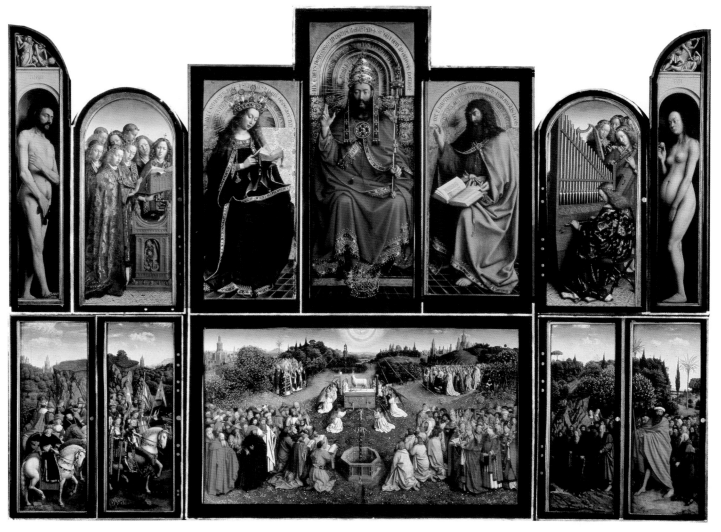

15-3. Hubert and Jan van Eyck. *Ghent Altarpiece* (open). Completed 1432. Oil on panel, 11'3" x 14'5" (3.4 x 4.4 m). Church of St. Bavo, Ghent, Belgium

colors. Thus the entire scene has a continuity and harmony beyond the pictorial range of Campin.

How did the Van Eycks achieve this effect? It is difficult to determine their exact technical process, but there can be no doubt that they used the oil medium with extraordinary refinement. By alternating opaque and translucent layers of paint, they were able to give their pictures a soft, glowing color that has never been equaled, probably because it depends as much on their individual sensibilities as it does on their skillful craftsmanship.

Seen as a whole, the *Crucifixion* seems to lack drama, as if the scene were calmed by some magic spell. Only when we concentrate on the details do we become aware of the violent expressions in the faces of the crowd beneath the Cross or the restrained but deeply touching grief of the Virgin Mary and her companions in the foreground. In the *Last Judgment* panel, this dual quality takes the form of two extremes. Above the horizon, all is order and calm symmetry; below it, on earth and in the realm of Satan, chaos prevails. The two states thus correspond to Heaven and Hell, contemplative bliss as against physical and emotional agitation. The lower half clearly was the greater challenge to the artists' imaginative powers. The dead rising from their graves with frantic gestures of fear and hope,

the damned being torn apart by monsters more terrifying than any we have seen before (compare fig. 10-24), all have the awesome reality of a nightmare. Yet it is all depicted with the same care as the natural world of the *Crucifixion* panel.

The *Ghent Altarpiece* (figs. 15-3, 15-4, and 15-6), the greatest monument of early Flemish painting, presents problems so complex that our discussion must be limited to essentials. Its basic arrangement is a triptych—a central body with two hinged wings—the standard format of altarpieces. Each of the three units consists of four panels. And since the wings are also painted on both sides, the altarpiece has a total of 20 panels of various shapes and sizes. It must originally have been placed in an elaborate architectural-style frame. This impressive "super-altar" could not have been planned this way, since it is far from harmonious. Apparently Jan took over a number of panels left unfinished by Hubert, completed them, added some of his own, and assembled them at the behest of the wealthy donor, Jodicus Vyd, whose portrait with that of his wife we see on the outer panels of the altar.

To reconstruct this train of events, and to determine each brother's share, is a fascinating but difficult game. Hubert's style, with retouches by Jan, can probably be found in the four central

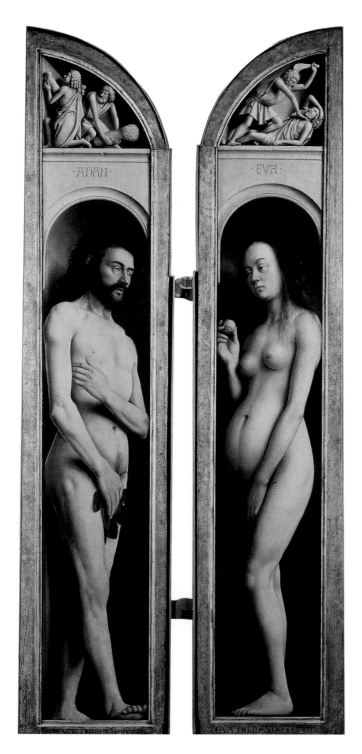

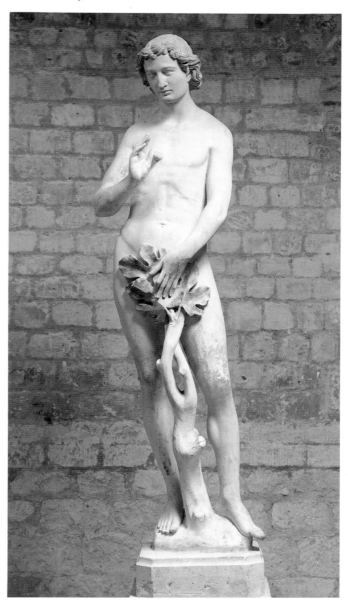

(LEFT) 15-4. *Adam and Eve,* details of *Ghent Altarpiece,* left and right wings

(BELOW) 15-5. *Adam,* from south transept, Notre-Dame, Paris. c. 1250. Stone, height 6'7¼" (2 m). Musée du Moyen Age, Hôtel de Cluny, Paris

panels inside, although they did not belong together originally. The upper three, showing the Lord between the Virgin Mary and St. John the Baptist, seem to have been intended as a self-contained triptych. The lower panel and the four flanking it probably formed a separate altarpiece: the Adoration of the Lamb, symbolizing Jesus' sacrificial death. The two panels with music-making angels may have been planned as a pair of organ shutters.

The two tall, narrow panels showing Adam and Eve (fig. 15-4) are certainly the most daring. These, the first monumental nudes of Northern panel painting (hardly less than lifesize), are magnificently observed and caressed by the most delicate play of light and shade. Although hardly different in pose from similar figures in Gothic

manuscripts (compare fig. 11-93), they were inspired mainly by statues like the *Adam* in fig. 15-5 (he was complemented by a missing Eve) from the middle of the thirteenth century, when Gothic realism was at its height (see pages 351–52). Painting and sculpture were closely allied in the fifteenth century. Wood carvings and panel paintings were often combined in altars (see page 378). Moreover, both Campin and Van Eyck painted **grisailles** (pictures done entirely in gray tones) to simulate stone sculpture. (Note the small, violently expressive scenes above Adam and Eve showing the story of Cain and Abel, which recall *The Kiss of Judas* on the Naumburg choir screen, fig. 11-52.) Still, Van Eyck's figures are revolutionary in their unprecedented realism, which is tied to a shift in attitude. Their

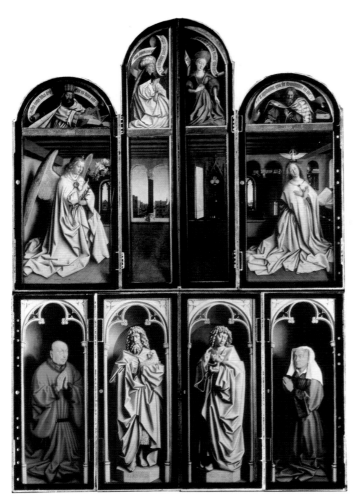

15-6. *Ghent Altarpiece* (closed)

Donors' portraits of convincing individuality occupy prominent positions in both the *Mérode* and the *Ghent Altarpieces*. A renewed interest in realistic portraiture had developed in the mid-fourteenth century, but until about 1420 its best achievements were in sculpture (see fig. 11-55). Painters usually confined themselves to profile views. Not until Campin, the first artist since antiquity to have real command of the human face in three-quarter view, did the portrait play a major role in Northern painting.

In addition to donors' portraits, we now begin to find a growing number of small likenesses whose intimacy suggests that they were keepsakes, pictorial substitutes for the sitter. One of the most impressive is Jan van Eyck's *Man in a Red Turban* of 1433 (fig. 15-7), which may well be a self-portrait. (The slight strain about the eyes seems to come from gazing into a mirror.) The face is bathed in the same gentle, clear light as Adam and Eve on the *Ghent Altarpiece*. Every detail has been recorded with minute precision. Yet, as in all of Jan's portraits, the personality remains a puzzle. It might be described as "even-tempered" in the most exact sense of the term. Since Jan was fully capable of expressing emotion, the stoic calm of his portraits surely reflects his ideal of human character.

The Flemish cities of Tournai, Ghent, and Bruges, where the new style of painting flourished, rivaled the great centers of international banking and trade in Italy. Their foreign residents included many Italian businessmen. Jan van Eyck painted the

quiet dignity and prominent place in the altar suggest that, unlike the Adam from Notre Dame, they should remind us not simply of Original Sin but also of our creation in God's own image. Actual evil, by contrast, is restricted to the grisailles. Even more extraordinary is the fact that the Adam and Eve were designed specifically for their present positions in the ensemble. Jan van Eyck has established a new, direct relationship between picture space and real space by depicting the two figures as they would really appear to the spectator, whose eye level is below the bottom of the panels.

The outer panels of the two wings (fig. 15-6) seem to have been planned as one unit. Here, as we would expect, the largest figures are in the lower tier, not above as they are inside, where they threaten to crush everything beneath them. The two St. Johns (painted in grisaille, like the scenes of Cain and Abel), the donor, and his wife, are each shown in a separate niche. The upper tier has two pairs of panels of different width. The artist has made a virtue of this awkward necessity by combining all four into one interior. Such an effect had first been created by Pietro Lorenzetti almost a century earlier (compare fig. 11-82). Not content with perspective devices alone, Jan heightens the illusion by painting the shadows cast by the frames of the panels on the floor of the Virgin's chamber. This Annunciation resembles, in its homely detail, the *Mérode Altarpiece*. It thus provides an important link between the two great pioneers of Flemish realism.

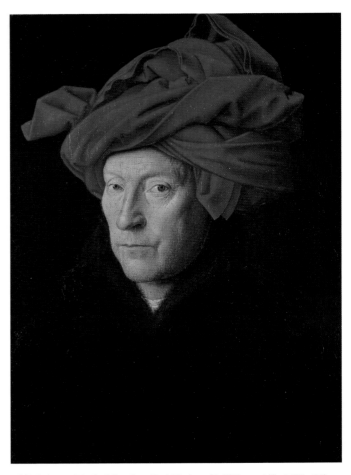

15-7. Jan van Eyck. *Man in a Red Turban (Self-Portrait?)*. 1433. Oil on panel, 10¼ x 7½" (26 x 19 cm). The National Gallery, London

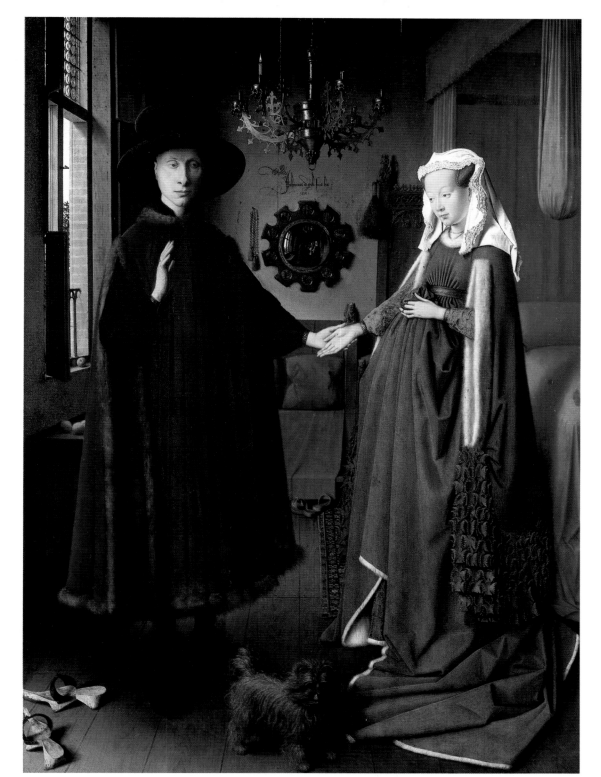

15-8. Jan van Eyck.
The Arnolfini Portrait.
1434. Oil on panel,
33 x 22½"
(83.7 x 57 cm).
The National Gallery,
London

(BELOW RIGHT)
15-9. Jan van Eyck.
The Arnolfini Portrait
(detail)

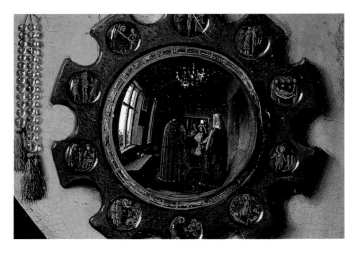

portrait in figure 15-8 to celebrate the alliance of two of these families that were active in Bruges and Paris. It probably shows the betrothal of Giovanni Arnolfini and Giovanna Cenami in the main room of the bride's house, rather than an exchange of marriage vows in the privacy of the bridal chamber, as usually thought. The young couple touches hands as he raises his right hand in solemn oath. (In accordance with Northern custom, the actual wedding took place later in front of a church, when the young couple's right hands were joined in holy matrimony.) They seem to be quite alone, but in the mirror behind them is the reflection of two other people who have entered the room (fig. 15-9). One of them is presumably the bride's father, who by tradition gives her to the groom. The other must be the artist, since the words above the mirror, in florid lettering, tell us that "Johannes de eyck fuit hic" (Jan van Eyck was here) in the year 1434.

Jan, then, acts as a witness to the engagement, which also entailed a legal and financial contract between the two families. The picture claims to show exactly what he saw. Given its secular nature, we may wonder whether the picture is filled with the same sort of disguised symbolism as the *Mérode Altarpiece*. Or does the realism serve simply as an accurate record of the event and its domestic setting? The elaborate bed, the main piece of furniture in the well-appointed living room of the day, was used not for sleeping but for greeting new mothers and paying final respects to the dead. May it not also refer to the physical consummation of marriage? Has the couple taken off their shoes merely as a matter of custom, or to remind us that they are standing on "holy ground"? (For the origin of the theme, see page 50.) By the same token, is the little dog a beloved pet, or an emblem of fidelity? (In Latin, *fides* is the root for the words *dog, fidelity,* and *betrothal.*) The other furnishings of the room pose similar questions. What is the role of the single candle in the chandelier, burning in broad daylight (compare page 513)? And is the convex mirror, whose frame is decorated with scenes from the Passion, not a **Vanitas** symbol

(see fig. 18-24)? Jan was so intrigued by its visual effects that he included it in two other paintings as well.

In the end, we are forced to conclude that here, too, the natural world contains the world of the spirit so completely that the two become one. As our detail of the mirror shows, the young couple are too far from the doorway to have removed their shoes simply out of habit. The mirror and its carved decorations convey a moral message: to think of spiritual values, not simply to enjoy the worldly pleasures represented by the luxurious interior. Nor can the placement of the dog directly below the mirror and squarely between the man and woman be simply a coincidence. As a sacrament, matrimony was holy and binding in a spiritual, not just a legal, sense. Yet, in questioning the traditional reading, we are reminded not to overinterpret the symbolic meaning of an image to the point where it would have been hopelessly obscure even to the artist's contemporaries.

ROGIER VAN DER WEYDEN. In the work of Jan van Eyck, the exploration of the reality made visible by light and color was not surpassed for another two centuries. Rogier van der Weyden (1399/1400–1464), the third great master of early Flemish painting,

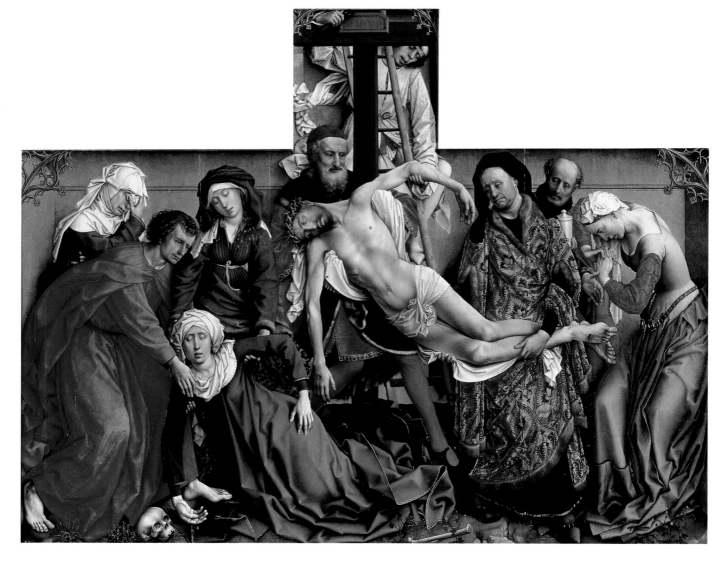

set himself a different but equally important task: to recapture the emotional drama and pathos of the Gothic past within the framework of the new style. We see this greater expressive immediacy in his early masterpiece, *Descent from the Cross* (fig. 15-10), which dates from about 1435. Here the modeling is sculpturally precise, with angular drapery folds recalling the work of Rogier's teacher, Robert Campin. The soft half-shadows and rich colors show his knowledge of Jan van Eyck, with whom he may also have been in contact. Yet Rogier is far more than a follower of the two older artists.

Whatever he owes to them (and it is clearly a great deal) he uses for his own purposes. The external event of lowering Jesus' body from the Cross concerns him less than the world of human feeling: "the inner desires and emotions . . . whether sorrow, anger, or gladness," in the words of an early account. The visible world in turn becomes a means toward that same end. Rogier's art has been well described as "at once physically barer and spiritually richer than Jan van Eyck's." Judged by its expressive content, this *Descent* could well be called a *Lamentation*. The Virgin's swoon echoes the pose and expression of her son. So intense are her pain and grief that they inspire the same compassion in the viewer. Rogier has

staged his scene in a shallow niche or shrine, not against a landscape. This bold device gives him a double advantage in heightening the effect of the tragic event. It focuses the viewer's attention on the foreground and allows the artist to mold the figures into a coherent group. It seems fitting that Rogier treats his figures as if they were colored statues, for the source of these grief-stricken gestures and faces is in sculpture rather than in painting. The panel descends from the Strasbourg *Death of the Virgin* (see fig. 11-45), to which it is similar in both composition and mood.

Truly Late Gothic, Rogier's art never departs from the spirit of the Middle Ages. Yet visually it belongs just as clearly to the new era, so that the past is restated in contemporary terms. *The Miraflores Altarpiece* (fig. 15-11) is full of archaic touches, yet it looks thoroughly up to date. By now the artist was in great demand, and his work involved the participation of assistants. Such is the case with our altar, named for the convent near Burgos that received it by 1445. (The composition is known in a second, equally fine version from his shop.) As the inscriptions on the scrolls tell us, the triptych celebrates the purity, faith, and perseverance of the Virgin, which are related in turn to the theme of her joys, sorrows, and glories.

(OPPOSITE) 15-10. Rogier van der Weyden. *Descent from the Cross.* c. 1435. Oil on panel, 7'2⅝" x 8'7⅛" (2.2 x 2.6 m). Museo del Prado, Madrid

Jan van Eyck had not so much resolved as negated the problems posed by the great painters of Tournai [for example, Robert Campin (Master of Flémalle), fig. 15-1]; he had eliminated the tensions and contradictions characteristic of the latter's manner by abolishing their very raison d'être. Where, as in Jan's mature style [see figs. 15-3, 15-4, 15-6, 15-7, and 15-8], all physical and emotional action was absorbed into pure existence there could be no conflict between movement and rest. Where all surface relations were transposed into space relations there could be no conflict between two-dimensional design and composition in depth. Where all details were perfectly integrated with total form there could be no conflict between a pictorial and a linear mode of presentation. Roger van der Weyden, however, set out to develop the expressive and calligraphical possibilities inherent in the style of the Master of Flémalle without forfeiting the consistency and purity attained by Jan van Eyck.

While Roger's figures are more dynamic than Jan's their movements are both more fluent and more controlled than the Master of Flémalle's, and while their grouping is denser and more diversified than in an Eyckian composition it is less crowded and more coordinated than in a Flémallesque one. It is as though a living chain of figures were thrown across the picture plane—a chain whose links remain distinct though conjoined by artful repetition and variation. And the component parts of every figure, body and garments alike, are both articulated in form and function and unified by an uninterrupted flow of energy. In short, Roger van der Weyden may be said to have introduced into Flemish fifteenth-century art the principle of rhythm in contradistinction to meter—definable as that by which movement is articulated without loss of continuity.

This rhythm unfolds within a kind of foreground relief neatly divorced from the space behind it. But both foreground relief and background space are what I should like to call "stratified" into a series of planes deliberately frontalized yet interconnected in depth. The entire picture space is thus made to obey a common principle analogous to the "rhythmical" organization of figure movement: articulation is accomplished without destroying continuity. . . .

As the principle of rhythm overcomes the tension between movement and rest in the behavior of the figures, and between surface and depth in the organization of space, so does it overcome the tension between the pictorial and the graphic in the presentation of plastic form as such; and this, I believe, is the very essence of Roger van der Weyden's "linearism." As in all Early Flemish painting, his lines are not abstract contours separating two areas of flat color, but represent a condensation or concentration of light or shade caused by the shape and texture of the objects. However, in Roger's paintings these forms assume a linear quality without relinquishing their luminary significance.

—Erwin Panofsky. *Early Netherlandish Painting: Its Origins and Character.* 2 vols. New York: Icon Editions, 1971. Originally published in 1953 by Harvard University Press.

ERWIN PANOFSKY (1892–1968), born and educated in Germany, established what was for several decades a mainstream methodology of art history, in which iconography and iconology dominated. Forced by the Nazi regime in 1934 to give up a full professorship at the university in Hamburg, Panofsky emigrated to the United States, where he spent most of the rest of his career at the Institute for Advanced Study, Princeton University. A brilliant scholar of medieval and Northern Renaissance art—he possessed an almost superhuman level of learning—Panofsky was a broad thinker for whom the relationship between the perception of images and the mental constructs elicited by those perceptions was a persistent fascination. For many American art historians, his *Early Netherlandish Painting* remains one of the most challenging and brilliant works ever written.

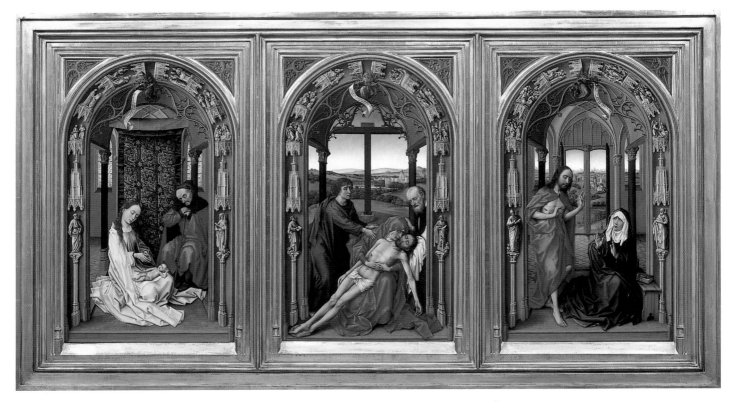

15-11. Rogier van der Weyden. *The Miraflores Altarpiece.* c. 1440–44. Oil on panel, each panel 28 x 16⅞" (71.1 x 42.8 cm). Staatliche Museen zu Berlin, Gemäldegalerie

A simulated portal provides the doorway into each scene, which is confined to the foreground of a small niche, despite the suggestion of deep space behind it. This old-fashioned device creates the impression of colored sculpture in an architectural setting (see the Naumburg *Crucifixion,* fig. 11-51). The effect is increased by the reliefs lining the archivolts. These reliefs carry much of the narrative and symbolic burden by depicting events from the life of Jesus related to the subject below. The Virgin adoring the Christ Child in the left panel brings to mind a traditional Nativity (compare fig. 11-97). Because it is transferred to an indoor setting, this Madonna of Humility is also the Queen of Heaven. The center panel combines the Byzantine motif of the Last Kiss with the German *Pietà* (see fig. 11-54). However, the Final Appearance of Jesus to his Mother, in the right panel, is unusual in both subject and treatment. It recalls the more familiar *Noli me tangere,* where he appears to the Magdalen.

The Miraflores Altar, like the *Descent,* may be thought of as an enlarged Gothic *Andachtsbild,* for it is meant to be an object of spiritual devotion. The figures continue the aristocratic ideal of the International Style. Slender and elegant, they represent Rogier's definitive type. He uses all these figures to convey a remarkable range of emotion not simply through gesture and expression but also through purely formal means—the precise quality of line, form, and color—which communicate their intent with powerful conviction.

Rogier was accessible to people who retained a medieval outlook. No wonder he set an example for countless other artists. When he died in 1464, after 30 years as the foremost painter of Brussels, his influence was supreme throughout Europe north

of the Alps. Its impact continued to be felt almost everywhere outside Italy, in sculpture as well as painting, until the end of the fifteenth century.

HUGO VAN DER GOES. Few Northern artists after Rogier van der Weyden escaped from his shadow. To them his paintings offered a choice between intense drama and delicate restraint. The vast majority chose the latter, and their work is marked by a fragile charm. The most dynamic of Rogier's disciples was Hugo van der Goes (c. 1440–1482), an unhappy genius whose tragic end suggests an unstable character. After a spectacular rise to fame in the cosmopolitan atmosphere of Bruges, he decided to enter a monastery as a lay brother in 1475, when he was about 35 years old. He continued to paint for some time, but increasing fits of depression drove him to the verge of suicide, and seven years later he was dead.

The huge altarpiece commissioned in 1475 by Tommaso Portinari, an agent of the Medicis in Bruges, is Van der Goes' most ambitious work (fig. 15-12). There is a tension between the artist's devotion to the natural world and his concern with the supernatural that suggests a nervous and restless personality. Hugo presents a wonderfully spacious and atmospheric landscape with a wealth of precise detail. Yet the difference in the size of the figures seems to contradict this realism. The angels and kneeling members of the Portinari family are dwarfed by the other figures, so that they appear abnormally small. The patron saints in the wings share the same huge scale with Joseph, the Virgin Mary, and the shepherds of the Nativity in the center panel. They are not meant to be larger than life, however. Their height is normal in

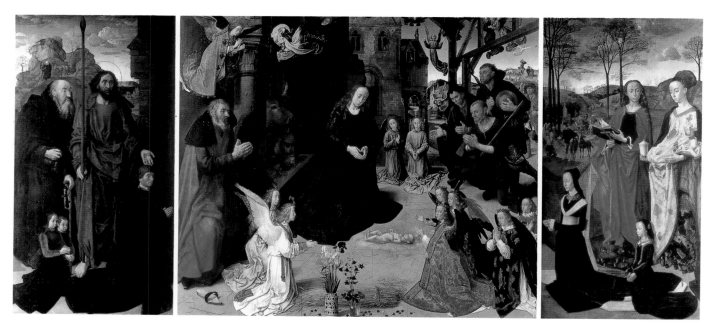

15-12. Hugo van der Goes. *The Portinari Altarpiece* (open). c. 1476. Tempera and oil on panel, center 8'3½" x 10' (2.5 x 3.1 m), wings each 8'3½" x 4'7½" (2.5 x 1.4 m). Galleria degli Uffizi, Florence

relation to the architecture and to the ox and ass. Instead, their gigantic size marks them as being of a higher order.

This change of scale stands outside the logic of everyday experience found in the setting that the artist has provided for his figures. Although it originated with Rogier van der Weyden and has a clear symbolic purpose, Hugo exploited this variation for expressive effect. There is another striking contrast between the hushed awe of the shepherds and the ritual solemnity of all the other figures. These field hands, gazing in breathless wonder at the newborn Christ child, react to the miracle of the Nativity with a wide-eyed directness new to Flemish art. They were especially admired by the Italian painters who saw the work after Portinari brought it to Florence in 1483.

GEERTGEN TOT SINT JANS. During the last quarter of the fifteenth century, there were no painters in Flanders comparable to Hugo van der Goes. The most original artists appeared farther north, in Holland. One of them, Geertgen tot Sint Jans of Haarlem, who died at the age of 28 around 1490–5, admired Hugo's work in Bruges. He then returned to his hometown to work for the Knights of St. John's, hence his name. His *Nativity* (fig. 15-13) is as daring in its quiet way as the center panel of the *Portinari Altarpiece*. The idea of a nighttime Nativity, lighted mainly by radiance from the Christ Child, goes back to the International Style (see fig. 11-98). But Geertgen applies the discoveries of Jan van Eyck to give new reality to the scene. The magic effect of his little panel is enhanced by the smooth, simplified shapes that record the play of light with striking clarity. The heads of the angels, the Infant, and the Virgin are all as round as objects turned on a lathe, while the manger is a rectangular trough.

HIERONYMUS BOSCH. Another Dutch artist, Hieronymus Bosch, appeals to our interest in the world of fantasy. Little is known about him except that he came from a family of painters

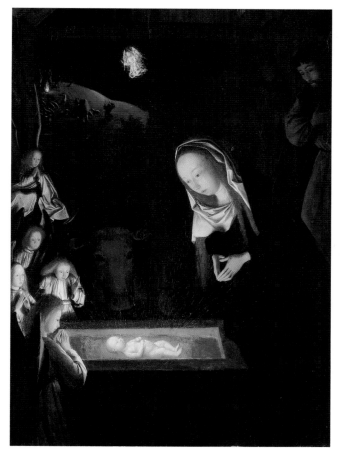

15-13. Geertgen tot Sint Jans. *Nativity*. c. 1490. Oil on panel, 13½ x 10" (34.3 x 25.7 cm). The National Gallery, London

named Van Aken, spent his life in the provincial town of 'sHerto-genbosch, and died, an old man, in 1516. His work, full of weird and seemingly irrational imagery, has proved difficult to interpret.

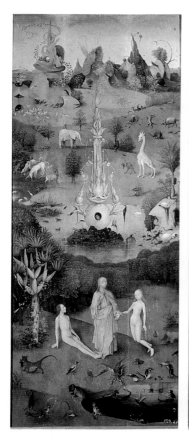
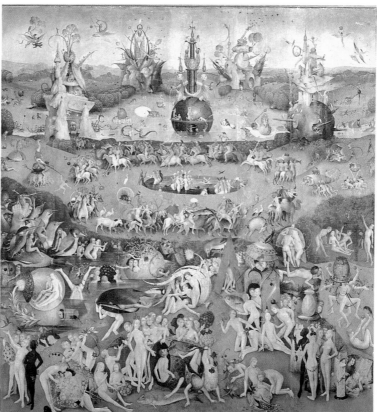
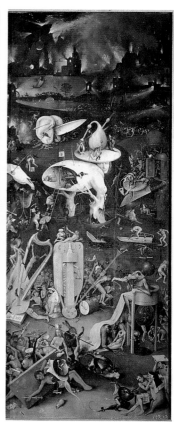

15-14. Hieronymous Bosch. *The Garden of Delights.* c. 1510–15. Oil on panel, center 7'2½" x 6'4½" (2.19 x 1.95 m); wings, each 7'2½" x 3'2" (2.19 x .96 m). Museo del Prado, Madrid

Bosch has all the makings of a landscape painter. There is character and grandeur in his wide and barren plains. Perhaps he is more entitled than Patenier, a professional landscape painter, to be included among the pioneers and innovators in this field.

However progressive in his intellectual independence and robust inventiveness the master may be, his formal idiom and manner of painting are still of the fifteenth century. By studying his terse sharp lines in their archaic ductus and the glazed clarity of the thinly applied paint (in well-preserved originals) we can avoid confusing his works with those of his imitators.

Primitive even in the circle of his contemporaries, Bosch composes like a carver in relief or a medallist; his profiled figures are thin, almost transparent, everything is flattened onto the surface. . . . A rapid smooth-flowing line, precisely directed, gives an ethereal quality to his pictures. . . .

The basic forms of the human figure, which is graceful and flexible in effect, are surely grasped but superficial intimations suffice him for

the details. We can expect little reverence for nature from one who tries to poach on the Creator. . . .

Bosch's human beings have thin, pale, elderly faces and generally participate in some sly feeble cunning. The pure and holy often have a foolish smile whilst evil lurks everywhere awaiting an opportunity to erupt.

—Max J. Friedlaender. *From Van Eyck to Bruegel.* Edited and annotated by F. Grossmann. Translated by Marguerite Kay. 2 vols. Ithaca: Cornell University Press, 1981, pp. 59–60. Originally published in 1956 by Phaidon Press Ltd.

MAX J. FRIEDLAENDER (1867–1958) was a specialist in Early Netherlandish and Northern Renaissance prints. His catalogue of Netherlandish prints, first published between 1924 and 1937 and reissued with updates in 1967, is still the seminal work in the field. However, he was far from a narrow specialist and published widely. His two-volume work *From Van Eyck to Bruegel* (1956/69), with annotations by Friedrich Grossmann, no mean scholar himself, bring Panofsky down to earth for the rest of us, so to speak, for it was meant to be accessible to nearly any reader. His observations on Bosch are among the most penetrating ever written.

Bosch's most famous work, the triptych known as *The Garden of Delights* (fig. 15-14) is the richest and most puzzling of all. [See Primary Sources, no. 50, page 650.] Its peculiar qualities may be due partly to the fact that this is not a traditional altarpiece but a secular work. It was probably commissioned by Henry III of Nassau for his palace in Brussels, where it was hanging just after

Bosch's death. (Henry would have been familiar with Bosch's work in Hertogenbosch, a royal residence.) Scholars have suggested many explanations for the painting: for example, that it represents the days of Noah, or that it is a heretical allegory of redemption through the acceptance of humanity's natural state before the Fall. Yet none of these explanations is wholly satisfactory. In the end, we must take the character of the painting itself into account. Moreover, any interpretation must be consistent with Bosch's work as a whole.

Of the three panels, only the left one has a clearly recognizable subject. It is the Garden of Eden, where the Lord introduces Adam to the newly created Eve. The airy landscape is filled with animals, including such exotic creatures as an elephant and a giraffe, as well as sinister hybrid monsters. The right wing, a nightmarish scene of burning ruins and instruments of torture, surely represents Hell. But what of the center panel? Here is a landscape much like that of the Garden of Eden, populated with countless nude men and women engaged in a variety of strange acts. In the center, they parade around a circular basin on the backs of all sorts of beasts. Many frolic in pools of water. Most of them are linked with huge birds, fruit, flowers, or marine animals. Only a few are openly engaged in lovemaking, but there can be no doubt that the birds, fruit, and the like are thinly disguised symbols of carnal desire. In the distance are the four rivers of Paradise, believed to be in India. The delights in this "garden" are an unending repetition of the Original Sin of Adam and Eve, which dooms us in our life on earth to be prisoners of our appetites.

The Garden of Delights derives in large part from *The Romance of the Rose*. This allegorical poem on love, modeled loosely after Ovid's *Art of Love,* was begun around 1230–40 by Guillaume de Lorris (named for his hometown near Orléans) and greatly expanded around 1275 by Jean Chopinel, better known as Jean de Meun (or Meung) for his birthplace, also in the vicinity of Orléans. It remained the most popular literary work in France for nearly three centuries. Bosch may well have known the version by Jean Molinet toward the end of the fifteenth century, but others would also have been available to him. (It is most familiar to English-speaking peoples in Geoffrey Chaucer's translation of the later 1360s.)

There are many parallels between *The Garden of Delights* and *The Romance of the Rose*. The title of Bosch's painting actually comes from the garden where the lover conquers his lady, whose symbol is the rose. As in the picture, the central feature is a fountain, where Narcissus fell in love with his reflection, thus giving rise to natural, or earthly, love. De Lorris' original poem begins in the garden after the Fall. It is cast as a sexual nightmare, which is further interpreted in de Meung's commentary covering a wide range of subjects, such as the sins of the clergy, that are treated in other works by Bosch as well. Both painting and poem use irony to teach moral lessons by horrid example. The difference is that in *The Romance of the Rose,* as in Neo-Platonism, earthly love may lead to a higher, spiritual love and thus to divine love and redemption. Nowhere, however, does Bosch even hint that salvation is possible. Corruption, on the animal level at least, was already found in the Garden of Eden before the Fall; hence we are all destined for Hell, the Garden of Satan, with its grisly instruments of torture.

Bosch, then, has not simply illustrated *The Romance of the Rose* but has given it a vigorous, highly personal reinterpretation. A good bit of the erotic imagery is based on popular sayings of the day. We also know that the shapes of the fountains and many other forms were taken from treatises on astrology and alchemy, which Bosch would have known through his father-in-law, a

MUSIC IN FIFTEENTH-CENTURY FLANDERS

The brilliance of the fifteenth-century Flemish painters had a close parallel in the field of music. After about 1420, the Netherlands produced a school of composers—Guillaume Dufay (c. 1400–1474), Johannes Ockeghem (c. 1420–1495), Josquin Des Prés (c. 1440–1521), and Adrian Willaert (c. 1490–1562)—so revolutionary as to dominate the development of music throughout Europe for the next 125 years. How much the new style was appreciated can be gathered from the words of the Flemish theorist Johannes Tinctoris (1446?–1511), who wrote of these composers in 1477: "Although it seems beyond belief, nothing worth listening to had been composed before their time." Except for the absence of any reference to the revival of antiquity, this remark, with its sweeping rejection of medieval music, shows a Flemish "Renaissance consciousness" much like that of the Italian humanists of the same period. In fact, Des Prés and Willaert held important positions in Italy, and Dufay had spent nearly a decade there early in his career. In Italy, during the High Renaissance, these Flemings were revered as the greatest composers of their day (see page 464). Their main contribution was the invention of the fugue: the passing of a short theme from one voice to another of equal weight (think of "Three Blind Mice"), a technique that was to become highly developed in the sixteenth century.

Tinctoris credited the English composer John Dunstable (c. 1385–1453), active in France between 1422 and 1435, with beginning a revolution that replaced the complexities of Gothic polyphony with a simpler style. Dufay carried Dunstable's innovations further by placing the main melody, which earlier had been sung by the tenor, in the soprano voice. This simple change gave greater prominence to the melodic line and emphasized its beauty. Dufay also led a movement to replace plainsong in sacred music with themes from secular songs, which were more flexible than chant and more appealing to contemporary taste. In the sixteenth century, these innovations evolved into a form called the parody mass, in which most of the themes were taken from popular songs, freely modified, and connected with newly composed passages. Ockeghem completed the musical revolution toward a more mellifluous style. Though less well known today than Dufay, Ockeghem was highly honored in his own time. The humanist Erasmus wrote of him, "His golden voice caressed the ears of the angels, and swayed the hearts of men to their depths," and his passing was mourned by his pupil Josquin in the lament "Nymphs of the Woods."

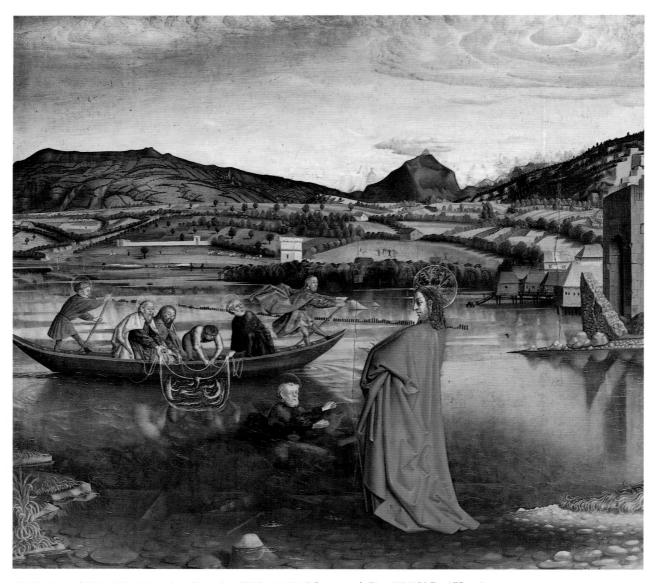

15-15. Conrad Witz. *The Miraculous Draught of Fishes.* 1444. Oil on panel, 51 x 61" (129.7 x 155 cm).
Musée d'Art et d'Histoire, Geneva, Switzerland

well-to-do pharmacist. Astrology and alchemy united the humors with the zodiac in a scheme of good and evil, death and rebirth paralleling Neo-Platonism, which also shared an interest in magic. In the context of *The Garden of Delights,* however, they represent earthly knowledge, which is the corruption of spiritual knowledge, just as earthly love is the sinful opposite of divine love in *The Romance of the Rose.*

Bosch certainly conveys a pessimistic attitude about humanity. Yet we sense a basic ambivalence in the central panel. There is an innocence, even a poetic beauty, in this panorama of human sinfulness. At the conscious level, Bosch was a moralist who intended his pictures to be visual sermons, so that every detail is packed with meaning. At the unconscious level, however, he must have been entranced by the sensuous world of the flesh, so that his images tend to celebrate what they are meant to condemn. That, surely, is the reason *The Garden of Delights* still provokes such a strong response today, even though we no longer understand every word of the visual sermon.

SWISS, GERMAN, AND FRENCH PAINTING

After about 1430 the new realism of the Flemish masters began to spread into France and Germany. By the middle of the century, its influence prevailed everywhere in Northern Europe, from Spain to the Baltic. Countless artists (including many whose names are unknown) turned out provincial versions of Netherlandish painting, but only a few were gifted enough to have a distinctive personality.

CONRAD WITZ. One of the earliest and most original of these painters was Conrad Witz of Basel (1400/10–1445/6). His altarpiece for Geneva Cathedral, painted in 1444, includes the panel shown in figure 15-15. To judge from the drapery, with its tubular folds and angular breaks, he must have had close contact with Campin. But it is the setting, rather than the figures, that attracts our interest, and here the influence of the Van Eycks seems dominant. Witz, however, did not simply follow these great masters.

An explorer himself, he was the first to depict this subject, and he knew more about the optical appearances of water than any other painter of his time. He accurately depicts every reflection on the water and its diminishing depth, so that we can see the bottom of the lake in the foreground. The landscape itself is an original contribution. Representing a specific part of the shore along the Lake of Geneva, it is among the earliest landscape "portraits" that have come down to us.

JEAN FOUQUET. In France the leading painter was Jean Fouquet (c. 1420–1481) of Tours. As the result of a lengthy visit to Italy around 1445, soon after he had completed his training, his work blends Flemish and Early Renaissance elements, although it remains basically Northern. *Étienne Chevalier and St. Stephen,* the left wing of the Melun Diptych (fig. 15-16), his most famous work, shows his mastery as a portraitist. The head of the saint seems no less individual than that of the donor. Italian influence can be seen in the style of the architecture and, less directly, in the statuesque solidity of the two figures. According to an old tradition, the Madonna in the right wing (fig. 15-17) is also a portrait: of Agnes Sorel, Charles VII's mistress. (Chevalier, the king's secretary and lord treasurer, served as executor of her estate upon her death in 1450, when our diptych may have been painted.) If so, it presents an idealized image of courtly beauty, as befits the Queen of Heaven, seen wearing a crown amid a choir of angels. (Her bared, ample breast signifies Mary nurturing the infant Jesus.)

Here we see the beginnings of the tendency toward intellectual clarity and visual abstraction that were to become distinctive to French art. This emphasis even extends to the background. The treatment of space is very different in the two panels, not out of disregard for visual perspective but in order to distinguish between the earthly and divine realms. Thus each half of the diptych is a self-contained world. In turn, pictorial space for Fouquet exists independently of the viewer's "real" space.

Manuscript painting continued to flourish on both sides of the Alps well into the sixteenth century, and Fouquet was the most famous illuminator of the day in the North. *The Fall of Jerusalem* (fig. 15-18) shows his debt to the Gothic. It comes from a copy of Josephus' *Les Antiquités Judaïques* that was started around 1410 for the duke of Berry and completed by Fouquet some 60 years later. The scene, which closely follows Josephus' text, depicts the forces of the Babylonian king Nebuchadnezzar under General Nebuzar-Adar overrunning the city and destroying the Temple of Solomon in 586 B.C. Fouquet's mastery of outdoor space and perspective is no less complete than in the *October* page of *Les Très Riches Heures du Duc du Berry* (see fig. 11-94). Yet Fouquet was more than an imitator of the Limbourg brothers, no matter how much he may have admired them.

The landscape is painted in the up-to-date style of Conrad Witz and presents a stunningly realistic description of a contemporary French town. It is hardly surprising that the page imitates effects found in panels, which had become the dominant form for painting. Yet the quality of the narrative itself belongs to the tradition of manuscript illustration. Even here Fouquet reveals himself an innovator. Precedents for the scene can be found in earlier illuminations, including some by Jan van Eyck, who excelled

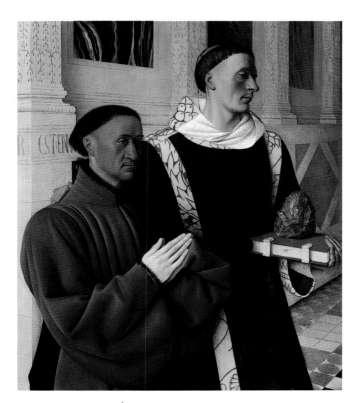

15-16. Jean Fouquet. *Étienne Chevalier and St. Stephen,* left wing of the Melun Diptych. c. 1450. Oil on panel, 36½ x 33½" (92.7 x 85 cm). Staatliche Museen zu Berlin, Gemäldegalerie

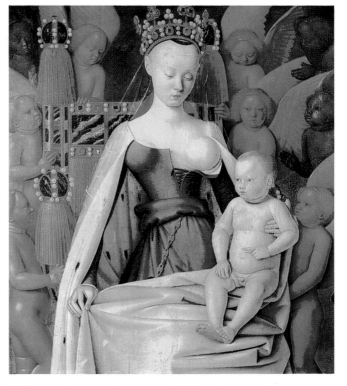

15-17. Jean Fouquet. *Madonna and Child,* right wing of the Melun Diptych. c. 1450. Oil on panel, 36⅝ x 33½" (93 x 85 cm). Musée Royal des Beaux-Arts, Antwerp, Belgium

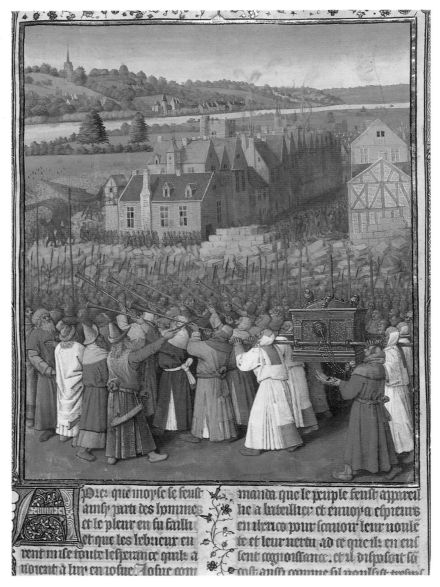

15-18. Jean Fouquet. *The Fall of Jerusalem,* from Josephus, *Les Antiquités Judaïques.*
c. 1470–75. Illumination, 16⅞ x 11¾" (42.8 x 29.8 cm). Bibliothèque Nationale, Paris

as a manuscript painter. Yet, surprisingly, its closest relative is *The Building of the Tower of Babel* at St.-Savin-sur-Gartempe (see fig. 10-36), which presents a similar subject in reverse, so to speak. They share the same monumental spirit, despite the vast difference in size—truly a remarkable achievement!

ENGUERRAND QUARTON. A Flemish style influenced by Italian art also appears in the most famous of all fifteenth-century French paintings, the *Avignon Pietà* (fig. 15-19). As its name indicates, the panel comes from the extreme south of France and is attributed to an artist of that region, Enguerrand Quarton (c. 1410–c. 1466). He must have been familiar with the art of Rogier van der Weyden, for the figure types and the expressive content of the *Avignon Pietà* could be derived from no other source. At the same time, the magnificently simple and stable design is Italian rather than Northern. We first saw these qualities

in the art of Giotto. Southern, too, is the bleak, featureless landscape that emphasizes the monumentality and isolation of the figures. The distant buildings behind the donor on the left have an unmistakably Islamic flavor, suggesting that the artist meant to place the scene in a Near Eastern setting. From these various features he has created an unforgettable image of pathos that unites Italian grandeur with Late Gothic feeling.

LATE GOTHIC SCULPTURE

If we had to describe fifteenth-century art north of the Alps in a single phrase, we might label it "the first century of panel painting." Panel painting was so dominant in the period between 1420 and 1500 that its standards apply to manuscript illumination, stained glass, and even sculpture. After the later thirteenth century, the emphasis had shifted from architectural sculpture to the

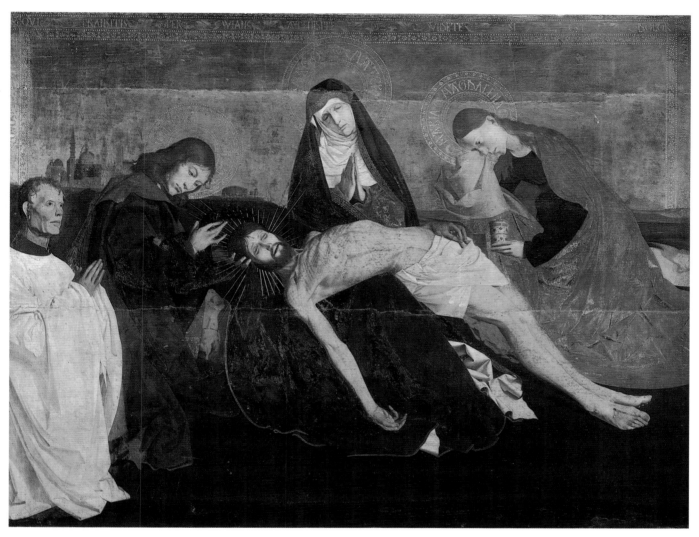

15-19. Enguerrand Quarton. *Avignon Pietà.* c. 1470. Oil on panel, 5'3¾" x 7'1⅞" (1.61 x 2.17 m). Musée du Louvre, Paris

more intimate scale of devotional images, tombs, pulpits, and the like. Claus Sluter, whose art is so impressive in weight and volume (see fig. 11-56), had briefly recaptured the monumental spirit of the High Gothic. However, he had no real successors, although echoes of his style can be felt in French art for the next 50 years. It was the influence of Campin and Rogier van der Weyden that ended the International Style in the sculpture of Northern Europe. The carvers, who quite often were also painters, reproduced the style of these artists in stone or wood until about 1500.

MICHAEL PACHER. The most important works of the Late Gothic carvers are wooden altarpieces, often large in size and intricate in detail. Such shrines were especially popular in the Germanic countries. One of the richest examples is the *St. Wolfgang Altarpiece* (fig. 15-20) by the Tyrolean sculptor and painter Michael

Pacher (c. 1435–1498). [See Primary Sources, no. 51, page 651.] Its lavishly gilt and colored forms make a dazzling spectacle as they emerge from the shadows under Flamboyant Gothic canopies. We enjoy it, but in pictorial rather than sculptural terms. We have no sense of volume, either positive or negative. The figures and setting in the central panel, showing the *Coronation of the Virgin,* seem to melt into a pattern of twisting lines that permits only the heads to stand out as separate elements.

Surprisingly, when we turn to the paintings of scenes from the life of the Virgin on the interior of the wings, we enter a different realm, one that already commands the vocabulary of the Northern Renaissance. Here the artist provides a deep space in scientific perspective that takes the viewer's vantage point into account, so that the upper panels are represented slightly from below. The figures, strongly modeled by the clear light, seem far more sculptural than the carved ones, even though they are a good deal smaller. It is as

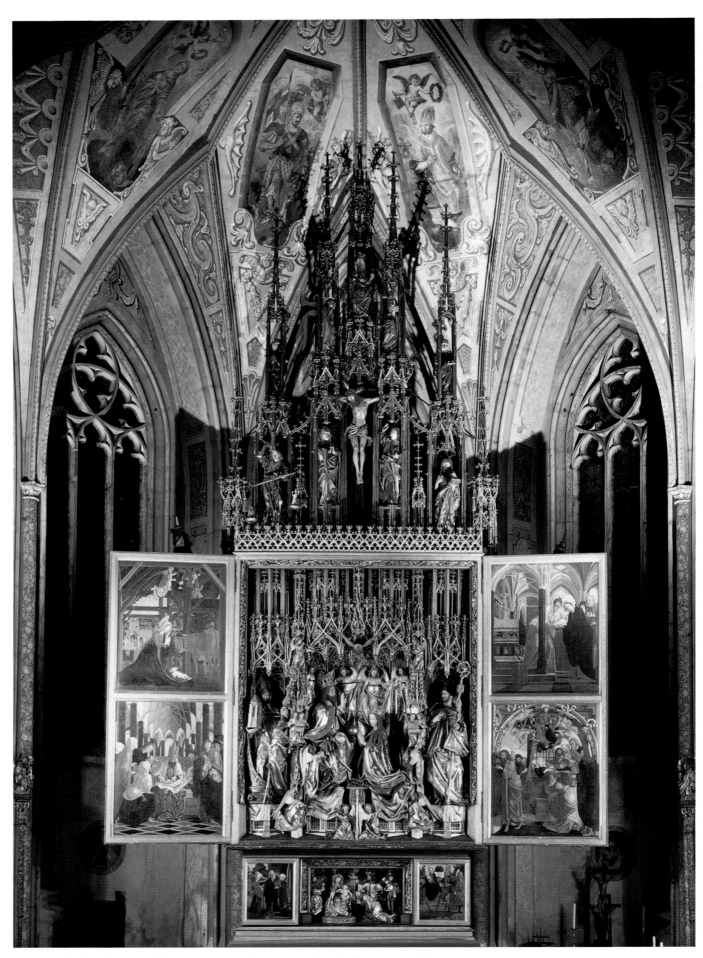

15-20. Michael Pacher. *St. Wolfgang Altarpiece.* 1471–81. Carved wood, figures about lifesize; wings, oil on panel.
Church of St. Wolfgang, Austria

if Pacher the sculptor felt unable to compete with Pacher the painter in rendering three-dimensional bodies, and therefore chose to treat the *Coronation of the Virgin* in pictorial terms by extracting the maximum of drama from contrasts of light and shade. The reason is that Pacher felt compelled here to adhere to the Northern tradition of carved altarpieces but was freer to follow the revolutionary developments in Italian Renaissance painting. He almost certainly crossed the Alps and visited northern Italy, where some of his works were commissioned, so that he was already Northern Renaissance in spirit.

THE GRAPHIC ARTS

WOODCUTS. We must now take note of another important event: the development of printmaking, which had a profound effect on Western civilization. Our earliest printed books in the modern sense were produced in the Rhineland soon after 1450. (It is not certain whether Johannes Gutenberg deserves the priority long claimed for him.) The new technique, which quickly spread all over Europe and developed into an industry, ushered in the era of increased literacy. Printed pictures had hardly less importance, for without them the printed book could not have replaced the work of the medieval scribe and illuminator so quickly and completely. The pictorial and the literary aspects of printing were, indeed, closely linked from the start. (For the various techniques of printing, for pictures as well as books, see page 532.) The idea of printing pictorial designs from blocks of wood onto paper seems to have originated in Northern Europe at the very end of the fourteenth century. Many of the oldest surviving examples of such prints, called woodcuts, are German, others are Flemish, and some may be French; but all are cast in the International Style. The designs were probably furnished by painters or sculptors. The actual carving of the wood blocks, however, was done by specially trained artisans, who also produced wood blocks for textile prints. As a result, early woodcuts, such as the St. Dorothy in figure 15-21, have a flat, ornamental pattern. Forms are defined by simple, heavy lines, and there is little concern for three-dimensional effects, as indicated by the lack of hatching or shading. Since the outlined shapes were meant to be filled in with color, these prints often recall stained glass (compare fig. 11-67) more than the miniatures they replaced.

Despite their appeal to modern eyes, fifteenth-century woodcuts were popular art, on a level that did not attract artists of great ability until shortly before 1500. A single wood block yielded thousands of copies, to be sold for a few pennies apiece, so that for the first time in history anyone could own pictures. What people did with these prints is shown in figure 15-22, a detail from a Flemish *Annunciation* panel of about 1435. We see a tattered woodcut of St. Christopher is pinned up above the mantel. Perhaps it is a hint at the Virgin's journey to Bethlehem (St. Christopher was the patron saint of travelers), but it is also a symbol of her humility, for only the poor would have such a print on their walls. The *St. Christopher* woodcut has two lines of lettering—presumably a short prayer—at the bottom. Similar woodcuts combining image and text were sometimes assembled into popular picture books, called **block books**.

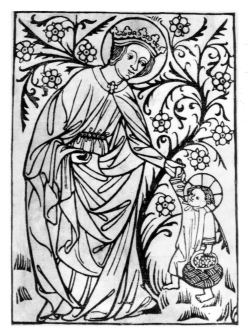

15-21. *St. Dorothy.* c. 1420. Woodcut, 10⅝ x 7½" (27 x 19 cm). Staatliche Graphische Sammlung, Munich

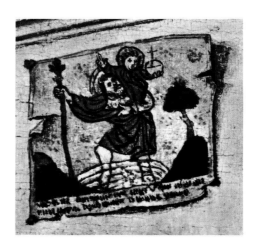

15-22. *Woodcut of St. Christopher,* detail from an *Annunciation* by Jacques Daret (?). c. 1435. Musées Royaux d'Art et d'Histoire, Brussels, Belgium

ENGRAVINGS. From the start, **engravings** appealed to a smaller and more sophisticated public. The oldest examples we know, dating from about 1430, already show the influence of the great Flemish painters. Their forms are systematically modeled with fine hatched lines and often convincingly foreshortened. Nor do engravings share the anonymity of early woodcuts. Individual hands can be distinguished almost from the beginning, dates and initials appear soon after; most of the important engravers of the last third of the fifteenth century are known to us by name. Although the early engravers were usually trained as goldsmiths, their prints are so closely linked to local painting styles that it is far easier to determine where they were made than it is for woodcuts. Especially in the Upper Rhine region, we can trace a continuous tradition of fine engravers from the time of Conrad Witz to the end of the century.

PRINTMAKING

The earliest printed books were produced in the Rhineland soon after 1450, and the technique spread quickly throughout Europe, with profound implications for Western civilization and literacy. Printed pictures were hardly less important, for without them the printed book could not have replaced the work of the medieval scribe and illuminator so quickly. The literary and pictorial aspects of printing were indeed closely linked from the start.

Johann Gutenberg (c. 1397–1468) is usually credited with inventing movable type, but the beginnings of printing actually lie in the ancient Near East 5,000 years ago. The Sumerians were the earliest "printers," for their relief impressions on clay from stone seals were carved with both pictures and inscriptions. From Mesopotamia the use of seals spread to India and eventually to China. The Chinese applied ink to their seals in order to impress them on wood or silk, and in the second century A.D. they invented paper. By the ninth century they were printing pictures and books from wooden blocks carved in relief, and 200 years later they developed movable type. Some of the products of Chinese printing surely reached the medieval West—although there is no direct evidence.

The technique of manufacturing paper, too, came to Europe from the East, though it gained ground as a cheap alternative to parchment very slowly. While printing on wood blocks was known in the later Middle Ages, it was used only for ornamental patterns on cloth. All the more astonishing, then, is the development, beginning about 1400, of a printing technology that within a century surpassed that of the Far East and proved of far wider cultural importance. After 1500, no basic changes were made in this field until the Industrial Revolution.

The printing technology of 1500 allowed for the reproduction of pictures by several methods, all developed in tandem with the printing of type.

WOODCUT: In a woodcut the design is cut into a woodblock so that the ridges will print. The thinner the ridges are, the more difficult they are to carve, and so this work was soon given over to specialists. Inscriptions are frequently found on early woodcuts, but to carve lines of text backward in relief on a wooden block must have been risky—a single slip could ruin an entire page. It is little wonder, then, that printers soon had the idea of putting each letter on its own small block. Wooden movable type carved by hand worked well for large letters but not for small ones, and the technique was too expensive for printing long texts such as the Bible. By 1450 this problem had been solved through the introduction of metal type cast from molds, and the stage was set for book production as it was practiced until very recently.

ENGRAVING: The success of metal type was no doubt attributable to the technical knowledge of armorers and especially goldsmiths, who had already entered the field of printmaking as engravers. The technique of engraving—of embellishing metal surfaces with incised pictures—was developed in classical antiquity (see fig. 6-11) and continued to be practiced throughout the Middle Ages (see fig. 10-41, where the engraved lines are filled in with enamel). Thus no new skill was required to engrave a plate that was to serve as the *matrix,* or recessed mold, for a paper print.

Engraved prints are more refined and flexible than woodcuts. In an engraving, lines are V-shaped grooves incised with a tool, called a burin, into metal plate, usually copper, which is relatively soft and easy to work with. The subsequent printing is done by rubbing ink into the grooves, wiping off the surface of the plate, covering it with a damp sheet of paper, and putting it through a press.

DRYPOINT: A variant of the technique of engraving is known as drypoint. It permitted artists to draw almost as freely as with a pen on a sheet of paper by scratching their designs into the copperplate with a fine steel needle. The needle, of course, did not cut grooves as deep as those made by the burin, so a drypoint plate wore out after a relative handful of impressions, whereas an engraved plate lasted through hundreds of printings. But the drypoint technique preserved the artist's personal "handwriting" and permitted soft, atmospheric effects—velvety shadows and delicate, luminous distances—unattainable with the burin.

ETCHING: Eventually creative printmakers came to prefer etching, often combined with drypoint, over the woodcut and engraving. The technique, too, must have originated with goldsmiths and armorers in the North. An etching is made by coating a copperplate with resin to make an acid-resistant "ground," through which the design is scratched with a needle, laying bare the metal surface underneath. The plate is then bathed in acid that etches (or "bites") the lines into the copper. The depth of these grooves varies with the strength and duration of the bath, and the biting is usually in stages. After a brief immersion in the acid bath the etcher applies a protective coating to the plate in those areas where the lines should be faint. The plate is then immersed until it is time to protect the next less delicate lines, and so on. To scratch a design into the resinous ground is, of course, an easier task than to scratch it into the copperplate itself. Hence an etched line is smoother and more flexible than a drypoint line. An etched plate is also more durable, yielding a far greater number of prints. But its chief virtue is its wide tonal range, including velvety dark shades not possible in a woodcut or an engraving.

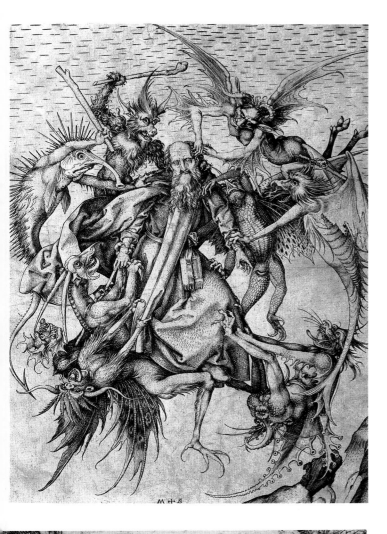

15-23. Martin Schongauer. *The Temptation of St. Anthony.*
c. 1480–90. Engraving, 11½ x 8⅝" (29.2 x 21.8 cm).
The Metropolitan Museum of Art, New York
ROGERS FUND, 1920

MARTIN SCHONGAUER. The finest of the Upper Rhenish engravers was Martin Schongauer of Colmar (c. 1430–1491). He was the first printmaker whom we also know as a painter, and the first to gain international fame. Schongauer might be called the Rogier van der Weyden of engraving. After learning the goldsmith's craft in his father's shop, he must have spent considerable time in Flanders, for his prints are filled with motifs and expressive devices that reveal a deep affinity to the great Fleming. Yet Schongauer was a highly original artist in his own right. His finest engravings have a complex design, spatial depth, and rich texture that make them equivalent to panel paintings. In fact, lesser artists often found inspiration in them for large-scale pictures. They were also copied by other printmakers.

The Temptation of St. Anthony (fig. 15-23), one of Schongauer's greatest works, masterfully combines intense expressiveness and formal precision, violent movement and ornamental stability. Schongauer was not surpassed by any later engraver in his range of tonal values, the rhythmic beauty of his engraved line, and his ability to render every conceivable kind of surface—spiky, scaly, leathery, furry—by varying the **burin**'s attack upon the plate. Although he remained Late Gothic in spirit, Schongauer paved the way for Albrecht Dürer, who was to become the greatest representative of the Renaissance in the North (see pages 507–10). Dürer had hoped to become a member of Schongauer's workshop but arrived shortly after the older artist's death, when he seems to have acquired some drawings from Schongauer's family.

THE MASTER OF THE HOUSEBOOK. Schongauer had only one rival among the printmakers of his time, the Master of the Housebook (so called after a book of drawings attributed to him). Although he was probably of Dutch origin, he seems to have spent most of his career, from about 1475 to 1490, in the Rhineland. The highly individual style of this artist is the opposite of Schongauer's. His prints—such as figure 15-24, the *Holy Family by the Rosebush*—are small, intimate in mood, and spontaneous, almost sketchy, in execution, which lends them a quaint charm that makes up for their naivité. Even his tools were different from the standard engraver's equipment, which demanded a somewhat impersonal discipline. The Master of the Housebook instead scratched his designs into the copperplate with a fine steel needle. This technique, known as **drypoint**, was to become the supreme instrument of Rembrandt's graphic art a century and a half later.

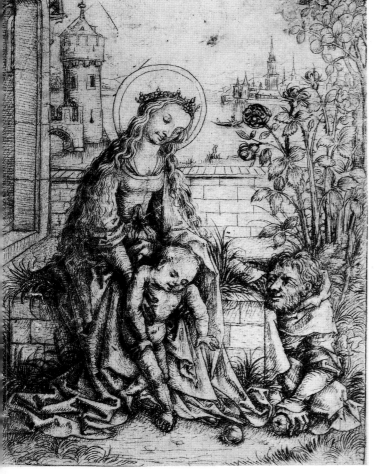

15-24. The Master of the Housebook. *Holy Family by the Rosebush.*
c. 1480–90. Drypoint, 5⅝ x 4½" (14.2 x 11.5 cm).
Rijksprentenkabinet, Rijksmuseum, Amsterdam

CHAPTER SIXTEEN
The Renaissance in the North

THE REFORMATION

The Protestant Reformation was launched in October 1517 by Martin Luther, a former Augustinian friar who had become professor of theology at the University of Wittenberg. There he enjoyed the protection of Frederick the Pious of Saxony. With Frederick's help, he escaped Wittenberg and lived for a while disguised as the aristocratic knight Junker Jörg (16-1). The artist Lucas Cranach the Elder (see below) became close friends with both Frederick and Luther, whose portraits he painted on several occasions. At face value, the 95 theses Luther nailed to the Wittenberg Castle church door on All Saints' Eve were a broadside against the sale of indulgences promising redemption of sins. More fundamentally they were a wholesale attack on Catholic dogma, for Luther claimed that the Bible and natural reason were the sole bases of religious authority, and that the intervention of clerics and saints was unnecessary for salvation, which was freely given by God. Thus authority was transferred from the pope to the individual conscience of each believer.

Freed from traditional doctrine, the Protestant movement rapidly developed splinter groups. Within a few years the Swiss pastor Huldreich Zwingli wanted to reduce religion to its essentials by preaching an even more radical fundamentalism. He denounced the arts as distractions and denied the validity of even the Eucharist as a rite, which led to a split with Luther that was never healed. Within Zwingli's camp there were also rifts: the Anabaptists accepted only adult baptism. What divided the reformers above all were the twin issues of grace and free will in attaining faith and salvation. By the time of Zwingli's death at the hands of the Catholic forces at the Battle of Kappel in 1531, the main elements of Protestant theology had nevertheless been defined. They were codified around mid-century by John Calvin of Geneva, who tried to mediate between Luther and Zwingli while adopting the puritanical beliefs of the Anabaptists.

The Reformation had its roots in the fourteenth century, when mystics like Johann Tauler and Gerhard Groote were inspired by the writings of St. Augustine. Tauler, who looked as well to the writings of St. Thomas Aquinas, exerted in turn a strong influence on Martin Luther. Groote became the founder of the Augustinian

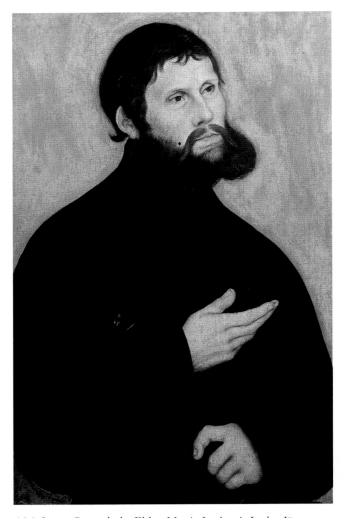

16-1. Lucas Cranach the Elder. *Martin Luther As Junker Jörg.* c. 1521. Oil on panel. 20½ x 13⅜" (53 x 34 cm). Kunstmuseum, Weimar, Germany

Brethren of the Common Life at Deventer, in today's Holland, which became, with the later community at Windesheim, the spearhead of the *devotio moderna* (modern devotion). This pietistic movement is best known for the *Imitation of Christ* by Thomas à Kempis (c. 1418), which enjoyed wide popularity throughout the north, as well as in Italy and Spain.

As in Italy, humanists played a vital role in the Reformation: Desiderius Erasmus of Rotterdam (see fig. 16-15), Philip Melancthon in Germany, and Thomas More in England, to name only the best known. The humanists at first had counted Luther and Zwingli among their number; however, many of them eventually turned against the Reformation because of its extreme views.

ITALIAN INFLUENCES

Italian forms and ideas, as we have seen, exerted little influence on artists north of the Alps during the fifteenth century. Since the time of Robert Campin and the Van Eycks they had looked to Flanders, rather than to Tuscany or Venice, for leadership. This relative isolation ended suddenly toward the year 1500. As if a dam had burst, Italian influence flowed northward in an ever wider stream, and Northern Renaissance art began to replace the Late Gothic. "Northern Renaissance," however, is far less well defined than "Late Gothic," which at least refers to a single, clearly recognizable stylistic tradition. During the sixteenth century the variety of trends in the North is even greater than in Italy. Nor does Italian influence provide a common denominator, since this influence is itself diverse: Early Renaissance, High Renaissance, and Mannerist, all are to be found in regional variants from Lombardy, Venice, Florence, and Rome. Its effects, too, vary greatly. They may be superficial or profound, direct or indirect, specific or general. The Late Gothic tradition remained very much alive, if no longer dominant. Its encounter with Italian art resulted in a conflict among styles that ended only when the Baroque emerged as an international movement in the early seventeenth century. Still, we may speak for the first time of a Renaissance proper in the North. As in Italy, it was marked by an interest in humanism, albeit with equally varied consequences. The course of both art and humanism was decisively affected by the Reformation (see page 534), which had an even greater impact north of the Alps than in Italy.

PAINTING AND THE GRAPHIC ARTS
Germany

It was in Germany, the home of the Reformation, that the earliest major stylistic developments took place during the first quarter of the century. Between 1475 and 1500, it had produced such important artists as Michael Pacher and Martin Schongauer (see figs. 15-20 and 15-23), but they hardly prepare us for the astonishing burst of creative energy that followed. This period was as brief and brilliant as the Italian High Renaissance. And like the High Renaissance, it was the creation of a handful of artists, whose finest works can stand beside those of Leonardo, Michelangelo, and Raphael. The range of its achievements can be measured by the contrasting personalities of its greatest masters: Matthias Grünewald and Albrecht Dürer. Both died in 1528, probably at about the same age, although we know only Dürer's birth date (1471). Dürer quickly became internationally famous, while Grünewald remained so obscure that his real name, Mathis Gothart Nithart, was discovered only at the end of the nineteenth

century. Thus his fame, like El Greco's, was developed almost entirely within the past century.

MATTHIAS GRÜNEWALD. We know little about Grünewald's training and early career, but he was born in Würzburg, probably in the early 1470s, and settled nearby shortly before 1503, the date of his earliest-known picture. He worked for the archbishop of Mainz, as well as other patrons, as a painter and maker of fountains from about 1510 until 1525. For reasons that are far from clear, he then moved to Frankfurt before going to Halle, where he died in 1528. Perhaps by that time he was in sympathy with Martin Luther. [See Primary Sources, no. 52, page 651.] If so, he continued to rely on Catholic patronage, since his paintings remain orthodox in content and show the same devout mysticism.

Grünewald's main work, the *Isenheim Altarpiece,* is unique in Northern Renaissance art in its ability to overwhelm us with the power of the Sistine ceiling. Long believed to be by Dürer, it was painted between about 1509/10 and 1515 for the monastery church of the Order of St. Anthony at Isenheim, in Alsace, not far from the former abbey that now houses it in the city of Colmar.

This extraordinary altarpiece is the cover of a huge shrine carved by Nicolas Hagenau around 1505. It has nine panels in two sets of movable wings, which give it three stages, or "views." The first of these views, when all the wings are closed, shows *The Crucifixion* in the center panel (fig. 16-2, page 536)—the most impressive ever painted. The figure of Christ, with its twisted limbs, its many wounds, its streams of blood, matches the vision of the fourteenth-century mystic St. Bridget as described in her book of Revelations, which had been published in a German edition in 1501–2. In one respect, however, the painting is very medieval. Jesus' terrible agony and the desperate grief of the Virgin, St. John the Evangelist, and Mary Magdalen recall the older German *Andachtsbild* (see fig. 11-54). But the body on the Cross is on a heroic scale that raises it beyond the human and thus reveals the two natures of Christ. The same message is conveyed by the flanking figures. The three historic witnesses on the left mourn Jesus' death as a man. John the Baptist, on the right, calmly points to him as the Savior foretold in the Bible he holds. Even the background suggests this duality. Golgotha (which means "Hill of Skulls") here is not a mere ridge outside Jerusalem, but a mountain towering above the other peaks. The Crucifixion, lifted from its familiar setting, becomes a lonely event silhouetted against a ghostly landscape and a blue-black sky. Darkness is over the land, in accordance with the Gospel, yet light bathes the foreground with the force of revelation. This union of time and eternity, of reality and symbolism, gives Grünewald's *Crucifixion* its awesome grandeur.

When the outer wings are opened, the mood of the *Isenheim Altarpiece* changes dramatically (fig. 16-3, page 536). All three scenes in this second view—the Annunciation, the Angel Concert for the Madonna and Child, and the Resurrection (fig. 16-4, page 536)—celebrate events as jubilant as the Crucifixion is somber. Most striking in comparison with Late Gothic painting is the sense of movement found throughout these panels. Everything twists and turns as if it had a life of its own. The angel of the Annunciation enters the room like a gust of wind that blows

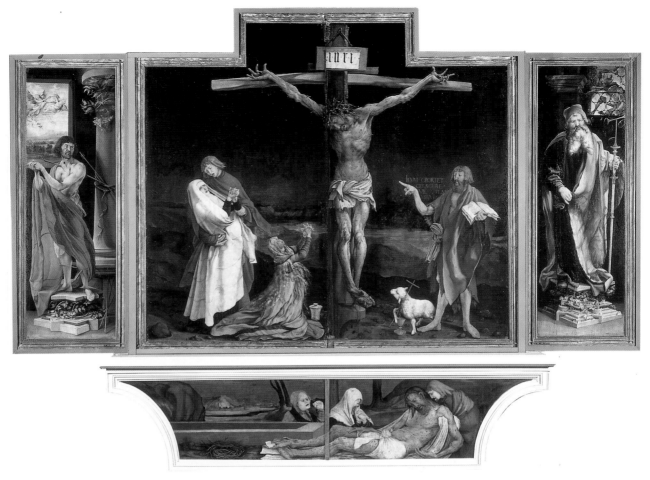

16-2. Matthias Grünewald. *St. Sebastian; The Crucifixion; St. Anthony Abbot;* predella: *Lamentation. Isenheim Altarpiece* (closed).
c. 1509/10–15. Oil on panel, main body 9'9½" x 10'9" (2.97 x 3.28 m), predella 2'5½" x 11'2" (0.75 x 3.4 m).
Musée Unterlinden, Colmar, France

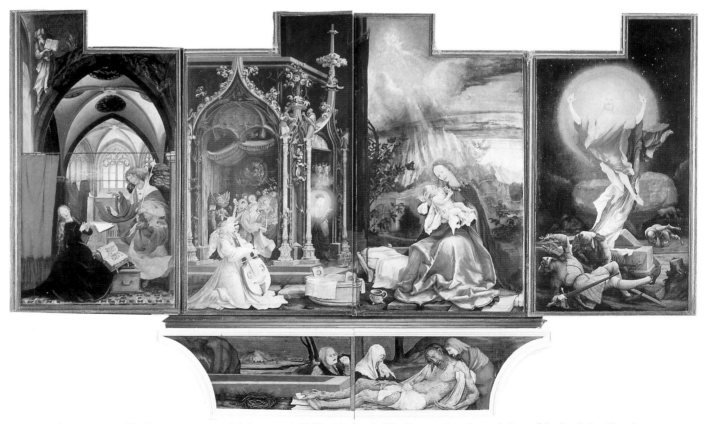

16-3. Matthias Grünewald. *The Annunciation; Madonna and Child with Angels; The Resurrection.* Second view of the *Isenheim Altarpiece.*
c. 1509/10–15. Oil on panel, each wing 8'10" x 4'8" (2.69 x 1.42 m); center panel 8'10" x 11'2½" (2.69 x 3.41 m).
Musée Unterlinden, Colmar, France

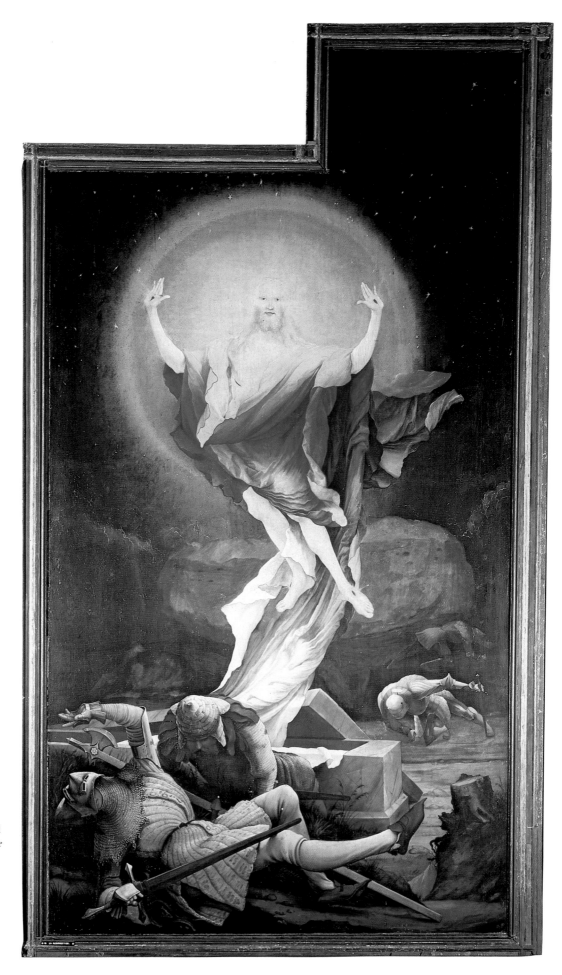

16-4. Matthias Grünewald.
The Resurrection, from second
view of the *Isenheim Altarpiece*

the Virgin backward, and the Risen Christ leaps from his grave with explosive force. This vibrant energy is matched by the ecstatic vision of heavenly glory in celebration of Jesus' birth, seen behind the Madonna and Child, who are the most tender and lyrical in all of Northern art.

In contrast to the brittle contours and angular drapery of Late Gothic art, Grünewald's forms are soft and fleshy. His light and color show a similar change. He employs the resources of Flemish art with extraordinary boldness and flexibility. The range of his color scale is matched only by the Venetians. Indeed, his use of colored light has no parallel at that time. Grünewald achieved unsurpassed miracles through light in the luminous angels of the *Madonna and Child,* the apparition of God the Father and the Heavenly Host above the Madonna, and the rainbow-hued radiance of the spectacular Risen Christ.

How much did Grünewald owe to Italian art? Nothing at all, we are first tempted to say, since his art remains Late Gothic in style and spirit. Yet he must have learned from the Renaissance in more ways than one. His knowledge of perspective (note the low horizons) and the vigor of his figures cannot be explained by the Northern tradition alone (compare fig. 15-19), and his later pictures show architectural details of Southern origin.

Perhaps the most important effect of the Renaissance on him, however, was psychological. As we have seen, he apparently did not lead the settled life of an artisan-painter controlled by guild rules. Like Leonardo, he was also an architect, an engineer, something of a courtier, and an entrepreneur. Moreover, he worked for many different patrons and stayed nowhere for very long. In a word, Grünewald seems to have shared the free, individualistic spirit of Italian Renaissance artists. The daring of his pictorial vision likewise suggests that he relied on his own abilities. The Renaissance, then, had a liberating influence on him but did not change the basic cast of his imagination. Instead, it helped him to heighten the expressive aspects of the Late Gothic in a uniquely intense and individual style.

ALBRECHT DÜRER. For Albrecht Dürer (1471–1528), the Renaissance held a richer meaning. Attracted to Italian art while still a young journeyman, he visited Venice in 1494/5 and returned to his native Nuremberg with a new view of the world and the artist's place in it. (He was to go again in 1505.) To him, the unbridled fantasy of Grünewald's art was "a wild, unpruned tree"—a phrase he used for painters who worked by rules of thumb, without theoretical foundations—that needed the discipline of the objective, rational standards of the Renaissance. He adopted the ideal of the artist as a gentleman and humanistic scholar, and took the Italian view that the fine arts belong among the liberal arts. By cultivating his artistic and intellectual interests, Dürer incorporated an unprecedented variety of subjects and techniques. And as the greatest printmaker of the time, he had a wide influence on sixteenth-century art through his woodcuts and engravings, which circulated all over Europe.

In Italy Dürer made copies after Mantegna and other Early Renaissance masters that show his eager grasp of their style. Equally remarkable are his watercolors painted on the way back

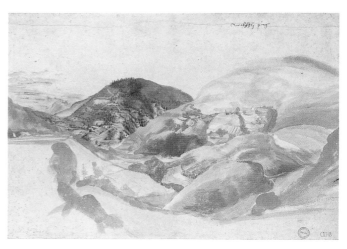

16-5. Albrecht Dürer. *Italian Mountains.* c. 1495 or 1505–6. Brush drawing in watercolor, 8¼ x 12¼" (21 x 31.2 cm). Ashmolean Museum, Oxford, England

from Venice, such as the one inscribed "Italian Mountains" (fig. 16-5). He was the first serious artist to work in watercolor, which gained new importance as a sketching medium thanks to his experiments. Yet Dürer did not record the name of the spot here or in his other sheets; the location had no interest for him. The title he jotted down seems exactly right, for this is not a "portrait," but a "study from the model." The calm rhythm of this panorama, with its softly rounded slopes, conveys an organic view of nature that was matched in those years only by Leonardo's landscapes (compare the background in the *Mona Lisa;* fig. 13-4).

After the breadth and lyricism of the *Italian Mountains,* the expressive violence of the woodcuts illustrating the Apocalypse is doubly shocking. This series was Dürer's most ambitious graphic work in the years following his return from Venice. The gruesome vision of *The Four Horsemen* (fig. 16-6) seems at first to return to the "Late Gothic" world of Martin Schongauer's *Temptation of St. Anthony* (see fig. 15-23). At this stage, Dürer's style still has much in common with Grünewald's. Yet the physical energy and full-bodied volume of these figures would have been impossible without Dürer's earlier experience in copying the works of such artists as Mantegna (compare fig. 12-59). Dürer has redefined his medium—the woodcut—by enriching it with the linear devices of engraving. In his hands, woodcuts lose their former charm as popular art (see fig. 15-21). In its place, they gain the precision of a mature graphic style. He set a standard that soon transformed the technique of woodcuts all over Europe.

Dürer was the first artist to be fascinated by his own image. In this respect he was more of a Renaissance personality than any Italian artist. His earliest known work, a drawing made at 13, is a self-portrait, and he continued to produce images of himself throughout his career. Most impressive, and uniquely revealing, is the panel of 1500 (fig. 16-7). In pictorial terms, it belongs to the Flemish tradition (compare Jan van Eyck's *Man in a Red Turban,* fig. 15-7), but the solemn pose and the idealization of the features have an authority not found in ordinary portraits. The panel

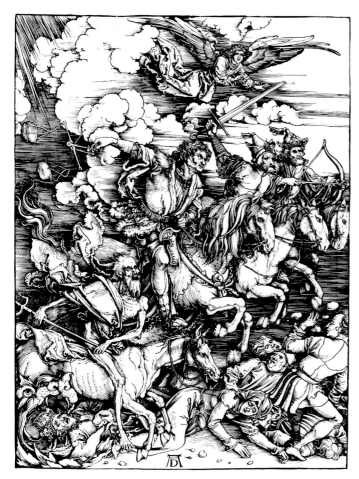

16-6. Albrecht Dürer. *The Four Horsemen of the Apocalypse.*
c. 1497–98. Woodcut, 15½ x 11⅛" (39.3 x 28.3 cm).
The Metropolitan Museum of Art, New York

GIFT OF JUNIUS S. MORGAN, 1919

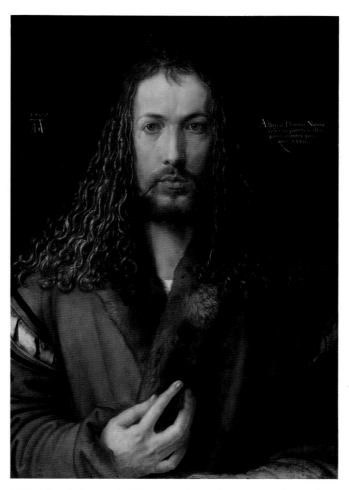

16-7. Albrecht Dürer. *Self-Portrait.* 1500. Oil on panel, 26¼ x 19¼"
(66.3 x 49 cm). Alte Pinakothek, Munich

looks, in fact, like a secularized icon, for it is patterned after images of Christ. It reflects not so much Dürer's vanity as the seriousness with which he viewed his mission as an artistic reformer.

The instructional side of Dürer's art is clearest in the engraving *Adam and Eve* of 1504 (fig. 16-8). Here the biblical subject allows him to display two ideal nudes: Apollo and Venus in a Northern forest (compare figs. 5-69 and 5-71). No wonder they look out of place. Unlike the picturesque setting and the animals in it, Adam and Eve are not observed from life. Instead, they are constructed according to what Dürer believed to be perfect proportions based on Vitruvius. [See Primary Sources, no. 53, page 652.] For the first time, both the form and the substance of the Italian Renaissance enter Northern art, but adapted to the unique cultural climate of Germany. That is why Dürer's ideal male and female figures, although very different from classical examples, were to become models in their own right to countless Northern artists.

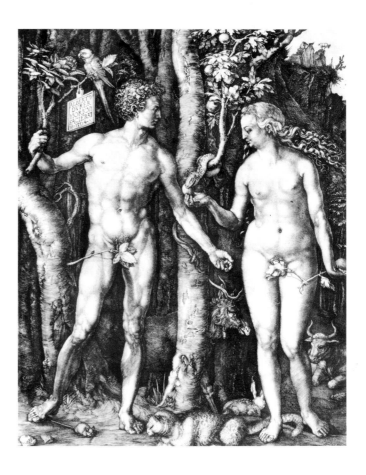

16-8. Albrecht Dürer. *Adam and Eve.* 1504. Engraving,
9⅞" x 7⅝" (25.2 x 19.4 cm). Museum of Fine Arts, Boston

CENTENNIAL GIFT OF LANDON T. CLAY

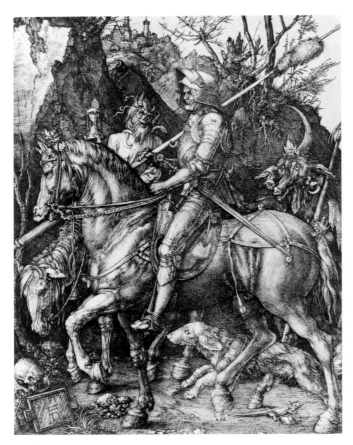

16-9. Albrecht Dürer. *Knight, Death, and Devil.* 1513. Engraving,
9⅞ x 7½" (25.2 x 19.4 cm). Museum of Fine Arts, Boston

GIFT OF MRS. HORATIO GREENOUGH CURTIS IN MEMORY OF HER HUSBAND

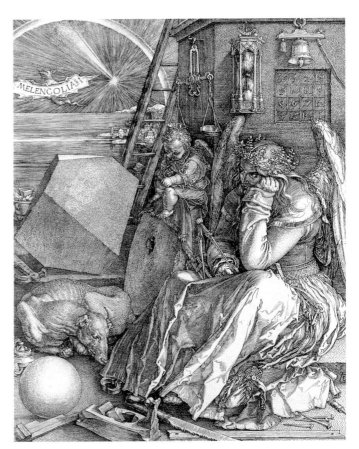

16-10. Albrecht Dürer. *Melencolia I.* 1514. Engraving, 9⅜ x 6⅝"
(23.8 x 16.8 cm). National Gallery of Art, Washington, D.C.

ROSENWALD COLLECTION

The same approach, now applied to a horse, can be seen in *Knight, Death, and Devil* (fig. 16-9), one of the artist's finest engravings. This time, however, there is no inconsistency. The knight on his mount, poised and confident as an equestrian statue (compare fig. 7-40), embodies an ideal that is both aesthetic and moral. He is the Christian Soldier, steadfast on the road of faith toward the Heavenly Jerusalem in the background and undeterred by the hideous rider threatening to cut him off or the grotesque devil behind him. The dog, a symbol of fidelity, loyally follows its master despite the lizards and skulls in their path. Italian Renaissance form, united with the heritage of Late Gothic symbolism (whether open or disguised), here takes on a new, characteristically Northern significance.

Dürer's convictions were essentially those of Christian humanism. He seems to have derived the subject of *Knight, Death, and Devil* from the *Manual of the Christian Soldier* by Erasmus of Rotterdam, the greatest of Northern humanists, whom he later met. It is the first of three engravings that were probably conceived as a unified program, since Dürer often sold them as a set. Taken together, they are an unusually personal statement. A *St. Jerome in His Study* complements the knight of action, who carries his faith into the world, with one who pursues his faith through private meditation.

The last of the suite, *Melencolia I* (fig. 16-10), is the very antithesis of the other two. One of the Four Temperaments, she holds the tools of geometry, yet is surrounded by chaos. She thinks

but cannot act, while the infant scrawling on the slate, who symbolizes Practical Knowledge, can act but not think. This is, then, the melancholia of an artist, perhaps Dürer himself. He cannot achieve perfect beauty, which is known only to God, because he cannot extend his thinking beyond the limits of space and the physical world. This image comes from the humanist Marsilio Ficino, who viewed melancholia (to which he was himself subject) as the source of divine inspiration. He tied it to Saturn, the Mind of the World, which, as the oldest and highest of the planets, he deemed superior even to Jupiter, the Soul of the World. It is clear, however, that in contrasting the ineffectiveness of *Melencolia,* who derives her tools from Saturn, to the spiritual achievements of the knight and saint, Dürer asserts the superiority of faith over reason.

Dürer became an early and enthusiastic follower of Martin Luther, although, like Grünewald, he continued to work for Catholic patrons. His new faith can be sensed in the growing austerity of style and subject in his religious works after 1520. The climax of this trend is represented by *The Four Apostles* (fig. 16-11). These paired panels have rightly been termed Dürer's artistic testament. He presented them in 1526 to the city of Nuremberg, which had joined the Lutheran camp the year before. These four apostles are fundamental to Protestant doctrine. John and Paul face one another in the foreground, with Peter and Mark behind. Quotations from their writings, inscribed below in Luther's translation, warn the city not to mistake human error and pretense for

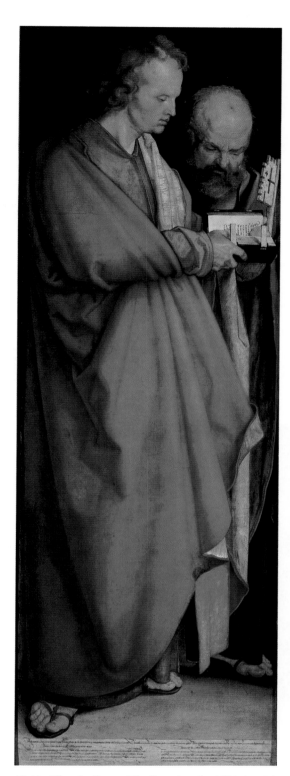
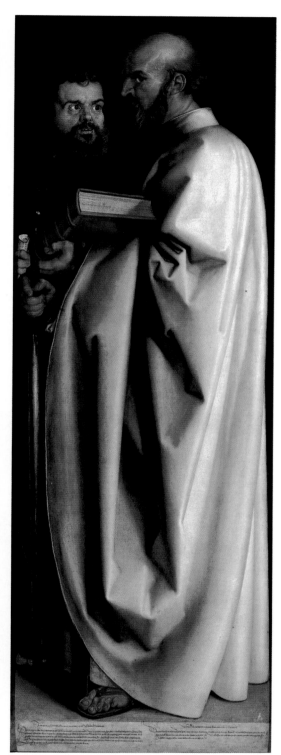

16-11. Albrecht Dürer. *The Four Apostles*. 1523–26. Oil on panel, each 7'1" x 2'6" (2.16 x .76 m).
Alte Pinakothek, Munich

the will of God. They plead against Catholics and Protestant radicals alike. But in another, more universal sense, the figures represent the Four Temperaments and, by implication, the other cosmic quartets—the seasons, the elements, the times of day, and the ages of life. Like the cardinal points of the compass, they encircle the Deity who is at the invisible center of this "triptych." In keeping with their role, the apostles have a sculptural solidity that brings to mind Nanni di Banco's *Quattro Coronati* (fig. 12-1). Not since Masaccio and Piero della Francesca have we seen such severity and grandeur. It is no coincidence that the style of *The Four Apostles* evokes the names of these great Italians. Dürer devoted a good part of his last years to the theory of art, including a treatise on geometry based on a thorough study of Piero della Francesca's book on perspective.

LUCAS CRANACH THE ELDER. Most of Dürer's religious paintings were done before the onset of the Reformation, and his hope for a monumental art embodying the Protestant faith was not fulfilled. Other German painters, notably Lucas Cranach the Elder (1472–1553), tried to cast Luther's doctrines into visual form but created no viable tradition. Such efforts were doomed, since the spiritual leaders of the Reformation looked upon religious images with indifference or, more often, hostility—even though Luther himself seems to have tolerated them. [See Primary Sources, no. 52, page 651.]

On his way to Vienna around 1500, Cranach had probably visited Dürer in Nuremberg. In any event, he fell under the influence of Dürer's work, which he turned to for inspiration throughout his career. In 1504 Cranach left Vienna for Wittenberg, then a center of humanist learning. There he became court painter to Frederick the Pious of Saxony (who also commissioned works by Dürer), as well as a close friend of Martin Luther, who became godfather to one of his children. Like Grünewald and Dürer, Cranach relied heavily on Catholic patronage for his religious paintings. Some of his altars have a Protestant content but, ironically, they lack the fervor of the panels he painted before his conversion.

Cranach is remembered today chiefly for his portraits and his delightfully incongruous mythological scenes. In *The Judgment of Paris* (fig. 16-12), nothing could be less classical than the three coy damsels, whose wriggly nakedness fits the Northern background better than does the nudity of Dürer's *Adam and Eve*. Cranach's Paris is a German knight clad in the fashionable armor of the nobles at the court of Saxony, who were among the artist's patrons. The playful eroticism, small size, and miniature-like detail make the picture a collector's item, attuned to the tastes of a provincial aristocracy. Cranach's many portraits hardly differ from the doll-like creatures in *The Judgment of Paris*.

Cranach's main contribution lies in the handling of the landscape, which lends Dürer's naturalism an element of fantasy (compare fig. 16-8). (Note the crinkly vegetation.) Cranach had developed this manner soon after arriving in Vienna. It played a critical role in the formation of the Danube School, which culminated in the work of Albrecht Altdorfer (c. 1480–1538), a somewhat younger artist who spent most of his career in Bavaria.

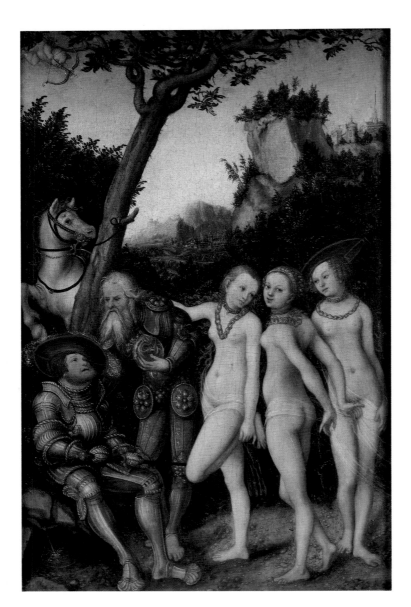

16-12. Lucas Cranach the Elder.
The Judgment of Paris. 1530.
Oil on panel, 13½ x 9½" (34.3 x 24.2 cm).
Staatliche Kunsthalle, Karlsruhe, Germany

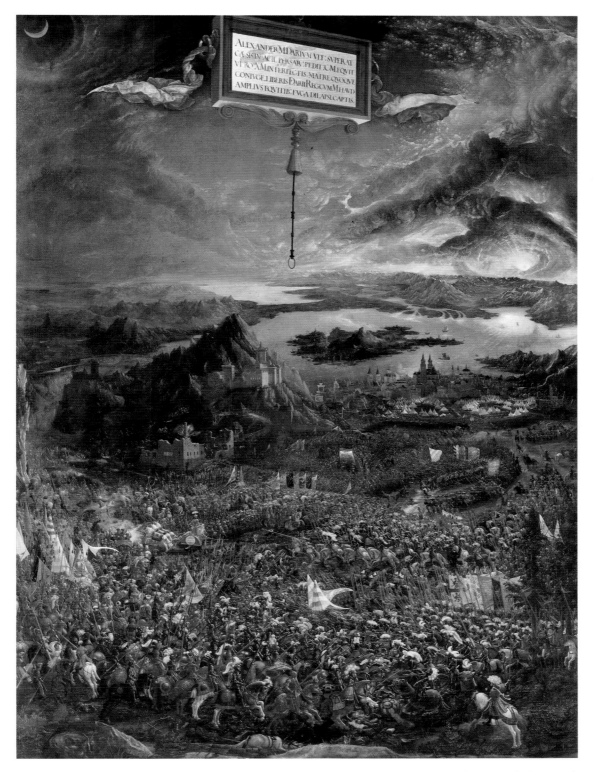

16-13. Albrecht Altdorfer. *The Battle of Issus.* 1529. Oil on panel, 62 x 47" (157.5 x 119.5 cm). Alte Pinakothek, Munich

ALBRECHT ALTDORFER. Altdorfer's *Battle of Issus* (fig. 16-13) is as remote from the classical ideal as Cranach's *The Judgment of Paris* but far more impressive. We could not possibly identify the subject, Alexander's victory over Darius, without the text on the tablet suspended in the sky and the inscriptions on the banners (they were probably written by the Regensburg court humanist Aventinus) and the label on Darius's fleeing chariot. The artist has tried to follow ancient descriptions of the actual number and kind of combatants in the battle. To fit everything in, he adopts a bird's-eye view, traditional in northern landscapes

(compare fig. 15-14), so that the two leaders are lost in the antlike mass of their own armies. (Compare the Hellenistic depiction of the same subject in fig. 5-62.)

However, the soldiers' armor and the fortified town in the distance are unmistakably of the sixteenth century. The panel commemorates a battle that took place in 1529, the year it was painted. At that time the Turks tried unsuccessfully to invade Vienna after gaining control over much of Eastern Europe. (They were to threaten the city repeatedly for another 250 years.) Neither the Hapsburg emperor Charles V nor Suleiman the

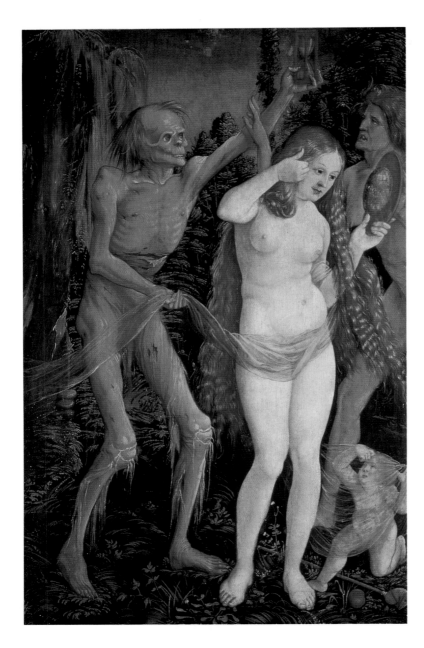

16-14. Hans Baldung Grien. *Death and the Maiden.*
c. 1510. Oil on panel, 15¾ x 12¾" (40 x 32.4 cm).
Kunsthistorisches Museum, Vienna

Magnificent, the Turkish sultan, was present at this battle. Yet the painting acclaims Charles a new Alexander in his victory over Suleiman, who, like Darius, became the ruler of a vast empire.

To suggest its importance, Altdorfer treats the event as an allegory. The sun triumphantly breaks through the clouds of the spectacular sky and "defeats" the moon, which represents the Turkish Crescent. We have seen the same battle of good versus evil symbolized by the sun and moon in the Zoroastrian relief of *Mithras Slaying the Sacred Bull* (see fig. 8-1). The celestial drama above a vast Alpine landscape, correlated with the human contest below, raises the scene to the cosmic level. This turbulent sky is strikingly similar to the vision of the Heavenly Host above the Virgin and Child in the *Isenheim Altarpiece* (see fig. 16-2) by Grünewald, who influenced Altdorfer early in his career.

Altdorfer, too, was an architect, and was thoroughly familiar with scientific perspective and Italian Renaissance style. However, his paintings show the same "unruly" imagination as Grünewald's. But Altdorfer differs in treating the human figure with ironic intent by making it incidental to the setting. Tiny

figures like the soldiers of *The Battle of Issus* also appear in his other late pictures, and he painted at least one landscape with no figures at all—the first "pure" landscape we know of since antiquity. (Dürer's sketch, *Italian Mountains,* see fig. 16-5, after all, is not a finished work of art.)

HANS BALDUNG GRIEN. Altdorfer's fantastic landscape shares imaginative qualities found in paintings by Hans Baldung Grien (1484/5–1545). This former apprentice of Dürer spent much of his career in Strasbourg, which is not far from Isenheim and, like Nuremberg and Wittenberg, was a center of humanism. Yet he was fascinated above all with the magical and the demonic—the dark side of the Renaissance. Humanism and the occult may be viewed as two sides of the same coin. Since the late thirteenth century, humanists had been nearly as interested in the treatises of the ancients on magic as in their literature and learning. (In fact, the key text of Renaissance magic, the *Corpus Hermeticum,* was translated by the humanist Marsilio Ficino.) But whereas the occult appears rarely in Italian art, it was a source of constant fascination in the North. Nowhere is this better seen than in Baldung Grien's *Death and the Maiden* (fig. 16-14). Clearly based on Dürer's *Eve* (see fig. 16-8), she is the personification of Vanitas, signifying the triumph of Death over Beauty. The three ages of life—infancy, adulthood, old age—are repeated in the mirror. Yet although the three heads stare out forlornly at the young woman, she examines her features with total serenity.

The painting illustrates the prophetic and demonic powers of the convex mirror. In antiquity mirrors had often served as attributes of goddesses and sometimes of mortal women, such as brides. The motif of a woman contemplating her beauty reappeared in Gothic cycles of the Vices and Virtues. This moralizing tradition was revived after 1500 as part of a renewal of piety and mysticism during the Reformation. It was closely linked to occultism at a time when rationalism seemed inadequate to explain the world. Because of their association with light, mirrors have had mystical connotations throughout history, and reflected images were widely valued as a source of revelation. At the same time, supernatural qualities were attributed to them in folklore as a means of effecting hexes and other forms of black magic.

At first the convex mirror expressed the Late Gothic fascination with the visible world. We saw this in Jan van Eyck's *Arnolfini Portrait* (see fig. 15-8), which was painted within a few decades after mirrors began to be made from polished metal. After 1500 the convex mirror came to be used almost exclusively as a Vanitas symbol (see page 520) because of its extreme distortions, which create a visionary reality; this, aspect, too, had its origin in a work by Jan van Eyck. In Baldung Grien's paintings, the characteristic image became a nude woman holding a convex mirror. Here it is used to convey a tragic vision of life to chilling effect through the striking contrast between the sensual nude and the grinning corpse, who holds an hourglass above her head as the horrified man vainly tries to stay the hand of Death.

HANS HOLBEIN THE YOUNGER. Gifted though they were, Cranach and Altdorfer both evaded the main challenge of the Renaissance so bravely faced, if not always mastered, by Dürer: the human image. Their miniature-like style set the pace for dozens of lesser masters. Perhaps the rapid decline of German art after Dürer's death was due to lack of ambition among artists and patrons alike. The career of Hans Holbein the Younger (1497–1543), the one painter of whom this is not true, confirms the general rule. The son of an important artist, he was born and raised in Augsburg, a center of international commerce in southern Germany that was particularly open to Renaissance ideas, but he left at the age of 18 with his brother to seek work in Switzerland. Thanks in large part to humanist patrons, he was well established in Basel by 1520 as a decorator, portraitist, and designer of woodcuts. Holbein took Dürer as his point of departure, but almost from the beginning his religious paintings and portraits show a keen interest in the Italian Renaissance, especially the latest tendencies from Venice and Rome.

Holbein's likeness of Erasmus of Rotterdam (fig. 16-15), painted soon after the famous author had settled in Basel, gives us a truly memorable image, at once intimate and monumental. This kind of profile view had been popular during the Early Renais-

sance and was adopted by Dürer late in his career. Here it is combined with a typical Northern realism to convey the sitter's personality in a way that is nonetheless in keeping with the High Renaissance. The very ideal of the scholar, this doctor of humane letters has a calm rationality that lends him an intellectual authority formerly reserved for Doctors of the Church. The similarity is intentional. Erasmus greatly admired St. Jerome, who translated the Bible into Latin (the Vulgate). In his biography of the saint, Erasmus praises him as "the best scholar, writer and expositor," who was "equally and completely at home in all literature, both sacred and profane" and "had the whole of Scripture by heart."

Holbein spent 1523–24 traveling in France, apparently with the intention of offering his services to Francis I. When he returned two years later, Basel was in the throes of the Reformation. Hoping for commissions at the court of Henry VIII, Holbein then went to England. He brought with him the portrait of Erasmus as a gift to the humanist Thomas More, who became his first patron in London. (Erasmus, in a letter recommending him to More, wrote: "Here [in Basel] the arts are out in the cold.") Ironically, Henry had More beheaded in 1525 for refusing to consent to the Act of Supremacy, which made the king the head of the Church of England. When Holbein returned to Basel in 1528, he saw Protestant mobs destroying religious images as "idols"; reluctantly, he abandoned Catholicism. Despite the entreaties of the city council, he left for London four years later, and visited Basel only

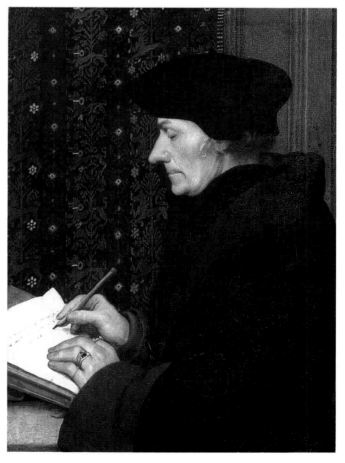

16-15. Hans Holbein the Younger. *Erasmus of Rotterdam.* c. 1523. Oil on panel, 16½ x 12½" (42 x 31.4 cm). Musée du Louvre, Paris

16-16. Hans Holbein the Younger. *Henry VIII*. 1540.
Oil on panel, 32 ½ x 29" (82.6 x 74.5 cm). Galleria Nazionale
d'Arte Antica, Rome

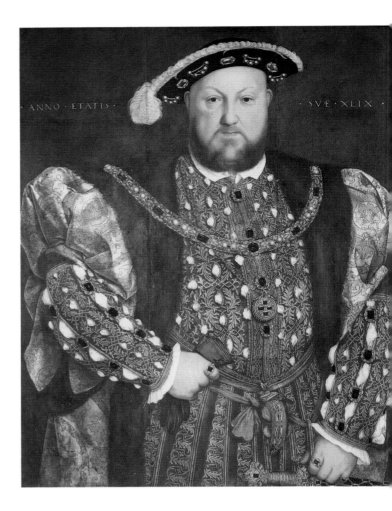

once, in 1538, while traveling on the Continent as court painter to Henry VIII. The city council made a last attempt to keep Holbein at home, but he had become an artist of international fame to whom Basel now seemed provincial indeed.

Holbein's style, too, had gained an international flavor. His portrait of Henry VIII (fig. 16-16) has the rigid frontality of Dürer's self-portrait (see fig. 16-7), but its purpose is to convey the almost divine authority of the absolute ruler. The king's physical bulk creates an overpowering sense of his ruthless, commanding personality. The portrait shares with Bronzino's *Eleanora of Toledo* (see fig. 14-8) the immobile pose, the air of unapproachability, and the precisely rendered costume and jewels. Holbein's picture does not reflect the Mannerist ideal of elegance, but both clearly belong to the same kind of court portrait. The link between them may lie in court portraits that Holbein could have seen on his travels. Between 1525 and 1550 the Mannerist portrait spread from Italy to other regions as the embodiment of a new aristocratic ideal. Although portraitists in France during the reign of Francis I, such as Jean Clouet (active 1516–1540/41), were largely of Flemish origin, the French court was especially hospitable to Italian artists and

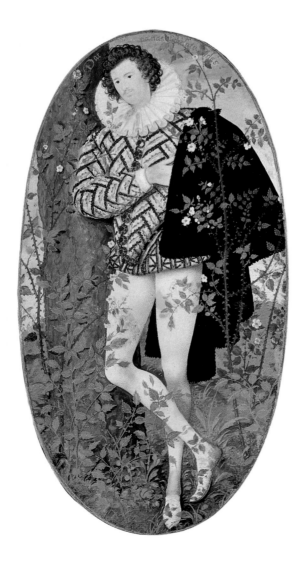

influences, and imported large numbers of paintings by the leading Italian masters. (For Francis I as a patron of Italian Mannerists, see pages 503–05.) Holbein's pictures molded British taste in aristocratic portraiture for decades, but he had no English disciples of real talent. The Elizabethan genius was more literary and musical than visual, and the English demand for portraits in the later sixteenth century continued to be filled largely by visiting foreign artists.

England

NICHOLAS HILLIARD. The most notable English painter of the period was Nicholas Hilliard (1547–1619), a goldsmith who also specialized in **miniature** portraits on parchment, tiny keepsakes often worn as jewelry. These "portable portraits" had been invented as **cameos** in antiquity and were revived in the fifteenth century. Holbein, too, produced miniature portraits, which Hilliard took as a model. We see this link in the even lighting and the careful detail of *A Young Man Among Roses* (fig. 16-17). However, the tall, slender proportions, elegant costume, and languorous grace come from Italian Mannerism, probably by way of Fontainebleau (compare figs. 14-6, 14-19, and 14-20). We can imagine our lovesick youth besieging his lady with sonnets and madrigals before presenting her with this token of devotion.

16-17. Nicholas Hilliard. *A Young Man Among Roses*. c. 1588.
Oil on parchment, shown at actual size, 5 ⅜ x 2 ¾" (13.7 x 7 cm).
Victoria & Albert Museum, London

MUSIC AND THEATER IN THE NORTHERN RENAISSANCE

The most significant musical development of the Reformation was the introduction of congregational singing in the services of the Protestant churches. The reformer Martin Luther, himself a singer and composer, admired the sophisticated polyphony of Josquin Des Prés, whose music he retained for use by choirs in the Latin Mass. Luther also believed strongly in the educational value of music, and he wanted every member of the church to participate in the service by singing. So in 1524 he wrote a German Mass with chorales—simple hymns to be sung by the congregation—based on traditional chants and secular songs for use especially in parishes without professional choirs. The Swiss reformer John Calvin, on the other hand, objected to hymns based on new poems and insisted that only the Word of God be sung in church. The result was the Calvinist psalter: Old Testament psalms set to traditional melodies and generally sung in unison. Another form of Protestant music was the English anthem, a kind of motet that could be "full" (sung by the choir *a cappella,* "without accompaniment") or "verse" (for soloists with chorus and instruments).

In secular music, the most popular form throughout Northern Europe was the madrigal. Its chief exponent was Roland de Lassus (1532–1594), a Fleming who had lived in Italy as a youth, but spent most of his career in Munich. Widely regarded as the leading composer of his day, he was the equal of Giovanni Palestrina as a writer of religious music; but because his temperament was more secular, many of his religious compositions are parody masses (see page 525). In his later years he devoted himself chiefly to madrigals and motets. In its impulsive leaps, irregular rhythms, and dramatic harmonies, his style anticipates the bold brilliance of Carlo Gesualdo (see page 569). During the reign of Elizabeth I (1558–1603), the English developed a distinguished madrigal school under Thomas Morley (1557–c. 1602), Thomas Weelkes (c. 1575–1623), John Wilbye (1574–1638), and John Dowland (1563–1626), whose lute songs are sensitive settings of poems by Shakespeare and his contemporaries.

It is utterly remarkable that English theater developed into greatness during the late sixteenth century. Its tradition was deeply rooted in medieval religious drama, and secular theater reached back only to about 1520. When Queen Elizabeth suppressed religious theater in the 1570s, secular theater came to the fore under humanist influence at schools, universities, and inns—colleges where young men completed their education—despite the fact that theater was strictly regulated by the Master of the Revels. Yet neither the decline of religious theater nor the influence of the humanists can account satisfactorily for the enthusiastic support of theater throughout the realm—ten public outdoor theaters were built in London between 1567 and 1642, in addition to numerous private indoor theaters—or the sudden appearance of four very fine playwrights within just a few years. Thomas Kyd (1558–1594) inaugurated the theme of revenge with *The Spanish Tragedy* (c. 1587); Christopher Marlowe (1564–1593) presented the great morality play of the day in *Dr. Faustus* (c. 1588);

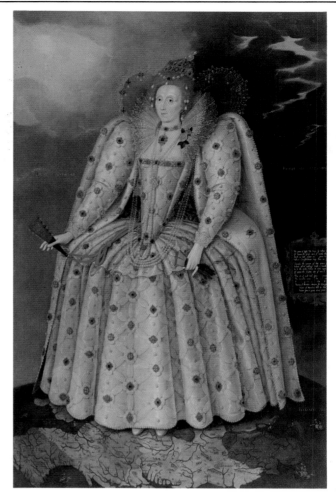

Marcus Gheeraerts the Younger. *Portrait of Elizabeth I.* c. 1592. Oil on canvas, 95 x 60" (241.3 x 152.4 cm). The National Portrait Gallery, London

John Lyly (c. 1553–1606) used classical mythology to flatter the queen in *Endimion* (c. 1588); and Robert Greene (c. 1558–1592) helped to introduce the history, or chronicle, drama with *James IV* (c. 1591). Shortly before, William Shakespeare (1564–1616) had written *Henry VI* (1590). Of these playwrights, Shakespeare was incomparably the finest. His plays featured bold plots (many of them drawn from English history and patterned after Roman dramas), and they refrained from conventional moralizing and traditional happy endings in favor of tragedy of unrelenting darkness. His greatness lies in his use of blank verse (unrhymed, although metrical composition), which he perfected into a poetic language of infinite richness and subtlety able to express any thought or mood on a transcendent, indeed universal, plane.

Shakespeare's only serious rival in popularity was Ben Jonson (1572–1637), the leading classicist of the 1590s, whose theories followed those of Julius Caesar Scaliger and Lodovico Castelvetro (see box pages 490–91). It was Jonson who published the first integrated edition of Shakespeare's works upon his death in 1616, thereby establishing the primacy of the playwright as a literary figure. Nevertheless, Jonson himself primarily wrote tragicomedies for reforming behavior based on Italian examples, which made him a great favorite at the court of James I, Elizabeth's successor.

The Netherlands

The Netherlands in the sixteenth century had the most turbulent history of any country north of the Alps. When the Reformation began, it was part of the empire of the Hapsburgs under Charles V, who was also king of Spain. Protestantism quickly gained strength in the Netherlands, and attempts to suppress it led to revolt against foreign rule. After a bloody struggle, the northern provinces (today's Holland) emerged at the end of the century as an independent state in all but name. The southern ones (roughly corresponding to modern Belgium) remained in Spanish hands.

The religious and political strife might have had catastrophic effects on the arts, but this, astonishingly, did not happen. The art of the period did not equal the fifteenth century's in brilliance, nor did it produce any pioneers of the Northern Renaissance comparable to Dürer and Holbein. This region absorbed Italian elements more slowly than Germany, but more steadily and systematically, so that instead of a few isolated peaks we find a continuous range of achievement. Between 1550 and 1600, their most troubled time, the Netherlands produced the major painters of Northern Europe, who in turn paved the way for the great Dutch and Flemish masters of the next century.

Two main concerns, sometimes separate, sometimes interwoven, characterize Netherlandish sixteenth-century painting: to assimilate Italian art from Raphael to Tintoretto (although in an often dry and academic manner), and to develop new genres that would supplement, and eventually replace, traditional religious subjects.

"MANNERISM" AND ROMANISM. Flanders passed from Burgundy to Spain in 1482, upon the death of Mary of Burgundy, heir of Charles the Bold, who had married the Hapsburg archduke Maximilian. Now Antwerp, with its deep harbor, replaced Ghent and Bruges as the political, commercial, and artistic capital of the Netherlands. Flemish artists spent the next quarter-century largely imitating earlier Netherlandish painting. Then, around 1507, we find two important new developments. "Antwerp Mannerism" is the misleading label applied to the school of largely anonymous painters which first arose in that city. Their preference for elongated forms, decorative surfaces, and arbitrary space seems a return to Late Gothic tendencies, although the similarities are superficial. Actually, the style was not directly related to either the Renaissance or to Mannerism in Italy. Still, the term has some basis. It suggests the odd flavor of their work, for it was a "mannered" response to the "classics" by Jan van Eyck, Rogier van der Weyden, and their successors. At almost the same time, a second group of Netherlandish artists, the so-called Romanists, began to visit Italy in the wake of Albrecht Dürer and returned home with the latest artistic tendencies. The preceding generation of Flemish painters had already shown a growing interest in Renaissance art and humanism, but none of them had ventured below the Alps, so that they had assimilated both at second hand.

JAN GOSSAERT. The greatest of the Romanists, Jan Gossaert (c. 1478–1532; nicknamed Mabuse, for his hometown), was also the first to travel south. In 1508 he accompanied Philip of Burgundy to Italy, where the Renaissance and antiquity made a deep impression on him. He nevertheless viewed this experience through Northern eyes. Except for their greater monumentality, his religious subjects were based on fifteenth-century Netherlandish art, and he often found it easier to assimilate Italian classicism through the intermediary of Dürer's prints.

Danaë (fig. 16-18), painted toward the end of Gossaert's career, is his most Italianate work. In true humanist fashion, Jupiter's seduction of the mortal is treated as a pagan equivalent of the Annunciation. (For the subject, see page 319.) Thus the picture may be seen as a chaste counterpart to Correggio's *Jupiter and Io* (see fig. 14-11). The god enters, disguised as a shower of gold analogous to the stream of light in the *Mérode Altarpiece* (see fig. 15-1). Despite her partial nudity, Danaë appears as modest as the Virgin in any Annunciation. Indeed, she hardly differs in type from Gossaert's paintings of the Madonna and Child, inspired equally by Van Eyck and Raphael. She even wears the blue robe traditional to Mary as Queen of Heaven. The linear perspective of the architectural fantasy, compiled largely from Italian treatises such as Serlio's, published in 1545 (see box page 490–91), marks a revolution. Never before have we seen such a systematic treatment of space in the Netherlands.

STILL LIFE, LANDSCAPE, GENRE. Later religious art in the Netherlands combined Antwerp Mannerism and Romanism to produce a distinctive strain of Northern Mannerism that lasted until the end of the century. After 1550, however, narrative painting was increasingly replaced by secular themes: landscape, still life, and genre (scenes of everyday life). The process was gradual—it began around 1500 and was not complete until a hundred years later—and was shaped less by the genius of individual artists than by the need to cater to popular taste as church commissions became scarcer. Protestant iconoclastic zeal was particularly widespread in the Netherlands. Under Calvin's instruction, sculpture, frescoes, and stained glass gave way to clear windows and whitewashed walls. Still life, landscape, and genre had been part of the Flemish tradition since the International Style (compare figs. 11-91 and 11-94) and became even more important under Robert Campin and the Van Eycks. We recall the objects grouped on the Virgin's table and the scene of Joseph in his workshop in the *Mérode Altarpiece* (see fig. 15-1). We may also think of the outdoor setting of the Van Eyck *Crucifixion* (see fig. 15-2). But these elements were subordinate to the devotional purpose of the whole and were often governed by the principle of disguised symbolism. Now they gained a new independence and grew in importance, until the religious subject could be relegated to the background.

JOACHIM PATINIR. We see the beginnings of this approach in the paintings of Joachim Patinir (c. 1485–1524). *Landscape with St. Jerome Removing the Thorn from the Lion's Paw* (fig. 16-19, page 550) shows that he is the heir of Bosch in both his treatment of nature and his choice of subject, but without the strange demonic overtones of *The Garden of Delights* (see fig. 15-14). Although the landscape dominates the scene, the figures are central to both

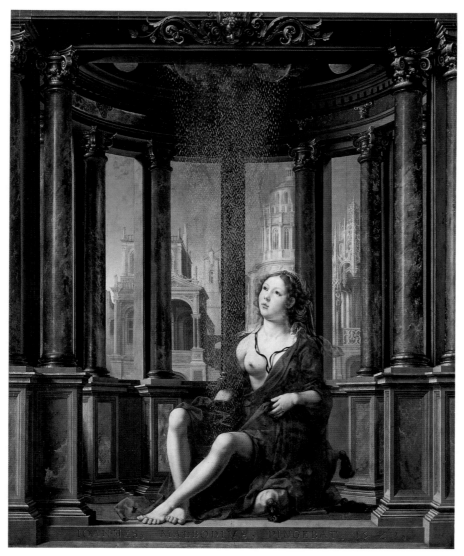

16-18. Jan Gossaert. *Danaë*. 1527. Oil on panel, 44½ x 37⅜" (113 x 95 cm).
Alte Pinakothek, Munich

its composition and subject. The landscape has been constructed around the hermit in his cave, which could exist happily in another setting, whereas the picture would be incomplete without it.

The painting is an allegory of the pilgrimage of life. It contrasts the way of the world with the road to salvation through ascetic withdrawal. (Note the two pilgrims wending their way up the hill to the right, past the lion hunt, which they do not notice.) The church on the mountain represents the Heavenly Jerusalem, which can be reached only by passing through the hermit's cave (compare fig. 11-86). Like Bosch, Patinir is ambivalent toward his subject. The vista in the background, with its well-kept fields and tidy villages, is enchanting in its own right. Yet, he seems to tell us, these temptations should not distract us from the path of righteousness.

PIETER AERTSEN. The Dutch painter Pieter Aertsen (1508/9–1575) is remembered today mainly as a pioneer of moralizing kitchen scenes and still lifes. However, he seems to have first

painted them as a sideline, until he saw many of his altarpieces destroyed by iconoclasts in 1566, a decade after moving back to Amsterdam from Antwerp, where he spent his early career. *The Meat Stall* (fig. 16-20, page 550), done while the artist was still in Antwerp, seems at first glance to be a purely secular picture. There is little interest in selection or formal arrangement. The food, piled in heaps or strung from poles, is meant to overwhelm us with its sensuous reality. (Aertsen lived near the city's meat market.) The tiny, distant figures are almost blotted out by the food in the foreground, which seems completely independent of the background. The still life so dominates the picture that it seems independent of the religious subject in the background. But in the distance to the left we see the Virgin on the Flight into Egypt giving bread to the poor, who are ignored by the worshipers lined up for church. To the right is a tavern scene with the prodigal son, who later repents his sins and returns to his forgiving father. The stall has a variety of Christian symbols, many of them disguised, some of them obvious, such as the two pairs of crossed fish signifying the Crucifixion.

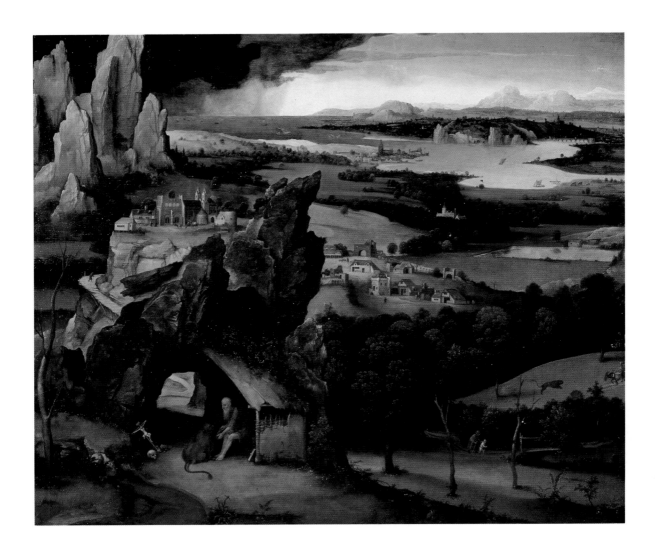

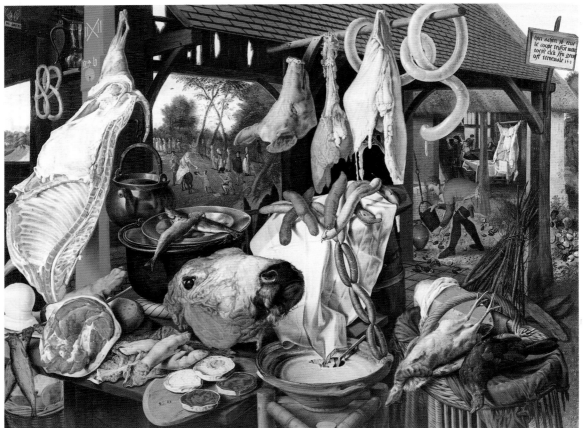

(ABOVE) 16-19. Joachim Patinir. *Landscape with St. Jerome Removing the Thorn from the Lion's Paw.* c. 1520. Oil on panel, 29⅛ x 35⅞" (74 x 91 cm). Museo del Prado, Madrid

(LEFT) 16-20. Pieter Aertsen. *The Meat Stall.* 1551. Oil on panel, 48½ x 59" (123.3 x 150 cm). University Art Collections, Uppsala University, Sweden

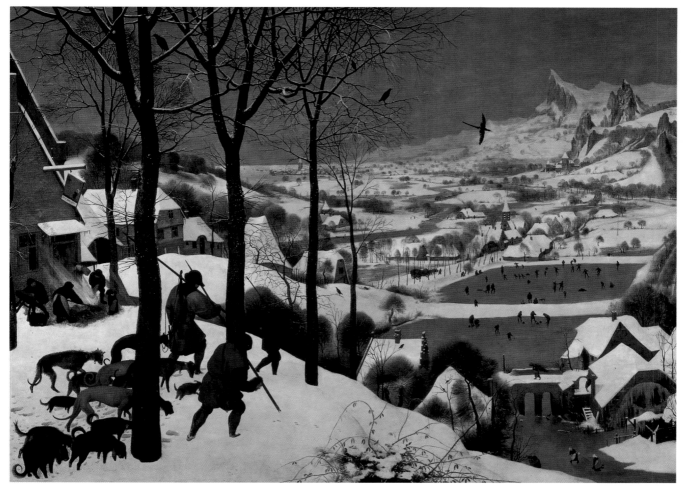

16-21. Pieter Bruegel the Elder. *The Return of the Hunters.* 1565. Oil on panel, 46 ½ x 63 ¾" (117 x 162 cm). Kunsthistorisches Museum, Vienna

The religious subject is not merely a pretext—it is central to the painting's meaning. Northern Mannerists often relegated the main subject matter to a minor position within their compositions. This "inverted" perspective was a favorite device of Aertsen's younger contemporary Pieter Bruegel the Elder, who treated it with ironic purpose in his landscapes. Aertsen belonged to the same tradition. It was an outgrowth of Northern humanist literature, whose greatest representative was Erasmus of Rotterdam (see above). *The Meat Stall* is, then, a moralizing sermon on gluttony, charity and faith, possibly relating to Lent, the time of fasting before Easter when meat and fish were traditionally forbidden. Not until around 1600 was this vision displaced as part of a larger change in worldview (see page 548). Only then did it no longer prove necessary to include religious or historical scenes in still lifes and landscapes.

PIETER BRUEGEL THE ELDER. Pieter Bruegel the Elder (1525/30–1569), the only genius among these Netherlandish painters, explored landscape, peasant life, and moral allegory. Although his career was spent in Antwerp and Brussels, he may have been born near 'sHertogenbosch, the home of Hieronymus Bosch. Certainly Bosch's paintings impressed him deeply, and in many ways his work is just as puzzling. What were his religious convictions, his political sympathies? We know little about him,

but his interest in folk customs and the daily life of humble people seems to have sprung from a complex philosophical outlook. Bruegel was highly educated, the friend of humanists, who, with wealthy merchants, were his main clients, although he was also patronized by the Hapsburg court. He apparently never worked for the Church, and when he dealt with religious subjects he treated them in a strangely ambiguous way.

Bruegel's attitude toward Italian art is also hard to define. A trip to the South in 1552–53 took him to Rome, Naples, and the Strait of Messina, but the famous monuments admired by other Northerners seem not to have interested him. He returned instead with a sheaf of magnificent landscape drawings, especially Alpine views. He was probably much impressed by landscape painting in Venice, above all the integration of figures and scenery and the continuous progression in space (see figs. 13-38 and 13-39).

Out of this experience came the sweeping landscapes of Bruegel's mature style. *The Return of the Hunters* (fig. 16-21) is one of a set depicting the months. (He typically composed in series; those in this group were owned by Niclaes Jonghelink in Antwerp by 1566, a year after they were painted.) Such scenes, we recall, had begun with medieval calendar illustrations, and Bruegel's still shows its descent from *Les Très Riches Heures du Duc de Berry* (see fig. 11-94). Now, however, nature is more than a setting for human activities. It is the main subject of the picture. The seasonal tasks

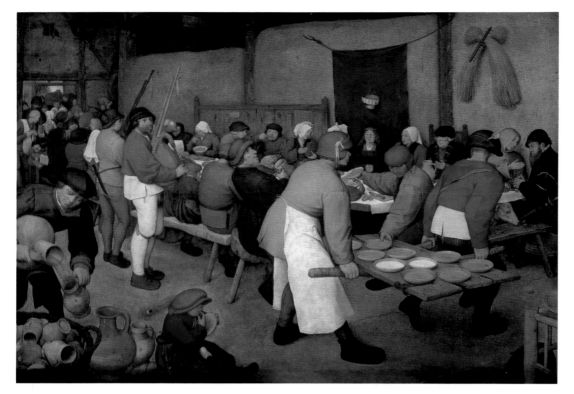

16-22. Pieter Bruegel the Elder. *Peasant Wedding*. c. 1565. Oil on panel, 44⅞ x 64" (114 x 162.5 cm). Kunsthistorisches Museum, Vienna

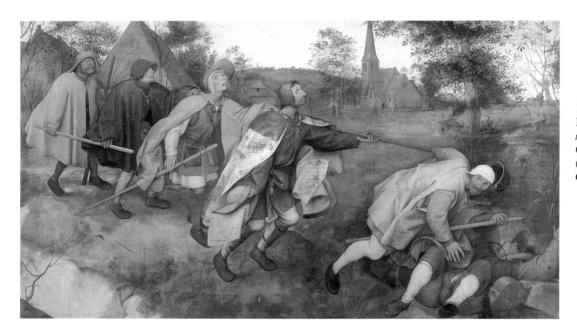

16-23. Pieter Bruegel the Elder. *The Blind Leading the Blind*. c. 1568. Oil on panel, 34½ x 60⅝" (85 x 154 cm). Museo di Capodimonte, Naples

of men and women are incidental to the majestic annual cycle of death and rebirth that is the rhythm of the cosmos.

The *Peasant Wedding* (fig. 16-22) is Bruegel's most memorable scene of peasant life. These are stolid, crude folk, heavy-bodied and slow, yet their very clumsiness gives them a strange gravity that commands our respect. Although painted in flat colors with little modeling and no cast shadows, the figures have a weight and solidity that remind us of Giotto. Space is created in assured perspective, and the composition is as monumental and balanced as in any Italian painting. Bruegel gives his peasant scene the seriousness of *The Last Supper* (compare fig. 14-15). Why, we wonder, did he endow this commonplace ceremony with the solemnity of a biblical event? It was first of all because marriage is one of the Seven Sacraments

and, as such, a sacred event (compare page 520). More important, he saw in the life of these rural people the natural condition of humanity. We know from his biographer, Karel van Mander ("the Netherlandish Vasari"), that Bruegel and his patron Hans Franckert often disguised themselves as peasants and joined in their revelries. [See Primary Sources, no. 48, page 649.] There Bruegel would draw them from life. In his hands, they become types whose follies he knew at first hand, yet whose dignity ultimately remains intact. For him, Everyman occupies an important place in the scheme of things.

Bruegel's philosophical detachment, which was shared by his fellow humanists, can also be seen in one of his last pictures, *The Blind Leading the Blind* (fig. 16-23). Its source is the Gospels (Matthew 15:12–19). Jesus, speaking of the Pharisees, says, "And if the blind lead the blind, both shall fall into the ditch." This parable recurs in humanistic as well as popular literature, and it appears in at least one earlier work. However, the tragic depth of Bruegel's image gives new urgency to the theme. He has used continuous narrative to ingenious effect. Each pose along the downward diagonal is more unstable than the last, thus leaving little doubt that everyone will end up in the ditch with the leader. (The gap between the two groups is especially telling.) Perhaps he found the meaning of the parable specially appropriate to his time, which was marked by religious and political fanaticism. Jesus continued: "Out of the heart proceed evil thoughts, murders . . . blasphemies." Could Bruegel have thought that this saying applied to the conflicts then raging over religious ritual?

ARCHITECTURE AND SCULPTURE
France

It took the Northern countries longer to absorb Italian forms in architecture and sculpture than in painting. France, however, was more closely linked with Italy than the rest. We will recall that it had conquered Milan in 1499. Earlier King Francis I had shown his admiration for Italian art by inviting Leonardo to Fontainebleau before luring several of the leading Mannerists—including Rosso, Primaticcio, and Cellini—to France (see pages 503–05). As a result, France began to assimilate Italian art and architecture somewhat earlier than the other countries and was the first to achieve a Renaissance style. Yet, although an important school of painting later flourished at Fontainebleau, the main achievement was in architecture and sculpture.

THE CHATEAU OF CHAMBORD. As we might expect, architects trained in the Gothic tradition could not adopt the Italian style all at once. They readily used its classical vocabulary, but its syntax gave them trouble for many years. At the Château of Chambord (fig. 16-24), however, the design, although greatly modified by later French builders, was originally by an Italian

pupil of Giuliano da Sangallo, probably Domenico da Cortona. His was surely the plan of the center portion (fig. 16-25), which is quite unlike earlier French châteaux. This square block, whose source is the keep of medieval castles (see page 337), has a central staircase fed by four corridors. These form a Greek cross that divides the interior into four square sections. Each section is subdivided into one large and two smaller rooms, and a closet. Together they form a suite (or apartment, as we call it today). This functional grouping, imported from Italy, was to become a standard pattern in France. It is the starting point of all modern "designs for living." However, the turrets, high-pitched roofs, elongated windows, and tall chimneys recall the old royal castle, the Louvre (see fig. 11-94), and the building is basically Gothic in style, despite the classical details.

GILLES LE BRETON. In 1528 Francis I, who built Chambord, decided to expand the medieval hunting lodge at Fontainebleau near Paris. What began as a modest enlargement soon developed into a vast palace. The original design, much altered over the years, was largely the work of the stonemason Gilles Le Breton (died 1553), whose father, Jean (died 1543/44) had helped design Chambord. It included the Gallery of Francis I, which Rosso was called from Italy to decorate a few years later. The Cour du Cheval Blanc (Court of the White Horse; fig. 16-26, page 554) is typical of the project as a whole. The design must have evolved in an organic fashion: the wing is surprisingly asymmetrical, and the forms are inconsistent. (The Italianate staircase was built by Jean Androuet du Cerceau in 1634.) Nevertheless, Fontainebleau is the point of departure for nearly all French châteaux for the next 250 years. Indeed, visiting Italian architects had to adapt their designs to the French taste. Thus classicism remained little more than a veneer applied to existing French types, although later structures followed its principles more closely.

This eclectic approach had such a strong appeal that it became, in effect, the basis of the national style. In his 1567 treatise, the architect Philibert de l'Orme (c. 1510–1570) actually proposed a new French classical order that was a variant of the five orders inherit-

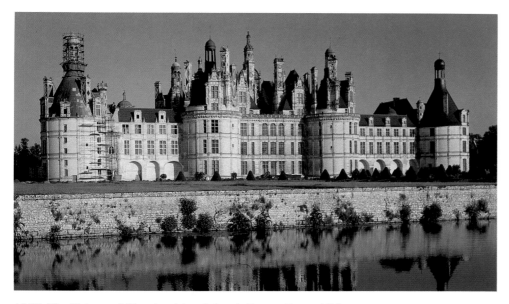

16-24. The Château of Chambord (north front), France. Begun 1519

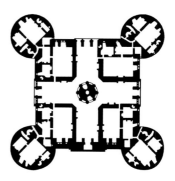

16-25. Plan of center portion, Château of Chambord (after Du Cerceau)

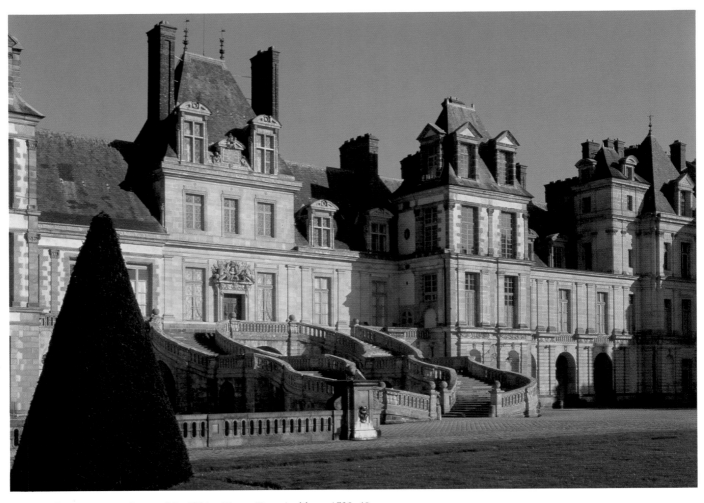

16-26. Gilles Le Breton, Court of the White Horse, Fontainebleau, 1528–40

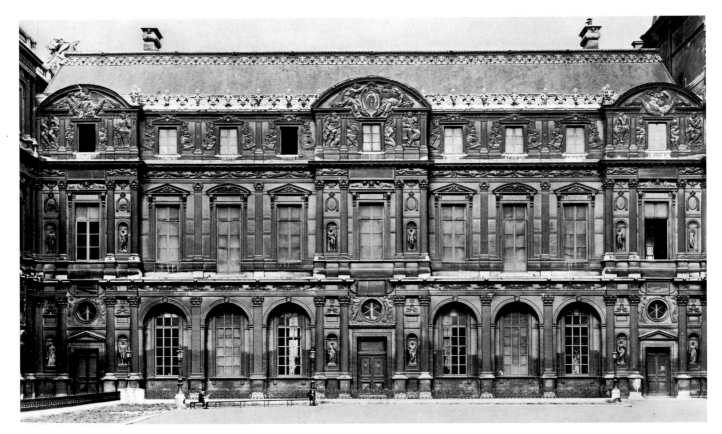

16-27. Pierre Lescot. Square Court of the Louvre, Paris. Begun 1546

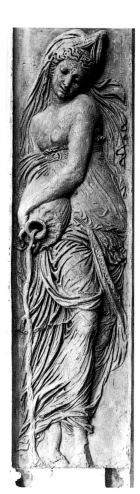
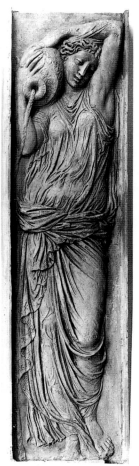
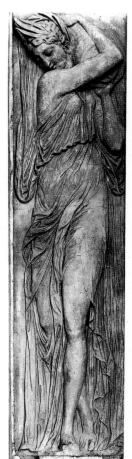
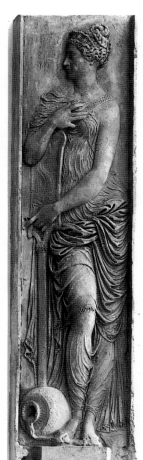
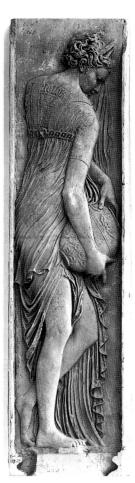

16-28. Jean Goujon. Reliefs from the Fontaine des Innocents, Paris (dismantled). 1548–49. Bas reliefs, each 6'4¾" x 2'4¾" (1.95 x .73 m). Musée du Louvre, Paris

ed from Greece and Rome. It added decorative bands to conceal the seams between column drums resulting from the limitations of French stone, which did not permit shafts as long as marble.

PIERRE LESCOT. In 1546 Francis I decided to replace the Gothic royal castle, the Louvre (see fig. 11-94), with a new palace on the old site. The project had barely begun at the time of his death, but his architect, Pierre Lescot (c. 1515–1578), continued it under Henry II, and quadrupled the size of the court. This enlarged scheme was not completed for more than a century. Lescot built only the southern half of the court's west side (fig. 16-27), which represents its "classic" phase, in contrast to the style of such buildings as Chambord. This distinction is well justified. The Italian vocabulary of Chambord is based on the Early Renaissance, whereas Lescot drew on the work of Bramante and his successors. Lescot's design is classic in another sense as well. It is the finest surviving example of Northern Renaissance architecture.

The details of Lescot's facade do indeed have a surprising classical purity, yet we would not mistake it for an Italian building. Its distinctive quality comes not from a superficial use of Renaissance forms but from a genuine synthesis of the traditional French château with the Italian palazzo. The superimposed classical orders, the pedimented window frames, and the arcade on the ground floor are Italian. But the continuity of the facade is broken by three projecting pavilions that have taken the place of the château turrets.

The high-pitched roof is also French. The vertical accents thus overcome the horizontal elements. (Note the broken architraves.) This effect is heightened by the tall, narrow windows, which descend from the Gothic. Lescot's solution proved so satisfying that the need for a purer classicism was not felt until the completion of the Louvre 120 years later under Louis XIV (see fig. 19-10).

GOUJON. Equally un-Italian is the rich sculptural decoration covering almost the entire wall surface of the Louvre's third story. These reliefs, beautifully adapted to the architecture, are by Jean Goujon (c. 1510–1565?), the finest French sculptor of the mid-sixteenth century, with whom Lescot often collaborated. Unfortunately, they have been much restored. To get a more accurate idea of Goujon's style, we must turn to the relief panels from the Fontaine des Innocents (fig. 16-28). They have survived intact, although the architectural framework by Lescot is lost. The graceful figures recall the Mannerism of Cellini and, even more, Primaticcio's Fontainebleau decorations (see figs. 14-19 and 14-20). Like Lescot's architecture at the Louvre (see fig. 16-27), however, they combine purely classical details with a slenderness that gives them a uniquely French air.

GERMAIN PILON. Germain Pilon (c. 1535–1590), the greatest sculptor of the later sixteenth century, was a more powerful artist. Whereas Goujon was mainly a relief carver, Pilon created

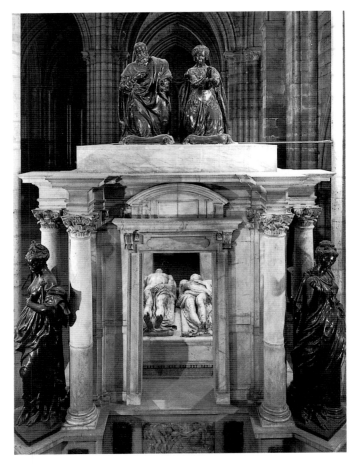

16-29. Francesco Primaticcio and Germain Pilon. Tomb of Henry II. 1563–70. Abbey Church of St.-Denis, Paris

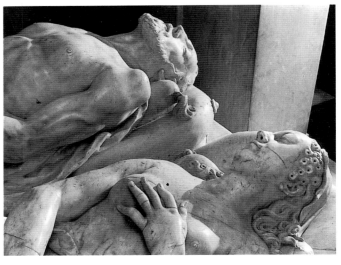

16-30. Germain Pilon. *Gisants* of the king and queen, detail of the Tomb of Henry II

monumental sculpture in every medium. In his early years Pilon, too, learned a good deal from Primaticcio, but he openly acknowledged his debt to Mannerism, instead of overlaying it with classicism. However, he soon developed his own style by merging the School of Fontainebleau with elements taken from ancient sculpture, the Gothic tradition, and Michelangelo and his school. His main works are tombs. The earliest and largest was for Henry II and Catherine de' Medici (fig. 16-29). Primaticcio designed the architectural framework, an oblong, freestanding

chapel on a platform decorated with bronze and marble reliefs. Pilon was responsible for all the sculpture. On the top of the tomb are bronze figures of the king and queen kneeling in prayer, while inside the chapel the couple reappear as recumbent marble ***gisants***, or nude corpses (fig. 16-30). The concept derives from the tomb of Francis I in St. Denis executed for Henry II in 1547 by the architect Philibert de l'Orme and the sculptor Pierre Bontemps (c.1507–c.1570).

This contrast of effigies had been a characteristic feature of Gothic tombs since the fourteenth century. The gisant expressed the transient nature of the flesh, usually by showing the body in an advanced stage of decay, sometimes with vermin crawling through its open cavities. That tradition remained popular in the North through the sixteenth century. How could this grim image be given Renaissance form without losing its emotional significance? Pilon's solution is brilliant. By idealizing the gisants he reverses their meaning, from the Gothic "prospective," which emphasizes the afterlife, to the classical "retrospective," which commemorates the deceased (see also pages 416–17). The queen is in the pose of a classical Venus and the king is like the dead Christ. They evoke neither horror nor pity. Instead, they have the pathos of a beauty that continues even in death.

England

In England the form of Late Gothic architecture known as the Perpendicular style (see fig. 11-27) proved extraordinarily persistent. Not until the middle of the sixteenth century did English buildings begin to absorb the vocabulary of the Italian Renaissance. It first appeared in 1563 with the publication of an architectural treatise by John Shute, which was based on a thorough study abroad of antique and contemporary architecture. Yet classicism was never applied consistently by Elizabethan architects. Instead, they relied on elements in pattern books from France, Italy, and Flanders, which they combined with the English vernacular tradition. Thus the Gothic lingered far longer in England than even in France. As late as 1600 the majority of English buildings still retained a "Perpendicular syntax"; that is to say, their stage of development corresponded to Chambord (see fig. 16-24). A major reason for this conservatism was the fact that English builders continued to be trained as masons and carpenters rather than as architects. They thus did not absorb the ideals of the Renaissance, merely its classical vocabulary, which they acquired almost entirely at second and third hand, beginning around 1550.

ROBERT SMYTHSON. Perhaps the only mason worthy of the title of architect in the proper sense of the term was Robert Smythson (c. 1536–1614). He designed several of the Elizabethan "prodigy" houses—country mansions built at enormous cost solely for the purpose of entertaining Queen Elizabeth and her court. The first and finest of these is Longleat (fig. 16-31), which went through several building campaigns. Perfectly symmetrical on all four sides and beautifully proportioned, it avoids the picturesque medieval effects of earlier English architecture. Instead, it achieves a classical harmony that makes it the most beautiful building in all of Britain before the time of Inigo Jones (see page 619). This

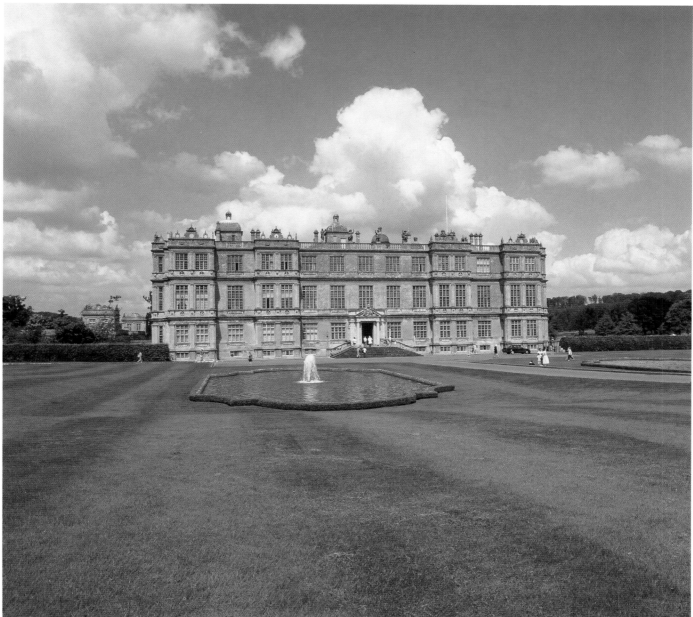

16-31. Robert Smythson, Allen Maynard, and others.
Longleat, Wiltshire, England. 1572–80

classicism, French rather than Italian in character (compare fig. 16-27), reflects the taste of its owner, John Thynne. (Thynne had already erected a somewhat similar building for Protector Edward Somerset.) The plan (fig. 16-32) had been established by another mason. However, the first two stories as we now see them were largely the responsibility of Smythson working with a French sculptor, Allen Maynard (active 1563–c. 1584), who carved the chimney pieces and ornamentation.

Begun in 1572 after a fire destroyed most of the existing house, the building envisioned by Smythson and Maynard was largely complete in time for a visit by the queen in 1574, but the third story was added by Thynne after they finished their work a year later. (The stairs are from the next century; compare fig. 16-26.) In contrast to later prodigy houses by Smythson and his contemporaries, Longleat preserves its classical character by omitting the elaborate crowns then in fashion, which freely juxtapose English and Flemish elements in wildly improbable combinations.

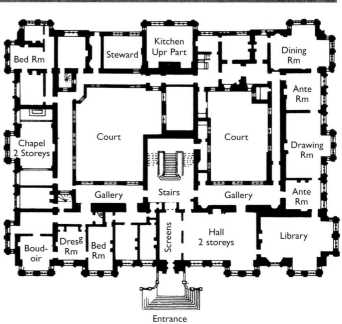

16-32. Plan of Longleat House, Wiltshire (after a plan from Sir Bannister Fletcher's *A History of Architecture*)

CHAPTER SEVENTEEN

The Baroque in Italy and Spain

What is Baroque? Like Mannerism, the term was originally coined to disparage the style it designates. It meant "irregular, contorted, grotesque." Art historians remain divided over its definition. Should Baroque be used only for the dominant style of the seventeenth century, or should it include other tendencies, such as classicism, to which it bears a complex relationship? Should the time frame include the period 1700 to 1750, known as the Rococo? More important, is the Baroque distinct from both Renaissance and modern? Although a good case can be made for viewing the Baroque as the final phase of the Renaissance, we shall treat it as a distinct era. The approach we choose is perhaps less important than understanding the factors that must enter into our decision.

The Baroque cannot be easily classified. It was a time full of contradictions and paradoxes, not unlike the present, which is why we find it so fascinating. It has been claimed that the Baroque style expresses the spirit of the Counter Reformation. However, by 1600 the Counter Reformation had largely run its course. Catholicism had regained much of its former territory and Protestantism was on the defensive, so that neither side had the power to upset the new balance. In 1622 the heroes of the Counter Reformation—Ignatius of Loyola, Francis Xavier (both Jesuits), Theresa of Ávila, Filippo Neri, and Isidoro Agricola—were named saints. (Carlo Borromeo had already been made one in 1610.) They began a wave of canonizations that lasted through the mid-eighteenth century. In contrast to the piety and good deeds of these reformers, the new princes of the Church who supported the growth of Baroque art were known mainly for their lives of worldly splendor.

Another reason we should avoid overemphasizing the Baroque's ties to the Counter Reformation is that, unlike Mannerism, the new style was not specifically Italian, even though it was born in Rome during the final years of the sixteenth century. Nor was it confined to religious art. Baroque elements quickly entered the Protestant North, where they were applied primarily to secular subjects.

Equally problematic is the idea that Baroque is "the style of absolutism," reflecting the centralized state ruled by an autocrat of unlimited powers. Although absolutism reached its climax during the reign of Louis XIV in the later seventeenth century, it had

been in the making since the 1520s under the Medicis in Tuscany, Francis I in France, the Hapsburgs in Austria and Spain, and Henry VIII in England. Moreover, Baroque art flourished in bourgeois Holland no less than in the absolutist monarchies, and the style sponsored under Louis XIV was a notably subdued, classicistic kind of Baroque.

It is nevertheless tempting to see the turbulent history of the era reflected in Baroque art, where the tensions of the era often seem to erupt into open conflict. The seventeenth century was one of almost continual warfare, which involved almost every European nation in a complex web of shifting alliances. The Thirty Years's War (1618–1648) was fueled by the ambitions of the kings of France, who sought to dominate Europe, and the Hapsburgs, who ruled not only Austria and Spain but also The Netherlands, Bohemia, and Hungary. Although fought largely in Germany, the war eventually engulfed nearly all of Europe. After the Treaty of Westphalia in 1648 ended the war and formally granted their freedom, the United Provinces—as the independent Netherlands was known—entered into a series of battles with England and France that lasted until 1679. Yet, other than in Germany, which was left in ruins, there is little correlation between these rivalries and the art of the period. In fact, the seventeenth century has been called the Golden Age of painting in France, Holland, Flanders, and Spain. Moreover, these wars had practically no effect on Baroque imagery. We see such an impact mainly in the etchings of Jacques Callot (see fig. 19-1), although we can catch indirect glimpses of it in Dutch militia scenes, such as Rembrandt's *Night Watch* (see fig. 18-16).

It is also difficult to relate Baroque art to the science and philosophy of the period. A direct link did exist in the Early and High Renaissance, when an artist could also be a humanist and a scientist. During the seventeenth century, however, scientific and philosophical thought became too complex, abstract, and systematic for the artist to share. Gravitation and calculus could not stir the artist's imagination any more than René Descartes's famous motto *Cogito, ergo sum* (I think, therefore I am).

There is nevertheless a relationship between Baroque art and science which is essential to an understanding of the age. The complex metaphysics of the humanists, which gave everything religious meaning, was replaced by a new physics. The change began with Nicholas Copernicus, Johannes Kepler, and Galileo Galilei, and culminated in Descartes and Isaac Newton. Their cosmology broke the ties between sensory perception and science. By placing the sun, not the earth (and humanity), at the center of the universe, it contradicted what our eyes (and common sense) tell us: that the sun revolves around the earth. Scientists now defined underlying relationships in mathematical and geometrical terms as part of the simple, orderly system of mechanics. Not only was the seventeenth century's worldview fundamentally different from the Renaissance's, but its understanding of visual reality was forever changed by the new science, thanks to advances in optical physics and physiology. Thus we may say that the Baroque literally saw with new eyes.

The attack on Renaissance science and philosophy, which could trace their origins and authority back to antiquity, also had the effect of displacing natural magic, a precursor of modern science that included both astrology and alchemy (see page 544). Unlike the new science, natural magic tried to control the world through prediction and manipulation; it did so by uncovering nature's "secrets" instead of her laws. Yet, because it was linked to religion and morality, natural magic lived on in popular literature and folklore long afterward.

In the end, Baroque art was not simply the result of religious, political, or intellectual developments. Let us therefore think of it as one among other basic features that distinguish the period: the strengthened Catholic faith, the absolutist state, and the new science. These factors are combined in volatile mixtures that give the Baroque its fascinating variety. Such diversity was well suited to express the expanding view of life. What ultimately unites this complex era is a reevaluation of humanity and its relation to the universe. Central to this image is the new psychology of the Baroque. Philosophers gave greater prominence to human passion, which encompassed a wider range of emotions and social levels than ever before. The scientific revolution leading up to Newton's unified mechanics responded to the same view, which presumes a more active role in people's ability to understand and affect the world around them. Remarkably, the Baroque remained an age of great religious faith, however divided it may have been in its loyalties. Newton, who was both the greatest scientist and the greatest philosopher of the era, never questioned the central position of god and religion. The interplay of passion, intellect, and spirituality may be seen as forming a dialogue that has never been truly resolved.

PAINTING IN ITALY

Around 1600 Rome became the fountainhead of the Baroque, as it had of the High Renaissance a century before, by attracting artists from other regions. The papacy patronized art on a large scale, with the aim of making Rome the most beautiful city of the Christian world "for the greater glory of God and the Church." This campaign had begun as early as 1585, but the artists then on hand were Late Mannerists with little talent. Soon, however, it attracted ambitious young artists, especially from northern Italy. It was they who created the new style.

CARAVAGGIO. Foremost among them was a painter of genius, Michelangelo Merisi (1571–1610), called Caravaggio after his birthplace near Milan. After finishing his training under a minor Milanese painter, he came to Rome sometime before 1590 and worked as an assistant to various artists before setting out on his own. His first important religious commission was a series of three monumental canvases devoted to St. Matthew that he painted for the Contarelli chapel in S. Luigi dei Francesi from 1599 to 1602 (fig. 17-1). The Church of the French (Francesi), founded in 1518 by Cardinal Giulio de' Medici (later Pope Clement VII) and designed by Giacomo della Porta (see pages 509–11), was finished in 1589. The Chapel of St. Louis (Luigi) was endowed by the French Cardinal Mathieu Contrel (Contarelli) in 1565, but despite a contract with the painter Girolamo Muziano of Brescia (1532-1592), the decorations were never carried out, probably because of procrastination and intrigues both before and after Contrel's death 20 years later. Caravaggio finally received the commission through the intervention of his patron, Cardinal del Monte.

As decorations the Contarelli paintings perform the same function that fresco cycles had in the Renaissance (compare fig. 12-47). Our view of the chapel includes *St. Matthew and the Angel,* in which the illiterate tax collector Matthew turns dramatically for inspiration to the angel who dictates the gospel. The main image illustrates *The Calling of St. Matthew* (fig. 17-2); a third canvas is

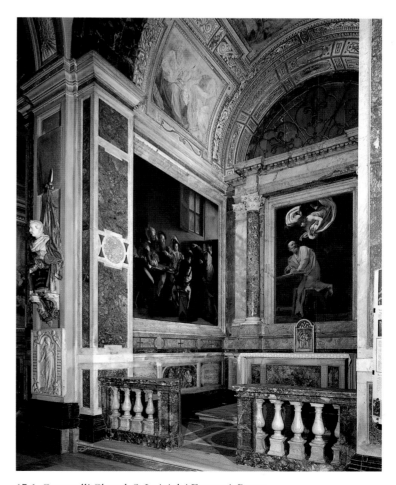

17-1. Contarelli Chapel, S. Luigi dei Francesi, Rome

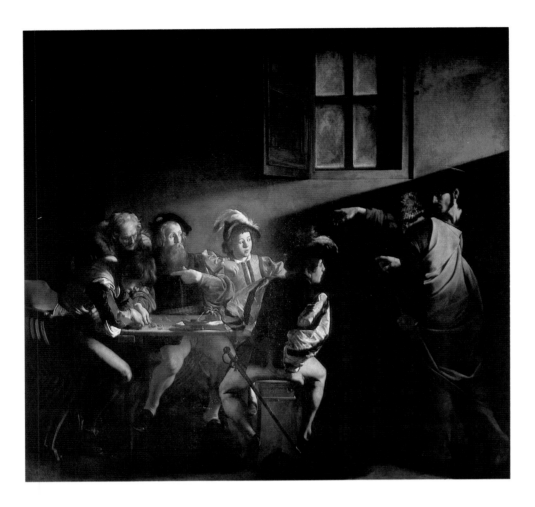

17-2. Caravaggio. *The Calling of St. Matthew.* c. 1599–1602.
Oil on canvas, 11'1" x 11'5" (3.4 x 3.5 m). Contarelli Chapel,
S. Luigi dei Francesi, Rome.

These costumes are certainly not the everyday dress of Caravaggio's time, and the explanation of them as the livery of pages (perhaps the pages of the Cardinal del Monte or of the Marchese Giustiniani). . . is most convincing. Saint Matthew, as he counts out the coins, is startled by the sudden appearance of Christ and his heavenly companion. The gesture of Christ's summoning hand at once calls to mind that of God the Father in Michelangelo's Creation of Adam *[see fig. 13-18] . . . .The psychological interrelation of the participants in the scene is expressed with the most careful and dramatic penetration; Christ's sudden appearance is like a flash of spiritual light in the midst of this worldly and rather suspect gathering. . . .*

The group of boys seated around the table continues both formally and psychologically the genre paintings of Caravaggio's early period . . . .Thus the Calling *represents the first use of such a group in a large-scale history painting charged with religious emotion. The momentary tension through which Caravaggio had made his everyday episodes interesting has now become a crisis affecting all humanity. To this end the stage, though still strictly limited, is now enlarged so that it no longer serves exclusively to display mere physiognomical studies but provides greater amplitude for the development of the drama. Caravaggio divides the surface of the painting horizontally into two parts which balance each other, the lower part filled with rich and colorful*

figures, the upper part almost empty. The bare wall is interrupted by a large high window permitting only a subdued light to enter through its oilskin pane. This division of space, which Caravaggio uses here for the first time, is of great importance for his own later work and for the painting of following centuries—one sees such a spatial arrangement for example in one of David's greatest compositions, the unfinished Jeu de Paume.

—Walter Friedlaender. *Caravaggio Studies.*
Princeton: Princeton University Press, 1975,
pp. 108–10. Originally published in 1955.

WALTER FRIEDLAENDER (1873–1966) taught at the University of Freiburg, Germany, before World War II, then at the Institute of Fine Arts, New York University until his death. He was, among other things, an authority on Caravaggio, and his monograph on the artist remains the touchstone for all later Caravaggio studies. He was known as "der heilige Walter" (The Holy Walter) by his small army of students because of his rare combination of genial charm, unhandsome physical appearance, and insightful intellect. His analysis of *The Calling of St. Matthew* is remarkable for its description of the emotional forces active throughout the picture, as if he and the reader had been present at the moment itself.

devoted to the saint's martyrdom. The style is remote from both Mannerism and the High Renaissance. Its only ancestor is the "North Italian realism" of artists such as Savoldo (see fig. 14-9). But Caravaggio's realism is of a new and radical kind. According to contemporary accounts, Caravaggio painted directly on the canvas, as had Titian, but he worked from the live model. [See Primary Sources, no. 55, page 653.] He depicted the world he knew, so that his canvases are filled with ordinary people. Highly argumentative, he carried a sword and was often in trouble with the law for fighting. When he killed a friend in a duel over a ballgame, Caravaggio fled Rome and spent the rest of his short life on the run. He first went to Naples, then spent several years in Malta before returning briefly to Naples. He died on his way back to Rome in the hope of gaining a pardon.

Caravaggio's pictures are often surprisingly autobiographical. *The Calling of St. Matthew* (fig. 17-2), the main image of the Contarelli chapel, shows this quality. Never before have we seen a sacred subject depicted so entirely in terms of contemporary lowlife. Matthew, the tax gatherer, sits with some armed men, who must be his agents, in a common Roman tavern. The setting and costumes must have been very familiar to Caravaggio. Two figures approach from the right. The arrivals are poor people whose bare feet and simple garments contrast strongly with the colorful costumes of Matthew and his companions.

For Caravaggio, however, naturalism is not an end in itself but a means of conveying profoundly spiritual content. Why do we sense a religious quality in this scene and not mistake it for an everyday event? The answer is that Caravaggio's North Italian realism is wedded to elements derived from his study of Renaissance art in Rome, which give the scene its surprising dignity. His style, in other words, is classical, without being classicizing. The composition, for example, is spread across the picture surface and its forms are sharply highlighted, much as in a relief (see fig. 7-32). What identifies one of the figures as Christ? It is surely not his halo, the only supernatural feature in the picture, which is a thin gold band that we might easily overlook. Our eyes fasten instead on his commanding gesture, borrowed from Michelangelo's *The Creation of Adam* (see fig. 13-18), which bridges the gap between the two groups and is echoed by Matthew, who points questioningly at himself.

Most decisive is the beam of sunlight above Jesus. By illuminating his face and hand in the gloomy interior, it carries his call across to Matthew. Without this light, so natural yet so charged with meaning, the picture would lose its power to make us aware of the divine presence. Caravaggio gives direct expression to an attitude shared by certain saints of the Counter Reformation: that the mysteries of faith are revealed not by speculation but through an inner experience that is open to all people. What separates the Baroque from the later Counter Reformation is the externalization of the mystic vision, which appears to us complete, without any signs of the spiritual struggle that characterizes El Greco's art (see pages 500–02).

Caravaggio's paintings have a quality of "lay Christianity" that appealed to Protestants no less than to Catholics. This quality made possible his strong, though indirect, influence on Rem-

brandt, the greatest religious artist of the Protestant North. In Italy, Caravaggio's work was praised by artists and connoisseurs, but the ordinary people for whom it was intended resented meeting their own kind in these paintings. They preferred religious imagery of a more idealized sort. Conservative critics, moreover, regarded Caravaggio as lacking decorum: the propriety and reverence demanded of religious subjects. For these reasons, Caravaggism largely ran its course by 1630, when it was absorbed into other Baroque tendencies.

RIBERA. Caravaggio's style lived on only in Naples, then under Spanish rule, where the artist lived after escaping from Rome. His main disciple in Naples was the Spaniard Jusepe Ribera (1591–1652), who settled there after having learned Caravaggio's style in Rome and who in turn spawned a school of his own. Especially popular were Ribera's paintings of saints, prophets, and ancient beggar-philosophers. Their asceticism appealed strongly to the otherworldliness of Spanish Catholicism. Such pictures also reflected the learned humanism of the Spanish nobility, who ruled Naples and were the artist's main patrons. Most of Ribera's figures are middle-aged or elderly men, who possess the unique blend of inner strength and intensity seen in *St. Jerome and the Angel of Judgment* (fig. 17-3, page 562), his masterpiece in this vein. The fervent characterization owes its expressive force to both the dramatic composition, inspired by Caravaggio (compare *St. Matthew and the Angel* in fig. 17-1), and the raking light, which gives the figure a powerful presence by heightening the realism and emphasizing the vigorous surface textures.

ARTEMISIA GENTILESCHI. So far, we have not discussed a woman artist, although this does not mean that there were none. Pliny, for example, in his *Natural History* (Book 35) documents the names and work of women artists in Greece and Rome, and there are records of women manuscript illuminators during the Middle Ages (see box page 318). We must remember, however, that the vast majority of *all* artists remained anonymous until the late fourteenth century. As a result, it has been possible to identify only a few works by women before that time. Women began to emerge as distinct artistic personalities about 1550, but it was not until the Baroque era that they first became prominent in the arts. Because it was difficult for them to obtain instruction in figure drawing and anatomy, women were effectively barred from painting narrative subjects. Hence, until the middle of the nineteenth century, women artists were largely restricted to painting portraits, genre scenes, and still lifes. Even so, many had successful careers, and often became the equals or superiors of the men in whose styles they were trained. The exceptions to this rule were certain Italian women born into artistic families, for whom painting came naturally.

The most important of them was Artemisia Gentileschi (1593–c. 1653). She was born in Rome, the daughter of Caravaggio's closest follower, Orazio Gentileschi, and became one of the leading painters of her day. She took great pride in her work but found the way difficult for a woman artist, despite her considerable fame. [See Primary Sources, no. 54, page 652.] Her

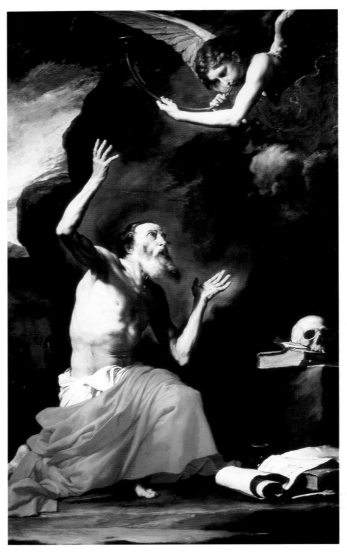

17-3. Jusepe Ribera. *St. Jerome and the Angel of Judgment*. 1626.
Oil on canvas, 8'7⅛" x 5'4½" (2.62 x 1.64 m).
Museo e Gallerie Nazionali di Capodimonte, Naples

characteristic subjects are Bathsheba, the tragic object of King David's passion, and Judith, who saved her people by beheading the Assyrian general Holofernes in his tent. Both themes were popular during the Baroque era, which delighted in erotic and violent scenes. Artemisia's frequent depictions of these biblical heroines suggest an ambivalence toward men that was rooted in her turbulent life. (She was raped by her teacher, who was convicted in a jury trial but given a light sentence that was never enforced.)

Gentileschi's early paintings of Judith rely heavily on her father's and Caravaggio's. Our example (fig. 17-4), however, is a fully mature, independent work that combines their best features in its unique blend of drama and restraint. Rather than the gruesome beheading itself, the artist shows the servant stuffing Holofernes' head into a sack. Momentarily distracted by something outside the tent, Judith gestures theatrically, heightening the air of mystery and intrigue. The hushed, candlelit atmosphere and the shadow across Judith's face convey her complex emotions with incomparable understanding. Clearly no mere follower, Artemisia emerged as a leader in her own right. Paintings such as this established her reputation throughout Italy. Her rich palette was to have a lasting influence in Naples, where she settled in 1631.

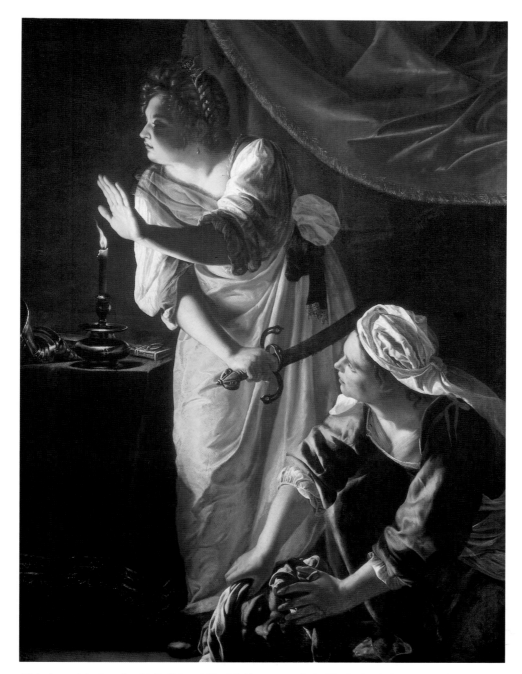

17-4. Artemisia Gentileschi. *Judith and Her Maidservant with the Head of Holofernes.* c.1625.
Oil on canvas, 6'1½" x 4'7" (1.84 x 1.41 m). The Detroit Institute of Arts

ANNIBALE CARRACCI. The conservative tastes of every-day people in Italy were met by artists who were less radical, and less talented, than Caravaggio. They took their lead instead from Annibale Carracci (1560–1609), who arrived in Rome in 1595. Annibale came from Bologna where, in the 1580s, he and two other members of his family had evolved an anti-Mannerist style based on North Italian realism and Venetian art. He was a reformer rather than a revolutionary. As with Caravaggio, who admired him, his experience of Roman classicism transformed his art. He, too, felt that painting must return to nature, but his approach emphasized a revival of the classics, which to him meant the art of antiquity. Anni-

bale also sought to emulate Raphael, Michelangelo, Titian, and Correggio. In his best work, he was able to fuse these diverse elements, although their union always remained somewhat unstable.

Between 1597 and 1604 Annibale produced a vast ceiling fresco in the gallery of the Farnese Palace (fig. 17-5, page 564), his most ambitious work, which soon became so famous that it ranked behind only the murals of Michelangelo and Raphael. [See Primary Sources, no. 55, page 653] Commissioned to celebrate a wedding in the Farnese family, it wears its humanist subject, the Loves of the Classical Gods, lightly. As on the Sistine ceiling, the narrative scenes are surrounded by painted architecture, simu-

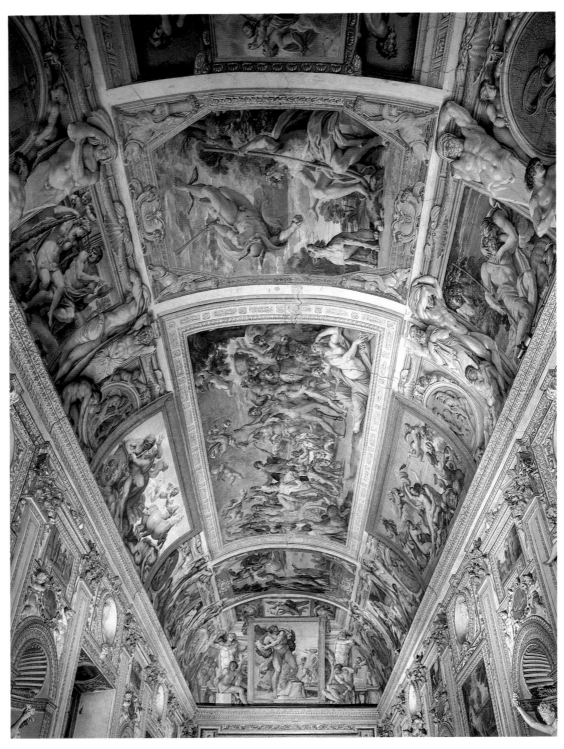

17-5. Annibale Carracci. Ceiling fresco. 1597–1601. Gallery, Palazzo Farnese, Rome

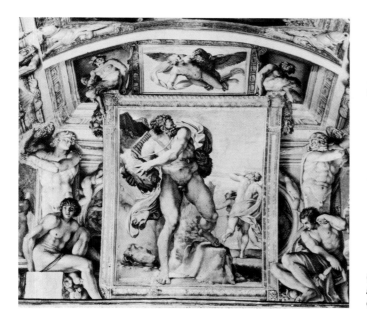

17-6. Annibale Carracci. Ceiling fresco (detail). Gallery, Palazzo Farnese

(BELOW) 17-7. Annibale Carracci. *Landscape with the Flight into Egypt.* c. 1603. Oil on canvas, 4'1/4" x 8'2 1/2" (1.22 x 2.50 m). Galleria Doria Pamphili, Rome

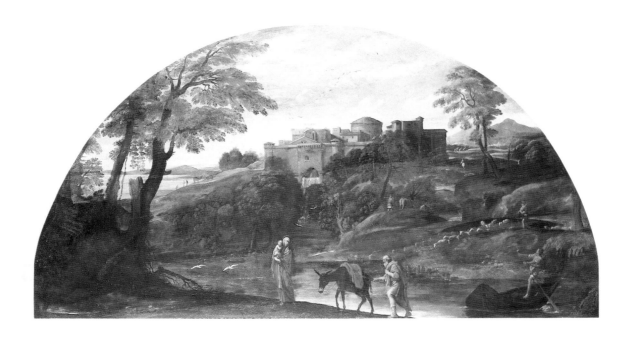

lated sculpture, and nude youths, which are carefully foreshortened and lit from below so that they appear real. But the fresco does not rely solely on Michelangelo's masterpiece. The main panels are presented as easel pictures (fig. 17-6), a solution adopted from Raphael. The style of these mythological scenes recalls Raphael's *Galatea* (see fig. 13-33), with a strong debt to Titian (compare the *Bacchanal* in fig. 13-39). The whole is held together by an illusionistic scheme that reflects Annibale's knowledge of Correggio (see fig. 14-10) and Veronese. Each of these levels of reality is handled with consummate skill, and the entire ceiling has an exuberance that sets it apart from both Mannerism and High Renaissance art.

The sculptured precision of the Farnese Gallery shows us only one side of Annibale Carracci's style. Another important aspect is his landscapes, such as the *Landscape with the Flight into Egypt*

(fig. 17-7). Its pastoral mood and the soft light and atmosphere hark back to Giorgione and Titian (see figs. 13-38 and 13-39). The figures, however, play a minor role here. They are as small and incidental as those in any Northern landscape (compare fig. 16-21). Nor does the landscape in any way suggest the Flight into Egypt. It would be equally suitable for almost any story. Still, we feel that the figures could not be removed altogether, although we can imagine them replaced by others. This is not the untamed nature of Northern landscapes. The old castle, the roads and fields, the flock of sheep, the ferryman with his boat, all show that this "civilized," hospitable countryside has been inhabited for a long time. Hence the figures, however tiny, do not appear lost or dwarfed. Their presence is implied by the orderly, domesticated quality of the setting. This firmly constructed "ideal landscape" evokes a vision of nature that is gentle yet austere, grand but not awesome.

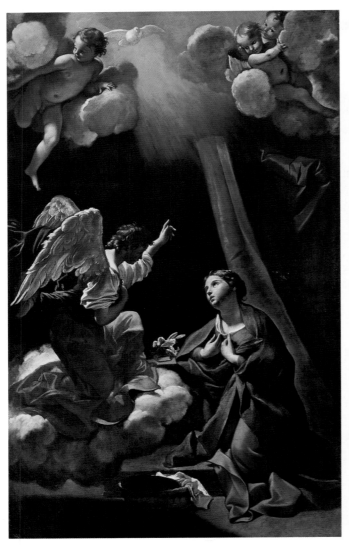

17-8. Giovanni Lanfranco. *Annunciation.* c. 1616. Oil on canvas, 9'8 ½" x 6' (2.96 x 1.83 m). S. Carlo ai Catinari, Rome

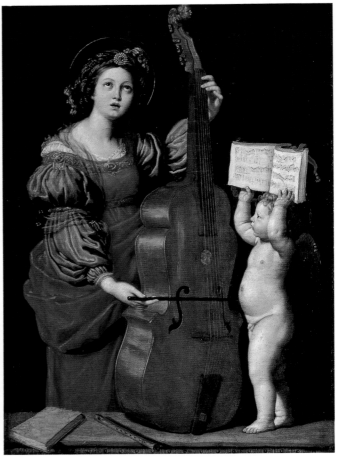

17-9. Domenichino. *St. Cecilia.* c. 1617–18. Oil on canvas, 62⅜ x 46⅛" (159 x 117 cm; enlarged). Musée du Louvre, Paris

GIOVANNI LANFRANCO; DOMENICHINO. The seeds of the reaction against Carracci's classicism were to be found within his own studio. The way was led by Giovanni Lanfranco (1582–1647), a native of Parma who worked for a while under Carracci. His *Annunciation* (fig. 17-8) unites Correggio's colorism with Caravaggio's drama. The result is an emotional style that signals the arrival of the High Baroque. Lanfranco's expressive intensity was the very opposite of the measured economy of Domenichino (1581–1641), Carracci's favorite pupil, who thought out every gesture and expression with impressive logic. Today, however, Domenichino is remembered more for his paintings of sweetly lyrical female figures, such as *St. Cecilia* (fig. 17-9), the patron saint of music. Inspired by Raphael, this subject inaugurates a long line of successors through the Rococo.

GUIDO RENI; GUERCINO. Lanfranco won out over Domenichino in fresco decoration, where the main development of Baroque painting was to take place through the 1630s. Their rivalry was repeated by two other pupils of the Carracci: Guido Reni

(1575–1642) and Guercino (Giovanni Francesco Barbieri; 1591–1666). Reni, who collaborated with Lanfranco for several years, exercised a widespread influence early on. (Domenichino may have known Raphael's painting of St. Cecilia through a copy by Reni.) Eventually he assumed leadership of the Bolognese school. Guercino succeeded Reni upon his death, but only after making major concessions to his refined style.

To artists who were inspired by it, the Farnese Gallery seemed to offer two alternatives. Using the Raphaelesque style of the mythological panels, they could arrive at a deliberate, "official" classicism; or they could take their cue from the illusionism of the framework. The approach varied according to personal style and the specific site. Among the earliest examples of the first alternative is Reni's ceiling fresco *Aurora* (fig. 17-10), which shows Apollo in his chariot (the Sun) led by *Aurora* (Dawn). Here grace becomes the pursuit of perfect beauty. The relieflike design would seem like little more than a pale reflection of High Renaissance art were it not for the glowing color and dramatic light, which gives it an emotional force that the figures alone could never achieve. This style is

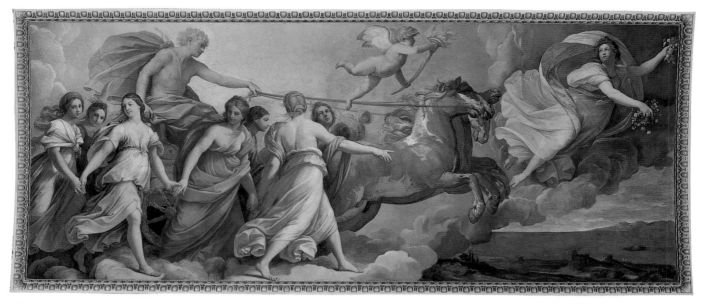

17-10. Guido Reni. Aurora. 1613. Ceiling fresco. Casino Rospigliosi, Rome

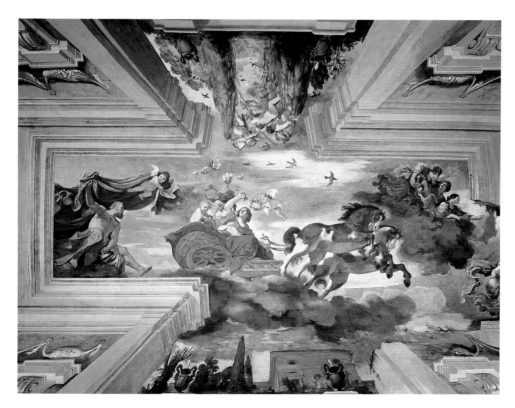

17-11. Guercino. *Aurora*. 1621–23. Ceiling fresco. Villa Ludovisi, Rome

called Baroque classicism to distinguish it from all earlier forms of classicism, no matter how much it may be indebted to them.

The *Aurora* ceiling (fig. 17-11) painted less than ten years later by Guercino is the very opposite of Reni's. Here architectural perspective, combined with the pictorial illusionism of Correggio and the intense light and color of Titian, converts the entire surface into one limitless space, in which the figures sweep past as if driven by the winds. With this work, Guercino started what became a flood of similar visions characteristic of the High Baroque after 1630.

PIETRO DA CORTONA. The most overpowering of these illusionistic ceilings is the fresco by Pietro da Cortona (1596–1669) in the great hall of the Barberini Palace in Rome (fig. 17-12, page 568). This enormous painting glorifies the reign of the Barberini pope, Urban VIII, in the form of a complex allegory. As in the Farnese Gallery, the ceiling area is subdivided by a painted framework that simulates architecture and sculpture, but beyond it we now see the limitless sky, as in Guercino's *Aurora*. Clusters of figures, perched on clouds or soaring freely, swirl above as well as below this framework. They create a dual illusion: some figures appear to hover inside the hall, close to us, while others recede into the distance. Cortona was familiar with a domed ceiling painted in Rome by Lanfranco nearly a decade earlier, based directly on Correggio's *The Assumption of the Virgin* (fig. 14-10), which creates a very similar effect.

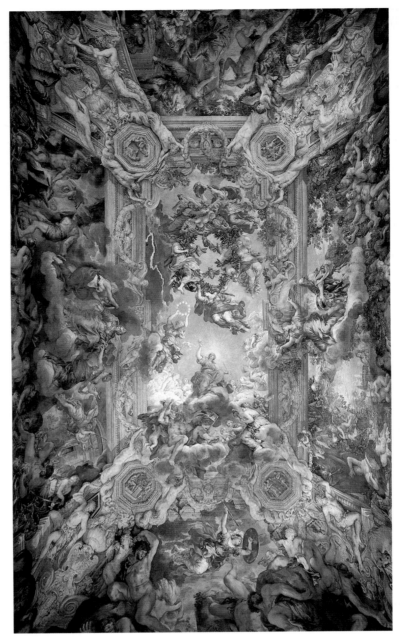

17-12. Pietro da Cortona. *The Glorification of the Reign of Urban VIII.*
1633–39. Portion of ceiling fresco. Palazzo Barberini, Rome

Cortona's frescoes were the focal point for the rift between the High Baroque and Baroque classicism that grew out of the Farnese ceiling. The classicists insisted that art serves a moral purpose and must observe the principles of clarity, unity, and decorum. And, supported by a tradition based on Horace's adage *ut pictura poesis* (see page 453), they maintained that painting should follow the example of tragic poetry in conveying meaning through a minimum of figures whose movements, gestures, and expressions can be easily read. Cortona, while not anticlassical, presented the case for art as epic poetry, with many actors and episodes that expand on the central theme and create a magnificent effect. He was also the first to argue that art has a sensuous appeal which exists as an end in itself.

Although it took place largely on a theoretical level, the debate over illusionistic ceiling painting involved more than opposing approaches to telling a story and expressing ideas in art. The issue lay at the very heart of the Baroque. Illusionism allowed artists to overcome the apparent contradictions of the era by fusing separate levels of reality into a pictorial unity of such overwhelming grandeur as to sweep aside any differences between them. Despite the intensity of the debate, in practice the two sides rarely came into conflict over easel paintings, where the differences between Cortona's and Carracci's followers were not always so clear-cut. Surprisingly, Cortona found inspiration in classical art and Raphael throughout his career. The leader of the reaction against the "excesses" of the High Baroque was neither a fresco painter nor an Italian, but a French artist living in Rome: Nicolas Poussin (see page 608), who moved in the same antiquarian circle as Cortona early on but drew very different lessons from it.

The most important contribution of the Baroque to music and theater was the invention of opera, which united all the theatrical elements of the period into a spectacular whole. It began modestly enough as a humanist exercise in Florence. Following the suggestion of Girolamo Mei of Rome, members of the Camerata of Florence, so called because it met *in camera* (behind closed doors) at the palace of Count Giorgio Bardi, set out to re-create ancient Greek drama, which they wrongly believed had been sung throughout a performance. Around 1590, Vincenzo Galilei (c. 1520–1591), the father of the astronomer Galileo, issued a polemic attacking the vocal counterpoint of madrigals as impersonal and artificial because it did not adhere to the Greek unity of text and music. Vincenzo experimented with monodies—short, dramatic monologues with continuo accompaniment—as part of an attempt to rediscover the power of music to move the soul. Along with the intermezzi that were performed between the acts of comedies, they were the direct forerunners of Baroque opera (short for *opera in musica*, " work in music"). The first opera was *Dafne,* produced privately in 1598 with a *libretto* (text) by Ottavio Rinuccini (1562–1621) and music mostly by Jacopo Peri (1561–1633). It was followed by *Euridice* from the same team, with additional arias by Giulio Caccini (c. 1546–1618), which was performed in 1600 in honor of the marriage of Henry IV and Marie de' Medici. Later that year and in 1601, Caccini and Peri, who were singers and professional rivals, published separate versions of the opera. Despite its limitations, the new declamatory style, called representative or theatrical style, made an extraordinary impression on listeners, and it was to remain the basis of classical opera in both Italy and France well into the eighteenth century.

Opera might nevertheless have remained of little more than antiquarian interest had it not been for Claudio Monteverdi (1567–1643). He has aptly been described as the "last great madrigalist and the first great opera composer." His *Orfeo,* produced in 1607 at Mantua with a libretto by Alessandro Striggio, enlarged the story of *Euridice* into the standard five acts demanded by the Roman poet Horace while increasing the variety of vocal music and giving a greater role to the instrumental accompaniment. Monteverdi was openly experimental. He was acutely aware of the conflict between the earlier style of the Netherlanders and the later Italian madrigalists such as Carlo Gesualdo (see page 547), and he fended off attacks by saying that he was working in an entirely new vein so that none of the old rules applied.

From then on, music took precedence over words in opera, which often emphasized extreme emotional states of mind *(affetti)* through violent contrasts, as did Baroque art. The future of the new form lay in Rome and Venice, which opened the first public opera house in 1637. Operas soon became wildly popular, not only in Italy but throughout Europe, and everyone vied for the services of the leading Italians. After 1650 the court in Vienna became the main center of theater and opera. Its zenith came with *The Golden Apple,* a huge spectacle staged there in 1668 to celebrate the wedding of Emperor Leopold I and the Infanta Margarita of

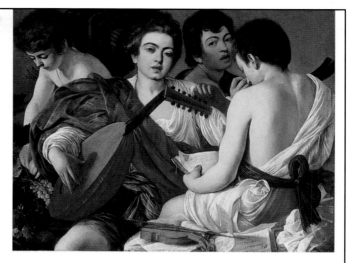

Caravaggio. *The Musicians.* c. 1595. Oil on canvas, 36¼ x 46⅝" (92.1 x 118.4 cm). The Metropolitan Museum of Art, New York
ROGERS FUND, 1952

Spain, with music by Pietro Antonio Cesti (1623–1669) and scenery by Ludovico Burnacini (1636–1707). The public wanted new operas as soon as they could be mounted, while star singers required virtuoso arias, solos to which they often added florid ornamentation to showcase their talents. Combined with the increasing emphasis on spectacle, these demands conspired to dilute opera as a dramatic form while the beauty of the music itself grew. The impact of opera was pervasive. Although it generally tried to adhere to tradition, even church music became operatic in the solo cantatas and oratorios of Giacomo Carissimi (1605–1674). These three vocal forms reached maturity in the compositions of Alessandro Scarlatti (1660–1725), who worked in Naples and Rome, so that he holds a position analogous to that of Francesco Solimena in painting (see page 571). In addition to being the outstanding Italian opera composer of his time, Scarlatti wrote religious music of great beauty. He was the pivotal figure in late Italian Baroque music, comparable in importance to Jean-Baptiste Lully of France (see box pages 612–13).

The Baroque was the first period in which instrumental music equaled vocal music in stature. While continuing the practice of imitating different dance types, it also began to mimic vocal style. The two approaches are exemplified in the trio sonatas of Arcangelo Corelli (1653–1713). His chamber sonatas use dance movements, while the church sonatas in principle do not, although they were in fact often mixed. Both employ two violins and a continuo consisting of a lower viol and a keyboard instrument. When expanded to a full string orchestra, the trio sonata became the *concerto grosso* (grand concerto), the most characteristic type of Baroque instrumental music, which began as overtures to and during Mass. Corelli alternated sprightly, dancelike movements with slow ones that have a uniquely plaintive, bittersweet quality similar to the laments in Monteverdi's madrigals. Virtuoso touches of ornamentation are treated discretely so as not to disrupt the singing line, which for the most part is kept well within the range of the human voice. Each movement generally has one or two alternating melodies developed in clear progressions that became the basis for modern harmony.

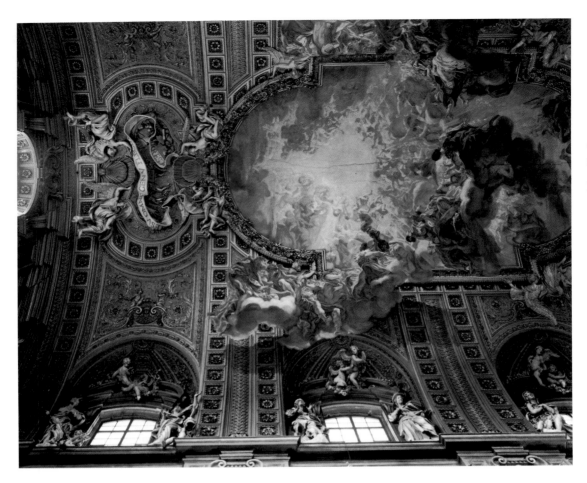

17-13. Giovanni Battista Gaulli. *Triumph of the Name of Jesus.* 1672–85. Ceiling fresco. Il Gesù, Rome

IL GESÙ. It is a strange fact that few ceiling frescoes were painted after Cortona finished his *Glorification of the Reign of Urban VIII.* Ironically the new style of architecture fostered by Francesco Borromini and Guarino Guarini (see pages 573–76) provided few opportunities for decoration. But after 1670 such frescoes enjoyed a revival in older buildings, which reached its peak in the interior of Il Gesù (fig. 17-13). Although his role in this case was only advisory, it is clear that the plan for this work must be by Gianlorenzo Bernini, the greatest sculptor-architect of the century (see below). At his suggestion, the commission for the ceiling frescoes went to his young protégé Giovanni Battista Gaulli, known as Baciccia (1639–1709). A talented assistant, Antonio Raggi (1624–1686), made the stucco sculpture. The program, which proved extraordinarily influential, shows Bernini's imaginative daring. As in the Cornaro Chapel (see fig. 17-30), the ceiling is treated as a single unit that evokes a mystical vision. The nave fresco, with its contrasts of light and dark, spills dramatically over its frame, then turns into sculptured figures. Here Baroque illusionism achieves its ultimate expression. [See Primary Sources, no. 54, page 652.]

LUCA GIORDANO. The greatest representative of the Late Baroque was the Neapolitan painter Luca Giordano (1634–1705). He began by imitating his teacher Ribera but eventually succeeded Pietro Cortona as the leading decorative painter in Italy. Legendary for his speed, Giordano was a virtuoso whose remarkable facility resulted in a vast and varied output. *The Abduction of Europa* (fig. 17-14) shows his spontaneous approach

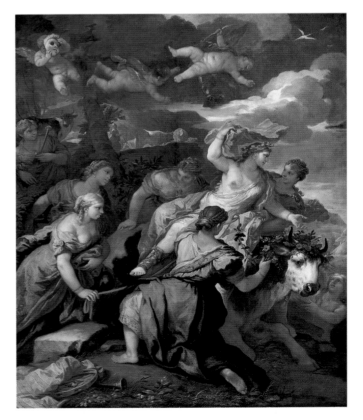

17-14. Luca Giordano. *The Abduction of Europa.* 1686. Oil on canvas, 7'5⅝" x 6'4¼" (2.27 x 1.93 m). Wadsworth Atheneum, Hartford, Connecticut

at its best. The composition is based on one by Veronese that also was to inspire François Boucher (see page 628). The painting shares the graceful style of Cortona but favors a rich tonalism inherited from Lanfranco, who worked in Naples during the 1630s. Although he never fully accepted colorism, Giordano set the stage for the great Venetian painters of the eighteenth century, even in his professional lifestyle, which was largely spent on the move. He became the first in a line of great Italian artists, culminating in Tiepolo (see page 641), to be called to the Spanish court.

Gaulli and Giordano mark the final flowering of Baroque extravagance. By this time the pendulum had swung in the opposite direction. Italian painting during the third quarter of the seventeenth century was marked by a conservative blend of the High Baroque and Baroque classicism. The result was an academic style that flourished in Rome and Naples, which were then firmly linked. It was developed chiefly by Carlo Maratta (1625–1713) of Rome, the most admired artist of his day, and Francesco Solimena (1657–1747), Giordano's successor in Naples. Maratta may be regarded as a less doctrinaire counterpart to Charles Lebrun in France (see pages 610–11). He wanted to revive the grand manner of the Carracci by emphasizing individual figures through a clear, even light without abandoning Cortona's color and drama. As might be expected, the results of such a compromise were generally not impressive. Surprisingly, Maratta's rival Gaulli also participated in this tendency, despite the differences between them.

ARCHITECTURE IN ITALY

CARLO MADERNO. The beginnings of the Baroque style in architecture cannot be defined as precisely as in painting. Carlo Maderno (1556–1629) was the most talented young architect to emerge in the vast ecclesiastical building program that got under way in Rome toward the end of the sixteenth century. In 1603 he was given the task of completing, at long last, the church of St. Peter's. Pope Clement VIII had decided to add a nave and narthex to the west end of Michelangelo's building (see fig. 13-28), thereby converting it into a basilica. The change of plan, which had already been proposed by Raphael in 1514, made it possible to link St. Peter's with the Vatican Palace to the right of the church (fig. 17-15).

Maderno's design for the facade follows the pattern established by Michelangelo for the exterior of the church. It consists of a colossal order supporting an attic, but with a dramatic emphasis on the portals. The effect can only be described as a crescendo that builds from the corners toward the center. The spacing of the supports becomes closer, the pilasters turn into columns, and the facade wall projects step by step. This quickened rhythm had been hinted at a generation earlier in Giacomo della Porta's facade of Il Gesù (see fig. 14-31). Maderno made it the dominant principle of his facade designs, not only for St. Peter's but for smaller churches as well. In the process, he replaced the traditional concept of the church facade as one continuous wall surface, which was not yet challenged by the facade of Il Gesù, with the "facade-in-depth," dynamically related to the open space before it. The possibilities of

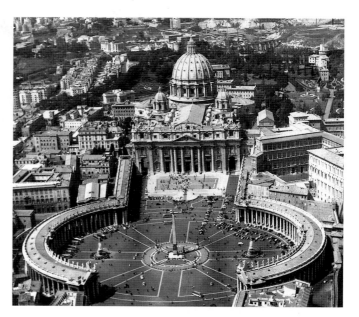

17-15. Aerial view of St. Peter's, Rome.
Nave and facade by Carlo Maderno, 1607–15;
colonnade by Gianlorenzo Bernini, designed 1657

this new treatment, which derives from Michelangelo's Palazzo dei Conservatori (fig. 13-26), were not to be exhausted until 150 years later.

GIANLORENZO BERNINI. After Maderna's death in 1629, his assistant Gianlorenzo Bernini (1598–1680) took over at St. Peter's. He considered himself Michelangelo's successor as both architect and sculptor. Thus he molded the open space in front of the facade into a magnificent oval piazza that is amazingly sculptural (see fig. 17-15). This "forecourt," which imposed a degree of unity on the sprawling Vatican complex, acts as an immense atrium framed by colonnades. The device, which Bernini himself likened to the motherly, all-embracing arms of the Church, is not new. It had been used at private villas designed by Jacopo Vignola for the Farneses in the 1550s; but these were, in effect, **belvederes** opening onto formal gardens to the rear. What is novel is the idea of placing it at the main entrance to a building. Also new is the huge scale. For sheer impressiveness, this integration of architecture and grandiose setting can be compared only with the ancient Roman sanctuary at Palestrina (see fig. 7-6).

The piazza can be thought of as a continuation on the exterior of the decoration program at St. Peter's, which occupied Bernini at intervals during most of his long career. The enormous size of St. Peter's made the treatment of its interior a difficult task. How could its vastness be related to the human scale and given a measure of emotional warmth? Bernini began by designing the bronze canopy for the main altar under the dome (fig. 17-16, page 572). The **tabernacle** is a splendid fusion of architecture and sculpture. Four ornate, spiral-shaped columns support an upper platform. At its corners are statues of angels and vigorously curved scrolls, which raise a cross high above a golden orb, the symbol of the victory of Christianity over the pagan world. The entire structure is so alive with expressive energy that it strikes us as the

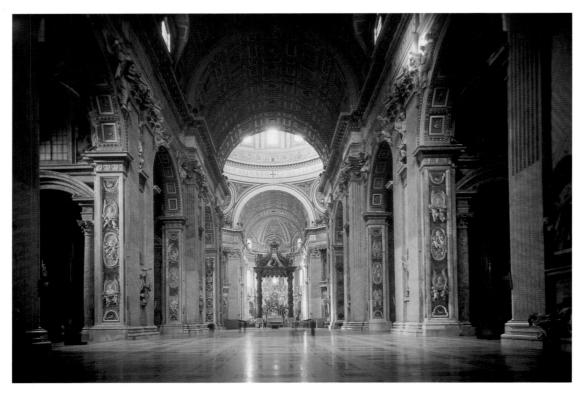

17-16. Carlo Maderno. Nave, with Bernini's Tabernacle (1624–33) at crossing, St. Peter's, Rome

epitome of Baroque style. Yet its most impressive feature, the corkscrew columns, had been invented in late antiquity and were even employed on a much smaller scale in the old basilica of St. Peter's. Thus Bernini could claim the best possible precedent for his own use of the motif. This is not the only instance of a kinship between seventeenth-century and ancient art. Several monuments of Roman architecture of the second and third centuries A.D. seem to anticipate the Baroque (see figs. 7-23 and 7-24).

PIETRO DA CORTONA. Like Michelangelo, Bernini sometimes attacked rivals out of professional and personal jealousy. Thus he was harshly critical of Pietro da Cortona, who established himself as one of the leading architects in Rome with the church of Ss. Luca e Martina (fig. 17-17). Cortona, the son of a stone mason, began his career as an architect and turned to painting only later. He had intended to renovate the existing church of the Academy of St. Luke, the artist's guild, at his own expense to provide a tomb for himself. When the remains of St. Martina were discovered, the project came under the patronage of Cardinal Francesco Barberini, who ordered it completely rebuilt in 1635. The two-tiered facade, with its submerged columns and ornate dome, recalls Mannerist architecture by Michelangelo's followers in Florence, where Cortona began his career (compare fig. 14-23). The massing of elements, however, is based on della Porta and Maderno, and the overall effect is strikingly Baroque. The facade has all the theatricality of a stage design. It disguises the plan of the church, a Greek cross with apses on each arm, although the grouping of the columns and pilasters is a preview of the interior. The

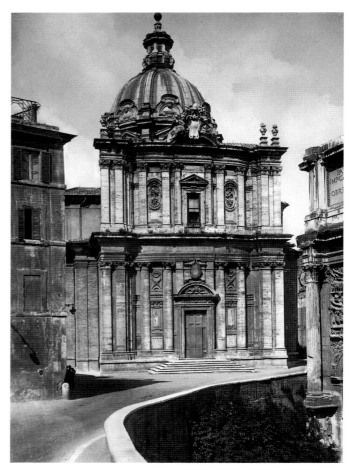

17-17. Pietro da Cortona. Facade of Ss. Luca e Martina, Rome. c. 1635–50

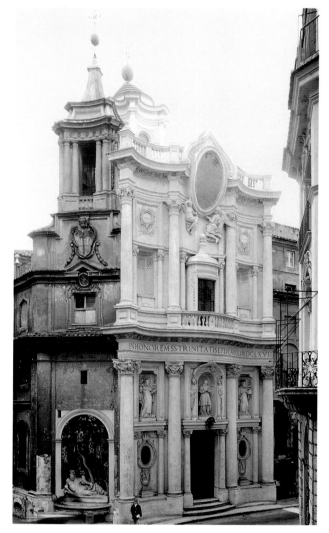

17-18. Francesco Borromini. Facade of S. Carlo alle Quattro
Fontane, Rome. 1665–67

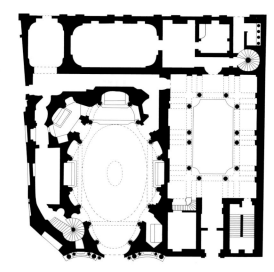

17-19. Plan of S. Carlo alle Quattro Fontane. Begun 1638

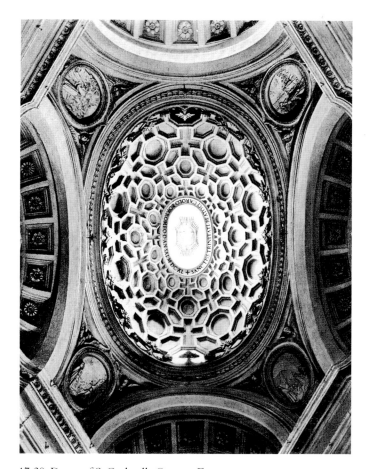

17-20. Dome of S. Carlo alle Quattro Fontane

surface bows outward, showing a new flexibility that became
characteristic of Italian Baroque architecture. Cortona occupies a
place of central importance. His S. Maria della Pace, begun in
1656, influenced the only major church Bernini built entirely himself, S. Andrea al Quirinale of two years later. And, as we shall see,
he was to have a decisive impact on Borromini.

FRANCESCO BORROMINI. As a personality, Bernini represents a type we first met among the artists of the Early Renaissance, a self-assured person of the world. His greatest rival in
architecture, Francesco Borromini (1599–1667), was just the opposite: a secretive and emotionally unstable genius who died by suicide. The Baroque heightened the tension between the two types.
The contrast between these two masters would be evident from
their works alone, even without the accounts by their contemporaries. Both represent the climax of Baroque architecture in Rome.
Yet Bernini's church designs are dramatically simple and unified,
while Borromini's structures are extravagantly complex. And
whereas the surfaces of Bernini's interiors are extremely rich,
Borromini's, like Cortona's, are surprisingly plain. They rely on

Borromini's phenomenal grasp of spatial geometry to achieve
their spiritual effects. Bernini himself agreed with those who
denounced Borromini for flagrantly disregarding the classical
tradition, enshrined in Renaissance theory and practice, that
architecture must reflect the proportions of the human body.

In Borromini's first major project, the church of S. Carlo alle
Quattro Fontane (figs. 17-18–17-20), it is the syntax, not the vocabulary, that is new and disquieting. The ceaseless play of concave

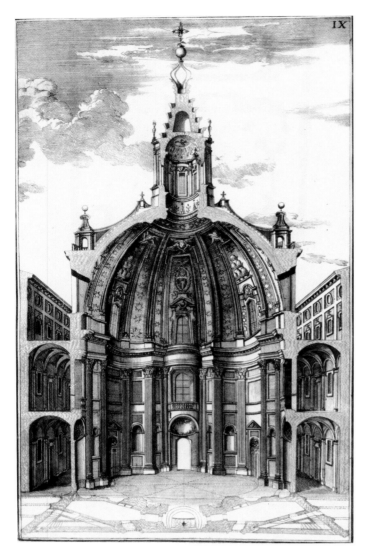

17-21. Francesco Borromini. Section, S. Ivo, Rome. Begun 1642

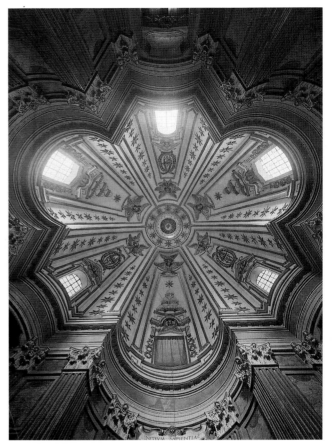

17-22. Dome of S. Ivo

and convex surfaces makes the entire structure seem elastic, as if pulled out of shape by pressures that no previous building could have withstood. The plan is a pinched oval that suggests a distended and half-melted Greek cross, as if it had been drawn on rubber. The inside of the coffered dome, like the plan, looks "stretched": if the tension were relaxed, it would snap back to normal. There is nevertheless an underlying logic, which follows a musical sequence very much like a fugue in structure.

The facade, designed almost 30 years later, shows the influence of Cortona's Ss. Luca e Martina, but here the pressures and counterpressures reach their maximum intensity. Borromini merges architecture and sculpture in a way that must have shocked Bernini. The statues above the entrance appear to emerge like actors entering a stage from behind a thin screen. We have caught a glimpse of this theatricality once before, on Vasari's Uffizi loggia (fig. 14-23), but the ensemble lacks the unity and dramatic presence created by Borromini's concentrated facade. (The sculp-

tures, interestingly enough, are by Bernini's assistant Antonio Raggi.) S. Carlo alle Quattro Fontane established the architect's fame. "Nothing similar," wrote the head of the religious order for which the church was built, "can be found anywhere in the world. This is attested by the foreigners who . . . try to procure copies of the plan. We have been asked for them by Germans, Flemings, Frenchmen, Italians, Spaniards, and even Indians."

The design of Borromini's next church, S. Ivo (figs. 17-21 and 17-22), is more compact but equally daring. He had originally been recommended for the project while working under Bernini but came to it only years later. The entire design is again dominated by a concave-convex "musical" rhythm, which focuses our attention on the altar. S. Ivo is a central-plan church based on a star-hexagon. Borromini may have been thinking of octagonal structures, such as S. Vitale, Ravenna (compare figs. 8-25–8-28), but the result is completely novel. The space is not subdivided into a tall, domed "nave" ringed by an ambulatory or chapels. Instead,

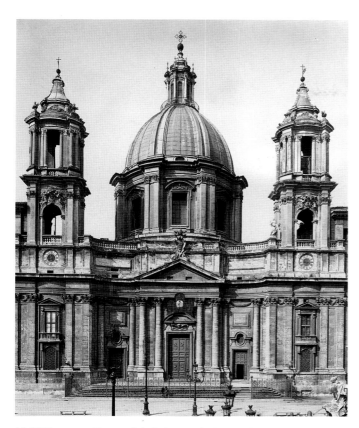

17-23 Francesco Borromini. S. Agnese in Piazza Navona, Rome. 1653–63

Borromini covered all of it with one great dome that continues the star-hexagon pattern up to the circular base of the lantern.

A third project by Borromini, S. Agnese in Piazza Navona (fig. 17-23), is of special interest as a High Baroque critique of St. Peter's. There were two problems that Maderno had been unable to solve. Although his facade forms an impressive unit with Michelangelo's dome when seen from a distance, the dome is gradually hidden by the new facade as we approach the church. Furthermore, the towers he planned for each end posed formidable structural difficulties. After his first attempt to overcome these problems failed, Bernini proposed making the towers freestanding but was forced to abandon the plan when it was heavily criticized on technical grounds by Borromini. The facade of S. Agnese is a brilliant solution to both of these issues. Borromini took over the project, which had been begun by another architect, Carlo Rainaldi (1611–1691), the year before, and completely recast it without completely abandoning the Greek-cross plan. The lower part is adapted from the facade of St. Peter's, but it curves inward, so that the dome (a tall, slender version of Michelangelo's) functions as the upper part of the facade. The dramatic juxtaposition of concave and convex, so characteristic of Borromini, is emphasized by the two towers, which form a monumental group with the dome. Such towers were also originally planned for St. Peter's by Bramante (see fig. 13-10) and also by

Bernini, but they would have been freestanding. Once again Borromini joins Gothic and Renaissance features—the two-tower facade and the dome—into a remarkably elastic compound.

CARLO RAINALDI; CARLO FONTANA. In the mid-1660s there was the beginning of the same kind of reconciliation between the High Baroque and Baroque classicism in Roman architecture that can be found in the painting of Carlo Maratta (see above); it also has a counterpart in the sculpture of Ercole Ferrata (1610–1686), who studied with both Algardi and Bernini (see below). Its leading representatives were Rainaldi and Carlo Fontana (1634–1714). Rainaldi was essentially an academic classicist, who discreetly combined Bernini's classicism with aspects of the High Baroque and even Mannerism. Because he was a chameleon who could adapt to the demands of any style, he was often commissioned to complete unfinished projects, such as the facade of S. Andrea della Valle, Rome (1661–65), which had been begun by Carlo Maderno and was left abandoned for over 30 years following his death. Despite his undeniable competence, he was replaced by architects of greater ability more than once—not only Borromini but also Bernini himself.

Fontana became the most important architect of his generation in Rome when he was appointed Bernini's successor at St. Peter's by Pope Innocent XI. Before becoming a master in 1665, he had worked in the studios of Cortona, Rainaldi, and Bernini. Perhaps he found the contrast between Cortona and Bernini too great, for it was the tepid manner of Rainaldi that affected him the most. Curiously enough, his church S. Marcello al Corso in Rome (1682–83) has sometimes been assigned to Rainaldi, and indeed it is very close to the latter's work in its ungainly combination of warring elements both inside and out. This détente style, which soon came to dominate Roman architecture, permitted little individuality. Fontana was nevertheless a gifted teacher, and some of the most important architects of the next generation—including Johann Fischer von Erlach and Filippo Juvarra (see pages 635 and 637)—studied with him, although there is hardly a trace of his influence on their work. The impact of Rainaldi and Fontana proved greatest in France, with its strong classical tradition and close ties to Rome.

GAURINO GAURINI. The new ideas introduced by Borromini were developed further not in Rome but in Turin, the capital of Savoy, which became the creative center of Baroque architecture in Italy toward the end of the seventeenth century. In 1666 Guarino Guarini (1624–1683), Borromini's most brilliant successor, was called to Turin as an engineer and mathematician by the duke Carlo Emanuele II. Guarini was a Theatine monk whose genius was grounded in philosophy and mathematics. His design for the facade of the Palazzo Carignano (figs. 17-24 and 17-25, page 576) for the House of Savoy repeats on a larger scale the undulating movement of S. Carlo alle Quattro Fontane (see fig. 17-18) using a highly individual vocabulary. Incredibly, the exterior of the building is entirely of brick, down to the last detail, as was Borromini's Oratory of S. Filippo Neri (1637–40), which Guarini had seen during his novitiate in Rome in 1639–47.

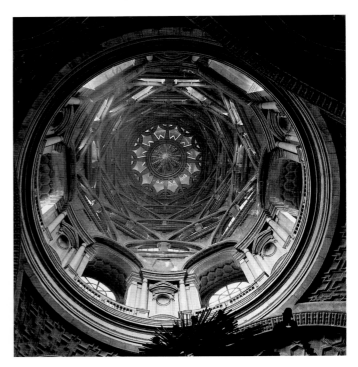

17-26. Guarino Guarini. Dome of the Chapel of the Holy Shroud, Turin Cathedral. 1668–94

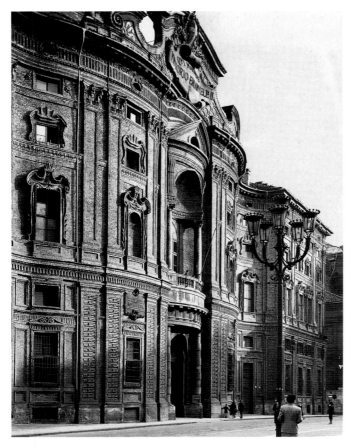

17-24. Guarino Guarini. Facade of Palazzo Carignano, Turin. Begun 1679

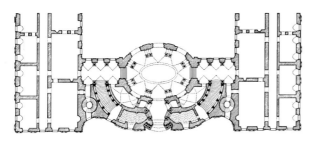

17-25. Plan of Palazzo Carignano

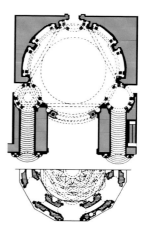

17-27. Plan of the Chapel of the Holy Shroud and of the dome

Even more extraordinary is Guarini's dome of the Chapel of the Holy Shroud, a round structure attached to Turin Cathedral (figs. 17-26 and 17-27). The tall drum, with alternating windows and tabernacles, consists of familiar Borrominian motifs. Yet it ushers us into a realm of pure illusion completely unlike anything by the earlier architect, for beyond it we enter a realm of pure illusion. The interior surface of the dome of S. Carlo alle Quattro Fontane, although dematerialized by light and a honeycomb of fanciful coffers, was still recognizable (see fig. 17-20). But here the surface has disappeared in a maze of ribs, inspired by Moorish architecture, which Guarini had studied while working in Messina, Sicily, during 1660–62. As a result, we find ourselves staring into a huge kaleidoscope. Above this seemingly endless funnel of space hovers the dove of the Holy Spirit within a 12-point star.

Guarini's dome retains the symbolic meaning of the Dome of Heaven in Sangallo's church of Sta. Maria delle Carceri (see page 430; figs. 12-35, 12-36, and 12-37). However, the objective harmony of the Renaissance has become subjective, a compelling experience of the infinite close to the Gothic mysticism of Abbot Suger's infinite (see pages 303–304). If Borromini's style at times suggests a fusion of Gothic and Renaissance, Guarini takes the next step. In his writings, Guarini contrasts the "muscular" architecture of the ancients with the effect of Gothic churches, which appear to stand only by means of some kind of miracle, and he expresses equal admiration for both. This attitude corresponds exactly to his own practice. By using the most advanced mathematical techniques of his day, he achieved wonders even greater than the seeming weightlessness of Gothic structures. The dome itself, for example, is on three pendentives instead of the usual four—a completely fresh approach to a traditional form that required a thorough command of structural engineering. He thus helped to pave the way for Soufflot and the rationalist movement in the next century (see pages 686–87).

SCULPTURE IN ITALY

GIANLORENZO BERNINI. We have already encountered Gianlorenzo Bernini as an architect. It is now time to consider him as a sculptor, although the two aspects are never far apart in his work. [See Primary Sources, no. 56, page 653.] He was trained by his father, Pietro Bernini (1562–1629), a sculptor of considerable ability who worked in Florence, Naples, and Rome. His work looks back further to statues by Leone Leoni, Annibale Fontana, and Guglielmo della Porta—artists whose names are all but forgotten today except by specialists but who made important contributions that paved the way for the Baroque. Bernini's style was thus a direct outgrowth of Mannerist sculpture in many ways, but this debt does not explain his revolutionary qualities.

As in the tabernacle for St. Peter's (see fig. 17-16), we can often see a strong relationship between Bernini's sculpture and antiquity. If we compare Bernini's *David* (fig. 17-28) with Michelangelo's (see fig. 13-12) and ask which is closer to the Pergamum frieze or *The Laocoön Group* (see figs. 5-76 and 5-78), our vote must go to Bernini, whose sculpture shares with Hellenistic works that unison of body and spirit, of motion and emotion, which Michelangelo so consciously avoids. This does not mean that Michelangelo (who had witnessed the Lacoön's unearthing) is more classical than Bernini. It shows, rather, that both the Baroque and the High Renaissance drew different lessons from ancient art.

Bernini's *David* is in no sense an echo of *The Laocoön Group.* What makes it Baroque is the implied presence of Goliath. Unlike earlier statues of David, including Donatello's (see fig. 12-6), Bernini's is conceived not as a self-contained figure but as half of a pair, his entire action focused on his adversary. Did Bernini, we wonder, plan a statue of Goliath to complete the group? He never did, nor did he need to. His *David* tells us clearly enough where he sees the enemy. Consequently, the space between David and his invisible opponent is charged with energy—it "belongs" to the statue.

Bernini's *David* shows us the distinctive feature of Baroque sculpture: its new, active relationship with the surrounding space. It rejects self-sufficiency in favor of the illusion of a presence or force implied by the action of the statue. Because it so often presents an "invisible complement" (like the Goliath of Bernini's *David*), Baroque statues attempt pictorial effects that were traditionally outside the realm of monumental sculpture. Such a charging of space with energy is, in fact, a key feature of Baroque art. Caravaggio had achieved it in his *St. Matthew* with the aid of a sharply focused beam of light. Indeed, Baroque art does not make a clear-cut distinction between sculpture and painting. And as we have seen on the ceiling of Il Gesù (fig. 17-13), both arts may even be combined with architecture to form a compound illusion, like that of the stage.

Bernini had a passionate interest in the theater and was an innovative scene designer. Thus he was at his best when he could merge architecture, sculpture, and painting. His masterpiece in this vein is the Cornaro Chapel in the church of Sta. Maria della Vittoria, containing the famous group *The Ecstasy of St. Theresa* (fig. 17-29, page 558). Theresa of Avila, one of the great saints of the Counter Reformation (see page 548), had described how an angel pierced her heart with a flaming golden arrow: "The pain

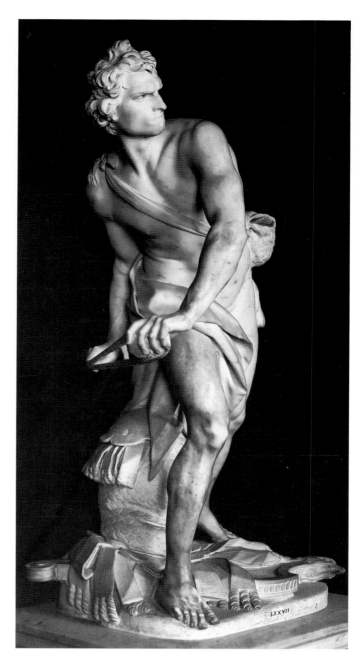

17-28. Gianlorenzo Bernini. *David.* 1623. Marble, lifesize. Galleria Borghese, Rome

was so great that I screamed aloud; but at the same time I felt such infinite sweetness that I wished the pain to last forever. It was not physical but psychic pain, although it affected the body as well to some degree. It was the sweetest caressing of the soul by God."

Bernini has made this visionary experience as sensuously real as Correggio's *Jupiter and Io* (see fig. 14-11), and the saint's rapture is obvious. (In a different context the angel could be Cupid.) The two figures on their floating cloud are lit from a hidden window above, so that they seem almost dematerialized. The viewer thus experiences them as visionary. The "invisible complement" here, less specific than David's but equally important, is the force that carries the figures toward heaven and causes the turbulence of their drapery. Its divine nature is suggested by the golden rays, which come from a source high above the altar. In an illusionistic fresco by Guidobaldo Abbatini on the vault of the chapel, the glory

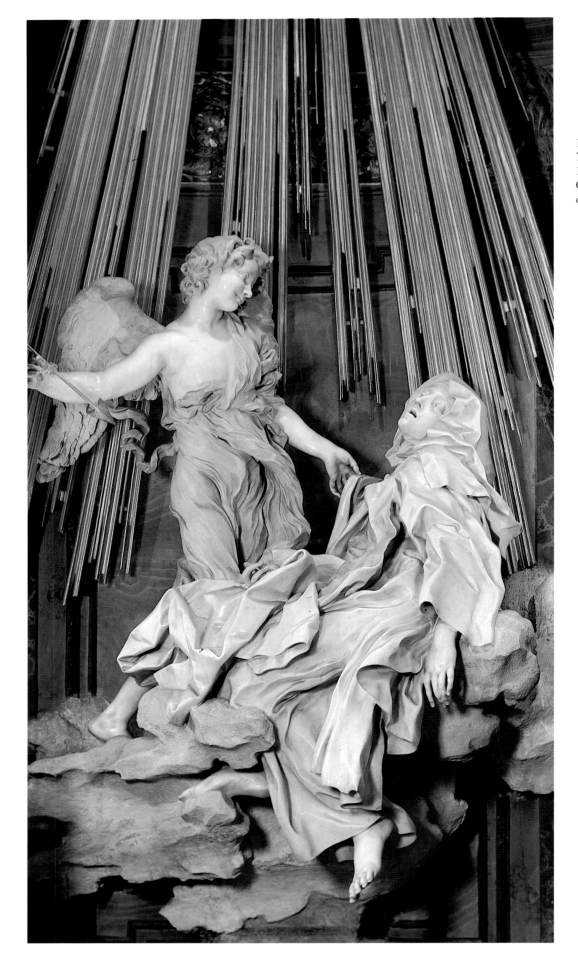

17-29. Gianlorenzo Bernini. *The Ecstasy of St. Theresa.* 1645–52. Marble, lifesize. Cornaro Chapel, Sta. Maria della Vittoria, Rome

of the heavens is revealed as a dazzling burst of light from which tumble clouds of jubilant angels (fig. 17-30). This celestial explosion gives force to the thrusts of the angel's arrow and makes the ecstasy of the saint believable.

To complete the illusion, Bernini even provides a built-in audience for his "stage." On the sides of the chapel are balconies resembling theater boxes that contain marble figures depicting members of the Cornaro family, who also witness the vision. Their space and ours are the same, and thus are part of everyday reality, while the saint's ecstasy, which is framed in a niche, occupies a space that is real but beyond our reach.

Finally, the ceiling fresco represents the infinite space of Heaven. We may recall that *The Burial of Count Orgaz* and its setting also form a whole that includes three levels of reality (see page 502). Yet there is a fundamental difference between the two chapels. El Greco's Mannerism evokes an ethereal vision in which only the stone slab of the sarcophagus is "real," in contrast to Bernini's Baroque staging, where the distinction nearly breaks down. It would be easy to dismiss *The Ecstasy of St. Theresa* as a theatrical display, but Bernini also was a devout Catholic who believed (as did Michelangelo) that he was inspired directly by God. Like the Spiritual Exercises of Ignatius of Loyola, which Bernini practiced, his religious sculpture is intended to help the viewer identify with miraculous events through a vivid appeal to the senses. Theatricality in the service of faith was basic to the Counter Reformation, which often referred to the Church as the theater of human life: it took the Baroque to bring this ideal to life.

Bernini was steeped in Renaissance humanism. Central to his sculpture is the role of gesture and expression in arousing emotion. While these devices were also important to the Renaissance (compare Leonardo), Bernini uses them with a freedom that seems anticlassical. However, he essentially followed the concept of decorum, and he planned his effects carefully by varying them in accordance with his subject (see box page 581). Unlike the Frenchman Nicolas Poussin (whom he respected, as he did Annibale Carracci), Bernini did this for the sake of expressive impact rather than conceptual clarity. The approaches of the two artists were diametrically opposed as well. For Bernini, antiquity served as no more than a point of departure for his own inventiveness, whereas for Poussin it was a standard of comparison. It is nevertheless characteristic of the Baroque that Bernini's theories were far more orthodox than his art. Thus he often sided with the classicists against his fellow High Baroque artists, especially Pietro da Cortona, who, like Raphael before him, also made an important contribution to architecture and was a rival in that sphere.

ALESSANDRO ALGARDI. It is no less ironic that Cortona was the closest friend of the sculptor Alessandro Algardi (1596–1654), who is regarded as the leading classical sculptor of the Italian Baroque and the only serious rival to Bernini in ability. His main contribution is *The Meeting of Pope Leo I and Attila* (fig. 17-31, page 580), done while he replaced Bernini at St. Peter's during the papacy of Innocent X. It introduces a new kind of high relief that soon became widely popular. The scene depicts the Huns under Attila being driven away from a threatened attack on Rome in 452, a fateful event in the early history

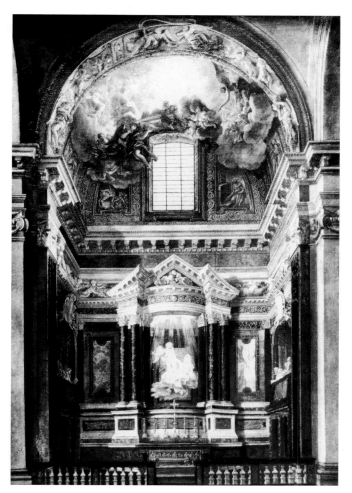

17-30. *The Cornaro Chapel.* 18th-century painting. Staatliches Museum, Schwerin, Germany

of Christianity when its very survival was at stake. (The actual event was very different: Leo persuaded the Huns not to attack, just as he did the Vandals three years later.) The subject revives one that is familiar to us from antiquity: the victory over barbarian forces (compare fig. 5-73). Now, however, it is the church, not civilization, that triumphs, and the victory is spiritual rather than military.

The commission was given for a sculpture, because water condensation caused by the location in an old doorway of St. Peter's made a painting impossible. Never before had an Italian sculptor attempted such a large relief—it stands nearly 28 feet high. The problems posed by translating a pictorial conception (it had been treated by Raphael in one of the Vatican Stanze) into a relief on this gigantic scale were formidable. If Algardi has not succeeded in resolving every detail, his achievement is stupendous nonetheless. By varying the depth of the carving, he nearly convinces us that the scene takes place in the same space as ours. The foreground figures are in such high relief that they seem detached from the background. To emphasize the effect, the stage on which they are standing projects several feet beyond its surrounding niche. Thus Attila seems to rush out toward us in fear and astonishment as he flees the vision of the two apostles defending the faith. The result is surprisingly persuasive in both visual and expressive terms.

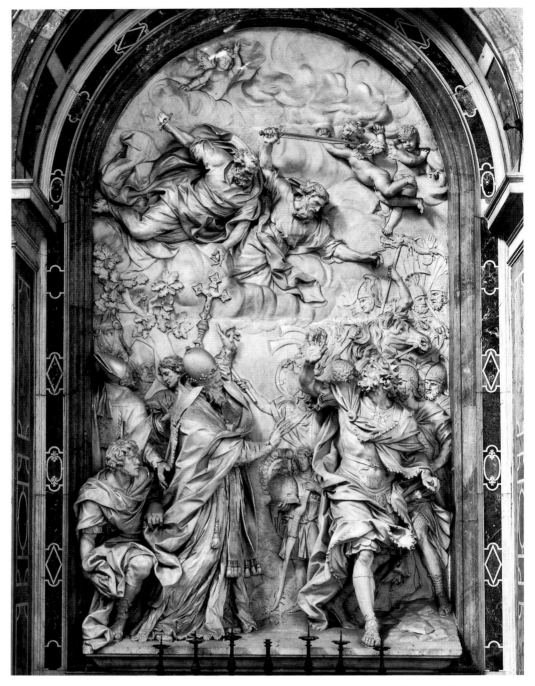

17-31. Alessandro Algardi. *The Meeting of Pope Leo I and Attila.* 1646. Marble, 28'1¾" x 16'2½"
(8.5 x 4.9 m). St. Peter's, The Vatican, Rome

Such illusionism is quintessentially Baroque. So is the intense drama, which is heightened by the twisting poses and theatrical gestures of the figures. Algardi was obviously touched by Bernini's genius. Strangely enough, the relief is partly a throwback to an *Assumption of the Virgin* of 1606–10 in Sta. Maria Maggiore by Bernini's father, Pietro. Only in his observance of the three traditional levels of relief carving (low, middle, and high, instead of continuously variable depth), his preference for frontal poses, and his restraint in dealing with the violent action can Algardi be called a classicist, and then purely in a relative sense. Clearly we must not draw the distinction between the High Baroque and Baroque classicism too sharply in sculpture any more than in painting.

PAINTING IN SPAIN

At the height of its political and economic power during the sixteenth century, Spain had produced great saints and writers, but no artists of the first rank. Nor did El Greco's presence stimulate native talent. The reason is that the Catholic church, the main source of patronage in Spain, was extremely conservative, while the Spanish court and most of the aristocracy held native artists in low esteem, so that they preferred to employ foreign painters whenever possible—above all Titian. Thus the main influences came from Italy and the Netherlands, which was then ruled by Spain.

JUAN SANCHEZ COTÁN. Inspired by the example of Aertsen and other Netherlandish painters, Spanish artists began to develop their own versions of still life in the 1590s. We see the distinctive character of this tradition in the example (fig. 17-32) by Juan Sanchez Cotán (1561–1627). This minor religious artist is remembered today as one of the first and most remarkable members of the Toledo school of still-life painters. In contrast to the lavish display of food or luxury objects often found in Northern pictures, our painting has such a clear order and stark simplicity that we cannot help wondering what symbolic significance the artist meant to convey. The combination of direct sunlight and impenetrable darkness, of painstaking realism and abstract form, creates a memorable image in which even these humble fruits and vegetables become sacred examples of God's work.

Although he probably used North Italian paintings as his point of departure, Sanchez Cotán's still lifes make one think of Caravaggio, whose effect on Spanish art, however, is not found until considerably later. We do not know exactly how Caravaggism was transmitted. The likeliest source was Naples, where Caravaggio had fled to safety, which was under Spanish rule. His principal follower there was Jusepe Ribera (see page 561), but too little is known of his activity before about 1625 for us to trace his influence on early Spanish Baroque art in detail. In any case, the impact of Caravaggism was felt especially in Seville, the home of the most important Spanish Baroque painters before 1640.

DIEGO VELÁZQUEZ. Diego Velázquez (1599–1660) painted in a Caravaggesque vein during his early years in Seville. His interests at that time centered on scenes of people eating and drinking

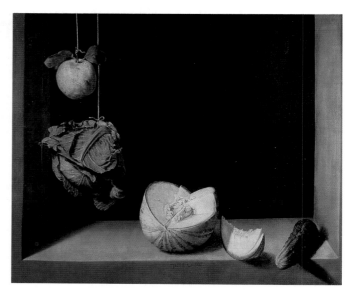

17-32. Juan Sanchez Cotán. *Quince, Cabbage, Melon, and Cucumber.* c. 1602. Oil on canvas, 27⅛ x 33¼" (68.8 x 84.4 cm). San Diego Museum of Art

rather than religious themes. Known as *bodegónes,* such paintings are the distinctive Spanish counterparts of Dutch breakfast pieces (see fig. 18-24). They evolved from the paintings of table-top displays brought to Spain by Flemish artists in the early seventeenth century. *The Water Carrier of Seville* (fig. 17-33, page 582), which Velázquez painted at age 20 under the apparent influence of Ribera, already shows his genius. His powerful grasp of

BAROQUE THEATER IN ITALY AND SPAIN

Besides the opera, the most popular form of Italian theater in the seventeenth century was the *commedia dell'arte,* which arose after 1570 as earlier sixteenth-century written farce declined. It then spread quickly throughout Europe, especially to France. The *commedia* actors improvised dialogue on a rough plot outline, taking the roles of stock characters—the innocent young girl, the impoverished youth, the braggart captain, the pedantic doctor—in age-old scenarios of love and intrigue. The comedic characters were clever servants, often called *zanni* ("Johnny" in the Venetian dialect—from which the English word *zany* is derived), who delighted their audiences by outwitting their masters and other figures of authority. The best known of these *zanni* were Harlequin, Mezzetin, and Pulcinella, whose name and huge nose survived into the twentieth century in the character of Punch of Punch-and-Judy puppet shows. The Italian *commedia* was also the source of modern slapstick and burlesque comedy. Its success depended on the close identification of the actors with their roles, which they rarely changed except in advanced age, so that they became one and the same in life and in art. Although the *commedia dell'arte* remained popular for 200 years, its heyday was over by 1650, when its creativity began to wane.

Under Philip III and Phillip IV the seventeenth century in Spain was the golden age of theater, as it was of art. It began around 1580 with the plays of Juan de la Cueva (c. 1543–1610) and Miguel de Cervantes (1547–1616), the author of *Don Quixote,* but its greatest writer was Lope de Vega (1562–1635), who claimed to have scripted more than 1,200 dramas and comedies. In its combination of worldliness and religion, Vega's work reflects the character and social order of Spain, which centered on the often-conflicting demands of love, honor, church, and responsibility among the social classes. The plots are lively and the writing fluid, but characters tend to be rather conventional because they conform to established codes. Tirso de Molina (1580–1648), a member of the Mercedarian order, was likewise prolific: he professed to have written 300 plays by 1621, of which 80 survive, but he is known primarily for introducing the legend of Don Juan in the *Trickster of Seville.* Vega's successor, Pedro Calderón de la Barca (1600–1681), wrote mainly cape-and-sword comedies for the court, which he served as Master of Revels, as well as religious dramas (called *autos sacramentales*) after he was ordained a priest toward the end of his life. Throughout the century, both types were performed at court and in public theaters by professional actors employed by local municipalities.

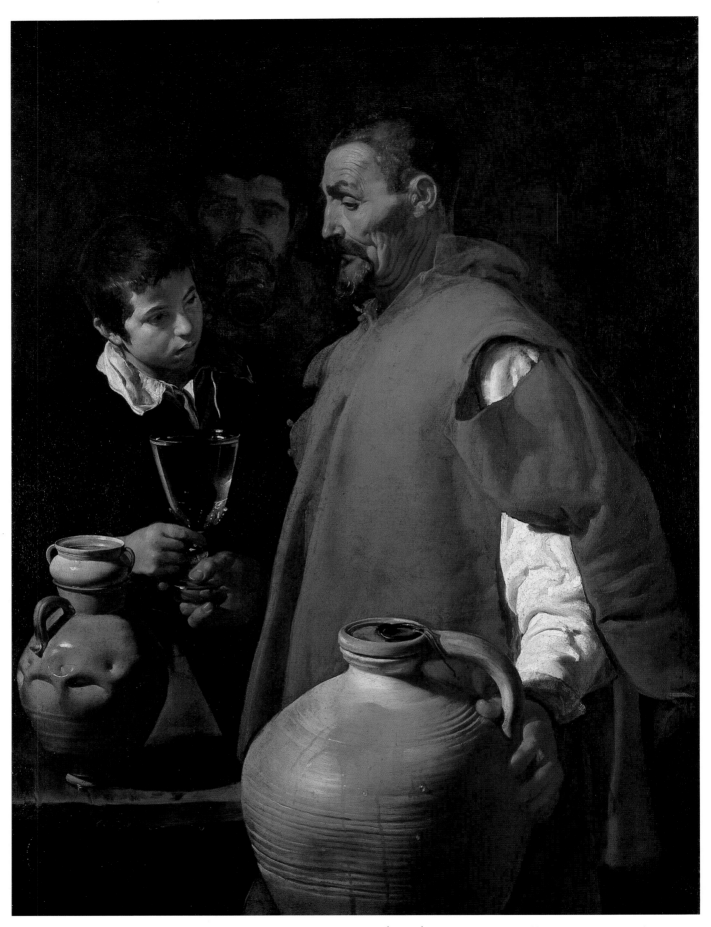

17-33. Diego Velázquez. *The Water Carrier of Seville*. c. 1619. Oil on canvas, 41½ x 31½" (105.3 x 80 cm). Wellington Museum, London

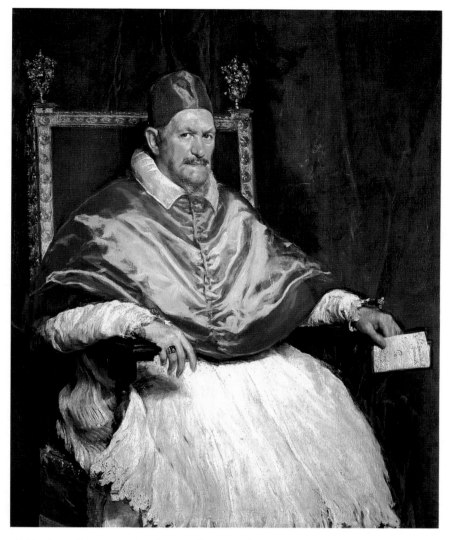

17-34. Diego Velázquez. *Pope Innocent X*. 1650. Oil on canvas,
55 x 45 ¼" (139.7 x 115 cm). Galleria Doria Pamphili, Rome

individual character and dignity gives this everyday scene the solemn spirit of a ritual—perhaps with good reason. The scene is related to Giving Drink to the Thirsty, one of the Seven Acts of Mercy, a popular theme among Caravaggesque painters of the day.

In the late 1620s Velázquez was appointed court painter to Philip IV, whose reign from 1621 to 1665 was the great age of painting in Spain. Much of the credit must go to the Duke of Olivares, who largely restored Spain's fortunes and supported an ambitious program of artistic patronage to proclaim the monarchy's greatness. Upon moving to Madrid, Velázquez quickly displaced the mediocre Florentines who had enjoyed the favor of Philip III and his minister, the Duke of Lerma. A skilled courtier, the artist soon became a favorite of the king, whom he served as chamberlain. Velázquez spent the rest of his life in Madrid painting mainly portraits of the royal family. The earlier of these still have the strong division of light and dark and the clear outlines of his Seville period, but his work soon acquired a new fluency and richness.

During his visit to the Spanish court on a diplomatic mission in 1628, the Flemish painter Peter Paul Rubens (see page 587) helped Velázquez discover the beauty of the many Titians in the king's collection. The magnificent portrait of Pope Innocent X

(fig. 17-34), painted in 1650 while Velázquez was visiting Italy, is meant to evoke the great tradition of the papal portraits of Raphael (see fig. 13-36). However, its fluid brushwork and vivid color are derived from Titian (compare fig. 13-42). The sitter's gaze, piercingly focused on the viewer, conveys a passionate and powerful personality so characteristic of the Baroque.

The Maids of Honor (fig. 17-35) shows Velázquez's mature style at its fullest. Both a group portrait and a genre scene, it might be subtitled "the artist in his studio," for Velázquez depicts himself at work on a huge canvas. In the center is the Princess Margarita, who has just posed for him, among her playmates and maids of honor. The faces of her parents, the king and queen, appear in the mirror on the back wall. They have just stepped into the room, to see the scene exactly as we do. Through their presence the canvas celebrates Velázquez's position as royal painter and his knighthood in the Order of Santiago, whose red cross he proudly wears on his tunic.

The painting reveals Velázquez's fascination with light. The varieties of direct and reflected light in *The Maids of Honor* are almost limitless. The artist challenges us to match the mirror image against the paintings on the same wall, and against the "picture"

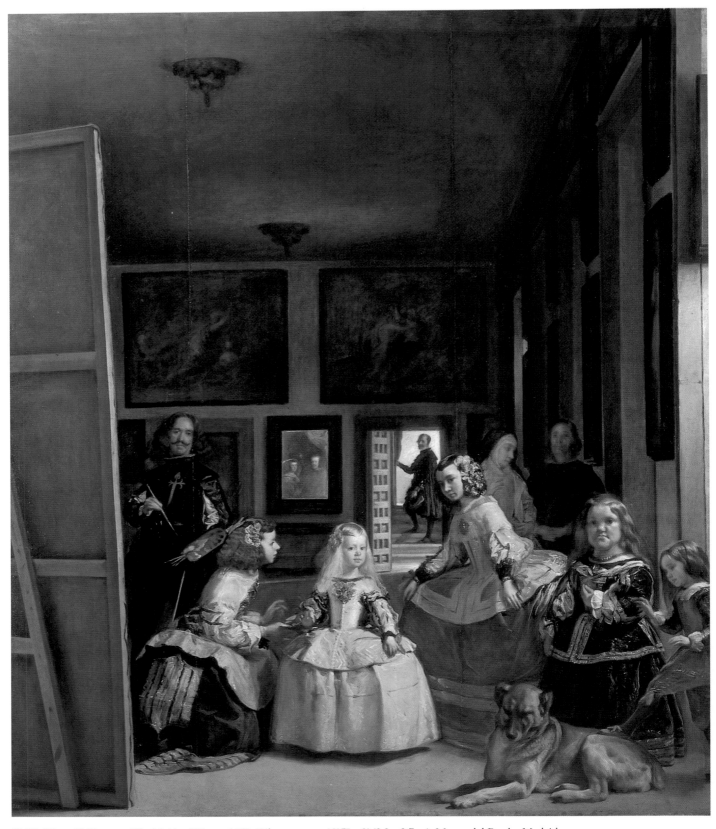

17-35. Diego Velázquez. *The Maids of Honor.* 1656. Oil on canvas, 10'5" x 9' (3.2 x 2.7 m). Museo del Prado, Madrid

of the man in the open doorway. Although the side lighting and strong contrasts of light and dark still suggest the influence of Caravaggio, Velázquez's technique is far more subtle, with delicate glazes setting off the impasto of the highlights. The glowing colors have a Venetian richness, but the brushwork is even freer and sketchier than Titian's. Velázquez explored the optical qualities of light more fully than any other painter of his time. His aim is to represent the movement of light itself and the infinite range of its effects on form and color. For Velázquez, as for Jan Vermeer in Holland (see page 605), light *creates* the visible world.

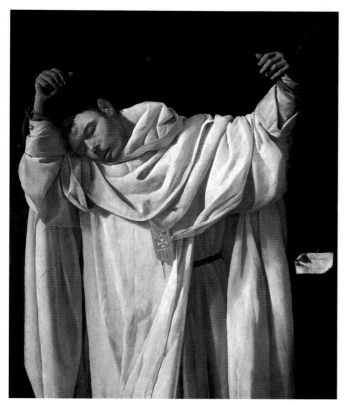

17-36. Francisco de Zurbarán. *St. Serapion.* 1628.
Oil on canvas, 47 1/2 x 41" (120.7 x 104.1 cm).
Wadsworth Atheneum, Hartford, Connecticut
ELLA GALLUP SUMNER AND MARY CATLIN SUMNER COLLECTION

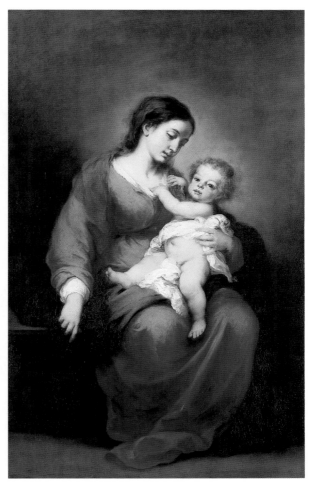

17-37. Bartolomé Esteban Murillo. *Virgin and Child.*
c. 1675–80. Oil on canvas, 65 1/4 x 43" (165.7 x 109.2 cm).
The Metropolitan Museum of Art, New York
ROGERS FUND, 1943

FRANCISCO ZURBARÁN. Francisco de Zurbarán (1598–1664) stands out among the painters of Seville for his quiet intensity. His most important works were done for monastic orders, and are filled with an ascetic piety that is uniquely Spanish. *St. Serapion* (fig. 17-36) shows an early member of the Mercedarians (Order of Mercy) who was brutally murdered by pirates in 1240 but canonized only a hundred years after this picture was painted. The canvas was placed as a devotional image in the funerary chapel of the order, which was originally dedicated to self-sacrifice.

The painting will remind us of Caravaggio. Zurbarán's saint, shown as a lifesize three-quarter-length figure, is both a hero and a martyr. The contrast between the white habit and the dark background gives the figure a heightened visual and expressive presence, so that the viewer contemplates the slain monk with a mixture of compassion and awe. Here pictorial and spiritual purity become one. The stillness creates a reverential mood that complements the stark realism. As a result, we identify with the strength of St. Serapion's faith rather than with his physical suffering. The absence of rhetorical pathos is what makes this image deeply moving.

BARTOLOMÉ ESTEBAN MURILLO. The work of Bartolomé Esteban Murillo (1617–1682), Zurbarán's successor as the leading painter in Seville, is the most cosmopolitan, as well as the most accessible, of any of the Spanish Baroque artists. For that reason, he had countless followers, whose pale imitations obscure his real achievement. He learned as much from Northern artists, including Rubens, Van Dyck, and Rembrandt, as he did from Italians such as Reni and Guercino. *The Virgin and Child* in figure 17-37 unites these influences in an image that nevertheless remains unmistakably Spanish in character. The haunting expressiveness of the faces has a gentle pathos that is more emotionally appealing than Zurbarán's austere pietism. This human warmth reflects a basic change in religious outlook. It is also an attempt to inject new life into standard devotional images that had been reduced to formulas in the hands of lesser artists. The extraordinary sophistication of Murillo's brushwork and the subtlety of his color show the influence of Velázquez. He succeeded so well that the vast majority of religious paintings in Spain and its South American colonies were derived from his for the next 150 years.

CHAPTER EIGHTEEN

The Baroque in Flanders and Holland

In 1581 the six northern provinces of the Netherlands, led by William the Silent of Nassau, declared their independence from Spain. Their rebellion had begun 15 years earlier against Catholicism and the attempt by Philip II to curtail local power. Spain soon recovered the southern Netherlands, called Flanders (now divided between France and Belgium). After a long struggle the United Provinces (today's Holland) gained their autonomy, which was recognized by the truce declared in 1609. Although hostilities broke out once more in 1621, the freedom of the Dutch was never again seriously in doubt. It was finally ratified by the Treaty of Münster, which ended the Thirty Years' War in 1648.

The division of the Netherlands had very different consequences for the economy, social structure, culture, and religion of the north and the south. After being sacked by Spanish troops in 1576, Antwerp, the leading port of the southern Netherlands, lost half its population. The city gradually regained its position as Flanders' commercial and artistic capital, although Brussels was the seat of government. As part of the Treaty of Münster, however, the Scheldt River leading to Antwerp's harbor was closed to shipping, thus crippling trade for the next two centuries. Because Flanders continued to be ruled by Spanish regents, who viewed themselves as the defenders of the true faith, its artists relied primarily on commissions from Church and State, but the aristocracy and wealthy merchants were also important patrons.

Holland, in contrast, was proud of its hard-won freedom. While the cultural links with Flanders remained strong, several factors encouraged the quick development of Dutch artistic traditions. Unlike Flanders, where all artistic activity radiated from Antwerp, Holland had a number of local schools of painting. Besides Amsterdam, the commercial capital, there were important artists in Haarlem, Utrecht, Leyden, Delft, and other towns. Thus Holland produced an almost bewildering variety of masters and styles.

The new nation was one of merchants, farmers, and seafarers, and its religion, Reformed Protestant, was iconoclastic. Hence Dutch artists rarely had the large-scale Church and State commissions that were available throughout the Catholic world. While city governments and civic bodies such as militias provided a certain amount of art patronage, their demands were limited. As a result, private collectors became the painters' chief source of support. This condition had already existed to some extent before (see page 548), but its full effect can be seen only after 1600. There was no shrinkage of output. On the contrary, the public developed such an appetite for pictures that the whole country became gripped by a kind of collector's mania. During a visit to Holland in 1641, the English traveler John Evelyn noted in his diary that "it is an ordinary thing to find a common farmer lay out two or three thousand pounds in this commodity. Their houses are full of them, and they vend them at their fairs to very great gain."

The result was an outpouring of artistic talent that can only be compared to Early Renaissance Florence. Pictures became a commodity, and their trade followed the law of supply and demand. Many artists produced for the market rather than for individual patrons. They were lured into becoming painters by hopes of success that often failed to materialize, and even the greatest masters were sometimes hard-pressed. (It was not unusual for an artist to keep an inn or run a small business on the side.) Yet they survived—less secure, but freer.

FLANDERS

PETER PAUL RUBENS. Although it was born in Rome, the Baroque style soon became international. The great Flemish painter Peter Paul Rubens (1577–1640) played a role of unique importance in this process. He finished what Dürer had started a hundred years earlier: the breakdown of the artistic barriers between North and South. Rubens' father was a prominent Antwerp Protestant who fled to Germany to escape Spanish persecution during the war of independence (see page 548). The family returned to Antwerp after his death, when Peter Paul was ten years old, and the boy grew up a devout Catholic. Trained by local painters, Rubens became a master in 1598, but developed a personal style only when he went to Italy two years later.

During his eight years in the south, he absorbed the Italian tradition far more completely than had any Northerner before him. He eagerly studied ancient sculpture, the masterpieces of the High Renaissance, and the work of Caravaggio and Annibale Carracci.

In fact, Rubens competed on even terms with the best Italians of his day and could well have made his career in Italy. When he returned to Flanders in 1608 because of his mother's illness, he meant the visit to be brief. His plans changed when he received a special appointment as court painter to the Spanish regent, which allowed him to set up a workshop in Antwerp that was exempt from local taxes and guild regulations. Rubens had the best of both worlds. Like Jan van Eyck (see page 514), he was valued at court not only as an artist but also as an adviser and emissary. Diplomatic errands gave him entry to the royal households of the major powers, where he received numerous commissions. Aided by a growing number of assistants, he was also free to carry out a huge volume of work for the city of Antwerp, the Church, and private patrons.

Rubens epitomized the Baroque ideal of the virtuoso for whom the entire universe is a stage. On the one hand, he was devoutly religious. On the other, he was a man of the world who succeeded in every arena by virtue of his character and ability. Rubens resolved the contradictions of the era through humanism, the union of faith and learning that was attacked by both the Reformation and the Counter Reformation. In his paintings as well, Rubens reconciled seemingly incompatible forces. His enormous intellect and vitality enabled him to unite the natural and supernatural, reality and fantasy, learning and spirituality. Thus his epic canvases defined the scope and the style of High Baroque painting. They possess a seemingly boundless energy and inventiveness, which, like his heroic nudes, express life at its fullest. The presentation of this heightened existence required the expanded arena that only Baroque theatricality could provide. Rubens' sense of drama was as highly developed as Bernini's. At the same time, he could be the most human of artists.

The Raising of the Cross (fig. 18-1), the first major altarpiece Rubens painted after his return to Antwerp, shows how much he was indebted to Italian art. The muscular figures, modeled to show their physical power and passionate feeling, recall the Sistine ceiling and the Farnese Gallery, while the lighting suggests Caravaggio's (see figs. 13-17, 17-1, and 17-2). In turn, the composition recalls that of Rosso's *Descent from the Cross* (fig. 14-1), but the greatest debt is ultimately to Titian (compare fig. 13-44). The panel nevertheless owes much of its success to Rubens' ability to combine Italian influences with Netherlandish ideas, which he updated in the process. The painting is more heroic in scale and conception than any previous Northern work, yet it is unthinkable without Rogier van der Weyden's *Descent from the Cross* (see fig. 15-10). Rubens is also a Flemish realist in such details as the foliage, the armor of the soldier, and the curly-haired dog in the foreground. These varied elements are integrated into a composition of tremendous force. The unstable pyramid of bodies, swaying precariously under the strain of the dramatic action, bursts the limits of the frame in a typically Baroque way, making the viewer feel like a participant in the action.

In the 1620s Rubens' style reached its climax in his huge decorative schemes for churches and palaces. The most famous is the cycle in the Luxembourg Palace in Paris glorifying the career of Marie de' Medici, the widow of Henri IV and mother of Louis XIII. Our illustration shows the artist's oil sketch for one episode: the young queen landing in Marseilles (fig. 18-2). This is hardly an exciting subject, yet Rubens has turned it into a spectacle of unpar-

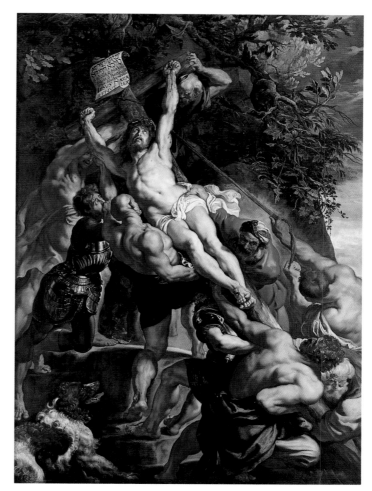

18-1. Peter Paul Rubens. *The Raising of the Cross.* 1609–10. Center panel of a triptych, 15'1" x 11'9⅝" (4.6 x 3.4 m). Antwerp Cathedral, Belgium

alleled splendor. As Marie de' Medici walks down the gangplank, Fame flies overhead sounding a triumphant blast on two trumpets. Neptune rises from the sea with his fish-tailed crew; having guarded the queen's journey, they rejoice at her arrival. Everything flows together here in swirling movement: heaven and earth, history and allegory. Even drawing and painting come together, for Rubens used oil sketches like this one to prepare his compositions. Unlike earlier artists, he preferred to design his pictures in terms of light and color from the start. (Most of his drawings are figure studies or portrait sketches.) This unified vision, which had been explored but never fully achieved by the great Venetians, was Rubens's most precious legacy to later painters.

Around 1630 the drama of Rubens' earlier work changed to a late style of lyrical tenderness inspired by Titian, whose work Rubens discovered anew in the royal palace while he visited Madrid in 1628 (see also page 583). *The Garden of Love* (fig. 18-3) is as glowing a tribute to life's pleasures as Titian's *Bacchanal* (see fig. 13-39). But these fashionable couples belong to the present, not to a golden age of the past, although they are playfully assaulted by swarms of cupids. The Garden of Love had been a feature of Northern painting ever since the courtly style of the International Gothic. The early versions, however, were genre scenes showing groups of young lovers in a garden. By merging this tradition with

Titian's classical mythologies, Rubens has created an enchanted realm where myth and reality become one.

The picture must have had special meaning for him, since he had just married a beautiful girl of 16. (His first wife died in 1626.) He also bought a country house, Château Steen, and led the leisurely life of a squire. This change renewed his interest in landscape painting, which he had practiced only occasionally before. Here, too, the power of his genius is undiminished. In *Landscape with the Château Steen* (fig. 18-4), a magnificent open space sweeps from the hunter and his prey in the foreground to the mist-veiled hills along the horizon. As a landscapist, Rubens again creates a synthesis from his Northern and Southern sources, for he is the heir of both Pieter Bruegel and Annibale Carracci (compare figs. 16-21 and 17-7).

ANTHONY VAN DYCK. Besides Rubens, only one Flemish Baroque artist won international stature. Anthony van Dyck (1599–1641) was that rarity among painters, a child prodigy. Before he was 20 he had become Rubens' most valued assistant. But like Rubens, he developed his mature style only after a stay in Italy.

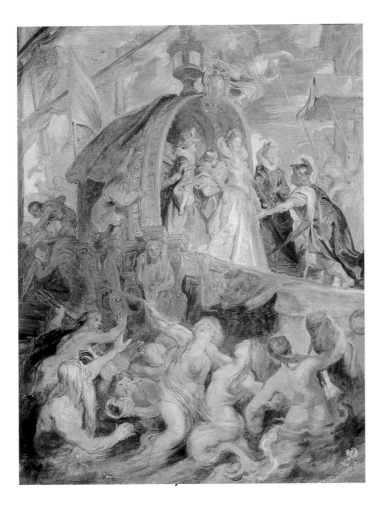

(LEFT) 18-2. Peter Paul Rubens. *Marie de' Medici, Queen of France, Landing in Marseilles.* 1622–23. Oil on panel, 25 x 19¾" (63.5 x 50.3 cm). Alte Pinakothek, Munich

(BELOW) 18-3. Peter Paul Rubens. *The Garden of Love.* c. 1638. Oil on canvas, 6'6" x 9'3½" (2 x 2.8 m). Museo del Prado, Madrid

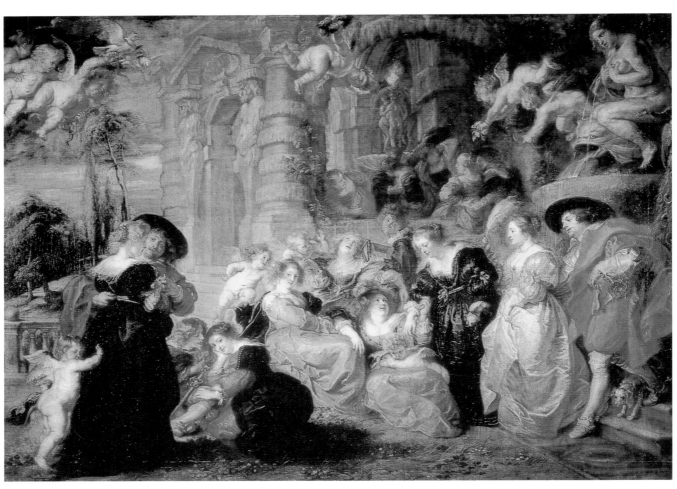

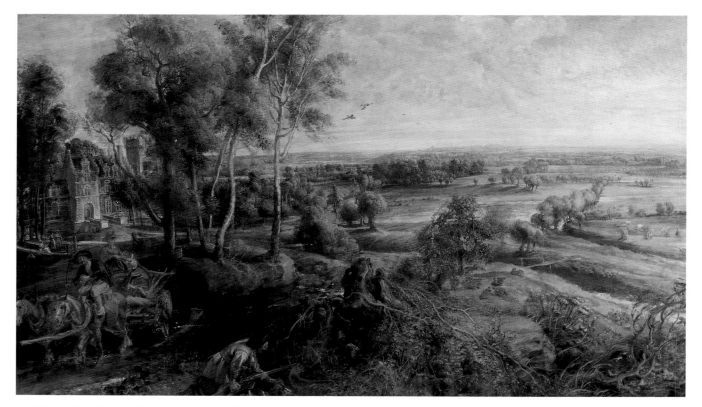

18-4. Peter Paul Rubens. *Landscape with the Château Steen.* 1636. Oil on panel, 4'5" x 7'9" (1.34 x 2.36 m). The National Gallery, London

As a history painter, Van Dyck was at his best in lyrical scenes of mythological love. *Rinaldo and Armida* (fig. 18-5) is taken from Torquato Tasso's immensely popular poem about the Crusades, *Jerusalem Freed* (1581), which gave rise to a new courtly ideal throughout Europe and inspired numerous operas as well as paintings (see box page 490). Van Dyck shows the sorceress falling in love with the Christian knight she had intended to slay. The canvas reflects the conception of the English monarch for whom it was painted. Charles I, a Protestant, had married the Catholic Henrietta Maria, sister of his main rival, the king of France. Charles found parallels in Tasso's epic. He saw himself as the virtuous ruler of a peaceful realm much like the Fortunate Isle where Armida brought Rinaldo. (Ironically, Charles' reign ended in civil war, and he was beheaded in 1649.) The artist tells his story of ideal love in the pictorial language of Titian and Veronese, but with an expressiveness and opulence that would have been the envy of any Venetian painter. The picture was so successful that it helped Van Dyck gain appointment to the English court two years later.

Van Dyck's fame rests mainly on the portraits he painted in London between 1632 and 1641. *Portrait of Charles I Hunting* (fig. 18-6) shows the king standing near a horse and two grooms against a landscape backdrop. Representing the sovereign at ease, the painting might be called a "dismounted equestrian portrait." It is less rigid than a formal state portrait, but hardly less grand, for the king remains in full command of the state, symbolized by the horse, which bows its head toward its master. The fluid movement of the setting complements the self-conscious elegance of the king's pose, which continues the stylized grace of Hilliard's

portraits (compare fig. 16-17). Van Dyck has brought the court portrait up to date by using Rubens and Titian as his points of departure. In the process, he created a new aristocratic portrait tradition that continued in England until the late eighteenth century and had considerable influence on the Continent as well.

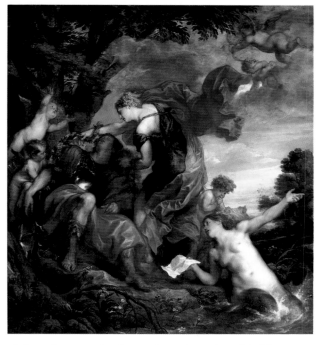

18-5. Anthony van Dyck. *Rinaldo and Armida.* 1629. Oil on canvas, 7'9" x 7'6" (2.36 x 2.24 m). The Baltimore Museum of Art

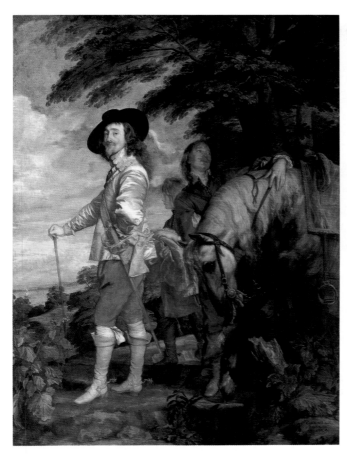

18-6. Anthony van Dyck. *Portrait of Charles I Hunting*. c. 1635. Oil on canvas, 8'11" x 6'11½" (2.7 x 2.1 m). Musée du Louvre, Paris

JACOB JORDAENS. Jacob Jordaens (1593–1678) was the successor to Rubens and Van Dyck as the leading artist in Flanders. Although he was never a member of Rubens' studio, he turned to Rubens for inspiration throughout his career. His most characteristic subjects are mythological themes depicting the revels of nymphs and satyrs. Like his eating and drinking scenes, which illustrate popular sayings, they reveal him to be a close observer of people. The dwellers of the woods in *Homage to Pomona (Allegory of Fruitfulness)* (fig. 18-7) inhabit an idyllic realm, untouched by human cares. The painterly execution shows a strong debt to Rubens, but the monumental figures lack Rubens' heroic vigor and instead possess a calm dignity distinctive to Jordaens.

JAN BRUEGHEL THE ELDER. Rubens' towering genius dominated Flemish painting. It touched every artist around him, including Jan Brueghel the Elder (1568–1625), the leader of the preceding generation, with whom he often collaborated. Brueghel was the principal heir to the tradition of his illustrious father, Pieter Bruegel the Elder (see page 551), whom he hardly knew. Jan also played an important role in the transition from Mannerism to the Baroque in the North. *Allegory of Earth* (fig. 18-8) shows one of his major contributions to Flemish art: the "paradise" landscape. It was part of a series devoted to the four elements, a common theme in Northern seventeenth-century painting, each with a biblical or mythological subject. Barely visible in the background is the expulsion of Adam and Eve from the Garden of Eden, a

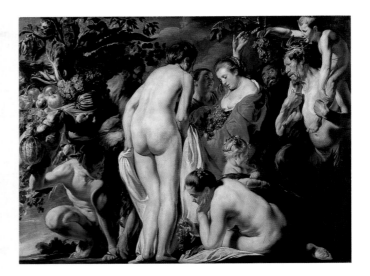

18-7. Jacob Jordaens. *Homage to Pomona (Allegory of Fruitfulness)*. c. 1623. Oil on canvas, 5'10⅞" x 7'10⅞" (1.8 x 2.4 m). Musées Royaux d'Art et d'Histoire, Brussels.

Besides scenes from fable and mythology, in the first half of the 1620s Jordaens painted two Allegories of fruitfulness: Homage to Pomona *and* Homage to Ceres. *The activities of country folk in their lush meadows or convivial farmsteads, together with the world of rural deities, satyrs and nymphs, were a favourite source of inspiration which Jordaens used again and again to produce paintings full of light and air and of healthy, quasi-animal life. The* Allegories of fruitfulness *are perhaps the clearest illustrations of this preference. True symbols of Jordaens's spiritual and artistic nature, they are admirably suited to convey his exuberant sense of earthly pleasures, his love of things in full bloom, his delight in voluptuous female forms and in the profusion of nature's bounty in fields, gardens and orchards. This theme attracted him from the beginning of his career, and he continued to celebrate it throughout his life. . . .its most perfect expression is in the Brussels* Homage to Pomona *[fig. 18-7]— Pomona, the glorious nymph who was wooed by all the gods of field and forest for her beauty and skill in gardening and fruit-growing. Jordaens does not take much trouble to depict her attributes, which Rubens would on no account have omitted. He confines himself to placing a few bunch of grapes in her arms, but her form and her whole attitude radiates such an impression of fertility that no symbols are needed to convey his meaning. Nymphs, satyrs and a country-woman surround her, filling the scene with a wealth of imagery. In this wonderful picture, all the elements of which are bound together in perfect harmony, Jordaens made use of several borrowed features. The work owes much to the many mythological and allegorical scenes in which Rubens introduced nymphs and satyrs to evoke a similar though more exalted world.*

—Roger-Adolf d'Hulst. *Jacob Jordaens.* Translated by P. S. Falla. Ithaca: Cornell University Press, 1982, p. 107.

Belgian art historian **ROGER-ADOLF D'HULST** (b. 1917) held a number of important posts in Belgium, including as a civil engineer, curator, and professor. A figure of singular charm and learnedness, d'Hulst carried on the grand tradition of scholarship on Flemish art, which reaches from Max Rooses (1839–1914) to Julius Held (b. 1905). His book on Jordaens is, for all intents and purposes, definitive. His passages on *Homage to Pomona* are moving testimony to his unique understanding of that artist.

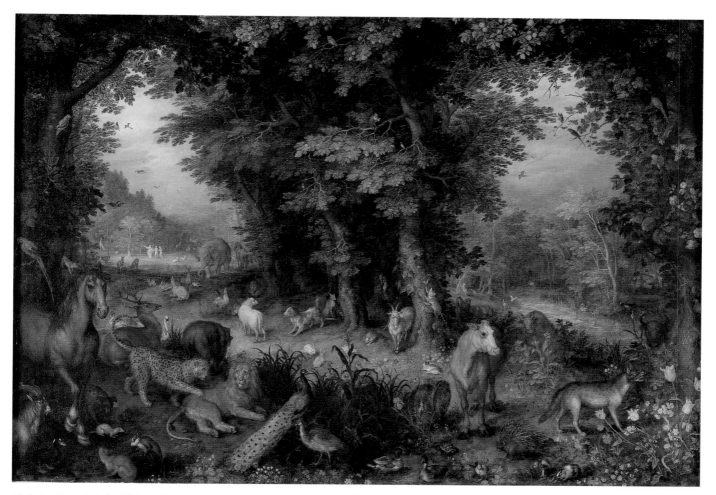

18-8. Jan Brueghel the Elder. *Allegory of Earth.* c. 1618. Oil on copper, 18⅛ x 26⅝" (46 x 67 cm). Musée du Louvre, Paris

remnant of the Mannerist inverted perspective (see page 551). Jan's meticulous realism makes his enchanting vision of this innocent realm utterly convincing. Like many older artists, he preferred painting on small copperplates, which offered a smooth, hard surface ideally suited to his jewel-like style.

FRANS SNYDERS. Brueghel also made an important contribution to flower painting. However, the development of the Baroque still life in Flanders was largely the responsibility of Frans Snyders (1579–1657), who studied with Jan's brother, Pieter Brueghel the Younger (1564–1638). Snyders concentrated on elaborate table still lifes piled high with food that express the Flemish gusto for life during the Baroque era. His splendid *Market Stall* (fig. 18-9, page 592) is a masterpiece of its kind. This early picture appeals frankly to the senses. The artist revels in the virtuoso application of paint to create the varied textures of the game. The scene is further enlivened by the youth picking the old man's pocket and the hens fighting in the foreground as a cat looks on from its safe retreat beneath the low bench.

Even here Rubens' influence can be found: the composition descends from one Snyders painted with Rubens, based on the latter's design, shortly after they had returned from Italy around 1609. *Market Stall* updates *The Meat Stall* of Pieter Aertsen (see fig. 16-20) into a Baroque style. Unlike Aertsen, Snyders subordinates every-

thing to the ensemble, which is characteristically Baroque in its lavishness and immediacy. There is a fundamental difference in content as well. No longer is there a religious subject in the background. Although an emblematic meaning has been suggested, the painting celebrates a time of peace and prosperity after the truce of 1609, when hunting was resumed in the replenished game preserves.

HOLLAND

HENDRICK TERBRUGGHEN. The Baroque style came to Holland from Antwerp through the work of Rubens, and from Rome through contact with Caravaggio's followers. Although most Dutch painters did not go to Italy, the majority of those who went in the early years of the century were from Utrecht, a town with strong Catholic traditions. It is not surprising that these artists were more attracted by Caravaggio's realism and "lay Christianity" than by Annibale Carracci's classicism. *The Calling of St. Matthew* by Hendrick Terbrugghen (1588–1629), the oldest and ablest of this group (fig. 18-10), recalls Caravaggio's earlier version (see fig. 17-2) in the sharp light, the dramatic timing, and the everyday detail. Missing, however, is the element of grandeur and simplicity. While it produced few major artists, the Utrecht School transmitted the style of Caravaggio to other Dutch masters, who then made better use of these new Italian ideas.

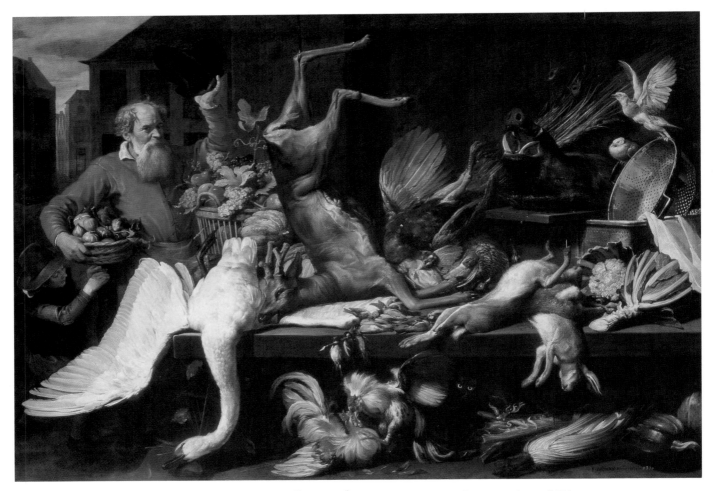

18-9. Frans Snyders. *Market Stall.* 1614. Oil on canvas, 6'11⅞" x 10'3⅝" (2.1 x 3 m). © 1991 The Art Institute of Chicago

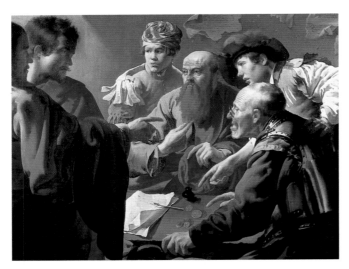

18-10. Hendrick Terbrugghen. *The Calling of St. Matthew.* 1621. Oil on canvas, 40 x 54" (101.5 x 137.2 cm). Centraal Museum, Utrecht, the Netherlands

FRANS HALS. One of the first to profit from this exchange was Frans Hals (1580/85–1666), the great portrait painter of Haarlem. He was born in Antwerp, and what little is known of his early work suggests the influence of Rubens. His mature style, however, is seen in *The Jolly Toper* (fig. 18-11), which perhaps represents an allegory of taste, one of the five senses, among the most popu-

lar themes in the seventeenth century. (The other senses are touch, sight, sound, and smell.) The painting combines Rubens' robustness with a focus on the dramatic moment that must be derived from the Caravaggesque artists of Utrecht. Everything here conveys complete spontaneity: the twinkling eyes and half-open mouth, the raised hand, the teetering wineglass, and—most important of all—the quick way of setting down the forms. Hals worked in dashing brushstrokes, each so clearly visible that we can almost count the total number of "touches." With this open, split-second technique, the completed picture has the immediacy of a sketch (compare our example by Rubens, fig. 18-2). The impression of a race against time is, of course, deceptive. Hals spent hours on this lifesize canvas, but he maintains the illusion of having done it all in the wink of an eye.

These qualities are even more forceful in the *Malle Babbe* (fig. 18-12), one of the artist's best genre pictures. A lower-class counterpart of *The Jolly Toper,* this folk character, half-witch (note the owl), half-village idiot, screams insults at other guests in a tavern. Hals seems to share their attitude of cruel amusement rather than sympathy, but his portrayal is masterfully sharp and his lightninglike brushwork has the brilliance of incredible skill.

In the artist's last canvases these pictorial fireworks are transformed into a severe style of great emotional depth. His group portrait, *The Women Regents of the Old Men's Home at Haarlem* (fig. 18-13), has an insight into human character matched only in

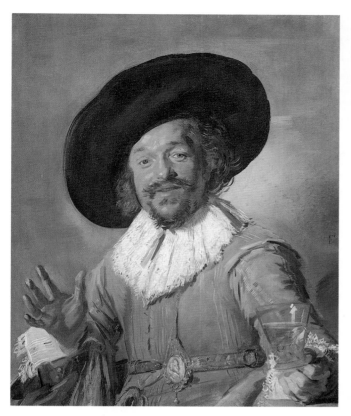

18-11. Frans Hals. *The Jolly Toper*. c. 1628–30. Oil on canvas, 31⅞ x 26¼" (81 x 66.6 cm). Rijksmuseum, Amsterdam

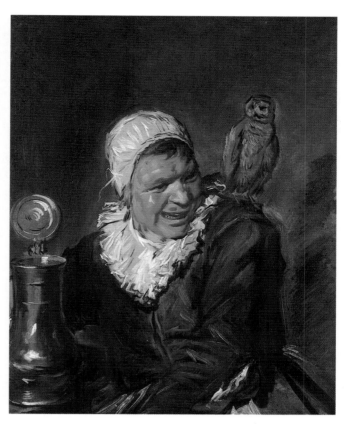

18-12. Frans Hals. *Malle Babbe*. c. 1650. Oil on canvas, 29½ x 25" (75 x 63.5 cm). Gemäldegalerie, Berlin

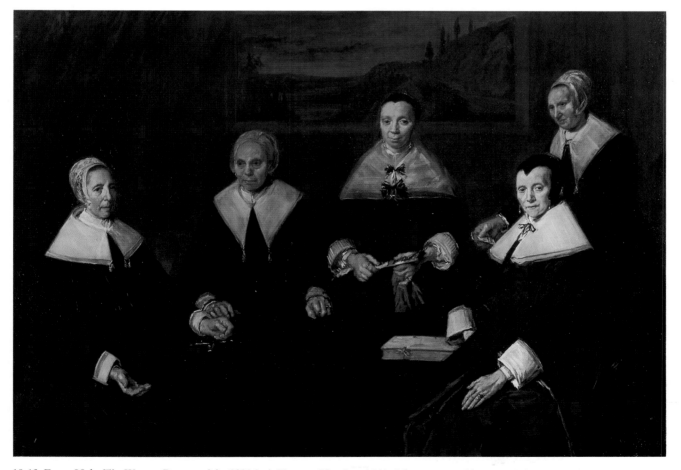

18-13. Frans Hals. *The Women Regents of the Old Men's Home at Haarlem*. 1664. Oil on canvas, 5'7" x 8'2" (1.70 x 2.49 m). Frans Halsmuseum, Haarlem, the Netherlands

Rembrandt's late style (compare figs. 18-18 and 18-19). The experience of suffering and death has so etched the faces of these women that they seem themselves to have become images of death—gentle, inexorable, and timeless.

JUDITH LEYSTER. Hals' virtuosity could not be readily imitated; hence he had few followers. The most important among them was Judith Leyster (1609–1660), who painted a number of works that long passed as Hals' own. Like many women artists before modern times, her career was curtailed by motherhood. (She married a fellow student of Hals'.) Leyster's *Boy Playing a Flute* (fig. 18-14) is her masterpiece. Significantly, its style is closer to Terbrugghen's than to Hals'. The rapt musician is a memorable expression of lyrical mood. To convey this spirit, Leyster explored the poetic quality of light with a quiet intensity that anticipates the work of Jan Vermeer a generation later (see page 605).

REMBRANDT. Like Hals, Rembrandt van Rijn (1606–1669), the greatest genius of Dutch art, was influenced indirectly by Caravaggio through the Utrecht School. His earliest pictures, painted in his native Leyden, are small, sharply lit, and intensely realistic. Many deal with Old Testament subjects, a lifelong preference. They show both his greater realism and his new emotional attitude. Since the beginning of Christian art, episodes from the Old Testament had often been represented as prefigurations of Christianity, rather than for their own sake. (The Sacrifice of Isaac, for example, foretold the sacrificial death of Christ.) This perspective not only limited the choice of subjects, it also colored their interpretation. Rembrandt, by contrast, viewed the stories of the Old Testament in much the same lay Christian spirit that governed Caravaggio's approach to the New Testament: as direct accounts of God's ways with his human creations.

How strongly these stories affected him is clear in *The Blinding of Samson* (fig. 18-15). Painted in the High Baroque style he

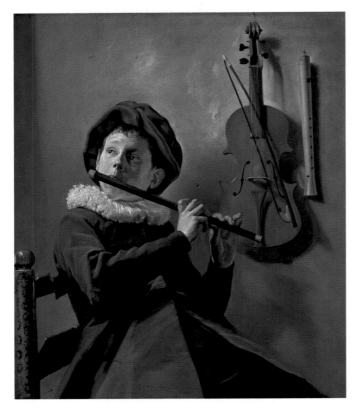

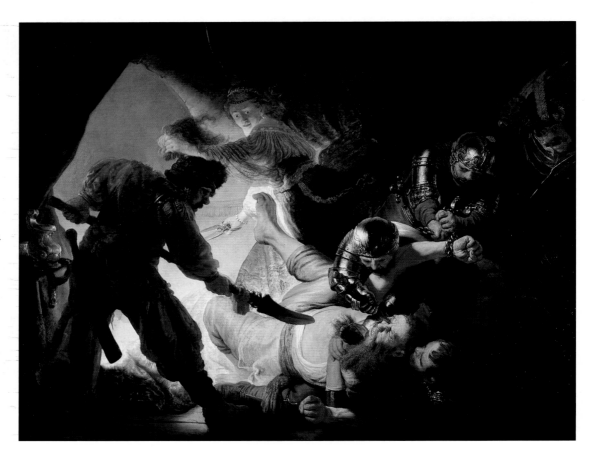

(ABOVE)
18-14. Judith Leyster. *Boy Playing a Flute.* 1630–35. Oil on canvas, 28⅛ x 24⅛" (73 x 62 cm). Nationalmuseum, Stockholm

(RIGHT)
18-15. Rembrandt. *The Blinding of Samson.* 1636. Oil on canvas, 7'9" x 9'11" (2.4 x 3 m). Städelsches Kunstinstitut, Frankfurt

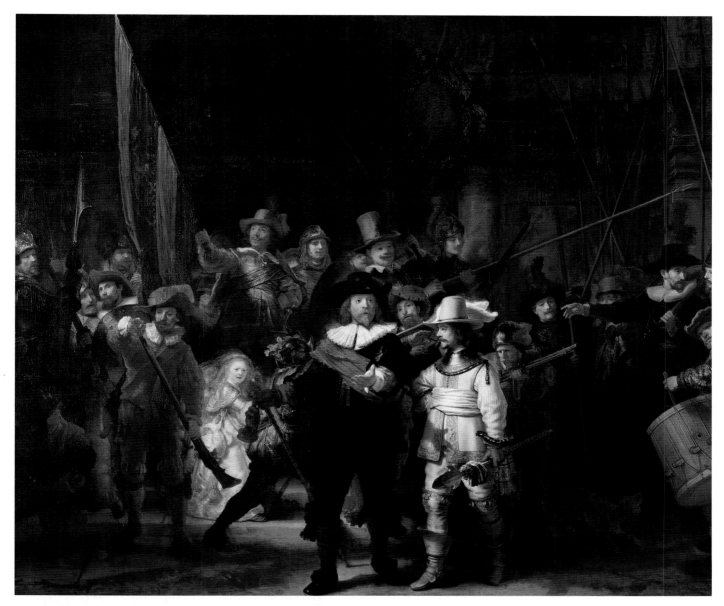

18-16. Rembrandt. *The Night Watch (The Company of Captain Frans Banning Cocq)*. 1642. Oil on canvas, 12'2" x 14'7" (3.8 x 4.4 m). Rijksmuseum, Amsterdam

developed in the 1630s after moving to Amsterdam, it shows Rembrandt as a master storyteller. The artist depicts the Old Testament world as full of Oriental splendor and violence. The theatrical light pouring into the dark tent heightens the drama to the pitch of *The Raising of the Cross* (see fig. 18-1) by Rubens, whose work, like Hals' before him, Rembrandt sought to rival.

Rembrandt was at this time an avid collector of Near Eastern objects, which served as props in these pictures. He had become Amsterdam's most sought-after portrait painter, and a man of considerable wealth. His famous group portrait known as *The Night Watch* (fig. 18-16), painted in 1642, shows a military company assembling for the visit of Marie de' Medici to Amsterdam. Although its members had each contributed toward the cost of the huge canvas (originally it was much larger), Rembrandt did not give them equal weight. He wanted to avoid the mechanically regular designs of earlier group portraits—a problem only Frans Hals had solved successfully. Instead, he made the picture a virtuoso performance filled with Baroque movement and light-

ing, which captures the excitement of the moment and gives the scene unique drama (compare fig. 17-2). Some of the figures were plunged into shadow, while others were hidden by overlapping. Legend has it that the people whose portraits he had obscured were not satisfied with the painting, but there is no evidence for this claim. On the contrary, we know that the painting was much admired in its time.

Like Michelangelo and, later, Van Gogh, Rembrandt has been the subject (one might say, the victim) of many fictionalized biographies. In them the artist's fall from public favor is usually explained by the "catastrophe" of *The Night Watch*. It is true that his prosperity petered out in the 1640s, as he was replaced by other, more fashionable artists, including some of his own pupils. Yet his fortunes declined less suddenly and completely than his romantic admirers would have us believe. A number of important people in Amsterdam continued to be his friends and supporters, and he received some major public commissions in the 1650s and 1660s. Actually, his financial problems were due largely to poor

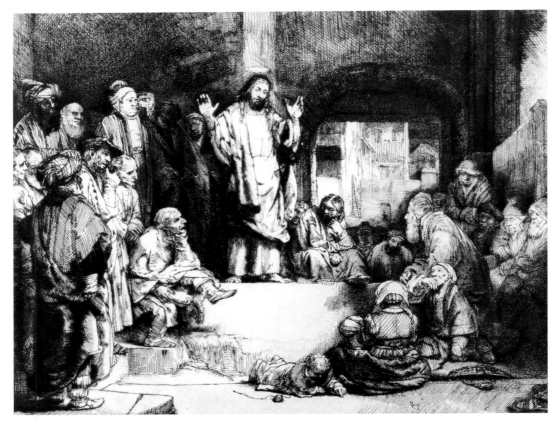

management and his own stubbornness, which alienated his patrons. Still, the 1640s were a time of inner uncertainty and external troubles, especially his wife's death.

As a result, Rembrandt's outlook changed profoundly. After about 1650, his style is marked by lyric subtlety and pictorial breadth. Some exotic trappings from the earlier years remain, but they no longer create an alien world. Rembrandt's etchings from these years, such as *Christ Preaching* (fig. 18-17), show this new depth of feeling. The sensuous beauty seen in *The Blinding of Samson* has yielded to a humble world of bare feet and ragged clothes. The scene is full of the artist's deep compassion for the poor and outcast who make up the audience. Rembrandt had a special sympathy for the Jews, both as heirs of the biblical past and as victims of persecution, and they were often his models. This print suggests some corner in the Amsterdam ghetto where the Jews found a haven and surely incorporates observations of life from the drawings he made throughout his career. Here it is the magic of light that gives *Christ Preaching* its spiritual significance. Rembrandt's importance as a graphic artist is second only to Dürer's, although we get no more than a hint of his virtuosity from this single example.

The many self-portraits Rembrandt painted over his long career reflect every stage of his inner development. They are experimental in the early Leyden years, theatrically disguised in the 1630s, and frank toward the end of his life. While our late example (fig. 18-18) is partially indebted to Titian's portraits (compare fig. 13-41), Rembrandt examines himself with a typically Northern candor (compare fig. 16-15). The bold pose and penetrating look bespeak a resigned but firm resolve in the face of adversity.

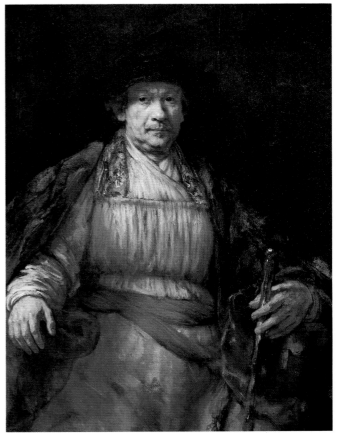

18-18. Rembrandt. *Self-Portrait.* 1658. Oil on canvas,
52⅝ x 40⅞" (133.6 x 103.8 cm). The Frick Collection, New York

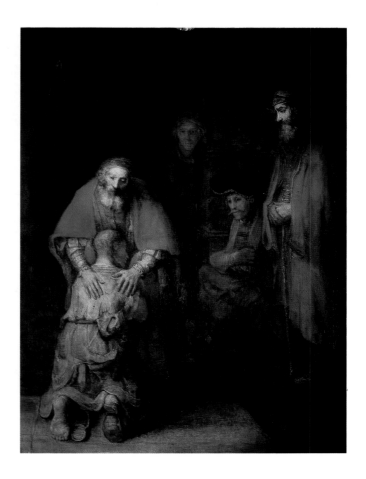

Rembrandt opened a new field in the history of painting. It is the world which lies behind visible appearances, but is, at the same time, implied. It is the sphere of the spirit, of the soul. . . .

It is worth noticing that Rembrandt usually does not express in the physiognomies of his subjects—especially in the mature stage of his art—either the power of the will or superficial emotions. . . .

Our inner spirit is a very elusive element. As the Latin word spiritus *suggests, it is a breath, deep-seated and concealed, easily disturbed and troubled by the forces of external activity. Nevertheless, the inner part of our life is the more basic one of our existence. And to this quality, which can be called the soul, the great religious leaders, above all Christ, have appealed. Rembrandt was born with a new, deep, and unique sense of it, and was able to probe with rare concentration through the external appearance of human beings, forcing us to participate with him in this, their most precious substance. . . .*

Rembrandt's final word is given in his monumental painting of the Return of the Prodigal Son *[fig. 18-19]. Here he interprets the Christian idea of mercy with an extraordinary solemnity, as though this were his spiritual testament to the world. It goes beyond the works of all other Baroque artists in the evocation of religious mood and human sympathy. The aged artist's power of realism is not diminished, but increased by psychological insight and spiritual awareness. Expressive lighting and colouring and the magic suggestiveness of his technique, together with a selective simplicity of setting, help us to feel the full impact of this event. The main group of the father and the Prodigal Son stands out in light against an enormous dark surface. . . . The observer is roused to a feeling of some extraordinary event. . . . The whole represents a symbol of homecoming, of the darkness of human existence illuminated by tenderness, of weary and sinful mankind taking refuge in the shelter of God's mercy.*

—Jakob Rosenberg, Seymour Slive, and E. H. ter Kuile.
Dutch Art and Architecture: 1600–1800.
Pelican History of Art Series. New Haven: Yale University
Press, 1997, pp. 66, 80–81. Originally published in 1966.

JAKOB ROSENBERG (1893–1980) left Germany in the mid-1930s and joined the faculty at Harvard University. He was one of the leading "old school" experts on Rembrandt, and he saw the artist through decidedly romantic lenses. The passages quoted above, from the Pelican History of Art volume he wrote with his younger colleague, Hals specialist Seymour Slive (b. 1920), and Belgian scholar E. H. ter Kuile, show his philosophy and approach to Rembrandt more closely than his monograph on the artist. Although often regarded as outmoded, Rosenberg's writing still has much to offer the thoughtful student of art history.

This approach helps to account for the dignity we see in the religious scenes that play so large a part in Rembrandt's work toward the end of his life. *The Return of the Prodigal Son* (fig. 18-19), created a few years before his death, may be his most moving painting. It is also his quietest—a moment stretching into eternity. So pervasive is the mood of tender silence that the viewer feels a kinship with this group. That bond is perhaps stronger and more intimate in this picture than in any earlier work of art. Here the understanding accumulated over a lifetime achieves a universal expression of sorrow and forgiveness.

Landscape, Still Life, and Genre Painters

Rembrandt's religious pictures demand an insight that was beyond the capacity of all but a few collectors. Most art buyers in Holland preferred subjects within their own experience: landscapes, architectural views, still lifes, and everyday (**genre**) scenes. These types, we recall, emerged in the latter half of the sixteenth century (see page 548). As they became fully defined, artists began to specialize. The trend was not confined to Holland. We find it everywhere to some degree, but Dutch painting was its fountainhead in both volume and variety.

JAN VAN GOYEN. *Pelkus-Poort* (fig. 18-20) by Jan van Goyen (1596–1656) is the kind of landscape that enjoyed great popularity because its elements were so familiar: the distant town under an overcast sky, seen through a moist atmosphere across an expanse of water. Such a view remains typical of the Dutch countryside to this day, and no one knew better than Van Goyen how to evoke the mood of these "nether lands," ever threatened by the sea.

Like other early Dutch Baroque landscapists, Van Goyen used only grays and browns highlighted by green accents, but within this narrow range he achieved an almost infinite variety of effects. The tonal landscape style in Holland was accompanied by radically simplified compositions, in which the complex constructions of Northern Mannerism were reduced to orderly arrangements. Van Goyen's scene is based on a clear scheme of parallel bands capped by a triangle. He discovered what Annibale Carracci had already learned from Giorgione and the Venetians: that the secret to depicting landscapes lay in geometry, which enabled the artist to gain visual control over nature as it did in architecture.

AELBERT CUYP. Other Northern artists learned this lesson in Rome, where they gathered in growing numbers. The Dutch Italianates who returned home in the 1640s brought with them new ideas that had an invigorating effect on landscape painting. Their impact can be seen in the work of Aelbert Cuyp (1620–1691), who never left his native soil. A follower at first of Van Goyen, he soon abandoned tonalism in favor of the radiant light seen in their views of the Roman Campagna, which parallel the work of Claude Lorraine (see fig. 19-7). The golden light of late afternoon gives Cuyp's *View of the Valkhof at Nijmegen* (fig. 18-21) a tranquil mood that suspends the scene in time and space. The classical structure of the composition and cubic handling of the architecture heighten the poetry created by Cuyp's grasp of even the subtlest atmospheric effects.

JACOB VAN RUISDAEL. The richest of the newly developed "specialties" was landscape, both as a portrayal of familiar views and as an imaginative vision of nature. Although nature was enjoyed for its own sake, it could also serve as a means of divine revelation through contemplation of God's work. Such is the case with *The Jewish Cemetery* (fig. 18-22) by Jacob van Ruisdael (1628/29–82), the greatest Dutch landscape painter. Natural forces dominate this wild scene, which is imaginary except for the tombs, depicting a Jewish cemetery near Amsterdam. The thunderclouds passing over a deserted mountain valley, the medieval ruin, the

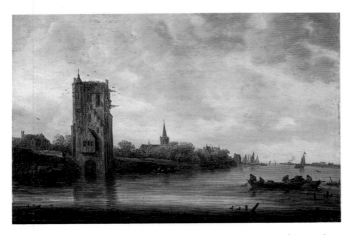

18-20. Jan van Goyen. *Pelkus-Poort.* 1646. Oil on panel, 14½ x 22½" (36.8 x 57.2 cm). The Metropolitan Museum of Art, New York

GIFT OF FRANCIS NEILSON, 1954

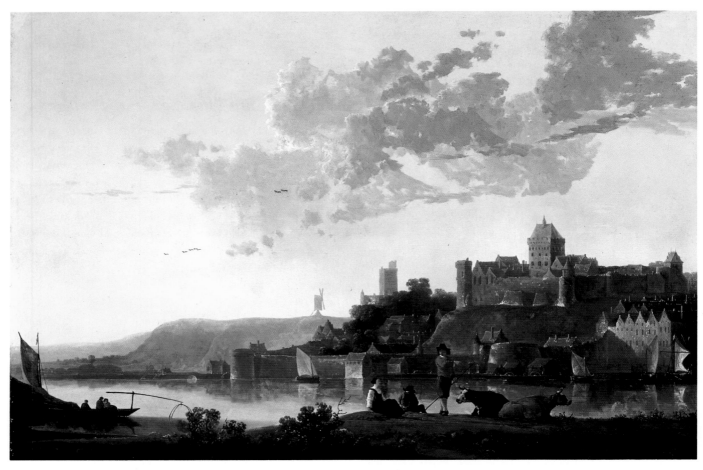

18-21. Aelbert Cuyp. *View of the Valkhof at Nijmegen.* c. 1655–65. Oil on panel, 19¼ x 29" (48.9 x 73.7 cm). © 1993 Indianapolis Museum of Art

GIFT OF MRS. JAMES W. FESLER

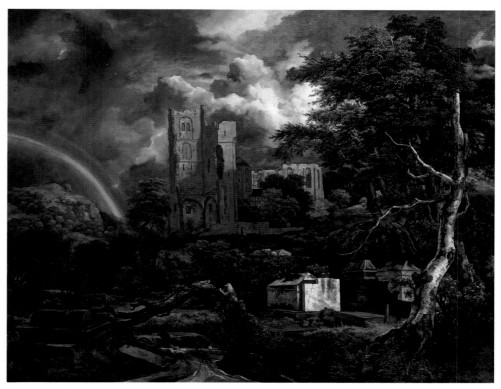

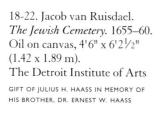

18-22. Jacob van Ruisdael. *The Jewish Cemetery.* 1655–60. Oil on canvas, 4'6" x 6'2½" (1.42 x 1.89 m). The Detroit Institute of Arts

torrent that has forced its way between ancient graves, all create a mood of melancholy. Nothing endures on this earth, the artist tells us: time, wind, and water grind all to dust—trees and rocks as well as the works of human hands. Even the massive tombs offer no protection from the same forces that destroy the church built in God's glory. In the context of this extended allegory, the rainbow may be understood as a sign of the promise of redemption through faith. Ruisdael's view of nature is thus the opposite of Annibale Carracci's civilized landscape (compare fig. 17-7). It harks back instead to Giorgione's tragic vision (see fig. 13-38). *The Jewish Cemetery* inspires that awe on which the Romantics, 150 years later, based their concept of the sublime. The difference is that for Ruisdael, God remains separate from his creation, instead of a part of it.

PIETER SAENREDAM. Nothing at first seems further removed from *The Jewish Cemetery* than the painstaking *Interior of the Choir of St. Bavo's Church at Haarlem* (fig. 18-23), painted by Pieter Saenredam at almost the same time. Yet it, too, is meant to serve as more than a mere record. (These architectural views were often freely invented as well.) The medieval structure, stripped of all furnishings and whitewashed under the Protestants, has acquired a crystalline purity that invites spiritual contemplation through the painting's quiet intensity.

STILL LIFES. Still lifes are meant above all to delight the senses, but even they can be tinged with a melancholy air. As a result of Holland's conversion to Calvinism, these visual feasts became vehicles for teaching moral lessons. Most Dutch Baroque still lifes

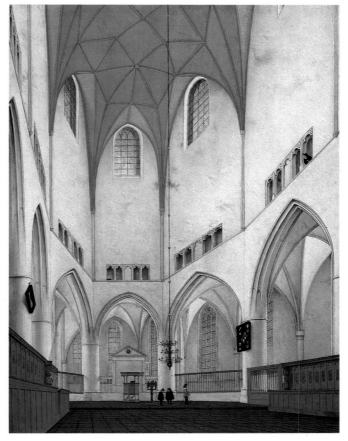

18-23. Pieter Saenredam. *Interior of the Choir of St. Bavo's Church at Haarlem.* 1660. Oil on panel, 27⅞ x 21⅝" (70.4 x 54.8 cm). Worcester Art Museum, Worcester, Massachusetts

Dutch Protestant conservatism regarding music in the church inhibited the development of music in the Netherlands. The only important Dutch composer in the seventeenth century was Jan Sweelinck (1562–1621), who succeeded his father as organist of the Oude Kerk (Old Church) in Amsterdam. He was particularly noted for his psalm music. Sweelinck's strongest influence was felt not in Holland but in Germany, where his best pupils, such as Samuel Scheidt (1587–1654), George Frideric Handel's distinguished predecessor in Halle (see pages 636–37), were able to find employment and where a love of church music, fostered by Lutheranism, was widespread.

German music was largely under the sway of the Italians. Its chief representative was Heinrich Schütz (1585–1672), who studied with Giovanni Gabrieli in Venice (see page 490), then spent most of his career as *Kapellmeister* (Master of the Chapel) to the Elector of Saxony in Dresden, where he composed large quantities of extremely beautiful church music, including several oratorios—notably *The Seven Last Words of Christ* of 1645—that are important precursors of Johann Sebastian Bach's (see page 636). The most daring German composer of the time between Schütz and Bach was Heinrich von Biber (1644–1704), Kapellmeister to the Archbishop of Salzburg. A noted violinist, he was a Northern counterpart to Arcangelo Corelli (see page 569), and his writing, though technically more demanding, shares an alternately bittersweet plaintive-

ness and dancelike sprightliness. Biber made extensive use of different tunings (*scordatura,* "mistuning") to lend a varied character to the 15 "mystery" sonatas he composed for violin and continuo around 1675–76. These visionary works are musical meditations on the Catholic rosary, written to celebrate its feast in early October.

In contrast to its rich musical heritage, Germany had little to offer in the way of theater, which relied heavily on imported Italian and French players at the more affluent courts in Vienna, Dresden, and Munich, where opera proved the most popular theatrical form (see page 569). The situation was just the opposite in Holland, which enjoyed a lively theatrical life, especially in Amsterdam. Dutch theater was partly an outgrowth of the societies of rhetoricians (*rederijkers*) that had sprung up during the fifteenth century and partly of the Dutch Academy, which was founded in 1617 as a "Netherlandish training school." The theater also flourished because under these promising conditions Holland produced a number of gifted playwrights, notably Joost van den Vondel (1587–1679), at a time when rising nationalism placed new emphasis on the Dutch language. The plots often drew on the Old Testament to glorify the Dutch as a new "chosen people." These dramas were an important inspiration to artists, particularly Rembrandt. Many of his paintings, especially those from his early years, depict scenes drawn directly from these plays. Moreover, Rembrandt's use of exotic costumes and stage properties shows a deep love of drama that helps account, in part, for the theatricality of his work.

treat the theme of Vanitas (the vanity of all earthly things). Directly or indirectly, they preach the typically Dutch virtues of temperance, frugality, and hard work by warning the viewer to contemplate the brevity of life, the inevitability of death, and the passing of all earthly pleasures. The medieval tradition of giving religious meaning to everyday objects was absorbed into popular culture through **emblem books** which, together with other forms of popular literature and prints, transmitted the Dutch ethic through words and pictures. The stern Calvinist outlook is represented by such mottos as, "A fool and his money are soon parted" (a saying that goes all the way back to ancient Rome), which is illustrated by flowers, shells, and other exotic luxuries. The very presence in Vanitas still lifes of precious goods, scholarly books, and objects appealing to the senses suggests an ambivalent attitude toward their subject. Such symbols usually take on multiple meanings which, although no longer readily understood today, were widely recognized at the time. In their most elaborate form, these moral allegories become visual riddles that rely on the very learning they sometimes ridicule.

WILLEM CLAESZ. HEDA. The **banquet** (or **breakfast**) **piece,** showing the remains of a meal, had Vanitas connotations almost from the beginning. The message may lie in such symbols as death's-heads and extinguished candles, or be implied by less

direct means. *Still Life* (fig. 18-24) by Willem Claesz. Heda (1594–1680) belongs to this widespread type. Food and drink are less emphasized here than luxury objects, such as crystal goblets

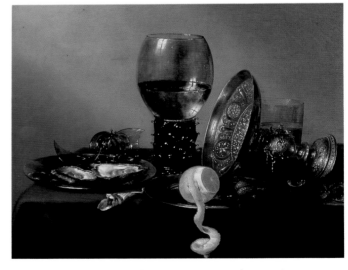

18-24. Willem Claesz. Heda. *Still Life.* 1634. Oil on panel, 16⅞ x 22⅞" (43 x 57 cm). Museum Boymans-van Beuningen, Rotterdam, the Netherlands

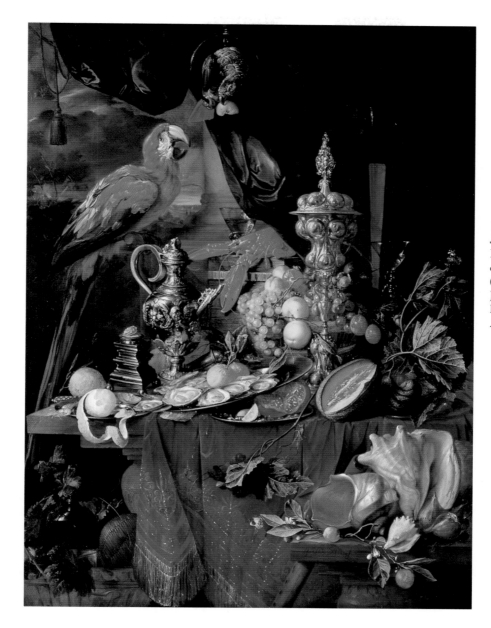

18-25. Jan de Heem. *Still Life with Parrots.* Late 1640s. Oil on canvas, 59¼ x 45½" (150.5 x 115.5 cm). John and Mable Ringling Museum of Art, Sarasota, Florida

and silver dishes, which are carefully chosen for their contrasting shapes, colors, and textures. How different this seems from the piled-up foods of Aertsen's *Meat Stall* (see fig. 16-20)! But virtuosity was not Heda's only aim. He reminds us that all is Vanity. His "story," the human context of these grouped objects, is suggested by the broken glass, the half-peeled lemon, the overturned silver dish. The unstable composition, with its signs of a hasty departure, suggests transience. Whoever sat at this table was suddenly forced to leave the meal. The curtain that time has lowered on the scene, as it were, gives the objects a strange pathos. The disguised symbolism of Late Gothic painting lives on here in a new form.

JAN DE HEEM. The breakfast piece soon developed into an even more lavish display, known as the "fancy" still life for its visual splendor. This type reached its peak in the work of Jan de Heem (1606–1684). De Heem began his career in Protestant Holland but he soon moved to Catholic Flanders. However, he traveled back

and forth between the two countries and eventually returned to his native land. He was able to synthesize the sober Dutch tradition with the flamboyant manner of Frans Snyders into a unique style that had equal influence on both sides of the border. In *Still Life with Parrots* (fig. 18-25), he depicts delicious food, exotic birds, and luxurious goods from around the world. The result is a stunning display of virtuosity. Despite the mountain of extravagant objects, the painting is unified by the balanced composition and brilliant colors. In keeping with the theme of appetite, the viewer is meant to enjoy the visual abundance, which celebrates the work of the Lord and humanity. At the same time, the picture has a hidden meaning. Many of these objects, including the oysters, melon, and shells (which commanded high prices), are also standard Vanitas symbols urging temperance. Also present in *Still Life with Parrots* is the time-honored theme of the four elements, as well as traditional Christian imagery. The parrot is identified with the Madonna as the mother of Christ, while the

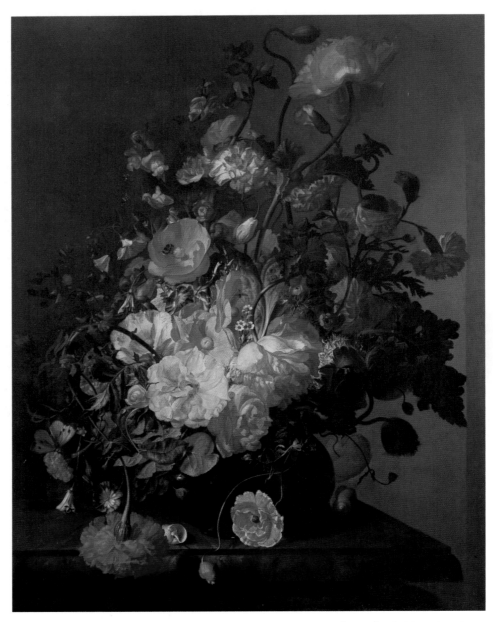

18-26. Rachel Ruysch. *Flower Still Life*. After 1700. Oil on canvas, 29¾ x 23⅞" (75.5 x 60.7 cm). The Toledo Museum of Art, Toledo, Ohio

grapes refer to the Eucharistic wine (and, hence, resurrection), as does the pomegranate, which stands for the Virgin's purity as well.

RACHEL RUYSCH. De Heem also defined the High Baroque floral still life so completely that flower painters were to feel his impact for the next 200 years. Many of them were women, including his pupil Maria van Oosterwijck (1630–1693), who became a famous artist in her own right. She was soon outstripped by Rachel Ruysch (1664–1750), who shared honors with Jan van Huysum (1682–1749) as the leading Dutch flower painters of the day. Was Ruysch aware of the significance of every blossom, and of the but-

terflies, moths, and snails she put into the piece in figure 18-26, each of which has a symbolic meaning? By this time their significance was taken for granted, and it is doubtful that she intended her bouquet to convey a moralizing message. Instead, the main purpose of the painting was surely to please the eye. She imparts such a sweeping vitality to the cascade of buds that they seem to leap from their vase.

JAN STEEN. Genre scenes are as varied as landscapes and still lifes. They range from tavern brawls to refined domestic interiors. In *The Feast of St. Nicholas* (fig. 18-27) by Jan Steen (1625/6–1679),

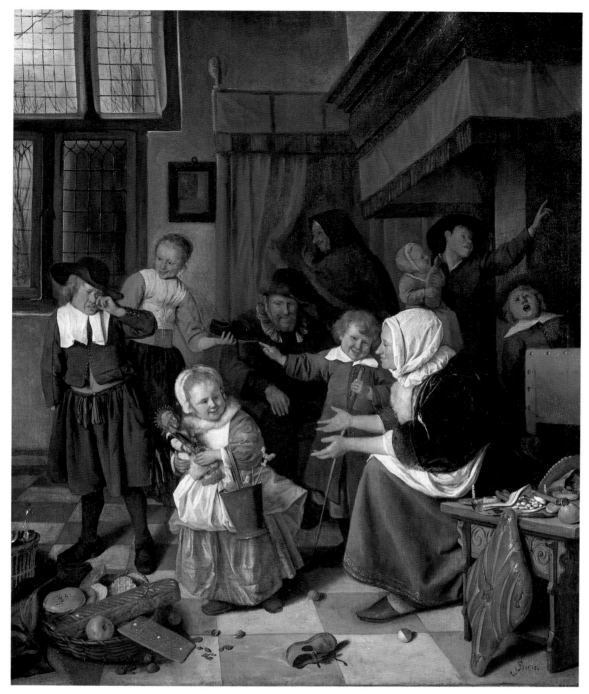

18-27. Jan Steen. *The Feast of St. Nicholas.* c. 1660–65. Oil on canvas, 32¼ x 27¾" (82 x 70.5 cm). Rijksmuseum, Amsterdam

St. Nicholas has just paid his pre-Christmas visit to the household and left toys, candy, and cake for the children. The little girl and boy are delighted with their presents. She holds a doll of St. John the Baptist and a bucket filled with sweets, while he plays with a golf club and ball. Everybody is jolly except their brother, on the left, who has received only a birch rod (held by the maidservant) for caning naughty children. Soon his tears will turn to joy, however: his grandmother, in the background, beckons to the bed, where a toy is hidden.

Steen tells the story with relish, embroidering it with many delightful details. Of all the Dutch painters of daily life, he was the sharpest and the most good-humored observer. To supplement his earnings he kept an inn, which may explain his keen insight into human behavior. His sense of timing and his characterizations often remind us of Frans Hals (compare fig. 18-12), while his storytelling stems from the tradition of Pieter Bruegel the Elder (compare fig. 16-22). Steen was also a gifted history painter, and although his pictures often contain parodies of well-known works by Italian artists, they usually convey a serious message as well. *The Feast of Saint Nicholas* has such a content: the doll of St. John is meant as a reminder of the importance of spiritual matters over worldly possessions, no matter how pleasurable.

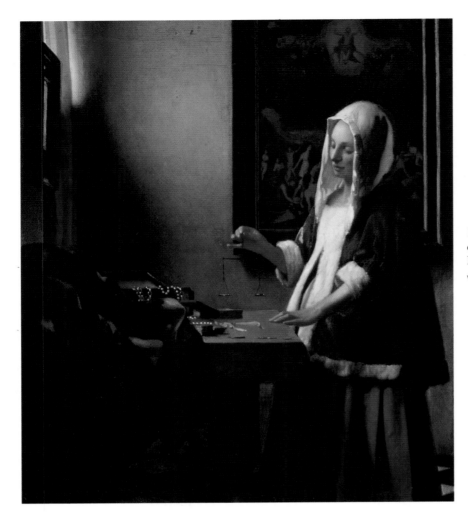

18-28. Jan Vermeer. *Woman Holding a Balance.*
c. 1664. Oil on canvas, 16¾ x 15" (42.5 x 38.1 cm).
National Gallery of Art, Washington, D.C.

JAN VERMEER. In the genre scenes of Jan Vermeer (1632–1675), by contrast, there is hardly any narrative. Single figures, usually women, are seemingly engaged in everyday tasks. They exist in a timeless "still life" world, as if becalmed by a spell. In *Woman Holding a Balance* (fig. 18-28), a young woman, richly dressed in the at-home wear of the day, is contemplating a balance in her hand, with strings of pearls and gold coins spread out on the table before her. The design is so perfect that we cannot move a single element without upsetting the delicate equilibrium. The vanishing point of the diagonals formed by the top of the mirror and the right side of the table lies near the juncture of the woman's hand and the picture frame. The bottom of the frame is actually lower on the right than on the left in order to guide our eye to the painting in the background, which depicts Christ at the Last Judgment, when every soul is weighed. Despite the obvious parallel of this subject to the woman's activity, the meaning is far from clear. The pans of the balance actually contain nothing, only beads of light.

What, then, is the woman doing? Is she weighing temporal against spiritual values? What accounts for her inner peace? Perhaps it is self-knowledge, symbolized here by the mirror. It may also be the promise of salvation through her faith. If so, light serves here not only to illuminate the scene but also to represent religious revelation. In the end, however, we cannot be sure, because Vermeer's approach to his subject proves as subtle as his pictorial treatment. He avoids any anecdote or symbolism that might limit us to a single interpretation. There can be no doubt, however, about his fascination with light. Vermeer's mastery of light's expressive qualities raises his concern for the reality of appearance to the level of poetry and includes all of its visual and symbolic possibilities. Here, then, we have found the real meaning of Vermeer's art. *Woman Holding a Balance* is also testimony to the artist's faith: he was a Catholic living in Protestant Holland, where his religion was officially banned, although worship in private houses was tolerated.

When there are two figures, as in *The Letter* (fig. 18-29), they do no more than exchange glances. The painting nonetheless does tell a story, but with unmatched subtlety. The "staged" entrance serves to establish our relation to the scene. The floor and chair tell us that we are seated just outside the doorway. We are more than bystanders: we become the bearer of the letter that has just been delivered to the young woman. Dressed in sumptuous clothing, she has been playing the lute, as if awaiting our visit. This instrument, filled with erotic meaning, traditionally signifies the harmony between lovers, who play each other's heart strings. Are we, then, her lover? The amused expression of the maid suggests such an interest. Moreover, the lover in Dutch art and literature is often compared to a ship at sea, whose calm waters shown in the painting on the wall indicate smooth sailing. As usual with Ver-

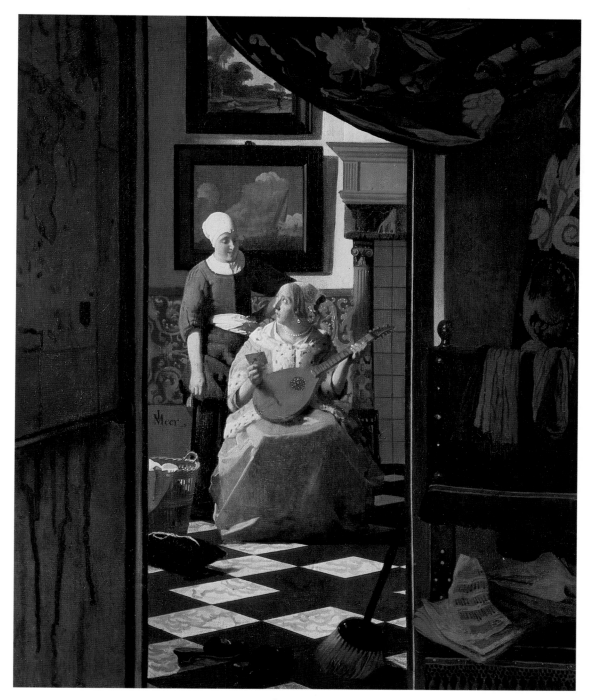

18-29. Jan Vermeer. *The Letter*. 1666. Oil on canvas, 17¼ x 15¼" (43.3 x 38.3 cm). Rijksmuseum, Amsterdam

meer, however, the picture refuses to yield a final answer, since he has depicted the moment before the letter is opened.

Here, too, Vermeer's real interest centers on the role of light. The cool daylight that filters in from the left in *The Letter* is the only active element, working its miracles upon all the objects in its path. As we look at the painting, we feel as if a veil had been pulled from our eyes. The everyday world shines with jewel-like freshness, more beautiful than we have ever seen before.

Vermeer, unlike earlier artists, perceives reality as a mosaic of colored surfaces—more accurately, he translates reality into a mosaic as he puts it on canvas. We see *The Letter* not only as a perspective "window," but as a "field" made up of smaller fields. Rectangles predominate, carefully aligned with the picture surface; there are no "holes," no undefined empty spaces. The interlocking shapes give Vermeer's work a uniquely modern quality. How did he acquire it? Although there is considerable documentary evidence relating to his life, we know very little about his training. Some of his works show the influence of Carel Fabritius (1622–1654), the most brilliant of Rembrandt's pupils. Others suggest his contact with the Utrecht School. But none of these sources really explains the origin of his style, which is so original that his genius was not recognized until the mid-nineteenth century. No painter since Jan van Eyck *saw* as intensely as this. Nor shall we meet his equal again until the Rococo artist Chardin (see figs. 20-8 and 20-9).

CHAPTER NINETEEN

The Baroque in France and England

FRANCE: THE AGE OF VERSAILLES

Under Henry IV (1553–1610), Louis XIII (1601–1643), and Louis XIV (1638–1715), France became the most powerful nation of Europe, militarily and culturally. These kings were aided by a succession of extremely able ministers and advisers: the Duc de Sully, Cardinal Richelieu, Cardinal Mazarin, and Jean-Baptiste Colbert. By the late seventeenth century, Paris was vying with Rome as the art capital of Europe. How did this change come about?

Sixteenth-century architecture in France, and to a lesser extent sculpture, were more closely linked with Italian Renaissance classicism than in any other Northern country, although painting continued to be governed by the Mannerist style of the later school of Fontainebleau until about 1625 (see pages 504–05). Classicism was also nourished by French humanism, with its intellectual heritage of reason and Stoic virtue: the values of the upper middle-class who gradually came to dominate cultural and political life. These factors slowed the spread of the Baroque in France and changed its course. Rubens' Medici cycle (see fig. 18-2), for example, had no effect on French art until the very end of the century. In the 1620s, when it was painted, the young artists in France were still assimilating the early Baroque. After 1640 French painting, too, fell under the spell of classicism. It became the official court style between 1660 and 1685, which corresponds with the climactic phase of Louis XIV's reign.

Because of the Palace of Versailles and other vast projects glorifying the king of France, we are tempted to think of French art in the age of Louis XIV as the expression of absolute rule. This is true of the period 1660–85, but by that time seventeenth-century French art had already attained its distinctive character. The French are reluctant to call this style Baroque. To them it is the Style of Louis XIV. Often they also describe the art and literature of the period as "classic." In this context, the word has three meanings. It is a synonym for "highest achievement," which suggests that the Style of Louis XIV is the equivalent of the High Renaissance in Italy or the age of Perikles in ancient Greece. It also refers to the imitation of the forms and subject matter of classical antiq-

uity. Finally, it suggests qualities of balance and restraint shared by ancient art and the Renaissance. The last two meanings describe what could more accurately be called "classicism." Since the Style of Louis XIV reflects Italian Baroque art, however modified, we may call it Baroque classicism.

Painting and Printmaking

JACQUES CALLOT. One of the most important among the transitional figures was Jacques Callot (1592/3–1635), an etcher and engraver whose prints inspired both Georges de La Tour (see below) and the young Rembrandt. Callot's work looks as much to past tradition as it does to the art of the present. Much of his early career was spent at the court of Cosimo II de' Medici in Florence, where he produced prints dealing mainly with the theater, especially the *commedia dell'arte* (see box page 581). After he returned to his native town of Nancy in 1621, his work underwent a major change. His prints now alternate between apocalyptic intensity, which links him directly with Hieronymus Bosch, and astonishing directness, which recalls the spirit of Pieter Bruegel the Elder. Yet he belongs fully to his own time in subject matter and outlook. These qualities merge in *Great Miseries of War,* which appeared in 1633, the year Richelieu conquered Nancy. This series of etchings represents a distillation of Callot's experience of the Thirty Years' War, but it also has a moralizing purpose. *Hangman's Tree* (fig. 19-1) depicts soldiers paying for their crimes. The inscription reads: "Finally these thieves, sordid and forlorn, hanging like unfortunate pieces of fruit from this tree, experience the justice of Heaven sooner or later." The style is Mannerist, except in the group to the right, which shows the same naturalism as the Le Nains' (compare fig. 19-33). This stark scene is far grimmer than Bosch's vision of Hell in *The Garden of Delights* (see fig. 15-14), for it is based on direct experience. The plate has a striking immediacy, gained from the artist's experience of the theater, that anticipates Goya's vivid imagery (see fig. 21-25).

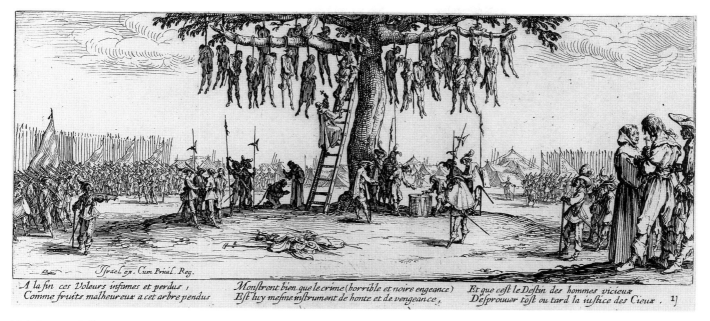

19-1. Jacques Callot. *Hangman's Tree,* from *Great Miseries of War.* 1633. Etching, 3½ x 9" (9 x 23 cm). The British Museum, London

GEORGES DE LA TOUR. Many early French Baroque painters were influenced by Caravaggio, although it is not clear how they absorbed his style. Most were minor artists toiling in the provinces but a few developed highly original styles. The finest of them was Georges de La Tour (1593–1652), whose importance was recognized only in the nineteenth century. Although he spent his career in Lorraine in northeast France, he was by no means a simple provincial artist. Besides being named a painter to the king, he received important commissions from the governor of Lorraine. He began his career painting picturesque genre figures, then turned to elaborate stock scenes from contemporary theater derived largely from Caravaggio's Northern followers.

Although these works are painted well enough, La Tour would arouse little more than passing interest were it not for his mature religious pictures, which possess both seriousness and grandeur. *Joseph the Carpenter* (fig. 19-2) might easily be mistaken for a genre scene, but its devotional spirit has the power of Caravaggio's *Calling of St. Matthew* (see fig. 17-2). La Tour's intensity of vision lends each gesture, each expression its maximum significance within this spellbinding composition. The boy Jesus holds a candle, a favorite device of the artist, which lights the scene with an intimacy and tenderness that recall the *Nativity* by Geertgen tot Sint Jans (see fig. 15-13). And like Geertgen, La Tour reduces forms to a geometric simplicity that raises them above the everyday world, despite their realism.

THE LE NAINS. The three Le Nain brothers—Antoine, Louis, and Mathieu—were rediscovered in the mid-nineteenth century, although they did not have to wait quite as long as La Tour. Their birth dates are not known, but all must have been born in Laon during the first decade of the century. By 1629 they were in Paris, where the two oldest died of the plague in 1648. Despite the fact that they shared the same style, signed their pictures simply "Le Nain," and worked on paintings together, each had a distinctive personality. Antoine was a miniaturist at heart,

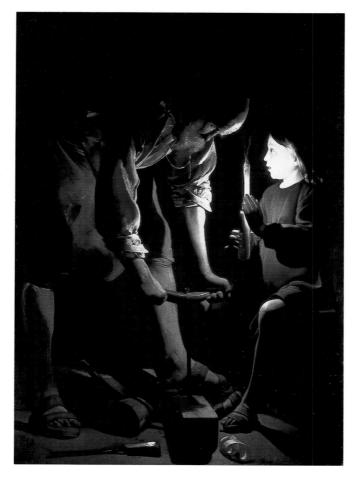

19-2. Georges de La Tour. *Joseph the Carpenter.* c. 1645. Oil on canvas, 51⅛ x 39¾" (130 x 100 cm). Musée du Louvre, Paris

Louis the most severe, and Mathieu the most robust. Louis' *Peasant Family* (fig. 19-3) nevertheless displays the main features of their family style and its virtues. Like the peasant scenes of seventeenth-century Holland and Flanders, with which it has much in

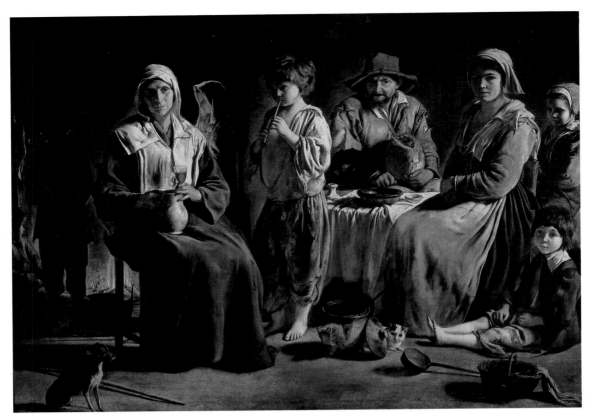

19-3. Louis Le Nain. *Peasant Family*. c. 1640. Oil on canvas, 44½ x 62½" (113 x 158.7 cm). Musée du Louvre, Paris

common, the picture stems from a tradition that goes back to Pieter Bruegel the Elder (see fig. 16-22). But whereas the Netherlandish scenes of lowlife are often humorous or satirical (see fig. 18-12), Le Nain gives his figures a dignity and solemnity that recall Velázquez' *Water Carrier of Seville* but on a smaller scale (see fig. 17-33).

NICOLAS POUSSIN. Why were De La Tour and the Le Nains forgotten so quickly? The reason is that classicism was supreme in France after the 1640s. The clarity, balance, and restraint of their art, when measured against other Caravaggesque painters, might be termed classical, but none was a "classicist." The artist who did the most to bring about the rise of classicism was Nicolas Poussin (1593/4–1665), the greatest French painter of the century. He nevertheless spent almost his entire career in Rome. There, under the influence of Raphael, he developed the style that was to become the model for French painters of the second half of the century.

At first Poussin was inspired by Titian's warm, rich colors and by his approach to classical mythology. In *Cephalus and Aurora* (fig. 19-4) he portrays the ancient past as a poetic dream world, although the bliss of Titian's *Bacchanal* (see fig. 13-39) is now tinged with melancholy. Like many of his early works, this is a tale of frustrated love drawn from the Roman poet Ovid's *Metamorphoses,* a favorite source for Baroque artists. However, as is typical of Poussin, the picture departs from the text. Aurora, the goddess of dawn, tries to embrace the mortal Cephalus, who spurns her love out of faithfulness to his wife, Procris. Cephalus' fidelity is shown by the charming device of a **putto** holding up a portrait of Procris to his gaze. The sleeping river-god to the left signifies night. In the background, the sun-god Apollo waits by his chariot for daybreak (see also fig. 17-10).

Poussin soon fell under the spell of Raphael. *The Rape of the Sabine Women* (fig. 19-5) shows his new allegiance to classicism. The painting has the severe discipline of Poussin's intellectual style, which developed in response to what he regarded as the excesses of the High Baroque (see page 568). The strongly modeled figures are "frozen in action," like statues. Many are, in fact, derived from Hellenistic sculpture, but the main group comes from Giovanni Bologna's *Abduction of the Sabine Woman* (fig. 14-21). Poussin has placed them before reconstructions of Roman architecture that he believed to be archaeologically correct. The scene has a theatrical air, and with good reason. It was worked out by moving wax figurines around a miniature stagelike setting until it looked right to the artist. [See Primary Sources, no. 55, page 653.] Emotion is abundantly displayed in the dramatic poses and expressions, but it is so calculated in its lack of spontaneity that it fails to touch us. The attitude reflected here is clearly Raphael's (see figs. 13-31 and 13-33). More precisely, it is Raphael as filtered through Annibale Carracci and his school (compare figs. 17-5 and 17-9). The Venetian qualities of his early work have been consciously suppressed.

Poussin now strikes us as an artist who knew his own mind only too well. This impression is confirmed by the numerous letters in which he stated his views to friends and patrons. The highest aim of painting, he believed, is to represent noble and serious human actions. [See Primary Sources, no. 57, pages 654–55.] This is true even in *The Abduction of the Sabine Women,* which, ironically, was admired as an act of patriotism that ensured the future of Rome. (According to the accounts of Livy and Plutarch, the Sabines otherwise escaped unharmed, and the young women abducted as wives by the Romans later became peacemakers between the two sides.) To Poussin, such actions must be shown in a logical and orderly way—not as they really happened, but as they

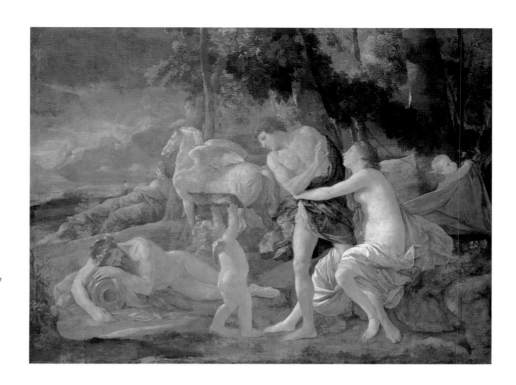

19-4. Nicolas Poussin.
Cephalus and Aurora. c. 1630.
Oil on canvas, 38 x 51" (96.7 x 129.7 cm).
The National Gallery, London

(BELOW) 19-5. Nicolas Poussin.
The Abduction of the Sabine Women.
c. 1633–34. Oil on canvas, 5'7⅞" x 6'10⅝"
(1.54 x 2.09 m). The Metropolitan
Museum of Art, New York

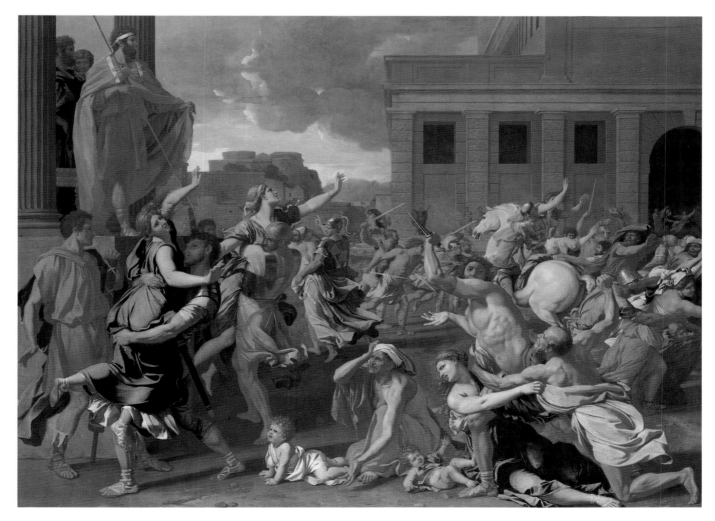

would have happened if nature were perfect. To this end, art must strive for the general and typical. In appealing to the mind rather than the senses, the painter should suppress such incidentals as color and instead emphasize form and composition. In a good picture, the viewer must be able to "read" the emotions of each figure and relate them to the story.

These ideas were not new. We recall Horace's motto *ut pictura poesis* and Leonardo's statement that the highest aim of painting is

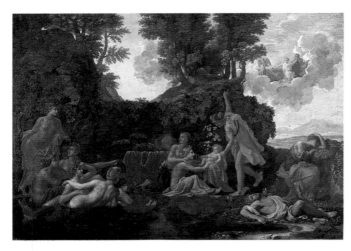

19-6. Nicolas Poussin. *The Birth of Bacchus*. c. 1657. Oil on canvas,
48¼ x 70½" (122.6 x 179.1 cm). Fogg Art Museum,
Harvard University Art Museums, Cambridge, Massachusetts
GIFT OF MRS. SAMUEL SACHS IN MEMORY OF HER HUSBAND

to depict "the intention of man's soul" (see page 453). Before
Poussin, however, no one made the analogy between painting and
literature so closely, or put it into practice so single-mindedly. His
method accounts for the cold rhetoric in *The Abduction of the Sabine
Women,* which makes the picture seem so remote.

Poussin also painted "ideal" landscapes with surprising success, for they have an austere beauty and somber calm. This severe
rationalism lasted until about 1650, when he began to paint landscapes that return to the realm of mythology he had abandoned in
middle age. They unite the Titianesque style of his early work
with his later, Raphaelesque classicism. The result is a new kind
of mythological landscape close in spirit to Claude Lorraine's (see
below) but rich in personal associations and levels of meaning.
Indeed, these late paintings have rightly been called transcenden-
tal meditations, for they contain archetypal imagery of universal
meaning. *The Birth of Bacchus* (fig. 19-6), among his most profound works, takes up the great Stoic theme (which Poussin had
treated twice as a young man) that death is to be found even in the
happiest realm. Bacchus, the god of wine, was created by Jupiter's
union with Semele, the moon-goddess, and born from his thigh to
protect the child from the wrath of his wife, Juno. The scene shows
the moment when the infant is brought by Mercury to the river-
goddess Dirce for safekeeping, while the satyr Pan plays the flute
in rapt inspiration. (Jupiter himself had been raised by nymphs on
Mount Ida in Crete to spare him from his father, Chronus.)

The picture is not beautifully executed. The act of painting
became difficult for Poussin in old age, so that the brushwork is
shaky. Yet he turned this difficulty to his advantage, and *The Birth
of Bacchus* represents the purest expressiveness. Its serene lyricism
conveys the joy of life on the one hand, and forebodings of death
on the other: to the right, the nymph Echo weeps over the dead
Narcissus, the youth who spurned her love and drowned kissing
his reflection. Like Cephalus and Aurora, the story of Echo and
Narcissus is taken from Ovid, but now it is the meaning, not the
narrative, that interests Poussin. He treats it as part of the eternal
cycle of nature, in which the gods embody natural forces and the

myths contain fundamental truths. The artist drew on the
pantheistic writings of Tommaso Campanella and the learned
commentaries of the Stoic Natale Conti, but it is his personal
understanding that brings these ideas to life.

CLAUDE LORRAINE. While Poussin developed the heroic
qualities of the ideal landscape, the great French landscapist
Claude Lorraine (1600–1682) brought out its idyllic aspects. He,
too, spent almost his entire career in Rome. Like many Northerners, Claude explored the surrounding countryside, the Campagna,
more thoroughly and affectionately than any Italian. Countless
drawings made on the spot reveal his powers of observation. He is
also the first artist known to have painted oil studies outdoors.
Sketches, however, were only the raw material for his landscapes.
Claude's paintings do not aim at topographic accuracy but evoke
the poetic essence of a countryside filled with echoes of antiquity.
Often, as in *A Pastoral Landscape* (fig. 19-7), the compositions have
the hazy, luminous atmosphere of early morning or late afternoon.
The space expands serenely, rather than receding step-by-step as
in Poussin's paintings. An air of nostalgia hangs over such vistas,
of past experience enhanced by memory. They had a special appeal
for many English who had seen Italy only briefly if at all.

SIMON VOUET. At an early age Simon Vouet (1590–1649), too,
went to Rome, where he became the leader of the French Caravaggesque painters. Unlike Poussin and Claude, who returned to
France only briefly, he settled in Paris. There he quickly shed all
traces of Caravaggio's manner and developed a colorful style based
on Carracci's, which won such acclaim that Vouet was named
First Painter to the king. He also brought with him memories of
the great north Italian precursors of the Baroque. *The Toilet of
Venus* (fig. 19-8) depicts a subject popular in Venice from Titian
(see fig. 13-43) to Veronese. Vouet's figure also recalls Correggio's
Io (see fig. 14-11), but without her frank eroticism. Instead, she has
been given an elegant sensuousness that is uniquely French.

The Toilet of Venus is far removed from Poussin's disciplined
art. It was painted about 1640, toward the beginning of Poussin's
ill-fated sojourn in Paris, where he had gone at the invitation of
Louis XIII. Poussin met with no more success than Bernini was to
have 20 years later (see pages 614 and 618). After several years he
left, deeply disillusioned by his experience at the court, whose taste
and politics Vouet understood far better. In one sense, their rivalry was to continue long afterward. Poussin's classicism soon dominated art in France, but Vouet's decorative style provided the basis
for Rococo painting. The two traditions vied with each other
through the Romantic era, alternating in succession without gaining the upper hand for long.

THE ROYAL ACADEMY. When young Louis XIV took over
the reins of government in 1661, Jean-Baptiste Colbert, his chief
adviser, built the administrative apparatus to support the power of
the absolute monarch. In this system, aimed at subjecting the
thoughts and actions of the entire nation to strict control from
above, the visual arts had the task of glorifying the king. As in
music and theater, which shared the same purpose, the official
"royal style" was classicism. Centralized control over the visual

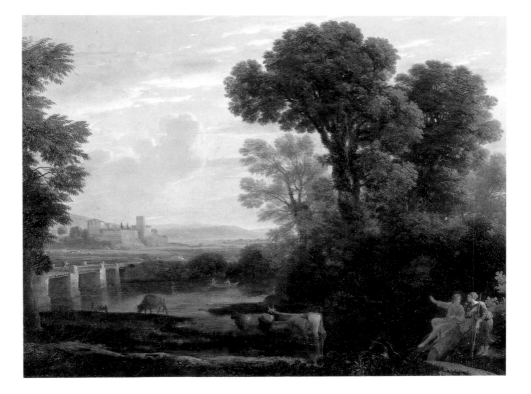

19-7. Claude Lorraine. *A Pastoral Landscape*. c. 1650. Oil on copper, 15½ x 21" (39.3 x 53.3 cm). Yale University Art Gallery, New Haven, Connecticut

LEO C. HANNA, JR., FUND

(BELOW) 19-8. Simon Vouet. *The Toilet of Venus*. c. 1640. Oil on canvas, 65¼ x 45" (165.7 x 114.3 cm). The Carnegie Museum of Art, Pittsburgh

GIFT OF MRS. HORACE BINNEY HARE

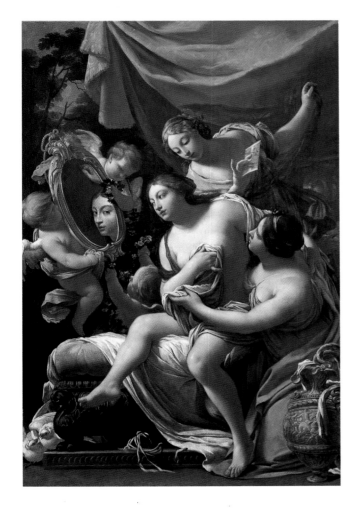

arts was exerted by Colbert and the artist Charles Lebrun (1619–1690), who became supervisor of all the king's artistic projects. As chief dispenser of royal art patronage, Lebrun had so much power that for all practical purposes he was the dictator of

the arts in France. His authority extended beyond the power of the purse. It also included a new system of educating artists in the officially approved style.

Throughout antiquity and the Middle Ages, artists had been trained by apprenticeship, and this practice still prevailed in the Renaissance. As painting, sculpture, and architecture gained the status of liberal arts, artists wished to supplement their "mechanical" training with theoretical knowledge. For this purpose, art academies were founded, patterned on the academies of the humanists. (The name *academy* is derived from the Athenian grove, dedicated to the legendary hero Akademos—Academus in Latin—where Plato met with his disciples.) Art academies appeared first in Italy in the later sixteenth century as an outgrowth of literary academies. They seem to have been private associations of artists who met to draw from the model and discuss art theory. These academies later became formal institutions that took over some functions from the guilds, but their teaching was limited and far from systematic.

This was the case as well with the Royal Academy of Painting and Sculpture in Paris, founded in 1648. But when Lebrun became its director in 1663, he established a rigid curriculum of instruction in practice and theory based on a system of rules. This set the pattern for all later academies, including the art schools of today. Much of this doctrine was derived from Poussin, with whom Lebrun had studied for several years in Rome, but it was carried to rationalist extremes. The Academy even devised a method for giving numerical grades to artists past and present in such categories as drawing, expression, and proportion. The ancients received the highest marks, of course, then came Raphael and his school, and Poussin. The Venetians, who "overemphasized" color, ranked low, the Flemish and Dutch even lower. Subjects were also classified, from history (that is, narrative subjects, be they classical, biblical, or mythological) at the top to still life at the bottom.

BAROQUE THEATER AND MUSIC IN FRANCE

The central fact of French culture in the seventeenth century was the taste for classicism, which had been established 50 years earlier. The Pléiade, a group of poets led by Pierre de Ronsard (1524–1585), was founded in 1550 to develop French literature along the lines of Greek and Roman poetry and plays, which had been published and studied since early in the century. Around the same time, court festivals became popular, as did *intermezzi* (also called *ballets de cour*), which combined song, dance, drama, and spectacle in the "antique" manner. Public theater was monopolized by the Confrérie de la Passion (Confraternity of the Passion), which was given control over secular drama. (Religious plays were banned in 1548.) These three factors—classical taste, antiquarianism, and court patronage—decisively shaped French theater and music. The preference for classicism and humanism was reinforced during the regency of Henry II's Italian queen, Catherine de' Medici (1560–1574). However, the development of the arts was disrupted by the Wars of Religion between Catholics and Protestants that broke out in 1562. Hostilities continued until the Protestants were defeated in 1629 by the soldiers of Louis XIII under the direction of his chief minister, Cardinal Richelieu (1585–1642).

The end of the Wars of Religion placed Richelieu in a position of immense power. A highly cultivated man, he now turned his attention not only to governing France but also to patronage of the arts. In 1629, the same year that the Protestants were defeated, the French Academy, a small group of intellectuals, began to meet informally to discuss literature. In 1636, at Cardinal Richelieu's behest, it became a state institution based on Italian models. The Academy required that theater teach moral lessons and adhere to the Italian concept of verisimilitude (see page 491). This was the first of a number of French academies that were to be founded during the course of the seventeenth century to foster painting and sculpture, music, architecture, and even dance. These state-controlled academies oversaw the training of young artists and were responsible for awarding royal commissions. As time went on, the academies became increasingly authoritarian, eventually exercising rigid control over all of the arts.

The first important French dramatist was Alexandre Hardy (c. 1572–1632), a prolific playwright who wrote some 700 tragicomedies (plays of serious subject that end happily) and pastoral plays for the Hôtel de Bourgogne, the only permanent playhouse in Paris before the end of the wars in 1629. Otherwise, plays were performed on tennis courts (*jeux de paume*), with a platform erected as a stage. In 1640 Cardinal Richelieu had a theater erected at his palace, the first in France to feature a proscenium (the arch separating the stage from the auditorium), an innovation from Italy that was soon to become standard throughout Europe. Richelieu took a particular interest in drama and personally employed five playwrights to work under his supervision. The only one to achieve lasting fame was Pierre Corneille (1606–1684), whose tragedies, drawn from ancient history and mythology, center on the hero who chooses death over dishonor. They are written in the ornate, emotional language that defined French classical drama before 1650. Yet when Corneille submitted *Le Cid* to the Academy for review the year it was founded, the play met with such harsh criticism that he stopped writing for four years. Corneille's younger brother, Thomas (1625–1709), was also a noted playwright whose finest works date from the 1670s.

French drama reached its zenith in the plays of Jean Racine (1639–1699), whose tragedies in the Greek manner revolved around the conflict of desire and duty, expressed in direct, simple language that quickly replaced the elaborate language of Pierre Corneille. Racine's plays embody the theories of Nicolas Boileau-Despréaux (1636–1711), who championed the three unities of action, time, and place, and decorum in speech, manner, and moral behavior. Early in his career Racine had been befriended by Molière (Jean-Baptiste Poquelin, 1622–1673), whose plays marked the high tide of French comedy. *The Misanthrope* (1666) and *Tartuffe* (1664), influenced by the commedia dell'arte, which enjoyed great success in France, are masterpieces of cynical wit written in the 12-syllable Alexandrine couplets that had become the standard verse form of French theater. The Comédie Française, formed by royal decree in 1680 from Molière's troupe and that of the rival Hôtel de Bourgogne, was granted a monopoly on all dramas in French, with the sole exception of the commedia dell'arte (see page 581), which was eventually banned in 1697 for an imagined slight of the king's mistress.

Cardinal Jules Mazarin, Richelieu's successor, who was an Italian by birth, had an abiding love of opera, which he actively promoted. Soon after taking the reins of full power upon

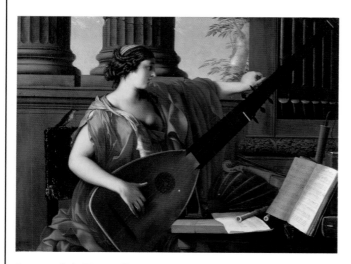

Laurent de la Hyre. *Allegory of Music.* 1645.
Oil on canvas, 41⅝ x 56¾" (105.7 x 144.1 cm).
The Metropolitan Museum of Art, New York

CHARLES B. CURTIS FUND, 1950

Mazarin's death in 1661, Louis XIV began construction of a new palace at Versailles, outside Paris. Even before the palace was completed in 1682 Louis staged huge spectacles, such as *The Pleasure of the Enchanted Land* (1664), an allegory of his reign. The arts during the age of Louis XIV were meant to glorify the king, and classicism had an essential role to play. Classicism was favored not only because of its learned humanism and elevated moral tone but also because it suggested that France was the successor to Greece and Rome. In the debates after 1688, known as the Battle of the Ancients and the Moderns, French academicians even sought to show the supremacy of French culture by using it to replace antiquity as the new standard.

During the 1650s, Louis XIV appeared regularly in ballets, which became great spectacles. Thereafter he continued to enjoy ballets and operas by his court composer and dancing master, Jean-Baptiste Lully (1632–1687). Lully had initially collaborated with Corneille and Molière on comic ballets for the court, but Molière refused to work with Lully in 1672 because of the latter's unscrupulous practices. Lully then forged a partnership with the playwright Philippe Quinault (1635–1688) that lasted a decade, from *Atys* (1676) through *Armide* (1686), based on Torquato Tasso's *Jerusalem Freed*. Their work, which emphasized the unity between text and music, was comparable in character to the tragedies of Corneille and Racine. Because he clung to the Florence *camerata*'s ideal of emphatic declamation (see page 569), Lully composed music of measured and stately simplicity. He was also considered a revolutionary for introducing additional choruses and ballets to the opera, which lent the performances a greater pageantry that benefited greatly from the costumes designed by Jean Bérain (1637–1711). The results were sober and pompous, but also colorful—perfectly suited to life at Versailles. Lully occupied a position in French music comparable to Charles Lebrun's in the arts. He was instrumental in founding the Royal Academy of Dance upon the king's retirement from active participation in ballets in 1661. In 1672, Lully merged the academies of music and dance to create the forerunner of the Opéra, the national opera company of France.

Lully was by far the most powerful force in French Baroque music. His only rival was Marc-Antoine Charpentier (1634–1704), a student of Carissimi, who as music director to the Jesuit order in Paris became the greatest French composer of religious music. Charpentier's secular music was also of high quality, particularly the opera *The Imaginary Illness* (1673), written with Molière after he had broken with Lully. The other major figure was the much younger François Couperin (1668–1733), organist to the king at Versailles, whose harpsichord and orchestral suites are notable for their lively invention. As a composer he straddled two eras: his most important compositions were written during the reign of Louis XV, although his music remained Late Baroque in style.

Architecture

FRANÇOIS MANSART. The foundations of Baroque classicism in architecture were laid by a group of designers of whom the best known was François Mansart (1598–1666). They form a continuous tradition with the sixteenth century that is unique in the history of architecture. The classicism introduced by Lescot at the Louvre (see fig. 16-27) reached its height around the middle of the sixteenth century under Henry II at the Château d'Anet, designed for Henry's mistress, Diane of Poitiers, by Philibert de l'Orme (see page 555); only the gateway, main entrance, and circular chapel are still intact. The tradition was continued at the Château of Ecouen by de l'Orme's chief disciple, Jean Bullant (c. 1520–1578), who is now known mainly for his books published in 1561 and 1563. The central position was occupied by the du Cerceau family, which worked on the Louvre and other royal projects through the middle of the seventeenth century.

The du Cerceau dynasty began with Jacques Androuet du Cerceau the Elder (c. 1515–c. 1585), a contemporary of de l'Orme and Bullant. Du Cerceau spent about a decade in Rome absorbing the High Renaissance style of Bramante before returning home to publish a series of treatises dealing mainly with town houses and their decoration. These preserve designs for lost buildings by de l'Orme and other architects of the period. Du Cerceau's grandson Salomon de Brosse (c. 1571–1626) continued the family style under the influence of Bullant. Mansart probably began his career under de Brosse in 1618; thus he belongs directly to this rich legacy. De Brosse's collaborators at the time included Mansart's brother-in-law, who may well have been responsible for the young man's training after the early death of his father. Mansart's talent was precocious, and within five years he had already established his reputation.

Apparently Mansart never visited Italy, but other French architects had already imported and adapted some aspects of the early Baroque. Chief among them was his rival, Jacques Lemercier (c. 1582–1654), who developed a rather dry and academic version of Vignola's and Della Porta's church designs as a result of his Roman stay in 1607–14. His works for Cardinal Richelieu, including the enlargement of the Square Court of the Louvre in 1624, are uninspired adaptations of earlier designs by Lescot, du Cerceau, and de Brosse. Lemercier was soon replaced by Mansart, who was the first architect of genius since Lescot.

Mansart clearly was familiar with the new Italian style. What he owed to it, however, is hard to determine. His most important buildings are châteaux, and in this field the French Renaissance tradition outweighed any Italian influences. For that reason his earlier designs are also the most classical. The Château of Maisons near Paris, built for the financier René du Longueil in the 1640s, shows Mansart's mature style. The exterior departs little from the precedents set by le Breton or de Brosse, although it possesses a classical logic and clarity that surpass any previous French design. It is the interior that breaks new ground. The vestibule leading to the grand staircase (fig. 19-9), among the most magnificent in all of French architecture, has a particularly beautiful effect, severe yet festive. On seeing the classically pure treatment of the white walls, one first thinks of Palladio (see page 508), whose treatise Mansart knew and admired. But sculpture is used here in a characteristically French way pioneered by

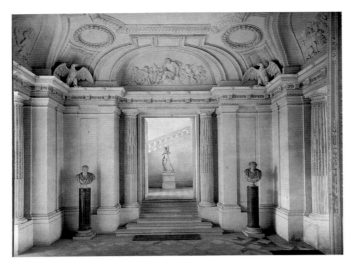

19-9. François Mansart. Vestibule of the Château of Maisons. 1642–50

de Brosse as an integral part of architectural design. The complex curves of the vaulting tell us that this structure, for all its classicism, belongs to the Baroque.

Mansart was at the height of his career at Maisons. Because of his difficult personality, however, he was replaced in 1646 after just one year at the church of the Val-de-Grâce in Paris by Lemercier. Lemercier then erected the most Baroque church ever built on French soil over Mansart's classical foundation. Mansart was also supplanted in the field of hôtels and châteaux by the younger and more adaptable Louis Le Vau (1612–1670). Le Vau was part of a team, including Charles Lebrun and the landscape architect André le Nôtre (1613–1700), who were called to the court by the king's minister Colbert in 1661 shortly before completing the château at Vaux-le-Vicomte outside Paris for the disgraced finance minister Nicolas Fouquet.

LOUIS XIV, COLBERT, AND THE LOUVRE. Mansart represents the early phase of French Baroque classicism. Its climactic stage, which may be compared with the heroic classicism of Poussin and the playwright Pierre Corneille (see box page 612), began with the first great project Colbert directed, the completion of the Louvre. Work on the palace had proceeded intermittently for over a century, along the lines of Lescot's design (see fig. 16-27). What remained to be done was to close the square court on the east side with an impressive facade. Colbert, however, was dissatisfied with the proposals of French architects, including Mansart, who submitted various designs not long before his death. He therefore invited Bernini to Paris in the hope that the most famous master of the Roman Baroque would do for the French king what he had already done for the Church. Bernini spent several months in Paris in 1665 and submitted three designs, all of them on a scale that would have dwarfed the existing palace. After much argument and intrigue, Louis XIV rejected these plans and turned over the problem to a committee of three: Charles Lebrun, his court painter; Louis Le Vau, his court architect, who had already done much work on the Louvre (including the Gallery of Apollo, Queen's court, and south facade); and Claude Perrault (1613–1688), who was an anatomist and student of ancient architecture, not a professional architect. All three were responsible for the structure that was actually built (fig. 19-10), but Perrault is rightly credited with the major share. Certainly his supporters and detractors thought so at the time, and he was often called upon to defend its design. [See Primary Sources, no. 58, page 655.]

The center pavilion is based on a Roman temple front, and the wings look like the sides of that temple folded outward. The temple theme required a single order of freestanding columns, but the Louvre had three stories. This problem was solved by treating the ground story as the podium of the temple and recessing the upper two behind the screen of the colonnade. The colonnade itself was

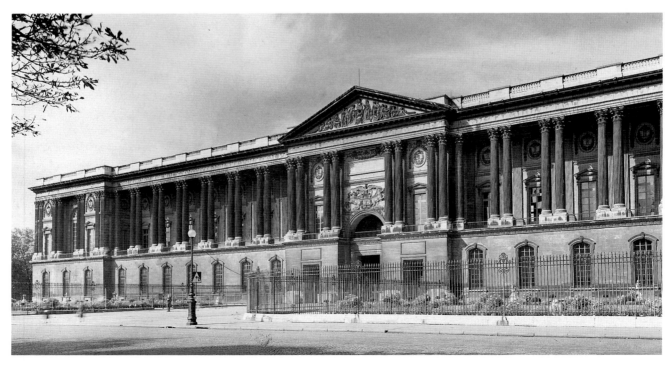

19-10. Claude Perrault. East Front of the Louvre, Paris. 1667–70

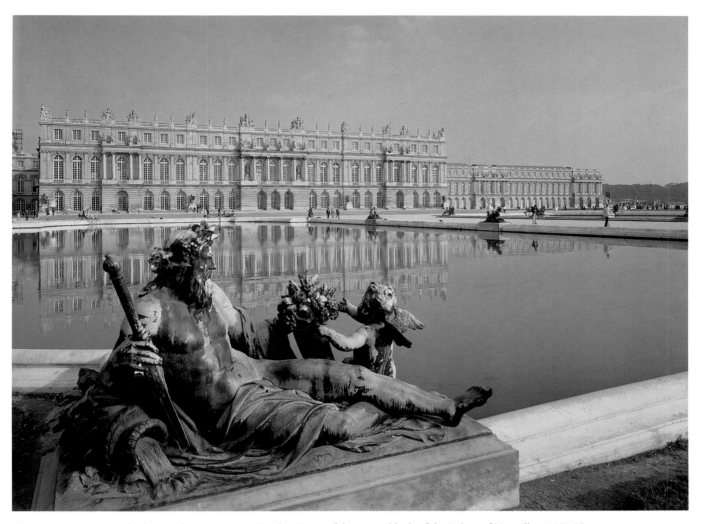

19-11. Louis Le Vau and Jules Hardouin-Mansart. Garden Front of the center block of the Palace of Versailles. 1669–85

controversial in its use of paired columns for aesthetic reasons, even though they were not needed for support.

The East Front of the Louvre signaled the victory of French classicism over the Italian Baroque as the royal style. It further proclaims France the new Rome, both politically and culturally, by linking Louis XIV with the glory of the Caesars. The design combines grandeur and elegance in a way that fully justifies its fame. In some ways it suggests the mind of an archaeologist, but one who knew how to choose those features of classical architecture that would be compatible with the older parts of the palace. This antiquarian approach was Perrault's main contribution.

Perrault owed his position to his brother, Charles Perrault (1628–1703), who, as Colbert's Master of Buildings under Louis XIV, had helped to undermine Bernini during his stay at the French Court. [See Primary Sources, no. 58, page 655.] It is likely that Claude shared the views set forth some 20 years later in Charles's *Parallels Between the Ancients and Moderns* (see page 667), which claimed "that Homer and Virgil made countless mistakes which the moderns no longer make [because] the ancients did not have all our rules. . . ." Thus the East Front of the Louvre presents not simply a classical revival but a vigorous distillation of what Claude Perrault considered the eternal ideals of beauty. As such, it was intended to surpass anything by the Romans themselves. Although it was attacked by strict classicists, this great example proved to be too pure and Perrault soon faded from favor.

THE PALACE OF VERSAILLES. The king's largest enterprise was the Palace of Versailles, located 11 miles from the center of Paris. It was built by Louis XIV to prevent a repeat of the civil rebellion known as the Fronde, which occurred in 1648–53 during his minority, by forcing the aristocracy to live under royal control outside of Paris. The project was begun in 1669 by Le Vau, who designed the elevation of the Garden Front (fig. 19-11), but he died within a year. Under Jules Hardouin-Mansart (1646–1708), a great-nephew and pupil of François Mansart (see above), it was greatly expanded to accommodate the ever-growing royal household. The Garden Front, intended by Le Vau to be the main view of the palace, was stretched to an enormous length with no change in the architectural elements. As a result, his original facade design, a less severe variant of the East Front of the Louvre, looks repetitious and out of scale. The whole center block contains a single room, the famous Galerie des Glaces (Hall of Mirrors, fig. 19-12). At either end are the Salon de la Guerre (War, fig. 19-13) and its counterpart, the Salon de la Paix (Peace). The sumptuous effect of the Galerie des Glaces imitates the Gallery of Francis I at Fontainebleau, which had been decorated by Primaticcio (see fig. 14-20).

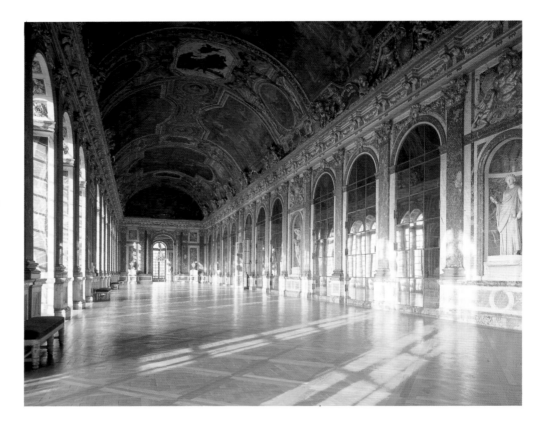

19-12. Hardouin-Mansart, Lebrun, and Coysevox. Galerie des Glaces (Hall of Mirrors), Palace of Versailles

19-13. Hardouin-Mansart, Lebrun, and Coysevox. Salon de la Guerre, Palace of Versailles. Begun 1678

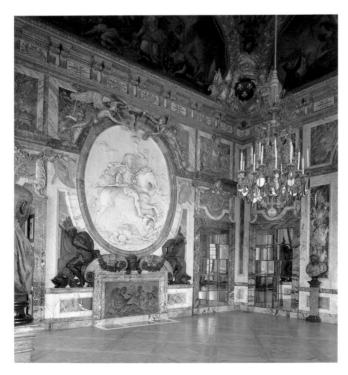

Baroque features, although not officially acknowledged, reappeared inside the Palace of Versailles. This shift reflected the king's own taste. Louis XIV was interested less in architectural theory and monumental exteriors than in the lavish interiors that would make suitable settings for himself and his court. Thus the man to whom he really listened was not an architect but the painter Lebrun. Lebrun's goal was in itself Baroque: to subordinate all the arts to the glorification of Louis XIV. To achieve it, he drew freely on his memories of Rome. The great decorative schemes of the Baroque that he saw there must also have impressed him.

They stood him in good stead 20 years later, both in the Louvre and at Versailles. Although a disciple of Poussin, he had studied first with Vouet, and became a superb decorator. Lebrun employed architects, sculptors, painters, and decorators to create ensembles of unprecedented splendor. The Salon de la Guerre at Versailles (fig. 19-13) is closer in many ways to the Cornaro Chapel than to the vestibule at Maisons (compare figs. 17-30 and 19-9). While Lebrun's ensemble is less adventurous than Bernini's, he has given greater emphasis to surface decoration. As in so many Italian Baroque interiors, the separate components are less impressive than the effect of the whole.

THE GARDENS OF VERSAILLES. Apart from the magnificent interior, the most impressive aspect of Versailles is the park extending west of the Garden Front for several miles (fig. 19-14). The design by André le Nôtre is so strictly correlated with the plan of the palace that it continues the architectural space. Like the interiors, these formal gardens, with their terraces, basins, clipped hedges, and statuary, were meant to provide a suitable setting for the king's public appearances. They form a series of "outdoor rooms" for the splendid fêtes and spectacles that Louis XIV so enjoyed. The spirit of absolutism is even more striking in the geometric regularity imposed upon an entire countryside than it is in the palace itself. This kind of formal garden had its beginnings in Renaissance Florence but had never been used on the scale achieved by Le Nôtre at Versailles and elsewhere.

JULES HARDOUIN-MANSART. At Versailles, where Jules Hardouin-Mansart worked as a member of a team, he was constrained by the design of Le Vau. His own style can be better seen in the Church of the Invalides (figs. 19-15 and 19-16), named after the institution for disabled soldiers of which it was a part.

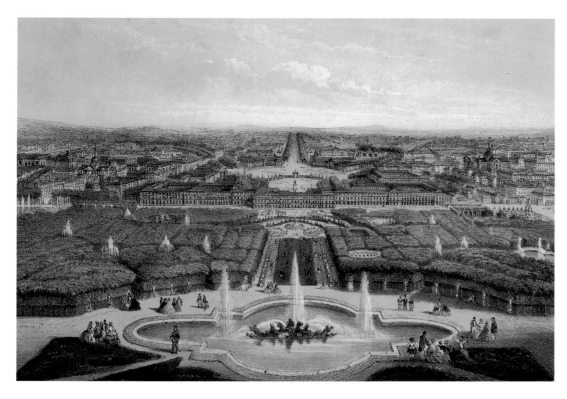

19-14. Charles Rivière. *Perspective View of the Château and Gardens of Versailles*. Lithograph after an 1860 photograph

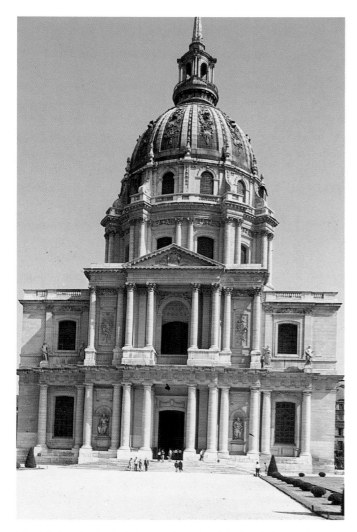

19-15. Jules Hardouin-Mansart. Church of the Invalides, Paris. 1680–91

The building combines Italian Renaissance and Baroque features, but they have been interpreted in a distinctly French manner that stretches back to de l'Orme's church for the castle at Anet (1549). The Invalides may be seen as Hardouin-Mansart's comment on its seventeenth-century predecessors in Paris: Lemercier's church of the College of the Sorbonne (1626), Mansart's Ste.-Marie de la Visitation (1632), the Val de Grâce (see above), and Le Vau's church at the College of Four Nations (1662) on the Seine across from the Louvre. The Visitation is an unsatisfactory effort from just before Mansart's maturity. However, Hardouin-Mansart incorporated features found in his grand-uncle's design of 1665 for the Bourbon dynasty chapel at St.-Denis. It may well be that the Invalides was intended to serve a similar purpose as Louis XIV's burial place.

In plan the Invalides consists of a Greek cross with four corner chapels. It is based (with various French intermediaries) on Michelangelo's and Bramante's plans for St. Peter's (see figs. 13-28 and 13-9). The only Baroque element is the oval choir. The dome, too, reflects the influence of Michelangelo (see fig. 13-27), but it consists of three shells, not the usual two, and the classicistic

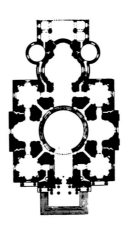

19-16. Plan of the Church of the Invalides

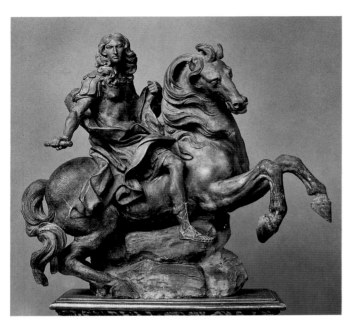

19-17. Gianlorenzo Bernini. *Model for Equestrian Statue of Louis XIV.* 1670. Terra-cotta, height 30" (76.3 cm). Galleria Borghese, Rome

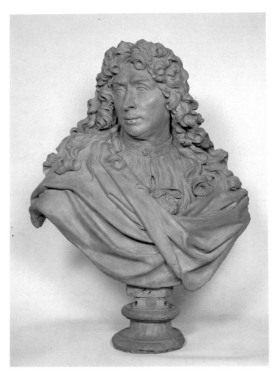

19-18. Antoine Coysevox. *Charles Lebrun.* 1676. Terra-cotta, height 26" (66 cm). The Wallace Collection, London

facade recalls the East Front of the Louvre. Nevertheless, the exterior as a whole is unmistakably Baroque. It breaks forward repeatedly in the crescendo effect introduced by Maderno (see fig. 17-15), and the facade and dome are as closely linked as at Borromini's S. Agnese in Piazza Navona (see fig. 17-23). The dome itself is the most original, as well as the most Baroque, feature of Hardouin-Mansart's design. Tall and slender, it rises in one continuous curve from the base of the drum to the spire atop the lantern. On the first drum rests a second, narrower drum. Its windows provide light for the painting inside the dome. The windows themselves are hidden behind a "pseudo-shell" with a large opening at the top, so that the vision of heavenly glory seems to be mysteriously illuminated and suspended in space. The bold theatrical lighting of the Invalides would do honor to any Italian Baroque architect.

Sculpture

Sculpture arrived at the official royal style in much the same way as architecture. While in Paris, Bernini carved a marble bust of Louis XIV. He was also commissioned to do an equestrian statue of the king, for which he made a terracotta model (fig. 19-17). However, the project shared the fate of Bernini's Louvre designs. Although he portrayed the king in classical military garb, the statue was rejected. Apparently the rearing horse, derived from Leonardo's design for the Battle of Anghiari (see page 456), was too dynamic to safeguard the dignity of Louis XIV. This decision was far-reaching. Equestrian statues of the king were later set up throughout France as

symbols of royal authority. Bernini's design, had it succeeded, might have set the pattern for these monuments. Adopted instead was a timid variation on the equestrian portrait of Marcus Aurelius (see fig. 7-40) executed in the 1680s by François Girardon (1628–1715), which was destroyed during the French Revolution.

ANTOINE COYSEVOX. Bernini's influence can nevertheless be felt in the work of Antoine Coysevox (1640–1720), one of the sculptors Lebrun employed at Versailles. The victorious Louis XIV in Coysevox's large stucco relief for the Salon de la Guerre (see fig. 19-13) retains the pose of Bernini's equestrian statue, although with a certain restraint. Coysevox is the first of a long line of distinguished French portrait sculptors. His terra-cotta portrait of Lebrun (fig. 19-18) repeats the general outlines of Bernini's bust of Louis XIV. The face, however, shows a realism and subtle characterization that are Coysevox's own.

PIERRE-PAUL PUGET. Coysevox approached the Baroque in sculpture as closely as Lebrun would permit. Pierre-Paul Puget (1620–1694), the most talented and most Baroque of seventeenth-century French sculptors, had no success at court until after Colbert's death, when Lebrun's power was on the decline. *Milo of Crotona* (fig. 19-19), Puget's finest statue, can be compared to Bernini's *David* (see fig. 17-28). Puget's composition is more contained than Bernini's, but the agony of the hero has such force that its impact is almost physical. The violent action fills the statue with an intense life that also recalls *The Laocoön Group* (see fig. 5-78). That, one suspects, is what made it acceptable to Louis XIV.

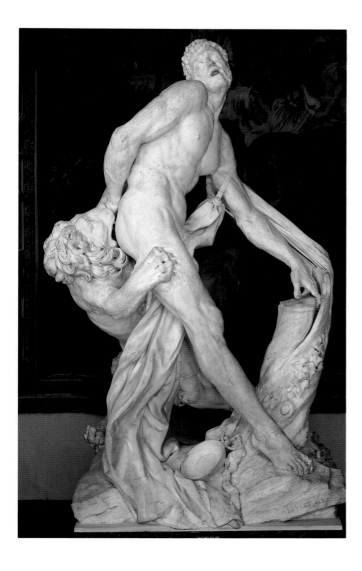

(LEFT) 19-19. Pierre-Paul Puget. *Milo of Crotona*. 1671–83. Marble, height 8'10½" (2.7 m). Musée du Louvre, Paris.

The "Milo" is perhaps Puget's most remarkable work. . . . The statue is Baroque in its violence of movement, in the sharp twist of the arm and head, in the naturalism of the tree trunk, which indicates that the artist must have known Bernini's "Apollo and Daphne." But the movement is so carefully controlled that, seen from the front as it is meant to be seen, the whole statue forms a simple silhouette composed of two sets of parallel axes: the legs and left arm forming one set, and the torso, drapery, and tree trunk forming the other. If this pattern is compared with say, the "David" of Bernini, which also depicts great strain, the difference is evident. In the "David" there is the maximum of contrapposto so that no straight line or plane survives; in the "Milo" the whole statue is based on straight lines and planes. And just as the physical strain is concentrated into a rigid and mathematical scheme, so the emotional expression is made to conform to a classical formula. For the head and the mask are based on the "Laocoon" and have the degree of restraint apparent even in the most Baroque of the ancient groups. Again this feature is brought out most clearly by a comparison with the "David," with its tense lips and down-drawn eyebrows.

—Anthony Blunt. *Art and Architecture in France 1500 to 1700.* Pelican History of Art Series. New Haven: Yale University Press, 1999, p. 376. Originally published in 1953 by Penguin Books Ltd.

SIR ANTHONY BLUNT (1907–1983) was a great connoisseur, especially of drawings, and possessed a singular grasp of French Baroque art. Poussin was his specialty. Much of his writing is dryly intellectual, but occasionally, as in his description of Puget's *Milo of Crotona,* an astonishing note of passion breaks out. Blunt left his position as Keeper of the Queen's Collection under the dark cloud of having been unmasked as a longtime spy for the KGB.

ENGLAND

The English made no significant contribution to Baroque painting and sculpture. They were content with feeble offshoots of Van Dyck's portraiture by imported artists such as the Dutch-born Peter Lely (1618–1680) and his German successor, Godfrey Kneller (1646–1723). The English achievement in architecture, however, was of genuine importance. This accomplishment is all the more surprising in light of the fact that England did not produce any buildings of note after the Gothic Perpendicular (see fig. 11-28) until the "prodigy" houses of Elizabethan times (see figs. 16-31 and 16-32).

INIGO JONES. The first English architect of genius was Inigo Jones (1573–1652), whose work developed from the country house tradition. He was also the leading English theatrical designer of the day. When he went to Italy about 1600 and again in 1613, he was influenced by the Baroque stage designs of Giulio Parigi (see box page 581). Surprisingly, he returned a disciple of Palladio (who had designed the theater of the Olympic Academy in Vicenza, one of the earliest of its kind; see illustration page 490). In 1615

Jones was appointed Surveyor of the King's Works, a post he held until 1643. The Banqueting House he built at Whitehall Palace in London (fig. 19-20) for the masques and other entertainment he presented at the court conforms in every way to the principles in Palladio's treatise, although it does not copy any specific design. It is essentially a Vitruvian "basilica" (a double-cube with an apse for the king's throne) treated as a Palladian villa, but with a breadth and consistency that remind us of Longleat (see fig. 16-31). Symmetrical and self-sufficient, it is more like a Renaissance palazzo than any other building north of the Alps designed at that time. Jones's spare style, supported by Palladio's authority as a theorist, stood as a beacon of classicist orthodoxy in England for 200 years.

CHRISTOPHER WREN. This classicism can be seen in some parts of London's St. Paul's Cathedral (figs. 19-21, 19-22, and 19-23) by Sir Christopher Wren (1632–1723), the great English architect of the late seventeenth century. Note the second-story windows and especially the dome, which looks like Bramante's Tempietto much enlarged (see fig. 13-7). St. Paul's is in other ways an up-to-date Baroque design that reflects a thorough knowledge of the Italian and French architecture of the day. Wren came close

BAROQUE THEATER AND MUSIC IN ENGLAND

In England, court masques adapted from Italian court pageants played a similar role to the French *ballets de cour* in that they promoted an idealized vision of monarchy presented through allegory and myth expressed in elegant speeches, music, and dance. Many of these masques were created for James I by the playwright Ben Jonson (1572–1637) and staged by Inigo Jones (see pages 619–20). Upon the overthrow in 1642 of Charles I by the Puritans—whose religious views demanded the most austere social standards—all theaters were closed, and remained so during the Commonwealth, the Puritan period of rule led by Oliver Cromwell; they were reopened only when the monarchy was restored in 1660. The Restoration, as the reign of the new king, Charles II, came to be known, was a period of great creativity for theater and music. There was an almost immediate demand for new plays, which were supplied by John Dryden (1631–1700), whose work was influenced by Shakespeare and the classi-cal Roman authors. The later plays by Dryden and William D'Avenant (1606–1668), Jonson's successor at court, are rather stilted, moralizing tragedies about people of noble birth. Comedy fared better, while adhering to the same goal of moral instruction. *The Rover: or the Banished Cavalier* (1677) by Mrs. Aphra Behn (1640–1689) and *The Way of the World* (1700) by William Congreve (1670–1729) and Sir John Vanbrugh (best known as the architect of Blenheim Palace; see fig. 19-25) are uproarious comedies of manners that reflect the cynicism—and what later critics called the licentiousness—of the age. The Restoration marked a revolution in English theater: not only did women begin to write plays but they also appeared on the legitimate stage for the first time. Some became enormously successful: one, Nell Gwyn, soon retired from the stage to become Charles II's mistress.

Theater gave rise to a new class of stage music by the leading composer of the Restoration, Henry Purcell (1659–1695). During the Commonwealth, English operas were plays set to music, which managed to avoid the ban against theater because

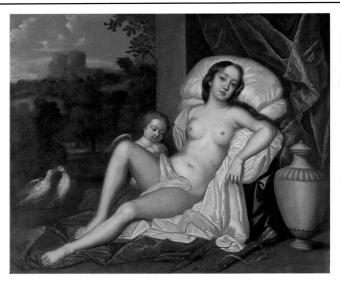

Sir Peter Lely and Studio. *Portrait of Nell Gwyn As Venus with Her Son Charles Beauclerk As Cupid.* 17th century. Oil on canvas, 47⅝ x 58½" (121 x 148.6 cm). Army and Navy Club, London

they were considered concerts. This practice continued even during the Restoration. Thus *Venus and Adonis,* by Henry Purcell's teacher John Blow (1649–1708), is essentially a masque in disguise. A large part of Purcell's output is theater music, such at *The Fairy Queen* (1692), which is a free adaptation of Shakespeare's *A Midsummer Night's Dream* (not Edmund Spencer's epic poem *The Faerie Queen,* published in 1596, which is an allegory of love and honor). The closest Purcell came to opera was *Dido and Aeneas* (1689), which is basically a concert opera reputedly composed for a girls' boarding school but perhaps given as a court entertainment instead. In the following decade, Purcell found an eager collaborator in Dryden, who supplied the composer with his finest "plays" set to music: notably *King Arthur* (1691), *Oedipus* (1692), and *The Indian Queen* (1695). Blow and Purcell also wrote numerous odes for the royal family and to celebrate other occasions, as well as many church anthems and a considerable body of chamber music and keyboard works.

to being a Baroque counterpart of the Renaissance artist-scientist. An intellectual prodigy, he first studied anatomy, then physics, mathematics, and astronomy, and was highly esteemed by Sir Isaac Newton for his understanding of geometry. He early on held a chair in astronomy at Gresham College, London, then at Oxford University. His serious interest in architecture did not begin until he was about 30. It is hard to determine if his technological knowledge affected the shape of his buildings. However, no previous architect went to such great lengths to conceal his structural supports. Only someone with an enormous grasp of geometry and mathematics could have achieved such results. Hence his great appeal to and importance for Soufflot (see pages 686–87), and why his work has confounded his critics.

For Wren as for Newton (who was appointed a Commissioner of St. Paul's in 1697), mathematics and geometry were central to the new understanding of the universe and humanity's place in it.

In his five Tracts, written toward the end of his life and presented in 1740 by his son to the Royal Society, Wren wrote that architecture must conform to "natural reason," which is the basis of eternal Beauty: it must use rational (that is, abstract) geometrical forms, such as the square and circle, among others, as well as proportion, perspective, and harmony, but not at the sacrifice of variety. Following Newton, he emphasized a dynamic space suggestive of the divine infinite through illusionism, not simply at the Greenwich Naval Hospital (1694), where he had previously constructed one of the first major observatories at the behest of Charles II (1675), but also, in a more limited way, at St. Paul's Cathedral.

If the great London fire of 1666 had not destroyed the Gothic cathedral of St. Paul and many lesser churches, Wren might have remained an amateur architect. But after that catastrophe, he was named to the short-lived royal commission for rebuilding the city, and a few years later began his designs for St. Paul's. [See Primary

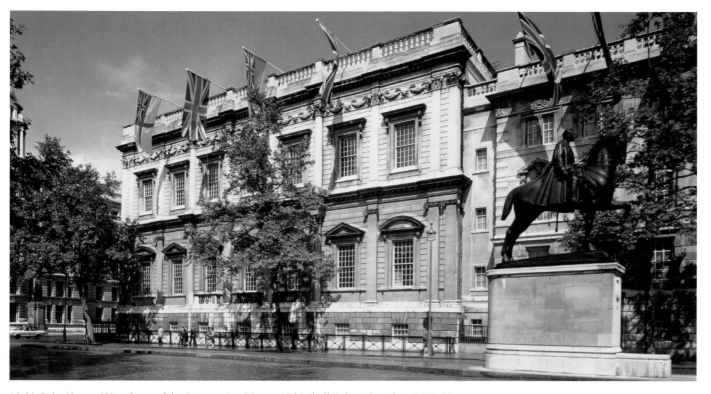

19-20. Inigo Jones. West front of the Banqueting House, Whitehall Palace, London. 1619–22

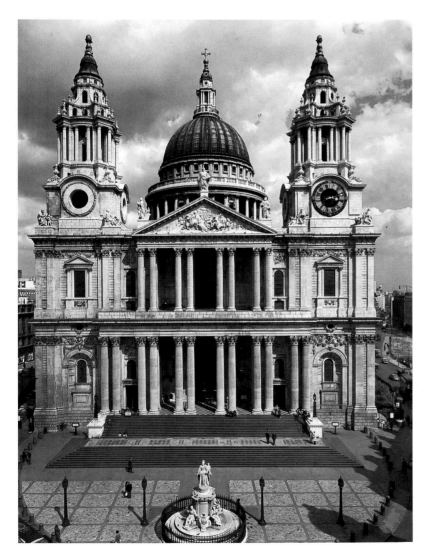

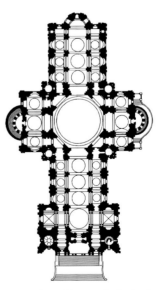

(Left) 19-21. Sir Christopher Wren.
Facade of St. Paul's Cathedral, London. 1675–1710

19-22. Plan of St. Paul's Cathedral

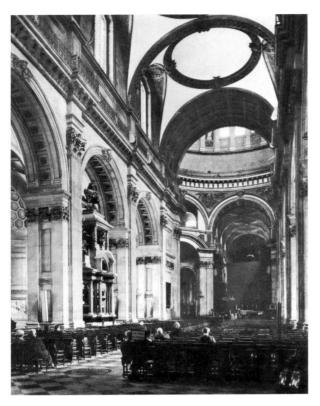

19-23. Interior of St. Paul's Cathedral

(BELOW) 19-24. William Clere. The "Great Model" for
St. Paul's Cathedral by Sir Christopher Wren.
1673. Wood, 13 x 14 x 17' (3.98 x 4.26 x 5.24 m).
Conway Library, The Courtauld Institute Library, London

Sources, no. 59, page 655.] Wren favored central-plan churches and originally conceived St. Paul's in the shape of a Greek cross (fig. 19-24), based on Michelangelo's plan of St. Peter's (see fig. 13-28), with a huge domed crossing. This idea was evidently inspired by a design by Inigo Jones, who had been involved with the restoration of the Gothic St. Paul's earlier in the century. Wren's proposal, however, was rejected as papist by church authorities, who favored a conventional basilica as more suitable for a Protestant structure.

The tradition of Inigo Jones provided no more than a starting point for Wren. He must have wanted the new St. Paul's to be the St. Peter's of the Church of England: soberer and not so large, but just as impressive. Like St. Peter's, St. Paul's dome has a diameter as wide as the nave and aisles combined, but it rises high above the rest of the building and dominates even our close view of the facade. The buttresses supporting the dome are ingeniously hidden behind a thick wall, which further helps to brace them.

The nave and the aisles consist of a series of domes on pendentives of novel design (see figs. 19-22 and 19-23). The effect can be compared only with the interior of St. Marks', Venice (fig. 8-46), as well as certain Romanesque examples inspired by it in the Perigord region of southern France, such as St. Front, Périgueux (c. 1120). Wren used polychromy to delineate the nave domes. Unlike Sangallo's dome at Prato (fig. 12-37), which appears to float above its squinches, the rings in St. Paul's seem tied by clamps to the arches and windows on either side, as if to assure us of the vaults' stability by bracing everything together. These domes and their supports are, however, completely disguised by the masonry walls and roofline of the exterior. Below the clerestory, echoes of the great Italian churches from Alberti's S. Andrea (fig. 12-33) through

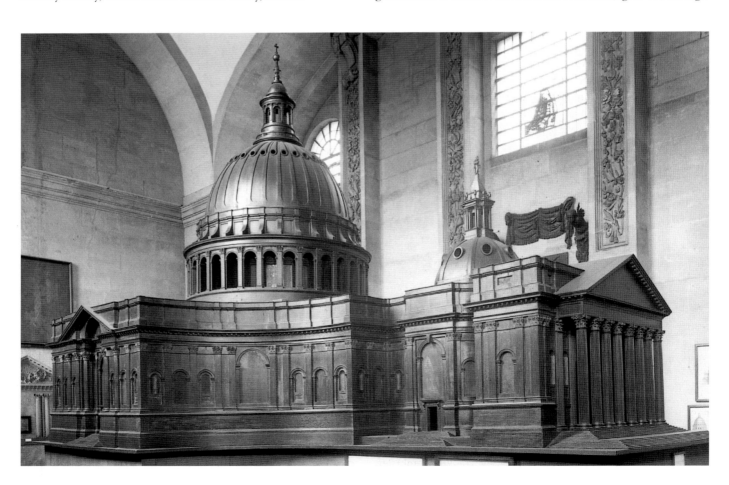

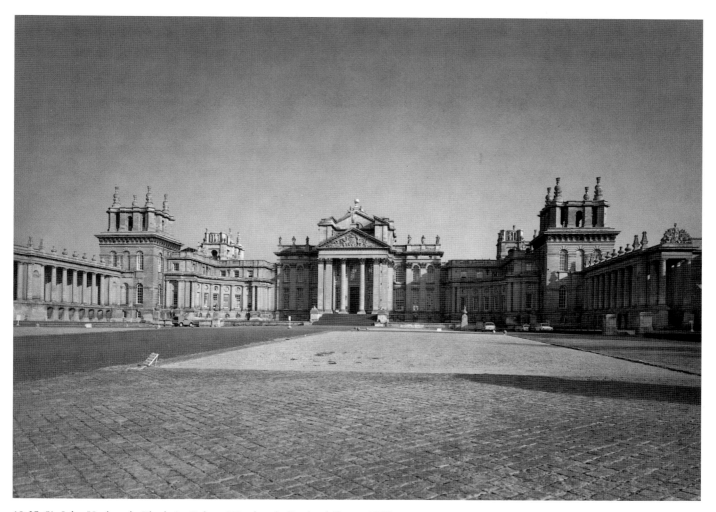

19-25. Sir John Vanbrugh. Blenheim Palace, Woodstock, England. Begun 1705

Vignola's Gesù (fig. 14-31) and Maderno's St. Peter's (fig. 17-16) abound throughout the vast interior. There is even a passing debt to the nave of Palladio's S. Giorgio Maggiore (see fig. 14-27).

Wren knew these Italian examples through prints. On his only trip abroad in 1665-6, he had visited France (and perhaps Flanders and Holland) at the time of the dispute over the completion of the Louvre. Wren must have sided with Perrault, whose design for the East Front is clearly reflected in the facade of St. Paul's. St. Paul's also bears a striking resemblance to Hardouin-Mansart's Church of the Invalides (see fig. 19-15), which inspired the three-part construction of the dome. Despite his belief that Paris provided "the best school of architecture in Europe," Wren was also affected by the Roman Baroque. The lantern and the upper part of the clock towers suggest that he knew Borromini's Sta. Agnese in Piazza Navona (see fig. 17-23), probably from drawings or engravings. The final result reflects not only the complex evolution of the design but also some needless changes made late in the construction by the commission overseeing it, which dismissed Wren in 1718.

JOHN VANBRUGH. The marriage of English, French, and Italian Baroque elements is even more evident in Blenheim Palace (fig. 19-25). This grandiose structure was designed by Sir John Vanbrugh (1664–1726), a gifted amateur, with the aid of Nicholas Hawksmoore (1661–1719), Wren's most talented pupil. Vanbrugh

owed his position to the Earl of Carlisle, which established him as Wren's rival and eventual successor. Blenheim, although his greatest work, caused Vanbrugh enormous problems. In the end he was left out in the cold like Wren, and the building had to be completed by Hawksmoore. It nevertheless shows no sign of this turbulent history. Blenheim skillfully combines the masses of an English castle with the breadth of a country house such as Longleat (see fig. 16-31); the rambling character of a French château such as Fontainebleau (see fig. 16-26); and a facade inspired, interestingly enough, by Vanbrugh's rival, Wren. However, when we compare Blenheim and its framing colonnade with the piazza of St. Peter's (see fig. 17-15), we can see that Vanbrugh's design is even closer to Bernini. The main block uses a colossal Corinthian order to wed a temple portico with a Renaissance palace (compare fig. 13-26), while the wings rely on a low-slung Doric order. Such an eclectic approach, extreme even by the relaxed standards of the period, is maintained even in the details. Vanbrugh, like Inigo Jones, had a strong interest in the theater. (He was a popular playwright; see box page 619.) The effect has both a theatricality and a massiveness that makes Blenheim a fitting counterpart to Versailles (see fig. 19-11) as a symbol of English power. Designed mainly for show and entertainment, it was presented by a grateful nation to the duke of Marlborough for his victories over French and German forces at the battle of Blenheim in 1704 during the War of Spanish Secession.

CHAPTER TWENTY

The Rococo

Much as the Baroque is often considered the final phase of the Renaissance, so the Rococo has been treated as the end of the Baroque: a long twilight, delicious but decadent, that was cleaned away by the Enlightenment and Neoclassicism. In France the Rococo is linked with Louis XV, because it roughly corresponds to his lifetime (1710–1774). However, it cannot be identified with the State or the Church any more than can the Baroque, even though they continued to provide the main patronage. The essential characteristics of Rococo style were defined largely during the regency phase of 1717–23. Moreover, its first signs appeared as much as 50 years earlier, during the Late Baroque. For that reason, the view of the Rococo as the final phase of the Baroque is well founded. As the philosopher Voltaire (François-Marie Arouet) pointed out, the eighteenth century lived in debt of the past. In art Poussin and Rubens cast their long shadows over the period. The controversy between their followers, in turn, goes back much further to the debate between the supporters of Michelangelo and of Titian over the merits of design versus color (see page 626). In this sense the Rococo, like the Baroque, still belongs to the Renaissance world.

There is, however, a fundamental difference between the Rococo and the Baroque. What is it? In a word, it is fantasy. If the Baroque presents theater on a grand scale, the Rococo stage is smaller and more intimate. At the same time, the Rococo is both more lighthearted and tender-minded, marked equally by playful whimsy and wistful nostalgia. Its artifice evokes an enchanted realm that presents a diversion from real life. Because the modern age is the product of the Enlightenment, the Rococo is still often criticized for its unabashed escapism and eroticism. To its credit, however, the Rococo celebrated the world of love and broadened the range of human emotion in art to include the family as a major theme.

FRANCE

THE RISE OF THE ROCOCO. After the death of Louis XIV in 1715, the administrative machine that Colbert had created ground to a stop (see pages 610–11). The nobility, formerly attached to the court at Versailles, were now freer from royal control. Many of them chose not to return to their châteaux in the provinces but to live in Paris, where they built elegant town houses, known as hôtels. Hôtels had been used as city residences by the landed aristocracy since about 1350, but during the seventeenth century they developed into social centers. As state-sponsored building activity was declining, the field of "design for private living" took on new importance. These city sites were usually cramped and irregular, so that they offered few opportunities for impressive exteriors. Hence the layout and décor of the rooms became the architects' main concern. The hôtels demanded an intimate style of interior decoration that gave full scope to individual fancy, uninhibited by the classicism seen at Versailles. To meet this need, French designers created the Rococo from Italian gardens and interiors. The name fits well: it was coined from *coquillage* and *rocaille* (echoing the Italian *barocco*), which meant the playful decoration of grottoes with irregular shells and stones.

The Decorative Arts

It was in the decorative arts that the Rococo flourished first and foremost. We have not discussed the decorative arts until now, because their conservative nature tended to limit creativity except in a few unusual cases. The later seventeenth century was a time of great change in French design. A central role was played by Colbert, who in the 1660s acquired the Gobelins (named after the brothers who founded them) for the crown. He turned them into a royal workshop that supplied luxurious furnishings, including tapestries, to the court under the direction of Charles Lebrun. After 1688 the War of the League of Augsburg forced the crown to economize. Reduced spending at the Gobelins gradually loosened central control of the decorative arts and opened the way to new stylistic developments. The situation paralleled the decline of the Academy's dominance over the fine arts, which gave rise to the Rococo in painting and sculpture.

This change does not explain the excellence of French décor, however. Crucial to its development was the importance assigned to designers. Their engravings established new standards of design that

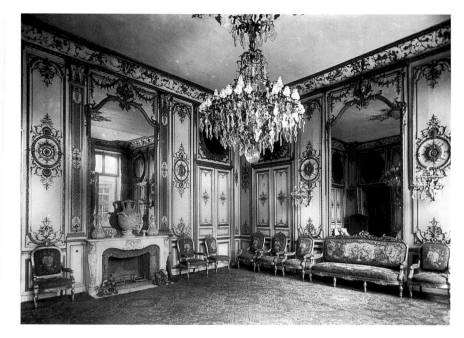

20-1. Robert de Cotte. Grand Salon of the Hôtel de Bourvallais, Paris. 1717
© GEORGES FESSY

(BELOW) 20-2. Claude Michel, known as Clodion. *Satyr and Bacchante.* c. 1775. Terra-cotta, height 23¼" (59 cm). The Metropolitan Museum of Art, New York
BEQUEST OF BENJAMIN ALTMAN, 1913

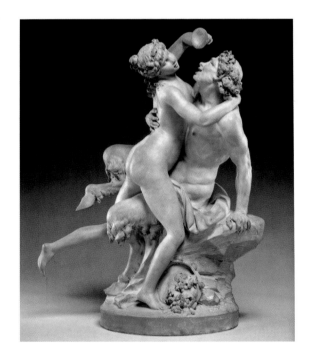

were expected to be followed by artisans, who thereby lost much of their independence. Let us note, too, the collaboration of architects, who became more involved in interior decoration. Along with sculptors, who often created the ornamentation, they helped to raise the decorative arts to the level of the fine arts, thus establishing a tradition that continued into modern times. The decorative and fine arts were most clearly joined in furniture. French cabinetmakers known as *ébénistes* (after ebony, their preferred wood veneer) helped to bring about the revolution in interior décor by introducing new materials and techniques. Many of these artisans came originally from Holland, Flanders, Germany, and even Italy.

The decorative arts played a unique role during the Rococo. Hôtel interiors were more than collections of objects. They were total environments put together with extraordinary care by discerning collectors and the talented architects, sculptors, decorators, and dealers who catered to their exacting taste. A room, like an item of furniture, could involve the services of a wide variety of artisans: cabinetmakers, wood carvers, gold- and silversmiths, upholsterers, porcelain makers. All were dedicated to producing the ensemble, even though each craft was, by tradition, a separate specialty subject to strict regulations. Together they fueled the insatiable hunger for novelty that swept Europe.

ROBERT DE COTTE. The vast majority of these rooms have been destroyed, heavily changed, or scattered. One of the few that survives intact is the Grand Salon of the Hôtel de Bourvallais in Paris (fig. 20-1) by Robert de Cotte (1656/7–1735), one of the leaders of the change to the Rococo. Dating from 1717 when the hôtel became the Chancellerie de France, it is in a transitional Regency style that still has some of the severe geometry of the Style of Louis XIV. (Compare the Salon de Guerre, fig. 19-13, designed in part by de Cotte's uncle, Jules Hardouin-Mansart.) It nevertheless anticipates the Rococo in its more generous planes and freer decorative forms. To create a sumptuous effect, the walls are encrusted with stucco ornamentation, and the elaborately carved furniture is embellished with gilt bronze. Everything swims in a sea of swirling patterns united by the most sophisticated sense of design and materials the world has ever known. Here there is no clear distinction between decoration and function in the richly designed fireplace and the opulent chandelier. The paintings, too, have been completely integrated into the decorative scheme.

Sculpture

CLODION. Because so much of it was done to adorn interiors, French Rococo sculpture generally took the form of small groups in a "miniature Baroque" style, designed to be viewed at close range. A typical example is *Satyr and Bacchante* (fig. 20-2) by Claude Michel (1738–1814), known as Clodion. Its coquettish

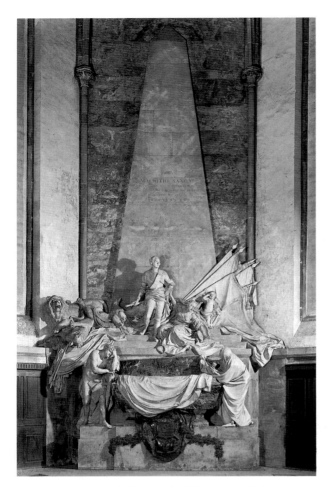

20-3. Jean-Baptiste Pigalle. Tomb of the Maréchal de Saxe. 1753–76. Marble. St. Thomas, Strasbourg, France

eroticism is a playful echo of the ecstasies of Bernini, whose work he studied during a nine-year stay in Italy (compare fig. 17-29). Although he undertook several large cycles in marble, Clodion was by nature a modeler who was at his best working on a small scale. He could work miracles with terra-cotta and he reigned supreme in this intimate medium.

JEAN-BAPTISTE PIGALLE. There were few monumental commissions for French sculptors. Lifesize statues were confined mainly to decorative figures of nymphs, goddesses, and the like, which are counterparts to the mythological creatures in the paintings of Boucher and his followers (see below). However, the Tomb of the Maréchal de Saxe (fig. 20-3) by Jean-Baptiste Pigalle (1714–1785), Clodion's teacher and the most gifted sculptor of the era, recaptures some of the grandeur of the Baroque. The Maréchal steps from a pyramid denoting immortality toward a casket held open for him by the figure of Death, as France tries in vain to intervene. He is mourned by the grief-stricken Hercules to the left, representing the French army, and, to the right, a weeping infant personifying the Genius of War, who extinguishes his torch before the fallen military standards. The strange menagerie on the left stands for the nations defeated by the Maréchal in combat: Holland, England, and the Holy Roman Empire.

If the allegory strikes us as heavy-handed, there can be no denying the effectiveness of the presentation, which is among the most astonishing in all of sculpture. The poses show the classicism required for official French art, but the spirit of the whole is unmistakably Baroque. Pigalle has mounted a tableau worthy of Bernini, whose works he came to know as a young man in Rome. The element of restraint also suggests the influence of Algardi (see fig. 17-31). The pyramid is not a three-dimensional structure but a low relief built against the wall of the church, while the steps leading to it and the figures standing on them are in the round, like actors performing before a backdrop. We may therefore view the monument as a kind of theatrical performance in marble. The artist has even set it apart from its surroundings by creating an elevated "stage space" that projects forcefully outward.

Painting

"POUSSINISTES" VERSUS "RUBÉNISTES." It is hardly surprising that the strict system of the French Academy (see pages 610–11) did not produce any major artists. Even Charles Lebrun, as we have seen, was far more Baroque in practice than we would expect from his classical theory. The rigidity of the official doctrine gave rise to a reaction that vented itself as soon as Lebrun's authority began to wane. Toward the end of the century, the members of the Academy formed two factions over the issue of drawing versus color: the "Poussinistes" versus the "Rubénistes." The conservatives defended Poussin's view that drawing, which appealed to the mind, was superior to color, which appealed to the senses. The Rubénistes (many of whom were of Flemish descent) favored color, rather than drawing, as being more true to nature. They also pointed out that drawing, admittedly based on reason, appeals only to the expert few, whereas color appeals to everyone. This argument had important implications. It suggested that the lay person should be the judge of artistic values, and challenged the Renaissance notion that painting, as a liberal art, could be appreciated only by the educated mind.

ANTOINE WATTEAU. By the time Louis XIV died in 1715, the power of the Academy had long been overcome, and the influence of Rubens and the great Venetians was everywhere. The greatest of the Rubénistes was Jean-Antoine Watteau (1684–1721), the only painter of the Rococo who can be considered a genius without reservation. His paintings broke many academic rules, while his subjects did not conform to any established category. To make room for Watteau, the Academy invented the new classification of *fêtes galantes* (elegant fêtes or outdoor entertainments). The term refers to the fact that his work mainly shows scenes of fashionable people or actors in parklike settings. His pictures often interweave theater and real life, so that there is no clear distinction between them. *A Pilgrimage to Cythera* (fig. 20-4), painted as his reception piece for the Academy, is an evocation of love that includes elements of classical mythology. Accompanied by swarms of cupids, young couples have come to Cythera, the island of love, to pay homage to Venus, whose garlanded image appears on the far right. The action unfolds in the foreground from right to left, like a continuous narrative, which tells us that they are about to board the boat. Two lovers are still engaged in their amorous tryst; behind them, another couple rises to follow a

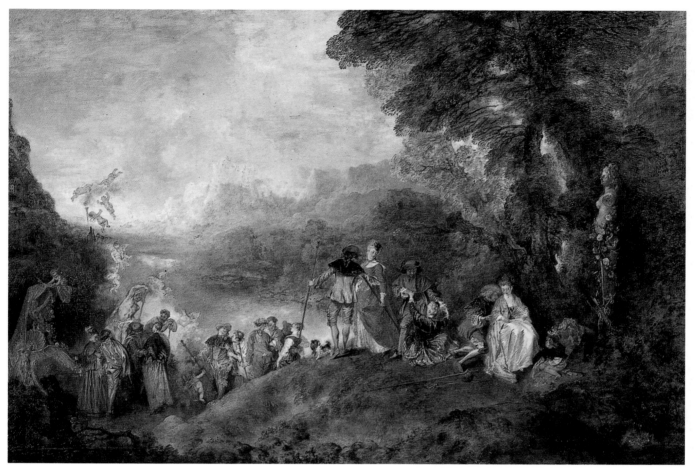

20-4. Jean-Antoine Watteau. *A Pilgrimage to Cythera*. 1717.
Oil on canvas, 4'3" x 6'4½" (1.3 x 1.9 m). Musée du Louvre, Paris

third pair down the hill as the reluctant young woman casts a longing look back at the goddess's sacred grove.

As a fashionable conversation piece, the scene recalls Rubens' *Garden of Love* (compare fig. 18-3), but Watteau has added a touch of poignancy that lends it a delicate poetry reminiscent of Giorgione and Titian (see figs. 13-39). Watteau's figures lack the vitality of Rubens'. Slim and graceful, they move with the assurance of actors who play their roles so well that they touch us more than reality ever could. They recapture an earlier ideal of mannered elegance.

Many of Watteau's paintings center on the commedia dell' arte, a form of improvisational comedy developed in Italy that uses stock characters (see box page 581). His treatment of this Italian theme is all the more remarkable because the commedia dell'arte was officially banned in France from 1697 until 1716 (see box page 612). Shortly before his death Watteau painted perhaps his most moving work: *Pierrot* (fig. 20-5), traditionally known as *Gilles* after a similar stock character in the commedia dell'arte. It was probably done as a sign for a café owned by a friend of the artist who retired from the stage after achieving fame in the racy role of the clown. The performance has ended, and the actor has stepped forward to face the audience. The other characters, all highly individualized, are probably likenesses of friends from the same circle.

Yet the painting is more than a portrait or an advertisement. Watteau approaches his subject with incomparable insight. Pierrot

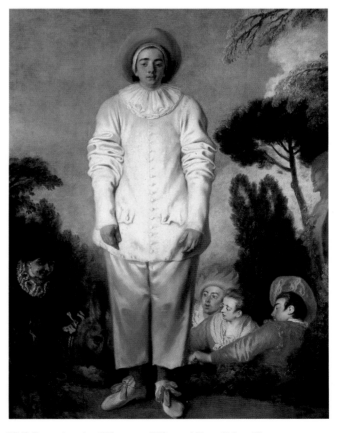

20-5. Jean-Antoine Watteau. *Gilles and Four Other Characters from the Commedia dell'Arte (Pierrot)*. c. 1719. Oil on canvas, 72½ x 58⅜" (184 x 149 cm). Musée du Louvre, Paris

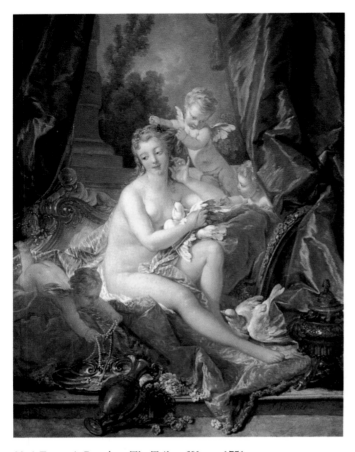

20-6. François Boucher. *The Toilet of Venus.* 1751.
Oil on canvas, 43 x 33½" (109.2 x 85.1 cm).
The Metropolitan Museum of Art, New York

is lifesize, so that he confronts us as a full human being, not simply as a stock character. In the process, Watteau transforms him into Everyman, with whom he evidently identified himself—a merger of identity basic to the commedia dell'arte. The face and pose have a poignancy that suggests a sense of alienation. Like the rest of the actors, except the doctor on the donkey who looks mischievously at us, he seems lost in his own thoughts. Still, it is difficult to define his mood, for the expression is as subtle as it is eloquent.

FRANÇOIS BOUCHER. The work of Watteau signals the decisive shift in French art to the Rococo. Although the term originally applied to the decorative arts, it suits the playful character of French painting before 1765 equally well. By about 1720 even history painting became intimate in scale and lighthearted in style and subject. The finest painter in this vein was François Boucher (1703–1770), who epitomized the age of Madame de Pompadour, the mistress of Louis XV. *The Toilet of Venus* (fig. 20-6), which was painted for her private retreat, is full of silk and perfume. Compared to Vouet's sensuous goddess (see fig. 19-8), from which she is descended, Boucher's Venus has been transformed into a coquette of enchanting beauty. In this cosmetic never-never land, she is an eternally youthful goddess with the same rosy skin as the cherubs who attend her. If Watteau elevated human love to the level of mythology, Boucher raised playful eroticism to the realm of the divine. What Boucher lacks in the emotional depth of Watteau, he makes up for in his understanding of the fantasies that enrich people's lives.

JEAN-HONORÉ FRAGONARD. *Bathers* (fig. 20-7), by Jean-Honoré Fragonard (1732–1806), Boucher's star pupil, shows him to be an even franker Rubéniste than Boucher. He paints with a fluid breadth and spontaneity that recall Rubens' oil sketches and even paraphrase the Flemish master's figures (see fig. 18-2). They

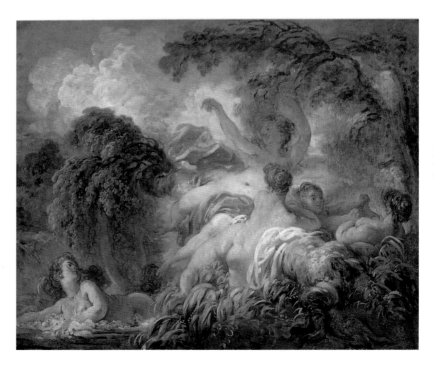

20-7. Jean-Honoré Fragonard. *Bathers.*
c. 1765. Oil on canvas,
25¼ x 31½" (64 x 80 cm).
Musée du Louvre, Paris

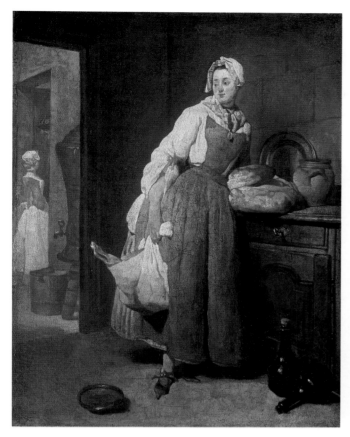

20-8. Jean-Baptiste-Siméon Chardin. *Back from the Market.*
1739. Oil on canvas, 18½ x 14¾" (47 x 37.5 cm).
Musée du Louvre, Paris

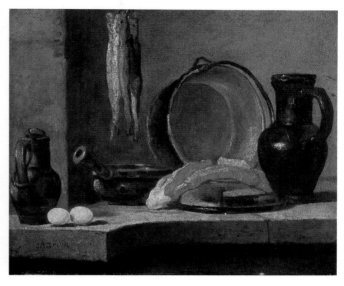

20-9. Jean-Baptiste-Siméon Chardin. *Kitchen Still Life.*
c. 1731. Oil on canvas, 12½ x 15⅜" (32 x 39 cm).
Ashmolean Museum, Oxford

BEQUEATHED BY MRS. W. F. R. WELDON

move with a floating grace that also links him with Tiepolo, whose work he had admired during a long stay in Italy (compare fig. 20-23). Fragonard's paintings range from erotic fantasies to intimate studies and pastoral landscapes, but all marked by the extraordinary virtuosity that made him the finest pure painter of his generation. He had the misfortune to outlive his era. His pictures became outdated as the French Revolution approached, and he was reduced to poverty after 1789. Later he was supported only by a curatorship to which he was appointed in 1793 by Jacques-Louis David (see pages 673–76), who recognized his achievement, although their styles were diametrically opposed. He died, virtually forgotten, in the heyday of the Napoleonic era.

JEAN-BAPTISTE CHARDIN. The style Fragonard practiced with such mastery was not the only one open to him and the other French painters of his generation. His art might have been different if he had followed the lead of his first teacher, Jean-Baptiste-Siméon Chardin (1699–1779). The Rubénistes had cleared the way for a renewed interest in still life and genre paintings by Dutch and Flemish masters. This revival was spurred by the presence of numerous artists from the Netherlands, especially Flanders, who settled in France in growing numbers after about 1550 but maintained ties to their native region. Chardin is the finest French painter in this vein. Yet he is far removed in spirit and style, if not in subject matter, from any Dutch or Flemish painter. His paintings act as moral lessons, not by conveying symbolic messages as

Baroque art often does (see pages 599–600), but by affirming the rightness of the existing social order and its values. To the rising middle class who were the artist's patrons, his genre scenes and kitchen still lifes proclaimed the virtues of hard work, frugality, honesty, and devotion to family.

Back from the Market (fig. 20-8) shows life in a Parisian middle-class household. Here we find such feeling for the beauty hidden in everyday life, and so clear a sense of spatial order, that we can compare him only to Vermeer (see fig. 18-28). However, Chardin's technique is very different from that of any Dutch artist. His brushwork renders the light on colored surfaces with a creamy touch that is both analytical and lyrical. To reveal the inner nature of things, he summarizes forms and subtly alters their appearance and texture, rather than describing them in detail.

Chardin's genius reveals a hidden poetry in even the most humble objects and endows them with timeless dignity. His still lifes usually depict the same modest environment and avoid the "object appeal" of their Dutch predecessors. In *Kitchen Still Life* (fig. 20-9), we see only the common objects that belong in any kitchen: earthenware jugs, a casserole, a copper pot, a piece of raw meat, smoked herring, two eggs. But how important they seem, each so firmly placed in relation to the rest, each so worthy of the artist's—and our—attention! Despite his concern with formal problems, seen in the beautifully balanced design, Chardin treats these objects with a respect close to reverence. Beyond their shapes, colors, and textures, they are to him symbols of the life of common people.

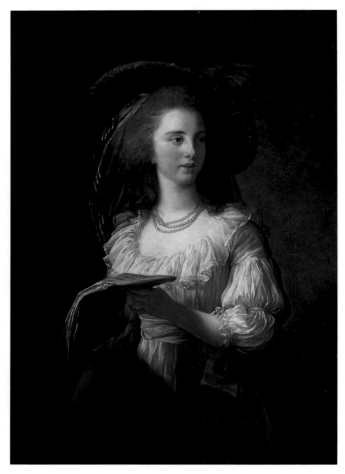

20-10. Marie-Louise-Élisabeth Vigée-Lebrun. *The Duchesse de Polignac*. 1783. Oil on canvas, 38¾ x 28" (98.3 x 71 cm). Waddesdon Manor, England

ÉLISABETH VIGÉE-LEBRUN. It is from portraits that we can gain the clearest understanding of the French Rococo, for the transformation of the human image lies at the heart of the age. In portraits of the aristocracy, men were endowed with the illusion of character as an attribute of their noble birth. But the finest Rococo portraits were those of women, hardly a surprising fact in a society that idolized love and feminine beauty. Indeed, one of the finest artists in this vein was herself a beautiful woman: Marie-Louise-Élisabeth Vigée-Lebrun (1755–1842), who has left us a fascinating autobiography. [See Primary Sources, no. 60, page 656.]

Vigée enjoyed great fame throughout her long career, which took her to every corner of Europe, including Russia, when she fled the French Revolution. *The Duchesse de Polignac* (fig. 20-10), painted a few years after Vigée had become the portraitist for Queen Marie Antoinette, is a descendant of Domenichino's *St. Cecilia* (see fig. 17-9). She has the youthful loveliness of Boucher's *Venus* (see fig. 20-6), made all the more persuasive by the artist's ravishing treatment of her clothing. At the same time, there is a sense of transience in the lyrical mood that shows the whimsical side of the Rococo. Interrupted in her singing, the duchesse becomes a real-life counterpart to the poetic creatures in Watteau's

A Pilgrimage to Cythera (see fig. 20-4). At the same time, she shares the delicate sentiment of the girl in Chardin's *Back from the Market* (see fig. 20-8).

ENGLAND
Painting

Across the English Channel, the Venetians were the dominant artists for more than a half-century (see page 639). However, the French Rococo had a major, although unacknowledged, effect. In fact, it helped to bring about the first school of English painting since the Middle Ages that had more than local importance.

WILLIAM HOGARTH. The earliest of these painters, William Hogarth (1697–1764), was the first English artist of genius since Nicholas Hilliard (see fig. 16-17). He began his career as an engraver and soon took up painting. Although he must have learned something about color and brushwork from Venetian and French examples, as well as Van Dyck, his work is so original that it has no real precedent. He made his mark in the 1730s with a new kind of picture, which he described as "modern moral subjects

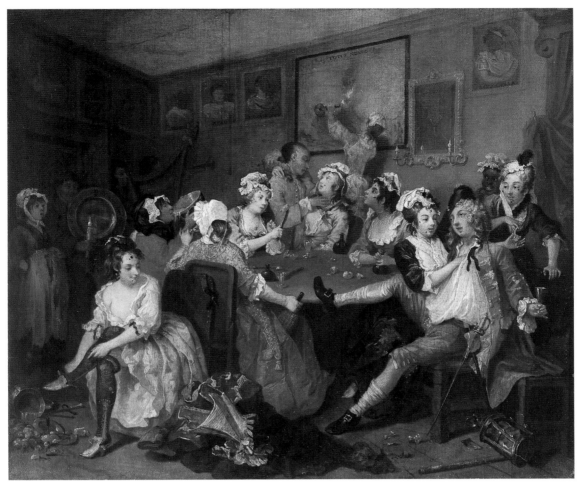

20-11. William Hogarth. *The Orgy,* Scene III of *The Rake's Progress.* c. 1734. Oil on canvas, 24½ x 29½" (62.2 x 74.9 cm). Sir John Soane's Museum, London

. . . similar to representations on the stage." It follows the vogue for sentimental comedies, such as the plays of Richard Steele, which attempted to teach moral lessons through satire (see box page 640). Hogarth's work is in the same vein as John Gay's *The Beggar's Opera* of 1728, a biting social and political parody that the artist illustrated in one of his paintings (see box page 637). He wished to be judged as a dramatist, he said, even though his "actors" could only "exhibit a dumb show." These pictures, and the prints he made from them for sale to the public, came in sets, with certain details repeated in each scene to unify the sequence. Hogarth's morality plays teach, by bad example, the solid middle-class virtues. They show a country girl who succumbs to the temptations of fashionable London; the evils of corrupt elections; and aristocratic rakes who live only for pleasure and marry wealthy women of lower status for their fortunes (marriage à la mode), which they soon squander. Hogarth is probably the first artist in history to become a social critic in his own right.

In *The Orgy* (figs. 20-11 and 20-12), from *The Rake's Progress,* the young wastrel is overindulging in wine and women. The scene is set in a famous London brothel, The Rose Tavern. The girl adjusting her shoe in the foreground is preparing for a vulgar dance involving the silver plate and candle behind her; to the left

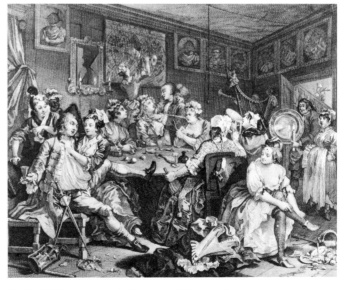

20-12. William Hogarth. *He Revels (The Orgy),* Scene III of *The Rake's Progress.* 1735. Engraving. The Metropolitan Museum of Art, New York

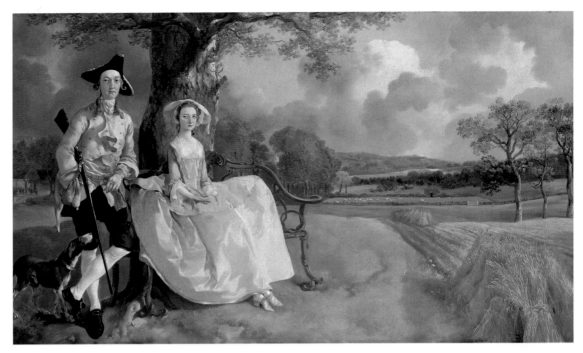

20-13. Thomas Gainsborough. *Robert Andrews and His Wife.* c. 1748–50. Oil on canvas, 27$\frac{1}{2}$ x 47" (69.7 x 119.3 cm). The National Gallery, London

a chamber pot spills its contents over a chicken dish; and in the background a singer holds sheet music for a bawdy song of the day. (The rogue is later arrested for debt, enters into a marriage of convenience, turns to gambling, goes to a debtor's prison, and dies in an insane asylum.) The scene is so full of visual clues that a full account would take pages, as well as constant references to other images in the series. However literal-minded, the picture has great appeal. Hogarth combines some of Watteau's sparkle with Jan Steen's narrative gusto (compare figs. 20-4 and 18-27), and entertains us so well that we enjoy his sermon without being overwhelmed by its message.

THOMAS GAINSBOROUGH. Portraiture remained the only constant source of income for English painters. Hogarth was a pioneer in this field as well. The greatest master, Thomas Gainsborough (1727–1788), began by painting landscapes but ended as the favorite portraitist of British high society. His early paintings, such as *Robert Andrews and His Wife* (fig. 20-13), have a lyrical charm that is not always found in his later pictures. The outdoor setting, although indebted to French art, was largely invented by Francis Hayman (1708–1766), whom Gainsborough came to know while an art student in London. Gainsborough even painted the backgrounds in some of Hayman's works during the 1750s but soon surpassed him. Compared to Van Dyck's artifice in *Charles I Hunting* (see fig. 18-6), this country squire and his wife are unpretentiously at home in their setting. The landscape is derived from Ruisdael and his school, but has a sunlit, hospitable air never achieved (or desired) by the Dutch masters. The casual grace of the two figures, which affects an air of naturalness, indirectly recalls Watteau's style. The newlywed couple do not till the soil themselves. She is dressed in the fashionable attire of the day, while he is

armed with a rifle to denote his status as a country squire. (Hunting was the privilege of wealthy landowners.) The painting nevertheless conveys the gentry's closeness to the land, from which the English derived much of their sense of identity. (Many private estates had been created in 1535, when Henry VIII broke with the Catholic church and distributed its property to his supporters.) Out of this attachment to place, a feeling for nature developed that became the basis for English landscape painting, to which Gainsborough himself made an important early contribution.

Gainsborough spent most of his career working in the provinces, first in his native Suffolk, then in the resort town of Bath. Toward the end of his career, he moved to London, where his work underwent a major change. The splendid portrait (fig. 20-14) of the famous actress Mrs. Siddons (see box page 640) has the virtues of the artist's late style: a cool elegance that translates Van Dyck's aristocratic poses into late-eighteenth-century terms, and a fluid, translucent technique reminiscent of Rubens' that renders the glamorous sitter, with her fashionable attire and coiffure, to ravishing effect.

JOSHUA REYNOLDS. Gainsborough painted Mrs. Siddons to outdo his great rival on the London scene, Sir Joshua Reynolds (1723–1792), who had portrayed her as the Tragic Muse (fig. 20-15). A less able painter, Reynolds had to rely on pose and expression to suggest the aura of character that Gainsborough was able to convey through color and brushwork alone. Reynolds, who had been president of the Royal Academy since its founding in 1768, championed the academic approach to art, which he had acquired during two years in Rome. [See Primary Sources, no. 61, page 656.] In his *Discourses,* delivered at the Academy, he set forth what he considered necessary rules and theories. His views were essentially those of

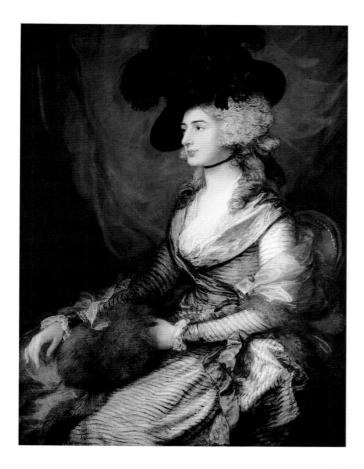

20-14. Thomas Gainsborough. *Mrs. Siddons.* 1785. Oil on canvas, 49½ x 39" (125.7 x 99.1 cm). The National Gallery, London.

Judged purely by the standards of portraiture the Mrs. Siddons of 1785 is perhaps his masterpiece. A serious critique of a picture of the English school by a foreigner of equal learning and taste is so rare, and the judgment so perceptive, that I will quote what Thoré-Burger said of the picture, when he saw it at the Manchester Exhibition of 1857: "The great tragic actress, who interpreted the passions with such energy and such feeling, and who felt them so strongly herself, is better portrayed in this simple half-length, in her day dress, than in allegorical portraits as the Tragic Muse or in character parts. This portrait is so original, so individual, as a poetic expression of character, as a deliberate selection of pose, as bold colour and free handling, that it is like the work of no other painter. It is useless to search for parallels, for there are none. Veronese a little—but no, it is a quite personal creation. This is genius."

—Ellis Waterhouse. *Gainsborough.*
London: Spring Books, 1966, p. 29.
Originally published in 1958 by Edward Hulton Limited.

SIR ELLIS WATERHOUSE (1905–1985) had a distinguished career in Birmingham, England, from 1952–72 as director of the Barber Insitute of Fine Arts. In his prime, he was the greatest living authority on British art before 1800 and was also an expert in Italian Baroque painting. He never flaunted his encyclopedic knowledge. Even with his vast erudition, his self-effacing temperament is evident here in his willingness to quote a nineteenth-century critic when discussing *Mrs. Siddons* by Gainsborough, a painter of whom Waterhouse was the leading authority.

Lebrun, tempered by British common sense, and like Lebrun, he found it difficult to live up to his theories in practice. Although he preferred history painting in the grand style, most of his works are portraits "enabled" by allegorical additions or disguises like those in his picture of Mrs. Siddons in order to ennoble them. His style owed a good deal more to the Venetians, the Flemish Baroque, and even Rembrandt (note the color and lighting in *Mrs. Siddons As the Tragic Muse*) than he was willing to admit, although he often recommended following the example of earlier masters.

Reynolds was generous enough to praise Gainsborough, whom he outlived by a few years, and whose instinctive talent he must have envied. He eulogized him as one who saw with the eye of a painter rather than a poet, even if the compliment was left-handed. Gainsborough's work epitomized the Enlightenment philosopher David Hume's idea that painting must incorporate both nature and art. Gainsborough himself was a simple and unpretentious person who exemplified Hume's "natural man," free of excessive pride or humility. Reynolds's approach, on the other hand, as stated in his *Discourses,* was based on Horace's

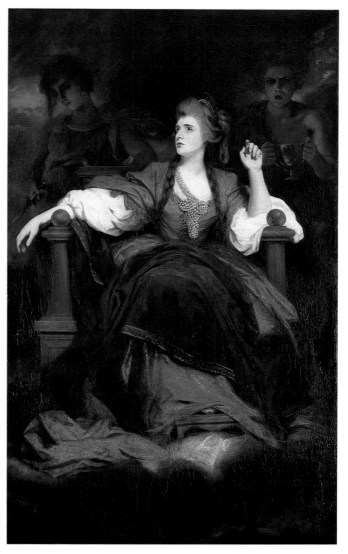

20-15. Sir Joshua Reynolds. *Mrs. Siddons As the Tragic Muse.* 1784. Oil on canvas, 7'9" x 4'9½" (2.36 x 1.46 m). Henry E. Huntington Library and Art Gallery, San Marino, California

saying *ut pictura poesis* (see page 453). His use of poses from the antique was intended to elevate the sitter from an individual to a universal type through association with the great art of the past and the noble ideals it embodied. This heroic model was closely related to the writings of the playwright Samuel Johnson and the practices of the actor David Garrick, both of whom were friends of Reynolds'. (Garrick sat for portraits by Hogarth and Gainsborough, as well as Reynolds; see illustration page 640.) In this respect, Reynolds was the opposite of Gainsborough. Yet, for all of the differences between them, the two artists had more in common, artistically and philosophically, than they cared to admit.

Reynolds and Gainsborough looked back to Van Dyck, while drawing different lessons from his example. Both emphasized in varying degrees the visual appeal and technical skill of their paintings. Moreover, their portraits of Mrs. Siddons are clearly related to the Rococo style of France—note their resemblance to Vigée's *Duchesse* (see fig. 20-10)—yet they remain distinctly English in character. Hume and Johnson were similarly linked by their skepticism. If anything, Johnson's writings, which inspired Reynolds, were more pessimistic than Hume's, which generally advocated a tolerant and humane ethical system.

Sculpture

English sculpture has not been discussed in these pages since the thirteenth century (see fig. 11-50). During the Reformation a great deal of sculpture was destroyed. This vandalism had so chilling an effect that for 200 years there was too little demand for statuary to sustain more than the most modest local production. With the rise of a vigorous English school of painting, however, sculptural patronage grew as well. During the eighteenth century, when portraits of famous people were all the rage, England set an example for the rest of Europe in creating the "monument to genius." Statues were set up in public places to honor cultural heroes such as Shakespeare, a privilege that in the past had been reserved for heads of state.

LOUIS-FRANÇOIS ROUBILIAC. One of the earliest and most delightful of these statues is the monument to the great composer George Frideric Handel (fig. 20-16) by the French-born Louis-François Roubiliac (1702–1762). It was the first monument to be made of a cultural hero within his lifetime. (The next to achieve this distinction was Voltaire in France a generation later; see fig. 21-12). Roubiliac (portrayed in fig. 21-6) carved the figure in 1738 for the owner of Vauxhall Gardens in London, a pleasure park with dining facilities and an orchestra stand where Handel's music was often performed. The statue thus served two purposes: homage and advertising. Handel is in the guise of Apollo, the god of music, playing a classical lyre, while a putto at his feet writes down the divine music. But Handel is a domestic Apollo, in slippers and dressing gown, with a soft beret on his head instead of a wig. These attributes mark him as a man of arts and letters. Although Roubiliac shows that he is well aware of the Baroque sculptural tradition, the informality of his *Handel* seems uniquely English. Touches such as the right foot resting upon rather than inside the slipper (a hint at the composer's gouty big

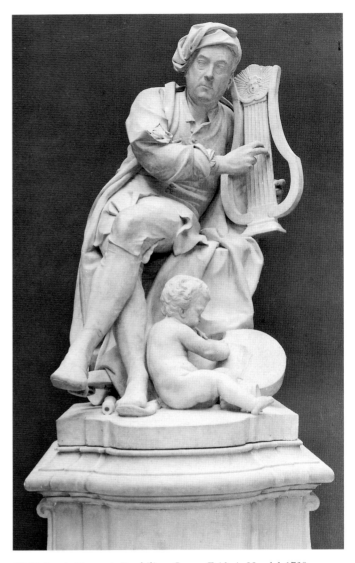

20-16. Louis-François Roubiliac. *George Frideric Handel.* 1738. Marble, lifesize. Victoria & Albert Museum, London

toe?) suggest that he sought advice from William Hogarth, with whom he was on excellent terms (see pages 630–32). *Handel* was Roubiliac's first big success in his adopted homeland, and it became the ancestor of countless monuments to cultural heroes everywhere (see fig. 22-28).

GERMANY AND AUSTRIA

Rococo architecture was a refinement in miniature of the curvilinear, "elastic" Baroque of Borromini and Guarini. It was readily united with the architecture of Central Europe, where the Italian Baroque had taken firm root. It is not surprising that the Italian style received such a warm response there. In Austria and southern Germany, which had been ravaged by the Thirty Years' War, the number of new buildings remained small until near the end of the seventeenth century. The Baroque was an imported style, practiced mainly by visiting Italians. Not until the 1690s did native architects come to the fore. There followed a period of intense activity that lasted more than 50 years and gave rise to some of the most imaginative creations in the history of architec-

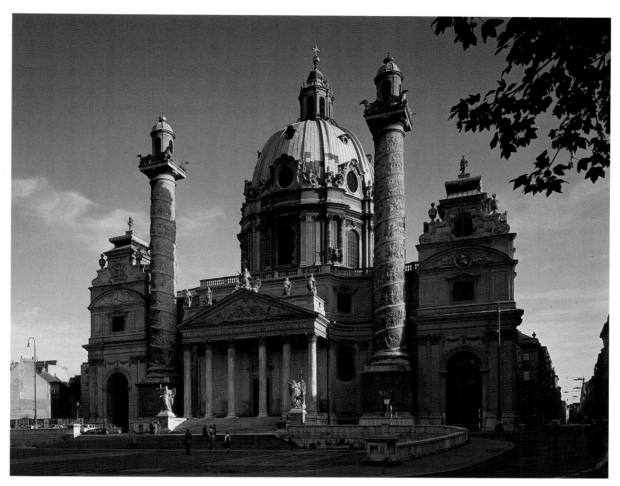

20-17. Johann Fischer von Erlach. Facade of St. Charles Borromaeus (Karlskirche), Vienna. 1716–37

ture. These monuments were built to glorify princes and prelates who are generally remembered only as lavish patrons of the arts. Rococo architecture in Central Europe is larger in scale and more exuberant than in France. Moreover, painting and sculpture are more closely linked with their settings. Palaces and churches are decorated with ceiling frescoes and sculpture unsuited to domestic interiors, however lavish, although they reflect the same taste that produced the Rococo French hôtels.

JOHANN FISCHER VON ERLACH. The Austrian Johann Fischer von Erlach (1656–1723), the first great architect of the Rococo in Central Europe, was closely linked to the Italian tradition: He had studied in Rome with Carlo Fontana (see page 575). But instead of following his teacher's tepid compromise between the High Baroque and Baroque classicism, similar to that found in Italian painting toward the end of the seventeenth century (see page 571), Fischer von Erlach was a bold genius who represents the decisive shift of the center of architecture from Italy to north of the Alps. His church of St. Charles Borromaeus in Vienna (figs. 20-17 and 20-18) combines the facade of Borromini's Sta. Agnese

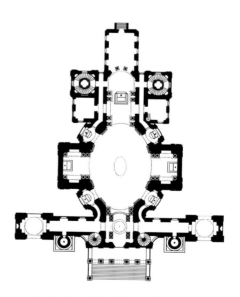

20-18. Plan of St. Charles Borromaeus

ROCOCO MUSIC

Although music after 1700 was the direct outgrowth of the previous century, it not only had a different sound but it was dominated by a handful of great composers. They were nevertheless surrounded by many others of equal ability who began to form recognizable schools. These phenomena were interrelated. They were made possible by the international circulation of printed scores and musical treatises and the codification of the modern major-minor harmonic system (see "Modern Harmony," page 638). Of course, we have encountered great composers before; yet when we listen to their music, it does not sound "modern" to our ears, no matter how beautiful or intricate it may be on its own terms.

The earliest of these eighteenth-century giants was Antonio Vivaldi (1678–1741). The son of a violinist at St. Mark's in Venice, he trained for the priesthood but was allowed to leave after one year for health reasons. From then on, he was employed chiefly as head of the Conservatory of the Pietà orphanage for girls. His vast body of work in virtually every instrumental and vocal form shows enormous versatility, one of the chief characteristics of the Rococo. Like the other great composers of the time, he was under constant pressure, due to his responsibilities and popularity, to write new music. He was, for example, the most successful composer of operas in Venice. He

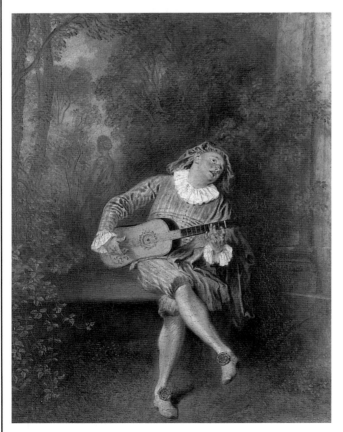

Jean Antoine Watteau. *Mezzetin*. 1718. Oil on canvas, 21¾ x 17" (55.3 x 43.2 cm). The Metropolitan Museum of Art, New York
MUNSEY FUND, 1942

claimed to have written 90 in all; of the 20 that survive relatively intact, some show signs of haste. (One of them was composed in only five days!) Nevertheless, *Orlando Furioso* (1727), inspired by Ariosto's epic poem, is unquestionably a masterpiece that is much superior to Handel's better-known opera of the same title (1733), and *Alcina* (1735), based on the same story. Today Vivaldi is known almost exclusively for his concertos, which number nearly 500, the large majority of them for the violin, of which *The Four Seasons,* set to verses probably written by Vivaldi himself, is justly the most famous.

Johann Sebastian Bach (1685–1750), trained as an organist and violinist, spent part of his early career as a court composer, then settled down as music director at the church of St. Thomas in Leipzig, a position that made huge demands on him for new music. As an organist, he was indebted to a virtuoso tradition that began in Italy with Girolamo Frescobaldi (1583–1643) and continued in Germany with Dietrich Buxtehude (1637–1707), whom he went out of his way to hear in Lübeck. Bach was influenced early on by Italian music, which helped to shape his sense of melody and harmony. His keyboard compositions show the impact of François Couperin as well (see box pages 612–13). Bach's music balances melody and polyphony, harmony and counterpoint, expressive power and supreme rationality. The instrumental works are built largely on fugues and variations, for he believed completely in his system of counterpoint, even when it forced unsatisfactory results. He is remembered chiefly for choral music, including the justly celebrated *Mass in B Minor,* several oratorios, which are nearly miniature operas, and voluminous cantatas, most of them early works. They owe their character to the revolution brought about in 1700 by Erdmann Neumeister (1671–1756) of Hamburg, a theologian and poet who introduced a new kind of sacred poetry, which he called a "cantata." It effectively reconciled the difference between the Lutheran chorale and Calvinist psalm by alternating biblical passages with original texts that expand on the scripture's meaning by offering personal responses and meditations.

Bach was hardly the most famous or prolific German composer of his time. That honor belonged to his friend Georg Philipp Telemann (1681–1767), who worked for a while in Leipzig but spent most of his life in Hamburg. New issues of his compositions were eagerly sought after, for they show the fertile imagination of Vivaldi, the technical mastery of Bach, and the cosmopolitan flair of Rameau. This is especially true of his overtures (which are really dance suites), trio sonatas, quartets, and concertos. These are combined in his justly celebrated *Tafelmusik* (1733) which, rather than being entertainment music for banquets (as the meaning of the German word *Tafel* suggests), are three chamber suites (or "productions") following a set format that shows off Telemann's mastery of every form.

George Frideric Handel (1685–1759), an admirer of Telemann, was likewise famous throughout almost his entire career. Born at Halle in Saxony, he first worked in Hamburg, then visited Italy between 1706 and 1710, when he met Arcangelo Corelli, Alessandro Scarlatti (1659–1725), and his son Domenico Scarlatti (1685–1757), a brilliant composer of harpsichord sonatas. The stay in Italy was decisive to Handel's formation, for it was there that he learned to compose operas and adopted the lyrical manner that distinguishes his work. Upon his return to Germany, he was appointed music director at Hanover but soon went to London on a leave of absence and never really returned. As fate would have it, the elector of Hanover then became King George I of England, and he continued to support Handel in London. Handel was both a composer and an impresario who made and lost fortunes in Italian opera. His masterpiece in this vein is *Julius Caesar,* put on in 1724. Four years later, however, John Gay's *The Beggar's Opera* (1728), a social and political satire written in English at the suggestion of the author Jonathan Swift (1667–1745), took England by storm. *The Beggar's Opera* used familiar songs culled from a variety of sources (including Purcell) and arranged by the German-born Johann Christoph Pepusch (1667–1752), who had settled in London in 1700 and no doubt enjoyed creating this spoof of his rival's music. (Ironically, the libretto for Handel's first opera was written by Gay with the poet Alexander Pope, a member of Lord Burlington's circle.) Handel, who by this time had become an English citizen, now turned increasingly to oratorios in his adopted tongue, though he continued to compose operas for another decade. The oratorios have a drama that makes them virtually concert operas, not church music, although many are based on biblical subjects. Their extroverted character expresses the confidence of the English as the new chosen people. His instrumental music, such as the *Concerti Grossi Opus 6,* is extremely appealing in its poetry, liveliness, and stateliness.

After failing to achieve success in Paris early in his career, Jean-Philippe Rameau (1683–1764) made his mark as a theorist in 1722 with the *Treatise on Harmony,* then returned the following year to Paris, where he gained the backing of a major patron and began to write operas, which established his reputation and earned him the support of the court. His style has the clarity and grace of Watteau and the intelligence of Voltaire. Despite the fact that Rameau's operas, such as *The Gallant Indes* (1735; a "heroic ballet" in several episodes) and *Castor and Pollux* (1737), are the direct descendants of Jean-Baptiste Lully's, they were attacked by the latter's supporters for their variety and drama. Ironically, the Lullyists later championed him against Italian opera, whose cause was being promoted by the Enlightenment philosopher Jean-Jacques Rousseau on the grounds that French was not fit for singing! Nevertheless, the revival of *Castor and Pollux* in 1754, after it had been heavily reworked by the composer, was an outstanding success that marked the defeat of Italian opera. The declamatory style satisfied the Lullyists, while the brilliant inventiveness, especially of the instrumental writing, pleased Rameau's partisans, who proclaimed the opera his masterpiece.

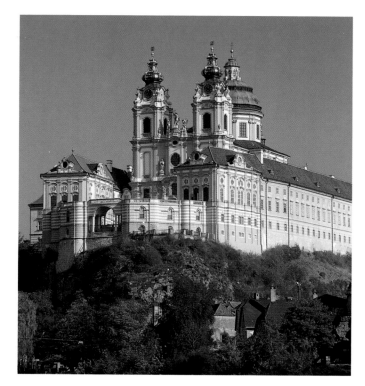

20-19. Jakob Prandtauer. Monastery Church, Melk, Austria. Begun 1702

and the Pantheon portico (see figs. 17-23 and 7-15). Here we find a pair of huge columns, derived from the Column of Trajan (see fig. 7-37) and decorated with scenes from the life of the saint. They take the place of towers, which have become corner pavilions reminiscent of Lescot's Louvre court facade (compare fig. 16-27). The church celebrates the emperor Charles VI as a Christian ruler. It reminds us that the Turks, who repeatedly menaced Austria and Hungary, had been defeated at the siege of Vienna only in 1683, thanks mainly to the intervention of John III of Poland, and that they remained a serious threat as late as 1718.

The extraordinary breadth of this ensemble is due to the site itself (fig. 20-18). It obscures the equally long main body of the church, which is a large oval with side chapels and a deep choir. With the inflexible elements of Roman Imperial art embedded into the elastic curves of his church, Fischer von Erlach expresses, more boldly than any Italian architect of the time, the power of the Christian faith to transform the art of antiquity. Indeed, it was now Italy's turn to respond to the North. The Superga, a monastery church overlooking Turin that was begun only a year later by Filippo Juvarra (1678–1736), another pupil of Fontana, was clearly influenced by Fischer von Erlach's design and by the Monastery of Melk.

JAKOB PRANDTAUER. The Monastery of Melk (fig. 20-19) was designed by Jakob Prandtauer (1660–1726), a stonemason rather than an architect by training. It owes much of its monumental effect to its site on the crest of a cliff above the Danube, from which it rises like a vision of heavenly glory. The polychromed buildings form a tightly knit unit that centers on the church. The wings, housing the library and imperial hall, are joined at the west by curving arms, which meet at a high balcony that provides a dramatic view onto the world beyond the monastery.

BALTHASAR NEUMANN. The next generation of architects favored lightness and elegance. Chief among them was Balthasar Neumann (1687–1753). Trained as a military engineer, he was named a surveyor for the Residenz (Episcopal Palace) in Würzburg after his return from a visit to Milan in 1720. The design is not wholly his. The basic plan was already established by Johann Maximilian von Welsch (1671–1745), and although Neumann greatly modified it, he was required to consult the leading architects of Paris and Vienna in 1723. The final result is a skillful blend of the latest German, French, and Italian ideas. The breathtaking Kaisersaal (fig. 20-20) is a great oval hall decorated in the favorite color scheme of the mid-eighteenth century: white, gold, and pastel shades. The structural importance of the columns, pilasters, and architraves has been minimized in favor of their decorative role. Windows and vault segments are framed by continuous, ribbon-like moldings, and the white surfaces are covered with irregular

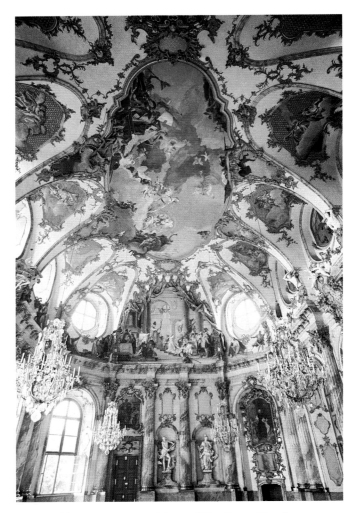

20-20. Balthasar Neumann. Kaisersaal, Residenz, Würzburg, Germany. 1719–44. Frescoes by Giovanni Battista Tiepolo, 1751-52

MODERN HARMONY

The development of eighteenth-century music was made possible by the codification of the modern system of harmony, which, after a gradual development over approximately 300 years, was spelled out in its final form in the *Treatise on Harmony* (1722) by the French composer Jean-Philippe Rameau. This system was based on the "tempered" diatonic scale, a progression of notes derived by equally spacing ("tempering") 12 tones within an octave (in essence, the black-and-white keys of a piano). The tonal distance, or interval, between any two of these one-twelfth-octave tones is called a semitone or "half step." Twice that interval is called a whole tone or "whole step." The diatonic system includes two principal scales, the major scale—the familiar "do-re-mi" that music students practice—and a modification of it called the minor scale. Both major and minor scales include a specific progression of five whole tones and two semitones, which start from the tonic, the note on which the scale is based, to the same note an octave above it. Like Greek modes, the major and minor scales communicate emotional qualities. Generally, a listener experiences the major scale as positive and optimistic and the minor scale as somber or plaintive.

The tempered scale allowed a keyboard to include a number of octaves, which in turn increased the range of music that could be written for keyboard instruments. The 48 pieces that Johann Sebastian Bach wrote in his *Well-Tempered Clavier* (1722, 1744) were one of the first series of compositions that exploited the possibilities of the newly expanded keyboard.

Another feature of the system as defined by Rameau were chords, sets of notes based on specific tones of the scale, sounded together in accompaniment to the melody. The major chord, for example, is derived from the major scale. It is made up of the tonic, the third note of the scale, and the fifth note of the scale. The chords for each scale were intended to create a full multivoice sound that is pleasing to the ear. Rameau's rules defined which chords were to be used in which musical circumstances; however, it was also understood that a composer might "break" the rules to create a deliberately discordant effect, or dissonance, for expressive purposes. Such dissonances were almost always "resolved" back to the notes of the scale in which the work was being played.

We need not be schooled in music theory to appreciate the virtues of the new system, which are readily apparent to the ear: its orderliness and flexibility, which not only permitted the fullest development of counterpoint but created new melodic possibilities as well. Modern harmony was an essential precondition for the work of the great composers of the eighteenth and nineteenth centuries, and it remained the basis of Western music composition until the end of World War I, when avant-garde composers began to seek other modes of musical expression.

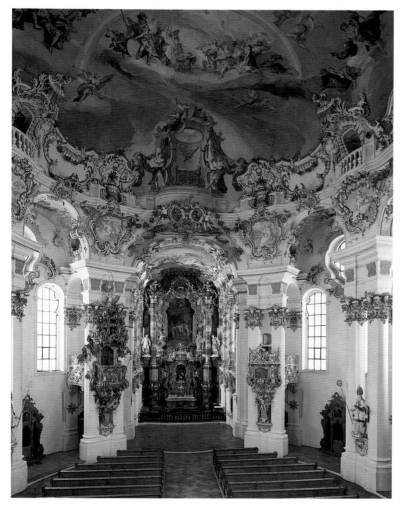

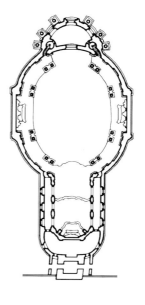

20-21. Dominikus Zimmermann. Interior of Die Wies,
Upper Bavaria, Germany. 1745–54

20-22. Plan of Die Wies

ornamental designs. These lacy, curling motifs, the hallmark of the French style (see fig. 20-1), are happily combined with German Rococo architecture. (The basic design recalls an early interior by Fischer von Erlach.) The abundant daylight, the play of curves and countercurves, and the weightless grace of the stucco sculpture give the Kaisersaal an airy lightness far removed from the Roman Baroque. The vaults and walls seem thin and pliable, like membranes easily punctured by the expansive power of space.

DOMINIKUS ZIMMERMANN. Dominikus Zimmermann (1685–1766), a contemporary of Balthasar Neumann, created what may be the finest design of the mid-eighteenth century: the Bavarian pilgrimage church nicknamed "Die Wies" ("The Meadow"). The exterior is so plain that the interior seems overwhelming (figs. 20-21 and 20-22). This richness is due to the fact that the architect and his brother, Johann Baptist Zimmermann (1680–1758), who was responsible for the frescoes, were trained as stucco workers. Like Fischer von Erlach's St. Charles Borromaeus, this church's basic shape is oval, but since the ceiling rests on paired, freestanding supports, the space is more fluid and complex. As a result, we are reminded of a German Gothic Hallenkirche. Even the way the Rococo décor tends to break up the

ceiling recalls the webbed vaults of Heiligenkreuz in Schwäbisch-Gmünd (see fig. 11-30). Here Guarini's prophetic revaluation of Gothic architecture has become reality.

ITALY

Just as the style of architecture invented in Italy achieved its climax north of the Alps, much Italian Rococo painting took place in other countries. The timid style of the Late Baroque in Italy was transformed during the first decade of the eighteenth century by the rise of the Rococo in Venice, which had been an artistic backwater for a hundred years. The Italian Rococo is distinguished from the Baroque by a revived appreciation of Veronese's colorism and pageantry, but with an airy sensibility that is new. The first artist to formulate this style was Sebastiano Ricci (1659–1734), who began his career as a stage painter and became an important artist only in mid-career. His skill at blending Venetian painterliness with High Baroque illusionism made Ricci and his later followers the leading decorative painters in Europe between 1710 and 1760. The Venetians were active in every major center throughout Europe, especially London, Dresden, and Madrid. They were not alone: many artists from Rome and other parts of Italy also worked abroad.

Theater throughout the Rococo period was marked by sentimentality, usually with a moralizing theme. In England this trend began with *Love's Last Shift* by Colley Cibber (1671–1757), which was presented even before the attacks of Jeremy Collier (1650–1726) in 1698 on the morality of the theater. The net result was a more conservative kind of domestic drama for the middle class, exemplified by *The Conscious Lovers* (1722) by Sir Richard Steele (1672–1729), in which people recant the folly of their ways. As a consequence of the political satires by Henry Fielding (1707–1754), which offended the prime minister, Sir Robert Walpole, theater was further constrained by the Licensing Act of 1737, which imposed strict censorship. England, which had been influenced by Molière and Racine during the seventeenth century, now made an important contribution to French theater. The counterpart to Steele's plays in France were the "tearful comedies" of Philippe Destouches (1680–1754), who served as a diplomat in London in 1716, Pierre-Claude Nivelle de La Chaussée (1692–1754), and Pierre Marivaux (1688–1763). Tragedy enjoyed a final resurgence in the plays of the writer and philosopher Voltaire (François-Marie Arouet, 1694–1778), who sought to liberalize classical drama after living as a refugee from 1726 to 1729 in England, where he came to know all the leading intellectuals and developed an admiration for Shakespeare. His later plays are no less sentimental than those of his peers, but the growing emphasis on spectacle led him in 1759 to banish spectators from the stage for the first time. Comedy was left in the hands of the Comédie Italienne, created in 1716 when the commedia dell'arte was invited back to France by the Duc d'Orléans upon the death of his brother, Louis XIV. In Italy, by contrast, the energies of the playwrights were absorbed by the mania for opera. The principal exception was Carlo Goldoni (1707–1793), a Venetian dramatist whose vivid comedies deliberately imitated those of Molière.

The major contributions of Rococo theater thus lay not in writing but in stagecraft: scenic design and acting. With the increased demand for spectacle, many artists were trained or employed as scenographers, including François Boucher and Canaletto. The affinity was natural, since the backgrounds in many paintings came to look increasingly like set designs after 1700. Boucher's pupil, Philippe-Jacques de Loutherbourg (1740–1812), who also trained under the scene designer Louis-René Boquet (1717–1814), brought French practices with him to England, where many painters, including Hogarth's father-in-law, James Thornhill (1676–1734), George Lambert (c. 1699–1765), and Francis Hayman (1708–1776), regularly worked for the theater.

De Loutherbourg, who became a friend of Thomas Gainsborough, had been invited to England by the actor David

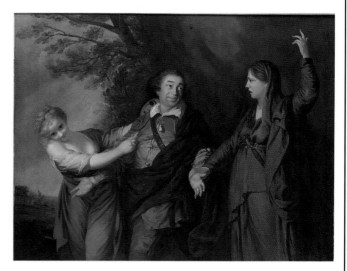

Sir Joshua Reynolds. *Garrick Between Tragedy and Comedy.* 1761. Oil on canvas, 48½ x 72" (125.2 x 182.9 cm). Collection the Royal National Theatre, London

Garrick (1717–1779) to supervise scene painting at his Drury Lane Theater, and both men introduced a number of innovations in the theater, especially in improved lighting. Garrick, whose portrait was painted by all the leading artists of the day, including Hogarth, Reynolds, and Gainsborough, dominated the English stage after his debut in 1741 and played a major role in theatrical reform on the Continent following his visits to France in 1763 and Italy and Germany two years later. Like Voltaire, he removed spectators from the stage. Nevertheless, Garrick had several rivals, chief among them Charles Macklin (1697?–1797) and Samuel Foote (1720–1777), who established the Haymarket as a rival to Drury Lane and Covent Garden, the two legitimate theaters in London. These three men were among the first English actors to show an awareness of period dress, which was also taken up by the French theater. Voltaire's main actor, Henri-Louis Lekain (1729–1778), and his leading lady, Mademoiselle Clairon (1723–1803), became the first French actors to use authentic costumes as part of the trend toward greater realism in theater.

Women had been acting in the Comédie-Française since the 1690s, but they never achieved the status of English actresses. Thus Adrienne Lecouvreur (1692–1730), who was the first to adopt formal court costumes for tragic heroines, was buried anonymously the same year that Anne Oldfield (1683–1730) was interred in Westminster Abbey. After 1780 the reigning actress was Sarah Siddons (1755–1831), the sister of the great impresario John Philip Kemble (1757–1823); like Garrick, she sat for both Gainsborough and Reynolds (see figs. 20-14 and 20-15). During the early decades of the eighteenth century, a number of women in England also became successful playwrights.

GIOVANNI BATTISTA TIEPOLO. The last and most refined stage of Italian illusionistic ceiling decoration can be seen in the works of Giovanni Battista Tiepolo (1696–1770). In his mastery of light and color, his grace and masterful touch, and his power of invention, Tiepolo easily surpassed his fellow Venetians. These qualities made him famous far beyond his home territory. When Tiepolo painted the Würzburg frescoes (figs. 20-20, 20-23, and 20-24), his powers were at their height. The tissuelike ceiling so often gives way to illusionistic openings, both painted and sculpted, that we no longer feel it to be a spatial boundary. Unlike Baroque ceilings (compare fig. 17-13), these openings do not reveal avalanches of figures propelled by dramatic bursts of light. Rather, we see blue sky and sunlit clouds, and an occasional winged creature soaring in this limitless expanse. Only along the edges of the ceiling are there solid clusters of figures.

At one end, replacing a window, is *The Marriage of Frederick Barbarossa* (see figs. 20-20 and 20-24). As a public spectacle, it is as festive as *Christ in the House of Levi* by Veronese (fig. 14-13). The artist has followed Veronese's example by putting the event, which took place in the twelfth century, in a contemporary setting. Its allegorical fantasy is "revealed" by the carved putti opening a gilt-stucco curtain onto the wedding ceremony. The result is a display of theatrical illusionism worthy of Bernini. Unexpected in this festive procession is the element of classicism, which gives an air of noble restraint to the main figures, in keeping with the solemnity of the occasion.

Tiepolo later became the last in the long line of Italian artists, beginning with Luca Giordano (see pages 570–71), who were invited to work at the Royal Palace in Madrid. There he encountered the German painter Anton Raphael Mengs, a champion of the classical revival whose presence signaled the end of the Rococo (see page 672).

CORRADO GIAQUINTO. The artist replaced by Mengs was Corrado Giaquinto (1703–1765), who left Madrid because of ill health. The only serious rival to Tiepolo in ability, he can be viewed as the last great painter in both Naples, where he trained under Francesco Solimena, and Rome, where he passed most of his career, for the two schools were closely related (see pages 570–71). At the Spanish court, where his power was similar to Lebrun's (see pages 610–11), Giaquinto was hailed as the successor to Giordano, whose work had a decisive impact on his art. *Justice and Peace* (fig. 20-25) clearly resembles Giordano's *Abduction of Europa* (see fig. 17-14), but with overtones of Boucher's style (see fig. 20-6). The painting unites the best of both worlds: the monumentality of Italy and the charm of France. The seemingly effortless brushwork and bold palette, which are unique to Giaquinto, set it apart. No other painter of the Rococo could apply such daring colors with such creamy consistency.

CANALETTO. During the eighteenth century, landscape in Italy evolved a new form in keeping with the character of the Rococo: **veduta** (view) painting. Its beginnings can be traced back to the seventeenth century with the many foreigners, such as Claude Lorraine (see fig. 19-7), who specialized in depicting the Roman countryside. After 1720, however, it took on a specifically

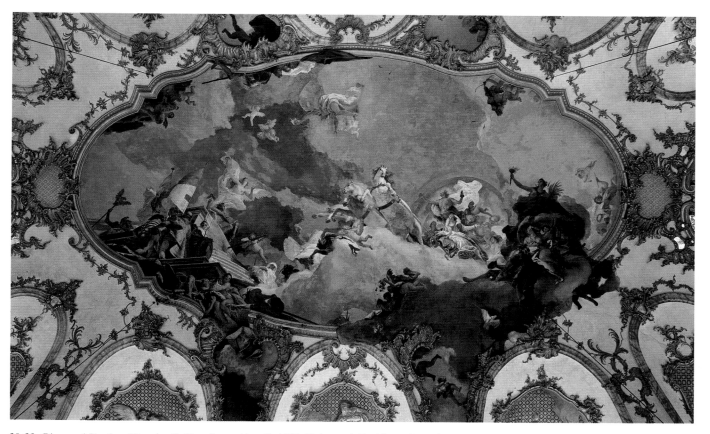

20-23. Giovanni Battista Tiepolo. Ceiling fresco (detail). 1751. Kaisersaal, Residenz, Würzburg

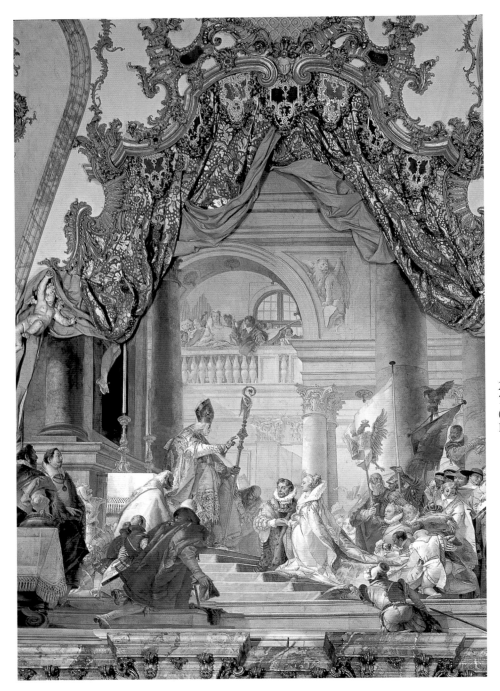

20-24. Giovanni Battista Tiepolo.
The Marriage of Frederick Barbarossa
(partial view). 1752. Fresco.
Kaisersaal, Residenz, Würzburg

20-25. Corrado Giaquinto. *Justice and Peace.*
c. 1753–54. Oil on canvas, 7'1" x 13'11¼"
(2.16 x 4.25 m). Museo del Prado, Madrid

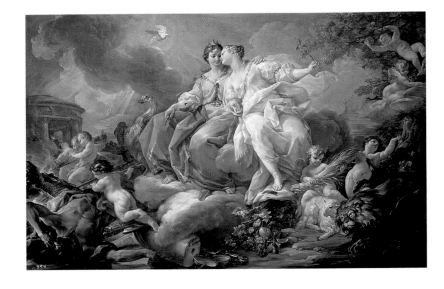

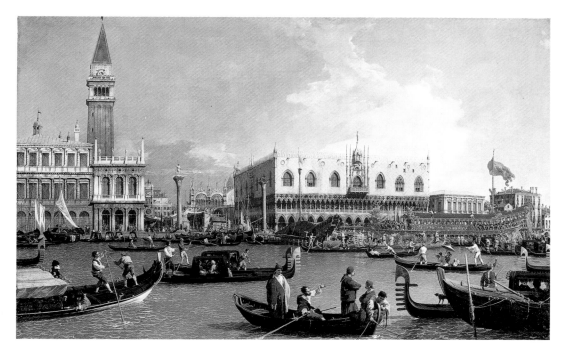

urban identity. The most famous of the vedutists was Canaletto (Giovanni Antonio Canal, 1697–1768) of Venice. His pictures were great favorites with the British, and he later became one of several Venetian artists to visit London for an extended period. *The Bucintoro at the Molo* (fig. 20-26) is one of a series of paintings commissioned by Joseph Smith, an English entrepreneur living in Venice, who later issued them as a suite of etchings to meet the demand for mementos of Venice from those who could not afford an original canvas by the artist. It shows a favorite subject: the Doge returning on his magnificent barge to the Piazza San Marco from the Lido (the city's island beach) on Ascension Day after celebrating the Marriage of the Sea. Canaletto has captured the pageantry of this great public celebration, which is presented as a brilliant theatrical display.

Canaletto's landscapes are, for the most part, topographically accurate. However, he was not above tampering with the truth. While he usually made only slight adjustments for the sake of the composition, he would sometimes treat scenes with considerable freedom or create composite views. He may have used a mechanical or optical device (perhaps a **camera obscura,** a forerunner of the photographic camera) to render some of his views, although he was a skilled draftsman who hardly needed such aids. However, the liveliness and sparkle of his pictures, as well as his sure sense of composition, sprang in large part from his training as a scenographer. As in our example, he often included vignettes of daily life in Venice that lend a human interest to his scenes and make them fascinating cultural documents as well.

GIOVANNI PIRANESI. Canaletto shared his background as a designer of stage sets with Ricci (see above) and with Giovanni Paolo Panini (1691–1765), his fellow vedutist in Rome who had a passion for classical antiquity (see fig. 7-12). They in turn are the forerunners of another Roman artist, Giovanni Battista Piranesi (1720–1778), whose *Prison Caprices* (fig. 20-27) are rooted in contemporary designs for theater and opera. Unlike the prints after

Canaletto's paintings, these masterful etchings were conceived as original works of art from the beginning, so that they have a gripping power. In Piranesi's imagery, the play between reality and fantasy, so fundamental to the theatrical Rococo, has been transformed into a romanticized vision of despair as terrifying as any nightmare. His bold imagination appealed greatly to many artists of the next generation, on whom he exercised a decisive influence.

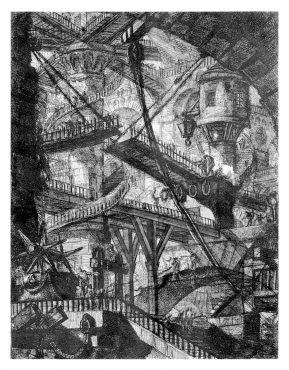

20-27. Giovanni Battista Piranesi.
Tower with Bridges, from *Prison Caprices.*
1760–61. Etching, 21¾ x 16⅜" (55.2 x 41.6 cm).
The Metropolitan Museum of Art, New York
ROGERS FUND

Primary Sources for Part Three

The following is a selection of excerpts, in modern translations, from original texts by artists, architects, religious figures, and historians from the Renaissance period through the Rococo period. These readings supplement the main text and are keyed to it. Their full citations are given in the Credits section at the end of the book.

40

LEONE BATTISTA ALBERTI (1404–1472)
From *On Painting*

Alberti's On Painting, *published in 1435, and his* On Sculpture, *which appeared in 1464, are among the most influential and revealing documents of the Early Renaissance. Alberti's was the first published account of linear perspective, though its relation to the system invented by Brunelleschi is problematic.*

I first draw a rectangle of right angles, where I am to paint, which I treat just like an open window through which I might look at what will be painted there, and then I decide how large I want the people in my picture, and I divide the length of a man of this size into three, which is proportionate to a two-foot measurement [a *braccio*], since a normal man measures almost six feet. And I mark these two-foot units on the bottom line of my rectangle, as many of them as it will take, and this line is for me proportional to the horizontal quantity I originally saw. Then inside the rectangle, where I like, I mark a point which will be where the middle ray hits, and I call it the midpoint. This should not be higher above the bottom line than a man I would paint there, so that the viewer and the things seen will appear to be on a level with each other. Then I draw straight lines from the midpoint to the divisions already marked in the bottom line. These lines will show how each transverse quantity might change from the one before almost to infinity. . . .

As for the transverse quantities . . . I take a little space and in it draw a straight line similar to the bottom line and divide it similarly, then above it I put a point, straight above one end of it, as high as the midpoint is above the bottom line, and thence I draw lines to each point in the first line. Then I fix the distance I want from the eye to the painting, and so draw a perpendicular line cutting every line it finds, and the places where I find all my parallels to be drawn, that is, the squares of the pavement in the painting. . . . When I have done this, I draw a horizontal straight line in the painting, parallel to the lower ones, passing through the midpoint, as a boundary that can be passed only by quantities higher than the observer's eye.

41

LEONE BATTISTA ALBERTI
From *On Architecture*

Modeled on Vitruvius' treatise on architecture (first century B.C.), On Architecture *was completed in 1452 but not published until 1485, after Alberti's death.*

The most expert Artists among the Ancients . . . were of [the] opinion that an Edifice was like an Animal, so that in the formation of it we ought to imitate Nature. . . . It is manifest that in those [animals] which are esteemed beautiful, the parts or members are not constantly all the same, . . . but we find that even in those parts

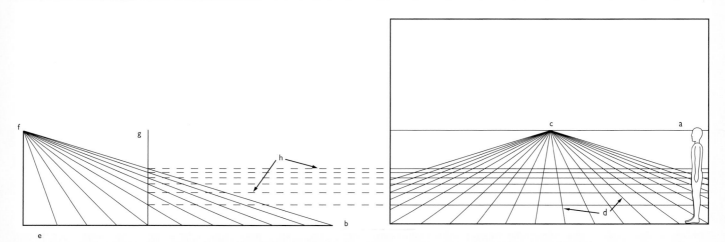

PS-40. Design of Leone Battista Alberti's Perspective Construction, according to recent discoveries: (a) height of human being; (b) base line; (c) vanishing point; (d) orthagonals; (e) "little space"; (f) distance point; (g) vertical intersection; (h) transversals

wherein they vary most, there is something inherent and implanted which tho' they differ extremely from each other, makes each of them be beautiful. . . . But the judgment which you make that a thing is beautiful, does not proceed from mere opinion, but from a secret argument and discourse implanted in the mind itself. . . . There is a certain excellence and natural beauty in the figures and forms of buildings, which immediately strike the mind with pleasure and admiration. It is my opinion that beauty, majesty, gracefulness and the like charms, consist in those particulars which if you alter or take away, the whole wou'd be made homely and disagreeable. . . . There is . . . something . . . which arises from the conjunction and connection of these other parts, and gives the beauty and grace to the whole: which we will call Congruity, which we may consider as the original, of all that is graceful and handsome. . . . Wherever such a composition offers itself to the mind either by the conveyance of the sight, hearing, or any of the other senses, we immediately perceive this Congruity: for by Nature we desire things perfect, and adhere to them with pleasure when they are offered to us; nor does this Congruity arise so much from the body in which it is found, or any of its members, as from itself and from Nature, so that its true Seat is in the mind and in reason. . . . This is what Architecture chiefly aims at, and by this she obtains her beauty, dignity and value.

42

LEONARDO DA VINCI (1452–1519)
From his undated manuscripts

Leonardo, the consummate High Renaissance man, wrote on a variety of intellectual topics. The comparison of the arts, or Paragone, *was a common subject in High Renaissance scholarship.*

He Who Depreciates Painting Loves Neither Philosophy nor Nature

If you despise painting, which is the sole imitator of all visible works of nature, you certainly will be despising a subtle invention which brings philosophy and subtle speculation to bear on the nature of all forms—sea and land, plants and animals, grasses and flowers—which are enveloped in shade and light. Truly painting is a science, the true-born child of nature. For painting is born of nature; to be more correct we should call it the grandchild of nature, since all visible things were brought forth by nature and these, her children, have given birth to painting. Therefore we may justly speak of it as the grandchild of nature and as related to God.

A Comparison Between Poetry and Painting

The imagination cannot visualize such beauty as is seen by the eye, because the eye receives the actual semblances or images of objects and transmits them through the sense organ to the understanding where they are judged. But the imagination never gets outside the understanding; . . . it reaches the memory and stops and dies there if the imagined object is not of great beauty; thus poetry is born in the mind or rather in the imagination of the poet who, because he describes the same things as the painter, claims to be the painter's equal! . . . The object of the imagination does not come from without but is born in the darkness of the mind's eye. What a difference between forming a mental image of such light in the darkness of the mind's eye and actually perceiving it outside the darkness!

If you, poet, had to represent a murderous battle you would have to describe the air obscured and darkened by fumes from frightful and deadly engines mixed with thick clouds of dust polluting the atmosphere, and the panicky flight of wretches fearful of horrible death. In that case the painter will be your superior, because your pen will be worn out before you can fully describe what the painter can demonstrate forthwith by the aid of his science, and your tongue will be parched with thirst and your body overcome by sleep and hunger before you can describe with words what a painter is able to show you in an instant.

On Painting and Poetry

Poetry is superior to painting in the presentation of words, and painting is superior to poetry in the presentation of facts. . . . For this reason I judge painting to be superior to poetry. But as painters did not know how to plead for their own art she was left without advocates for a long time. For painting does not talk; but reveals herself as she is, ending in reality; and Poetry ends in words in which she eloquently sings her own praises.

43

GIORGIO VASARI (1511–1574)
From *The Lives of the Most Excellent Italian Architects, Painters, and Sculptors from Cimabue to Our Times*

Vasari was inspired to write The Lives *by his patron, Cardinal Farnese, later Pope Paul III. The book, first published in 1550 and expanded in 1568, was based on interviews conducted throughout Italy. Vasari personally knew many of the artists about whom he wrote, including Michelangelo, whom he idolized at the expense of others, most notably Raphael, who becomes his rival's student—a claim effectively refuted by Pietro Bellori at the end of the seventeenth century. Although art historians have spent entire careers disproving details of Vasari's narrative, they remain the starting point for the study of Italian Renaissance art. Because of the length of the biographies, only brief excerpts are possible here.*

This marvellous and divinely inspired Leonardo…would have been proficient at his early lessons if he had not been so volatile and unstable; for he was always setting himself to learn many things only to abandon them almost immediately. . . . Clearly, it was because of his profound knowledge of painting that Leonardo started so many things without finishing them; for he was convinced that his hands, for all their skill, could never perfectly express the subtle and wonderful ideas of his imagination. . . .

For Francesco del Giocondo Leonardo undertook to execute the portrait of his wife, Mona Lisa. He worked on this painting for four years, and then left it still unfinished. . . . If one wanted to see how faithfully art can imitate nature, one could readily perceive it from this head; for here Leonardo subtly reproduced every living detail. . . . Leonardo also made use of this device: while he was painting Mona Lisa, who was a very beautiful woman, he employed singers and musicians or jesters to keep her full of merriment and so chase away the melancholy that painters usually give to portraits. As a result, in this painting of Leonardo's there was a smile so pleasing that it seemed divine rather than human; and those who saw it were amazed to find that it was as alive as the original.

. . . Raphael Sanzio of Urbino, an artist as talented as he was gracious, . . . was endowed by nature with the goodness and modesty to be found in all those exceptional men whose gentle humanity is enhanced by an affable and pleasing manner, expressing itself in courteous behaviour at all times and towards all persons. . . . Raphael [had] the finest qualities of mind accompanied by such grace, industry, looks, modesty, and excellence of character as would offset every defect, no matter how serious, and any vice, no matter how ugly. . . .

At the time when Raphael determined to change and improve his style he had never studied the nude as intensely as it requires, for he had only copied it from life, employing the methods he had seen used by Perugino, although he gave his figures a grace that he understood instinctively. . . . Nonetheless, Raphael realized that in this manner he could never rival the accomplishments of Michelangelo, and...being unable to compete with Michelangelo in the branch of painting to which he had set his hand, resolved to emulate and perhaps surpass him in other respects. So he decided not to waste his time by imitating Michelangelo's style but to attain a catholic excellence in the other fields of painting. . . .

When Michelangelo had finished the statue [of Pope Julius II, later destroyed], Bramante, the friend and relation of Raphael and therefore ill-disposed to Michelangelo, seeing the Pope's preference for sculpture, schemed to divert his attention, and told the Pope that it would be a bad omen to get Michelangelo to go on with his tomb, as it would seem to be an invitation to death. He persuaded the Pope to get Michelangelo, on his return, to paint the vaulting of the Sistine Chapel. In this way Bramante and his other rivals hoped to confound him, for by taking him from sculpture, in which he was perfect, and putting him to colouring in fresco, in which he had had no experience, they thought he would produce less admirable work than Raphael. . . . Thus, when Michelangelo returned to Rome, the Pope was disposed not to have the tomb finished for the time being, and asked him to paint the vaulting of the chapel. Michelangelo tried every means to avoid it, and recommended Raphael. . . . At length, seeing that the Pope was resolute, [he] decided to do it. . . . Michelangelo then made arrangements to

do the whole work singlehanded. . . . When he had finished half, the Pope . . . daily became more convinced of Michelangelo's genius, and wished him to complete the work, judging that he would do the other half even better. Thus, singlehanded, he completed the work in twenty months, aided only by his mixer of colours. He sometimes complained that owing to the impatience of the Pope he had not been able to finish it as he would have desired, as the Pope was always asking him when he would be done. On one occasion Michelangelo replied that he would be finished when he had satisfied his own artistic sense. "And we require you to satisfy us in getting it done quickly," replied the Pope, adding that if it was not done soon he would have the scaffolding down. . . . Michelangelo wanted to retouch some parts of the painting *a secco,* as the old masters had done on the scenes below...in order to heighten the visual impact. The Pope, learning that this ornamentation was lacking...wanted him to go ahead. However, he lacked the patience to rebuild the scaffolding, and so the ceiling stayed as it was. . . .

Gian. Bellini and other painters of [Venice], through not having studied antiquities, employed a hard, dry and laboured style, which Titian acquired. But in 1507 arose Giorgione, who began to give his works more tone and relief, with better style, though he imitated natural things as best he could, colouring them like life, without making drawings previously, believing this to be the true method of procedure. He did not perceive that for good composition it is necessary to try several various methods on sheets, for invention is quickened by showing these things to the eye, while it is also necessary to a thorough knowledge of the nude. . . .

On seeing Giorgione's style Titian abandoned that of Bellini, although he had long practised it, and imitated Giorgione so well that in a short time his works were taken for Giorgione's. . . . Titian's methods in these paintings differ widely from those he adopted in his youth. His first works are executed with a certain fineness and diligence, so that they may be examined closely, but these are done roughly in an impressionist manner, with bold strokes and blobs, to obtain the effect at a distance. This is why many in trying to imitate him have made clumsy pictures, for if people think that such work can be done without labour they are deceived, as it is necessary to retouch and recolour them incessantly, so that the labour is evident. The method is admirable and beautiful if done judiciously, making paintings appear alive and achieved without labour.

. . . In 1546, at the summons of Cardinal Farnese, [Titian] went to Rome where he found Giorgio Vasari who...was working for the cardinal on the hall of the Palazzo della Cancellaria. The cardinal recommended Titian to Vasari, who then lovingly kept him company and took him to see the sights of Rome. After Titian had rested for some days he was given rooms in the Belvedere [Palace] so that he could set his hand to painting once more the portrait of Pope Paul. . . . Then one day Michelangelo and Vasari went along to visit Titian in the Belvedere, where they saw a painting he had finished of a woman, representing Danäe, who had in her lap Jove transformed into a rain of gold; and naturally, as one would do with the artist present, they praised it warmly. After they had gone, they started to discuss Titian's method and Buonarroti commended it highly, saying that his colouring and his style pleased him very much, but that it was a shame that in Venice they did not learn to draw well from the beginning and that those painters did not pursue their studies with more method. For the truth was, he went on, that if Titian had been assisted by art and design as much as he was by nature, and especially in reproducing living subjects, then no one could achieve more or work better, for he had a fine spirit and a lively and entrancing style.

44
From the Canons and Decrees of the Council of Trent

The Catholic church responded to the growth in northern Europe of independent "Reformed" churches (inaugurated by Martin Luther's 1517 critique of the Church) by attempting to stop the Reformation and win back the territories and peoples lost to the Roman Church. These various measures of the sixteenth and early seventeenth centuries are collectively called the Counter Reformation. One agency of this development was the Council of Trent, a series of three meetings of church leaders in 1545–47, 1551–52, and 1562–63. The following is from one of the council's last edicts, dated December 3–4, 1563, a response to ongoing Protestant attacks against religious images.

The holy council commands all bishops and others who hold the office of teaching and have charge of the *cura animarum,* that in accordance with the usage of the Catholic and Apostolic Church, received from the primitive times of the Christian religion, and with the unanimous teaching of the holy Fathers and the decrees of sacred councils, they above all instruct the faithful diligently in matters relating to intercession and invocation of the saints, the veneration of relics, and the legitimate use of images. . . . Moreover, that the images of Christ, of the Virgin Mother of God, and of the other saints are to be placed and retained especially in the churches, and that due honor and veneration is to be given them; not, however, that any divinity or virtue is believed to be in them by reason of which they are to be venerated, or that something is to be asked of them, or that trust is to be placed in images, as was done of old by the Gentiles who placed their hope in idols; but because the honor which is shown them is referred to the prototypes which they represent, so that by means of the images which we kiss and before which we uncover the head and prostrate ourselves, we adore Christ and venerate the saints whose likeness they bear. That is what was defined by the decrees of the councils, especially of the Second Council of Nicaea, against the opponents of images.

Moreover, let the bishops diligently teach that by means of the stories of the mysteries of our redemption portrayed in paintings and other representations the people are instructed and confirmed in the articles of faith, which ought to be borne in mind and constantly reflected upon; also that great profit is derived from all holy images, not only because the people are thereby reminded of the benefits and gifts bestowed on them by Christ, but also because through the saints the miracles of God and salutary examples are set before the eyes of the faithful, so that they may give God thanks for those things, may fashion their own life and conduct in imitation of the saints and be moved to adore and love God and cultivate piety. But if anyone should teach or maintain anything contrary to these decrees, let him be anathema.

If any abuses shall have found their way into these holy and salutary observances, the holy council desires earnestly that they be completely removed, so that no representation of false doctrines and such as might be the occasion of grave error to the uneducated be exhibited. . . . Finally, such zeal and care should be exhibited by the bishops with regard to these things that nothing may appear that is disorderly or unbecoming and confusedly arranged, nothing that is profane, nothing disrespectful, since holiness becometh the house of God.

45
From a session of the Inquisition Tribunal in Venice of Paolo Veronese

Because of the liberal religious atmosphere of Venice, Veronese was never required to make the various changes to his painting of the Last Supper *(see fig. 14-13) asked for by the tribunal of the Inquisition in this interrogation. All parties seem to have been satisfied with a mere change of title to* Supper in the House of Levi *(now* Christ in the House of Levi*).*

Today, Saturday, the 18th of the month of July, 1573, having been asked by the Holy Office to appear before the Holy Tribunal, Paolo Caliari of Verona, . . . Questioned about his profession:
Answer: I paint and compose figures.
Q: Do you know the reason why you have been summoned?
A: No, sir.
Q: Can you imagine it?
A: I can well imagine.
Q: Say what you think the reason is.
A: According to what the Reverend Father, the Prior of the Convent of SS. Giovanni e Paolo, . . . told me, he had been here and Your Lordships had ordered him to have painted [in the picture] a Magdalen in place of a dog. I answered him by saying I would gladly do everything necessary for my honor and for that of my painting, but that I did not understand how a figure of Magdalen would be suitable there. . . .
Q: What picture is this of which you have spoken?
A: This is a picture of the Last Supper that Jesus Christ took with His Apostles in the house of Simon. . . .
Q: At this Supper of Our Lord have you painted other figures?
A: Yes, milords.
Q: Tell us how many people and describe the gestures of each.
A: There is the owner of the inn, Simon; besides this figure I have made a steward, who, I imagined, had come there for his own

pleasure to see how the things were going at the table. There are many figures there which I cannot recall, as I painted the picture some time ago. . . .

Q: In this Supper which you made for SS. Giovanni e Paolo what is the significance of the man whose nose is bleeding?

A: I intended to represent a servant whose nose was bleeding because of some accident.

Q: What is the significance of those armed men dressed as Germans, each with a halberd in his hand? . . .

A: We painters take the same license the poets and the jesters take and I have represented these two halberdiers, one drinking and the other eating nearby on the stairs. They are placed there so that they might be of service because it seemed to me fitting, according to what I have been told, that the master of the house, who was great and rich, should have such servants.

Q: And that man dressed as a buffoon with a parrot on his wrist, for what purpose did you paint him on that canvas?

A: For ornament, as is customary.

Q: Who are at the table of Our Lord?

A: The Twelve Apostles.

Q: What is St. Peter, the first one, doing?

A: Carving the lamb in order to pass it to the other end of the table.

Q: What is the Apostle next to him doing?

A: He is holding a dish in order to receive what St. Peter will give him.

Q: Tell us what the one next to this one is doing.

A: He has a toothpick and cleans his teeth. . . .

Q: Did anyone commission you to paint Germans, buffoons, and similar things in that picture?

A: No, milords, but I received the commission to decorate the picture as I saw fit. It is large and, it seemed to me, it could hold many figures.

Q: Are not the decorations which you painters are accustomed to add to paintings or pictures supposed to be suitable and proper to the subject and the principal figures or are they for pleasure—simply what comes to your imagination without any discretion or judiciousness?

A: I paint pictures as I see fit and as well as my talent permits.

Q: Does it seem fitting at the Last Supper of the Lord to paint buffoons, drunkards, Germans, dwarfs, and similar vulgarities?

A: No, milords.

Q: Do you not know that in Germany and in other places infected with heresy it is customary with various pictures full of scurrilousness and similar inventions to mock, vituperate, and scorn the things of the Holy Catholic Church in order to teach bad doctrines to foolish and ignorant people?

A: Yes that is wrong. . . .

After these things had been said, the judges announced that the above named Paolo would be obliged to improve and change his painting within a period of three months from the day of this admonition and that according to the opinion and decision of the Holy Tribunal all the corrections should be made at the expense of the painter and that if he did not correct the picture he would be liable to the penalties imposed by the Holy Tribunal. Thus they decreed in the best manner possible.

46

ANDREA PALLADIO (1518–1580)
From *The Four Books of Architecture*

Published in 1570, Palladio's The Four Books of Architecture *made an enormous impression on his European contemporaries. His book provided the basis for much French and English architecture of the seventeenth and eighteenth centuries.*

Guided by a natural inclination, I gave myself up in my most early years to the study of architecture: and as it was always my opinion, that the ancient Romans, as in many other things, so in building well, vastly excelled all those who have been since their time, I proposed to myself Vitruvius for my master and guide, who is the only ancient writer of this art, and set myself to search into the reliques of all the ancient edifices, that, in spight of time and the cruelty of the Barbarians, yet remain; and finding them much more worthy of observation, than at first I had imagined, I began very minutely with the utmost diligence to measure every one of their parts; of which I grew at last so sollicitous an examiner, (not finding any thing which was not done with reason and beautiful proportion) that I have very frequently not only travelled in different parts of Italy, but also out of it. . . .

Whereupon perceiving how much this common use of building was different from the observations I had made upon the said edifices, and from what I had read in Vitruvius, Leon Battista Alberti, and in other excellent writers . . . it seemed to me a thing worthy of a man, who ought not to be born for himself only, but also for the utility of others, to publish the de-signs of those edifices, (in collecting which, I have employed so much time, and exposed myself to so many dangers) and concisely to set down whatever in them appeared to me more worthy of consideration; and moreover, those rules which I have observed, and now observe, in building; that they who shall read these my books, may be able to make use of whatever will be good therein, and supply those things in which . . . I shall have failed; that one may learn, by little and little, to lay aside the strange abuses, the barbarous inventions, the superfluous expence, and (what is of greater consequence) avoid the various and continual ruins that have been seen in many fabricks. . . .

47

CAREL VAN MANDER (1548–1606)
From *The Painter's Treatise*

Van Mander's biographies of distinguished Dutch and Flemish painters, published in 1604, are a counterpart to the lives of Italian artists by Giorgio Vasari, which first appeared in 1550. Van Mander, a painter himself, begins his biographies with Jan van Eyck because he was considered the inventor of oil painting and consequently the originator, with his brother Hubert, of the Netherlandish tradition of painting. Among the works described by Van Mander are the Ghent Altarpiece (see figs. 15-3, 15-4, 15-6) and a painting that is probably The Arnolfini Portrait *(see figs. 15-8 and 15-9).*

It is supposed that the art of painting with a glue and egg medium [tempera painting] was imported into the Netherlands from Italy, because, as we have noted in the biography of Giovanni of Cimabue, this method was first used in Florence, in 1250. . . .

According to the people of Bruges, Joannes [Jan] was a learned man, clever and inventive, who studied many subjects related to painting: He examined many kinds of pigment; he studied alchemy and distillation. At length, he worked out a method of varnishing his egg and glue paintings with oil, so that these shining and lustrous pictures exceedingly delighted all who saw them. . . .

Joannes had painted a panel on which he had spent much time. . . . He varnished the finished panel according to his new invention and placed it in the sunlight to dry. . . . The panel burst at the joints and fell apart. Joannes . . . took a resolve that the sun should not damage his work ever again.

Accordingly, . . . he set himself to discover or invent some kind of varnish which would dry within the house, away from the sunlight. He had already examined many oils and other similar materials supplied by nature, and had found that linseed oil and nut oil had the best drying ability of them all. . . .

Joannes found, after many experiments, that colors mixed with these oils could be handled easily, that they dried well, became hard, and, once dry, could resist water. The oil made the color appear more alive, owing to a lustre of its own, without varnish. And what surprised and pleased him most was that paint made with oil could be applied more easily and mixed more thoroughly than paint made with egg and glue. . . .

Joannes . . . had created a new type of painting, to the amazement of the world. . . . This noble discovery, of painting with oil, was the only thing the art of painting still needed to achieve naturalistic rendition.

If the ancient Greeks, Apelles and Zeus [Zeuxis] had come to life again in this country and had seen this new method of painting, they would not have been any less surprised than if war-like Achilles [had] witnessed the thunder of cannon fire. . . .

The most striking work which the Van Eyck brothers did together is the altar-piece in the church of St John, in Ghent. . . .

The central panel of the altar-piece represents a scene from the Revelation of St John, in which the elders worship the Lamb. . . . In the upper part, Mary is represented; she is being crowned by the Father and the Son. . . .

Next to the figure of Mary are little angels singing from sheets of music. They are painted so exquisitely and so well that one can detect readily, from their facial expressions, who is singing the higher part, the high counter part, the tenor part, and the bass. . . .

Adam and Eve are represented. One may observe that Adam has a certain fear of breaking the command of the Lord, for he has a worried expression. . . .

The altar painting of the Van Eyck brothers was shown only to a few personages of high standing or to someone who would reward the keeper very well. Sometimes it was shown on important holidays, but then there was usually such a crowd that it was difficult to come near it. Then the chapel containing the altarpiece would be filled with all kinds of people—painters young and old, every kind of art lover, swarming like bees and flies around a basket of figs or raisins. . . .

Some Florentine merchants sent a splendid painting, made in Flanders, by Joannes to King Alphonso I of Naples. . . . A huge throng of artists came to see this marvelous painting, when it reached Italy. But although the Italians examined the picture very carefully, touching it, smelling at it, scenting the strong odor produced by the mixture of the colors with oil, and drawing all kinds of conclusions, the secret held until Antonello of Messina, in Sicily, went to Bruges to learn the process of oil-painting. Having mastered the technique, he introduced the art into Italy, as I have described in his biography. . . .

Joannes had once painted in oil two portraits in a single scene, a man and a woman, who give the right hand to each other, as if they had been united in wedlock by *Fides*. This little picture came through inheritance into the hands of a barber in Bruges. Mary, aunt of King Philip of Spain and widow of King Louis of Hungary, . . . happened to see this painting. The art loving princess was so pleased with this picture that she gave a certain office to the barber which brought him a yearly income of a hundred guilders.

48

CAREL VAN MANDER
From *The Painter's Treatise*

Van Mander's biography of Pieter Bruegel the Elder remains an important source of information about the artist, whose talent he appreciated fully.

He did a great deal of work [in Antwerp] for a merchant, Hans Franckert, a noble and upright man, who found pleasure in Breughel's company and met him every day. With this Franckert, Breughel often went out into the country to see peasants at their fairs and weddings. Disguised as peasants they brought gifts like the other guests, claiming relationship or kinship with the bride or groom. Here Breughel delighted in observing the droll behavior of the peasants, how they ate, drank, danced, capered, or made love, all of which he was well able to reproduce cleverly and pleasantly. . . . He represented the peasants—men and women of the Campine and elsewhere—naturally, as they really were, betraying their boorishness in the way they walked, danced, stood still, or moved.

. . . When the widow of Pieter Koeck [van Aelst, with whom van Mander says Breughel studied] was living in Brussels, he courted her daughter who . . . he had often carried about in his arms, and married her. The mother, however, demanded that

Breughel should leave Antwerp and take up residence in Brussels, so as to give up and put away all thoughts of his former girl. And this indeed he did. He was a very quiet and thoughtful man, not fond of talking, but ready with jokes when in the company of others. . . . He left behind him two sons who are also good painters. One is called Pieter. He was a pupil of Gillis van Coninxloo. . . . Jan, who had learned the use of water color from his grandmother, the widow of Pieter van Aelst, was instructed in the art of painting in oils by Pieter Goedkindt. . . .

49

GASPAR OFHUYS (c. 1456–1523)
From an account of the illness of Hugo van der Goes

Gaspar Ofhuys entered the "Red Cloister" monastery near Brussels together with Hugo van der Goes in 1475. Ofhuys was perhaps jealous of the special privileges Van der Goes enjoyed because of his status as a painter, and intimates that his mental illness was an affliction brought on by the sin of pride. This sin was often attributed to artists in the Middle Ages.

About five or six years after he had taken the vows it fell to our brother [Hugo van der Goes] to make a journey which—if I remember right—took him to Cologne. . . . Hugo, during one night of his journey home, was seized by a strange illness of his mind; he uttered unceasing laments about being doomed and sentenced to eternal damnation. He even wanted to lay murderous hands on himself and had to be prevented by force from doing so. Because of this strange illness that journey came to an extremely sad end. However, thanks to efficient help, Brussels was safely reached, and prior Thomas was immediately summoned. When he saw and heard all that had happened he suspected that Hugo was vexed by the same illness which had befallen King Saul; and remembering that Saul was relieved when David played the harp he at once permitted plenty of music to be made in the presence of Hugo and also other soothing performances to be arranged in order to chase away those fantasies. But with all this, Hugo's health did not improve; he continued to rave and to pronounce himself a child of perdition. In this sad state he came home to the monastery. . . .

We can speak of two possible assumptions concerning the illness of our painter-brother converse. The first is that it was a natural one, a kind of frenzy. There exist various natural species of this disease: sometimes it is caused by "melancholy" victuals, sometimes by imbibing strong wine; then again by passions of the soul such as anxiety, sadness, overwork, or fear. . . . As regards those passions of the soul, I know for certain that this converse brother was much afflicted by them. For he was deeply troubled by the thought of how he could ever finish the works of art he wanted to paint, and it was said at that time that nine years would hardly suffice for it. . . .

The second possibility of explaining this disease is that it was sent by Divine Providence which, as it is written in the second Epistle of St. Peter, ch. 3, "is long-suffering to us-ward, not willing that any should perish, but that all should come to repentance." For this converse brother was highly praised in our order because of his special artistic achievements—in fact, he thus became more famous than he would have been outside our walls; and since he was only human—as are all of us—the various honors, visits, and accolades that came to him made him feel very important. Thus, since God did not want him to perish, He in His compassion sent him this humiliating disease which indeed made him very contrite. This our brother understood very well, and as soon as he had recovered he became most humble.

50

FRAY JOSÉ DE SIGÜENZA (1544?–1606)
From the *History of the Order of St. Jerome*

The works of Hieronymus Bosch were collected by the Spanish king Philip II (ruled 1556–98) and were displayed in his Escorial Palace near Madrid, where Sigüenza was the librarian. The interpretation of Bosch's work was as difficult then as it is today and caused just as much disagreement. This passage is Sigüenza's attempt to interpret the painting that we call The Garden of Delights *(see fig. 15-14).*

Among these German and Flemish pictures . . . there are distributed throughout the house many by a certain Geronimo Bosch. Of him I want to speak at somewhat greater length for various reasons: first, because his great inventiveness merits it; second, because they are commonly called the absurdities of Geronimo Bosque by people who observe little in what they look at; and third, because I think that these people consider them without reason as being tainted by heresy. . . .

The difference that, to my mind, exists between the pictures of this man and those of all others is that the others try to paint man as he appears on the outside, while he alone had the audacity to paint him as he is on the inside. . . .

The . . . painting has as its basic theme and subject a flower and the fruit of [a] type that we call strawberries. . . . In order for one to understand his idea, I will expound upon it in the same order in which he has organized it. Between two pictures is one large painting, with two doors that close over it. In the first of the panels he painted the Creation of Man, showing how God put him in paradise, a delightful place . . . and how He commands him as a test of his obedience and faith not to eat from the tree, and how later the devil deceived him in the form of a serpent. He eats and, trespassing God's rule, is exiled from that wondrous place and deprived of the high dignity for which he was created. . . . This is [shown] with a thousand fantasies and observations that serve as warnings. . . .

In the large painting that follows he painted the pursuits of man after he was exiled from paradise and placed in this world, and he shows him searching after the glory that is like hay or straw, like a plant without fruit, which one knows will be cast into the oven the next day, . . . and thus uncovers the life, the activities, and the thoughts of these sons of sin and wrath, who, having forgotten the commands of God . . . strive for and undertake the glory of the flesh. . . .

In this painting we find, as if alive and vivid, an infinite number of passages from the scriptures that touch upon the evil ways of man, . . . many allegories or metaphors that present them in the guise of tame, wild, fierce, lazy, sagacious, cruel, and bloodthirsty beasts of burden and riding animals. . . . Here is also demonstrated the transmigration of souls that Pythagoras, Plato, and other poets . . . displayed in the attempt to show us the bad customs, habits, dress, disposition, or sinister shades with which the souls of miserable men clothe themselves—that through pride they are transformed into lions; by vengefulness into tigers; through lust into mules, horses, and pigs; by tyranny into fish; by vanity into peacocks; by slyness and craft into foxes; by gluttony into apes and wolves; by callousness and evil into asses; by stupidity into sheep; because of rashness into goats. . . .

One can reap great profit by observing himself thus portrayed true to life from the inside. . . . And he would also see in the last panel the miserable end and goal of his pains, efforts, and preoccupations, and how . . . the brief joys are transformed into eternal wrath, with no hope or grace.

51
From the contract for the St. Wolfgang Altarpiece

It took Michael Pacher ten years (1471–81) to complete this elaborate altarpiece for the pilgrimage church of St. Wolfgang. The altarpiece is still in its original location (see fig. 15-20).

Here is recorded the pact and contract concerning the altar at St. Wolfgang, concluded between the very Reverend, Reverend Benedict, Abbot of Mondsee and of his monastery there, and Master Michael, painter of Bruneck, on St. Lucy's day of the year 1471.

ITEM, it is first to be recorded that the altar shall be made conforming to the elevation and design which the painter has brought to us at Mondsee, and to its exact measurements.

ITEM, the predella shrine shall be guilded on the inside and it shall show Mary seated with the Christ Child, Joseph, and the Three Kings with their gifts; and if these should not completely fill the predella shrine he shall make more figures or armored men, all gilt.

ITEM, the main shrine shall show the Coronation of Mary with angels and gilt drapery—the most precious and the best he can make.

ITEM, on one side St. Wolfgang with mitre, crozier, church, and hatchet; on the other St. Benedict with cap, crozier, and a tumbler, entirely gilded and silvered where needed.

ITEM, to the sides of the altar shall stand St. Florian and St. George, fine armored men, silvered and gilded where needed.

ITEM, the inner wings of the altar shall be provided with good paintings, the panels gilded and equipped with gables and pinnacles, representing four subjects, one each. . . .

ITEM, the outer wings—when the altar is closed—shall be done with good pigments and with gold added to the colors; the subject from the life of St. Wolfgang. . . .

ITEM, at St. Wolfgang, while he completes and sets up the altar, we shall provide his meals and drink, and also the iron work necessary for setting up the altar, as well as help with loading wherever necessary.

ITEM, the contract is made for the sum of one thousand two hundred Hungarian guilders or ducats. . . .

ITEM, if the altar is either not worth this sum or of higher value, and there should be some difference of opinion between us, both parties shall appoint equal numbers of experts to decide the matter.

52
MARTIN LUTHER (1483–1546)
From *Against the Heavenly Prophets in the Matter of Images and Sacraments*

Luther inaugurated the Protestant Reformation movement in 1517 with a public critique of certain Church practices, especially the sale of indulgences. His actions soon inspired a number of similar reformers in the north, some of whom were more extreme in their denunciations of the conventional artistic and musical trappings of the Church. The ideas of one of these, Andreas Bodenstein, inspired this writing of 1525.

I approached the task of destroying images by first tearing them out of the heart through God's Word and making them worthless and despised. . . . For when they are no longer in the heart, they can do no harm when seen with the eyes. But Dr. Karlstadt [Andreas Bodenstein], who pays no attention to matters of the heart, has reversed the order by removing them from sight and leaving them in the heart. . . .

I have allowed and not forbidden the outward removal of images, so long as this takes place without rioting and uproar and is done by the proper authorities. . . . And I say at the outset that according to the law of Moses no other images are forbidden than an image of God which one worships. A crucifix, on the other hand, or any other holy image is not forbidden. Heigh now! you breakers of images, I defy you to prove the opposite! . . .

Thus we read that Moses' Brazen Serpent remained (Num. 21:8) until Hezekiah destroyed it solely because it had been worshiped (II Kings 18:4). . . .

However, to speak evangelically of images, I say and declare that no one is obligated to break violently images even of God, but everything is free, and one does not sin if he does not break them with violence. . . .

Nor would I condemn those who have destroyed them, especially those who destroy divine and idolatrous images. But images for memorial and witness, such as crucifixes and images of saints, are to be tolerated. This is shown above to be the case even in the Mosaic law. And they are not only to be tolerated, but for the sake of the memorial and the witness they are praiseworthy and honorable, as the witness stones of Joshua (Josh. 24:26) and of Samuel (I Sam. 7:12).

53

ALBRECHT DÜRER (1471–1528)
From the draft manuscript for
The Book on Human Proportions

Dürer made two trips to Italy and was exposed to the new art theories being discussed there, which impressed him greatly. He did not accept them uncritically, however. His rethinking of Italian ideas often appears only in preliminary form, in drafts such as this one, written in 1512–13.

How beauty is to be judged is a matter of deliberation.... In some things we consider that as beautiful which elsewhere would lack beauty. "Good" and "better" in respect of beauty are not easy to discern, for it would be quite possible to make two different figures, neither of them conforming to the other, one stouter and the other thinner, and yet we scarce might be able to judge which of the two may excel in beauty. What beauty is I know not, though it adheres to many things. When we wish to bring it into our work we find it very hard. We must gather it together from far and wide, and especially in the case of the human figure.... One may often search through two or three hundred men without finding amongst them more than one or two points of beauty which can be made use of. You therefore, if you desire to compose a fine figure, must take the head from some and the chest, arm, leg, hand, and foot from others....

Many follow their taste alone; these are in error. Therefore let each take care that his inclination blind not his judgment. For every mother is well pleased with her own child....

Men deliberate and hold numberless differing opinions about these things and they seek after them in many different ways, although the ugly is more easily attained than the beautiful. Being then, as we are, in such a state of error, I know not how to set down firmly and with finality what measure approaches absolute beauty....

It seems to me impossible for a man to say that he can point out the best proportions for the human figure; for the lie is in our perception, and darkness abides so heavily within us that even our gropings fail....

However, because we cannot altogether attain perfection, shall we therefore wholly cease from our learning? This bestial thought we do not accept. For evil and good lie before men, wherefore it behooves a rational man to choose the better.

54

ARTEMISIA GENTILESCHI (1593–c.1653)
From a letter to Don Antonio Ruffo

Being a woman in what was considered until very recently a man's field was not easy, as this letter of November 13, 1649, only begins to suggest. Ruffo was one of Artemisia's patrons.

I have received a letter of October 26th, which I deeply appreciated, particularly noting how my master always concerns himself with favoring me, contrary to my merit. In it, you tell me about that gentleman who wishes to have some paintings by me, that he would like a Galatea and a Judgment of Paris, and that the Galatea should be different from the one that Your Most Illustrious Lordship owns. There was no need for you to urge me to do this, since by the grace of God and the Most Holy Virgin, they [clients] come to a woman with this kind of talent, that is, to vary the subjects in my painting; never has anyone found in my pictures any repetition of invention, not even of one hand.

As for the fact that this gentleman wishes to know the price before the work is done, ... I do it most unwillingly.... I never quote a price for my works until they are done. However, since Your Most Illustrious Lordship wants me to do this, I will do what you command. Tell this gentleman that I want five hundred ducats for both; he can show them to the whole world and, should he find anyone who does not think the paintings are worth two hundred scudi more, I won't ask him to pay me the agreed price. I assure Your Most Illustrious Lordship that these are paintings with nude figures requiring very expensive female models, which is a big headache. When I find good ones they fleece me, and at other times, one must suffer [their] pettiness with the patience of Job.

As for my doing a drawing and sending it, I have made a solemn vow never to send my drawings because people have cheated me. In particular, just today I found ... that, having done a drawing of souls in Purgatory for the Bishop of St. Gata, he, in order to spend less, commissioned another painter to do the painting using my work. If I were a man, I can't imagine it would have turned out this way....

I must caution Your Most Illustrious Lordship that when I ask a price, I don't follow the custom in Naples, where they ask thirty and then give it for four. I am Roman, and therefore I shall act always in the Roman manner.

55

GIOVANNI PIETRO BELLORI (1613–1696)
From *Lives of the Modern Painters, Sculptors, and Architects*

Unlike Vasari's Lives, *Bellori's book is more selective and critical. He often ignores or gives minimal treatment to those artists and architects who offended his classical taste. Bellori's account was published in Rome in 1672.*

When the divine Raphael with the ultimate outlines of his art used its beauty to the summit, restoring it to the ancient majesty of all those graces and enriching the merits that once made it most glorious in the presence of the Greeks and the Romans, painting was most admired by men and seemed descended from Heaven. But since things of the earth never stay the same, and whatever gains the heights inevitably must with perpetual vicissitude fall back again, so art, which from Cimabue and Giotto had slowly advanced over the long period of two hundred and fifty years, was seen to decline rapidly and from a queen become humble and common. Thus, with the passing of that happy century, all of its beauties quickly vanished. The artists, abandoning the study of nature, corrupted art with the *maniera,* that is to say, with the fantastic idea based on practice and not on imitation. This vice, the destroyer of painting, first began to appear in masters of honored acclaim. It rooted itself in the schools that later followed. . . .

Thus, when painting was drawing to its end. . . . It pleased God that in the city of Bologna, the mistress of sciences and studies, a most noble mind was forged and through it the declining and extinguished art was reforged. He was that Annibale Carracci, of whom I now mean to write. . . .

Annibale continued in the [Farnese] gallery [see fig. 17-5] . . . ordering various myths toward an end: the theme . . . is human love governed by Heaven. Thus the theme of love . . . displays its power, subjecting the breasts of the strong, the chaste, and the savage: the loves, that is to say, of Hercules, Diana, and of Polyphemus. . . . The amours of Jupiter, Juno, Aurora, and Galatea reveal its power in the universe. The white wool that Diana receives from the god Pan and the golden apples given to Paris by Mercury are the gifts by which Amor sways human minds, and the discords provoked by beauty. The Bacchanal is the symbol of drunkenness, the source of impure desires. And since the end of all irrational pleasures is sorrow and punishment, . . . he painted Andromeda bound to the rock to be devoured by the sea monster, symbolizing that the soul bound to emotion becomes the food of vice if Perseus—that is to say, reason and the love of the worthy—does not come to her assistance.

Now [Caravaggio] began to paint according to his own genius. He not only ignored the most excellent marbles of the ancients and the famous paintings of Raphael, but he despised them, and nature alone became the object of his brush. . . . [He] was making himself more and more notable for the color scheme which he was introducing, not soft and sparingly tinted as before, but reinforced throughout with bold shadows and a great deal of black to give relief to the forms. He went so far in this manner of working that he never brought his figures out into the daylight, but placed them in the dark brown atmosphere of a closed room, using a high light that descended vertically over the principal parts of the bodies while leaving the remainder in shadow in order to give force through a strong contrast of light and dark. The painters then in Rome were greatly impressed by his novelty and the younger ones especially gathered around him and praised him as the only true imitator of nature. Looking upon his works as miracles, they outdid each other in following his method. . . .

. . . Having thought up his inventions, [Poussin] then made a rough sketch of what he had in mind; he then made small wax models, half a hand's breadth in height, of all the figures striking their attitudes, and then constructed the story of the fable in relief in order to study the natural effects of the light and the shadow of the bodies. He then made larger models, which he dressed, so as to make a separate study of their attire and the folds of material on the naked form, and for this purpose he used fine canvas, or wet cambric, with just a few pieces of cloth providing a variety of colors. Thus he gradually sketched nude life studies, and the drawings emanating from his imaginings were done with simple lines, using simple chiaroscuro watercolours, which nonetheless effectively conveyed movement and expression. He continually sought action in historical subjects, and maintained that it was the painter himself who had the right to choose the subject matter and that he should avoid subjects that had no meaning. . . . He read Greek and Latin histories and made notes, which he then used when the occasion arose.

56

FILIPPO BALDINUCCI (1625–1696)
From *The Life of Bernini*

In 1681 Baldinucci, a Florentine theorist and scholar, was commissioned by Queen Christina of Sweden, who spent her life in Rome after converting to Catholicism, to write a biography of Bernini shortly after his death. Carefully researched, it is still the main source of information about the artist.

The opinion is widespread that Bernini was the first to attempt to unite architecture with sculpture and painting in such a manner that together they make a beautiful whole. This he accomplished by removing all repugnant uniformity of poses, breaking up the poses sometimes without violating good rules, although he did not bind himself to the rules. . . . He knew from the beginning that his strong point was sculpture. Thus, although he felt a great inclination toward painting, he did not wish to devote himself to it altogether. . . . Bernini declared that painting was superior to sculpture, since sculpture shows that which exists with more dimensions, whereas painting shows that which does not exist, that is, it shows relief where there is no relief and gives an effect of distance where there is none. . . . [I]t is not surprising at all that a man of Bernini's excellence in the three arts, whose common source is drawing, also possessed in high measure the fine gift of composing excellent and most ingenious theatrical productions. . . . Bernini was, then, outstanding in dramatic actions and in composing plays. He put on many productions, which were highly applauded for scope and creativity. . . . Bernini's ability to blend his talents in the arts for the invention of stage machinery has never been equalled in my opinion.

---

5 7

NICOLAS POUSSIN (c. 1593–1665)
From an undated manuscript

Poussin's ideas on art were central to the formation of the French Academy in 1648 and, because of the preemi- *nence of that academy, therefore to the entire European academic movement of the seventeenth through the nineteenth centuries.*

The magnificent manner consists of four things: subject, or topic, concept, structure and style. The first requirement, which is the basis for all the others, is that the subject or topic should be great, such as battles, heroic actions and divine matters. However, given the subject upon which the painter is engaged is great, he must first of all make every effort to avoid getting lost in minute detail, so as not to detract from the dignity of the story. He should describe the magnificent and great details with a bold brush and disregard anything that is vulgar and of little substance. Thus the painter should not only be skilled in formulating his subject matter, but wise enough to know it well and to choose something that lends itself naturally to embellishment and perfection. Those who choose vile topics take refuge in them on account of their own lack of ingenuity. Faintheartedness is therefore to be despised, as is baseness of subject matter for which any amount of artifice is useless. As for the concept, it is simply part of the spirit, which concentrates on things, like the concept realized by Homer and Phidias of Olympian Zeus who could make the Universe tremble with a nod of his head. The drawing of things

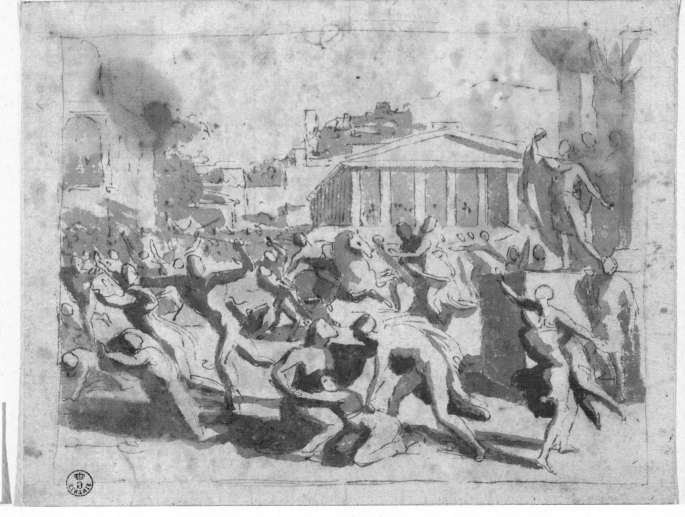

PS-55. Nicolas Poussin. *The Rape of the Sabines.* c. 1630. Brush drawing, 6¼ x 8⅛" (16.1 x 20.7 cm). Archive of Drawings and Prints, Uffizi Gallery, Florence

should be such that it expresses the concept of the things themselves. The structure, or composition of the parts, should not be studiously researched, and not sought after or contrived with effort but should be as natural as possible. Style is a particular method of painting and drawing, carried out in an individual way, born of the singular talent at work in its application and in the use of ideas. This style, and the manner and taste emanate from nature and from the mind.

58

CHARLES PERRAULT (1628–1703)
From *Memoirs of My Life*

Charles Perrault, a poet, critic, and adviser to Colbert on arts and letters, helped his brother, Claude, get the assignment to design the East Front of the Louvre (see fig. 19-10).

Since the Cavaliere Bernini's design was not very well conceived, and could only be carried out to the shame of France, I made a listing of only a few of the incongruities with which it was ridden, because I thought it inappropriate to point out too many of them the first time. I sent this memorandum to Monsieur Colbert, who was then at Saint-Germain. The first time he came to Paris, after having received my list, he had me step into the garden with him, and even cut short the audience he was granting to someone else, in order to talk to me. . . .

"You did well," he told me; "continue doing so, because one cannot be too well informed on a matter of this importance. I don't understand," he added, "how this man believes he can give us a design in which so many things are misunderstood."

From that moment on, Monsieur Colbert undoubtedly saw that he had approached the wrong party, but he believed he had to follow through on his gamble. Perhaps he thought also that with good advice, he could redirect the Cavaliere to the right way of doing things, and that by showing him his mistakes, he would have him produce something excellent; but he still did not know the Cavaliere. . . .

I am persuaded that as an architect he hardly excelled at all, except with the decor and machinery of the theater. . . .

59

SIR CHRISTOPHER WREN (1632–1723)
From *Proposals for Rebuilding the City of London After the Great Fire*

The manner of building in the city of London, practised in the former ages, was commonly with timber, a material easily procured, and at little expense when the country was overburthened with woods. This often subjected the town to great and destructive fires, sometimes to the ruin of the whole, as happened, for instance, in the year 1083, and reign of William the Conquerer. . . . Notwithstanding these incidents, this mode continued until the two fatal years 1665 and [166]6; but then the successive calamities of plague and fire gave all people occasion seriously to reflect on the causes of the increase of both to that excessive . . . closeness of buildings, and combustible materials; and hence the wishes for the necessary amendment of both, by widening the streets, and building with stone and brick, became universal.

Some intelligent persons went farther, and thought it highly requisite the city in the restoration should rise with beauty, by the straightness and regularity of buildings, and convenience for commerce, by the well disposing of streets and public places, and the opening of wharfs, &c. which the excellent situation, wealth, and grandeur of the metropolis of England did justly deserve. . . . In order therefore to a proper reformation, Dr. Wren (pursuant to the royal commands) immediately after the fire, took an exact survey of the whole area . . . and designed a plan or model of a new city in which the deformity and inconveniences of the old town were remedied. . . .

The observations of a late critic (allowing for some mistakes in his description of [my] scheme for rebuilding the city) are judicious and right.

"Towards the end of King James the First's reign, and in the beginning of his son's, taste in architecture made a bold step from Italy to England at once, and scarce staid a moment to visit France by the way. From the most profound ignorance in architecture, the most consummate night of knowledge, Inigo Jones started up, a prodigy of art, and vied even with his master, Palladio himself. From so glorious an outset there was not any excellency that we might not have hoped to attain; Britain had a reasonable prospect to rival Italy. . . . But in the midst of these sanguine expectations, the fatal civil war commenced. . . . What followed was all darkness and obscurity. . . .

"Wren was the next genius that arose, to awake the spirit of science. . . .

"The fire of London furnished the most perfect occasion that can ever happen in any city, to rebuild it with pomp and regularity. This Wren foresaw, and . . . offered a scheme for that purpose, which would have made it the wonder of the world. He proposed to have laid out one large street from Aldgate to Temple Bar, in the middle of which was to have been a large square, capable of containing the new church of St. Paul [see figs. 19-21–19-24], with a proper distance for the view all round it; whereby that huge building would not have been cooped up, as it is at present, in such a manner as nowhere to be seen to advantage at all; but would have had a long and ample vista at each end. . . . He further proposed to rebuild all the parish churches in such a manner as to be seen at the end of every vista of houses. . . . Lastly, he proposed to build the houses uniform, and supported on a piazza, . . . and by the water-side . . . he had planned a long and broad wharf . . . with proper warehouses for merchants between, to vary the edifices, and make it at once one of the most beautiful and most useful ranges of structure in the world. But the hurry of rebuilding, and the disputes about property, prevented this glorious scheme from taking place."

60
MARIE-LOUISE-ÉLISABETH VIGÉE-LEBRUN
(1755–1842)
From the *Memoirs of Vigée-Lebrun*

Vigée-Lebrun published three volumes of memoirs (1835 and 1837) when she was in her eighties. Female portraits and the painting of flowers were considered the most appropriate subjects for women artists in the eighteenth and nineteenth centuries.

M. Le Brun asked for my hand in marriage. Nothing could have been further from my thoughts than my marrying Le Brun. . . . I was then twenty years old; I had few worries about my future since I was already earning a substantial amount of money. In short, I had no inclination to wed at all. . . . Finally, I accepted, goaded on by the desire to escape the torment of living with my stepfather. . . . So little inclined was I to sacrifice my freedom, that even as I approached the church on my wedding day, I was still asking myself, "Shall I say yes or no?" Alas, I said yes and merely exchanged my old problems for new ones. . . . His overwhelming passion for extravagant women, combined with a love of gambling, decimated both his fortune and my own, of which he made very free use. So, by the time I left France in 1789 I had less than twenty francs to my name, in spite of the fact that I had earned more than a million from my work: he had squandered the lot! . . .

When I finally announced my marriage officially . . . I was not as downcast as I might have been, for I still had my beloved painting. I was overwhelmed with commissions from every quarter and although Le Brun took it upon himself to appropriate my earnings, this did not prevent him from insisting that I take pupils in order to increase our income even further. I consented to this demand without really taking time to consider the consequences and soon the house was full of young ladies learning how to paint "eyes, noses and faces." I was constantly correcting their efforts and was thus distracted from my own work, which I found very irritating indeed. . . .

I believe the strain of having to leave my precious brushes for several hours each day only increased my eagerness to paint. I refused to leave my easel until nightfall and the number of portraits I painted at this period is quite astonishing. As I had a horror of the current fashion, I did my best to make my models a little more picturesque. I was delighted when, having gained their trust, they allowed me to dress them after my fancy. No-one wore shawls then, but I liked to drape my models with large scarves, interlacing them around the body and through the arms, which was an attempt to imitate the beautiful style of draperies seen in the paintings of Raphael and Dominichino. . . .

Happy as I was at the idea of becoming a mother, after nine months of pregnancy, I was not in the least prepared for the birth of my baby. The day my daughter was born, I was still in the studio, trying to work on my *Venus Binding the Wings of Cupid* in the intervals between labour pains.

61
SIR JOSHUA REYNOLDS (1723–1792)
From "A Discourse, Delivered at the Opening of the Royal Academy, January 2, 1769"

An Academy, in which the Polite Arts may be regularly cultivated, is at last opened among us by Royal Munificence. This must appear an event in the highest degree interesting, not only to the Artists, but to the whole nation.

It is indeed difficult to give any other reason, why an empire like that of Britain, should so long have wanted an ornament so suitable to its greatness, than that slow progression of things, which naturally makes elegance and refinement the last effect of opulence and power. . . .

The principal advantage of an Academy is, that . . . it will be a repository for the great examples of the Art. These are the materials on which Genius is to work, and without which the strongest intellect may be fruitlessly or deviously employed. By studying these authentick models, that idea of excellence which is the result of the accumulated experience of past ages may be at once acquired, and the tardy and obstructed progress of our predecessors, may teach us a shorter and easier way. The Student receives, at one glance, the principles which many Artists have spent their whole lives in ascertaining. . . . How many men of great natural abilities have been lost to this nation, for want of these advantages? . . .

Raffaelle, it is true, had not the advantage of studying in an Academy; but all *Rome,* and the works of Michael Angelo in particular, were to him an Academy. . . .

One advantage, I will venture to affirm, we shall have in our Academy, which no other nation can boast. We shall have nothing to unlearn. . . .

But as these Institutions have so often failed in other nations . . . I must take leave to offer a few hints, by which those errors may be rectified. . . .

I would chiefly recommend, that an implicit obedience to the *Rules of Art,* as established by the practice of the great Masters, should be exacted from the *young* Students. That those models, which have passed through the approbation of ages, should be considered by them as perfect and infallible Guides; as subjects for their imitation, not their criticism.

I am confident, that this is the only efficacious method of making a progress in the Arts; and that he who sets out with doubting, will find life finished before he becomes master of the rudiments. For it may be laid down as a maxim, that he who begins by presuming on his own sense, has ended his studies as soon as he has commenced them. Every opportunity, therefore, should be taken to discountenance that false and vulgar opinion, that rules are the fetters of Genius.

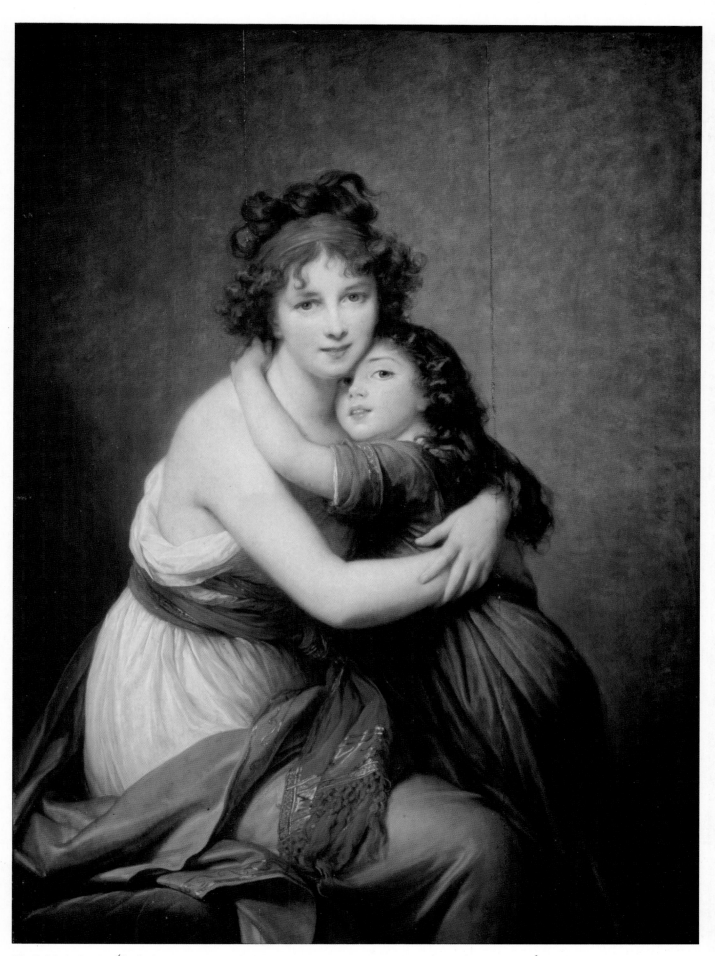

PS-60. Marie-Louise-Élisabeth Vigée-LeBrun. *Self-Portrait with Her Daughter, Julie.* c. 1789. Oil on canvas, 51³⁄₁₆ x 37" (130 x 94 cm).
Musée du Louvre, Paris

Timeline Three: 1350 to 1800

	1350–1375	1375–1400	1400–1425
HISTORY AND POLITICS	**1356** Edward, the "Black Prince," son of Edward III of England, defeats the French at Poitiers and takes prisoner Jean le Bon, king of France **c. 1358** Foundation of the powerful Hanseatic League of Baltic mercantile cities **Peasant uprisings:** 1358, Jacquerie revolt in France; 1381, Wat Tyler's rebellion in England, London sacked **1368** In China, the Buddhist monk Chu Yüan-chang leads a peasants' revolt, driving the Mongols out of Beijing and founding the Ming dynasty, taking the title Hungwu **Timur (Tamerlane, c. 1369–1405),** Mongol leader with capital at Samarkand, establishes the Timurid Empire, conquering much of the Mideast and Persia and invading India		**1410** Teutonic Knights defeated by Poles and Lithuanians at battle of Tennenberg, ending their sole jurisdiction over Prussia **Philip the Good of Burgundy (ruled 1419–67)** inherits the Northern Provinces; including Holland, Flanders, and Luxembourg, it is one of the largest and richest holdings in Europe and a threat to France

SOURCES OF RENAISSANCE NEO-PLATONISM Neo-Platonic ideas of harmony, balance, proportion, and spirituality appeared in Western thought throughout the Middle Ages, but the source texts of Plato, Plotinus, and their followers were little known. In 1394 the Greek scholar Manuel Chrysoloras visited Italy from Constantinople and remained to teach Greek in Florence. In 1439 other Greek scholars from the Byzantine Empire attended the ecclesiastical Council of Florence, which attempted to unite the Eastern and Western churches, and they further exposed local writers and artists to the intellectual heritage of classical Greece, especially its idealism. The work

	1350–1375	1375–1400	1400–1425
RELIGION		**1378** Papal court returns to Rome from Avignon. Great Papal Schism begins, in which several candidates compete for the papacy **c. 1382** John Wycliffe, English theologian and religious reformer, initiates first complete translation of the Bible into English	**1405–15** Jan Hus, influenced by Wycliffe, leads the Hussite movement to reform the church in Bohemia and denounces sale of indulgences; 1415, burned at the stake as a heretic at the Council of Constance **1417** Pope Martin V ends Great Schism

BOHEMIAN MASTER
Death of the Virgin, Prague, 1355–60

Florence Cathedral, begun by Arnolfo di Cambio, 1296; dome by Filippo Brunelleschi, 1420–36

CLAUS SLUTER
The Moses Well, Dijon, 1395–1406

DONATELLO
St. Mark, 1411–13

GENTILE DA FABRIANO
The Adoration of the Magi, Italy, 1423

	1350–1375	1375–1400	1400–1425
MUSIC, LITERATURE, AND PHILOSOPHY	**1361** Foundation of the University of Pavia in northern Italy **Christine de Pisan (c. 1363–c. 1430),** French writer of poems on courtly love, best known for her spirited defense of women in *The Book of the City of Ladies*, c. 1404–5 **Leonardo Bruni (1370–1444),** prominent humanist and classical scholar in Florence, author of *Praise of the City of Florence,* 1402–3	**1395–98** Manuel Chrysoloras, a Byzantine Greek scholar, teaches Greek in Florence; translates Plato's *Republic* into Latin; author of first Greek grammar used in western Europe	**Leone Battista Alberti (1404–72)** writes influential treatises *On Painting,* 1435, *On Architecture,* 1452, and *On Sculpture,* 1464
SCIENCE, TECHNOLOGY, AND EXPLORATION	**1355** Death of Jacopo Dondi (b. 1298), creator of an early clock run by weights	**1375** Charles V of France commissions the *Carta catalana,* an accurate map of Europe, North Africa, and western Asia **Prince Henry the Navigator of Portugal (1394–1460)** sponsors exploration, especially of the African coasts, an observatory, a school of navigation, and improvements in ship design, the compass, and cartography **1398** Cennino Cennini writes the *Libro dell' arte,* a technical manual for painters	**1406** King Edward IV of England founds the Society of Merchant Adventurers to encourage trade and commerce **1407** Establishment of Bank of St. George, first public bank, in Genoa **1410** Ptolemy's *Geography* translated into Latin **c. 1413** Pictorial perspective invented in Italy by Filippo Brunelleschi

1438 Hapsburg rule of the Holy Roman Empire (later Germany and Austria) begins (until 1806)

By 1450 Medici family, founded by Cosimo the Elder (1389–1464), gains power in Florence; 1469–92, Lorenzo the Magnificent virtually rules the city

1453 Constantinople falls to the Turkish army of Mohammed II; Ottoman Empire founded

Matthias the Just (ruled 1458–90) establishes Hungary as dominant power in central Europe

1469 Marriage of Ferdinand of Aragon and Isabella of Castile unites Spain

1477 French army defeats Charles the Bold of Burgundy at Nancy. Northern Provinces pass to Maximilian, Hapsburg emperor; 1488, Flemish cities revolt against his rule

1478 Pazzi Conspiracy in Florence; Giuliano de' Medici assassinated during Easter mass, and Pazzi family decimated in revenge; 1480, turmoil among Tuscan city-states quelled by Lorenzo's leadership

1492 Defeat of Muslim Grenada by the Spanish Christian powers; 1502, expulsion of Jews and Moors

1493–94 Territories of South America divided between Spain and Portugal by the pope

1494 Medici rulers expelled for the first time from Florence; a republic declared

1495–96 Charles VIII of France invades Italian peninsula and claims the kingdom of Naples; repulsed by the Holy League (the papacy, Spain, and Holy Roman Empire)

---

of the Early Renaissance architects Leone Battista Alberti (1404–72) and Filarete (c. 1400–c. 1469) reflects this influence to a certain degree.

After the fall of Constantinople to the Turks in 1453, many scholars fled permanently to the West. Their ideas, and the precious manuscripts they brought, stimulated interest in humanist studies. Neo-Platonism was particularly influential at the erudite Florentine court of Lorenzo de' Medici, known as the Platonic Academy. The philosopher Marsilio Ficino (1433–99) and the artists Sandro Botticelli (1444/5–1510) and Michelangelo (1475–1564) were prominent members of this circle.

1431 Joan of Arc burned at the stake in Rouen, accused of heresy and witchcraft

1439 Council of Florence attempts to reunite the Eastern Orthodox church with the Western Catholics; its success is short-lived

1464 Pope Pius II, humanist and patron of learning, dies during a failed Crusade against the Turks

Pope Sixtus IV (ruled 1471–84) condemns the excesses of the Spanish Inquisition and tries to reunite Russian church with Rome

1494 Rise in Florence of Fra Girolamo Savonarola (1452–98), monk and religious radical advocating moral and governmental reform; 1498, he is burned at the stake for heresy

---

(LEFT) JAN VAN EYCK
Arnolfini Portrait, detail, 1434
(RIGHT) LORENZO GHIBERTI
Panel of the *"Gates of Paradise,"* c. 1435

HUGO VAN DER GOES
The Portinari Altarpiece, center panel, c. 1476

SANDRO BOTTICELLI
The Birth of Venus, c. 1480

François Villon (born c. 1431), French poet

Marsilio Ficino (1433–99), humanist and philosopher, undertakes a translation of Plato, under the patronage of the Medici in Florence

Josquin Des Prés (c. 1440–1521), Flemish composer of madrigals

Pope Nicholas V (ruled 1447–55) founds Vatican Library

Desiderius Erasmus of Rotterdam (c. 1466–1536), scholar and satirical author (*Praise of Folly,* 1509), epitomizes the humanist intellectual concerns of the Northern Reformation

1481 A commentary on Dante's *Divine Comedy* is published, with illustrations by Botticelli and a preface by Marsilio Ficino

1494 Sebastian Brant (1458?–1521), German humanist, writes *The Ship of Fools,* a satirical poem

---

c. 1425 Discovery and proliferation in northern Europe of the technique of painting with oil

c. 1440 Earliest record of a suction pump

c. 1450 Movable type for printing invented in Germany (by Johann Gutenberg?); books become more readily available; literacy gradually spreads

Leonardo da Vinci (1452–1519) performs dissections of human cadavers; his experiments in hydraulics, mechanics, engineering, flight, and optics, recorded in coded manuscripts, address a dazzling range of intellectual and scientific problems

1487–88 Bartholomew Diaz of Portugal rounds Cape of Good Hope and circumnavigates African continent

1490 First Latin edition of Galen's works on medicine published in Venice

1492 Columbus lands in the Bahamas

1497–1501 Voyages of Vasco da Gama and Pedro Cabral establish Portuguese dominance of trade with India, utilizing both Atlantic and Pacific sea passages

Timeline Three: 1350 to 1800

	1500–1525	1525–1550	1550–1575
HISTORY AND POLITICS	**Francis I of France (ruled 1515–47),** a popular king. His rich and cultured court introduces Italian ideas and art to the North **1519–21** The Spaniard Hernán Cortés defeats Aztecs in Mexico; 1532, Francisco Pizarro conquers Peru **Charles V of Spain** elected Holy Roman Emperor (ruled 1519–56); founder of Hapsburg Dynasty **Suleiman I, Turkish sultan (ruled 1520–66),** raids the European continent, threatening Hungary, Austria, and Italy; begins a gradual Turkish conquest of the eastern Mediterranean islands over the next century **1524–25** Peasants' War in Germany, inspired by Martin Luther	**1527** Henry VIII of England, seeking a divorce from his first wife, Catherine of Aragon, breaks with the Catholic church; 1534, his Act of Supremacy establishes the Church of England and confiscates Catholic church property **1527** Charles V of Spain sacks Rome, demoralizing the Italian states and signaling the end of Roman dominance **1533–84** Ivan the Terrible rules in Russia	**Wars of Lutheran against Catholic princes in Germany;** 1555, Peace of Augsburg lets each sovereign decide the religion of his subjects **1556** Philip II reigns in Spain; territories include lands in the Americas, Italy, France, and the Netherlands as well as the Iberian peninsula **Elizabeth I (ruled 1558–1603)** succeeds to the English throne, fostering a period of prosperity, international trade, and exploration **1562–98** Henry IV's persecution of Protestants in France leads to religious wars **1568–1648** The Netherlands revolt against Spain; 1579, Union of Utrecht affirms the unification of the northern Netherlands; 1581, they declare independence from Spain **1571** Battle of Lepanto, off the Greek coast. Spanish and Venetian fleets defeat the Turks, beginning the decline of Turkish naval power
RELIGION	**1517** Martin Luther (1483–1546) posts "95 Theses," against Catholic practice of selling indulgences, on door of Wittenberg church, signaling the beginning of the Protestant Reformation	**1534** Ignatius of Loyola (1491–1556) founds Society of Jesus (Jesuits) **1541** John Calvin (1509–64) brings Reformation to the Swiss city of Geneva. His writings establish the rigorous Calvinist branch of Protestantism **1545** Pope Paul III (ruled 1534–49), in response to the threat of Protestantism, calls the Council of Trent, the first major conference on church reform. Its tenets provide the basis for the Catholic Counter Reformation, including a number of rules for artists depicting religious subjects. The council meets periodically until 1563	**1560** John Knox, Scottish minister, founds Presbyterian branch of Protestant church

MICHELANGELO
David, 1501–4

HIERONYMUS BOSCH
The Garden of Delights, center panel, c. 1510–15

PONTORMO
Deposition, c. 1526–28

TITIAN
Christ Crowned with Thorns, c. 1570

	1500–1525	1525–1550	1550–1575
MUSIC, LITERATURE, AND PHILOSOPHY	**Sir Thomas Wyatt (1503–42),** English poet and courtier under Henry VIII, translates Petrarch's sonnets and creates the English sonnet form **1516** Ludovico Ariosto (1474–1533), Italian poet and diplomat, publishes *Orlando Furioso*, an epic poem	**1528** Baldassare Castiglione (1478–1529) writes *The Book of the Courtier* **1532** Niccolò Machiavelli (1469–1527) writes *The Prince*, examining Renaissance political practice and thought **1534** François Rabelais (1483–1553) authors the satires *Gargantua* and *Pantagruel* **1547** Henry Howard translates Vergil's *Aeneid* into English blank verse	**1550** Giorgio Vasari (1511–74), Italian painter, publishes *The Lives of the Artists* **Felix Lope de Vega (1562–1635),** Spanish poet and playwright **William Shakespeare (1564–1616),** English dramatist and poet **Ben Jonson (1572–1637),** English dramatist and poet; **John Donne (1573–1631),** English master of metaphysical poetry and prose
SCIENCE, TECHNOLOGY, AND EXPLORATION	**1501** Amerigo Vespucci, a Florentine navigator in the service of Portugal, explores coast of Brazil **1511** First road map of Europe **1513** The Spaniard Vasco Nuñez de Balboa crosses Panama and finds the Pacific Ocean **1516** Portuguese sailors reach China; 1543, Japan **1519–22** Ferdinand Magellan of Portugal circumnavigates the globe	**1543** Nicolaus Copernicus (1473–1543), Polish astronomer, publishes theory of the solar system in which the planets revolve around the sun; beginning of modern astronomy **1543** Andreas Vesalius (1514–64), court physician to Emperor Charles V, publishes first scientific study of human anatomy based on dissections	**1556** Georgius Agricola (1494–1555) publishes *De re metallica*, on metallurgy **1569** Gerhard Mercator (1512–94) designs correct projection of the earth onto a flat map for accurate navigation charts **c. 1572** Tycho Brahe (1546–1601), Danish astronomer, produces a catalogue of stars; Johannes Kepler (1571–1630), German astronomer, discovers the elliptical orbits of the planets

1588 Spanish Armada, aiming to attack England, defeated by English navy

1607 Colony of Jamestown, Virginia, first permanent settlement in North America, founded by English; 1620, Pilgrims arrive at Plymouth, in New England

1613 Romanov dynasty comes to power in Russia (deposed 1917)

1618–48 Thirty Years' War; much of Protestant Europe erupts in political and religious struggles against Catholic regimes

1625 Charles I rules England. Disputes with Parliament and autocratic measures lead, in 1642, to Civil War; 1649, Charles beheaded, ending the war and founding the Commonwealth (1649–53) under Oliver Cromwell

1630–42 Large-scale emigration of English settlers to North American colonies: 16,000 arrive in Massachusetts

1639 Japanese enforce policy of isolation from all Europeans, except a token Dutch trading post

1648 Treaty of Westphalia ends Thirty Years' War; Spain acknowledges the sovereignty of the northern Netherlands

---

THE PROTESTANT REFORMATION The history of European Christianity before the Renaissance was punctuated by periodic movements to reform corrupt practices within the Catholic church. In the Middle Ages these were usually local and short-lived. But the fifteenth century saw the spread of literacy and education, growing economic power, a much-envied rise in the wealth of the papacy, and persistent quarrels between the pope and secular princes; these forces made criticism of the Church especially fierce. In 1517, the German cleric Martin Luther proclaimed his "95 Theses" condemning abuses of the Church and sparked a popular revolt, soon joined by rulers who saw the pope as a rival and who coveted the vast territories held by the papacy. The movement grew dramatically, especially in northern Europe. What had begun as a protest with mixed political, pious, and social aims developed into a detailed reformulation of the Christian religion itself; this restructuring is generally called Protestantism.

Protestantism focused on the relationship of the individual believer to God and was characterized by an austerity of taste that signified a rejection of the corrupt and worldly opulence of Rome. Use of images in churches was strictly prohibited. Renaissance taste for the personal, the contemporary, and the material was to some degree a product of Protestant culture, which patronized secular arts. For this new market, artists began to create small images for personal use. A new vocabulary of subject matter developed: landscape, still life, and scenes of daily life. In the North such paintings were sold directly to the public in a free-market system, rather than solely by patronage or commission.

Publications of Cornelius Jansenius (*Augustinus,* **1640**) lead to conflict with Jesuits. Preoccupied with internal strife, the papacy loses its dominant position in European politics

ARTEMISIA GENTILESCHI
Judith and Maidservant with the Head of Holofernes, c. 1625

JACQUES CALLOT
Detail of *Hangman's Tree,* from *Great Miseries of War,* 1633

1588 St. Theresa of Avila writes *Interior Castle,* a visionary text; Michel de Montaigne, French thinker, writes *Essays*

1590 Edmund Spenser, English poet, publishes *The Faerie Queene*

1604 Carel van Mander publishes biographical history of Dutch and Flemish painting

1605 Miguel de Cervantes Saavedra (1547–1616) writes *Don Quixote*

1607 Claudio Monteverdi's *Orpheus* is performed in Mantua, one of the first operas

Baruch Spinoza (1632–77), Dutch philosopher

Molière (1622–73) and **Jean Racine (1639–99),** French playwrights

1636 Pierre Corneille (1606–84), French dramatist, writes *Le Cid*

1637 René Descartes (1596–1650), French philosopher and scientist, writes *Discourse on Method*

1649 Francisco Pacheco (1564–1654), Spanish historian, publishes *The Art of Painting*

---

c. 1575 Potatoes, maize, tobacco, cocoa, coffee imported from the Americas to Europe

1578 Li Shih-chen, Chinese physician, publishes an illustrated compendium of medicines

1582 Pope Gregory XIII reforms the calendar, aligning it more accurately with astronomy; in order to do so, he decrees that Thursday, October 4, be followed by Friday, October 15

c. 1600 Invention of the telescope and microscope, based on new lens-grinding techniques developed in Holland

1610 Galileo Galilei (1564–1642), in Italy, first uses the telescope to view the stars and planets; his conclusions support the Copernican system and are banned by the Catholic church in 1633

1628 William Harvey, English physician (1575–1657), describes the circulation of blood

1636 Founding of Harvard College, Boston

1642 Blaise Pascal (1623–62) invents first adding machine

Antonio Stradivari (1644–1737), Italian designer of fine stringed instruments

1648 Royal Academy of Painting and Sculpture founded in Paris

Timeline Three: 1350 to 1800

	1650–1675	1675–1700	1700–1725
HISTORY AND POLITICS	**1652–54** Naval and mercantile competition between English and Dutch leads to war **1659** Louis XIV of France marries Maria Teresa, daughter of Philip IV of Spain; 1661, establishes autocratic regime (ruled 1661–1715) with his influential adviser Jean-Baptiste Colbert **1660** Parliament proclaims Charles II king, restoring English monarchy **1666** Great Fire in London destroys more than 450 acres of the city **1672–78** France and England wage war against the Netherlands. William III of Orange beats back invasion of French forces	**1679** English Parliament passes Habeas Corpus Act, which sets foundation for fair judicial procedure and prisoners' rights **1685** Louis XIV revokes Edict of Nantes (1598), which had granted Protestants some religious freedom. Mass emigration of educated Protestants ensues, a blow to French industry and commerce. In England, James II, a Catholic, succeeds to the throne and attempts to restore Catholicism **1688** The so-called Glorious Revolution in England: James II flees; Parliament passes Declaration of Rights, limiting the power of the monarchy **1689** Protestants William III of Orange and Mary rule England; new laws protect freedom of religion, establish annual parliaments, and guarantee individual liberty **Peter the Great (ruled 1689–1725)** rules Russia, with a program of westernization **1692** Witchcraft trials in Salem, Massachusetts	**1701** Frederick III crowns himself king of Prussia. Prussia gains international power through military strength **1702–13** War of Spanish Succession: extinction of the Hapsburg line in Spain leads to war among major European powers. At conclusion, Philip of Anjou, grandson of Louis XIV, takes the Spanish throne as Philip V; beginning of Bourbon rule in Spain **1704** Defeat of French at Blenheim by English and allies, led by John Churchill, Duke of Marlborough **1707** Union of England and Scotland as the United Kingdom of Great Britain **Louis XV (ruled 1715–74)**, king of France, consolidates absolute power of the monarchy
RELIGION	**c. 1667** Russian church changes liturgy and ritual to conform to Greek practice. Secession from the church of the conservative "Old Believers" **1668** Society of Friends (Quakers) officially established in England	**1682** Louis XIV's Four Articles are adopted in France, placing secular power over religious authority. Vehemently opposed by Pope Innocent XI (ruled 1676–89)	**John Wesley (1703–91)**, with his brother, Charles, founds the Methodist branch of Protestantism in England **1721** Peter the Great reforms Russian church government

DIEGO VELÁZQUEZ
The Maids of Honor, 1656

FRANS HALS
The Women Regents of the Old Men's Home at Haarlem, 1664

BARTOLOMÉ ESTEBAN MURILLO
Virgin and Child, c. 1675–80

SIR CHRISTOPHER WREN
Facade of St. Paul's Cathedral, London, 1675–1710

RACHEL RUYSCH
Flower Still Life, after 1700

	1650–1675	1675–1700	1700–1725
MUSIC, LITERATURE, AND PHILOSOPHY	**1667** John Milton (1608–74), English poet, writes *Paradise Lost* **Joseph Addison (1672–1719)**, English essayist, editor with the writer and statesman **Sir Richard Steele (1672–1729)** of the *Spectator,* a literary and satirical periodical **1672** Giovanni Pietro Bellori (1613–96), Italian commentator on Baroque art, publishes *Lives of the Modern Painters*	**John Locke (1632–1704)**, founder of English school of empirical philosophy **Baroque composers:** Alessandro Scarlatti (1659–1725) and Antonio Vivaldi (1678–1741), Italian; Johann Sebastian Bach (1685–1750) and George Frideric Handel (1685–1759), German **François-Marie Voltaire (1694–1778)**, French critical writer	**1711** Alexander Pope (1688–1744), English poet, writes *The Rape of the Lock* **David Hume (1711–76)**, Scottish philosopher **Jean-Jacques Rousseau (1712–78)**, French philosopher and novelist **Denis Diderot (1713–84)**, editor of first *Encyclopedia,* in France **Johann Joachim Winckelmann (1717–68)**, German art theorist and antiquarian
SCIENCE, TECHNOLOGY, AND EXPLORATION	**1662** Royal Society of London founded by Charles II, a forum for scientific activity for two centuries; 1662, Boyle's Law describes the properties of gas pressure **1663** Charles Lebrun, at Royal Academy in Paris, institutes strict guidelines for art **1665** In England Robert Hooke publishes his discovery of cells and microorganisms **1673** Pendulum clock invented by the Dutchman Christiaan Huygens	**1687** Isaac Newton (1642–1727) publishes theory of the laws of motion, including the principle of gravity, in England; 1704, his *Optics* investigates the nature and behavior of light **1698** Steam engine invented in England by Thomas Savery	**1705** Edmund Halley (1656–1742), in England, discovers similarities in the paths of comets **Benjamin Franklin (1706–90)**, American statesman and inventor, invents bifocal lens, lightning rod, and Franklin stove and publishes observations on electricity in Philadelphia **1717** Temperature gradation system proposed by Gabriel Fahrenheit in Holland

SCIENCE, TECHNOLOGY, AND EXPLORATION

1725–1750

1744 Geographical survey of France begun, the first such topographical survey

1745 Discovery of Pompeii and Herculaneum

1749 George Leclerc (1707–88) writes a treatise on natural history in England

1750–1775

1753 Carl Linnaeus, Swedish botanist (1707–78), writes the *Species Plantarum*, the definitive modern classification system for plants

1764 Invention of the spinning jenny and cotton gin (1793) hastens mechanization of textile production

1768–79 Captain James Cook (1728–79) explores the islands of the Pacific

1774 Joseph Priestly (1733–1804), English chemist, isolates oxygen

1775–1800

1783 First flight in a hot-air balloon, France

1789 Antoine Lavoisier (1743–94) publishes his systematic study of chemistry in France

1790–1801 Revolutionary government of France instates metric system

1798 Edward Jenner (1749–1823) demonstrates first vaccination against smallpox

1798 Alois Senefelder (1771–1834), Hungarian inventor, develops lithography

MUSIC, LITERATURE, AND PHILOSOPHY

1725–1750

1726 Jonathan Swift (1667–1745), Irish political satirist, writes *Gulliver's Travels*

1750–1775

1755 Samuel Johnson (1709–84) compiles a *Dictionary of the English Language*

Wolfgang Amadeus Mozart (1756–91), innovative Austrian composer of symphonies, operas, and church music

1774 Johann von Goethe (1749–1832) publishes *The Sorrows of Young Werther* in Germany, extolling naturalism and sentimentality; it inspires numerous suicides

1775–1800

1776 Adam Smith (1723–90), Scottish economist, writes *The Wealth of Nations*

1781 Immanuel Kant (1724–1804), German critical philosopher, writes the *Critique of Pure Reason*

1792 Mary Wollstonecraft (1759–1836) writes *Vindication of the Rights of Women*, first English feminist treatise

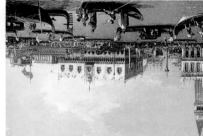

CANALETTO
The Bucintoro at the Molo, c. 1732

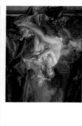

FRANÇOIS BOUCHER
The Toilet of Venus, 1751

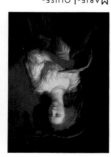

GIOVANNI BATTISTA TIEPOLO
The Marriage of Frederick Barbarossa, 1752

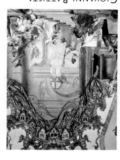

MARIE-LOUISE-ELISABETH VIGÉE-LEBRUN
The Duchesse de Polignac, 1783

(LEFT) JOHN HENRY FUSELI
The Nightmare, c. 1790

(RIGHT) FRANCISCO GOYA, *The Sleep of Reason Produces Monsters*, from *Los Caprichos*, c. 1798

RELIGION

1775–1800

1793 French government, under Robespierre, outlaws the worship of God; Cult of Reason established

1798 Napoleon abolishes papal rule and establishes a French-dominated Roman Republic in the Papal States

THE ENLIGHTENMENT The European eighteenth century was a time of colonial expansion and development of new methods in industry, farming, financial markets, and government. Constitutions and parliamentary systems weakened monarchs and the church and offered the vote to broader populations. English parliamentary monarchy, American representative democracy, and the various forms of the French government after the Revolution were all attempts to remake the political system more inclusive, while radical discoveries in the sciences and technology encouraged a new definition of society itself. Thinkers such as Rousseau, Hume, Voltaire, Diderot, Kant, and Swift sought to use reason and scientific method in their inquiries and took experience as the measure of knowledge. Coupled with this skeptical, modernist attitude was a taste for sentimentality and idealism, expressed as a commitment to the perfectibility of humanity. This led, in public life, to reforms in education, medicine, taxation, and religious tolerance, as well as movements to abolish slavery. The Neoclassical and Romantic movements in art are both a reflection of and reaction to this impulse.

HISTORY AND POLITICS

1750–1775

1756–66 Seven Years' War: England and Prussia fight Austria and France on land and sea and throughout the colonies, called the French and Indian Wars in North America; 1759, French defeated at Quebec

Catherine the Great (ruled 1762–96) increases the power, territory, and influence of Russia

1775–1800

1775–83 American Revolution: 1776, Declaration of Independence; 1787–88, United States Constitution ratified

1789 French Revolution begins. Declaration of a National Assembly dedicated to producing a constitution. Mobs storm Bastille prison and riot in Paris, 1792, French monarchy is abolished; 1793, Louis XVI is beheaded. European states declare war against the French Republic, whose radical ideas are feared to encourage unrest

1793–95 Reign of Terror in France, dominated by Maximilien Robespierre, with as many as 350 executions per month

1793–95 Partition of Poland by Russia, Prussia, and Austria completely erases the country

1796–97 Napoleon Bonaparte's Italian campaign conquers most of Italy; after his Egyptian campaign (1798–99), his reputation as soldier and diplomat is established; 1799, he controls France

ART HISTORY, ACCORDING TO THE CLASSICAL MODEL OF JOHANN WINCKELMANN, UNFOLDS IN AN ORDERLY PROGRESSION IN WHICH ONE PHASE FOLLOWS ANOTHER AS INEVITABLY AS NIGHT FOLLOWS DAY.

In addition, the concept of period style implies that the arts march in lockstep, sharing the same characteristics and developing according to the same inner necessity. The thoughtful reader will already suspect, however, that any attempt to synthesize the history of art and place it in a broader context must inevitably mask a welter of facts that do not conform to such a systematic model and may indeed call it into question. So far as the art of the distant past is concerned, we may have little choice but to see it in larger terms, since so many facts have been erased that we cannot possibly hope to reconstruct a full and accurate historical record. Hence it is arguably the case that any reading is an artificial construct inherently open to question. As we approach the art of our times, these become more than theoretical issues. They take on a new urgency as we try, perhaps vainly, to understand modern civilization and how it came to be this way.

It is suggestive of the difficulties facing the historian that the period which began 250 years ago has not acquired a name of its own. Perhaps this does not strike us as peculiar at first. We are, after all, still in its midst. Considering how promptly the Renaissance coined a name for itself, however, we may well

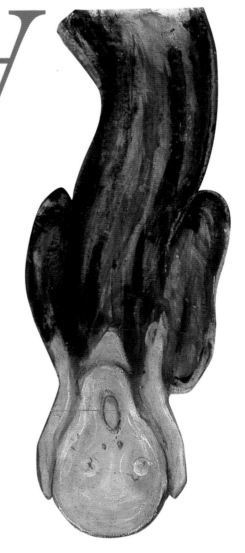

PART FOUR

The Modern World

wonder why no key concept comparable to the "rebirth of antiquity" has yet to emerge. It is tempting to call this "The Age of Revolution," for it has been characterized by rapid and violent change. It began with revolutions of two kinds: the Industrial Revolution, symbolized by the invention of the steam engine; and a political revolution, under the banner of democracy, inaugurated in America and France. Both of these revolutions are still going on. Industrialization and democracy are sought over much of the world. Western science and Western political thought (and, in their wake, all the other prod- ucts of modern civilization: food, dress, art, music, literature) will eventually belong to all peoples, although they have been challenged by other ideologies that command allegiance—nationalism, reli- gion, even tribalism. Industrialization and democracy are so closely linked today that we tend to think of them as different aspects of one process, with effects more far-reaching than any basic shift since the Neolithic Revolution 10,000 years ago. Still, the twin revolutions are not the same. Indeed, we cannot find a common impulse behind these developments, despite attempts to relate them to the rise of capitalism. The more we try to explain their relationship and trace their historic roots, the more paradoxical they seem. Both are founded on the idea of progress. But whereas progress in science and technology during the past two centuries has been more or less continuous and measurable, we can hardly make this claim for our pursuit of happiness, however we choose to define it. Here, then, is a fundamental conflict that continues to this very day.

If we nevertheless accept "The Age of Revolution" as a convenient name for the era as a whole, we must still make a distinction for the era since 1900. For lack of a better word, we shall call it modernity. It is a problematic term, *modernity*. What is it? When did it begin? These questions are not unlike those posed by the Renaissance, and so perhaps is the answer. No matter how many different opinions there may be about its nature—and scholars remain deeply divided over the issues—the modern era clearly began when people acquired "modern consciousness." Around 1900 the Western world became aware that the character of the new age was defined by the machine, which brought with it a different sense of time and space, as well as the promise of a new kind of humanity and society.

It is difficult for us to appreciate from our vantage point just how radical the technological revolution seemed to people of the time, for it has since become commonplace and been outstripped by even more far-reaching changes. The advances that took place in science, mathematics, engineering, and psychology during the 1880s and 1890s laid the foundation for the Machine Age. The diesel and turbine engines, electric motor, tire, automobile, light bulb, phonograph, radio, box camera: all these were invented before 1900, and the airplane shortly thereafter. They forever transformed the quality of life—its very feel—but it was not until these changes reached a "critical mass" in the opening years of the twentieth century that their sweeping magnitude was fully realized. Of course, this was by no means the first time that people have felt "modern," which simply means contemporary. Yet modern consciousness has been so fundamental to our identity that we can hardly hope to understand civilization for the past 100 years without it.

The word *modern* has its origins in the early medieval *modernus*, meaning that which is present, of our time, and, by extension, new or novel. Surprisingly, classical antiquity lacked a comparable expression, even though the word *modern* derives ultimately from the Latin *modo* (now). As this odd fact suggests, modernity is based on the Christian view of history as a break in time (before and after Christ), instead of the concept of recurring cycles that had prevailed in Greece and Rome. It is to Petrarch that we owe the idea of history as a succession of periods, which he separated into eras of light, dark, and rebirth. For him, history was linear and progressive, permitting humanity to play an active part in shaping its outcome. In his veneration for antiquity Petrarch was indebted partly to Bernard of Chartres, who in the early twelfth century argued that we are puny dwarfs who see farther than our predecessors because we are standing on the shoulders of giants. However, such a position did not allow the authority of the past, no matter how great, to go unchallenged. The end of the twelfth century witnessed the first dispute between disciples of ancient versus modern poetry; ever since, literature and criticism have taken the lead in framing the central issues of modernity. The controversy was revived in late-seventeenth-century

France by Charles Perrault as the Quarrel of Ancients and Moderns (satirized by the English writer Jonathan Swift in *The Battle of the Books*). Throughout the debate, *modern* generally held negative connotations, for it was taken as the opposite of *classic,* whose original antonym in Latin was "vulgar." Yet not even the most conservative voices recommended the slavish imitation of antiquity. Moreover, the moderns saw themselves as adhering to eternal values even more faithfully than had the ancients themselves! As Christians, they held the advantage over the ancients on another count as well, since religious truth was deemed superior to scientific truth or aesthetic beauty, the only area where the pagans had excelled.

The nineteenth century gave birth to two conflicting views of modernity that have continued to compete with each other to this day: one based on scientific and material progress, which arose out of the Enlightenment, with its belief in reason and freedom, and is identified with the middle class; and a radical alternative regarding the bourgeois as enemies of culture—in a word, philistines. Although its roots lie in eighteenth-century German thought, the second of these conceptions is a peculiarly Romantic notion first formulated by the French writer Stendhal (Marie-Henri Beyle). Not only did he relate modernity specifically to Romanticism as a reaction against classicism, he regarded the Romantic as a warrior in the service of modernity. But why should modernity need such a warrior in the first place? Because the times were slow to accept the new, which could therefore only be validated by the future, not the present. We will recognize in Stendhal's warrior the forerunner of the avant-garde.

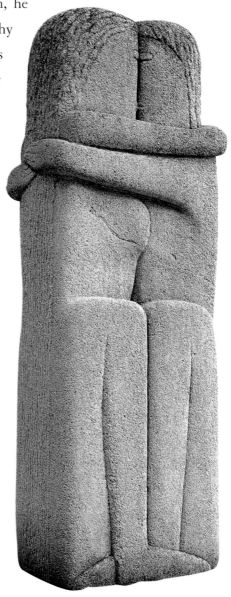

It was nevertheless the French poet and critic Charles Baudelaire who gave modernity its current meaning. "Modernity," he wrote, "is the transitory, the fugitive, the contingent, the half of art, of which the other half is the eternal and the immutable. . . ." And "since all centuries and all peoples have had their own form of beauty, so inevitably we have ours. The particular element in each manifestation comes from the emotions; and just as we have our own particular emotions, so we have our own beauty." Perceptively, he located the source of that beauty in urban existence: "The life of our city is rich in poetic and marvelous subjects. We are enveloped and steeped as though in an atmosphere of the marvelous; but we do not notice it." In this he relied partly on his fellow critic Théophile Gautier, who said that modern beauty is based on accepting modern civilization as it is. To do so, however, artists must go against tradition and rely on their own imaginations, which requires taking enormous risks.

Baudelaire had the distinction of being the first to use mechanical metaphors for beauty in place of the organic ones favored by the Romantics. Yet he also denounced the material progress of modern civilization, thereby helping to create the schism between modernity and

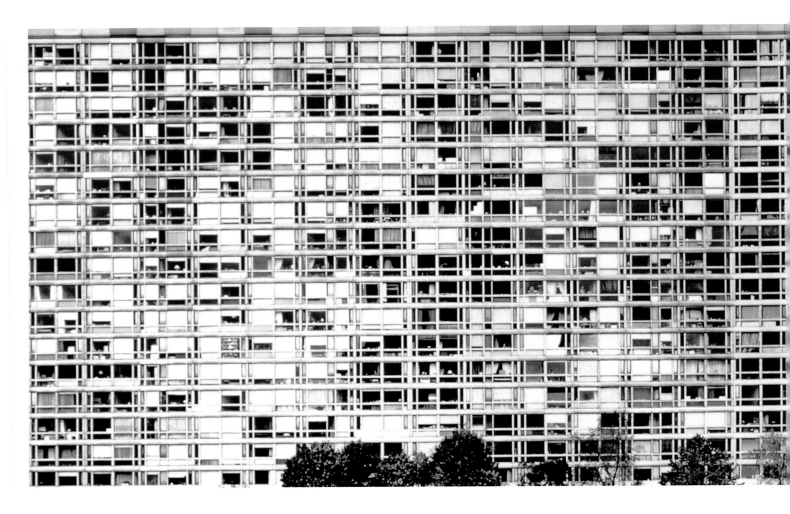

modernism. What is the difference between them? Paradoxically, modernism looks to the future, whereas modernity is concerned with the present, which can stand in the way of progress. To artists, modernism is a trumpet call that both asserts their freedom to create in a new style and provides them with the mission to define the meaning of their times—and even to reshape society through their art. To be sure, artists have always responded to the changing world around them, but rarely have they risen to the challenge as they have under the banner of modernism, or with so fervent a sense of personal cause.

This is a role for which the "avant-garde" (literally, vanguard) is hardly sufficient. Although both arose as part of the decadent movement toward the end of the nineteenth century, the term *avant-garde,* like modernism, has a long history reaching back to the Middle Ages. The word originated in French warfare and was first applied to the arts in the sixteenth century, but began to acquire its modern definition only under the Romantics. The Socialist reformer Comte de Saint-Simon included artists with scientists and industrialists in the elite group that would rule the ideal state, because as people of imagination they can foresee the future and therefore help to create it. As Baudelaire realized, however, there is an inherent contradiction between Romantic individualism and the discipline necessary for political action.

Although its scope was subsequently limited mainly to culture, the avant-garde has sometimes played an active part in politics. Despite the fact that they are closely linked, the avant-garde is by no

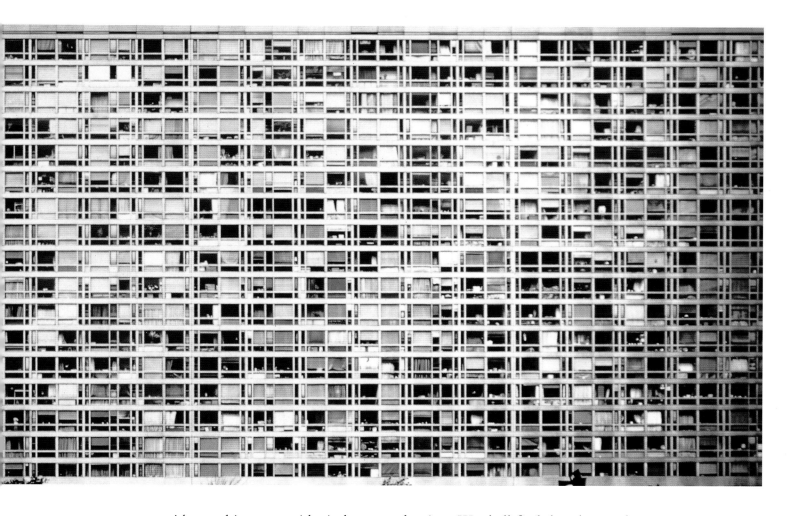

means synonymous with—and is even antithetical to—modernism. We shall find that the two have held very different meanings for different artists—and produced surprisingly different results in each of the visual arts. Both run counter to their times. But whereas modernism remains dedicated to a utopian vision of the future that stems from the Enlightenment, the avant-garde is bent solely on the destruction of bourgeois modernity. Judged by this standard, few of the twentieth-century's leading artists were members of a self-styled avant-garde.

Today, having cast off the framework of traditional authority which confined and sustained us before, we can act with a latitude that is both frightening and exhilarating. The consequences of this freedom to question all values are everywhere around us. Our knowledge about ourselves is now vastly greater, but this has not reassured us as we had hoped. In a world without fixed reference points, we search constantly for our own identity and for the meaning of human existence, individual and collective.

Modern civilization doesn't proceed by readily identifiable periods; nor are there clear period styles to be discerned in art or in any other form of culture. Instead, we find a continuity of another kind: that of movements and countermovements. Spreading like waves, these "isms" defy national, ethnic, and chronological boundaries. Never dominant anywhere for long, they compete or merge with each other in endlessly shifting patterns. Hence our account of modern art is guided more by movements than by countries. Only in this way can we hope to do justice to the fact that modern art, all regional differences notwithstanding, is as international as modern science.

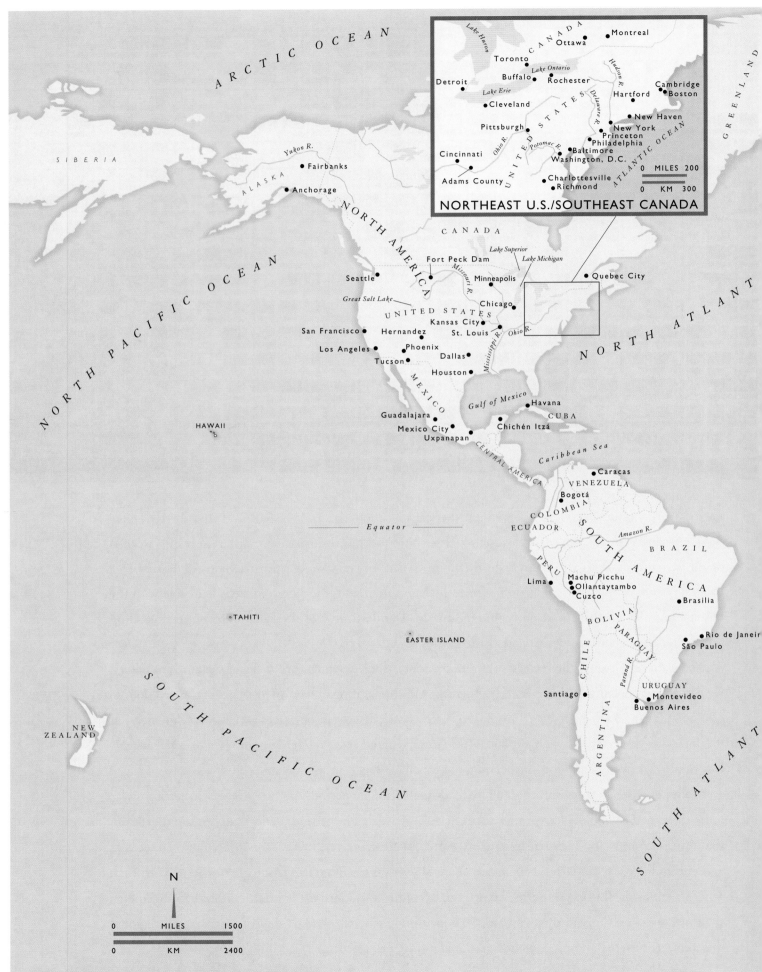

ARCTIC OCEAN

SIBERIA

NORTHEAST U.S./SOUTHEAST CANADA

CANADA

Lake Huron

Montreal

Ottawa

Toronto
Buffalo   Lake Ontario
Detroit   Rochester
Lake Erie   Hartford   Cambridge
Cleveland   Boston
Pittsburgh   UNITED STATES   New Haven

Ohio R.   New York
Princeton
Cincinnati   Potomac R.   Philadelphia
Baltimore
Adams County   Washington, D.C.

Charlottesville   ATLANTIC OCEAN
Richmond

Hudson R.
Delaware R.

GREENLAND

0   MILES   200
0   KM   300

ALASKA
NORTH AMERICA
Yukon R.

Fairbanks
Anchorage

CANADA

Lake Superior
Fort Peck Dam   Lake Michigan
Seattle   Missouri R.   Minneapolis   Quebec City

Great Salt Lake   UNITED STATES   Chicago
San Francisco   Hernandez   Kansas City   St. Louis   Ohio R.
Los Angeles   Phoenix   Dallas   Mississippi R.
Tucson   Houston

NORTH PACIFIC OCEAN

MEXICO

Gulf of Mexico   Havana
Guadalajara   CUBA
Mexico City   Chichén Itzá
Uxpanapan

CENTRAL AMERICA   Caribbean Sea

HAWAII

NORTH ATLANT

NORTH ATLANTIC OCEAN

Caracas
VENEZUELA
Bogotá
COLOMBIA
ECUADOR   SOUTH AMERICA
Amazon R.   BRAZIL

Equator

Lima   PERU   Machu Picchu
Ollantaytambo   Brasilia
Cuzco

TAHITI

EASTER ISLAND

BOLIVIA
PARAGUAY
Parana R.   Rio de Janeir
São Paulo

NEW
ZEALAND

SOUTH PACIFIC OCEAN

CHILE   URUGUAY
Santiago   Montevideo
ARGENTINA   Buenos Aires

SOUTH ATLANT

0   MILES   1500
0   KM   2400

N

THE MODERN WORLD

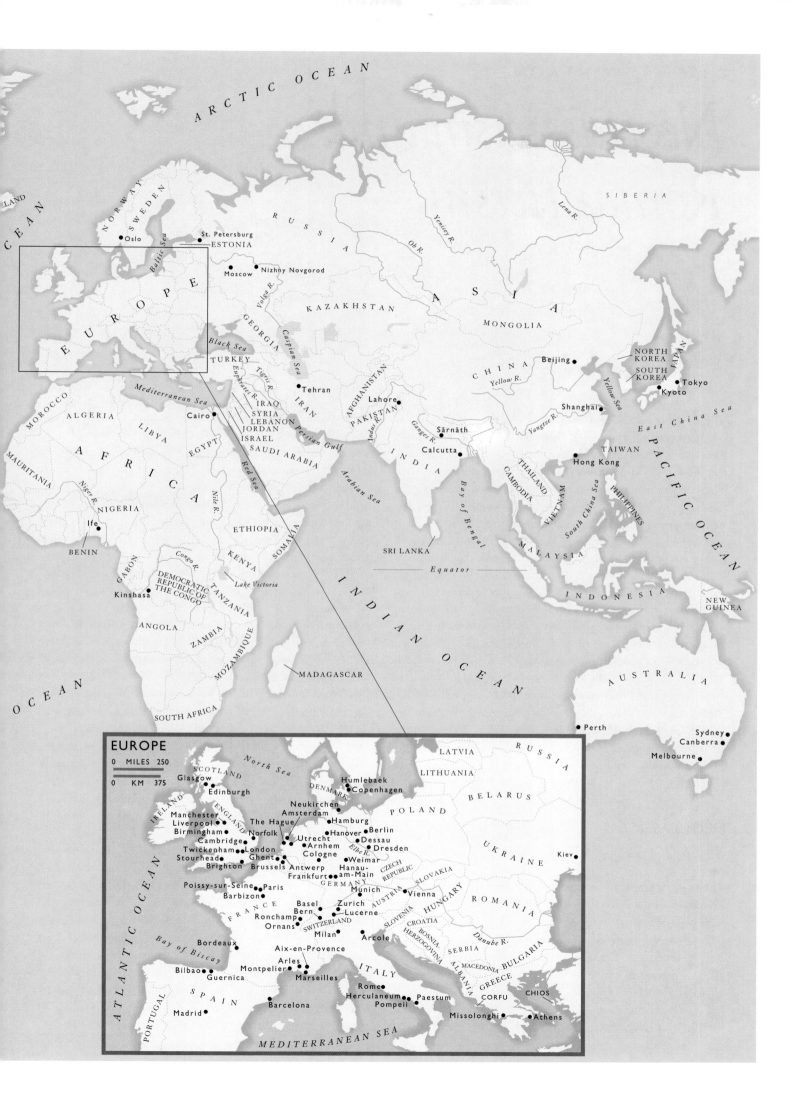

ARCTIC OCEAN

OCEAN

SIBERIA

NORWAY
SWEDEN
• Oslo
RUSSIA
Lena R.
Yenisey R.
Ob R.
St. Petersburg
ESTONIA
Baltic Sea
Moscow •
• Nizhny Novgorod
Volga R.
KAZAKHSTAN
ASIA
EUROPE
GEORGIA
Caspian Sea
MONGOLIA
Black Sea
TURKEY
Euphrates R.
Tigris R.
CHINA
Yellow R.
Beijing •
NORTH KOREA
SOUTH KOREA
JAPAN
Mediterranean Sea
Tehran •
IRAN
AFGHANISTAN
Yangtse R.
Yellow Sea
Tokyo •
Kyoto •
MOROCCO
ALGERIA
LIBYA
Cairo •
IRAQ
SYRIA
LEBANON
JORDAN
ISRAEL
EGYPT
SAUDI ARABIA
Persian Gulf
PAKISTAN
Lahore •
Indus R.
Ganges R.
Sārnāth •
INDIA
Calcutta •
Shanghai •
East China Sea
TAIWAN
Hong Kong •
PACIFIC OCEAN
AFRICA
Red Sea
Nile R.
MAURITANIA
Niger R.
NIGERIA
Ife •
BENIN
GABON
ETHIOPIA
SOMALIA
Arabian Sea
Bay of Bengal
THAILAND
CAMBODIA
VIETNAM
South China Sea
PHILIPPINES
DEMOCRATIC REPUBLIC OF THE CONGO
Congo R.
KENYA
Lake Victoria
TANZANIA
SRI LANKA
Equator
MALAYSIA
Kinshasa •
ANGOLA
ZAMBIA
MOZAMBIQUE
INDONESIA
NEW GUINEA
OCEAN
MADAGASCAR
INDIAN OCEAN
AUSTRALIA
SOUTH AFRICA
Perth •
Sydney •
Canberra •
Melbourne •

EUROPE

0 MILES 250
0 KM 375

North Sea
SCOTLAND
Glasgow •
Edinburgh •
IRELAND
ENGLAND
Manchester •
Liverpool •
Birmingham •
Cambridge •
Twickenham •
Stourhead •
Norfolk •
The Hague •
Amsterdam •
Neukirchen •
DENMARK
Humlebaek •
Copenhagen •
LATVIA
LITHUANIA
RUSSIA
BELARUS
POLAND
Hamburg •
Hanover •
Berlin •
Dessau •
Dresden •
Utrecht •
Arnhem •
Elbe R.
Cologne •
Weimar •
London •
Ghent •
Brighton •
Brussels •
Antwerp •
Hanau-am-Main •
Frankfurt •
CZECH REPUBLIC
GERMANY
SLOVAKIA
UKRAINE
Kiev •
Poissy-sur-Seine •
Paris •
Barbizon •
FRANCE
Munich •
AUSTRIA
Vienna •
HUNGARY
ROMANIA
Basel •
Zurich •
Bern •
Lucerne •
Ronchamp •
Ornans •
SWITZERLAND
SLOVENIA
CROATIA
BOSNIA HERZOGOVINA
SERBIA
Danube R.
BULGARIA
Bordeaux •
Milan •
Arcole •
MACEDONIA
ALBANIA
GREECE
Bay of Biscay
Aix-en-Provence •
Arles •
Montpelier •
Marseilles •
ITALY
Bilbao •
Guernica •
Rome •
Herculaneum •
Pompeii •
Paestum •
CORFU
CHIOS
SPAIN
PORTUGAL
Madrid •
Barcelona •
Missolonghi •
Athens •
ATLANTIC OCEAN
MEDITERRANEAN SEA

CHAPTER TWENTY-ONE

Neoclassicism and Romanticism

The history of the two movements to be dealt with in this chapter covers roughly a century, from about 1750 to 1850. Paradoxically, Neoclassicism has been seen both as the opposite of Romanticism on the one hand, and as no more than one aspect of it on the other. The problem is that the two terms are not directly comparable. Neoclassicism was a new revival of classical antiquity, although it was no more consistent than earlier classicisms. It was linked, at least initially, to Enlightenment thought. Romanticism, in contrast, refers not to a specific style but to an attitude that manifested itself in a number of ways, including classicism. Romanticism is therefore a far broader concept and thus harder to define. To complicate matters further, the Neoclassicists and early Romantics were exact contemporaries, who in turn overlapped the preceding generation of Rococo artists. The Neoclassicist David and the Romantic Goya, for example, were born within a few years of each other. And in England the leading representatives of the Rococo, Neoclassicism, and Romanticism—Reynolds, West, and Fuseli—shared many of the same ideas; nor were they always separated by clear differences in style or approach. Finally, Romanticism lasted far longer in sculpture and architecture than it did in painting: it continued well into the era of Realism and Impressionism, with vestiges lingering as late as 1900.

NEOCLASSICISM

The Enlightenment

The modern era was born during the American Revolution of 1776 and the French Revolution of 1789. These political upheavals were preceded by a revolution of the mind that had begun half a century earlier. Its standard-bearers were those thinkers of the Enlightenment in England, France, and Germany—David Hume, François-Marie-Arouet Voltaire, Jean-Jacques Rousseau, Denis Diderot, and Heinrich Heine, to name only the most important—who proclaimed that human affairs ought to be ruled by reason and the common good, rather than by tradition and established authority. As in economics, politics, and religion, this rationalist movement turned against the prevailing practice in the arts: the ornate and aristocratic Rococo. In the mid-eighteenth century there was a widespread call for a return to reason, nature, and morality in art. Such terms proved highly problematic, because their definition was deliberately vague and varied according to the intent of the user. Nevertheless, this demand in effect meant a return to the ancients. After all, had not the classical philosophers been the original "apostles of reason"?

The first to express this view was Johann Joachim Winckelmann (1717–1768), the German art historian and theorist who popularized the concept of the "noble simplicity and calm grandeur" of Greek art (in *Thoughts on the Imitation of Greek Works . . . ,* published in 1755). [See Primary Sources, no. 62, page 962.] His ideas deeply impressed two painters then living in Rome, the German Anton Raphael Mengs (1728–1779) and the Scotsman Gavin Hamilton (1723–1798). Both had strong antiquarian leanings but otherwise limited artistic ability. This shortcoming may explain why they accepted Winckelmann's doctrine so readily. Mengs' importance lies mainly in his role as a proselytizer of the "Winckelmann program," since most of his paintings are weak paraphrases of Italian art. He left Rome in 1761 after painting his major work, a ceiling fresco of Parnassus inspired by Raphael's mural in the Stanza della Segnatura, and went to Spain, where he vied with the aging Tiepolo (see page 626).

It is an indication of Italy's decline that artistic leadership passed to the Northerners who gathered in Rome. The only Roman painter who could compete on even terms with the foreigners was Pompeo Batoni (1708–1787), a splendid technician who practiced the eclectic classicism of Carlo Maratta (see page 560), but is remembered today chiefly for portraits of his English patrons. This vacuum helps to account for the astonishing success of Mengs and Hamilton. Toward the end of Batoni's career the Italian school was eclipsed once and for all by the French Academy in Rome under Joseph-Marie Vien (1716–1809), its head from 1775 to 1781. To French artists, a return to the classics meant the style of Poussin

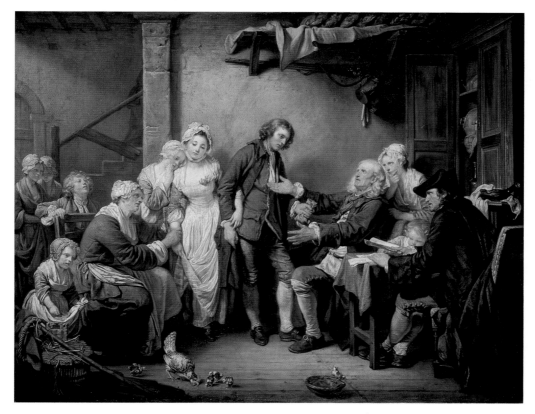

21-1. Jean-Baptiste Greuze. *The Village Bride*. 1761. Oil on canvas, 36 x 46 ½" (91.4 x 118.1 cm). Musée du Louvre, Paris

and the "academic" theory of Lebrun, with a maximum of archaeological detail gleaned from the excavations of Pompeii and Herculaneum in 1737 and 1748. Vien himself was a minor artist who reduced history painting to genre scenes of ancient life, but he was a gifted teacher. It was his pupils who were to establish French painting as the self-proclaimed guardian of the great tradition of Western art.

PAINTING

France

JEAN-BAPTISTE GREUZE. In France, the anti-Rococo trend in painting was at first a matter of content rather than style, which accounts for the sudden fame around 1760 of Jean-Baptiste Greuze (1725–1805). *The Village Bride* (fig. 21-1) is a scene of lower-class family life. It differs from earlier genre paintings (compare fig. 18-27) in its contrived, stagelike character, borrowed from Hogarth's "dumb show" narratives (see figs. 20-11 and 20-12). But Greuze had neither wit nor satire. His pictorial sermon illustrates the social gospel of Jean-Jacques Rousseau: that the poor, in contrast to the immoral aristocracy, are full of "natural" virtue and honest sentiment. Everything is intended to remind us of this point, from the theatrical gestures and expressions of the actors to the smallest detail: one of the chicks gathered around the hen in the foreground has left the brood and sits alone on a saucer, like the bride who is about to leave her own "brood."

The Village Bride was acclaimed a masterpiece. The loudest praise came from Denis Diderot, that apostle of Reason and Nature. Here at last was a painter with a social mission who appealed to the viewer's moral understanding, instead of merely giving pleasure like the frivolous works of Boucher (see fig. 20-6)! In his first flush of enthusiasm, Diderot accepted the narrative of Greuze's pictures as "noble and serious human action" in Poussin's sense. [See Primary Sources, no. 63, page 962.] Diderot's extravagant praise of Greuze is understandable. *The Village Bride* is a pictorial counterpart to Diderot's own melodramas, which attempted to add domestic tragedy and the comedy of virtue to the accepted classifications of theater (see box page 683).

JACQUES-LOUIS DAVID. Greuze was less successful at painting historical subjects, and Diderot modified his views later when a far more gifted and rigorous "Neo-Poussinist" appeared on the scene: Jacques-Louis David (1748–1825). A disciple of Vien, David had developed his Neoclassical style in Rome between 1775 and 1781. Upon his return to France, he quickly established himself as the leading Neoclassical painter. He overshadowed all others by far, so that our conception of the movement is largely based on his work. In *The Death of Socrates* (fig. 21-2) of 1787, David seems more "Poussiniste" than Poussin himself (compare fig. 19-5). The composition unfolds parallel to the picture plane like a relief, and the figures are as solid and immobile as statues. David has added one unexpected element. The lighting, which is sharply focused and casts precise shadows, is derived from Caravaggio. So is the firmly realistic detail. (Note the hands and feet, the furni-

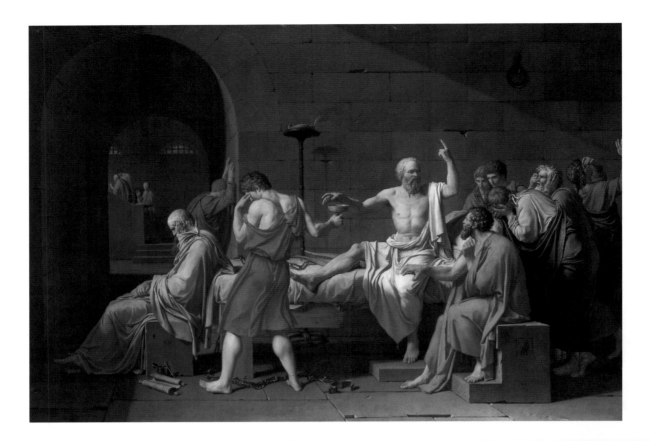

21-2. Jacques-Louis David. *The Death of Socrates.* 1787.
Oil on canvas, 4'3" x 6'5¼" (1.3 x 1.96 m). The Metropolitan
Museum of Art, New York. Wolfe Fund, 1931

David's Socrates *depends on dramatic motifs familiar to the late eighteenth century but elevates them to greatness through pictorial genius
and moral rigor. . . .David's lofty idealism of style and drama is conspicuous. The spongy swaying figures of Sané's* Socrates *[lost, known
through engraving] are crystallized here. . .into figures of marmoreal
firmness, disposed upon a ground plane marked out with perspectival
exactitude; and in keeping with this vigorous lucidity of style, the sto-
icism of the subject is dramatically underscored. Instead of. . .Greuz-
ian despair. . .David offers a firm moral paradigm of uncommon nobility. For dramatic foils to Socrates' steadfast resolution, he uses the
philosopher's own disciples. . . .*

*Combined with David's idealism of form and morality, this literal-
ism of detail, which extends here to the chips in the blocks of the*

*masonry wall. . .produces the new kind of classicism inaugurated in
the late eighteenth century as one facet of Historicism—an image of a
lost Greco-Roman past optimistically retrievable through exact arche-
ological reconstruction.*

—Robert Rosenblum. *Transformations in Late
Eighteenth Century Art.* Princeton: Princeton University
Press, 1970, pp. 74–76. Originally published in 1967.

ROBERT ROSENBLUM (b. 1927) is one of today's most productive and most
published art historians. He was educated at Queens College in New York and
taught at Princeton University for ten years before H. W. Janson brought him to
New York University's Washington Square College. (Janson and Rosenblum later
collaborated in *Nineteenth Century Art,* 1984, which is a standard text still today.)
Rosenblum's *Transformations in Late Eighteenth Century Art* became an almost
instant classic when it was published in 1967 and remains essential reading for students of the period. The treatment of David's *The Death of Socrates* is a model of
its kind.

ture, and the texture of the stone surfaces.) As a result, the picture
has a lifelike quality that is astonishing in such a doctrinaire statement of the new style. After refusing to compromise his principles,
Socrates was convicted of a trumped-up charge of teaching heresy
and sentenced to death. He is shown about to drink poison hem-
lock from the cup. Thus he becomes not only an example of
Ancient Virtue, but also the founder of the "religion of Reason."
Here he is a Christlike figure amid his 12 disciples, although fewer
people were actually present at his death and his wife is omitted
from the scene.

The very harshness of the design suggests that David was
passionately involved in the issues of his age, artistic as well as

political. In fact, he took an active part in the French Revolution,
and for some years he controlled the artistic affairs of the nation
much as Lebrun had a century before (see pages 610–11). During
this time he painted his greatest picture, *The Death of Marat*
(fig. 21-3). David's deep emotion has made a masterpiece from a
subject that would have embarrassed a lesser artist. Marat, one of
the political leaders of the Revolution, had been murdered in his
bathtub. A painful skin condition required immersion, and he did
his work there, with a wooden board serving as his desk. One day
a young woman named Charlotte Corday burst in with a personal petition, and plunged a knife into his chest while he read it.
David has composed the scene with a stark directness that is

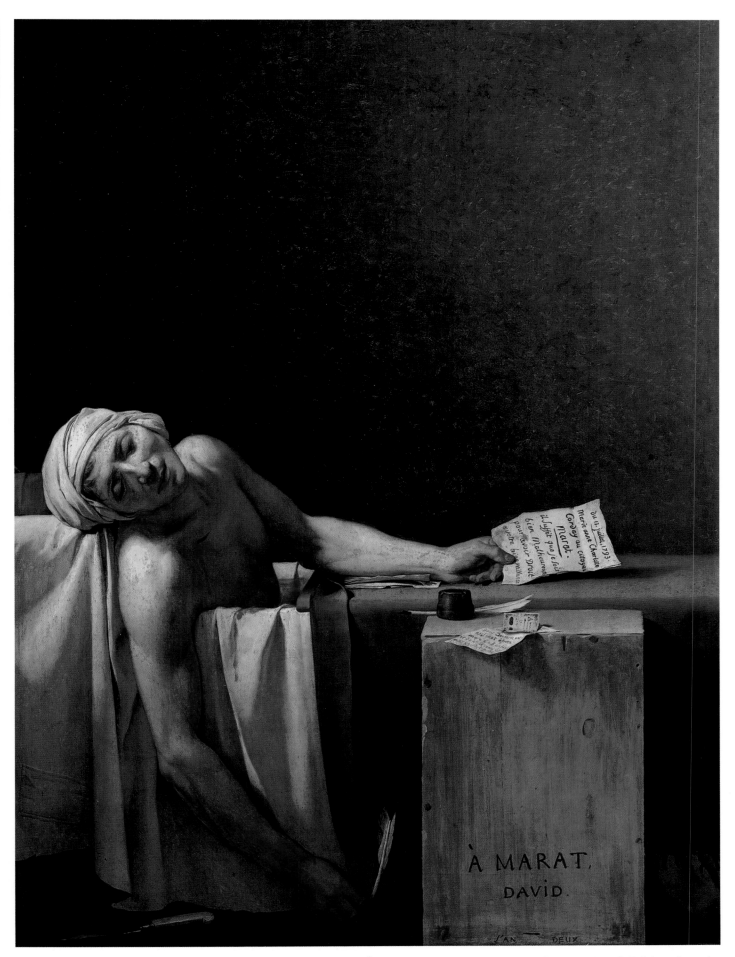

21-3. Jacques-Louis David. *The Death of Marat.* 1793. Oil on canvas, 65 x 50½" (165 x 128.3 cm). Musées Royaux des Beaux-Arts de Belgique, Brussels

awe-inspiring. In this canvas, which was planned as a public memorial to the martyred hero, classical art combines with devotional image and historical account. However, classical art could offer little specific guidance for such a work, even though the slain figure probably was derived from an antique source. The artist has drawn on the Caravaggesque tradition of religious art far more than in *The Death of Socrates*. It is no accident that his Marat reminds us so strongly of Zurbarán's *St. Serapion* (see fig. 17-36).

England

The leading role of artists such as Gavin Hamilton in formulating Neoclassicism was a result of England's enthusiasm for classical antiquity since the early years of the century. This appreciation was political, philosophic, and literary. Because it was motivated by a new nationalism, this admiration soon turned into a demand that England become "the principal seat of the arts" as well. In 1748 King George III established the Royal Academy of Arts as a way of encouraging painting, sculpture, and architecture in Great Britain. (It is still under the patronage of the Crown.)

BENJAMIN WEST. Among the founding members of the Royal Academy was Benjamin West (1738–1820), who succeeded Sir Joshua Reynolds as its president. Largely self-taught, West went to Rome from Pennsylvania in 1760 and caused a sensation, since no American painter had appeared in Europe before. He relished his role of frontiersman. On being shown the *Apollo Belvedere* (see fig. 5-71) he reportedly exclaimed, "How like a Mohawk warrior!" He also quickly absorbed the lessons of Neoclassicism, so that he was in command of the most up-to-date style when he left a few years later. West stopped in London for what was intended to be a brief stay on his way home, but decided to remain there. He enjoyed phenomenal success and became the most important history painter in England. His career was thus

European rather than American, but he always took pride in his New World background.

The Death of General Wolfe (fig. 21-4), West's most famous work, is the first painting to immortalize the martyrdom of a secular hero. It represents an incident that had aroused considerable feeling in London. Wolfe's death in 1759 occurred in the siege of Quebec during the French and Indian War. When West decided to represent this event 11 years later, two methods were open to him. He could give a factual account, with the maximum of historical accuracy, or he could use "the grand manner," based on Poussin's ideal of history painting (see fig. 19-5), with figures in "timeless" classical costume. Although he had been influenced by Mengs and Hamilton, he did not follow them in this painting, because he knew the American scene too well. Instead, he merged the two approaches. His figures wear contemporary dress, and the figure of the Indian places the scene in the New World. Yet all the attitudes and expressions are "heroic." The composition, in fact, recalls the lamentation over the dead Christ (compare fig. 11-79). The artist has dramatized it with Baroque lighting, drama, and brushwork (see fig. 18-1). West thus endowed the death of a modern military hero with both the classical pathos of "noble and serious human actions," as defined by academic theory, and the trappings of a real event. He created an image that expresses an attitude basic to modern times: the shift of allegiance from religion to nationalism. No wonder his picture had countless successors during the nineteenth century.

JOHN SINGLETON COPLEY. West's gifted countryman, John Singleton Copley of Boston (1738–1815), moved to London just two years before the American Revolution. As New England's outstanding portrait painter, he had adapted the formulas of the British portrait tradition to the cultural climate of his hometown. *Paul Revere,* painted around 1768–70 (fig. 21-5), is deservedly his most famous painting in this vein. Silversmith, printmaker, busi-

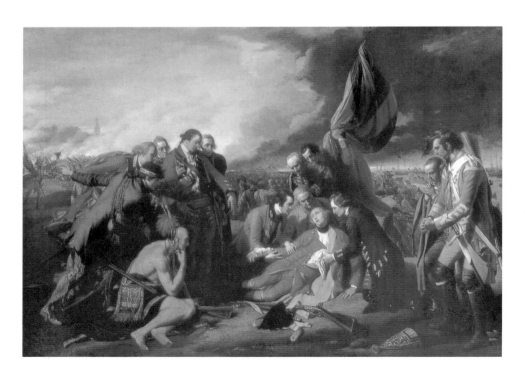

21-4. Benjamin West.
The Death of General Wolfe.
1770. Oil on canvas, 4' 11 ½" x 7'
(1.51 x 2.13 m). National Gallery
of Canada, Ottawa
GIFT OF THE DUKE OF WESTMINSTER

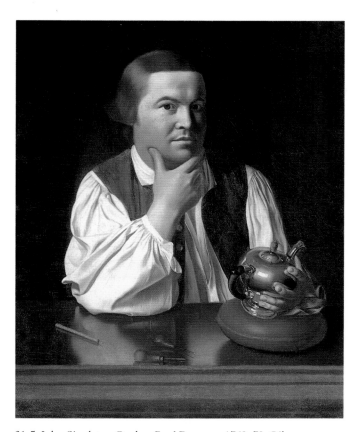

21-5. John Singleton Copley. *Paul Revere.* c. 1768–70. Oil on canvas, 35 x 28½" (88.9 x 72.3 cm). Museum of Fine Arts, Boston

nessman, and patriot, Revere has acquired legendary status thanks to Henry Wadsworth Longfellow's famous poem about his midnight ride. Copley's painting, in turn, has become virtually an American icon. It is usually treated as a workingman's portrait, so to speak. However, this is not Revere's working outfit but his best business clothes. Revere looks out at us with astonishing directness, as if he were examining us with the same intensity as we read his strongly modeled features. The sharp light gives him an unusually forceful presence and heightens the thoughtful mood. Revere is a thinker who possesses a keen intelligence, and we will recognize the pose of hand on chin as an old device used since antiquity to represent philosophers. Clearly this is no ordinary craftsman. Why, then, did Copley show Revere at a workbench with his engraving tools spread out before him? And why is he holding a teapot as the object of his contemplation and offering it to us for our inspection? Revere's work as a silversmith is not a sufficient explanation, natural as it might seem.

Paul Revere belongs to a type of informal portrait that originated in France in the early eighteenth century and soon became popular as well in England. Reserved originally for artists, writers, and other cultural figures, it soon gave rise to a variant showing a sculptor at work in his studio with his tools prominently displayed. In fact, the sitter shown in our example (fig. 21-6), Louis-François Roubiliac, helped to popularize the image of the culture hero in England through his statue of the composer George Frideric Handel (fig. 20-16). Sometimes an engraver is seen instead. There is another source as well: moralizing portraits,

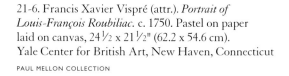

21-6. Francis Xavier Vispré (attr.). *Portrait of Louis-François Roubiliac.* c. 1750. Pastel on paper laid on canvas, 24½ x 21½" (62.2 x 54.6 cm). Yale Center for British Art, New Haven, Connecticut

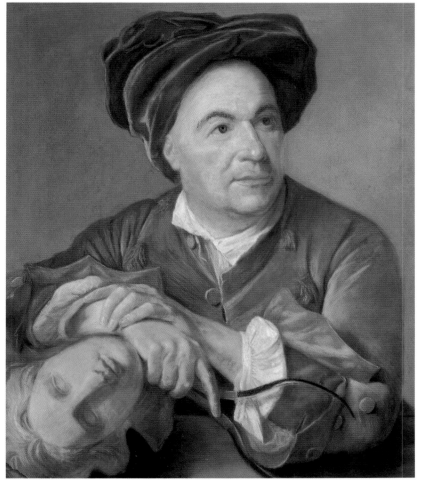

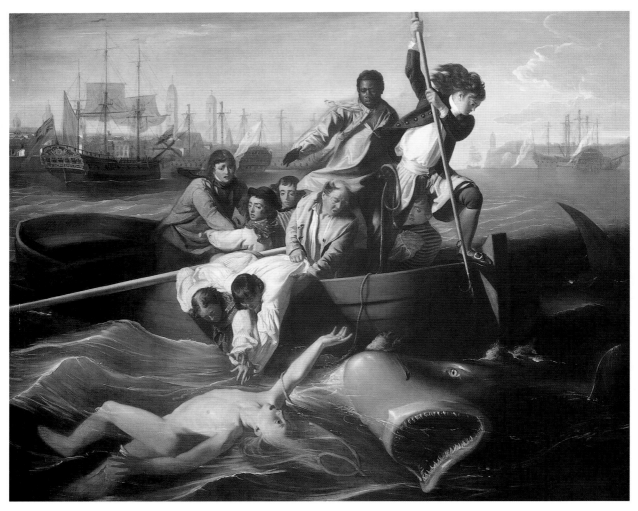

21-7. John Singleton Copley. *Watson and the Shark*. 1778. Oil on canvas, 7'6¼" x 6'½" (2.29 x 1.84 m). Museum of Fine Arts, Boston

the descendants of pictures of St. Jerome holding or pointing to skulls, much as Revere has the teapot in his hand. Copley was surely familiar with both images from the portrait engravings he collected, although the exact sources for the Revere painting remain unknown. Copley thus transformed Revere from a craftsman into an artist-philosopher—and with good reason: Revere's portrait probably dates from around the time of his first engravings. The painter and the silversmith must have known each other well. (Copley ordered various pieces of silver, and even false teeth, from Revere.) The portrait is exceptional for its penetrating characterization, which goes far beyond the genteel conventions of the day. The painting thus stands as a compelling tribute to a fellow artist—and as an invaluable document of Colonial culture.

In Europe Copley was at last able to achieve his goal of history painting in the manner of West, who encouraged him to come to London. His most memorable work is *Watson and the Shark* (fig. 21-7). As a young man, Watson had been dramatically rescued from a shark attack while swimming in Havana harbor, but not until he met Copley did he decide to have this gruesome experience memorialized. Perhaps he thought that

only an artist newly arrived from America would do full justice to the exotic flavor of the incident. Copley, in turn, must have been fascinated by the task of translating the story into pictorial terms. Following West's example, he made every detail as authentic as possible. (Here the black man has the same purpose as the Indian in *The Death of General Wolfe*.) He also used all the resources of Baroque painting to invite the viewer's participation. The composition is indebted partially to a hunting scene by Rubens. Copley may also have remembered representations of Jonah and the Whale, which include the elements of his scene, except that the action is reversed. (In the Bible, the prophet is thrown overboard into the jaws of the sea monster, which eventually spits him out.) The shark becomes a monstrous embodiment of evil; the man with the boat hook recalls the Archangel Michael fighting Satan; and the nude youth, resembling a fallen gladiator, flounders helplessly between the forces of doom and salvation. This kind of moral allegory is typical of Neoclassicism as a whole, and despite its charged action and emotion, the picture has the same logic and clarity found in David's *Death of Socrates* (see fig. 21-2).

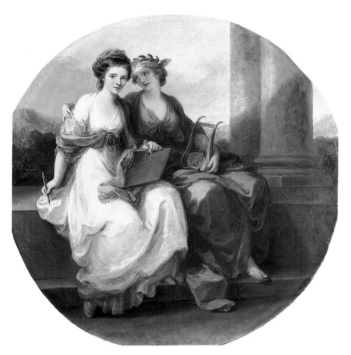

21-8. Angelica Kauffmann. *The Artist in the Character of Design Listening to the Inspiration of Poetry.* 1782. Oil on canvas, diameter 24" (61 cm)

ANGELICA KAUFFMANN. One of the leading Neoclassicists in England was the Swiss-born painter Angelica Kauffmann (1741–1807), who had been a disciple of Mengs'. A founding member of the Royal Academy, she spent 15 years in London among the group that included Reynolds and West, whom she had met in Winckelmann's circle in Rome (see page 672). From the antique she developed a delicate style admirably suited to the interiors of Robert Adam (see page 724), which she was often commissioned to decorate. Kauffmann's most ambitious works are narrative paintings, of which the artist John Henry Fuseli (see page 705) observed, "Her heroines are herself." *The Artist in the Character of Design Listening to the Inspiration of Poetry* (fig. 21-8) combines both aspects of her art. The subject must have held particular meaning for her. The artist is shown in the guise of Design, suggesting her strong sense of identification with the muse. The painting became the prototype of the allegorical "friendship" pictures showing two female figures that remained popular into the Romantic era (see fig. 21-54).

GEORGE STUBBS. George Stubbs (1724–1806), who painted portraits of racehorses (and sometimes their owners) for a living, developed a new type of animal picture full of feeling for the grandeur and violence of nature that looks forward to Romanticism. On a visit to North Africa, he is said to have seen a horse being killed by a lion. Certainly this image haunted his imagination. *Lion Attacking a Horse* (fig. 21-9) can be thought of as an animal counterpart to Copley's *Watson and the Shark,* and it has similar allegorical overtones. People have no place in this realm. The artist identifies himself emotionally with the horse, whose pure whiteness contrasts so dramatically—and symbolically—with the sinister rocks of the lion's domain. Thunderclouds racing across the sky reinforce the mood of doom. Frightened as well by the approaching storm, the horse seems doubly defenseless against these forces of destruction. We respond to its plight with the same mixed fascination and horror as we do Watson's.

Stubbs' depiction of animals with nearly human action and emotion was the beginning of a larger investigation so characteristic of the Enlightenment. He later made a series of drawings for a book of comparative anatomy—including one that could well be used to illustrate Plato's famous observation that humans are

21-9. George Stubbs. *Lion Attacking a Horse.* 1770. Oil on canvas, 40⅛ x 50¼" (102 x 127.6 cm). Yale University Art Gallery, New Haven, Connecticut

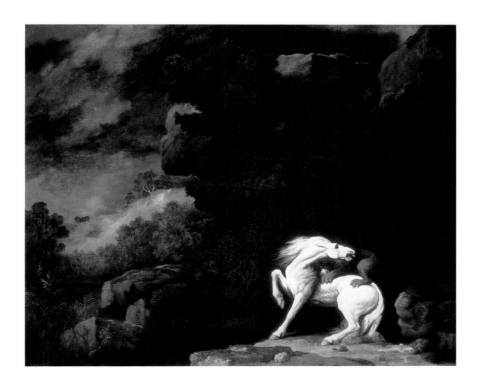

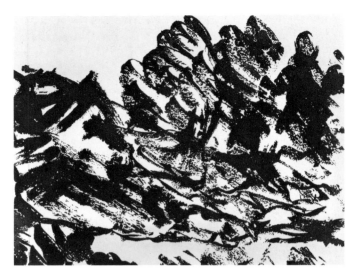

21-10. Alexander Cozens. *Landscape,* from *A New Method of Assisting the Invention in Drawing Original Compositions of Landscape.* 1784–86. Aquatint. The Metropolitan Museum of Art, New York

featherless bipeds. In them he emphasized the similarities in physiology and psychology between people and animals. His scientific curiosity and comprehensive approach relate his study to Diderot's attempt to unite all knowledge and philosophy in his massive *Encyclopédie*.

THE PICTURESQUE AND THE SUBLIME. Picturesque landscape painting was as distinctive to the Enlightenment as the English garden (see pages 684–85), to which it was closely related. As the term implies, the picturesque was a way of looking at nature through the eyes of landscape painters. The scenery of Italy and the idyllic landscapes of Claude contributed to the English appreciation of nature. In expressing emotions inspired by these examples, English nature poets such as James Thomson further validated the aesthetic response to nature, often through references to mythology. The picturesque was soon joined by wilder scenes reflecting a taste for the sublime—that delicious sense of awe experienced before grandiose nature. The idea had been around since the beginning of the eighteenth century, but it was defined once and for all by Edmund Burke in *Inquiry into the Origin of Our Ideas of the Sublime and the Beautiful* of 1756, which held that the sublime is the opposite of beauty. After touring the rugged lake region of England in 1780, Reverend William Gilpin claimed that the picturesque lay somewhere between Burke's extremes, since it is neither vast nor smooth but finite and rough. The picturesque later came to include a topographical mode as well as a rustic mode, but it remained essentially a way of manipulating nature to conform to art.

ALEXANDER COZENS. Alexander Cozens (c. 1717–1786), who helped to originate the picturesque, soon tired of these models. He felt they could produce only conventional variations on a standard theme. The direct study of nature, important though it was, could not be the new starting point either. It did not supply the imaginative, poetic quality that for him was the essence of landscape painting. As a teacher Cozens developed what he called "a new method of assisting the invention in drawing original compositions of landscapes," which he published, with illustrations such as figure 21-10, shortly before his death. Leonardo da Vinci, Cozens noted, had observed that an artist could stimulate his imagination by trying to find recognizable shapes in the stains on old walls. Why not produce such chance effects on purpose, to be used in the same way? Crumple a sheet of paper, smooth it. Then, while thinking generally of landscape, blot it with ink while using as little conscious control as possible. (Our example is such an "ink-blot landscape.") With this as the point of departure, representational elements may be picked out among the blots and developed into a finished picture. Cozens' blotscape, then, is not a work of nature but a work of art. Even though only half-born, it shows a highly individual graphic style.

Because it relies on art, the Cozens method still falls within the picturesque, while the scope of his attempt places it within the Enlightenment, with its love of systems. It has far-reaching implications, theoretical as well as practical, but these could hardly have been understood by his contemporaries, who regarded the "blot-master" as ridiculous. Nevertheless, the method was not forgotten. Its memory was kept alive partly by its very notoriety. The two great masters of Romantic landscape in England, John Constable and William Turner, both benefited from it, although they differed in almost every other way. But it was in the twentieth century that Cozens' approach was to bear its most important fruit (see page 832).

SCULPTURE

Neoclassicism is distinguished from Romanticism far more clearly in sculpture than in painting. Unlike painters, Neoclassical sculptors were overwhelmed by the authority granted since Winckelmann to ancient statues, which were praised as supreme manifestations of the Greek genius. Most of them were in fact mechanical Roman copies of no great distinction after Greek originals (see fig. 5-44 and 5-69). (Goethe, upon seeing the newly discovered late Archaic sculpture from Aegina, pronounced it clumsy and inferior; see figs. 5-23 and 5-24.)

When Winckelmann published his essay advocating the imitation of Greek works, enthusiasm for classical antiquity was already well established among the intellectuals of the Enlightenment. In Rome from 1760 on, the restoring of ancient sculpture and its sale, especially to wealthy visitors from abroad, was a flourishing business. To these patrons, "classics" such as the *Apollo Belvedere* or *The Laocoön Group* (see figs. 5-71 and 5-78), to cite only two of the most famous, belonged to a different world. They were admired as embodiments of an aesthetic ideal that was undisturbed by the demands of time and place. To enter this world, modern sculptors set themselves the goal of creating "modern classics"—sculpture demanding to be judged on a basis of equality with its ancient predecessors. This was not just a matter of style and subject matter. It meant that sculptors had to hope that critical acclaim would establish such works as classics in their own right and attract buyers. Exhibiting original plasters enabled them to present major works to the public without investing in expensive marble or bronze. Plaster sculpture thus became a feature at the Salons, the exhibitions sponsored by the French Academy, where success was crucial for young artists. Without the original plaster, the Neoclassical revolution in sculpture would have been impossible.

If Paris was the artistic capital of the Western world during the second half of the eighteenth century, Rome became the birthplace and spiritual home of Neoclassicism. As we have seen, however, the new style was pioneered by the resident foreigners from north of the Alps, rather than by Italians. That Rome should have been an even stronger magnet for sculptors than for painters is hardly surprising. Rome had an abundance of antique sculpture but only a limited choice of ancient painting. (The city also had many skilled artisans in both marble and bronze.) In the shadow of these monuments, Northern sculptors trained in the Baroque tradition awakened to a new conception of what sculpture ought to be. They paved the way for Antonio Canova, whose success as a creator of modern classics was the ultimate fulfillment of their ambitions (see page 719).

England

Spurred in part by the mania for collecting antique statues, England played the leading role before 1780 in developing Neoclassicism in sculpture as it did in painting. This precocious appreciation was at first political, philosophical, and literary. Because it was also motivated by nationalism, this admiration soon turned into a demand that England become "the principal seat of the arts."

THOMAS BANKS. Thomas Banks (1735–1805) came closest to achieving the sculptor's goal of creating modern classics. Little is known of Banks' career before he went to Rome in 1772 for seven years on a traveling fellowship from the Royal Academy. *The Death of Germanicus* (fig. 21-11), a large relief of 1774, shows his close study of classical art, yet it is not in the least archaeological in flavor. While the faces and drapery derive from classical sources, the strained poses, the emphatic linear rhythms, and the emotional intensity of the scene have no counterpart in ancient sculpture. They reflect Banks' admiration for the painters Gavin Hamilton (who had treated the same subject) and Henry Fuseli (see page 707).

Unfortunately, Banks found little demand for his "new classics" on his return to England, although they were enthusiastically received by the Royal Academy. He was forced instead to seek commissions for funerary monuments, which were the main source of steady employment for sculptors in England.

France

JEAN-ANTOINE HOUDON. Jean-Antoine Houdon (1741–1828), unlike most of his contemporaries, built his career on portrait sculpture. He would have been glad to accept state commissions had they been available. However, he soon discovered his special gift for portraits, for which there was a growing demand. Indeed, portraiture proved the most viable field for Neoclassical

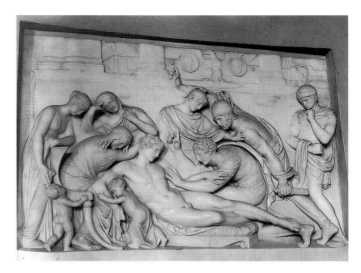

21-11. Thomas Banks. *The Death of Germanicus.* 1774. Marble, height 30" (76.2 cm). Holkham Hall, Norfolk, England

sculpture. How else could modern artists rise above the quality of the Greek and Roman classics? Houdon's portraits retain the keen sense of individual character introduced by Antoine Coysevox (see fig. 19-18), but they establish entirely new standards of physical and psychological realism. Houdon, more than any other artist of his time, knew how to give visible form to Enlightenment ideals while still relying on Rococo devices. His portraits have an apparent lack of style that is deceptive. Houdon had an uncanny ability to make all his sitters into Enlightenment personalities while remaining conscientiously faithful to their individual features. He even managed this on the rare occasions when he had to make portrait busts of people long dead, or when he had to work only from a death mask.

With Voltaire, he was more fortunate. Houdon modeled him from life a few weeks before the famous author's death in May 1778, and then made a death mask as well. From these studies he created *Voltaire Seated*. The original plaster has not survived, but we have a terra-cotta cast of it, retouched by Houdon (fig. 21-12), that offers a close approximation. The statue was immediately acknowledged the greatest masterpiece of its kind. As contemporary critics quickly pointed out, the *Voltaire Seated* was a "heroicized" likeness. The sculptor enveloped the frail old man in a Roman toga and even added some hair he no longer had in order to justify the classical headband. Yet the effect is not disturbing, for Voltaire wears the toga as casually as a dressing gown. His facial expression and the turn of his head, so reminiscent of Rococo portraiture (compare fig. 20-10 of about the same time), suggest an intimate conversation. Thus Voltaire is not merely cast in the role of classical philosopher—he becomes the modern counterpart of one, a modern classic in his own right! In him, we recognize ourselves. Voltaire is the image of modern life: unheroic, skeptical, with his own unique mixture of rationality and emotion. That is surely why Voltaire strikes us as so "natural." We are, after all, the heirs of the Enlightenment, which coined this ideal type.

Aside from *Voltaire Seated,* the Virginia *George Washington* (fig. 21-13) is Houdon's finest work. In 1778, the year he portrayed

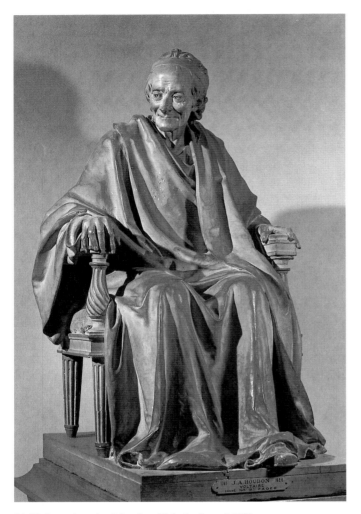

21-12. Jean-Antoine Houdon. *Voltaire Seated*. 1781.
Terra-cotta model for marble original, height 47" (119.3 cm).
Musée Fabre, Montpellier, France

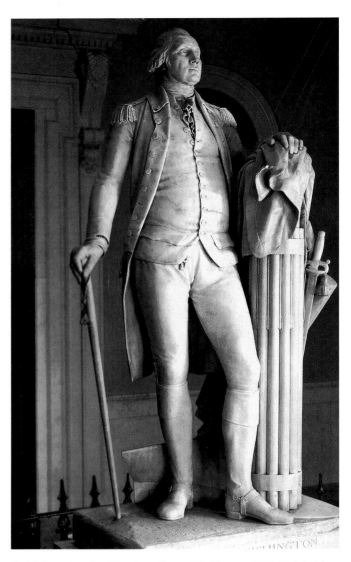

21-13. Jean-Antoine Houdon. *George Washington*. 1788–92. Marble,
height 6'2" (1.88 m). State Capitol, Richmond, Virginia

Voltaire, Houdon became a Freemason and modeled Benjamin Franklin. Replicas of the Franklin bust spread the artist's fame in the New World. American colonial sculpture hardly existed aside from weathervanes, tombstone carvings, and cigar-store Indians. Public monuments were few, and were imported from England rather than produced at home. Thus the newborn republic had to look to France for a sculptor to immortalize its first president. After all, it could not be entrusted to an Englishman. There was, it seems, no contact with British sculpture from 1776 until after the fall of Napoleon. Thus when the Virginia legislature decided to commission a marble statue of George Washington, the natural choice was Houdon. Houdon insisted on coming over to model his sitter directly, and in October 1785 he spent two weeks at Mount Vernon as Washington's guest. The figure was placed at long last in the rotunda of the State Capitol 11 years later.

Houdon initially made two versions, one in classical garb and one in modern costume. Even in its final form, the statue has a classical pose, and we can feel the chill breath of the *Apollo Belvedere* (see fig. 5-71), as it were, on the tranquil, smooth surfaces. Houdon has given Washington a general's uniform, but the sword, no longer needed in peacetime, is suspended from a bun-

dle of 13 rods (the fasces, representing the original states of the Union) and his right hand rests on a cane. Behind his feet is a plow, the symbol of peace. These attributes, with their classical allusions, blend easily with the contemporary dress, which is thoroughly up-to-date in detail, while the contrapposto stance of the figure is so natural that the viewer is hardly aware of its antique origin. The statue is more than a record of Washington's physical appearance. Above all, Houdon has created a powerful impression of Washington's character, but within the framework of the ideal personality type of the Enlightenment. Houdon's statue, and the busts derived from it, did much to determine how the nation visualized the Father of His Country.

ARCHITECTURE

England

THE PALLADIAN REVIVAL. England was the birthplace of Neoclassicism in architecture, just as it had been in the forefront of painting and sculpture. The earliest sign was the Palladian revival. It was sparked by the publication of the treatise *Vitruvius*

NEOCLASSICAL THEATER

In France, around the middle of the eighteenth century, the philosopher and encyclopedist Denis Diderot (1713–1784) attempted to add domestic tragedy and the comedy of virtue (the so-called middle genres) to the accepted classifications of theater through his sentimental plays *The Illegitimate Son* (1757) and *The Father of a Family* (1758). They were quickly forgotten, with good reason. The only important French playwright of the later Enlightenment was Pierre-Augustin Caron de Beaumarchais (1732–1799), whose comedies *The Barber of Seville* (1775) and *The Marriage of Figaro* (1783) became the basis for operas by Rossini and Mozart. While the *Barber* is a lighthearted farce derived from the commedia dell'arte about the triumph of young lovers over lecherous old men, *Figaro* was a critique of the aristocracy, whose ranks Beaumarchais joined, thanks to the wealth he amassed through his inventions and business ventures.

Neoclassicism in German theater was represented chiefly by the playwright, critic, and university professor Johann Christoph Gottsched (1700–1766), who modeled his plays on French examples and who based his ideas on the classical theories of the French critic Nicolas Boileau (1636–1711); however, their success depended heavily on his close association with the actress Caroline Neuber (1697–1760). His theories were attacked by Gotthold Ephraim Lessing (1729–1781) in *Laokoon* (1766) and in the journal *Hamburgische Dramaturgie* (1767–68). Lessing argued that the goal of drama is to arouse compassion, thereby fulfilling an important moral and social function. Although he belittled his own work, Lessing's plays, such as *Minna von Barnhelm* (1767), embody his principles very capably.

Lessing helped pave the way for the *Sturm und Drang* (Storm and Stress) period (1770–87), which constituted a rebellion against the restrictions of the Neoclassical drama and Enlightenment philosophy and was the first attempt to create a distinctive German form of theater. Although this literary movement took its name from a play of that title (1776) by F. M. Klinger (1752–1831), it centered on the young poet Johann Wolfgang von Goethe (1749–1832), whose drama *Goetz van Berlichingen* (1773), inspired by the memoirs of a famous sixteenth-century German knight, launched the movement in theater. The extreme subjectivity of *Sturm und Drang* writing was epitomized by Goethe's novel *The Sorrows of Young Werther,* published the following year. *Sturm und Drang* in theater was poorly received but widely discussed; it was finally legitimized by August von Kotzebue (1761–1819), who became the most popular playwright in Europe. The late eighteenth century was notable for the establishment of national theaters throughout Germany, as well as Austria; important examples are the Hamburg National Theater, which employed Lessing as its artistic adviser (dramaturge) when it opened in 1767, and the Burgtheater in Vienna of 1776.

After the publication of *The Sorrows of Young Werther,* which established his reputation, Goethe was invited to the court in Weimar, where he spent the rest of his career and even served as minister of state for ten years. During a sojourn to Italy in 1786–88 he became a convert to classicism and rejected *Sturm und Drang*. In 1791 he was appointed director of the theater at Weimar, in which he showed little interest until he became friends with the poet Friedrich von Schiller (1759–1805). Schiller had written some early dramas before turning to the study of history, which led to a professorship at the university in Jena, not far from Weimar. The friendship was so close that Schiller moved to Weimar in 1799. From then until his death he wrote his great dramas, which were a direct outgrowth of his abiding interest in history. They center on the Thirty Years' War, about which he wrote the first major treatise, particularly on General Albrecht Wallenstein (1583–1634). His other plays concern William Tell, Mary Stuart, and Joan of Arc. Under Goethe and Schiller, Weimar became home to the leading theater on the Continent. They argued that theater should transform experience through harmony and grace rather than create an illusion of real life; hence, they instituted stylized conventions designed to lead the viewer to ideal truth.

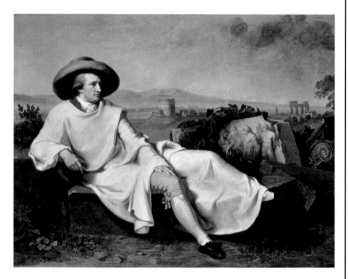

Johann Heinrich Wilhelm Tischbein. *Goethe in the Campagna.* 1787. Oil on canvas, 64⅝ x 81⅛" (164 x 206 cm). Städelsches Kunstinstitut, Frankfurt

Brittanicus (1715–17; 1725) by Colin Campbell (1676–1729), which advocated a return to the style of Palladio and Inigo Jones and rejected Wren's Baroque. However, it was the wealthy amateur Richard Boyle, Lord Burlington (1694–1753), who emerged as the leader of the movement in the 1720s. To carry out his designs, he employed his friend William Kent (c. 1685–1748), a painter-decorator among his considerable circle of artists and writers. (They included the poet Alexander Pope, who urged a classical reform of literature.) Palladio appealed to the English partly because his designs for villas were well-suited to English country houses and

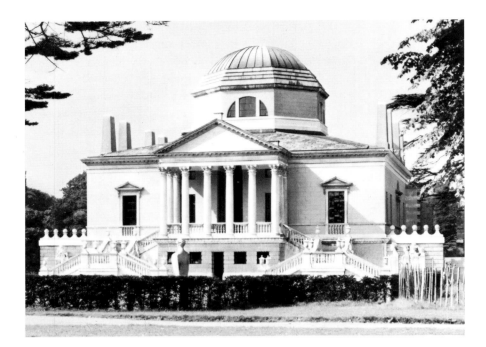

21-14. Lord Burlington and William Kent. Chiswick House, near London. Begun 1725

partly because his style conformed to the Rule of Taste promoted by the Enlightenment philosopher Anthony Ashley Cooper, Third Earl of Shaftesbury (1617–1713). What distinguishes the Palladian revival from earlier classicisms, however, is less its style than its motivation. Instead of merely reasserting the superior authority of the ancients, it claimed to satisfy the demands of reason, and thus to be more "natural" than the Baroque. At the time, the Baroque style was identified with papist Rome by English Protestants, with absolutist France by George I, and with Tory policies by the Whig opposition. Thus began an association between Neoclassicism and liberal politics that was to continue through the French Revolution. The appeal to reason found support in Palladio's writings. Basing himself on Alberti and Vitruvius, he condemned abuses "contrary to natural reason" on the grounds that "architecture, as well as all other arts, being an imitation of nature, can suffer nothing that either alienates or deviates from that which is agreeable to nature."

This rationalism helps to explain the abstract, segmented look of Chiswick House on Burlington's estate (fig. 21-14). Adapted by Burlington and Kent from the Palladio's Villa Rotonda (see fig. 14-26), as well as other Italian sources, it is compact, simple, and geometric—the antithesis of the Baroque pomp of Blenheim Palace (see fig. 19-25). The concept was not new to England. It had been used on a larger scale just a couple of years earlier at Mereworth Castle by Campbell. Chiswick is at once bolder and more rigorous, yet less derivative than Mereworth. Campbell himself acknowledged Burlington as "not only a great Patron of all Arts, but the first Architect." The exterior surfaces of Chiswick are flat and unbroken, the ornament is meager, and the temple portico juts out abruptly from the blocklike body of the structure. The interior, probably by Kent, is more luxurious, in the manner of Jones, but with a clarity that looks forward to Robert Adam.

THE ENGLISH GARDEN. Should such a villa be set in a geometric, formal garden, like Le Nôtre's at Versailles (see fig. 19-14)? Lord Burlington and Kent maintained that such a setting would

be unnatural, hence contrary to reason. At Chiswick they invented what became known all over Europe as the English landscape garden. It was carefully planned to look unplanned, with winding paths, irregularly spaced clumps of trees, and little lakes and rivers instead of symmetrical basins and canals. The "reasonable" garden must seem as unbounded, as full of surprise and variety, as nature itself. It must, in a word, be picturesque, a term that applies equally well to Burlington's villa, which would look out of place in other surroundings. English landscape architects took the landscapes of Claude Lorraine (see fig. 19-7) as their source of inspiration. A standard feature was the inclusion of little temples half concealed by the shrubbery, or artificial ruins, "to draw sorrowful reflections from the soul."

Such sentiments were not new. They had often been expressed before in poetry and painting. But to project them onto nature itself through planned irregularity was a new idea. The landscape garden is a work of art intended not to look like a work of art, which blurred the long-established boundary between artifice and reality. It thus set an important precedent for the revival styles to come. After all, the landscape garden stands in the same relation to nature as a synthetic ruin to an authentic one, or a Neoclassical or Neo-Gothic building to its ancient or medieval model. When the fashion spread to the other side of the Channel, it was welcomed not only as a new way to lay out gardens but as a vehicle of Romantic emotion.

STOURHEAD. Of all the landscape gardens laid out in England in the mid-eighteenth century, the one at Stourhead most nearly retains its original appearance. Its creators, the banker Henry Hoare and the architect Henry Flitcroft (1697–1769), were both enthusiastic followers of Lord Burlington and William Kent. Stourhead is unique not only for its fine preservation but also for the owner's active role in planning every detail of its development. Our view (fig. 21-15) is across a small lake made by damming the river Stour. High on the far shore is the Temple of Apollo modeled

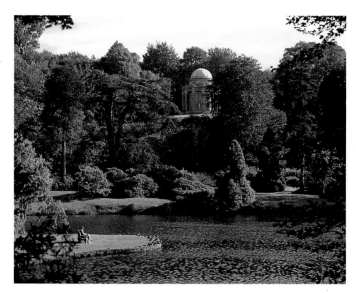

21-15. Henry Flitcroft and Henry Hoare. Landscape garden with Temple of Apollo, Stourhead, England. 1744–65

on the recently discovered Temple of Venus at Baalbek. Other focal points at Stourhead are a grotto, a Temple of Venus, a Pantheon, a genuine Gothic cross, and a neo-medieval tower built to commemorate King Alfred the Great, the "Father of His People."

France

THE RATIONALIST MOVEMENT. The rationalist movement came somewhat earlier in France as far as theory is concerned, but was first achieved in actual buildings only in the middle years of the century. It was made up of several factions that were united only by their rejection of the Rococo as heavy and ornate.

Structural rationalism was initiated by the pro-Greek rigorists, who were theorists rather than practicing architects. The first, Abbé Jean-Louis de Cordemoy (active 1706–1712), argued in his *New Treatise on All Architecture* (1708, 1714) against the representative and expressive use of architectural elements. He favored a simple, clear system based on freestanding columns surmounted by an entablature and stripped of all unnecessary ornament. For him good architecture depended not on Vitruvius' utility, solidity, and beauty but on order, arrangement, and appropriateness (akin to the concept of decorum). He therefore warned against the unnecessary decorative use of classical elements. He was further important for helping to initiate the French fascination with the Gothic by calling for an architecture combining classical forms and Gothic construction principles. This idea had first been introduced, however cautiously, by the great classicist Claude Perrault himself, who wrote, "Gothic architecture may not be the best kind, but it is not to be rejected out of hand [simply because things are] different in Gothic and ancient architecture. And (here comes the heresy) Gothic is not therefore to be thought the worse for it. . . ." Perreault's proposal in 1676 for a new church of St. Geneviève featured a barrel vault over a classical peristyle—a design so prophetic that several churches were later erected along those very lines.

De Cordemoy was an early but inconsistent voice. The central figure was the Jesuit Abbé Marc-Antoine Laugier (1713–1769), whose *Essay on Architecture* (1753) acknowledged a debt to de Cordemoy's treatise but was far more systematic. The difference was essentially one of a perceptive critic as against a true philosopher of the Enlightenment whose faith in reason was complete. Following Vitruvius, Laugier accepted that the beautiful in architecture, as in art, must proceed from nature. And like Jean-Jacques Rousseau, he believed that early people lived in an idyllic state of harmony with nature. In needing shelter from the elements, they built primitive huts of trees using the simplest possible—and therefore the "truest"—system of vertical and horizontal elements. (They were later discovered to have been made of bowed trees.) This post-and-lintel method Laugier believed to be the forerunner of the columns and entablatures found in Classical Greek architecture, where every element performed a clear role and ornament was held to a minimum (compare page 127). He therefore totally rejected the Roman use of arches, pilasters, and compound orders. Despite his insistence on clarity and logic, Laugier, too, was fascinated by the lightness, gracefulness, and spaciousness of Gothic architecture. He proposed a union of these two ideal systems in which glass would fill the voids between columns.

Laugier was probably familiar with the ideas of the Franciscan theologian Carlo Lodoli (1690–1761) of Venice, who was an even purer structuralist. Lodoli argued that architecture was a science based on the nature of materials, specifically stone, and the laws of statics. Designs should be determined by function (the relationship between structure and purpose) and representation (the way material is disposed to fulfill the intended purpose). Beauty must proceed not from aesthetics but from the dictates of materials. To him the Greek orders, and by extension Roman and Renaissance architecture, were dishonest because they substituted marble for wood. Thus the only true models of masonry architecture were Stonehenge and Egyptian temples, even though they actually employed the same post-and-lintel system as Greek architecture.

The actual attack on the Rococo style began in 1737 with a treatise by the architect Jacques-François Blondel (1705–1774), the leader of the traditionalists. He argued for a return to the French classical style of Perrault and Mansart out of nostalgia for the age of Louis XIV. The offensive was joined eight years later by the theorist Abbé Jean-Bernard Leblanc, whose *Letters from England* (1745) endorsed a Neoclassical style under the influence of Lord Burlington's ideas. The antiquarians, centering on the collector the Comte de Caylus (1692–1765), attracted the younger generation of French architects who returned from studies in Rome during the 1740s and 50s filled with new ideas based on antiquity and the Renaissance. The most prominent was Jean-Laurent Legeay (c. 1710–c.1786), a visionary who influenced first Piranesi in Rome (see page 629) and then a generation of architects in Paris (including Boullée; see below) after being appointed to a position at the Academy in 1742. The archaeological neoclassicists of the 1760s proved even more radical. Chief among them were Marie-Joseph Peyre (1730–1785) and Charles-Louis Clérisseau (1721–1820),

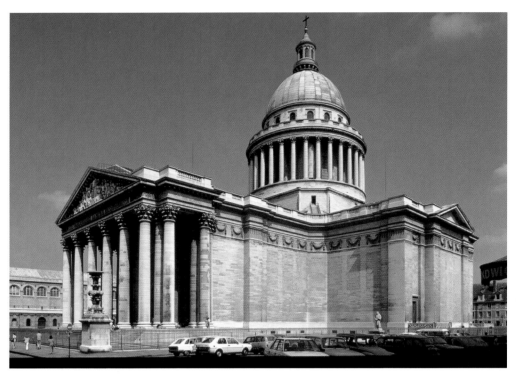

21-16. Jacques-Germain Soufflot. The Panthéon (Ste.-Geneviève), Paris. 1757–92

a pupil of Blondel's who was also inspired by Piranesi and Johann Winckelmann (see page 672). They believed that the Romans had perfected the Greek orders by extending and combining them in boldly imaginative ways.

It is characteristic of the Enlightenment that utility and necessity replaced beauty, which came to be measured by reason, not aesthetics. However, practicing architects found it impossible to follow such an approach in every respect, and they mounted a vigorous counteroffensive. The net result was that French architecture in the 1750s and 60s was dominated by the conscious return to the Style of Louis XIV, but "corrected" and overlaid with new ideas of such boldness that they provided the foundation for modern architecture.

JACQUES-GERMAIN SOUFFLOT. The first great monument of the rationalist movement was the Panthéon in Paris (fig. 21-16), by Jacques-Germain Soufflot (1713–1780). It was begun in 1757 as the Church of Ste-Geneviève, but was secularized during the Revolution. The architect owed his position to his close relationship with the Marquis de Marigny, the brother of Louis XV's mistress, Madame du Pompadour, with whom he toured Italy in 1749–51. Upon his return he settled in Lyons, the home of Laugier, where he quickly established himself as a leading architect of the day. As with so much else in eighteenth-century France, the Church of Ste.-Geneviève looks back to the previous century, in this case Hardouin-Mansart's Church of the Invalides (see fig. 19-15). The huge east portico, however, is modeled directly on Perrault's Louvre facade (see fig. 19-10), as well as ancient Roman temples. (Soufflot had spent seven years studying architecture in Italy as a winner of the French Academy's Prix de Rome at the beginning of his career.) The plan, unusual for France, is in the shape of a Greek cross. Although

Hardouin-Mansart's Invalides also uses a Greek-cross plan (see fig. 19-16), the overall shape strongly suggests a debt to Wren's initial proposal for St. Paul's in London (see fig. 19-24). From the beginning, Soufflot intended his church to have long arms and to treat the interior as a classical colonnade supporting an entablature, rather than as a traditional arcade. He eventually resolved to enlarge the dome. This decision posed formidable problems of vaulting, which he solved with characteristic ingenuity. Interestingly enough, the dome in its final form is also derived from Wren's St. Paul's (see fig. 19-21), not Hardouin-Mansart's Invalides as one might expect, which further indicates England's new importance for Continental architects. Although he never crossed the Channel, Soufflot had personal ties to England, and could easily have known Wren's designs from engravings issued in 1726 and 1756. In fact, the resemblance between Ste.-Geneviève and the initial proposal for St. Paul's becomes obvious when the illustration in figure 19-24 is viewed in mirror-image, which reverses the design just as the engraving after it does. The English connection also helps to explain why the smooth, sparsely decorated facade is closer to Chiswick House (which was published by its co-designer, William Kent, in his book on Inigo Jones of 1727) than to any French building. It is an indication of the appeal Chiswick had for French rationalists that Voltaire had admired it during his English exile of 1721–26.

From this coolly precise exterior we would never suspect that Soufflot also had a strong interest in Gothic churches. He admired them, not for the seeming miracles they perform but for their structural elegance—a rationalist version of Guarini's point of view (see fig. 17-26). Ste.-Geneviève fulfills Soufflot's ideal, conceived early in his career, "to combine the classic orders with the lightness so admirably displayed by certain Gothic buildings." In this regard, he was responding partly to Laugier and other theorists who advocated a union of these seemingly incompatible styles. Soufflot studied Gothic architecture and its proportions in detail. He even constructed a special device to test the strength of stone in order to understand the Gothic structural system, which he used to support the massive dome. However, the buttresses at the four corners remain completely hidden from view by a parapet in order not to disturb the insistent classicism inside and out.

Ste.-Geneviève remains the great architectural statement of the rationalist movement. Unfortunately, the windows were walled in at the suggestion of the critic-theorist Antoine Quatremère de Quincy (1755–1849) in 1791–93 to make the building more "appropriate" for a national monument. The remodeling destroyed the light-filled interior and emphasized the abstract severity of the facade. Soon after being rededicated as the Panthéon, it received the ashes of the Enlightenment philosophers Voltaire and Rousseau, and eventually those of the author Victor Hugo. As the Panthéon, the building underwent numerous modifications during the nineteenth century that reflect the turbulent politics of the era. At the direction of Napoleon, Soufflot's pupil Jean-Baptiste Rondelet (1743–1829) redesigned the marble flooring and made changes to the crypt so that it could accommodate the remains of military heroes. Under the Restoration the building was reconsecrated as a church, and a fresco, *The Apotheosis of Louis XVIII,* was added to the dome by Baron Gros (see page 694). Finally, during the July Monarchy it was restored to its role as the Panthéon, and the pediment was replaced in the 1830s with an entirely new one by Pierre-Jean David d'Angers (1788–1856) representing The Nation Distributing Laurel Wreaths to Great Men with the Help of Liberty and History.

ÉTIENNE-LOUIS BOULLÉE.

Étienne-Louis Boullée (1728–1799) was half a generation younger than Soufflot and even more daring. A painter who retired early, he built little other than private residences, but his teaching at the Royal Academy, where he was Legeay's student and successor, helped to create a tradition of visionary architecture that flourished during the last third of the century and the early years of the next. [See Primary Sources, no. 64, page 963.] Boullée's ideal was an architecture of "majestic nobility," an effect he sought to achieve by combining huge, simple masses. Most of his designs were for structures on a scale so enormous that they could hardly be built even today. His ideas were strongly influenced by the theories of Jacques-François Blondel, with whom he also studied, particularly the concept of varying the compositions of different building types according to their social character.

Boullée hailed the sphere as the perfect form, since no trick of perspective can alter its appearance, except its apparent size. Thus he designed a memorial to Isaac Newton as a gigantic hollow sphere, mirroring the universe (fig. 21-17). "O Newton!" he exclaimed, "I conceived the idea of surrounding you with your discovery, and thus, somehow, of surrounding you with yourself." The interior was to be bare, apart from an empty sarcophagus symbolizing the mortal remains of the great man. However, the surface of its upper half would be pierced by countless small holes, allowing points of light meant to create the illusion of stars. Bathed in deep shadow, Boullée's plan for the memorial to Newton has a striking pictorialism inspired in part by the *Prison Caprices* of Piranesi (see fig. 20-27). Plans such as this have a utopian grandeur that dwarfs the boldest ambitions of earlier architects. Largely forgotten during most of the nineteenth century, Boullée was rediscovered in the early twentieth, when architects again dared to "think the unthinkable."

CLAUDE-NICOLAS LEDOUX.

Although he, too, was a pupil of Blondel, Claude-Nicolas Ledoux (1736–1806) was the opposite of Boullée. He was an architect who built much and turned to theory only late in his career. Yet his work quickly developed visionary qualities that are readily apparent in his most important achievement, the 50 tollgates he designed for the new walls around Paris in 1785–89, of which only four still exist. (The rest were torn down during the French Revolution.) Our example (fig. 21-18) shows a remarkable sense of geometry placed at the service of an extraordinary imagination. Ledoux has mounted a huge rotunda on a square base, which is entered through a Greek portico supported by pillars instead of columns. (All four sides are identical in appearance.) Although the structure was derived from antiquity via Palladio, the effect is anything but classical. Visually the portico seems almost crushed by the burden of the rotunda,

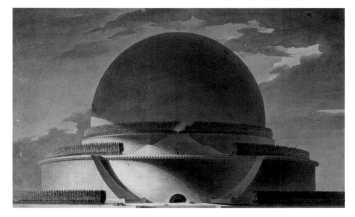

21-17. Étienne-Louis Boullée. *Project for a Memorial to Isaac Newton.* 1784. Ink and wash drawing, 15½ x 25½" (39.4 x 64.8 cm). Bibliothèque Nationale, Paris

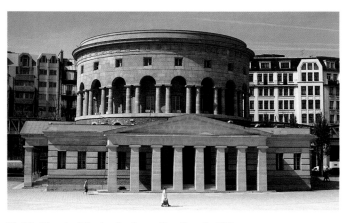

21-18. Claude-Nicolas Ledoux. Barrière de Villette (after restoration), Paris. 1785–89

whose massiveness is barely relieved by the strangely medieval-looking screen of arches over paired columns (compare fig. 10-17). The radically simplified forms and decidedly odd proportions are a critique of all earlier examples of the same type, from the Pantheon (see fig. 7-15) through Soufflot's Ste.-Geneviève (see fig. 21-16). (Compare also figs. 12-22, 14-26, 19-15, and 21-14.) The building, nearly Mannerist in its gestures, is among the most peculiar of any before Frank Lloyd Wright's Guggenheim Museum (see fig. 26-39), which may be regarded as its spiritual descendant.

Neoclassicism and the Antique

The mid-eighteenth century was greatly stirred by two experiences: the rediscovery of Greek art as the original source of classical style, and the excavations at Herculaneum and Pompeii in 1738 and 1748, which for the first time revealed the daily life of the ancient Romans and the full range of their arts and crafts. Richly illustrated books about the Akropolis at Athens, the temples at Paestum, and the finds at Herculaneum and Pompeii were published in England and France. Archaeology caught everyone's imagination. From this enthusiasm came a new revival style of interior decoration. The Greek phase proved necessarily limited, as only a narrow range of household furnishings was known at

second hand from vase paintings and sculpture, such as the *Grave Stele of Hegeso* (see fig. 5-60). When they wanted to work in a Greek style, designers turned chiefly to architecture, whose vocabulary could be readily adapted to large pieces of furniture, where it was combined with Roman elements. Thus decorators employed, for the most part, a classicism of particulars.

ROBERT ADAM. The Neoclassical style was epitomized by the work of the Englishman Robert Adam (1728–1792). His friendship with Piranesi in Rome reinforced Adam's goal of arriving at a personal style based on the antique without slavishly imitating it. He was also influenced by Clérisseau, with whom he measured the palace of Diocletian at Split (see fig. 7-24). His genius is seen most fully in the interiors he designed in the 1760s for palatial homes, which take the style of Lord Burlington and William Kent as their point of departure. Most are remodelings of or additions to existing homes. Because Adam commanded an extraordinarily wide vocabulary, including the Gothic, each room is different in both shape and design. Yet the syntax, which treats classicism with remarkable richness and flexibility, remains distinctive to him. The library wing he added to Kenwood (fig. 21-19) shows Adam at his finest. It is covered with a barrel vault connected at either end to an apse that is separated by a screen of Corinthian columns.

NEOCLASSICAL MUSIC

Neoclassicism and *Sturm und Drang* (see box page 683) were as important to music as they were to theater and literature. The leading representative of the former was Christoph Willibald Glück (1714–1787). Glück wrote two operas, *Orfeo ed Euridice* (1762) and *Alceste* (1767) with the poet Raniero Calzabigi (1714–1795), who was influenced by Rameau's operas during a sojourn in Paris. They sought to correct the excesses of Italian opera through "a beautiful simplicity" and to "confine music to its proper function of serving the poetry for the expression and the situation of the plot." Though originally produced in Vienna, which had become the opera capital of Europe, the two operas enjoyed greater success in Paris, where classicism was an uninterrupted tradition. Glück's operas have a nobility and depth of feeling that hark back to Monteverdi, and a classicism and pageantry worthy of Lully and Rameau. The subject of both works is the immortality of love, which conquers even death. Thanks in good measure to the *Orfeo's* popularity, Jean-François Peyron (1744–1814), the only serious rival of Jacques-Louis David (see pages 673–76), made it the subject of his first important commission from Louis XVI in 1785. (The painting is now in the Louvre.)

Carl Philipp Emanuel Bach (1714–1788), a son of Johann Sebastian Bach (see box page 636), served for nearly 30 years at the Berlin court of Frederick the Great (1712–1786), himself a very able composer. Unlike his illustrious father, the younger Bach loathed counterpoint. The widespread reaction against the complexities of counterpoint may be likened to the call for natural morality by Bach's exact contemporary, the philosopher

Jean-Jacques Rousseau (1712–1778). Bach nevertheless adopted a conservative style that suited his patron's taste. Upon being appointed music director of Hamburg, one of the most important posts in Germany, he felt free to pursue a direct, expressive style that sometimes shows a debt to his predecessor there, Georg Philipp Telemann. His first Hamburg symphonies exemplify *Sturm und Drang* in music: they are full of extremes, with brooding, sighing, slow movements sandwiched between dynamic fast ones characterized by irregular rhythms and emotional outbursts that startle the listener. Their limitation, and it is a significant one, is the composer's disregard for form, which prevented him from developing them further.

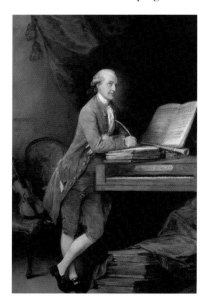

Thomas Gainsborough. *Portrait of Johann Christian Fischer.* 1780. Oil on canvas, 90 x 59½" (228.6 x 150.5 cm). The Royal Collection, London

© HER MAJESTY ELIZABETH II

The basic scheme, although Roman in origin (compare fig. 7-21), comes from Palladio (see pages 500–502). Amazingly, it had been anticipated more than 40 years earlier by Johann Fischer von Erlach (see pages 621–22), who no doubt used the same source.

Adam was concerned above all with movement, but this idea must be understood not in terms of Baroque dynamism or Rococo ornamentation but as the careful balance of varied shapes and proportions. The play of semicircles, half-domes, and arches lends an air of festive grace to the room. The library thus provides an apt setting for "the parade, the convenience, and the social pleasures of life," since it was also a place "for receiving company." This intention was in keeping with Adam's personality, which was at ease with the aristocratic circles in which he moved. The ceiling owes much of its charm to the paintings by Antonio Zucchi (1762–1795), later the husband of Angelica Kauffmann (see page 679), who also worked for Adam, and to the stucco ornament by Adam's plasterer Joseph Rose, which was adapted from newly discovered Roman examples. The color, too, was in daring contrast to the stark white that was widely preferred for interiors at the time. The effect, stately yet intimate, echoes the delicacy of Roco-

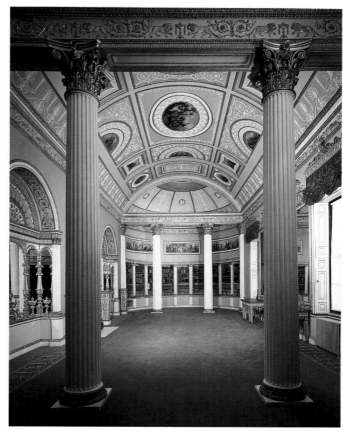

(RIGHT) 21-19. Robert Adam. The Library, Kenwood, London. 1767–69

Sturm und Drang influenced the middle symphonies written by Franz Joseph Haydn (1732–1809) in 1771–74. He spent almost his entire career at the estate of the Esterházys south of Vienna, where he had a small but excellent ensemble of instrumentalists and singers in the service of an enlightened if demanding patron. Haydn became the most famous composer of his era and was called to Paris (1785–86) and London (1790, 1794), where he created symphonies of unrivaled sophistication and richness. He was no less a master of the string quartet, which he invented and wrote in large numbers, all of them marked by unprecedented variety, formal mastery, and refined feeling. Although less perfectly formed than Mozart's (see below), Haydn's late piano sonatas show considerable daring and imagination, qualities that had a marked impact on the "lesser" ones of his most celebrated pupil, Ludwig von Beethoven (see box page 722). Also surprisingly influential on Beethoven's choral works were Haydn's oratorios, which were modeled on Handel's (see box pages 636–37), with German texts by Baron Gottfried von Swieten of Vienna, who commissioned them: *The Creation* (1798), based on John Milton's *Paradise Lost,* and *The Seasons* (1801), adapted from James Thomson's poem (1726–30) of the same name. They maintain the eighteenth-century view of an orderly cosmos and natural social order created by a benevolent God for the good of humanity, although it is open to question whether the composer himself shared this belief.

Haydn became a close friend of Wolfgang Amadeus Mozart (1756–1791), despite their great difference in age, temperament, and outlook. A child prodigy, Mozart received a rigorous training from his father, Leopold (1719–1787), who took him on tour through the great courts of Europe, where he was exposed to the full range of contemporary music. Mozart failed in his efforts to gain a major court appointment; deprived of this measure of security, he became a prolific composer for the open market, putting the stamp of his individual genius on nearly everything he wrote. His finest quartets are the six dedicated to Haydn, who declared him the greatest composer alive, while the late symphonies blaze new territory that foreshadow those of the young Beethoven. His numerous concertos for piano, of which he was a virtuoso, combine enchanting lyricism with brilliant technical display. Mozart was a supreme vocal composer, and it is the singing quality of the human voice that underlies his mature work, regardless of instrument. He was also a master of compositional technique, including counterpoint (he had discussed Bach's music with his successor at Leipzig), and his works depend for much of their success on their formal perfection. Indeed, for Mozart, form was the vehicle of expression, which it served to contain, so that there was an ideal, "classical" balance between the two. He was fully sympathetic with the Enlightenment. Its philosophy both informs and burdens his operas, including his acknowledged masterpieces, *The Marriage of Figaro* (1787), based on the play by Pierre-Augustin Beaumarchais (1732–1799), and *Don Giovanni* (1787). Both are a new type of comic opera, called *opera buffa* to distinguish it from traditional serious operas *(opera seria)*, but unlike others of their kind, they have a wonderful humanity and substantial content, thanks in part to the librettos by Mozart's collaborator, Lorenzo Da Ponte (1749–1838).

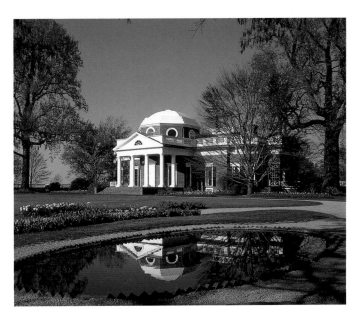

21-20. Thomas Jefferson. Monticello, Charlottesville, Virginia. 1770–84; 1796–1806

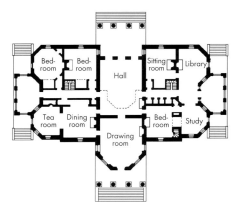

21-21. Plan of Monticello

co interiors (Adam had stayed in Paris in 1754 before going to Rome) but with a characteristically Neoclassical insistence on planar surfaces, symmetry, and geometric precision.

THOMAS JEFFERSON. The Palladianism launched by Lord Burlington spread overseas to the American Colonies, where it became known as the Georgian style after the kings of England who reigned 1714–1830. An example of great distinction is the house of Thomas Jefferson (1743–1826), Monticello (figs. 21-20 and 21-21). Built of brick with wood trim, it is not so doctrinaire a design as Chiswick House. (Note the less compact plan and the numerous windows.) It nevertheless stands as a monument to the Enlightenment ideals of order and harmony, with which Jefferson was fully in agreement. The original plan was adapted from a book of English designs, then gradually modified as Jefferson was exposed to other treatises. The scheme of about 1770 featured an Ionic portico placed over a Doric one and crowned by a pediment. However, the house was remodeled during Jefferson's presidency, and in its final form Monticello has a facade inspired by Palladio (compare fig. 14-26), although the plan itself was modified only slightly. There is a clear separation between the private quarters in the wings and the public areas for receiving and entertaining visitors, which are described by the porch and dome.

Instead of using the Corinthian order favored by Lord Burlington, Jefferson chose the Roman Doric, which Adam had helped to legitimize, although the late eighteenth century came to favor the heavier and more austere Greek Doric. Jefferson was linked indirectly to Adam through Clérisseau, whom he came to know while serving as the American ambassador to France in 1784–88 and whose help he sought in designing the state capitol of Virginia in Richmond in 1785. Jefferson thought out every detail of Monticello, including its relation to the rest of the plantation. The building is carefully placed in its setting, thanks to Jefferson's study of landscape gardening during a visit to England.

THE ROMANTIC MOVEMENT

Of all the "isms" found in Western art of the past two centuries, Romanticism has always been the most difficult to define. It deserves to be termed an "ism" only because its followers (or at least some of them) thought of themselves as being part of a movement. However, they did not leave us anything approaching a definition. Romanticism, it seems, was a certain state of mind rather than the conscious pursuit of a goal or a style. If we try to analyze this state of mind, it breaks down into a series of attitudes, none of which, taken individually, is unique to Romanticism. It is only their particular combination that seems characteristic of the Romantic movement.

How did Romanticism come about? The Enlightenment, paradoxically, liberated not only reason but also its opposite. It helped to create a wave of emotionalism that lasted for the better part of a half-century. The word *Romanticism* derives from the late-eighteenth-century vogue for medieval tales of adventure (such as the legends of King Arthur or the Holy Grail), called "romances" because they were written in a Romance language, not Latin. This interest in the long-neglected "Gothick" past was the sign of a general trend. Those who shared a revulsion against the established social order and religion—against established values of any sort—could either try to found a new order based on their faith in the power of reason, or they could seek release in a craving for emotional experience.

Their common goal was a desire to "return to Nature." The rationalists revered nature as the ultimate source of reason, while the Romantics worshiped it as unbounded, wild, and ever changing. The Romantics believed that evil would disappear if people were only to behave "naturally" and give their impulses free rein. In the name of nature, the Romantics acclaimed liberty, power, love, violence, classical civilization, the Middle Ages, or anything else that stirred them, although actually they exalted emotion as an end in itself. This attitude has motivated some of the noblest, as well as vilest, acts of the modern era. In its most extreme form, Romanticism could be expressed only through direct action, not through works of art. No artist, then, can be a wholehearted Romantic, for the creation of a work of art demands some detachment, self-awareness, and discipline. What William Wordsworth (1770–1850), the great Romantic poet, said of poetry in 1798—that it is "emotion recollected in tranquility"—applies also to the visual arts.

To cast fleeting experience into permanent form, Romantic artists needed a style. But since they were in revolt against the old order, this could not be the established style of the time. It had to come from some phase of the past to which they felt linked by "elective affinity" (another Romantic concept). Romanticism thus favored the revival not of one style but of a potentially unlimited number of styles. In fact, the rediscovery and use of forms that previously had been neglected or scorned evolved into a stylistic principle in itself. Revivals thus became the "style" of Romanticism in art, as they did, to a certain degree, in literature and music.

Seen in this context, Neoclassicism was simply the first phase of Romanticism, a revival that continued all the way through the nineteenth century and thus ultimately came to represent conservative taste. Perhaps it is best, then, to think of the two as sides of the same modern coin. If we maintain the distinction between them, it is because Neoclassicism overshadowed the other Romantic revivals until about 1800, and because the Enlightenment was dedicated to the cause of liberty as against the cult of the individual, represented by the Romantic hero.

PAINTING

It is one of the many contradictions of Romantic art that, despite the desire for complete freedom of individual creativity, it became art for the rising professional and commercial class. The upper middle class dominated nineteenth-century society and replaced state commissions and aristocratic patronage as the most important source of support for artists. Painting remains the greatest creative achievement of Romanticism in the visual arts because, being less expensive, it was less dependent than architecture or sculpture on public approval. It held a greater appeal for the individualism of the Romantic artist as well. Moreover, it could better accommodate the themes and ideas of Romantic literature. Romantic painting was not essentially illustrative. Nevertheless, the literature of both past and present became a more important source of inspiration for painters than ever before. It provided a new range of subjects, emotions, and attitudes. Romantic writers, in turn, often saw nature with a painter's eye. Many had a strong interest in art criticism and theory. Some, notably the German poet Johann Wolfgang von Goethe and the French novelist Victor Hugo, were capable draftsmen. And William Blake cast his visions in both pictorial and written form (see page 707). Art and literature thus have a complex relationship within the Romantic movement.

Spain

FRANCISCO GOYA. We begin with the great Spanish painter Francisco Goya (1746–1828), David's contemporary and the only artist of the age who may be called a genius without hesitation. When Goya first arrived in Madrid in 1766, he found both Mengs and Tiepolo working there. He was much impressed with Tiepolo (see page 626), whom he must have recognized immediately as the greater of the two artists. (Spain had produced no painters of significance for more than a century.) Goya's early works are in a delightful late Rococo vein that reflects the influence of Tiepolo,

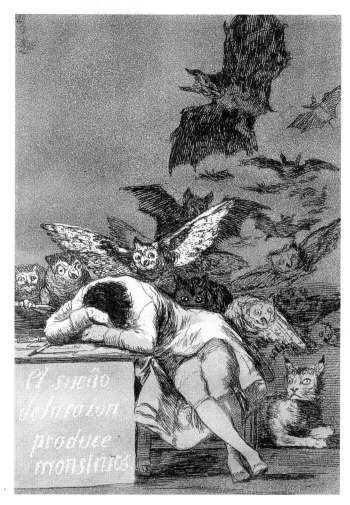

21-22. Francisco Goya. *The Sleep of Reason Produces Monsters,* from *Los Caprichos.* c. 1798. Etching and aquatint, 8½ x 6" (21.6 x 15.2 cm). The Metropolitan Museum of Art, New York

as well as the French Rococo. He ignored the growing Neoclassical trend during his brief visit to Rome five years later.

In the 1780s, however, Goya became more of a libertarian. His involvement with Enlightenment thought is best seen in his etchings, which made him the most important printmaker since Rembrandt. Published in series at intervals throughout his career, they ridicule human folly from the same moral viewpoint as Hogarth. But what a vast difference separates the two artists! Although suggested by proverbs and popular superstitions, many of Goya's prints defy exact analysis. He creates terrifying scenes such as *The Sleep of Reason Produces Monsters* from the series *Los Caprichos* of the late 1790s (fig. 21-22). The subtitle, added later, expands on the meaning of the image without entirely explaining it. "Imagination abandoned by reason produces impossible monsters; united with her, she is the mother of the arts." The artist, shrinking from the assault of his visions, suffers from the same disorder as the figure in Dürer's *Melencolia I* (see fig. 16-9), but his paralysis is psychological rather than conceptual. The image belongs to that realm of imagined horror which we will meet in Fuseli's *The Nightmare* (see fig. 21-43) but is infinitely more compelling. Goya's etching owes part of its success to the technique of **aquatint**, which he was the first to take advantage of fully, although he did not invent it (see box page 694).

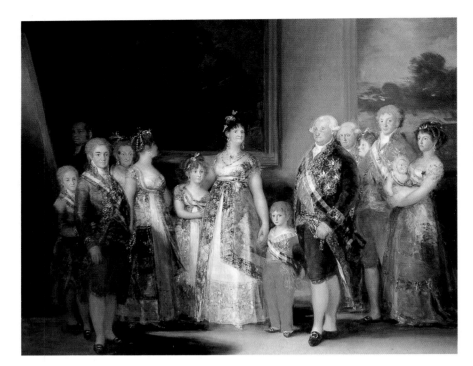

21-23. Francisco Goya. *The Family of Charles IV.* 1800. Oil on canvas, 9'2" x 11' (2.79 x 3.35 m). Museo del Prado, Madrid

Goya surely sympathized with the French Revolution, and not with the king of Spain, who had joined other monarchs in war against the young Republic. Yet he was highly regarded at court, where he was appointed painter to the king in 1799. Goya now abandoned the Rococo for a Neo-Baroque style based on Velázquez and Rembrandt, the masters he had come to admire most. It is this Neo-Baroque style that announces the arrival of Romanticism.

The Family of Charles IV (fig. 21-23), Goya's largest royal portrait, echoes Velázquez's *The Maids of Honor* (see fig. 17-35). The entire clan has come to visit the artist, who is painting in one of the picture galleries of the palace. As in Velázquez's painting, shadowy canvases hang behind the group and the light pours in from the side. The brushwork has a sparkle, the color a radiance rivaling Velázquez's. Goya does not use the Caravaggesque Neoclassicism of David, but his painting has more in common with David's work than we might think. Like David, he practices a revival style and, in his way, is equally devoted to the unvarnished truth: he uses the Neo-Baroque of Romanticism to unmask the royal family.

Psychologically, *The Family of Charles IV* is almost shockingly modern. No longer shielded by the polite conventions of Baroque court portraiture, the inner being of these individuals has been laid bare with pitiless honesty. They are like a collection of ghosts. We see the frightened children, the bloated king, and—in a master stroke of sardonic humor—the grotesquely vulgar queen, posed like Velázquez's Princess Margarita. (Note the left arm and the turn of the head.) How could Goya get away with this seeming caricature? Was the royal family so dazzled by the splendid painting of their costumes that they failed to realize what he had done to them? Goya, we realize, must have painted them as they saw themselves, while unveiling the deeper truth for all the world to see.

When Napoleon's armies occupied Spain in 1808, Goya and many other Spaniards hoped that the conquerors would bring the liberal reforms so badly needed. The barbaric behavior of the French troops crushed that dream and led to a popular resistance of equal savagery. Many of Goya's works from 1810 to 1815 reflect this bitter experience. The greatest is a pair of large paintings done in 1814 at his request for the newly restored king Ferdinand VII. Their purpose was to commemorate the heroic actions of the Spanish people during the struggle for independence from France. He chose two events that ignited the prolonged guerrilla war against the occupying forces. *The Second of May, 1808* (fig. 21-24) shows a group of Madrid citizens attacking a detachment of French troops. The soldiers took revenge by murdering the family of bankers (to whom the artist was related by marriage) and servants of the house from which the shot that killed the fallen Mamaluke on horseback was fired. *The Third of May, 1808* (fig. 21-25) represents the execution of rioters the following night. It is doubtful that Goya witnessed either incident, although he made some attempt at topographical accuracy. In characteristically Romantic fashion, he has taken liberties with both scenes for the sake of a higher, "poetic" truth. Together these canvases are the models for the scenes of violence and combat taken up by the French painters Théodore Géricault and Eugène Delacroix (compare figs. 21-28 and 21-33). In *The Second of May,* the blazing color, and broad, fluid brushwork are more Neo-Baroque than ever in order to heighten the drama. In *The Third of May,* the dramatic nocturnal light, so reminiscent of El Greco (compare fig. 14-11), gives the picture the emotional intensity of religious art, but these martyrs are dying for Liberty, not the Kingdom of Heaven. Nor are their executioners the agents of Satan but of political tyranny. They are a formation of faceless killers, completely indifferent to their victims' defiance and despair. The same scene was

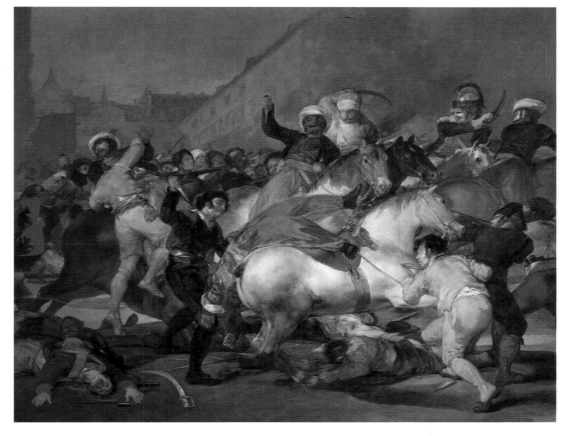

21-24. Francisco Goya.
The Second of May, 1808.
1814. Oil on canvas,
8'9" x 11'4"
(2.67 x 3.45 m).
Museo del Prado,
Madrid

(BELOW) 21-25.
Francisco Goya.
The Third of May, 1808.
1814. Oil on canvas,
8'9" x 13'4" (2.67 x 4.06 m).
Museo del Prado,
Madrid

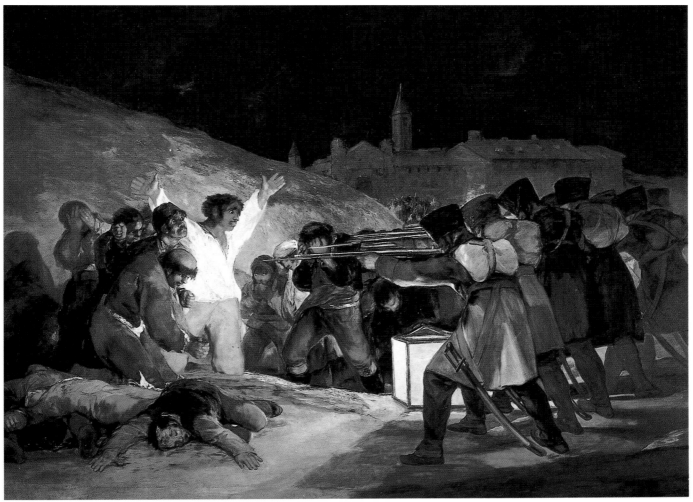

During the eighteenth century, the range of printmaking was enlarged by the addition of two techniques on copperplates. The first, aquatint, is an extension of etching. It involves melting resin powder on the plate, which leaves a fine crackle pattern exposed to the acid bath. The result is an even, medium tone similar to that of a wash drawing. The other, called mezzotint, is found almost exclusively in portrait and other reproductive engravings. It utilizes a cylindrical rocker covered with tiny teeth to pit the surface of the plate, providing velvety grays and rich blacks on the finished print.

The first completely new print medium, however, was lithography. Invented in Germany shortly before 1800 by Alois Senefelder, it is the most important of the planographic processes, that is, processes that produce prints from a flat surface. Using a greasy crayon or ink, called *tusche,* the artist draws or brushes the design onto a special lithographic stone; alternatively, it can be transferred from paper. (Zinc and aluminum plates have also been used for lithographic printing.) Once the design is fixed by an acid wash, the surface is dampened, then rolled with oily ink, which adheres to the greasy design but is repelled by water. The print is made by pressing moistened paper under light pressure against the stone. Because this technique allows for a limitless number of prints to be pulled relatively cheaply, lithography has been closely associated from the beginning with commercial printing and the popular press.

to be repeated countless times in modern history. With the prophecy of genius, Goya created an image that has become a terrifying symbol of our era.

After the defeat of Napoleon, the Spanish monarchy instituted a new wave of repression, and Goya withdrew more and more into a private world, isolated as well by his growing deafness. Finally, in 1824, he went into voluntary exile. After a brief stay in Paris, Goya settled in Bordeaux, where he died a few years later. His importance for the Neo-Baroque Romantic painters of France is affirmed by Delacroix, the greatest of them all (see pages 698–702), who said that the ideal style would be a combination of Michelangelo's and Goya's art. Later, Edouard Manet turned to him as a source as well (see page 740).

France

ANNE-LOUIS GIRODET. By 1795 Neoclassicism in France had largely run its course, and rapidly lost its purity and rigor. Within a few years French Romantic painting began to emerge among the Primitif faction of Jacques-Louis David's studio. These rebellious students simplified his severe Neoclassicism even more by turning to the linear designs of Greek and Etruscan vase painting, and to the unadorned style of the Italian Early Renaissance. They further undermined Neoclassicism by preferring subjects whose appeal was primarily emotional rather than intellectual. Their sources were not the classical authors such as Horace or Ovid but the Bible, Homer, Ossian (the legendary Gaelic bard whose poems were forged by James Macpherson in the eighteenth century), and Romantic literature—anything that excited the imagination.

The ablest, as well as most radical, member of the group was Anne-Louis Girodet-Trioson (1767–1824), whose *Funeral of Atala* (fig. 21-26) has all the hallmarks of the Primitif style. Without abandoning his teacher's demanding technique, he reduces the composition to a rhythmic play of lines across the picture plane. The artist emphasizes simple shapes with strong contours, which are further accentuated by the strong highlights. The scene is taken from the wildly popular *Atala, or The Love of Two Savages*

in the Desert by François-René de Chateaubriand, one of the first Romantic authors and later foreign minister of France. In typical Romantic fashion, the novel was never intended to be finished; instead, it was published as "excerpts" in 1801. The story has the character of a classical idyll, but with a Romantic taste for the exotic and a religious theme that reflects the Catholic renewal in France. These elements are seen in Girodet's canvas, which treats the burial of the virtuous young woman in the cave like the entombment of a Christian martyr. (Note the cross on the hillside.) Yet unlike the secular martyrdom memorialized by David in *The Death of Marat* (see fig. 21-3), the painting is a celebration of sentiment. Girodet uses an eerie light to evoke the elegiac mood that is his real aim.

ANTOINE GROS. With its exciting glamour and its adventurous conquests in remote parts of the world, the reign of Napoleon (which lasted from 1799 to 1815, with one interruption) gave rise to French Romanticism. David became an ardent admirer of Napoleon and executed several large pictures glorifying the emperor. As a portrayer of the Napoleonic myth, however, he was partially eclipsed by artists who had been his students. Some of them found the style of David too confining and fostered a Baroque revival to capture the excitement of the age. Antoine-Jean Gros (1771–1835), David's favorite pupil, shows us Napoleon as a Christlike leader and healer (fig. 21-27). During the siege of Jaffa on the Mediterranean coast in 1799, the bubonic plague broke out. To calm the panic that followed, the general entered the pesthouse and walked fearlessly among the patients—an event that soon became legendary. The painting is a carefully calculated piece of propaganda, which ignores the fact that Napoleon had ordered the execution of hundreds of prisoners during the epidemic.

The central group is a play on the Doubting of St. Thomas (see figs. 9-29 and 12-18), but now the roles are reversed. This simple but ingenious device raises Napoleon to an almost godlike status even before he became emperor toward the end of 1804, the year the picture was painted. The focus is on the general's courage in touching the sick and the dying. (Note the officer covering his face

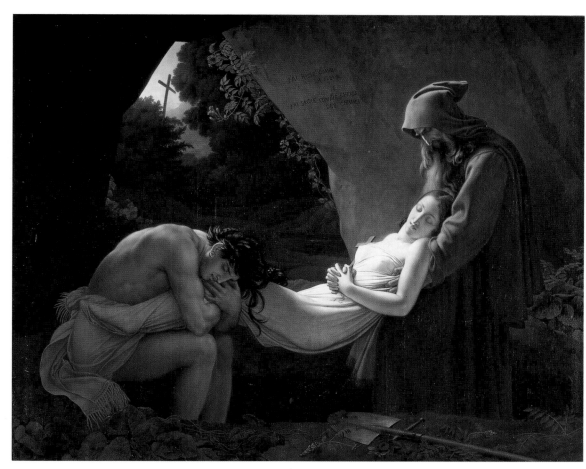

21-26. Anne-Louis Girodet-Trioson. *The Funeral of Atala.* 1808. Oil on canvas, 5'5¾" x 6'10⅝" (1.67 x 2.10 m). Musée du Louvre, Paris

(BELOW) 21-27. Antoine-Jean Gros. *Napoleon in the Pesthouse at Jaffa, 11 March 1799.* 1804. Oil on canvas, 17'5½" x 23'7½" (5.32 x 7.20 m). Musée du Louvre, Paris

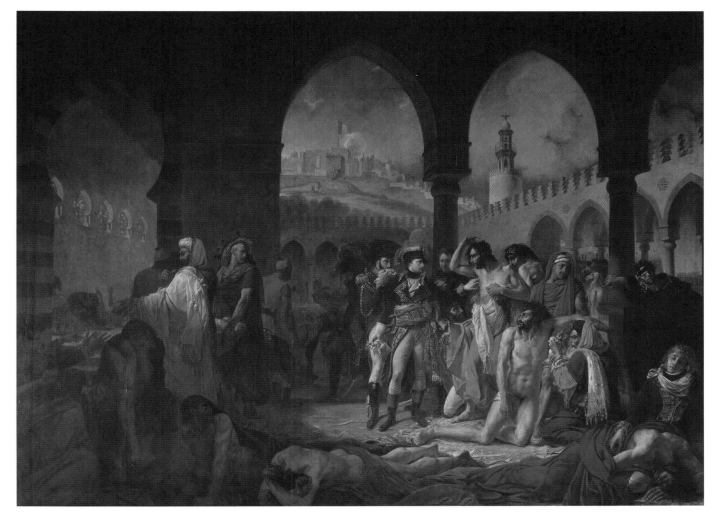

with a kerchief against the odor.) Many of them are paraphrased from Michelangelo's *Last Judgment* (see fig. 13-20). The burning ruins in the background heighten the apocalyptic aura of the scene. But what really excited the artist's imagination was the alien surroundings. Napoleon opened up Egypt and the Near East for the first time in centuries, and this led to the European colonization of North Africa. *Napoleon in the Pesthouse at Jaffa, 11 March 1799,* is one of the first symptoms of Orientalism: the Romantic fascination with the Arab world that preoccupied European artists and writers throughout most of the nineteenth century. The artist cannot resist dwelling on the foreign costumes and architecture, which, strangely enough, paraphrases the classical setting in an early canvas by his master, David.

After Napoleon's empire collapsed, David spent his last years in exile in Brussels. There his major works were playfully amorous subjects, which were drawn from ancient myths and legends and painted in a coolly sensuous Neo-Mannerist style he had developed in Paris. He turned his pupils over to Gros, whom he urged to return to Neoclassical orthodoxy. Much as Gros respected his teacher's doctrines, his emotional nature drew him to the color and drama of the Baroque. He remained torn between academic principles and his pictorial instincts. As a result, he never achieved David's authority and ended his life by suicide.

THÉODORE GÉRICAULT. The Neo-Baroque trend initiated in France by Gros stirred the imagination of many talented younger artists. The chief heroes of Théodore Géricault (1791–1824), apart from Gros, were Michelangelo and the great Baroque masters. Géricault painted his most ambitious work, *The Raft of the "Medusa"* (fig. 21-28), in response to a political scandal and a modern tragedy of epic proportions. The *Medusa,* a government vessel, had foundered off the West African coast with hundreds of men on board. Only a handful were rescued, after many days on a makeshift raft that had been set adrift by the ship's heartless captain and officers. The event attracted Géricault's attention because, like many French liberals, he opposed the monarchy, which was restored after Napoleon. He went to extraordinary lengths in trying to achieve a maximum of authenticity. He interviewed survivors, had a model of the raft built, and even studied corpses in the morgue. This search for uncompromising truth is like David's, and *The Raft of the "Medusa"* is indeed remarkable for its powerfully realistic detail. Yet these preparations were subordinate in the end to the spirit of heroic drama that dominates the canvas.

Géricault depicts the moment when the rescue ship is first sighted. From the bodies of the dead and dying in the foreground, the composition is built up to a climax in the group that supports

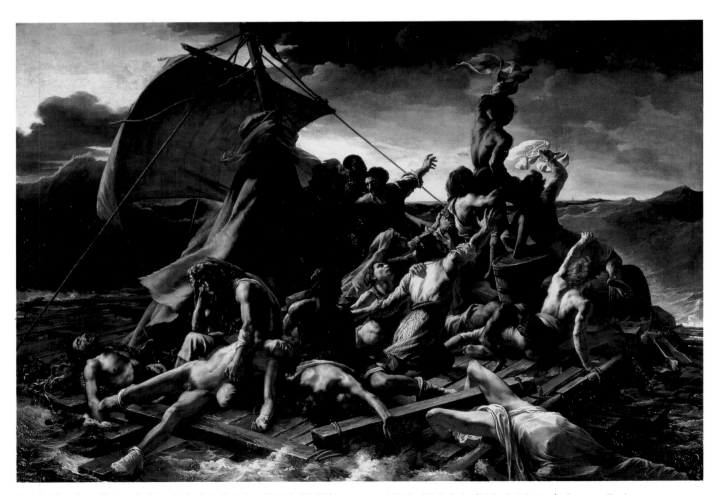

21-28. Théodore Géricault. *The Raft of the "Medusa."* 1818–19. Oil on canvas, 16'1" x 23'6" (4.9 x 7.16 m). Musée du Louvre, Paris

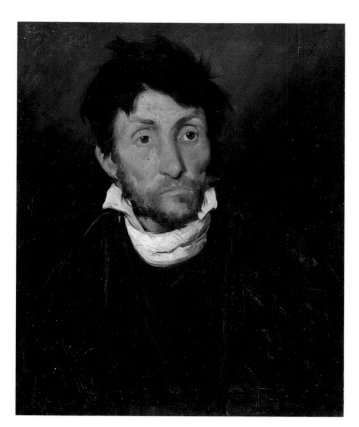

21-29. Théodore Géricault. *The Madman.* 1821–24. Oil on canvas, 24 x 20" (61 x 50.8 cm). Museum voor Schone Kunsten, Ghent, Belgium

the frantically waving black man, so that the forward surge of the survivors parallels the movement of the raft itself. In 1820 the artist took the monumental canvas on a traveling exhibit to England, in the hope that this theme of "man against the elements" would have strong appeal across the Channel, where Copley had painted *Watson and the Shark* 40 years before (see fig. 21-7).

Géricault's numerous studies for *The Raft of the "Medusa"* had taught him how to explore extremes of the human condition scarcely touched by earlier artists, even Gros. He went now not only to the morgue, but also to the insane asylum of Paris. There he became a friend of Dr. Georget, a pioneer in modern psychiatry, and painted for him a series of portraits of individual patients to illustrate various types of derangement. The study in figure 21-29 has an immediacy that recalls Frans Hals, but Géricault's sympathy toward his subject is in sharp contrast with *Malle Babbe* (see fig. 18-12). This ability to see the victims of mental disease as fellow human beings, not as accursed or bewitched outcasts, is one of the noblest fruits of the Romantic movement.

Goya, too, had ventured into an insane asylum a few years earlier, but rendered it as a madhouse, in keeping with his pessimistic view of human nature. The two artists shared other subjects that few had taken up before, including horses and blacksmiths. Géricault, himself an enthusiastic horseman, became interested in the British animal painters such as George Stubbs (see fig. 21-9) during his stay in England. Sadly, he was to die at an early age after a riding accident.

JEAN-AUGUSTE INGRES. The leadership of David's school ultimately fell to his pupil Jean-Auguste-Dominique Ingres (1780–1867), whose early sympathies were with the Primitifs. Although he painted impressive portraits of Napoleon early in his career, Ingres largely missed out on the formation of Romantic painting in France, because he went to Italy in 1806 and remained for 18 years. After his return he became the high priest of the Davidian tradition, which he defended from the attacks of younger artists. [See Primary Sources, no. 65, page 964.] What had been a revolutionary style only half a century earlier now became rigid dogma, endorsed by the government and backed by the weight of conservative opinion.

Ingres is usually called a neoclassicist, and his opponents Romantics. Actually, both factions stood for aspects of French Romanticism after 1800: the Neoclassical phase, with Ingres as the last important survivor, and the Neo-Baroque, announced by Baron Gros. Indeed, the two seem so interrelated that we should prefer a single name for both if a suitable one could be found. ("Romantic Classicism," which is appropriate only to the classical camp, has not won wide acceptance.) The two sides seemed to revive the old quarrel between Poussinistes and Rubénistes (see page 612). The original Poussinistes had never quite practiced what they preached, and Ingres' views, too, were far more doctrinaire than his pictures.

Ingres always held that drawing was superior to painting, yet his canvas *Odalisque with a Slave* (fig. 21-30) reveals an exquisite sense of color. Instead of merely tinting his design, he sets off the petal-smooth limbs of this Oriental Venus (**odalisque** is a Turkish word for a harem slave girl) with a dazzling array of transparent tones and rich textures. The poetic mood, filled with the enchantment of the *Thousand and One Nights,* is as important as the finely balanced composition in holding the picture together. The exotic subject is characteristic of the Romantic movement. Despite Ingres' professed worship of Raphael, this nude hardly embodies a classical ideal of beauty. Her elongated proportions, languid grace, and strange mixture of coolness and voluptuousness remind us of Parmigianino's figures (compare fig. 14-4). Whether he admitted it or not, Ingres was just as Romantic as his great rival, Eugène Delacroix, only in a different way (compare fig. 21-34).

History painting as defined by Poussin remained Ingres' lifelong ambition, but he had great difficulty with it. Portraiture, which he pretended to dislike, was his strongest gift and his steadiest source of income. He was, in fact, the last great professional in a field soon to be dominated by the camera. Ingres' portrait of the banker Louis-François Bertin (fig. 21-31) at first glance looks like a kind of "super-photograph," but this impression is deceptive. Comparing it with the preliminary pencil drawing (fig. 21-32), we realize how much interpretation the portrait contains. The drawing, quick, sure, and precise, is a masterpiece of detached observation. However, the painting gives the sitter a massive presence and forceful personality by using a few simple devices to adjust the figure. Bertin's pose is shifted slightly to the left, his jacket open to lend the figure greater weight. The position of his powerful hands, which are barely indicated in the drawing, has been changed to convey an almost lionlike strength. Ingres further uses the Caravaggesque Neoclassicism he had inherited from David to introduce slight

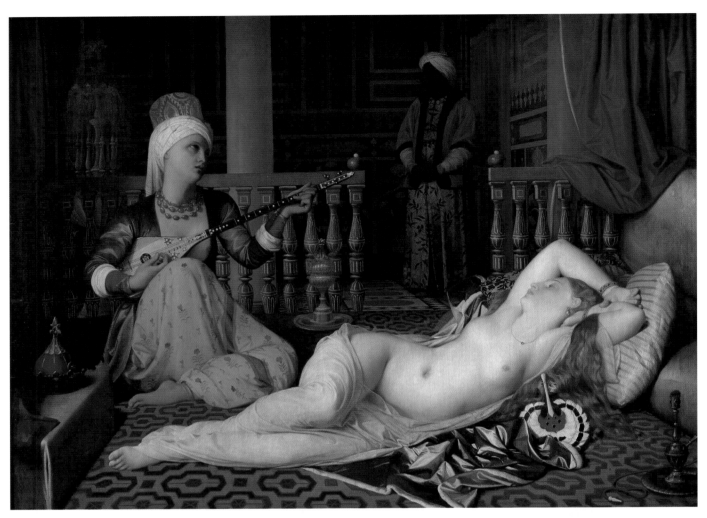

21-30. Jean-Auguste-Dominique Ingres. *Odalisque with a Slave*. 1839–40. Oil on canvas, 28³⁄₈ x 39¹⁄₂" (72.1 x 100.3 cm). Fogg Art Museum, Harvard University Art Museums, Cambridge, Massachusetts

GRENVILLE L. WINTHROP REQUEST

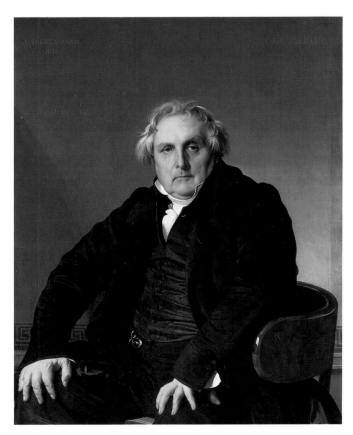

21-31. Jean-Auguste-Dominique Ingres. *Louis-François Bertin*. 1832. Oil on canvas, 46 x 37¹⁄₂" (116.8 x 95.3 cm). Musée du Louvre, Paris

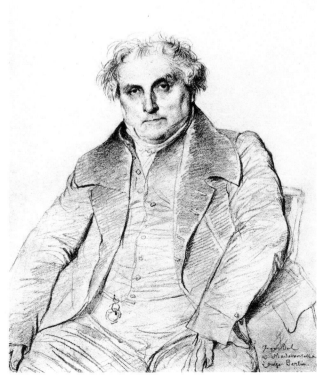

21-32. Jean-Auguste-Dominique Ingres. *Louis-François Bertin*. 1832. Pencil drawing. Musée du Louvre, Paris

changes of light and to emphasize selectively certain features in the face, which now has an almost frightening intensity.

Only Ingres among the Romantics could unify psychological depth and physical accuracy so completely. His followers focused on detailed realism alone and competed vainly with the camera. The Neo-Baroque Romantics, in contrast, emphasized the psychological aspect, so that their portraits tended to become records of the artist's private emotional relationship with the sitter. These are often interesting and moving, but they are no longer portraits in the proper sense of the term.

EUGÈNE DELACROIX. The year 1824 was a turning point for French painting. Géricault died after a riding accident. The first showing in Paris of works by the English Romantic painters, especially John Constable, was a revelation to many French artists (see pages 708–09). Ingres returned to France from Italy and had his first public success. And Eugène Delacroix (1798–1863) established himself as the foremost Neo-Baroque Romantic painter. For the next quarter-century he and Ingres were bitter rivals, and their opposition, fostered by supporters, dominated the artistic scene in Paris. [See Primary Sources, no. 66, page 964.]

To French critics, who had recently begun to struggle with the problem of defining Romanticism in art, Delacroix seemed the first indisputably Romantic painter, and his work helped to crystallize the issues. As a result, Romanticism, which previously had been identified largely with the Germanic theories of the writer Madame de Staël (see box page 714), now became virtually synonymous with modernism. Delacroix occupied a position at its artistic center. As a painter he was comparable to Hector Berlioz in music and to Victor Hugo and Stendhal in literature (see boxes on pages 714 and 722). Like his model Rubens, Delacroix is such a challenging artist that it is not easy to take the full measure of his accomplishments.

Although he studied with a pupil of David, his early paintings reflect his admiration for Gros (who nevertheless called Delacroix's *The Massacre at Chios* "the massacre of painting" when it was exhibited in 1824) and Géricault, whom he knew well. His first mature work is *The Death of Sardanapalus* (fig. 21-33), inspired by Lord Byron's drama in free verse of 1821. Delacroix was above all a literary painter. (He also became the most original—and controversial—illustrator of the age.) If the military hero inspired the early Romantics, it was the cultural hero who touched the imagination

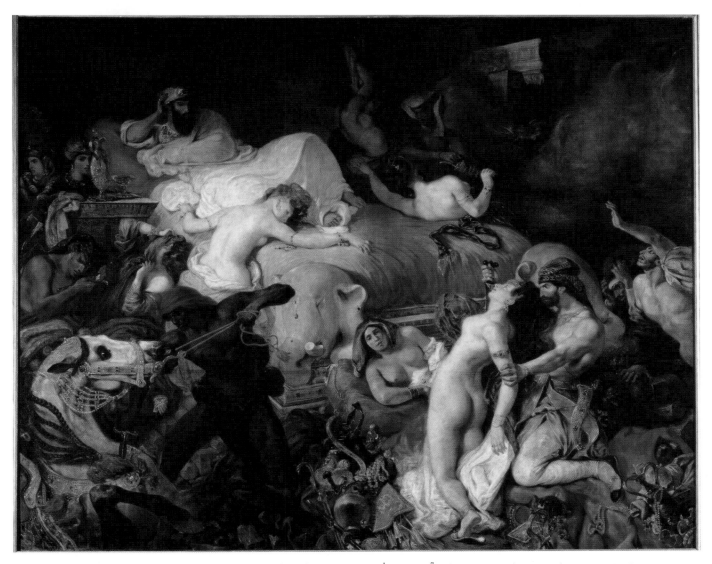

21-33. Eugène Delacroix. *The Death of Sardanapalus*. 1827. Oil on canvas, 12'1½" x 16'2⅞" (3.69 x 4.94 m). Musée du Louvre, Paris

of the generation that arose in the mid-1820s. The glamorous days of Napoleon and his Empire were now only a memory, so that Delacroix had either to go to some remote place or turn to exotic history and literature for the kind of subject that excited his imagination. He often chose writers favored by other Romantic artists: Dante, Shakespeare, Goethe, and Sir Walter Scott. But he was inspired above all by Byron, the archetype of the Romantic, whose valiant death as commander of a regiment at Missolonghi in 1824 during the Greek war of independence from the Turks was mourned by Delacroix as a tragedy. The artist's fascination with all things English was fired by the flood of literature that began to be published in French translations in 1816. It was further kindled by his friendship with Géricault and Gros' pupil Richard Bonington (1802–1828), who also helped to awaken his interest in the Orient. This enthusiasm was cemented when Delacroix, who had learned English as a schoolboy, visited London in 1825.

His journal records that when stuck for a subject, he would turn to the same authors again and again for inspiration. "I should want to spread out some good thick, fat paint on a brown or red canvas. What I would need, then, in finding a subject is to open a book that can inspire me and let its mood guide me. There are those that never fail. The same with engravings. Dante, Lemar-

tine, Byron, Michelangelo." Exactly this sort of thing seems to have happened with the *Sardanapalus,* which, strangely enough, does not illustrate the final scene in Lord Byron's literary play. It instead evokes the hero's death as the artist imagined it. Delacroix's vision of the Orient was based nevertheless almost entirely on Byron's poetry: "The Giaour," "The Bride of Abydos," and "The Siege of Corinth" (which inspired one of Berlioz's operas, as did "The Corsair").

The picture has the apocalyptic intensity of Michelangelo's *Last Judgment* (see fig. 13-20), the nearly superhuman power of Rubens' *Raising of the Cross* (see fig. 18-1), and the extraordinary freedom of Velázquez's late works (see fig. 17-35). Such sources have been combined into an intoxicating mixture of sensuousness and cruelty. As in Rubens' painting, the sea of writhing figures is loosely organized along a rising diagonal. In both, virtually every square inch is covered with action, save for a glimpse into the distant background. The rich color and fluid brushwork show Delacroix to be a Rubéniste of the first order. Earlier he had maintained the primacy of line to enclose form. Here he is more concerned with setting up linear rhythms across the canvas, which requires him to adjust contours in response to each other. As a result, there is a ceaseless movement in which the main organizing

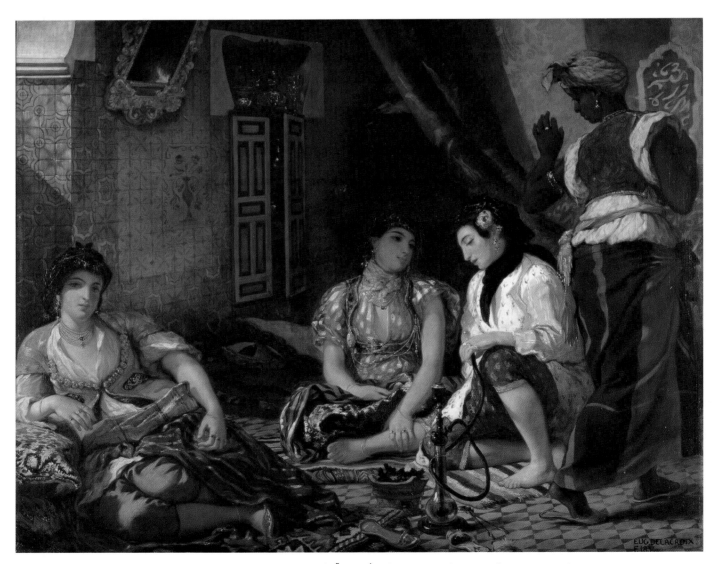

21-34. Eugène Delacroix. *Women of Algiers.* 1834. Oil on canvas, 70⅞ x 90⅛" (180 x 229 cm). Musée du Louvre, Paris

role is played by the cascades of red cloth. No wonder the painting was severely criticized by conservatives for its poor draftsmanship and inconsistent space, for it violates every classical rule. Delacroix realized its flaws, but was willing to sacrifice everything for the sake of effect. While we do not quite accept the scene as authentic, we revel in the sheer splendor of the painting.

Delacroix's sympathy with the Greeks did not prevent him from sharing the enthusiasm of other Romantics for the Orient. He was enchanted by a visit in 1832 to North Africa, where he found a living counterpart of the violent, chivalric, and picturesque past evoked in Romantic literature. His sketches from this trip supplied him with a large repertory of subjects: harem interiors, street scenes, lion hunts. It is fascinating to compare his *Women of Algiers* (fig. 21-34) with Ingres' *Odalisque with a Slave* (see fig. 21-30). In his version, Ingres also celebrates the exotic world of the Near East—alien, seductive, and violent—but how different the result! Delacroix's is based on studies made during a visit to an actual harem in Algiers. The painting has an authenticity even in the details that is clearly missing in Ingres' aromatic confection, although the Arab women were carefully posed using a model in Delacroix's studio and the costumes were reworked. No less important, the intense colors and bright light of Northern Africa made an indelible impression on the artist, whose palette underwent a major change.

Delacroix's creativity reached its peak in the years around 1840. During this extraordinarily fertile period, he established many of the great themes that were to preoccupy him for the rest of his career. Thereafter he introduced only a few new subjects. Among them is *The Abduction of Rebecca* (fig. 21-35). Taken from Sir Walter Scott's novel *Ivanhoe,* it shows the beautiful Jewish woman being taken from the burning castle of Front-de-Boeuf by two Saracen slaves of the Knight Templar Bois-Gilbert. Although Delacroix harbored doubts about the literary quality of Scott's work, it provided the violent subjects so dear to his own Romantic sensibility, and he treated it often. The scene is similar to Oriental combats inspired by Lord Byron's poems. What mattered to the artist was its exotic quality.

The painting shows Delacroix at the height of his powers. It is the direct outgrowth of the change initiated by *The Women of Algiers.* The color is lighter and more expressive. Above all, the brushwork has a nervous energy that animates the entire surface. Not since Rubens have we seen such virtuosity. How did he achieve it? Ironically, at the very moment that his inventiveness seemed to wane, he turned his attention to the formal qualities of art. He arrived, in a word, at pure painting.

When it was exhibited at the Salon of 1846, the painting was favorably reviewed by the young critic Charles Baudelaire (1821–1867):

> The admirable thing about *The Abduction of Rebecca* is the perfect ordering of its colors, which are intense, close-packed, aligned, and logical; the result of this is a thrilling effect. With almost all painters who are not colorists, you will always notice vacuums, that is to say great holes, produced by tones which are below the level of the rest, so to speak. Delacroix's painting is like nature: it has a *horror vacuii.*

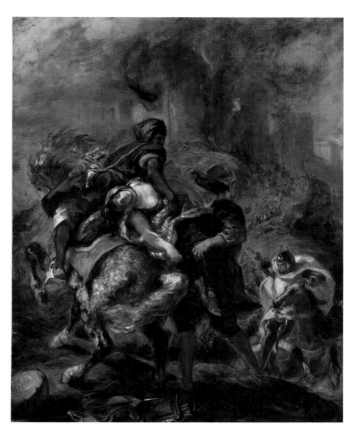

21-35. Eugène Delacroix. *The Abduction of Rebecca.* 1846. Oil on canvas, 39½ x 32¼" (100.3 x 81.9 cm). The Metropolitan Museum of Art, New York

Baudelaire devoted a long section of his Salon review to Delacroix, whose art he worshiped and understood more deeply than any other critic of the day. Discussing one of the artist's important state commissions, he noted perceptively, "Delacroix had decorations to paint, and he solved the great problem. He discovered pictorial unity without doing harm to his trade as a colorist. We have the Palais Bourbon to bear witness to this extraordinary *tour de force.*" This commission, which absorbed the artist between 1838 and 1847, brought him into renewed contact with the tradition of Western art. His work now showed a preference for classical and biblical themes, without abandoning his earlier subjects. He was, as Baudelaire observed, that rarity in the nineteenth century: an artist who could paint moving religious works, even though he was not a believer himself.

The time frame of the Bourbon Palace decorations coincides with a general crisis of tradition that gripped French art beginning in about 1840 and climaxed eight years later, when revolution was in the air everywhere. Delacroix came to be seen, with Ingres, as the last great representative of the mainstream of European painting. Baudelaire put it best. "Delacroix is the latest expression of progress in art. Heir to the great tradition . . . and a worthy successor of the old masters, he has even surpassed them in his command of anguish, passion and gesture! But take away Delacroix, and the great chain of history is broken and slips to the ground. It is true that the great tradition has been lost, and that the new one is not yet established." There is every indication that Delacroix himself was aware of his new status. He nevertheless stands at the head of a new tradition, one that Baudelaire could not yet have foreseen. Not only did the Impressionists take his palette and technique as their point of departure, but he became, in effect, the founder of what came to be called Expressionism. Thus the course of modern art is unthinkable without him.

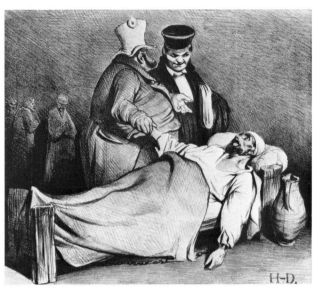

21-36. Honoré Daumier. *It's Safe to Release This One!* 1834. Lithograph

HONORÉ DAUMIER. The later work of Delacroix reflects the attitude that eventually doomed the Romantic movement: its growing detachment from contemporary life. History, literature, the Bible, and the Near East were the realms of the imagination where he sought refuge from the turmoil of the Industrial Revolution. Honoré Daumier (1808–1879), one of the few Romantic artists who did not shrink from reality, remained practically unknown as a painter in his day. A biting political cartoonist, he contributed satirical drawings to various Paris weeklies for most of his career. Nearly all of Daumier's cartoons were done with lithography (see box page 694). He turned to painting in the 1840s but found no public for his work. Only a few friends encouraged him and, a year before his death, arranged his first solo exhibition. Thus his pictures had little impact during his lifetime.

Although Daumier is sometimes called a realist, his work falls entirely within the range of Romanticism. The neat outlines and systematic crosshatching in Daumier's early cartoons (fig. 21-36) show his conservative training. He quickly developed a bolder and more personal style of draftsmanship, however, and his paintings of the 1850s and 1860s are Neo-Baroque. Their subjects vary widely. Many deal with aspects of everyday urban life also found in his cartoons, now viewed with a painter's eye rather than from a satirist's angle. In *The Third-Class Carriage* (fig. 21-37), which repeats the composition found in one of his lithographs, Daumier's forms reflect the compactness of Jean-François Millet's (compare fig. 21-41), but are painted so freely that they must have seemed raw and "unfinished" even by Delacroix's standards. The power of the image derives from this very freedom. Daumier's concern is not for the visible surface of reality but for the emotional meaning behind it. In *The Third-Class Carriage,* he has

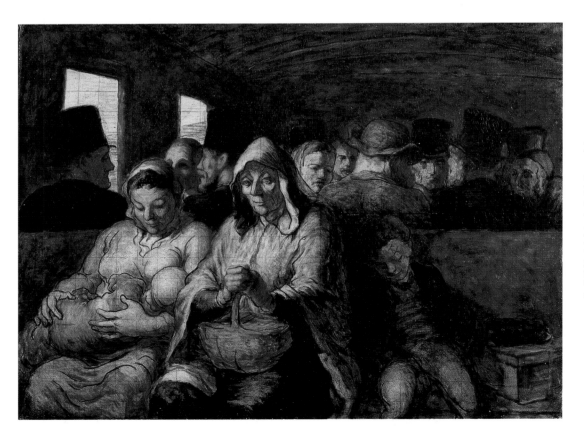

21-37. Honoré Daumier. *The Third-Class Carriage.* c. 1862. Oil on canvas, 25¾ x 35½" (65.4 x 90.2 cm). The Metropolitan Museum of Art, New York

BEQUEST OF MRS. H. O. HAVEMEYER, 1929. THE H. O. HAVEMEYER COLLECTION

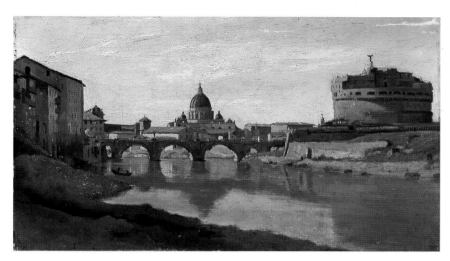

21-38. Camille Corot. *View of Rome: The Bridge and Castel Sant'Angelo with the Cupola of St. Peter's.* 1826–27. Oil on paper mounted on canvas, 10½ x 17" (22 x 38 cm). Fine Arts Museums of San Francisco

captured a peculiarly modern human condition: "the lonely crowd." The only thing these people have in common is the fact that they are traveling together in a railway car. Although they are physically crowded, they take no notice of one another, for each is alone with his or her own thoughts. Daumier explores this state with an insight and sympathy worthy of Rembrandt, whose work he admired. His feeling for the dignity of the poor also suggests the Le Nains, who had recently been rediscovered by French critics. Indeed, the old woman on the left in Louis Le Nain's *Peasant Family* (fig. 19-3) seems the direct ancestor of the central figure in *The Third-Class Carriage.*

LANDSCAPE PAINTING. Thanks to the cult of nature, landscape painting became the most characteristic form of Romantic art. While it arose out of Enlightenment ideas, the Romantic landscape lies outside the descriptive and emotional range of the eighteenth century. The Romantics believed that God's laws could be seen written in nature. Their faith, known as *pantheism,* was based not on rational thought but on subjective experience, and the appeal to the emotions rather than the intellect made those lessons all the more compelling. In order to express the feelings inspired by nature, the Romantics transcribed landscape as faithfully as possible, in contrast to the neoclassicists, who forced landscape to conform to prescribed ideas of beauty and linked it to historical subjects. At the same time, the Romantics felt free to modify nature's appearance as a means of evoking heightened states of mind in accordance with dictates of the imagination, the only standard they ultimately recognized. Landscape inspired the Romantics with passions so exalted that only in the hands of the greatest history painters could the human figure equal nature in power.

CAMILLE COROT. The first and undeniably greatest French Romantic landscape painter was Camille Corot (1796–1875). In 1825 he went to Italy for two years and explored the countryside

around Rome, like a latter-day Claude Lorraine. What Claude recorded in his drawings—the quality of a particular place at a particular time—Corot made into small canvases done on the spot in an hour or so (fig. 21-38). In size and immediacy, these quickly executed pictures are comparable to oil sketches by John Constable (see page 708), yet they stem from different traditions. Whereas Constable's view of nature, which emphasizes the sky as "the chief organ of sentiment," is derived from Dutch seventeenth-century landscapes, Corot's instinct for architectural clarity and stability recalls Poussin and Claude. But he, too, insists on "the truth of the moment." His exact observation and his readiness to seize upon any view that attracted him during his excursions show the same commitment to direct visual experience that we find in the English artist. The neoclassicists had also painted oil sketches out-of-doors. Unlike them, Corot did not transform his sketches into idealized pastoral visions. His willingness to accept them as independent works of art marks him unmistakably as a Romantic.

After returning from his second visit to Italy in 1834, Corot began to paint historical landscapes which combine stylistic and topographical features from Italy and the North. But during the 1840s he gradually developed a unique style that appears in its definitive form in *Morning: Dance of the Nymphs* (fig. 21-39). The canvas has rightly been called a souvenir of the opera, especially the ballets traditional in the Parisian productions which he habitually sketched. He found in them a common bond of feeling with painting that provided inspiration for his work. The landscape shows a new unity between the figures and their setting. The silvery light creates a veiled atmosphere that envelops the forms and lends the painting a poetic mood that recalls Poussin's late works (see fig. 19-6). In this way, Corot reconciles romantic sentiment and classical content.

Morning: Dance of the Nymphs was the outgrowth of the crisis of tradition in French art and of a personal crisis. When he painted it, Corot was approaching old age with increasing anxiety, and

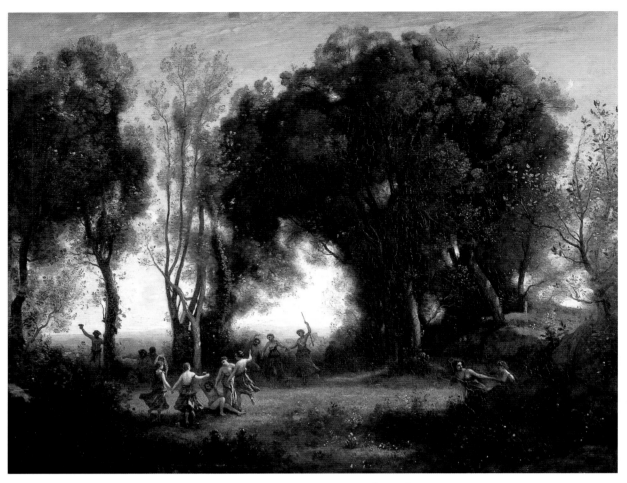

21-39. Camille Corot. *Morning: Dance of the Nymphs*. 1850. Oil on canvas, 38⅝ x 51⅝" (97.1 x 130 cm). Musée d'Orsay, Paris

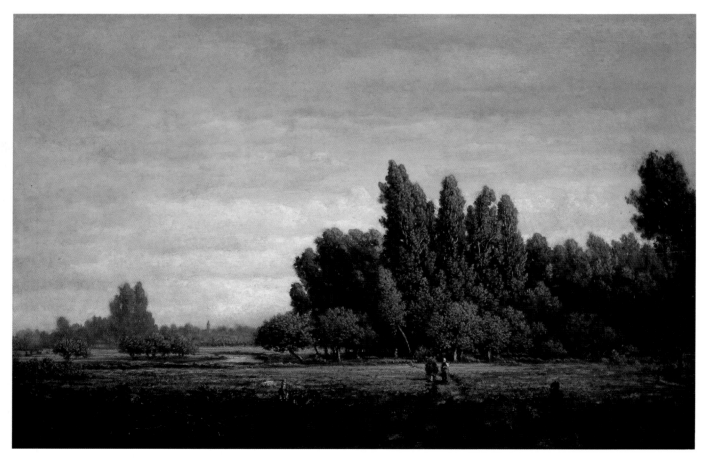

21-40. Théodore Rousseau. *A Meadow Bordered by Trees*. c. 1840–45. Oil on panel, 16⅜ x 24⅜" (41.6 x 61.9 cm).
The Metropolitan Museum of Art, New York

in Poussin he discovered a kindred spirit burdened with similar fears. Thus it was Corot's own development that enabled him to unlock the secret of the late Poussin and learn how to interpret nature in a deeply personal way.

THÉODORE ROUSSEAU. Corot's early fidelity to nature was an important model for the Barbizon School, although he was not actually a member. This group of younger artists, centering on Théodore Rousseau (1812–1867), is named for the village of Barbizon on the edge of the forest of Fontainebleau near Paris, where they painted landscapes and scenes of rural life. Enthused by Constable, whose work had been exhibited in Paris in 1824, they turned to the Northern Baroque landscape as an alternative to the classical tradition. From Ruisdael's example (see fig. 18-22), Rousseau learned how to give his encrusted forms and gnarled trees a sense of inner life. It was, however, the hours of solitary contemplation in the forest of Fontainebleau that made it possible for him to unlock nature's secrets. *A Meadow Bordered by Trees* (fig. 21-40) is a splendid example of his landscapes, which are filled with a simple reverence that admirably reflects the rallying cry of the Romantics—sincerity.

JEAN-FRANÇOIS MILLET. Jean-François Millet (1814–1875) became a member of the Barbizon School the same year that the Revolution of 1848 swept across France and the rest of Europe. Although he was no radical, *The Sower* (fig. 21-41) was championed by liberal critics, because it was the very opposite of the Neoclassical history paintings endorsed by the establishment. Millet's archetypal image nonetheless has a self-consciously classical flavor that reflects his admiration for Poussin. Blurred in

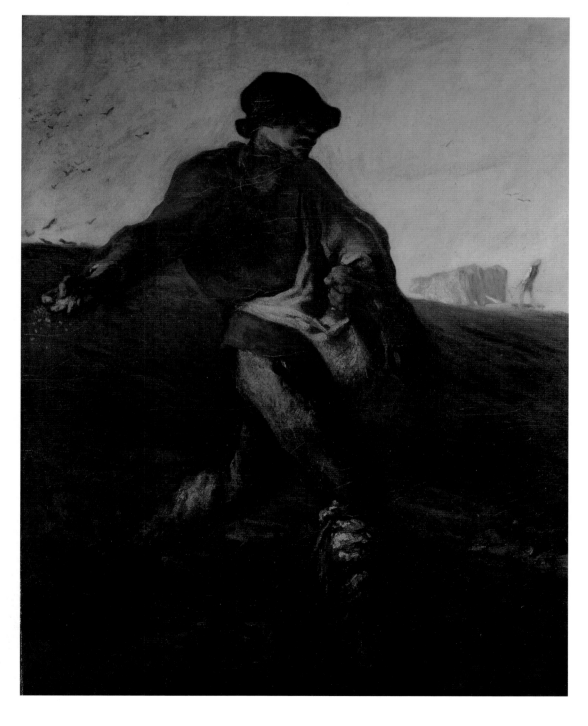

21-41. Jean-François Millet. *The Sower.* c. 1850. Oil on canvas, 40 x 32½" (101.6 x 82.6 cm). Museum of Fine Arts, Boston

GIFT OF QUINCY ADAMS SHAW THROUGH QUINCY A. SHAW, JR., AND MRS. MARION SHAW HAUGHTON

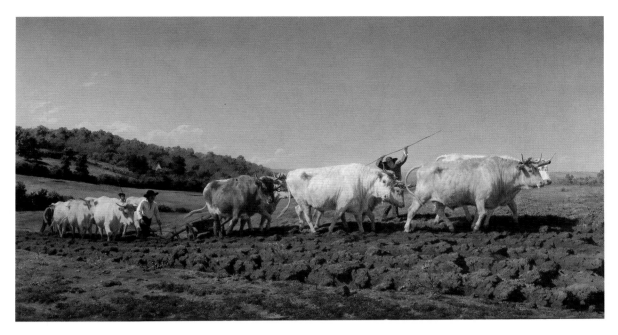

21-42. Rosa Bonheur. *Plowing in the Nivernais.* 1849. Oil on canvas, 5'9" x 8'8" (1.75 x 2.64 m). Musée d'Orsay, Paris

the hazy atmosphere, this "hero of the soil" is a timeless symbol of the unending labor that the artist viewed as the peasant's inescapable lot. (Could Millet have known the pathetic sower from the October page of *Les Très Riches Heures du Duc de Berry?* Compare fig. 11-94.) The painting monumentalizes a rural way of life that was rapidly disappearing as a result of the Industrial Revolution. For that very reason, however, the peasant—not the downtrodden industrial workers championed by Karl Marx—was seen as the chief victim of the evils arising from the Machine Age.

ROSA BONHEUR. The Barbizon School generally advocated a return to nature as a way of fleeing the social ills brought on by industrialization and urbanization. Despite their conservative outlook, these artists were raised to a new prominence in French art by the Revolution of 1848. That same year Rosa Bonheur (1822–1899), another artist who worked outdoors, received a French government commission that led to her first great success. She established herself as a leading painter of animals—and eventually as the most famous woman artist of her time. [See Primary Sources, no. 67, page 965.] Her painting *Plowing in the Nivernais* (fig. 21-42) was exhibited the following year, after a winter spent making studies from life. The theme of humanity's union with nature had already been popularized in the country romances of the French writer George Sand, among others (see box page 714). Bonheur's picture shares Millet's reverence for peasant life, but the real subject here, as in all her work, is the animals within the landscape. She depicts them with a convincing naturalism that later placed her among the most influential realists.

England

JOHN HENRY FUSELI. England was as precocious in fostering Romanticism as it had been in promoting Neoclassicism. In fact, one of its first representatives, John Henry Fuseli (1741–1825), was a contemporary of West and Copley. This Swissborn painter (originally named Johann Heinrich Füssli) had an

extraordinary impact on his time, more perhaps because of his adventurous and forceful personality than the quality of his work. Ordained a minister at 20, he left the Church by 1764 and went to London in search of freedom. Encouraged by Reynolds, he spent the 1770s in Rome, where he met Gavin Hamilton and studied classical art. Fuseli, however, based his style on Michelangelo and the Mannerists, not on Poussin and the antique. A German

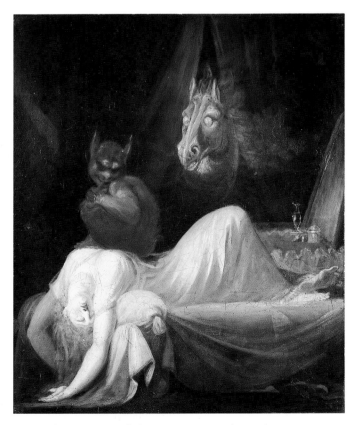

21-43. John Henry Fuseli. *The Nightmare.* c. 1790. Oil on canvas, 29½ x 25¼" (74.9 x 64.1 cm). Freies Deutsches Hochstift-Frankfurter Goethe-Museum, Frankfurt

acquaintance of those years described him as "extreme in every-thing, Shakespeare's painter." Shakespeare and Michelangelo were indeed his twin gods. He even envisioned a Sistine Chapel with Michelangelo's figures transformed into Shakespearean characters. The sublime would be the common denominator for "classic" and "Gothic" Romanticism. This concept marks Fuseli as a transitional figure. He espoused many of the same Neoclassical theories as Reynolds, West, and Kauffmann (he translated Winckelmann's writings into English) but bent their rules virtually to the breaking point.

We see this mixture in *The Nightmare* (fig. 21-43). The sleeping woman, more Mannerist than Michelangelesque in proportions, is Neoclassical in style. The grinning devil and the luminescent horse, however, come from the demon-ridden world of medieval folklore, while the Rembrandtesque lighting reminds us of Reynolds (compare fig. 20-14). Here the Romantic quest for terrifying experiences leads not to physical violence but to the dark recesses of the mind.

What was the genesis of *The Nightmare?* Nightmares often have strong sexual overtones, sometimes openly expressed, at other times disguised. We know that Fuseli originally conceived the subject not long after his return from Italy. He had fallen violently in love with a friend's niece who soon married a merchant, much to the artist's distress. We may see in the picture a projection of his "dream girl," with the demon taking the artist's place, while the impassioned horse, a well-known erotic symbol, looks on.

WILLIAM BLAKE. Fuseli later befriended the poet-painter William Blake (1757–1827), who had an even greater creativity and stranger personality than his own. A recluse and visionary, Blake produced and published his own books of poems with engraved text and hand-colored illustrations. Although he never left England, he acquired a large repertory of Michelangelesque and Mannerist motifs from engravings, as well as through the influence of Fuseli. He also had a tremendous admiration for the Middle Ages, and came closer than any other Romantic artist to reviving pre-Renaissance forms. (His books were meant to be the successors of illuminated manuscripts.)

These elements are all present in Blake's memorable image *The Ancient of Days* (fig. 21-44). The muscular figure, radically foreshortened and fitted into a circle of light, is taken from Mannerist sources (fig. 21-45), while the symbolic compasses come from medieval representations of the Lord as Architect of the Universe. We might therefore expect the Ancient of Days to signify Almighty God. In Blake's esoteric mythology, however, he stands for the power of reason, which the poet regarded as destructive, since it stifles vision and inspiration. To Blake, the "inner eye" of the imagination was all-important; he felt no need to copy nature.

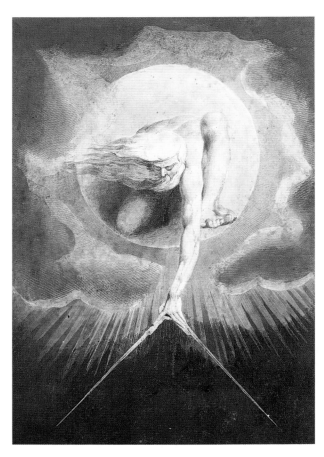

21-44. William Blake. *The Ancient of Days,* frontispiece of *Europe, A Prophesy.* 1794. Metal relief etching, hand-colored illustration, 9⅛ x 6⅝" (23.2 x 16.8 cm). Library of Congress, Washington, D.C.

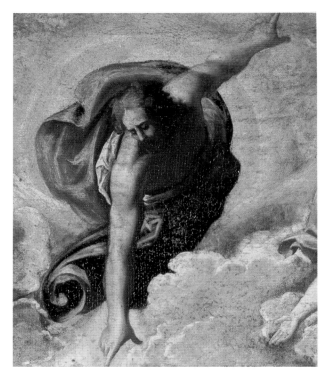

21-45. Taddeo Zuccaro. *The Conversion of St. Paul* (detail). c. 1555. Oil on canvas. Galleria Doria Pamphili, Rome

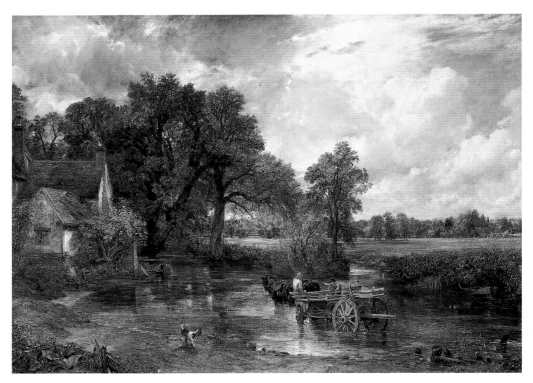

21-46. John Constable. *The Haywain.* 1821. Oil on canvas, 4'3¼" x 6'1" (1.3 x 1.85 m). The National Gallery, London

JOHN CONSTABLE. It was nevertheless in landscape rather than in narrative scenes that English Romantic painting reached its fullest expression. During the eighteenth century, landscape paintings consisted largely of imaginary scenes conforming to Northern and Italian Baroque examples. John Constable (1776–1837) admired both Ruisdael and Claude, yet he opposed all flights of fancy. Landscape painting, he believed, must be based on observable facts and aim at "embodying a pure apprehension of natural effect." Toward that end, he painted countless oil sketches outdoors. They were not the first such studies. However, Constable was more concerned than his predecessors with the intangible qualities—sky, light, and atmosphere—than the concrete details of the scene. Often the land serves as no more than a foil for the ever-changing drama overhead, which he studied with a meteorologist's accuracy. In order to record these fleeting effects, he arrived at a painting technique as broad, free, and personal as that of Cozens' "ink-blot landscapes," even though his point of departure was nature, not the imagination.

All of Constable's pictures show familiar views of the English countryside. It was, he later claimed, the scenery around his native Stour Valley that made him a painter. [See Primary Sources, no. 68, page 965.] Although he painted the final versions in his studio, he prepared them by making oil studies based on sketches from nature. The sky, to him, was a mirror of those sweeping forces so dear to the Romantic view of nature. It remained "the key note, standard scale, and the chief organ of sentiment." In *The Haywain* (fig. 21-46), he has caught a particularly splendid moment. A great expanse of wind, sunlight, and clouds plays over the spacious land-scape. The earth and sky have become vehicles of sentiment imbued with the artist's poetic attitude. At the same time, there is an intimacy in this monumental composition that reveals Constable's deep love of the countryside. This new, personal note is characteristically Romantic. Since Constable has painted the landscape with such conviction, we see the scene through his eyes and accept it as real, even though it looks back to paintings by Gainsborough and Ruisdael.

In 1829 a marked change came over Constable's work. Deeply affected by his wife's death a year earlier, he was subject to dark moods. *Salisbury Cathedral from the Meadows* (fig. 21-47), begun that summer, is his most personal statement. When the canvas was exhibited two years later, he added nine lines from *The Seasons* by the eighteenth-century poet James Thomson that reveal its meaning: the rainbow is a symbol of hope after a storm that follows on the death of the young Amelia in the arms of her lover Celadon. Although a political intent has sometimes been attributed to the landscape, there can be little doubt of its autobiographical significance. To the left of the huge ash tree, a symbol of life, is a grave marker, emblem of death. To the right stands the great church, one of his major themes, a symbol of faith and resurrection. The rainbow, added late in the composition's development and inspired by a version of Ruisdael's *The Jewish Cemetery (*see fig. 18-22), suggests the artist's renewed optimism. Thus the painting reflects his changing state of mind.

Constable continued to work on *The Rainbow,* as he called it, on and off for several more years. He attached great importance to the canvas. He regarded the painting as the fullest expression of

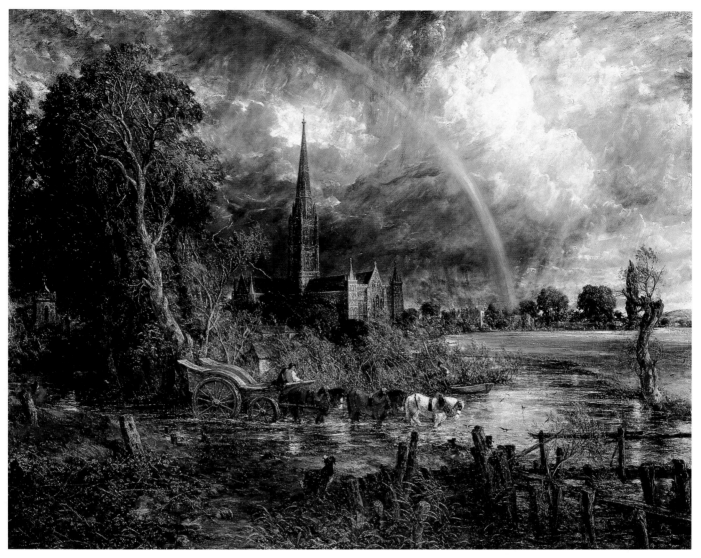

21-47. John Constable. *Salisbury Cathedral from the Meadows.* 1829–34. Oil on canvas, 59¾ x 74¾" (151.8 x 189.9 cm).
PRIVATE COLLECTION, ON LOAN TO THE NATIONAL GALLERY, LONDON

his art and felt it would be considered his finest work by future generations. It is indeed an astonishing achievement. The amazingly free application of paint (much of it done with a palette knife) and rich, somber colors convey an agitation not seen before in his landscapes. All nature is caught up in the fury of a catastrophic event beyond human comprehension. Every leaf, every branch acts as an index of feeling to express the artist's turbulent emotions. Once again it is the sky that provides the keynote: now the storm has clearly passed. No other painter before or since was able to capture the clash of the elements with such power. Even paintings by his great rival Joseph Mallord William Turner seem tame by comparison.

J. M. W. TURNER. Joseph Mallord William Turner (1775–1851) arrived at a style that Constable disdainfully but accurately described as "airy visions, painted with tinted steam." Turner began as a watercolorist, and the use of translucent tints on white

paper may help to explain his obsession with colored light. Like Constable, he made extensive studies from nature (although not in oils), but the scenery he chose satisfied the Romantic taste for the picturesque and the sublime—mountains, the sea, or places linked with historic events. In his full-scale pictures he often changed these views so freely that they became unrecognizable.

Many of Turner's landscapes are linked with literary themes and bear such titles as *The Destruction of Sodom,* or *Snowstorm: Hannibal Crossing the Alps,* or *Childe Harold's Pilgrimage: Italy.* When they were exhibited, he would add appropriate quotations from ancient or modern authors to the catalogue. Sometimes he would make up some lines himself and claim to be citing his own unpublished poem, "Fallacies of Hope." These canvases are nevertheless the opposite of history painting as defined by Poussin. The titles indeed indicate "noble and serious human actions," but the tiny figures, who are lost in the seething violence of nature, suggest the ultimate defeat of all endeavor—"the fallacies of hope."

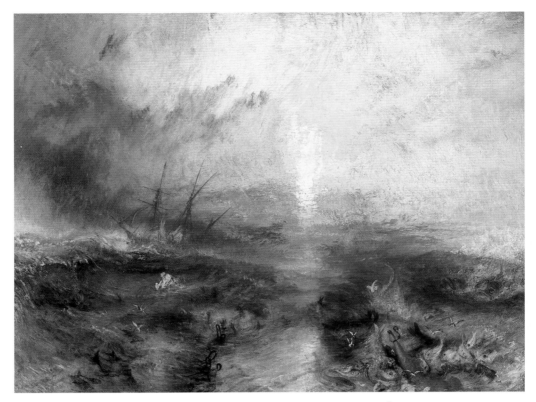

21-48. Joseph Mallord William Turner. *The Slave Ship*. 1840. Oil on canvas, 35¾ x 48" (90.8 x 121.9 cm). Museum of Fine Arts, Boston

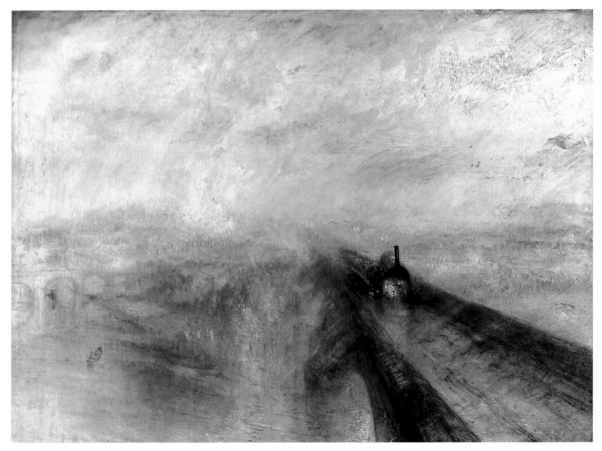

21-49. Joseph Mallord William Turner. *Rain, Steam and Speed—The Great Western Railway*. 1844. Oil on canvas, 35¾ x 48" (90.8 x 122 cm). The National Gallery, London

The Slave Ship (fig. 21-48) is one of Turner's most spectacular visions and illustrates how he translated his literary sources into "tinted steam." First entitled *Slavers Throwing Overboard the Dead and Dying—Typhoon Coming On,* the painting has several levels of meaning. Like Géricault's *The Raft of the "Medusa"* (see fig. 21-28), which had been exhibited in England in 1820, it has to do, in part, with a specific incident that Turner had recently read about.

When an epidemic broke out on a slave ship, the captain threw his human cargo overboard because he was insured against the loss of slaves at sea, but not by disease. Turner also thought of a relevant passage from James Thomson's poem *The Seasons* that describes how sharks follow a slave ship during a typhoon, "lured by the scent of steaming crowds, or rank disease, and death." But what is the relation between the slaver's action and the typhoon? Are the dead and dying slaves being cast into the sea against the threat of the storm, perhaps to lighten the ship? Is the typhoon nature's retribution for the captain's greed and cruelty? Of the many storms at sea that Turner painted, none has quite this apocalyptic quality. A cosmic catastrophe seems about to engulf everything, not merely the "guilty" slaver but the sea itself, with its crowds of fantastic and oddly harmless-looking fish.

While we still feel the force of Turner's imagination, most of us enjoy the tinted steam for its own sake rather than as a vehicle of the awesome emotions the artist meant to evoke. Even in terms of the values he himself acknowledged, Turner strikes us as "a virtuoso of the sublime," led astray by his own enthusiasm. He must have been pleased by praise from the critic and theorist John Ruskin (1819–1900), who saw in *The Slave Ship* (which he owned) "the true, the beautiful, and the intellectual"—all qualities that raised Turner above older landscape painters in Ruskin's eyes. Still, Turner may have come to wonder if his tinted steam had its intended effect. Soon after finishing *The Slave Ship,* he read in his copy of Goethe's *Color Theory,* recently translated into English, that yellow has a "gay, softly exciting character," while orange-red suggests "warmth and gladness." These are hardly the emotions aroused by *The Slave Ship* in a viewer, even one who does not know its title. Interestingly enough, Turner soon modified his approach to take Goethe's ideas into account. He even painted a pair of canvases about the Deluge that were meant to illustrate Goethe's theory of positive (light and warm) and minus (dark and cold) colors. They nevertheless differ little from the rest of his work.

Many of Turner's later paintings originated in watercolors called "color beginnings" that are as abstract as American Color Field Painting (see pages 852–54). However, they always retained a basis in the artist's actual experiences. Turner sought out the unusual. *Rain, Steam and Speed—The Great Western Railway* (fig. 21-49) shows the recently completed Maidenhead railway bridge looking across the Thames River toward London. It was painted after Turner had stuck his head out of a window on the Exeter express for some nine minutes during a rainstorm. One could hardly ask for a more vivid impression of speed and atmospheric turbulence. The train pursues the hare (barely visible in our illustration) running vainly ahead of it just as a hound chases its prey.

WATERCOLORS. Turner was the greatest watercolorist of his time. Watercolors were first introduced into Britain by visiting Northerners, who had used them as a means of recording on-the-spot observations since the time of Dürer (see fig. 16-4). The English soon made the medium their own. Because they became an indispensable part of the genteel person's education, watercolors are often thought of as an amateur's medium. After the middle of the eighteenth century, however, they attracted gifted painters like Thomas Gainsborough (see page 618). Important contributions were made by Alexander Cozens' talented son, John Robert Cozens (1752–1797), who was the first to introduce poetic melancholy into watercolors, and Thomas Girtin (1752–1802), Turner's brilliant contemporary, who during his brief career revolutionized the English landscape by investing it with a Romantic mood. The full potential of watercolors was realized only in the nineteenth century, when artists like Turner and Constable, who turned to them late in his career, greatly extended the range of subjects, techniques, and expression. Many of the most famous watercolorists are all but forgotten today, while others, such as John Sell Cotman (1782–1842), who were largely ignored, are now seen as major artists.

JOHN SELL COTMAN. Cotman started out in London, where he moved in the same circles as Turner. However, most of his career was spent as a drawing master in the north of England, as much out of a weakness in his character as out of the force of circumstances. Although he achieved modest local recognition as a leader of the Norwich landscape school, he died in obscurity and was only rediscovered in the 1920s, when his highly unusual style

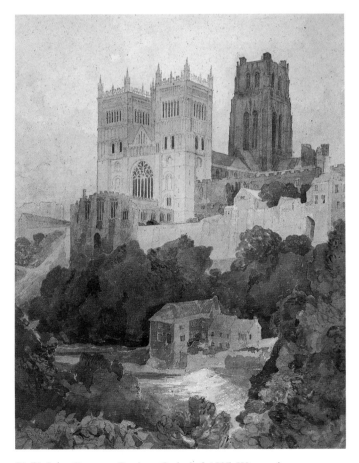

21-50. John Cotman. *Durham Cathedral.* 1805. Watercolor on paper, 17¼ x 13" (43.8 x 33 cm). The British Museum, London

suddenly appeared remarkably modern. Cotman's watercolors are notable for an economy of means that endows even the simplest subject with monumentality and dignity. His formalism grew out of the landscape tradition of Nicolas Poussin and Claude Lorraine, but he was no classicist. And although he was affected by the Dutch and Flemish Baroque artists who so influenced Constable, Cotman's watercolors are among the most original creations of the English Romantic landscape school during its early phase.

Durham Cathedral (fig. 21-50), a watercolor painted in the studio from nature studies, bears the stamp of his genius. The artist has concentrated on the essential elements, so that the scene is reduced to a flat, nearly abstract pattern. The result is an expressiveness of astonishing intensity. Cotman emphasizes the massiveness of the great church, which looms over the house below as if threatening to crush it. The landscape shows the English Romantic fascination with the Gothic. It inspired the artist with much the same sentiment found in Ruisdael's *The Jewish Cemetery* (see fig. 18-22). Did Cotman intend it as a testimony of his personal faith? Of man's works, he seems to say, only the cathedral, a house of worship, will endure. Yet we know little about his beliefs.

Germany

CASPAR DAVID FRIEDRICH. In Germany, as in England, landscape was the finest achievement of Romantic painting. The underlying ideas, too, were often strikingly similar. In about 1800 German artists rediscovered the Gothic, which they regarded as their native heritage. For the most part, this Gothic Revival remained limited in subject matter and scope, but in the hands of Caspar David Friedrich (1774–1840), the most important German Romantic artist, it acquired a haunting mystery. A devout Protestant, he had a pantheistic love of nature, which he imbued with deep religious feeling. In *Abbey in an Oak Forest* (fig. 21-51) all is death—the ancient graves, the barren trees, and ruined church silhouetted against the somber winter sky at twilight. We contemplate the forlorn burial scene with the same hushed reverence as the solemn procession of monks. Hardly distinguishable from the tombstones, they seek the crucifix enshrined in the arched portal, which offers eternal life to the faithful. The frozen stillness is in marked contrast to the painting by Ruisdael that probably inspired it (a variant of fig. 18-22). Infinitely lonely, the bleak landscape is a reflection of the artist's own melancholy.

When Friedrich painted *The Polar Sea* (fig. 21-52), he may have known of Turner's "Fallacies of Hope." In an earlier picture on the same theme (now lost) he had inscribed the name "Hope" on the crushed vessel. In any case, he shared Turner's attitude toward human fate. The painting, too, was inspired by a specific event, to which the artist gave symbolic significance: a dangerous moment in William Parry's Arctic expedition of 1819–20.

One wonders how Turner might have depicted this scene. Perhaps it would have been too static for him. Friedrich, however, was attracted by this very immobility. He has visualized the piled-up slabs of ice as a kind of megalithic monument to human defeat built by nature itself. There is no hint of tinted steam—the very

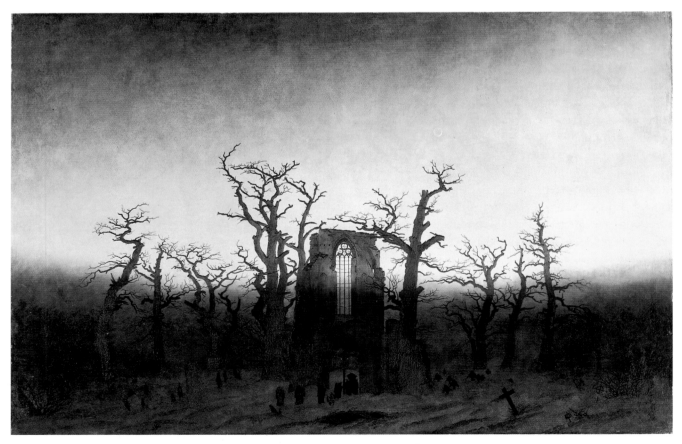

21-51. Caspar David Friedrich. *Abbey in an Oak Forest.* 1809–10. Oil on canvas, 44 x 68½" (111.8 x 174 cm). Schloss Charlottenburg, Berlin

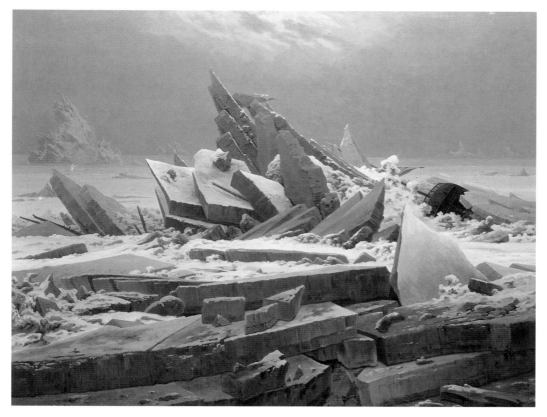

21-52. Caspar David Friedrich. *The Polar Sea*. 1824. Oil on canvas, 38½ x 50½" (97.8 x 128.3 cm). Kunsthalle, Hamburg, Germany

air seems frozen—nor any subjective handwriting. We look right through the paint-covered surface at a reality that seems created without the painter's intervention.

This technique, impersonal and exacting, is peculiar to German Romantic painting. It stems from the early neoclassicists, but the Germans, whose tradition of Baroque painting was weak, adopted it more wholeheartedly than the English or the French. Friedrich learned this approach at the Royal Academy in Copenhagen, and although in his hands it yielded extraordinary effects, the results proved disappointing for most German artists, who lacked his lofty imagination.

PHILIPP OTTO RUNGE. Philipp Otto Runge (1777–1810), who attended the Copenhagen academy soon after Friedrich, shared many of the same ideas but expressed them very differently. His most important work was a series of four allegorical landscapes devoted to the times of day, which occupied him throughout his brief career and was left incomplete at his death. The paintings incorporate an ambitious program having several levels of meaning. They stand for, among other things, the seasons and the ages of life. The set was intended for a Gothic chapel of Runge's own design, where poetry and music by his friends would be heard.

Morning, the only picture to be finished, was later cut up and survives only in fragments, but a slightly earlier, smaller version (fig. 21-53) gives a good idea of its appearance. The landscape represents spring and childhood. Within Runge's program, it also signifies "the boundless illumination of the universe."

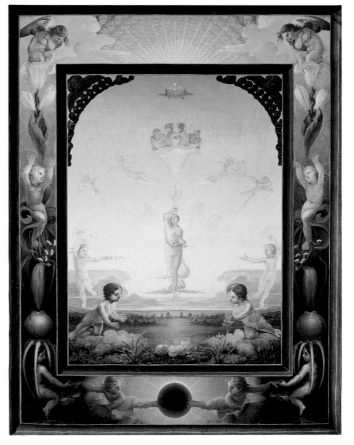

21-53. Philipp Otto Runge. *Morning*. 1808. Oil on canvas, 42⅞ x 33⅝" (109 x 85.4 cm). Kunsthalle, Hamburg

THE ROMANTIC MOVEMENT IN LITERATURE AND THE THEATER

Romanticism in art had an exact counterpart in literature and the theater. It was inextricably entwined with Johann Wolfgang von Goethe, whose dramatic poem *Faust* (Part 1, 1808; Part 2, 1832) remains the greatest monument of the Romantic movement. Goethe was interested in a vast range of subjects, including botany and architecture. His book on color theory (1810), which constituted an attack on Newtonian optics, exercised widespread influence on painters. He was also a gifted amateur musician who conducted operas and wrote librettos, as well as lyrical poems that inspired some of the finest songs by Beethoven and Schubert. Romanticism in the theater began in Germany just before the turn of the nineteenth century as an outgrowth of the work of Friedrich von Schiller and Goethe. It centered on August Wilhelm von Schlegel (1767–1845), the editor of the literary journal *Athenäum* from 1798 to 1800, and his brother Friedrich (1772–1829), a noted philosopher. Together they promoted Romanticism as an all-embracing vision. An early admirer of Shakespeare, whose plays he began to translate, August Schlegel emphasized mood and character over plot in literature and championed the revival of such medieval works as the twelfth-century German epic *Nibelungenlied (The Song of the Niebelungs)*. The Schlegels were part of a small, tightly knit group that included Ludwig Tieck (1773–1853), who completed the job of translating Shakespeare after August's death. Tieck, who wrote both comedies and tragedies, was also an important theorist, especially later in life, and exercised considerable influence on German Romantic painting through his friendship with Philipp Otto Runge (see pages 713 and 715). In the heady early days of Romanticism he collaborated with Wilhelm Heinrich Wackenroder (1773–1798), who stated that "the Gothic church and the Greek temple are equally pleasurable in the sight of God." Medievalism, with its reverence for Christian ideals, was also taken up in 1799 by the writer Novalis (Friedrich von Hardenberg, 1772–1801). The writings of the Schlegel circle inspired not only the landscape painter Caspar David Friedrich but also the Nazarenes, who were to establish the mainstream of German Romantic art (see pages 712 and 715). Though he was generally overlooked during his lifetime, the finest playwright of the early nineteenth century in Germany was Heinrich von Kleist (1777–1811), a poet and novelist, whose tragedies and comedies are filled with the conflict of extreme emotions typical of Romanticism.

German ideas were first introduced into France by Madame de Staël (Germaine Necker, 1760–1817), the daughter of Louis XVI's finance minister and the wife of the Swedish ambassador to France, who detested Napoleon. She went into exile in Germany, where she wrote *Of Germany,* which presented many of the Schlegels' theories. The book, initially suppressed upon its publication in 1810, was reissued after Napoleon's exile to Elba in 1813. Equally important for French Romanticism was the enthusiasm for all things English, which reached its height dur-

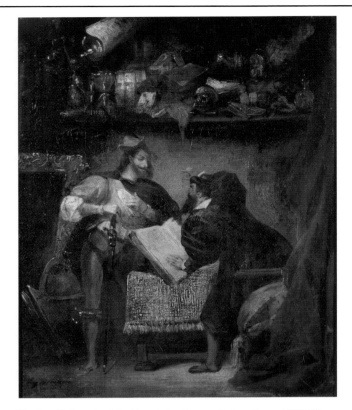

Eugène Delacroix. *Mephistopheles Appears Before Faust.* 1826–27. Oil on canvas, 17⅞ x 14⅞" (45.5 x 37.7 cm). The Wallace Collection, London

ing the following decade. The novels of Sir Walter Scott sparked the taste for medieval legends, while an English troupe caused a sensation in Paris with its performances of Shakespeare four years after his plays had been declared superior to Racine's by Marie-Henri Beyle, known as Stendhal (1783–1842), in 1823.

The central figure among the French Romantics was the novelist Victor Hugo (1802–1885). The introduction to his play about Oliver Cromwell (1827), the puritan who ruled England after the execution of King Charles II, was a broadside attack on classical drama. In 1830 Hugo's drama *Hernani* announced the triumph of Romanticism. It reversed the shopworn triumph of young lovers (so dear to classical French theater) by ending in tragedy and broke from the stilted literary conventions of French drama by altering the length of the poetic line. Perhaps fittingly, it was the failure of Hugo's *The Burgraves* in 1843 that signaled the end of Romantic theater. The other leading dramatist of the 1830s was Alexandre Dumas the Elder (1802–1870), who wrote a number of successful historical and domestic plays before turning to the novels for which he is best known today: *The Three Musketeers* (1844) and *The Count of Monte Cristo* (1845). George Sand (Amandine-Aurore-Lucile Dupin Dudevant, 1804–1876), who adopted a male pen name to help gain acceptance of her work, was a favorite novelist as well as a prolific playwright. Her apartment was also host to one of the most glittering *salons*—gatherings of writers, artists, and musicians that formed the center of cultural life in nineteenth-century Europe.

It was popular theater that enjoyed the greatest success, fueled by the huge growth of cities spawned by the Industrial Revolution. Much of it took the form of bourgeois melodramas, which owed their appeal to their simple plots and morality. New kinds of spectacle were made possible by the same technology that gave rise to the Industrial Revolution itself: for example, the invention in 1816 of gaslight and limelight, which involved heating lime with compressed oxygen and compressed hydrogen. They were superseded by Thomas Edison's invention of the electric light in 1879, which led to the improved carbon arc lamp a year later. Among the favorite spectacles were large paintings of panoramas and dioramas, which created special effects through changes of light and color. The leader in this field was Louis Daguerre, who was also an important scene designer before he turned to the invention of photography (see page 734).

In England, all the important Romantic poets tried their hand at plays but with little success: Samuel Taylor Coleridge (1772–1834), William Wordsworth (1770–1850), John Keats (1795–1821), Percy Bysshe Shelley (1792–1822), and even Robert Browning (1812–1889). The most important among them was Lord Byron (George Gordon, 1788–1824), the very prototype of the Romantic writer. His impact was immediate— Delacroix painted canvases inspired by Byron's dramas *Marino Faliero* and *Sardanapalus* (see fig. 21-33)—and lasted well beyond his own brief lifetime. The novelist Sir Walter Scott (1771–1832) also wrote plays, but mainly his novels were adapted to the stage by others to great acclaim. The most popular productions in England were translations of middle-class plays by the German Kotzebue; these were superseded by the works of George Bulwer-Lytton (1803–1873)—famous for the opening "It was a dark and stormy night"—who invented the "gentlemanly" melodrama that gave an air of Victorian respectability to the theater.

Philadelphia was the theater capital in the United States, as it was of art, before 1815. The most important house, the Chestnut Street Theater, was designed by the great English architect Inigo Jones. New York City soon surpassed Philadelphia. The close ties between art and theater in America are illustrated by William Dunlap (1766–1839), who was the nation's leading playwright before turning to painting in 1812; toward the end of his long life he also wrote the first histories of American theater and art. Many artists, particularly aspiring younger ones along the frontier, found their first employment painting stage scenery. As in Europe, the growth of cities in America created a demand for larger and more numerous theaters around the country. Especially popular were Native American and Yankee plays as symbols of the young nation. They were soon joined by African-American minstrel shows (the term *Jim Crow* comes from a song introduced by Thomas D. Rice in 1829), which featured the "end men" Tambo and Bones, and a "middle" man who functioned as a master of ceremonies. The 1840s saw the rise of a new type, the city boy, who was often pitted against his country cousin.

Aurora-Venus (combining the rising sun and the morning star) hovers over the Christlike infant while child genii sprout from a lily above. (Flowers in Runge's personal system become symbols of universal life through emotional identification with their forms.) The decorated frame, inspired by medieval manuscripts (compare fig. 10-38), expands on the meaning of the central image. The light of revelation, eclipsed by darkness below, liberates the soul trapped beneath the earth within the roots of the bulb. Above, the soul rises as a genius from the lily to the heavens and is transformed into an angel.

Morning is an extraordinary synthesis of classical mythology and Christian faith, Romantic attitudes and Neoclassical technique. Painting for Runge was a deeply spiritual act revealing the divinity of nature. To him abstraction was essential to express the poetic idea. The artist communicates his concepts through the stylized forms and symmetrical composition. More generally, *Morning* represents the mystical yearning of the soul for the infinite so dear to the German Romantic. This ecstatic vision, the "chord" of harmony as he put it, is depicted using the same method as Friedrich's. Every detail has been precisely observed. The picture surface, transparent as glass, makes us look at nature with the same innocence as the newborn child. As a result, the landscape has an appealing simplicity, despite the complexity of its program. In the end, it is the painting technique that validates Runge's ideas and makes them convincing.

THE NAZARENES. In 1809 a group of young German painters at the Vienna Academy banded together to form the Guild of St. Luke (also known as the Brotherhood), after the artists' guilds of old. They equated simplicity with pious virtue, and avoided all virtuosity, which they felt worked against the heartfelt sincerity that was their goal. Two years later they decided to lead the life of artist-monks at an abandoned monastery near Rome, where they became known as the Nazarenes. At first their paintings and drawings had a striking purity, achieved by imitat-

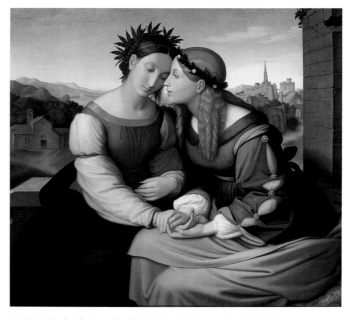

21-54. Friedrich Overbeck. *Italia and Germania*. 1811–28. Oil on canvas, 37¾ x 41⅞" (96 x 106.4 cm). Bayerische Staatsgemäldesammlungen, Neue Pinakothek, Munich

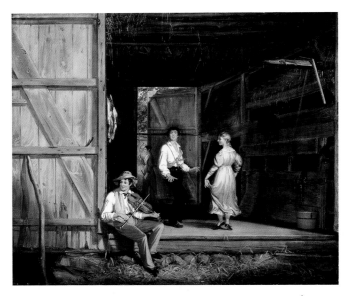

21-55. William Sidney Mount. *Dancing on the Barn Floor.*
1831. Oil on canvas, 25 x 30" (63.5 x 76.2 cm). Collection of
The Museums at Stony Brook

ing the painstaking precision of the old German masters and the style of the Early Renaissance. Over time their work suffered from the Neoclassic emphasis on form at the expense of color and from inflated rhetoric. The Nazarene movement gradually petered out as its members died or returned to Germany, where they established the mainstream of German Romanticism.

FRIEDRICH OVERBECK. The Nazarenes were at their best in intimate subjects, such as *Italia and Germania* (fig. 21-54) by Friedrich Overbeck (1789–1869). This manifesto by the movement's "priest" expresses the North's long-standing love-hate relationship with the South. It shows personifications of the two countries, so different in every respect, reconciled in tender friendship. The painting is at once a nostalgic reminiscence of the artist's homeland and a celebration of the beauty he found around him in Rome, here united in harmony and mutual respect. Its source was Angelica Kauffmann's self-portrait (see fig. 21-8) by way of German portraiture.

United States

Painting after the American Revolution was dominated by followers of Benjamin West, who took every young artist from the New World under his wing. The only ones to enjoy much success were portraitists such as Gilbert Stuart (1755–1828). Using the fashionable conventions of Joshua Reynolds, they conferred the aura of established aristocracy on the Federalists, who were only too eager to forget the recent revolutionary past enshrined by the history painters. What Americans wanted was an art based not on the past but on the present. Romantic painting in the United States rode the tidal wave of nationalism fostered by Jacksonian democracy. Collectors now began to support artists who could express their vision of the United States. For perhaps the only time in the country's history, artists, patrons, and intellectuals shared a common point of view.

WILLIAM SIDNEY MOUNT. During the 1820s America found its history painting in genre scenes descended from Dutch and English examples. The first native genre painter of real talent, William Sidney Mount (1808–1868), spent his career on rural Long Island, which provided him with a rich vein of subjects. Although he began as a history painter, Mount quickly turned to scenes of everyday life, which he invested with the humor of Jan Steen. *Dancing on the Barn Floor* (fig. 21-55), one of his first efforts, projects the ideal of the United States as a land of contentment in which its fun-loving people enjoy a simple, happy life as the fruit of their honest labor. The carefully observed violinist testifies to the artist's love of music, his favorite theme. This ingenious inventor and theoretician wrote considerable "fiddle" music himself, and later patented a violin of unusual design.

THE HUDSON RIVER SCHOOL. It was at this time that Americans began to discover landscape painting. Before then, settlers were far too busy carving out homesteads to pay much attention to the poetry of nature's moods. The attitude toward landscape began to change only as the surrounding wilderness was gradually tamed. The spread of civilization allowed Americans for the first time to see nature as the escape from urban life that had long inspired European painters. As in England, the contribution of the poets proved essential to shaping American ideas about nature. By 1825 they were calling on artists to depict the wilderness as the most distinctive feature of the New World and its emerging culture. Pantheism virtually became a national religion during the Romantic era. While it could be terrifying, nature was everywhere and was believed to play a special role in determining the American character. Led by Thomas Cole (1801–1848), the founder of the Hudson River School, which flourished from 1825 until the Centennial celebration in 1876, American painters elevated the forests and mountains to symbols of the United States.

THOMAS COLE. Like many early American landscapists, Cole came from England, where he was trained as an engraver, but learned the basics of painting from an itinerant artist in the Midwest. After a summer sketching tour up the Hudson River, he invented the means of expressing the elemental power of the country's primitive landscape by transforming the formulas of the English picturesque into Romantic hymns based on the direct observation of nature. Because he also wrote poetry, the artist was uniquely able to create a visual counterpart to the literary ideas of the day. His painting *View of Schroon Mountain, Essex County, New York, After a Storm* (fig. 21-56) shows the peak rising majestically like a pyramid from the forest below. It is treated as a symbol of permanence surrounded by death and decay, signified by the autumnal foliage, passing storm, and dead trees. Stirred by sublime emotion, the artist has heightened the dramatic lighting behind the mountain, so that the broad landscape becomes a revelation of God's eternal laws.

GEORGE CALEB BINGHAM. *Fur Traders Descending the Missouri* (fig. 21-57), by George Caleb Bingham (1811–1879), shows this close identification with the land in a different way.

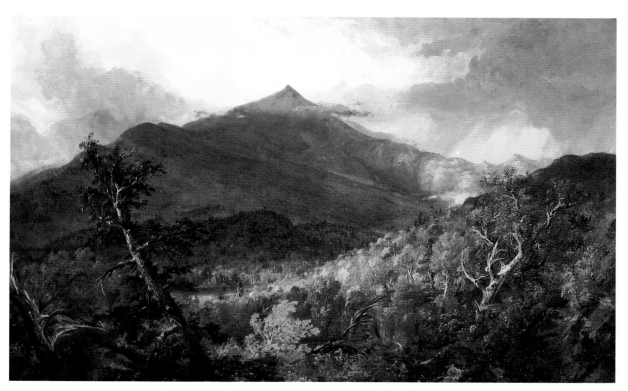

21-56. Thomas Cole. *View of Schroon Mountain, Essex County, New York, After a Storm.* 1838. Oil on canvas, 39⅜ x 63" (100 x 160 cm). The Cleveland Museum of Art

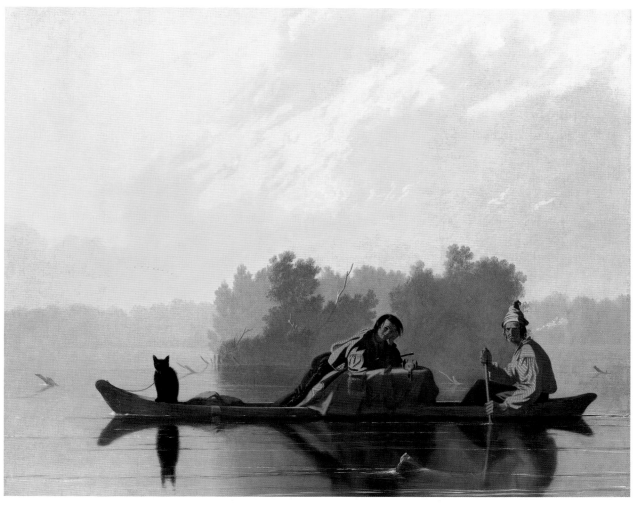

21-57. George Caleb Bingham. *Fur Traders Descending the Missouri.* c. 1845. Oil on canvas, 29 x 36½" (73.7 x 92.7 cm). The Metropolitan Museum of Art, New York

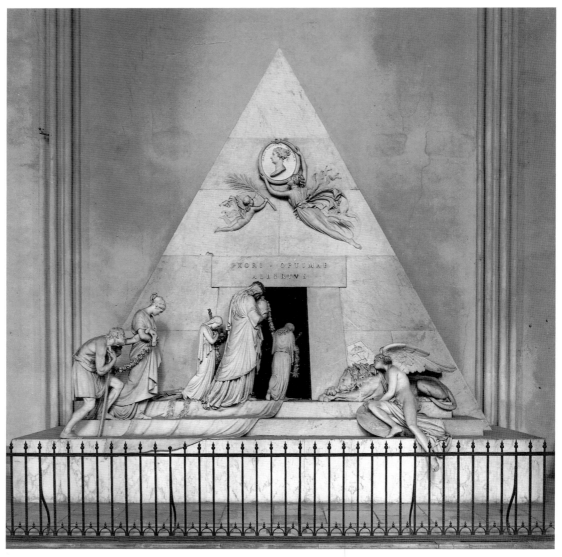

21-58. Antonio Canova. Tomb of the Archduchess Maria Christina. 1798–1805. Marble, lifesize. Augustinerkirche, Vienna

The picture, both a landscape and a genre scene, is full of the vastness and silence of the wide-open spaces. The two trappers in their dugout canoe, gliding downstream in the misty sunlight, are entirely at home in this idyllic setting. Bingham portrays the United States as a benevolent Eden in which settlers assume their rightful place. Rather than being dwarfed by a vast and often hostile continent, these hardy pioneers live in an ideal state of harmony with nature, symbolized by the waning daylight. The picture carries us back to the innocent era of Mark Twain's *Tom Sawyer* and *Huckleberry Finn*. It reminds us of how much Romantic adventurousness went into the westward expansion of the United States. The scene owes much of its haunting charm to the silhouette of the black cub chained to the prow and its reflection in the water. This masterstroke adds a note of primitive mystery that we shall not meet again until the work of Henri Rousseau (see pages 785–86).

SCULPTURE

In attempting to define Romanticism in sculpture, we are immediately struck by an extraordinary fact. In contrast to the abun-

dance of theoretical writings that accompanied Neoclassical sculpture from Winckelmann on, there exists only one piece of writing that sets forth a general theory of sculpture from the Romantic point of view: Baudelaire's essay of 1846, "Why Sculpture Is Boring," which occupies only a few pages of his long review of the Salon of that year. Actually, Baudelaire was less concerned with the state of French sculpture at that moment, which struck him as deplorable, than he was with the limitations of sculpture as a medium. To him, there can be no such thing as Romantic sculpture. Every piece of sculpture is a "fetish" whose objective existence prevents the artist from expressing his subjective view of the world, his personal sensibility, because its three-dimensionality presents a hundred different points of view that prevent him from taking up a unique point of view. It can overcome this limitation only if it is placed in the service of architecture, where it becomes part of a larger whole, such as in a Gothic cathedral. As soon as it is detached from this context, sculpture returns to its primitive status.

Fortunately, Baudelaire's theory was not taken at face value by either artists or patrons. It does, however, suggest the difficulty Romantic sculptors had in finding a self-image they could live

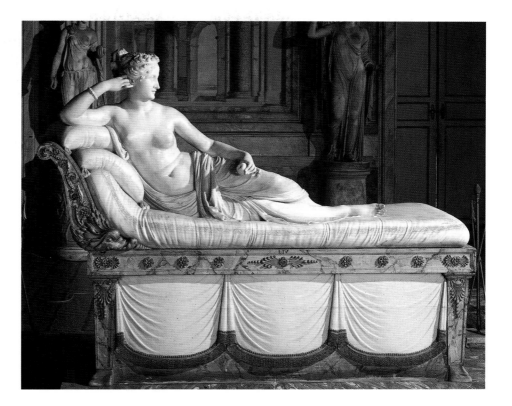

21-59. Antonio Canova. *Pauline Borghese As Venus.* 1808. Marble, lifesize. Galleria Borghese, Rome

with. The unique virtue of sculpture—its solid, space-filling reality (its "idol" quality)—was not compatible with the Romantic temperament. To defy established society, its values and institutions, was easier for writers and painters than for sculptors. The rebellious and individualistic urges of Romanticism could find expression in rough, small-scale sketches but rarely survived the laborious process of translating the sketch into a permanent, finished monument.

Italy

ANTONIO CANOVA. At the beginning of the Romantic era, we find an adaptation of the Neoclassical style to new ends by sculptors. They were led by Antonio Canova (1757–1822), who was not only the greatest sculptor of his generation but also the most famous artist of the Western world from the 1790s until long after his death. Both his work and his personality became a model for every sculptor during those years. Canova's meteoric rise led to numerous commissions. The Tomb of Maria Christina, archduchess of Austria, in the Church of the Augustinians in Vienna (fig. 21-58), was commissioned by her husband soon after her death in 1798. It is remarkable as much for its "timeless" beauty as for its gentle melancholy. The framework had been anticipated in a monument to Titian planned by Canova several years before. This ensemble, in contrast to the tombs of earlier times (such as fig. 12-14), does not include the real burial place. Moreover, the archduchess appears only in a portrait medallion framed by a snake biting its own tail (a symbol of eternity) and sustained by two floating **genii**. Presumably, but not actually, the urn carried by the woman in the center contains her ashes. This is an ideal burial service performed by mostly allegorical figures: a mourning winged genius on the right, and the group about

to enter the tomb on the left who represent the Three Ages of Life. The slow procession, directed away from the beholder, stands for "eternal remembrance." All references to Christianity are notably absent.

Canova must have known of Pigalle's tomb for the maréchal de Saxe (see fig. 20-3), which looks forward to it in so many respects. The differences are equally striking, however. Canova's design looks surprisingly like a very high relief. Most of the figures are seen in strict profile, so that they seem to hug the wall plane despite the deep space. Gestures are kept to a minimum, and the allegorical trappings that clutter Pigalle's monument have been swept away, so that nothing distracts us from the solemn ritual being acted out before us. It is this intense concentration that distinguishes Canova's Romantic classicism from the Baroque classicism of Pigalle.

Canova's friends included Jacques-Louis David (see pages 673–76), who helped to spread his fame in France. In 1802, Canova was invited to Paris by Napoleon, who wanted his portrait done by the greatest sculptor of the age. With Napoleon's approval, he made a colossal nude figure in marble showing the conqueror as a victorious and peace-giving Mars. (Fittingly enough, the statue was given to the Duke of Wellington after he defeated Napoleon at Waterloo.) Not to be outdone, Napoleon's sister Pauline Borghese had Canova sculpt her as a reclining Venus (fig. 21-59). The statue is so obviously idealized as to quiet any gossip. We recognize it as a forerunner, more classically proportioned, of Ingres' *Odalisque* (see fig. 21-30). It is equally characteristic of early Romanticism, which incorporated Rococo eroticism but in a less sensuous form. Strangely enough, Pauline Borghese seems less three-dimensional than the painting. She is designed like a "relief in the round," for front and back view only. Her charm comes almost entirely from the fluid grace of her contours.

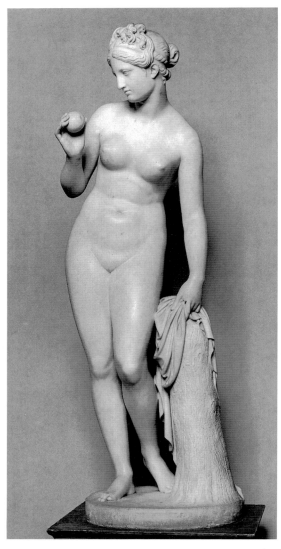

21-60. Bertel Thorvaldsen. *Venus*. 1813–16. Marble, lifesize. Thorvaldsens Museum, Copenhagen

BERTEL THORVALDSEN. The Napoleonic era was not favorable for those who wanted to be like Canova: independent, obligated to no single patron, free to create "modern classics." The only sculptor who achieved that goal was Bertel Thorvaldsen (1770–1844), a Dane who came to Rome in 1797 on a scholarship from the Royal Academy in Copenhagen and became Canova's successor. For all of Europe except France and Spain, he remained the model of sculptural perfection until the 1850s. Germans, Scandinavians, and many Italians viewed him as more "truly Greek" than Canova. Although he established his reputation early, Thorvaldsen had to live through some difficult years before he could feel artistically and financially secure.

Thorvaldsen became the first to revive the most heroic phase of Greek art, but he soon underwent a basic change not only of style but also of outlook. His *Venus* (fig. 21-60) is closer to a living model than to any ancient source, although its immediate ancestor is a statue by Houdon. Thorvaldsen shows her in a moment of triumph, holding the golden apple awarded by Paris in the beauty contest that started the Trojan War. Yet she contemplates the apple in a way that might lead us to mistake her for Eve in the Temptation, were it not for the garment in her left hand. The statue shows Thorvaldsen's new emphasis on poetic sentiment, as well as his reawakened religious feeling, which he shared with the Nazarenes, many of whom were his friends (see page 715). Thus his *Venus* is far more Romantic than Neoclassic, despite its style.

France

It was in France that the main development of Romantic sculpture took place. Although the doctrine of the Academy came to be broadened and modified in the course of time, it lasted until Rodin late in the century. Its core belief was that the human body is nature's noblest creation and hence the sculptor's noblest subject. Translated into practice, this idea meant that every student of sculpture received a rigorous training. The course of study was especially demanding at the Paris École des Beaux-Arts. In 1819 it opened as the successor to both the Académie Royale de Peinture et Sculpture and the Académie Royale d'Architecture under the Académie des Beaux-Arts, which in turn was part of the Institut de France. Since the level of teaching at the École was far higher

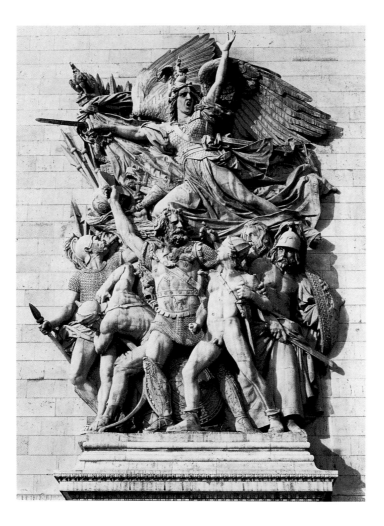

21-61. François Rude.
La Marseillaise. 1833–36.
Stone, approx. 42 x 26'
(12.8 x 7.9 m).
Arc de Triomphe, Paris

in sculpture than it was in painting, the limitations of the academic sculptural tradition became apparent only much later.

The Romantic reaction against the ideal of the "modern classic" first asserted itself in the sculpture sections of the French Salons after the Revolution of 1830, which brought about the fall of the restored Bourbon regime. However, antiacademic tendencies did not dominate until the last two decades of the century, when Michelangelo, Rodin's ideal, at last won out over Canova. What ultimately destroyed the modern classic was the cult of the fragmentary and the unfinished.

That the Romantic rebellion started so much later in sculpture than in painting also indicates how closely the medium was linked to politics in nineteenth-century France. Artists were often passionately involved in politics, but because the state remained the largest single source of commissions for sculptors, their fortunes were more directly affected than those of the painters by changes in regime. French sculpture was by no means dominated by its social and political environment. Yet, to the extent that it was a public art, sculpture responded to the pressure of these forces, directly or indirectly, far more than did painting. It was shaped by them in varying degrees, depending on local circumstances. Thus we cannot understand its development without reference to the changing politics around it.

FRANÇOIS RUDE. François Rude (1784–1855), who enthusiastically took Napoleon's side after the emperor's return in 1815

from exile on the island of Elba, sought refuge in Brussels from Bourbon rule, as had Jacques-Louis David, whom he knew and admired. After returning to Paris in 1827, Rude must have felt that artistically he had reached a dead end and decided to strike out in fresh directions. He acquired a new interest in the French Renaissance tradition of the School of Fontainebleau and Giovanni Bologna (see pages 496–98), which would eventually lead him back to Claus Sluter (see page 210). This rediscovery of national sculptural traditions, so characteristic of Romantic revivalism, was part of a new wave of nationalism, which was also manifested by a passion for historical portraits as "morally elevating for the public."

These concerns are seen in Rude's masterpiece, *The Departure of the Volunteers of 1792,* commonly called *La Marseillaise* (fig. 21-61). It was carved for Napoleon's unfinished Arc de Triomphe on the Place de l'Étoile. The new king, Louis-Philippe, and his energetic minister of the interior, Adolphe Thiers, saw the triumphal arch's completion as an opportunity to demonstrate that the July Monarchy was a government of national reconciliation. Hence the sculptural program had to offer something to every segment of the French political spectrum. Rude received a commission for one of the four groups that flank the opening. He raised his subject—the French people rallying to defend the Republic against attack from abroad—to the level of mythic splendor. The volunteers surge forth, some nude, others in classical armor, inspired by the great forward movement of the winged genius of Liberty above them.

ROMANTICISM IN MUSIC

Many music historians still view the early nineteenth century as part of the Classical period. To them, the Romantic era proper did not arrive until the 1860s, by which time Romanticism in painting had run its course. Music proved the ideal Romantic art form because it was widely believed to allow the fullest expression of pure feeling, without the hindrance of literal meaning or the reality of appearance. The archetype of the early Romantic composer was Ludwig van Beethoven (1770–1827). He sympathized strongly with the American and French Revolutions, which fed his restless Romantic spirit, and in his personal relations he bowed to no one, least of all to his aristocratic patrons. Nevertheless, he was closest spiritually to Goethe, a member of the previous generation whom he revered. After being trained at the piano by his father, Beethoven wanted to study with Mozart, who was then terminally ill; he had to settle for Haydn. Although Haydn was a tough task master who tolerated no mistakes, he had little time for Beethoven, who secretly took lessons in theory from two minor composers. Beethoven's early works belong to the Neoclassical period of music (see box page 688). Except for the piano sonatas, which take Haydn's as their point of departure, his style has more affinities with that of C. P. E. Bach than of Mozart or Haydn. Beethoven was a virtuoso whose only rival at the piano was Mozart's pupil Johann Nepomuk Hummel (1778–1837), who introduced the cascades of notes that were to become characteristic of later Romantics, such as Chopin and Lizst (see below). Like Mozart, Beethoven was a universal genius. Beethoven greatly expanded the expressive range of the forms he inherited. His works are more explosive and dynamic, and by emphasizing content over form, they pushed classical music to its limits, and often beyond. Mercilessly self-critical, he composed far fewer works than his predecessors, but they are mostly substantial contributions to the literature. The most striking aspect of Beethoven's music is its novelty, which made it controversial to many of his contemporaries, such as the composer Carl Maria von Weber (1786–1826), who was his harshest critic. It features heroic expression counterbalanced by melting lyricism. No other composer could scale the heights or plumb the depths of the soul to such stirring effect. Extremely public during his youth and early maturity, his music became increasingly private over time, perhaps as the result of his growing deafness, which was largely complete by 1816, as well as of his troubled personal life. Yet its complexity was a consistent outgrowth of the composer's personality, and makes the late works demanding for interpreter and listener alike.

Beethoven was the essential point of departure for most Romantic composers of the next generation. Yet, no matter how awed they were by his commanding presence, they remained independent personalities determined to make their own contributions.

The dreamy sensibility of Franz Schubert (1797–1828) found its ideal outlet in German art songs (*Lieder*; singular, *Lied*), inspired by the poetry of Goethe and Schiller among others, which he wrote in vast quantity and variety that occasionally provides a glimpse of the stormy side of his personality. Lieder remained the heart and soul of his chamber music, which is pure enchantment: the first piano trio, the octet, and the last three quartets, including the well-known *Death and the Maiden,* which is based on one of his most memorable songs. Schubert's piano sonatas in turn present an ideal combination of intimate lyricism and large scale, although he had some difficulty handling extended symphonic form.

Orchestral writing presented no difficulties to Felix Mendelssohn-Bartholdy (1809–1847). Like Mozart, he was a child prodigy who was writing significant music by late adolescence. (His sister, Fanny, was also gifted and remains unjustly neglected.) His five symphonies and numerous overtures are notable for their vitality and colorism, which "paint" vivid images in sound. Mendelssohn, too, was stirred by literature, above all by the plays of Shakespeare. For an 1843 production by Ludwig Tieck he set Shakespeare's *A Midsummer Night's Dream* to music that perfectly captures its impish spirit. Mendelssohn, like Schubert, succumbed early to syphilis (the AIDS of the time), which also claimed the lives of numerous other people in the arts.

The most characteristic music of Robert Schumann (1810–1856) was piano and vocal music. But although he lacked the facility for orchestration of his friend Mendelssohn, his four symphonies were of major importance for the next generation of German composers. They breathe an innocence and love of nature that make them the musical counterparts of Romantic landscape paintings. Schumann was also inspired by Romantic writers, and undertook a series of large-scale vocal works: incidental music for *Manfred* (1849), incorporating the poem by Lord Byron; the opera *Genoveva* (1850), taken from Ludwig Tieck's drama; and *Scenes from Faust* (1853), based on Goethe's poetry. Schumann's wife, Clara Wieck (1819–1896), was also an excellent pianist and composer, but she put her career second to her husband's, so that only recently has her music come to the fore. Schumann died young after suffering from two years of madness, perhaps brought on by syphilis.

The only composer to equal Beethoven's heroic stature was the Frenchman Hector Berlioz (1803–1869), whose music employs the full force of a very large orchestra. Despite being mainly self-taught, Berlioz was a masterful composer in

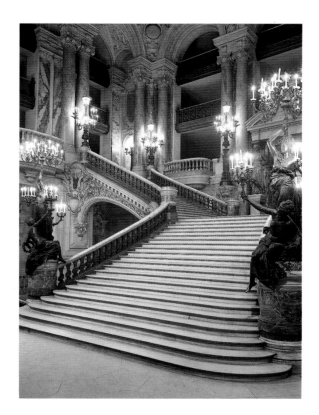

(LEFT) 21-75. Charles Garnier. Grand Staircase, the Opéra, Paris. 1861–74

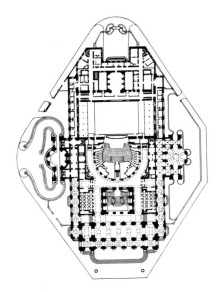

21-76. Plan of the Opéra

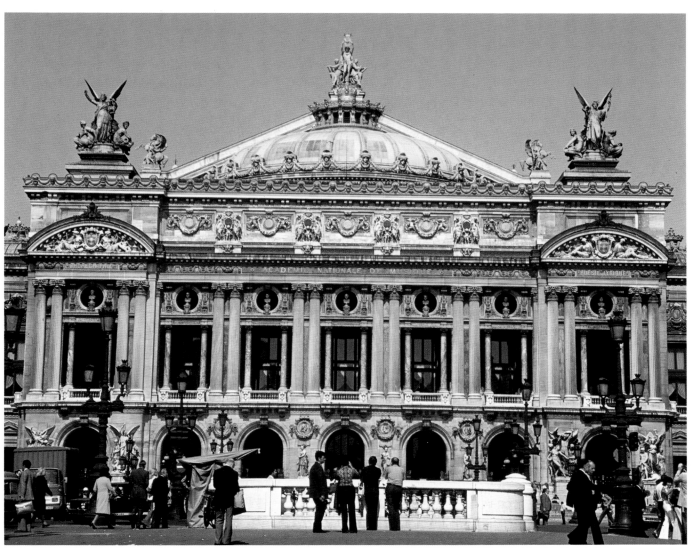

21-77. The Opéra

thorough command of orchestration—the technique of specifying which instruments should play which parts of a musical composition. Berlioz's music is programmatic, that is, it tells a story, or at least suggests a sequence of incidents, and this emphasis on story line over pure form is one of his most Romantic qualities. Berlioz's *Symphonie fantastique* (1830) is a morbid account of unrequited love. Shakespeare made a deep impression on him, and his most successful work is a dramatic realization of *Romeo and Juliet* (1839). No one, not even Verdi and Tchaikovsky later in the century, understood better the magic of love or the power of tragedy in Shakespeare. Although they were little performed during his lifetime, Berlioz's operas were important for successfully reviving the grand tradition of Lully and Rameau.

Paris was the opera capital of Europe during the first half of the nineteenth century. The most prolific and popular composer of opera was Giacchino Rossini (1792–1868), who adapted his Italian style to suit the French taste. While his operas generally have ridiculous plots, the music itself is beautiful and, given a libretto of quality, the result is a masterpiece: *The Barber of Seville* (1816), based on Beaumarchais' play, and *William Tell* (1829), Rossini's last opera, inspired by Schiller's drama of 1804. By the time he arrived in Paris in 1824, Rossini had the field to himself. His only potential rival, Luigi Cherubini (1760–1842), another Italian who had settled there in 1788, turned his attention largely to church music after 1813. A later academic counterpart to Christoph Willibald Glück (see page 688), Cherubini provided the classical antithesis to Rossini's unabashed Romanticism. During his day, he was regarded as the equal of Beethoven, who is known to have admired him. Indeed, Beethoven's lone opera, *Fidelio,* was influenced by Cherubini's "rescue" operas. *Medea* (1797), based on the Greek tragedy by Euripides, remains Cherubini's finest achievement, though modern performances are marred by a later orchestration of the spoken dialogue.

With Rossini's departure for Paris in 1824, Italian opera was left in the capable hands of Gaetano Donizetti (1797–1848). Most of his 70 operas are potboilers, but the best have spirited drama and appealing music. *Lucia di Lammermoor* (1835), freely adapted from a historical novel by Sir Walter Scott (see box page 714), might be considered the perfect opera: it spins its tale through a succession of glorious arias that bring the characters, centering on a tragic heroine of epic proportions, vividly to life. Donizetti's style largely determined the character of Italian opera before Giuseppe Verdi. His chief competition, Vincenzo Bellini (1801–1835), died too young to achieve his full potential, only a few years after writing *Norma* and *La Somnambula* in 1831.

Among the most unusual musical personalities of the Romantic movement was the Polish composer Frédéric Chopin (1810–1849), who was drawn to Paris at an early age. A celebrated virtuoso of the piano, Chopin introduced a wide range of new types of composition for the keyboard, most of them—such as the *polonaise* and the *mazurka*—based on the national music of Poland, although John Field (1782–1837) helped to pave the way for his nocturnes, and there is a debt to Hummel, Schubert, and Mendelssohn as well. These compositions are so free and inventive that they seem to be entirely new forms spun as if by magic from Chopin's endlessly fertile imagination. Although mostly small in scale, they yielded not only poetic intimacy, at which he excelled, but also heroic grandeur. Chopin and his companion, the novelist George Sand (see box page 714), sat for a famous portrait by Delacroix.

For Chopin, music remained an expressive vehicle first, a technical display second. With the Italian violinist Niccolò Paganini (1782–1840), who also spent much of his life in Paris, virtuosity became an end in itself, which greatly enlarged the scope of violin playing. He was one of the first great music stars to be idolized by an adoring public. Paganini became the model in turn for the Hungarian piano virtuoso Ferenc Liszt (1811–1886), a friend of Chopin's who came to Paris for a while, but later traveled widely.

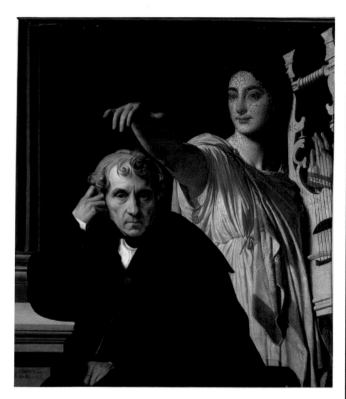

Jean-Auguste-Dominique Ingres. *Cherubini and the Muse of Lyric Poetry.* 1842. Oil on canvas, 41⅜ x 37" (105.1 x 94 cm). Musée du Louvre, Paris

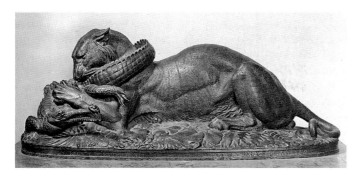

21-62. Antoine-Louis Barye. *Tiger Devouring a Gavial of the Ganges*. 1831–32. Bronze, length 39½" (100.3 cm). Musée du Louvre, Paris

ANTOINE-LOUIS BARYE. *La Marseillaise* brings to mind certain paintings by Delacroix and, in fact, its ultimate source is pictorial. In a similar way, Stubbs' *Lion Attacking a Horse* (see fig. 21-9) is the forerunner of animal groups by Antoine-Louis Barye (1795–1875). Barye followed in his father's footsteps as a goldsmith, but spent all his free hours at the Paris zoo, sketching live animals and studying their anatomy. He also became a friend of Delacroix, who shared these interests and sometimes treated the same themes. Barye scored his first public success at the Salon of 1831 with the plaster model of *Tiger Devouring a Gavial of the Ganges* (fig. 21-62). His group displays a realism based on thorough scientific knowledge. What really impressed critics and public alike was the ferocity of the tiger, the pitiless display of "nature red in tooth and claw" so exciting to the Romantic imagination. Animal combats had a long tradition in Western art going all the way back to classical antiquity. Found often in Roman mosaics, these followed well-established formal conventions that governed both the choice of animals and their compositional relationship. Barye disregarded all such precedents. Not only did he study his animals directly from nature, he chose exotic species and unusual combinations, no matter how implausible. (Gavials are unlikely prey for tigers.) What counted was the group's expressive power, intensified here by the compact monumentality of the design.

No wonder the work aroused an emotional response that made people identify the group with the national anthem itself. For Rude the group had a deeply felt personal meaning: his father had been among those volunteers. When the arch was officially unveiled in 1836, there was almost unanimous agreement that Rude's group made the other three pale into insignificance. Despite its great public acclaim, *La Marseillaise* failed to gain Rude the official honors he so clearly deserved. He found himself more and more in opposition to the regime, and his most important works between 1836 and 1848 were direct expressions of his Bonapartist political beliefs.

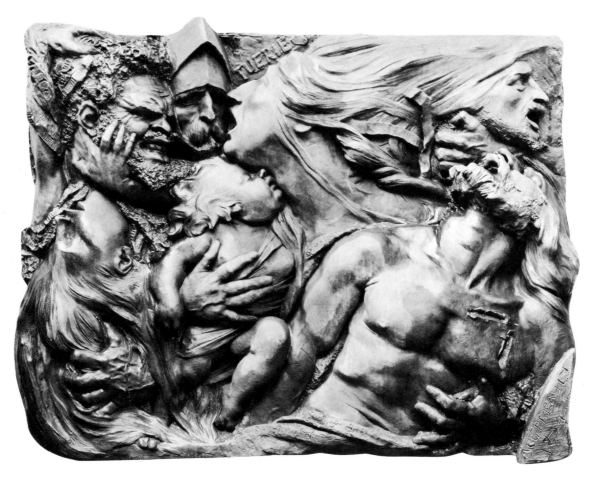

21-63. Auguste Préault. *Tuerie (Slaughter)*. 1834. Bronze, 43 x 55" (109.2 x 139.7 cm). Musée des Beaux-Arts, Chartres, France

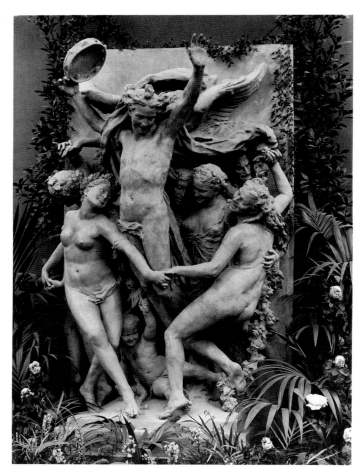

21-64. Jean-Baptiste Carpeaux. *The Dance*. 1867–69. Plaster model, approx. 15' x 8'6" (4.6 x 2.6 m). Musée de l'Opéra, Paris

AUGUSTE PRÉAULT. Besides bringing Rude and Barye into prominence, the Salons of the early 1830s served as showcases for sculptors still in their twenties. What separated them from the generation of their teachers was that none was old enough to have experienced the Napoleonic era. As it happened, there was not a single first-rate artist in this group. Auguste Préault (1809–1879), the most interesting of them, may have been the first to earn the title "a genius without talent," as he was called by one of his contemporaries. His ambitious relief titled *Tuerie (Slaughter)* (fig. 21-63), sent to the Salon of 1834, shows that his interest centered on extreme physical and emotional states. He submitted the panel as the fictitious fragment of a larger composition, probably to ease it past the jury. The design is actually quite self-contained, even though every figure in it is indeed a fragment, except for the baby. The style of *Tuerie* must be termed Neo-Baroque, yet it is brimming with a physical and emotional violence far exceeding seventeenth-century art. Its expressive distortions and its irrational space, filled to the bursting point with writhing shapes, evoke memories of Gothic sculpture. In fact, the helmeted knight's face next to that of the screaming mother hints that the subject itself—some dread apocalyptic event beyond human control—is medieval. But in true Romantic fashion, Préault does not define it.

Tuerie established Préault's reputation as the prototype of the Romantic sculptor. It was praised by avant-garde critics as a radical attack on the rules of classical relief. (What conservatives thought of it can easily be imagined.) Its very extremism, however, condemned *Tuerie* to being a dead end. Neither Préault nor anyone else could make it the starting point of a new development.

JEAN-BAPTISTE CARPEAUX. If the high tide of Romanticism is to be found among the French sculptors born during the first decade of the century, those born during the second may, with some hesitation, be designated late Romantics, but we again look in vain for a major talent among them. The third decade, in contrast, saw the birth of several important sculptors. Of these, the best known was Jean-Baptiste Carpeaux (1827–1875). Carpeaux's masterpiece came at the end of the Second Empire, which succeeded the short-lived Second Republic in 1852. In 1861 Carpeaux's old friend the architect Charles Garnier began the Paris Opéra (see pages 731–33) and entrusted him with one of the four sculptural groups across the facade. *The Dance* (fig. 21-64) perfectly matches Garnier's Neo-Baroque architecture. (The plaster model in our illustration is both livelier and more precise than the final stone group in fig. 21-77, lower right.)

The group created a scandal after its unveiling in 1869. The nude bacchantes dancing around the winged male genius in the center were denounced as drunk, vulgar, and indecent—and small wonder, for their coquettish gaiety derives from small Rococo groups such as Clodion's (see fig. 20-2). But Carpeaux's enormous figures (they are 15 feet tall) look undressed rather

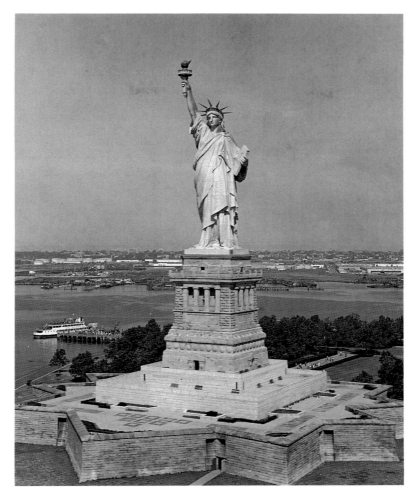

21-65. Auguste Bartholdi. *Statue of Liberty (Liberty Enlightening the World)*.
1875–84. Copper sheeting over metal armature, height of figure 151'6" (46 m).
Liberty Island, New York Harbor

than nude, because of their naturalism, so that we do not accept them as inhabiting the realm of mythology. Public opinion insisted that the group be replaced. After the war with Germany ended in 1871, the old complaints were forgotten and *The Dance* was recognized as a masterpiece. It is as obviously superior to the other three Opéra groups by more conservative sculptors as Rude's *Marseillaise* is to its neighbors on the Arc de Triomphe. (Carpeaux had studied for a while with Rude.) *The Dance* established the Beaux-Arts style, as it is called, in sculpture for the rest of the century, much as Garnier's Opéra did in architecture (see page 731).

AUGUSTE BARTHOLDI. The late nineteenth century offered enormous opportunities for official commissions to sculptors. It is a safe guess that the great majority of monuments in the Western world were produced, or at least begun, between 1872 and 1905. The most ambitious of these was the *Statue of Liberty* (or, to use its official title, *Liberty Enlightening the World*) by Auguste Bartholdi (1834–1904). This monument (fig. 21-65) in memory of French support for America during the War of Independence was a gift of the French people, not of the government. Its enormous cost was raised by public subscription, which took ten years. The sculpture was placed on a tall pedestal built with funds raised by the American public.

Bartholdi developed the *Statue of Liberty* from a previous concept for a gigantic lighthouse in the form of a woman holding a lamp that was intended to be erected at the northern entry to the Suez Canal. All he had to do was exchange the Egyptian headdress for a radiant crown and the lantern for a torch. The final work shows an austere, classically draped young woman holding the torch in her raised right hand and a tablet in her left. She steps on the broken shackles of tyranny with her left foot, on which her weight rests. The right leg (the free one, in accordance with the rules of classical contrapposto) is set back, so that the figure seems to be advancing when seen from the side but looks stationary from the front. As a piece of sculpture, the *Statue of Liberty* is less original than one might think. It derives from a well-established ancestry reaching back to Canova and beyond. Its conservatism, however, was Bartholdi's conscious choice. He sensed that only a "timeless" statue could embody the ideal he wanted to glorify.

The figure, which stands more than 150 feet tall, presented severe structural problems that called for the skills of an architectural engineer. Bartholdi found the ideal collaborator in Gustave Eiffel, the future builder of the Eiffel Tower (see fig. 22-36). The project took more than a decade to complete. The *Statue of Liberty* was inaugurated at last in the fall of 1886. Its fame as the symbol—one is tempted to say "trademark"—of the United States has been worldwide ever since.

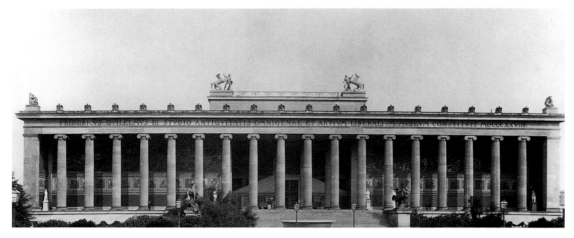

21-66. Karl Friedrich Schinkel. Altes Museum, Berlin. 1824–28

ARCHITECTURE

Given the individualistic nature of Romanticism, we might expect the range of revival styles to be widest in painting, the most personal and private of the visual arts, and narrowest in architecture, the most communal and public. Yet the opposite is true. Painters and sculptors were unable to abandon Renaissance habits of representation, and never really revived medieval art or ancient art before the Classical Greek era. Architects were not subject to this limitation. Because they felt free to draw on a wider range of sources, the revival styles lasted longer in architecture than in the other arts.

The Classical Revival

The Greek revival phase of Neoclassicism was pioneered on a small scale in England, but was quickly taken up everywhere. The Greek Doric was believed to embody more of the "noble simplicity and calm grandeur" of Classical Greece than the later, less "masculine" orders. However, the Greek Doric was also the least flexible order and the most difficult to adapt to modern purposes. Hence only rarely could Greek Doric architecture furnish a direct model for Neoclassical structures. We instead find variations of it combined with elements taken from the other Greek orders.

KARL FRIEDRICH SCHINKEL. The Altes Museum (Old Museum; fig. 21-66) by Karl Friedrich Schinkel (1781–1841) is a spectacular example of the Greek revival. The main entrance resembles a Doric temple seen from the side (see fig. 5-28), but with Ionic columns strung across a Corinthian order (compare figs. 5-25 and 5-39). (Strictly speaking, it is like a Greek **stoa**; see page 137.) The plan is based on a contemporary treatise by the French architect Jean-Nicolas Durand (1760–1834), a pupil of Boullée and professor at the recently established engineering school in Paris. Durand reduced classical architecture to a set of geometric formulas based on function and economy, an idea that goes back to Blondel (see page 685). Schinkel's building, however, has none of Durand's utilitarianism. On the contrary, it is notable for its bold design and refined proportions.

Schinkel, an architect of great ability, began as a painter in the style of Caspar David Friedrich (see pages 712–13). He then worked as a stage designer before being appointed to the Berlin public works office, which he later headed. (He owed his appointment to Wilhelm von Humboldt, the Prussian statesman and Minister of Education, who was a friend of Goethe and Schiller; see box page 683.) Thus he knew how to instill architecture with Romantic associations and a theatrical flair worthy of Piranesi. Schinkel's first love was the Gothic, but although most of his public buildings are in a Neoclassical style, they retain a strong element of the picturesque. He could admire both styles because he shared the Enlightenment belief in the moral and educational functions of architecture.

Here the measured rhythm of the monumental facade establishes a contemplative mood appropriate to viewing the art of antiquity. The Altes Museum expresses the veneration of ancient Greece in the land of Winckelmann and Mengs. To the poet Goethe, Greece remained the peak of civilization. The Altes Museum testifies, furthermore, to the informed attitude that gave rise to art museums, galleries, and academies on both sides of the Atlantic during the nineteenth century. At the same time, the Greek style served the imperial ambitions of Prussia, which emerged as a major power at the Congress of Vienna in 1815 following the defeat of Napoleon. The imposing grandeur of the Altes Museum proclaims Berlin as the new Athens, with Kaiser Wilhelm III as a modern Perikles.

LEO VAN KLENZE. Schinkel was the tutor and friend of Crown Prince Friedrich Wilhelm, an amateur architect who wanted to combine Greek and Gothic architecture into a new style expressing his dream of a united Germany. This same ambition was shared by Crown Prince Ludwig of Bavaria, an ally of Napoleon who nevertheless conceived a monument to German unity during a visit to occupied Berlin in 1807. To achieve his vision, Ludwig turned to another Prussian, Leo von Klenze (1784–1864). Like Schinkel he had been a pupil in Berlin of Friedrich Gilly (1772–1800). Von Klenze was actually the first to design neoclassical museums as temples of art: the Glyptothek in

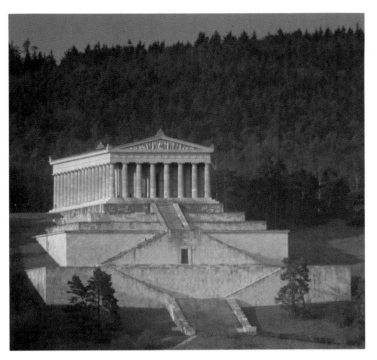

21-67. Leo von Klenze. Walhalla, near Regensburg, Germany. 1821–42

structural rationalist at heart, preferred it because it was "true according to the program and true according to the methods of construction." Certain English writers, notably John Ruskin, regarded Gothic as superior for ethical or religious reasons on the grounds that it was "honest" and "Christian."

HORACE WALPOLE. England played a key role in the Gothic revival, as it did in the development of Romantic literature and painting. Gothic forms had never wholly disappeared in England. They were used on occasion for special purposes, even by Sir Christopher Wren and Sir John Vanbrugh (see pages 619–23), but these were survivals of an authentic, if outmoded, tradition. The conscious revival was begun by William Kent in the 1730s, partly at the prompting of Robert Walpole, one of the most important politicians of the day. It soon became linked with the cult of the picturesque, and with the vogue for medieval (and pseudo-medieval) romances.

Horace Walpole (1717–1797), Robert's son, started the medieval craze with the publication in 1764 of his novel *The Castle of Otranto: A Gothic Story*. It was in this spirit that he enlarged and "gothicized" Strawberry Hill, his country house outside London (figs. 21-68 and 21-69). The process, which began midway in the eighteenth century, took more than 25 years and involved Wal-

Munich (1816), which houses the sculpture from Aegina (see figs. 5-22 and 5-23), followed by the Alte Pinakothek (1822), which holds the collection of Old Master paintings. Such an association could find support in the Classical past, specifically the small pinakotheke (picture gallery) at the entrance to the Akropolis (see fig. 5-34). Whereas Schinkel merely referred to a plan by Durand, von Klenze actually studied with him, as well as with Napoleon's architects Percier and Fontaine (see page 733).

In 1821 von Klenze designed his masterpiece Walhalla, overlooking the Danube near Regensburg (fig. 21-67). Named for the resting place of heroes in ancient Teutonic mythology, it served as a pantheon of German notables whose portrait busts line the interior. The design owes a great deal to a proposed monument to Frederick the Great by Gilly, which was as grandiose as anything conceived by Boullée, but it has been tamed by von Klenze's academic classicism. The building nevertheless fulfills its intended purpose, as stated by Prince Ludwig: "The Walhalla was erected so that the German might depart from it more German and better than when he had arrived."

The Gothic Revival

It is characteristic of Romanticism that at the time architects launched the classical revival, they also started a Gothic revival. The appeal of the Gothic was chiefly as a means for creating picturesque effects and expressing Romantic feeling. After 1800 the choice between classical and Gothic modes was often resolved in favor of Gothic. Nationalist sentiments, strengthened by the Napoleonic wars, became important factors. England, France, and Germany each believed that Gothic expressed its national genius. The French theorist Eugène Viollet-le-Duc (1814–1879), a

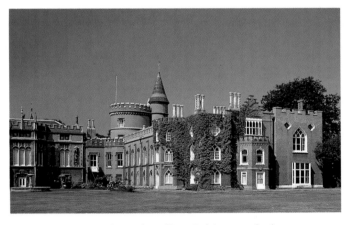

21-68. Horace Walpole, with William Robinson and others. Strawberry Hill, Twickenham, England. 1749–77

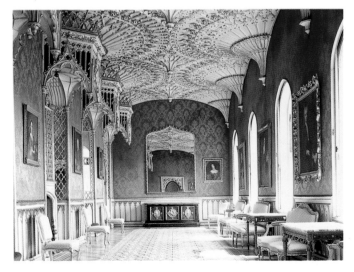

21-69. Interior of Strawberry Hill

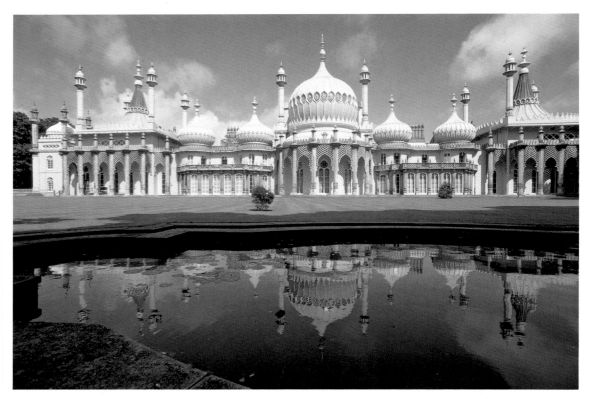

21-70. John Nash. The Royal Pavilion, Brighton, England. 1815–18

pole's circle of friends. Those who worked on the project included John Chute (1701–1776), William Robinson (c. 1720–1775), Richard Bentley (1708–1782), Thomas Pitt (c. 1737–1793), and Robert Adam, who was responsible for the round tower. The rambling structure has a studied irregularity, due mainly to Chute, that is decidedly picturesque. Inside, however, most of the elements were faithfully copied or closely adapted from authentic Gothic sources. The gallery in figure 21-69, designed by Pitt in 1759–62 with fire-places by Chute, is a splendid imitation of the English Perpendicular style found in the chapel of Henry VII at Westminster Abbey, with its conical vaults (compare fig. 11-28). The richly brocaded, yet dainty wall surfaces look almost as if they were decorated with lace-paper doilies. Although Walpole associated the Gothic with the pathos of the sublime, he acknowledged that the house was "pretty and gay." This playfulness, so free of dogma, gives Strawberry Hill its special charm. Gothic here is still an "exotic" style. It appeals because it is strange. But for that very reason it must be "translated," like a medieval romance or like the Chinese motifs that crop up in Rococo decoration.

JOHN NASH. The Romantic imagination saw the Gothic and the mysterious East in much the same light, and did not hesitate to mix and match elements. The masterpiece in this vein is the Royal Pavilion at Brighton (fig. 21-70), created half a century later by John Nash (1752–1835). The greatest architect of the English picturesque, he mastered the full range of revival styles, which here have been combined to brilliant effect. This "stately pleasure dome" is a cream-puff version of the Taj Mahal. Over a Neo-Palladian building Nash imposed a cast-iron armature supporting a facade of sheet-iron domes, minarets, and lacy screens. Chinese and even Gothic motifs were thrown in for good measure. Hence the style was known as Indian Gothic.

BENJAMIN LATROBE. By 1800 the Gothic was a fully acceptable alternative to the Greek revival as a style for major churches. The result was often a mixture in keeping with the eclectic bent of Romanticism. Benjamin Latrobe (1764–1820), an Anglo-American who became the most influential architect of Federal Neoclassicism under Jefferson, submitted a design in each style among the seven or eight he worked up for the Cathedral in Baltimore. In this respect he was a disciple of the English architect John Soane (1753–1837), who also worked in a variety of revival styles. The Neoclassical one was chosen, but it might just as well have been the Neo-Gothic. The present building is, in fact, a combination of the two. The exterior (fig. 21-71) has walls that resemble Soufflot's Panthéon (see fig. 21-16), which also provided the model for Latrobe's initial design in the shape of a Greek cross. It, too, features a dome and a temple front, but adds bell towers of disguised Gothic-Baroque ancestry. (The bulbous crowns are not his work.)

The interior (fig. 21-72) is far more distinguished. It was inspired by the domed and vaulted spaces of ancient Rome, especially the Pantheon (see fig. 7-12). Latrobe, however, was not interested in archaeological correctness. The "muscularity" of Roman structures has been subdued. The delicate moldings, profiles, and coffers are derived straight from Robert Adam (compare fig. 21-19). They are no more than linear accents that do not disturb the continuous, abstract surfaces. Here Latrobe shows how much he had learned from Soane's masterpiece, the Bank of

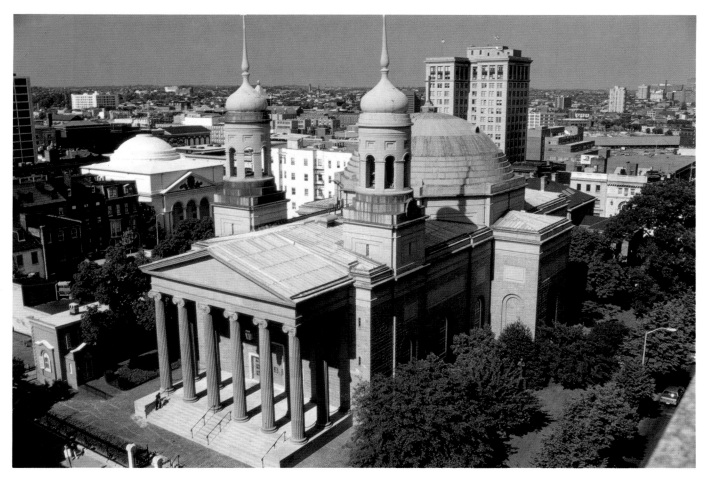

21-71. Benjamin Latrobe. Baltimore Cathedral (Basilica of the Assumption), Baltimore, Maryland. Begun 1805

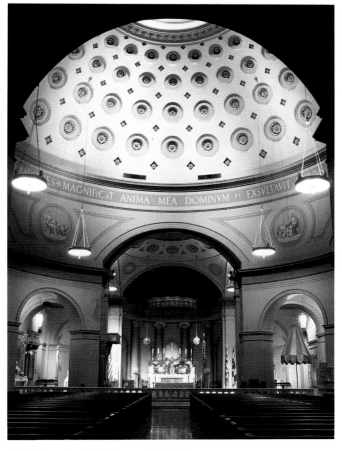

21-72. Interior of Baltimore Cathedral

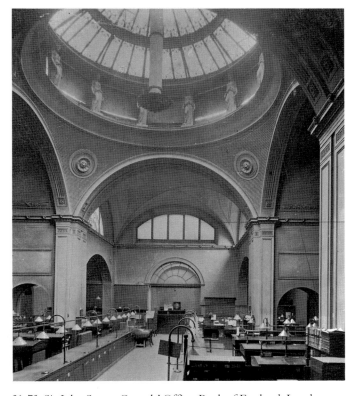

21-73. Sir John Soane. Consols' Office, Bank of England, London. 1794. Destroyed

England in London, before his departure for America in 1796. Unfortunately, the bank was largely destroyed in 1927, but it is still known from photographs (fig. 21-73). Like Adam, Soane was enthused by Piranesi's architectural fantasies, which he joined with the latest French theories. Soane's eclecticism is seen in the "Byzantine" dome on pendentives (compare fig. 8-34), which he used to picturesque effect. Soane relied heavily on the designs and advice of his teacher, George Dance (1741–1825), but was a far more capable architect.

In Latrobe's interpretation, the spatial qualities of ancient architecture have acquired the visionary character of Boullée's memorial to Isaac Newton (see fig. 21-17)—vast, pure, sublime. The seemingly weightless interior nearly presents that combination of classic form and Gothic lightness first proposed by Soufflot. It also shows the free and imaginative look of the mature Neoclassical style, when handled by a gifted architect. Had the Gothic design been chosen, the exterior might have been more striking, but the interior would probably have been less impressive. Like most Romantic architects seeking the sublime, Latrobe viewed Gothic churches "from the outside in"—as mysterious, looming structures silhouetted against the sky—but based his spatial fantasy on Roman monuments.

CHARLES BARRY AND A. N. WELBY PUGIN. The largest monument of the Gothic revival is the Houses of Parliament in London (fig. 21-74), designed by Sir Charles Barry (1785–1860) and A. N. Welby Pugin (1812–1852). As the seat of government and a focus of patriotic feeling, it presents a curious mixture: repetitious symmetry governs the main body of the structure and picturesque irregularity its silhouette. The building is a contradiction in terms. It imposes Pugin's Gothic vocabulary,

inspired by the English Perpendicular style (compare fig. 11-28), onto the classically conceived structure by Barry, with results that satisfied neither. Nevertheless, the Houses of Parliament admirably convey the grandeur of Victorian England at the height of its power.

Neo-Renaissance and Neo-Baroque Architecture

CHARLES GARNIER. Meanwhile, the stylistic alternatives were continually increased for architects by other historical revivals. When the Renaissance, then the Baroque, returned to favor by mid-century, the revival movement had come full circle: Neo-Renaissance and Neo-Baroque replaced the Neoclassical. This final phase of Romantic historicism dominated French architecture during the years 1850–75 and lingered through 1900. It is epitomized in the Paris Opéra (figs. 21-75, 21-76, and 21-77), designed by Charles Garnier (1825–1898). He had graduated from the École des Beaux-Arts and won the Prix de Rome, which enabled him to spend six years studying in Italy and Greece. The Opéra was the culmination of Baron Georges-Eugène Haussmann's (1809–1891) plan to modernize Paris under Napoleon III. It is the focal point for a series of main avenues that converge on it from all sides. Although the building was not completed until after the fall of the Second Empire, its extravagance typifies the Beaux-Arts style of the new Paris at its height.

The building is a masterpiece of eclecticism. The fluid curves of the Grand Staircase, for example, recall the Vestibule of the Laurentian Library (see fig. 13-23). The massing of the main entrance for those arriving on foot is reminiscent of Lescot's

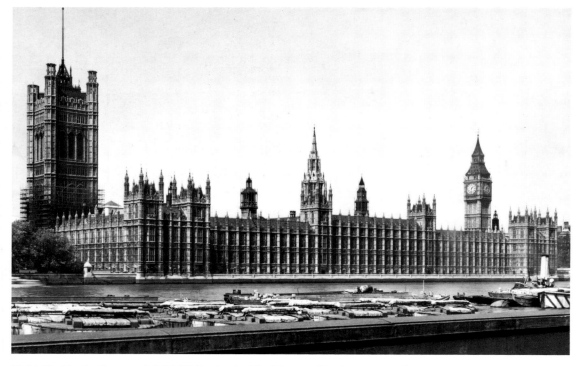

21-74. Sir Charles Barry and A. N. Welby Pugin. The Houses of Parliament, London. Begun 1836

Square Court of the Louvre (see fig. 16-26). But the paired columns of the facade, "quoted" from Perrault's East Front of the Louvre (see fig. 19-10), are combined with a smaller order in a fashion first suggested by Michelangelo's Palazzo dei Conservatori (see fig. 13-26). The rear entrance consists of a temple front. On the east side is the emperor's entrance with a sweeping staircase like that of the Cour de Cheval Blanc at Fontainebleau (see fig. 16-25), and on the west side a carriage entrance. The Opéra used the latest building materials and techniques, including iron. The stagecraft, too, was state-of-the-art. Garnier nevertheless went to great lengths to conceal the technology, which for him remained a means, not a principle.

The Opéra consciously suggests a palace of the arts combined with a temple of the arts. The theatrical effect captures the festive air of a crowd gathering before the opening curtain. Its Neo-Baroque quality derives more from the abundance of ornament and sculpture—including Carpeaux's *The Dance* (see fig. 21-64)—than from its architectural vocabulary. The whole building looks "overdressed," its luxurious vulgarity so naïve as to disarm all criticism. It reflects the taste of the capitalist tycoons, newly rich and powerful, who saw themselves as the heirs of the old aristocracy. For a display of comparable extravagance, we must turn to Sansovino's Library of St. Mark's (see fig. 14-25), which celebrates the wealth of Venice. Small wonder, then, that captains of industry found the styles before the French Revolution more appealing than Neoclassical or Neo-Gothic.

DECORATIVE ARTS

THE EMPIRE STYLE. During the Romantic era the decorative arts followed much the same course as architecture, with which they were intertwined, but they were, if anything, even more eclectic. The classical revival sparked by the discoveries at Pompeii and Herculaneum reached its climax during the early nineteenth century with the Empire style. This late form of Neoclassicism spread throughout Europe in the wake of Napoleon's conquests. As the term suggests, the style drew heavily on Roman art and associated Napoleon with the Caesars by borrowing imperial imagery. At first Roman examples were copied more or less faithfully, but such imitations are the least important contribution of the Empire style. Far more interesting are the free adaptations of those sources to glorify the Bonapartes. These often incorporate Egyptian motifs to commemorate Napoleon's invasion in 1798.

CHARLES PERCIER AND PIERRE-FRANÇOIS FONTAINE. We have already caught a glimpse of the Empire style in the bed of Canova's *Pauline Borghese As Venus* (see fig. 21-59). We see it at its fullest in the Château de Malmaison, Napoleon's private residence near Paris, which was remodeled after 1798 by the architects Charles Percier (1764–1838) and Pierre-François Fontaine (1762–1853). They were also entrusted with its furnishings, and their book on interior decoration, printed in 1812, set the standard for the Empire style. The bedroom of Napoleon's wife, Joséphine, reveals her taste for the ornate, which was characteristic of the Empire style as a whole (fig. 21-78). Its lavish splendor tells us a great deal about the First Empire and

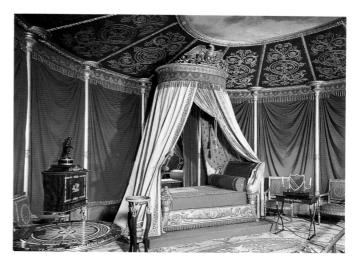

21-78. François-Honoré Jacob-Desmalter (after a design by Charles Percier and Pierre-François Fontaine). Bedroom of Empress Joséphine Bonaparte. c. 1810. Château de Malmaison, Rueil-Malmaison, France

its ambitions. As at Versailles (see fig. 19-13), the décor here serves the purpose of propaganda, for this is a state bedroom. (The empress usually slept in an ordinary one nearby.) The remarkable bed—made by François-Honoré Jacob-Desmalter (1770–1841), the leading furniture manufacturer under Napoleon, from a design by Percier and Fontaine—became the centerpiece of a total redecoration in 1810. Ordered previously, it proclaimed Joséphine empress even after her marriage had been annulled earlier that year. The ornamentation incorporates swans and cornucopias, standard Napoleonic devices, while the canopy resembles a military tent surmounted by an imperial eagle. Nearby is a tripod washstand, with basin and jug, based on Pompeiian examples. Like everything else about the bedroom, it is faithful to archaeological fact in details. Yet nothing in antiquity looked quite like this, and the effect is surprisingly close to the style of Louis XVI on the eve of the French Revolution.

THE INDUSTRIAL REVOLUTION. The rise of the Industrial Revolution led to the degeneration of the decorative arts. Everything from porcelain and silverware to drapery and furniture became mass-produced to meet the needs of the rapidly expanding middle class. Despite attempts to preserve the craftsmanship of the past, the machine won out after the Revolution of 1848. This decline was also seen in the standards of design, which catered to the largest number of customers. During the Restoration and July Monarchy—1814–1848—the decorative arts were intended to evoke the earlier glory of France through indiscriminate imitation. There were even revivals of revival styles! By 1840 furnishings began to disappear in a sea of bric-a-brac that provided a luxurious setting for the wealthy. Only rarely did the decorative arts rise above the ordinary. Among the few exceptions are the enormous torchères for the Grand Staircase of the Paris Opéra (see fig. 21-75) by the gifted sculptor Albert-Ernest Carrier-Belleuse (1824–1887). In the end, however, the only thing that could reverse the trend was another revolution in the decorative arts: the Arts and Crafts Movement (see page 766).

PHOTOGRAPHY

Is photography art? The fact that we still pose the question testifies to the continuing debate. The answers have varied with the changing definition and understanding of art. In itself, photography is simply a medium, like oil paint or pastel, used to make art and has no inherent claim to being art. What distinguishes any art from a craft is why, not how, it is done. Photography shares creativity with art because, by its very nature, it necessarily involves the imagination. Any photograph, even a casual snapshot, represents both an organization of experience and the record of a mental image. The subject and style of a photograph thus tell us about the photographer's inner and outer worlds. Furthermore, photography participates in the same seek-and-find process as painting or sculpture. Photographers may not realize what they respond to until after they see the image in printed form.

Like woodcut, etching, engraving, and lithography, photography is a form of printmaking that depends on mechanical processes. But in contrast to the other graphic mediums, photography has always been tainted as the product of a new technology. Apart from pushing a button or lever, setting up special effects, or creating them in the darkroom, no active intervention is required of the artist's hand to guide an idea. For this reason, the camera has usually been considered little more than a recording device. Photography, however, is by no means a neutral medium. Its reproduction of reality is never completely faithful. Whether we realize it or not, the camera alters appearances. Photographs thus reinterpret the world around us, making us see it in new terms.

Photography and painting represent parallel responses to their times and have generally expressed the same worldview. Sometimes the camera's power to extend our way of seeing has been realized first by the painter's creative vision. The two mediums nevertheless differ fundamentally in their approach. Painters communicate their understanding through techniques that represent their cumulative response over time, whereas photographers recognize the moment when the subject before them corresponds to the mental image they have formed of it.

It is hardly surprising that photography and art have enjoyed an uneasy relationship from the start. Artists have generally treated the photograph as a preliminary sketch: a convenient source of ideas or record of motifs fleshed out and incorporated into a finished work. Academic painters found the detail provided by photographs in keeping with their own precise naturalism. Many other kinds of artists have used photographs, without always admitting it. Photography has in turn been heavily influenced throughout its history by the painter's mediums. Photographs are often still judged according to how well they imitate paintings and drawings. To understand photography's place in the history of art, we must recognize the medium's particular strengths and inherent limitations.

The Founders of Photography

In 1822 the French inventor Joseph Nicéphore Niépce (1765–1833) succeeded in making the first permanent photographic image, although his earliest surviving example (fig. 21-79) dates from four years later. He then joined forces with a younger man, Louis-Jacques-Mandé Daguerre (1789–1851), who had invented an improved camera. After ten more years of chemical and mechanical research, the **daguerreotype**, using positive exposures, was unveiled publicly in 1839, and the age of photography was born. The announcement spurred the Englishman William Henry Fox Talbot (1800–1877) to complete his own photographic process, involving a paper negative from which positives could be made, which he had been pursuing independently since 1833.

What motivated the earliest photographers? They were searching for an artistic medium, not for a practical device. Although Niépce was a research chemist rather than an artist, his achievement was an outgrowth of his efforts to improve the lithographic process. Daguerre was a skilled painter, and he probably turned to the camera to heighten the illusionism of his huge painted dioramas, which were the sensation of Paris during the 1820s and 1830s. Fox Talbot saw in photography a substitute for drawing, as well as a means of reproduction, after he used a camera obscura as a tool to sketch landscapes while on a vacation. The interest that all of the founders had in the artistic potential of the medium they had created is reflected in their photographs. Daguerre's first picture (fig. 21-80) imitates a type of still life originated by Chardin, while Fox Talbot's *Sailing Craft* (fig. 21-81) looks like the English marine paintings of his day.

That the new medium should have a mechanical aspect was particularly appropriate. It was as if the Industrial Revolution, having forever altered civilization's way of life, now had to invent its own method for recording itself, although the transience of modern existence was not captured by "stopping the action" until the 1870s. Photography underwent a rapid series of improvements, including better lenses, glass-plate negatives, and new chemical processes that provided faster emulsions and more stable images. Because many of the initial limitations of photography were overcome around mid-century, it would be misleading to tell the early history of the medium in terms of technological developments, important though they were.

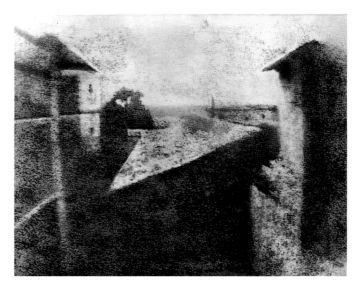

21-79. Joseph Nicéphore Niépce. *View from His Window at Le Gras.* 1826. Heliograph, 6½ x 7⅞" (16.5 x 20 cm). Gernsheim Collection, Harry Ransom Research Center, University of Texas at Austin

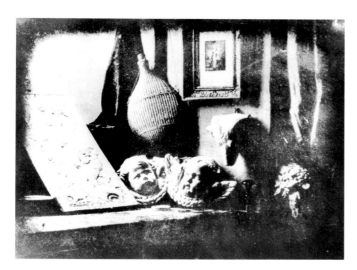

21-80. Louis-Jacques-Mandé Daguerre. *Still Life*. 1837.
Daguerreotype, 6½ x 8½" (16.5 x 21.7 cm).
Société Française de Photographie, Paris

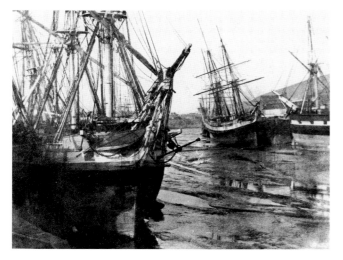

21-81. William Henry Fox Talbot. *Sailing Craft*. c. 1845.
Calotype. Science Museum, London

The basic mechanics and chemistry of photography had been known for a long time. The camera obscura, a box with a small hole in one end, dates back to antiquity. In the sixteenth century, it was widely used for visual demonstrations. The camera was fitted with a mirror and then a lens in the Baroque period, which saw major advances in optical science culminating in Newtonian physics. By the 1720s it had become an aid in drawing architectural scenes. At the same time, silver salts were discovered to be light-sensitive.

Why, then, did it take another hundred years for someone to put this knowledge together? Much of the answer lies in the nature of scientific revolutions. As a rule, they combine old technologies and concepts with new ones in response to changing worldviews that they, in turn, influence. Photography was neither inevitable in the history of technology, nor necessary to the

history of art; yet it was an idea whose time clearly had come. If we try for a moment to imagine that photography had been invented a hundred years earlier, we will find this to be impossible simply on artistic, let alone technological, grounds. The early eighteenth century was too devoted to fantasy to be interested in the literalness of photography. Rococo portraiture, for example, was more concerned with providing a flattering image than an accurate likeness. Hence the camera's straightforward record would have been totally out of place. Even in architectural painting, extreme liberties were often taken with topographical truth (see pages 628–29).

The invention of photography was a response to the artistic urges and historical forces that underlie Romanticism. Much of the impulse came from a quest for the True and the Natural. The desire for "images made by Nature" can already be seen, on the one hand, in Cozens' ink-blot compositions (see fig. 21-10), which were "natural" because they were made by chance; and, on the other, in the late-eighteenth-century vogue for silhouette portraits (traced from the shadow of the sitter's profile), which led to attempts to record such shadows on light-sensitive materials. David's harsh realism in *The Death of Marat* (see fig. 21-3) had already proclaimed the cause of unvarnished truth. So did Ingres' *Louis Bertin* (see fig. 21-31), which established the standards of physical reality and character portrayal that photographers were to follow. [See Primary Sources, no. 69, page 965.]

Portraiture

Like lithography, which was invented in 1797, photography met the growing demand for images of all kinds. By 1850 large numbers of the middle class were having their likenesses painted, and it was in portraiture that photography found its readiest acceptance. Soon after the daguerreotype was introduced, photographic studios sprang up everywhere, especially in America, and multi-image *cartes de visites,* invented in 1854 by Adolphe-Eugène Disdéri (1818–1889), became ubiquitous. Anyone could have a portrait taken cheaply and easily. In the process, the average person became memorable. Photography thus became an outgrowth of the democratic values fostered by the American and French revolutions. There was also keen competition among photographers to get the famous to pose for portraits.

NADAR. Gaspard Félix Tournachon (1820–1910), better known as Nadar, managed to attract most of France's leading personalities to his studio. Like many early photographers, he started out as an artist but came to prefer the lens to the brush. He initially used the camera to capture the likenesses of the 280 sitters whom he caricatured in an enormous lithograph, *Le Panthéon Nadar.* The actress Sarah Bernhardt posed for him several times, and his photographs of her (fig. 21-82) are the direct ancestors of modern glamour photography (compare fig. 27-11). With her romantic pose and expression, she is a counterpart to the soulful maidens found throughout nineteenth-century painting. Nadar has treated her in remarkably sculptural terms. Indeed, the play of light and sweep of drapery are reminiscent of the sculptured portrait busts that were so popular with collectors at the time.

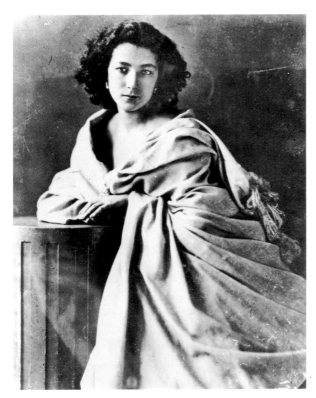

21-82. Nadar. *Sarah Bernhardt.* 1859. George Eastman House, Rochester, New York

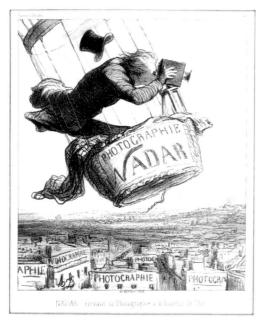

21-83. Honoré Daumier. *Nadar Elevating Photography to the Height of Art.* 1862. Lithograph. George Eastman House, Rochester, New York

The Restless Spirit

Early photography reflected the outlook and temperament of Romanticism. Indeed, the entire nineteenth century had a pervasive curiosity and an abiding belief that everything could be discovered. While this fascination sometimes showed a serious interest in science—witness Charles Darwin's voyage on the

Beagle from 1831 to 1836—it typically took the form of a restless quest for new experiences and places. Photography had a remarkable impact on the imagination of the period by making the rest of the world widely available in visual form, or by simply revealing it in a new way. Sometimes the search for new subjects was close to home. Nadar, for example, took aerial photographs of Paris from a hot-air balloon. This feat was wittily parodied by Daumier (see fig. 21-83) in a lithograph whose caption, "Nadar Elevating Photography to the Height of Art," expresses the prevailing skepticism about the aesthetics of the new medium.

A love of the exotic was fundamental to Romantic escapism, and by 1850 photographers began to cart their equipment to faraway places. The same restless spirit that we saw in George Caleb Bingham's *Fur Traders Descending the Missouri* (see fig. 21-57) drew photographers to the frontier. They documented the westward expansion of the United States, often for the U.S. Geological Survey, with pictures that have primarily historical interest today.

TIMOTHY O'SULLIVAN. An exception is the landscape photography of Timothy O'Sullivan (c. 1841–1882), who often preferred scenery that contemporary painters had overlooked. He practically invented his own aesthetic in photographing the *Cañon de Chelle* (fig. 21-84), which conforms to no established pictorial type. The view filling the entire photograph allows no visual escape and lends the scene an awesome force. The composition is held together by the play of lines of the displaced strata of

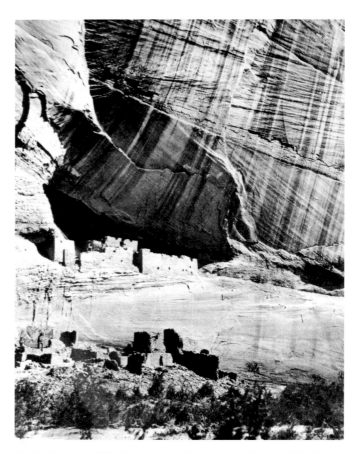

21-84. Timothy O'Sullivan. *Ancient Ruins in the Cañon de Chelle, N.M., in a Niche 50 Feet above the Present Cañon Bed* (now Canyon de Chelly National Monument, Arizona). 1873. Albumen print. George Eastman House, Rochester, New York

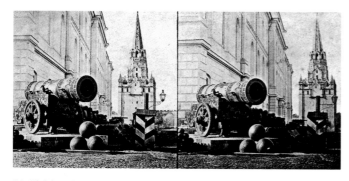

21-85. *Tsar Cannon Outside the Spassky Gate, Moscow* (cast 1586; presently inside the Kremlin). Second half of 19th century. Stereophotograph

COURTESY CULVER PICTURES

the rock, which creates a strikingly abstract design. O'Sullivan's control of tonal relations is so masterful that even color photographs taken since then of the same site have far less impact.

Stereophotography

The unquenchable thirst for vicarious experiences accounts for the great popularity of stereoscopic photographs. Invented in 1849, the two-lens camera produced two photographs comparable to the slightly different images perceived by our two eyes. When seen through a special viewer called a **stereoscope**, stereoptic photographs fuse to create a remarkable illusion of three-dimensional depth. Two years later, stereoscopes became the rage at the Crystal Palace exposition in London (see fig. 22-34). Countless thousands of double views, such as the example in figure 21-85, were taken over the next 50 years. Virtually every corner of the earth became accessible to practically any household, with a vividness second only to being there.

Stereophotography was an important breakthrough. Its binocular vision marked a major departure from perspective in the pictorial tradition and demonstrated for the first time photography's potential to enlarge human vision. Nevertheless, its success waned, except for special uses. People were simply too accustomed to viewing pictures as if with one eye. Later on, when the halftone plate was invented in the 1880s for reproducing images on a printed page, stereophotographs revealed another drawback. As our illustration demonstrates, they were unsuitable for illustrations. From then on, single-lens photography was closely linked with the mass media of the day.

Photojournalism

Fundamental to the rise of photography was the widespread nineteenth-century sense that the present was already history in the making. Only with the advent of the Romantic hero did great acts, other than martyrdom, become popular subjects for contemporary painters and sculptors. It is hardly surprising that photography was invented a year after the death of Napoleon, who had been the subject of more paintings than any previous secular leader. At about the same time, Géricault's *The Raft of the "Medusa"* (see fig. 21-28) signaled a decisive shift in the Romantic attitude toward representing contemporary events. This outlook brought with it a new kind of photography: photojournalism.

MATHEW BRADY. Its first great representative was Mathew Brady (1823–1896), who covered the Civil War in the United States. Other wars had already been photographed, but Brady and his 20 assistants (including Timothy O'Sullivan) were able to bring home the horrors of that war with unprecedented directness, despite using cameras too slow and cumbersome to show actual combat.

ALEXANDER GARDNER. *Home of a Rebel Sharpshooter, Gettysburg* (fig. 21-86) by Alexander Gardner (1821–1882), a former assistant of Brady who formed his own photographic team in 1863, is a landmark in the history of art. Never before had both the grim reality and, above all, the significance of death on the battlefield been conveyed so fully in a single image. Compared with the heroic act celebrated by Benjamin West (see fig. 21-4), this tragedy is as anonymous as the slain soldier himself. The photograph is all the more convincing for having the same harsh realism found in David's *The Death of Marat* (see fig. 21-3), and the limp figure, hardly visible between the rocks framing the scene, is no less moving. In contrast, the paintings and engravings by the artists—such as Winslow Homer (see pages 755–56)—who illustrated the Civil War for magazines and newspapers were mostly genre scenes that kept the reality of combat safely at arm's length.

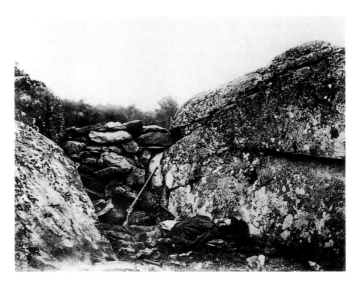

21-86. Alexander Gardner. *Home of a Rebel Sharpshooter, Gettysburg*. July 1863. Wet-plate photograph. Chicago Historical Society

CHAPTER TWENTY-TWO

Realism and Impressionism

PAINTING

France

"Can Jupiter survive the lightning rod?" asked Karl Marx, not long after the middle of the nineteenth century. The question suggests that the ancient god of thunder and lightning was now threatened by science. In 1846 Charles Baudelaire addressed the problem in a different way when he called for paintings that expressed "the heroism of modern life." [See Primary Sources, no. 70, page 966, for more.]

> To prove that our age is no less fertile in sublime themes than past ages, we may assert that since all centuries and all peoples have had their own form of beauty, so inevitably we have ours . . . just as we have our own particular emotions, so we have our own beauty.
>
> The pageant of fashionable life and the thousands of floating existences—criminals and kept women—which drift about in the underworld of a great city . . . all prove to us that we have only to open our eyes to recognize our heroism. . . .
>
> The life of our city is rich in poetic and marvellous subjects. We are enveloped and steeped as though in an atmosphere of the marvellous; but we do not notice it.
>
> The *nude*—that darling of the artists, that necessary element of success— is just as frequent and necessary today as it was in the life of the ancients; in bed, for example, or in the bath, or in the anatomy theater. The themes and resources of painting are equally abundant and varied; but there is a new element—modern beauty.

GUSTAVE COURBET AND REALISM. At that time, only one painter was willing to follow this artistic doctrine: Baudelaire's friend Gustave Courbet (1819–1877). Courbet was born in Ornans, a village near the French-Swiss border, and remained proud of his rural background. He had begun as a Neo-Baroque Romantic in the early 1840s. By 1848, under the impact of the revolutionary upheavals then sweeping through Europe, he had come to believe that the Romantic emphasis on feeling and imagination was merely an escape from the realities of the time. Truth became the rallying cry of the Realists, their motto Baudelaire's precept, "It is necessary to be of one's time." Modern artists must rely on direct experience—they must be Realists. "I cannot paint an angel because I have never seen one," Courbet wrote. [See Primary Sources, no. 71, page 966.] As a term, *Realism* is not very precise. For Courbet, it meant something akin to the realism of Caravaggio (see page 559). As an admirer of Louis Le Nain and Rembrandt, Courbet had, in fact, strong links with the Caravaggesque tradition. Moreover, his work, like Caravaggio's, was denounced for its supposed vulgarity as well as its lack of spiritual content. What ultimately defines Courbet's Realism, however, and distinguishes it from Romanticism, is his devotion to radical (as against merely liberal) politics. His Socialist views were the result of his close friendship with the theorist Pierre-Joseph Proudhon, ten years his senior, who was from the same region in southern France, and they colored his entire outlook. Although Socialism did not determine the specific content or appearance of Courbet's pictures, it does help to account for his choice of subject matter and style, which went against the grain of tradition.

Burial at Ornans (fig. 22-1), from 1849, fully embodies Courbet's programmatic Realism. Here is a picture that disregards the academic hierarchy by treating an apparent genre scene with the same seriousness and monumentality as a history painting. It was executed with a heavy impasto that violated accepted standards of finish, so that it had a hostile reception from the public and most critics. Courbet asked 50 people to pose for him in his studio. He painted them lifesize, solidly and matter-of-factly. The canvas is much larger than anything by Millet, and with none of

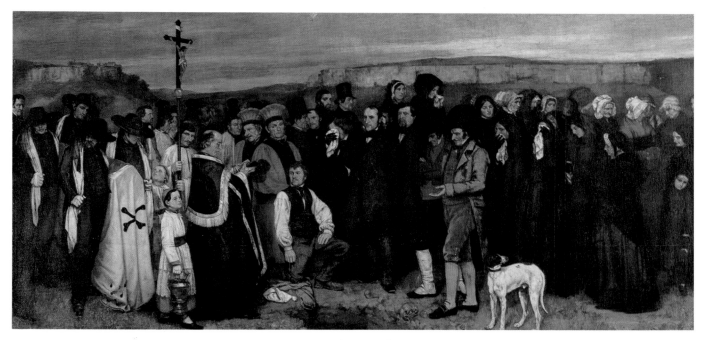

22-1. Gustave Courbet. *Burial at Ornans.* 1849–50. Oil on canvas, 10'3½" x 21'9½" (3.13 x 6.64 m). Musée d'Orsay, Paris

Millet's overt pathos (compare fig. 21-41). Its nearest relatives are Dutch group portraits of the seventeenth century. *Burial at Ornans* rivals Rembrandt's *The Night Watch* (see fig. 18-16) in scale and ambition. Courbet has adopted the Dutch master's dark palette and thick brushwork as well. The picture consciously avoids any trace of Baroque dynamism, however. It has instead a classical gravity worthy of Masaccio and Raphael (see fig. 12-38 and fig. 13-31).

In contrast to other funerary scenes, such as El Greco's *The Burial of Count Orgaz* (see fig. 14-14), this is not the apotheosis of a great man or woman (compare also fig. 7-38). In fact, the identity of the deceased is never revealed—nor is it important—although the painting is sometimes said to have been inspired by the funeral of Courbet's grandfather. It is not even a religious scene, let alone one about death. The real subject is the gathering as social ritual, to which the burial itself seems almost incidental. The composition is divided into three groups of clergy, men, and women, each of whom is carefully observed. Many of the faces are partially obscured, however, so that they remain as anonymous as the person they have come to mourn. The artist's main intention was to record the dress and customs of his hometown. By rigorously excluding anything that might distract our attention, he prevents us from reading any further significance into the painting. Yet it has a grandeur and solemnity that are deeply moving, precisely because of the factual presentation. In this way, *Burial at Ornans* fulfills Baudelaire's "heroism of modern life."

During the 1855 Paris Exposition, where works by Ingres and Delacroix were prominently displayed, Courbet brought attention to his pictures by organizing a private exhibition in a large shed and by distributing a "manifesto of Realism." The show, which included *Burial at Ornans,* centered on another huge canvas, titled *Studio of a Painter: A Real Allegory Summarizing My Seven Years of Life As an Artist* (fig. 22-2). (Fittingly enough, the two paintings now hang opposite each other in the Musée d'Orsay in Paris.) "Real allegory" is something of a teaser. Allegories, after all, are unreal by definition. Courbet meant either an allegory couched in the terms of his particular Realism, or one that did not conflict with the "real" identity of the figures or objects embodying it.

The framework is familiar. Courbet's composition clearly belongs to the type seen in Velázquez's *The Maids of Honor* and Goya's *The Family of Charles IV* (see figs. 17-35 and 21-23). But now the artist has moved to the center, and the visitors here are his guests, not royal patrons who enter whenever they wish. He has invited them specially for a purpose that becomes apparent only upon further thought. The picture does not yield its full meaning unless we take the title seriously and consider Courbet's relation to this assembly.

There are two main groups. On the left are "the people." They are types rather than individuals, drawn largely from the artist's home town of Ornans: hunters, peasants, workers, a Jew, a priest, a young mother with her baby. On the right we see groups of portraits representing the Parisian side of Courbet's life: clients, critics, intellectuals. (The man reading is Baudelaire; the black woman, his mistress.) All of them are strangely passive, as if they are waiting for something to happen. Some are quietly talking among themselves, others seem lost in thought. Yet hardly anyone looks at Courbet. They are not his audience, but a representative sampling of his social environment.

Only two people watch the artist at work: a small boy, intended to suggest "the innocent eye," and the nude model. What is her role? In a more conventional picture, we would identify her as Inspiration, or Courbet's Muse, but she is no less "real" than the others here. Courbet probably meant her to be Nature, or that undisguised Truth which he proclaimed to be the guiding

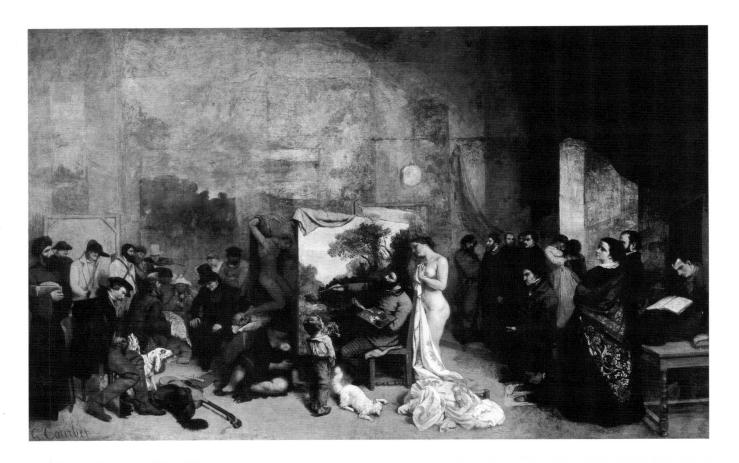

22-2. Gustave Courbet. *Studio of a Painter: A Real Allegory Summarizing My Seven Years of Life as an Artist.* 1854–55. Oil on canvas, 11'10" x 19'7" (3.6 x 6 m). Musée d'Orsay, Paris

It is the artist, Courbet, of course, who plays the central role in the monumental Painter's Studio, *yet he envisions his role as one both socially more humble and ideologically more grandiose than the usual conception of the term. Courbet sees himself at once as the earthy, matter-of-fact master-painter, a popular craftsman working with the tools of brush and canvas and, at the same time, in the iconographic context of the* Studio, *as the Harmonian Leader, the immovable, active, generating centre from which the Fourierist implications of the whole work radiate. For the generating impulse behind Courbet's modern allegory is most probably Fourierist. The* Studio *may be interpreted as a pictorial statement, in contemporary, concrete, personal terms, of Fourierist ideals and doctrine—the Association of Capital, Labour and Talent. . . .*

—Linda Nochlin. *Realism.* New York: Viking Press, 1993, p. 130. Originally published in 1971.

LINDA NOCHLIN (b. 1931), the first great feminist art historian in the United States, taught for many years at Vassar College in Poughkeepsie, New York, at Hunter College in New York City, and at the Institute of Fine Arts of New York University, where she got her Ph.D. in 1963. Her writings on Courbet and Realism remain the foundation of the modern view of the artist and the movement, for they are backed with brilliant intellect, commanding scholarship, and disarming wit.

principle of his art. (Note the emphasis on the clothing she has just taken off.) Significantly enough, the center group is lighted by clear, sharp daylight, but the background and the side figures are veiled in shadow. This device underlines the contrast between the artist—the active creator—and the world around him that waits to be brought to life.

EDOUARD MANET AND THE "REVOLUTION OF THE COLOR PATCH." Courbet's *Studio* helps us to understand a picture that shocked the public even more: *Luncheon on the Grass*

(Le Déjeuner sur l'Herbe) (fig. 22-3), showing a nude young woman next to two gentlemen in frock coats, by Édouard Manet (1832–1883). Manet was the first artist to grasp Courbet's full importance; his *Luncheon* is, among other things, a tribute to the older artist. There is a long tradition of such picnic scenes stretching back to an outdoor concert by Titian that Manet copied in the Louvre while an art student. He nevertheless offended the morality of the day by placing the nude and nattily attired figures in an outdoor setting without allegorical overtones. Even worse, the neutral title offered no "higher" significance.

People assumed that Manet had intended to represent an actual event; yet the group's poses are too formal. Not until many years later was the source of these figures discovered: a group of classical deities from an engraving after Raphael that was in turn derived from a classical Roman sarcophagus, (see figs. 13-34 and 13-35). In both we see the Judgment of Paris to the left, and to the right Mars accompanying Venus to Olympia, where they are greeted by Zeus holding his thunderbolt. While Raphael has taken obvious liberties with the composition, the debt is obvious enough. Had Manet's contemporaries known of this origin in the revered work of Raphael, the *Luncheon* might have seemed less disreputable to them. Furthermore, the girl washing in the distance was inspired by a painting of *Diana Bathing* by Watteau. (Manet originally titled his canvas *The Bath,* which would have shocked the public even more.)

The comparison makes the cool, formal quality of Manet's figures even more obvious. The unembarrassed gaze and frank realism of the nude are not simply a witty parody of classical art. Far more than Courbet's *Studio of a Painter, Luncheon on the Grass* fulfills all the conditions set down in "The Heroism of Modern Life" by Baudelaire. [See Primary Sources, no. 70, page 966.] By borrowing freely from the past and clothing his figures in modern urban dress, Manet both updated tradition and gave fresh meaning to the nude. These, he seems to say, are the gods and goddesses of today, and they are no less worthy of our attention—or respect—than those of the past. Nevertheless, the scene fits neither everyday experience nor mythology. Perhaps the meaning of the canvas lies in this very denial of plausibility. For that reason, Manet could be championed by two seemingly opposite literary giants: the Realist novelist Émile Zola, who found in the artist's paintings a counterpart to his own writings; and the Symbolist poet Stéphane Mallarmé, who appreciated Manet's economy and artfulness (see box pages 788–89).

As a visual manifesto of artistic freedom, the *Luncheon* is much more revolutionary than Courbet's *Studio*. It asserts the painter's privilege to combine whatever elements he pleases for aesthetic effect alone. The nudity of the model is "explained" by the contrast between her warm, creamy flesh tones and the cool black-and-gray of the men's attire. To put it another way, the world of painting has "natural laws" that are different from those of everyday reality, and the painter's first loyalty is to his canvas, not to the outside world. Here begins an attitude that became a bone of contention between progressives and conservatives for the rest of the century. It was later summed up in the doctrine of Art for Art's

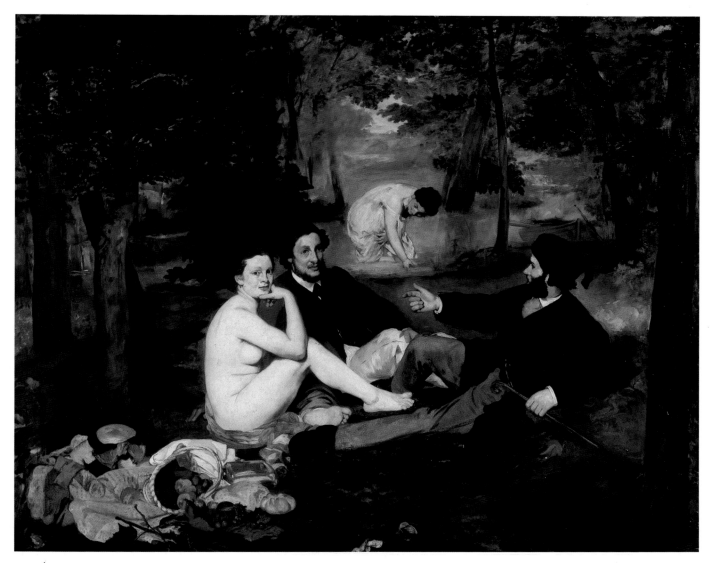

22-3. Édouard Manet. *Luncheon on the Grass (Le Déjeuner sur l'herbe).* 1863. Oil on canvas, 7' x 8'10" (2.1 x 2.6 m). Musée d'Orsay, Paris

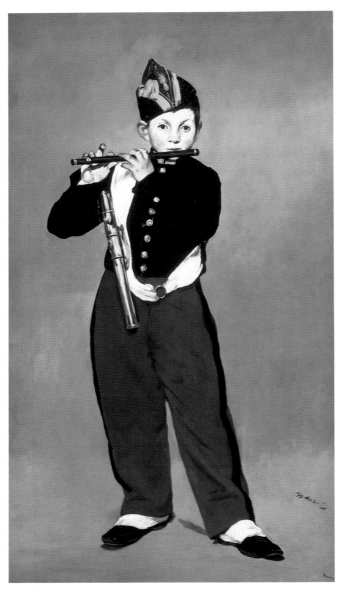

22-4. Édouard Manet. *The Fifer*. 1866. Oil on canvas, 63 x 38¼" (160 x 97.5 cm). Musée d'Orsay, Paris

few but it takes a real effort to find them.) The figure looks three-dimensional only because it is rendered in realistic foreshortening. Otherwise Manet avoids all the methods invented since Giotto's time for transforming a flat surface into a pictorial space. The nearly undifferentiated light-gray background seems as near to us as the figure and just as solid. If the fifer stepped out of the picture, he would leave a hole, like the cutout shape of a stencil.

Here, then, the canvas itself has been redefined. It is no longer a "window," but a screen made up of flat patches of color, like a child's jigsaw puzzle. Just how radical a step this is can be seen if we compare *The Fifer* to Delacroix's *The Death of Sardanapalus* (see fig. 21-33) and to a Cubist work such as Picasso's *Three Dancers* of 1925 (see fig. 24-27). Manet's painting obviously resembles Picasso's in its structure, whereas Delacroix's still follows the "window" tradition of the Renaissance. The revolutionary qualities of Manet's art could already be seen in the *Luncheon,* even if they were not yet so obvious. The three main figures are almost as shadowless and flat as *The Fifer.* They would be more at home on a screen, and the chiaroscuro of the setting, inspired by the landscapes of Courbet, no longer fits them, so that they look out of place in more ways than one.

What brought about this "revolution of the color patch"? We do not know, and Manet himself surely did not reason it out in advance. It is tempting to think that he was spurred to create the new style by the challenge of photography. The "pencil of nature," then known for a quarter-century, had demonstrated the objective truth of Renaissance perspective, but it established a standard of accuracy that no handmade image could hope to rival. Painting needed to be rescued from competition with the camera. Manet accomplished this task by insisting that a painted canvas is, above all, a material surface covered with pigments—that we must look *at* it, not *through* it. Unlike Courbet, he gave no name to the style he had created. When his followers began calling themselves Impressionists, he refused to adopt the term for his own work. His aim was to be accepted as a Salon painter, a goal that eluded him until late in life.

CLAUDE MONET AND IMPRESSIONISM. The word *Impressionism* was coined in 1874, after a hostile critic had looked at a picture entitled *Impression: Sunrise* by Claude Monet (1840–1926). It certainly fits Monet better than it does Manet. Monet had adopted Manet's approach to painting and applied it to landscapes done outdoors. Monet's *On the Bank of the Seine, Bennecourt* of 1868 (fig. 22-5) is flooded with sunlight so bright that conservative critics claimed it made their eyes hurt. In this flickering network of color patches, shaped like mosaic tesserae, the reflections on the water are as real as the banks of the Seine. [See Primary Sources, no. 72, page 967.] Even more than *The Fifer,* Monet's painting is a "playing card." Were it not for the woman and the boat in the foreground, the picture would be just as effective upside-down, like the Queen of Hearts in a deck. The mirror image here serves the opposite purpose of earlier ones (compare fig. 15-15). Instead of adding to the illusion of real space, it strengthens the unity of the painted surface. This internal consistency sets *On the Bank of the Seine, Bennecourt* apart from Romantic "impressions" such as Constable's *The Haywain* (fig.

Sake (see page 753). Manet himself avoided such controversies. His work nevertheless shows his lifelong devotion to "pure painting": to the belief that brushstrokes and color patches themselves—not what they stand for—are the artist's primary reality. Among the painters of the past, he found that Hals, Velázquez, and Goya had come closest to this ideal. He admired their broad, open technique and their fascination with light and color values. Many of his canvases are, in fact, "pictures of pictures": they translate into modern terms those older works that particularly fascinated him. Yet Manet always filtered out the expressiveness or symbolism of his models to avoid distracting the viewer's attention from his pictorial concerns. His paintings always have an emotional reserve that can easily be mistaken for emptiness unless we understand its purpose.

Courbet is said to have remarked that Manet's pictures were as flat as playing cards. Looking at *The Fifer* (fig. 22-4), we can see what he meant. Painted three years after the *Luncheon,* it has very little modeling, no depth, and hardly any shadows. (There are a

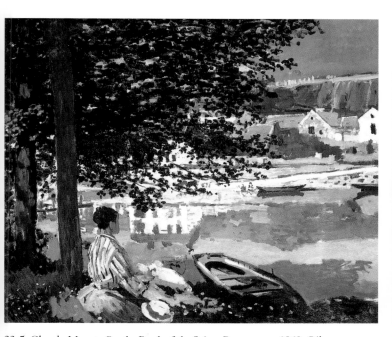

22-5. Claude Monet. *On the Bank of the Seine, Bennecourt.* 1868. Oil on canvas, 32⅛ x 39⅝" (81.5 x 100.7 cm). The Art Institute of Chicago

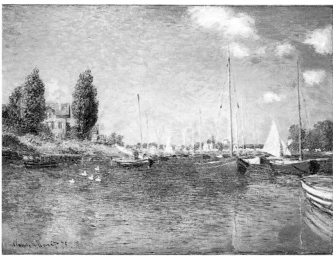

22-6. Claude Monet. *Red Boats, Argenteuil.* 1875. Oil on canvas, 23½ x 31⅝" (59.7 x 80.3 cm). Fogg Art Museum, Harvard University Art Museums, Cambridge, Massachusetts

21-46) or Corot's *View of Rome* (fig. 21-38), even though all three share the same on-the-spot immediacy.

In the late 1860s and early 1870s, Monet and his friend Auguste Renoir worked together closely to develop Impressionism into a fully mature style, one that proved ideally suited to painting outdoors. Monet's *Red Boats, Argenteuil* (fig. 22-6) captures to perfection the intense sunlight along the Seine near Paris, where the artist was spending his summers. Now the flat brushstrokes have become flecks of paint that convey an extraordinary range of visual effects. The amazingly free brush weaves a tapestry of rich color inspired by the late paintings of Delacroix (compare fig. 21-35). Despite its spontaneity, Monet's technique retains an underlying logic in which each color and brushstroke has its place. As an aesthetic, then, Impressionism was hardly the straightforward realism it first seems. It nevertheless remained an intuitive approach, even in its color, although the Impressionists were familiar with many of the optical theories that were to provide the basis for Seurat's Divisionism (see pages 772–74).

CAMILLE PISSARRO. The method that Monet and Renoir developed was soon adopted by other members of the group. The landscapes of Camille Pissarro (1830–1903) have a straightforward naturalism that places him close to the Barbizon School, and a firm, almost classical structure that was shared by his friend Paul Cézanne (see pages 768–72). We see these qualities in *The Côte des Boeufs at l'Hermitage, near Pontoise* (fig. 22-7). The painting has a real feel for rural life and scenery, which concerned Pissarro more than any other Impressionist. The overgrown landscape evokes the rebirth of life in early springtime through the tangled network of forms embedded in the dense surface texture. Yet the majestic procession of trees and the blocklike buildings establish a clear structure that gives the picture a timeless quality.

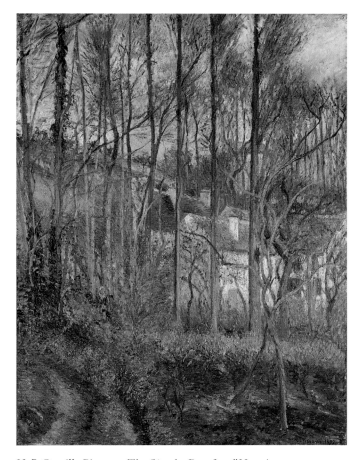

22-7. Camille Pissarro. *The Côte des Boeufs at l'Hermitage, near Pontoise.* 1877. Oil on canvas, 45¼ x 34½" (114.9 x 87.6 cm). The National Gallery, London

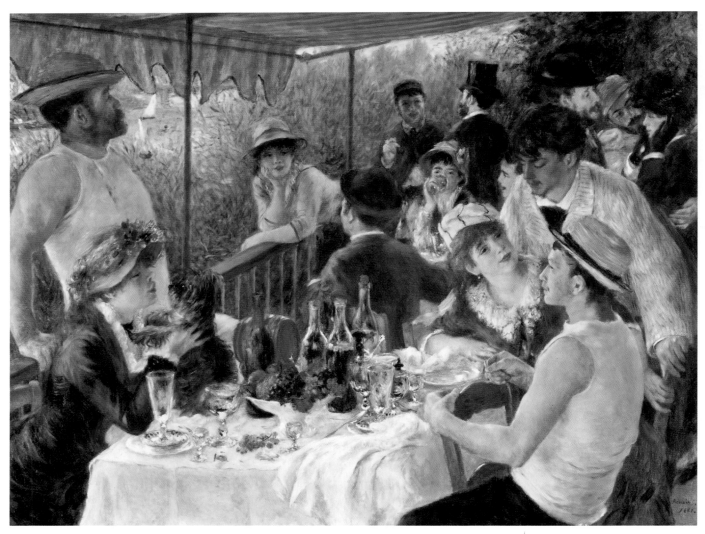

22-8. Auguste Renoir. *Luncheon of the Boating Party, Bougival.* 1881. Oil on canvas, 51 x 68" (129.5 x 172.7 cm). The Phillips Collection, Washington, D.C.

AUGUSTE RENOIR. The Impressionist painters answered Baudelaire's call to artists to capture the "heroism of modern life" by depicting its dress and its pastimes. Scenes from the world of entertainment—dance halls, cafés, concerts, the theater—were favorite subjects for them. These carefree views of bourgeois pleasure are flights from the cares of daily life. Although he helped to create the Impressionist landscape style, Auguste Renoir (1841–1919) began as a figure painter who took Manet as his point of departure, and his finest works after 1875 focus on people. *Luncheon of the Boating Party, Bougival* (fig. 22-8) is filled with the joy of life. The group of merrymakers are all friends of the artist. (The young woman with a dog was soon to become his wife.) Renoir used amazingly free brushwork to create a masterful orchestration of color and light. (Note the reflections on the glasses and bottles.) The painting has an air of abandon worthy of Steen or Hogarth (compare figs. 18-27 and 20-11). Yet the composition is actually controlled by a strong underlying geometry. This firm structure lends stability to the apparent informality and fixes our position, so that we become participants in the festive gathering.

Thus we can easily imagine ourselves leaning against a railing and surveying the scene with the same casualness as the man in the straw hat.

MANET AND IMPRESSIONISM. Such spontaneity came less easily to Manet. In 1869, however, he became a convert to Impressionism under Monet's influence and soon developed into the greatest of all the Impressionists. His last major work, *A Bar at the Folies-Bergère* (fig. 22-9), was painted about the same time as Renoir's *Boating Party,* and they have much in common. The canvas is a display of dazzling virtuosity. It shows a single figure as calm and as firmly fixed within the pictorial field as the fifer (see fig. 22-4), but the background is no longer neutral. A huge shimmering mirror image now fills most of the picture. Set close behind the barmaid, it shows the whole interior of the nightclub. The artist, however, denies the three-dimensionality of the scene by taking certain liberties. For example, the reflection of the barmaid and customer is shown off to one side, something that is obviously impossible and creates a subtle aura of unreality. The

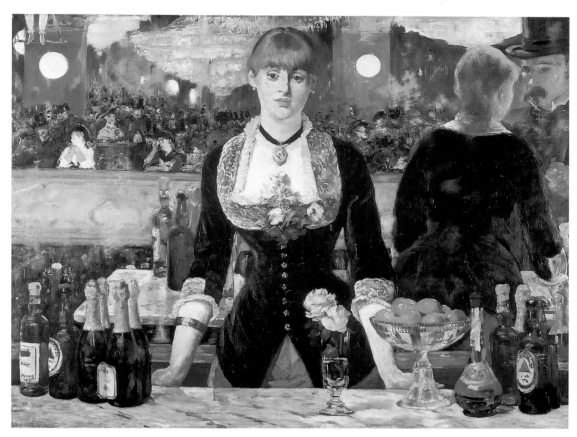

22-9. Édouard Manet. *A Bar at the Folies-Bergère.* 1881–82. Oil on canvas, 37½ x 51" (95.3 x 129.7 cm). Courtauld Institute Galleries, Home House Trustees, London

foreground is just as fascinating. Manet was a superb still life painter. With only a few deft strokes of the brush, he creates a miniature self-contained world in the water glass with a rose and the fruit bowl filled with oranges. The barmaid's attitude, detached and touched with melancholy, contrasts poignantly with the gaiety of her setting, which she is not permitted to share. Thus the mood of the painting reminds us of Daumier's *The Third-Class Carriage* (see fig. 21-37).

EDGAR DEGAS. Edgar Degas (1834–1917), a wealthy aristocrat by birth, had a deep understanding of human character that lends significance even to seemingly casual scenes such as *The Glass of Absinthe* (fig. 22-10). He makes us look steadily at the disenchanted pair in his café scene, but out of the corner of our eye, so to speak. The design of this picture at first seems as unstudied as a snapshot. (Degas practiced photography, although it was not yet capable of capturing an instant on the fly.) However, a closer look shows us that everything here dovetails precisely. The zigzag of empty tables between us and the unfortunate couple reinforces

their brooding loneliness, for example. Compositions as boldly calculated as this set Degas apart from other Impressionists. The artist had been trained in the tradition of Ingres, whom he greatly admired, and did not abandon his early loyalty to draftsmanship. When he joined the Impressionists, he always stood slightly outside the movement by refusing to adopt its name.

His finest works were often done in pastels (powdered pigments molded into sticks), which allowed him to create effects of line, tone, and color simultaneously. *Prima Ballerina* (fig. 22-11, page 747) shows the advantages of this flexible medium. The oblique view of the stage, from a box near the proscenium arch, has been shaped into another deliberately off-center composition. The dancer floats above the steeply tilted floor like a butterfly caught in the glare of the footlights. *The Tub* (fig. 22-12), of a decade later, is another oblique view, but now severe, almost geometric, in design. The tub and the crouching woman, both strongly outlined, form a circle within a square, and the rest of the rectangular format is filled by a shelf so sharply tilted that it almost shares the plane of the picture. Yet on this shelf Degas has placed

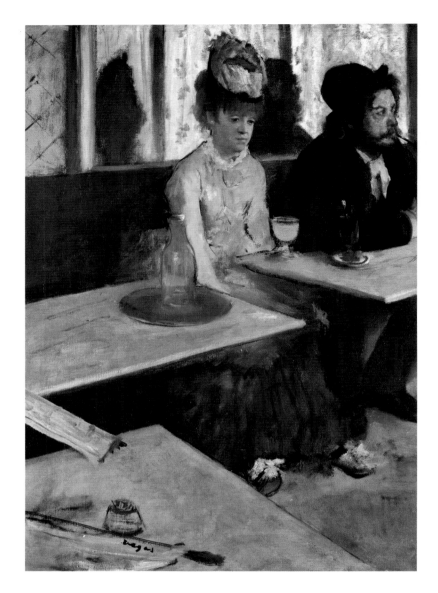

22-10. Edgar Degas. *The Glass of Absinthe.* 1876.
Oil on canvas, 36 x 27" (91.3 x 68.7 cm).
Musée d'Orsay, Paris

(OPPOSITE) 22-11. Edgar Degas. *Prima Ballerina.*
c. 1876. Pastel, 23 x 16½" (58.3 x 42 cm).
Musée d'Orsay, Paris

two pitchers that are hardly foreshortened at all. (Note how the curve of the small one fits the handle of the other.) Here the tension between the "two-D" surface and "three-D" depth comes close to the breaking point. *The Tub* is Impressionist only in its shimmering, luminous colors. Its other qualities are more characteristic of the 1880s, the first Post-Impressionist decade, when many artists showed a renewed concern with problems of form (see Chapter 23).

BERTHE MORISOT. The Impressionists' ranks included several women of great ability. The subject matter of Berthe Morisot (1841–1895), a member of the group from its beginning, was the world she knew: the domestic life of the French upper middle class, which she depicted with rare sympathy. Morisot's early paintings, centering on her mother and her sister Edma, were directly influenced by Manet, whose brother she later married. Her mature work is altogether different in character.

Morisot's characteristic themes are women and children, sometimes alone, sometimes together. Usually her figures are engrossed in reading or lost in thought but they always stay in their private world. Morisot's pictures at first convey a subtle sense of

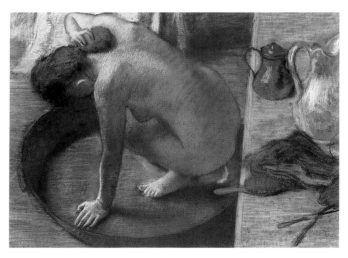

22-12. Edgar Degas. *The Tub.* 1886. Pastel, 23½ x 32⅜"
(59.7 x 82.3 cm). Musée d'Orsay, Paris

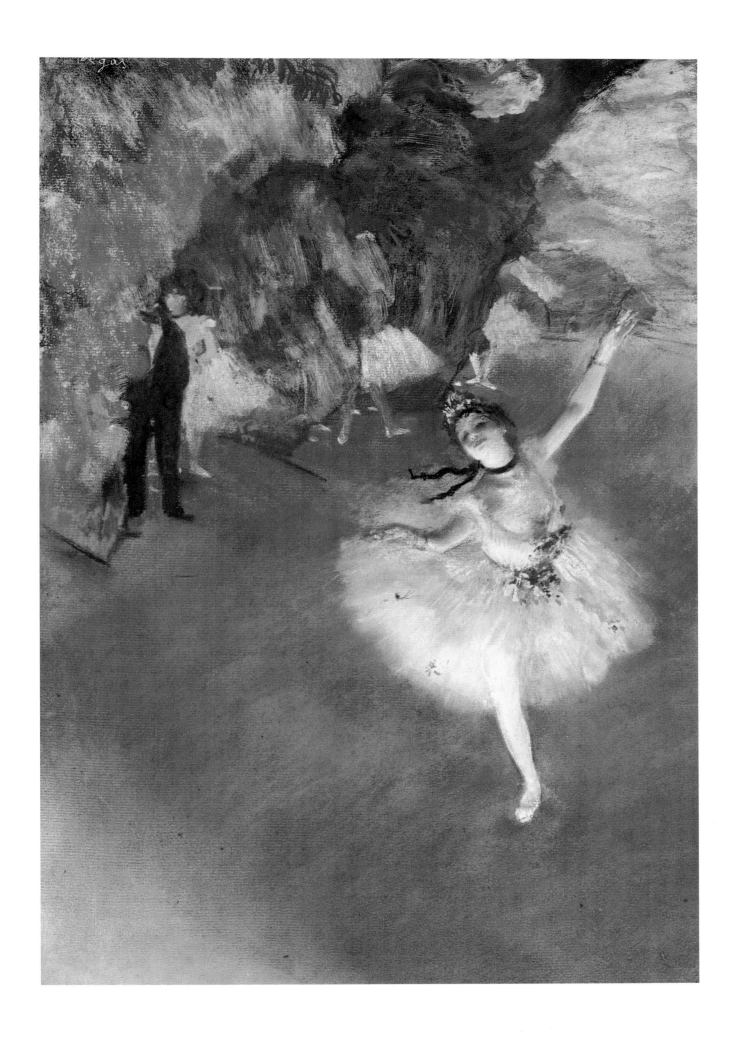

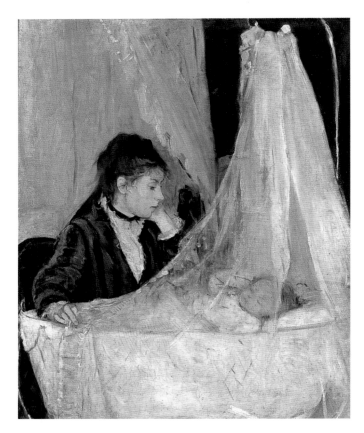

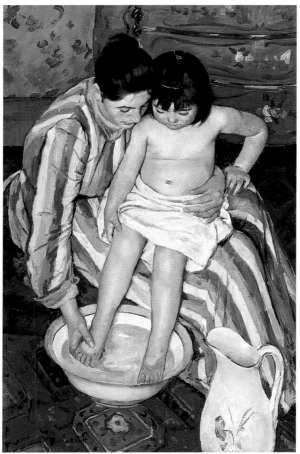

22-14. Mary Cassatt. *The Bath*. 1891–92.
Oil on canvas, 39½ x 26" (100.3 x 66 cm).
The Art Institute of Chicago

22-13. Berthe Morisot. *The Cradle*.
1872. Oil on canvas.
22 x 18⅓" (55.9 x 46 cm).
Musée d'Orsay, Paris

alienation through activities undertaken together, yet not shared—of experiences encountered in a world from which they remain isolated. Later it is human relationships that are the real subjects of her canvases, even when a single figure is shown, for the artist is always present in a subtle way.

The Cradle (fig. 22-13) shows Edma looking tenderly at her daughter Blanche. Although asleep, the infant is her mother's sole object of attention. It is the maternal bond that fascinates Morisot—and that was not fulfilled until the birth of her own daughter, Julie, in 1878. Morisot applied her brushstrokes with a sketchlike brevity that omits unessential details, yet captures a complete impression of the scene through the careful balance of the compositional elements. The serene painting radiates an air of tenderness free of the sentimentality that often affects genre paintings of the period.

MARY CASSATT. Surprisingly, Americans responded to the new style sooner than Europeans did and became the first patrons of the Impressionists. At a time when no French museum would have them, Impressionist works entered public collections in the United States. American painters such as Mary Cassatt (1845–1926) and James McNeill Whistler (see below) were among the earliest followers of Manet and his circle. Cassatt joined the Impressionists in 1877 and became a tireless champion of their work. She had received a standard academic training in Philadelphia but had to struggle to overcome traditional barriers. At a time when painting was viewed as an unsuitable occupation for a woman, Cassatt, like Morisot, was able to pursue her career as an artist because she was independently wealthy. She helped to gain early acceptance for Impressionist paintings in the United States through her social contacts with rich private collectors. She never married or had children, yet maternity provided the thematic and formal focus for most of her work. *The Bath* (fig. 22-14) is a masterpiece from her mature period. The tilted view, simplified color forms, and flat composition show the impact of her mentor, Degas, as well as her study of Japanese prints. Despite the complexity of its design, the painting has a directness that lends simple dignity to motherhood.

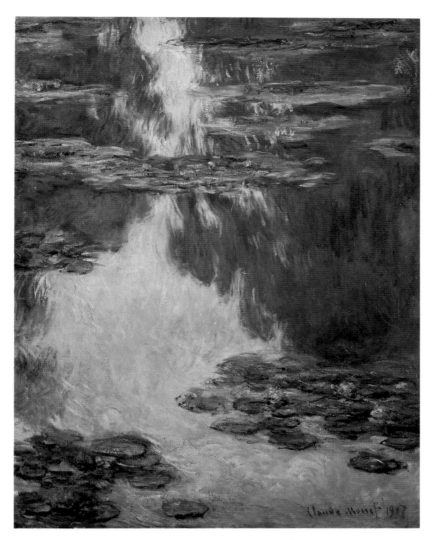

22-15. Claude Monet. *Water Lilies*. 1907. Oil on canvas, 36½ x 29" (92.7 x 73.7 cm).
Kawamura Memorial Museum of Art, Sakura City, Chiba Prefecture, Japan

MONET'S LATER WORKS. By the mid-1880s Impressionism had become widely accepted. Its technique was imitated by conservative painters and practiced as a fusion style by a growing number of artists worldwide. However, the movement now underwent a deep crisis. Manet died in 1883. Renoir, already beset by doubts, moved toward a more classical style. Racked by internal dissension fostered by Degas, the group held its last show in 1886. At that time Pissarro abandoned Impressionism for several years in favor of Seurat's Divisionism (see pages 772–74). Among the major figures of the movement, only Monet remained faithful to the Impressionist view of nature. Although his work became more subjective over time, he never ventured into fantasy, nor did he forsake the basic approach of his earlier landscapes.

Around 1890 Monet began to paint pictures in series, showing the same subject under different conditions of light and atmosphere. These tended increasingly to resemble Turner's "airy visions, painted with tinted steam," as Monet concentrated on the effects of colored light. (He had visited London in 1870 during the German invasion of France and knew Turner's work; see pages 709–11.) *Water Lilies* (fig. 22-15) is a fascinating sequel to *On the Bank of the Seine, Bennecourt* (see fig. 22-5), painted almost 40 years earlier. The surface of the pond now takes up the entire canvas, so that the effect of a weightless screen is stronger than ever. The artist's brushwork, too, has greater variety and a more individual rhythm. While the scene is still based on nature, this is no ordinary landscape but one entirely of his making. On the estate at Giverny, given to him late in life by the French government, Monet created a self-contained world for purely personal and artistic purposes. The subjects he painted there are as much reflections of his imagination as they are of reality. They convey a very different sense of time as well. Instead of the single moment captured in *On the Bank of the Seine,* his *Water Lilies* summarizes a shifting impression of the pond in response to the changing water as breezes play across it.

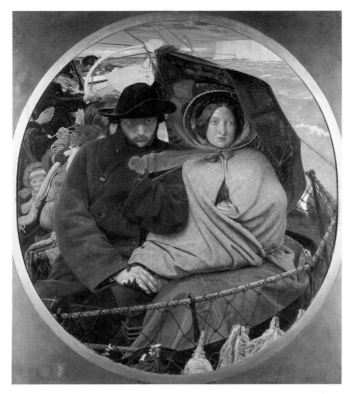

22-16. Ford Madox Brown. *The Last of England*. 1852–55. Oil on panel, 32½ x 29½" (82.5 x 74.9 cm). City Museum and Art Gallery, Birmingham, England

BY PERMISSION BIRMINGHAM MUSEUM AND ART GALLERY

England

REALISM. By the time Monet came to admire his work, Turner's reputation was at a low ebb in his own country. In 1848, when Courbet launched his revolutionary doctrine of Realism, a concern with "the heroism of modern life" arose independently in English painting, although the movement lacked a leader of Courbet's stature and boldness.

Perhaps the best-known example of English Realism is *The Last of England* (fig. 22-16) by Ford Madox Brown (1821–1893), a picture that enjoyed enormous popularity throughout the latter half of the nineteenth century in the English-speaking world. The subject—a group of emigrants as they set out on their long overseas journey—may be less obvious today; nor does it carry the same emotional charge. There can be no question, however, that the artist has treated an important theme taken from modern experience, and that he has done so with touching seriousness.

The painting is intended to dramatize the conditions that made the emigrants decide to leave England. The pathos of the scene may strike us as a bit theatrical: note the contrast between the "good riddance" gesture of the man at the upper left and the brooding young family in the foreground. (Brown used himself, his wife, and daughter as the models.) We recognize its source in the "dumb shows" of Hogarth, whom Brown admired (see fig. 20-11). Their styles, however, have nothing in common. The extreme detail strikes us as almost photographic. There is no hint of personal "handwriting" in the scene. Brown had developed this painstaking technique after meeting the Nazarenes, the group of

German painters in Rome who practiced what they regarded as a "medieval" style (see page 715). He in turn taught it to his three pupils who together in 1848 helped to found an artists' society called the Pre-Raphaelite Brotherhood: William Holman Hunt (1827–1910), John Everett Millais (1829–1896), and Dante Gabriel Rossetti (1828–1882).

THE PRE-RAPHAELITES. Brown himself never actually joined the Pre-Raphaelites, but he shared their basic aims: to do battle against the frivolous art of the day by having "genuine ideas to express" and by producing "pure transcripts . . . from nature," an objective inspired by the writings of John Ruskin. As the name of the Brotherhood proclaims, its members took their inspiration from the "primitive" masters of the fifteenth century. To that extent, they belong to the Gothic revival, which had long been an important aspect of the Romantic movement. What set the Pre-Raphaelites, like the Nazarenes, apart from Romantics was a desire to reform the ills of modern civilization through art. This ambition of the Pre-Raphaelites was inspired by Chartism, the democratic working-class movement that reached its peak in the revolutionary year 1848.

WILLIAM HOLMAN HUNT. *The Awakening Conscience* (fig. 22-17) by William Holman Hunt, the artist who remained truest to the Brotherhood's ideals, is the quintessential Pre-Raphaelite statement. It, too, is a morality play in the tradition of Hogarth and one that addresses a very real social problem of the time, although Hunt treated it as a personal crisis. Inspired by an episode in

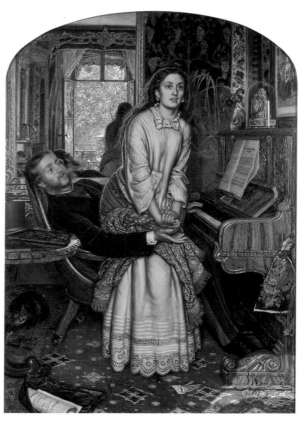

22-17. William Holman Hunt. *The Awakening Conscience*. 1853. Oil on canvas, 30 x 20" (76.2 x 50.8 cm). The Tate Gallery, London

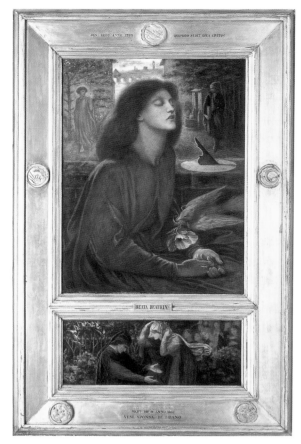

22-18. Dante Gabriel Rossetti. *Beata Beatrix*. 1872. Oil on canvas, 34½ x 27¼" (87.5 x 69.3 cm); predella 10½ x 27¼" (26.5 x 69.3 cm). The Art Institute of Chicago

CHARLES L. HUTCHINSON COLLECTION

Charles Dickens' *David Copperfield,* the painting shows a young woman stirred to the realization by the music she sings that she has been living in sin. The scene is presented in obsessive detail, which is filled with symbolic meaning. The print above the piano, for example, shows Christ and the Woman Taken into Adultery, while the reflection in the mirror represents the light of religious revelation. Here the artist looked to the example of Jan van Eyck's *Arnolfini Portrait* (see fig. 15-8), which had recently been acquired by the National Gallery in London.

DANTE GABRIEL ROSSETTI. Unlike Hunt, Dante Gabriel Rossetti was not concerned with social issues. He thought of himself as a reformer of aesthetic sensibility. The vast majority of his work consists of watercolors or pastels showing women taken from literary sources, but all bear a striking resemblance to his wife, Elizabeth Siddal. *Beata Beatrix* (fig. 22-18), created as a memorial to Siddal, imposes her features on the beloved wife of his namesake, the Italian poet Dante, whose account of her death inspired the painting. Rossetti explained the program in detail: "The picture illustrates the 'Vita Nuova,' embodying symbolically the death of Beatrice as treated in that work. The picture is not intended at all to represent death, but to render it under the semblance of a trance. . . . I have introduced . . . the figures of Dante and Love passing through the street and gazing ominously on one another, conscious of the event; while the bird, a messenger of

death, drops the poppy between the hands of Beatrice. She, through her shut lids, is conscious of a new world." In this version, the artist has expressed the hope of seeing his beloved Elizabeth again by adding a second panel showing Dante and Beatrice meeting in Paradise and inscribing the dates of their deaths on the frame. For all its apparent spirituality, the painting has an aura of repressed eroticism that is the hallmark of Rossetti's work. It exerted a powerful influence on other Pre-Raphaelites as well.

EDWARD BURNE-JONES. Rossetti's pupil Edward Burne-Jones (1833–1898) came to be identified most completely with the Brotherhood in the public's mind, although he was too young to have been a member. *The Wheel of Fortune* (fig. 22-19) is an allegorical painting that was initially planned as part of a large pseudo-triptych devoted to the story of Troy. The project, which remained unfinished, was based on a poem by William Morris that likewise was never completed. It was divided into four sections representing Fortune, Fame, Oblivion, and Love. The figures chained to the wheel of fortune, from which they cannot

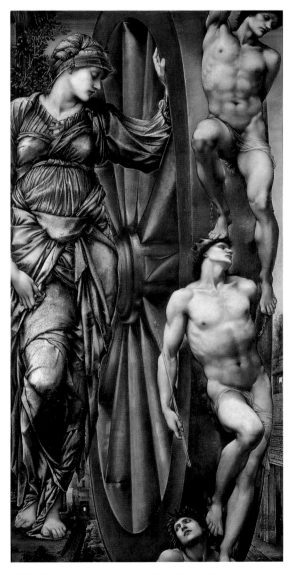

22-19. Edward Burne-Jones. *The Wheel of Fortune*. 1877–83. Oil on canvas, 6'6¾" x 3'3⅜" (2 x 1 m). Musée d'Orsay, Paris

NATIONALISM IN MID-NINETEENTH-CENTURY MUSIC

In the mid-nineteenth century, composers turned for inspiration to their native heritages. The fascination with folk music, as well as folklore, was an outgrowth of nationalism, an intrinsic part of Romanticism that became nearly universal after mid-century. Among the first to take up this interest was Johannes Brahms (1833–1897), an equally ardent nationalist and fervent admirer of Count Otto von Bismarck, the Prussian minister who unified Germany. Although he was one of the first composers to show an interest in folk music, Brahms owed much to his teacher, Robert Schumann, for whose widow, Clara, he developed an abiding but unrequited love (see page 722). Brahms' development was slow: his first symphony was not completed until 1876, but it is cast in the heroic mold of Beethoven. No other composer of his generation wrote masterpieces in such a wide range of music. The works are characteristically intense, with writing high in the string sections, but with slow movements of astonishingly tender lyricism. They are nevertheless without the bombast found in the work of other composers from the same time and are held together by a thorough command of composition and a strong, classical structure.

Brahms was one of the first to appreciate the Czech composer Antonin Dvořák (1841–1904), whose career he encouraged. Whereas Brahms' music is alternately brooding and rapturous, Dvořák's is almost uniformly sunny and uniquely Czech in flavor—he proclaimed himself "a happy Bohemian." Love of nature and homeland fill his music. Dvořák was proud of his national music, but he was affected by that of other cultures, especially during his sojourn in New York as head of the National Conservatory of Music (1892–95), when he produced his celebrated *New World Symphony* and *American Quartet*. He left behind a body of chamber music even more substantial than Brahms' and a splendid cello concerto that is the greatest of its kind. The late tone poems, inspired mostly by folktales, became important models for the next generation of Czech composers centering on Leo Janáček (1854–1928).

Perhaps the most distinctive national school was to be found in Russia. The group known as The Five sought to infuse their music with the sound of their country and often took folk melodies as the basis for their work. They also revived the system of modes, which had remained intact in Orthodox music and was indigenous to large parts of Russia. The most original member of the Russian school was Modest Moussorgsky (1839–1881), despite his being the least trained. His opera *Boris Godunov* (1868–72), written about the same time as Aleksei Tolstoy's drama but taken from an earlier play by Aleksandr Pushkin (1799–1837) and a history of Russia by Nikolai Karamzin, is the undisputed masterpiece of the entire movement. It is generally performed in a version reworked by the very professional composer Nikolai Rimsky-Korsakov (1844–1908), who rescued it from oblivion, although Moussorgsky's original score is far bolder, if uneven. His large output of songs, some of them orchestrated by others, is extremely high in quality and varied in subject, drawing from a wide range of literary sources by the leading Russian writers of the day. Unfortunately, the language barrier has prevented this rich trove from becoming as well-known as it deserves to be.

The greatest Russian composer remains Peter Ilyich Tchaikovsky (1840–1893), who began as a student of the traditionalist Anton Rubinstein (1829–1894) but was decisively influenced early in his career by The Five, and was a close friend of Rimsky-Korsakov. Tchaikovsky's tone poems, all based on literature, pulsate with Romantic yearning and adventure, while his six symphonies, several of which incorporate Russian themes, are programmatic—especially the last three, which are virtually autobiographical. Indeed, the final one (the *Pathétique*, 1893) is a valedictory statement of the composer's life, with its struggles and triumphs. Its undeniable Russian elements notwithstanding, Tchaikovsky's music owes its enduring appeal to its internationalism. Despite its physical isolation, Russia was closely linked to the musical capitals of western Europe. Thus Tchaikovsky's three great ballets build on the French tradition and possess a sophistication that is extraordinarily cosmopolitan. The first and finest, *Swan Lake* (1875–76), grew out of a short work for his sister's children. The other two (*Sleeping Beauty*, 1888–89, and *The Nutcracker*, 1891–92) are based on fairy tales by Charles Perrault and E. T. A. Hoffmann respectively; both were written for Marius Petipa (1819–1910), under whom Russian ballet reached its zenith. They share the same literary bent and uncanny understanding of human nature, combined with a sophisticated understanding of Russian and Polish folk music, that is found in the later symphonies and the tone poems *Francesca da Rimini* (1876) and *Hamlet* (1888), and the *Manfred Symphony* (1882). Tchaikovsky had a special affinity for childhood and its difficulties, and for the joys and torments of love, for he was a discreet homosexual.

escape, include a slave, a king, and a poet. The composition was inspired by one of Mantegna's altarpieces, while Dame Fortune reflects the artist's admiration for Botticelli (compare fig. 12-53). The figures also show the impact of the sibyls and nudes on the ceiling of the Sistine Chapel (fig. 13-19), which he studied in detail during a visit to Rome, as well as Michelangelo's "slaves"

(see figs. 13-14, 13-15, and 13-16). His principal interest, however, lies in the decorative design. Inspired by Early Renaissance paintings, it has the flatness and luxuriance of a tapestry. Even more than Whistler's, Burne-Jones' work represents an escape from reality into a dreamlike world of heightened beauty and rarefied feeling.

With Richard Wagner (1813–1883), nationalist rhetoric came to express the growing expansionist mood of Germany that led ultimately to the rise of Nazism during the 1930s. Wagner manned the barricades in Dresden during the revolutionary upheavals that struck Europe throughout 1848–49 and was forced into exile for 13 years, until he won the support of Ludwig II of Bavaria. His operas, such as *Tristan and Isolde* (1859), written under the influence of the philosophy of Arthur Schopenhauer (1788–1860), and the enormous four-part cycle *The Ring of the Niebelungen* (1853–74), which dates from about the same time as Christian Hebbel's plays, expand greatly on medieval Germanic legends. Wagner's goal was a total work of art that united music, literature, and theater. His texts reflect the influence of Goethe in their literary, declamatory style. One of Wagner's characteristic devices is the leitmotif (pronounced "light moteef," from German, "leading motif"), a melodic line that represents a person, idea, or situation. If, for example, the music brings together the leitmotif for Tristan with one that signifies Fate, the informed listener understands that Tristan is being drawn toward his destiny. Add the motif for Isolde, and we know that his fate is intertwined with hers. Music of such sophistication demanded a highly educated audience, which the prosperous cities of nineteenth-century Europe could readily supply.

Despite the enormous demands Wagner placed on singers, it was the orchestra that carried the largest part of the musical burden. His highly unconventional orchestration techniques and integrated drama set an important example for the Italian composer Giuseppe Verdi (1813–1901), who nevertheless denied their influence. Verdi's early operas often have patriotic subjects espousing the cause of Italian independence (the *risorgimento*). Although his arias remained vehicles of virtuoso singing, the last five operas broke decisively with the style of Donizetti and Bellini under the influence of Wagner's integrated approach. Dating from 1862 to 1893, they are the culmination of the entire Italian tradition stretching back to Monteverdi. Like Berlioz and Tchaikovsky, Verdi was attracted above all to the plays of Shakespeare—*Macbeth, Othello,* and *The Merry Wives of Windsor*—which brought out the best in him.

The main contribution of French music was the comic operas by the German-born composer Jacques Offenbach (1819–1880), most notably *Orpheus in Hell* (1859; rev. 1874) and *La Belle Hélène* (1864), which wreak playful havoc with classical myths. They depend heavily on the librettos by Offenbach's main collaborators, Lodovic Halèvy (1834–1908) and Henri Meilhac (1831–1897), who also supplied the book for the only great success by the Viennese waltz and operetta king Johann Strauss (1825–1899), *Die Fledermaus (The Bat)* (1874). Offenbach built on the French Romantic and comic operas of another German-born composer, Giacomo Meyerbeer (1791–1864), who relied equally on his prolific librettist, Eugène Scribe (1791–1861). When Offenbach matched musical wits with his writers, the results were at once hilarious and tuneful.

As in art and architecture, revivalism was an important factor in music, although it never became a guiding principle. Mendelssohn resuscitated Bach's *St. Matthew Passion,* for which every serious music lover must be eternally grateful, as it is Bach's greatest masterpiece; Wagner rediscovered Palestrina and Glück (his very antitheses as composers); and Brahms helped to prepare complete editions of the works of Handel, C. P. E. Bach, and Mozart that mark the beginning of modern musicology.

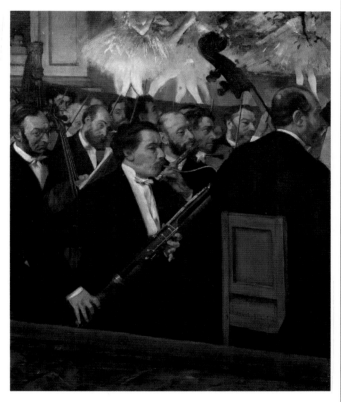

Edgar Degas. *Orchestra of the Opera.* c. 1870. Oil on canvas, 22¼ x 18³⁄₁₆" (56.5 x 46.2 m). Musée d'Orsay, Paris

JAMES MCNEILL WHISTLER. James Abbott McNeill Whistler (1834–1903) came to Paris from America in 1855 to study painting. Four years later he moved to London, where he spent the rest of his life, but he visited France during the 1860s and was in close touch with the rising Impressionist movement. *Arrangement in Black and Gray: The Artist's Mother* (fig. 22-20), his best-known painting, reflects the influence of Manet in its flat, geometric design, while the likeness has the precision of Degas. Its fame as an icon of today's "mother cult" would have horrified Whistler, who wanted the canvas to be appreciated for its formal qualities alone.

Whistler was a witty, sharp-tongued advocate of Art for Art's Sake, the rallying cry of the Aesthetic movement, which removes

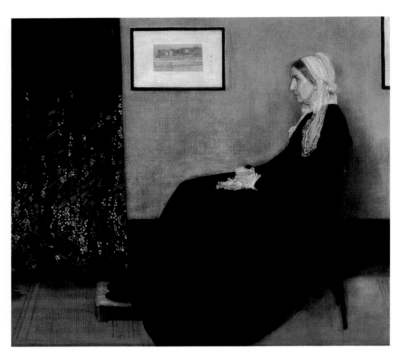

22-20. James Abbott McNeill Whistler.
Arrangement in Black and Gray: The Artist's Mother.
1871. Oil on canvas, 57 x 64½" (144.6 x 163.8 cm).
Musée d'Orsay, Paris

22-21. James Abbott McNeill Whistler.
Nocturne in Black and Gold: The Falling Rocket.
c. 1874. Oil on panel, 23¾ x 18⅜" (60.2 x 46.8 cm).
The Detroit Institute of Arts

GIFT OF DEXTER M. FERRY, JR.

art and its content from its times. He thought of his pictures as comparable to pieces of music and often called them "symphonies" or "nocturnes." [See Primary Sources, no. 73, page 967.] The boldest example, painted about 1874, is *Nocturne in Black and Gold: The Falling Rocket* (fig. 22-21). Without the explanatory subtitle, we would have real difficulty making out the subject. Although Art for Art's Sake originated with the French writers Gustave Flaubert and Charles Baudelaire, no French painter had yet dared to produce a picture so "nonrepresentational," so reminiscent of Cozens' "blotscapes" and Turner's "tinted steam" (see figs. 21-10 and 21-49). It was this canvas, more than any other, that prompted John Ruskin to accuse Whistler of "flinging a pot of paint in the public's face." (Since the same critic had highly praised Turner's *The Slave Ship,* we must conclude that what Ruskin admired was not the tinted steam itself but the Romantic feeling behind it.)

Whistler successfully sued Ruskin for libel in 1878, but the victory was purely moral: he was awarded only one farthing, and the legal costs helped drive him into bankruptcy a year later. During his testimony he offered a definition of his aims that is particularly relevant to *The Falling Rocket:* "I have perhaps meant rather to indicate an artistic interest alone in my work, divesting the picture from any outside sort of interest. . . .It is an arrangement of line, form, and color, first, and I make use of any incident of it which shall bring about a symmetrical result." The last phrase has special significance, since Whistler acknowledges that in using chance effects, he does not look for resemblances but for a purely formal harmony. While he rarely practiced what he preached to quite the same extent as he did in *The Falling Rocket,* his statement reads like a prophecy of American abstract painting (see fig. 24-59).

United States

THE AMERICAN BARBIZON SCHOOL. After the Civil War, the United States underwent unprecedented industrial growth, immigration, and westward expansion. These changes led to not only a new range of social and economic issues but also a different outlook and taste. As the nation became more like the Old World, Americans traveled abroad in growing numbers and found their cultural models in Europe, particularly France, which led to a new cosmopolitanism in art. There was an equally dramatic shift in the attitude toward nature. The uneasy balance between civilization and nature shifted once and for all in favor of progress by the end of the Centennial Celebration in 1876. The loss of the twin Romantic visions of the virgin wilderness and a pastoral Eden left nature as little more than a sentimental vestige to be preserved in parks. Since landscape ceased to be a teacher of moral truths as well, the viewer was left only with a personal reaction to a total impression of scenery. In this way, the mystery of nature kept its spiritual significance but required a different mode of expression. The American Barbizon painters answered the need for a new form of landscape by turning inward. Their canvases embody the altered mentality of the United States by evoking a poetic state of mind with increasing freedom.

GEORGE INNESS. The leader of the American Barbizon School was George Inness (1825–1894), who had been deeply

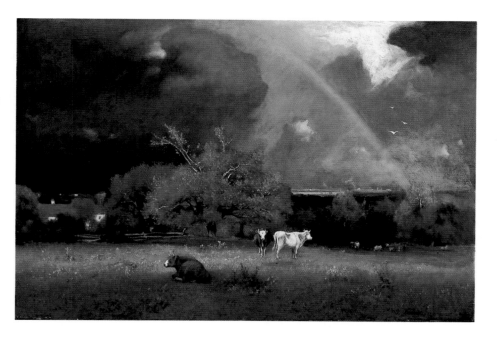

22-22. George Inness. *The Rainbow.*
c. 1878–79. Oil on canvas, 30¼ x 45¼"
(76.8 x 114.9 cm). © 1993
Indianapolis Museum of Art

impressed by the work of Théodore Rousseau and his followers during visits to France. *The Rainbow* (fig. 22-22) shows one of the storm scenes so characteristic of this artist. The contrast of nature's bounty with the tumultuous sweep of cosmic forces is reminiscent of Cole's *View of Schroon Mountain* (see fig. 21-56). Instead of depicting the wilderness, however, this former member of the Hudson River School has followed a rustic scene by Millet. Inness gives his landscape a sense of divine presence by freely rearranging nature according to formulas that act as indexes of personal feelings. Deeply religious, he had converted to the spiritualism of Emanuel Swedenborg, who believed in an immaterial but light-filled realm of departed souls that is visually similar and parallel

to our own. Although only a few of his landscapes have a specific symbolic meaning, rainbows had great spiritual significance for Inness. Swedenborg's ideas confirmed and intensified his approach, which relied increasingly on light and color to impart his vision of a deeper reality lying hidden from people's eyes but not their souls.

WINSLOW HOMER. Winslow Homer (1836–1910) was a pictorial reporter during the Civil War and continued as a magazine illustrator until 1875. He went to Paris in 1866, but although he left too soon to feel the full impact of Impressionism, French art had an important effect on his work. *Snap the Whip* (fig. 22-23)

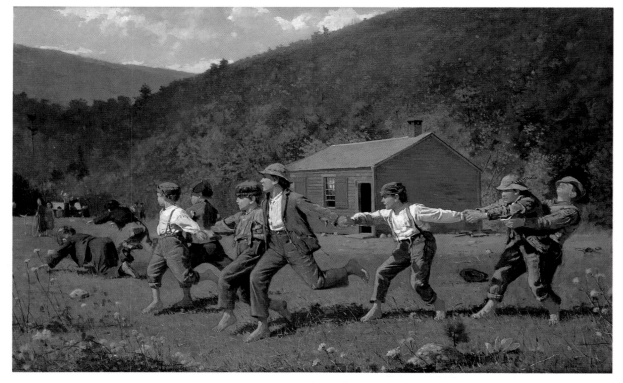

22-23. Winslow Homer. *Snap the Whip.* 1872. Oil on canvas, 22¼ x 36½" (56.5 x 92.7 cm).
The Butler Institute of Art, Youngstown, Ohio

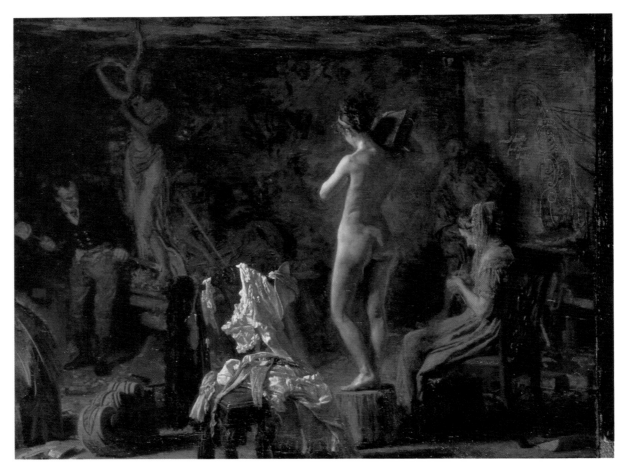

22-24. Thomas Eakins. *William Rush Carving His Allegorical Figure of the Schuylkill River.* 1877. Oil on canvas, 20⅛ x 26½" (51.1 x 67.3 cm). Philadelphia Museum of Art

conveys a nostalgia for a simpler era of America before the Civil War (see fig. 21-57). The sunlit scene might be called "pre-Impressionist," as its fresh delicacy lies halfway between Corot and Monet (compare figs. 21-39 and 22-5). The composition, with its air of youthful innocence, was inspired by the bacchanals then popular in French art (compare fig. 21-64). Homer's design shows the same subtle understanding of movement as Bruegel's *The Blind Leading the Blind* (see fig. 16-22), which also ends in a fallen figure.

THOMAS EAKINS. Thomas Eakins (1844–1916) arrived in Paris from Philadelphia about the same time as Homer. He went home four years later after studying with leading academic painters but with decisive impressions of Velázquez and Courbet. Elements from both these artists are combined in *William Rush Carving His Allegorical Figure of the Schuylkill River* (fig. 22-24; compare figs. 17-35 and 22-2). Eakins had met with stiff opposition for advocating traditional life studies at the Pennsylvania Academy of the Fine Arts. To him, Rush was a hero for basing his 1809 statue for the Philadelphia Water Works on the nude model, although the figure itself was draped in a classical robe. Eakins must have known contemporary European paintings of sculptors

carving from the nude; these were closely related to the theme of Pygmalion and Galatea, popular at the time among academic artists. Conservative critics nevertheless denounced the picture for its nudity, despite the presence of the chaperon knitting quietly to the right. Today the painting's declaration of unvarnished truth seems a courageous fulfillment of Baudelaire's demand for pictures that express the "heroism of modern life."

HENRY OSSAWA TANNER. Eakins encouraged women and blacks to study art seriously at a time when professional careers were closed to them. Thanks in large part to his enlightened attitude, Philadelphia became the leading center of minority artists in the United States. African-Americans had no chance to enter the arts before Emancipation, and after the Civil War the situation improved only gradually. Henry Ossawa Tanner (1859–1937), the first important black painter, studied with Eakins in the early 1880s. Tanner's masterpiece, *The Banjo Lesson* (fig. 22-25), painted after he moved permanently to Paris, shows Eakins' unmistakable influence. The scene is rendered with the same direct realism as *William Rush Carving His Allegorical Figure of the Schuylkill River,* so that it avoids the sentimentalism of similar subjects by other American painters.

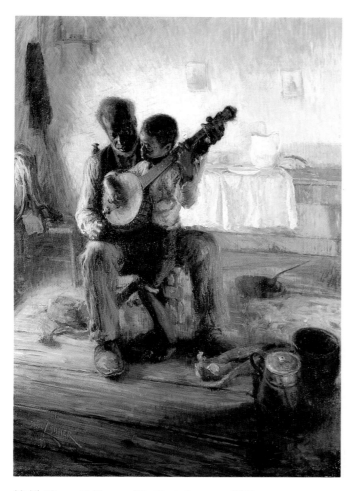

22-25. Henry O. Tanner. *The Banjo Lesson.* c. 1893.
Oil on canvas, 48 x 35" (121.9 x 88.9 cm). Hampton University
Museum, Hampton, Virginia

SCULPTURE

Impressionism, it is often said, revitalized sculpture no less than painting. The statement is at once true and misleading. Auguste Rodin (1840–1917) redefined sculpture during the same years that Manet and Monet revolutionized painting. However, he did not follow their lead. How indeed could the effect of such pictures as The Fifer (fig. 22-4) or *On the Bank of the Seine, Bennecourt* (fig. 22-5) be reproduced in three dimensions and without color?

AUGUSTE RODIN. What Rodin did accomplish can be seen in the first piece he tried to exhibit at the Salon, figure 22-26, *The Man with the Broken Nose* of 1864. (It was rejected on the grounds that it conformed to no established category of sculpture.) Earlier, he had worked briefly under Carrier-Belleuse and Barye, whose influence help to explain the vigorous surface (compare fig. 21-62). These welts and wrinkles produce, in polished bronze, an ever-changing pattern of reflections. But is this effect borrowed from Impressionist painting? Does Rodin actually dissolve three-dimensional form into flickering patches of light and dark? These fiercely exaggerated shapes pulsate with sculptural energy, and they have this quality under whatever conditions the piece is

viewed. Rodin did not, of course, work directly in bronze; he modeled in wax or clay. How then could he calculate in advance the reflections on the cast bronze surfaces?

His working method was intended not to capture elusive optical effects, but to emphasize the process of "growth"—the miracle of dead matter coming to life in the artist's hands. As the color patch for Monet is the primary reality, so for Rodin are the malleable lumps from which he builds his forms. Conservative critics rejected *The Man with the Broken Nose* on the same grounds as Impressionist painting: it was "unfinished," a mere sketch.

The Man with the Broken Nose was Rodin's confession of aesthetic faith. Later on, he said of it: "That mask determined all my future work." The head, on which he had worked for about a year, represented a revolutionary insight. What matters in sculpture is not whether it is "finished" or "complete" but whether it conveys the way it grew. *The Man with the Broken Nose* certainly does, and that is why Rodin thought of it as the cornerstone of his entire future output. He was the first to make "unfinishedness" an aesthetic principle that governed both his handling of surfaces and the whole shape of the work. (*The Man with the Broken Nose* is not a bust but a head "broken off" at the neck.) By discovering the independence of the fragment, he rescued sculpture from mechanical naturalism, just as Manet rescued painting from photographic realism.

Rodin still believed that the sculptor's noblest task was to show the nude human figure, although now it could be done in fragmentary form. He also continued to believe that the sculptor's purpose was to create "new classics"— but without regard to traditional standards of beauty and ugliness. [See Primary Sources,

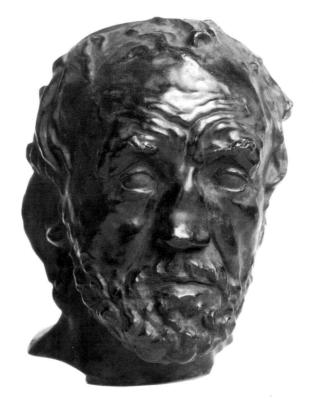

22-26. Auguste Rodin. *The Man with the Broken Nose.* 1864. Bronze, height 9½" (24 cm). Rodin Museum, Philadelphia Museum of Art

no. 74, page 967.] In 1880 he was at last given a major commission, the entrance of the École des Arts Décoratifs in Paris. Rodin developed it into an ambitious ensemble called *The Gates of Hell,* which, characteristically enough, he never finished. The symbolic program was inspired by Dante's *Inferno,* but it was equally indebted to Baudelaire's book of poetry *The Flowers of Evil.* Its common denominator is a tragic view of the human condition: guilty passions, desire forever unfulfilled here and in the beyond, the vain hope of happiness. The perceptive critic Gustave Geffroy, writing of *The Gates of Hell* in 1889, defined their subject as the endless reenactment of the sufferings of Adam and Eve. Indeed, Rodin had tried in 1881 to persuade the government to let him flank *The Gates* with statues of the first man and woman.

   The Gates of Hell served as the framework for countless smaller pieces that eventually became independent works. The most famous of these separate fragments is *The Thinker* (fig. 22-27). The figure was intended for the lintel of the *Gates,* where he could contemplate the panorama of despair below. It derives partly from a statue by Carpeaux of another subject from *The Inferno,* Ugolino

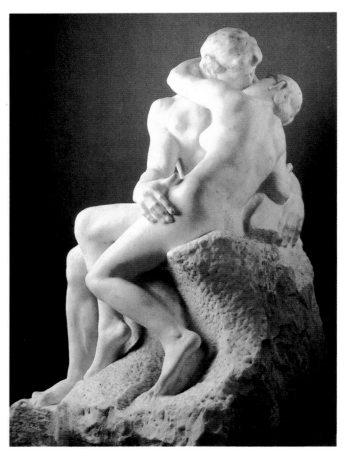

22-28. Auguste Rodin. *The Kiss.* 1886–98. Marble, over-lifesize. Rodin Museum, Paris

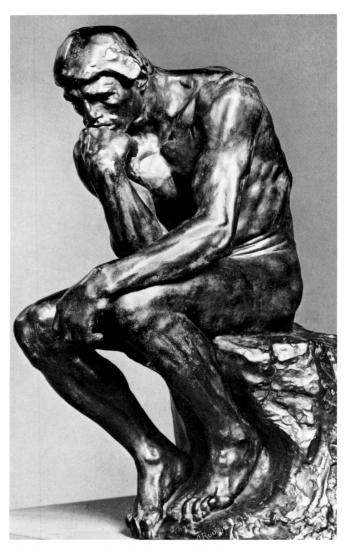

22-27. Auguste Rodin. *The Thinker.* 1879–89. Bronze, height 27½" (69.8 cm). The Metropolitan Museum of Art, New York
GIFT OF THOMAS F. RYAN, 1910

and his sons. The ancestry of *The Thinker* can be traced back much further, however, to depictions of Adam in early Christian art. It also includes the action-in-repose of Michelangelo's superhuman bodies (see figs. 13-13, 13-18, and 13-22) and the tension in Puget's *Milo of Crotona* (see fig. 19-19; note especially the feet).

   Who is *The Thinker?* In the context of *The Gates of Hell,* he was originally conceived as a generalized image of Dante (see page 251), the poet who in his mind's eye sees what goes on all around him. Once Rodin decided to detach him from *The Gates,* he became *The Poet-Thinker,* and finally just *The Thinker.* But what kind of thinker? Partly Adam, no doubt (although there is also a different Adam by Rodin, another outgrowth of the Gates), partly Prometheus, and partly the brute imprisoned by the passions of the flesh. Rodin wisely refrained from giving him a specific name, for the statue fits no established type. In this new image of a man, form and meaning are united, instead of being separated as in Carpeaux's *The Dance* (see fig. 21-64). Carpeaux's naked figures pretend to be nude. *The Thinker,* by contrast, is a true nude, like Michelangelo's: it is no longer bound to the undressed model.

   Unlike Michelangelo, Rodin was by instinct a modeler, not a carver. We nevertheless have a number of excellent marbles by his hand. Among the finest is *The Kiss* (fig. 22-28), an over-lifesize group that also evolved from *The Gates.* It was meant to portray Dante's Paolo and Francesca, but Rodin rejected it as unsuitable. Evidently he realized that *The Kiss* shows the ill-fated pair succumbing to their illicit desire for each other here on earth, not as tortured souls in Hell. Knowing its original title helps us to understand a striking aspect of the group: passion reigned in by hesitancy, for the embrace is not yet complete. Less powerful than *The Thinker*, it exploits another kind of artful unfinishedness. Rodin had been impressed by the struggle of Michelangelo's *"Slaves"* against the remnants of the blocks that imprison them (compare fig. 13-16). *The Kiss* was planned from the start to include the mass of rough-hewn marble. The effect approximates the sense of growth seen in his bronzes. The lovers emerge from, yet remain attached to the base, which thus symbolizes their earthbound passion. The contrast of textures emphasizes the sensuous softness of the bodies.

The Monument to Balzac was Rodin's last, as well as most daring and controversial, creation (fig. 22-29). The sculpture was rejected by the writers' association that had commissioned it, and remained in plaster for many years. He had been asked at the insistence of the author Émile Zola to take over the project when the first sculptor died after producing only a sketch. Rodin declared it to be "the sum of my whole life.... From the day of its conception, I was a changed man." Outward appearance did not pose a problem (Balzac's features were well known). But Rodin wanted far more than that. He was searching for a way to express Balzac's whole personality, without adding allegorical figures or symbolic attributes, which were the usual props of monuments to genius. The final version gives no hint of the many alternative solutions he tried. (More than 40 have survived.) The element common to them all is that Balzac is standing, in order to express the virile energy Rodin saw in his subject.

The sculpture shows the writer clothed in a long dressing gown—described by his contemporaries as a "monk's robe"—which he liked to wear while working at night. Here was a "timeless" costume, much like the toga in Houdon's portrait of Voltaire (see fig. 21-12), that permitted Rodin to conceal and simplify the contours of the body. Seized by a sudden creative impulse, Balzac awakens in the middle of the night. Before he settles down to record his thoughts on paper, he hastily throws the robe over his shoulders without putting his arms through the sleeves. But, of course, Balzac is not about to write. He looms before us with the awesome power of a phantom, completely unaware of his surroundings. The entire figure leans backward to stress its isolation from the viewer.

The statue is larger than life, physically and spiritually: it has an overpowering presence. Like a huge monolith, the man of genius towers above the crowd. He shares "the sublime egotism of the gods" (as the Romantics put it). From a distance we see only the great bulk of the figure. The head thrusts upward—one is tempted to say, erupts—with elemental force from the mass formed by the shroudlike cloak. When we are close enough to make out the features clearly, we sense beneath the disdain an inner agony that stamps *Balzac* as the descendent of *The Man with the Broken Nose*.

To this day the *Balzac* remains a startling sight. Rodin had indeed reached the outer limits of his art, as he himself realized. The question remains, Why did he never have the sculpture cast in bronze, the medium he chose for most of his greatest works, even

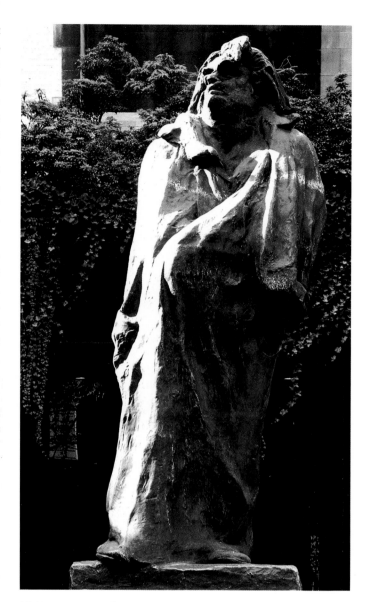

22-29. Auguste Rodin. *Monument to Balzac*. 1897–98. Bronze (cast 1954), height 9'3" (2.82 m). The Museum of Modern Art, New York
PRESENTED IN MEMORY OF CURT VALENTIN BY HIS FRIENDS

though a wealthy private collector offered to pay for it? Perhaps the reason can be found in its compact shape, which certainly lent itself to a marble statue. Can it be that he visualized the monument in marble all along?

CAMILLE CLAUDEL. Rodin employed various assistants throughout his career. One of them, Camille Claudel (1864–1943), has been recognized in recent years as an important artist in her own right. She entered Rodin's studio as a 19-year-old, and for the next decade was his artistic collaborator and mistress. Her sculpture is strongly in her mentor's style, and her best pieces might pass for his. Much of her work is autobiographical. *Ripe Age* (fig. 22-30) depicts a grisly Rodin, his features clearly recognizable, being led away reluctantly by his longtime companion, Rose Beuret, whom Claudel sought to replace in his affections. Beuret is shown as a sinister, shrouded figure who first appears in Claudel's work as

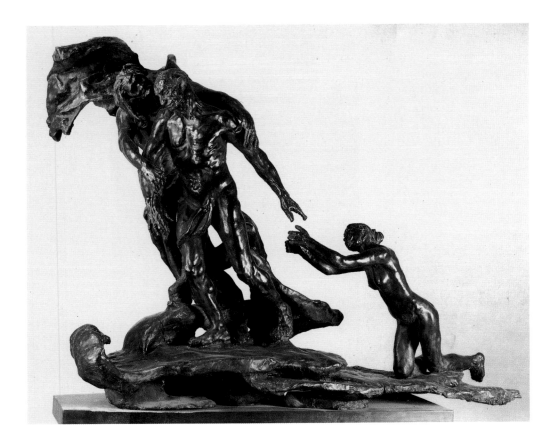

22-30. Camille Claudel. *Ripe Age.* c. 1907. Bronze, 34½ x 20½" (87.6 x 21.9 cm). Musée d'Orsay, Paris

(BELOW) 22-31. Edgar Degas. *The Little Fourteen-Year-Old Dancer.* 1878–80. Bronze with gauze tutu and satin hair ribbon, height 38" (96.5 cm). Norton Simon Art Foundation, Pasadena, California

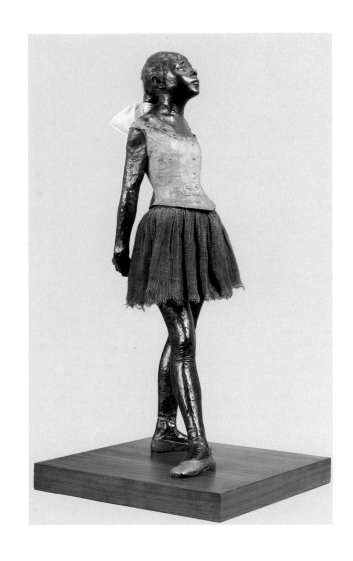

Clotho, one of the three Fates, caught in the web of life she has woven. The nude figure is a self-portrait of Claudel, which likewise evolved from an earlier work, *Entreaty.*

EDGAR DEGAS. The fundamental difference between painting and modeling is illustrated by the fact that only Degas among the Impressionists produced sculpture. He made dozens of small-scale wax figurines that explore the same themes as his paintings and drawings. (Renoir's late sculptures were actually done by an assistant according to his instructions and thus do not qualify.) These are private works made for his own interest. Few of them were exhibited during the artist's lifetime, and none were cast until after his death in 1917.

During the 1870s there was a growing taste for casts made from artists' working models. It reflected the same appreciation for spontaneity and inspiration found in drawings and oil sketches, which had long appealed to collectors. This preference, which dates back to Rodin's ideal, Michelangelo, was essentially an outgrowth of the Romantic cult of originality, not of Impressionism. It was felt that quick, unfinished, even fragmentary works conveyed the force of the artist's vision more directly than any finished piece could.

For the first time sculptors felt free to violate time-honored standards of naturalism and craftsmanship for statuettes, and to leave the impress of their fingers on the soft material as they molded it. Nevertheless, when Degas showed the wax original of *Prima Ballerina (The Little Fourteen-Year-Old Dancer)* at the Impressionist exhibitions of 1880 and 1881, the public was scandalized by its lack of traditional finish and its uncompromising observance of unvarnished truth. (The response from critics was less harsh.) The statue, reproduced here in a posthumous cast (fig. 22-31), is nearly as rough in texture as the slightly smaller nude study from life on which it is based.

Instead of sculpting her costume, Degas used real cotton and silk, a revolutionary idea for the time but something the Romantics, with their insistent naturalism, must often have felt tempted to do. Degas was intrigued by the contrast between the soft material and the hard surface of the bronze, and by the tension between the outfit and the directional forces beneath it. The ungainliness of the young adolescent's body is subtly emphasized by the pose of a dancer at "stage rest." In Degas' hands this pose becomes extremely stressful, so full of sharply opposing angles that no dancer could maintain it for more than a few moments. Yet, rather than awkwardness, the figure conveys a simple dignity and grace that are irresistible. The openness of the stance, with hands clasped behind the back and legs pointing in opposite directions, demands that we walk around the statuette to arrive at a complete image of it. As we view the work from different angles, the surface provides a constantly shifting impression of light that recalls Degas' paintings and pastels of the ballet (compare fig. 22-11). Yet the similarity serves to emphasize the distinctions between these pictorial media and sculpture.

ARCHITECTURE

From the mid-eighteenth to the late nineteenth century, architecture had been dominated by a succession of "revival styles" (see pages 727–33). This term does not mean that these were slavish copies. The best work of the time has both individuality and distinction. Moreover, each revival mirrored a different side of Neoclassical and Romantic thought. Yet the architecture of the past, however freely interpreted, proved in the long run inadequate to the practical demands of the Industrial Age. (See box page 794; materials of modern architecture.) The problem became one not simply of how to use a host of new inventions in utilitarian structures such as factories and warehouses, but also how to apply them to the stores, apartments, libraries, and other city buildings that made up most construction.

HENRI LABROUSTE. A famous early example of Industrial Age design is the Bibliothèque Ste.-Geneviève in Paris by Henri Labrouste (1801–1875). Labrouste entered the École des Beaux-Arts in 1819, the year it opened, and was quickly recognized for his brilliance. In 1824 he won the Prix de Rome and spent five years in Italy studying classical architecture on a government stipend. Labrouste's radical ideas established him among the leaders of the younger generation after his return during the turbulent year 1830, when the French government was overthrown. The Bibliothèque Ste.-Geneviève was his first important commission, and it made his reputation.

The exterior (fig. 22-32) represents the early Beaux-Arts style at its finest. It conforms to the historicism of architecture at mid-century. The facade is drawn chiefly from Italian Renaissance banks, libraries, and churches (compare fig. 12-28), but the two-tiered elevation also looks back to Perrault's East Front of the Louvre (see fig. 19-10). At the last minute, Labrouste hit on the brilliant idea of inscribing the names of great writers around

the facade to identify the building as a library. (The letters were originally painted red for legibility.) What led him to use this simple but ingenious device was the library's location just behind Soufflot's church of Ste.-Geneviève, which, as we have seen, had been secularized during the French Revolution and renamed the Panthéon (see fig. 21-16). Labrouste, in effect, has turned his library into a pantheon as well—but one dedicated to literary and intellectual, not national, heroes. The facade has also been interpreted as an expression of Auguste Comte's positivism, in which the rows of names act like so many rows of newsprint, with embossed decoration, to denote the library as the setting for human activity.

The reading room (fig. 22-33), in contrast, recalls the nave of a French Gothic cathedral (compare fig. 11-17). The combination of the classical and the Gothic again pays homage to Soufflot, whose goal was to combine them. Barrel vaults supported by columns, although derived from Romanesque churches (see fig. 10-6), had been introduced into Renaissance libraries by Michelozzo (see page 422) and soon became a common feature of reading rooms. The type was revived by Boullée in a characteristically visionary project for a huge library in the Palais Mazarin surmounted by a coffered vault, and there can be little doubt, in fact, that Labrouste's design is partly indebted to Boullée's. Barrel-vaulted libraries enjoyed renewed popularity in England and on the Continent during the 1830s (compare also fig. 21-19). To Labrouste, barrel vaults undoubtedly looked "Gothic." (The term "Romanesque" had not yet been coined.) They had the further advantage of acquiring literary associations through the addition of the classical columns. In uniting the two main systems of Western architecture, the Bibliothèque Ste.-Geneviève fulfills the program of Soufflot and the structural rationalists.

Labrouste's enthusiasm for the Gothic arose from his contact with the writer Victor Hugo, who consulted him on technical questions for his novel Notre-Dame de Paris (The Hunchback of Notre-Dame). Hugo believed that architecture was originally a form of writing, which had reached its zenith in the Greek and Gothic eras. In a similar vein, Labrouste once wrote that the Temple of Hera at Paestum (see fig. 5-27) had been "covered with painted notices, serving as a book." Hugo, and most likely Labrouste himself, was strongly influenced by the Socialist followers of the Comte de Saint-Simon (see page 655). They

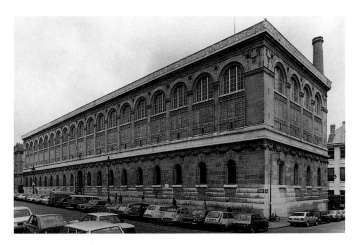

22-32. Henri Labrouste. Bibliothèque Ste.-Geneviève, Paris. 1843–50

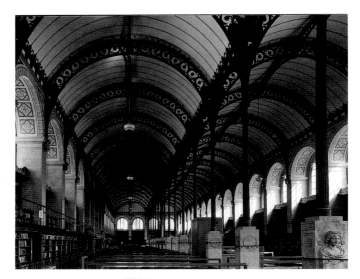

22-33. Henri Labrouste. Reading Room,
Bibliothèque Ste.-Geneviève

regarded Greek and Gothic architecture as ideal "organic" phases, to be succeeded by a third one expressing a new social philosophy, moral values, and religious beliefs. Such egalitarian ideas, further shaped by Charles Fourier, were appropriate to the library, which was for general use by the public. But why did Labrouste choose cast-iron columns and arches? Cast iron was not necessary to provide support for the two barrel roofs—this function could have been filled using other materials. Rather, it was essential to the completion of the building's symbolic program. With the Bibliothèque Ste.-Geneviève he announced that technology would provide the new tradition to succeed the classical and the Gothic.

Labrouste boldly left the interior iron skeleton uncovered, rather than disguising it. His solution does not fully integrate the two systems but lets them coexist. The iron supports, shaped like

Corinthian columns, are as slender as the new material permits. Their collective effect is that of a space-dividing screen that denies their structural importance. To make them appear weightier, Labrouste has placed them on tall pedestals of solid masonry, instead of directly on the floor. Aesthetically the arches presented greater difficulty, since there was no way to make them look as powerful as their masonry ancestors. Here Labrouste has gone to the other extreme and perforated them with lacy scrolls as if they were pure ornament, so that the vaulting has a fanciful and delicate quality. This daring expressive (as against merely structural) use of exposed iron members created a sensation and placed Labrouste in the forefront of French architecture, although it had already been tried 30 years earlier in England (see page 728). The reading room featured another innovation as well. It was the first of its kind to be lit by gas, making it usable at night. Although iron was later replaced by **structural steel** and **ferroconcrete**, Labrouste's wedding of historicism and engineering proved so satisfying that most libraries, railroad stations, and the like were indebted to the Bibliothèque Ste.-Geneviève, directly or indirectly, for the rest of the century.

The authority of revival styles nevertheless had to be broken if the industrial era was to produce a truly contemporary style. It proved extraordinarily persistent, however. Labrouste, pioneer though he was of cast-iron construction, could not think of architectural supports as anything but columns having proper capitals and bases, rather than as metal rods or pipes (see pages 789–93). The "architecture of conspicuous display" practiced by Garnier (see pages 731–33) was divorced even more from the needs of the present. It was only in structures that were not considered architecture at all that new building materials and techniques could be explored without restrictions.

JOSEPH PAXTON. The Crystal Palace (fig. 22-34) was built in London within a year of the completion of the Bibliothèque

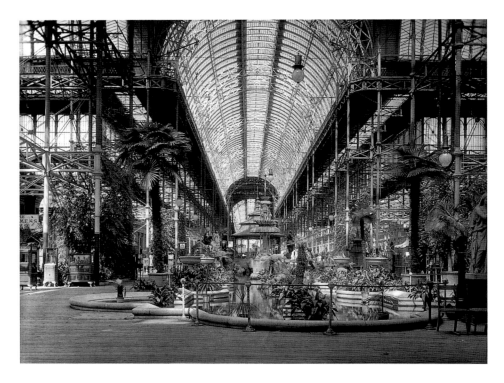

22-34. Sir Joseph Paxton.
The Crystal Palace, London. 1851;
reerected in Sydenham 1852;
destroyed 1936

Ste.-Geneviève. A pioneering achievement far bolder in conception than Labrouste's library, it housed the first of the great international expositions that continue in our day. The designer, Sir Joseph Paxton (1801–1865), was an engineer and builder of greenhouses. The Crystal Palace was, in fact, a gigantic greenhouse—so large that it enclosed some old trees growing on the site—with its iron skeleton freely on display. In exhibition halls, ease and cost of construction were paramount, since they were not intended to stay up for very long. Paxton's design was such a success that it set off a wave of similar commercial buildings, such as public markets. However, the notion that products of engineering might have beauty, not just utility, made very slow headway, even though it found supporters from the mid-nineteenth century on. Hence most such buildings have decorations that follow the eclectic taste of the period.

JOHN AND WASHINGTON ROEBLING. Only rarely could an engineering feat express the spirit of the times. One of the few to achieve this was the Brooklyn Bridge, built by John (1806–1869) and Washington (1837–1926) Roebling (fig. 22-35), which remains one of the outstanding achievements of the Indus-

trial Revolution. It was referred to, appropriately enough, as America's Arch of Triumph. The massive towers incorporate aspects of Egyptian, Roman, and Gothic architecture (note the pointed arches) to express a combination of eternal strength, civic pride, and soaring spirituality. Small wonder it came to be celebrated by poets and artists alike (see fig. 24-35).

GUSTAVE EIFFEL. What was needed for products of engineering to be accepted as architecture was a structure that would capture the world's imagination through its bold conception. The breakthrough came with the Eiffel Tower, named after its designer, Gustave Eiffel (1832–1923). As shown in a contemporary photograph (fig. 22-36), it was erected at the entrance to the Paris World's Fair of 1889, where it served as a "triumphal arch" of science and industry. It has become such a visual cliché beloved of tourists—much like the *Statue of Liberty,* which also involved Eiffel (see fig. 21-65)—that we can hardly appreciate what a revolutionary impact it had at the time. [See Primary Sources, no. 75, page 968.] The tower, with its frankly technological aesthetic, so dominates the city's skyline that it provoked a storm of protest by the leading intellectuals of the day. Eiffel used the same principles of

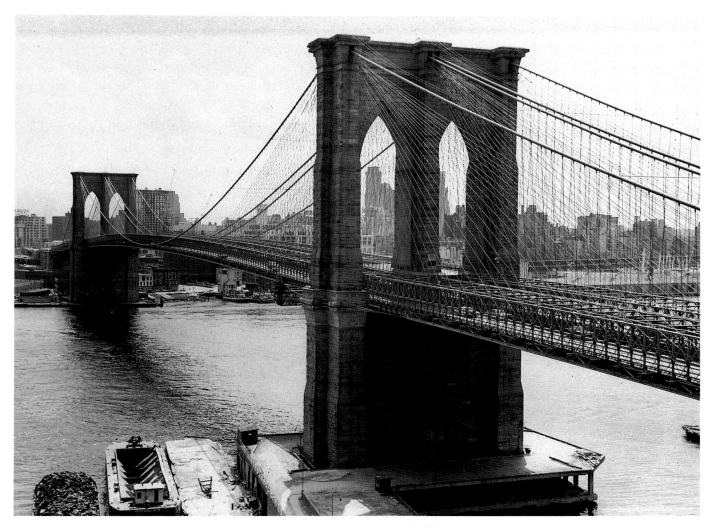

22-35. John and Washington Roebling. The Brooklyn Bridge, New York. 1867–83

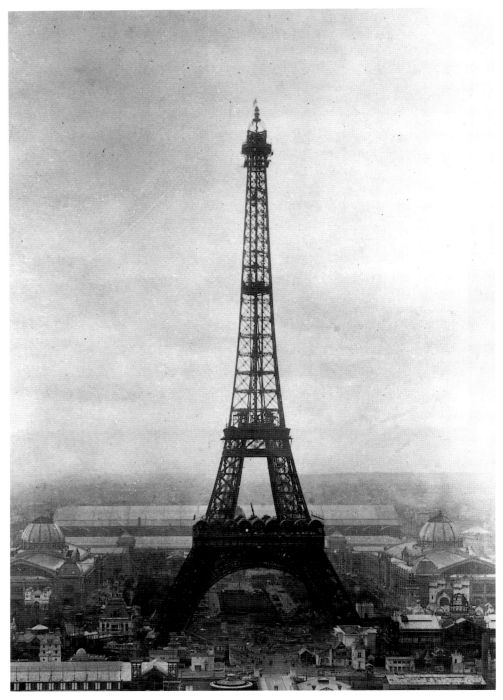

22-36. Gustave Eiffel. The Eiffel Tower, Paris. 1887–89

structural engineering that he had already applied successfully to bridges. Yet the result was so novel in appearance and so daring in construction that nothing quite like it has ever been built, before or since.

The Eiffel Tower owed much of its success to the fact that for a small sum anyone could take its elevators to see a view of Paris that was previously reserved for the privileged few able to afford hot-air balloon rides (see fig. 21-83). It thus helped to define a distinctive feature of modern architecture, one that it shares with modern technology as a whole: it acts on large masses of people, without regard to social or economic class. Although this capacity, which was shared only by the largest churches and public buildings of the past, has also served the aims of extremists at both ends of the political spectrum, modern architecture has tended by its very nature to function as a vehicle of democracy. We can readily understand, then, why the Eiffel Tower quickly became a popular symbol of Paris itself. It could do so, however, precisely because it serves no practical purpose whatsoever.

REALISM IN MID-NINETEENTH-CENTURY THEATER

Realism was the dominant style in mid-nineteenth-century theater, as it was in painting. In part, theatrical Realism was a reflection of the pragmatic character of the Industrial Revolution. Its principal theorist was the French philosopher Auguste Comte (1798–1857), the founder of a system of thought known as Positivism, which called for a material explanation of truth based on objective observation and scientific analysis. As in art, Realism in drama covered a wide range of tendencies, from simple adherence to historic fact, social reality, or physical appearance to highly emotional treatments that have much in common with Romanticism.

The Realist playwright best known today is Alexandre Dumas the Younger (1824–1895), whose drama *Camille* (1852) was the first to treat the now-familiar theme of the prostitute with a heart of gold. While a modern audience might find *Camille* somewhat melodramatic, in its own time the play was considered an unflinching depiction of life at the fringes of Parisian society. In response to the criticism of *Camille* contained in *Olympe's Marriage* (1855) by Émile Augier (1820–1889), Dumas abandoned Realism three years later in *The Demi-Monde,* his first attempt at social and moral criticism. The most popular playwright of the period was Victorien Sardou (1831–1908), whose drama *La Tosca* (1887) was later turned into a well-known opera by the Italian composer Giacomo Puccini (see box page 778). This story of love, treachery, and revenge during the Italian struggle for independence was an important starring role for the great British tragic actress Sarah Bernhardt (1844–1923; see fig. 21-82). A gifted sculptor as well, Bernhardt specialized in tragic heroines such as Camille and Adrienne Lecouvreur. Her only rival was the English actress Ellen Terry (1847–1928), who came from a long line of actors (see fig. 23-45). She was the leading lady to Henry Irving (1838–1905), by far the most important actor and manager in England during the later nineteenth century, who commissioned Edward Burne-Jones (see page 751) and other prominent artists to design stage sets for him. Irving was knighted in 1895, while Terry was made a Dame Commander of the British Empire only in 1925.

Germany produced few major dramatists during the third quarter of the century. Instead, it was content to rely on the plays of Shakespeare, Goethe, and Schiller and on translations of Sardou and the younger Dumas. Vienna became the main theater center under Heinrich Laube (1806–1884), a former member of Young Germany, and Franz Dingelstedt (1814–1881), who had produced Christian Friedrich Hebbel's (1813–1863) trilogy *The Nibelungen* in 1861 at Weimar. A fascination with old Germanic legends that was fueled by growing nationalism helped to make historical accuracy the goal of German theater. The chief contributors to theater in Germany at this time were Duke George II of Saxe-Meiningen (1826–1914) and his wife, the actress Helene Franz (1839–1923), who elevated the quality of acting through careful preparation and emphasis on ensemble. Attention was also paid to costumes and scenery.

Russian authors of the time had a particular affinity for psychological Realism. The first Russian professional playwright, Aleksandr Ostrovsky (1823–1886), had an abiding interest in characters and their relationships. However, the major plays were written by the great novelists of the era. Ivan Turgenev (1818–1883) wrote a number of dramas that are remarkable for their portrayal of their characters' inner lives and complex relationships. Leo Tolstoy (1828–1910) also tried his hand at plays, notably *The Power of Darkness,* which was produced in 1895, some 30 years after it was written. Aleksei Tolstoy (1817–1875), a distant relative, established himself as the leading Realist with a strong interest in the history of Russia. *The Death of Ivan the Terrible* and *Tsar Boris,* both of 1870, were based on the historical research of Nikolai Karamzin (1766–1826), which did much to stimulate Russian nationalism.

In the United States, the favorite dramas before the Civil War were various adaptations of the novel *Uncle Tom's Cabin* by Harriet Beecher Stowe (1811–1896). This portrayal of the life of slaves on southern plantations helped fuel abolitionist sentiment. The years before the war were also a time of great actors. The Englishman William Burton (1804–1860) headed the finest company in New York, the undisputed theater capital of America, although the Boston Museum also staged many plays after 1850. Burton had been preceded by another English performer, Junius Booth (1796–1852), whose son Edwin Booth (1833–1893) became the greatest actor America has ever produced. Unfortunately, the family remains notorious for another son, John Wilkes Booth (1838–1865), the assassin of President Abraham Lincoln. The most popular form of theater was the burlesque extravaganza. Over time it came to appeal mainly to men by featuring beautiful women, although striptease was added only in 1929. Vaudeville, a more genteel form of family entertainment that reached its height between 1890 and 1930, was defined largely by Tony Pastor (1837–1908).

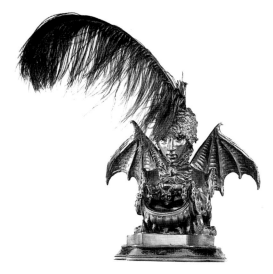

Sarah Bernhardt. *Fantastic Inkwell, Self-Portrait As a Sphinx.* After 1880. Patinated bronze. Height: 12½" (31.8 cm); base: 7½" (19.1 cm). Museum of Fine Arts, Boston

HELEN AND ALICE COLBURN FUND

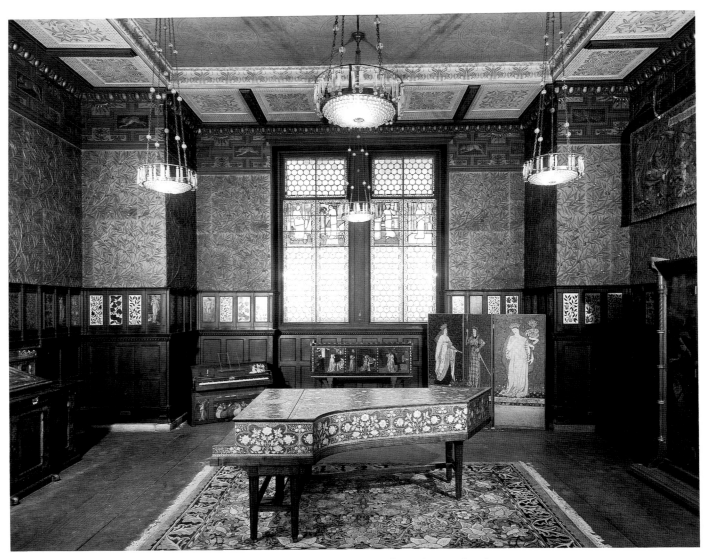

22-37. William Morris (Morris & Co.). Green Dining Room. 1867. Victoria & Albert Museum, London

DECORATIVE ARTS

WILLIAM MORRIS. The decorative arts played a vital role in England during the second half of the nineteenth century. William Morris (1834–1896), the early leader in what came to be known as the Arts and Crafts Movement, started out with William Holman Hunt as a student of the Pre-Raphaelite painter Dante Gabriel Rossetti (see page 751) but soon shifted his interest to "art for use": domestic architecture and interior decoration such as furniture, tapestries, and wallpapers. He wanted to displace the shoddy products of the Machine Age by reviving the handicrafts of the preindustrial past, an art "made by the people, and for the people, as a happiness to the maker and the user."

Morris was an apostle of simplicity. Architecture and furniture ought to be designed in accordance with the nature of their materials and working processes. Surface decoration must be flat and simple. His interiors (fig. 22-37) are total environments that create an effect of quiet intimacy. Despite Morris' self-proclaimed championship of the medieval tradition, he never imitated its forms directly but tried to capture its spirit. His achievement was to invent the first original system of ornament since the Rococo.

Through the many enterprises he sponsored, as well as his skill as a writer and publicist, Morris became a tastemaker without equal in his day. Toward the end of the century his influence had spread throughout Europe and America. Nor was he content to reform the arts of design alone. He saw them as a lever by which to reform modern society as a whole. As a result, he played an important part in the early history of Fabianism—a gradualist form of socialism invented in England as an alternative to the revolutionary kind on the Continent.

JAMES MCNEILL WHISTLER. In the 1860s the reform ideas of William Morris began to influence domestic architecture and decoration. The boldest innovations, however, came not from members of his immediate circle but from Whistler and his followers. Whistler himself created one of the masterpieces of nineteenth-century design: the Peacock Room (fig. 22-38), which housed the blue-and-white porcelain collection of Frederick Leyland. What began as a modest project to remedy the previous decorations soon grew into an ambitious overhaul by Whistler, who spared no expense to achieve his lavish scheme while his patron was away.

The results were inevitably mixed, as the room itself originally embodied basically the same sensibility as Morris' Green Dining Room (see fig. 22-37). In contrast, Whistler's fanciful decorations, with gilt everywhere, exemplify the Aesthetic Movement, which sought refuge from the tawdry reality of the Industrial Revolution by retreating into a realm of the utmost elegance and refinement. The peacock motif, which reflects Whistler's fascination with Japanese art, seems a uniquely appropriate symbol of his aestheticism, which regarded beauty as an end in itself, without regard to social responsibility. Leyland, a Liverpool shipping magnate, was Whistler's main patron in the 1870s. When he and Whistler had a falling out over the excessive costs of the Peacock Room, Whistler was forced to declare bankruptcy.

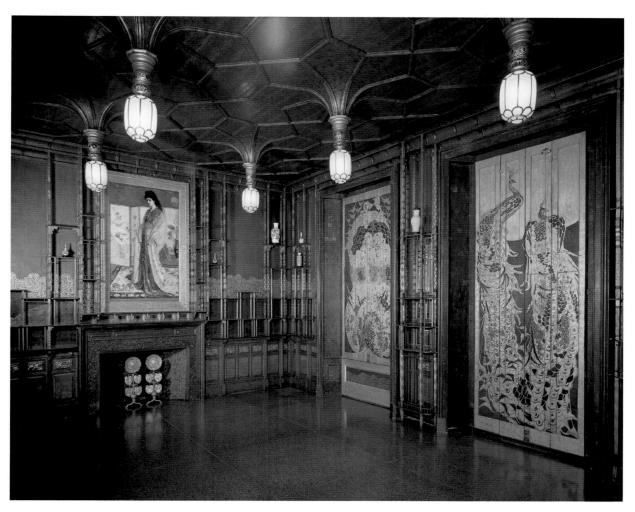

22-38. James Abbott McNeill Whistler. *Harmony in Blue and Gold: The Peacock Room.* 1876–77. Oil color and gold on leather and wood. The Freer Gallery of Art, Smithsonian Institution, Washington, D.C.

CHAPTER TWENTY-THREE

Post-Impressionism, Symbolism, and Art Nouveau

PAINTING

The three movements that came to the fore after 1884—Post-Impressionism, Symbolism, and Art Nouveau—bore complex, shifting relationships to each other. At face value, they had little in common other than the time period they shared (the mid-1880s to around 1910). Post-Impressionism encompassed a wide range of styles, from the severely analytical to the highly expressive. Thus it could be readily adapted to different outlooks on art and life. Symbolism was not a style at all but an intensely private world-view based on the literary movement of the same name. Like the Romantics, the Symbolists were free to adopt any style that suited their purposes, including Post-Impressionism. Art Nouveau, by contrast, was both a style and an attitude toward life and art. It was closely linked to the Aesthetic Movement and the Arts and Crafts Movement. The adherents of Post-Impressionism, Symbolism, and Art Nouveau were united by a desire to be new and by the need to respond to the profound social and economic changes brought on by the Industrial Revolution.

Post-Impressionism

In 1882, just before his death, Édouard Manet was made a knight of the Legion of Honor by the French government. This honor marks the turning of a tide. Impressionism had gained wide acceptance among artists and the public, but by the same token it was no longer a pioneering movement. When the Impressionists held their last group show four years later, the future already belonged to the Post-Impressionists. Taken literally, this colorless label applies to all painters of any significance in the 1880s and 1890s. More specifically, it designates a group of artists who passed through an Impressionist phase but became dissatisfied with the limitations of the style and pursued a variety of other directions. Although they did not share a common goal, they were not "anti-Impressionists," no matter how much they may have challenged Monet's goals. Far from trying to undo the effects of Impressionism, they wanted to carry it further. Thus Post-Impressionism was a later stage, although a very important one, of the "Manet Revolution" that had begun in the 1860s.

PAUL CÉZANNE. Paul Cézanne (1839–1906), the oldest of the Post-Impressionists, was born in Aix-en-Provence, near the Mediterranean coast. There he formed a close friendship with the writer Émile Zola, later a champion of the Impressionists. A man of intensely emotional temperament, Cézanne came to Paris in 1861 filled with enthusiasm for the Romantics. Delacroix was his first love among painters, and he never lost his admiration for him. Cézanne, however, quickly grasped the nature of the "Manet Revolution." He also completely transformed it.

A Modern Olympia (fig. 23-1) was painted in response to a work by Manet titled *Olympia* which featured a prostitute whose frank nakedness scandalized the art world. Like the women in *Luncheon on the Grass* (see fig. 22-3), painted by Manet the same year as *Olympia,* Cézanne's nude shares the company of a man wearing contemporary clothing. His features are plainly those of the artist himself (see fig. 23-2). Like many of Cézanne's early works, *A Modern Olympia* is sexually charged, although in a curiously ambivalent way that suggests why he never formed a lasting relationship. While the setting is a boudoir, the picture is one of the first to treat what was to become one of the favorite themes in modern art: the artist and his model, a subject often filled with erotic overtones. The artist sits in silent adoration of the young woman, whose sumptuous surroundings suggest that she is indeed a modern goddess. Yet the relationship between the two figures is strange indeed. Although separated in space, they are placed so near each other on the picture plane that she seems almost to recoil from his dark presence! Equally disturbing is the brushwork, which communicates the turbulent passion repressed by the seemingly impassive artist in the picture. Never before have we seen such brusqueness, not even in Cézanne's ideal, Delacroix. The subtitle *The Pasha* pays homage to the Orientalism of Delacroix, whose *The Death of Sardanapalus* (see fig. 21-33) nevertheless has a sensuousness missing from Cézanne's *Olympia.* This artist-as-potentate can admire, but not possess, his "harem girl."

After passing through a Neo-Baroque phase, Cézanne began to paint bright outdoor scenes with Pissarro, but he never shared

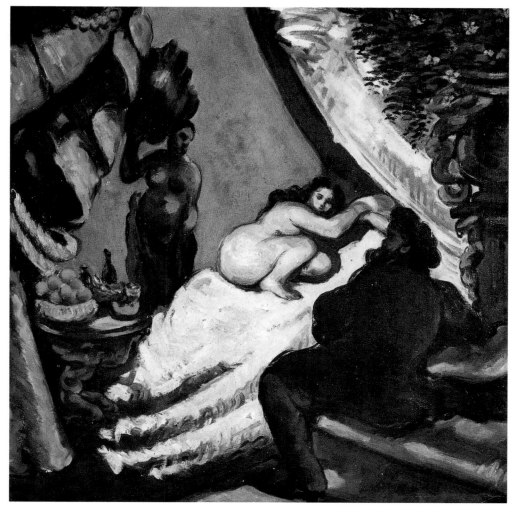

23-1. Paul Cézanne. *A Modern Olympia (The Pasha)*. Early 1870s.
Oil on canvas, 22 x 21⅝" (56 x 55 cm). Private collection

his fellow Impressionists' interest in "slice-of-life" subjects or in movement and change. About 1879, when he painted the *Self-Portrait* in figure 23-2, he had decided "to make of Impressionism something solid and durable, like the art of the museums." His Romantic impulsiveness gave way to a patient, disciplined search for harmony of form and color. Every brushstroke became like a building block, firmly placed within the pictorial architecture, which creates a subtle balance between the two dimensional picture plane and the three-dimensional forms. (Note how the pattern of wallpaper in the background frames the rounded shape of the head.) The colors, too, are carefully controlled so as to produce "chords" of warm and cool tones that echo throughout the canvas.

This quest for the "solid and durable" can be seen most clearly in Cézanne's still lifes, such as *Still Life with Apples in a Bowl* (fig. 23-3). Not since Chardin have simple everyday objects assumed such importance in a painter's eye. The ornamental backdrop is integrated with the three-dimensional shapes, and the brushstrokes have a rhythmic pattern that helps to organize the canvas. We also notice another aspect of Cézanne's style that may puzzle us at first. The forms are deliberately simplified and outlined with dark contours. Also the perspective is "incorrect," for both the fruit bowl and the horizontal surfaces seem to tilt upward. Yet the longer we study the picture, the more we realize the rightness of

these apparently arbitrary distortions. When Cézanne took these liberties with reality, his purpose was to uncover the permanent qualities beneath the accidents of appearance. All forms in nature, he believed, were based on abstractions such as the cone, the sphere, and the cylinder. [See Primary Sources, no. 76, page 968.] This underlying order was the real subject of his pictures, but he had to interpret it to fit the separate, closed world of the canvas.

To apply this method to landscape became the greatest challenge of Cézanne's career. From 1882 on he lived in isolation near his hometown of Aix-en-Provence, and explored its surroundings as thoroughly as Claude Lorraine and Camille Corot had explored the Roman countryside. One subject, a distinctively shaped mountain called Mont Ste.-Victoire, seemed to obsess him. Its craggy profile looming against the blue Mediterranean sky appears in a long series of compositions culminating in monumental late works such as figure 23-4. There are no hints of human presence here—houses and roads would only disturb the lonely grandeur of the view. Above the wall of rocky cliffs that bar our way like a chain of fortifications, the mountain rises in triumphant clarity, infinitely remote, yet as solid as the shapes in the foreground. For all its architectural stability, the scene is alive with movement. But the forces at work here have been brought into balance, subdued by the greater power of the artist's will. This disciplined energy,

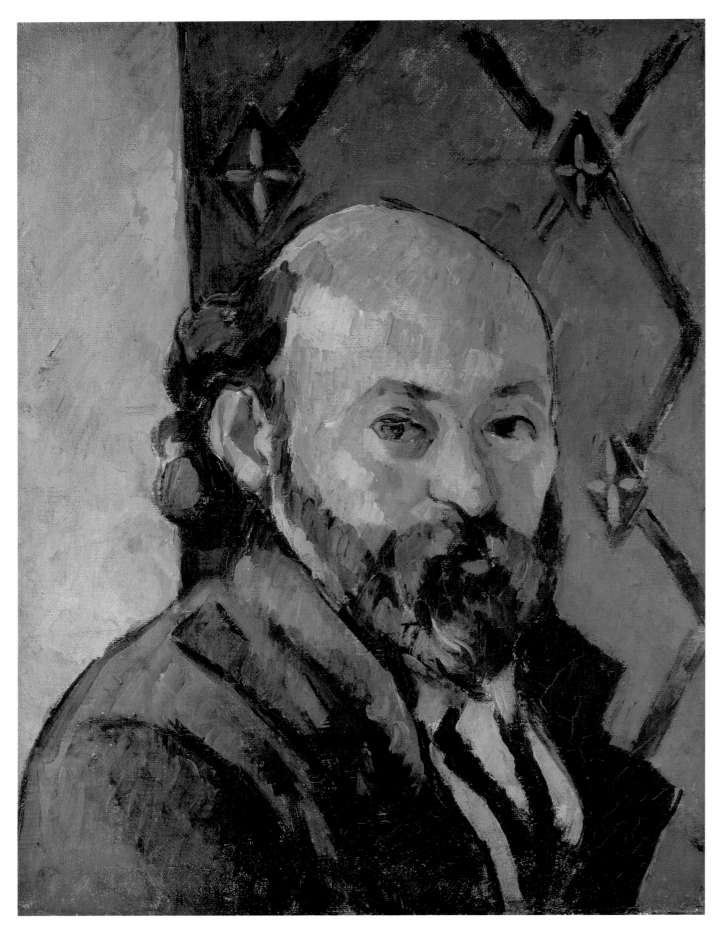

23-2. Paul Cézanne. *Self-Portrait*. c. 1879. Oil on canvas, 13¾ x 10⅝" (35 x 27 cm). The Tate Gallery, London

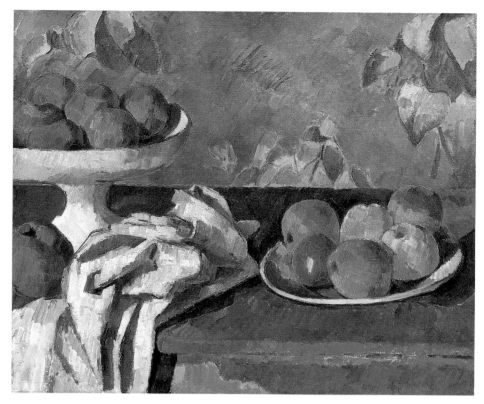

23-3. Paul Cézanne. *Still Life with Apples in a Bowl.* 1879–82. Oil on canvas, 17⅛ x 21¼" (43.5 x 54 cm). Ny Carlsberg Glyptotek, Copenhagen, Denmark

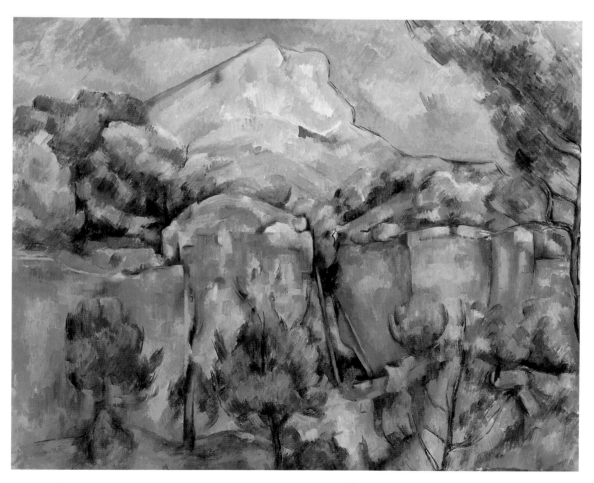

23-4. Paul Cézanne. *Mont Ste.-Victoire Seen from Bibemus Quarry.* c. 1897–1900. Oil on canvas, 25½ x 31½" (65.1 x 80 cm). The Baltimore Museum of Art

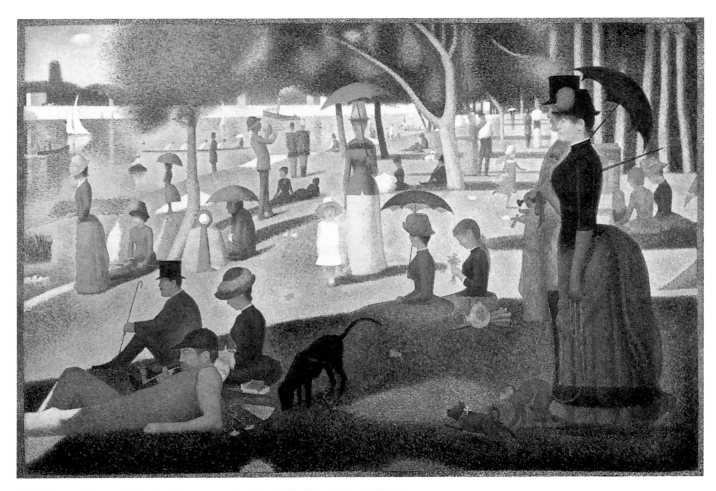

23-5. Georges Seurat. *A Sunday Afternoon on the Island of La Grande Jatte*. 1884–86.
Oil on canvas, 6'10" x 10'1¼" (2.08 x 3.08 m). The Art Institute of Chicago

distilled from the trials of a stormy youth, gives Cézanne's mature style its enduring strength.

GEORGES SEURAT. Georges Seurat (1859–1891) shared Cézanne's aim to make Impressionism "solid and durable," but he went about it very differently. His goal, he once stated, was to make "modern people, in their essential traits, move about as if on friezes, and place them on canvases organized by harmonies of color, by directions of the tones in harmony with the lines, and by the directions of the lines." Seurat's career was as brief as those of Masaccio, Giorgione, and Géricault, and his achievement just as remarkable. Although he participated in the last Impressionist show, thereafter he exhibited with an entirely new group, the Society of Independents.

Seurat devoted his main efforts to a few very large paintings. He would spend a year or more on each, and make endless series of preliminary studies before he felt sure enough to tackle the final version. *A Sunday Afternoon on the Island of La Grande Jatte* of 1884–86 (fig. 23-5), his greatest masterpiece, had its genesis in this painstaking method. The subject is the kind that had long been popular among Impressionist painters. Impressionist, too, are the brilliant

colors and the effect of intense sunlight. Otherwise the picture is the exact opposite of a quick "impression." The firm contours, simple forms, and motionless figures give the scene a timeless stability that recalls Piero della Francesca (see fig. 12-48) and shows a clear awareness of Puvis de Chavannes (see page 781).

In *La Grande Jatte* modeling and foreshortening are reduced to a minimum. The figures appear mostly in either strict profile or in frontal views, as if Seurat had adopted the rules of ancient Egyptian art. He has fitted them into the composition as tightly as the pieces of a jigsaw puzzle. So exactly are they fixed in relation to each other that not a single one could be moved by even a millimeter. Frozen in time and space, they act out their roles with ritualized solemnity, in contrast to the joyous abandon of the relaxed figures in Renoir's *Luncheon of the Boating Party, Bougival* (see fig. 22-8), who are free to move about. Thus we read this cross section of Parisian society as timeless, despite the period costumes.

Even the brushwork shows Seurat's passion for order and permanence. The surface is covered with systematic, impersonal dots of brilliant color that were supposed to merge in the beholder's eye and produce intermediary tints more luminous than pigments mixed on the palette. This procedure was variously known as

Neo-Impressionism, Pointillism, or Divisionism (the term preferred by Seurat). The actual result, however, does not follow the theory. Looking at *La Grande Jatte* from a comfortable distance (seven to ten feet from the original), we find that it does not create the intended effect: the mixing of colors in the eye remains incomplete. The dots do not disappear but are as clearly visible as the tesserae of a mosaic (compare figs. 8-28 and 8-29). Seurat himself must have liked this unexpected effect, which gives the canvas the quality of a shimmering, translucent screen. Otherwise, he would have reduced the size and spacing of the dots. These "flicks" make Cézanne's architectural brushstrokes seem dynamic and temperamental by comparison.

The painting has a dignity and simplicity that suggest a new classicism, but it is a distinctly modern classicism based on scientific theory. Seurat adapted the laws of color discovered by Eugène Chevreul, O. N. Rood, and David Sutter, as part of a comprehensive approach to art. Like Degas, he had studied with a follower of Ingres, and his theoretical interests grew out of this experience. He came to believe that art must be based on a system. With the help of his friend Charles Henry (who was, like Rood and Sutter, an American), he formulated a series of artistic "laws" based on early experiments in the psychology of visual perception. These principles helped him to control every aesthetic and expressive aspect of his paintings. But, as with all artists of genius, Seurat's theories do not really explain his pictures. It is the pictures, rather, that explain the theories. In fact, the theories were devised, along with their "proofs," to support Seurat's paintings.

Strange as it may seem, color was an adjunct to form in Seurat's work—the very opposite of the Impressionists' technique. Much of his output consists of drawings done in conté crayon, which is made of graphite and clay and provides rich, velvety blacks (fig. 23-6). These sheets have a haunting mystery in contrast to the festive character of his paintings. The forms have a machine-like quality achieved through rigorous abstraction. This is the first expression of a peculiarly modern outlook that led to Futurism (see page 815). Seurat's systematic approach to art has the logic of modern engineering, which he and his followers hoped would transform society for the better. This social consciousness was linked to a form of anarchism descended from Courbet's friend Pierre-Joseph Proudhon, and contrasts with the general political indifference of the Impressionists. The fact that the Impressionists and Seurat shared the same subject matter serves only to emphasize the fundamental difference in their attitudes.

Toward the end of his brief career, Seurat's paintings acquired a new liveliness, seen in *Chahut* (fig. 23-7). True, everything is held tightly in place by a system of vertical and horizontal lines that defines the canvas as a self-contained rectilinear field. Only in the work of Vermeer have we encountered a similar "area-consciousness" (compare fig. 18-29). But while these dancers move in lockstep, the decorative arabesques within the flat design have an unexpected energy. Consciously or unconsciously, Seurat here moves close to the world of commercial art. The speckled surface resembles the cheap offset printing then coming into use. The subject and composition, too, directly anticipate the posters of Henri de Toulouse-Lautrec—even in the marvelous wit and insight of the facial expressions.

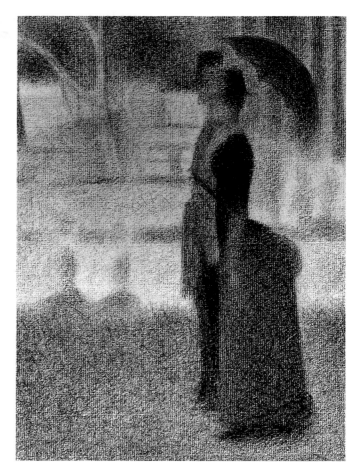

23-6. Georges Seurat. *The Couple*. c. 1884–85. Conté crayon on paper, 11½ x 9" (29.2 x 22.8 cm). Private collection, Paris

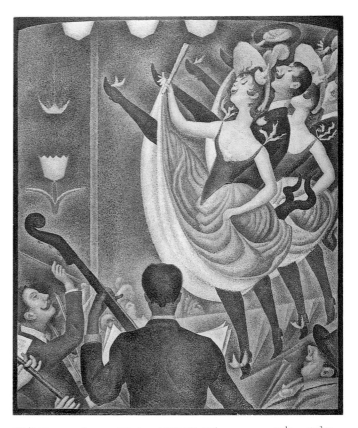

23-7. Georges Seurat. *Chahut*. 1889–90. Oil on canvas, 66½ x 54¾" (169 x 139 cm). Rijksmuseum Kröller-Müller, Otterlo, Holland

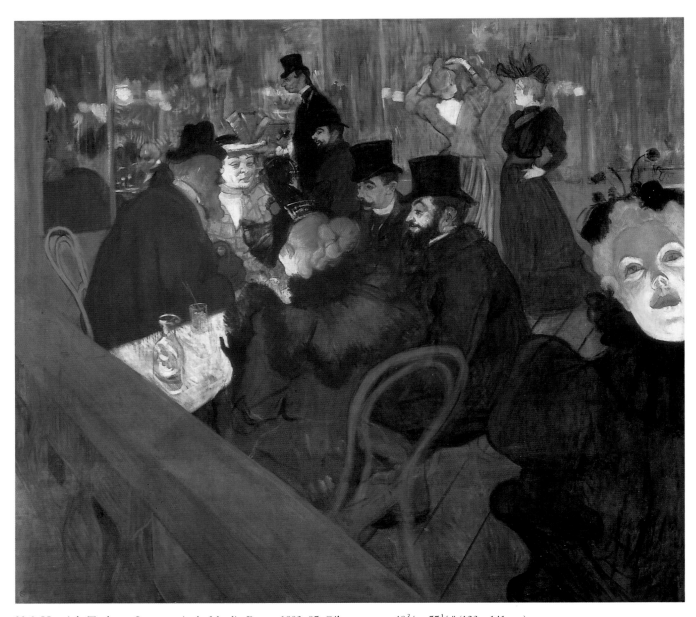

23-8. Henri de Toulouse-Lautrec. *At the Moulin Rouge.* 1893–95. Oil on canvas, 48³⁄₈ x 55¹⁄₂" (123 x 141 cm).
The Art Institute of Chicago

HENRI TOULOUSE-LAUTREC. Henri de Toulouse-Lautrec (1864–1901) was an artist of superb talent but he led a dissolute life in the night spots and brothels of Paris and died of alcoholism. He was a great admirer of Degas; *At the Moulin Rouge* (fig. 23-8) recalls the zigzag pattern in Degas' *The Glass of Absinthe* (see fig. 22-10). Yet this view of the well-known nightclub is no Impressionist slice of life. Toulouse-Lautrec sees through the apparent cheerfulness of the scene. He views performers and customers alike with a sharp eye for character—including his own: he is the tiny, bearded man (he was born a dwarf) next to the very tall man in the back of the room. The large areas of flat color and the emphatic, curving outlines reflect the influence of Paul Gauguin (compare fig. 23-13). The Moulin Rouge that Toulouse-Lautrec shows has an atmosphere so joyless and oppressive that we have to wonder if the artist did not regard it as a place

of evil. This scene, no less than Manet's *Luncheon on the Grass* (see fig. 22-3), fulfills Baudelaire's definition of "the heroism of modern life." It includes "the spectacle of fashionable life and of thousands of roaming existences—criminals and kept women—drifting about in the undergrounds of a great city." [See Primary Sources, no. 70, page 966.]

If his paintings bring to mind Degas and Gauguin, Toulouse-Lautrec's graphic art is without precedent. His posters, done in a distinctive style, are ideally suited to inexpensive lithography, which imposes economy of form and color. His first poster, *La Goulue* (fig. 23-9), established his fame. The artist gives this seedy demimonde an air of glamour that is at once captivating and mysterious. As advertising it sets a standard that has rarely been matched. The design is wed to the text so seamlessly that neither can live without the other.

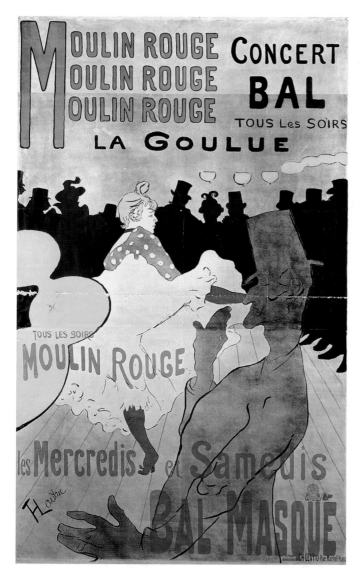

23-9. Henri de Toulouse-Lautrec. *La Goulue*. 1891.
Colored lithographic poster, 6'3" x 3'10" (1.90 x 1.16 m)

VINCENT VAN GOGH. While Cézanne and Seurat were making Impressionism into a more rigorous, classical style, Vincent van Gogh (1853–1890) moved in the opposite direction. He believed that Impressionism did not provide artists with enough freedom to express their emotions. Since this was his main concern, he is sometimes called an Expressionist, although the term ought to be reserved for certain twentieth-century painters (see page 802). Van Gogh, the first great Dutch master since the seventeenth century, did not become an artist until 1880; he died only ten years later, so that his career was even briefer than Seurat's. His early interests were in literature and religion. Profoundly dissatisfied with the values of industrial society and filled with a strong sense of mission, he worked for a while as a lay preacher among poverty-stricken coal miners in Belgium. This intense feeling for the poor dominates the paintings of his pre-Impressionist period, 1880–85. In *The Potato Eaters* (fig. 23-10), the last and most ambitious work of those years, there is a naïve clumsiness that comes

from his lack of training. This awkwardness only adds to the expressive power of his style. [See Primary Sources, no. 77, page 968.] We are reminded of Daumier and Millet (see figs. 21-37 and 21-41), and of Rembrandt and Le Nain (see figs. 18-19 and 19-3). For this peasant family, the evening meal has the solemn importance of a ritual.

When he painted *The Potato Eaters,* Van Gogh had not yet discovered the importance of color. A year later in Paris, where his brother Theo had a gallery devoted to modern art, he met Degas, Seurat, and other leading French artists. Their effect on him was electrifying. His pictures now blazed with color, and he even experimented briefly with Seurat's Divisionism. This phase, however, lasted less than two years. Although it was vitally important for his development, he had to integrate it with the style of his earlier years before his genius could fully unfold. Paris had opened his eyes to the sensuous beauty of the visible world and had taught him the pictorial language of the color patch. Painting nevertheless continued to be a means for expressing his personal emotions. To investigate his deeper spiritual reality with these new means, he went to Arles, in the south of France. It was there, between 1888 and 1890, that he produced his greatest canvases.

Like Cézanne, Van Gogh now devoted his main energies to landscape painting, but the sun-drenched Mediterranean countryside evoked a very different response in him than it did in Cézanne. He saw it filled with ecstatic movement, not architectural stability and permanence. In *Wheat Field and Cypress Trees* (fig. 23-11), the earth and sky pulsate with an overpowering turbulence. The wheat field resembles a stormy sea, the trees spring flamelike from the ground, and the hills and clouds heave with the same undulating motion. The blazing color is applied with a dynamism that makes each brushstroke an incisive graphic gesture. The artist's personal "handwriting" is even more dominant than in the canvases of Daumier (compare fig. 21-37). Yet to Van Gogh it was the color, not the form, that determined the expressive content of his pictures. The letters he wrote to his brother include many eloquent descriptions of his choice of hues and the emotional meanings he attached to them. He had learned about

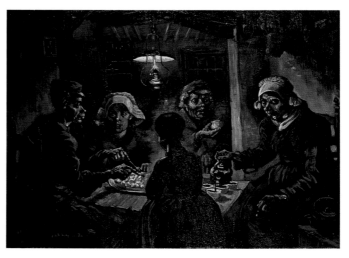

23-10. Vincent van Gogh. *The Potato Eaters*. 1885.
Oil on canvas, 32¼ x 45" (82 x 114.3 cm).
Vincent van Gogh Foundation/Van Gogh Museum, Amsterdam

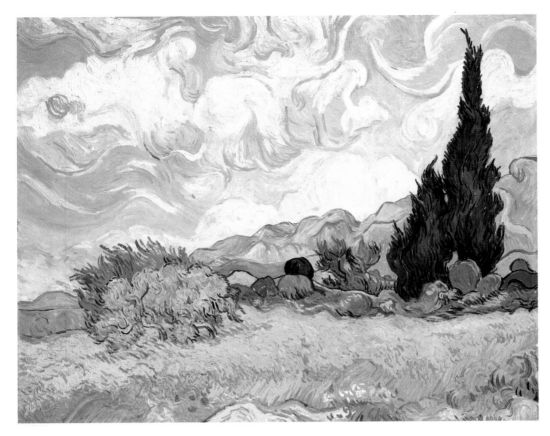

23-11. Vincent van Gogh. *Wheat Field and Cypress Trees.* 1889. Oil on canvas, 28½ x 36" (72.4 x 91.4 cm). The National Gallery, London

Impressionist color from Pissarro, but his personal color symbolism probably stemmed from discussions with Paul Gauguin (see below), who stayed with Van Gogh at Arles for several months. (Yellow, for example, meant faith or triumph or love to Van Gogh. Carmine was a spiritual color; cobalt, a divine one. Red and green, however, stood for the terrible human passions.) Although he acknowledged that his desire "to exaggerate the essential and to leave the obvious vague" made his colors look arbitrary by Impressionist standards, he remained deeply committed to the visible world. [See Primary Sources, no. 78, page 969.]

Compared to Monet's *On the Bank of the Seine, Bennecourt* (see fig. 22-5), the colors of *Wheat Field and Cypress Trees* are stronger, simpler, and more vibrant, but in no sense "unnatural." They speak to us of that "kingdom of light" Van Gogh had found in the south and of his mystic faith in a creative force animating all forms of life—a faith no less ardent than the sectarian Christianity of his early years.

His *Self-Portrait* (fig. 23-12) reminds us of Dürer's (see fig. 16-6), and with good reason: the missionary had now become a prophet. Van Gogh's luminous head, with its emaciated features and burning eyes, is set off against a whirlpool of darkness. "I want to paint men and women with that something of the eternal which the halo used to symbolize," the artist had written, in an attempt to define for his brother the human essence that was his aim in pictures such as this. At the time of the *Self-Portrait,* he had already begun to suffer from a severe form of mental illness that made painting increasingly difficult. Despairing of a cure, Van Gogh committed suicide a year later, for he felt that art alone made his life worth living.

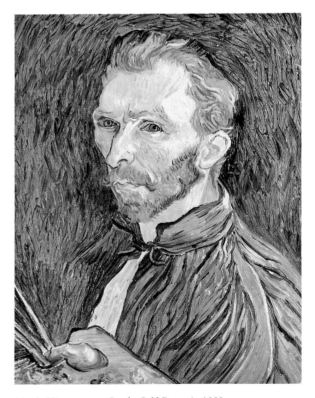

23-12. Vincent van Gogh. *Self-Portrait.* 1889. Oil on canvas, 22½ x 17" (57.2 x 43.2 cm). Collection Mrs. John Hay Whitney, New York

PAUL GAUGUIN. The quest for religious experience also played an important part in the work, if not in the life, of another great Post-Impressionist, Paul Gauguin (1848–1903). He began as a prosperous stockbroker in Paris, and became an amateur painter and collector of modern pictures. At the age of 35, however, Gauguin decided to devote himself entirely to art. He abandoned his business career, separated from his family, and by 1889 was the central figure of a new movement called Synthetism or Symbolism.

Gauguin started out as a follower of Cézanne and once owned one of his still lifes. He then developed a style that, although less intensely personal than Van Gogh's, was in some ways an even bolder advance beyond Impressionism. Gauguin believed that Western civilization was spiritually bankrupt, because industrial society had forced people into an empty life dedicated to material gain, while their emotions lay neglected. To rediscover the hidden world of feeling, Gauguin left Paris in 1886 to live among the peasants of Brittany at Pont-Aven in western France. There, two years later, he met the painters Émile Bernard (1868–1941) and Louis Anquetin (1861–1932), who had rejected Impressionism and had begun to evolve a new style, which they called *Cloissonism* (after an enamel technique), for its strong outlines and bright colors. Gauguin incorporated their approach into his own and emerged as the most forceful member of the Pont-Aven group, which quickly came to center on him.

The Pont-Aven style was first developed fully in the works Gauguin and Bernard painted there during the summer of 1888.

Gauguin noticed particularly that religion was still part of the everyday life of the country people. In pictures such as *The Vision after the Sermon (Jacob Wrestling with the Angel)* (fig. 23-13), he tried to depict their simple, direct faith. Here at last is what no Romantic artist had achieved: a style based on pre-Renaissance sources. Modeling and perspective have given way to flat, simplified shapes outlined heavily in black, while the brilliant colors are equally "unnatural." This style, inspired by folk art and medieval stained glass, is meant to re-create both the imagined reality of the vision and the trancelike rapture of the peasant women. The painting fulfills the goal of Synthetism: by treating the canvas in this decorative manner, the artist has turned it from a straightforward representation of the external world into an aesthetic object that projects an inner idea without using narrative or literal symbols. Yet we sense that, while he tried to share this experience, Gauguin remained an outsider. He could paint pictures about faith but not from faith.

Two years later, Gauguin's search for the unspoiled life led him to Tahiti—he had already visited Martinique in 1887—as a sort of "missionary in reverse," to learn from the natives instead of teaching them. [See Primary Sources, no. 79, page 969.] He spent the rest of his life in the South Pacific and returned home only once, from 1893 to 1895. Yet he never found the virgin Eden he was seeking. Instead, he often had to rely on the writings and photographs of those who had recorded the culture before him. His Tahitian canvases nonetheless conjure up an ideal world filled with the beauty and meaning he sought so futilely in real life.

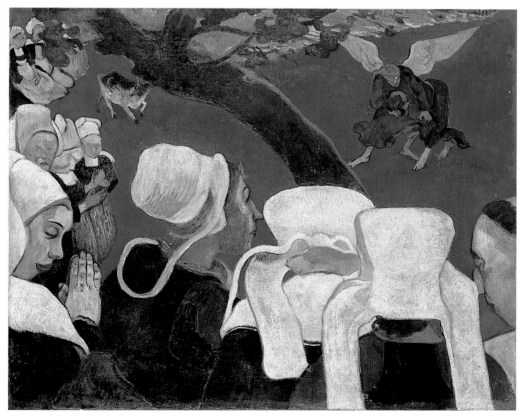

23-13. Paul Gauguin. *The Vision after the Sermon (Jacob Wrestling with the Angel)*. 1888. Oil on canvas, 28¾ x 36½" (73 x 92.7 cm). The National Galleries of Scotland, Edinburgh

Gauguin's masterpiece in this vein is *Where Do We Come From? What Are We? Where Are We Going?* (fig. 23-14). It was painted as a summation of his art shortly before he was driven by despair to attempt suicide. Even without the suggestive title, we would recognize the painting's allegorical purpose from its monumental scale, pensive air, static poses, and careful placement of the figures in the tapestry-like landscape. Although Gauguin intended the surface to be the sole conveyer of meaning, we know from his letters that the huge canvas represents an epic cycle of life. The scene unfolds from right to left. It begins with the sleeping girl, continues with the beautiful young woman (a Tahitian Eve) in the center picking fruit, and ends with "an old woman approaching death who seems reconciled and resigned to her thoughts." Gauguin has cast the answer to his title in distinctly Western terms. In effect, the picture is a variation on the three ages of life found in *Death and the Maiden* by Hans Baldung Grien (see fig. 16-13). The mysterious Maori god overseeing everything is a counterpart to the figure of Death in Baldung Grien's painting. Gauguin painted the composition in response to Puvis de Chavannes' classical allegories, especially *The Sacred Grove* (see fig. 23-16, left). The real secret to the central mystery of life, Gauguin tell us, lies in this primitive Eden, not in some mythical past.

The renewal of Western art and Western civilization as a whole, Gauguin believed, must come from outside its traditions. He advised other Symbolists to shun Graeco-Roman forms and to turn instead to Persia, the Far East, and ancient Egypt for inspiration. This idea itself was not new. It stems from the Romantic myth of the Noble Savage, which had been proclaimed by the thinkers of the Enlightenment more than a century before. Its ultimate source is the age-old tradition of an earthly paradise where people once dwelled—and might one day live again—in a state of nature and innocence. However, no one before Gauguin had gone as far to put the doctrine of primitivism into practice. His pilgrimage to the South Pacific had more than a purely private meaning. It symbolized the end of the 400 years of expansion that had brought most of the world under Western domination.

Symbolism

Van Gogh's and Gauguin's discontent with the spiritual ills of Western civilization was part of a widely shared sentiment at the end of the nineteenth century. It reflected an intellectual and moral upheaval that rejected the modern world and its materialism in favor of irrational states of mind. A preoccupation with the realm of dreams and other emanations of the subconscious, despite the air of childlike innocence.

The music of Debussy and Ravel was in many respects the conscious antithesis of Neo-Romanticism, that late phase of

---

MUSIC IN THE POST-IMPRESSIONIST ERA

The late nineteenth century presents a welter of musical tendencies no less perplexing than the diversity found in Post-Impressionism. Strictly speaking, the term *Impressionism* cannot be applied to music because music, by its very nature, cannot describe, it can only evoke. The term has nevertheless often been used to characterize the works of the Frenchman Claude Debussy (1862–1918), such as *La Mer* (1905), which successfully conveys the contrasting moods of the sea. In reality, however, his compositions are much closer in spirit to Symbolist poetry. (His closest friends, such as Pierre Louÿs, were writers.) This is especially evident in his lone opera, *Pelléas et Mélisande* (1893–1902), which was derived from a play by the Franco-Belgian Symbolist Maurice Maeterlinck (1862–1949); despite the vast difference between them, the opera reveals a debt to Wagner's music, which Debussy first heard at Bayreuth in 1888. Early in his career, Debussy summered in Russia as the guest of Tchaikovsky's patron, Madame von Meck, and it must have been at that time that he first became interested in modes, as well as other "lost" and exotic musical forms. This interest was reinforced by hearing Javanese music at the Universal Exposition in Paris in 1889. As a consequence, he began to employ such unusual devices as the pentatonic scale (the five black notes on the piano), which in his later years pushed conventional tonality virtually to its breaking point.

Symbolism also touched Debussy's fellow "Impressionist," Maurice Ravel (1875–1937), particularly in such early works as *Gaspard de la nuit* (1908) for piano, which was inspired by a poem by Aloysius Bertrand (1807–1841). It also underlies the enchanting *Mother Goose,* originally composed that same year as a piano duet for the daughters of a close friend and later orchestrated as a ballet: the choice of stories and their musical treatment revel in

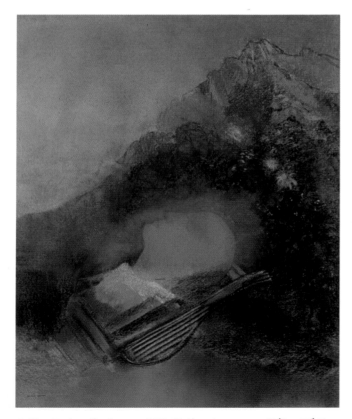

Odilon Redon. *Orpheus.* c. 1903-10. Pastel on paper, 27⅛ x 22⅜" (68.8 x 56.8 cm). The Cleveland Museum of Art

GIFT FROM J. H. WADE, 1926

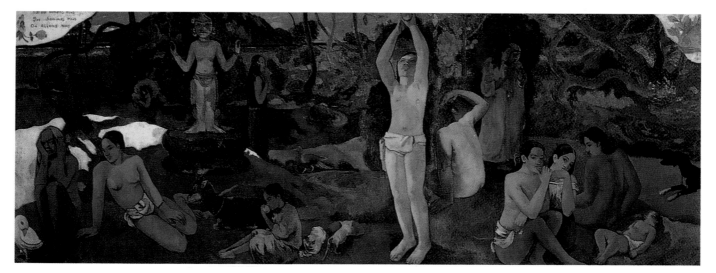

23-14. Paul Gauguin. *Where Do We Come From? What Are We? Where Are We Going?* 1897.
Oil on canvas, 4'6¾" x 12'3½" (1.3 x 3.7 m). Museum of Fine Arts, Boston

ARTHUR GORDON TOMPKINS RESIDUARY FUND

Romanticism that is identified particularly with the German composers Gustav Mahler (1866–1911) and Richard Strauss (1864–1949). Strauss started out as a classicist but through his friendship with the poet Alexander Ritter (1833–1896) became a disciple of Wagner and Liszt. While pursuing a career as a conductor, he first gained fame for his tone poems, such as *Death and Transfiguration* (1889). From 1905 on, however, Strauss devoted himself primarily to operas, notably *Der Rosenkavalier* (*The Cavalier of the Rose;* 1911), which, like all his finest efforts, was the result of his collaboration with the Austrian Neo-Romantic poet and dramatist Hugo von Hofmannsthal (1874–1929). The composer later supported the Nazis and served for a while as head of musical affairs under Hitler, although he was officially exonerated of collaboration shortly before his death.

If Strauss represents the final glory of German Romanticism, the symphonies and orchestrated song cycles by his friend and fellow conductor Gustav Mahler of Vienna can be seen as the musical counterpart to the morbid sensitivity of Gustav Klimt and the Vienna Secession movement, with which he was personally involved. His works' enormous scale makes huge demands on orchestra and singers alike, while the extremes of hypersensitive introspection and almost hysterical bombast go beyond the expressive limits of Romanticism. Mahler's late works, sparser in character, were the point of departure for the next generation of Viennese composers, whose work he encouraged: Arnold Schoenberg, Anton Webern, and Alban Berg, who were to revolutionize twentieth-century music (see boxes on pages 812 and 840).

This fact points to an anomaly, namely, that a number of Late Romantics had the unfortunate fate of living well beyond the advent of modern music. Both Ravel and the Finnish composer Jean Sibelius (1865–1957) responded by virtually ceasing to write music after 1925. Sibelius was a throwback to the nationalist composers of the mid-nineteenth century. His early works are tone poems, based on Nordic legends, that are filled with a brooding melancholy. His major contribution, however, lies in the seven symphonies, which build short motifs into large structures of decidedly unconventional form that nearly stand Romanticism on its ear. Although passionate at times, his compositions lack the lush, sentimental appeal of those by the other great nationalist composer of the era, the Russian Sergei Rachmaninov (1873–1943), who wrote piano concertos as showcases for his virtuosity, in addition to three symphonies that follow in a direct line of descent from Tchaikovsky's.

Just as there was no true Impressionism in music, so the term *realism* in late-nineteenth-century opera is something of a misnomer. It was applied to a small group of operas—including *Carmen* (1875) by Georges Bizet (1838–1875) and *Pagliacci* (1892) by Ruggiero Leoncavallo (1858–1919), which is often produced on the same bill with *Cavalleria Rusticana* (1889) by Pietro Mascagni (1863–1945)—set in contemporary Europe that are nonetheless sentimental melodramas. *La Bohème* (1896) and *Tosca* (1900) by Giacomo Puccini (1858–1924), Verdi's successor as the leading composer of this genre in Italy, partake of this *verismo,* as it was called, although they are set earlier in the century; however, they owe their success to their combination of melting lyricism and pungent drama. The later operas, such as *Madame Butterfly* (1904) and *Girl of the Golden West* (1910), based on successful melodramas by the American playwright David Belasco (c. 1853–1931), exploit the European taste for the exotic, although they were failures initially. Belasco's plays, however, were considered examples of realism by audiences in the United States, to whom their setting and moral meaning were instantly recognizable. Their realism was heightened by spectacular staging and special effects.

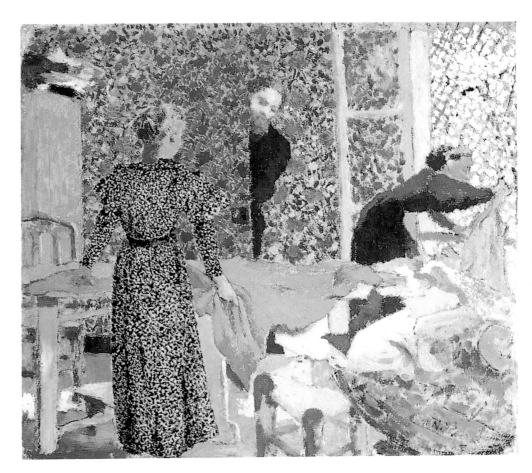

23-15. Édouard Vuillard. *The Suitor.*
1893. Oil on millboard panel,
12½ x 14" (31.8 x 35.6 cm).
Smith College Museum of Art,
Northampton, Massachusetts

decadence, evil, and darkness pervaded the artistic and literary climate. Even those who saw no escape from the problems of modern life analyzed their predicament in fascinated horror. Yet this very awareness proved to be a source of strength that gave birth to the movement known as Symbolism.

Symbolism in art was at first an outgrowth of the literary movement that arose in 1885–86 with Jean Moréas and Gustave Kahn at its helm. Reacting against the Naturalism (the matter-of-fact observation of life) of the novelist Émile Zola, they reasserted the primacy of subjective ideas and championed the *poètes maudits* ("doomed poets") Stéphane Mallarmé and Paul Verlaine (see box page 788). There was a natural sympathy between the Pont-Aven painters and the Symbolist poets, and in a long article defining Symbolism published in April 1892, the writer G. Albert Aurier insisted on Gauguin's leadership of the movement. However, unlike Post-Impressionism, which embodies several stylistic tendencies, Symbolism was a general outlook, one that allowed for a wide variety of styles—whatever would embody its peculiar frame of mind.

THE NABIS. Gauguin's Symbolist followers called themselves Nabis, from the Hebrew word for prophet. They were less remarkable for their creative talent than for their ability to spell out and justify the aims of Post-Impressionism in theoretical terms. One of them, Maurice Denis, coined the statement that was to become the first article of faith for modernist painters of the twentieth century: "A picture—before being a war horse, a female nude, or some anecdote—is essentially a flat surface covered with colors in a particular order." He added that "every work of art is a transposition, a caricature, the passionate equivalent of a received sensation." The theory of equivalents gave the Nabis their independence from Gauguin: "We supplemented the rudimentary teaching of Gauguin by substituting for his over-simplified idea of pure colors the idea of beautiful harmonies, infinitely varied like nature; we adapted all the resources of the palette to all the states of our sensibility; and the sights which caused them became to us so many signs of our own subjectivity. We sought equivalents, but equivalents in beauty!"

ÉDOUARD VUILLARD. We can now understand why paintings by the Nabis soon came to look so different from Gauguin's. The Nabis became involved with decorative projects which, like Whistler's Peacock Room (see fig. 22-38), participate in the late-nineteenth-century retreat into a private realm of beauty. The pictures done in the 1890s by Édouard Vuillard (1868–1940), the most gifted member of the Nabis, are mostly domestic scenes, small in scale and intimate in effect. They combine the flat planes and strong contours of Gauguin with the Divisionist color mosaic and geometric surface organization of Seurat. *The Suitor* (fig. 23-15) presents a seemingly casual view of the workroom in Vuillard's mother's corset shop. The artist probably derived the flat patterns from the fabrics themselves. The picture's quiet magic makes us think of Vermeer and Chardin (compare figs. 18-29 and 20-8), whose subject matter, too, was the snug life of the middle class.

In both subject and treatment, the painting has counterparts in Symbolist literature and theater: in the poetry of Paul Verlaine, the

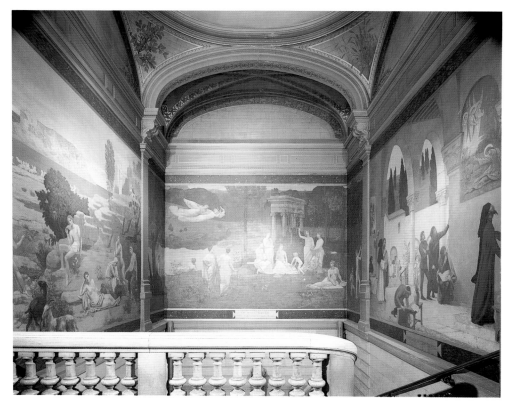

23-16. Pierre-Cécile Puvis de Chavannes. *The Sacred Grove,* c. 1883–84; *Vision of Antiquity,* c. 1888–89; and *Christian Inspiration,* c. 1888–89. Painting cycle, Grand Staircase, Musée des Beaux-Arts, Lyons, France

novels of Stéphane Mallarmé, and in the productions of Aurélian-Marie Lugné-Poë, for whom Vuillard designed stage sets (see box page 788). It evokes a wide range of feelings through purely formal means that could never be conveyed by naturalism alone. The Nabis established an important precedent for Henri Matisse a decade later (see fig. 24-2). By then, however, the movement had disintegrated as its members became more conservative. Vuillard himself turned more toward naturalism, and he never recaptured the delicacy and daring of his early canvases.

PIERRE PUVIS DE CHAVANNES. The Symbolists discovered that there were some older artists, descendants of the Romantics, whose work, like their own, placed inner vision above the observation of nature. Many Symbolists, as well as other Post-Impressionists, found inspiration in the classicism of Pierre Puvis de Chavannes (1824–1898), a follower of Ingres who became the leading muralist of his day. Rejecting academic conventions, he pursued a radical simplification of style, which at first seemed out of place but was soon hailed by critics and artists of every outlook. The effectiveness of the murals he executed in the 1880s for the museum at Lyons (fig. 23-16) relies in large part on formal devices—the compressed space, schematic forms, and restricted palette—which imitate in oil the chalky surface of old frescoes. The antinaturalism of Puvis' style emphasizes the allegorical quality of the scene, which has a gravity and mystery missing from other mural paintings of the day. Storytelling is replaced by nostalgia for an idealized, mythical past. The stiff, ritualistic poses freeze time and convey a poetry that is both melancholy and serene. Puvis' economy of means was intended to present his ideas with maximum clarity, but it has just the opposite effect: it heightens the suggestiveness of his paintings. His popularity resulted precisely from this ambiguity, which allowed a wide variety of interpretations. Symbolists from Gauguin through the young Picasso could thus claim him as one of their own. Nevertheless, he vehemently protested any association with the movement.

GUSTAVE MOREAU. One of the Symbolists, Gustave Moreau (1826–1898), a recluse who admired Delacroix, created a world of personal fantasy that has much in common with the medieval reveries of the English Pre-Raphaelites Rossetti and Burne-Jones. *The Apparition* (fig. 23-17) shows one of his favorite themes. The head of John the Baptist, in a blinding light, appears to Salome, whose seductive dance has brought about his death. The painting combines the dreams of Oriental splendor and cruelty so dear to the Romantic imagination with a belief in the supernatural. Moreau summons up this exotic realm through the odalisque-like sensuousness of the girl, the stream of blood pouring from the severed head, and the vast, mysterious space of the setting, which suggests an exotic temple rather than Herod's palace. Moreau gained recognition only late in life. Suddenly his art was in tune with the times. During his last six years he even held a professorship at the conservative École des Beaux-Arts, the successor of the official art academy founded under Louis XIV (see pages 610–11). There he attracted the most gifted students, among them Henri Matisse and Georges Rouault (see pages 803–04).

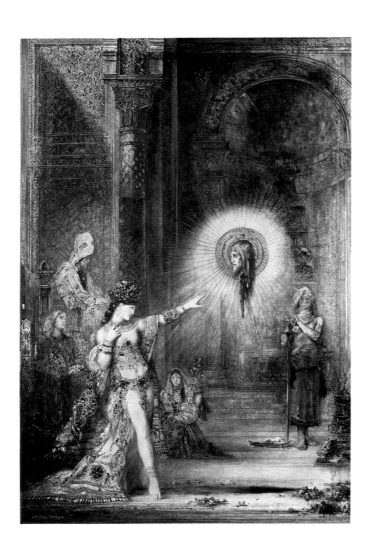

23-17. Gustave Moreau. *The Apparition (Dance of Salomé)*.
c. 1876. Watercolor, 41¾ x 28⅜" (106 x 72 cm).
Musée du Louvre, Paris.

Delacroix, as a painter, was fiery and dramatic; Gustave Moreau strove to be cold and static. The former painted gestures, the latter attitudes. Although far apart in artistic merit (after all, Delacroix in his best work is a great painter), they are highly representative of the moral atmosphere of the two periods in which they flourished—of Romanticism, with its fury of frenzied action, and of Decadence, with its sterile contemplation. The subject-matter is almost the same—voluptuous, gory exoticism. But Delacroix lives inside his subject, whereas Moreau worships his from outside, with the result that the first is a painter, the second a decorator.

—Mario Praz. *The Romantic Agony.* Translated by
Angus Davidson. London: Oxford University Press, 1978,
page 103. Originally published in 1951.

Cultural historian and professor of English at the University of Rome from 1934 to 1982, **MARIO PRAZ** (1896–1982) is remembered and respected for his ability to synthesize a vast range of material into a coherent and compelling narrative and for his powerful characterizations of literary and artistic figures. *The Romantic Agony* (1933), from which our excerpt is taken, is unique in its understanding of the morbid fascination with evil and decadence of late Romanticism. This is the more remarkable because Praz was an expert on Neoclassicism, which shared none of these preoccupations.

AUBREY BEARDSLEY. How prophetic Moreau's work was of art at the end of the century can be seen from a comparison with black-and-white drawings by the talented young Englishman Aubrey Beardsley (1872–1898). Among Beardsley's graphic work—which was the height of "elegantly decadent" taste—is an illustration (fig. 23-18) for Oscar Wilde's *Salome* (see box page 788) that might well be the final scene of the drama depicted by Moreau. Salome has taken up John's severed head and triumphantly kissed it. Whereas Moreau's intent remains ambiguous, Beardsley's erotic meaning is plain: Salome is passionately in love with John and has asked for his head because she could not have him any other way. The thematic parallel is striking, and there are formal similarities as well, such as the "stem" of trickling blood from which John's head rises like a flower. Yet Beardsley's *Salome* was not derived from Moreau's. The sources of his style are English—specifically, the graphic art of the Pre-Raphaelites—but with a strong Japanese influence.

ODILON REDON. Another solitary artist whom the Symbolists discovered and claimed as one of their own was Odilon Redon (1840–1916). Like Moreau, he had a haunted imagination, but his imagery was even more personal and disturbing. A master of etching and lithography, he drew inspiration from the fantastic visions of Goya (see fig. 21-22) as well as Romantic literature. The lithograph shown in figure 23-19 is one of a set Redon issued in 1882 and dedicated to Edgar Allan Poe. The American poet had been dead for 33 years, but his tormented life and his equally tortured imagination made him the very model of the poète maudit. His works, translated by Baudelaire and Mallarmé, were greatly admired in France. Redon's lithographs do not illustrate Poe. They are instead "visual poems" in their own right that evoke the morbid, hallucinatory world of Poe's imagination. Here the artist has revived an ancient device, the single eye representing the all-seeing mind of God. But, in contrast to the traditional form of the symbol, Redon shows the whole eyeball removed from its socket and converted into a balloon that drifts aimlessly in the sky. The disquieting visual puzzles in Redon's prints express the pessimism of a troubled mind struggling to find meaning. Only after 1900 did this remarkably pervasive general outlook give way to a new serenity filled with spiritual overtones.

JAMES ENSOR. In the paintings of the Belgian artist James Ensor (1860–1949), Redon's cynical view of the human condition reaches obsessive intensity, and for much the same reason. In *Christ's Entry into Brussels in 1889* (fig. 23-20), the demon-ridden world of Bosch and Schongauer has come to life again in modern form (compare figs. 15-14 and 15-23). The painting, showing the Second Coming of Christ in contemporary Belgium, is a grotesque parody of a subject familiar to us since the Gothic (compare figs. 11-75 and 11-77). Here Christ is virtually lost in a sea of leering faces, which are treated as the personifications of evil. As we examine these masks we become aware that they are the crowd's true faces, revealing the depravity ordinarily hidden behind the facade of everyday appearances. At the time, Ensor

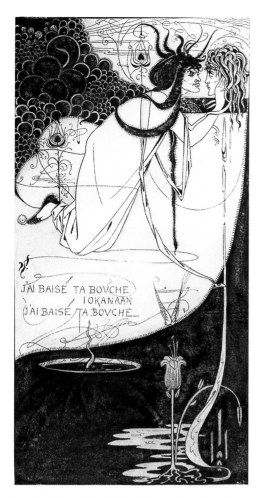

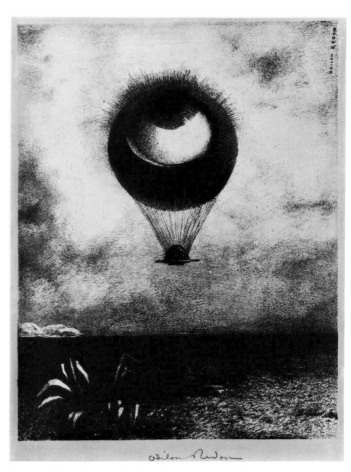

23-18. Aubrey Beardsley. *Salomé*. 1892. Pen drawing,
10⅝16 x 5³⁄₁₆" (27.8 x 14.8 cm). Aubrey Beardsley Collection.
Manuscripts Division, Department of Rare Books and
Special Collections, Princeton University Library, New Jersey

23-19. Odilon Redon. *The Eye Like a Strange Balloon Mounts Toward
Infinity,* from the series *Edgar A. Poe.* 1882. Lithograph, 10¼ x 7¹¹⁄₁₆"
(25.9 x 19.6 cm). The Museum of Modern Art, New York

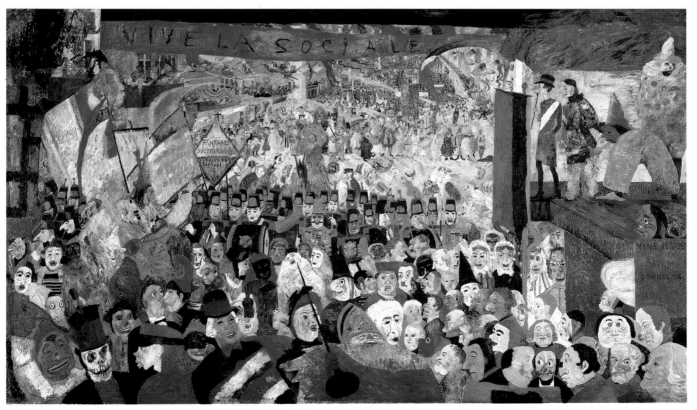

23-20. James Ensor. *Christ's Entry into Brussels in 1889.* 1888. Oil on canvas, 8'6½" x 14'1½" (2.6 x 4.3 m).
Collection of the J. Paul Getty Museum, Malibu, California

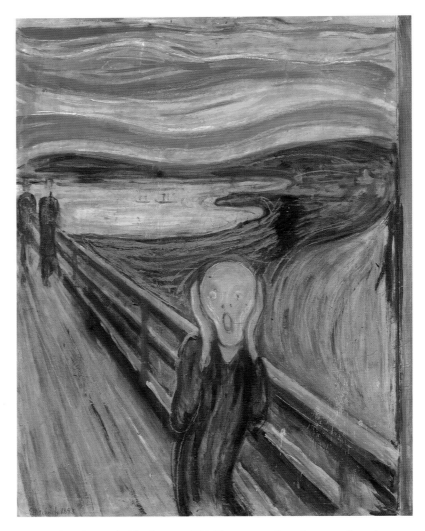

23-21. Edvard Munch. *The Scream*. 1893. Tempera and casein on cardboard, 36 x 29" (91.4 x 73.7 cm). Nasjonalgalleriet, Oslo, Norway

identified with Christ, whose suffering he felt paralleled his own at the hands of hostile critics and an indifferent public. Later, when his art began to gain wide acceptance, he abandoned this bitter attitude.

EDVARD MUNCH. A macabre quality also pervades the early work of Edvard Munch (1863–1944), a far more gifted artist who came to Paris from Norway in 1889 and based his starkly expressive style on Toulouse-Lautrec, Van Gogh, and the Nabis. *The Scream* (fig. 23-21) shows their influence. It is an image of fear—the terrifying, unreasoned fear we feel in a nightmare. Unlike Goya and Fuseli (see figs. 21-22 and 21-43), Munch visualizes this experience without the aid of frightening apparitions, and his picture is the more persuasive for that very reason. [See Primary Sources, no. 80, page 969.] The rhythm of the long, wavy lines seems to carry the echo of the scream into every corner of the picture, so that earth and sky become one great sounding board of fear.

GUSTAV KLIMT. Munch's pictures created such controversy when they were exhibited in Berlin in 1892 that a number of

young radicals broke from the local artists association and formed the Berlin Secession, which took its name from a similar group that had been founded in Munich earlier that year. The Secession quickly became a loosely allied international movement. In 1897 it spread to Austria, where Gustav Klimt (1862–1918) established the Vienna Secession with the purpose of raising the level of quality of the arts and crafts through close ties to Art Nouveau (see pages 789–93). *The Kiss* (fig. 23-22) by Klimt expresses a different kind of anxiety from Munch's *The Scream*. The image will remind us of Beardsley's *Salome* (see fig. 23-18), but here the barely suppressed eroticism has burst into desire. (It shows the artist with his lover Emilie Flöge.) Engulfed in robes inspired by Byzantine mosaics (compare figs. 8-28 and 8-29) that create an illusion of rich beauty, the angular figures embrace in a moment of passion. The atmosphere is nevertheless curiously oppressive, expressive of an anxiety that overrides joy.

PABLO PICASSO. When he came to Paris from his native Spain in 1900, Pablo Picasso (1881–1973) felt the spell of the same artistic atmosphere that had given rise to the style of Munch. His

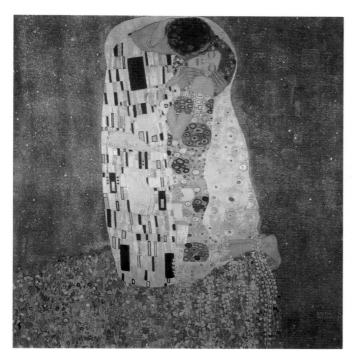

23-22. Gustav Klimt. *The Kiss.* 1907–8. Oil on canvas, 70⅞ x 70⅞" (180 x 180 cm). Österreichische Galerie, Vienna

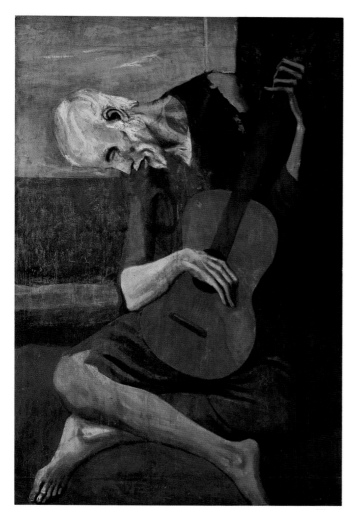

23-23. Pablo Picasso. *The Old Guitarist.* 1903. Oil on panel, 48⅝ x 32½" (122.9 x 82.6 cm). The Art Institute of Chicago

HELEN BIRCH BARTLETT MEMORIAL COLLECTION

so-called *Blue Period* (the term refers to the dominant color of his canvases as well as to their mood) consists almost exclusively of pictures of beggars and other outcasts, such as *The Old Guitarist* (fig. 23-23). These victims of society have a pathos that reflects the artist's own sense of isolation. Yet these figures convey poetic melancholy more than outright despair. The aged musician accepts his fate with a resignation that seems almost saintly, and the attenuated grace of his limbs reminds us of El Greco (compare fig. 14-16). *The Old Guitarist* is a strange fusion of Mannerism, Gauguin, and Toulouse-Lautrec, imbued with the personal gloom of a 22-year-old genius. We will return to Picasso again and again, for he was one of the most important figures of modern art.

HENRI ROUSSEAU. A few years later, Picasso and his friends discovered Henri Rousseau (1844–1910), a retired customs collector who had started to paint in middle age without training of any sort. He had been exhibiting his work since 1886 to public ridicule, but he attracted the attention of Renoir, Degas, and Toulouse-Lautrec. His ideal (which fortunately he never achieved) was the dry academic style of the followers of Ingres. Rousseau is that paradox, a folk artist of genius. Here at last was the innocent directness that Gauguin thought so necessary for the age. His painting *The Dream* (fig. 23-24) depicts an enchanted world that needs no explanation—and indeed none is possible. Perhaps for that very reason its magic becomes believably real to us. Rousseau himself described the scene in a little poem worthy of the Symbolist Alfred Jarry (1873–1907), who admired him (see box pages 788–89):

> Yadwigha, peacefully asleep
> Enjoys a lovely dream:
> She hears a kind snake charmer
> Playing upon his reed.
> On stream and foliage glisten
> The silvery beams of the moon.
> And savage serpents listen
> To the gay, entrancing tune.

PAULA MODERSOHN-BECKER. The inspiration of primitivism that Gauguin had traveled so far to find was discovered by Paula Modersohn-Becker (1876–1907) in the village of Worpswede, near her family home in Bremen, Germany. Among the artists and writers who gathered there was the Symbolist lyric poet Rainer Maria Rilke, Rodin's friend and briefly his personal secretary. Rilke had visited Russia and had been deeply impressed with what he viewed as the purity of Russian peasant life, which he idolized. His influence on the colony at Worpswede particularly affected Modersohn-Becker, whose last works are direct forerunners of modern art. Her gentle but powerful *Self-Portrait* (fig. 23-25), painted in 1906, the year before her death, presents a transition to Expressionism (see Chapter 25) from the Symbolism of Gauguin and his followers, which she absorbed during several stays in Paris. The color has the intensity of Matisse's and the Fauves' (see page 802), while her simplified treatment of forms parallels the experiments of Picasso that led to *Les Demoiselles d'Avignon* (see fig. 24-12).

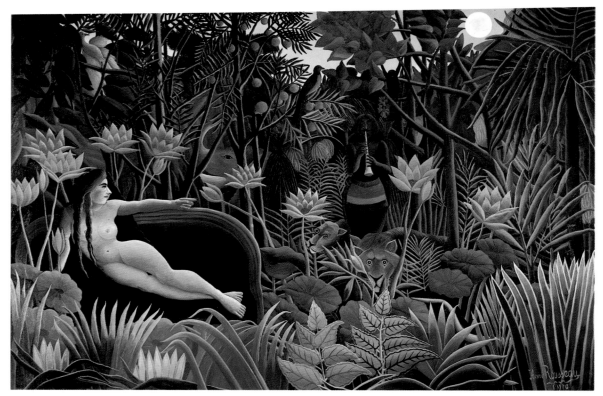

23-24. Henri Rousseau. *The Dream*. 1910. Oil on canvas, 6'8½" x 9'9½" (2.05 x 2.96 m). The Museum of Modern Art, New York

GIFT OF NELSON A. ROCKEFELLER

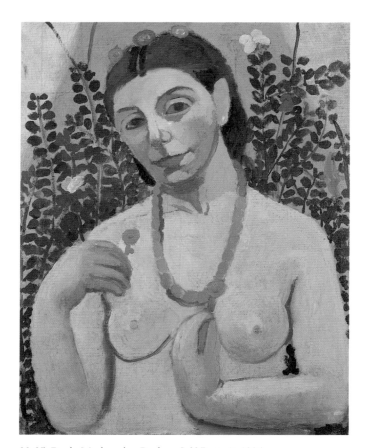

23-25. Paula Modersohn-Becker. *Self-Portrait*. 1906. Oil on canvas, 24 x 19¾" (61 x 50.2 cm). Öffentliche Kunstsammlung Basel, Kunstmuseum, Switzerland

SCULPTURE

ARISTIDE MAILLOL. In sculpture there was nothing comparable to Post-Impressionism, but a form of Symbolism appeared around 1900. Younger French sculptors who had been trained under the dominant influence of Rodin were ready by then to go their own ways. The finest of these, Aristide Maillol (1861–1944), began as a Symbolist painter, although he did not share Gauguin's anti-Greek attitude. Maillol might be called a classical primitivist. He admired the simplified strength of early Greek sculpture but rejected its later phases. *Seated Woman* (fig. 23-26) recalls the Archaic and Severe styles rather than Pheidias and Praxiteles. The clearly defined forms also bring to mind Cézanne's statement that everything in nature is based on the cone, the sphere, and the cylinder. But the most striking quality of the figure is its harmonious, self-contained tranquillity, which the outside world cannot disturb. A statue, Maillol thought, must above all be "static": structurally balanced like a piece of architecture. It must further represent a state of being that is detached from external circumstance, with none of the restless, thrusting energy of Rodin's work. In this respect, the *Seated Woman* is the exact opposite of *The Thinker* (see fig. 22-27). Maillol later gave it the title *La Méditerranée—The Mediterranean*—to suggest the source from which he drew the timeless serenity of his figure.

CONSTANTIN MEUNIER. If Maillol sought to transcend his epoch, the Belgian Constantin Meunier (1831–1905) was thoroughly engaged with it. Politically and socially, Belgium exemplified all the tensions of the later nineteenth century. A conservative government, insensitive to the extremes of wealth and poverty, seemed determined to suppress all protests or attempts at reform.

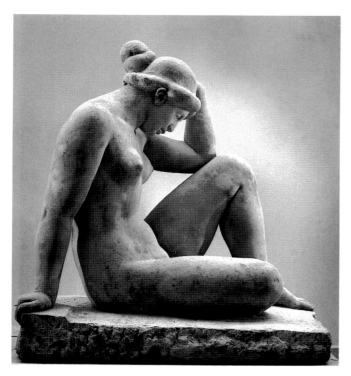

23-26. Aristide Maillol. *Seated Woman (La Méditerranée).* c. 1901. Stone, height 41" (104.1 cm). Collection Oskar Reinhart, Winterthur, Switzerland

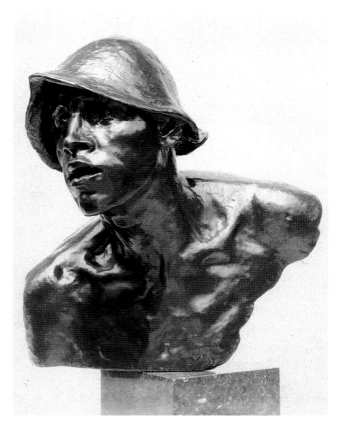

23-27. Constantin Meunier. *Bust of a Puddler.* c. 1885–90. Bronze, lifesize. Private collection

The workers' movement thus had a late start. Not until 1885 were labor unions strong enough to found the Belgian Workers' Party. By that time many writers and artists had become supporters of social reform. Meunier began as a painter but soon began to model in clay. From 1885 until the end of his life, his output was made up almost entirely of sculpture. The change was an outgrowth of his search for a more "monumental" medium. The heroism of labor, its pride and its pathos, was to be his theme as a sculptor. He treated it with the seriousness of his earlier religious subjects. He shared this concern with Vincent van Gogh, who had had an unforgettable experience of human misery in the mining district of Belgium (see page 775). The lifesize *Bust of a Puddler* (fig. 23-27) has an air of noble suffering that makes him a "martyr of labor." It also shows Meunier's considerable debt to Rodin, for whom he always expressed the greatest admiration.

ERNST BARLACH. The German sculptor Ernst Barlach (1870–1938), who reached maturity in the years before World War I, is the very opposite of Maillol: he is a "Gothic primitivist." What Gauguin had experienced in Brittany and the tropics, and Moder-sohn-Becker in Worpswede, Barlach found by going to Russia: the simple humanity of a preindustrial age. Human beings, to Barlach, are humble creatures at the mercy of forces beyond their control; they are never masters of their fate. His figures, such as *Man Drawing a Sword* (fig. 23-28), embody elementary emotions—wrath, fear, grief—that seem imposed upon them by invisible presences. When they act, they appear to be unaware of their own impulses.

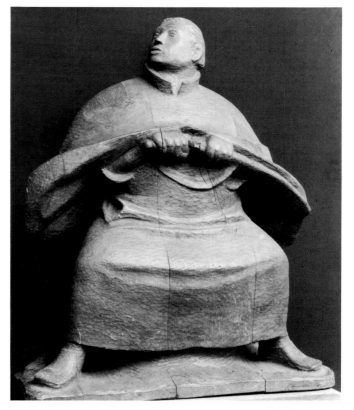

23-28. Ernst Barlach. *Man Drawing a Sword.* 1911. Wood, height 31" (78.7 cm). Private collection

The major competing tendencies of the late nineteenth century were Realism and Symbolism, which were sometimes found in the work of the same author. The most important Realist was the French novelist Émile Zola (1840–1902). Inspired by Charles Darwin's theory of evolution and Auguste Comte's socialism, he argued that the dramatist should observe the human condition with the detachment of the scientist and illustrate the "inevitable laws of heredity and environment." However, Zola's plays, like those of the Goncourt brothers, Edmond (1822–1896) and Jules (1830–1870), were more important in theory than in practice, and Realism found its main ex-pression in the plays of Henri Becque (1837–1899), which are pessimistic to the point of cynicism. Even so, Realism's success depended in the end on the determination of André Antoine (1858–1943), who established the Théâtre Libre (Free Theater) in 1887 and a decade later the Théâtre Antoine, both of which became proving grounds for Realist drama and experimental staging techniques until Antoine was appointed head of the state-supported Odéon in 1906.

Antoine also mounted productions of foreign playwrights, notably the Norwegian Henrik Ibsen (1828–1906), who first established his reputation with verse-dramas about the legendary past, notably *Peer Gynt* (1867), which is still considered the great national saga of Norway. In the 1870s, however, he turned to Realism in such plays as *The Doll's House* (1879), then began making greater use of Symbolism beginning with *The Wild Duck* (1884). The basic theme of his mature works nevertheless remained the same: the conflict between duty and self, which finally sees the consequences of its actions in a moment of revelation. However, Ibsen's treatment of this theme changed considerably over time, almost reversing itself: whereas at first he condemned excessive devotion to duty, in the end he came to criticize unbridled self-interest.

Like the Norwegian painter Edvard Munch, Ibsen enjoyed considerable influence in Germany, thanks in part to the productions mounted by Otto Brahm (1856–1912), who was president of the Freie Bühne (Free Theater) in Berlin in 1889–94 and then director of the Deutsches Theater (German Theater) for a decade before taking over the Lessing Theater until his death. The most important German playwright associated with the Freie Bühne was Gerhart Hauptmann (1862–1946), whose drama *The Weavers* (1892) shows the same social conscience as the early paintings of Van Gogh (see fig. 23-10) and the sculpture of Constantin Meunier (see fig. 23-27). Psychological, not social, realism was the particular interest of Arthur Schnitzler (1862–1931), whose major play, *Anatol* (1893), follows the ideas of his friend Sigmund Freud, the founder of modern psychiatry, in treating human sexuality through a series of affairs that inevitably give way to boredom because ego gratification cannot give rise to enduring love. Owing in good measure to heavy government funding, it was in Germany that most of the major technical innovations in stagecraft were devised, including the revolving stage, the elevator stage, the rolling platform, and the sliding platform.

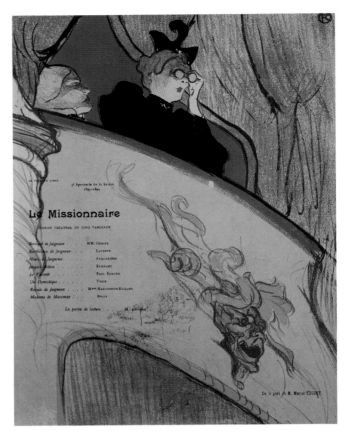

Henri de Toulouse-Lautrec. *Le Missionnaire.* 1894. Four-color lithograph on wove paper, sheet: 12¹/₁₆ x 9⁷/₁₆" (30.6 x 24 cm). National Gallery of Art, Washington, D.C.
GIFT OF THE ALTAS FOUNDATION

In England, the counterpart of the Théâtre Libre and the Freie Bühne was the Independent Theater, where George Bernard Shaw (1856–1950) first achieved critical acclaim in 1892. Shaw used sharp wit to illustrate philosophical propositions in the guise of national and social issues. His belief in human progress through moral persuasion and exercise of free choice found its highest expression in *Man and Superman* (1901), in which a socialist intellectual representing man as spiritual creator outwits his rivals but succumbs to a woman who exemplifies the life force.

The leading Realist in Russia at the turn of the century was Anton Chekhov (1860–1904), whose fame rests on the four plays about ennui in the upper class that he wrote for the Moscow Art Theater during the last five years of his life, especially *The Three Sisters* (1901). Like Chekhov, who befriended him, Maxim Gorky (1868–1936) was at first better known as a writer of short stories; his plays, likewise written mainly for the Moscow Art Theater and centering on class conflict, reflect his political activism.

The antithesis of Zola's Realism was the Symbolism of Stéphane Mallarmé (1842–1898), a poet who was affected by Edgar Allan Poe's macabre writings, Charles Baudelaire's poetry and art criticism, and Richard Wagner's operas. Mallarmé proposed theater that evoked the mystery of life through poetic metaphor. Symbolism was championed first by the short-lived Théâtre d'Art of Paul Fort (1872–1962) and then by the Théâtre de l'Oeuvre under Aurélian-Marie Lugné-Poë (1869–1940). Lugné-Poë drew many of his ideas about scenery from his friends Édouard Vuillard, Maurice Denis, and Pierre Bonnard, whom he also employed to create sets, along with Odilon Redon and Henri de Toulouse-Lautrec (see pages 782 and 774). The most important French dramatist associated with Lugné-Poë was the Belgian-born Maurice Maeterlinck (1862–1949), whose masterpiece, *Pelléas et Mélisande* (1892), which was to inspire Debussy's opera ten years later (see box page 778), relies heavily on symbolic devices to create an air of mystery. Lugné-Poë also staged *Ubu Roi* by Alfred Jarry (1873–1907), which sparked a riot on opening night in 1896. Originally written as a schoolboy satire of a chemistry teacher, this play about an unscrupulous bourgeois king and his wife who give in to every appetite and depraved whim later exercised great influence on the absurdist theater of the Surrealists. A year later Lugné-Poë abandoned Symbolism out of admiration for Ibsen, whose dramas offered far richer content.

After establishing his reputation as a Realist in the late 1880s with *Miss Julie,* the Swedish playwright August Strindberg (1849–1912) began to write "dream plays" in which he tried, as he put it, "to imitate the disconnected but seemingly logical form of the dream. Anything may happen; everything is possible and probable. Time and space do not exist. But one consciousness reigns above them all—that of the dreamer." Unlike Schnitzler's plays, Strindberg's dramas arose not from Freudian theory but from the dramatist's own bout with madness during the 1890s, when he was living in Berlin, from which he recovered with the aid of Emanuel Swedenborg's spiritualist belief in a higher reality.

Closely related to Strindberg as a dramatist was the German Benjamin Franklin Wedekind (1864–1918), whose two major plays, *Earth Spirit* and *Pandora's Box* (both 1895), deal with frankly sexual themes through the prostitute Lulu, who inspired the subject of Alban Berg's unfinished opera (see box page 840). After becoming disillusioned with the power of words, Hugo von Hofmannsthal (1874–1929) actually gave up theater almost entirely to write librettos for Richard Strauss' operas (see box page 778). Another leader in the reaction against Realism was the Swiss-born Adolphe Appia (1861–1928), who emphasized the staging of Wagner's operas through three-dimensional scenery and carefully calculated light effects that made full use of recent advances in lighting technology.

The only serious experiment with Symbolism by an English dramatist was *Salomé* (1892) by Oscar Wilde (1856–1900), but it can hardly be called an English play. It had been written in French during the previous decade and was published in Paris with illustrations by Aubrey Beardsley (see fig. 23-18). Moreover, the work, which was banned in England until 1931, was first produced in Paris by Lugné-Poë in 1896 with Sarah Bernhardt in the lead role. Wilde was otherwise a writer of extremely clever, albeit conventional, comedies; his main connection to Symbolism was his involvement with the Aesthetic Movement, whose dandyism he personified.

Characteristically, these figures do not fully emerge from their material substance (often, as here, a massive block of wood). Their clothing is like a hard shell that hides the body, as in medieval sculpture. Barlach's art is severely restricted in both form and feeling, yet within these limits its quiet intensity is not easily forgotten.

ARCHITECTURE

Art Nouveau

During the 1890s and early 1900s, a movement usually known as Art Nouveau (New Art) arose throughout Europe and the United States. It takes its name from a shop opened in Paris in 1895 by the entrepreneur Siegfried Bing, who employed most of the leading designers of the day and helped to popularize their work. By the time Bing's shop opened, however, the movement had already been in full force for several years. Art Nouveau has various other names as well: it is called Jugendstil (Youth Style) in Germany and Austria, Stile Liberty (after the well-known London store that helped to launch it) in Italy, and Modernista in Spain.

Like Post-Impressionism and Symbolism, Art Nouveau is not easy to characterize. It was primarily a decorative style, inspired by Rococo forms and based on sinuous curves that often suggest organic shapes. Its favorite pattern was the whiplash line; its typical shape, the lily. The ancestors of Art Nouveau were the ornament of William Morris (see page 766) and Whistler's enthusiasm for Japanese art (see page 767). Other influences were the styles of Gauguin, Beardsley, Munch, and Klimt, among others, and the Aesthetic, Socialist, and Symbolist movements. There was also a severely geometric side that proved of even greater importance in the long run.

The goal of Art Nouveau was to raise the crafts to the level of the fine arts in order to eliminate the distinction between them. In this respect, it was meant to be a "popular" art, available to everyone. Yet it often became so extravagant that only the wealthy could afford it. Art Nouveau had a great impact on public taste; its widespread influence on the applied arts can be seen in wrought-iron work, furniture, jewelry, glass, typography, and even women's fashions. Historically, Art Nouveau may be regarded as a prelude to modernism, but its preciousness was perhaps the most obvious symptom of the anxiety that afflicted the Western world at the end of the nineteenth century.

While highly influential in the realm of the decorative arts, Art Nouveau did not lend itself easily to large-scale architectural designs. Indeed, wags aptly called it book-decoration architecture, after the origin of its ornamental designs, which were best suited to two-dimensional surface effects. But in the hands of architects seeking a modern style, Art Nouveau undermined the authority of revival styles once and for all—in Europe, at least, but not in America.

VICTOR HORTA. The first architect to explore the full potential of Art Nouveau was Victor Horta (1861–1947), the founder of the movement in Brussels. After studying in Paris, he brought the latest ideas back to Belgium. There he gained the patronage of wealthy industrialists who were surprisingly liberal in their

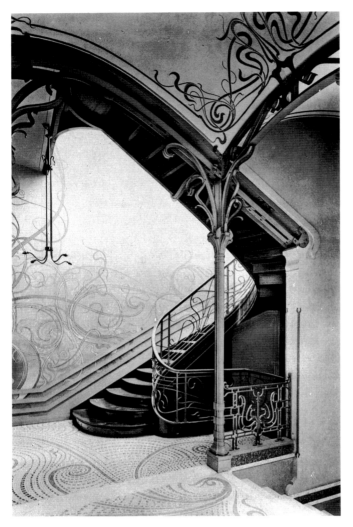

23-29. Victor Horta. Interior Stairwell of the Tassel House, Brussels. 1892–93

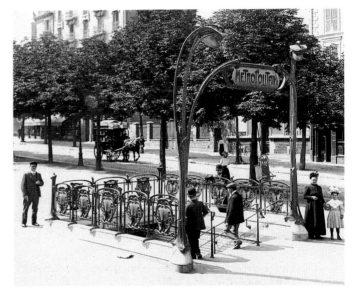

23-30. Hector Guimard. Métro Station, Paris. 1900

political and cultural views. The stairwell in Tassel House (fig. 23-29), built in 1892–93 for a mathematics professor, has an amazingly fluid grace. Horta has made maximum use of wrought iron, which could be drawn out into almost any shape, although his interior presents no structural advance. The supporting role of the column is frankly acknowledged, although it has been made as slender as possible. But in a charming play on the Corinthian capital (compare fig. 5-39), it sprouts ribbonlike tendrils that dissolve the arches—an effect that is enhanced by continuing the vegetal motif in the vault above. Similarly the banister, which is light and supple, uncoils with taut springiness. The linear patterns extend to the floor and walls, where they further integrate the space visually. The ensemble has a litheness and airiness that make the grand staircase of Garnier's Opéra seem heavy and vulgar (see fig. 21-75).

HECTOR GUIMARD. Although Art Nouveau's designs lie mainly on the surface, the same devices could be turned into inde-

pendent three-dimensional forms whose role was largely sculptural. The entrances for the Métro (the Paris subway) designed in 1900 for the Paris Exposition by Hector Guimard (1867–1942) are just such a case (fig. 23-30). Like Horta, whose work he admired, Guimard was a designer rather than an engineer, and it is this background in the applied arts that makes these stations appealing even today. The functional purpose is so thoroughly disguised by the fanciful forms that we readily overlook the role of the plantlike posts springing like strange hybrids from the sidewalk in providing safety and light.

ANTONÍ GAUDÍ. The most remarkable example of Art Nouveau architecture is the Casa Milá in Barcelona, a large apartment house designed by Antoní Gaudí (1852–1926) (figs. 23-31 and 23-32). Gaudí, who began his career working in the Gothic Revival style, shows an almost maniacal avoidance of all flat surfaces, straight lines, and symmetry of any kind. As a result, the building looks as if it had been freely modeled of some flexible

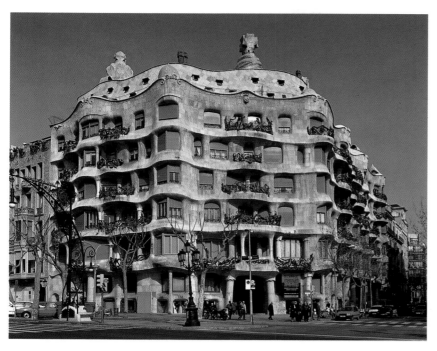

23-31. Antoní Gaudí. Casa Milá Apartments, Barcelona. 1905–7

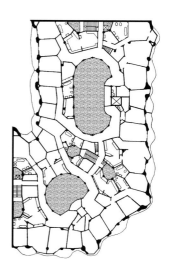

23-32. Floor plan of typical floor, Casa Milá

material, even though the structure is built of steel. The "skin" is not stucco or cement, as we might suppose, but cut stone. The softly rounded facade, with its "eroded" openings, undulates as freely as Guarini's Palazzo Carignano (see fig. 17-24). The roof has the rhythmic motion of a wave, while the chimneys seem to have been squeezed from a pastry tube. The Casa Milá expresses one architect's fanatical devotion to the ideal of natural form. It could never be repeated, let alone developed further. Rather, its combination of modern structure and old-fashioned craftsmanship was an attempt at reform from the edges, rather than from the center, through aesthetics rather than engineering.

CHARLES RENNIE MACKINTOSH. Gaudí represents one extreme of Art Nouveau architecture. The Scot Charles Rennie Mackintosh (1868–1928) represents the other. Although they stood at opposite poles, both strove for the same goal—a contemporary style independent of the past. Mackintosh's basic outlook was so close to the functionalism of Louis Sullivan (see below) that at first glance his work hardly seems to belong to Art Nouveau at all. The north facade of the Glasgow School of Art (fig. 23-33), designed as early as 1896 while Mackintosh was an assistant in a local architectural firm, might be mistaken for a building done 30 years later. The walls have been replaced by huge, deeply recessed studio windows, leaving only a framework of undecorated cut stone (which he preferred for its mass). The entrance, however, is "sculptured" in a style related to Gaudí's, despite its preference for angles over curves. Another Art Nouveau feature is the wrought-

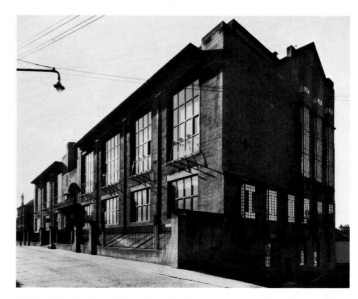

23-33. Charles Rennie Mackintosh. North facade of the Glasgow School of Art, Glasgow, Scotland. 1896–1910

iron grillwork (here with a minimum of ornament). Even more surprising is the two-story library (fig. 23-34), so different from Labrouste's revivalist mixture (see fig. 22-33). With its rectangular wooden posts and lintels supporting the balcony, it anticipates early twentieth-century interiors.

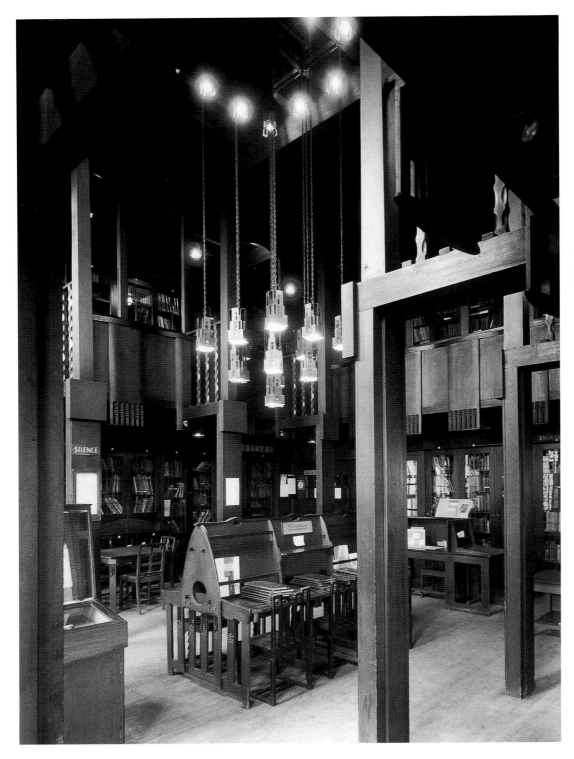

23-34. Interior of the Library, Glasgow School of Art

HENRY VAN DE VELDE. Mackintosh's work came to be widely known abroad through architectural magazines and exhibitions. Its clarity and force had a profound effect on one of the leaders of Art Nouveau in Belgium, Henry van de Velde (1863–1957), who began as a Divisionist painter. Then, under the influence of William Morris, he became a designer of posters, furniture, silverware, and glass, first for Siegfried Bing in Paris and later in Berlin. After 1900 Van de Velde worked mainly as an architect. In 1908 he founded the Weimar School of Arts and Crafts in Germany, which became famous after World War I as the Bauhaus (see pages 902–03).

Van de Velde's most ambitious building was the theater he designed in Cologne for an exhibition sponsored by the Werkbund (Arts and Crafts Association) in 1914 (figs. 23-35 and 23-36). It makes a striking contrast with the Paris Opéra, completed only 40 years before (see figs. 21-76 and 21-77). Whereas Garnier's building tries to evoke the splendors of the Louvre through its ornate facade, Van de Velde's exterior is a tightly stretched, plain "skin" that covers—and reveals—the individual units of the internal space. The theater, constructed of concrete, bears a curious resemblance to Mesopotamian ziggurats (compare fig. 3-4), which had greatly impressed the architect during

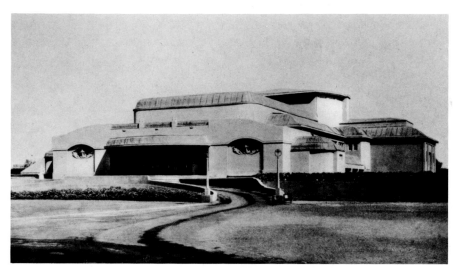

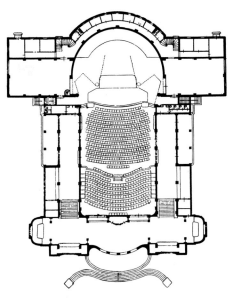

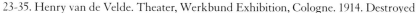

23-35. Henry van de Velde. Theater, Werkbund Exhibition, Cologne. 1914. Destroyed

23-36. Plan of the Theater, Werkbund Exhibition

a visit to the Middle East and Greece in 1903. He held theater as sacred, for to him it was the ultimate expression of social and spiritual life—a conception that was influenced heavily by the director Max Reinhardt and the stage designer Gordon Craig (see box pages 818–19).

The Werkbund Exhibition was a watershed in the development of modern architecture. It provided a showcase for a whole generation of young German architects who were to achieve prominence after World War I (see Chapter 26). Many of the buildings they designed for the fairgrounds anticipate ideas of the 1920s.

United States

The search for a modern architecture began in earnest around 1880. It required marrying the ideas of William Morris to a new machine aesthetic—tentatively explored some 15 years earlier in the decorative arts—and to new construction materials and techniques. The process itself took several decades, while architects experimented with a variety of styles. It is significant that the symbol of modern architecture became the skyscraper and that its first home was Chicago, then a flourishing city unburdened by loyalty to the styles of the past.

HENRY HOBSON RICHARDSON. The Chicago fire of 1871 had opened enormous opportunities to architects from older cities such as Boston and New York. Among them was Henry Hobson Richardson (1838–1886), who as a young man studied at the École des Beaux-Arts in Paris, where he was in contact with Labrouste (see fig. 22-32). Most of his work along the eastern seaboard shows a massive Neo-Romanesque style. There are still echoes of this historicism in his last major project for Chicago, the

Marshall Field Wholesale Store, designed in 1885 (fig. 23-37). The huge building filled an entire city block. In its symmetry and the treatment of masonry, it may remind us of Italian Early Renaissance palaces (see fig. 12-27) as interpreted through the Beaux-Arts style (compare fig 22-32). Yet the complete lack of ornament announces its utilitarian purpose.

As commercial building types, warehouses and factories had a history dating back to the later eighteenth century. Richardson

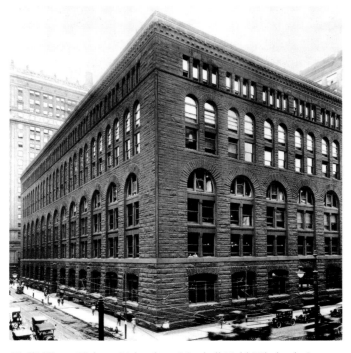

23-37. Henry Hobson Richardson. Marshall Field Wholesale Store, Chicago. 1885–87. Demolished 1930

must have been familiar with this tradition, which on occasion had produced impressive "stripped-down" designs (fig. 23-38). In contrast to those earlier structures, however, the walls of the Marshall Field Wholesale Store do not present a continuous surface pierced by windows. Except for the corners, which have the effect of heavy piers, they show a series of superimposed arcades, like a Roman aqueduct (see fig. 7-9). This impression is strengthened by the absence of decoration and the thickness of the masonry. (Note how deeply the windows are recessed.) These arcaded walls are as functional and self-sustaining as their ancient ancestors. They give the building a sense of strength and dignity unrivaled in any earlier commercial building. Behind them is an iron skeleton that actually supports the seven floors, but the exterior does not depend on it, either structurally or aesthetically.

THE MATERIALS OF MODERN ARCHITECTURE

After about 1780 the gradual introduction of new techniques and materials—especially iron, steel, and concrete—had a profound effect on architectural style, especially commercial architecture. Of these by far the most important was iron, which was used as early as the fourth millennium B.C. and began to be made on a large scale beginning in the fourteenth century. Pig iron, smelted in blast furnaces, can be poured into molds to make cast iron. Cast iron is brittle because it has relatively high amounts of carbon and impurities (slag), but is stronger and more fire-resistant than wood. A new form of iron, wrought iron, was introduced around 1820. Because it contains less carbon and slag than cast iron, it is soft and malleable (hence its name) and possesses greater tensile strength, making it ideal for bolts, ties, and trusses.

Cast iron was first mass-produced for rails by Abraham Darby in 1767. Ten years later, in 1777–79, the first iron bridge was built at Coalbrookdale by Abraham Darby III from a design by the architect Thomas F. Pritchard. Fires at textile mills led to the use of cast-iron pillars in the 1780s, then beams during the following decade. Cast-iron columns were also introduced in churches as early as the 1780s. Soon the structural elements in a number of English churches were being built almost entirely of iron, beginning with St. George at Merseyside, erected in 1812–13 by the architect Thomas Rickman and the iron founder John Cragg, which uses an extremely sophisticated structural system, including tension rods to tie it together (see illustration). The idea was also taken up in the 1850s by the Frenchman Louis-Auguste Boileau.

Iron construction was greatly improved during the first half of the nineteenth century by the introduction of new **truss** systems and the riveted I-beam. Within a few decades of their first appearance, iron columns and arches became the standard means of supporting roofs over the large spaces required by railroad stations. The first railway shed, built in 1830, was a modest structure using straight beams; the arch became an important form only in the 1840s, as rail lines became increasingly common first throughout Europe, then in America, and large terminals began to be erected.

Because it can be manufactured with great consistency, iron can be used in predictable ways that can be calculated using standard mathematical formulas. This property gave rise to new structural systems (notably those by James Bogardus in the 1840s and 50s) that are extremely stable yet lightweight. Although these systems almost always remained completely hidden from view, technology produced a fundamental change in the practice of architecture, which became increasingly dependent on engineering. As a consequence, the tradition of artists and gifted amateurs practicing as architects was over by 1880. The Universal Exposition held in Paris in 1889 announced the triumph of the iron age with the Eiffel Tower and the Hall of Machines (seen behind the Eiffel Tower in figure 22-36). The tower itself was a miracle of engineering, manufacturing, and construction. In addition to being extremely lightweight, it was precast so precisely that no fabrication or cutting was done on the site, only riveting, and planned so carefully that not a single worker was killed. Interestingly enough, Eiffel added the arches at the base, similar to those on his bridges, to assure the viewer that the tower would stand, even though they were not structurally necessary.

By this time, iron was already being rapidly supplanted by steel. Steel is an even stronger alloy of iron and carbon that is also ductile and corrosion-resistant. (Technically, most nineteenth-century steel was really a form of wrought iron, since it lacked other elements, such as nickel, chromium, and aluminum, which were added after 1900 for greater hardness.) Steel was handmade until the 1850s, when the Englishman Henry Bessemer and the American William Kelly independently invented a commercial process to remove the impurities by introducing oxygen while heating the iron in a converter of steel lined with silica. The open hearth furnace, devised in 1864 by William and Ernst Siemens, used regenerative preheating of air to smelt a combination of iron ore and pig iron at extremely high temperatures. Steel mills sprang up everywhere after 1865 to serve the rail industry, but it was not until the 1880s that long rolled-steel beams began to be produced in large quantities, thanks to the widespread use of the open-hearth furnace. This innovation in turn made possible steel-frame construction, essential to skyscrapers, whose potential was first explored during the same decade in New York and Paris, and then in Chicago. The only major advances since then in steel production have been the basic-oxygen process and the electric furnace.

The difficulty with iron and steel is that they rust and can be damaged by fire. To overcome these limitations, they can be embedded in concrete to form ferroconcrete. Concrete used on its own is fire- and water-resistant, but has low tensile strength and is subject to erosion. It is made by heating limestone and clay till they almost fuse, then grinding and mixing them with water and stone, sand or gravel. Used widely by the Romans, it was rediscovered in 1774 by John Smeaton of England. Portland Cement,

LOUIS SULLIVAN. Richardson's Marshall Field building stands midway between the old and the new. Its severe logic embodies a concept of monumentality derived from the past, but its opened-up walls, divided into vertical "bays," look forward to the work of Louis Sullivan (1856–1924), who also received part of his training at the École des Beaux-Arts. In 1879 Sullivan became an assistant to the engineer Dankmar Adler (1844–1900);

two years later they formed a partnership that lasted till 1895. The Wainwright Building in St. Louis (fig. 23-39), their first skyscraper, was built only five years after the Marshall Field Store. It, too, is monumental, but in a very untraditional way. The organization of the exterior reflects and expresses the internal steel skeleton. The total effect of the slender brick piers rising between the windows is like a vertical grating encased by

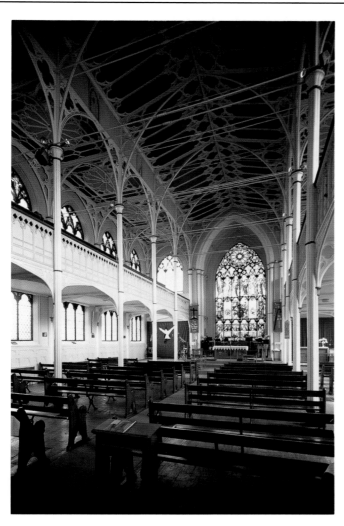

Thomas Rickman and John Cragg. Interior, St. George's Church, Everton, Liverpool, England. 1812–13

which is stronger and more durable, was invented in 1824 by another Englishman, Joseph Aspdin. The process of making it is similar to that of concrete but uses different materials. Lime, silica, alumina, sulfates, and iron oxide are heated until they nearly coalesce before being ground up and mixed with gypsum. Though a concrete house was built as early as 1837 by J. B. White of England, cement did not become widely adopted until the 1850s and 60s for sewer systems. It nevertheless remained too expensive for large-scale use before the early 1900s.

Ferroconcrete unites the best of concrete and metal. Ferroconcrete incorporating tension rods was first patented in 1856 by François Coignet. Iron beams were substituted in patents issued in 1867 and 1878 to Joseph Monier, whose system was improved

further by Gustav Adolf Wayss in his important publication of 1887. In 1892 the Belgian François Hennebique replaced iron with steel, and enclosed girders in cement, for the first time, to protect them from fire and corrosion, as well as from the chemical fumes found in factories; equally important, he combined all supports, walls, and ceilings into a single unit using hooked connections that was far more stable. The final step was taken in the early 1900s by Eugène Freyssinet, who recalculated all the formulas for reinforced concrete and in the process invented prestressed concrete, which enables curved supports to carry much greater loads and counteracts deterioration of the concrete itself under pressure.

As important as these developments were, modern architecture would not have been possible without other innovations that we now take for granted. Plate glass was introduced in the 1820s, followed by cheaper sheet glass around 1835. The repeal of the excise tax on glass in 1845 in England finally made sheet glass an affordable material on a large scale. Used in conjunction with cast iron, ever-larger panes of glass gave rise to the modern store front, which became ubiquitous after mid-century. Massive windows, used serially, were also incorporated first into department stores and eventually skyscrapers from the late 1870s onward. Equally essential to the skyscraper was the invention of the passenger elevator by Elisha Otis in 1857. The humble brick became an important building material in the 1850s with the advent of the modern kiln, which produced it cheaply in vast quantities. Other amenities included gas lighting (1840s), toilets (c. 1870), electricity (1880s), telephones (1880s), and central heat (1890s).

Finally, we should mention rubber. It was limited chiefly to waterproofing as the result of a process for applying it to fabrics devised by Samuel Peale in 1791, though it was the chemist Charles Mackintosh who opened the first factory in Glasgow in 1823. Its widespread use as insulation and in other applications was made possible only in 1839, when Charles Goodyear, relying on the work of the German chemist Friedrich Ludersdorf and the American chemist Nathaniel Hayward, discovered vulcanization, which involved cooking the rubber with sulfur to prevent it from melting in hot weather and becoming brittle in cold. Synthetic rubber was initially developed in Germany during World War I because natural rubber was hard to come by, but it was not commercially viable until after 1930, when the chemistry of polymers was finally understood by Wallace Hume Carothers of America and Hermann Staudinger of Germany. The result was neoprene (1931), Buna (1935), butyl rubber (1940), and GR-S (Government Rubber-Styrene, used in World War II).

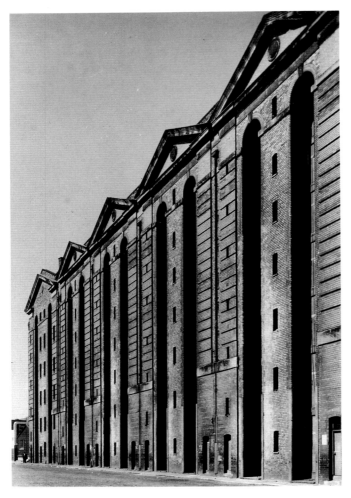

23-38. Warehouses on New Quay, Liverpool. 1835–40

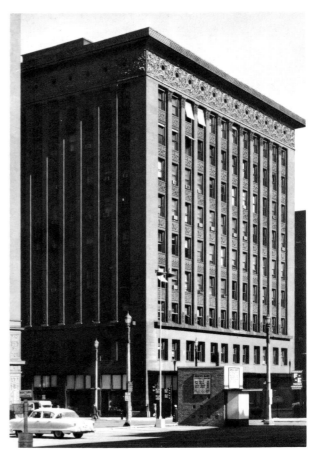

23-39. Louis Sullivan. Wainwright Building,
St. Louis, Missouri. 1890–91. Destroyed

the corner piers and by the emphatic horizontals of attic and mezzanine.

This is, of course, only one of the many possible "skins" that could be stretched over the structural framework. What counts is that we immediately feel this wall is derived from the skeleton underneath and that it is not self-sustaining. Skin is perhaps too weak a term to describe this brick casing. To Sullivan, who often thought of buildings as comparable to the human body, it was more like the "flesh" and "muscle" attached to the "bone," yet capable of an infinite variety of expressive effects. He coined the phrase "form follows function," but to him it meant something very different from the modernist creed of the twentieth century: "It is the pervading law of all things organic, and inorganic, of all things physical and metaphysical, of all things human and all things superhuman, of all true manifestations of the head, of the heart, of the soul, that the life is recognizable in its expression, that form ever follows function." Clearly he intended a flexible relationship between the two, not rigid dependence. [See also Primary Sources, no. 81, page 969.]

The range of Sullivan's invention can be seen by comparing the Wainwright Building with his last building, the Schlesinger and Meyer (later the Carson Pirie Scott & Company) Department Store in Chicago, begun nine years later (fig. 23-40). The white terra-cotta on the upper stories follows the grid of the steel frame

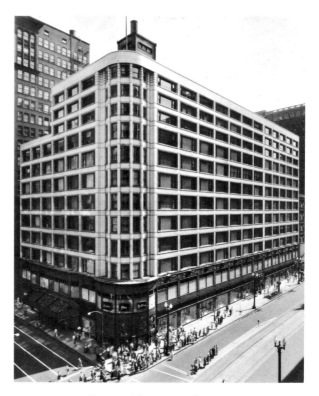

23-40. Louis Sullivan. Schlesinger and Mayer
Department Store, Chicago. 1899–1904

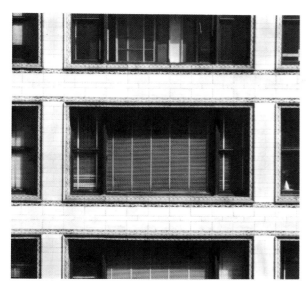

23-41. Detail of facade, showing window,
Schlesinger and Mayer Department Store

far more closely, and the overall effect, enhanced by the simple molding around the windows (fig. 23-41), is light and crisp. The contrast between the horizontal continuity of the sides and the vertical accent at the corner provides a clear end point to the facade.

Sullivan's buildings are based on a lofty idealism inspired by the poetry of Walt Whitman and the philosophy of Friedrich Nietzsche. Their ornamentation remains firmly rooted in the nineteenth century, even as they point the way to twentieth-century architecture. From the beginning, Sullivan's geometry carried a spiritual meaning, derived partly from the theosopher Emanuel Swedenborg (1688–1772), that centered on birth, flowering, decay, and regeneration. It was tied to a highly original style of decoration embodying Sullivan's theory that ornament must give expression to structure—not by reflecting it literally but by interpreting the same concepts through organic abstraction. The soaring verticality of the Wainwright Building, for example, stands for growth, which is developed further by the vegetative motifs of the moldings along the cornice and between the windows. The clean articulation of the windows on the upper stories of the Schlesinger and Meyer building gives way on the ground floor and mezzanine to an elaborate ironwork entrance—designed largely by George G. Elmslie (1871–1952) using Sullivan's system—that increases the storefront's attraction to shoppers.

PHOTOGRAPHY
Documentary Photography

During the second half of the nineteenth century, the press played a leading role in the social movement that brought the harsh realities of poverty to the public's attention. The camera became an important instrument of reform through the photodocumentary, which tells the story of people's lives in a pictorial essay. It responded to the same conditions that had stirred Courbet (see pages 738–40), and its factual reportage likewise fell within the realist tradition—only its response came a quarter-century later. Before then, photographers had been content to present romanticized images of the poor like those in genre paintings of the day. The first photodocumentary was John Thomson's illustrated sociological study *Street Life in London,* published in 1877. To get his pictures, he had to pose his figures, since exposures took minutes, not a split second as they do today.

JACOB RIIS. The invention of gunpowder flash ten years later allowed Jacob Riis (1849–1914) to rely for the most part on the element of surprise. Riis was a police reporter in New York City, where he learned at first hand about the crime-infested slums and their appalling living conditions. He kept up a vigorous campaign of illustrated newspaper exposés, books, and lectures, which in some cases led to major revisions of the city's housing codes and labor laws. Even today his photographs' unflinching realism has lost none of its force. Certainly it would be difficult to imagine a more nightmarish scene than *Bandits' Roost* (fig. 23-42). With good reason we sense a pervasive air of danger in the eerie light. The notorious gangs of New York City's Lower East Side looked for their victims by night and killed them without hesitation. Although almost certainly posed, the motionless figures seem to look us over with the practiced casualness of hunters coldly sizing up potential prey.

Pictorialism

The raw subject matter and realism of documentary photography had little impact on art and were shunned by most other photographers. Through such organizations as the Photographic Society

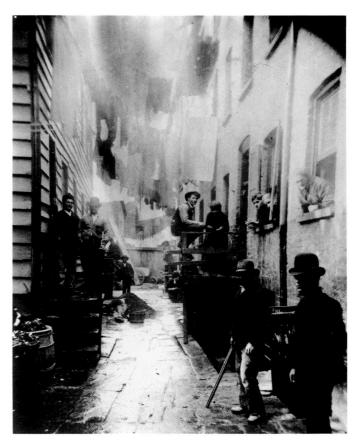

23-42. Jacob Riis. *Bandits' Roost.* c. 1888. Gelatin-silver print. Museum of the City of New York

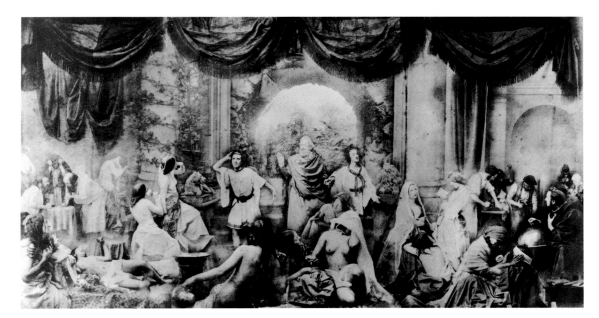

23-43. Oscar Rejlander. *The Two Paths of Life*. 1857. Combination albumen print, 16 x 31" (40.6 x 78.7cm). George Eastman House, Rochester, New York

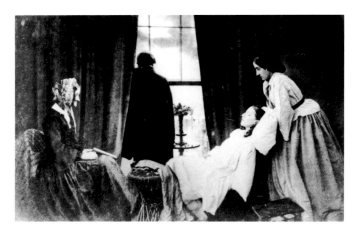

23-44. Henry Peach Robinson. *Fading Away.* 1858. Combination print. Royal Photographic Society, London

of London, founded in 1853, England became the leader of Pictorialism. The movement aimed to convince doubting critics that by imitating painting and printmaking, photography could indeed be art. To Victorian England, beauty meant, above all, art with a high moral purpose or noble sentiment, preferably in a classical style.

OSCAR REJLANDER. *The Two Paths of Life* (fig. 23-43) by Oscar Rejlander (1818–1875) fulfills these ends by presenting an allegory clearly descended from Hogarth's *Rake's Progress* series (see figs. 20-11 and 20-12). This amazing photomontage, almost three feet wide, combines 30 negatives through composite printing. We see a young man (in two images) choosing between the paths of virtue and vice, the latter represented by a half-dozen nudes. The picture created a sensation in 1857, and Queen Victoria herself purchased a print. Rejlander, however, never enjoyed the same success again. He was the most adventurous photographer of his time and soon turned to other subjects less in keeping with popular taste.

HENRY PEACH ROBINSON. The mantle of art photography fell to Henry Peach Robinson (1830–1901), who became the most famous photographer in the world. He established his reputation with *Fading Away* (fig. 23-44), which appeared a year after Rejlander's *The Two Paths of Life*. The photograph, with six lines from Shelley's "Queen Mab" printed below on the mat, is typical of Robinson's sentimental scenes. Like *The Two Paths of Life,* it is a photomontage, but made of only five negatives. The scene is as carefully staged as any Victorian melodrama. At first Robinson made detailed drawings before photographing the individual components. He later renounced multiple-negative photography, but still tried to imitate contemporary genre painting in his pictures. In treating this subject matter, he continued to distinguish between fact and truth, which to him was a mixture of the real and the artificial.

JULIA CAMERON. The photographer who pursued ideal beauty with the greatest passion was Julia Margaret Cameron (1815–1879). An intimate friend of leading poets, scientists, and artists, she took up photography at the age of 48 when she was given a camera. She went on to create a remarkable body of work. In her own day Cameron was known for her allegorical and narrative pictures, but now she is remembered chiefly for her portraits of the men who shaped Victorian England. Many of her finest photographs, however, are of the women who were married to her closest friends. An early study of the actress Ellen Terry (fig. 23-45; see box page 765) has the lyricism and grace of the Pre-Raphaelite aesthetic that shaped Cameron's style (compare fig. 22-18).

Naturalistic Photography

PETER HENRY EMERSON. The attack against art photography was taken up by Peter Henry Emerson (1856–1936), who became the bitter enemy of Robinson. Emerson championed what he called naturalistic photography, based on scientific principles and Constable's landscapes. Nevertheless he, too, contrasted

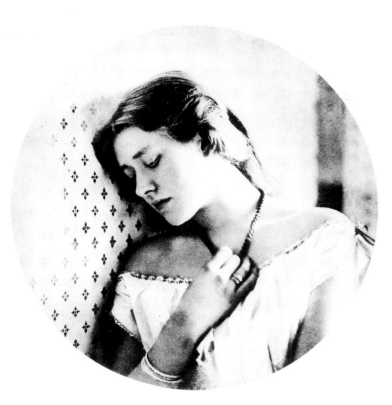

23-45. Julia Margaret Cameron. *Ellen Terry, at the Age of Sixteen.* c. 1863. Carbon print, diameter 9½" (24 cm). The Metropolitan Museum of Art, New York

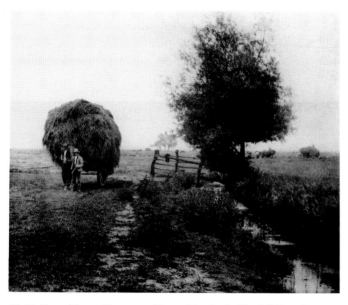

23-46. Peter Henry Emerson. *Haymaking in the Norfolk Broads.* c. 1890. Platinum print. Société Française de Photographie, Paris

realism with truth, which he defined in terms of sentiment, aesthetics, and the selective arrangement of nature. Using a single negative, Emerson composed his scenes with the greatest care. The results were sometimes similar to Robinson's, which of course he never acknowledged. Most of Emerson's work was devoted to scenes of rural and coastal life that are not far removed from those captured in early documentary photographs.

In his best prints, nature predominates. He was a master at distributing tonal masses across a scene, and his photographs (fig. 23-46) are the equivalents of fine English landscape paintings of the period. Although the effect is rarely apparent in his images, Emerson advocated putting the lens slightly out of focus, in the belief that the eye sees only the central area of a scene sharply. When he gave up this idea a few years later, he decided that because it was machine-made, not personal, photography was indeed a science.

PHOTO-SECESSION. The issue of whether photography could be art came to a head in the early 1890s with the Secession movement (see page 784), which was spearheaded in 1893 by the founding in London of the Linked Ring, a rival group to the Royal Photographic Society of Great Britain. Stimulated by Emerson's ideas, the Secessionists wanted a pictorialism independent of science and technology. They steered a course between idealism and naturalism by imitating every form of late Romantic art that did not involve narrative. Equally incompatible with their aims were Realist and Post-Impressionist painting, then at their zenith. In its approach to photography as Art for Art's Sake, the Photo-Secession had the most in common with Whistler's aestheticism.

GERTRUDE KÄSEBIER. To resolve the dilemma between art and mechanics, the Secessionists tried to make their photographs look as much like paintings as possible. Rather than resorting to composite or multiple images, however, they exercised total control over the printing process, chiefly by adding special materials to their printing paper in order to create different effects. Pigmented gum brushed on coarse drawing paper yielded a warm-toned, highly textured print that in its way approximated Impressionist painting. Paper impregnated with platinum salts was especially popular among the Secessionists because of its clear grays. The subtlety and depth of the platinum print lend a remarkable ethereality to *The Magic Crystal* (fig. 23-47) by the American photographer Gertrude Käsebier (1854–1934), in which spiritual forces almost visibly sweep across the photograph.

EDWARD STEICHEN. The Linked Ring had close ties with America through Käsebier and Alfred Stieglitz, who opened his Photo-Secession gallery in New York in 1905. [See Primary Sources, no. 82, page 970.] Among his protégés was the young Edward Steichen (1879–1973), whose photograph of Rodin in his sculpture studio (fig. 23-48) is the finest achievement of the entire Photo-Secession movement. The head in profile contemplating *The Thinker* expresses the essence of the confrontation between the sculptor and his work of art. His brooding introspection hides the inner turmoil evoked by the ghostlike monument to Victor Hugo, which rises dramatically like a genius in the background. Not since *The Creation of Adam* by Michelangelo (see fig. 13-18), Rodin's ideal, have we seen a more telling use of space or an image that penetrates the mystery of creativity so deeply.

The Photo-Secession movement achieved its goal of gaining wide recognition for photography as an art form, but by 1907 its approach was regarded as stilted. Although the movement lasted for a few more years, it was becoming clear that the future of photography did not lie in the imitation of painting, which was then being reformed by modernists. The legacy of the Photo-Secession was valuable nonetheless, for it taught photographers much about the control of composition and the response to light.

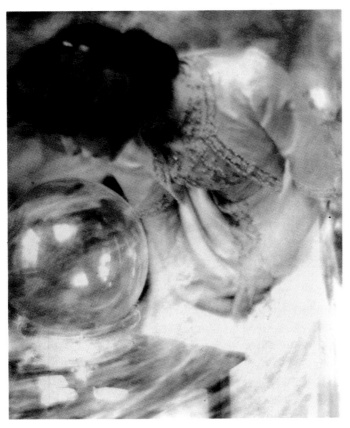

23-47. Gertrude Käsebier. *The Magic Crystal.* c. 1904. Platinum print. Royal Photographic Society, Bath

Motion Photography

EADWEARD MUYBRIDGE. An entirely new direction was charted by Eadweard Muybridge (1830–1904), who arrived in America from England at the age of 22 and became the founder of motion photography. He wedded two different technologies in devising a set of cameras capable of photographing action at successive points. From the beginning, photography had grown from such marriages; another instance had occurred when Nadar used a hot-air balloon to take aerial shots of Paris (see fig. 21-83). After some trial efforts, Muybridge managed in 1877 to produce a set of pictures of a trotting horse that forever changed artistic depictions of the horse in movement. Of the 100,000 photographs he devoted to the study of animal and human locomotion, the most astonishing were those taken from two or three vantage points at once (fig. 23-49). The idea was surely in the air, for the art of the period occasionally shows similar experiments, but Muybridge's photographs must nevertheless have come as a revelation to artists. The simultaneous views present an entirely new treatment of motion across time and space that challenges the imagination. Like a complex visual puzzle, they can be combined in any number of ways that are endlessly fascinating.

Muybridge left it to others to pursue these possibilities further. Much of his later work was conducted at the University of Pennsylvania in Philadelphia with the support of Thomas Eakins, then the head of the Academy of the Fine Arts (see page 756). Eakins was already adept at using a camera, and photographs provided the subjects for several of his paintings. Soon his interest in science led him to take up motion photography as well. Unlike Muybridge's succession of static images, Eakins' multiple exposures show sequential motion on one plate. In the

23-48. Edward Steichen.
*Rodin with His Sculptures
"Victor Hugo" and "The Thinker."* 1902.
Gum print, 14¼ x 12¾" (36.3 x 32.4 cm).
The Art Institute of Chicago

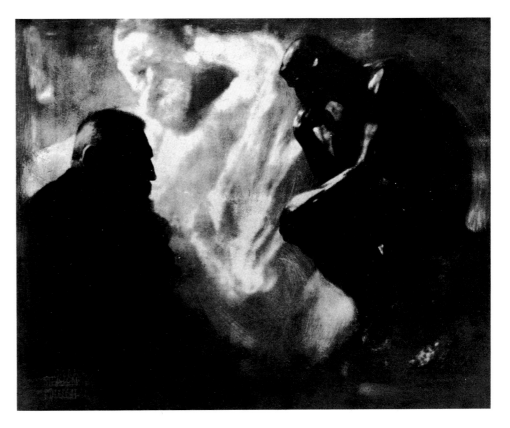

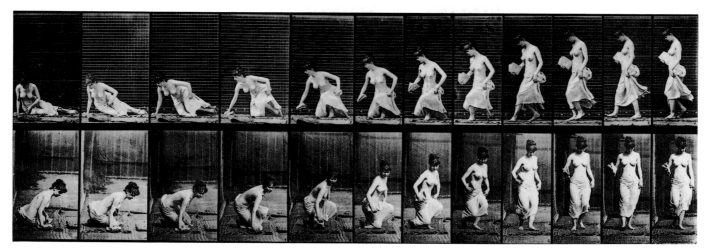

23-49. Eadweard Muybridge. *Female Semi-Nude in Motion,* from *Human and Animal Locomotion,* vol. 2, pl. 271. 1887. George Eastman House, Rochester, New York

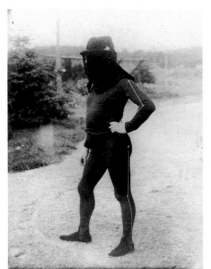 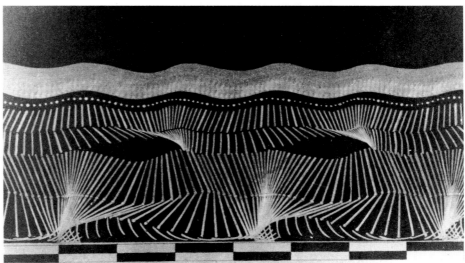

23-50a and b. Étienne-Jules Marey. *Man in Black Suit with White Stripes Down Arms and Legs, Walking in Front of a Black Wall.* c. 1884. Chronophotograph

end, however, photography for Eakins was simply a means of depicting figures more realistically.

ÉTIENNE-JULES MAREY. It was Étienne-Jules Marey (1830–1904) who developed motion photography into an art. A noted French physiologist, Marey (like Muybridge, with whom he was in direct contact) saw the camera as a tool for demonstrating the mechanics of bodily movement. Soon he began to use it so creatively that his photographs have a perfection not equaled for another 60 years (compare fig. 27-30). Indeed, his multiple exposure of a man walking (fig. 23-50a and b) satisfies both scientific and aesthetic truth in a way that Emerson and the Secessionists never imagined.

The photographs of Muybridge and Marey convey a uniquely modern sense of dynamics reflecting the tempo of life in the Machine Age. However, because the gap was then so great between scientific fact on the one hand and visual perception and artistic representation on the other, their far-reaching aesthetic implications were first realized by the Futurists (see page 815).

THE IMPACT OF PHOTOGRAPHY ON ART. The full implications of photography were not felt by artists immediately. Although they continued to use it as a storehouse of images, it took some time for them to fully appreciate that photography's realism posed a challenge to which they could respond in either of two ways. They could imitate its precision by packing their work with minutely detailed forms. Or they could admit defeat on the grounds that no picture can match the exactness of a photograph and turn instead to styles that emphasize painting as art. To those painters, an image became first and foremost an aesthetic object independent of nature, one that demands to be judged on its artistic and expressive merits alone. While meticulous verism remained widely popular among the large mass of conservative painters and collectors, modernists increasingly chose what came to be known as art for art's sake. However, for the most part, they, too, continued to depict the world around them until 1905, when modern art was born. Within ten years art became independent of even subject matter.

CHAPTER TWENTY-FOUR

Twentieth-Century Painting

PAINTING BEFORE WORLD WAR I

In our account of art in the modern era, we have already discussed a succession of "isms": Neoclassicism, Romanticism, Realism, Impressionism, Post-Impressionism, Divisionism, and Symbolism. There are many more in art since 1900, but we can disregard all but the most important. Like the terms we have used for the styles of earlier periods, they are merely labels to help us sort things out. If an "ism" fails the test of usefulness, we need not keep it. Thus we can omit many of the numerous obscure doctrines, especially in contemporary art. The movements they relate to either cannot be seen as clearly separate or have so little importance that they are of interest only to the specialist. It has always been easier to invent new labels than to create a movement in art that truly deserves a new name. Still, we cannot do without "isms" altogether. Since the start of the modern era, the West (and, increasingly, the rest of the world) has faced the same basic problems everywhere, and local artistic traditions have steadily given way to international trends. Surprisingly, this remains true, even though we live in a different world after the terrorist attack on New York's World Trade Center on September 11, 2001.

During the rise of modern art, we can distinguish three main currents, each made up of a number of "isms," that began among the Post-Impressionists and developed further in the early twentieth century: Expressionism, Abstraction, and Fantasy. Expressionism stresses artists' emotional attitude toward themselves and the world; abstraction focuses on the formal structure of the work of art; and fantasy explores the realm of the imagination, especially its spontaneous and irrational sides. Feeling, order, and imagination, however, are present in every work of art. Without imagination, art would be deadly dull; without order, it would be chaotic; and without feeling, it would leave us unmoved.

These currents are not mutually exclusive, and we shall find them interrelated in many ways. An artist's work often belongs to more than one, which may in turn embrace a wide range of approaches, from the realistic to the completely nonrepresentational (or "nonobjective"). Our three currents, then, do not correspond to specific styles but to general attitudes. They represent parallel responses to the realization, intuitive as well as intellectual, that

after 1900 people were living in a different age. Expressionism is concerned mainly with the human community; abstraction is interested in the structure of reality; and fantasy is occupied with the labyrinth of the mind. We shall also find that realism, which is concerned with the appearance of the world around us, has continued to exist independently of the other three, especially in the United States, where art has often pursued a separate course. The shifting relationships between these strands reflect the complexity of modern life. To be understood, each must be seen in its proper historical context. Beginning in the mid-1930s, the distinction between them begins to break down, so that it is no longer meaningful to trace their evolutions separately after 1945. Despite their limitations, these terms are still useful, for they reflect the critical thinking of the kind that surrounded early modernism.

In examining twentieth-century art, we shall find it anything but tidy. We quickly discover that painting, architecture, sculpture, and photography are like soldiers marching to different drummers. A purely chronological approach would reveal just how out of step they have generally been with one another, but at the cost of losing sight of the internal development of each. Does this mean that they have shared none of the same concerns? On the contrary, expressionism, abstraction, and fantasy can be found in all these art forms before 1945. However, they are present in different measure and do not always carry the same meaning. For that reason, the parallels between them should not be overemphasized.

EXPRESSIONISM

The Fauves

The twentieth century may be said to have begun five years late as far as painting is concerned. Between 1901 and 1906, comprehensive exhibitions of the work of Van Gogh, Gauguin, and Cézanne were held in Paris and Germany. For the first time the achievements of these masters became available to a broad public. The young painters who had grown up in the "decadent," morbid mood of the 1890s (see pages 781–82) were deeply impressed by what they saw. Several of them created a radical new style, full of

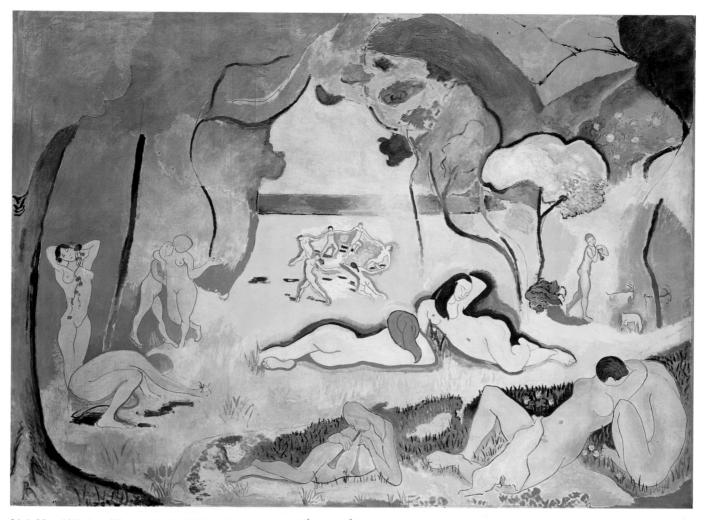

24-1. Henri Matisse. *The Joy of Life*. 1905-6. Oil on canvas, 5'8½" x 7'9¾" (1.74 x 2.38 m). The Barnes Foundation, Merion, Pennsylvania

the violent color of Van Gogh and the bold distortions of Gauguin, which they freely altered for pictorial and expressive effects. When their work first appeared in 1905, it so shocked the critic Louis Vauxcelles (1870–1943) that he dubbed these artists *Fauves* (wild beasts), a label they wore with pride. It was not a common program that brought them together, but their shared sense of liberation and experimentation. As a movement, Fauvism included a number of loosely related individual styles, and the group dissolved after a few years. Most of its members were unable to sustain their inspiration or to adapt successfully to the challenges posed by Cubism (see page 811). Fauvism was nevertheless a decisive breakthrough. It constituted the first unquestionably modern movement of the twentieth century in both style and attitude, one to which every important painter before World War I owed a debt.

HENRI MATISSE. The leader of the Fauves was Henri Matisse (1869–1954), the oldest of the founders of twentieth-century painting. *The Joy of Life* (fig. 24-1), probably the most important picture of his long career, sums up the spirit of Fauvism better than any other single work. It obviously derives its flat planes of color, heavy, undulating outlines, and the "primitive" flavor of its forms from Gauguin (see fig. 23-14). Even its subject suggests the vision of humanity in a state of nature that Gauguin had sought in Tahi-

ti. But Matisse's figures are not Noble Savages under the spell of a native god. The subject is a pagan scene in the classical sense: a bacchanal like Titian's (compare fig. 13-39). The poses of the figures have a classical origin for the most part, and behind the apparently careless draftsmanship lies a profound knowledge of the human body. (Matisse, a pupil of Gustave Moreau, had been trained in the academic tradition.) What makes the picture so revolutionary is its radical simplicity, its "genius of omission." As much as possible, everything has been left out or stated only indirectly. The scene nevertheless retains the essentials of three-dimensional form and spatial depth. What holds the painting together is its firm underlying structure, which reflects Matisse's admiration for Cézanne.

Painting, Matisse seems to say, is not a representation of observed reality but the rhythmic arrangement of line and color on a flat plane. He explores how far the image of nature can be pared down without destroying its basic properties and thus reducing it to mere surface ornament. "What I am after, above all," Matisse once explained, "is expression. . . . [But] . . . expression does not consist of the passion mirrored upon a human face. . . . The whole arrangement of my picture is expressive. The placement of figures or objects, the empty spaces around them, the proportions, everything plays a part." [See Primary Sources, no. 83, pages 970–71.] What, we wonder, does *The Joy of Life* express?

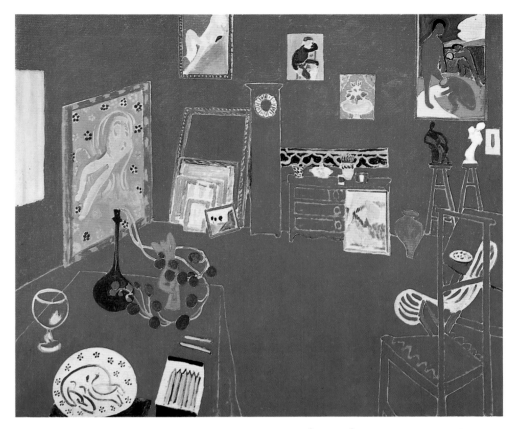

24-2. Henri Matisse. *The Red Studio.* 1911. Oil on canvas, 5'11¼" x 7'2¼" (1.81 x 2.19 m).
The Museum of Modern Art, New York

Exactly what its title says. Whatever his debt to Gauguin, Matisse was never stirred by the same discontent with the decadence of Western civilization. He instead shared the untroubled outlook of the Nabis, with whom he had previously associated, and the canvas owes its decorative quality to their work (compare fig. 23-15). Matisse was concerned above all with the act of painting. This to him was an experience so joyous that he wanted to share it with the viewer.

Matisse's "genius of omission" is seen again in *The Red Studio* (fig. 24-2). By reducing the number of tints to a minimum, he makes color an independent structural element. The result is to emphasize the radical new balance he struck between the two-dimensional and three-dimensional aspects of painting. Matisse spreads the same flat red color on the tablecloth and wall as on the floor, yet he distinguishes the horizontal from the vertical planes with complete assurance, using only a few lines. Equally bold is Matisse's use of pattern, seemingly casual yet perfectly calculated. He harmonizes the relationship of each element with the rest of the picture by repeating a few basic shapes, hues, and decorative motifs around the edges of the canvas. Cézanne had pioneered this integration of surface ornament into the design of a picture (see fig. 23-2), but here Matisse makes it a mainstay of his composition.

GEORGES ROUAULT. For Georges Rouault (1871–1958), the other important member of the Fauves, expression still had to include "the passion mirrored upon a human face," as it had in the past. The expressiveness of *Head of Christ* (fig. 24-3) does not come only from its "image quality." The savage slashing brushstrokes speak eloquently of the artist's rage and compassion. If we cover the upper third of the picture, it is no longer a recognizable image. Yet the expressive effect is hardly less.

Rouault was the true heir of Van Gogh's and Gauguin's concern for the corrupt state of the world. However, he hoped for spiritual renewal through a revitalized Catholic faith. His pictures, whatever their subject, are personal statements of that ardent hope. Trained in his youth as a stained-glass worker, he was better prepared than the other Fauves to share Gauguin's enthusiasm for medieval art. Rouault's later work, such as *The Old King* (fig. 24-4), has glowing colors and broad, black-bordered shapes inspired by Gothic stained-glass windows (compare fig. 11-67). Within this framework he maintains a good deal of the freedom we saw in the *Head of Christ,* which he uses to express his profound understanding of the human condition. The old king's face conveys a mood of resignation and inner suffering that reminds us of Rembrandt, Daumier, and Van Gogh.

German Expressionism

Fauvism had a decisive influence on the Expressionist movement, which arose at the same time in Germany. Because Expressionism had deep historical roots that made it especially appealing to the Northern mind, it lasted far longer in Germany than in France. It also proved broader and more varied. For these reasons, *expressionism* is sometimes applied to German art alone, but such a limit

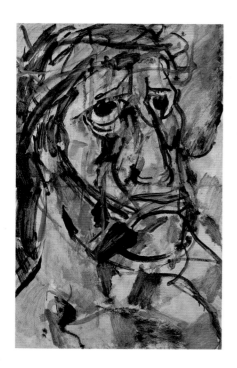

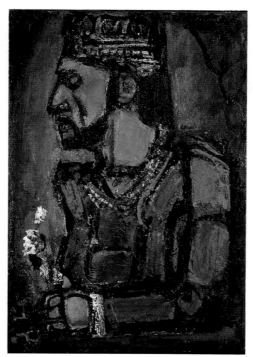

(FAR LEFT) 24-3. Georges Rouault. *Head of Christ.* 1905. Oil on paper, mounted on canvas, 39 x 25¼" (99.1 x 64.2 cm). The Chrysler Museum, Norfolk, Virginia

GIFT OF WALTER P. CHRYSLER, JR.

(LEFT)24-4. Georges Rouault. *The Old King.* 1916-37. Oil on canvas, 30¼ x 21¼" (76.8 x 54 cm). The Carnegie Museum of Art, Pittsburgh

PATRONS ART FUND

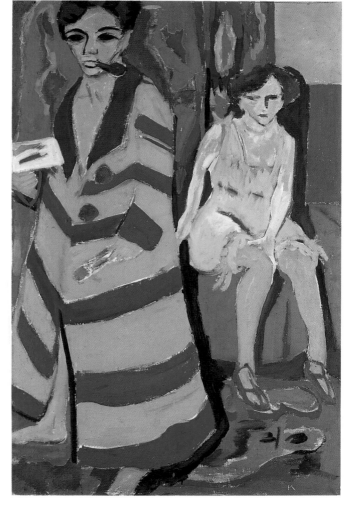

ignores its close ties to Fauvism and the numerous similarities between them. Of the two, German Expressionism was characterized by greater emotional extremes and a more spontaneous approach, while Fauvism was for the most part less openly neurotic and morbid. But the two movements were not separated by any fundamental difference in style or content.

DIE BRÜCKE. Expressionism in Germany began with *Die Brücke* (The Bridge), a group of like-minded painters who lived in Dresden in 1905. Through its bohemian lifestyle, *Die Brücke* cultivated a sense of imminent disaster that is one of the hallmarks of the modern avant-garde. Their early work reveals not only the direct impact of Van Gogh and Gauguin but also of Munch, who was living then in Berlin. It was an exhibition of Matisse that proved decisive, however. *Self-Portrait with Model* (fig. 24-5) by Ernst Ludwig Kirchner (1880–1938), the group's leader, reflects Matisse's simplified, rhythmic line and bright color. Yet the contrast between the coldly aloof artist and the brooding model, who looks as if she has been violated, has a peculiar expressiveness that comes from Munch, whose work was often filled with sexual tension.

ERICH HECKEL. The artists of *Die Brücke* were idealists who wanted to revive German art. Toward that end, they took up woodcuts, which they regarded as a uniquely national medium. The first to begin working on woodblocks was Kirchner, but the finest printmaker of the group was Erich Heckel (1883–1970).

24-5. Ernst Ludwig Kirchner. *Self-Portrait with Model.* 1907. Oil on canvas, 59¼ x 39⅜" (150.5 x 100 cm). Kunsthalle, Hamburg

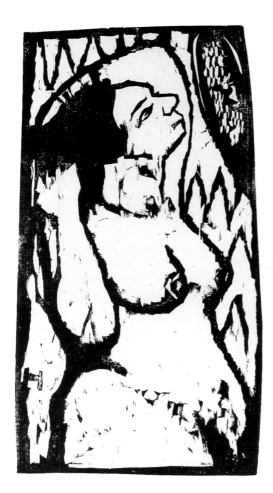

24-6. Erich Heckel. *Woman Before a Mirror.*
1908. Woodcut, 16⅝ x 8⅞" (42.2 x 22.5 cm).
Brücke Museum, Berlin

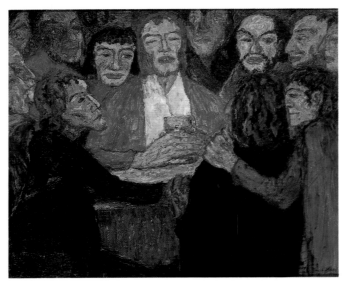

24-7. Emil Nolde. *The Last Supper.* 1909.
Oil on canvas, 32½ x 41¾" (82.6 x 106.1 cm).
Stiftung Seebüll Ada und Emil Nolde, Neukirchen,
Schleswig, Germany

Under the influence of ethnographic art and Gauguin's woodcuts, Heckel's prints, such as *Woman Before a Mirror* (fig. 24-6), imitate the simplified style of the early German "primitives" instead of Dürer's (compare figs. 15-21 and 16-5), which had originally inspired *Die Brücke.* Heckel's figure is "primitive" in another sense as well: her massive fleshiness lends her the primeval quality of ancient fertility goddesses (see fig. 1-12), but with a sensuous charm that is utterly irresistible.

EMIL NOLDE. One *Brücke* artist, Emil Nolde (1867–1956), stands somewhat apart. Older than the rest, he was already working in an Expressionist style when he was invited in 1906 to join the movement, which he left two years later. Nolde shared Rouault's preference for religious subjects, and his figures show a like sympathy for the suffering of humanity. The thickly encrusted surfaces and deliberately clumsy draftsmanship of *The Last Supper* (fig. 24-7) reject pictorial refinement in favor of a primeval, direct expression inspired by Gauguin. Ensor's grotesque masks, too, come to mind (see fig. 23-20), as does the blocklike monumentality of Barlach's peasants (see fig. 23-28). But it is the impact of ethnographic art that we feel the most. Nolde admired the "primitive" artist's ability "to express delight in form and the love of creating it," the "absolute originality, the intense and often grotesque expression of power and life in very simple forms. . . ."

OSKAR KOKOSCHKA. An Expressionist of even greater talent was the Austrian painter Oskar Kokoschka (1886–1980), who began his career as a member of the Vienna Secession (see page 782). In 1910, he was invited to Berlin by Herwarth Walden, the publisher of the art journal *Der Sturm* (The Storm; see box page 834), which soon attracted members of *Die Brücke* and *Der Blaue Reiter* (see below). Kokoschka's most memorable work, *The Bride of the Wind* (fig. 24-8), celebrates his love for Alma Mahler, the "muse" who inspired so many of Germany's and Austria's leading cultural figures. (Besides the composer-conductor Gustave Mahler, she married the poet Franz Werfel and the architect Walter Gropius.) Based on Romantic paintings of Dante's tragic lovers Paolo and Francesca, it was originally conceived as Tristan and Isolde after Wagner's opera but received its present title from the poet Georg Trakl (1887–1914). The awesome canvas is a monument to the power of love: echoing the impassioned brushwork, the entire universe resounds in a great chord of exaltation at the pair's embrace. Its ecstatic vision forms a fascinating contrast to Gustav Klimt's *The Kiss* (see fig. 23-22). The painting achieves that state of mind when "one's perception reaches out towards the Word, towards awareness of the vision," which was Kokoschka's ideal. "It is love, delighting to lodge itself in the mind."

VASSILY KANDINSKY. The most daring and original step beyond Fauvism was taken by the Russian artist Vassily Kandinsky (1866–1944). He was the leading member of a group of Munich artists called *Der Blaue Reiter* (The Blue Rider) after one of his early paintings. Formed in 1911, it was a loose alliance united only by its mystical tendencies. Kandinsky began to abandon representation as early as 1910 and gave it up altogether several years later. Using the rainbow colors and the free, dynamic brush-

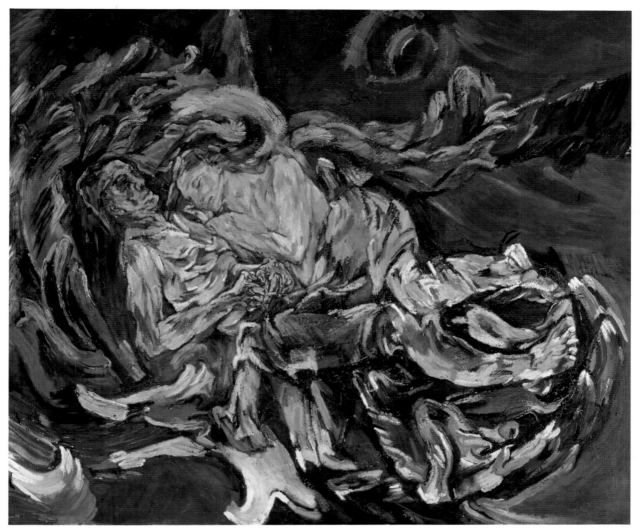

24-8. Oskar Kokoschka. *The Bride of the Wind.* 1914. Oil on canvas, 5'11¼" x 7'2⅝" (1.81 x 2.20 m).
Öffentliche Kunstsammlung Basel, Kunstmuseum, Switzerland

work of the Fauves, he created a completely nonobjective style charged with extraordinary energy. These works have titles as abstract as their forms: our example, one of the most striking, is called *Sketch I for "Composition VII"* (fig. 24-9). Perhaps we should avoid the term *abstract,* because it is often taken to mean that the artist has analyzed and simplified visible reality into geometric forms. (Compare Cézanne's assertion that all natural forms are based on the cone, sphere, and cylinder.) Kandinsky did indeed derive his shapes from the world around him—in landscapes that he freely invented—but by transforming rather than reducing them. (Not until after his return from Russia in 1922 were the implications of his discussion of form fulfilled when he adopted geometric abstraction; see fig. 24-32).

Kandinsky's aim is made clear in the first part of his book *Concerning the Spiritual in Art,* written in 1910 but only published two years later. His intention was to charge form and color with a "purely spiritual meaning," one that expressed his deepest feelings by eliminating all resemblance to the physical world. [See Primary Sources, no. 84, page 971.] To him the only reality that mattered was the artist's inner reality. Thus Kandinsky regarded the Symbolists as his ancestors. Like Gauguin, he wanted to create an art of spiritual renewal. But in contrast to Rouault or Nolde, he had

no specific spiritual program, although his views were similar to those of the theosophist Rudolf Steiner (1861–1925), who influenced many early-twentieth-century artists in Germany. Kandinsky, like Steiner, believed that humanity had lost touch with its spirituality through attachment to material things, and he wanted to rekindle a dreamlike consciousness through his art.

The second part of the book is concerned exclusively with the formal aspects of painting—above all, color. Kandinsky studied the color theories of Seurat and his followers (see page 772), as did many other Expressionists, but the meaning he gave to specific hues was as individual as Van Gogh's (see page 775). Kandinsky's theory of color relationships is strikingly similar to the tonal relationships spelled out in *Theory of Harmony* (1911) by the Expressionist composer Arnold Schoenberg (see box page 812), an ally of Der Blaue Reiter with whom the artist was in close contact.

What does all this have to do with Kandinsky's paintings themselves? The character of his art is best summed up by his later statement: "Painting is the vast, thunderous clash of many worlds, destined, through a mighty struggle, to erupt into a totally new world, which is creation. And the birth of a creation is much akin to that of the Cosmos. There is the same vast and cataclysmic quality belonging to that mighty symphony—the Music of the Spheres."

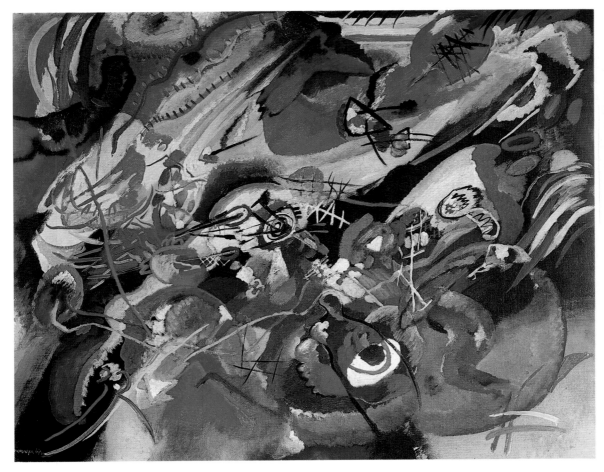

24-9. Vassily Kandinsky. *Sketch I for "Composition VII."* 1913. Oil on canvas, 30¾ x 39⅜" (78 x 100 cm). Private collection

Kandinsky's antinaturalism was inherent in Expressionist theory from the very beginning. Whistler, too, had spoken of "divesting the picture from any outside sort of interest." He even anticipated Kandinsky's "musical" titles (see fig. 22-21). But it was the liberating influence of the Fauves that permitted Kandinsky to put this approach into practice.

How valid is the analogy between painting and music? Although Kandinsky was careful to acknowledge the differences between the two art forms, he sought a painting style that, like music, was absolute, because it was divorced entirely from the "objective," material realm. While acknowledging that music can say far more than words, Schoenberg (who was also a competent painter) wrote, "I cannot unreservedly agree with the distinction between color and pitch. I find that a note is perceived by its color, one of whose dimensions is pitch. Color, then, is the great realm, pitch one of its provinces. . . . If the ear could discriminate between differences of color, it might be feasible to invent melodies that are built of colors." When a painter like Kandinsky carries such an approach through so completely, does he really lift his art to another plane? Kandinsky's supporters like to point out that representational painting has a "literary" content, and they object to such dependence on another art. But they do not explain why the "musical" content of non-objective painting should be superior. They believe music is a higher art than literature or painting because it is inherently nonrepresentational. This point of view has an ancient tradition that goes back to Plato and includes Plotinus, St. Augustine, and their medieval successors.

The case is difficult to argue, and it does not matter whether this theory is right or wrong, for the proof of the pudding is in the eating, not the recipe. Kandinsky's—or any artist's—ideas are not important to us unless we are convinced of the importance of the work itself. The painting reproduced here impresses us with its radiant freshness and vitality, even though we may be uncertain what exactly the artist has expressed.

FRANZ MARC. The subject matter of Franz Marc (1880–1916), another member of *Der Blaue Reiter,* was the unconscious life of animals in nature. The artist was motivated by the pantheistic feeling of the Romantics, which was heightened by his association with Kandinsky. His paintings represent humanity's desire to return to a state of harmony with the universe—a central concept of Rudolf Steiner's theosophy. Marc's color symbolism is as personal as that of Van Gogh, who had inspired his early work (see page 775). He wrote: "Blue is the masculine principle, robust and spiritual. Yellow is the feminine principle, gentle, serene, sensual. Red is matter, brutal and heavy." But it was the Orphism of Robert Delaunay (see page 814), with whom he formed a friendship in 1912, that showed Marc the full potential of color to express his mystical beliefs. Later that year, his discovery of Futurism (see page 815) enabled him to depict the dynamism of nature by creating rhythms that echo those of the cosmos, or so he believed. Marc's poetic vision attained apocalyptic intensity in *Animal Destinies* (fig. 24-10), with its interpenetrating crystalline forms looking like so many pieces of jagged stained glass. The picture is even more powerful than Stubbs'

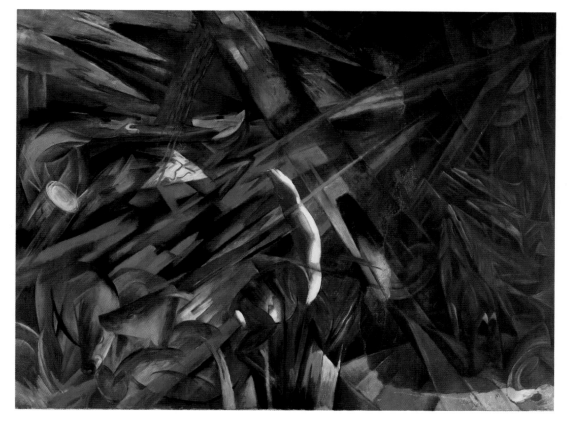

24-10. Franz Marc. *Animal Destinies*. 1913. Oil on canvas, 6'4½" x 8'7" (1.94 x 2.62 m). Öffentliche Kunstsammlung Basel, Kunstmuseum, Switzerland

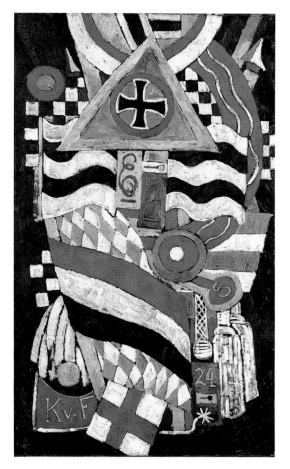

24-11. Marsden Hartley. *Portrait of a German Officer*. 1914. Oil on canvas, 68¼ x 41⅜" (173 x 104 cm). The Metropolitan Museum of Art, New York

Lion Attacking a Horse (see fig. 21-9) in evoking the terrifying forces of nature that overwhelm these uncomprehending beasts. Here the artist was indeed on the verge of depicting the "higher" symbolic reality he sought. A year later he abandoned representation almost entirely for an abstract style no less advanced than Kandinsky's. Soon, however, he was drafted into World War I, which claimed his life.

MARSDEN HARTLEY. Americans became familiar with the Fauves through exhibitions from 1908 onward. After the pivotal Armory Show of 1913, which introduced the latest European art to New York, there was a growing interest in the German Expressionists as well (see page 804). The driving force behind the modernist movement in the United States was the photographer Alfred Stieglitz (see page 925), who almost single-handedly supported many of its early members. To him modernism meant abstraction and its related concepts. Among the most important works by the Stieglitz group are the canvases painted by Marsden Hartley (1887–1943) in Munich during the early years of World War I under the direct influence of Kandinsky. *Portrait of a German Officer* (fig. 24-11) is a masterpiece of design from 1914, the year Hartley was invited to exhibit with *Der Blaue Reiter*. He had already been introduced to Futurism and to several offshoots of Cubism, including Orphism (see page 814), which he used to discipline Kandinsky's supercharged surface. The emblematic image is an allusion to Hartley's lover, who was killed during the war. It includes the insignia, epaulets, Maltese cross, and other details from an officer's uniform of the day.

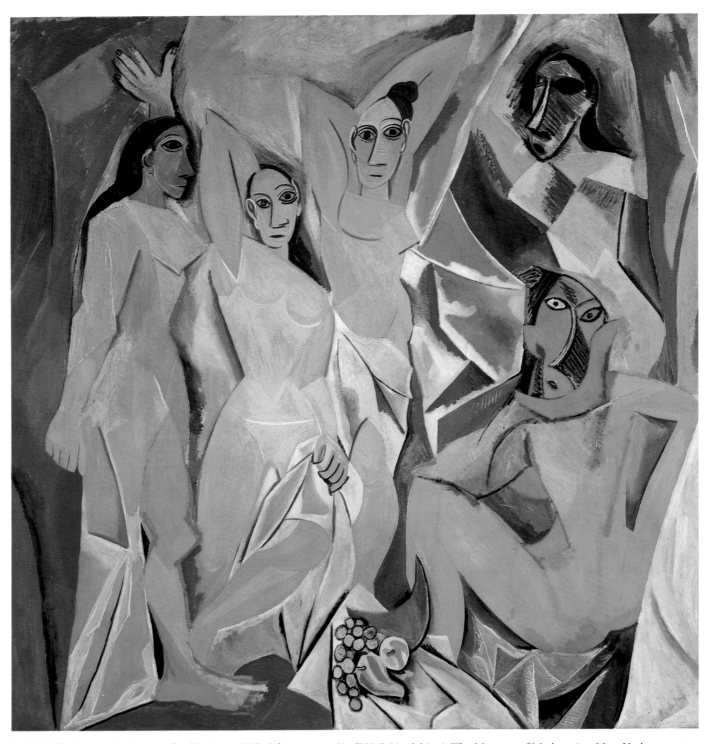

24-12. Pablo Picasso. *Les Demoiselles d'Avignon.* 1907. Oil on canvas, 8' x 7'8" (2.44 x 2.34 m). The Museum of Modern Art, New York
ACQUIRED THROUGH THE LILLIE P. BLISS BEQUEST

ABSTRACTION

The second of our main currents is abstraction. When discussing Kandinsky, we said that the term is usually taken to mean analyzing and simplifying observed reality into geometric shapes. Literally it means "to draw away from, to separate." Actually, abstraction goes into the making of any work of art, whether the artist knows it or not, since even the most painstakingly realistic portrayal can never be an entirely faithful replica. The process was not conscious and controlled, however, until the Early Renaissance, when artists first analyzed the shapes of nature in terms of mathematical bodies (see pages 438–40). Cézanne and Seurat revived this approach and explored it further. They are the direct ancestors of the abstract movement in twentieth-century art. The difference, as one critic has noted, is that after 1900 abstraction became both a premise and a goal, not simply a reductive refinement. Abstraction was the most distinctive and consistent feature of twentieth-century painting, to which even its most outspoken opponents responded.

PICASSO'S DEMOISELLES D'AVIGNON. It is difficult to imagine the birth of modern abstraction without Pablo Picasso. About 1905 he gradually abandoned the melancholy lyricism of his Blue Period (see fig. 23-23) for a more robust style that was stimulated as much by the Fauves as by the retrospective exhibitions of the great Post-Impressionists. Picasso shared Matisse's enthusiasm for Gauguin and Cézanne, but he viewed these masters very differently. In 1907 he produced his own counterpart to *The Joy of Life,* a monumental canvas (fig. 24-12) so challenging that it outraged even Matisse. (They nevertheless remained lifelong friends and rivals who learned much from each other's example.) The title, *Les Demoiselles d'Avignon* (The Young Ladies of Avignon), which came from Picasso's friend André Salmon, does not refer to the town of that name but to Avignon Street in a notorious section of Barcelona near where the artist grew up. When Picasso started the picture, it was to be a temptation scene in a brothel, but he ended up with a composition of five nudes and a still life. But what nudes! Their savage aggressiveness makes Matisse's generalized figures in *The Joy of Life* (see fig. 24-1) seem incredibly innocent.

The three on the left are angular distortions of classical figures, but the violently dislocated features and bodies of the other two have all the "barbaric" qualities of ethnographic art. Following Gauguin's lead, the Fauves had discovered African and Oceanic sculpture, and in turn had introduced Picasso to it. Nonetheless it was Picasso, not the Fauves, who used primitivist art as a battering ram against the classical conception of beauty. Not only the proportions but also the organic integrity of the human body are denied here, so that the canvas (in the apt description of one critic) "resembles a field of broken glass."

Picasso, then, has destroyed a great deal. What has he gained in the process? Once we recover from the initial shock, we begin to see that the destruction is quite methodical. Everything—the figures as well as their setting—is broken up into angular wedges or facets. These, we will note, are not flat, but shaded in a way that gives them a certain three-dimensionality. We cannot always be sure whether they are concave or convex. Some look like chunks of solidified space, others like fragments of translucent bodies. They constitute a unique kind of matter, which imposes a new continuity on the entire canvas. *Les Demoiselles,* unlike *The Joy of Life,* can no longer be read as an image of the external world. Its world is its own, analogous to nature but constructed along different principles. Picasso's revolutionary "building material," made up of voids and solids, is hard to describe exactly. After seeing an exhibition of paintings by Picasso's friend Georges Braque (see below) in 1909, Louis Vauxcelles, the same critic who named Fauvism, dubbed the new style Cubism after Matisse described the pictures as consisting of little cubes.

Analytic Cubism

Les Demoiselles owes a great deal to Cézanne. The artist had carefully studied Cézanne's late work, and found in his abstract treatment of volume and space the structural units from which to derive the faceted shapes of what became known as Analytic (or Facet) Cubism. The link is clearer in *Portrait of Ambroise Vollard*

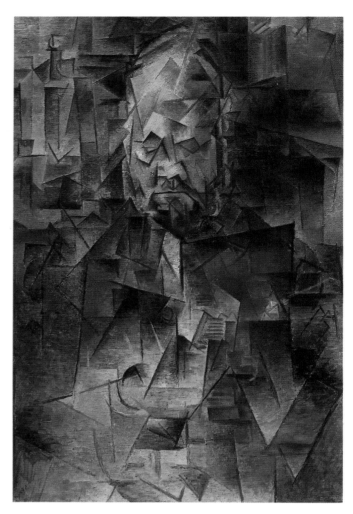

24-13. Pablo Picasso. *Portrait of Ambroise Vollard.* 1910.
Oil on canvas, 36¼ x 25⅝" (92 x 65 cm).
The Pushkin State Museum of Fine Arts, Moscow

(fig. 24-13), which Picasso painted three years later. (Vollard [1865–1939] was one of the leading print publishers and dealers of the time.) The facets are small and precise, more like prisms, and the canvas has the balance and refinement of a fully mature style.

Contrasts of color and texture, so pronounced in *Les Demoiselles,* are now reduced to a minimum. The subdued tonality of the picture approaches monochrome, so as not to compete with the design. The structure has become so complex and systematic that it would seem entirely calculated if the "imprismed" sitter's face did not emerge with such dramatic force. Indeed, this is as commanding a portrait as Ingres' *Louis Bertin* (see fig. 21-31), one that fully conveys the power of Vollard's complex personality. There is no trace of the "barbaric" distortions in *Les Demoiselles;* they had served their purpose. Cubism had become an abstract style in the purely modern sense, but it was not any further removed from observed reality. Picasso may have been playing an elaborate game of hide-and-seek with nature, but he still needed the visible world to stimulate his creative powers. The nonobjective realm held no appeal for him, then or later.

Just as the art of the twentieth century was distinguished by abstraction from an early date, so its music has often been marked by atonality, a rejection of the major and minor diatonic scales, the rules of harmony in general, and especially the importance of the tonic (the first tone of the scale in which a given piece was written; see box page 606). From about 1550, most European music had centered around the tonic note, in effect a musical "home base" to which the melody tended to return. However, a frequent return to the tonic note is not actually required by the rules of harmony or the tempered scale (see page 606)—a fact that had already been exploited by a number of German Romantic composers, starting with Wagner, who emphasized chromaticism (musical color) at the expense of tonality (which stresses the importance of the tonic). It was almost inevitable that the final break with tonality would be made by a post-Romantic.

The final step was taken by Arnold Schoenberg (1874–1951). The hypersensitive content of his early work, like Mahler's, sometimes brings to mind the world of neurosis explored by his great contemporary in Vienna Sigmund Freud, the pioneer of modern psychology. His *Transfigured Night* (1899) has the sensuality of the famous Liebestod duet in Wagner's opera *Tristan and Isolde*. Schoenberg, an Expressionist by inclination, later became a friend of Kandinsky and a capable artist in his own right. Schoenberg, however, moved almost immediately into complete atonality and dissonance with *Erwartung* (Expectation), a one-act stage work for soprano that stands the Liebestod on its ear thematically and musically. In 1912 he took the further step of abandoning the pitches used in normal singing for "speech-song" (German, *Sprechstimme*) in the song-cycle *Pierrot Lunaire*. Commissioned and first performed by the actress Albertine Zehme, it was based partly on the performance practices of contemporary German melodrama and cabaret, with which Schoenberg was thoroughly familiar, having written a cycle of cabaret songs at the beginning of his career. Schoenberg nevertheless continued to make use of other traditional techniques of composition, which he built into pieces of extraordinary intricacy.

If any one event announced the arrival of twentieth-century music, it was the ballet *The Rite of Spring* (1913) by the Russian-born composer Igor Stravinsky (1882–1971), the last of three scores commissioned in 1910–13 by the impresario Sergei Diaghilev for his Ballets Russes (see box page 818). While a pupil of the nationalist composer Nikolai Rimsky-Korsakov (1844–1908) in St. Petersburg, Stravinsky had revealed a striking gift for melody in the Russian tradition and an unusual sense of rhythm. These were evident in his first two ballets, *The Firebird* and *Petrushka*, which created a sensation in Paris because of their exoticism. The primitivism and overt eroticism of *The Rite of Spring* caused a famous riot at its premiere, although there is evidence that it was staged. Stravinsky was the musical counterpart to Picasso as a giant of his time. Indeed, not only was *The Rite* similar to Picasso's *Les Demoiselles d'Avignon* (see fig. 24-12) in its impact, but Stravinsky's rhythmic "cells" were analogous to the facets in Analytic Cubism: both served as building blocks to create dynamic compositions of unprecedented complexity. Like Picasso, Stravinsky turned to classicism after 1920, cultivating a lean style that stressed clarity and balance while rejecting any concession to Romanticism. His position in music was comparable to Picasso's in art: until the end of World War II, he was by far the leading composer in the world. The culmination of this phase of Stravinsky's career is the *Symphony in C* (1940) and *Symphony in Three Movements* (1945), which restored melody and rhythm to prominence in his work. Finally, toward the end of his long life, he successfully adopted the serialism of his contemporary Arnold Schoenberg, who emerged as the world's most influential composer only after 1945.

Synthetic Cubism

By 1910 Cubism was well established as an alternative to Fauvism, and Picasso had been joined by a number of other artists. The most important was Georges Braque (1882–1963), who had started out as a Fauve painter and then helped to create Cubism. The two collaborated so closely that their work at times is difficult to tell apart. Both of them (it is not clear who deserves the main credit) launched the next phase of Cubism, which was even bolder than the first. Usually called Synthetic Cubism because it puts forms back together, it is also known as Collage Cubism, after the French word for "paste-up," the technique that started it all. We see its beginnings in Picasso's *Still Life with Chair Caning* of 1912 (fig. 24-14). Most of the painting consists of facets. Because they were already abstract signs, the letters could not be translated into prismatic shapes. But beneath the still life is a piece of imitation chair caning, which was pasted onto the canvas, and the picture is "framed" by a piece of rope. This inclusion of found materials has a most remarkable effect: the abstract still life appears to rest on a real surface (the chair caning) as if it were on a tray, and the reality of this tray is further emphasized by the rope.

Within a year, Picasso and Braque were producing still lifes composed almost entirely of cut-and-pasted scraps of material, with only a few painted lines added to complete the design. In *Le Courrier* by Braque (fig. 24-15) we recognize strips of imitation wood graining, part of a tobacco wrapper with a contrasting stamp, half of the masthead of a newspaper, and a bit of newsprint made into a playing card (the ace of hearts). Why did Picasso and

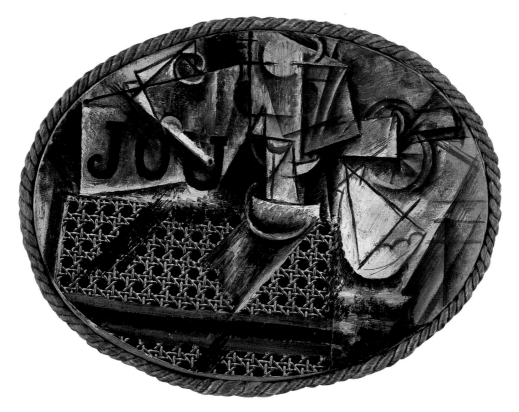

24-14. Pablo Picasso. *Still Life with Chair Caning.* 1912. Collage of oil, oilcloth, and pasted paper simulating chair caning on canvas, 10½ x 13¾" (26.7 x 35 cm). Musée Picasso, Paris

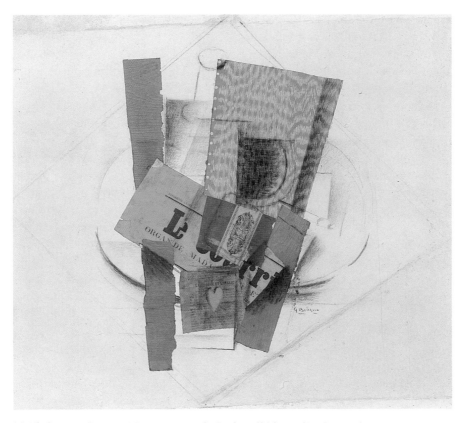

24-15. Georges Braque. *Newspaper, Bottle, Packet of Tobacco (Le Courrier).*
1914. Collage of charcoal, gouache, pencil, ink, and pasted paper on cardboard,
20⅝ x 25" (52.4 x 63.5 cm). Philadelphia Museum of Art

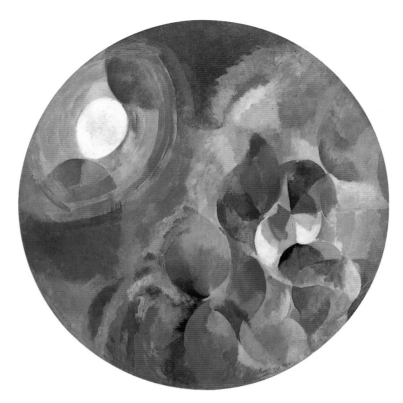

24-16. Robert Delaunay. *Simultaneous Contrasts: Sun and Moon*. 1913. Oil on canvas, diameter 53" (134.5 cm). The Museum of Modern Art, New York

Braque suddenly prefer the contents of the wastepaper basket to brush and paint? They wanted to explore their new idea of the picture as a tray on which to "serve" the still life, and found that the best way was to put real things on the tray. The ingredients of a collage play a double role. They have been shaped and combined, then drawn or painted upon to give them a representational meaning. Yet they do not lose their original identity as scraps of material, they remain "outsiders" in the world of art. Their function is both to represent (to be a part of an image) and to present (to be themselves). Thus they give the collage a self-sufficiency that no Analytic Cubist picture can possibly have. A tray, after all, is a self-contained area, detached from the rest of the physical world. Unlike a painting, it cannot show more than is actually on it.

The difference between the two phases of Cubism may also be defined in terms of picture space. Analytic Cubism still has a certain depth, so that the painted surface acts as a window through which we perceive the remains of the perspective space of the Renaissance. Although fragmented and redefined, this space lies behind the picture plane and has no visible limits. Potentially, it may even contain objects that are hidden from our view. In Synthetic Cubism, on the contrary, the picture space lies in front of the plane of the "tray." Space is not created by illusionistic devices, such as modeling and foreshortening, but by the overlapping of layers of pasted materials. This nonperspective space is not violated even when, as in *Le Courrier,* the apparent thickness of these materials and their distance from each other are increased by a bit of shading here and there. Synthetic Cubism, then, offers a basi-

cally new concept of space, the first since Masaccio. It is a true landmark in the history of painting.

Before long Picasso and Braque discovered that they could maintain this new pictorial space without the use of pasted materials. They only had to paint as if they were making collages. World War I, however, put an end to their collaboration and delayed the further development of Synthetic Cubism, which thus did not reach its height until the following decade.

Orphism

The Cubism of Picasso and Braque was little concerned with color—an issue addressed finally by Robert Delaunay (1885–1941) and his wife, Sonia Delaunay-Terk (1885–1979). They evolved a totally abstract style called Orphism (after the legendary Orpheus) by the poet Apollinaire (1880–1918), the chief theorist of the movement. Following the concepts of Chevreul, Seurat, and Gauguin, the Delaunays wanted to produce pure color harmonies as independent of nature as music. Late in 1912 Delaunay began to paint his series *Simultaneous Contrasts* (fig. 24-16), in which the swirling movement is meant to evoke the rhythms pulsating throughout the universe. The idea was in the air. At almost the same time, the Czech painter Frantisek Kupka (1871–1957), working independently in Paris, came to the identical solution. It was soon taken up as well by the Americans Stanton Macdonald-Wright (1890–1973) and Morgan Russell (1886–1953), who were also active in Paris and who called their movement Synchromism. Orphism proved to be short-lived, however. Even the Delaunays were able to maintain

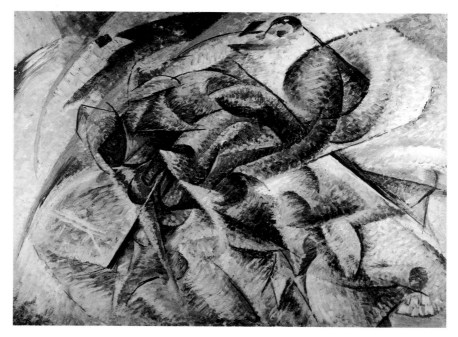

24-17. Umberto Boccioni. *Dynamism of a Cyclist*. 1913.
Oil on canvas, 27⅝ x 37⅜" (70 x 95 cm). Collection Gianni Mattioli, Milan

this nonobjective style for only a few years and soon turned to Futurism. Nevertheless, the movement was of great importance. Among its early members were Marcel Duchamp and his brother Raymónd Duchamp-Villon. In addition to Franz Marc, it affected Fernand Léger, Marc Chagall, and Paul Klee.

Futurism

As originally conceived by Picasso and Braque, Cubism was a subtle formal discipline applied to traditional subjects: still life, portraiture, the nude. Other painters, however, saw in the new style a strong affinity with the geometric precision of engineering that made it uniquely attuned to the dynamism of modern life. The short-lived Futurist movement in Italy represents this attitude. In 1909–10 its disciples, led by the poet Filippo Tommaso Marinetti (1876–1944), issued a series of manifestos violently rejecting the past and exalting the beauty of the machine. [See Primary Sources, no. 85, page 971.]

At first they used techniques developed from Post-Impressionism to convey the surge of industrial society, but these were otherwise static compositions, still dependent upon representational images. By adopting the simultaneous views of Analytic Cubism in *Dynamism of a Cyclist* (fig. 24-17), Umberto Boccioni (1882–1916), the most original of the Futurists, was able to communicate the energy of rapid pedaling across time and space far more tellingly than if he had actually depicted the human figure. In traditional art the subject could be seen in only one time and place. Boccioni was partly inspired by the motion photogra-

phy of Eadweard Muybridge and his successors (see pages 800–01). But in the flexible vocabulary provided by Cubism, he found the means of expressing what Albert Einstein had defined in 1905 in his special theory of relativity—the twentieth century's new sense of time, space, and energy. Moreover, Boccioni suggests the unique quality of the modern experience. With his pulsating movement, the cyclist has become an extension of his environment, from which he is now indistinguishable.

Futurism died out in World War I. Its leading artists were killed by the same vehicles of destruction they had glorified only a few years earlier in their revolutionary manifestos. However, their legacy was soon taken up in France, the United States, and, above all, Russia.

Cubo-Futurism

As its name implies, Cubo-Futurism took its style from Picasso and Braque, and based its theories on Futurist tracts. The movement arose in Russia a few years before World War I as the result of close contacts with the leading European art centers. The Russian Futurists were, above all, modernists. They welcomed industry, which was spreading rapidly throughout Russia, as the foundation of a new society and the means for conquering that old Russian enemy, nature. Unlike the Italian Futurists, however, the Russians rarely extolled the machine, least of all as an instrument of war.

Central to Cubo-Futurist thinking was the concept of *zaum,* a term that has no counterpart in English. Invented by Russian poets, *zaum* was a "trans-sense" (as opposed to the Dadaist "nonsense"; see page 831) language based on new word forms and syntax. In theory *zaum* could be understood universally, since it was thought that meaning was implicit in the basic sounds and patterns of speech. When applied to painting, *zaum* provided the artist with complete freedom to redefine the style and content of art. The picture surface was now seen as the sole conveyer of meaning through its appearance. Hence the subject of a work of art became its visual elements and their formal arrangement. However, because Cubo-Futurism was concerned with means, not ends, it failed to provide the actual content that is found in modernism. The Cubo-Futurists were more important as theorists than as artists, but they provided the springboard for later Russian movements.

The new world envisioned by the Russian modernists redefined roles of man and woman, and it was in Russia that women emerged as artistic equals in a way that was not achieved in Europe or America until considerably later. The finest painter among the Cubo-Futurists was Liubov Popova (1889–1924), who studied in Paris in 1912 and visited Italy in 1914. The combination of Cubism and Futurism that she absorbed abroad is seen in *The Traveler* (fig. 24-18). The treatment of forms remains essentially Cubist, but the painting shares the Futurist obsession with representing dynamic motion in time and space. The jumble of image fragments creates the impression of objects seen in rapid succession. The tumultuous interaction of forms with their environment across the plane threatens to extend the painting into the surrounding space. At the same time, the strong modeling draws attention to the surface and gives it a relief-like quality that is enhanced by the vigorous texture.

Suprematism

The first purely Russian art of the twentieth century was Suprematism. It was devised by Kazimir Malevich (1878–1935), who wanted to reduce painting to a "supreme" reality based on geometry, because it is an independent abstraction—hence the movement's name. According to the artist, Suprematism was also a philosophical color system constructed in time and space. His space was an intuitive one, with both scientific and mystical overtones. The flat plane replaces volume, depth, and perspective as a means of defining space. Each side or point represents one of the three spatial dimensions, while the fourth stands for the fourth dimension: time. Like Einstein's formula $E=mc^2$ for the theory of relativity, Suprematism has an elegant simplicity that belies the intense effort required to synthesize a complex set of ideas and reduce them to a fundamental "law." The relationship between art and science is closer than we might think, for despite the differences in approach, they are united by the imagination. In fact, the key to solving the theory of relativity came to Einstein as a visual image.

When it first appeared in 1915 in Malevich's painting of a black quadrilateral within a white border, Suprematism had much the same impact on Russian artists that Einstein's theory had on scientists. It unveiled a world never seen before, one that

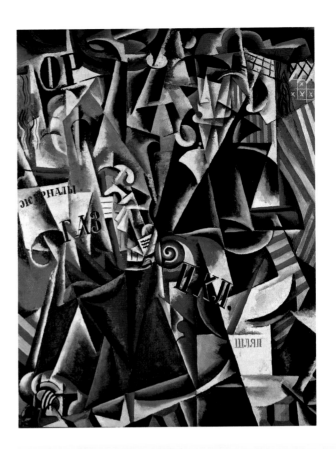

24-18. Liubov Popova. *The Traveler.* 1915.
Oil on canvas, 56 x 41 ½" (142.2 x 105.4 cm).
Norton Simon Art Foundation, Pasadena California.

During this time, the pre-Revolutionary movement of Suprematism and the post-Revolutionary school of Constructivism emerged and became crystallized. . . . so that when movement and exchange of ideas with the outside world again became possible in the early twenties, these two unknown movements made a tremendous impact on post-war Western Europe. . . .

Yet in many ways the mood in war-time Russia, reflected in Futurism and Non-sense Realism, resembled the German Dada movement. There was the same feeling of uselessness, the same sense of victimization in a hostile, senseless world. The ludicrous masks that the Futurists wore or painted on their faces. . .the guy-like costume they adopted, the undignified public brawls and vociferous street language of their paintings and poetry, all these typical Russian Futurist traits indicate a Dada-like rejection of reality, a bitter mocking of themselves as useless misfits in a decadent society. This mood was essentially non-creative, negative, passive.

—Camilla Gray. *The Russian Experiment in Art, 1863–1922.*
The World of Art. New York: Thames & Hudson, 1986, p. 182.
Originally published in 1962 by Harry N. Abrams, Inc.

CAMILLA GRAY (1936–1971), a British scholar who died of hepatitis when she was thirty-five years old, wrote *The Great Experiment: Russian Art 1863–1922* (*The Russian Experiment in Art, 1863–1922*) when she was in her mid-twenties. Gray was composer Sergei Prokofiev's daughter-in-law. Published in 1962, it was the first comprehensive survey of the Russian avant-garde to demonstrate how it evolved out of late nineteenth-century art. Other books have since appeared, but none has replaced Gray's as the best book on the subject.

was unmistakably modern. Malevich later began to tilt his quadrilaterals and to simplify his paintings still further in search of the ultimate work of art. These efforts culminated in *Suprematist Composition: White on White* (fig. 24-19), his most famous composition, which limits art to its fewest possible components. It is tempting to dismiss such a radical reduction as an absurdity. Seen in person, however, the canvas is surprisingly persuasive. The shapes, created by two subtly different shades of white, have a visionary purity that makes other paintings seem needlessly complex.

The heyday of Suprematism was over by the early 1920s. In response to the growing diversity and fragmentation of Russian art, its followers defected to other movements, especially the Constructivism led by Vladimir Tatlin (see pages 871–72).

FANTASY

Fantasy follows a less clear-cut course than expressionism or abstraction, because it depends on a state of mind more than on any particular style. The one thing all painters of fantasy have in common is the belief that imagination, "the inner eye," is more important than the outside world. We must be careful how we use the term *fantasy*. It originated in psychoanalytic theory and meant something very different in the early twentieth century than it does now. Fantasy was thought of as mysterious and pro-

found—anything but the lighthearted and superficial view we take of it today.

Why did private fantasy come to loom so large in early-twentieth-century art? There were several causes. First, the rift that developed between reason and imagination in the wake of the Enlightenment tended to dissolve the heritage of myth and legend that had been the common channel of private fantasy in earlier times. Second, artists had greater freedom—and insecurity—within society, giving them a sense of isolation and favoring an introspective attitude. Finally, the Romantic cult of emotion prompted the artist to seek out subjective experience and to accept its validity. We saw the process beginning at the end of the eighteenth century in the art of Goya and Fuseli (see figs. 21- 22 and 21-43). In early-nineteenth-century painting, private fantasy was still a minor current, but by 1900 it had become a major trend, thanks to Symbolism on the one hand and the naive vision of artists like Henri Rousseau on the other.

GIORGIO DE CHIRICO. The heritage of Romanticism can be seen most clearly in the pictures painted in Paris just before World War I by the Italian artist Giorgio de Chirico (1888–1978). Illuminated by the cold light of the full moon, the deserted square in *Mystery and Melancholy of a Street* (fig. 24-20), with its tilted perspective and rapidly diminishing arcades, has all the poetry of

24-19. Kazimir Malevich. *Suprematist Composition: White on White*. 1918. Oil on canvas, 31¼ x 31¼" (79.4 x 79.4 cm). The Museum of Modern Art, New York

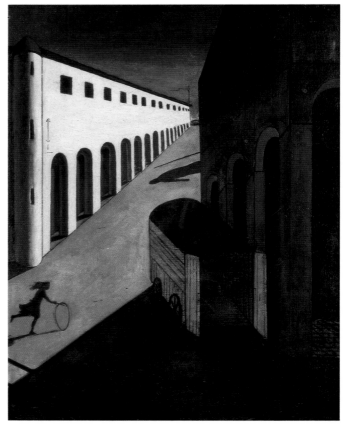

24-20. Giorgio de Chirico. *Mystery and Melancholy of a Street*. 1914. Oil on canvas, 34¼ x 28½" (87 x 72.4 cm). Private collection

By far the most adventurous theater before World War I was to be found in Russia, thus preparing the way for even more radical experiments after the Russian Revolution of 1917. The most famous of the Russian reformers remains Konstantin Stanislavsky (1863–1938), who was a cofounder of the Moscow Art Theater with Vladimir Nemirovich-Danchenko (1858–1943). Stanislavsky's legacy is clouded by a lack of fully authentic texts, but in general he placed greatest emphasis on the actor, despite the fact that he never adopted the "star" system. Stanislavsky insisted on a rigorous training of body, voice, and mind based on a thorough understanding of stagecraft, reality, and the drama itself, so that the action would unfold naturally and convincingly, although he was by no means a Realist. Stanislavsky's theories were later practiced in the modified American form known as "method acting" (see box page 850).

The key figure in early Russian modernism, however, was Vsevelod Meyerhold (1874–1940), who considered the director the main creative force in the theater. He was employed by every Russian avant-garde theater, including Stanislavsky's Moscow Art Theater, but never lasted very long in any position because his experiments were regarded as too bold. For example, he dispensed with the theatrical curtain and set his productions in symbolic scenery or even on a bare stage. Alexander Tairov (1885–1950) adopted a centrist position: like Stanislavsky, he stressed the importance of the actor but followed Meyerhold in treating the play as the point of departure for the director's creativity. At the same time, he maintained that there is no relationship between art and life and that theater should be like the sacred dances of ancient temples. The ritual effect of his productions, which stressed unity of word, music, and dance, was similar in intent to Classical Greek theater. At the opposite end of the spectrum was the equally innovative Nikolai Evreinov (1879–1953), whose "monodramas," such as *The Theater of the Soul* (1912), sought to lead the audience to a greater understanding by drawing on what he believed was humanity's innate theatricality, which leads people to seek a higher reality.

The Russians had a great impact on French theater. The first to exercise his influence was Sergei Diaghilev (1872–1929), whose publication *The World of Art* promoted Symbolist art, literature, and theater. The ballet company he took to Paris in 1909 met with such success that he formed the Ballets Russes, featuring the great dancer Vasily Nijinsky (1890–1950), the choreography of Mikhail Fokine (1880–1942), the music of Igor Stravinsky and his teacher Nikolai Rimsky-Korsakov, and the designs of Aleksandr Benois (1870–1960) and Léon Bakst (1866–1924). With the onset of the Russian Revolution the company remained in Paris; it later employed Picasso, Braque, and De Chirico, among other artists, as stage and costume designers.

Under Russian influence, Jacques Rouché (1862–1957) launched the periodical *Modern Theater* simultaneously with the Théâtre des Arts in 1910. His ideas were to bear fruit at the Paris Opéra, where he was appointed director four years later and remained until 1936. It was at the Théâtre des Arts that Jacques Copeau (1879–1949), who became the leading figure in French theater between the wars, got his start. He adopted the opposite position of Meyerhold's in arguing that only the actor was essential and that the director's primary responsibility was the faithful translation of the script into a "poetry of the theater." And whereas Rouché thought primarily in visual terms, Copeau argued for a return to the bare stage.

For all of its inventiveness, early-twentieth-century theater contributed little in the way of new plays. The main impetus in

---

Romantic reverie. It also has a strangely sinister air. This is an "ominous" scene in the full sense of the term: everything here suggests an omen, a portent of unknown and disquieting significance. The artist himself could not fully explain the illogical elements in these paintings—the empty furniture van or the girl with the hoop—that trouble and fascinate us. De Chirico called this *Metaphysical Painting:* "We who know the signs of the metaphysical alphabet are aware of the joy and the solitude which are enclosed by a portico, by the corner of a street, or even in a room, on the surface of a table, or between the sides of a box. . . . The minutely accurate and prudently weighed use of surfaces and volumes constitutes the canon of the metaphysical aesthetic." [See also Primary Sources, no. 85, page 971.] Later, after he had returned to Italy, De Chirico adopted a conservative style and disowned his early works, as if embarrassed at having put his dream world on display. He nevertheless secretly continued to paint copies to meet commercial demand.

MARC CHAGALL. The power of nostalgia, so apparent in *Mystery and Melancholy of a Street,* also dominates the work of Marc Chagall (1887–1985), a Russian Jew who went to Paris in 1910. *I and the Village* (fig. 24-21) weaves dreamlike memories of Russian folk tales, Jewish proverbs, and the look of Russia into a glowing Cubist vision:

But please defend me against people who speak of "anecdote" and "fairy tales" in my work. A cow and woman to me are the same—in a picture both are merely elements of a composition [which] have different values of plasticity, but not different poetic values. In the large cow's head in *I and the Village* I made a small cow and woman milking visible through its muzzle because I needed that sort of form, there, for my composition. Whatever else may have grown out of these compositional arrangements is secondary. The fact that I made use of cows, milkmaids, roosters, and provincial Russian architecture as my source forms is because they are part of the environment from which I spring. . . .

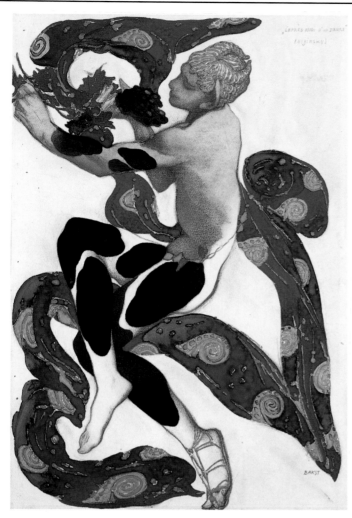

Leon Bakst. *Nijinsky in L'Après-midi d'un Faune* (costume design). 1912. Watercolor, paper, and gouache, sheet: 15⅜ x 10½" (39.1 x 26.7 cm). Wadsworth Atheneum, Hartford, Connecticut

dramatic writing came from Ireland. There plays with a Gaelic focus were produced by the Irish National Theater Society, better known as the Abbey Theater, where it was housed after 1904. The most important playwrights were the poet William Butler Yeats (1865–1939), Lady Augusta Gregory (1863–1935), and John Millington Synge (1871–1909). Yeats' early work sprang from the writing of the French Symbolists he had met in Paris. He was primarily concerned with restoring the importance of writing to theater; thus, his poetic-mythic approach was the opposite of Lady Gregory's, whose style was realistic-domestic. It was Yeats who convinced Synge to return from Paris to write about Irish peasant life. Synge successfully synthesized the best features of Yeats and Lady Gregory in the two finest dramas staged by the Abbey: *Riders to the Sea* (1904) and *The Playboy of the Western World* (1907). Synge was fearless in tackling controversial subjects that went against customary beliefs—*Playboy* caused riots wherever it played—but the real secret of his success was his unique form of poetic prose.

In England, the most important theorist was the director and designer Edward Gordon Craig (1872–1966), the son of Ellen Terry and Edward Goodwin, whose thinking laid the ground for many of the key concepts of modern directing. Like Meyerhold, he conceived of the director as an artist who created theater as a work of art independent of the drama itself by utilizing lights and simply painted screens. No one, however, had more impact on theater than Max Reinhardt (1873–1943), who succeeded Otto Brahm as director of the Deutsches Theater in Berlin. He realized that each play demanded a different approach, without adhering to any single system. In place of the conventions of the day he insisted that the director rethink and control every detail of the production, which was prepared in close collaboration with his actors and designers.

The experiences of Chagall's childhood were so important to him that his imagination shaped and reshaped them for years.

MARCEL DUCHAMP. In Paris shortly before World War I we meet another artist of fantasy, the French painter Marcel Duchamp (1887–1968). After basing his early style on Cézanne, he created a dynamic version of Analytic Cubism similar to Futurism by superimposing successive phases of movement on one another, much like multiple-exposure photography (see fig. 23-50a, b). His *Nude Descending a Staircase* (fig. 24-22) caused a scandal at the Armory Show because it went against all traditional notions of what a nude should look like. Although his objective was simply to paint "a static representation of movement," this parody of the human figure already shows the ironic wit that was to underlie his later work.

Duchamp's development soon took a far more disturbing turn. In *The Bride* (fig. 24-23) from 1912, we look in vain for any

resemblance, however remote, to the human form. What we see instead is a mechanism that seems part motor, part distilling apparatus. It is beautifully engineered to serve no purpose whatsoever. The title cannot be irrelevant: by lettering it right onto the canvas, Duchamp has emphasized its importance. Yet it remains truly puzzling. Evidently the artist intended the machine as a kind of modern fetish that acts as a metaphor of human sexuality. He satirizes the scientific outlook on humanity by "analyzing" the bride until she is reduced to a complicated piece of plumbing that seems totally dysfunctional, physically and psychologically. Thus the picture represents the negative counterpart of the glorification of the machine so stridently proclaimed by the Futurists. We may further see in Duchamp's pessimistic outlook a response to the gathering forces that were soon to be unleashed in World War I and topple the political order that had been created a hundred years earlier at the Congress of Vienna following Napoleon's final defeat.

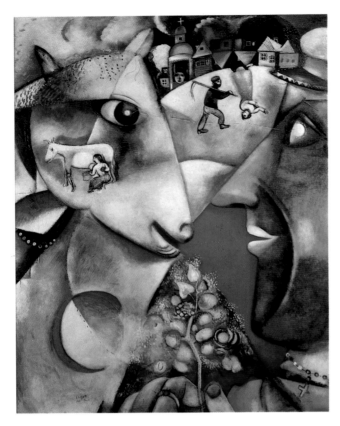

24-21. Marc Chagall. *I and the Village*. 1911.
Oil on canvas, 6'3⅝" x 4'11½" (1.92 x 1.51 m).
The Museum of Modern Art, New York

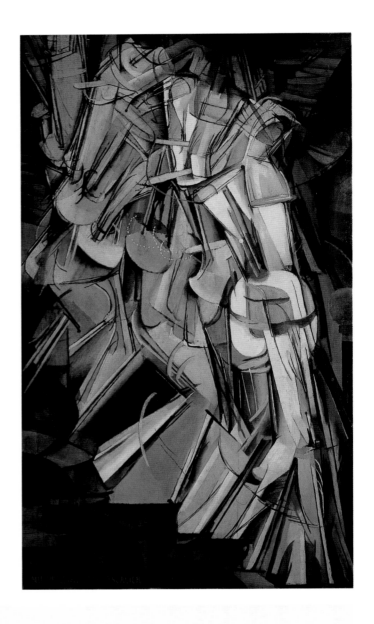

(ABOVE RIGHT) 24-22. Marcel Duchamp. *Nude Descending a Staircase No. 2*. 1912. Oil on canvas, 58 x 35" (147.3 x 89 cm). Philadelphia Museum of Art

One reason why public interest centered on the Nude, *I suspect, is that while obviously avant-garde, it was, paradoxically, less advanced, more gimmicky, than the Analytic Cubist pictures of the same date. With aid of its title, spectators could make out the cinematic action of the painting and, grasping it by that handle, could compare it in turn with their presumptive notions of what a nude descending a staircase should look like. Such possibilities are obviated by the greater abstractness of a Picasso or Braque of 1912. The* Nude's *place in modern painting is not far from that of Futurist painting. Its novel element— the "representation" of movement by the depiction, in one picture, of successive phases of an object in movement—was a* narrative, *not a* plastic, *innovation, and it did not open a new direction for painting.*

Yet if the "mechanism" of Nude Descending a Staircase *is like that of Futurism, its spirit is quite different. Looking not to its manifestoes but at the paintings themselves, particularly those of Umberto Boccioni, we become aware that Futurism frequently appeals to nostalgia and mystery (see Boccioni's* Farewells *or* The Forces of a Street; *fig. D-28). Duchamp's* Nude, *on the other hand, is unsentimental and ironic, and has an undercurrent of mordant wit. This last is rarely found in Futurism. . . .Duchamp had grasped Bergson's insight that humor is inherent to the image of man momentarily deprived of his human status and reduced to the state of an automaton or machine (for example, a man slipping on a banana peel). This kind of humor, as well as its converse, the humanization of the machine, was to be more deliberately explored in Duchamp's later creations.*

—William S. Rubin. *Dada and Surrealist Art.*
New York: Harry N. Abrams, Inc., 1968, [p. TK]

WILLIAM S. RUBIN (b. 1927), Director of Painting and Sculpture at the Museum of Modern Art, New York, from 1968 to 1973, is an authority on Dada and Surrealism. Like Werner Haftmann (see fig. 24-32), Rubin's acquaintance with many of the twentieth century's most important artists give his scholarly writing an unusually sympathetic understanding of artists and artworks. This passage on Duchamp's *Nude Descending the Staircase* is particularly perceptive in identifying the painting's strengths and limitations as an avant-garde work.

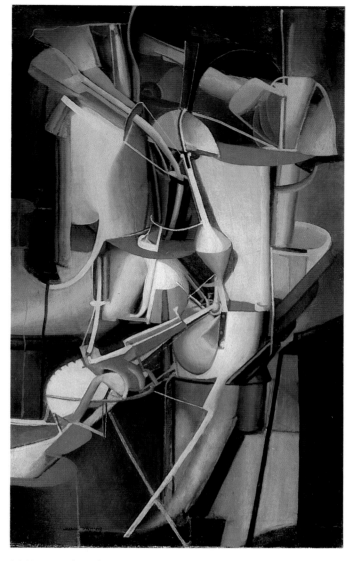

24-23. Marcel Duchamp. *The Bride*. 1912. Oil on canvas, 35⅛ x 21¾" (89.4 x 55.2 cm). Philadelphia Museum of Art

GEORGE BELLOWS. Although not among its founders, George Bellows (1882–1925) became the leading representative of the Ash Can School in its heyday. His greatest work, *Stag at Sharkey's* (fig. 24-24), shows why. No American artist had expressed such heroic energy. The painting continues the Realist tradition of Eakins' *William Rush Carving His Allegorical Figure of the Schuylkill River* (see fig. 22-24). Both place us in the scene as if we were present and use the play of light to pick out the figures against a dark background. Bellows' canvases were fully as shocking as Eakins' had been. Most late-nineteenth-century American artists had all but ignored urban life in favor of landscapes and genteel interiors. Compared with such works, the subjects and surfaces of the Ash Can School pictures had a disturbing rawness.

THE ARMORY SHOW. The Ash Can School was quickly eclipsed by the rush toward a more radical modernism set off by the Armory Show. Held in New York in 1913, this exhibition was an outgrowth of the Independents Show three years earlier, which had showcased the talents of a group of rising young artists known as the Eight. The Armory Show was intended to foster a "new spirit in art" by introducing the public to the latest trends in Europe and the United States. The exhibition began with a survey of French painting from the Romantics to the Post-Impressionists, and featured the Symbolists. The modern section was also heavily French, with a strong emphasis on Matisse and Picasso. There were curious lapses as well: Orphism had a prominent place while German Expressionism was poorly represented and Futurism was omitted completely. The selection of sculpture was haphazard at best. American art, which made up by far the largest part of the exhibition, included works by members of the Ash Can School, the Stieglitz group, and the Eight. While it failed to promote the interests of its organizers, the Armory Show did succeed in its goal of introducing a new cosmopolitanism into the American art scene. It also proved a success with collectors, who bought an astonishing number of works from the exhibition.

REALISM

THE ASH CAN SCHOOL. In the United States, the first wave of change began with the Ash Can School, which flourished in New York just before World War I. Centering on Robert Henri (1865–1929), who had studied with a pupil of Thomas Eakins at the Pennsylvania Academy, this group of artists was made up mainly of former illustrators for Philadelphia and New York newspapers. They were fascinated with the teeming life of the city slums and found an endless source of subjects in the everyday urban scene, to which they brought a reporter's eye for color and drama. Despite the socialist outlook that many of them shared, theirs was not an art of social commentary but one that felt the pulse of the city, in which they discovered vitality and richness while ignoring poverty and squalor. To capture these qualities they relied on rapid execution, inspired by Baroque and Post-Impressionist painting. This technique lends their canvases a sense of directness and spontaneous observation.

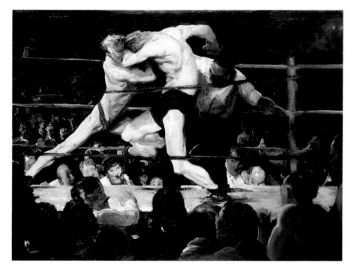

24-24. George Bellows. *Stag at Sharkey's*. 1909. Oil on canvas, 36¼ x 48¼" (92.1 x 122.6 cm). The Cleveland Museum of Art

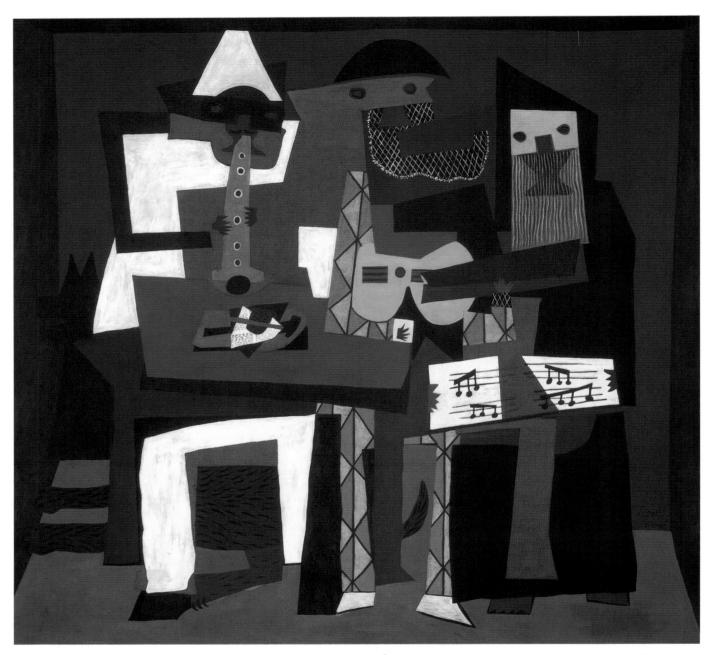

24-25. Pablo Picasso. *Three Musicians*. Summer 1921. Oil on canvas, 6'7" x 7'3¾" (2 x 2.3 m). The Museum of Modern Art, New York

PAINTING BETWEEN THE WARS

The Founders

As we examine painting between the wars, we shall find anything but an orderly progression. World War I had completely disrupted the evolution of modernism, and its end unleashed an unprecedented outpouring of art after a four-year creative lull. The responses were equally varied. Because they were already fully formed artists, the founders of modern painting—Picasso, Braque, Matisse, Kirchner, and Kandinsky—followed very different paths from those who had not yet reached maturity by 1914. Responding only to the dictates of their imaginations, they broke the rules they had established earlier; hence their development defies convenient categories. Rather than a simple linear develop-

ment, we must think in terms of multiple layers of varying depths that bear a shifting relation to one another.

PABLO PICASSO. We begin with Picasso, whose genius towers over the period. As a Spanish national living in Paris, he was not involved in World War I, unlike many French and German artists who served in the military and even lost their lives. This was a time of quiet experimentation that laid the foundation for Picasso's art of the next several decades. The results did not become fully apparent, however, until the early 1920s, following a period of intense development. *Three Musicians* (fig. 24-25) shows the fruit of that labor. It utilizes the "cut-paper style" of Synthetic Cubism so consistently that we cannot tell from the reproduction whether it is painted or pasted. The canvas revives a favorite

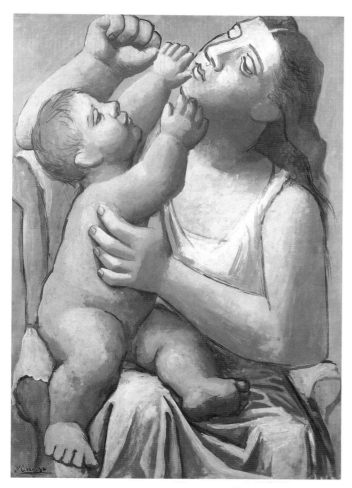

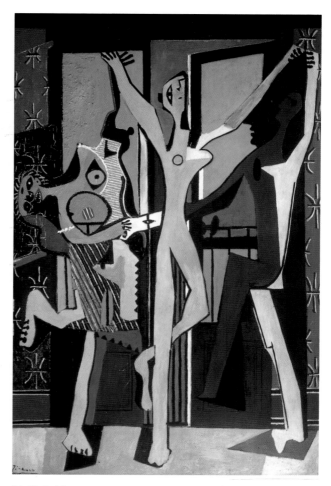

24-26. Pablo Picasso. *Mother and Child*. 1921–22.
Oil on canvas, 38 x 28" (96.7 x 71 cm).
The Alex L. Hillman Family Foundation, New York

24-27. Pablo Picasso. *Three Dancers*. 1925.
Oil on canvas, 7'1½" x 4'8¼" (2.15 x 1.43 m).
The Tate Gallery, London

theme of the artist's early years, the Italian commedia dell'arte (see box page 613). The shapes are locked together as tightly as the pieces of a jigsaw puzzle to create a colorful, almost jaunty composition. The effect is by no means lighthearted, however. On the contrary, the painting is a haunting evocation of the tragic mood following World War I. These musicians wear mysterious masks, like those of a primitive rite, which lend them a peculiar anonymity that is strangely unsettling. The piece they play must be anything but joyous, for the somber palette invests the scene with brooding solemnity.

By now Picasso was internationally famous. Cubism had spread throughout the Western world. It influenced not only other painters but sculptors and even architects. However, Picasso was already striking out in a new direction. Soon after the invention of Synthetic Cubism, he had begun to do realistic drawings reminiscent of Ingres'. By 1920 he was working simultaneously in two separate manners: the Synthetic Cubism of the *Three Musicians,* and a Neoclassical style with the strongly modeled, heavy-bodied figures seen in *Mother and Child* (fig. 24-26). To many of his admirers, this seemed a kind of betrayal, but in hindsight the reason for Picasso's two-pronged approach is clear. Having reached the limits of Synthetic Cubism, he wanted to resume contact with the classical tradition. In fact, Picasso had

never entirely abandoned the "art of the museums." The painting was part of a much broader return to classicism by artists who felt a need to reaffirm their belief in an orderly world following the cataclysmic upheavals of World War I. The figures in *Mother and Child* have a mock-monumental quality that suggests colossal statues rather than flesh-and-blood human beings, yet the theme is treated with surprising tenderness. The forms are carefully dovetailed within the frame, not unlike the way the *Three Musicians* is put together.

A few years later the two tracks of Picasso's style began to converge into an extraordinary synthesis that was to become the basis of his art. *Three Dancers* of 1925 (fig. 24-27) shows how he accomplished this seemingly impossible feat. Structurally the picture is pure Synthetic Cubism. It even includes painted imitations of specific materials, such as patterned wallpaper and samples of various fabrics cut out with pinking shears. The figures, a wildly fantastic version of a classical scheme (compare the dancers in Matisse's *Joy of Life,* see fig. 24-1), are an even more violent assault on convention than the figures in *Les Demoiselles d'Avignon* (see fig. 24-12). Human anatomy is here simply the raw material for Picasso's incredible inventiveness. Limbs, torsos, breasts, and faces are handled with the same freedom as the fragments of external reality in Braque's *Le Courrier* (see fig. 24-15). Their original identity no longer matters. Breasts may turn into eyes, profiles merge with frontal views, shadows become objects, and vice versa, in an endless flow of metamorphoses. They are "visual puns," offering wholly unexpected possibilities of expression—humorous, grotesque, macabre, even tragic.

Three Dancers marks a transition to Picasso's experiment with Surrealism (see page 831). He had been in close contact with the Surrealists since 1924; his art, in turn, was a point of departure for theirs. He nevertheless denied that he was affected by Surrealism until a decade later, and with good reason. His prodigious imagination notwithstanding, Picasso did not practice automatism; hence his work did not arise spontaneously from the subconscious. Instead, the paintings of the 1920s address formal concerns in the free transformation of objects, which are worked out with great care.

Three Dancers is one of the few canvases from this period that is so boldly expressive. It is only with *Girl Before a Mirror* (fig. 24-28) of 1932 that he began to reinvest his paintings with the psychological content that had marked his early work. In fact, the picture is an outgrowth of two canvases from 1905-6. The motif of a young woman contemplating her beauty goes all the way back to antiquity, but rarely has it been depicted with such disturbing overtones. In contrast to Baldung-Grien's *Death and the Maiden* (fig. 16-13), Picasso's girl is anything but serene. She reaches out to touch the image in the mirror with a mixture of longing and apprehension. We all feel a jolt when we unexpectedly see ourselves in a mirror, which often gives back a reflection that upsets our self-conception. Picasso here suggests this visionary truth in several ways. He has treated his shapes much like the enclosed, flat panes of a stained-glass window. Just as a real mirror introduces changes of its own and does not reflect the simple truth, so this one alters the way the girl looks in order to reveal a deeper reality. She appears not so much to be examining her physical appearance as to be exploring her sexuality. Her face is divided into two parts, one with a somber expression, the other with a masklike appearance whose color nevertheless betrays passionate feeling. The mirror is a sea of conflicting emotions signified above all by the color scheme of her reflection. Framed by strong blue, purple, and green hues, her features stare back at her with fiery intensity. Clearly discernible is a tear on her cheek. But it is the masterstroke of the green spot, shining like a beacon in the middle of her forehead, that conveys the anguish of the girl's confrontation with her inner self. Picasso was probably aware of the theory that red and green are complementary colors which intensify each other. However, this "law" can hardly have dictated his choice of green to stand for the girl's psyche. That was surely determined as a matter of pictorial and expressive necessity.

Although Picasso never developed into a true follower of Surrealism, the impact of his fellow Spaniard Joan Miró (see page 833) can be seen in the biomorphism of Picasso's mural *Guernica* (fig. 24-29). Picasso did not show any interest in politics during World War I or the 1920s, but the Spanish Civil War stirred him to ardent support of the Loyalists. The mural, executed in 1937 for the Pavilion of the Spanish Republic at the Paris International Exposition, has truly monumental grandeur. It was inspired by the

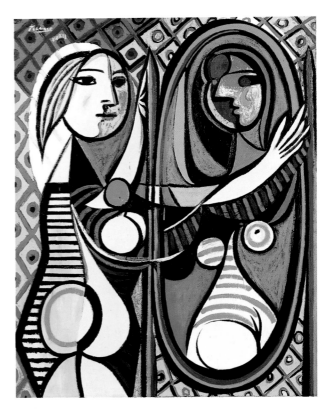

24-28. Pablo Picasso. *Girl Before a Mirror. March 1932.* Oil on canvas, 64 x 51¼" (162.3 x 130.2 cm). The Museum of Modern Art, New York

terror-bombing of Guernica, the ancient capital of the Basques in northern Spain. The destruction of Guernica was the first demonstration of the technique of saturation bombing that was later used on a huge scale during World War II. The mural was thus a prophetic vision of doom.

The canvas does not represent the carnage itself. Rather, it evokes the agony of the event with a series of powerful images that make it the greatest visual statement about war since Goya's *The Third of May, 1808* (see fig. 21-25), which Picasso must have partly had in mind while painting *Guernica*. Like Préault's *Tuerie* (see fig. 21-63), which is also its ancestor, the symbolism of the scene resists exact interpretation, despite several traditional elements: the mother and her dead child are the descendants of the *Pietà* (see fig. 11-54), the woman with the lamp recalls the *Statue of Liberty* (see fig. 21-65), and the dead fighter's hand, still clutching a broken sword, is a familiar emblem of heroic resistance (compare fig. 21-61). We also sense the contrast between the menacing, human-faced bull, which we know Picasso intended to represent the forces of brutality and darkness, and the dying horse, which stands for the people. He insisted, however, that the mural was not a political statement about fascism, though "there is a deliberate appeal to people, a deliberate sense of propaganda. . . . " These figures owe their terrifying eloquence to what they are, not to what they mean. The anatomical dislocations, fragmentations, and transformations, which in the *Three Dancers* seemed fantastic, now express the stark reality of unbearable pain. The ultimate test of the validity of collage construction (shown here in superimposed flat "cutouts" lim-

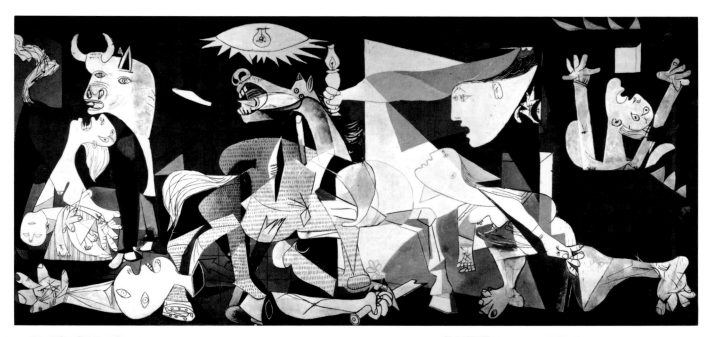

24-29. Pablo Picasso. *Guernica.* 1937. Oil on canvas, 11'6" x 25'8" (3.5 x 7.8 m). Museo Nacional Centro de Arte Reina Sofía, Madrid. On permanent loan from the Museo del Prado, Madrid

ited to black, white, and gray) is that it could express such over-powering emotions.

HENRI MATISSE. From 1911 on, Matisse was influenced increasingly by Cubism, but after World War I he, like Picasso, returned to the classical tradition. The lessons he absorbed from Cubism nevertheless had a far-reaching effect on his style. Their impact can be seen in *Decorative Figure Against an Ornamental Background* (fig. 24-30). The painting has a new richness, but there is also an underlying discipline resulting from his study of Cubism. The carpet provides a firm geometric structure for organizing the composition, so that everything has its place, although the system itself is entirely intuitive. Only in this way could Matisse control all the elements of his complex picture. It is among the finest in a long series of odalisques (harem girls) that he painted during the 1920s and 1930s. In them the artist emerges as the heir of the French academic tradition, which he had assimilated through his teacher Gustave Moreau (see page 761). The visual splendor would be worthy of Delacroix himself. Yet in the calm pose and strong contours of the figure, Matisse reveals himself to be a classicist at heart, closer to Ingres than to the Romantics (compare figs. 21-30 and 21-33). The picture also has overtones of Degas (see fig. 22-12), who had been trained by a disciple of Ingres' and thus formed an important link in the chain of tradition. Nevertheless, Matisse's is a distinctly modern classicism. *Decorative Figure* breathes the classical serenity of *Seated Woman* by his friend Maillol (see fig. 23-26), who early in his career had also been inspired by Gauguin.

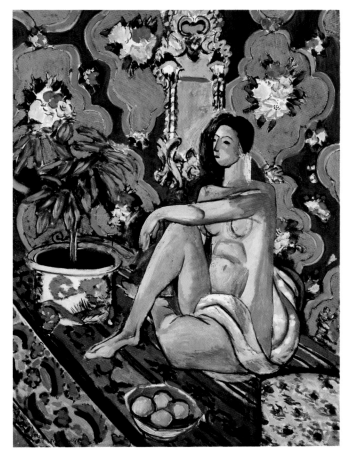

24-30. Henri Matisse. *Decorative Figure Against an Ornamental Background.* 1927. Oil on canvas, 51⅛ x 38½" (129.9 x 97.8 cm). Musée National d'Art Moderne, Paris

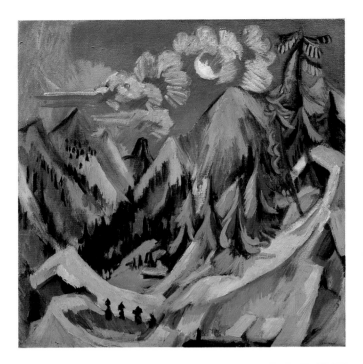

24-31. Ernst Ludwig Kirchner. *Winter Landscape in Moonlight.* 1919. Oil on canvas, 47⅝ x 47⅝" (121 x 121 cm). The Detroit Institute of Arts

The true genius among the Brücke painters—E. L. Kirchner—took another path, leading to a far deeper knowledge of nature. In 1917 Kirchner had been brought to Davos, desperately ill. Then, after a long stay in various sanatoria, he had made his home in a lonely hut at the entrance to the Sertig Valley. . . .Released from the sanatorium with its Magic Mountain *atmosphere and alone beneath the snug low ceiling of his hut—the sick city-dweller with his exacerbated sensibility acquired a serene, hopeful patience and entered into a new relationship with nature. His surroundings filled him with wonderment. He had only to open the door to find himself face to face with an overpowering, elemental world—the high mountains. Little by little he familiarized himself with the vast, eternal face of nature—gigantic and overwhelming but not hostile. Each step he took into this mountain world gave him a share in its power, its permanence and peace, appeasing the unrest of his soul. . . .*

This simple power could not be expressed by any copying of appearances; it could only be signified by a bold runic script. Things must be replaced by signs and with these signs the epic of reality must be written. Kirchner had always known the hieroglyphic, "signifying" character of form. But hitherto the agitation of his soul had given his forms a lyrical, dramatic character; they had stood for psychological states. Only now, with his new-found epic vision, was he able to conceive "objective" forms, capable of signifying things.

—Werner Haftmann. *Painting in the Twentieth Century.* Translated by Ralph Manheim. Cambridge: International Thomson Publishing, 1965, p. 134. Originally published in 1960 by Percy Lund, Humphries and Company Limited.

WERNER HAFTMANN (1912–1999) was a director of the Nationalgalerie, Berlin, and co-founder, in 1955, of Documenta, the contemporary art event staged in Kassel, Germany, every five years since 1972. He was, above all, an art historian whose knowledge of modern painting still astonishes. His great work, *Painting in the Twentieth Century,* from which our extract on Kirchner is drawn, is typical Haftmann. Illuminated by his personal knowledge of many of the artists he wrote about, his writing is animated by an understanding of the inner lives and artistic intentions of his subjects.

ERNST KIRCHNER. Kirchner, too, was influenced by Cubism after 1911, when he joined the other members of *Die Brücke* in Berlin. Four years later he was drafted into World War I, which ruined his physical and mental health. Released from the army after six months to recover from tuberculosis, he moved to Switzerland, where he turned increasingly to landscapes, as did many other German Expressionists following the war. *Winter Landscape in Moonlight* (fig. 24-31), painted in the Swiss Alps, is filled with a sense of peace and wonderment before nature. The painting has the ecstatic rhythms of the young Kandinsky (compare fig. 24-9), whose work Kirchner came to know while participating in exhibitions of *Der Blaue Reiter* following the demise of *Die Brücke.*

VASSILY KANDINSKY. Kandinsky himself spent the war years in Russia, where he participated enthusiastically in the Revolution and played an important role in shaping artistic policy. When his teaching reforms met with growing hostility, he returned to Germany in 1921 and soon accepted an invitation from Walter Gropius to teach at the Bauhaus (see page 902). Kandinsky had begun to experiment with a more geometric style in Russia under the influence of Constructivism and other related avant-garde movements (see page 871), some of which shared his mystical tendencies, but his output was small. It was only after he assumed his position at Weimar that he fully adopted geometric abstraction. The lessons and exercises he developed for his students helped to crystallize his theories of form and structure. These he set out systematically in *Point and Line to Plane,* published in 1926, which spells out concepts that were present only in elementary form in his earlier book, *Concerning the Spiritual in Art* (see pages 806–08). His development was reinforced by the presence at the Bauhaus after 1923 of Laszlo Moholy-Nagy, who came from a Constructivist background, although his approach was otherwise the opposite of Kandinsky's (see page 934). Looking at a typical example of Kandinsky's work from this time (fig. 24-32), we seem to have entered a totally different world than that of his earlier work (see fig. 24-9). Only when we analyze the painting do we realize that it, too, embodies a clash of cosmic forces. The artist has clarified the shapes and lines that had been buried in a sea of swirling forms. Yet the attitude is still the same, and Kandinsky admitted that he remained a Romantic to the end. (Later, his forms became increasingly biomorphic in the manner of Miró; see page 833.)

Abstraction

Picasso's abandonment of pure Cubism signaled the broad retreat of abstraction after 1920. The utopian ideals associated with modernism, which abstraction embodied, had been largely dashed by "the war to end all wars." In retrospect, abstraction can be seen as a necessary phase through which modern painting had to pass, but it was not essential to modernism as such, even though it was the dominant tendency of the twentieth century.

FERNAND LÉGER. The Futurist spirit continued to find followers on both sides of the Atlantic. Buoyant with optimism and excitement, *The City* (fig. 24-33) by the Frenchman Fernand

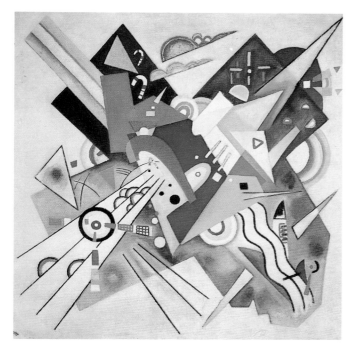

24-32. Vassily Kandinsky. *Accented Corners, No. 247.* 1923. Oil on canvas, 51¼ x 51¼" (130 x 130 cm). Private collection

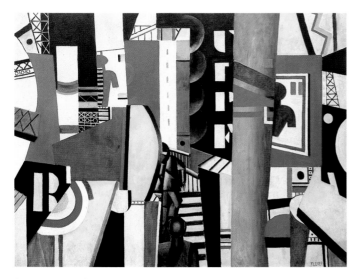

24-33. Fernand Léger. *The City.* 1919. Oil on canvas, 7'7" x 9'9" (2.31 x 2.98 m). Philadelphia Museum of Art

A. E. GALLATIN COLLECTION

Léger (1881–1955) creates a vision of a mechanized utopia that reflects his Communist political views. This beautifully controlled industrial landscape is stable without being static and reflects the clean geometric shapes of modern machinery. In this instance, the term *abstraction* applies mainly to the choice of design elements and their manner of combination. The shapes themselves are "prefabricated," except for the two figures on the staircase, who hardly differ from their surroundings.

CHARLES DEMUTH. The modern movement in the United States proved short-lived. Charles Demuth (1883–1935) was one of the few artists to continue working in an abstract vein after

World War I. A member of the Stieglitz group (see pages 925–26), he had been friendly with Marcel Duchamp and the exiled Cubists in New York during World War I. A few years later, under the impact of Futurism, he developed a style known as Precisionism to depict urban and industrial architecture. Influences from all of these movements can be seen in *I Saw the Figure 5 in Gold* (fig. 24-34). The title is taken from the poem "The Great Figure" by Demuth's friend William Carlos Williams, whose name also forms part of the design as "Bill," "Carlos," and "W. C. W." In the poem the figure 5 appears on a red fire truck, but in the painting it has become the dominant feature, repeated three times to reinforce its echo in our memory as the fire truck rushes on through the night:

> Among the rain
> and lights
> I saw the figure 5 in gold
> on a red
> firetruck
> moving
> tense
> unheeded
> to gong clangs
> siren howls
> and wheels rumbling
> through the dark city

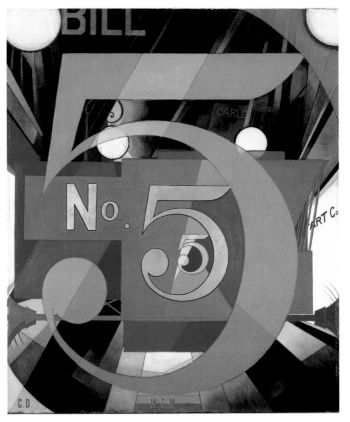

24-34. Charles Demuth. *I Saw the Figure 5 in Gold.* 1928. Oil on composition board, 36 x 29¾" (91.4 x 75.6 cm). The Metropolitan Museum of Art, New York

THE ALFRED STIEGLITZ COLLECTION, 1949

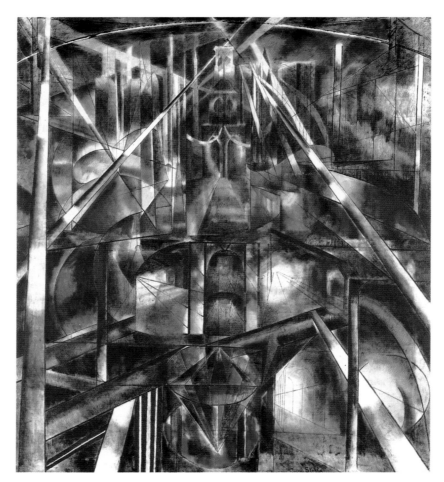

24-35. Joseph Stella. *Brooklyn Bridge.* 1917.
Oil on bedsheeting, 7' x 6'4" (2.13 x 1.93 m).
Yale University Art Gallery, New Haven, Connecticut
GIFT OF COLLECTION SOCIÉTÉ ANONYME

JOSEPH STELLA. Poetry was also central to *Brooklyn Bridge* (fig. 24-35) by the Italian-American Joseph Stella (1877–1946). To Stella, who emigrated to America as a young man, the bridge became a symbol of his adopted land, which provided his boldest theme. He wrote in his autobiography: "To realize this towering imperative vision in all its integral possibilities . . . I appealed for help to the soaring verse of Walt Whitman and to the fiery Poe's plasticity. Upon the swarming darkness of the night, I rung all the bells of alarm with the blaze of electricity scattered in lightnings down the oblique cables, the dynamic pillars of my composition, and to render more pungent the mystery of the metallic apparition, through the green and red glare of the signals I excavated here and there caves as subterranean passages to infernal recesses." His painting achieves what a contemporary critic perceptively called the apotheosis of the bridge through a synthesis of Futurism, which he had been exposed to during a visit to Paris in 1912, and Precisionism, which he experimented with as early as 1917. With its maze of luminescent cables, vigorous diagonal thrusts, and crystalline cells of space, the painting is a striking visual counterpart to Hart Crane's famous hymn of 1930, "To Brooklyn Bridge":

O harp and altar, of the fury fused,
(How could mere toil align thy choiring strings!)
Terrific threshold of the prophet's pledge,
Prayer of pariah, and the lover's cry,—
Again the traffic lights that skim thy swift
Unfractioned idiom, immaculate sigh of stars,
Beading thy path—condense eternity:
And we have seen night lifted in thine arms.

PIET MONDRIAN. The most radical abstractionist of the twentieth century was the Dutch painter Piet Mondrian (1872–1944). Nine years older than Picasso, he arrived in Paris in 1912 as a mature Expressionist in the tradition of Van Gogh and the Fauves. Under the influence of Analytic Cubism, his work soon underwent a complete change, and within the next decade Mondrian developed an entirely nonrepresentational style that he called Neo-Plasticism. The short-lived movement as a whole is also known as *De Stijl,* after the Dutch magazine advocating his ideas, which were formulated with Theo van Doesburg (1883–1931) and Bart van der Leck (1876–1958). [See Primary

Sources, no. 87, page 972.] Mondrian became the center of the abstract movement in Paris, where he returned from the Netherlands in 1919 and remained until the onset of World War II. Indeed, the School of Paris in the 1930s was made up largely of foreigners like him—especially the Abstraction-Création group, which included artists of every outlook. As a result, the differences between the various movements soon became blurred, although Mondrian himself remained true to his principles.

Composition with Red, Blue, and Yellow (fig. 24-36) shows Mondrian's style at its most severe. He restricts his design to horizontals and verticals and his palette to the three primary colors—red, yellow, and blue—plus black and white. Representation is completely eliminated. Yet his canvases remain paintings in every sense of the term. Mondrian never hid his brushwork or the texture of the canvas, and the pigments have surprising density. Like Kandinsky, Mondrian was affected by theosophy, albeit the distinctive Dutch branch founded during World War I by the mathematician M. J. H. Schoenmaekers. Unlike Kandinsky, however, he did not strive for pure, lyrical emotion. His goal, he asserted, was "pure reality," which he defined as equilibrium "through the balance of unequal but equivalent oppositions"—especially between line and color. [See Primary Sources, no. 88, page 972.] "Plastic" for Mondrian, as for many other early-twentieth-century artists, meant the formal structural relationships underlying both art and nature. The term *Neo-Plasticism* itself was coined by Schoenmaekers, for whom yellow symbolized the vertical movement of the sun's rays; blue, the horizontal line of the earth's orbit around the sun; and red, the union of both. For all of their analytic calm, Mondrian's paintings are highly idealistic. He believed, "When we realize that equilibriated relationships in society signify what is just, then we shall realize that in art, likewise, the demands of life press forward when the spirit of the age is ready."

Perhaps we can best understand what Mondrian meant by equilibrium if we think of his work as "abstract collages" that use black bands and colored rectangles instead of recognizable fragments of chair caning and newsprint. He was interested solely in visual relationships and wanted no distracting elements or accidental associations. By establishing the "right" relationship among his bands and rectangles, he transformed them as thoroughly as the snippets of pasted paper in Braque's *Le Courrier* (see fig. 24-15). How did he discover the "right" relationship? And how did he determine the shape and number for the bands and rectangles? In Braque's collage the ingredients are to some extent "given" by chance. Apart from his self-imposed rules, however, Mondrian constantly faced the problem of unlimited possibilities. He could not change the relationship of the bands to the rectangles without changing the bands and rectangles themselves. When we consider his task, we begin to realize its infinite complexity.

Looking again at *Composition with Red, Blue, and Yellow*, we find that when we measure the various units, only the proportions of the canvas itself are truly rational: an exact square. Mondrian has arrived at all the rest "by feel," and must have undergone endless trial and error. How often, we wonder, did he change the dimensions of the red rectangle to bring it and the other elements

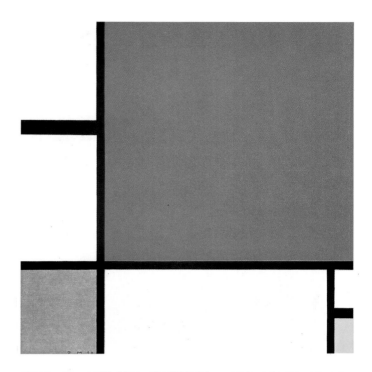

24-36. Piet Mondrian. *Composition with Red, Blue, and Yellow.* 1930. Oil on canvas, 20 x 20" (50.8 x 50.8 cm). Private Collection

Mondrian was surely aware that in those venerated works the old masters considered every detail a necessary part in the order and harmony of the whole.

Yet one may speak of certain relations of the geometric units in Mondrian's paintings as "abstracted" or transposed from the previous art of representation, without assuming that the units themselves are reductions of complex natural forms to simple regular ones. These elements are indeed new, as concrete markings of pigments on the tangible canvas surface with distinctive qualities—straightness, smoothness, firmness—which may be called physiognomic and are grasped as such, rather than as illustrative presentations of the ideal concepts of mathematical or metaphysical thought, although we may use the terms of geometry in talking about them. The position of Mondrian's straight line (which on the diamond field is a bar with mitred ends), its length and thickness, its precise distance from a neighboring line, are no more nor less constitutive of the painting as a unique aesthetic whole than are the complex image-forms that Mondrian wished to supplant by his "pure relations". . . .

—Meyer Schapiro. *Modern Art: Nineteenth and Twentieth Centuries.* New York: George Braziller, Inc., 1982, p. 242. Originally published in 1978.

MEYER SCHAPIRO (1904–1996) emigrated from Lithuania with his family when he was two years old. He spent most of his career at Columbia University, where students considered it the greatest good fortune to be admitted to one of his classes or to hear him lecture. Regarded as one of the greatest art historians of all time, he was a brilliant medievalist and a modernist. His reputation was larger than his published output, yet no one disputes his brilliance or the inspiring influence he had on a generation of artists and art historians, among them Robert Motherwell, Willem de Kooning, and H. W. Janson.

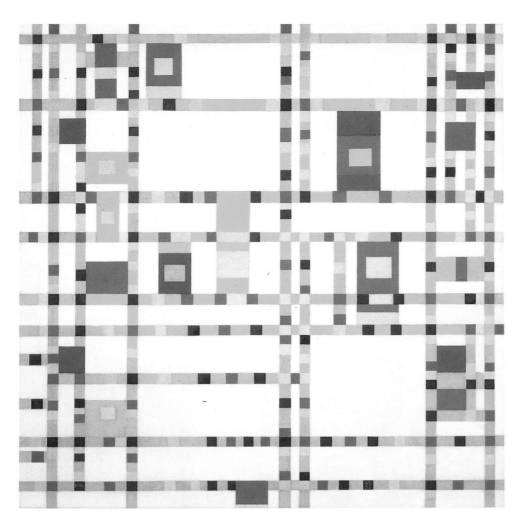

24-37. Piet Mondrian. *Broadway Boogie Woogie*. 1942–43. Oil on canvas, 50 x 50" (127 x 127 cm). The Museum of Modern Art, New York

into self-contained equilibrium? Strange as it may seem, Mondrian's exquisite sense for nonsymmetrical balance is so specific that experts have no difficulty in distinguishing fakes from genuine pictures. People who work with nonfigurative shapes, such as designers, architects, and typographers, are likely to be most sensitive to this quality. Mondrian has had a greater influence on them than on artists (see page 907).

At the beginning of World War II, Mondrian left Paris for London and then New York, where he arrived in 1940. He now began to give to his works such titles as *Trafalgar Square* or *Broadway Boogie Woogie* (fig. 24-37), which hint at a relationship, however indirect, with observed reality. *Broadway Boogie Woogie* immortalizes Mondrian's fascination with the culture he found in America. The artist uses white and the three primary colors to signify radiant light. The play of color evokes with striking success the jaunty rhythms of music and light found in New York's nightclub district during the Jazz Age. As in a medieval manuscript decoration (see fig. 9-5), the composition relies entirely on surface pattern. *Broadway Boogie Woogie* seems as flat as the canvas it is painted on. Although Mondrian abandons his system of black lines, he has laid out his colored "tiles" along a grid system that closely resembles a city map.

This sense of order seems typically Dutch. If we analyze the surface geometry in Jan Steen's *The Feast of St. Nicholas* (see fig. 18-27), we find that it is basically similar to *Broadway Boogie Woogie*. Each part of the room is treated as a separate element to be integrated into the design as a whole. Thus, although Steen depicted three-dimensional space, the problems he faced in composing his work were not very different from those confronted by Mondrian 200 years later.

BEN NICHOLSON. Mondrian did have a number of followers among painters. By far the most original was the English artist Ben Nicholson (1894–1982). A rigorous abstractionist, he bent Mondrian's rules without breaking them in his painted reliefs (fig. 24-38). These also show the inspiration of his wife, the sculptor Barbara Hepworth (see page 878). The overlapping shapes violate the integrity of the rectangle and overcome the tyranny of the grid maintained by Mondrian. The geometry is further altered by the introduction of the circle. Yet Nicholson's work, too, relies on the delicate balance of elements. The effect is enhanced by the subdued palette and matte finish, which create harmonies of the utmost refinement. In comparison, Mondrian's primary colors seem astonishingly bright and exuberant.

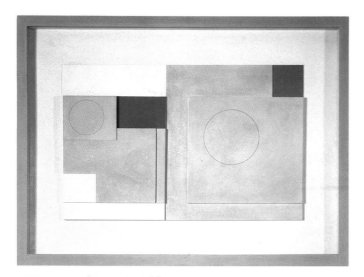

24-38. Ben Nicholson. *Painted Relief.* 1939. Synthetic board mounted on plywood, painted, 32⅞ x 45" (83.5 x 114.3 cm). The Museum of Modern Art, New York

Fantasy

DADA. Out of despair over the mechanized mass killing of World War I, a number of artists in Zurich and New York, including Marcel Duchamp, simultaneously launched a protest movement called *Dada* (or Dadaism), which then spread to other cities in Germany and France. The term *dada,* which means hobbyhorse in French, was reportedly picked at random from a dictionary, although it had actually been used as the title of a Symbolist journal. As an infantile, all-purpose word, however, it perfectly suited the spirit of the movement. Dada has often been called nihilistic, and it was indeed the very prototype of an avant-garde movement. Its declared purpose was to make clear to the public at large that all established values—political, moral, or aesthetic—had been rendered meaningless by the catastrophe of the Great War. Dada's program was closely linked to Communism, which it hoped would overthrow bourgeois society and substitute a proletarian paradise. Such political activism was the norm. Between 1915 and 1950 most avant-garde artists on both sides of the Atlantic, even Picasso, were associated with Communism or Socialism at one time or another.

During its short life (c. 1915–22) Dada preached "non-sense" and antiart with a vengeance. [See Primary Sources, no. 89, page 973.] As Hans Arp wrote, "Dadaism carried assent and dissent ad absurdum. In order to achieve indifference, it was destructive." Marcel Duchamp once "improved" a reproduction of Leonardo's *Mona Lisa* with a mustache and the abbreviation LHOOQ, which makes an off-color pun when pronounced in French. Not even modern art was safe from the Dadaists' assaults. One example exhibited a toy monkey inside a frame with the title "Portrait of Cézanne." Yet Dada was not a completely negative movement. In its calculated irrationality there was also liberation, a voyage into

unknown provinces of the creative mind. The only law respected by the Dadaists was that of chance, and the only reality, that of the imagination.

MAX ERNST. Although their most characteristic art form was the readymade (see page 874), the Dadaists adapted the collage technique of Synthetic Cubism for their purposes. Figure 24-39 by the German Dadaist Max Ernst (1891–1976), an associate of Duchamp, is largely composed of snippets from illustrations of machinery. The caption pretends to enumerate these mechanical ingredients, which include (or add up to) "1 Piping Man." Actually there is also a "piping woman." These offspring of Duchamp's prewar *Bride (*see fig. 24-23), staring at us blindly through goggles, are strangely haunting and disturbing.

SURREALISM. In 1924, after Duchamp's retirement from Dada, a group led by the poet André Breton founded Surrealism, Dada's successor, which also took up Communism. The members of the Surrealist group defined their aim as "pure psychic automatism . . . intended to express . . . the true process of thought . . . free from the exercise of reason and from any aesthetic or moral purpose." [See Primary Sources, no. 90, page 973.] Surrealist

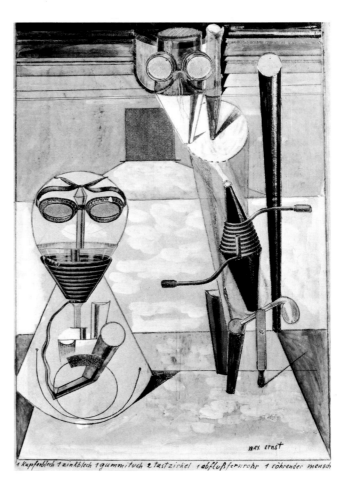

24-39. Max Ernst. *1 Copper Plate 1 Zinc Plate 1 Rubber Cloth 2 Calipers 1 Drainpipe Telescope 1 Piping Man.* 1920. Collage, 12 x 9" (30.5 x 23 cm). Estate of Hans Arp

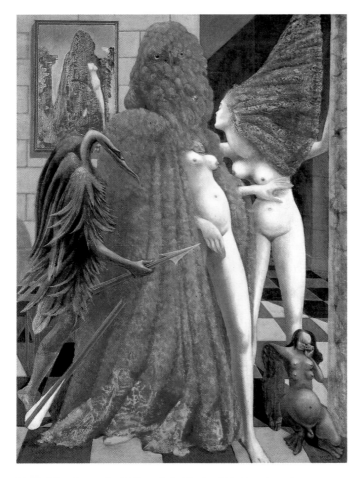

24-40. Max Ernst. *La Toilette de la Mariée (The Dressing of the Bride)*. 1940. Oil on canvas, 51 x 37⅞" (129.5 x 96.2 cm). Peggy Guggenheim Collection, Venice

theory was filled with concepts borrowed from psychoanalysis, and its rhetoric cannot always be taken seriously. The notion that a dream can be transferred by "automatic handwriting" directly from the unconscious mind to the canvas did not work in practice. It was impossible to bypass the conscious awareness of the artist altogether, since some degree of control was unavoidable.

ERNST'S DECALCOMANIA. Surrealism gave rise to several novel techniques for stimulating and exploiting chance effects. Max Ernst, the most inventive member of the group, often combined collage with "frottage." (Frottage involves making rubbings from pieces of wood, pressed flowers, and other relief surfaces. It is the process we all know from the children's pastime of rubbing with a pencil on a piece of paper covering, say, a coin.) In *La Toilette de la Mariée (The Dressing of the Bride)* (fig. 24-40), he produced fascinating shapes and textures by "decalcomania," which uses pressure to transfer oil paint to the canvas from some other surface. This technique is in essence another variant of one recommended by Leonardo da Vinci and Alexander Cozens (see fig. 21-10). Ernst relied on chance effects produced by his stains, but he further developed them into an image of extraordinary wealth. The end result has some of the qualities of a dream, but it is a dream born of a strikingly romantic imagination.

SALVADOR DALÍ. The same can be said of *The Persistence of Memory* (fig. 24-41) by Salvador Dalí (1904–1989). The most notorious of the Surrealists because of his self-promotion, he used a painstaking realism to render a "paranoid" dream in which time, forms, and space have been distorted in a frighteningly convincing way.

RENÉ MAGRITTE. The Belgian artist René Magritte (1898–1967) employed detailed realism for completely different ends. Although he found his early inspiration in the work of De Chirico, his style comes from the tradition of Magic Realism that flourished in Belgium in the late nineteenth and early twentieth centuries. Magritte's goal was "poetic painting." His illusionistic pictures transform objects into images having completely different meaning through astonishing metamorphoses, changes in scale, juxtapositions, and the like. *Les Promenades d'Euclid* (fig. 24-42) shows one of his favorites devices, the picture within a picture. The title, added after the fact through free association, only compounds the mystery of the painting by failing to explain it. This divorce of word and image prevents us from finding any literal (or literary) meaning. The painting's charm lies not simply in this visual and verbal puzzle but in the presentation itself: the beautifully simple, abstract design, and the artist's way of subtly heightening reality while ultimately denying its plausibility.

FRIDA KAHLO. A number of women, Meret Oppenheim among them (see page 874), were associated with the Surrealist movement. Today the best known is Frida Kahlo (1910–1954), who was first discovered by the poet André Breton during a visit to Mexico in 1938 and then rediscovered in recent years by feminist art historians. She owes her reputation to her troubled life as well as to her work, for they are inseparable. Her paintings are frankly autobiographical. However, they are presented in such enigmatic terms and are so full of personal meaning that the exact circumstances must be known in order to understand their content.

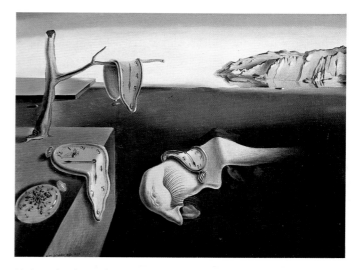

24-41. Salvador Dalí. *The Persistence of Memory*. 1931. Oil on canvas, 9½ x 13" (24.1 x 33 cm). The Museum of Modern Art, New York
GIVEN ANONYMOUSLY

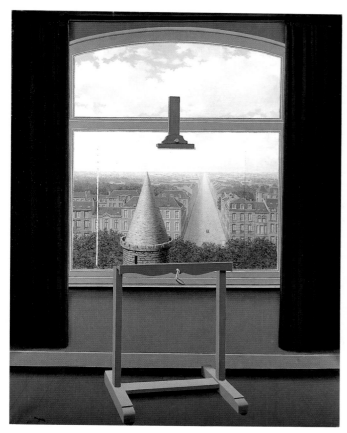

24-42. René Magritte. *Les Promenades d'Euclid.* 1955.
Oil on canvas, 64⅛ x 51⅛" (163 x 130 cm).
The Minneapolis Institute of Arts

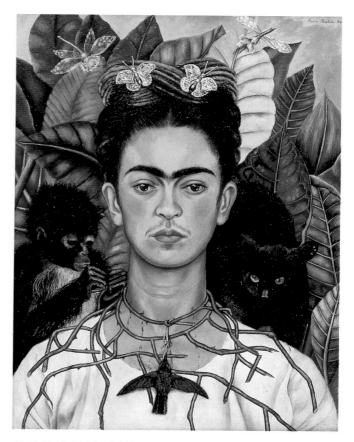

24-43. Frida Kahlo. *Self-Portrait with Thorn Necklace.*
1940.Oil on canvas, 24½ x 18¾" (62 x 47.5 cm).
Art Collection, Harry Ransom Research Center,
University of Texas at Austin

Self-Portrait with Thorn Necklace (fig. 24-43) is similar to traditional Mexican religious images. It was painted in 1940, when her
tempestuous marriage to the painter Diego Rivera (1886–1957)
was interrupted by divorce for a year. The necklace, an allusion
to the crown of thorns worn by Christ during the Passion, is a
symbol of her humiliation. From it hangs a dead hummingbird,
a traditional amulet worn in Mexico by people seeking love. On
her shoulders are two demons in the guise of the artist's pets: death,
who appears as a black cat, and the devil, seen as a monkey. She is
shown as a martyr to love hoping for a resurrection like the Lord's,
as signified by the butterflies overhead. In the context of the
moment, it seems likely that Kahlo was thinking of suicide.

JOAN MIRÓ. Surrealism had an even more boldly imaginative
branch. Some works by Picasso, such as *Three Dancers* (see fig.
24-27), have affinities with it, and its greatest representative was
also Spanish: Joan Miró (1893–1983). His style has been labeled
biomorphic abstraction, since his forms are fluid and organic,
rather than geometric. Biomorphic concretion might be a more
suitable name. Like the sculptures of Hans Arp (see fig. 25-13), the
shapes in Miró's pictures (fig. 24-44) have their own vigorous life.
They seem to change before our eyes, expanding and contracting like amoebas until they approach human individuality. Their
spontaneous "becoming" is the very opposite of abstraction as we

have defined it (see page 810). Once he conceived his forms, however, Miró subjected them to a formal discipline no less rigorous
than that of Picasso's. In fact, he began as a Cubist and turned to
Surrealism only in 1924, five years after moving to Paris.

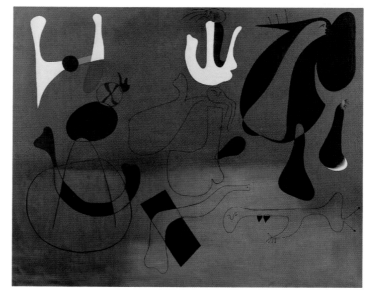

24-44. Joan Miró. *Composition.* 1933. Oil on canvas, 51¼ x 63½"
(130.5 x 161.3 cm). Wadsworth Atheneum, Hartford, Connecticut

German Expressionism in art had a counterpart in Expressionist drama, which compressed as much emotion as possible into a play, eliminating anything not needed to convey the central message of the piece. It initially took the form of subjective truth and utopian vision in *The Beggar* (1912) by Reinhard Sorge (1892–1916) but soon turned to antiwar sentiment in *One Race* (1918) by Fritz von Unruh (1885–1970). Expressionist theater was also promoted by Herwarth Walden (1878–1941), publisher of the journal *Der Sturm,* which attracted many of the leading painters to Berlin, including Oskar Kokoschka, who was also a dramatist. The trilogy *Gas* (1917–20) by Georg Kaiser (1878–1945) characteristically expressed utopian ideals by reducing its characters to symbols of social forces, such as the Engineer and the Billionaire's Son.

Under the Weimar Republic (1920–33), Germany was the most vibrant center of theater in all of Europe, with a dazzling variety that reflected the turmoil of the postwar years. The most important German drama produced between the wars was *Man and the Masses* (1921) by Ernst Toller (1893–1939), featuring a kaleidoscopic production by the director Jürgen Fehling (1890–1968). The play already shows the pessimism that led to the decline of Expressionism a few years later. In its place rose Epic Theater, promoted by Erwin Piscator (1893–1966), who championed proletarian drama. He instituted a deliberately episodic style of drama that, in contrast to Expressionism, encouraged psychological distance in the viewer through using divided stages, incorporating film clips, and having characters speak to the audience directly. These devices, later to become standard, thus broke the traditional theatrical illusion that the audience is watching actual events as they are taking place.

The main exponent of Epic Theater was Bertolt Brecht (1898–1956), a confirmed Communist who spent much of his career in exile in America. He remains best known for *The Three Penny Opera* (1928), with cabaret-style music by Kurt Weill (1900–1950), which is even more profoundly cynical than the original opera by John Gay on which it is based (see page 605). The collaborations of Brecht and Weill are, in effect, modern-day morality plays but with an anticapitalist bent. Brecht's best play, however, is *Mother Courage and Her Children* (1938–39), the story of the destruction of a family during the Thirty Years' War. It provoked viewers to think about its meaning by setting contemporary events in the past (a process known as historification) and presenting them as a series of disjointed episodes, while adding strange effects to induce a sense of alienation.

The 1920s were also a time of technical innovation in Germany. The Bauhaus conducted important experiments under its longtime director Walter Gropius, who devised a stage that could be reconfigured to place the audience in the center of the action. Oskar Schlemmer (1888–1943), head of the theater workshop, designed abstract costumes that made actors into architectural units to be placed at will within the stage space by rigorously controlling their every movement. *Neue Sachlichkeit* (New Objectivity) also found an outlet in theater in documentary dramas dealing with a variety of social issues, but the only notable playwright of this genre was Ferdinand Bruckner (1891–1958).

In France, the major contribution was Surrealist theater. In addition to Jarry's *Ubu Roi, The Breasts of Tiresias* (1903–17) by Guillaume Apollinaire (1880–1918) was the early prototype of Surrealist drama, mingling popular theater with music and dance in an illogical free form. The poet Jean Cocteau (1892–1963) used many of these devices in *Parade* (1917), a ballet presented by Diaghilev's Ballets Russes that was one of the great collaborations of the time, with costumes by Picasso and music by Erik Satie (1866–1925). Cocteau's finest efforts were restatements of Classical Greek dramas transposed to modern times and treated with all kinds of Surrealist effects. He also worked for the Ballet Suédois (Swedish Ballet), a rival company active in the early 1920s that attracted the painters Léger and De Chirico.

Although the Surrealists mounted numerous absurdist events in the 1920s and '30s, the most important work was done by André Breton's disciple Antonin Artaud (1896–1948) after he abandoned Surrealism in 1931. Rather than appealing to the mind, his Theater of Cruelty rejected language as impotent and mounted a concerted assault on all the senses to drain the "abscesses" of civilization by "providing the spectator with the true sources of his dreams, in which his taste for crime, his erotic obsessions, his savagery . . . would surge forth." Surrealism also stimulated Henri-René Lenormand (1882–1951) to write *Time Is a Dream* (1919) and *The Eater of Dreams* (1922), whose distortions of time and space anticipate effects seen later in Dalí's *The Persistence of Memory* (see fig. 24-41). Perhaps the most interesting Surrealist play was *No Exit* (1944), written during World War II by the existentialist philosopher Jean-Paul Sartre (1905–1980). It is a drama about interpersonal relations in which a man and two women pursue each other vainly as they seek self-validation in the eyes of others, whom they try to control but who in turn have their own agenda. Sartre's "theater of situations" sought to "explore the state of man in its entirety, and to present to modern man a portrait of himself" through his choices and actions.

Although it was short-lived, Italian Futurism was notable for its extreme rejection of traditional staging through the use of multimedia techniques to promote its glorification of the machine, achieve simultaneous effects, and break down barriers between the arts. World War I saw the equally brief Theater of the Grotesque in the plays of Luigi Chiarelli (1880–1947). By far the greatest Italian playwright of the century was Luigi Pirandello (1867–1936), a novelist who turned his hand to drama only after 1910. *Six Characters in Search of an Author* (1921) intermixes fantasy and reality so completely that truth becomes entirely subjective and unknowable, since it varies according to the perspective of each character and spectator. The finest dramatist in Spain was the novelist and poet Federico García Lorca (1898–1936). He worked with the theater group La Barraca in the early 1930s to create updated versions of popular theater dealing with the time-honored Spanish themes of love and honor, as did Alejandro Casona (1903–1966), who directed a similar touring group, the People's Theater.

After the revolution, theater in Russia continued to be a hotbed of experimentation. The most powerful director was Meyerhold, who now emphasized biomechanics—machinelike movement—as the chief means of expression. His sets, designed by the Constructivists, were the most boldly imaginative the world has ever seen. In 1918 Meyerhold collaborated on *Mystery Bouffe* with Kazimir Malevich and Vladimir Mayakovsky (1893–1930)—the only true literary genius produced by the Communist Revolution in which Malevich, like Tatlin, believed wholeheartedly. However, Mayakovsky's last plays, such as *The Bedbug* (1929), were acerbic satires on Soviet bureaucracy that were received so badly that he committed suicide. Yevgeny Vakhtangov (1883–1922), who trained many of the leaders of the next generation, managed to successfully combine the seemingly opposite approaches of Meyerhold and Stanislavsky.

Theater thrived in England after World War I. Not since the Elizabethan era were there so many great directors and actors or so many major theaters. The list of legendary stars includes Tyrone Guthrie, Barry Jackson, Laurence Olivier, John Gielgud, Michael Redgrave, Alec Guinness, Elsa Lanchester, Charles Laughton, and Sybil Thorndike, to name only the most famous. English playwriting of the time is remembered now chiefly for comedies by the novelist W. Somerset Maugham (1874–1965) and Noël Coward (1899–1973), who was a consummate man of the theater. There was considerable dramatic writing by serious authors as well. A notable example is *I Have Been Here Before* (1937) by the novelist J. B. Priestley (1894–1984), which deals with the effect of previous incarnations on the present. The poet W. H. Auden (1907–1973) and the novelist Christopher Isherwood (1904–1986) collaborated on several plays in expressionistic verse, including *The Dog Beneath the Skin* (1935), which was presented at the Group Theater. The American-born poet T. S. Eliot (1888–1965) was also a founder of the Group Theater, which staged his *Sweeney Agonistes* (1932), an "Aristophanic melodrama" that he considered a poem in dialogue, and *Murder in the Cathedral* (1935), about the death of Thomas à Becket. Both were attempts to restore verse to theater using popular forms and music-hall techniques, though Eliot abandoned this approach toward the end of the decade. The early dramas written for the Abbey Theater in the mid-1920s by Sean O'Casey (1880–1964) dealt with the impact of the Irish rebellion on people's lives, but his style later veered toward Expressionism in the pacifist play *The Silver Tassie* (1928), which led to a break with the Abbey, despite support from Yeats.

In the United States, new groups sprang up everywhere, many of them later subsidized by the government during the Great Depression under the Federal Theater Project. Stagecraft underwent radical changes at the hands of the designers Lee Simonson (1888–1967) and Robert Jones (1887–1954) and the producers Arthur Hopkins (1878–1950) and Norman Bel Geddes (1893–1958), all of whom were well versed in the latest European techniques. The Group Theater, begun in 1931 by Lee Strasberg (1901–1982) and others along the lines of the Moscow Art Theater, included such stars as Stella Adler (1904–1992) and

Elia Kazan (b. 1909). It was also the golden age of Hollywood films. Orson Welles, Laurence Olivier, Vivien Leigh, John Gielgud, Elsa Lanchester, Vincent Minelli, and Judy Garland were among the actors and directors who were equally successful on stage and screen.

For the first time in its history, America had writers who were fully the equal of those in Europe, and many of them wrote for the stage. The finest was unquestionably Eugene O'Neill (1888–1953), the son of the actor James O'Neill (1846–1920), whose powerful dramas *Desire under the Elms* (1925), *Mourning Becomes Electra* (1931), and *The Iceman Cometh* (1940/46) remain the great American classics of the era. Their only rivals are the plays written by Clifford Odets (1906–1963) in 1935 for the Group Theater—*Waiting for Lefty, Awake and Sing,* and *Paradise Lost*—all scripted in intense, graphic language. Odets' most popular work remains *Golden Boy* (1937), about a young violinist who becomes a boxer to earn money, which is a thinly veiled reference to his own decision to move to Hollywood, where his talents soon petered out. The novelist John Steinbeck (1902–1968) adapted three of his own books for the stage. The best is *Of Mice and Men,* done in collaboration with George S. Kaufman (1889–1961), a story of strength, weakness, and human dignity among migrant workers in a Midwest farming town during the Depression. Maxwell Anderson (1888–1959) achieved critical acclaim during the 1930s when he won the Pulitzer Prize for *Both Your Houses* (1933) and the Drama Critics' Circle Award for *Winterset* (1935). Much of his work dealt with war or the great monarchs and political leaders of the past. Other notable contributions to the American theater were *Street Scene* (1929) by Elmer Rice (1892–1967), about oppression and dehumanization; *The Time of Your Life* (1939) by William Saroyan (1908–1981), a witty and colorful story about life in San Francisco; *Mulatto* (1935) by Langston Hughes (1902–1967), the great writer of the Harlem Renaissance; and *The Cradle Will Rock* (1937) by Marc Blitzstein (1905–1964), whose rejection by the Federal Theater Project led Orson Welles and John Houseman (1902–1988) to form the Mercury Theater.

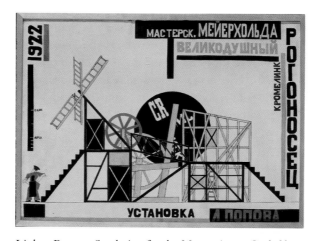

Liubov Popova. Set design for the *Magnanimous Cuckold.* 1922. India ink, gouache, and collage on varnished paper, 19⅝ x 27⅛" (50 x 69 cm). Trétiakov Gallery, Moscow
GIFT OF GEORGE COSTAKIS

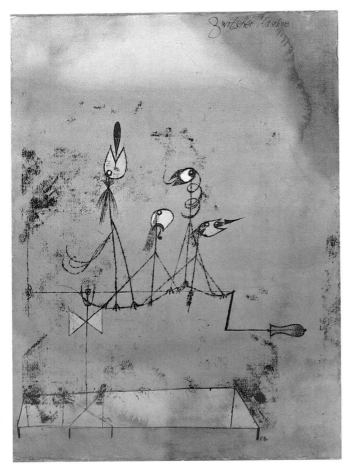

24-45. Paul Klee. *Twittering Machine.* 1922.
Watercolor and pen and ink on oil transfer drawing
on paper, mounted on cardboard, 25¼ x 19" (64.1 x 48.3 cm).
The Museum of Modern Art, New York

PAUL KLEE. Miró's work shows the impact of the German-Swiss painter Paul Klee (1879–1940). Klee in turn had been decisively influenced early in his career by *Der Blaue Reiter,* and shared many of the same ideas as his friends Kandinsky and Marc. He was fascinated with music, for example, and was himself a talented violinist. His theories of art also have much in common with Kandinsky's. (They were colleagues at the Bauhaus during the 1920s; see page 902.) Klee nevertheless went in the opposite direction. Instead of seeking a higher reality, he wanted to illuminate a deeper one from within the imagination. Thus natural forms were essential to his work, but as pictorial metaphors conveying hidden meaning rather than as representations of nature. He was affected, too, by Cubism and Orphism, but Egyptian and ethnographic art—and especially the drawings of small children—held an equally strong interest for him.

During World War I he molded these elements into a pictorial language that was marvelously economical and precise. *Twittering Machine* (fig. 24-45), a delicate pen-and-ink drawing tinted with watercolor, demonstrates the unique flavor of Klee's art. With a few simple lines, he has created a ghostly mechanism that mocks both our faith in the miracles of the Machine Age and our senti-mental appreciation of bird song. The quality of the line itself evokes the raspy sound made by this strange device. The little contraption is not without its sinister aspect: the heads of the four wiry birds look like fishing lures that might entrap any real birds that flew too near. It thus condenses into one striking invention a complex set of ideas about present-day civilization.

The title has an essential role. It is characteristic of Klee's works that the image, no matter how appealing, does not reveal its full content unless the artist tells us what it means. The title, in turn, needs the picture. The witty concept of a twittering machine does not fire our imagination until we are shown such a thing. This interdependence is familiar to us from cartoons, but Klee lifts it to the level of high art without giving up the playful character of these verbal-visual puns. To him art was a language of signs, of shapes that are images of ideas—just as the shape of the letter S stands for a specific sound or an arrow is the sign of a one-way street. He also realized that in any conventional system the sign is no more than a "trigger." The instant we see it, we automatically give it meaning without stopping to consider its shape. Klee wanted his signs to be perceived as visual facts and also to act as triggers.

How did Klee create *The Twittering Machine?* His writings confirm what we can sense from the drawing itself. He started with a point, which grew organically into a line that became a plane and then evolved into spaces; taken together they define the form. This process, although based on "pure artistic craftsman-ship," gives the drawing its air of fresh inspiration and accounts for its whimsical character. He admitted as much: "The legend of the childishness of my drawing must have originated from those linear compositions of mine in which I tried to combine a con-crete image . . . with the pure representation of the linear element. Always combined with the more subconscious dimensions of the picture."

Toward the end of his life, Klee became absorbed in the study of ideographs of all kinds, such as hieroglyphics, hex signs, and the mysterious markings in prehistoric caves—simplified representa-tional images that appealed to him because they had the twin quality he strove for in his own graphic language. This "ideo-graphic style" is clearly stated in figure 24-46, *Park near Lu(cerne).* As a lyric poet may use the plainest words, these deceptively simple shapes sum up a wealth of experience and sensation: the innocent gaiety of spring, the clipped orderliness peculiar to captive plant life in a park. Has it not also a relationship, in spirit if not in fact, with the Romanesque *Summer Landscape* in the manuscript of *Carmina Burana* (see fig. 10-42)? Klee's attitude soon changed. Shortly before his death, the artist's horror at World War II led him to abandon this lighthearted approach in favor of a pessimistic manner similar to Miró's darkest fantasies of the same time.

Expressionism

KÄTHE KOLLWITZ. The experience of World War I filled German artists with a deep anguish at the state of modern civi-lization, which found its principal outlet in Expressionism. The work of Käthe Kollwitz (1867–1945) consists almost exclusively of prints and drawings that are comparable to those of Kokoschka,

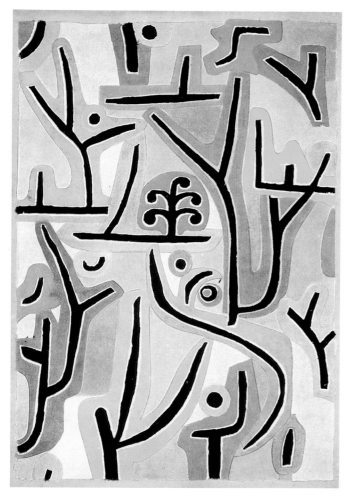

24-46. Paul Klee. *Park near Lu(cerne)*. 1938. Oil and newsprint on burlap, 39½ x 27½" (100.3 x 69.7 cm). Foundation Paul Klee, Kunstmuseum, Bern, Switzerland

COPYRIGHT 1986 COSMOPRESS, GENEVA

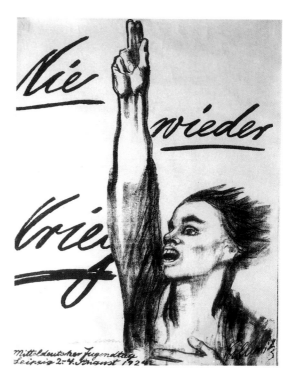

24-47. Käthe Kollwitz. *Never Again War!* 1924. Lithograph, 37 x 27½" (94 x 70 cm). Courtesy Galerie St. Etienne, New York

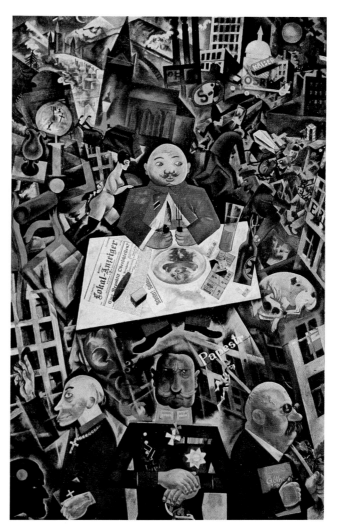

24-48. George Grosz. *Germany, a Winter's Tale*. 1918. Formerly Collection Garvens, Hanover, Germany

whom she admired. Her graphics had their sources in the nineteenth century. Munch, Klimt, and the German artist Max Klinger (1857–1920) were early inspirations, as was her friend Ernst Barlach (see page 768). However, Kollwitz pursued a resolutely independent course by devoting her art to themes of inhumanity and injustice. To articulate her social and ethical concerns, she adopted an intensely expressive yet naturalistic style that is as unrelenting in its bleakness as her choice of subjects. Gaunt mothers and exploited workers provided many of Kollwitz's themes, but her most impassioned statements were reserved for war. World War I, which cost her oldest son his life, made her an ardent pacifist. Her lithograph *Never Again War!* (fig. 24-47) is an unforgettable image of protest.

GEORGE GROSZ. George Grosz (1893–1959), a painter and graphic artist who had studied in Paris in 1913, joined the Dadaist movement in Berlin after the end of the war. Inspired by the Futurists, he developed a dynamic form of Cubism for his bitter and often savage satires, which expressed the disillusionment of his generation. In *Germany, a Winter's Tale* (fig. 24-48), the city of Berlin forms the kaleidoscopic and chaotic background for several large figures, which are superimposed on it as in a collage. They

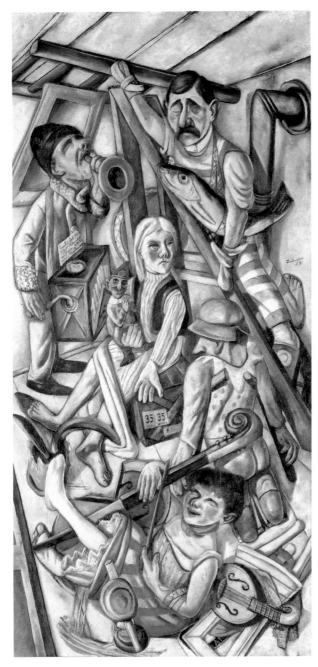

24-49. Max Beckmann. *The Dream*. 1921. Oil on canvas,
71 x 35" (180.3 x 89 cm). Collection Morton D. May,
St. Louis, Missouri

painting to "reproach God for his errors." *The Dream* (fig. 24-49) is a mocking nightmare, a tilted, zigzag world as disquieting as Bosch's Hell (see fig. 15-14). It is crammed with maimed, puppet-like figures that reflect the artist's experience in the army medical corps. We see the handless swimmer carrying a fish and climbing a ladder that leads only to another ladder on the ceiling; the crippled clown whose open hat protects his eyes but not his head from the nonexistent sun; the woman singing ecstatically to herself as she plays a stringless cello; and the beggar frantically cranking his hurdy-gurdy and blaring his trumpet to this unreceptive audience. All are blind except the blond girl in the center. (Note the mirror that reflects nothing and the lantern that illuminates nothing.) A recent arrival, to judge from her trunk, she observes everything with detachment and gestures as if to say, "Behold this Ship of Fools," while the puppet in her hand mockingly applauds the absurd performance. Her innocence is underscored by the plant, which rudely pushes aside her dress as she tries to stop its advance with one foot. The forms show the inspiration of the early German prints, which Beckmann shared with the members of *Die Brücke* (compare figs. 15-21–15-24).

The claustrophobic space, derived from the same source, is essential to the image, which radiates an oppressive aura. It was, he said, "how I defend myself against the infinity of space . . . the great spatial void and uncertainty that I call God." [See Primary Sources, no. 91, page 944.] Beckmann has created a powerful image whose meaning is conveyed by symbolism that is necessarily subjective. How indeed could Beckmann have expressed the chaos in Germany after the war with the worn-out language of traditional symbols? "These are the creatures that haunt my imagination," he seems to say. "They show the true nature of the modern condition—how weak we are, how helpless against ourselves in this proud era of so-called progress."

Some elements from this grotesque and sinister sideshow recur in altered form more than a decade later in the wings of Beckmann's triptych *Departure* (fig. 24-50), which reflects his admiration for Grünewald (compare figs. 16-1 and 16-2). The two wings show a nightmarish world crammed with puppetlike figures, as disquieting as those in Bosch's hell (see fig. 15-14). The right panel incorporates a blind man holding a fish, a lantern that illuminates nothing, and a mad musician, while the left one shows a scene of almost unimaginable torture. What are we to make of these brutal images? We know from letters written by the artist and a close friend that they represent life itself as endless misery filled with all kinds of physical and spiritual pain. The woman trying to make her way in the dark with the aid of the lamp is carrying the corpse of her memories, evil deeds, and failures, from which no one can ever be free so long as life beats its drum. The center panel signifies the departure from life's illusions to the reality behind appearances. The crowned figure seen from behind recalls the legendary Fisher King from the legend of the Holy Grail, whose health and that of his land is restored by Parsifal.

Departure proved remarkably prophetic. It was completed when the artist was on the verge of leaving his homeland under Nazi pressure. The topsy-turvy quality of the two wing scenes, full of mutilations and meaningless rituals, well captures the flavor of Hitler's Germany. The stable design of the center panel, in con-

include the marionette-like "good citizen" at his table and the sinister forces that molded him: a hypocritical clergyman, a brutal general, and an evil schoolmaster. This, Grosz tells us, is the decadent world of the bourgeoisie that he, like many German intellectuals, hoped would be overthrown by Communism. His bitter parodies are counterparts to the Expressionist dramas of Georg Kaiser and the nihilistic early Dadaist plays of Bertolt Brecht, who shared a Marxist outlook (see box page 834).

MAX BECKMANN. Max Beckmann (1884–1950), a descendant of *Die Brücke* artists, did not become an Expressionist until after he had lived through World War I, which filled him with such despair at the state of modern civilization that he took up

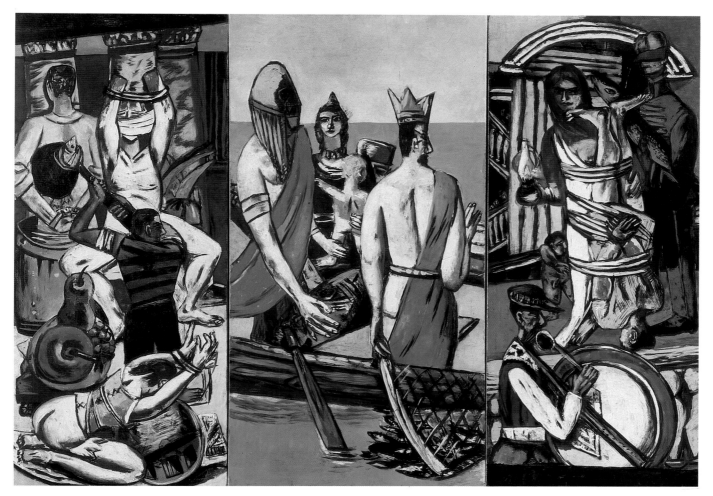

24-50. Max Beckmann. *Departure.* 1932–33. Oil on canvas, center panel 7'3⁄4" x 3'9 3⁄8" (2.15 x 1.15 m); side panels each 7'3⁄4" x 3'3 1⁄4" (2.15 x 1 m). The Museum of Modern Art, New York

trast, with its expanse of blue sea and its sunlit brightness, conveys the hopeful spirit of an embarkation for distant shores. After living through World War II in occupied Holland under the most difficult conditions, Beckmann spent the final three years of his life in America.

ARTHUR DOVE. In the United States after 1920, most of the original members of the Stieglitz group concentrated on landscapes, which they treated in representational styles derived from Expressionism. Alone among them Arthur G. Dove (1880–1946) consistently maintained a form of abstraction, one loosely related to Kandinsky's. The difference between the two artists is that Dove wanted to reveal the inner life of nature, whereas Kandinsky tried to rid his images of readily recognizable subject matter. Dove was a natural-born painter, with a sure touch and flawless sense of design. His paintings have a monumental spirit that belies their often modest size. *Foghorns* (fig. 24-51) shows the intelligence and economy of his mature work. To evoke the diffusion of sound, Dove used the simple but ingenious device of irregular concentric circles of color that grow paler as they radiate outward.

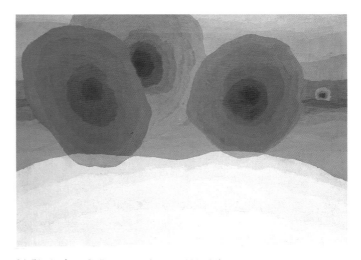

24-51. Arthur G. Dove. *Foghorns.* 1929. Oil on canvas, 18 x 26" (42.7 x 66 cm). Colorado Springs Fine Arts Center

MUSIC BETWEEN THE WARS

In 1923 Arnold Schoenberg (see also box page 812) had made the decisive final step from dissonance to complete atonality when he produced his first "serial" works based on the so-called twelve-tone row (also called series). Each row uses all the notes of the tempered scale just once, except for a few "free" notes that do not conform to the sequence. It thus constitutes a self-contained musical realm representing the final overthrow of tonalism. By subjecting it to various traditional techniques for modifying and extending it (including such as devices as retro-grades, inversions, and transpositions), the row can be built into a large-scale composition without repeating any sequence. Serialism was, then, simply a means of organizing Schoenberg's compositions, which were often conventional in form, notably the concertos for cello, violin, and piano written between 1932 and 1942. *A Survivor from Warsaw* (1948), written after the com-poser, like Stravinsky, had fled Austria and settled in California, conveys the nightmare of the Holocaust with almost unbearable anguish. By this time he had emerged as the most influential composer in the West. Even Stravinsky (see box page 812) adopt-ed serialism toward the end of his long life. Early on Schoenberg's music had a dissonance and liveliness comparable to Stravinsky's, while in the late 1920s it acquired an equal astringency.

Needless to say, Schoenberg's music made extraordinary demands on musician and listener alike. Yet he was able to attract talented disciples almost as soon as he settled in Vienna in 1903. Chief among them was Anton Webern (1883–1945), who, like Gustav Mahler before him, was better known as a conduc-tor during his lifetime. Webern's mature compositions, all small in scale, are miracles of rigor, conciseness, and purity. For over a decade his music retained aspects of Schoenberg's expression-ism, making it a counterpart to the hypersensitive manner of his friend Oscar Kokoschka. Hence serialism initially had little impact on his style and, as was the case with Schoenberg, was lit-tle more than a convenient means of organizing compositions more coherently. However, he gradually began to apply its prin-ciples to other aspects of music, not just tone rows. Much of Webern's work consists of songs and choral music that treat the voice as simply another instrument, for he was as devoted to his serial system as Bach had been to counterpoint. At first Webern's literary sources differed little in character from those of Mahler, but his terse atonality can be regarded as the antidote to the inflated rhetoric of his predecessor's song cycles,—*The Youth's Magic Horn,* for instance. Webern's later songs in the serial tech-nique are remarkably successful settings of mystical poems by his friend Hildegard Jone.

The main contributions of Alban Berg (1885–1935), Schoen-berg's other important pupil, are the Expressionist operas *Wozzeck* (1923), based on the play by Georg Büchner (1813–1837), and the unfinished *Lulu* (1935), derived from two plays of 1895 by Franklin Wedekind. Both are emotionally har-rowing explorations of the dark side of human existence in a world of unrelenting evil. *Wozzeck* becomes a terrifying symbol of modern man trapped by forces he cannot comprehend that ultimately destroy him, while *Lulu* traces the descent of the pro-tagonist into prostitution and her murder at the hands of Jack the Ripper as a tragic metaphor for the unbridled lust and avarice in contemporary society. In Berg's vocal writing one can still hear the last vestiges of Wagnerian opera, stripped of its mythical trappings so that it evokes a disturbing, yet haunting, vision of twentieth-century life.

The most important composer to emerge between the world wars was Béla Bartók (1881–1945). In 1905 he met the composer Zoltán Kodály (1882–1967); together they began to collect the ethnic music of Hungary and ran the Budapest Academy of Music. While utilizing folk melodies, rhythms, and modes, Bartók incorporated the complex rhythms and the percussive effects of Stravinsky, as well as the dissonance and atonality of Schoenberg. His music was intensely personal, uniting Expressionism and Surrealism to convey the searing emotionalism apparent in the opera *Bluebeard's Castle* (1918), the ballet *The Mandarin Prince* (1926), and especially the six string quartets (1908–39), which equal Beethoven's in profun-dity and innovation. Bartók was a famous piano virtuoso, whose three concertos (1926–45) exploit the full percussive potential of that instrument. The final piano concerto and the *Concerto for Orchestra* (1943), both written in the United States, are more melodic and accessible to a wide audience, without diluting the composer's unique vision.

The Czech composer Leo Janáček (1854–1928) did not achieve prominence until the last decade or so of his life, when most of his best music was written. Because of the language bar-rier, his late operas, such as *The Makropulos Affair* and *From the House of the Dead,* present serious obstacles for performance that have hindered their wider acceptance, but they are compa-rable to Bartók's *Bluebeard's Castle* in their innovation, fervent nationalism, and uncompromising tough-mindedness. More approachable are the orchestral pieces: the justly famous *Sinfonietta* (1926) combines swirling passion with brilliant, imaginative touches that make it one of the greatest master-pieces of the twentieth century.

Sergei Prokofiev (1891–1953), the greatest Russian compos-er of the twentieth century, became a member of the avant-garde even before completing his studies in composition and piano at the St. Petersburg Conservatory of Music. His early contact with modernist poets, the Cubo-Futurists (see pages 815–16), Sergei Diaghilev, and Vsevelod Meyerhold (see box page 818, as well as his study of Igor Stravinsky's early ballets (see box page 812), led him to investigate dissonance with increasing boldness. The heart of his music nevertheless remained melody coupled with strong rhythmic impulses. Prokofiev was a noted virtuoso, and much of his piano music, including five sonatas and two concer-tos, as well as numerous shorter pieces, were written prior to the Russian revolution, along with his first efforts at ballet and opera, which became lifelong interests. In 1918, he left with the blessings of the authorities for a concert tour that took him to the United States and Europe. He settled eventually in Paris, where he gained the support of Diaghilev and the Russian expatriate conductor Serge Koussevitsky. These years were devoted mainly to ballets and an opera, *The Stone Flower*, which together provided the basis for much of his symphonic output as well. This was nevertheless a relatively fallow period. In 1933 Prokofiev decided to return to Russia, which he had visited several times on tour. The result was an outpouring of the music for which he is best known today: the great ballet *Romeo and Juliet*, the enchanting orchestral fairy tale for children *Peter and the Wolf*, scores for Sergei Eisenstein's films *Alexander Nevsky* and *Ivan the Terrible*, the *Second Violin Concerto*, the *Fifth Symphony*, and the magnificent *Eighth Piano Sonata*. Mention should also be made here of the composer Nikolai Miaskovsky (1881–1950), whose vast output of symphonies, quartets, and piano sonatas form a bridge to those of the younger Dmitri Shostakovich (see box page 812). Although they tried to accommodate the demands of Soviet musical authorities, Prokofiev, Miaskovsky, and Shostakovich all suffered terrible privation and repression after the war. Fittingly enough, no one today listens to the composers who were approved by Russian officials.

The most prominent German composer to emerge after World War I was Paul Hindemith (1895–1963), who nevertheless occupies a problematic place in history. His finest works are the chamber music pieces from the 1920s —mostly in the form of concertos for various instruments—which have the vitality of a young composer reveling in his growing mastery. Thereafter Hindemith became increasingly absorbed by theory and pedagogy. He devised a comprehensive, yet still modern, tonal system that reflected his moral and spiritual idealism. The fullest statements of the composer's principles are *The Life of the Virgin (Das Marienleben)* (1948), which is a complete reworking of the song cycle for soprano after poems by Rainer Maria Rilke; and *The Harmony of the Universe* (1951), which is based on a poem by Hindemith himself on the life of the 17th-century astronomer Johannes Kepler, whose treatise bears the same title. Although these works undeniably achieve the complete integration he sought, most lack the lively interest of his early works.

The United States produced two composers of note during the first part of the twentieth century: Charles Ives (1874–1954) and Henry Cowell (1897–1965). Ives received a conventional academic music training at Yale University, but even before then he had begun to experiment with effects that were to become the hallmarks of his music. They reach their height in *Symphony no. 4* (1916), which employs several themes played simultaneously in different keys by different groups under separate conductors that create a clashing, kaleidoscopic effect; and in the *Piano Sonata no. 2 (Concord)* (1920), which requires the pianist to use elbows as well as wood blocks to play the notes. Ives was nevertheless a gifted melodist. *Three Places in New England* (1914) is a consciously American piece in its choice of themes and alternately festive and haunting atmosphere.

Ives did little composing after 1918. He spent the rest of his life as a successful insurance salesman, and shared his music with only a few friends, such as Cowell and Carl Ruggles (1876–1971). Cowell, like Ives, was a pioneer in experimental music for the piano. He wrote several pieces for "prepared piano," an instrument made ready for performance by having objects attached to or placed on its strings, some of which might also be tuned unconventionally. He was the first American composer to show a consistent interest in the music of other cultures, which he incorporated into his numerous symphonies. Ruggles was a resolute individualist whose few works, such as *Sun Treader (1932)*, deal with Symbolist themes. Although their treatment sometimes has a nearly post-Romantic massiveness, they consistently show an obsession with perfection of form and sound achieved through the most concentrated means. (He once spent the afternoon repeating the same note on the piano in search of "the perfect C.")

Aaron Copland (1900–1990) studied under Nadia Boulanger (1887–1979) during the early 1920s in Paris, where he came under the influence of Stravinsky. Upon his return to the United States, he adopted themes and rhythms inspired by jazz. Enthused by liberal ideology, he sought to create music that would speak to all the people, not simply those of one region. As a result, Copland, more than any other composer, defined our concept of "American" music across a wide spectrum, including Latin, Mexican, Appalachian, and Western. His three ballets—*Billy the Kid* (1838), *Rodeo* (1942), and above all *Appalachian Spring* (1944)—are justifiably popular works that combine touching lyricism with rhythmic vivacity of almost irresistible appeal. Copland's work also includes a number of challenging serious works, such as *Variations* for piano (1930) and the *Third Symphony* (1946), composed in the Neoclassical manner of Stravinsky.

England also had an important school of composers before 1945, starting with the Victorian Romantic Edward Elgar (1857–1934). Elgar's cantata, *A Dream of Gerontius* (1900), based on a poem about a soul's journey to heaven by the theologian John Henry Newman, conveys the idealism of the English school, which reaches all the way back to George Frideric Handel (see pages 636–37), although Elgar himself largely retired in bitter disillusionment after completing his well-known *Cello Concerto* in 1919. Equally characteristic was the love of nature found in the work of Gustav Holst (1874–1934), best-known for *The Planets* (1916). Perhaps the finest composer representative of the English school between the wars was Ralph Vaughan Williams (1872–1958). His most characteristic orchestral works, such as the Fifth Symphony (1938-43, rev. 1951) and *The Lark Descending (*1914, rev. 1920), are in the pastoral vein unique to the British school. However, the *Fourth* and *Eighth Symphonies* (1931–34; 1953–56) reveal a more turbulent side, as does the brilliant *Partita for Double String Orchestra* (1946-8). His masterpiece is the choral work *Serenade to Music,* which incorporates the full expressive range of Vaughn Williams' music. Composed in 1938 for sixteen singers and orchestra under the conductor Henry Wood, it is set to a text from Shakespeare's *Merchant of Venice* that expresses the mysterious power of music over the human spirit.

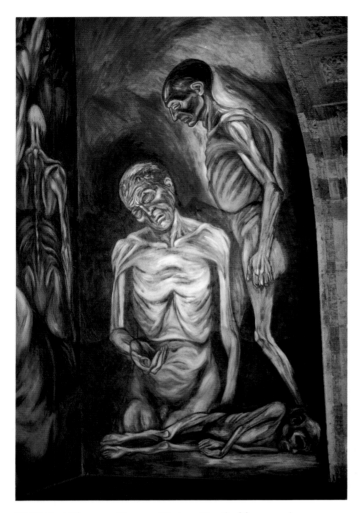

24-52. José Clemente Orozco. *Victims*. Detail of fresco cycle.
1936. University of Guadalajara, Mexico

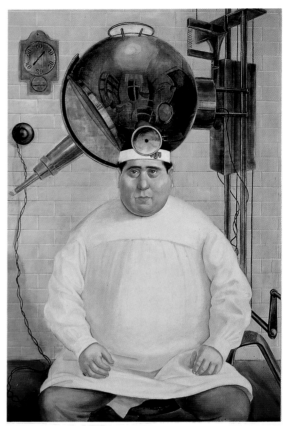

24-53. Otto Dix. *Dr. Mayer-Hermann*. 1926.
Oil and tempera on wood, 58¾ x 39" (149.2 x 99.1 cm).
The Museum of Modern Art, New York

JOSÉ CLEMENTE OROZCO. During the 1930s, the center of Expressionism in the New World was Mexico. The Mexican Revolution began in 1911 with the fall of the dictator Porfirio Díaz (1830–1915) and continued for more than two decades. It inspired a group of young painters to search for a national style incorporating the great native heritage of Pre-Columbian art. They also felt that their art must be "of the people," and must express the spirit of the Revolution in large mural cycles in public buildings. Although each developed his own distinctive style, they shared a common point of departure: the Symbolist art of Gauguin, which had shown how non-Western forms could be integrated into the Western tradition. The flat, decorative quality of Symbolism was well suited to murals. However, the involvement of these painters in the political turmoil of the day often led them to overburden their works with ideology. Only José Clemente Orozco (1883–1949), a passionately independent artist, refused to get embroiled in factional politics. The detail from the mural cycle at the University of Guadalajara (fig. 24-52) illustrates his most powerful trait: a deep humanitarian sympathy with the silent, suffering masses.

Realism

OTTO DIX. In 1923 the director of the Mannheim museum in Germany organized an exhibition with the title *Die Neue Sachlichkeit* (The New Objectivity; sometimes also known as *Magic Realism*). This, he explained, was "a label for the new realism bearing a socialist flavor. Cynicism and resignation are the negative side of New Objectivity; the positive side expresses itself in the enthusiasm for immediate reality." Its principal representatives were George Grosz, who by this time had abandoned his slashing style for a more realistic manner no less biting in its sarcasm, and Max Beckmann, whose naturalism was simply a means for expressing his disillusionment. But it was the meticulous realism of Otto Dix (1891–1969), another Expressionist who had also been a member of Dada, that defined the main characteristics of the New Objectivity. Its roots lay in German Renaissance art and the Romanticism of Runge, which Dix used to expose the ills of modern Germany with obsessive detail. His best works are his portraits, such as one of Dr. Mayer-Hermann (fig. 24-53). The image has a supernatural clarity that lends an almost nightmarish intensity to

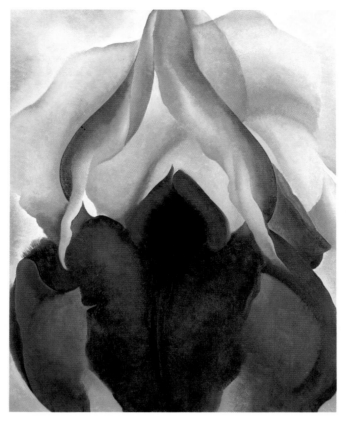

24-54. Georgia O'Keeffe. *Black Iris III*. 1926.
Oil on canvas, 36 x 29⅞" (91.4 x 75.9 cm).
The Metropolitan Museum of Art, New York

this image of a doctor seated impassively before his instruments, which echo his bulbous shape. In the process, these medical instruments have acquired the alien quality of the devices in Max Ernst's *1 Piping Man* (see fig. 24-39), so that they become strangely menacing. For an equally compelling portrayal, we must turn to Ingres' *Louis Bertin* (see fig. 21-31). That the portrait by Dix compares favorably shows Dix's powers of characterization. It also testifies to his desire to extend "those forms of expression already present in the Old Masters. For me, the object is primary and determines the form. I have therefore always felt it vital to get as close as possible to the thing I see." Such an approach was necessary for Dix, because the object both stood for and provided the subject of art.

GEORGIA O'KEEFFE. The New Objectivity soon gave way to realism for its own sake. Tinged with Romantic nostalgia, it was part of a widespread conservative reaction on both sides of the Atlantic. The most important realist in American art during the 1920s was Georgia O'Keeffe (1887–1986). Throughout her long career, she experimented with a wide range of subjects and styles. Like Arthur Dove, she practiced a form of organic abstraction indebted to Expressionism, but she also adopted the Precisionism of Charles Demuth (see fig. 24-34), so that she is sometimes considered an abstract artist. Her work often combined aspects of both approaches: as she absorbed a subject into her imagination, she would alter and simplify the image to invest it with personal meaning. O'Keeffe nevertheless remained a realist at heart. *Black Iris III* (fig. 24-54) is the kind of painting for which she is best known. The image is marked by a strong sense of design unique to her. The decorative quality of the flower is deceptive, however. Observed close-up and magnified to large scale, it is a thinly disguised symbol of female sexuality.

AMERICAN SCENE PAINTING. The dominance of realism during the 1930s signaled the retreat of progressive art everywhere in response to the economic depression and social turmoil that gripped both Europe and the United States. Realism was often linked to political propaganda or the reaffirmation of traditional values. Most American artists split into two camps, the Regionalists and the Social Realists. The Regionalists wanted to revive idealism by updating the American myth, which was largely defined, however, in Midwestern terms. The Social Realists, by contrast, captured the dislocation and despair of the Depression era, and were often concerned with social reform. Although bitterly opposed to each other, both movements drew freely on the Ash Can School (see page 821).

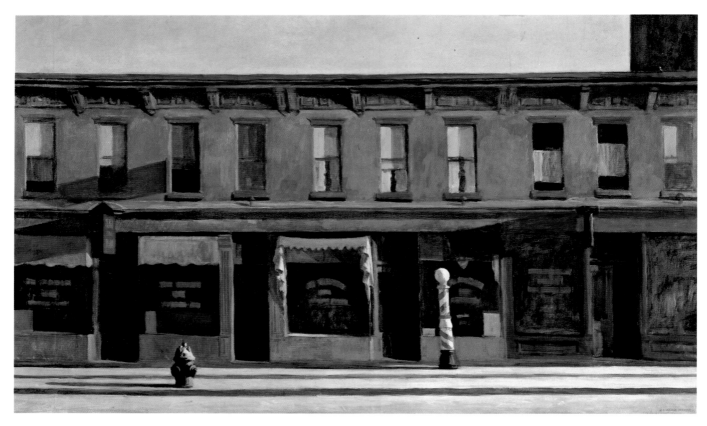

24-55. Edward Hopper. *Early Sunday Morning.* 1930. Oil on canvas, 35 x 60" (88.9 x 152.4 cm).
WHITNEY MUSEUM OF AMERICAN ART, NEW YORK

EDWARD HOPPER. The one artist who appealed to all factions, including the few remaining abstractionists, was Edward Hopper (1882–1967), a former pupil of Robert Henri (see page 821; Ash Can School). He focused on what has since become known as the vernacular architecture of American cities—store fronts, movie houses, all-night diners—which no one else had thought worthy of attention. *Early Sunday Morning* (fig. 24-55) finds a haunting sense of loneliness in the familiar elements of an ordinary street. Its quietness, we realize, is temporary; there is hidden life behind these facades. We almost expect to see one of the window shades raised as we look at them. Apart from its poetic appeal, the picture also has remarkable formal discipline. We note the careful placement of the fireplug and barber pole, the subtle variations in the treatment of the row of windows, and the precisely defined slant of the sunlight. The delicate balance of verticals and horizontals clearly shows Hopper's awareness of Mondrian.

JACOB LAWRENCE. The 1920s brought about a cultural revival among African-Americans known as the Harlem Renaissance. Although its promise was shattered by the economic disaster of the Great Depression, this brief flowering, which included literature and music, produced the first black artists to gain national recognition. By far the most famous remains Jacob Lawrence (1917–2000), who rose to prominence around 1940. Motivated by rage at the injustices inflicted on African-Americans, Lawrence treated historical themes and the major social issues of the day. His series "From Every Southern

Town . . ." (see fig. 24-56) focuses on the mass exodus of blacks from the south. Despite its small size, our panel has an impressive monumentality, thanks to the simplified forms and flat colors. So powerful was Lawrence's impact that his art continues to define African-American painting for many people, although he retired in 1983.

PAINTING SINCE WORLD WAR II
Abstract Expressionism: Action Painting

Having survived the most serious economic disaster and the greatest threat to civilization in all of history, the Western world now faced a potentially even greater danger: nuclear holocaust. This central fact conditioned the entire Cold War era, which began when the Soviet Union exploded its own nuclear bomb in 1948 and came to an end only with the fall of Russian Communism in 1985. Ironically, it was also a period of unprecedented prosperity in the West, but not for much of the rest of the world, which, with the notable exception of Japan, has struggled to compete successfully until very recently and still lags in many areas.

The painting that prevailed for about 15 years after the end of World War II arose in direct response to the anxiety brought on by these dramatic changes. The term *Abstract Expressionism* is often applied to this style, which was initiated by artists living in New York City. Under the influence of Surrealism and existentialist philosophy, Action painters, the first of the Abstract Expressionists, developed a new approach to art. Painting became a counterpart

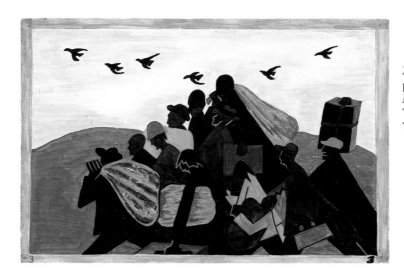

24-56. Jacob Lawrence. *The Migration of the Negro,* panel 3, from the series *From Every Southern Town Migrants Left by the Hundreds to Travel North.* 1940–41. Tempera on Masonite, 11½ x 17½" (29.2 x 44.4 cm). The Phillips Collection, Washington, D.C.

to life itself. It was seen as an ongoing process in which risks are faced and overcome through a series of conscious and unconscious decisions in response to dictates of the imagination and the demands imposed by their canvases. The Color Field painters in turn dissolved the frenzied gestures and intense hues of the Action painters in broad forms of poetic color, which sometimes reflect the influence of Oriental spirituality. In a sense, Color Field Painting resolved the conflicts expressed by Action Painting. They are, however, two sides of the same coin, separated by the thinnest differences of approach.

ADOLPH GOTTLIEB. During World War II the poet André Breton and other Surrealists found refuge in New York, where their work was enthusiastically received by critics and exhibited at museums and galleries such as Peggy Guggenheim's Art of This Century. Soon the early Abstract Expressionists developed their own form of Surrealism that allowed them to convey their sense of horror at the pervasive evil of a chaotic world. Deeply troubled by the massive bloodshed, they became myth-makers whose images expressed their sense of impending disaster. Their approach was strongly affected by the theory of the collective subconscious formulated by Freud's disciple Carl Jung, who believed that universal archetypes are imbedded in the "collective subconscious" of our psyches.

The breakthrough came in a discussion between Adolph Gottlieb (1903–1974) and Mark Rothko (see below), who suggested they try Classical themes. Gottlieb then began to paint pictographs based on Sophokles and the other Greek tragedians. Pictographs are a form of picture writing found in prehistoric art; no longer intelligible to us, they nevertheless exercise a mysterious, instinctive appeal. Few prehistoric images, however, have the impact of Gottlieb's pictographs (fig. 24-57), which conjure up something more elemental than even the most ancient relic. The canvas owes its power to his uncanny ability to cast the viewer back into the dark, primitive realm of the human mind. Painted in an uncompromisingly severe style, it radiates a menacing evil that is a truly frightening evocation of the war. Composed in a grid system derived from Mondrian, the painting has Surrealist forms influ-

enced by the grimmest works of Picasso, Miró, and Klee from the same years. At face value the picture seems a confusing jumble of human anatomy cut up and reassembled by a maniac. It demands to be read section by section, yet it does not yield a literal meaning. Instead, the accumulation of intuitive responses through free association provides an experience at once overwhelming and profoundly disturbing.

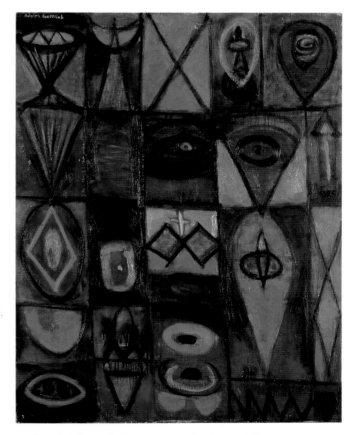

24-57. Adolph Gottlieb. *Descent into Darkness.* 1947. Oil on Masonite, 30 x 25" (76.2 x 63.5 cm). Smith College Museum of Art, Northampton, Massachusetts

ACQUIRED BY EXCHANGE, 1951

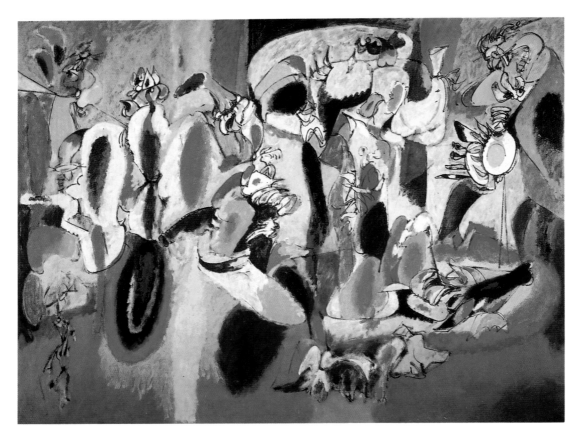

24-58. Arshile Gorky.
*The Liver Is the
Cock's Comb.* 1944.
Oil on canvas, 6¼" x 8'2"
(1.86 x 2.49 m).
Albright-Knox Art
Gallery, Buffalo,
New York

ARSHILE GORKY. Arshile Gorky (1904–1948), an Armenian who came to America at 16, was the pioneer of the Abstract Expressionist movement and the single most important influence on its other members. It took him 20 years, painting first in the manner of Cézanne, then Picasso, to arrive at his mature style. We see it in *The Liver Is the Cock's Comb* (fig. 24-58), his greatest work. The enigmatic title suggests the artist's close contact with the Surrealists during the war. A personal mythology underlies Gorky's work; each form represents a private symbol within this self-contained realm. Everything here is in the process of turning into something else. The treatment reflects his own experience in camouflage, gained from a class he conducted during the war. The biomorphic shapes clearly owe much to Miró, while their spontaneous handling and the glowing color reflect Gorky's enthusiasm for Kandinsky (see fig. 24-9). The differences are equally striking. The dynamic interlocking of the forms, their aggressive power of attraction and repulsion, are unique to Gorky.

JACKSON POLLOCK. The most important of the Action painters proved to be Jackson Pollock (1912–1956). His huge canvas titled *Autumn Rhythm: Number 30, 1950* (fig. 24-59) was executed mainly by pouring and spattering the colors, instead of applying them with a brush. [See Primary Sources, no. 92, page 974.] The result, especially when viewed at close range, suggests both Kandinsky and Max Ernst (compare figs. 24-9 and 24-40). Kandinsky's nonrepresentational Expressionism and the Surrealists' exploitation of chance effects were indeed the main sources of Pollock's work, but they do not account for his revolutionary technique and the emotional appeal of his art. Why did Pollock

"fling a pot of paint in the public's face," as Ruskin had accused Whistler of doing? It was surely not to be more abstract than earlier artists, for the strict control implied by abstraction is exactly what Pollock gave up when he began to dribble and spatter. Rather, he came to regard paint itself not as a passive substance to be manipulated at will but as a storehouse of pent-up forces for him to release.

The actual shapes visible in our illustration were largely determined by the internal dynamics of his material and his process: the viscosity of the paint, the speed and direction of its impact upon the canvas, its interaction with other layers of pigment. The result is a surface so alive, so sensuously rich, that all earlier American painting looks pale in comparison. Pollock did not simply "let go" and leave the rest to chance when he "aimed" the paint at the canvas instead of "carrying" it on the tip of his brush. He released the forces within the paint by giving it a momentum of its own. He himself was the source of energy for these forces, and he "rode" them as a cowboy might ride a wild horse, in a frenzy of psychophysical action. He did not always stay in the saddle; yet the thrill of this contest, which strained his entire being, was worth the risk.

Our simile, though crude, points up the main difference between Pollock and previous artists: his total commitment to the *act* of painting. Thus he preferred to work on huge canvases that provided a "field of combat" large enough for him to paint not merely with his arms but with his whole body. The term *Action Painting* conveys the essence of this distinctive approach far better than does Abstract Expressionism. Although Pollock gave up a good deal of control over his medium, this loss was

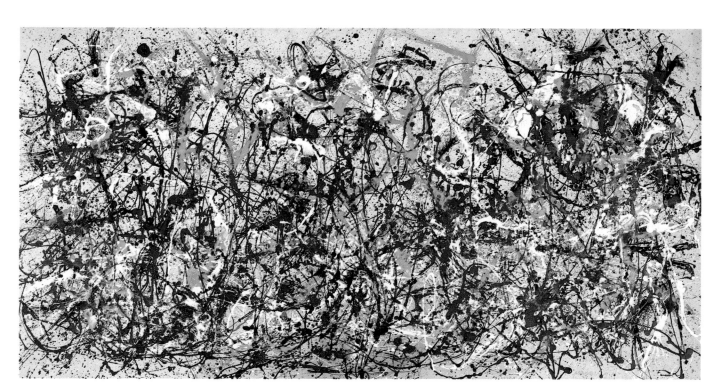

24-59. Jackson Pollock. *Autumn Rhythm: Number 30, 1950*. 1950. Oil on canvas, 8'8" x 17'3" (2.64 x 5.26 m).
The Metropolitan Museum of Art, New York

GEORGE A. HEARN FUND, 1957

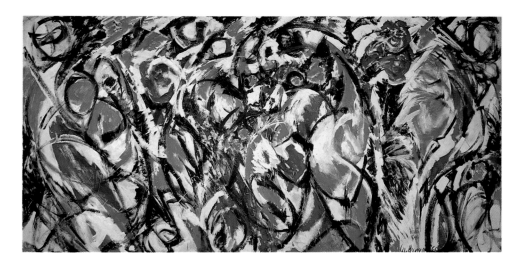

24-60. Lee Krasner.
Celebration. 1959–60.
Oil on canvas, 7'8¼" x 16'4½"
(2.3 x 4.9 m). Private collection

COURTESY ROBERT MILLER GALLERY, NEW YORK

more than offset by a gain: the new continuity and expansiveness in the creative process, which gave his work its distinctive mid-twentieth-century stamp. Pollock's drip technique, however, was not in itself essential to Action Painting, and he stopped using it in 1953 as part of a personal and artistic crisis—including acute alcoholism—that ended his life.

LEE KRASNER. Lee Krasner (1908–1984), who was married to Pollock, never abandoned the brush, although she was unmistakably influenced by him. She struggled to establish her artistic identity and emerged from his shadow only after undergoing several changes in direction and destroying much of her early work. Following Pollock's death, she succeeded in doing what he had been attempting to do for the last three years of his career: to reintroduce the figure into Abstract Expressionism while retaining the automatic handwriting that was a hallmark of the style. The poten-

tial had always been there in Pollock's work: we can easily imagine wildly dancing people in *Autumn Rhythm*. In *Celebration* (fig. 24-60), Krasner defines these rudimentary shapes from within the tangled network of lines by using the broad gestures of Action Painting to suggest human forms without actually depicting them.

WILLEM DE KOONING. The work of Willem de Kooning (1904–1997), another prominent member of the group and a close friend of Gorky, always maintains a link with the visible world, whether or not it has a recognizable subject. In some paintings, such as *Woman II* (fig. 24-61), the image emerges from the jagged welter of brushstrokes. De Kooning shares with Pollock the furious energy of the painting process, the sense of risk, of a challenge successfully—but barely—met. The picture looks as if it had been executed in an afternoon. In reality, the artist worked on the canvas for two years and constantly repainted it until he got it right.

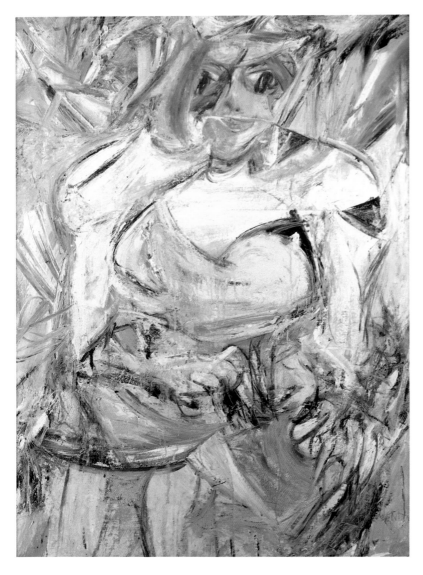

24-61. Willem de Kooning. *Woman II.*
1952. Oil on canvas, 59 x 43" (149.9 x 109.2 cm).
The Museum of Modern Art, New York
GIFT OF MRS. JOHN D. ROCKEFELLER 3RD

What are we to make of his wildly distorted *Woman II*? She was actually intended as a caricature of modern movie stars such as Marilyn Monroe, but the result is anything but humorous. It is as if the flow of psychic impulses during the process of painting unleashed this nightmarish specter from deep within the artist's subconscious, much as it did in Adolph Gottlieb's pictographs (compare fig. 24-57). For that reason, De Kooning has sometimes been accused of being a woman-hater, a charge he denied. Rather, his figure is like a primordial goddess, frightening yet seductive, who represents the primitive side of our makeup. We have met her before, for example, in *"The Mistress of the Animals"* from Thera (see fig. 4-8). De Kooning, who emigrated to America from Holland as a young man, shared with Max Beckmann an Old World horror of empty space, which to him signified the existential void. Only after he moved to Long Island from the confines of New York City was he able to overcome this deep-seated anxiety, which led him to cover every inch of canvas.

Expressionism in Europe

Action Painting marked the international coming-of-age of American art. The movement had a powerful impact on European art, which in those years had nothing to show of comparable force and conviction. One French artist, however, was of such amazing originality as to constitute a movement all by himself: Jean Dubuffet (1901–1985), whose first exhibition soon after the Liberation electrified and antagonized the Paris art world.

JEAN DUBUFFET. Although he had formal instruction in painting as a young man, Dubuffet responded neither to the various trends he saw around him nor to the art of the museums. All struck him as divorced from real life, and he turned to other pursuits. Only in middle age did he experience the breakthrough that permitted him to discover his creative gifts. Dubuffet suddenly realized that for him true art had to come from outside the ideas and traditions of the artistic elite, and he found inspiration in the art of children and the insane. The distinction between "normal" and "abnormal" struck him as no more justifiable than established notions of beauty and ugliness. Not since Marcel Duchamp (see page 874) had anyone attempted so radical a critique of art.

Dubuffet made himself the champion of what he called *l'art brut* ("art-in-the-raw") but he also created a paradox. While exalting the directness and spontaneity of the amateur over the refinement

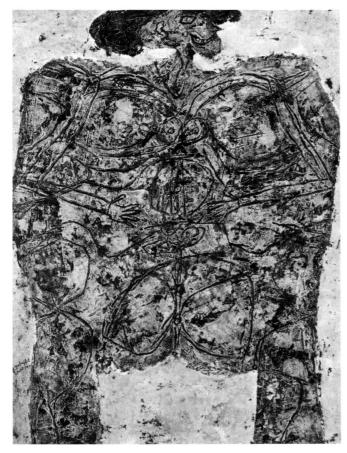

24-62. Jean Dubuffet. *Le Métafisyx,* from the *Corps de Dames* series. 1950. 45¾ x 35¼" (116.2 x 89.5 cm). Private collection

stitute another and vaster beauty, touching all objects and beings, not excluding the most despised . . . I would like people to look at my work as an enterprise for the rehabilitation of scorned values, and . . . a work of ardent celebration."

FRANCIS BACON. The English artist Francis Bacon (1909–1992) was allied not with Abstract Expressionism, although he was clearly related to it, but with the Expressionist tradition. For his power to translate sheer anguish into visual form he had no equal among twentieth-century artists except perhaps Rouault (see fig. 24-3 and fig. 24-4). Bacon often derived his imagery from other artists. He freely combined several sources while transforming them in order to give them new meaning. *Head Surrounded by Sides of Beef* (fig. 24-63) reflects Bacon's obsession with Velázquez's *Pope Innocent X* (compare fig. 17-34), a picture that haunted him for years. It is, of course, no longer Innocent X we see here but a screaming ghost, inspired by a scene from Sergei Eisenstein's film *The Battleship Potemkin,* that is materializing out of a black void. The two glowing sides of beef are taken from a painting by Rembrandt. Knowing the origin of the imagery does not help us to understand it, however. Nor does comparison with earlier works such as Grünewald's *Crucifixion,* Fuseli's *Nightmare,* Ensor's *Christ's Entry into Brussels in 1889,* or Munch's *The Scream,* which are its ancestors (see figs. 16-1, 21-43, 23-20, and 23-21). Bacon was a gambler, a risk-taker, in real life as well as in art. What he wanted were images that, in his own words, "unlock the deeper possibilities of sensation." Here he competes with Velázquez, but on his own terms, which are to set up an almost unbearable tension between the shocking violence of his vision and the luminous beauty of his brushwork.

of professional artists, he became a professional artist himself. Duchamp's questioning of established values had led him to cease artistic activity altogether, but Dubuffet became incredibly prolific, second only to Picasso in output. Compared with the work of Paul Klee, who had first used the style of children's drawings (see page 836), Dubuffet's art is "raw" indeed. Its stark immediacy, its explosive, defiant presence, are the opposite of Klee's discipline and economy. Did Dubuffet perhaps fall into a trap of his own making? If his work merely imitated the *art brut* of children and the insane, would not these self-chosen conventions limit him as much as those of the artistic elite?

We may be tempted to think so on first sight of *Le Métafisyx* (fig. 24-62) from his *Corps de Dames* series. Even De Kooning's wildly distorted *Woman II* (see fig. 24-61) seems gentle when matched against this shocking assault on our inherited cultural sensibilities. The paint is as heavy and opaque as a rough coating of plaster, and the lines describing the blocklike body are scratched into the surface like graffiti made by an untrained hand. Appearances are deceiving, however. The fury and concentration of attack in Dubuffet's demonic female is by no means "something any child can do." In an eloquent statement the artist explained the purpose of such images: "The female body . . . has long . . . been associated with a very specious notion of beauty which I find miserable and most depressing. Surely I am for beauty, but not that one. . . I intend to sweep away everything we have been taught to consider——without question——as grace and beauty [and to] sub-

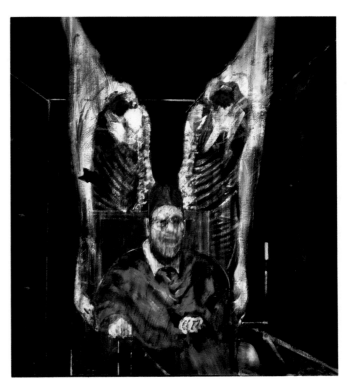

24-63. Francis Bacon. *Head Surrounded by Sides of Beef.* 1954. Oil on canvas, 50¾ x 48" (129 x 122 cm). The Art Institute of Chicago
HARRIOTT A. FOX FUND

The end of World War II brought an explosion of theater in response to pent-up cultural energy and popular demand. In Europe heavy government subsidies were used to restore national theaters and establish new ones. French theater initially adhered to concepts and practices that had been developed during the war years. The majority of new dramas were by established writers, such as Jean Anouilh (1910–1987), the most popular playwright in France through the 1970s, whose work centered on the dilemma of maintaining youthful integrity in an adult world based on compromise. But the essential contribution of postwar France was the Theater of the Absurd, which, appropriately enough, was never an organized movement and was named by the critic Martin Esslin only in 1961, when its heyday was over. The term derives from the essay "The Myth of Sisyphus" written in 1943 by Albert Camus (1913–1960), who considered the universe to be chaotic and irrational and thus regarded the search for meaning to be as "absurd" as the futile task of the Corinthian king who was condemned to pushing the same boulder up a hill in Hades forever. Camus' outlook was closely related to the existentialism of Jean-Paul Sartre (1905–1980), which held that truth in any absolute sense is unknowable and that meaning must be self-created by each individual. Camus, however, rejected Sartre's call for political engagement as a necessary, albeit irrational, act, thereby prompting a long and bitter feud between the two men.

This attitude was a response to the horrors of the war and the anxiety created by the ensuing Cold War, with its omnipresent threat of nuclear holocaust. In fact, *End Game* (1957) by Samuel Beckett (1906–1989), the greatest of the absurdists, takes place at the end of the world and uses the metaphor of chess to represent the human condition through four characters who alternately torment and console each other in their incomprehensible predicament, over which they have no control. Although he was Irish, Beckett spent much of his career in Paris, and *End Game* was originally written in French. Paris was also home to the Romanian-born Eugène Ionesco (1912–1994), whose early one-act dramas, such as *The Bald Soprano* (1949), which was inspired by an English phrase book, were "antiplays" using the conventions of language to convey irrational, anguished states of mind. His later works, notably *Rhinoceros* (1960), are more conventional in form and character delineation, but they are no less hallucinatory in their effect. Of all the absurdists, the most disturbing was Jean Genet (1910–1986). Like many of his plays, Genet's masterpiece, *The Balcony* (1956), deals with outcasts—he himself was a criminal and a homosexual—caught in a web of perverse and destructive relationships, but nevertheless it reveals a surprisingly compassionate, if

pessimistic, view of humanity. Genet's plays are extremely powerful in their impact on the viewer. In this he reveals himself a disciple of Artaud's Theater of Cruelty, which exercised a pervasive influence on French theater after the war, including on the director Roger Blin (1907–1984), who staged numerous absurdist plays in experimental theaters across the country. By far the most important recent development has come from the Théâtre du Soleil, founded in 1964, with Ariane Mnouchkine (b. 1940) at its helm. Her productions of Shakespeare, Euripides, and Aeschylus freely incorporate elements from India, Japan, and Asia to striking effect.

In Germany, the most powerful influence came from Bertolt Brecht; his Berlin Ensemble, directed by his wife, Helene Weigel (1900–1971), was widely regarded as among the finest of the time in Europe. Despite heavy state support on both sides of the iron curtain, not until the 1960s did Germany produce its first postwar dramatist of note: Peter Weiss (1916–1982), whose *Marat/Sade* (the customary shortened title) unites Brecht and Artaud to treat an insane asylum as a metaphor of the world. Of the German playwrights born around the end of the war, the foremost is Botho Strauss (b. 1944). Strauss' drama *Big and Little* (1978), in which characters try unsuccessfully to establish contact with one another, is close to absurdist theater but replete with political overtones. Throughout the 1970s German theater was heavily leftist in its orientation, especially the productions of director Peter Stein (b. 1937), which were critiques of the ideologies underlying traditional plays and examinations of their historical roots. Since then a more conventional ideology and approach have been adopted, as much out of self-preservation as conviction.

After the war, England rebuilt its fabled theater system, including the Old Vic and the Stratford Festival Company, and reestablished the important festivals such as Glyndebourne. Experimental theater, however, came only in the mid-1950s, when the English Stage Company, under George Devine (1910–1966), was established and produced two epoch-making plays by John Osborne (1929–1994): *Look Back in Anger* (1956), an attack on the inherited class system and its injustices, and *The Entertainer* (1957), starring Laurence Olivier as the fading music-hall actor Archie Rice, who symbolizes the decline of England. At about the same time, the Theatre Workshop began to reach its height under Joan Littlewood (1914–2002), its director until 1961, who wanted to create a working-class theater. Her most famous productions were *The Quare Fellow,* written in 1945 by the Irish poet and novelist Brendan Behan (1923–1964), about the impending execution of an Irish Republican Army sympathizer; and *A Taste of Honey* (1958), written at the age of 17 by Shelagh Delaney (b. 1939), about a teenaged mother who rears her child with the help of a gay man. Under

Peter Hall (b. 1930) and Peter Brook (b. 1925), the most experimental of all English directors, the newly chartered Royal Shakespeare Company became the leading venue for avantgarde theater in the 1960s. By far the most significant English playwright of the postwar era has been Harold Pinter (b. 1930), whose enigmatic "comedies of menace," such as *The Caretaker* (1960), have more than a little in common with Beckett's dramas but are filled with a sense of mystery and fear that makes them psychologically gripping. The generation born in the 1930s continues to dominate English drama. Typically their work is radical, both socially and morally. Among them, Edward Bond (b. 1935) gained particular notoriety for the shock value of his early plays written in 1965–68, which use violence and bizarre plots to emphasize the moral depravity of modern existence.

Poland's contribution to contemporary theater has been as important as its role in contemporary music. Jerzy Grotowski (b. 1933) emerged as a leading director in the mid-1960s when the Polish Laboratory Theater toured Europe, but it was as a theorist that he made his mark with the publication in 1968 of *Towards a Poor Theater,* which advocated eliminating every nonessential element from theater until it was reduced to the only components that could not be omitted without destroying theater itself—the actor and the audience. The heavy physical and psychic demands of Grotowski's acting method drew mainly on the Russians, while his approach to stagecraft makes the audience play a role in the drama unselfconsciously through its psychological response. Eventually he took the final step of eliminating theater itself in favor of rituals re-creating the archetypal experiences on which he believed theater was ultimately based.

In contrast to Europe, the United States government gave little support to theater after the war. American theater nonetheless prospered in small houses across the land, thanks to a revival of the Little Theater movement, which had struggled during the Great Depression. In New York experimental theater thrived off-Broadway. Major new regional companies were formed as well, particularly the Tyrone Guthrie Theater in Minneapolis, established in 1963. The most prominent organization was the Actors Studio, which was cofounded in 1947 by the director Elia Kazan, although Lee Strasberg soon became the key figure. It was the first theater to promote "method acting," a modified form of Stanislavsky's practices (see page 818), which dominated the American stage into the 1960s. It also staged the first classics of American postwar drama: *A Streetcar Named Desire* (1947) by Tennessee Williams (1911–1983) and *Death of a Salesman* (1949) by Arthur Miller (b. 1916). The former, featuring the actor Marlon Brando in his first important role as the brutish Stanley Kowalski, is an unforgettable play about sex, madness, and violence in the South, while the latter, which focuses on the

American dream of success, was written as a classical tragedy about the common man. As in the other arts, the period since 1945 has witnessed the high tide of writing for the American stage.

The most important playwright of the 1960s was Edward Albee (b. 1928), who began as an absurdist, then turned to dramas (*Who's Afraid of Virginia Woolf,* 1962) about how people deal psychologically with inner and external reality, before he became an iconoclast whose meanings are ambiguous (*The Marriage Play,* 1987). In 1964 Sam Shepard (b. 1943) won an Obie Award for his first play, *Cowboy,* centering on his favorite theme, the American West, treated in archetypal terms. The late 1960s and early 1970s were a time of turmoil everywhere. In addition to student and race riots in France and America in 1968, there were protests against the Vietnam War, which found expression in such plays as *America Hurrah!* (1967) by Jean-Claude van Itallie (b. 1936) and *Sticks and Bones* (1971) by David Rabe (b. 1940). At the same time the distinction between art and theater was dissolved in the Happenings staged by Alan Kaprow and Jean Tinguely (see page 893).

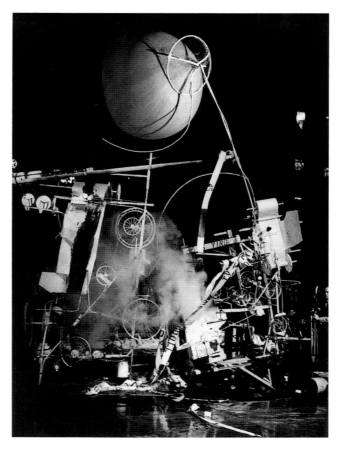

Jean Tinguely. *Hommage to New York.* 1960. Mixed media. Self-destructing installation in the garden of the Museum of Modern Art, New York

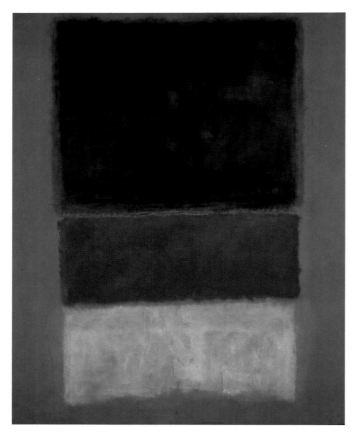

24-64. Mark Rothko. *White and Greens in Blue*. 1957.
Oil on canvas, 8'4" x 6'10" (2.5 x 2.1 m).
Collection of Mr. and Mrs. Paul Mellon, Virginia

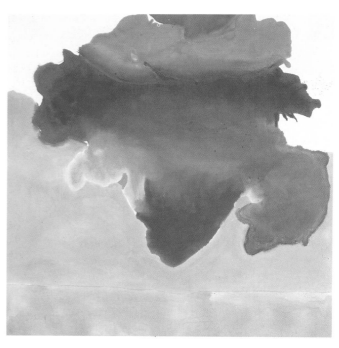

24-65. Helen Frankenthaler. *The Bay*. 1963. Acrylic on canvas,
6'8¾" x 6'9¾" (2.05 x 2.08 m). The Detroit Institute of Arts

Color Field Painting

By the late 1940s, a number of artists began to transform Action Painting into a style called Color Field Painting, in which the canvas is stained with thin, translucent color washes. These may be oil or even ink, but the favored material quickly became acrylic, a plastic suspended in a polymer resin, which can be thinned with water so that it flows freely.

MARK ROTHKO. In the mid-1940s Mark Rothko (1903–1970) worked in a style derived from the Surrealists, then adopted the gestures of early Action Painting using block-like colored forms that act like characters in a dream. Within a few years, however, he sought maximum concentration for greatest clarity. Toward 1947 his forms began to merge, until he subdued the aggressiveness of Action Painting so completely that his pictures radiated the purest contemplative stillness. *White and Greens in Blue* (fig. 24-64) consists of three rectangles with blurred edges on a blue field. The darker forms seem immersed in the blue ground, so that the white rectangle stands out all the more vividly. The canvas is very large, almost eight and one-half feet high, and the thin washes of color permit the texture of the cloth to be seen in places.

This description hardly begins to touch the essence of the work or its mysterious power to move us. The reasons are to be found in the delicate equilibrium of the shapes, their strange interdependence, and the subtle variations of hue, which seem to immerse the viewer in the monumental painting. The bold, simplified forms and somber colors are intended as universal symbols. They express the meaning of life by condensing the drama of human existence to its very essence.

For those attuned to the artist's special vision, the experience can be akin to a trancelike rapture. Yet Rothko wanted to convey anything but a mystical experience. He possessed a philosophical cast of mind born of his melancholy outlook. The overarching theme of his work is the tragedy of the human condition in the face of inevitable death. This meaning is inescapable in several series painted toward the end of his life, which ended in suicide.

HELEN FRANKENTHALER. The stained canvas was also pioneered by Helen Frankenthaler (b. 1928), who was inspired by Rothko's example as early as 1952. In *The Bay* (fig. 24-65), Frankenthaler uses the same biomorphic forms basic to early Action Painting but eliminates the personal handwriting found in the brushwork of Gorky and De Kooning. The results are reminiscent of O'Keeffe's paintings in their lyrical and decorative qualities, and are no less impressive (compare fig. 24-54).

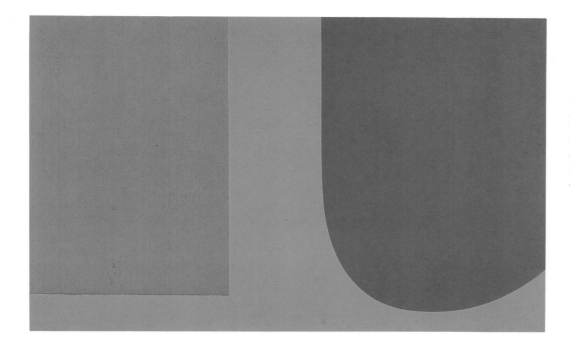

24-66. Ellsworth Kelly. *Red Blue Green*. 1963. Oil on canvas, 7'8" x 11'4" (2.34 x 3.45 m). Museum of Contemporary Art, San Diego, La Jolla, California

GIFT OF JACK AND CAROLYN FARRIS

Minimalism

ELLSWORTH KELLY. Many artists who came to maturity in the 1950s turned away from Action Painting altogether in favor of "hard-edge" painting. *Red Blue Green* (fig. 24-66) by Ellsworth Kelly (b. 1923), an early leader of this movement, abandons Rothko's impressionistic softness. Instead, flat areas of color are contained within carefully delineated shapes as part of the formal investigation of color and design for its own sake.

This radical abstraction of form is known as Minimalism, which implies an equal reduction of content. It was a quest for basic elements representing the fundamental aesthetic values of art, without regard to issues of content. Minimalism was a necessary, even valuable phase, of modern art. At its most extreme, it reduced art not to an eternal essence but to an arid simplicity. In the hands of a few artists of genius like Kelly, however, it yielded works of unequaled formal perfection.

FRANK STELLA. The ancestry of Minimalism can be traced back to Mondrian. In fact, Frank Stella (b. 1936) began as an admirer of Mondrian, then soon evolved an even more self-contained style. Unlike Mondrian (see pages 828–30), Stella did not concern himself with the vertical-horizontal balance that connects the older artist's work to the world of nature. Logically enough, he also abandoned the traditional rectangular format to make quite sure that his pictures bore no resemblance to windows. The shape of the canvas had now become an indispensable part of the design. In one of his largest works, the majestic *Empress of India* (fig. 24-67), this shape is determined by the thrust and counterthrust of four huge chevrons. They are identical in size and shape but sharply different in color and in their relationship to the whole. The paint, moreover, contains powdered metal, which gives it an iridescent sheen. This is yet another way to stress the impersonal precision of the surfaces and to remove the work from any comparison with the "handmade" look of easel pictures.

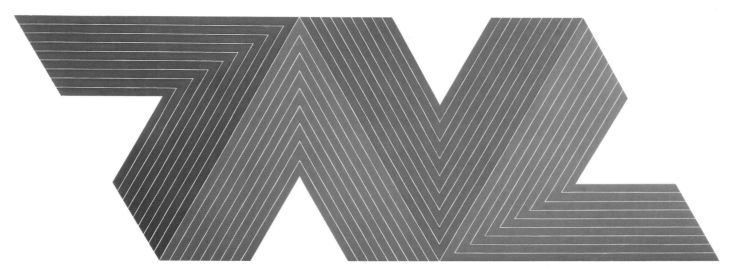

24-67. Frank Stella. *Empress of India*. 1965. Metallic powder in polymer emulsion on canvas, 6'5" x 18'8" (1.9 x 5.7 m). The Museum of Modern Art, New York

GIFT OF S. I. NEWHOUSE, JR.

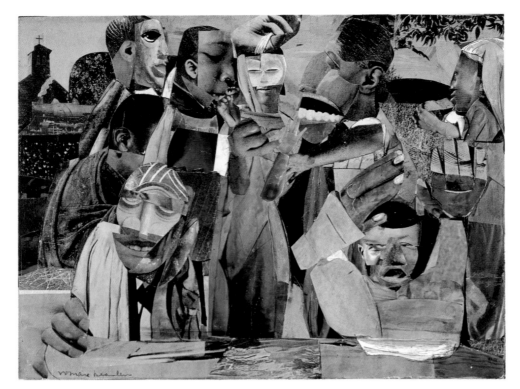

24-68. Romare Bearden.
The Prevalence of Ritual: Baptism.
1964. Collage of photochemical
reproduction, synthetic polymer,
and pencil on paperboard, 9⅛ x 12"
(23.2 x 30.5 cm). Hirshhorn Museum
and Sculpture Garden, Smithsonian
Institution, Washington, D.C.

GIFT OF JOSEPH H. HIRSHHORN. 1966

In fact, *Empress of India* is hardly a picture in the traditional sense. It demands to be thought of as an object, sufficient in itself.

African-American Painting

Blacks began to attend art schools in growing numbers after World War II, at the very time that Abstract Expressionism marked the maturation of American painting. The civil rights movement helped them to establish their personal identities and to seek artistic styles for expressing them. The turning point proved to be the assassinations of Malcolm X in 1965 and Martin Luther King, Jr., in 1968, which led to an unprecedented out-pouring of African-American art.

Since then, black artists have pursued three major tendencies. Mainstream abstractionists, particularly those of the older genera-tion, tend to be concerned primarily with seeking a personal aesthetic. They maintain that there is no such thing as African-American, or black, art, only good art. Consequently they have been denounced by radical artists. Stirred by social consciousness as well as by political ideology, these activists have adopted highly expressive representational styles to communicate a black per-spective to people in their communities. Mediating between these two approaches is a more decorative form that frequently incor-porates African, Caribbean, and even Mexican motifs. Abstraction has nevertheless proved the most fruitful path because it allows black artists to achieve a universal, not only an ethnocentric, state-ment. No hard-and-fast rules separate these alternatives, however, and artists have often combined aspects of each into their work.

ROMARE BEARDEN. The most successful synthesis was achieved by Romare Bearden (1911–1988). Although he got his start in the 1930s, it was not until the mid-1950s that he decided to devote his career entirely to art. Over the course of his long life, he pursued interests in mathematics, philosophy, and music that enriched his work. Bearden was affected by Abstract Expression-ism, but, dissatisfied with the approach, he abandoned it in favor of a collage technique. Although his work is representational, abstraction remained the underpinning of his art. His reputation was established during the mid-1960s by photomontages such as *The Prevalence of Ritual: Baptism* (fig. 24-68). Bearden's aim, as he put it, was to depict "the life of my people as I know it, passion-ately and dispassionately as Brueghel. My intention is to reveal through pictorial complexities the life I know." [See Primary Sources, no. 93, pages 944–45.] He had a full command of the resources of Western and African art. Our example is as complex as Terbrugghen's *The Calling of St. Matthew* (see fig. 18-10), but it is couched in the forms of tribal masks. No wonder Bearden's work appeals to people of all races. His widespread popularity was a breakthrough that inspired other African-American artists.

WILLIAM T. WILLIAMS. William T. Williams (b. 1942) belongs to the generation of African-Americans born around 1940 who have brought black painting and sculpture to artistic maturi-ty. He was initially a member of the "lost" generation of the lyrical Expressionists from the early 1970s whose contribution has been largely overlooked. After a period of intense self-scrutiny, he developed the sophisticated technique seen in *Batman* (fig. 24-69). His method can be compared to jazz improvisation, a debt that the artist himself has acknowledged. He interweaves his color and brushwork within a contrasting two-part structure that permits endless variations on the central theme. Although Williams is con-cerned mainly with formal issues, the play of color across the encrusted surface evokes memories of landscapes in the rural South where he spent his childhood.

24-69. William T. Williams. *Batman*. 1979. Acrylic on canvas, 6'8" x 5' (2.03 x 1.52 m). Collection the artist

RAYMOND SAUNDERS. With Williams, it is the intense effort to build up meaning through dense layers of paint that impresses us. By contrast, the work of Raymond Saunders (b. 1934) relies on spontaneity, yet it, too, arises from memory. He was among the first artists to explore the urban African-American environment. His subjects are provided by graffiti, church facades, store signs, restaurant menus, and other commercial images. Despite the suggestive title, *White Flower Black Flower* (fig. 24-70) holds no specific meaning, which comes purely through free association. By the same token, there is no precise order, even though the painting has an underlying geometry. A brilliant technician, Saunders feels at liberty to juxtapose the representational and the abstract, "real" collage elements and "imitation" graffiti, pure geometry and painterly gesture. These components are nevertheless related thematically and aesthetically through Saunders' experience, which determines the specific combination. This approach permits him to have the best of both worlds, by uniting the distinctive features of black culture with mainstream abstraction in a way that resists all stereotypes.

Op Art

A trend that arose in the mid-1950s was known as Op Art because of its concern with optics: the physical and psychological process of vision. Op Art has been devoted primarily to optical illusions. In one sense or another, all representational art from the Old Stone Age onward has been involved with illusion. What is new about Op Art is that it is rigorously nonrepresentational. It evolved partly from hard-edge abstraction, although its ancestry can be traced back still further to Mondrian (see page 828). Op Art extends the realm of

24-70. Raymond Saunders. *White Flower Black Flower*. 1986. Mixed media on canvas, 6'7" x 8'9¾" (2 x 2.53 m). Private collection

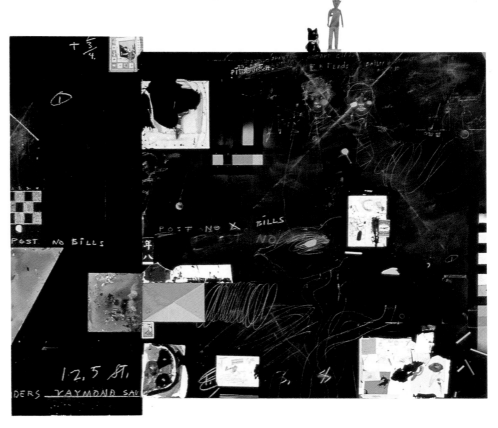

At first glance, postwar music, like postwar art, seems almost chaotic in its diversity. Composers after 1945 have vastly extended the experiments of their early-twentieth-century predecessors. Many have resorted to extreme dissonance, incorporated chance (called aleatory, from the Latin work for dice) events, treated music as a form of noise, and abandoned traditional notation. Others have written for newly invented electronic instruments, turned to repetitive motifs, or looked to non-Western music for inspiration. While these innovations have widened the scope of contemporary music, they often, like Abstract Expressionist painting, place extreme demands on the audience, requiring its listeners to discard traditional standards to judge each work on its own terms. Nevertheless, certain sounds, textures, intervals, and rhythms are so widely used as to be virtual signatures of later twentieth-century music. Moreover, contemporary music is no more alien to most twentieth-century ears than that of the late Middle Ages or Early Renaissance.

The most important composer of the postwar era was the Frenchman Olivier Messiaen (1908–1992). Like his predecessor Francis Poulenc (1899–1963), Messiaen was a devout Catholic, and his music bears witness to his faith, which remained remarkably pure even in the face of great adversity. Despite his position as a leader of the avant-garde, Messiaen created music of a haunting beauty that makes it remarkably accessible. Nowhere is Messiaen's cosmic vision more fully realized than in *Colors of the Heavenly City* (1963) for piano and ensemble, a kaleidoscopic yet ethereal evocation of the Apocalypse that uses exotic instruments and compositional modes from India and the Orient to suggest a universal spirituality. His music radiates an enchantment with God's creation that led him to incorporate transcriptions of bird songs in the delightful *Exotic Birds* (1955–56), for he delighted in and revered these simple creatures much as St. Francis of Assisi had before him. There is an intimate connection between these works: Messiaen associated the colors of the heavenly city with the brilliant plumage of birds, whose songs provided the inspiration for his music.

Messiaen was one of the first composers to apply the principles of serialism to timbre (tone color), time, rhythm, and dynamic level. His interest in twelve-tone techniques was stimulated by his pupils Pierre Boulez (b. 1925) and Karlheinz Stockhausen (b. 1928), on whom he in turn exerted a decisive influence. Boulez, the most intellectual composer on the scene today, has likewise extended serialism in all directions, but came to reject the twelve-tone row for a themeless (athematic) style that also permits carefully calculated "chance" effects and sometimes incorporates "concrete" (recorded) music (see below). *The Hammer Without a Master* (1954), inspired by the Surrealist poetry of René Char (1907–1988), has a rhythmic liveliness that belies its highly theoretical conception; by contrast, *Pli selon pli (Fold by Fold; 1957–62)*, a sustained work for soprano and orchestra utilizing poems by Mallarmé, requires the utmost concentration to absorb its subtleties. The choice of Mallarmé is significant in itself. Not only was his Symbolist poetry the point of departure for Surrealists such as Char, but he was the first to allow reciters

the opportunity to vary the choice and sequence of poems at will, a technique that Boulez used in *Pli selon pli* and that Stockhausen exploited around the same time.

Stockhausen's compositions, though no less complex than Boulez's, are more visceral in their power. He became associated early on with Pierre Schaeffer (b. 1910), the leading composer of "concrete" music consisting of recorded natural sounds. Soon after the electronic synthesizer was invented in Germany in 1950, Stockhausen turned to it while continuing to compose for traditional instruments. These strands merged in the mid-1950s, when he experimented with multiple orchestras and choruses placed in different arrays under separate conductors. He also explored a succession of moments in time as a replacement for form, which he subsequently abandoned for free form that allowed players to improvise on brief texts.

The Polish composer Witold Lutoslawski (1913–1994) turned to serialism and aleatory music in 1958, despite the fact that such Western techniques were officially frowned on by Communist authorities. His mature instrumental and orchestral works, such as *Venetian Games* (1961), accord well with the music of Messiaen and Boulez, and he became among the most respected composers of the European avant-garde. After 1975 he pursued a more personal style that culminated in his fourth and final symphony, written in 1992, which begins with an evocation of haunting mystery and ends with a thunderous climax. Lutoslawski began his career in the mold of Bartók, who exercised considerable influence on other members of the Polish school as well. Krzysztof Penderecki (b. 1933) is a miniaturist at heart noted for his discrete use of dissonance. He shares spiritual concerns with Henryk Górecki (b. 1933), whose tonalism and traditional religious emphasis have made him very popular in the West in recent years.

The preeminent English composer of the second half of the century was Benjamin Britten (1913–1976), who came to maturity during World War II. He is principally known for vocal music, including operas, of which *Peter Grimes* (1945) and *Death in Venice* (1973) are the outstanding examples; choral works, most notably the large-scale *War Requiem* (1962), which is rooted in the idealistic English tradition; and assorted songs, many written for the tenor Peter Tears, which reveal the dark, almost quirky side of his imagination. His collaborations with the poet W. H. Auden were especially successful. Britten was also an excellent writer of music for the cello, string quartet and chamber orchestra. The Violin Concerto and Cello Symphony are Britten's finest orchestral works. They reveal the influence of the Russians Prokofiev and Shostakovich. Late in life, after the two composers became friends, Shostakovich returned the compliment in his last symphonies (see below). Britten was a musician's musician, and he collaborated with many of the great instrumentalists of the day. He was further important for helping to revive interest in Henry Purcell (see page 620), whose work he greatly admired. Britten's contemporary Michael Tippett (1905–1997) possessed comparable abilities, and in addition was a fine symphonic composer; but because he was an iconoclast who broke the rules in such works as the oratorio *A Child of Our Time* (1939–41), recognition came to him only later.

Dmitri Shostakovich (1906–1975) became a tool of the Soviets in order to survive. His symphonies, written under the influence of Tchaikovsky, Rachmaninov and Mahler, are rousing post-romantic works for public consumption. Only two late symphonies are free of bombast: the Thirteenth (1962), set to Yevgeny Yevtushenko's poetry cycle *Baba Yar,* and the *Fourteenth* (1969), dedicated to the English composer Benjamin Britten, which incorporates poems by Apollinaire and Carl Maria Rilke, among others. It is for his string quartets, however, that Shostakovich earned immortality. Written for the Beethoven Quartet of Moscow, whose cellist was a close friend and collaborator, these are private works of uncompromising integrity, close in both character and quality to those of Beethoven and Brahms. Shostakovich wrote little for the piano, his own instrument. His main contributions are the preludes (1932–33) and preludes and fugues (1950–51), which use forms favored by Bach in a most personal way.

From the beginning the French-born composer Edgar Varèse (1883–1965) was a consummate maverick. Influenced by the "Brutism" of the Futurists, he became fascinated by sounds of all sorts, and soon began to utilize sirens and unusual percussion instruments to create novel effects. His major early contributions were three works written between 1918 and 1927 after he emigrated to the United States—*Amériques, Arcana, and Intégrales*—that treat the orchestra as a form of organized noise. All are marked by extreme dynamism in rhythm and volume. Though he was a ceaseless experimenter, he never developed a system, which he considered a sign of impotence. It was not until the invention of the tape recorder in 1948 and the synthesizer two years later that Varèse found a medium ideally suited to his extraordinary vision. (He had tried to convince Bell Laboratories to set up an experimental research center around 1930, and even stopped composing around 1937 because he could not achieve the sounds he wanted.) Electronics allowed him to create and mix sounds of every conceivable sort into a new kind of total sound experience: the *poème électronique,* for the 1958 Brussels World's Fair, which stands as the first great masterpiece of American electronic music.

Varèse was precocious not only in coming to America at an early date but also in advocating experimental techniques far in advance of their time. American music reached maturity simultaneously with American art in the early 1950s and for many of the same reasons. During World War II many of Europe's leading composers—Stravinsky, Bartók, Hindemith, and Schoenberg among them—came to the United States, where they exercised considerable influence. The most important American composer of the postwar era was John Cage (1912–1992), who studied with Cowell, Varèse, and Schoenberg. Cage nevertheless owed his unique approach to music primarily to his wide range of interests: he made prints, composed scores for and toured with the avant-garde choreographer Merce Cunningham (b. 1919), and organized light shows, among his many activities. During the 1940s he extended Cowell's use of the "prepared" piano by adding bits of "debris" from everyday life to produce unusual sounds. Like many American intellectuals during the 1950s he became interested in Zen Buddhism, which helped stimulate his fascination with chance events. "Chance" for Cage, however, must be understood not as total randomness but as improvisation within a defined context, since Cage considered music a kind of organized noise within the stream of life itself. For example, *Imaginary Landscape No. 4* (1951) uses 12 radios tuned to different frequencies established by the score, though the final result was unpredictable because what each radio was playing could cannot be predetermined. Such an attitude, we realize, comes very close to that of the Abstract Expressionists, particularly Jackson Pollock, who also relied on chance as a reflection of life. Like Messiaen, Cage sought a spiritual experience in his music; toward that end, silence—what is not there—is often just as important as the sounds themselves.

The foremost disciple of the synthesizer in America has been Milton Babbitt (b. 1916), who helped to found the Columbia-Princeton Electronic Music Center in 1959. Like Boulez, he seeks to apply serialism to all aspects of music, including his quartets and compositions for orchestra, which incorporate syn-

(box continues on following page)

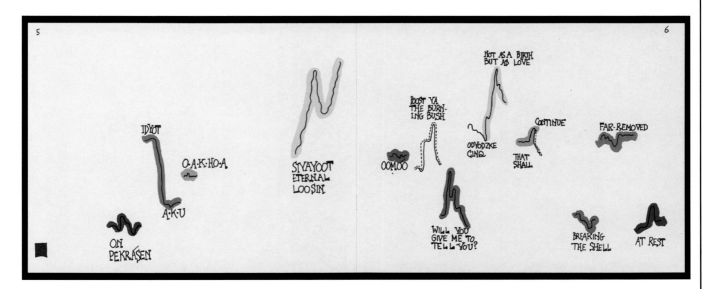

John Cage. *Aria, Voice (any range).* 1960. Score for a multilingual solo vocal work

thesized sounds. Despite its profoundly logical basis, his music can be surprisingly expressive, almost in spite of itself. Babbitt studied under Roger Sessions (1896–1985), an early pioneer of modernism with Copland. The symphonies and chamber music Sessions composed after adopting the twelve-tone system in 1953 established him as one of America's leading composers. His masterpiece is the cantata *When Lilacs Last in the Dooryard Bloom'd* (1970), a haunting evocation of verses by Walt Whitman (1819–1892), the greatest American poet. Whitman's poem was written as "A Requiem for Those We Love" in memory of Abraham Lincoln and those who had fallen during the American Civil War. Of equal stature is *Time Cycle* (1960) by Lukas Foss (b. 1922), who was born in Europe and educated in Paris but came at the age of 15 to the United States, where he completed his training in Philadelphia. Perhaps the most gifted member of the American school to emerge since World War II is Elliott Carter

(b. 1908). His four quartets are the finest since Bartók's, while *Variations for Orchestra* (1954–66) is the outstanding contribution to orchestral music in the United States from the 1950s.

The compositions of Luciano Berio (b. 1925), a former associate of Stockhausen who emigrated to the United States, are mini-dramas (he often composes for the stage as well), which utilize every available modernist technique. He often treats the human voice as another instrument while employing speechlike sounds to suggest different emotional states. Of particular interest are the works he wrote for his wife, the soprano Cathy Berberian (1925–1983), notably *Recital* (1971), which deals with the nervous collapse of a singer. George Crumb (b. 1929), the most important American composer to emerge in the 1960s, has also used the human voice in new ways. *Ancient Voices of Children* (1970), one of the great masterpieces of the twentieth century, incorporates motifs similar to those of South and Central American Indians to conjure up a primeval state with unforgettable power. Like almost all of Crumb's vocal works, it is based on the

illusion by using the latest materials and processes of science, including laser technology. Much of it consists of constructions or "environments" (see page 891) that depend on light and motion for their effect and cannot be reproduced satisfactorily in a book.

Because it relies so heavily on science and technology, Op Art's possibilities seem unlimited at first glance. However, the movement matured within a decade and developed little thereafter.

The difficulty lies mainly with its subject. Op Art seems overly cerebral and calculated, closer to the sciences than to the humanities. It often engages the viewer in a truly novel, dynamic way. But its effects, although often fascinating, involve a relatively narrow range of interests that for the most part lie outside the tradition of modern art. Only a handful of artists have enriched it with the variety and expressiveness necessary for great art.

24-71. Josef Albers. *Apparition,* from *Homage to the Square series.* 1959. Oil on Masonite, 47½ x 47½" (120.7 x 120.7 cm). Solomon R. Guggenheim Museum, New York

poetry of Federico García Lorca, the early Spanish modernist (1892–1936) whose work was inspired as much by music and art as it was by poetic tradition. One of the great masterpieces of the twentieth century, it utilizes motifs similar to those of South and Central American Indians to conjure up a primeval state with unforgettable power. Crumb's work belongs to no school. Neither did that of Samuel Barber (1910–1981), a romantic with an extraordinary gift for melody. Although he felt the influence of Stravinsky's Neoclassicism, Barber's compositions for voice use dissonance discreetly to emphasize the text, to which he had a unique sensitivity. *Knoxville: Summer of 1915* (1947), commissioned by the soprano Eleanor Steber and set to a famous poem by James Agee, is surely the most purely beautiful vocal work by any American composer of the twentieth century.

The main tendency to emerge in recent years has been dubbed Minimalism, which uses many of the same devices as the art movement of the same name, albeit for different ends. It relies on the repetition of simple motifs that are gradually varied over time to create a hypnotic, almost mystical, effect, as in *Drumming* (1970–71) by Steve Reich (b. 1936) and *In C* (1964) by Terry Riley (b. 1943). These techniques were first explored by Stockhausen, whose music shares with Riley's an inspiration in Eastern religion. The most sophisticated products of Minimalism are the operas of Philip Glass (b. 1937), above all *Satyagraha* ("truth-force," a Sanskrit word that refers to the philosophy of nonviolent resistance practiced by Mahatma Gandhi and Martin Luther King). Minimalism is ideally suited to the text, which is drawn from the *Bhagavad-Gita,* a part of the major Hindu religious epic known as the *Mahabharata.* Minimalism responds to the music and philosophy of other cultures, from Africa to Asia, but it is also "crossover" music that incorporates jazz and popular music, including rock and roll. It reinvests contemporary music with a tonality and accessibility that have won new audiences for the concert hall. In the process, it has enjoyed increasing influence—the recent symphonies of Górecki use Minimalist devices, for example.

JOSEF ALBERS. The founder of mainstream Op Art was Josef Albers (1888–1976), who came to America in 1933 when the Bauhaus school at Dessau was closed by the Nazis (see page 902). He preferred to work in series, so that he could explore each theme fully before moving on to a new subject. Albers devoted his later career to color theory. *Homage to the Square* (fig. 24-71), his final series, is concerned with color relationships using simple geometric shapes, which he reduced to a few basic compositions. Within these limits, he was able to invent almost endless combinations based on rules he devised through ceaseless experimentation. Basically Albers relied on color scales in which primary hues are desaturated in perceptually even gradations by giving them higher values (that is, by diluting them with white or gray). A step from one color scale can be substituted for the same step in another; these in turn can be combined by following the laws of color mixing, complementary colors, and so forth. This approach requires the utmost sensitivity to color, and even though the paint is taken directly from commercially available tubes, the colors bear a complex relation to each other. In our example, the artist creates a strong optical push-pull through the play of colors of contrasting value. The exact spatial effect is determined not only by the hue and the intensity of the pigments but by their sequence and the relative size of the squares.

RICHARD ANUSZKIEWICZ. Albers was an important teacher as well as theorist. His gifted pupil Richard Anuszkiewicz (b. 1930) developed his art by relaxing the self-imposed restrictions of Albers' color system and varying the geometry. In *Entrance to Green* (fig. 24-72), the decreasing rectangles create a sense of infinite recession toward the center. This rhythm is counterbalanced by the color pattern, which brings the center close to us by the gradual shift from cool to warm tones as we move inward

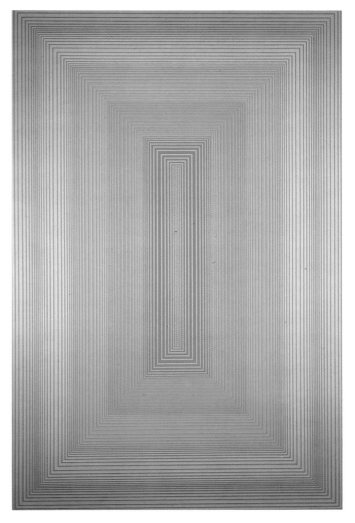

24-72. Richard Anuszkiewicz. *Entrance to Green.* 1970.
Acrylic on canvas, 9 x 6' (2.74 x 1.83 m). Collection the artist

from the periphery. The resonance of the colors within the strict geometry heightens the optical push-pull. What is surprising for such a theoretical work is its expressive intensity. In fact, the painting can be likened to a modern icon, for it is capable of having an almost mystical effect on the viewer.

Pop Art

Other artists who made a name for themselves in the mid-1950s rediscovered what the public continued to take for granted, despite all efforts to persuade otherwise: that a picture is *not* "essentially a flat surface covered with colors," as Maurice Denis had insisted, but an image wanting to be recognized. If art is representational by its very nature, then the modern movement, from Manet to Pollock, had been based on a delusion, no matter how impressive its achievements. Painting, it seemed, had been on a kind of voluntary starvation diet for the past hundred years, feeding upon itself rather than on the world around us. It was time to give in to the "image-hunger" that had built up. The public at large had never suffered from this craving, since its appetite for images was satisfied by a constant stream of photography, advertising, magazine illustrations, and comic strips.

The artists who felt this way seized on the products of commercial art catering to popular taste. Here, they realized, was an essential aspect of our visual environment that had been almost entirely ignored as vulgar and anti-aesthetic by the representatives of "highbrow" culture. It was a presence that cried out to be examined. Only Marcel Duchamp and some of the Dadaists, with their contempt for all orthodox opinion, had dared to enter this realm (see page 819). It was they who now became the patron saints of Pop Art, as the new movement came to be called, because of its basis in the art of popular culture.

RICHARD HAMILTON. Pop Art actually began in London in the mid-1950s with the Independent Group of artists and intellectuals. They were fascinated by the impact on British life of the American mass media, which had been flooding England since the end of World War II. The first unmistakable statement of Pop Art was a small collage (fig. 24-73) made in 1956 by Richard Hamilton (b. 1922), a follower of Duchamp. It already incorporates most of the subject matter that was taken up by later artists: comic strips, cinema, commercial design, nudes, cheap decor, appliances—all tokens of modern materialistic culture. Hamilton wrote that "popular culture abstracted from Fine Art its role of mythmaker. If the artist is not to lose much of his ancient purpose, he may have to plunder the popular arts to recover the imagery which is his rightful inheritance. Pop-Fine-Art . . . upholds a respect for culture of the masses and a conviction that the artist in twentieth-century urban life is inevitably a consumer of mass culture and potentially a contributor to it." [See Primary Sources, no. 94, page 975.]

It is not surprising that the new art had a special attraction for America, and that it reached its fullest development there during the following decade. In retrospect, Pop Art in the United States was an expression of the optimistic spirit of the 1960s, which began with the election of John F. Kennedy and ended at the height of the Vietnam War. Unlike Dada, Pop Art was not motivated by despair or disgust at contemporary civilization. It viewed commercial culture as its raw material, an endless source of pictorial subject matter, rather than as an evil to be attacked. Nor did Pop Art share Dada's aggressive attitude toward the established values of modern art.

JASPER JOHNS. The work of Jasper Johns (b. 1930), one of the pioneers of Pop Art in America, raises questions that go beyond the boundaries of the movement. Johns began by painting such familiar objects as flags, targets, numbers, and maps. His *Three Flags* (fig. 24-74) presents an intriguing problem: just what is the difference between image and reality? We instantly recognize the Stars and Stripes, but if we try to define what we actually see here, we find the answer surprisingly elusive. The flags, instead of waving or flopping, stand at attention, rigidly aligned with each other in a kind of reverse perspective. There is movement of another sort as well. The reds, whites, and blues are not areas of solid color but are subtly modulated and remarkably painterly. Can we really say, then, that this is an image of three flags? Clearly no such flags can exist anywhere except in the artist's head. The more we think about it, the more we begin to recognize the picture as a feat of the imagination, which is probably the last thing we expected to do when we first looked at it.

ROY LICHTENSTEIN. Revolutionary though it was, Johns' use of flags, numerals, and similar elements as pictorial themes had been anticipated to some extent 30 years earlier by Charles Demuth in *I Saw the Figure 5 in Gold* (see fig. 24-34). In contrast, Roy Lichtenstein (1923–1997) turned to comic strips—or, more

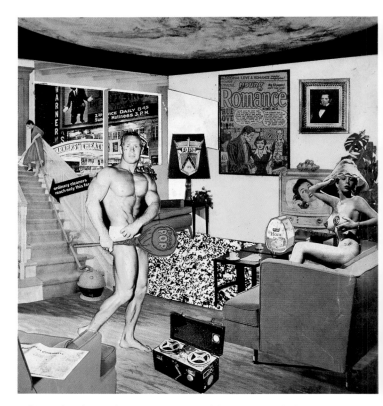

24-73. Richard Hamilton. *Just What Is It That Makes Today's Home So Different, So Appealing?* 1956. Collage on paper, 10¼ x 9¼" (26 x 24.8 cm). Kunsthalle Tübingen. Sammlung Zundel, Germany

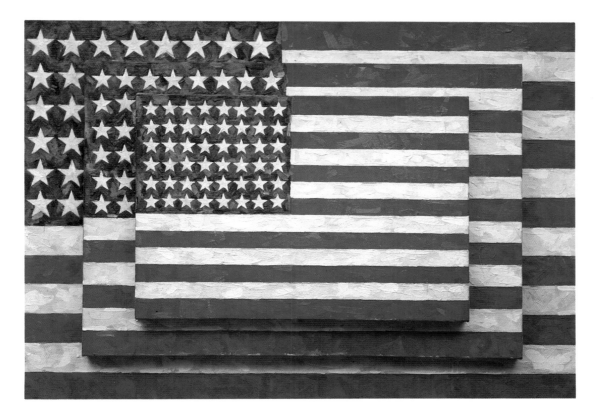

24-74. Jasper Johns. *Three Flags.* 1958. Encaustic on canvas, 30⅞ x 45½ x 5" (78.4 x 115.6 x 12.7 cm). Whitney Museum of American Art, New York

precisely, to the standardized imagery of the traditional strips devoted to violent action and sentimental love, rather than those bearing the stamp of an individual creator. His paintings, such as *Drowning Girl* (fig. 24-75), are greatly enlarged copies of single frames, including the speech balloons, the impersonal, simplified black outlines, and the dots used for printing color on cheap paper. [See Primary Sources, no. 95, page 845.]

These pictures are perhaps the most paradoxical in all of Pop Art. Unlike any other paintings past or present, they cannot be accurately reproduced in this book, for they then become indistinguishable from real comic strips. Enlarging a design meant for an area only a few inches square to one several hundred times larger gave rise to a host of problems: how, for example, to draw the girl's nose so it would look "right" in comic-strip terms, or how to space the colored dots so that they would have the proper weight in relation to the outlines.

Clearly our picture is not a mechanical copy but an interpretation. In fact, it is excerpted from the original panel. It nevertheless remains faithful to the spirit of the model, because of the countless changes and adjustments the artist has introduced. How is it possible for images of this sort to be so instantly recognizable? Why are they so "real" to millions of people? What fascinates Lichtenstein about comic strips—and what he makes us see for the first time—are the rigid conventions of their style, as firmly set and as remote from life as those of Byzantine art (compare fig. 8-55).

ANDY WARHOL. Andy Warhol (1928–1987) used this very quality in ironic commentaries on modern society. A former commercial artist, he made the viewer consider the aesthetic qualities of everyday images, such as soup cans, that we readily overlook. He did much the same thing with the subject of death, an

obsession of his. In silk-screened pictures of electric chairs and gruesome traffic accidents, he reduced dying to the same commonplace level as in the mass media. Warhol had an uncanny understanding of how newspapers and television shape our view of people and events, how they create their own reality and larger-than-life figures. He became a master at manipulating the

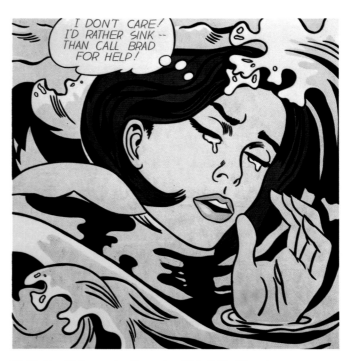

24-75. Roy Lichtenstein. *Drowning Girl.* 1963. Oil and synthetic polymer paint on canvas, 67⅝ x 66¾" (171.6 x 169.5 cm). The Museum of Modern Art, New York

PHILIP JOHNSON FUND AND GIFT OF MR. AND MRS. BAGLEY WRIGHT

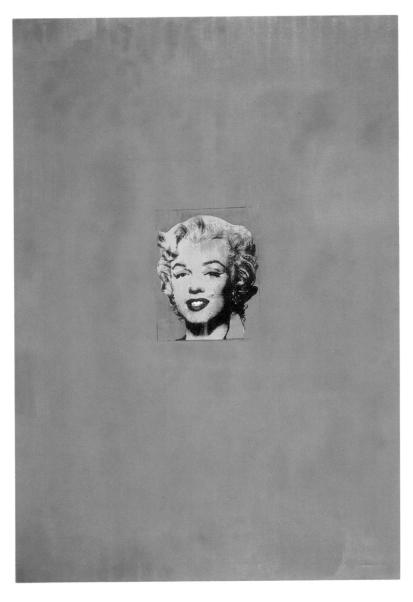

24-76. Andy Warhol.
Gold Marilyn Monroe.
1962. Synthetic polymer paint,
silk-screened, and oil on canvas,
6'11¼" x 4'7" (2.12 x 1.4 m).
The Museum of Modern Art,
New York

GIFT OF PHILIP JOHNSON

media to project a public image that disguised his true character. These themes come together in his *Gold Marilyn Monroe* (fig. 24-76). Set against a gold background, like a Byzantine icon, the famous movie star becomes a modern-day Madonna. Yet Warhol conveys a sense of the tragic personality that lay behind her glamorous facade. The color, lurid and off-register like a reproduction in a sleazy magazine, makes us realize that she has been reduced to a cheap commodity. Through mechanical means, she has become as impersonal as the Virgin who stares out from the thousands of icons produced by hack artists through the ages.

Photorealism

Although Pop Art was sometimes referred to as "the new realism," the term hardly seems to fit the painters we have discussed. To be sure, they remained true to their sources. However, their material was rather abstract: flags, numerals, lettering, signs, badges, comic strips. A later offshoot of Pop Art was the trend called Photorealism because of its fascination with camera images. Photographs had been used by nineteenth-century painters soon after the "pencil of nature" was invented (one of the earliest to

adopt them was Delacroix), but they were no more than convenient substitutes for reality. For the Photorealists, in contrast, the photograph itself became the reality on which to build their pictures, yet they adhere no less strongly to abstraction.

RICHARD ESTES. The acknowledged grand master of Photorealism is Richard Estes (b. 1936). His work is marked by its technical perfection, which turns Photorealism into a form of Magic Realism, a tendency that has flourished periodically since the late nineteenth century. This ability, however exact, is no better than that of any competent illustrator; nor does it distinguish Estes from the Precisionists, who often used photographs as the basis for their paintings. What, then, is the key to his success? It lies in his choice of subject and composition. Estes has a preference for store fronts of an earlier time that evoke nostalgic memories. In this respect he is like an archaeologist of modern urban life. His best paintings, such as *Food Shop* (fig. 24-77), show the same uncanny ability to strike a responsive chord as Hopper's *Early Sunday Morning* (see fig. 24-55). The more we look at it, the more we realize that the gridlike composition is as subtly balanced as a painting by Mondrian (compare fig. 24-36). Unlike the photo-

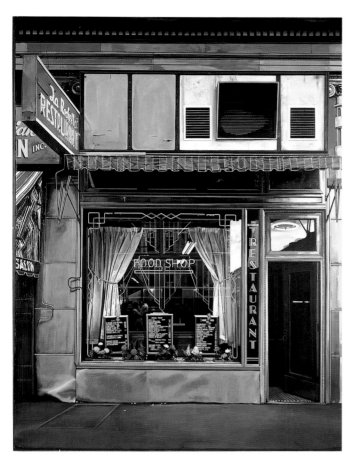

24-77. Richard Estes. *Food Shop*. 1967. Oil on linen, 65⅝ x 48½" (166.7 x 123.2 cm). Museum Ludwig, Cologne

graph on which it was based, Estes' canvas shows everything in uniformly sharp focus and defines details lost in the shadows. In this way Estes makes his humble store front an arresting visual experience fully worthy of our attention.

FEMINISM. Photorealism was part of the resurgence of realism that marked American painting in the 1970s. This tendency incorporated a wide range of themes and techniques, from the most personal to the most detached, depending on the artist's vision of objective reality and its subjective significance. Such flexibility made realism an ideal vehicle for feminism, which came to the fore in the same decade. Beyond organizing groups dedicated to a wider recognition for women artists, feminism in art has shown little of the unity that initially characterized the social movement. Many feminists, for example, turned to "traditional" women's crafts, particularly textiles, or incorporated crafts into a collage approach known as Pattern and Decoration. In painting, however, the majority pursued different forms of realism for a variety of artistic ends.

AUDREY FLACK. Women artists such as Audrey Flack (b. 1931) have used realism to explore their world from a personal as well as a feminist viewpoint. Like most of Flack's paintings, *Queen* (fig. 24-78) is an extended allegory. The queen is the most powerful figure on the chessboard, yet she remains expendable in defense of the king. Equally apparent is the meaning inherent in the queen of hearts, but here the card also refers to the passion for gambling in Flack's family, represented by photos of the artist and her mother in the open locket. The contrast of youth and age is cen-

24-78. Audrey Flack. *Queen*. 1975–76. Acrylic on canvas, 6'8" (2.03 m) square. Private collection

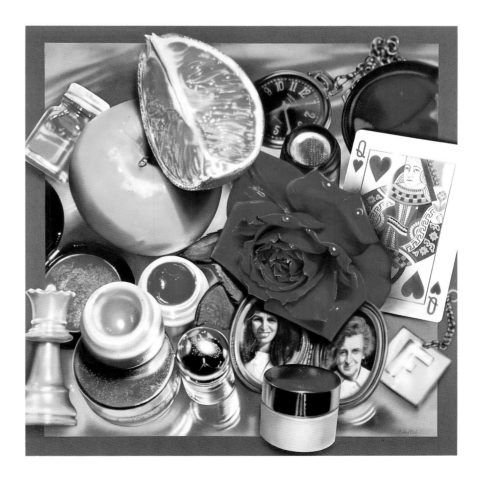

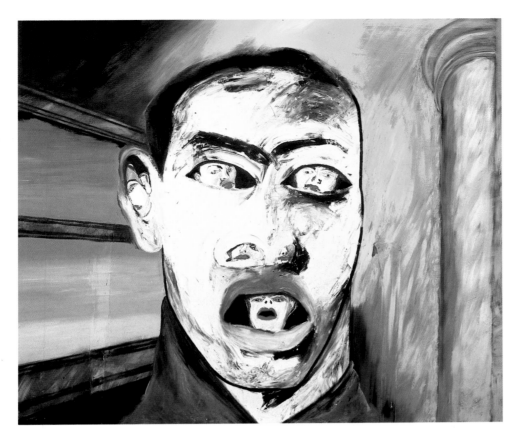

24-79. Francesco Clemente. *Untitled*. 1983. Oil and wax on canvas, 6'6" x 7'9" (1.98 x 2.36 m)

COURTESY THOMAS AMMANN, ZURICH

tral to *Queen.* The watch is a traditional emblem of life's brevity, and the dewy rose stands for the transience of beauty, which is further conveyed by the makeup on the dressing table. The suggestive shapes of the bud and fruits can also be seen as symbols of feminine sexuality.

Queen is successful not so much for its statement, no matter how interesting, as for its imagery. Flack creates a purely artistic reality by superimposing two separate photographs. Critical to the illusion is the gray border, which acts as a framing device and also establishes the central space and tonal scale of the painting. The objects that seem to project from the picture plane are shown in a different perspective from those on the tilted tabletop behind. The picture space is further enlivened by the active play of brilliant colors within the neutral gray zone.

LATE MODERNISM
Neo-Expressionism

The art we have looked at since 1945, although distinctive to the postwar era, is so closely related to what came before it that it was clearly cut from the same cloth. Hence we do not hesitate to call it modernist. At long last, however, twentieth-century painting, to which everything from Abstract Expressionism to Photorealism had made such a vital contribution, began to lose strength. The first sign of decline came in the early 1970s with the widespread use of *Neo-* to describe the latest tendencies, which came and went in rapid succession and are all but forgotten today. Only one of these movements has made a lasting contribution: Neo-Expressionism, which arose toward the end of the '70s and became

the dominant current of the 1980s. Imagery of all kinds completely overshadowed the tendency called Neo-Abstraction (also known as Neo-Geo). Indeed, abstraction itself was declared all but dead by critics. In its place was left a feeble imitation, which indicated that painting had turned its back to the mainstream of modern art. And despite the fact that Neo-Expressionism is deeply rooted in modernism, it, too, represents the end of the tradition we have traced in this chapter.

Europe

FRANCESCO CLEMENTE. The Italian Francesco Clemente (b. 1952) is in many respects representative of his artistic generation in Europe. As a result of his association with the *Arte Povera* ("Poor Art") movement in Italy, he developed a potent Neo-Expressionist style. Clemente's career took a decisive turn in 1982, when he decided to go to New York in order "to be where the great painters have been." But he has also spent a great deal of time in India, where he has been inspired by Hinduism. His canvases and wall paintings sometimes have the ambitiousness of allegorical cycles in the manner of the Italian painters who worked on a grand scale, starting with Giotto. His most compelling works, however, are those that take the artist's moods, fantasies, and appetites as their subjects. Clemente is fearless in recording urges and memories that the rest of us repress. Art becomes for him an act of cathartic necessity that releases, but never resolves, the impulses that assault his acute self-awareness. His self-portraits (fig. 24-79) suggest a soul bombarded by drives and sensations that can never be truly enjoyed. Alternately fascinating and repellent, his pictures remain curiously unsensual, yet their expressiveness is riveting. Clemente uses what-

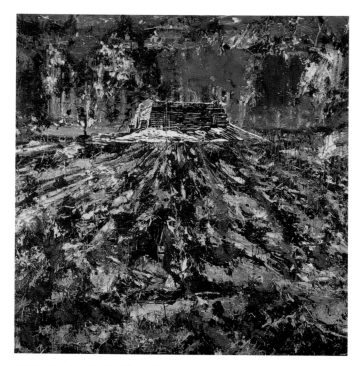

24-80. Anselm Kiefer. *To the Unknown Painter.* 1983.
Oil, emulsion, woodcut, shellac, latex, and straw on canvas,
9'2" (2.79 m) square. The Carnegie Museum of Art, Pittsburgh

ever style or medium seems appropriate to capture the fleeting states of mind emanating from his inner world. He is unusual among Italians in being heavily influenced by northern European Symbolism and Expressionism, with an occasional reminiscence of Surrealism. Our example is indeed a vivid nightmare, combining the masklike features of Ensor, the psychological terror of Munch, and the haunted vision of De Chirico.

ANSELM KIEFER. The German artist Anselm Kiefer (b. 1945) is the direct heir to Northern Expressionism, but rather than investigating personal moods he confronts moral issues posed by Nazism and its cultural foundations that have been evaded by other postwar artists in his country. By exploring the major themes of German Romanticism from a modern perspective, he has attempted to reweave the threads broken by history. That tradition, which began as a noble ideal for a national identity based on a longing for a mythical past, ended as a perversion in the hands of Hitler and his followers. It is uniquely fitting that Kiefer adopted Expressionism: ironically, some of the most important Expressionists (notably Kirchner and Nolde) had begun as admirers of Hitler before their work was condemned as "decadent" by the Nazis.

To the Unknown Painter (fig. 24-80) is a powerful statement of the human and cultural catastrophe created by World War II. Conceptually as well as compositionally, it was inspired by the paintings of Caspar David Friedrich (see page 692), to which it is a worthy successor. To express the epic tragedy of the war, Kiefer works on a vast scale. Painted in jagged strokes of predominantly earth and black tones, the charred landscape is made tangible by the inclusion of pieces of straw. Amid this destruction stands a somber ruin that is shown in woodcut to proclaim Kiefer's alle-

giance to the German Renaissance and to Expressionism. The fortresslike monument for fallen heroes recalls the tombs and temples of ancient civilizations (see figs. 2-6 and 3-4). But instead of being dedicated to soldiers killed in combat, it is a memorial to the painters whose art was no less a casualty of the war.

United States

SUSAN ROTHENBERG. Neo-Expressionism has found its most gifted American representative in Susan Rothenberg (b. 1945). She once said, "In terms of goals, I'd like to be like Mondrian in the control I'd exert." Yet her painting *Mondrian* (fig. 24-81) hardly pays homage to that artist, for it is a highly charged commentary on his rigorous discipline, which is so contrary to her painterly freedom. The composition has been pared down to a figure and a shadow placed uncomfortably close to the edge of the canvas. "It all comes back to trying to invent new forms to stand in for the body since I don't want to make a realist painting. I wanted to get that body down in paint, free it from its anatomical confines. A lot of my work is about body orientation, both in the making of the work and in the sensing of space, comparing it to my own physical orientation." The sheer beauty of the surface belies the intensity of the image. The figure emerges from

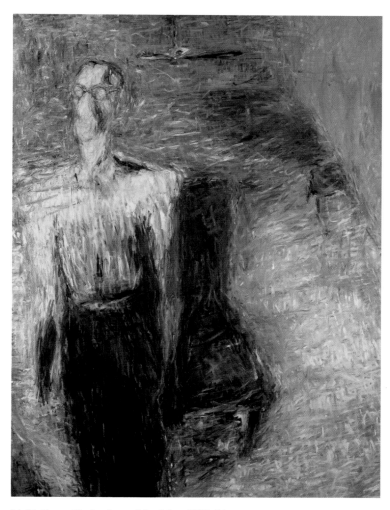

24-81. Susan Rothenberg. *Mondrian.* 1983–84.
Oil on canvas, 9'1" x 7' (2.8 x 2.1 m). Private collection

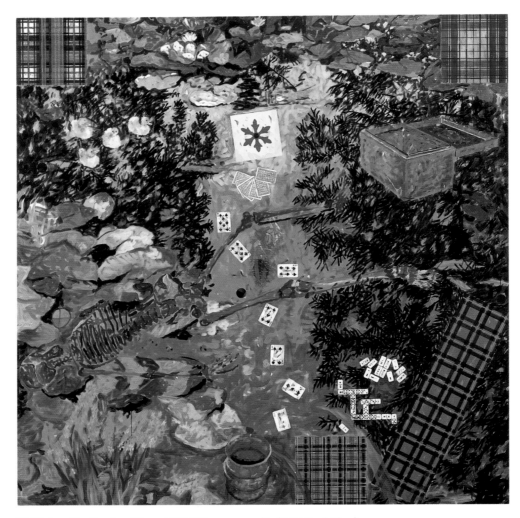

24-82. Jennifer Bartlett. *Water.* 1990. Oil on canvas, 7 x 7' (2.13 x 2.13 m). Private collection, Honolulu, Hawaii

the feathery brushstrokes like an apparition from a nightmare. The face, which bears Mondrian's unmistakable features, is a vision of madness. We have seen its like before in Bacon's *Head Surrounded by Sides of Beef* (see fig. 24-63). The painting thus declares Rothenberg's loyalty to the Expressionist tradition.

JENNIFER BARTLETT. Jennifer Bartlett (b. 1941) has long been recognized as a talented artist; missing, however, was a content worthy of her ability. Like Audrey Flack before her (see page 863), she eventually turned to a traditional subject for material. The four elements, a popular theme during the Baroque and Rococo, provided the focus for an extensive series of canvases that are as rich in meaning as they are in appearance. Although reminiscent of Monet's *Water Lilies* (see fig. 22-15), *Water* (fig. 24-82) is no mere evocation of nature. Floating half-in, half-above the water is a skeleton. The real subject here is **Vanitas,** another theme associated with the elements as well as with the senses and the seasons (see pages 599–600). References to Fate, inexorable and quixotic, are found in the cards, dominoes, and other devices used in games and fortune-telling. Seemingly "stuck" onto the canvas, along with illusionistic swatches of plaid material, they serve to deny the illusionism of the scene and emphasize the surface as an independent realm; hence, too, the red container that seems to

hover nonsensically in midair. This play between two- and three-dimensionality has much the same effect as it did in Flack's *Queen* (see fig. 24-78), and it shares a similar purpose. While charging the painting visually, it also places it at one remove from everyday reality. We are thus forced to contemplate its message instead of seeing it simply as a picture.

ELIZABETH MURRAY. Neo-Expressionism has a counterpart in Neo-Abstraction, which has yielded less impressive results, however. The greatest successes have come from artists who invest Neo-Abstraction with the personal meaning of Neo-Expressionism. Elizabeth Murray (b. 1940) has emerged since 1980 as the leader of this crossover style in the United States. *More than You Know* (fig. 24-83) makes a fascinating comparison with Audrey Flack's *Queen* (see fig. 24-78) for both are packed with autobiographical references. While it is at once simpler and more abstract than Flack's painting, Murray's composition seems about to fly apart under the pressure of barely contained emotions. The table will remind us of the one in Picasso's *Three Musicians* (see fig. 24-25), a painting she referred to in other works from the same time. The contradiction between the flattened collage perspective of the table and chair on the one hand, and the allusions to the distorted three-dimensionality of the surrounding room on

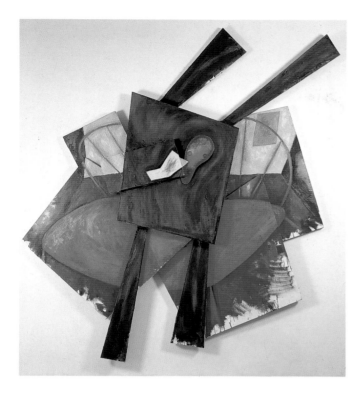

24-83. Elizabeth Murray. *More Than You Know.* 1983.
Oil on ten canvases, 9'3" x 9' x 8" (2.8 m x 2.7 m x 20.3 cm).
The Edward R. Broida Trust

COURTESY PACEWILDENSTEIN, NEW YORK

24-84. Kay WalkingStick. *On the Edge.* 1989. Acrylic, wax, and
oil on canvas, 32 x 64 x 31½" (81.3 x 162.6 x 9 cm)

COURTESY M-13 GALLERY, NEW YORK

the other, create a disquieting pictorial space. Indeed, the more
we look at the painting, the more we begin to realize that it radiates an almost unbearable tension. The table threatens to turn
into a figure, with a skull-like head, that moves with the explosive force of Picasso's *Three Dancers* (see fig. 24-27). What was
Murray thinking of? She has said that the room reminds her of
the place where she sat with her ill mother. At the same time, the
demonic face was inspired by Munch's *The Scream* (see fig. 23-21),
while the sheet of paper recalls Vermeer's paintings of women
reading letters (see fig. 18-29), which to her express a combination
of serenity and anxiety.

KAY WALKINGSTICK. Kay WalkingStick (b. 1935) has managed to combine Neo-Expressionism and Neo-Abstraction in a
deeply personal and emotionally satisfying way. Part Cherokee,
she was strongly affected by her Native-American spiritual heritage, especially its reverence for the earth, although she was raised
among whites. The death of her husband in 1989 brought forth
the outpouring of grief seen in *On the Edge* (fig. 24-84), which
combines two kinds of landscapes in a format that she had experimented with briefly several years earlier. The two halves respond
to entirely different impulses. The left panel, built up in thick coats
of paint applied mainly with her hands, continues the abstract
manner she had developed successfully over more than a decade.
In the center is a fan shape, which suggests a man-made feature
in a primitive landscape—like those of the ancient mound
builders—and acts as a "sign" that lends the canvas a mysterious
emblematic significance with erotic overtones. The right half,
painted with intense color in an Expressionist style, unleashes a
torrent of anguish. This duality has several layers of meaning. It
suggests the contrasting aspects of nature as spiritual center and
generative force, the opposing forces of order and chaos, and the
dichotomy between calm contemplation and powerful feeling.
Thus both parts of the diptych are necessary to give the painting
its full meaning.

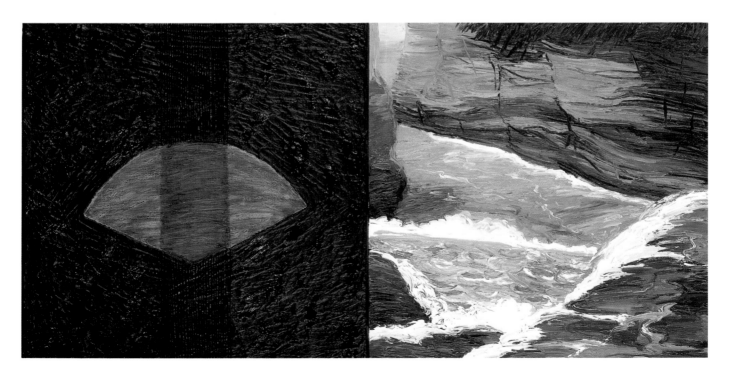

CHAPTER TWENTY-FIVE
Twentieth-Century Sculpture

SCULPTURE BEFORE WORLD WAR I

Sculpture, the most conservative of the arts throughout most of the nineteenth century, found it difficult to escape tradition. As a result, twentieth-century sculpture remained far less adventurous on the whole than painting, which often influenced it. The American sculptor David Smith (see page 880) even claimed that modern sculpture was created by the painters, and to a remarkable degree he was right. Sculpture successfully challenged the leadership of painting only when it followed a separate path.

We shall find that twentieth-century sculpture followed two main trends: primitivism and abstraction. Although they were not mutually exclusive and are often found in combination, the two used different means for fundamentally different aims. Primitivism was found most commonly before 1945. After World War II, abstraction became the dominant (but hardly exclusive) mode of modern sculpture. Primitivism should be understood here not simply as sculpture inspired by ethnographic art, which attracted many painters and sculptors during the early decades of the century but largely died out thereafter. It should be broadened to include any piece that emphasizes the "idol" quality of sculpture, so that it is not, as Baudelaire put it, "a humble associate of painting and architecture." What do we mean by *idol*? The usual dictionary definition is an image of a deity, usually a false god, used as an object of worship. Such a view, however, is based on the Judeo-Christian tradition, such as the Adoration of the Golden Calf described in Genesis. If we examine prehistoric sculpture (see figs. 1-7, 1-12, and 1-15), we realize that this definition is far too narrow. Baudelaire himself came closer to the truth when he emphasized primitive sculpture as fetish: something worshiped for its magical, especially sexual, powers or inhabited by a nature or ancestor spirit. While few of the works we shall discuss in this chapter are intended as objects of devotion, a surprising number of them retain the quality of a fetish. They seem possessed of magical powers, often with erotic overtones, as if bestowed by an inner demon. For that reason, the "primitive" sculptures in this larger sense grab the imagination in a way that abstract sculpture rarely does.

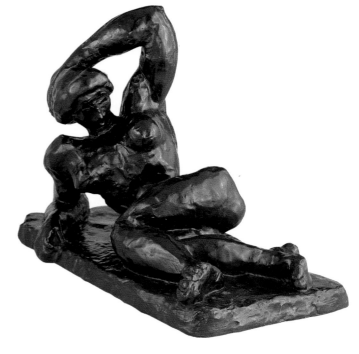

25-1. Henri Matisse. *Reclining Nude I*. 1907. Bronze, 13⁹⁄₁₆ x 19⁵⁄₈ x 11" (34.5 x 49.9 x 28 cm). The Baltimore Museum of Art

THE CONE COLLECTION, FORMED BY DR. CLARIBEL CONE AND MISS ETTA CONE OF BALTIMORE, MARYLAND

HENRI MATISSE. Some of the most important experiments in sculpture were conducted by Matisse. During the years 1907–14, he was inspired by ethnographic sculpture. There had been a growing interest in "primitive" art on the part of Gauguin and other painters even before the first major public collections began to be formed in 1890. *Reclining Nude I* (fig. 25-1) is a counterpart to Matisse's painting *Blue Nude* from the same year, which shares its "savage" element. Sculpture was a natural complement to Matisse's pictures. It allowed him to investigate problems of form that in turn provided important lessons for his canvases. The bulging distortions in *Reclining Nude* create an astonishing muscular tension. Yet the artist was concerned above all with what he called *arabesque,* and it is the rhythmic contours that define the nude. We will recognize

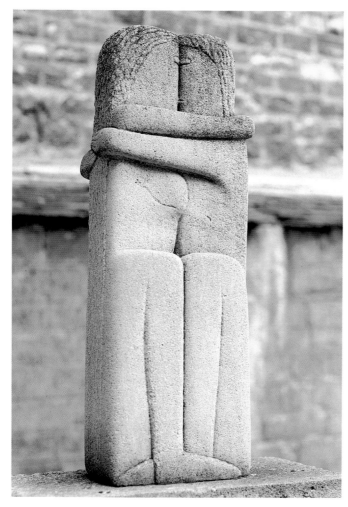

25-2. Constantin Brancusi. *The Kiss*. 1909.
Stone, height 35¼" (89.5 cm). Tomb of T. Rachevskaia,
Montparnasse Cemetery, Paris

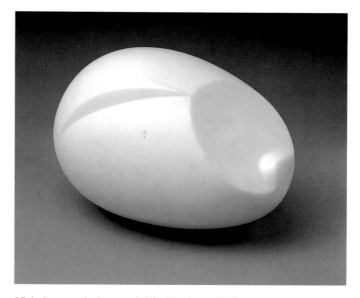

25-3. Constantin Brancusi. *The Newborn*. 1915.
Marble, length 8⅛" (20.7 cm). Philadelphia Museum of Art
LOUISE AND WALTER ARENSBERG COLLECTION

the statuette's kinship with the reclining figures in *The Joy of Life* (see fig. 24-1), which were also conceived in outline. Now, however, these rhythms are explored in the round and manipulated for expressive effect. Remarkably, Matisse accomplished this aim without diminishing the fundamentally classical character of the nude.

CONSTANTIN BRANCUSI. Sculpture remained only a sideline for Matisse. Perhaps for that reason, Expressionism was much less important in sculpture than in painting. This fact may seem surprising, since the rediscovery of ethnographic art by the Fauves might have been expected to have a strong impact on sculptors. The only one who shared this interest, however, was Constantin Brancusi (1876–1957), a Romanian who went to Paris in 1904. However, he was fascinated with the formal simplicity and coherence of primitive carvings rather than with their untamed expressiveness.

This concern is evident in *The Kiss* (fig. 25-2), executed in 1909 and now placed over a tomb in a Paris cemetery. The compactness and self-sufficiency of the group are a radical step beyond Maillol's *Seated Woman* (see fig. 23-26), to which it is related much as the Fauves are to Post-Impressionism. Brancusi has a "genius of omission" comparable to Matisse's, and his attitude toward art expresses the same optimistic faith so characteristic of early modernism: "Don't look for mysteries," he said. "I give you pure joy."

To him a monument was a permanent marker, like the steles of the ancients—an upright slab, symmetrical and immobile. He disturbed this basic shape as little as possible in *The Kiss* by differentiating between the two figures just enough to make them separately identifiable. The embracing lovers seem more primeval than primitive. Innocent and anonymous, they are a timeless symbol of generation—the exact opposite of Rodin's *The Kiss* (see fig. 22-28), where the contrast of flesh and stone mirrors the dualism of guilt and desire. Brancusi's genius posed the first successful alternative to Rodin, whose authority overwhelmed the creativity of many younger sculptors. In the process, Brancusi gave modern sculpture its independence.

Brancusi's work took another daring step about 1910, when he began to produce nonrepresentational pieces in marble or metal. (He reserved his "primeval" style for wood and stone.) They fall into two groups: variations on the egg shape, and soaring, vertical "bird" motifs. In concentrating on two basic forms of such uncompromising simplicity, Brancusi strove for essences, not for Rodin's illusion of growth. He was fascinated by the contrast of life as potential and as kinetic energy: the self-contained perfection of the egg, which hides the mystery of all creation, and the pure dynamics of the creature released from this shell. *The Newborn* (fig. 25-3) is a marvelously concise and witty, yet surprisingly sympathetic, portrayal of an infant's first cry upon entering the world (compare fig. 27-12).

Bird in Space (fig. 25-4), made more than a decade later, is the culmination of Brancusi's art. It began as the figure of a mythical bird that talks, which he gradually simplified until it was no longer the abstract image of a bird. Rather, it is flight itself, made visible and concrete. "All my life I have sought the essence of flight," Brancusi stated, and he repeated the motif in variants of ever greater refinement. Its disembodied quality is emphasized by the high polish, which gives the surface the reflectivity of a mirror and thus establishes a new continuity between the molded space of the sculpture and the surrounding free space.

CUBISM. In the second decade of the century a number of artists tackled the problem of object-space relationships with the formal tools of Cubism. This was no simple task, since Cubism was a painter's approach, more suited to shallow relief and not easily adapted to sculpture in the round. Most of the Cubist painters attempted at least a few pieces, but the results were generally timid. Although they were of fundamental importance, even Picasso's attempts to translate the Analytic Cubism seen in *Portrait of Ambroise Vollard* (see fig. 24-13) into three-dimensional form succeeded only partially in breaking up the solid surface. Because its facets are ambiguous in both density and location, Cubism in painting provided an infinitely richer experience both visually and expressively.

RAYMOND DUCHAMP-VILLON. The boldest solution to the problems posed by Analytic Cubism in sculpture was achieved in *The Great Horse* (fig. 25-5) by the sculptor Raymond Duchamp-Villon (1876–1916), an older brother of Marcel Duchamp. He began with abstract studies of the animal, but his final version is

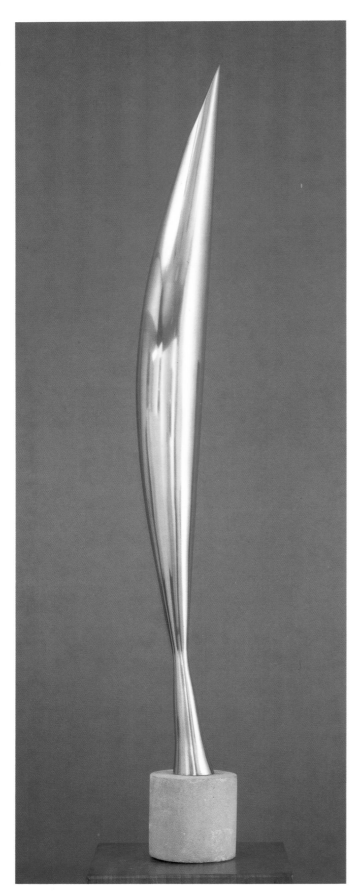

25-4. Constantin Brancusi. *Bird in Space* (unique cast). 1928. Bronze, 54 x 8½ x 6½" (137.2 x 21.6 x 16.5 cm). The Museum of Modern Art, New York

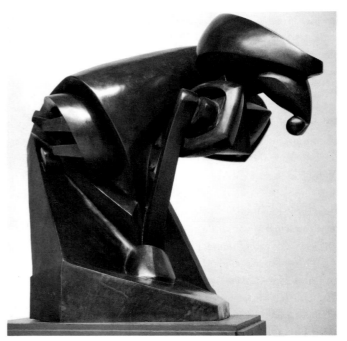

25-5. Raymond Duchamp-Villon. *The Great Horse.* 1914. Bronze, height 39¼" (99.7 cm). The Art Institute of Chicago

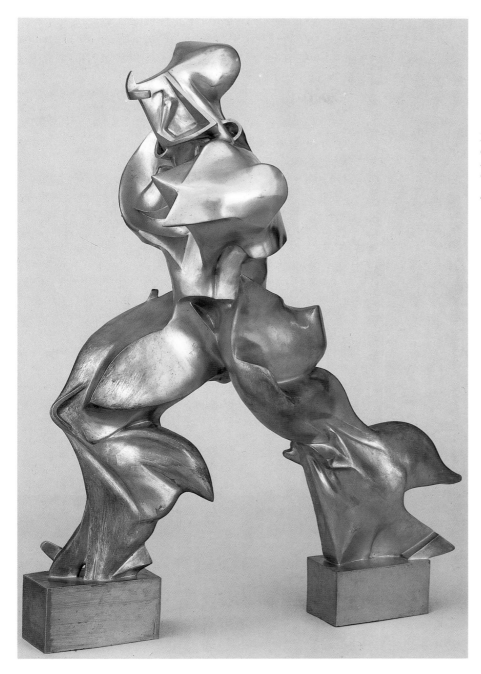

25-6. Umberto Boccioni. *Unique Forms of Continuity in Space.* 1913. Bronze (cast 1931), 43⅞ x 34⅞ x 15¾" (111.4 x 88.6 x 40 cm). The Museum of Modern Art, New York

an image of "horsepower." The body has become a coiled spring and the legs resemble piston rods. These quasi-mechanical shapes have a dynamism that is entirely convincing precisely because they are so removed from real anatomy.

UMBERTO BOCCIONI. In 1912 the Futurists suddenly became absorbed with making sculpture, which they wanted to redefine as radically as painting. They used "force-lines" to create an "arabesque of directional curves" as part of a "systematization of the interpenetration of planes." Hence, as Umberto Boccioni declared, "We break open the figure and enclose it in environment." His running figure titled *Unique Forms of Continuity in Space* (fig. 25-6) is as breathtaking in its complexity as Brancusi's *Bird in Space* is simple. Boccioni has attempted to represent not the human form itself, but the imprint of its motion upon the surrounding air. The figure itself remains concealed behind its

"garment" of atmospheric turbulence. The picturesque statue recalls the famous Futurist statement that "the roaring automobile is more beautiful than the *Winged Victory,*" although it obviously owes more to the *Winged Victory* (the *Nike of Samothrace;* see fig. 5-77) than to the design of motor cars. (In 1913, fins and streamlining were still to come.)

SCULPTURE BETWEEN THE WARS

CONSTRUCTIVISM. In Analytic Cubism, concave and convex were treated as equivalents. All volumes, whether positive or negative, were "pockets of space." The Constructivists, a group of Russian artists led by Vladimir Tatlin (1895–1956), applied this principle to relief sculpture and arrived at what might be called three-dimensional collage. Eventually they took the final step of making the works freestanding. According to Tatlin and his

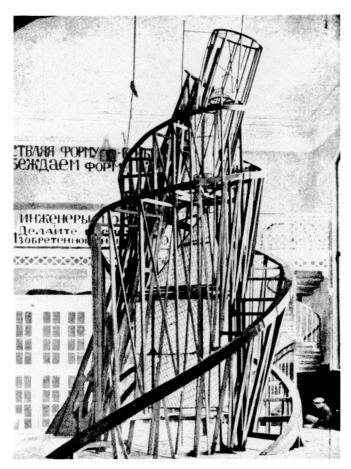

25-7. Vladimir Tatlin. *Project for Monument to the Third International.* 1919–20. Wood, iron, and glass, height 20' (6.1 m). Destroyed; contemporary photograph

followers, these "constructions" were actually four-dimensional. Since they implied motion, they also implied time.

For Tatlin, art was not the Suprematists' spiritual contemplation (see page 816) but an active process of formation that was based on material and technique. He believed that each material dictates specific forms that are inherent in it, and that these laws must be followed if the work of art is to be valid according to the laws of life itself.

VLADIMIR TATLIN. Cut off from artistic contact with Europe during World War I, Constructivism developed into a uniquely Russian art that was little affected by the return of some of the country's most important artists, such as Kandinsky and Chagall. The Russian Revolution galvanized the modernists, who celebrated the overthrow of the old regime with a creative outpouring throughout Russia. Tatlin's model for a *Monument to the Third International* (fig. 25-7) captures the dynamism of the technological utopia envisioned under Communism. Pure energy is expressed as lines of force that establish new time-space relationships. The work also implies a new social structure, for the Constructivists believed in the power of art literally to reshape society. This extraordinary tower revolving at three speeds was conceived on an enormous scale, complete with Communist Party offices. Like other such

projects, however, it was wildly impractical in a society still recovering from the ravages of war and revolution, and was never built.

Constructivism proceeded to a Productivist phase, which ignored any contradiction between true artistic creativity and purely utilitarian production. After the movement was suppressed as "bourgeois formalism," a number of its members emigrated to the West, where they joined forces with the few movements and artists still espousing abstraction.

NAUM GABO. The most important of these was Naum Gabo (1890–1977), who went first to Berlin, then to England, before settling in America after World War II. His main contribution came in the early 1940s, when he created a new kind of plastic construction strung with nylon filament (fig. 25-8) that comes very close to mathematical models. Although he arrived at it through intuition, the parallels to contemporary scientific theory are astonishing, for his work embodies much the same spatiality as modern physics. Gabo was fascinated by the links between art and science, which, he said, "arise from the same creative source and flow into the same ocean of the common culture." Like Kandinsky's, his motives were purely spiritual, and he saw Constructivism as an instrument of change. None of this theory, however, accounts for the elegance of Gabo's linear constructions, which embody a strikingly modern sensibility.

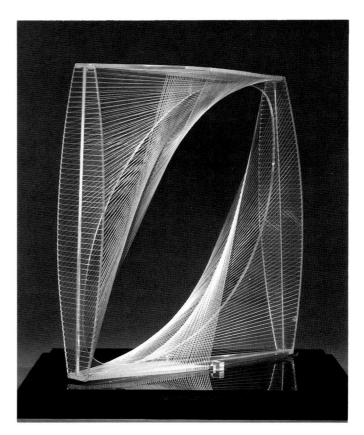

25-8. Naum Gabo. *Linear Construction #1* (smaller version). 1942–43. Plexiglas and nylon thread on plexiglass base, 12 1/4 x 12 1/4 x 2 3/4" (31.1 x 31.1 x 6.9 cm). Hirshhorn Museum and Sculpture Garden, Smithsonian Institution, Washington, D.C.

GIFT OF JOSEPH H. HIRSHHORN, 1966

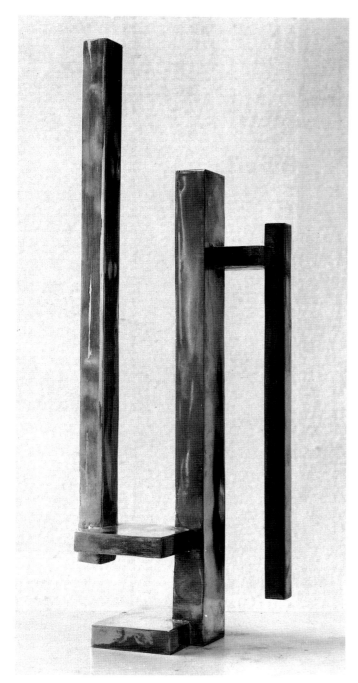

25-9. Georges Vantongerloo. *Métal: y=ax3-bx3+cx.* 1935. Argentine, height 15" (38 cm). Emanuel Hoffmann Foundation, Basel, on loan to Kunstmuseum Basel

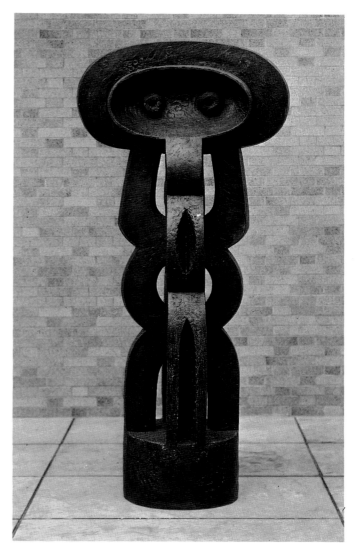

25-10. Jacques Lipschitz. *Figure.* 1926–30 (cast 1937). Bronze, height 7'1¼" (2.17 m). The Museum of Modern Art, New York

GEORGES VANTONGERLOO. Soon after arriving in Berlin, Gabo was in touch with *De Stijl,* the Dutch group. Its only true sculptor was the Belgian Georges Vantongerloo (1886–1965), who settled in Paris. He, too, was obsessed with the problem of how to represent space. *Métal: y=ax3-bx3+cx* (fig. 25-9) is a daring prefiguration of Minimalist sculpture of the 1950s and 1960s (compare fig. 25-23). Whereas Mondrian's grids were never governed by strict ratios, Vantongerloo used the same bands to articulate space by establishing precise relationships as defined by algebraic formulas. The artist, however, saw this method as a means of expressing an intuition of creation, which is infinite and is perceived only through our sensitivity. His was indeed an ecstatic

vision. "O! The incommensurable is never the same; if it were, it would be commensurable. And as the universe is incommensurable, what we need is an expression that would have neither end nor beginning; and this too exists." Ultimately this realization led him to abandon his sparse forms for a curvilinear approach, based not on classical Euclidian geometry but on Cartesian analytical geometry to describe parabolic equations.

JACQUES LIPSCHITZ. Surprisingly, the everyday materials of Synthetic Cubism proved of far greater interest to painters than to Cubist sculptors, who maintained a traditional loyalty to bronze. After World War I sculptors in France largely deserted abstraction and abandoned Expressionism altogether. Only the Lithuanian-born Jacques Lipschitz (1891–1973), a friend of both Picasso and Matisse, continued to explore the possibilities offered by Cubism. He also shared in Brancusi's primevalism, and in the mid-1920s he achieved a remarkable synthesis of these two tendencies. With its intently staring eyes, *Figure* (fig. 25-10) is a haunting evocation in Cubist terms of African sculpture. Consisting of two interlocking figures, it creates a play of open and closed forms that relieves Brancusi's austere simplicity through arabesque rhythms akin to Matisse's. The patron who commissioned *Figure* as a garden sculpture understandably found it difficult to live with. No other sculptor at the time was able to rival Lipschitz for sheer power, and he set an important example for the generation of sculptors that reached maturity a decade later (see pages 877–79).

MARCEL DUCHAMP. Lipschitz's disciplined abstraction was the very opposite of Dada, which fostered nontraditional approaches that have both enriched and confounded modern sculpture ever since. Playfulness and spontaneity are the motives behind the **readymades** of Marcel Duchamp, which he created by shifting the context of everyday objects from the utilitarian to the aesthetic. The artist would put his signature and a provocative title on found ("readymade") objects, such as bottle racks, and exhibit them as works of art. In *Advance of the Broken Arm* (fig. 25-11) pushed the spirit of readymades even further. Duchamp "re-created" the lost original version of 1915 with this one made in 1945. [See Primary Sources, no. 96, page 975.] Some of Duchamp's examples consist of combinations of found objects. These "assisted" readymades approach the status of constructions or of three-dimensional collage. This technique, later baptized "assemblage" (see pages 888–91), proved to have unlimited possibilities, and many artists have explored it since World War II, especially in junk-ridden America.

SURREALISM. Readymades are certainly extreme demonstrations of a principle: that artistic creation depends neither on established rules nor on manual craft. The principle itself was an important discovery, although Duchamp abandoned readymades after only a few years. The Surrealist contribution to sculpture is harder to define. It was difficult to apply the theory of "pure psychic automatism" to painting, but still harder to live up to it in sculpture. How could solid, durable materials be given shape without the sculptor being consciously aware of the process?

MERET OPPENHEIM. A breakthrough came in 1930, when the Surrealists met in response to a growing crisis caused in part by André Breton's insistence on tying the movement to Leon Trotsky's Communist faction. They issued a new manifesto drafted by Breton that called for the "profound and veritable occultation of Surrealism." It further required "uncovering the strange symbolic life of the most ordinary and clearly defined objects." The result was a new class of Surrealist object. Neither readymade nor sculpture, it constituted a kind of three-dimensional collage. However, it was assembled not out of aesthetic concerns using traditional techniques but according to "poetic affinity" following dictates of the subconscious. *Object* (fig. 25-12) by Meret Oppenheim (1913–1985), one of several gifted women associated with the movement, created a sensation when it was exhibited in 1936. Like others of its kind, it was intended to be repulsive and unsettling in the extreme, yet proves all the more fascinating for that very reason.

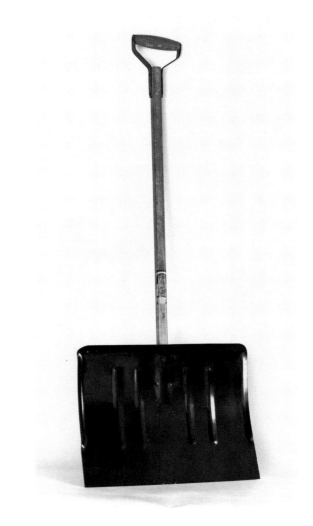

25-11. Marcel Duchamp. *In Advance of the Broken Arm.* 1945, from the original of 1915. Snow shovel, length 46¾" (118.7 cm). Yale University Art Gallery, New Haven, Connecticut
GIFT OF KATHERINE S. DREIER FOR THE COLLECTION SOCIÉTÉ ANONYME

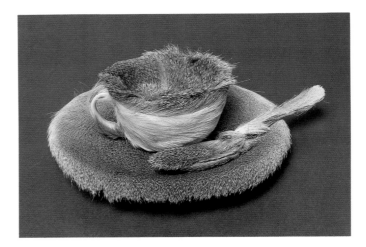

25-12. Meret Oppenheim. *Object.* 1936. Fur-covered teacup, saucer, and spoon; diameter of cup 4¾" (12.1 cm); diameter of saucer 9⅜" (23.8 cm); length of spoon 8" (20.3 cm). The Museum of Modern Art, New York
PURCHASE

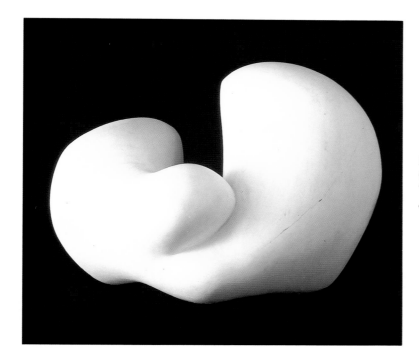

25-13. Hans Arp. *Human Concretion*. 1935.
Original plaster, 19½ x 18¾ x 25½" (49.5 x 47.6 x 64.7 cm).
The Museum of Modern Art, New York

HANS ARP. Perhaps the purest form of Surrealist sculpture was created by Hans Arp (1887–1966). Around 1930 he began to translate his reliefs, which arose from his experiments with collage, into three-dimensional forms. A few years later they evolved into the *Human Concretion* series (fig. 25-13), a term that aptly describes their character (see also page 878). In contrast to Brancusi's abstractions, which reduce things to their absolute essence, Arp's biomorphic forms seem to grow organically as they are built up during the modeling process. The concretions were almost always done first in clay or plaster; many were later carved in marble or wood, and sometimes cast in bronze, by skilled artisans. They have influenced countless sculptors ever since.

PABLO PICASSO. As in painting, Picasso's genius was the driving force for much of the sculpture made during the 1930s. The painter developed a serious interest in three-dimensional forms in 1928, and for the next five years he concentrated intensively on making sculptures of all sorts. The amazing variety testifies to his fertile imagination. *Head of a Woman* (fig. 25-14) is an especially appealing example of his work from this period. This arresting figure, made from a colander and other discarded materials, shows Picasso's fascination with the "primitive" quality of ethnographic sculpture. Its kinship with the head in *Girl Before a Mirror* of about the same time (see fig. 24-28) suggests why the artist turned to sculpture in the first place. On the one hand, his painted shapes have a solidity that practically demands translation into three-dimensional form. On the other, his work is so full of startling transformations that the process of metamorphosis involved in sculpture became highly intriguing. Picasso's involvement with Surrealism also stimulated his imagination and allowed him to approach sculpture without preconceived ideas. As he put it, "One should be able to take a bit of wood and find it's a bird."

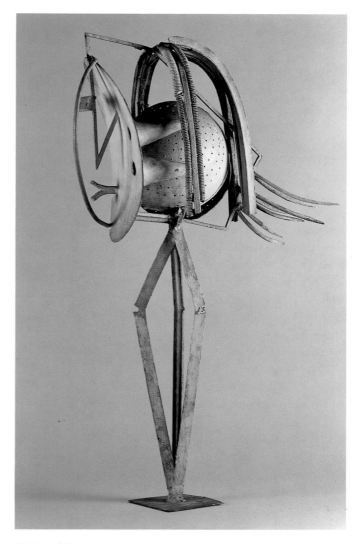

25-14. Pablo Picasso. *Head of a Woman*. 1930-31. Painted iron, sheet metal, springs, and colanders, 39⅜ x 14½ x 23¼"
(100 x 37 x 59 cm). Musée Picasso, Paris

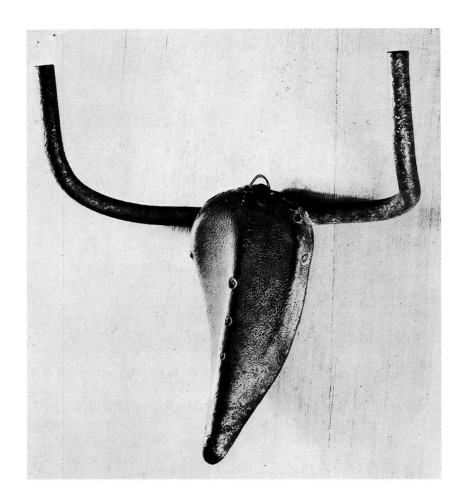

25-15. Pablo Picasso. *Bull's Head.* 1943. Bronze cast bicycle parts, height 16⅛" (41 cm). Musée Picasso, Paris

This freedom of association allowed Picasso to see the possibilities hidden in the debris of modern civilization—an attitude that culminated in *Bull's Head* (fig. 25-15). It is a work of disarming simplicity that at face value consists of nothing but the seat and handlebars of an old bicycle. What is far from simple is the leap of the imagination by which Picasso recognized a bull's head in these unlikely objects. While we feel a certain jolt when we first recognize the ingredients of this visual pun, we also sense that it was a stroke of genius to put them together in this unique way. The handiwork was ridiculously simple: once the seat had been properly placed on the handlebars, it was cast in bronze, and the job was done. Nevertheless, the artist's hands, however modest the task, played an essential part in the creative process. Once he had conceived his *Bull's Head,* he could not be sure that it would really work unless he actually made the work of art.

JULIO GONZÁLEZ. Picasso also galvanized the creative energies of Julio González (1872–1942). Trained as a wrought-iron craftsman in his native Catalonia, González had gone to Paris in 1900. Although he was a friend of both Brancusi and Picasso, he produced little of importance until the 1930s, when Picasso called on him for technical advice in working with wrought iron. By taking advantage of the technical difficulties that had discouraged its use before, González established this medium as important for sculpture. *Head* (fig. 25-16), produced on the eve of World War II, combines extreme economy of form

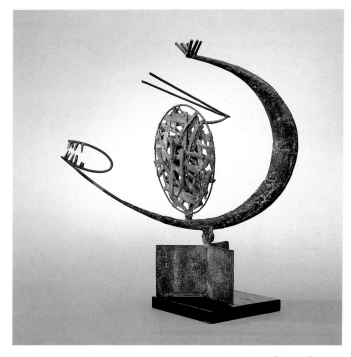

25-16. Julio González. *Head.* c. 1935. Wrought iron, 17¾ x 15¼" (45.1 x 38.7 cm). The Museum of Modern Art, New York

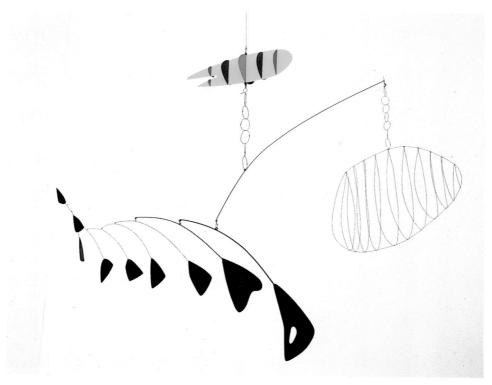

25-17. Alexander Calder. *Lobster Trap and Fish Tail*. 1939. Painted steel wire and sheet aluminum, approx. 8'6" x 9'6" (2.6 x 2.9 m). The Museum of Modern Art, New York

COMMISSIONED BY THE ADVISORY BOARD FOR THE STAIRWELL OF THE MUSEUM

with an aggressive reinterpretation of anatomy that is derived from Picasso's work after the mid-1920s. As in the head of the figure on the left in Picasso's *Three Dancers* (see fig. 24-27), the mouth is an oval cavity with spikelike teeth, the eyes two rods that converge upon an "optic nerve" linking them to the tangled mass of the "brain." González has produced a gruesomely expressive metaphor, as if the violence of his working process mirrored the violence of modern life.

ALEXANDER CALDER. Surrealism in the early 1930s produced still another important development: the mobile sculptures of the American Alexander Calder (1898–1976). Called *mobiles* for short, they are delicately balanced constructions of metal wire, hinged together and weighted so as to move with the slightest breath of air. Unpredictable and ever-changing, such mobiles incorporate the fourth dimension as an essential element. They may be of any size, from tiny tabletop models to the huge *Lobster Trap and Fish Tail* (fig. 25-17). Kinetic sculpture had been conceived first by the Constructivists. Their influence is evident in Calder's earliest mobiles, which were motor-driven and tended toward abstract geometric forms. Calder was also affected early on by Mondrian, whose use of primary colors he adopted. Like Mondrian, he initially thought of his constructions as self-contained miniature universes. But it was his contact with Surrealism that made him realize the poetic possibilities of "natural" rather than fully controlled movement. He borrowed biomorphic shapes from

Miró and began to conceive of mobiles as counterparts to organic structures: flowers on flexible stems, foliage quivering in the breeze, marine animals floating in the sea. Infinitely responsive to their environment, they seem amazingly alive.

ENGLAND. Two English sculptors represent the culmination of the modern sculptural tradition before 1945: Henry Moore (1898–1986) and Barbara Hepworth (1903–1975). The presence of Gabo, Kokoschka, Mondrian, Gropius, and other émigrés helped give rise to modern art in England during the mid-1930s, when Moore and Hepworth were emerging as mature artists. As a result, they absorbed the full spectrum of earlier twentieth-century sculpture but in different measure, reflecting their contrasting personalities. The two were closely associated as leaders of the modern movement in England, and influenced each other. Moore was the more boldly inventive artist, but Hepworth was arguably the better sculptor.

HENRY MOORE. The majestic *Two Forms* (fig. 25-18), an early work by Moore, may be regarded as the second-generation offspring of Brancusi's *The Kiss* of a quarter-century before (see fig. 25-2), although there is no direct connection between them. [See Primary Sources, no. 97, page 975.] Abstract and subtle in shape, they are "persons" in much the same vein as Lipschitz's *Figure* (see fig. 25-10). This family group—the forked slab evolved from the artist's studies of the mother-and-child theme—is mysterious

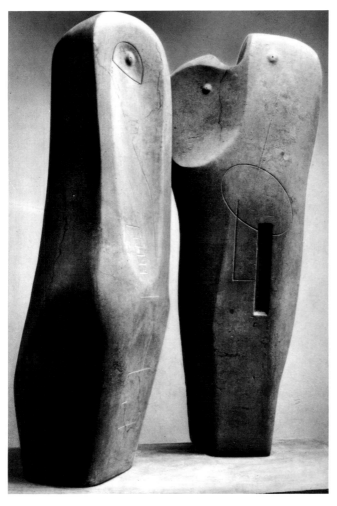

25-18. Henry Moore. *Two Forms*. 1936. Stone, height approx. 42" (106.7 cm). Collection Mrs. H. Gates Lloyd, Haverford, Pennsylvania

and remote like the monoliths of Stonehenge, which greatly impressed the sculptor (see fig. 1-18). And like Stonehenge, Moore's figures are meant to be placed in a landscape, so architectural are they in character.

Recumbent Figure (fig. 25-19), perhaps Moore's finest sculpture, retains both a classical motif—one thinks of a reclining river-god (see fig. 13-35)—and a primeval look. The design is in complete harmony with the natural striations of the stone, as if the forms had resulted from slow erosion over a thousand years. Through biomorphic abstraction, Moore has evoked the essence of the human figure with striking success. If we were to follow the natural temptation to run our hand over the sculpture, the swelling forms would seem filled with inner life. Moore was originally inspired by a Mayan statue of the rain spirit Chac Mool. Interestingly enough, the nearest relative of Brancusi's *The Kiss* is a Pre-Columbian pottery figurine group—which the artist cannot have known, however, since it was a later discovery. The coincidence nevertheless underscores the fundamental kinship between Brancusi and Moore. Moore's figure also suggests an awareness of Arp's *Human Concretion* from about the same time (see fig. 25-13). The difference is that Arp suggests anatomical forms without specifically referring to them, as Moore does. The undulating effect recalls the arabesques achieved by Matisse in *Reclining Nude I* (see fig. 25-1). Moore also takes liberties with the human figure that would be unthinkable without Picasso (compare fig. 24-29). In this way, Moore weaves the strands of early modern sculpture into a seamless unity of incomparable beauty and subtlety.

BARBARA HEPWORTH. Hepworth was the greatest woman sculptor of the twentieth century. In common with Moore's, her work had a biomorphic foundation, but her style became more

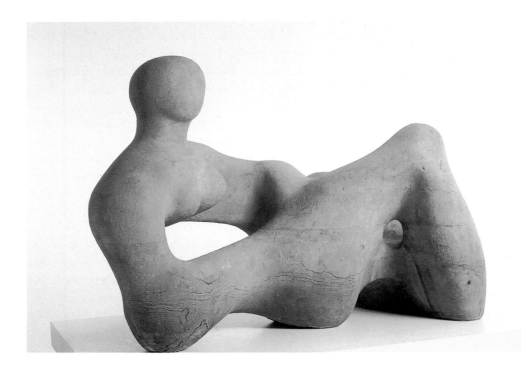

25-19. Henry Moore. *Recumbent Figure*. 1938. Green Hornton stone, length approx. 54" (137.2 cm). The Tate Gallery, London

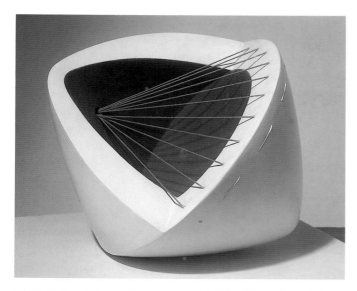

25-20. Barbara Hepworth. *Sculpture with Color (Deep Blue and Red)*. 1940-42. Wood, painted white and blue, with red strings, on a wooden base, 11 x 10¼" (27.9 x 26 cm). Collection Alan and Sarah Bowness, London

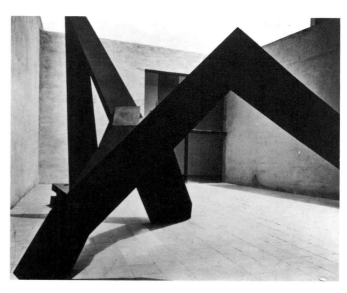

25-21. Mathias Goeritz. *Steel Structure*. 1952–53. Height 14'9" (4.5 m). The Echo (Experimental Museum), Mexico City

abstract after her marriage to the painter Ben Nicholson (see page 830), her association with the Constructivist Naum Gabo, and her contact in Paris with Brancusi and Arp. For a time she was practicing several modes at once under these influences. At the onset of World War II, she went to St. Ives in Cornwall, where she initiated a style that emerged fully in the early 1940s. *Sculpture with Color (Deep Blue and Red)* is a flawless synthesis of painting and sculpture, Surrealist biomorphism and organic abstraction, the molding of space and the shaping of mass (fig. 25-20). Carved from wood and immaculately finished, it transforms the shape of an egg into a timeless ideal that has the lucid perfection of a classical head, yet the elemental expressiveness of a primitive mask. Hepworth's egg shape undoubtedly owes something to Brancusi's (see fig. 25-3), although their work is very different. The colors accentuate the play between the interior and exterior of the hollowed-out form, while the strings, a device first used by Moore, seem to suggest a life force within. As a result of its open forms, *Sculpture with Color* enters into an active relationship with its surroundings.

Like Moore, Hepworth was concerned with the relationship of the human figure in a landscape, but in an unusually personal way. After moving to a house that overlooked St. Ives Bay, she wrote, "I was the figure in the landscape and every sculpture contained to a greater or lesser degree the ever-changing forms and contours embodying my own response to a given position in that landscape. I used colour and strings in many of the carvings of this time. The colour in the concavities plunged me into the depth of water, caves, or shadows deeper than the carved concavities themselves. The strings were the tension I felt between myself and the sea, the wind or the hills."

SCULPTURE SINCE 1945

PRIMARY STRUCTURE AND ENVIRONMENTAL SCULPTURE. Like painting, sculpture since 1945 has been characterized by epic proportions. Indeed, scale became fundamental for a sculptural movement that extended the scope—the very concept—of sculpture in an entirely new direction. Primary Structure, the most suitable name suggested for this type, conveys its two chief characteristics: extreme simplicity of shapes and a kinship with architecture. Another term, Environmental Sculpture (not to be confused with the mixed-medium "environments" of Pop art; see page 860), refers to the fact that many Primary Structures are designed to envelop the viewer, who is invited to enter them. It is this space-defining function that distinguishes Primary Structures from all previous sculpture and relates them to architecture. They are the modern successors to prehistoric monuments such as Stonehenge (see figs. 1-17 and 1-18).

MATHIAS GOERITZ. The first to explore these possibilities was Mathias Goeritz (1915–1981), a German working in Mexico City. As early as 1952–53 he established an experimental museum, The Echo, for displaying massive geometric sculptures, some so large that they occupy an entire patio (fig. 25-21). On this scale, Primary Structures virtually become architecture in their own right. Goeritz collaborated five years later with the architect Luis Barragán (1902–1987) on a group of colored office towers in Mexico City, which are themselves Primary Structures.

RONALD BLADEN. Goeritz's ideas were soon taken up on both sides of the Atlantic. Often sculptors of Primary Structures

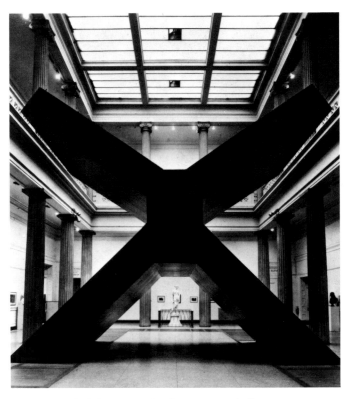

25-22. Ronald Bladen. *The X* (in the Corcoran Gallery, Washington, D.C.). 1967. Painted wood, later constructed in steel, 22'8" x 24'6" x 12'6" (6.9 x 7.3 x 3.8 m)

COURTESY FISCHBACH GALLERY, NEW YORK

limited themselves to the role of designer and left the execution to others, in order to emphasize the impersonality and repeatability of their invention. If no patron could be found to foot the bill for carrying out these costly structures, they remained on paper, like unbuilt architecture. Sometimes such works reached the mock-up stage. *The X* (fig. 25-22), by the Canadian Ronald Bladen (1918–1988), was originally built with painted wood substituting for metal for an exhibition inside the two-story hall of the Corcoran Gallery in Washington, D.C. Its commanding presence, dwarfing the Neoclassical colonnade of the hall, seems doubly awesome in such a setting.

DAVID SMITH. Most Primary Structures are not Environmental Sculptures but freestanding works independent of the sites that contain them. Bladen's *The X,* for example, was later constructed of painted steel as an outdoor sculpture. Primary Structures and Environmental Sculptures nevertheless share the same massive scale and simplified forms. The artist who played the most influential role in defining them was David Smith (1906–1965). His earlier work had been strongly influenced by the wrought-iron constructions of Julio González (see fig. 25-16), but during the last years of his life he developed a singularly impressive form of Primary Structure in his *Cubi* series. Figure 25-23 shows three of them against the open sky and rolling hills of the artist's farm at Bolton Landing, New York. (All are now

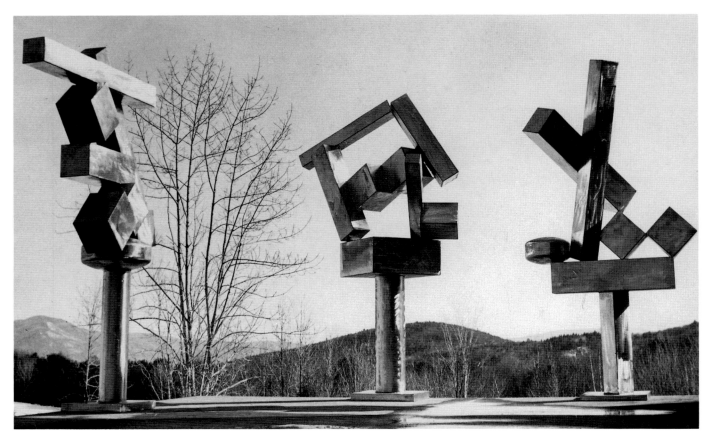

25-23. David Smith. *Cubi* series (at Bolton Landing, New York). Stainless steel. (left) *Cubi XVIII.* 1964. Height 9'8" (2.9 m). Museum of Fine Arts, Boston; (center) *Cubi XVII.* 1963. Height 9'2" (2.7 m). Dallas Museum of Fine Arts; (right) *Cubi XIX.* 1964. Height 9'5" (2.9 m). The Tate Gallery, London

in major museums.) Only two basic components are used: cubes and cylinders. Yet Smith created a seemingly endless variety of configurations. The forms are balanced upon each other as if held in place by a magnetic force, so that each sculpture represents a fresh triumph over gravity. Unlike many members of the Primary Structure movement, Smith executed these pieces himself. They are welded stainless steel sheets whose shiny surfaces he finished by hand. As a result, his work displays an "old-fashioned" subtlety of touch that reminds us of the polished bronzes of Brancusi.

DONALD JUDD. A younger generation of Minimalists, Bladen among them, carried the implications of Primary Structures to their logical conclusion. In search of the ultimate unity, they reduced their geometry to the fewest possible components, and used mathematical formulas to establish precise relationships. They further eliminated any hint of personal expression by contracting out the work to industrial fabricators. Unlike Environmental Sculpture, the work of Donald Judd (1928–1994) defined interior space without shaping it. In search of the ultimate unity, he separated Smith's *Cubi* into its two components by reducing the geometry to a single cube or cylinder. Like other Minimalist sculptors, he had them made to order by custom shops after using simple ratios to establish the design. Having gained total control over all his elements, he soon began to elaborate on them. His most involved pieces have a decorative richness, achieved by repeating the shape serially at set intervals and adding an intense primary color to one or more sides (fig. 25-24). Judd's strict guidelines permitted few variations, only greater refinement. Within these limitations, however, the results are often surprisingly impressive. Why this should be so is not easily explained, although the artist was an eloquent spokesman. In the end, the success of his work depends on its subtle proportions and flawless finish, which enabled him to attain a degree of perfection equaled by few other sculptors who shared the same approach.

JOEL SHAPIRO. A number of sculptors gradually began to move away from Minimalism without abandoning it altogether. This trend is called Post-Minimalism to denote its continuing debt to the earlier style. Its leading representative is Joel Shapiro (b. 1941). After producing small pieces having great conceptual intensity and aesthetic power, he suddenly began to make sculptures of simple wood beams that refer to the human figure but do not directly represent it. They assume active "poses," some standing awkwardly off-balance, others dancing or tumbling, so that they charge the space around them with energy. Shapiro soon began casting them in bronze, which retains the texture of the rough wood grain (fig. 25-25). These pieces reassert the traditional craft of sculpture in being hand-finished with a beautiful patina by skilled artisans. By freely rearranging the vocabulary of David Smith, who experimented with such a figure before his death, Shapiro gave Minimalist sculpture a new lease on life. Nevertheless, his work remains one of the few successful attempts at reviving contemporary sculpture, which as a whole has found it difficult to chart a new direction.

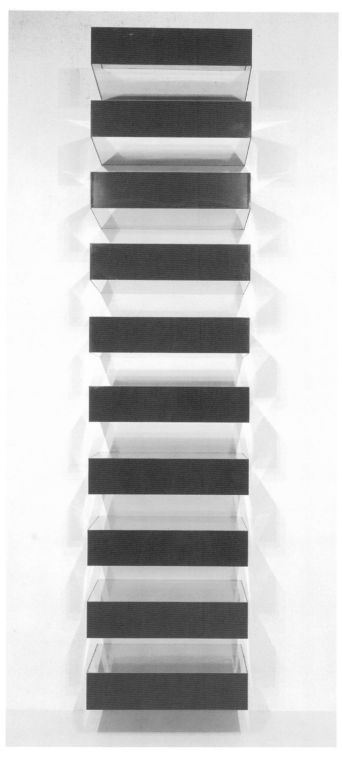

25-24. Donald Judd. *Untitled.* 1989. Copper with red Plexiglas; ten units, each 9 x 39½ x 31" (23 x 100.3 x 78.8 cm)
COURTESY THE PACEWILDENSTEIN GALLERY, NEW YORK

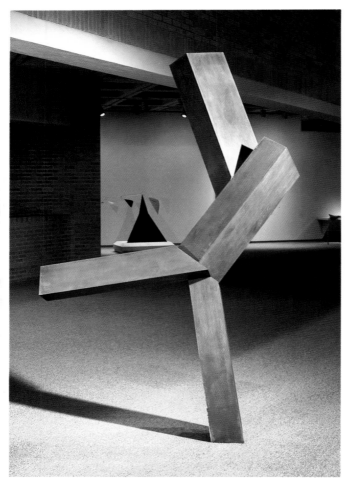

25-25. Joel Shapiro. *Untitled*. 1989-90. Bronze, 8'5½" x 3'6" x 6'6" (2.57 x 1.06 x 1.98 m). North Carolina Museum of Art, Raleigh

PURCHASED WITH FUNDS FROM VARIOUS DONORS, BY EXCHANGE

AFRICAN-AMERICAN SCULPTURE. Minimalism and Post-Minimalism were decisive influences on a group of talented African-American sculptors who came to maturity in the 1960s. Their work has helped to make the late twentieth century the first great age of African-American art. While these sculptors show a variety of styles, subjects, and approaches, all address the black experience in America within a contemporary abstract aesthetic. Thus they have the advantage over African-American painters, who have often been burdened by representationalism and traditional styles.

MARTIN PURYEAR. Martin Puryear (b. 1941), the leading black sculptor on the scene today, draws on his experience with woodworkers in Sierra Leone in western Africa, where he spent several years in the Peace Corps, and in Sweden, where he attended the Royal Academy. Puryear manages to weld these very different sources into a unified personal style. He adapts African motifs and materials to the modern Western tradition by relying on careful craftsmanship to bridge the gap. His forms, at once bold and refined, have an elegant simplicity that contrasts the natural and man-made, the finished and unfinished. They may evoke a saw, bow, fishnet, anthill, or in this case a basket (fig. 25-26)—whatever his memory suggests—but each is restated in whimsical fashion.

TYRONE MITCHELL. Dogon culture had a profound impact on Tyrone Mitchell (b. 1944) during a pivotal stay in Africa. Like Puryear's, his mature work combines Western and African sources. *Horn for Wifredo* (fig. 25-27) reduces an antelope to its essence using Minimalist forms and the spare simplicity of Bran-

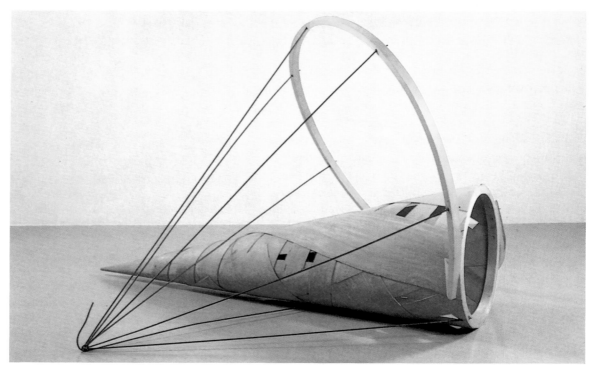

25-26. Martin Puryear. *The Spell*. 1985. Pine, cedar, and steel, 4'8" x 7' x 5'5" (1.42 x 2.13 x 1.65 m). Collection the artist

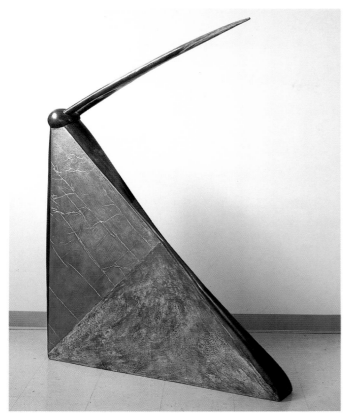

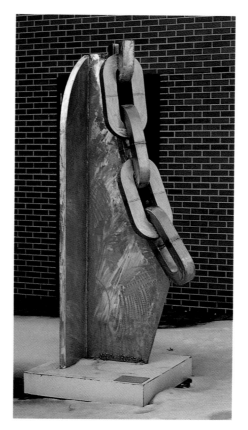

25-27. Tyrone Mitchell. *Horn for Wifredo*. 1987. Wood, copper, plaster, and pigment, 65 x 49 x 7" (165 x 124.5 x 17.8 cm). Collection of the Schomburg Center for Research in Black Culture, The New York Public Library, Art and Artifacts Division

25-28. Melvin Edwards. *To Listen*. 1990. Stainless steel, 7'5½" x 1'3½" x 3'1" (2.27 x .39 x .93 m)

cusi, who influenced him at the beginning of the 1980s. The diversity of materials creates a rich array of textures and colors that shows the artist's respect for time-honored materials and craftsmanship. This compound object, we realize, has a vital energy that makes of it a Surrealist creature. In fact, the title refers to the Cuban-born Surrealist Wifredo Lam (1902–1982), an important early inspiration for Mitchell.

MELVIN EDWARDS. Melvin Edwards (b. 1937), who also paid homage to Lam, was equally affected by visits to Africa. He may be regarded as the purist among contemporary African-American sculptors. An artist in the mold of David Smith, he continues to maintain an allegiance to the Primary Structure and the vocabulary of Minimalism. He invests them, however, with uniquely personal meaning and social content. *To Listen* (fig. 25-28) is a totemic figure reminiscent of Moore's *Two Forms* (see fig. 25-18) in its elemental shape but with the rugged strength that defines Edwards' work. Attached to it is the fragment of a chain. This is a favorite motif which recurs in his "Lynch Fragment Series"—small works that radiate a truly frightening menace. In addition to denoting slavery, the chain has a positive meaning for the artist: it signifies links with the past and the larger community. Edwards finds that abstraction helps him get in touch with his roots while providing a common ground of experience. In this respect he is close to his friend the painter William T. Williams (see page 854). He revels in the labor of sculpture, the very feel of metal, which is reflected

in the vigorous, handmade finish, a further debt to Smith. The result is a powerful monument to the African-American struggle for freedom and equality. The sculpture has the dignity of the man himself and reflects his strong sense of social responsibility.

ALISON SAAR. A late bloomer is Alison Saar (b. 1956). The daughter of the famous artist Betye Saar (b. 1929), who has parodied such white-created black icons as Aunt Jemima with unerring wit and sarcasm. Alison Saar spent much of her early career playing the role of "artist as professional angry black woman," which earned her praise from liberals and leftists but gained her little genuine artistic recognition outside that limited circle. In the 1990s, however, there was a major change in her work. It showed not only a more mature attitude but also adopted a more professional, mainstream approach, while addressing African-American issues no less seriously.

A splendid example of this new direction is *Compton Nocturne* (fig. 25-29). The title refers to an area south of Los Angeles and a piece by Duke Ellington. We have met her like often before: in the Eve by Giselbertus (fig. 10-25), the sleeping bacchante in Titian's *Bacchanal* (fig. 13-39), the Eve-like figure in the lower left of Gauguin's *Where Do We Come From? What Are We? Where Are We Going?* (fig. 23-14), the nude in Rousseau's *The Dream* (fig. 23-24), and Matisse's *Reclining Nude* (fig. 25-1; compare also fig. 24-1). All evoke a primeval paradise as a lost Golden Age. Saar takes up this timeless theme from a distinctly modern African-American point

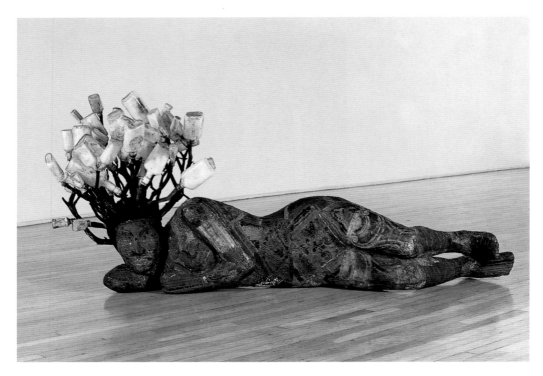

of view. Hers is no gentle, passive ideal, however. On the contrary, this over-lifesize black figure, covered with primitive painted decorations, looks out at the viewer with startling directness and barely suppressed anger that make a mockery of the classical tradition. Her hair, made of sticks dipped in tar, is a play on traditional "pickininny" braids, with their colorful ribbons that here are cheap bottles. The glass and plastic bottles come from on old Southern tradition of decorating trees with bottles, but they also suggest the rollers that many blacks use to straighten their hair. At the same time, *Compton Nocturne* evokes the realm of classical mythology, such as the snaky locks of the Medusa (compare fig. 28-10) and the story of Apollo and Daphne, who is turned into a tree by Aphrodite to escape the god. Saar's success in packing so many layers of complex meaning into such a compelling figure places her at the forefront of contemporary artists.

MONUMENTS. On a large scale, most Primary Structures are obviously monuments. But just as obviously they are not monuments commemorating or celebrating anything except their designer's imagination. They offer no ready frame of reference, nothing to be reminded of, even though the original meaning of *monument* is "a reminder." Monuments in the traditional sense died out when contemporary society could no longer agree on what ought to be publicly remembered or how; yet the belief in the possibility of such monuments has not been abandoned altogether.

CLAES OLDENBURG. The Pop artist Claes Oldenburg (b. 1929) has proposed a number of imaginative solutions to the problem of the monument. He is, moreover, an exceptionally persuasive commentator on his ideas. All his monuments are heroic in size, though not in subject matter. And all share one feature: their origin in humble objects of everyday use.

In 1969 Oldenburg conceived his most unusual project. For a piece of outdoor sculpture he wanted a form that combined hard and soft and did not need a base. An ice bag met these demands, so he bought one and started playing with it. He soon realized, he says, that the object was made for manipulation, "that movement was part of its identity and should be used." He then executed a work shaped like a huge ice bag (fig. 25-30) with a mechanism

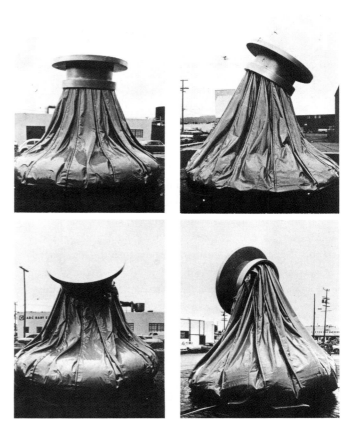

25-30. Claes Oldenburg. *Ice Bag-Scale B.* 1970. Programmed kinetic sculpture of polyvinyl, fiberglass, wood, and hydraulic and mechanical movements, 16 x 18 x 18' (4.9 x 5.5 x 5.5 m). National Gallery of Art, Washington, D.C.

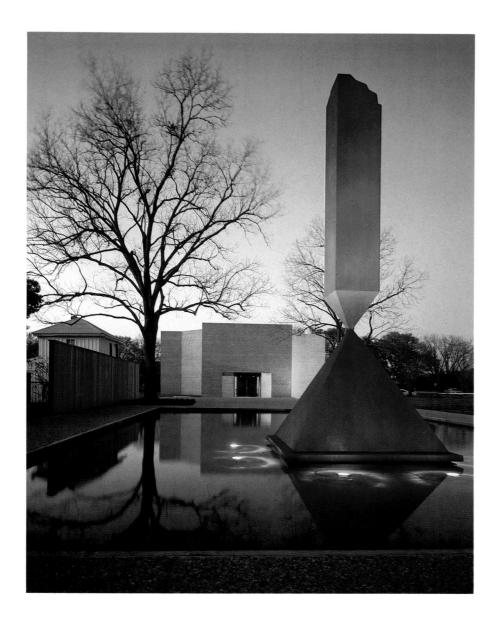

25-31. Barnett Newman. *Broken Obelisk.*
1963–67. Steel, height 25'1" (7.7 m).
Rothko Chapel, Houston

inside to make it produce "movements caused by an invisible hand," as the artist described them. He sent the *Giant Ice Bag* to the U.S. Pavilion at EXPO 70 in Osaka, Japan, where crowds were endlessly fascinated to watch it heave, rise, and twist like a living thing, then relax with an almost audible sigh.

What do such monuments celebrate? Part of their charm, which they share with readymades and Pop Art, is that they reveal the aesthetic potential of the ordinary and all-too-familiar. They also have an undeniable grandeur. There is one dimension, however, that is missing in Oldenburg's monuments. Wholly secular, wedded to the here and now, they delight, astonish, amuse— but they do not move us.

BARNETT NEWMAN. The few monuments that touch our deepest emotions have generally been inspired by profound religious beliefs and philosophical ideas. One of the most successful in this respect is *Broken Obelisk* (fig. 25-31) by Barnett Newman (1905–1970). Rising from the center of a shallow reflecting pool, it consists of a pyramid whose tip supports an up-ended, broken obelisk. Obelisks are slender, four-sided pillars of stone erected by the ancient Egyptians. The Romans brought many of them to Italy; one marks the center of the piazza of St. Peter's (see fig.

17-15). These obelisks gave rise to a number of later monuments in Europe and America. The two tips in Newman's sculpture have exactly the same angle (53 degrees, borrowed from Egyptian pyramids, which had long fascinated the artist). Hence their juncture forms a perfect X.

Why this monument has such power to stir our feelings is difficult to put into words. Is it the daring juxtaposition of two age-old shapes that have contrary meanings, the one symbolizing timeless stability, the other a thrust toward the heavens (compare figs. 20-3 and 21-58)? Surely, but what if the obelisk were intact? Would that not reduce the whole to an improbable balancing feat? The brokenness of the obelisk, then, is essential to the pathos of the monument. (Broken columns were traditional symbols of mortality; see fig. 13-38.) It speaks to us of our unfulfilled spiritual yearnings, of a quest for the infinite and universal that endures today as it has for thousands of years.

ISAMU NOGUCHI. The search for meaning absorbed the Japanese-American sculptor Isamu Noguchi (1904–1988). Influenced early on by the Surrealists, as well as by Brancusi, he did not confront Asian culture until a prolonged stay in Japan in 1952 that proved decisive to his formation. From then on he developed into

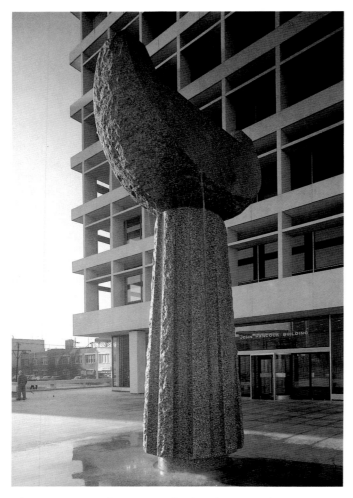

one of the most varied sculptors of this century whose rich imagination fed on both heritages. His role in mediating between East and West was of incalculable importance. To the Japanese he introduced modern Western ideas of style; to Americans he made traditional Japanese concepts of art comprehensible at a time when there was a growing fascination with Zen Buddhism.

We see this union in Noguchi's fountain for the John Hancock Insurance Company in New Orleans (fig. 25-32). Like much of Zen thought, it is an elegantly simple statement of a paradoxical idea. A "capital" rather like the wood-beam supports in a Japanese temple sits atop a grooved column recalling the primitive Doric of ancient Greece, where the Western sculptural tradition, of which Noguchi felt himself a part, originated. Except for the flat faces on either side of the capital, the finish has been left rough, out of the age-old Japanese respect for natural materials and unadorned simplicity in the crafts. It gives the fountain a primeval look that emphasizes the stone's origin in the earth, for which Noguchi acquired an Oriental veneration. The contrast to the sleek modern lines of the Hancock building could hardly be greater. Yet the placement of the fountain shows not only a Japanese sensitivity to space but a fundamental understanding of the logic of modern architecture that Japanese critics recognized as distinctly Western.

25-32. Isamu Noguchi. Fountain for the John Hancock Insurance Company, New Orleans. 1961–62. Granite, 16' (4.88 m)

MAYA LIN. Part of the problem confronting the monument maker in our era has been that, unlike a century ago, there have been so few things worth commemorating in the first place—no event or cause has galvanized our fragmented world, despite the momentous changes going on everywhere. Furthermore, there is no artistic vocabulary that we readily agree on. It is all the more ironic that the best-known memorial to American soldiers killed in Vietnam should turn out to be not an embarrassing reminder of one of the most bitterly divisive chapters in recent history, but an eloquent testimony to the universal tragedy of war (fig. 25-33). Designed by Maya Lin (b. 1959), it casts a spell on all those who

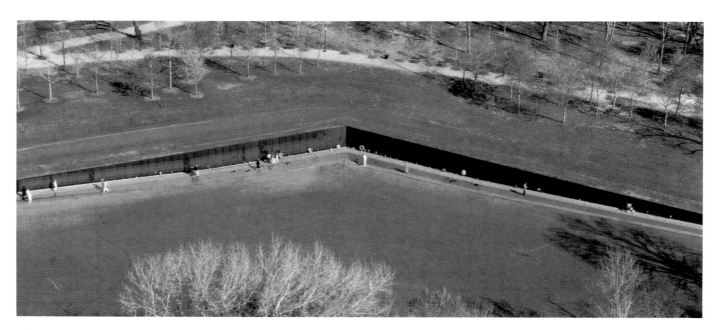

25-33. Maya Lin. *Vietnam Veterans Memorial.* 1982. Black granite, length 500' (152 m). The Mall, Washington, D.C.

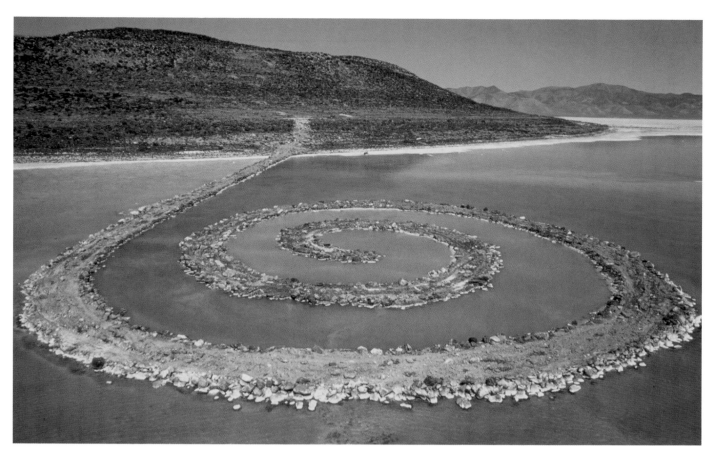

25-34. Robert Smithson. *Spiral Jetty.* As built in 1970. Total length 1,500' (457.2 m); width of jetty 15' (4.6 m). Great Salt Lake, Utah

see it. Its secret lies in the very simplicity of the architectural form and its setting.

By comparison, all other war memorials of recent times seem trite and needlessly complex, especially those incorporating realistic figures. It evokes a solemn mood without the inflated rhetoric that mars most memorials. The triangular shape, although embedded in tradition and rich in historical connotations (compare fig. 21-58), permits viewers to form their own associations because of its abstractness. Moreover, the reflective quality of the polished granite draws the viewer into the work. Yet these attributes alone cannot account for its extraordinary impact. Like Labrouste before her (see pages 761–62), Lin seized on the simple but brilliant idea of inscribing names—thousands of them—whose cumulative effect is to bring home the full enormity of the tragedy with awesome power. This device does not tell the story either, since other sculptors have inscribed names on monuments. In the end, the *Vietnam Veterans Memorial* is that rare instance of perfect harmony between form and idea. So unique is this achievement that no artist has been able to duplicate its success, although Lin herself has come close.

EARTH ART. Because of its space-defining function we might be tempted to call the *Vietnam Veterans Memorial* a work of architecture, like Stonehenge; yet it is so sculptural that it belongs equally well to Primary Structures. The two categories merge in "Earth Art," which is the ultimate medium for Environmental Sculpture, since it provides complete freedom from the limitations of the human scale. Logically enough, some designers of Primary Structures have turned to it. In some instances they have invented projects that stretch over many miles. These latter-day successors to the mound-building Indians of Neolithic times have the advantage of modern earth-moving machinery, but this is more than outweighed by the problem of cost and the difficulty of finding suitable sites on our crowded planet.

ROBERT SMITHSON. The few projects that have actually been carried out are mostly found in remote regions of western America, so that the finding is itself often difficult. *Spiral Jetty,* the work of Robert Smithson (1938–1973), jutted out into Great Salt Lake in Utah (fig. 25-34). Its appeal rests in part on the Surrealist irony of the concept: a spiral jetty is as self-contradictory as a straight corkscrew. But it can hardly be said to have grown out of the natural formation of the terrain like the Great Serpent Mound (see fig. 1-20). No wonder it has not endured long, nor was it intended to. The process by which nature is reclaiming *Spiral Jetty,* already twice submerged, was part of Smithson's design from the start. The project nevertheless lives on in photographs. How can such a thing be called art? To Smithson, "The strata of the Earth is a jumbled museum. When one scans the ruined sites of prehistory one sees a heap of wrecked maps that upsets our present art historical limits . . . there is only an uncertain disintegrating order that transcends the limits of rational separations. The brain itself resembles an eroded rock from which ideas and ideals leak."

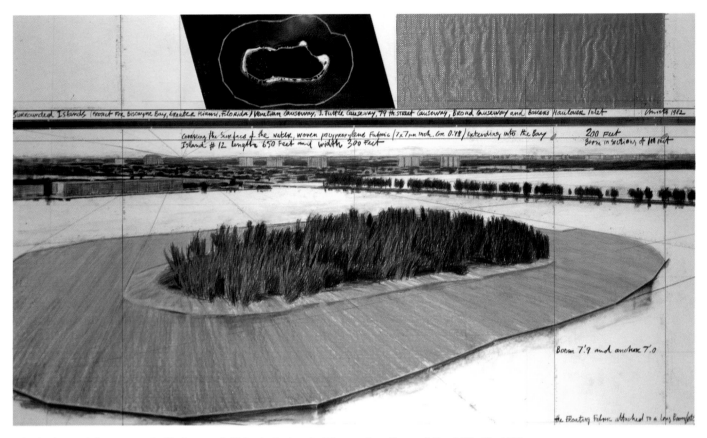

25-35. Christo (Christo Javacheff). *Surrounded Islands, Project for Biscayne Bay, Greater Miami, Florida.* 1982. Drawing in two parts, 1'3" x 8' (.38 x 2.44 m) and 3'6" x 8' (1.06 x 2.44 m). Pencil, charcoal, pastel, crayon, enamel paint, aerial photograph, and fabric sample. Private collection

COPYRIGHT CHRISTO 1982

CHRISTO. The projects of Christo (Christo Javacheff, b. 1935), who has gained notoriety for wrapping things, are deliberately short-lived. They enhance the environment only temporarily instead of altering it permanently. *Surrounded Islands, Biscayne Bay, Miami,* his most satisfying project, was installed for all of two weeks in the spring of 1983. Part Conceptual Art, part Happening (see pages 893–95), this ambitious repackaging of nature was a public event involving a small army of assistants. While the emphasis was on the campaign itself, the outcome was a triumph of epic fantasy.

Photographs hardly do justice to the results. Our collage of Christo's drawings, an aesthetic object in its own right, gives a clearer picture of the artist's intention by presenting the project in different ways and suggesting the complex experience it provided (fig. 25-35). (The sale of drawings such as this helped to fund the project.) In effect, Christo turned the islands into inverse lily pads of pink fabric. If Smithson's *Spiral Jetty* suggests the futility of grandiose undertakings, Christo's visual pun is as festive and decorative as Monet's water-lily paintings (see fig. 22-15), an inspiration the artist has acknowledged.

CONSTRUCTIONS AND ASSEMBLAGE. Constructions present a difficult problem. If we agree to limit the term *sculpture* to objects made of a single material, then we must put assemblages (constructions using mixed mediums) in a class of their own. This is probably a useful distinction, because of their relationship to readymades (see fig. 25-11). But what of Picasso's *Bull's Head* (see fig. 25-15)? Is it not an instance of assemblage, and have we not called it a piece of sculpture? Actually, there is no inconsistency here. The *Bull's Head* is a bronze cast, even though we cannot tell this by looking at a photograph of it. Had Picasso wished to display the actual handlebars and bicycle seat, he would surely have done so. Since he chose to have them cast in bronze, it must have been because he wanted to "dematerialize" the components of the work by having them reproduced in a single material. Apparently he felt it necessary to clarify the relation of image to reality in this way—the sculptor's way—and he almost always used the same procedure whenever he worked with found objects.

Nevertheless, we must not apply the "single-material" rule too strictly. Calder's mobiles, for instance, often combine metal, string, wood, and other substances. Yet they do not strike us as being assemblages, because these materials are not allowed to assert their separate identities. Conversely, an object may deserve to be called an assemblage even though composed of essentially the same material. Such is often true of works known as "junk sculpture." These are made of fragments of old machinery, parts of wrecked automobiles, and similar discards, which constitute a broad class that can be called sculpture, assemblage, or environment, depending on the work itself.

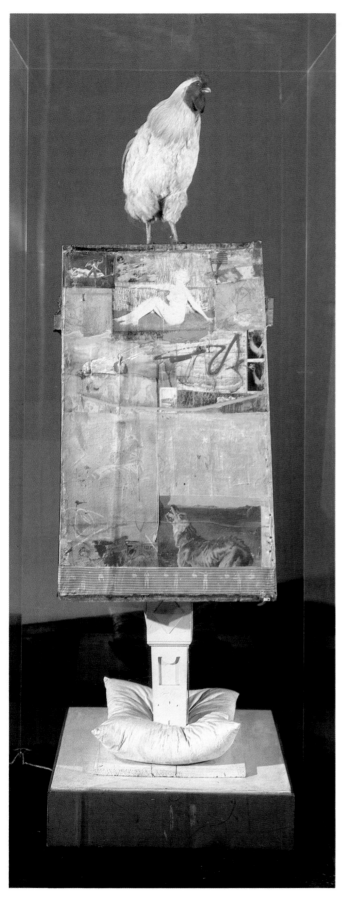

25-36. Robert Rauschenberg. *Odalisk.* 1955–58. Construction, 6'9" x 2'1" x 2'1" (2.06 x .64 x .64 m). Museum Ludwig, Cologne

ROBERT RAUSCHENBERG. Robert Rauschenberg (b. 1925) pioneered assemblage as early as the mid-1950s. Much like a contemporary composer making music out of the noises of everyday life (see box page 856), he constructed works of art from the trash of urban civilization. *Odalisk* (fig. 25-36) is a box covered with an assortment of pasted images—comic strips, photos, clippings from picture magazines—held together only by the network of brushstrokes the artist has painted on them. The box perches on a foot improbably anchored to a pillow on a wooden platform, and is topped by a stuffed chicken.

The title is a witty blend of "odalisque" and "obelisk." It refers both to the nude girls among the collage of clippings as modern "harem girls" and to the shape of the construction as a whole, for the box shares its verticality and slightly tapering sides with real obelisks. Rauschenberg's unlikely "monument" has at least some qualities in common with its predecessors: compactness and self-sufficiency. We will recognize in this improbable juxtaposition the same ironic intent as the readymades of Duchamp, whom Rauschenberg had come to know well in New York.

LOUISE NEVELSON. Although it is almost always made entirely of wood, the work of Louise Nevelson (1900–1988) must be classified as assemblage; when extended to a monumental scale, it acquires the status of an environment (see page 888). Before Nevelson, there had not been any important American women sculptors in the twentieth century. Sculpture had traditionally been reserved for men because of the manual labor involved. Thanks to the women's suffrage movement in the second half of the nineteenth century, Harriet Hosmer (1830–1908) and her "White Marmorean Flock" (as the novelist Henry James (1843–1916) called her and her followers in Rome) had succeeded in legitimizing sculpture as a medium for women. This school of sculpture waned, however, when the sentimental, idealizing Neoclassical style fell out of favor after the Philadelphia Centennial of 1876.

In the 1950s Nevelson rejected external reality and began to construct a private world from her collection of found pieces of wood, both carved and rough. At first these self-contained realms were miniature cityscapes, but they soon grew into large environments of freestanding "buildings," complete with decorations that were inspired by the sculpture on Mayan ruins. However, Nevelson's work generally took the form of large wall units that flatten her architecture into reliefs (fig. 25-37). Assembled from individual compartments, the whole is always painted a single color, usually a matte black to suggest the shadowy world of dreams. Each unit is elegantly designed and is itself a metaphor of thought or experience. While the organization is governed by an inner logic, the statement remains an enigmatic monument to the artist's imagination.

BARBARA CHASE-RIBOUD. Nevelson's success has encouraged other American women to become sculptors. Barbara Chase-Riboud (b. 1939), a prize-winning novelist and poet who lives in Paris and Rome, belongs to a generation of remarkable black women who have made significant contributions to several of the arts at once. She is heir to a unique American tradition. It is a

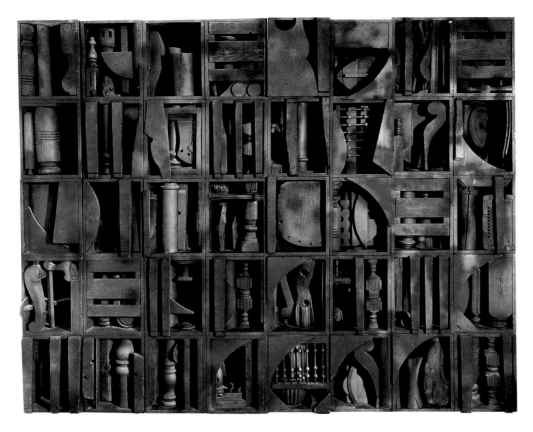

25-37. Louise Nevelson.
Black Chord. 1964. Painted wood,
8' x 10' x 11½" (2.44 x 3.05 x .29 m).
Collection Joel Ehrenkranz

(BELOW) 25-38.
Barbara Chase-Riboud.
Confessions for Myself. 1972. Bronze,
painted black, and black wool,
10' x 3'4" x 1' (3.05 x 1.02 x .30 m).
University Art Museum,
University of California
at Berkeley

PURCHASED WITH FUNDS FROM THE
H. W. ANDERSON CHARITABLE FOUNDATION

paradox that whereas black women almost never carve in traditional African cultures, in America they found their first artistic outlet in sculpture. They were attracted to it by the example set by Harriet Hosmer at a time when abolitionism and feminism were closely allied liberal causes.

Chase-Riboud received her initial training in her native Philadelphia, the first center of minority artists. The monumental sculpture she developed in the early 1970s, after graduating from Yale University, makes an indelible impression. In *Confessions for Myself* (fig. 25-38) she has envisioned a demonic archetype of awesome power. Her approach uses the principle of assemblage to combine bronze, either polished or with a black patina, and braided fiber. Similar qualities can be found in cast bronze figures from Benin and in carved wooden masks by the Senufo tribe, which are sometimes decorated with textiles. *Confessions for Myself* can be compared to a poem: each form, made by folding flat sheets of wax, is like a strophe that contributes to the total meaning of the work. Nor is the analogy an accident, for Chase-Riboud's growth as an artist coincided with her development as a poet. The title in this case comes from one of the poems that she wrote around the same time. She began *Confessions for Myself* with the poem in mind, which accounts for the extremely personal nature of the work.

Her sculpture expresses a distinctly ethnic sensibility and feminist outlook. At the same time, she is like an archaeologist, peeling back layer after layer of personal memory to reveal a meaning from deep within our collective subconscious. Thus she achieves a universality in keeping with her cosmopolitan view of art and life. Because it transcends barriers of race and culture, Chase-Riboud has found wider acceptance in Europe than in the United States, where her work does not meet popular stereotypes of black art.

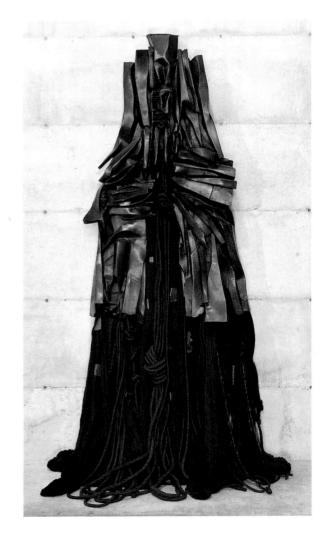

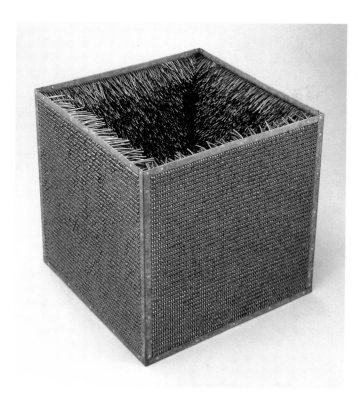

25-39. Eva Hesse. *Accession II*. 1967. Steel and rubber tubes, 30¾ x 30¾ x 30¾" (78 x 78 x 78 cm). The Detroit Institute of Arts
FOUNDERS SOCIETY PURCHASE, FRIENDS OF MODERN ART AND MISCELLANEOUS GIFTS FUND

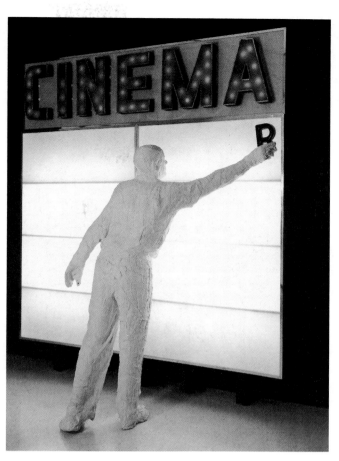

25-40. George Segal. *Cinema*. 1963. Plaster, metal, Plexiglas, and fluorescent light, 9'10" x 8' x 3'3" (3 x 2.4 x .99 m). Albright-Knox Art Gallery, Buffalo, New York
GIFT OF SEYMOUR H. KNOX

EVA HESSE. A special case is provided by Eva Hesse (1936–1970) who had just begun to hit her stride when her life was cut short by cancer. It is impossible to separate her work from her life, which is known in considerable detail, thanks to her diaries and many interviews. [See Primary Sources, no. 98, page 976.] While not a feminist, she has been treated as a heroine by the women's liberation movement because of her personal and artistic struggles. In many respects she represented the prototype of the feminist artist, one who was later to provide inspiration to others. Her sculpture nevertheless defies convenient categories. It began to develop rapidly only in 1966 as the result of a stay in Germany, where she was influenced by Joseph Beuys and his Zero Group (see below). For Hesse as for Beuys, art had the ability to heal through its power of revelation, only for her it was private rather than social. Her artistic environment was the New York circle of Minimalists that included her closest friends. Her work derives its best features from both circles, but is entirely individual.

To look at Hesse's sculpture is to see a central mystery unveiled through its often paradoxical, mythic character. *Accession II* (fig. 25-39) has been aptly described as "suggesting a stylistic collision between one of Donald Judd's minimalist aluminum boxes and Meret Oppenheim's Surrealist fur-covered teacup of 1936." (Compare figs. 25-24 and 25-12.) Aesthetically it has the spareness of Minimalist art, but with infinitely richer meaning. It possesses all the enigma of Pandora's box and the piquancy of an erotic fetish.

This quality is found throughout Hesse's mature work, which is saturated with unmistakable sexual overtones.

ENVIRONMENTS AND INSTALLATIONS. A number of artists associated with Pop Art have also turned to assemblage because they find the flat surface of the canvas too confining. In order to bridge the gap between image and reality, they often introduce three-dimensional objects into their pictures. Some even construct full-scale models of everyday things and real-life situations, utilizing every conceivable material in order to embrace the entire range of their physical environment, including people, in their work. These environments combine the qualities of painting, sculpture, collage, and stagecraft. Being three-dimensional, they can claim to be considered sculpture. However, environments form a separate category, distinct from both painting and sculpture, because they combine different materials ("mixed mediums") and blur the borderline between image and reality. The differences are underscored in "installations," which are environments expanded into room-size settings.

GEORGE SEGAL. George Segal (1924–2000) created three-dimensional lifesize environments showing people and objects in everyday situations. The subject of *Cinema* (fig. 25-40) is ordinary enough to be instantly recognizable: a man changing the letters on a movie theater marquee. The relation of image and reality is

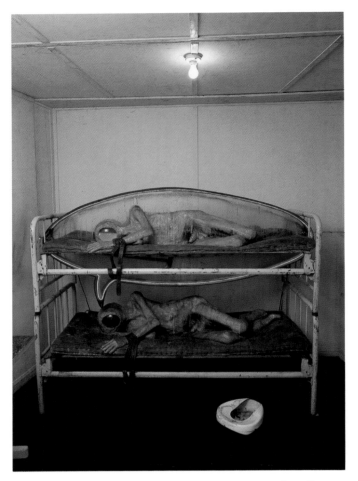

25-41. Edward Kienholz. *The State Hospital*. 1966. Mixed media, 8 x 12 x 10' (2.4 x 3.7 x 3.1 m). Moderna Museet, Stockholm

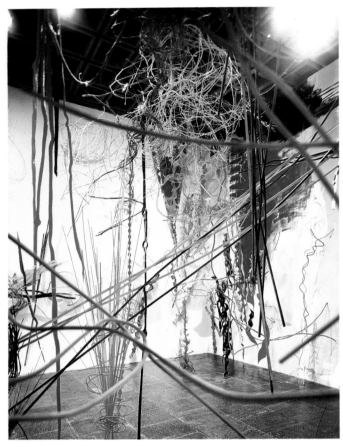

25-42. Judy Pfaff. *Dragons*. 1965. Installation at the Whitney Biennial, February–April 1981. Mixed media. Whitney Museum of American Art, New York

COURTESY HOLLY SOLOMON GALLERY, NEW YORK

far more subtle and complex than the scene first suggests. The man's figure is cast from a live model by a technique of Segal's invention and retains its ghostly white plaster surface. Thus it is one crucial step removed from our world of daily experience. The neon-lit sign has been carefully designed to complement and set off the shadowed figure. Moreover, the scene is brought down from its normal place high above the entrance to the theater, where we might have seen it in passing, and is shown at eye level, isolated from its natural context, so that we grasp it completely for the first time.

EDWARD KIENHOLZ. Some environments can have a shattering impact on the viewer. This is certainly true of *The State Hospital* (fig. 25-41) by the West Coast artist Edward Kienholz (1927–1994), which shows a cell in a ward for senile patients with a naked old man strapped to the lower bunk. He is the victim of physical cruelty, which has reduced what little mental life he had in him almost to the vanishing point. His body is little more than a skeleton covered with leathery, discolored skin, and his head is a glass bowl with live goldfish, of which we catch an occasional glimpse. The horrifying realism of the scene is completed by the sense of smell. When the work was displayed at the Los Angeles County Museum of Art, it emitted a sickly hospital stench.

But what of the figure in the upper bunk? It almost duplicates the one below, with one important difference: it is a mental image, since it is enclosed in the outline of a comic-strip balloon rising from the goldfish bowl. It represents, then, the patient's awareness of himself. The abstract devices of the balloon and the metaphoric goldfish bowl are both alien to the realism of the scene; yet they play an essential part in it, for they help to break the grip of horror and pity. They make us think as well as feel. Kienholz's means may be Pop, but his goal is that of Greek tragedy. His environments have no equal as witnesses to the unseen miseries beneath the surface of modern life.

JUDY PFAFF. The work of Judy Pfaff (born 1946) is as exuberant as Kienholz's is somber. Her constructions and environments bring to mind the fantasies of Robert Rauschenberg, but they are characterized by playfulness rather than ironic wit. Pfaff's installations mix painting with sculpture and found materials to activate architectural space. *Dragons* (fig. 25-42) is aptly named for its fiery forms and brilliant colors, which make it as festive as a Chinese New Year's celebration. Her spontaneous energy is the equivalent of Jackson Pollock's, and the swirling profusion of materials is like an Action Painting brought to life. It is as if the paint had been released from the canvas and left free to roam in space. The experience is one of enchantment as the viewer wanders this exotic indoor jungle.

CONCEPTUAL ART. Conceptual Art has the same "patron saint" as Pop Art: Marcel Duchamp. It arose during the 1960s out of the Happenings staged by Alan Kaprow (b. 1927) and Jean Tinguely (1925–1991), in which the event itself became the art (see illustration page 819). Conceptual Art challenges our definition of art more radically than Pop by insisting that the leap of the imagination, not the execution, is the art. According to this view, works of art can be dispensed with altogether, since they are incidental by-products of the imaginative leap. So, too, can galleries and, by extension, even the artist's public. The creative process need only be documented in some way. Sometimes the evidence is in verbal form, but more often it is still photography, video, or cinema exhibited within an installation.

Conceptual Art is related to Minimalism as a phenomenon of the 1960s, but instead of abolishing content, it eliminates aesthetics from art. This deliberately antiart approach, stemming from Dada (see page 831), poses a number of stimulating paradoxes. As soon as the documentation takes on visible form, it begins to come perilously close to more traditional forms of art (especially if it is placed in a gallery, where it can be seen by an audience). In fact, it is almost impossible to divorce the imagination fully from aesthetic matters.

JOSEPH KOSUTH. We see this dilemma in *One and Three Chairs* (fig. 25-43) by Joseph Kosuth (b. 1945), which is clearly indebted to Duchamp's readymades (see fig. 25-11). It "describes" a chair by combining in one installation an actual chair, a full-scale photograph of that chair, and a printed dictionary definition of the word. Whatever the Conceptual artist's intention, this making of the work of art, no matter how minimal the process, is as essential as it was for Michelangelo. In the end, all art is the final document of the creative process, because without execution, no idea can ever be fully realized. Without such "proof of performance," the Conceptual artist becomes like the emperor wearing new clothes that no one else can see. And, in fact, Conceptual Art has embraced all of the mediums in one form or another.

JOHN BALDESSARI. Like Dada, Conceptual Art is notable for its ironic humor—whose bark is admittedly worse than its bite. It reached a high point with *Art History,* from *Ingres and Other Parables* by John Baldessari (b. 1931). The image is both a witty spoof on art-history texts such as this book and a telling commentary on the difficulties young artists face in finding acceptance (fig. 25-44). The juxtaposition of a great monument, mock-serious narrative, and absurd moral is meant to deride traditional value judgments about art. Yet it remains strangely innocuous, as if the artist were too self-consciously aware of his mischievous role.

PERFORMANCE ART. Performance Art, which originated in the early decades of the twentieth century, belongs for the most part to the history of theater. However, the form that arose in the 1970s combines aspects of Happenings and Conceptual Art with

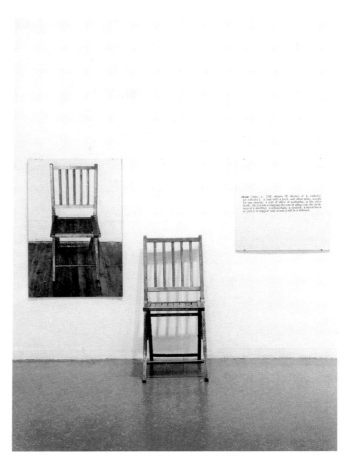

25-43. Joseph Kosuth. *One and Three Chairs.* 1965.
Wooden folding chair, photographic copy of chair, and photographic enlargement of dictionary definition of chair; chair 32 3/8 x 14 7/8 x 20 7/8" (82.2 x 37.8 x 53 cm); photo panel 36 x 24 1/8" (91.5 x 61.1 cm); text panel 24 x 24 1/8" (61 x 61.3 cm). The Museum of Modern Art, New York
LARRY ALDRICH FOUNDATION FUND

installations. In reaction to Minimalism, artists now wanted to reassert their presence by becoming, in effect, living works of art. The results have relied mainly on the shock value of irreverent humor or explicit sexuality. Nonetheless, Performance Art emerged as perhaps the most characteristic art form of the 1980s.

JOSEPH BEUYS. The German artist Joseph Beuys (1921–1986) managed to overcome these limitations, but he, too, was a controversial figure who incorporated an element of parody into his work. Life for Beuys was a creative process in which everyone is an artist, and he made up many of the "facts" of his life to enhance his role as myth-maker. To him, art was capable of transforming society itself, and thus acquired a political mission as well. Beuys assumed the guise of a modern-day shaman intent on healing the spiritual crisis of contemporary life caused, he believed, by the rift between the arts and sciences.

To find the common denominator behind such divisions, he created objects and scenarios which, though often intellectually baffling, were meant to appeal to the imagination. In 1974, Beuys spent one week caged up in a New York gallery with a coyote (fig. 25-45), an animal sacred to the American Indian but persecuted by the white man. His goal in this "dialogue" was to ease the trauma

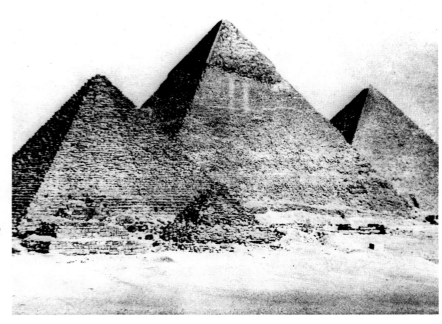

ART HISTORY

A young artist had just finished art school. He asked his instructor what he should do next. "Go to New York," the instructor replied, "and take slides of your work around to all the galleries and ask them if they will exhibit your work." Which the artist did.

He went to gallery after gallery with his slides. Each director picked up his slides one by one, held each up to the light the better to see it, and squinted his eyes as he looked. "You're too provincial an artist," they all said. "You are not in the mainstream." "We're looking for Art History."

He tried. He moved to New York. He painted tirelessly, seldom sleeping. He went to museum and gallery openings, studio parties, and artists' bars. He talked to every person having anything to do with art; travelled and thought and read constantly about art. He collapsed.

He took his slides around to galleries a second time. "Ah," the gallery directors said this time, "finally you are historical."

Moral: Historical mispronounced sounds like hysterical.

25-44. John Baldessari. *Art History, from Ingres and Other Parables.* 1972. Photograph and typed text. Collection Angelo Baldassarre, Bari, Italy

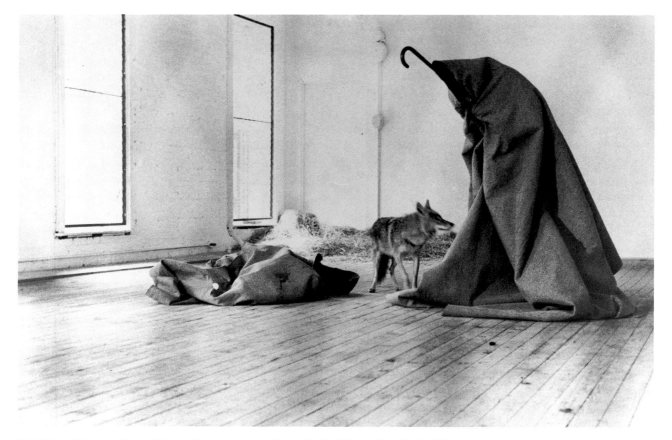

25-45. Joseph Beuys. *Coyote.* Photo of performance at Rene Block Gallery, New York, 1974

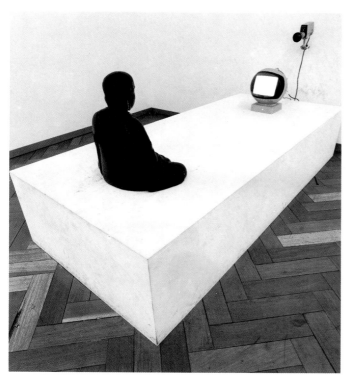

25-46. Nam June Paik. *TV Buddha*. 1974.
Video installation with statue. Stedelijk Museum, Amsterdam

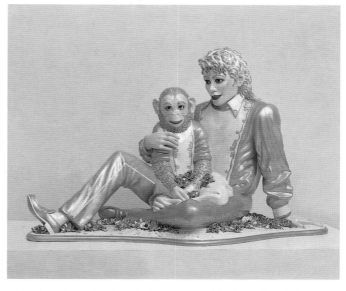

25-47. Jeff Koons. *Michael Jackson and Bubbles*. 1988. Porcelain
ceramic blend. 42 x 70½ x 32½". Broad Gallery, New York

caused to an entire nation by the schism between the two opposing
worldviews. That the attempt was inherently doomed to failure
does not in any way reduce the sincerity of this act of conscience.

NAM JUNE PAIK. The notes and photographs that document
Beuys' performances hardly do them justice. His chief legacy today
lies perhaps in the stimulation he provided his many students,
including Anselm Kiefer (see page 865), and his collaborators,
among them Nam June Paik (b. 1932). The sophisticated video
displays of the Korean-born Paik belong to cinema and thus fall
outside the scope of this book. His installation with a Buddha contemplating a television (fig. 25-46) is nevertheless a memorable
image uniquely appropriate to our age, in which the fascination
with electronic mediums often seems to have replaced spirituality
as the focus of modern life.

LATE MODERN. A great deal of late twentieth-century sculpture was concerned with "objects of desire": consumer goods as
status symbols, which are displaced through changes in location,
scale, materials, and recombination. Such shifts in context call into
question the aesthetic value and social meaning of these articles
and, by extension, our materialistic culture, sometimes with
bizarre results. These artists are the descendants of Marcel
Duchamp (see fig. 25-11), Robert Rauschenberg (see fig. 25-36),
and Andy Warhol (see fig. 24-76), as well as the Conceptualists.

JEFF KOONS. A leading representative of this international
trend is Jeff Koons (b. 1955), who makes sculpture rich in concep-

tual issues, although he is not a conceptual artist as such. This, in
part, accounts for why his work constantly changes in both style
and medium, and it is the thread that ties this diverse output
together. Continuously pushing the limits of sculpture, Koons
makes objects that range from two basketballs suspended in water
in fish tanks to a cast-bronze aqualung, from a chrome rabbit balloon to a 43-foot-high puppy made of flowers.

His sculpture epitomizes the 1980s concern with making art
that both draws and comments on other art, as well as exploring
the relationship of high and low art. For example, the ornateness
of *Michael Jackson and Bubbles* (fig. 25-47) evokes seventeenth-
century Italian Baroque sculpture (see Bernini's *The Ecstasy of
St. Theresa* fig. 17-29) and eighteenth-century French porcelain,
while the tawdry gold paint and rouged lips, along with the popular culture imagery, give the work a crass look associated with
mass-produced, gift-shop figurines, both plastic and ceramic. The
sculpture was, in a sense, factory produced, for it was made in a
limited edition by craftsmen in Italy to Koons' specifications. The
image in turn was based on a publicity photograph of the singer
with his pet chimpanzee. Despite its Pop subject and mass-appeal
aesthetics, the sculpture is magically powerful. Koons realized
that presenting his subject on a lifesize scale, he transformed it
from a **kitsch** souvenir into a compelling statement about the difference between fine art and a gift-shop trinket. The work also
captures the glamour and glitz of celebrity promotion of its times.
But the tawdriness and the porcelain itself give *Michael Jackson
and Bubbles* a poignant sense of fragility and impermanence, suggesting how temporary life and fame really are.

CHAPTER TWENTY-SIX

Twentieth-Century Architecture

Modernism in twentieth-century architecture meant first and foremost an aversion to historicism and ornamentation. Instead it favored a clean functionalism that expressed the Machine Age, with its insistent rationalism. In this regard, it can be regarded as the successor to classicism and, more specifically, the tradition of structural rationalism (see page 685). Yet modern architecture demanded far more than a reform of architectural vocabulary and grammar. A new philosophy was needed to take full advantage of the latest building techniques and materials that the engineer had made available to the architect.

The leaders of modern architecture to the present have been vigorous and eloquent thinkers, in whose minds architectural theory is closely linked with ideas of social reform to meet the challenges posed by industrial civilization. To them, architecture's ability to shape human experience brings with it the responsibility to play an active role in molding modern society for the better. Architecture since 1900 has nevertheless been characterized as much by conservative counter-movements and dead ends as by modernism, although it is the latter that defines the age. Moreover, modernism has created as many problems as it has solved, from faulty structures caused by engineering flaws to inhuman buildings based on abstract ideals.

ARCHITECTURE BEFORE WORLD WAR I

The Quest for a Modern Architecture

FRANK LLOYD WRIGHT. The first indisputably modern architect was Frank Lloyd Wright (1867–1959), Louis Sullivan's great disciple. If Sullivan, Gaudí, Mackintosh, and Van de Velde could be called the Post-Impressionists of architecture, Wright took architecture to its Cubist phase. This is certainly true of his brilliant early style, which he developed between 1900 and 1910 and which had broad international influence. In the beginning, Wright's main activity was the design of suburban homes in the upper Midwest.

These were known as Prairie houses, because their low, horizontal lines were meant to blend with the flat landscape around them.

The last, and most successful, residence in this series is the Robie House of 1909 (figs. 26-1 and 26-2). The exterior, so unlike anything seen before, instantly proclaims the building's modernity. However, its "Cubism" is not just a matter of the clean-cut rectangular elements composing the structure but also of Wright's handling of space. Robie House is designed as a number of "space blocks," similar to the building blocks the architect played with as a child, arranged around a central core, the chimney. Some of the blocks are closed and others are open, but all are defined with equal precision. Thus the space that has been architecturally shaped includes the balconies, terrace, court, and garden, as well as the house itself. As in Analytic Cubism, voids and solids are regarded as equivalents, and the entire complex enters into an active and dramatic relationship with its surroundings.

Wright did not aim simply to design a house; he wanted to create a complete environment. In the Francis W. Little House (fig. 26-3), he even took command of the details of the interior and designed stained glass, fabrics, and furniture. The controlling factor here was not the client's special wishes. Wright acted out of a conviction that buildings have a profound influence on those who live, work, or worship in them, thus making the architect, consciously or unconsciously, a molder of people.

ADOLF LOOS. In Europe modern architecture developed slowly and unevenly. One of the first priests of modernism, Adolf Loos (1870–1933), the son of a Moravian stonemason, spent three years in Chicago during the 1890s and returned to Vienna a convert to functionalism. Architecture to him served a practical purpose as building, not art. Hence he was violently opposed to the Art Nouveau style of the Secession movement. His credo was, "Modern man, the man with modern nerves, does not need ornamentation; it disgusts him." It was based in part on the socialist view of the craftsman as a slave to the rich bourgeoisie. Oddly

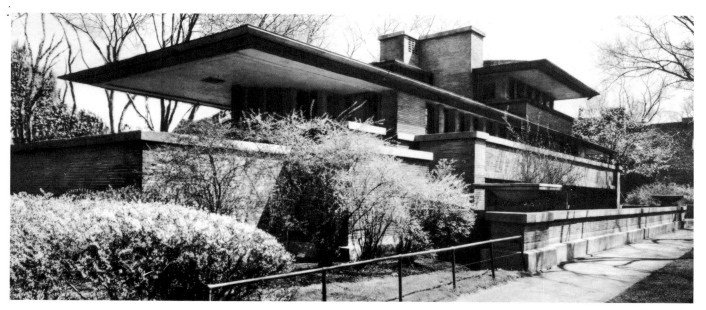

26-1. Frank Lloyd Wright. Robie House, Chicago. 1909

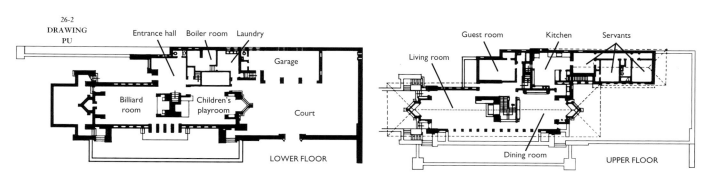

26-2. Plan of Robie House

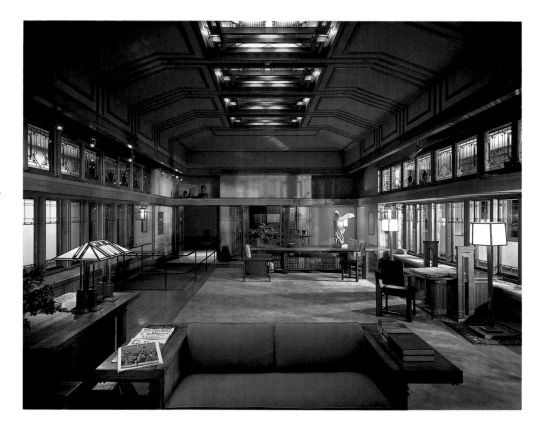

26-3. Frank Lloyd Wright.
Installation of the living room
from Francis W. Little House.
The Metropolitan Museum of Art,
New York

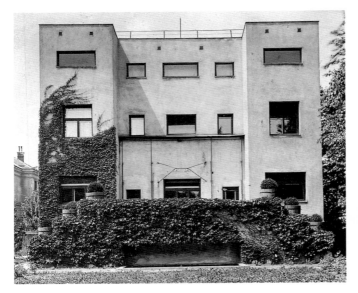

26-4. Adolf Loos. Steiner House, Vienna. 1910

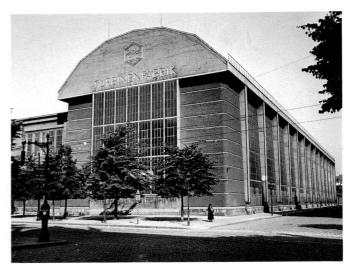

26-5. Peter Behrens. A.E.G. Turbine Factory, Berlin. 1909–10

enough, this distaste for ornament was confined to the exterior; rich materials were used on the inside to make up for this lack of decoration, much as at Chiswick (see page 684). The garden side of Loos' Steiner House from 1910 (fig. 26-4), one of the first private houses built of **ferroconcrete** (concrete reinforced with steel), is free of decoration, and retains its striking modern appearance to this very day. (The front represents an awkward compromise with local building authorities.) In its insistent logic, Steiner House embodies Loos' statement, made the same year, that "like almost every town dweller, the architect possesses no culture. He does not have the security of the peasant to whom this culture is innate. The town dweller is an upstart. I call culture that balance of inner and outer man, which alone can guarantee reasonable thought and action."

DEUTSCHER WERKBUND. The Deutscher Werkbund (Artisans Community) was pivotal to the early development of modernism in Germany. This alliance of "the best representatives of art, industry, crafts and trades" was founded in 1907 to upgrade the quality and value of German goods to the level of England's. Its leader was Hermann Muthesius (1861–1927), whose mission was to translate the Arts and Crafts Movement into a machine style using the most advanced techniques of industrial design and manufacturing. The membership consisted of 12 leading industrial firms and a like number of artists, designers, and architects from Germany and Austria.

PETER BEHRENS. The way was led by Peter Behrens (1869–1940), the chief architect and designer for the electrical firm A.E.G. His Turbine Factory of 1909–10 (fig. 26-5) transforms the factory shed into a monument to industry through the unmistakable reference to Greek temples (compare fig. 5-28). Yet it does so without resorting to a historicist veneer. Rather, it defines a modern style stemming from Mackintosh's Glasgow School of Art (see fig. 23-33). For Behrens the key to monumentality was not size but "proportionality, the regularity that expresses itself in architectural relationships." The result is an even greater simplicity

than in Sullivan's Schlesinger and Mayer department store (see fig. 23-40). Structurally there is little new here. Reinforced concrete had been in use since the later nineteenth century. Even the wall of glass does not advance beyond Paxton's Crystal Palace (see fig. 22-34). Nor does the building promote a machine aesthetic or enforce structural rationalism. It was nevertheless of critical importance for Behrens' three disciples, who became the founders of modern architecture: Walter Gropius, Ludwig Mies van der Rohe, and Le Corbusier.

WALTER GROPIUS. The first to cross that threshold fully was Gropius (1883–1969), who came from a well-known family of architects. The Fagus Shoe Factory (fig. 26-6), designed in 1911 with his partner Adolf Meyer (1881–1929), represents the critical step toward modernism in European architecture. The most dramatic

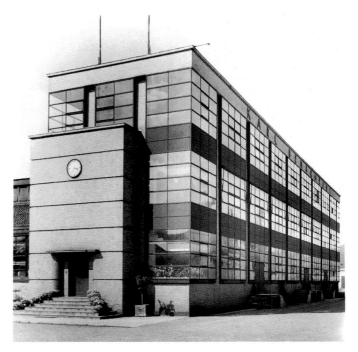

26-6. Walter Gropius and Adolf Meyer. Fagus Shoe Factory, Alfeld, Germany. 1911–14

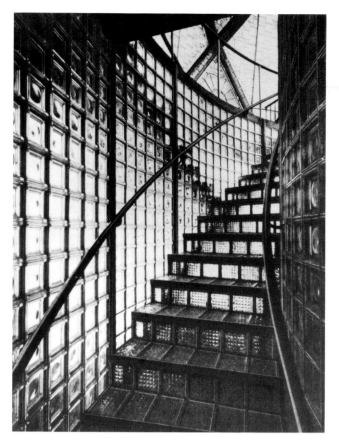

26-7. Bruno Taut. Staircase of the "Glass House," Werkbund Exhibition, Cologne. 1914

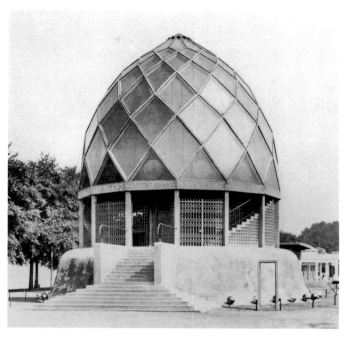

26-8. Bruno Taut. The "Glass House," Werkbund Exhibition, Cologne. 1914

feature is the walls, which are a nearly continuous surface of glass. This radical innovation had been possible ever since the introduction of the structural steel skeleton several decades before, which relieved the wall of any load-bearing function. Sullivan had approached it, but he could not yet free himself from the traditional notion of the window as a "hole in the wall." Far more radically than Sullivan or Behrens, Gropius frankly acknowledged, at last, that in modern architecture the wall is no more than a curtain or climate barrier, which may consist entirely of glass if maximum daylight is wanted. Only in the classical entrance did he give a nod to the past.

Expressionism

BRUNO TAUT. The Werkbund exhibition of 1914, which featured Van de Velde's theater (see fig. 23-35), was a showcase for a whole generation of young German architects who were to achieve prominence after World War I. Many of the buildings they designed for the fairgrounds anticipate ideas of the 1920s. Among the most adventurous is the staircase of the "Glass House" (fig. 26-7) by Bruno Taut (1880–1938). It was made magically translucent by the use of glass bricks, then a novel material. The structural steel skeleton was as thin and unobtrusive as the great strength of the metal permits. The total effect precociously suggests Stella's *Brooklyn Bridge (*see fig. 24-35) translated into three dimensions.

If the interior seems astonishingly prophetic, the exterior of the "Glass House" (fig. 26-8) was shaped like a faceted bulbous crystal, with a multicolored bonnet not unlike those on John Nash's Brighton pavilion (see fig. 21-70). It was inspired not by technology but by the widespread mystical interest in crystal. This enthusiasm was started by the poet Paul Schneebart, whose aphorisms, such as "Colored glass destroys hatred," ring the "Glass House."

Taut's mysticism was shared by the Expressionist movement. After the war he helped to establish the short-lived Workers Council for Art, whose members included Emil Nolde and other painters of *Die Brücke.* Its purpose was to unite all the arts under the umbrella of architecture. Through his journals *The Glass Chain* and *Early Light,* Taut became the center of a loose network of architects, including Behrens, Gropius, Erich Mendelsohn (see below), and even Mies van der Rohe, who had the same fascination with crystalline glass. To Taut architecture "consists exclusively of powerful emotions and addresses itself exclusively to the emotions." We may call this approach Expressionism, because it stresses the artist's feelings toward himself and the world (see page 802). Does modern architecture not incorporate the spontaneous and irrational qualities of fantasy as well? Indeed it does. But because the modern architect shares the Expressionist's primary concern with the human community, rather than the labyrinth of the imagination, fantasy plays a much smaller role than Expressionism, which has incorporated it.

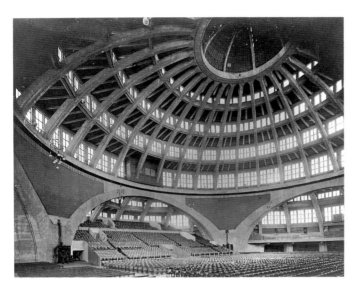

26-9. Max Berg. Interior of the Centennial Hall, Breslau, Germany. 1912–13

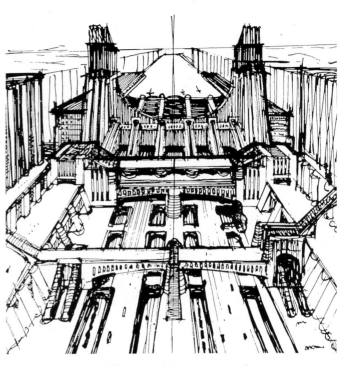

26-10. Antonio Sant'Elia. Central Station project for Città Nuova (after Banham). 1914

MAX BERG. The romantic side of Expressionist architecture is best seen in the Centennial Hall (fig. 26-9) designed by Max Berg (1870–1948) in Breslau to celebrate Germany's liberation from Napoleon in 1812. Berg was the first to take full advantage of reinforced concrete's incredible flexibility and strength. The vast scale is not simply an engineering marvel; it encloses a visionary space that fulfills the grandest dream of Boullée (compare fig. 21-17). The immediate ancestry of Centennial Hall can be traced back to the Bank of England by John Soane (see fig. 21-73), while the exterior is reminiscent of Ledoux's tollgate (see fig. 21-18). Ultimately the interior looks back to the Pantheon (see fig. 7-12), but with the solids and voids reversed, so that we are reminded of nothing so much as the interior of Hagia Sophia (see fig. 8-34). That Centennial Hall further recalls the soaring spirituality of a Gothic cathedral (such as our fig. 11-17) is not a coincidence. Berg shared with Rouault and Nolde an intense religiosity, which later led him to abandon his profession for Christianity.

Utopianism

ANTONIO SANT'ELIA. The final component of modernist architecture—its utopian side—was added by the Futurist Antonio Sant'Elia (1888–1916). He declared that "we must invent and reconstruct the Futurist city as an immense, tumultuous yard and the Futurist house as a gigantic machine." The Central Station project for his Città Nuova (New City; fig. 26-10) is treated in terms of circulation patterns that determine the relationships between buildings. They establish a restless perpetual motion that fulfills the Futurist vision announced in Boccioni's work (see figs. 24-17 and 25-6). But it is the enormous scale, dwarfing even the largest complexes of the past, that makes this a uniquely modern conception. It even includes a runway for airplanes. (The scheme is not as impractical as that may seem; it anticipates the huge Fiat-Lingotto automobile factory in Turin designed by Giacomo Matté-Trucco just two years later.) Although Sant'Elia's style remained basically Secessionist, his program was resolutely forward-looking: "Modern structural materials and our scientific concepts do not lend themselves to the disciplines of historical styles. . . . We no longer feel ourselves to be the men of the cathedrals and ancient moot halls, but men of the Grand Hotels, railway stations, giant roads . . . . The house of cement, iron and glass, without carved or painted ornament, rich only in the inherent beauty of its lines and modelling, extraordinarily brutish in its mechanical simplicity . . . must rise from the brink of a tumultuous abyss. . . ."

ARCHITECTURE BETWEEN THE WARS

By the onset of World War I, the stage was set for a modern architecture. But which way would it go? Would it follow the impersonal standard of the machine aesthetic advocated by Muthesius or the artistic creativity espoused by Van de Velde? The issue was decided by Van de Velde's choice of Behrens' disciple Walter Gropius as his successor as director of the Bauhaus

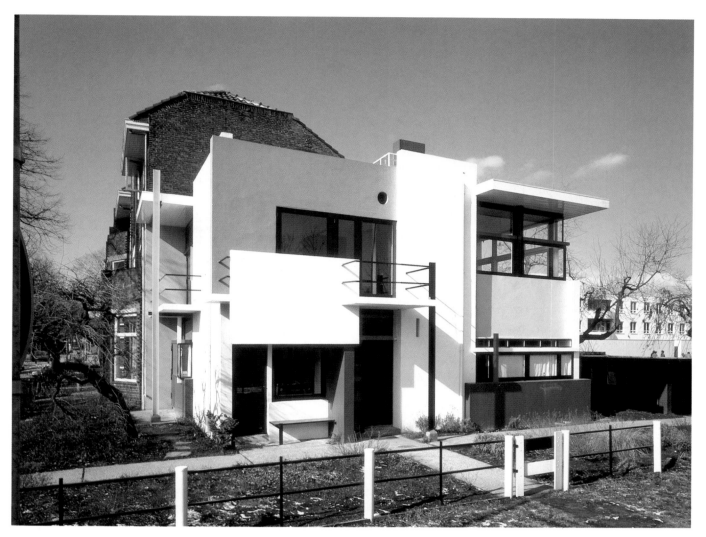

26-11. Gerrit Rietveld. Schröder House, Utrecht, Holland. 1924

at Weimar in 1915, when Van de Velde, who had founded the school in 1907, was forced to resign because he was not a German. However, the war effectively postponed the further evolution of modern architecture for nearly a decade. When this development resumed in the 1920s, the outcome of the issues posed at the Cologne Werkbund exhibition in 1914 was no longer clear-cut. Rather than a simple linear progression, we find a complex give-and-take between modernism and competing tendencies representing traditional voices and alternative visions. This varied response has its parallel in the art of the period, which largely rejected abstraction in favor of fantasy, Expressionism, and Realism.

De Stijl

GERRIT RIETVELD. The work of Frank Lloyd Wright attracted much attention in Europe through German publications of 1910 and 1911 featuring his buildings. Among the first to recognize Wright's importance were some young Dutch architects who, a few years later, joined forces with Mondrian in the *De Stijl* movement (see page 828). The classic statement of the group's principles is Schröder House by Gerrit Rietveld (1888–1964), which was tacked on to an existing apartment house in 1924. The facade (fig. 26-11) looks like a Mondrian painting projected into three dimensions, for it uses the same rigorous geometry (compare fig. 24-36). The arrangement of floating panels and intersecting planes is based on Mondrian's principle of dynamic equilibrium: the balance of unequal but equivalent oppositions, which expresses the mystical harmony of humanity with the universe. Steel beams, rails, and other elements are painted in bright, primary colors to articulate the structure. Unlike the elements of a painting by Mondrian, the exterior components of Schröder House look as if they can be shifted at will, although in fact they fit as tightly as the interlocking pieces of a jigsaw puzzle. Not a single element could be moved without destroying the delicate balance of the whole.

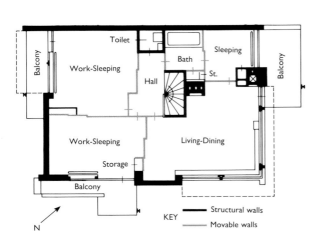

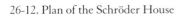

26-12. Plan of the Schröder House

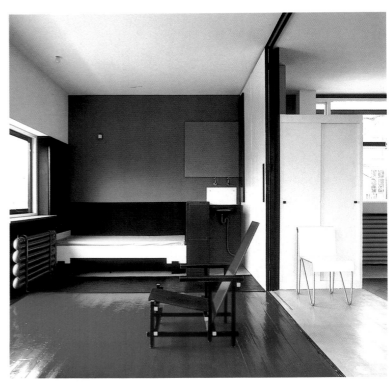

26-13. Interior, Schröder House

Rietveld's treatment of the living quarters (fig. 26-12) reveals his background as a cabinetmaker in the use of "boxes" of space. Far from being impersonal, the simple, clean design is remarkably intimate. This effect is achieved not simply through the small scale but also the architect's allegiance to traditional materials and craftsmanship, even though they were equated by *De Stijl* with the self-indulgent materialism of the past. The upper story incorporates a continuous, "universal" space, which can be left open or configured into different work and sleeping areas through a system of sliding partitions that fit neatly together or can be moved out of the way (fig. 26-13). This flexible approach to the interior was devised with the owner, Truss Schröder, herself an artist, to suit her individual lifestyle.

Schröder House proclaims a utopian ideal widely held in the early twentieth century. The machine would hasten humanity's spiritual development by liberating people from nature, with its imperfection and conflict, and by leading them to the higher order of beauty reflected in the architect's clean, abstract forms. The harmonious design of Schröder House owes its success to the insistent logic of this aesthetic, which we respond to even without being aware of its ideology.

The International Style

THE BAUHAUS. Schröder House was recognized immediately as one of the classic statements of modern architecture. Rietveld and the *De Stijl* architects represented the most advanced ideas in European architecture in the early 1920s. They had a decisive influence on so many architects abroad that the movement soon

became international. The largest and most complete example of this International Style is the group of buildings created in 1925–26 by Walter Gropius for the Bauhaus in Dessau, the famous German art school of which he was the director. The most dramatic is the shop block, which is a fully mature statement of the principles announced more than a decade earlier in the Fagus Shoe Factory (see fig. 26-6). The building is a four-story box with walls of continuous glass (fig. 26-14). Since the glass walls reflect as well as transmit light, their appearance depends on the interplay of these two effects. They respond to any change of conditions outside and inside, which lends a surprising quality of life to the surface. The result is very similar to the interaction between the mirrorlike finish of Brancusi's *Bird in Space* and its surroundings (see fig. 25-4).

More important than this individual structure is the complex as a whole and what it stood for. The Bauhaus was the result of merging two separate schools, one devoted to art and the other to crafts. This union happened in Weimar in 1919—the same year the national assembly established the government there known as the Weimar Republic. Hence the Bauhaus occupied a politically sensitive position from the beginning. At first it tried to fulfill the goals of the Arts and Crafts Movement, but traditional attitudes toward the two branches were too different for this romantic dream to succeed. A deep split developed between the Workshop Masters, who were responsible for practical crafts, and the Masters of Form, such as Kandinsky and Klee, who were invited by the artist Johannes Itten (1888–1967) in the early 1920s to teach theory. The curriculum was given a far more rational and pragmatic basis by the arrival first of László Moholy-Nagy (see page 934, a

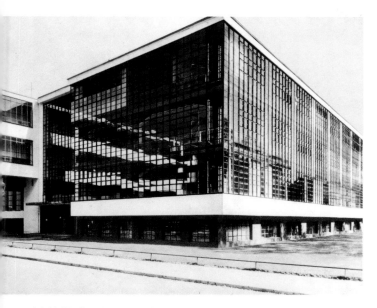

26-14. Walter Gropius. Shop Block, the Bauhaus, Dessau, Germany. 1925–26

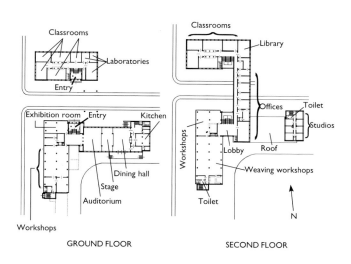

26-15. Plan of the Bauhaus

Hungarian follower of Tatlin's Constructivism (see page 872) who replaced Itten in 1922, and then of Josef Albers (see page 859). Also important was the visit in 1921 of Theo van Doesburg, a founder of the De Stijl movement (see page 828), whose ideas galvanized faculty and students alike. But it was the move to Dessau that proved decisive. The city invited the school to transfer there in 1925, when it was closed down for a while by Weimar during a period of political turmoil.

The definitive character of the Bauhaus in Dessau is reflected in Gropius' design. The plan consists of three major blocks (fig. 26-15) for classrooms, shops, and studios, which were interconnected. (There was also a student center.) The curriculum embraced all the visual arts, linked by the root concept of "structure" (Bau). It included, in addition to an art school, departments of industrial design under Marcel Breuer (see page 907), graphic art under Herbert Bayer (see page 933), and architecture, whose chief representative was Mies van der Rohe (see below), the Bauhaus' last director.

Gropius' buildings at Dessau incorporate elements of *De Stijl* and Constructivism, just as the school accommodated a range of temperaments and approaches. The Shop Block proclaims the Bauhaus' frankly practical approach, which was closely allied to The New Objectivity movement (see page 842). The complex as a whole promoted a remarkable community spirit based on a utopian Socialist dream. Gropius' philosophy was surprisingly humanist. [See Primary Sources, no. 100, page 977.] Under Gropius' leadership, the Bauhaus at Dessau was very different in character than it had been during Van de Velde's directorship at Weimar, although the two men shared much the same vision.

The program embodied Gropius' tolerant, yet unified vision. Not surprisingly, the school did not last long after his departure in 1928 to pursue architecture full time. His hand-picked successor, Hannes Meyer (1889–1954), the first architect appointed to the faculty, was forced to resign in 1930 because of his Marxist leanings, even though he had prevented the formation of a Communist student cell. Mies van der Rohe tried vainly to revive the school's fortunes, but it was shut down by the Dessau parliament in 1932. By then, most of its leaders had left. After a final attempt to reopen it as a private school in Berlin, the Bauhaus was closed by the Nazis in 1933.

LUDWIG MIES VAN DER ROHE. The early career of Ludwig Mies van der Rohe (1886–1969) followed a highly varied path. As a young architect in Berlin, where he worked several years for Behrens, Mies started out as a neoclassicist under the sway of the Schinkel school (see page 727), then became a Structural Rationalist after meeting the Dutch architect Hendrik Berlage (1856–1934) in 1912. Following the war, he joined the radical November Group, which was allied with Taut's Workers Council for Art, and as a result became an Expressionist. He also came into contact with *De Stijl* and Constructivism. In 1927, as vice-director of the Deutscher Werkbund, Mies was charged with organizing the highly experimental Weissenhof Estate exhibition in Stuttgart. Held in response to the need for vast amounts of inexpensive but comfortable housing in Germany during the Weimar Republic, it became a showcase for all the leading modernist architects of the day. As a result, Mies himself became a convert to rationalization and standardization as the most

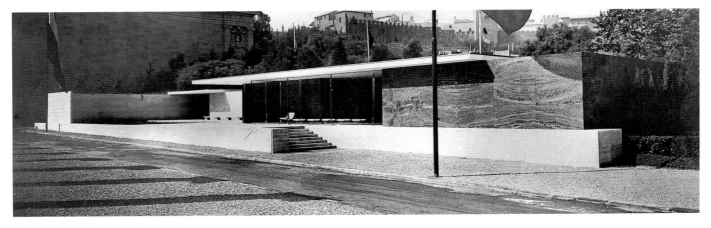

26-16. Ludwig Mies van der Rohe. German Pavilion, International Exposition, Barcelona. 1929

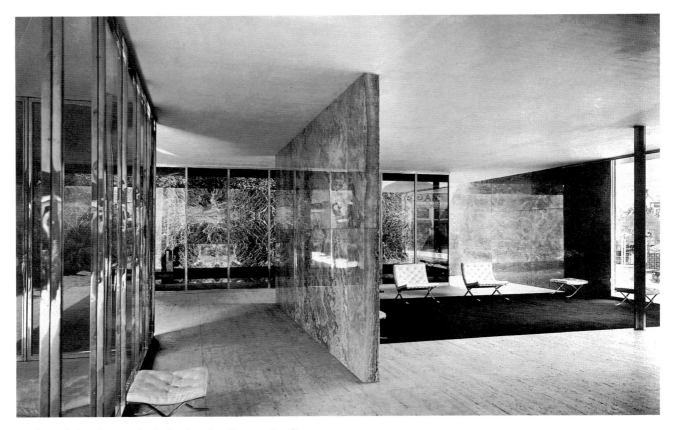

26-17. Ludwig Mies van der Rohe. Interior, German Pavilion

effective means to attain that end. However, he never achieved the spartan functionalism of the leftist New Objectivity movement.

In 1929 Mies designed the prophetic German Pavilion for the International Exposition in Barcelona (figs. 26-16 and 26-17). (Unfortunately it was dismantled soon after the fair closed.) The pavilion, which proceeded from ideas he began to develop around 1923, was a daringly low-slung structure elevated on a marble base, with enclosed courtyards at the front and rear. It was even more radically simple in appearance than Wright's Robie House (see figs. 26-1 and 26-2), out of which it clearly developed. Its walls were constructed of different-colored marble slabs, arranged with

great precision like so many dominoes in a grid system. Here is the great spiritual counterpart to Mondrian among contemporary designers, possessed of the same "absolute pitch" in determining proportions and spatial relationships. Flooded with light from the great expanse of windows, the pavilion's interior was wonderfully open and fluid, yet with a sparse cleanness that still seems irrepressibly modern.

LE CORBUSIER'S EARLY WORK. In France the most distinguished representative of the International Style during the 1920s was the Swiss-born architect Le Corbusier (Charles

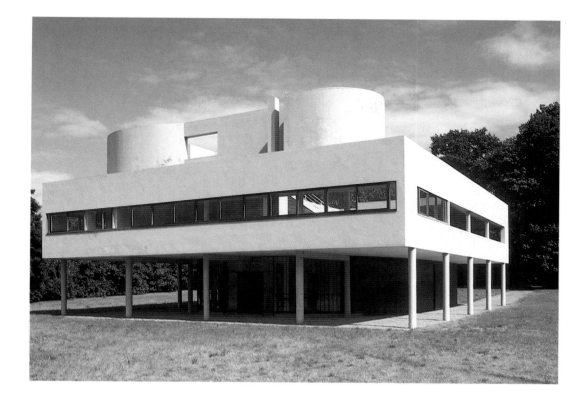

26-18. Le Corbusier. Savoye House, Poissy-sur-Seine, France. 1928–29

Édouard Jeanneret, 1886–1965). His training under Peter Behrens and Auguste Perret (see below), from whom he acquired a preference for reinforced concrete, made him a disciple of structural rationalism. His style was further shaped by his experience as a painter. In 1918 he and the artist Amédée Ozenfant (1886–1966) cofounded the movement known as Purism, which advocated a machine aesthetic similar to that of Le Corbusier's friend Fernand Léger (see fig. 24-33) and promoted the ideas of Henry van de Velde and Adolf Loos. Le Corbusier worked with his cousin Pierre Jeanneret (1896–1967) from 1922 until 1940, when the latter joined the French resistance against the Germans. Before 1940 Le Corbusier built only private houses— from necessity, not choice—but these are as important as Wright's Prairie houses. Le Corbusier called them *machines à habiter* ("machines to live in"). This term was intended to suggest his admiration for the clean, precise shapes of machinery, not the Futurist desire for "mechanized living." [See Primary Sources, no. 99, page 976.]

Le Corbusier evidently wanted to imply that his houses were so different from conventional homes as to constitute a new species. Such is indeed our impression as we approach the most famous of them, the Villa Savoye at Poissy-sur-Seine (fig. 26-18), built in 1928–29. It is an outgrowth of the "Dom-Ino" houses he developed during World War I. The structure resembles a low, square box resting on stilts. These pillars of reinforced concrete (called *pilotis*) form part of the structural skeleton and reappear to divide the "ribbon windows" running along each side of the box. The flat, smooth surfaces deny all sense of weight. They stress Le Corbusier's preoccupation with abstract "space blocks," which he derived in part from Loos' designs of the early 1920s.

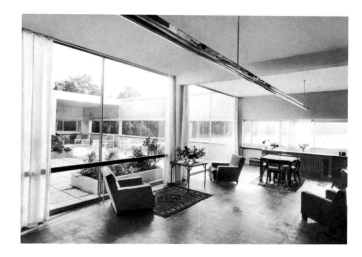

26-19. Interior, Savoye House

In order to find out how the box is subdivided, we must enter it (fig. 26-19). We then realize that this simple structure contains living spaces that are open as well as closed, separated by glass walls. Views of the sky and the surrounding landscape are available from every side. Yet we enjoy complete privacy, since we cannot be seen from the ground unless we stand next to a window. The functionalism of Villa Savoye is governed by a "design for living," not by mechanical efficiency. It fulfills Le Corbusier's statement that "Architecture is the masterly, correct, and magnificent play of masses brought together in light . . . Cubes, cones, cylinders, and pyramids are the primary forms which light reveals to advantage. . . . These are . . . the most beautiful forms."

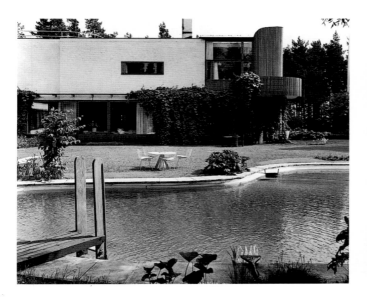

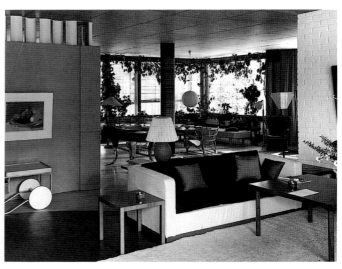

26-20. Alvar Aalto. Villa Mairea, Noormarkku, Finland. 1937–38

26-21. Interior, Villa Mairea

ALVAR AALTO. Although its aesthetic and philosophy were codified about 1930 by a committee of Le Corbusier and his followers, the International Style was by no means monolithic. Soon all but the most confirmed purists among them began to depart from this standard. One of the first to break ranks was the Finnish architect Alvar Aalto (1898–1976), whose Villa Mairea (figs. 26-20 and 26-21) reads at first glance like a critique of Le Corbusier's Villa Savoye of a decade earlier. Like Rietveld's Schröder House, Villa Mairea was designed for a woman artist. Her second-story studio, covered with wood slats, dominates the view of the house from three directions. This time, however, the architect was given a free hand by his patron, and the building is a summation of ideas he had been developing for nearly ten years.

Aalto adapted the International Style to the traditional architecture, materials, lifestyle, and landscape of Finland. He took an approach opposite to Le Corbusier's in order to arrive at a similar end. Aalto's primary concern was human needs, both physical and psychological, which he sought to harmonize with functionalism. The modernist heritage, which extends back to Wright, is unmistakable in his vocabulary of forms and massing of elements. Yet everywhere there are romantic touches that add a warmth missing from Villa Savoye. Wood, brick, and stone are used in combination throughout the interior and exterior of the house, in contrast to Le Corbusier's pristine classicism. Free forms are introduced at several places to break up the cubic geometry and smooth surfaces of the International Style, as well as add an element of playfulness.

Aalto's importance is undeniable, but his place in twentieth-century architecture remains unclear. His inclusion of nationalist elements in Villa Mairea has been interpreted both as a rejection of modernism and as a fruitful regional variation on the International Style. Today his work can also be seen as a forerunner of Late Modern architecture (see pages 916–21).

Expressionism

EXPRESSIONISM. Architecture between the wars is sometimes labeled Expressionist if it does not conform to the International Style. Such a view is valid only insofar as it represents the assertion of the right of the individual to express a personal point of view against the norms of modernism. The International Style based its ideals on standardization for the sake of universality. As such, it represents the triumph of classicism and structural rationalism. In reality, however, it was never the dominant approach after 1917, any more than abstraction was in painting. It seems best, then, to limit the use of *Expressionism* to buildings that have specific expressionist characteristics created between the end of World War I and the early 1920s.

ERICH MENDELSOHN. Inspired by the Arts and Crafts Movement's liberal politics and utopian ideals, a number of German architects gave free rein to their imaginations. The most eccentric building from this period is the Einstein Tower at Potsdam (fig. 26-22) by Erich Mendelsohn (1887–1953). It has an amazing organic quality that looks back to the Art Nouveau architecture of Antoní Gaudí and Henry van de Velde (see figs. 23-31 and 23-35). Because of a lack of materials, it was built of brick with a cement veneer instead of reinforced concrete, as the architect originally planned. Despite its retrospective element, Mendelsohn was no reactionary, and the Einstein Tower, which functioned as an observatory and laboratory, has also been hailed as the forerunner of Le Corbusier's later work (see fig. 26-31).

AUGUSTE PERRET. Auguste Perret (1874–1954) was even more important for Le Corbusier. Early in the century he had been among the first to make effective use of recent advances in reinforced concrete and to define its architectural character. Perret

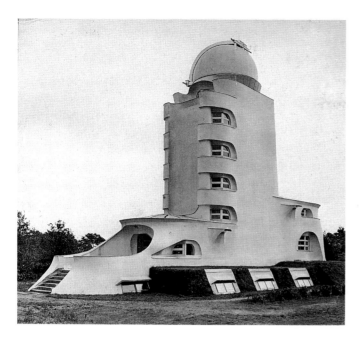

26-22. Erich Mendelsohn. Einstein Tower, Potsdam, Germany. 1921

hard to find. They have had a unique, even privileged, understanding of modernism, its meaning, materials, and techniques. Their designs, like their buildings, have generally expressed the Machine Age through clean lines and cubic shapes stripped of unnecessary decoration. This was particularly true of the Bauhaus, where architecture and design were closely linked. The Bauhaus nevertheless failed in its goal of unifying the arts and putting the decorative arts on the same level as the fine arts. The main reason was that its members were far more gifted in architecture and painting than in design, despite the considerable emphasis placed on this area.

Gropius himself considered Bauhaus designs models for the future that would fulfill his goal of providing high-quality wares to everyone through mass manufacturing techniques. However, Hannes Meyer placed design at the service of people's practical needs. The interiors of the Masters' Houses designed by Marcel Breuer (1902–1981) reflect the school's approach (fig. 26-24). As in Wright's Prairie Houses, space is treated as building

was a pupil of the last great French academicians. His teachers included Julien Guadet (1834–1908), professor at the École des Beaux-Arts and a pupil of Labrouste, who maintained a traditional approach to architectural composition using modern materials; and the theoretician Auguste Choisy (1841–1909), professor at the School of Bridges and Roads, whose *History of Architecture* (1899) maintained that style, be it Greek or Gothic, properly proceeds from construction technique.

Thus Perret was a structural rationalist from the beginning. For him concrete provided the means to reconcile classical form and Gothic structural authenticity. His greatest achievement must nevertheless be labeled Expressionist: the Church of Notre Dame, built as a war memorial at Le Raincy outside Paris (fig. 26-23). It is an astonishingly successful translation of medieval architectural forms (compare fig. 10-6) into unadorned ferroconcrete.

The structure is supported entirely by grooved classical columns, so that the "walls" become vast expanses of glass, like the stained-glass windows of Gothic cathedrals (see fig. 11-1). In this way, Perret created a modern-day counterpart to Soufflot's Panthéon before the walls were filled in (see fig. 21-16). The idea can be traced back even earlier to Laugier (see page 685). This feat is not important in itself. It could, after all, readily be dismissed as mere historicism. Yet Perret has brilliantly solved one of the most difficult problems facing architects after 1900: how to express religious faith using the materials and forms of our secular society. Le Raincy is so pivotal that nearly all modern church architecture in the West is indebted to its example, no matter how different the results.

Design

THE BAUHAUS. Many of the great architects since Gaudí, Mackintosh, and Van de Velde have also been important designers who exercised a great influence on others. The reason is not

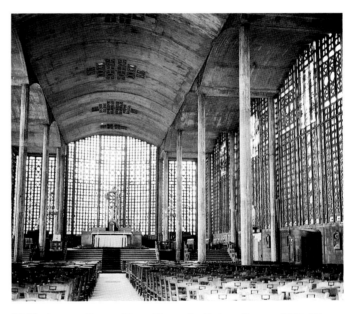

26-23. Auguste Perret. Notre Dame, Le Raincy, France. 1923–24

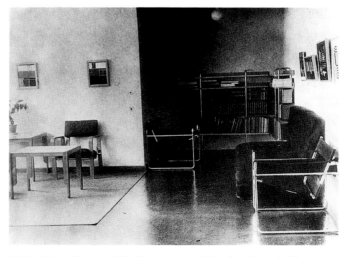

26-24. Marcel Breuer. The living room of Josef and Anni Albers, Masters' House, Dessau, Germany. c. 1929

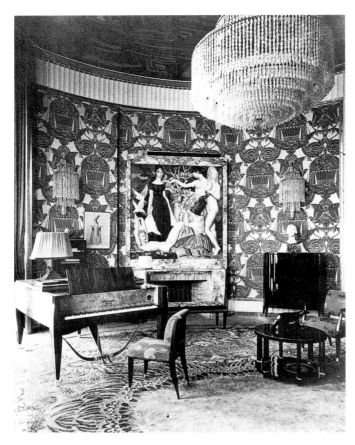

26-25. Emil-Jacques Ruhlmann. Grand Salon of the Hôtel du Collectionneur at the 1925 Exposition, Paris

blocks, but the grouping of these units is much simpler. The houses have an almost monastic asceticism that is further emphasized by the stark simplicity of the furnishings. Breuer's famous chair in the right foreground is a marvel of elegant geometry for its own sake—without regard to comfort, as anyone who has ever sat in one can attest. Here, then, is the chief limitation of so much of twentieth-century design: the tyranny of form over human considerations (a field known as ergonomics).

ART DECO. The Bauhaus style was not the only major form of early-twentieth-century design. Art Deco is the name commonly given to the style that dominated the decorative arts between the world wars. (In France it was called *Le Style Moderne*.) Like the Bauhaus, Art Deco arose out of the work of the Glasgow School. Charles Rennie Mackintosh (see page 791), his wife Margaret Macdonald-Mackintosh (1865–1933), and her sister Frances Macdonald (1874–1921) had a great impact after 1900 on the Secession movements in Munich and especially Vienna, where the next phase of modern design took place (see page 784). Art Deco received its official introduction at the Exhibition of Decorative and Industrial Arts held in Paris in 1925, two years after the Bauhaus scored a great success at its initial design show in Weimar. The event had actually been conceived ten years earlier, but like the development of the style itself, was postponed by World War I, when the movement was already well under way. Every leading designer and architect, including Le Corbusier, exhibited at the Paris exposition. The hit of the show was undoubtedly the

Hôtel du Collectionneur assembled by Emil-Jacques Ruhlmann (1879–1933), the last of the great French furniture designers (fig. 26-25).

In common with the Bauhaus, Art Deco attempted to resolve the dilemma between quality design and mass production, which both the Arts and Crafts Movement, and Art Nouveau, had failed to reconcile. It, too, created a geometric style that could be applied to anything from teacups to building facades. This tendency reached its climax in the following decade when everything became streamlined. The difference is that Art Deco never made the decisive break from Art Nouveau, of which it was a direct outgrowth.

Art Deco cannot be called a modernist movement in the same sense as the International Style, because it never developed a fully defined machine aesthetic, although the two evolved in parallel to each other and sometimes achieved strikingly similar results. With its idealistic program of social and artistic reform, the International Style proved far bolder in redefining the decorative arts, despite its failure to achieve those goals. Art Deco, in contrast, was a decorative veneer that did not address the substance of modern existence. Instead, it responded to the changing taste of society during the "Jazz Age," without consciously intending to shape it. Whereas the Bauhaus adhered to rigorous abstraction, Art Deco was broadly eclectic in scope. It included a taste for the exotic, ranging from ancient Egyptian and Native American art to the Ballets Russes of Sergei Diaghilev (see box page 818)—whatever could be incorporated into its geometric framework. The virtue of Art Deco is that it embodied the very feature so obviously lacking in the International Style: fantasy, which gave vent to individual expression. Perhaps for that reason it proved widely popular. Moreover, it enjoyed the commercial backing of major manufacturers and department stores. Needless to say, much of what filtered down to everyday objects catered to the lowest common denominator. But at its finest, Art Deco could be brilliantly innovative.

Because it was essentially a decorative "skin," Art Deco lent itself readily to architecture. (The streamlined style associated with it was adapted from Dutch architecture of the early 1920s.) It was especially widespread in the United States, where it reached its most flamboyant phase during the 1930s. A spectacular example is the interior of the Union Trust Company in Detroit (fig. 26-26). Resembling nothing so much as a gigantic Indian feather headdress, the ceiling of ceramic tiles has the honeycomb pattern of a beehive to symbolize Thrift and Industry.

THE SKYSCRAPER IN AMERICA. The United States, despite its early position of leadership, did not share the exciting growth that took place in European architecture during the 1920s. The impact of the International Style did not begin to be felt in America until the very end of the decade. A pioneer example is the Philadelphia Savings Fund Society Building of 1931–32 (fig. 26-27) by George Howe (1886–1954) and William E. Lescaze (1896–1969). It is the first skyscraper anywhere to incorporate many of the concepts developed in Europe after the end of World War I. The skyscraper was a compelling attraction to modernist architects in Europe as the embodiment of the idea of America, and during the 1920s Gropius and Mies van der Rohe designed several prototypes that were remarkably advanced for their time.

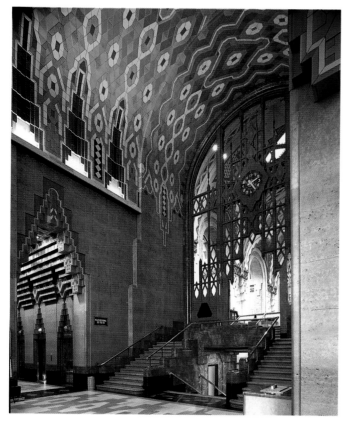

26-26. Wirt Rowland, with Smith, Hinchman & Grylls, Associates, Inc. (Tiles designed by Thomas Dilorenzo and made by Rookwood, Cincinnati.) Main Lobby, Union Trust Company, Detroit. 1929

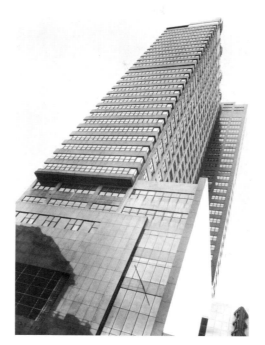

26-27. George Howe and William E. Lescaze. Philadelphia Savings Fund Society Building, Philadelphia. 1931–32

Yet none were erected, while those built in the United States were encased in a variety of revivalist styles. (The Gothic was preferred.) Although they quickly became the most characteristic form of American architecture, even the skyscrapers of the 1930s—when many of the most famous ones, such as the Empire State Building, were constructed—are in the tradition of Sullivan, and do little to expand on the Wainwright Building (see fig. 23-39) except to make it bigger. Despite the fact that it is not entirely purist, the skyscraper of Howe and Lescaze is a landmark in the history of architecture, one that was not surpassed for 20 years (compare fig. 26-28). The only building of comparable importance is Raymond Hood's McGraw-Hill Building in New York, which was built at the same time.

ARCHITECTURE SINCE 1945
High Modernism

After the rise of the Nazis, the best German architects, whose work Hitler condemned as "un-German," came to the United States and stimulated the development of modern American architecture. Walter Gropius was appointed chairman of the architecture department at Harvard University, where he had an important educational influence. Ludwig Mies van der Rohe, his former colleague at Dessau, settled in Chicago as a practicing architect. Following the war, they were to realize the dream of modern architecture, contained in germinal form in their buildings of the 1930s

but never fully implemented. We may call the style that dominated architecture for 25 years after World War II High Modernism. It was indeed the culmination of the developments that had taken place during the first half of the twentieth century.

Even at its zenith High Modernism never arrived at a single, universal style. Nevertheless, its unified spaces embodied a harmonious vision that developed in a consistent way as the style came to be used in countless buildings throughout the world. Like the International Style before it, High Modernism permitted considerable local variation within established guidelines, although such departures led almost inevitably to its decline.

MIES VAN DER ROHE AND THE SKYSCRAPER. The crowning achievement of American architecture in the postwar era was the modern skyscraper, defined largely by Mies van der Rohe. The Seagram Building in New York (fig. 26-28), designed with his disciple Philip Johnson (b. 1906), carries the principles announced in Gropius' design for the Bauhaus to their ultimate conclusion. It uses the techniques developed by Louis Sullivan and Frank Lloyd Wright, Mies van der Rohe's great predecessors in Chicago, to extend the structure to an enormous height. Yet the building looks like nothing before it. Although not quite a pure box, it illustrates Mies van der Rohe's famous saying that "less is more." This alone does not explain the difference, however. He discovered the perfect means to articulate the skyscraper in the I-beam, its basic structural member, which rises continuously along nearly the entire height of the facade. (The actual skeleton of

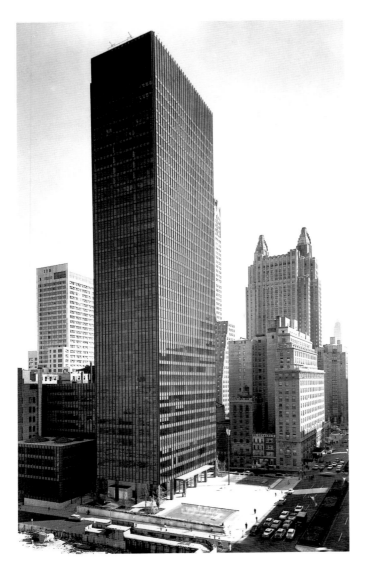

26-28. Ludwig Mies van der Rohe and Philip Johnson.
Seagram Building, New York. 1954–58

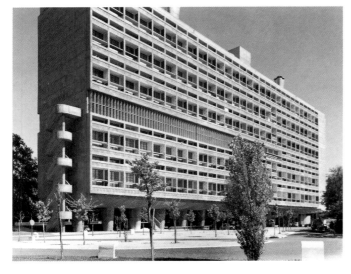

26-29. Le Corbusier. Unité d'Habitation
Apartment House, Marseilles, France. 1947–52

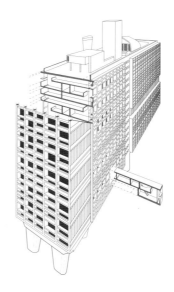

26-30. Le Corbusier.
Isometric projection
and cross section of
Unité d'Habitation
(after a drawing in
Kenneth Frampton's
Modern Architecture)

the structure remains completely hidden from view.) The effect is
as soaring as the responds inside a Gothic cathedral (compare fig.
11-5)—and with good reason, for Mies van der Rohe believed that
"structure is spiritual." He achieved it through the lithe proportions, which create a perfect balance between the play of horizontal
and vertical forces. This harmony expresses the idealism, social as
well as aesthetic, that underlies High Modernism in architecture.

LE CORBUSIER'S LATE WORK. After the war, Le Corbusier abandoned the strict purism of the International Style. His
work began to show a growing preoccupation with sculptural,
even anthropomorphic, effects. The Unité d'Habitation, a large
apartment house in Marseilles (fig. 26-29), is a "box on stilts" like
the Savoye House, but the pillars are not thin rods. (Because of
a shortage of materials, the building is constructed of unfaced
concrete, called *béton brut;* hence the term "Brutalism" for this
aesthetic.) Their shape, which the architect said "should be
like the strong curvaceous thighs of a woman," expresses their
muscular strength in a way that makes us also think of Doric
columns. The exposed staircase on the flank, too, is vigorously
sculptural. The flat plane of the all-glass facade incorporates a
honeycomb screen of louvers and balconies that forms a sunbreak
but also enhances the three-dimensional quality of the structure.
This screen (known as a *brise soleil*) has proved to be an invention
of great importance, practically and aesthetically. It became a
standard feature of modern architecture throughout the tropics.
(Le Corbusier himself introduced it in India and Brazil.) In many
respects the Unité d'Habitation represents the culmination of the
architect's thinking about housing as well as urban design. It realizes his utopian vision of integrating families within a tightly knit
society while preserving their privacy. The precast apartments,
each one and one-half stories high and extending the full depth
of the building, are linked on every fourth floor by a tunnel-like
hall. They thus form complex interlocking units that are slotted
like "bottles into a wine rack" (see fig. 26-30). As so often happens
with Le Corbusier's buildings, however, theory and design over-
ride practical considerations. For example, the ceiling height
is only about 7½ feet high, based on a "Modular" of his own
devising. Moreover, the shops and other facilities on the seventh

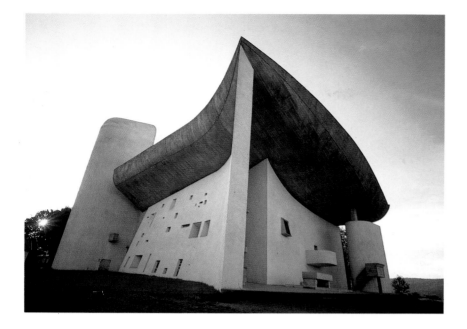

26-31. Le Corbusier. Notre-Dame-du-Haut (from the southeast), Ronchamp, France. 1950–55

26-32. Interior, Notre-Dame-du-Haut

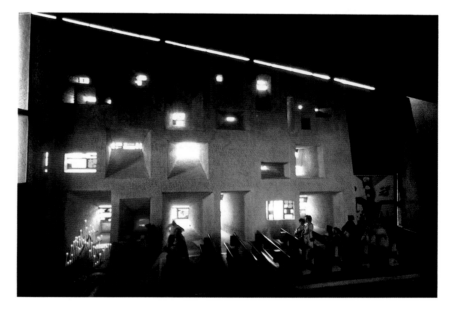

and eighth floors, like the garden and swimming pool on the roof, do not adequately fulfill their communal functions.

Le Corbusier's most revolutionary building from the mid-twentieth century is the church of Notre-Dame-du-Haut at Ronchamp in eastern France (figs. 26-31 and 26-32), which is constructed of reinforced concrete. Its design is so irrational that it defies analysis, even with the aid of perspective diagrams. The play of curves and countercurves is as insistent as in Gaudí's Casa Milá, although the shapes are simpler and more dynamic. The massive walls seem to obey an unseen force that makes them slant and curl like paper. And the overhanging roof suggests the brim of an enormous hat over a ship split lengthwise by the sharp-edged buttress at its prow.

Le Corbusier was asked to create a sanctuary on a hilltop, which makes it a counterpart to depictions of the Heavenly Jerusalem on Mount Zion (compare fig. 12-62). He must nevertheless have felt that this was the primeval task of architecture, which placed him in a direct line of succession with the builders of Stonehenge, the ziggurats of Mesopotamia, and the Greek temples. Hence he also consciously avoids any correlation between exterior and interior. The doors are concealed; we must seek them out like clefts in a hillside. To pass through them is much like entering a secret—and sacred—cave. This evocation of the dim, prehistoric past is quite intentional.

Only inside do we sense the specifically Christian aspect of Ronchamp. The light, channeled through stained-glass windows so tiny that they seem hardly more than slits or pinpricks on the exterior, cuts widening paths through the thickness of the wall. It thus becomes once more what it had been in medieval architecture: the visible counterpart of the Light Divine. There is true magic in the interior of Ronchamp, but also a strangely disquieting quality, a nostalgia for the certainties of a faith that is no longer unquestioned. In this way, Ronchamp mirrors the spiritual condition of the modern age, which is a measure of its greatness as a work of art.

LOUIS KAHN. Le Corbusier belongs to the same heroic generation as Gropius and Mies van der Rohe: all were born in the 1880s. It was these giants who in the course of their long, fruitful careers coined the language of twentieth-century architecture.

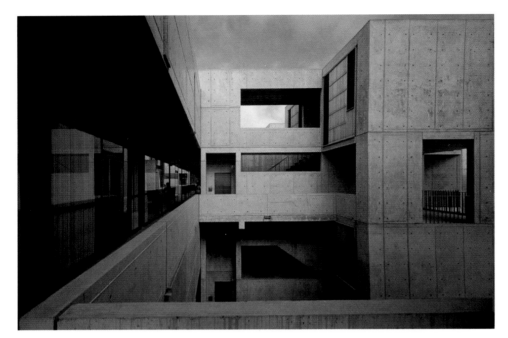

26-33. Louis Kahn. Jonas Salk Institute of Biological Studies, La Jolla, California. 1959–65

Their successors continued to use many aspects of its vocabulary in new building types and materials. Nor did they forget its fundamental logic.

Louis Kahn (1901–1974), the foremost representative of Brutalism in the United States, used bare concrete to great effect in the Jonas Salk Institute of Biological Studies in La Jolla (fig. 26-33). Salk, inventor of the first polio vaccine, had been deeply impressed by his visit to Assisi and conceived of the center as similar to the Franciscan monastery there. Kahn, who was in complete sympathy with his patron's views, carried out this scheme brilliantly. He treated the offices as a series of monastic cells attached to the central work spaces formed by the laboratories—or, as he put it, servant and server spaces. With its spartan surfaces, concrete expressed the asceticism of this scientific retreat. Like so many others, the ambitious project proved too costly. (It included, among other things, separate living quarters for the scientists and their families.) It was halted before it could be completed. The Salk Institute nevertheless remains the fullest embodiment of Kahn's principles.

EERO SAARINEN. There is an alternate tradition of reinforced concrete dating back to Berg's Centennial Hall (see fig. 26-9). This Expressionist vision continued to provide a dialogue with the International Style that enriched modern architecture. The Trans World Airlines Terminal at Kennedy Airport in New York (figs. 26-34 and 26-35) by Eero Saarinen (1910–1961) is the great statement of postwar Expressionism. Saarinen, whose father had also been a well-known architect, was a skilled practitioner of the International Style. Here he has used the full potential of concrete in order to express the very essence of flight. Yet the inspiration, rather than mechanical, was purely organic. The swelling, sail-like forms of the four "flying" roofs create the impression of a gigantic bird, while the free-flowing spaces pull visitors through the graceful interior with astonishing force.

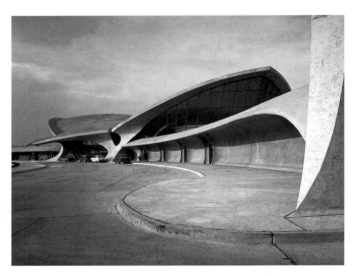

26-34. Eero Saarinen. Trans World Airlines Terminal, John F. Kennedy Airport, New York. 1956–63

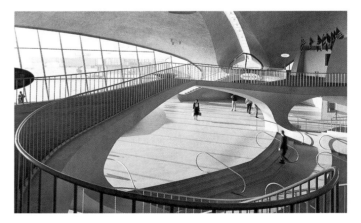

26-35. Interior, Trans World Airlines Terminal, John F. Kennedy Airport

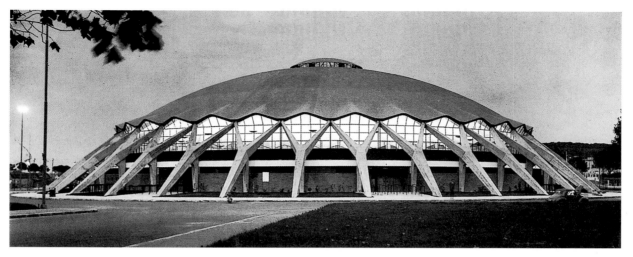

26-36. Pier Luigi Nervi and Annibale Vitellozzi. Sports Palace, Rome. 1956–57

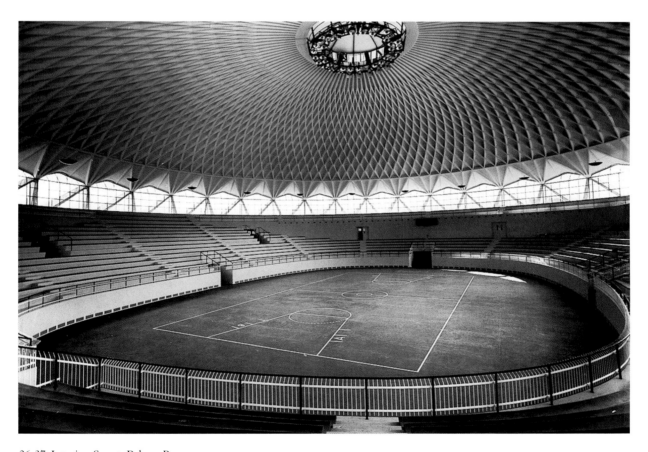

26-37. Interior, Sports Palace, Rome

PIER LUIGI NERVI. Saarinen is linked to Berg by Pier Luigi Nervi (1891–1979), who during the 1930s and 1940s pioneered the use of ferroconcrete in designs for aircraft hangars that provided the point of departure for all future developments in this vein. Nervi was a structural engineer with a bold sense of form and an even more daring vision. He was the successor to Eugène Freyssinet (see box page 795), whose enormous reinforced concrete airship hangars at Orly near Paris (1916–24) were the first of their kind. The climax of Nervi's efforts was the Sports Palace designed with Annibale Vitellozzi for the 1960 Olympics in Rome (figs. 26-36 and 26-37). From the outside, the roof appears as a thin covering whose light weight and flexibility are emphasized by the scalloped edges. It gives the impression of having been draped over the Y-shaped supports that radiate outward like flying buttresses. The effect inside is even more remarkable. The honeycombed roof, nearly 200 feet in diameter, recalls the interior of the Pantheon, with its great oculus (see fig. 7-12). A marvel of engineering, it seems to float effortlessly, like the dome of Hagia Sophia, in a pool of light without visible support (compare fig. 8-34).

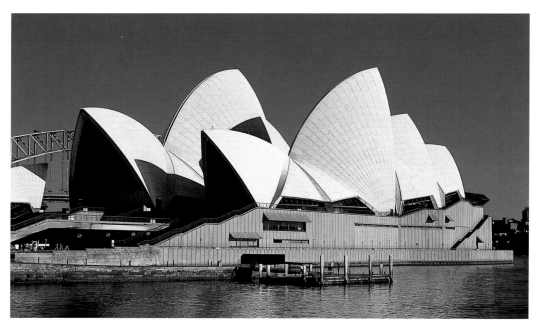

26-38. Jørn Utzon with Hall, Todd, and Littlemore. Sydney Opera House, Sydney, Australia. 1957–73

JØRN UTZON. The Sydney Opera House (fig. 26-38) combines the expressionism of Saarinen and the engineering of Nervi in spectacular fashion to create something that transcends both. It was designed in 1956 by the Danish architect Jørn Utzon (b. 1918), who had worked briefly under Aalto and Wright in the years right after World War II. From the former he acquired a respect for local materials and traditions, and from the latter a fascination with organic forms based on nature. Nervi perceptively called the shell roofs, which bear no relation to the auditoriums, "the most straightforward anti-functionalism from the point of view of statics as well as construction," something that might be said as well of Wright's Guggenheim Museum (see below). They required the most advanced engineering of the day, which was provided by Ove Arup (1895–1988). Second only to Nervi as an innovator, Arup was to work as a consultant on some of the most important late modern and postmodern buildings. Indeed, the Sydney Opera House has sometimes been called a forerunner of Postmodern architecture (compare fig. 28-7).

The project was problematic from the start and was completed in altered form only after Utzon resigned. Built on an abandoned wharf as part of a larger port and urban renewal plan, it became an instant classic. The opera house is justly famous throughout the world as a symbol of Sydney, as instantly recognizable as the Eiffel Tower or the Statue of Liberty. Utzon intended it to sit in splendid isolation as a gateway to the harbor. Today there are plans to develop the jetty commercially with apartments and shops, which will destroy the building's unique character.

WRIGHT'S GUGGENHEIM MUSEUM. An extreme case of Expressionism at mid-century is the Solomon R. Guggenheim Museum in New York by that apostle of modernism, Frank Lloyd Wright. Scorned when it was first erected in the late 1950s, it is a brilliant, if idiosyncratic, creation by one of the most original architectural minds of the century. The sculptural exterior (fig. 26-39) announces that this can only be a museum, for it is self-consciously a work of art in its own right. As a piece of design, the Guggenheim Museum is remarkably headstrong. In shape it is as defiantly individual as the architect himself and refuses to conform to the boxlike apartments around it. From the outside, the structure looks like a gigantic snail, reflecting Wright's interest in organic shapes. The office area forming the "head" to the left is connected by a narrow passageway to the "shell" containing the main body of the museum.

The outside gives us some idea of what to expect inside (fig. 26-40), yet nothing quite prepares us for the extraordinary sensation of light and air in the main hall after we are ushered through the unassuming entrance. The radical design makes it clear that Wright completely rethought the purpose of an art museum. The exhibition area is a kind of inverted dome with a huge glass-covered eye at the top. The vast, fluid space creates an atmosphere of quiet harmony while actively shaping our experience by determining how art shall be displayed. After taking an elevator to the top of the building, visitors begin a leisurely descent down the gently sloping ramp. The continuous spiral provides for uninterrupted viewing, favorable to the study of art. At the same time, the narrow galleries prevent viewers from becoming passive observers, by forcing them into direct confrontation with the works of art. Paintings acquire a new prominence by protruding slightly from the curved walls, instead of receding into them. Sculpture takes on a heightened physical presence as well which demands that viewers look at it. Viewing exhibitions at the Guggenheim is like being led through a predetermined stream of consciousness, where everything merges into a total unity. Whether one agrees with this approach or not, the building testifies to the strength of Wright's vision by precluding any other way of seeing the art.

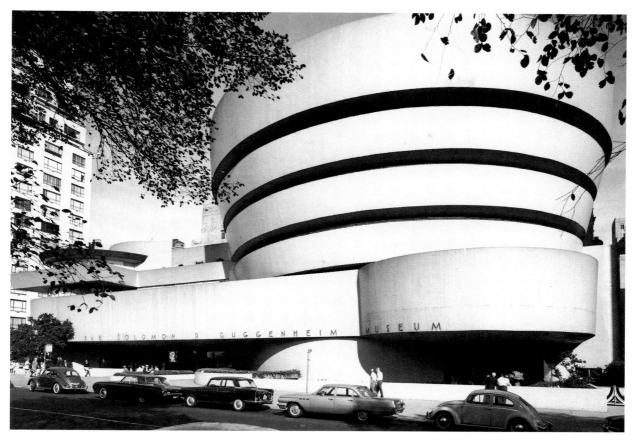

26-39. Frank Lloyd Wright. Solomon R. Guggenheim Museum, New York. 1956–59

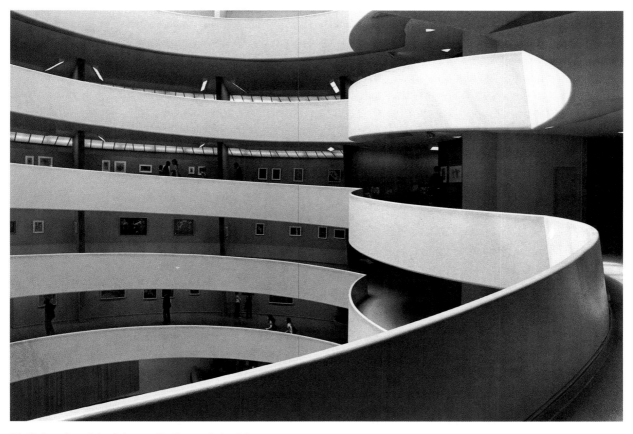

26-40. Interior of the Solomon R. Guggenheim Museum

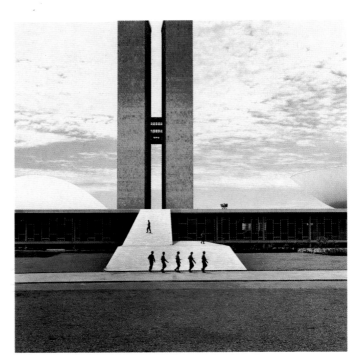

26-41. Oscar Niemeyer. Brasilia, Brazil. Completed 1960

URBAN PLANNING. To some architects, the greatest challenge is not the individual structure but urban design. Urban planning is probably as old as civilization itself (which, we recall, means "city life"). We have caught only occasional glimpses of it in this book, since its history is difficult to trace by direct visual evidence. Cities, like living organisms, are ever-changing, and to reconstruct their pasts is the task of archaeology.

Since the arrival of the industrial era two centuries ago, cities have grown explosively. Much of this growth was uncontrolled, beyond laying out a network of streets. Worse, housing standards were poor or badly enforced. The unfortunate result can be seen in the overcrowded, crumbling apartment blocks that blight huge urban areas. They were taken over by the poor, while those who could afford it fled to the bedroom communities of suburbia. This exodus, accelerated by the automobile, has produced the societal tensions that make the need for urban renewal so urgent. Such renewal, needless to say, must involve the political, social, and economic resources of an entire society, rather than the architect alone. Yet architects play an essential role in the process by translating the schemes of planning agencies into reality. However, they have generally failed in their mandate to replace the slums of our decaying cities with housing that will provide a healthful environment for very large numbers of people.

OSCAR NIEMEYER. Nowhere are the issues facing modern civilization put into sharper focus than in the vast urban projects conceived by twentieth-century architects. These utopian visions may be regarded as laboratory experiments, which redefine the role of architecture in shaping our lives and pose new solutions to social problems. Because of their enormous scope, few of these ambitious proposals make it off the drawing board. Among the

rare exceptions is Brasilia, the inland capital of Brazil built entirely since 1960. Presented with a unique opportunity to design a major city from the ground up and with enormous resources at its disposal, the design team, headed by the Brazilian Oscar Niemeyer (b. 1907), achieved spectacular results (fig. 26-41). Like most projects on this massive scale, however, Brasilia has an unrelenting, oppressive quality that makes it seem a chilling glimpse of the future despite its grandeur (compare fig. 26-10). Moreover, it is plagued by maintenance problems.

Late Modernism

Since 1970 architecture has been obsessed with breaking the tyranny of the cube—and the High Modernism it stands for. Consequently, a wide range of tendencies has arisen, representing almost every conceivable point of view. Like so much else in contemporary art, architecture has become theory-bound. Yet once the dust has settled, we may simplify its bewildering categories, with their equally confusing terminology, into Late Modernism, Postmodernism, and Deconstructivism (see also Chapter 28). They are separated only by the degree to which they challenge the basic principles of High Modernism. Indeed, it may well happen that what once seemed separate tendencies will merge into one or two dominant trends by 2010.

RICHARD MEIER. Late Modernism began innocently enough as an attempt to introduce greater variety of form and material, but it ended in the segmentation of space and use of high-tech finishes that are the hallmarks of late-twentieth-century buildings. An important early example of this process is The Atheneum at New Harmony, Indiana (fig. 26-42), by Richard Meier (b. 1934).

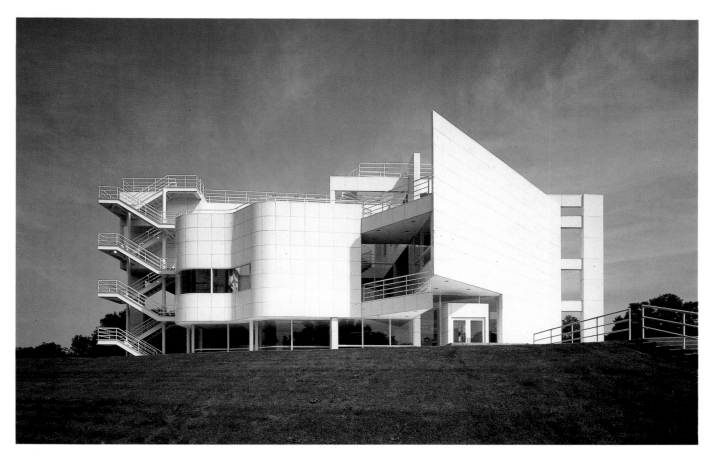

26-42. Richard Meier. The Atheneum, New Harmony, Indiana. 1975–79

In its departure from the idealism of High Modernism, it seems an ironic commentary on the utopian vision of this historic settlement. New Harmony was founded in 1815 by George Rapp (1757–1847) and sold ten years later to the Scottish reformer Robert Owen (1771–1858), who established a short-lived socialist society. The Atheneum reflects Meier's principal concerns: program and site, entry and circulation, structure and enclosure. Its placement within the landscape has been carefully calculated, with equal consideration given to its function as a visitors' center. The inspiration of Le Corbusier's Villa Savoye (see fig. 26-18) of nearly a half-century earlier is evident in the pristine white surfaces, which lend the building a sense of clarity. The vocabulary, too, remains essentially Cubist (compare fig. 24-26).

To that extent, the Atheneum falls well within the modern tradition. Yet it looks like Le Corbusier's classic statement exploded from within. The building bristles with external stairways and ramps, intersecting planes and jutting walls, and false structural elements that "frame" the view. These disrupt the facade and dissolve the boundary with the surrounding environment, so that the structure lacks the self-containment of the International Style. As we might expect, the interior is an equally dynamic play on Villa Savoye. Spatial relations are skewed by distorting forms and rotating them off-axis. Clearly Meier has pushed the syntax of High Modernism to its limits. Beyond this lies only Postmodernism.

GUSTAV PEICHL. In contrast to the centralized authority proclaimed by the Seagram Building, Late Modernist corporate architecture may be seen as a reflection of today's global economy, in which major companies are based on rapid technological advances and are dispersed in far-flung smaller units. The Austrian Radio and Television studios designed by Gustav Peichl (b. 1928) in the early 1970s are among the most imaginative Late Modernist statements. Our example has sharply contrasting wings radiating out from a central core to suggest their different functions (fig. 26-43). The core itself has been treated as a witty parody of spaceships, while the astonishing interior (fig. 26-44) looks like a futuristic movie set. Everything gleams with polished metal tubing clustered like the pipes of a rocket, which "blasts off" through the skylight. This space-age motif is continued on the rear of the auditorium, which sports exhaust pipes that curiously resemble the artillery of an aircraft carrier, as if to protect its flanks from some imaginary attack.

ROGERS AND PIANO. Among the freshest statements of Late Modernism is the Centre Georges Pompidou, the national arts and cultural center in Paris, which rejects the formal beauty of the International Style without abandoning its functionalism (fig. 26-45). Selected in an international competition, the design by the Anglo-Italian team of Richard Rogers (b. 1933) and Renzo

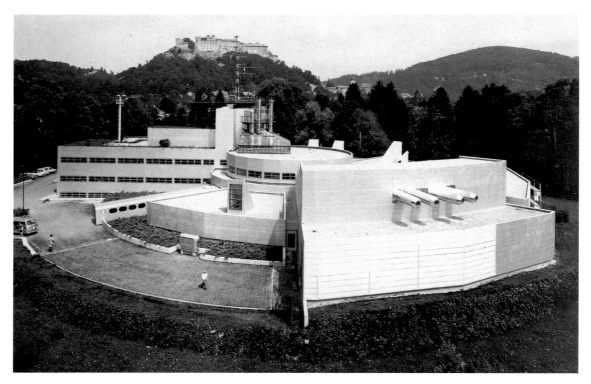

26-43. Gustav Peichl. Austrian Radio and Television Studio, Salzburg. 1970–72

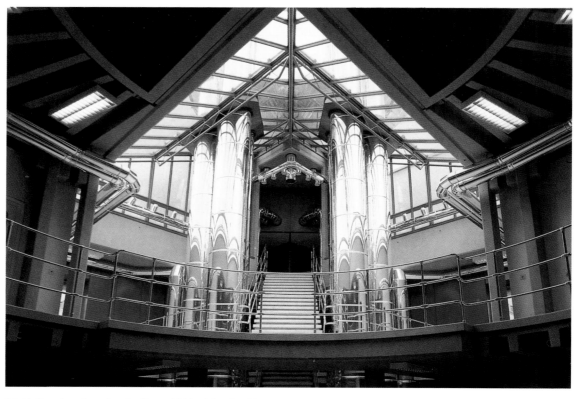

26-44. Interior, Austrian Radio and Television Studio

Piano (b. 1937) looks like a High Modern building turned inside-out. The architects have eliminated any trace of Le Corbusier's elegant facades (see fig. 26-18) by exposing the building's inner mechanics while disguising the underlying structure. The interior itself has no fixed walls, so that temporary dividers can be arranged to meet any need. This stark utilitarianism, sometimes termed Productivism, expresses a populist sentiment widespread in France. The exterior features eye-catching colors, each keyed to a different function. The festive display is as lively and imaginative as Léger's *The City* (see fig. 24-33), which, with Paris's Eiffel

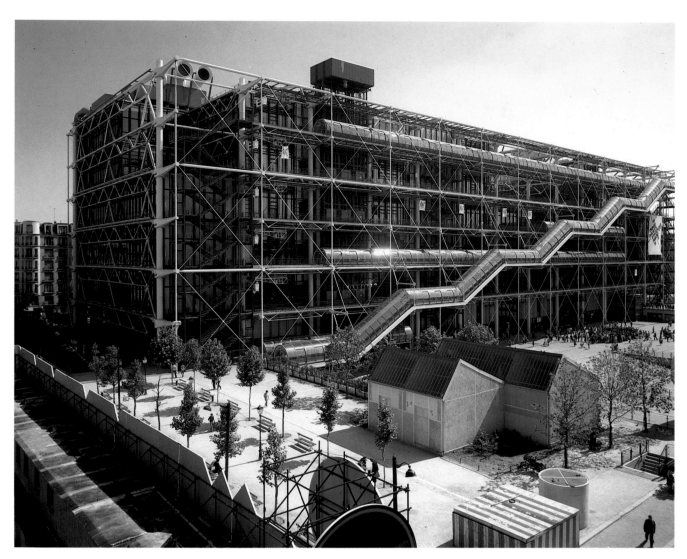

26-45. Richard Rogers and Renzo Piano. Centre National d'Art et Culture Georges Pompidou, Paris. 1971–77

Tower (see fig. 22-36), can be regarded as the Pompidou Center's true ancestors.

NEO-EXPRESSIONISM. It can be argued that Late Modernism actually fulfills the agenda mapped at the beginning of the century, when architecture pursued not one but several paths. There is a certain truth to this paradoxical notion. Since 1985 architecture has also seen the rise of Neo-Expressionism and Neo-Modernism, which may be regarded as counterparts of the similarly named movements in painting (see page 866). The difference is that they have helped to make architecture the most vibrant and innovative of all art forms on the scene today, whereas painting and sculpture seem adrift. Indeed, the architecture of the past fifteen years is among the richest in variety and quality of any period since the Baroque. At present there are more than two dozen great architects at work around the world. (See also pages 944–52).

SANTIAGO CALATRAVA. Neo-Expressionism utilizes the same high-tech materials and techniques as Late Modernism, but creates fantasies that are more sculptural than architectural. Thus

architecture has replaced sculpture as the giver of contemporary form. Santiago Calatrava (b. 1951), Spanish-born but Swiss-based, has created a "flight" of fancy for the futuristic TGV Station at Satolas, Lyons (fig. 26-46), which suggests some sort of mechanized prehistoric creature out of a science-fiction movie. The entrance to the central hall looks like the Concorde supersonic plane constructed on a birdlike skeleton but with a tail echoing the French Super Train (Train à Grande Vitesse). Through this seemingly mixed metaphor, the structure helps to link the railroad station with a nearby airport. In this innovative design, Calatrava has updated the image of flight in contemporary terms (compare figs. 26-34 and 26-35).

NEO-MODERNISM. Neo-Modernism, in contrast, looks back consciously to the tradition created by Gropius, Mies van der Rohe, and Le Corbusier. Within it we may discern several separate, yet closely related, strands. The first is a revival of structural rationalism, which is especially characteristic of Italian architects, such as Mario Botta (b. 1943) and Aldo Rossi (1931–1997), as well as the Frenchman Jean Nouvel (b. 1945). The second is a conscious

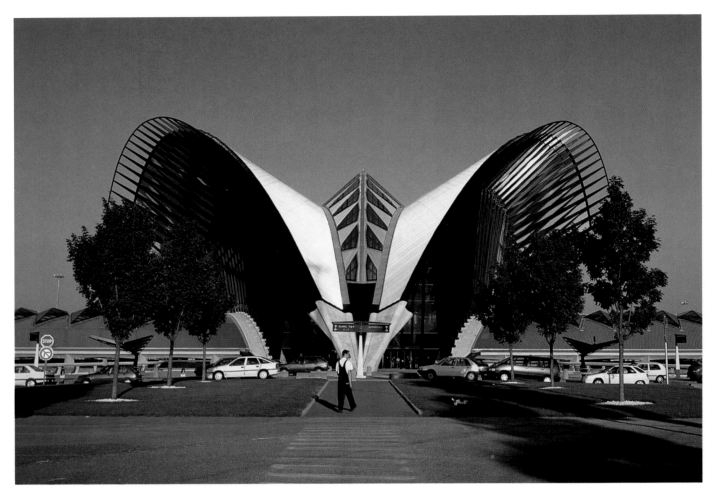

26-46. Santiago Calatrava. TGV (Très Grande Vitesse) Super Train Station, Satolas, Lyons. 1988–94

return on the part of certain English architects, most notably Nicholas Grimshaw (b. 1939), to the functional engineering of Paxton's Crystal Palace (see fig. 22-34). And the third, taken up by a new school of Dutch architects, among whom Rem Koolhaas (b. 1944) is the best-known, questions the legacy of High Modernism and tries to give it new life by reconsidering its potential in light of present-day realities. The theories and approaches of these three overlap not only with each other, but also with Postmodernism's, so that in recent years there has been a gradual merging of previously independent trends.

REM KOOLHAAS. An issue that concerns all schools is how to deal with the blight of unplanned urban growth in the late twentieth century, although each has faced it somewhat differently. Unlike earlier architects, they have generally avoided attempting to cure social ills, since most of the utopian schemes put forward by the High Modernists were generally failures. Instead of sweeping urban renewal proposals, they have been interested primarily in making architectural statements under the difficult conditions imposed by the sites themselves.

Koolhaas and his OMA group focus on modern chaos theory and the "culture of congestion" epitomized by New York City, which has led to a recent preoccupation with size. For Koolhaas,

it is the architect's role to resist chaos and instead find a new modernism reflecting the urban existence of our time, so full of paradoxes and contradictions. For that reason, Koolhaas combines "architectural specificity with programmatic instability," in which goals are treated in terms of strategy. Far from rejecting modernism, Koolhaas builds on it, while discarding many of its underlying assumptions. Although he has been influenced by Frank Gehry and the Deconstructionists (compare pages 950–52), especially in his preference for corrugated metal and other standard industrial building supplies, he has rejected the return to the style of the early Russian moderns as imitative and irrelevant to our age.

What all this theorizing in effect means is a new functionalism in which the facade is no more than an envelope that coexists with its surroundings. In fact, his exteriors are deceptively bland, effectively disguising the purposes and spaces they enclose. The real action takes place inside. If the Neo-Expressionists and the Sculptural Architects (see page 950) are masters of form, Koolhaas is the master of interior space. The facade of the Netherlands Dance Theater, which is grafted onto an existing concert hall, is extremely modest. However, the foyer (fig. 26-47) is that rarity in modern architecture: a genuinely engaging interior, although it deliberately breaks no new ground. Despite Koolhaas' importance as a

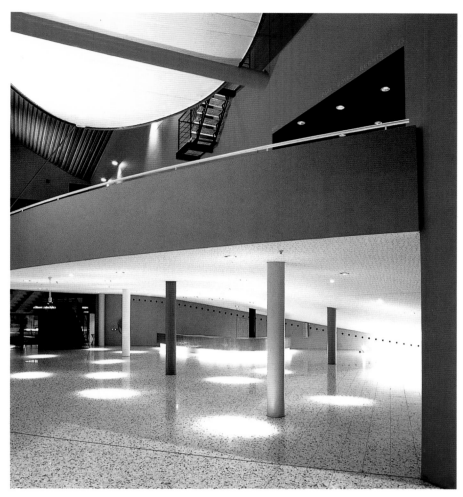

26-47. Rem Koolhaas.
Foyer of the Netherlands
Dance Theater, Amsterdam. 1987.

(BELOW) 26-48. Foster Associates.
Hearst Corporation, New York. Begun 2000

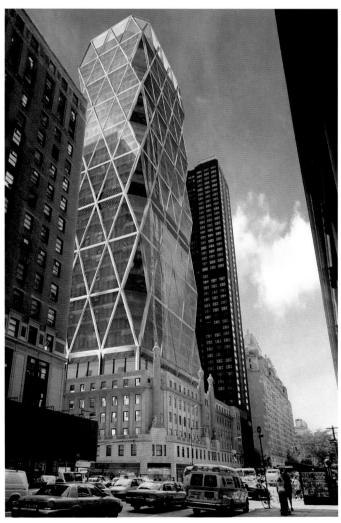

theorist, his design refrains from the didacticism that made High Modernism seem so cold and barren. He instead rescues modernism from itself by investing it with a new humanism through festive colors and dynamic space, which are strikingly reminiscent of Léger's paintings (compare fig. 24-33). It is this kind of thoughtful reappraisal of the modernist legacy that offers perhaps the best hope for its continued vitality.

NORMAN FOSTER. Koolhaas has proved remarkably prophetic. Architects around the world have recently become obsessed with exploring the origins of modern architecture, as if to discover its inner secret, which they hope will lead them to the new architecture of the twenty-first century. One of these is Norman Foster (b. 1935), who wants to transform the Hearst Corporation's New York headquarters at 8th Avenue near 57th Street (it was built in 1928 by Joseph Urban and George Post) by encasing most of it in a transparent crystalline structure (fig. 26-48). The architect claims a descent from Paxton's Crystal Palace (fig. 22-34) but, in fact, the greatest debt is to Bruno Taut and the mystical fascination with crystals that engrossed many architects in the first decades of the early twentieth century (see page 899). This brilliant design, which underwent a complex approval process, was rewarded the coveted Pritzker Prize for architecture.

CHAPTER TWENTY-SEVEN

Twentieth-Century Photography

THE FIRST HALF-CENTURY

During the nineteenth century, photography struggled to establish itself as art but failed to find an identity. Only under extraordinary conditions of political upheaval and social reform did it address the most basic subject of art, which is life itself. To create an independent vision, photography after 1900 combined the aesthetic principles of the Secession and the documentary approach of photojournalism with lessons learned from motion photography. At the same time, modern painting, with which it soon became allied, forced a decisive change in photography. Mod-

ernism undermined the theoretical assumptions of photography and challenged its credentials as art. Like the other arts, photography responded to the three main artistic currents of the early twentieth century: Expressionism, Abstraction, and Fantasy. But because it has concentrated for the most part on the world around us, modern photography has generally followed a separate course marked by realism. We must therefore discuss twentieth-century photography primarily in terms of different schools and how they have dealt with those often-conflicting currents.

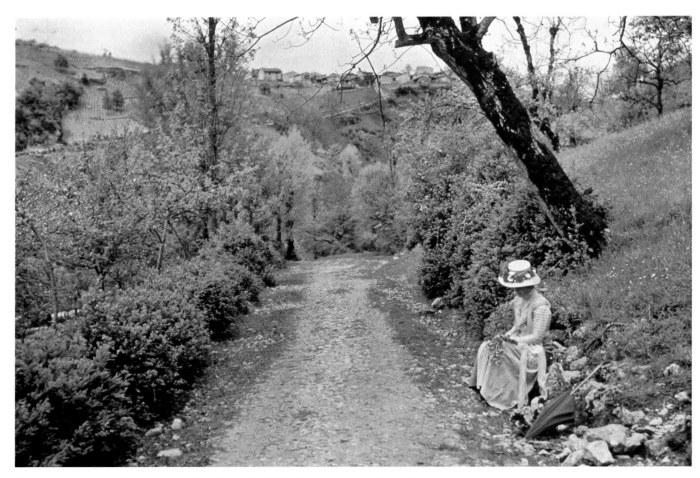

27-1. Louis Lumière. *Young Lady with an Umbrella*. 1906–10. Autochrome. Société Lumière

Modern photography was aided by technological advances. It must be emphasized, however, that these innovations have increased but not dictated the photographer's options. George Eastman's invention of the hand-held camera in 1888 and the advent of 35mm photography with the Leica camera in 1924 made it easier to take pictures that had been difficult but by no means impossible to take with the traditional view camera.

Surprisingly, color photography did not have revolutionary importance. It began in 1907 with the introduction of the **autochrome** by Louis Lumière (1864–1948) who, with his brother Auguste, had created a new art form, the cinema, in 1894. The autochrome was a glass plate covered with grains of potato starch dyed in three colors that acted as color filters, over which was applied a coating of silver bromide emulsion. It yielded a positive color transparency upon development, and was not superseded until Kodak began to make color film in 1932 using the same principles but more advanced materials. The autochrome was based on the color theories used by Seurat. It even achieved Divisionist effects, as we can see if we look hard enough at Lumière's *Young Lady with an Umbrella* (fig. 27-1), an early effort. Except for its color, the picture differs little from photographs by the Photo-Secessionists, who were the first to turn to the new process. Color, in fact, had little impact on the content, outlook, or aesthetic of

photography until the 1930s, even though it removed the last barrier cited by nineteenth-century critics of photography as art.

France

EUGÈNE ATGET. Modern photography began quietly in Paris with Eugène Atget (1856–1927), who turned to the camera only in 1898 at the age of 42. From then until his death, he toted his heavy equipment around Paris to record the city in all its variety. Atget was all but ignored by the art photographers, for whom his commonplace subjects had little interest. He himself was a humble man whose studio sign read simply, "Atget—Documents for Artists." His patrons included the founders of modern art: Braque, Picasso, Duchamp, and Man Ray (see below), to name only the best known. It is no accident that these artists were also admirers of Henri Rousseau. Rousseau and Atget shared a naïve vision, although Atget found inspiration in unexpected corners of his environment rather than in magical realms of the imagination.

Atget's pictures are characterized by a subtle intensity and technical perfection that heighten the reality, and hence the significance, of even the most mundane subjects. Few photographers have equaled his ability to compose simultaneously in two- and three-dimensional space. Like *Versailles* (fig. 27-2), his scenes

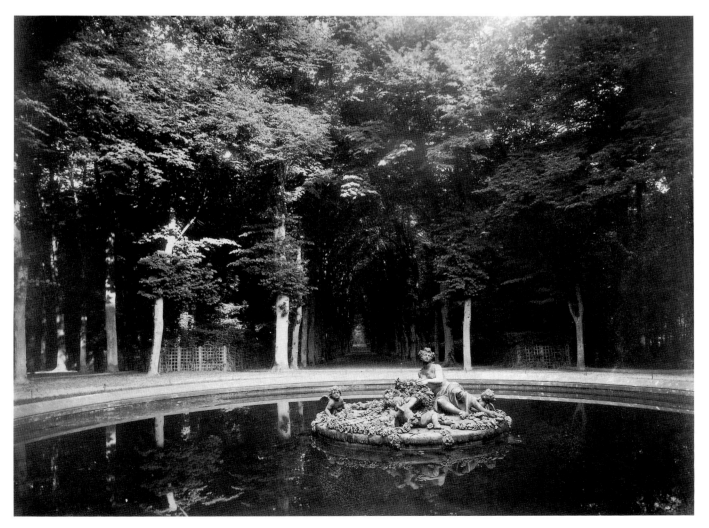

27-2. Eugène Atget. *Versailles*. 1924. Albumen-silver print, 7 x 9⅜" (17.8 x 23.9 cm). The Museum of Modern Art, New York

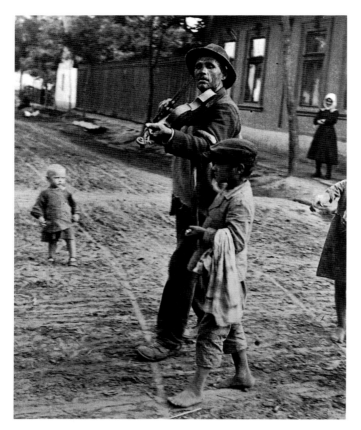

27-3. André Kertész. *Blind Musician.* 1921.
Gelatin-silver print, 16⅜ x 13¼" (41.6 x 33.7 cm).
The Museum of Modern Art, New York

BRASSAÏ. Brassaï's photographic style was conditioned by Paris, its views and its habits. He was born in Transylvania and studied art in Budapest, but was a Frenchman at heart even before arriving in Paris in 1923. Several years later, while working as a journalist, he borrowed a camera from Kertész and took a series of evocative photographs of the city by night. He soon turned to the nightlife of the Parisian cafés, and had an unerring eye for the exotic characters who haunt them. *"Bijou" of Montmartre* (fig. 27-4) shows the same appreciation of the abnormal as *At the Moulin Rouge* (see fig. 23-8) by Toulouse-Lautrec, whose art clearly influenced Brassaï.

HENRI CARTIER-BRESSON. The greatest photographer of the Paris school was Henri Cartier-Bresson (b. 1908). The son of a wealthy thread manufacturer, he studied under a Cubist painter in the late 1920s before taking up photography in 1932. Strongly affected at first by Atget, Man Ray (see page 934), Kertész, and the cinema, he soon developed into the most influential photojournalist of his time. His purpose and technique were nevertheless those of an artist and his photographs have universal appeal.

Cartier-Bresson was the master of what he has termed "the decisive moment." This to him meant the instant recognition and visual organization of an event at the most intense moment of

are often desolate, bespeaking a strange and haunted outlook. The viewer has the peculiar sensation that time has been frozen by the majestic composition and the photographer's obsession with textures. While Atget's work is related to the journalistic tradition of Nadar, Brady, and Riis (see pages 715, 717, and 774), it is distinctly different from earlier photography. This departure can only be explained in relation to late-nineteenth-century art. His pictures of neighborhood shops and street vendors, for example, are nearly identical with slightly earlier paintings by minor realists whose names are all but forgotten. Moreover, his photographs are directly related to a strain of Magic Realism that was a forerunner of Surrealism. Indeed, Atget has sometimes been called a Surrealist. While this label is misleading, it is easy to understand why he was rediscovered by Man Ray, the Dada and Surrealist artist-photographer, and championed by Ray's former assistant Berenice Abbott (see page 935).

ANDRÉ KERTÉSZ. Atget's direct successors were two East Europeans: André Kertész (1894–1985) and Gyula Halasz, known simply as Brassaï (1899–1984). Kertész began photographing in his native Hungary as early as 1915, and his style was already defined when he came to Paris ten years later. *Blind Musician* (fig. 27-3), made in Hungary in 1921, is the kind of picture Atget sometimes took, and it uses many of the same devices. The careful composition isolates the subject, with just enough of the surroundings to set the scene.

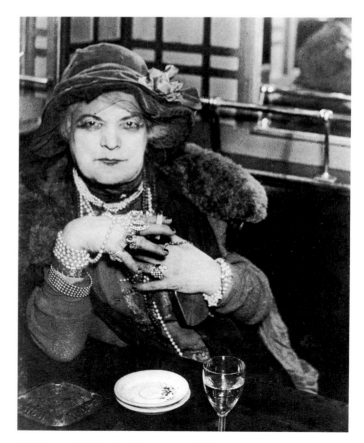

27-4. Brassaï. *"Bijou" of Montmartre.* 1933.
11⅞ x 9¼" (30.2 x 23.5 cm).
The Museum of Modern Art, New York

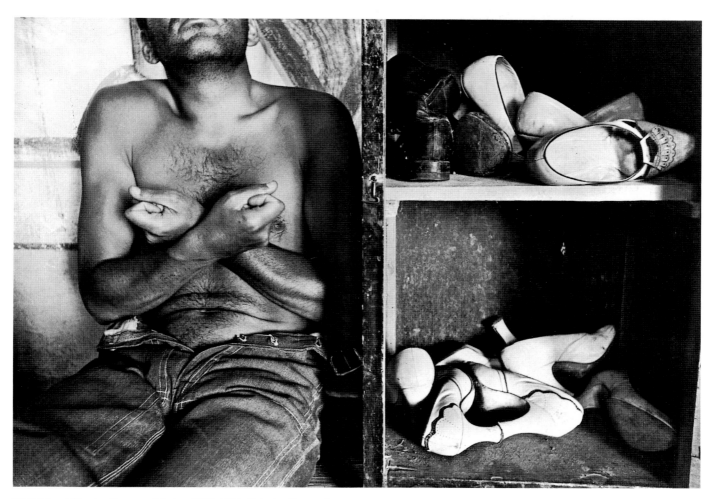

27-5. Henri Cartier-Bresson. *Mexico, 1934.* 1934. Gelatin-silver print

action and emotion in order to reveal its inner meaning, not simply to record its occurrence. Unlike other members of the Paris school, Cartier-Bresson was at home anywhere in the world and always seemed in sympathy with his subjects. His photographs show an interest in composition for its own sake, derived from modern abstract art. He also had a fascination with motion, which he invested with all the dynamism of Futurism and the irony of Dada.

The key to his work is his use of space to establish relations that are suggestive and often astonishing. Although he dealt with reality, Cartier-Bresson was a Surrealist at heart and admitted as much. The results can be disturbing, as in *Mexico, 1934* (fig. 27-5). By omitting the man's face and surroundings, Cartier-Bresson prevents us from identifying the meaning of the gesture, so that we respond to its tension even more powerfully.

The United States

ALFRED STIEGLITZ. The founder of modern photography in the United States was Alfred Stieglitz, and he remained the dominant figure throughout his long life (1864–1946). From his involvement with the Photo-Secession onward (see page 799), he was a tireless spokesman for photography-as-art, which he defined more broadly than did other members of the movement. He backed up his words by publishing the magazine *Camera Work*. He also supported the other pioneers of American photography by exhibiting their work in his New York galleries, especially the first one, known as "291." Most of his early work follows Secessionist conventions by treating photography as a pictorial equivalent to painting. During the mid-1890s, however, he took some pictures of street scenes that are forerunners of his mature photographs.

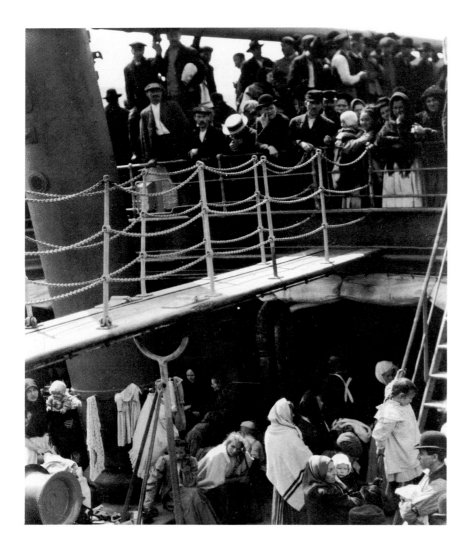

27-6. Alfred Stieglitz. *The Steerage*.
1907. Chloride print, 4⅜ x 3⅝" (11.1 x 9.2 cm).
The Art Institute of Chicago

His classic statement, and the one he regarded as his finest photograph, is *The Steerage* (fig. 27-6), taken in 1907 on a trip to Europe. Like Ford Madox Brown's *The Last of England* (see fig. 22-16), painted more than a half-century earlier, it captures the feeling of a voyage by letting the shapes and composition tell the story. The scene is divided visually by the gangway in order to emphasize the contrasting activities of the observers on the upper deck and the people below in steerage, which was reserved for the cheapest fares. What it lacks in obvious sentiment it makes up for by remaining true to life.

This kind of "straight" photography is deceptive in its simplicity: the image mirrors the feelings that stirred Stieglitz. For that reason, *The Steerage* marks an important step in his evolution and a turning point in the history of photography. Its importance emerges only in comparison with earlier photographs such as Steichen's *Rodin* (see fig. 23-48) and Riis' *Bandits' Roost* (see fig. 23-42). *The Steerage* is a pictorial statement independent of painting on the one hand and free from social commentary on the other. It represents the first time that documentary photography achieved the level of art in the United States.

Stieglitz's straight photography shaped the American school. It is therefore ironic that Stieglitz, with the encouragement of Edward Steichen, became America's first champion of abstract art. He attacked the members of the Ash Can school (see page 821), whose paintings were often similar in subject and appearance to his photographs. The resemblance is misleading, however. For Stieglitz, photography was less a means of recording things than of expressing his experience and philosophy of life, much as a painter does.

This attitude culminated in his Equivalents. In 1922 Stieglitz began to photograph clouds to show that his work was independent of subject and personality. A remarkably lyrical cloud photograph from 1930 (fig. 27-7) corresponds to a state of mind waiting to find expression rather than merely responding to the moonlit scene. The study of clouds is as old as Romanticism itself, but no one before Stieglitz had made them a major theme in photography. Like Käsebier's *The Magic Crystal* (see fig. 23-47), *Equivalent* evokes unseen forces that also make it a counterpart to Kandinsky's *Sketch I for "Composition VII"* (see fig. 24-9).

EDWARD WESTON. Stieglitz's concept of the Equivalent opened the way to "pure" photography as an alternative to straight photography. The leader of this new approach was Edward Weston (1886–1958), who was decisively influenced by Stieglitz. During the 1920s Weston pursued abstraction and realism as

27-7. Alfred Stieglitz. *Equivalent*. 1930. Chloride print. The Art Institute of Chicago

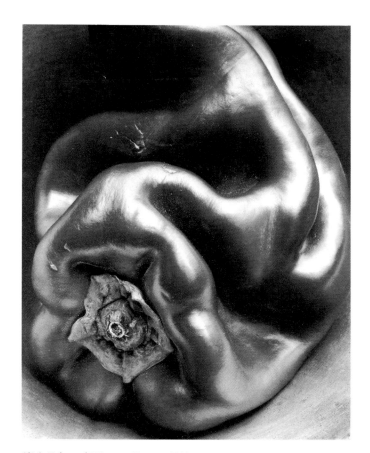

27-8. Edward Weston. *Pepper*. 1930. Center for Creative Photography, Tucson, Arizona

separate paths, but by 1930 he united them in images that are wonderful in their design and miraculous in their detail.

Pepper (fig. 27-8) is a splendid example of Weston's photography. The image is anything but a straightforward record of this familiar fruit. Like Stieglitz's "Equivalents," it makes us see the ordinary with new eyes. [See Primary Sources, no. 101, pages 977–78.] The pepper is shown with incredible sharpness and so close up that it seems larger than life. Thanks to the tightly cropped composition, we are forced to contemplate the familiar form anew. *Pepper* has the sensuousness of *Black Iris III* by O'Keeffe (see fig. 24-54), which lends the Equivalent a new meaning. Every undulation is revealed by the dramatic lighting. The shapes suggest the female nude, a subject that Weston also pioneered in photography.

ANSEL ADAMS. To achieve uniform detail and depth, Weston worked with the smallest possible camera lens openings. His success led to the formation in 1932 of the West Coast society known as Group f/64, for the smallest aperture. Among its founders was Ansel Adams (1902–1984), who soon became the foremost nature photographer in the United States. He is regarded as the successor to Timothy O'Sullivan (see fig. 21-84), and his landscapes often hark back to nineteenth-century American painting and photography.

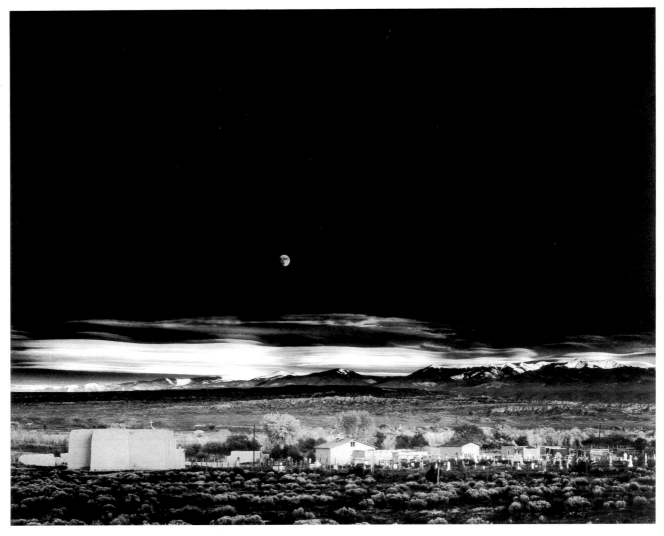

27-9. Ansel Adams. *Moonrise, Hernandez, New Mexico.* 1941. Gelatin-silver print, 15 x 18½" (38.1 x 47 cm).
The Museum of Modern Art, New York

Adams was a meticulous technician, planning every step from the composition and exposure to the final print. His famous work *Moonrise, Hernandez, New Mexico* (fig. 27-9) is a perfect marriage of straight and pure photography. The image came from pure chance, which could never be repeated. The key to the photograph lies in the low cloud that divides the scene into three zones, so that the moon appears to hover effortlessly in the early evening sky. As in all of Adams' pictures, there is a full range of tonal nuances, from clear whites to inky blacks.

MARGARET BOURKE-WHITE. Stieglitz was among the first to photograph skyscrapers, the new architecture that came to dominate America's growing cities. He also championed the Precisionist painters (see pages 826–28), who began to depict urban and industrial architecture around 1925 under the inspiration of Futurism. Several of them soon took up the camera as well and used it as the basis of their canvases. Thus painting and photography once again became closely linked. Both responded to the revitalized economy after World War I, which led to unprecedented industrial expansion on both sides of the Atlantic. During the Great Depression that followed, photography continued to grow with the new mass-circulation magazines that ushered in the great age of photojournalism and, with it, of commercial photography. In the United States, most of the important photographers were employed by the leading journals and corporations.

Margaret Bourke-White (1904–1971) was the first staff photographer hired by *Fortune* magazine and then by *Life* magazine, both published by Henry Luce (1898–1967). Her cover photograph of Fort Peck Dam in Montana for the inaugural November 23, 1936, issue of *Life* remains a classic example of the new photojournalism (fig. 27-10). The decade witnessed enormous building campaigns. With her keen eye for composition, Bourke-White drew a visual parallel between the dam and the massive constructions of ancient Egypt (compare fig. 2-32). (This idea had already appeared in *My Egypt,* a painting of grain elevators from 1927 by Charles Demuth.) In addition to their architectural power, Bourke-White's columnar forms have a remarkable sculptural quality. They loom like colossal statues at the entrance to a temple, so that they assume a nearly human presence. But unlike the passive timelessness of the pharaohs at Luxor (fig. 2-33), these

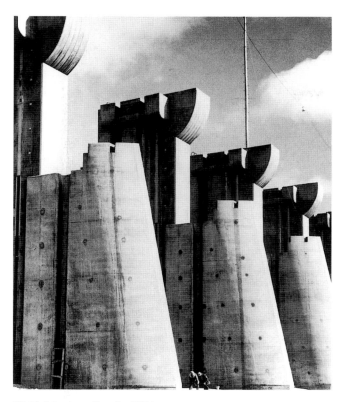

27-10. Margaret Bourke-White.
Fort Peck Dam, Montana. 1936. Time-Life, Inc.

"guardian figures" have the peculiar alertness of Henry Moore's abstract monoliths (see fig. 25-18). Bourke-White's rare ability to suggest multiple levels of meaning made this cover and her accompanying photo essay a landmark in photojournalism.

EDWARD STEICHEN. The flourishing magazine business also gave rise to fashion and glamour photography, which was developed into an art by Edward Steichen, America's most complete photographer. Steichen's talent for portraiture, seen in his early Photo-Secession photograph of Rodin (see fig. 23-48), makes *Greta Garbo* (fig. 27-11) a worthy successor to Nadar's *Sarah Bernhardt* (see fig. 21-82). The young film actress had her picture taken countless times, despite her desire "to be alone," but none captures better the magnetic presence and complex character seen in her movies. The photograph owes much to its abstract black-and-white design, which focuses attention on her wonderfully expressive face. But Steichen's stroke of genius was to have Garbo put her arms around her head to suggest her enigmatic personality.

WAYNE MILLER. One of Steichen's contributions to photography was to organize the "Family of Man" exhibition, which opened at the Museum of Modern Art in New York in 1955.

27-11. Edward Steichen. *Greta Garbo.*
1928 (for *Vanity Fair* magazine).
The Museum of Modern Art, New York

GIFT OF THE PHOTOGRAPHER

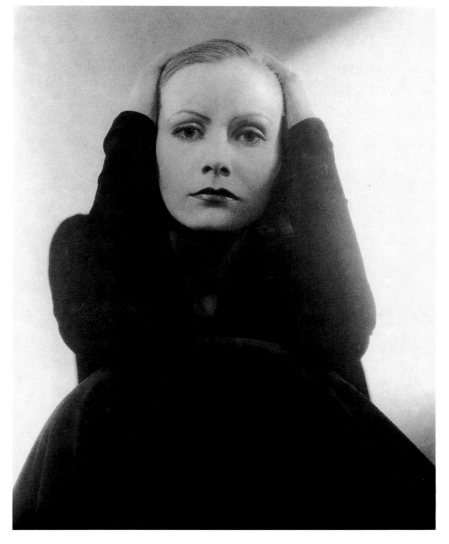

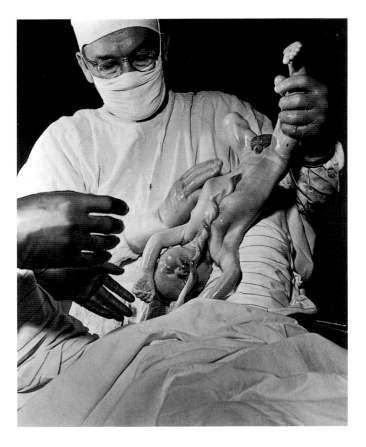

Wayne Miller's picture of childbirth (fig. 27-12) from this epoch-making show captures the miracle of life in one dramatic image. It records with shocking directness the newborn infant's abrupt entry into the world we all share (compare fig. 25-3). At the same time, the hands that reach out to help him are a moving affirmation of human existence.

JAMES VANDERZEE. The nature of the Harlem Renaissance, which flourished in the 1920s (see page 818), was hotly debated by black critics even in its own day. While its achievement in literature is beyond dispute, the photography of James VanDerZee (1886–1983) is often regarded as the movement's chief contribution to the visual arts. Much of his work is commercial and variable in quality, yet it remains of great documentary value. The best examples provide a compelling portrait of the era. VanDerZee had a deep understanding of settings as reflections of people's sense of place in the world, and he used them to bring out each sitter's character and dreams. *At Home* (fig. 27-13) shows VanDerZee's unique ability to capture the pride of African-Americans during a period when their dreams seemed on the verge of being realized. Posed in imitation of fashionable photographs of white society, it is a portrait of the

27-12. Wayne Miller. *Childbirth.* "Family of Man" exhibition. 1955

27-13. James VanDerZee. *At Home.* 1934. James VanDerZee Estate

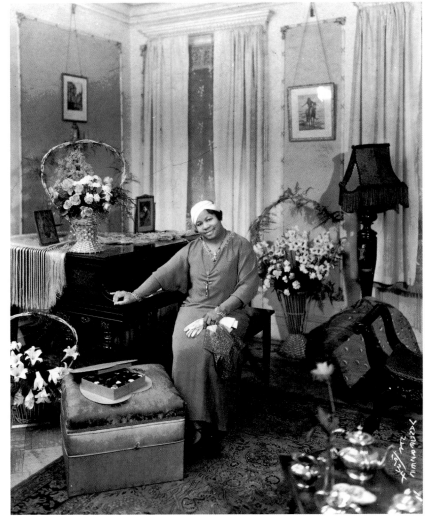

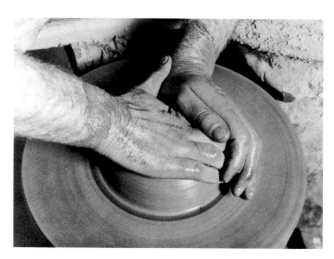

27-14. Albert Renger-Patzsch. *Potter's Hands.* 1925.
Gelatin-silver print, 11¾ x 15⅛" (29.8 x 38.2 cm).
The Museum of Modern Art, New York

GIFT OF THE PHOTOGRAPHER

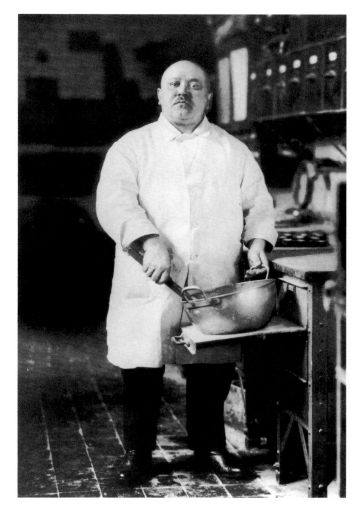

27-15. August Sander. *Pastry Cook, Cologne.* 1928.
August Sander Archiv/SK-Stiftung Kultur, Cologne, Germany

wife of the Reverend George Wilson Becton, taken two years after the popular pastor of the Salem Methodist Church in Harlem was murdered.

Germany

With the New Objectivity movement in Germany during the late 1920s and early 1930s (see page 815), photography achieved a degree of excellence that has not been surpassed. Fostered by the invention of superior German cameras and the boom in publishing everywhere, this German version of straight photography emphasized materiality at a time when many other photographers were turning away from the real world. The intrinsic beauty of things was brought out through clarity of form and structure. This approach accorded with Bauhaus principles of design.

ALBERT RENGER-PATZSCH. *Potter's Hands* (fig. 27-14) by Albert Renger-Patzsch (1897–1966), New Objectivity's leading exponent, is a marvel of technique and design that deliberately avoids any personal statement by reducing the image to an abstraction. The content lies solely in the cool perfection of the presentation and the orderly world it suggests.

AUGUST SANDER. When applied to people rather than things, the New Objectivity could be deceiving in its results. August Sander (1876–1964), whose *Face of Our Time* was published in 1929, concealed his intentions behind a disarmingly straightforward facade. The 60 portraits provide a devastating survey of Germany during the rise of the Nazis, who later suppressed the book. Clearly proud of his position, the man in Sander's *Pastry Cook, Cologne* (fig. 27-15) is the very opposite of the timid figure in George Grosz's *Germany, a Winter's Tale* (see fig. 24-48). Despite their curious resemblance, this "good citizen"

seems oblivious to the evil that Grosz has depicted so vividly. While the photograph passes no individual judgment, in the context of the book the chef's lack of concern stands as a strong indictment of the era as a whole.

Czechoslovakia

JOSEF SUDEK. The work of Josef Sudek (1896–1976) was the most varied of its time. It shows the full range of modern photography before 1945, except photojournalism, which is concerned with passing moments that were merely incidental to him. Sudek was the Atget of Prague, which provided his main subject matter. This photographer lost his right arm in World War I and had to struggle to take his pictures. From pictorialism he learned to become a master of light, which he invested with the poetry of Vermeer, while the New Objectivity taught him to photograph simple objects with the reverence of Chardin. A romantic at heart, he wanted to reveal the secret life of nature. Sudek preferred to work in series over the years. He would often return to the same place to document its changing face and

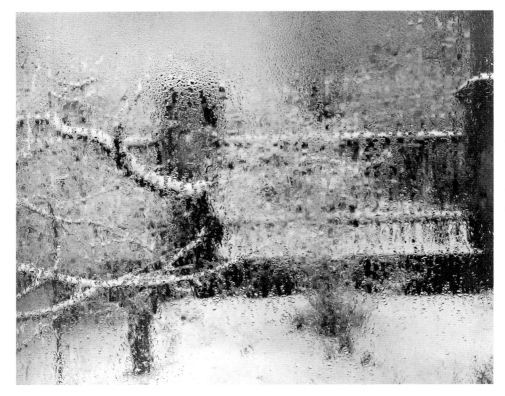

27-16. Josef Sudek.
View from Studio Window in Winter.
1954. Gelatin-silver print,
8½ x 11 1/16" (21.6 x 28.1 cm).
The Museum of Modern Art, New York

uncover new meanings. He was a recluse who became even more secretive during World War II, when his movement was severely restricted by the German occupation of Czechoslovakia. The most characteristic photographs from his later years are of private worlds, be they the cluttered studio where he lived, or gardens, his own as well as those of the artists, writers, and musicians who were his friends. Branches of a tree in snow seen through his window (fig. 27-16) may be taken as a metaphor of the photographer himself. To Sudek, trees were primordial symbols of life; they weathered nature's difficulties much as he had survived personal tragedy.

The Heroic Age of Photography

ROBERT CAPA. The period from 1930 to 1945 can be called the heroic age of photography for its response to the challenges of the times. The physical bravery of photographers was illustrated by Robert Capa (1913–1954), who covered wars around the world for 20 years before being killed by a land mine in Vietnam. While barely adequate technically, his picture of a Loyalist soldier being shot during the Spanish Civil War (fig. 27-17) captures fully the horror of death at the moment of impact. Had it been taken by someone else, it might seem an accident, but it is typical of Capa's

27-17. Robert Capa.
Death of a Loyalist Soldier.
September 5, 1936

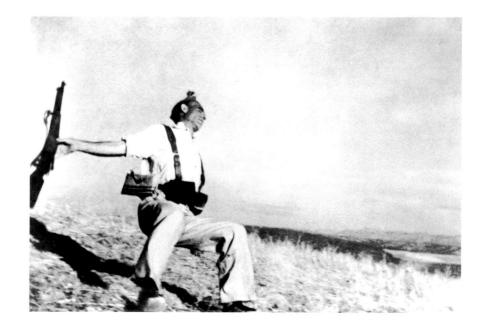

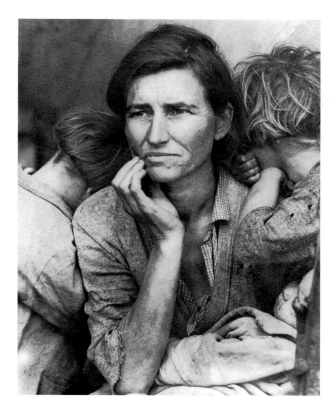

27-18. Dorothea Lange. *Migrant Mother, California.*
February 1936. Gelatin-silver print.
Library of Congress, Washington, D.C.

battle close-ups. He was as fearless as the Civil War photographers Mathew Brady and Alexander Gardner (fig. 21-86).

DOROTHEA LANGE. Photographers in those difficult times demonstrated moral courage as well. Under Roy Stryker, staff photographers of the Farm Security Administration compiled a comprehensive photodocumentary archive of rural America during the Depression. While the FSA photographers presented a balanced and objective view, most of them were also reformers whose work responded to the social problems they confronted daily in the field. The concern of Dorothea Lange (1895–1965) for people, and her sensitivity to their dignity, made her the finest documentary photographer of the time in America.

At a pea-pickers' camp in Nipomo, California, Lange discovered 2,500 nearly starving migrant workers and took several pictures of a young widow with her children. (She was identified much later as Florence Thompson, and she resented all the attention the photographs received.) When *Migrant Mother, California* (fig. 27-18) was published in a news story about their plight, the government rushed in food, and eventually migrant relief camps were opened. More than any Social Realist or Regionalist painting (see page 843), *Migrant Mother, California* has come to stand for that entire era. Unposed and uncropped, this photograph has an unforgettable immediacy no other medium can match.

Fantasy and Abstraction

"Impersonality," the very disadvantage that had hindered the acceptance of photography in the eyes of many critics, became a virtue in the 1920s. Precisely because photographs are produced by mechanical devices, the camera's images now seemed to some artists the perfect means for expressing the modern era. This change in attitude did not stem from the Futurists. Surprisingly, they never fully grasped the camera's importance for modern art, despite the influence of motion photography on their paintings (see page 801). The new view of photography arose as part of the Berlin Dadaists' assault on traditional art. Toward the end of World War I, the Dadaists "invented" the photomontage and the photogram. (Actually, these processes had been practiced early in the history of photography.) In the service of antiart they lent themselves equally well to Fantasy and to Abstraction, despite the differences between these two modes.

PHOTOMONTAGE. Photomontages are simply pieces of photographs cut out and recombined into new images. Composite negatives originated with the art photography of Rejlander and Robinson (see page 798), but by the 1870s they were already being used in France to create witty impossibilities that are the ancestors of Dada photomontages. Like *1 Piping Man* (see fig. 24-39) by Max Ernst (who, not surprisingly, became a master of the genre), Dadaist photomontages use the collage techniques of Synthetic Cubism to ridicule social and aesthetic conventions.

These imaginative parodies destroy all pictorial illusionism. They therefore stand in direct opposition to straight photographs, which use the camera to record and probe the meaning of reality. Dada photomontages might be called "ready-images," after Duchamp's readymades. Like other collages, they are literally torn from popular culture and given new meaning. Although the photogram relies more on the laws of chance, the Surrealists later claimed that the photomontage was a form of automatic handwriting on the grounds that it responds to a stream of consciousness.

Most Surrealist photographers have been influenced by the Belgian painter René Magritte, whose mystifying fantasies (see fig. 24-42) are treated with a magic realism that is the opposite of automatic handwriting. Magritte's pictorial style was already highly naturalistic, and he experimented little with the camera. Nevertheless, he had a considerable impact on photography because his illusionistic paradoxes can be readily imitated in photographs. An excellent example of how photomontage can be used to challenge our conception of reality is *lonely metropolitan* (fig. 27-19) by the German-born Herbert Bayer (1900–1985). The purpose of such visual riddles is to show up the discrepancy between our perception of the world and our irrational understanding of its significance.

POSTERS. Photomontages were soon incorporated into posters. These became a double-edged sword in political propaganda in Germany, where they were used by Hitler's sympathizers and enemies alike. The most bitter anti-Nazi commentaries were

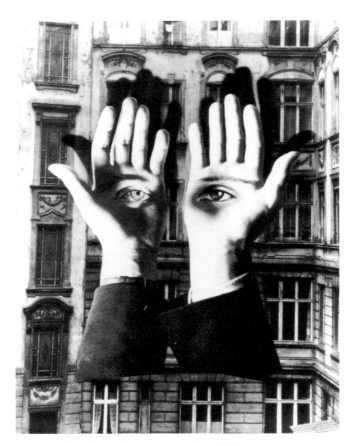

27-19. Herbert Bayer. *lonely metropolitan.* 1932.
Photomontage, 14 x 11" (35.6 x 28 cm).
Collection the artist (copyright)

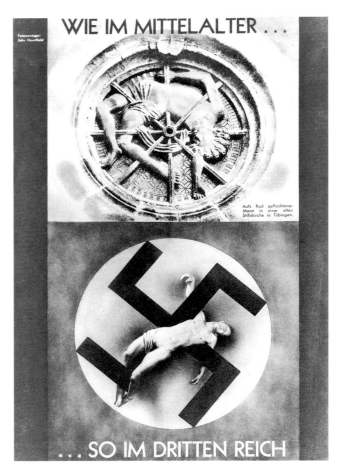

27-20. John Heartfield. *As in the Middle Ages, So in the Third Reich.*
1934. Poster, photomontage. Akademie der Künste,
John Heartfield Archiv, Berlin

created by John Heartfield (1891–1968), who changed his name from the German Herzfeld as a sign of protest. His horrific poster of a Nazi victim crucified on a swastika (fig. 27-20) appropriates a Gothic image of humanity punished for its sins on the wheel of divine judgment. Obviously Heartfield was not concerned about reinterpreting the original meaning in his montage, which communicates its message with overwhelming power.

PHOTOGRAMS. The photogram does not take pictures but makes them. Objects are placed directly onto photographic paper and exposed to light. This technique was not new. Fox Talbot (see pages 734–35) had used it to make negative images of plants, which he called *photogenic drawings.* Like their photomontages, however, Dadaist photograms were intended to alter nature's forms, not to record them, and to substitute impersonal technology for the handwork of the individual. Since the results of photograms are so unpredictable, making one involves even greater risks than does a photomontage.

MAN RAY. Man Ray (1890–1976), an American working in Paris, was not the first to make photograms, but his name is most closely linked to them through his "Rayographs." Fittingly enough, he discovered the process by accident. The amusing face in figure 27-21 was made according to the laws of chance by dropping a string, two strips of paper, and a few pieces of cotton onto the photographic paper, then coaxing them here and there before making the exposure. The resulting image is a witty creation that shows the playful, spontaneous side of Dada and Surrealism in contrast to Heartfield's grim satire.

THE CONSTRUCTIVISTS. Because the Russian Constructivists had a mechanistic view of society, they soon followed Dada's lead in using photograms and photomontages as a means to integrate industry and art, but for very different purposes. László Moholy-Nagy (1895–1946), a Hungarian teaching at the Bauhaus, was deeply affected by Constructivism. He successfully combined the best features of both approaches in his photographs. By removing the lens to make photograms, he transformed his camera from a reproductive into a productive instrument. In theory if not in practice, photography could now become a technological tool for fostering creativity in mass education.

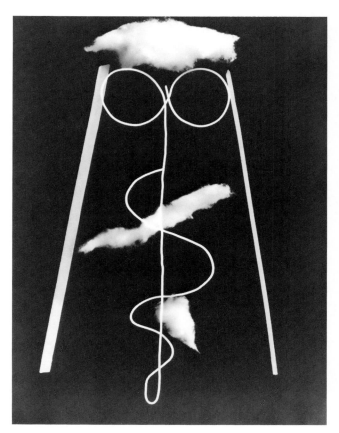

27-21. Man Ray. *Untitled* (Rayograph). 1928.
Gelatin-silver print, 15½ x 11⅝" (39.4 x 29.5 cm).
The Museum of Modern Art, New York

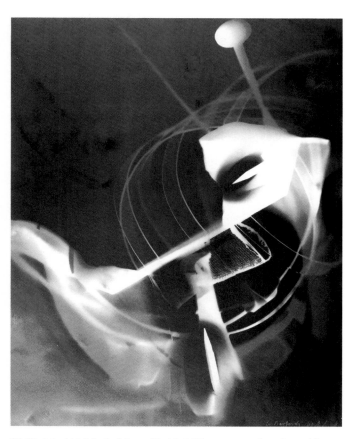

27-22. László Moholy-Nagy. *Untitled.* Photogram, silver-bromide
print, 19½ x 15¾" (49.5 x 40 cm). The Art Institute of Chicago

Like many of the Russian artists in the 1920s, Moholy-Nagy also saw light as the embodiment of dynamic energy in space. The effects created by the superimposition and interpenetration of forms in his photographs are fascinating (fig. 27-22). We feel transported in time and space to the edges of the universe. Here the artist's imagination gives shape to a play of cosmic forces that is no less astonishing than photographs from the Hubbell space telescope.

BERENICE ABBOTT. One of the main educational purposes of Moholy-Nagy's images was to extend sense perception in new ways. Similar goals have been achieved by taking pictures through microscopes and telescopes. Such photographs have helped to open our eyes to the invisibly small and the infinitely far. Wondrous scientific photographs were taken from 1939 to 1958 by Berenice Abbott (1898–1991), Man Ray's former pupil and assistant, to demonstrate the laws of physics (fig. 27-23). Like Marey's motion photographs of 50 years earlier (see fig. 23-50a and b), they are arresting images, literally and visually. Their formal perfection makes them aesthetically compelling and scientifically valid. As a result, they have proved to be even more educational than Moholy-Nagy's photograms.

PHOTOGRAPHY SINCE 1945
Abstraction

AARON SISKIND. Photography after World War II was marked by abstraction for nearly two decades, particularly in the United States. Aaron Siskind (1903–1991), a close friend of the Abstract Expressionist painters, recorded modern society's debris and decaying signs. Hidden in these details he discovered cipherlike figures (fig. 27-24) which are reminiscent of the ideographs from some forgotten civilization that are no longer intelligible to us.

MINOR WHITE. The work of Minor White (1908–1976) is close in spirit to that of the Abstract Expressionists. An associate of Adams and Weston, he was decisively influenced by Stieglitz's concept of the Equivalent. During his most productive period, from the mid-1950s to the mid-1960s, White used the alchemy of the darkroom to transform reality into a mystical metaphor. His *Ritual Branch (*fig. 27-25) evokes a primordial image. What it shows is not as important as what it stands for, but the meaning we sense must be there remains elusive.

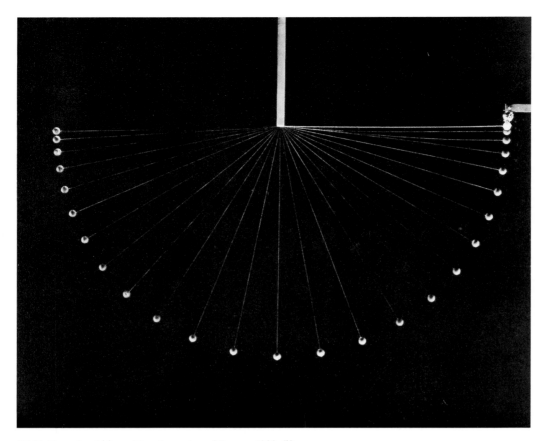

27-23. Berenice Abbott. *Transformation of Energy.* 1939–58

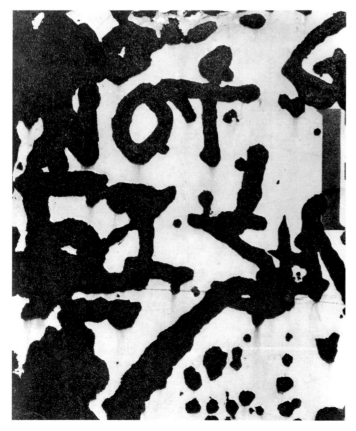

27-24. Aaron Siskind. *New York 2.* 1951.
Collection the artist

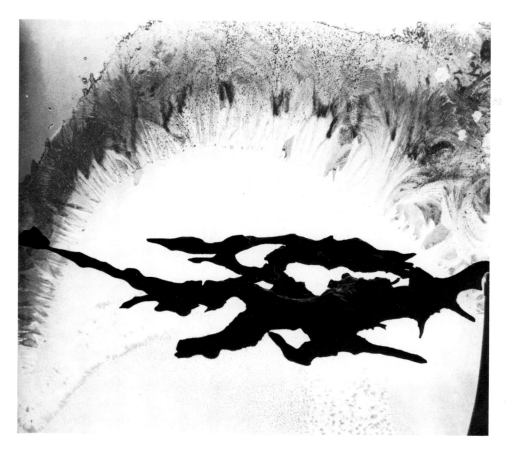

27-25. Minor White. *Ritual Branch.*
1958. Gelatin-silver print,
10⅜ x 10⅝" (26.4 x 27 cm).
THE INTERNATIONAL MUSEUM OF PHOTOGRAPHY AT
GEORGE EASTMAN HOUSE, ROCHESTER, NEW YORK

Documentary Photography

W. EUGENE SMITH. The continuing record of misery that photography provides has often been the means for making strong personal statements. W. Eugene Smith (1918–1978), the foremost photojournalist of the later twentieth century, was a cynic who commented on the human condition with "reasoned passion," as he put it. *Tomoko in Her Bath* (fig. 27-26), taken in 1971 in the Japanese fishing village of Minamata, shows a child crippled by mercury poisoning being bathed by her mother. Not simply the subject itself but Smith's treatment of it makes this an intensely moving work. The imagery lies deep in our heritage. The mother holding her child's body goes back to the theme of the German Gothic *Pietà* (see fig. 11-54), while the dramatic lighting and vivid realism recall a painting of another martyr in his bath, Jacques-Louis David's *The Death of Marat* (see fig. 21-3). But what engages our emotions above all and makes the photograph memorable is the infinite love conveyed by the mother's tender expression.

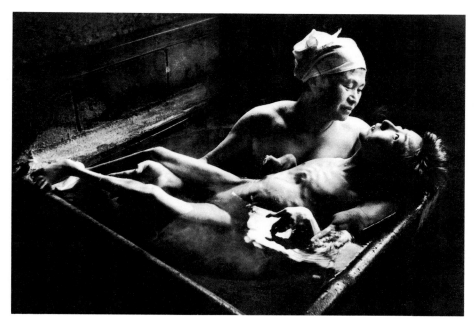

27-26. W. Eugene Smith.
Tomoko in Her Bath. December 1971.
Gelatin-silver print.
Aileen and W. Eugene Smith

ROBERT FRANK. The birth of a new form of straight photography in the United States was due largely to Robert Frank (b. 1924). His book *The Americans,* compiled from a cross-country journey made in 1955–56, created a sensation upon its publication in 1959. It expressed the same restlessness and alienation as *On the Road* by his traveling companion, the Beat poet Jack Kerouac, published in 1957. As this friendship suggests, words have an important role in Frank's photographs, which are as loaded in meaning as Demuth's *I Saw the Figure 5 in Gold* (fig. 24-34). Yet Frank's social point of view is often hidden behind a facade of bland neutrality. It is a shock when we recognize the ironic intent of *Santa Fe, New Mexico* (fig. 27-27). The gas pumps face the sign *SAVE* in the barren landscape like members of a religious cult vainly seeking salvation at a revival meeting. Frank, who was born in Switzerland and later turned to film, holds up an image of American culture that is as sterile as it is joyless. Even spiritual values, he tells us, become meaningless in the face of vulgar materialism.

Fantasy

Fantasy gradually reasserted itself on both sides of the Atlantic in the mid-1950s. Photographers first manipulated the camera for the sake of extreme visual effects by using special lenses and filters to alter appearances, sometimes virtually beyond recognition. Since about 1970, however, they have turned mainly to printing techniques, with results that are frequently even more startling.

BILL BRANDT. Manipulation of photography was pioneered by Bill Brandt (1904–1983). Although regarded as the quintessen-tial English photographer, he was born in Germany and did not settle in London until 1931. He decided on a career in photography during psychoanalysis and was apprenticed briefly to Man Ray. Brandt remained a Surrealist who altered visual reality in search of a deeper truth charged with mystery. His work was marked consistently by a literary, even theatrical, cast of mind that drew on the cinema for some of its effects. His early photodocumentaries were often staged as re-creations of personal experience to make social commentaries based on Victorian models. Brandt's fantasy images show a strikingly romantic imagination. Yet there is an oppressive anxiety implicit in his landscapes, portraits, and nudes. *London Child* (fig. 27-28) has the haunting mood of novels by the Brontë sisters (Charlotte, Emily, and Anne). At the same time, this is a classic dream image filled with troubling psychological overtones. The spatial dislocation, worthy of De Chirico, suggests a person who is alienated from both herself and the world.

JERRY UELSMANN. The American Jerry Uelsmann (b. 1934), a recent leader of this movement, was inspired by Oscar Rejlander's multiple-negative photographs, as well as by Stieglitz's Equivalents. While Uelsmann's work also has a playful side, for the most part he involuntarily expresses archetypal images from deep within the subconscious. The nude lying within the soil in *Untitled* (fig. 27-29) identifies the fertility of nature, signified by the tree of life, with woman as earth goddess. The photograph also conveys a dream in which the psyche retreats into the womblike sanctuary of primal nature. The print is utterly convincing because each part is a faithful record. It is the astonishing juxtaposition of unrelated elements that transforms the image into a new reality.

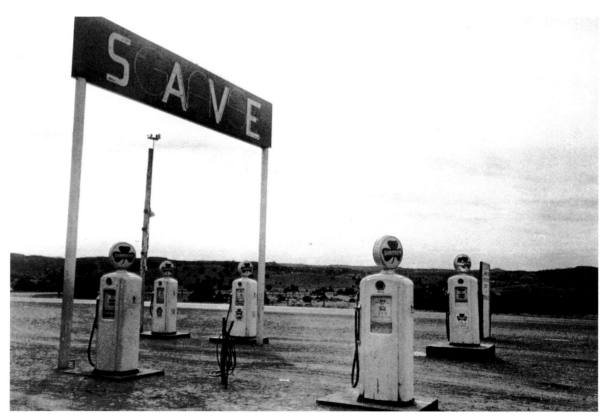

27-27. Robert Frank. *Santa Fe, New Mexico.* 1955–56. Gelatin-silver print.
COLLECTION PACEWILDENSTEIN GALLERY, NEW YORK

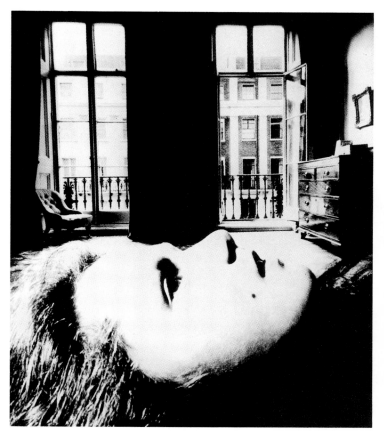

27-28. Bill Brandt. *London Child.* 1955
COPYRIGHT MRS. NOYA BRANDT

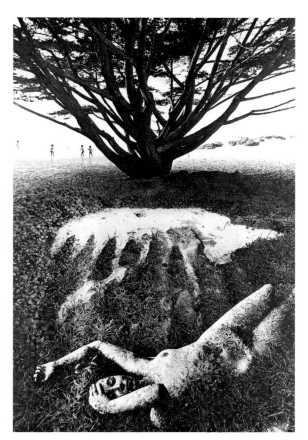

27-29. Jerry Uelsmann. *Untitled.* c. 1972.
Collection the artist

Uelsmann once participated in one of Minor White's classes, and their photographs are not as far removed visually or expressively from each other as they might seem. The main difference lies in their approach to the Equivalent as a means of achieving a poetical inner truth. White, like Stieglitz, recognizes his symbols in images received from nature. Uelsmann, however, creates his symbols from his imagination in the dark room. [See Primary Sources, no. 113, page 948.] Paradoxically, it is Uelsmann's imagery, not *Ritual Branch,* that is instantly recognizable. But like the paintings of Magritte (see fig. 24-42) that inspired him, it refuses to yield a clear meaning.

Artists As Photographers

DAVID HOCKNEY. The most recent demonstrations of photography's power to extend our vision have come, fittingly enough, from artists. The photographic collages that the English painter David Hockney (b. 1937) began making in 1982 are like revelations. They overcome the traditional limitations of a unified image, fixed in time and place, by closely approximating how we actually see. In *Gregory Watching the Snow Fall, Kyoto, Feb. 21, 1983* (fig. 27-30), each frame is similar to a movement of the eye: it contains a piece of visual data that must be stored in our memory and synthesized by the brain. Just as we process only essential information, so there are gaps in the matrix of the image, which becomes more fragmentary toward its edges, though without the loss of sharpness experienced in vision itself.

The collage, with its unusual shape, is a masterpiece of design. The scene appears to bow oddly as it comes toward us. This ebb and flow is more than simply the result of optical physics. In the perceptual process, space and its corollary, time, are not linear but fluid. Hockney includes his own feet as reference points to establish our position clearly. As a result, he helps us to realize that vision is less a matter of looking outward than an egocentric act that defines the viewer's visual and psychological relationship to the surrounding world. Hockney has recorded his friend several times to suggest his reactions to the serene landscape outside the door.

Hockney's picture shows a clear awareness of earlier twentieth-century art. It combines the faceted views of Picasso (see fig. 24-13) and the sequential action of Duchamp (see fig. 24-22) with the dynamic energy of Popova (see fig. 24-18). *Gregory Watching the Snow Fall* is nonetheless a distinctly contemporary work, for it also incorporates the fascinating effects of Photorealism and the illusionistic potential of Op Art. Hockney later explored the implications of these photo collages, such as continuous narrative. Some of his photographs have even shown an object or scene simultaneously from multiple vantage points to let us see it completely for the first time.

JOANNE LEONARD. Contemporary photographers have often turned to fantasy as autobiographical expression. Both the image and the title of *Romanticism Is Ultimately Fatal* (fig. 27-31) by Joanne Leonard (b. 1940) suggest a meaning that is personal in its reference: it was made during the breakup of her marriage.

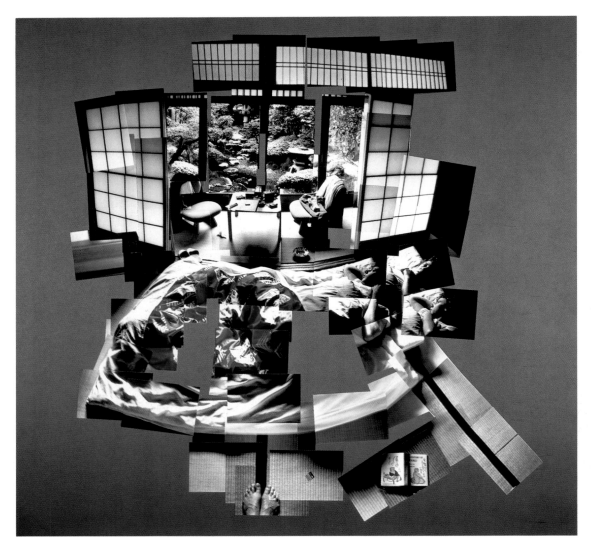

27-30. David
Hockney. *Gregory
Watching the Snow
Fall, Kyoto,
Feb. 21, 1983.* 1983.
Photographic collage,
43½ x 46½"
(110.5 x 118 cm).
Collection the artist

© 1983 DAVID HOCKNEY

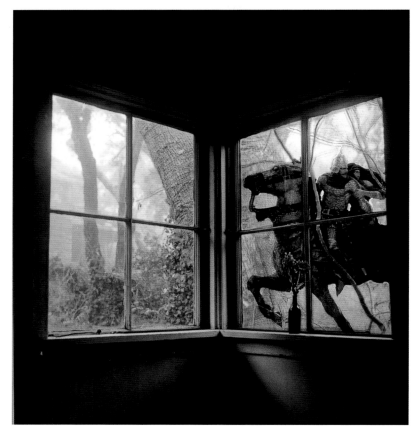

27-31. Joanne Leonard.
Romanticism Is Ultimately Fatal,
from *Dreams and Nightmares.* 1982.
Positive transparency selectively opaqued
with collage, 9¾ x 9¼" (24.8 x 23.5 cm).
Collection M. Neri, Benicia, California

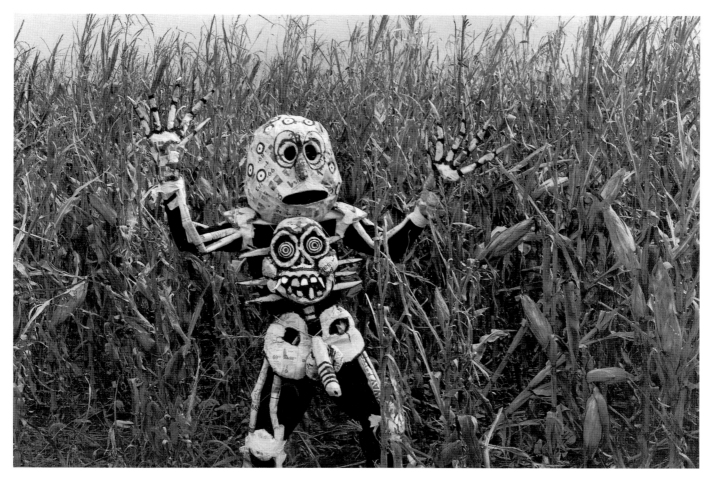

27-32. David Wojnarowicz. *Death in the Cornfield.* 1990. Silver print, 26 x 38" (66 x 96.5 cm)
COURTESY OF P.P.O.W. GALLERY, NEW YORK

We will recognize in this disturbing vision the tortured emotions of Fuseli's *The Nightmare* (see fig. 21-43). The clarity of the presentation turns the phantom at the window into a real and terrifying personification of despair. This is no romantic knight in shining armor, but a grim reaper whose ancestors can be found in Dürer's woodcut *The Four Horsemen of the Apocalypse* (see fig. 16-5).

DAVID WOJNAROWICZ. Even more shocking is *Death in the Cornfield* (fig. 27-32) by David Wojnarowicz (1954–1992). Gifted with a singularly bizarre imagination, he was obsessed with the horrific, which is found throughout his work, both artistic and literary. At the time of this photograph, Wojnarowicz was already suffering from AIDS, which claimed his life two years later. Of the countless images devoted to this dread disease by painters and photographers, none so fully captures its nightmarish terror. The macabre costume, made by Wojnarowicz himself, makes this grim reaper an awesome demon of death from some primitive tribal ritual that appears out of nature as if by magic. Like Munch's *The Scream* (fig. 23-21), here is an expression of irrational fear so gripping in its power as to lift personal suffering to a universal plane. It serves as an unforgettable reminder of how many people, not just in the art world, have been touched by the loss of family members, cherished friends, and colleagues to AIDS.

THE GREAT AGE OF PHOTOGRAPHY. The photographs we have seen since the rise of Romanticism form the great age of photography. These images are each, in their own way, "classics." What follows is the breakdown of this tradition in Postmodernism, which may be called the Age of Rephotography, because the image is seldom, if ever, original, but lifted from another source and placed in a new context to convey a radical social or political message. The relationship between form and content of traditional art hardly seems to exist, although it is there if one looks hard enough. This new form challenges our preconceptions not only about art but also about the world around us.

CHAPTER TWENTY-EIGHT
Postmodernism

Postmodernism

We began Part Four with a discussion of modernism. It is appropriate that we end, for now, with its opposite: postmodernism. We live in the "postmodern" era. How can that be, if modern is what is happening today? The term itself suggests the peculiar nature of postmodernism, which seeks out incongruity. To resolve this contradiction, we must understand modern in a dual sense: modernity and modernism. Postmodernism is a trend that not only supersedes modernism; it is also opposed to the world order as it exists today and to the values that created it.

What is postmodernism and when did it begin? Generally speaking, postmodernism is characterized by a total skepticism that rejects modernism as an ideal defining twentieth-century culture. In challenging tradition, however, it deliberately refuses to provide a new meaning or impose a different order in its place. Postmodernism represents a generation consciously *not* in search of its identity. Hence it is not a unified movement at all, but a loose collection of tendencies that reflect a new sensibility. Taken together, these pieces provide a jigsaw puzzle of our times. Each country has a somewhat different outlook and vocabulary; nevertheless all may be considered forms of postmodernism. We must therefore paint a broad picture, one that will provide us with a general idea of postmodernism's unique character. Our treatment of Postmodern art is likewise intended to be suggestive in discussing representative examples, while admittedly omitting much that is of interest. The following discussion is intended to characterize the nature of the debate, which is often bitter.

As the prefix *post* suggests, our world is in a state of transition—without telling us where we will land. Although the term *postmodern* was coined by a historian in the late 1940s to denote a late stage of the civilization initiated by the Renaissance, it has been used mainly by literary critics since the mid-1960s, a significant fact in itself. We may indeed trace the first postmodern symptoms back to that time. However, in hindsight they appear to have been mostly a late phase of modernism, without making a decisive break from the mainstream of the twentieth century.

What is the difference between modernism and postmodernism? Postmodernism springs from post-industrial society, which is passing rapidly into the Information Age (the so-called Third Wave). According to postmodern theorists, the political, economic, and social structures that have governed the Western world since the end of World War II are either changing, undergoing attack from within, or breaking down altogether, ironically at the same time as the collapse of Communism in eastern Europe. This institutional erosion has resulted in a corresponding spiritual crisis that reflects the chaos of people's lives.

Postmodernism is a product of the disillusion and alienation afflicting the middle class. At the same time, bourgeois culture has exhausted its possibilities by absorbing its old enemy, the avant-garde, whose mission was ended by its very success. During the 1950s the media made the avant-garde so popular that the middle class accepted it and began to hunger for ceaseless change for its own sake. By the following decade, modernism was reduced to a "capitalist" mode of expression by large corporations, which adopted it not just in architecture but in the painting and sculpture that decorate it.

Postmodernism celebrates the death of modernism, which it regards as not only arrogant in its claim to universality but also as responsible for the evils of contemporary civilization. Democracy, based on Enlightenment values, is seen as a force of oppression to spread the West's dominance around the world. In common with most earlier avant-garde movements (including existentialism), postmodernism is antagonistic to humanism, which it dismisses as bourgeois. Reason, with its hierarchies of thought, is abandoned in order to liberate people from the established order. This rejection opens the way for nontraditional approaches, especially those from the Third World, that emphasize emotion, intuition, fantasy, contemplation, mysticism, and even magic. In this view, Western science is no better than any other system, since it has failed to solve today's problems. And because scientific reality does not conform to human experience, it is irrelevant to daily life.

Truth is rejected as neither possible nor desirable on the grounds that it is used by its creators for their own power ends. Subjective and conflicting interpretations are all that can be offered, and these may vary freely according to the context. Since no set of values can have more validity than any other, everything becomes relative. Deprived of traditional guidelines, the postmodernist drifts aimlessly in a sea without meaning or reality. To the extent that the world makes any sense, it is at the local level, where the limited scale makes understanding possible in human terms.

The only escape from an existence in which nothing has inherent worth is inaction, hedonism, or spirituality. Spirituality is rarely an option, however, since religions impose their own authority and self-discipline. For that reason, only the most extreme forms of mysticism, lacking all rational control, are acceptable. Postmodern people are thus fated to become pleasure-seeking narcissists lacking any strong identity, purpose, or attachments. Cynical and amoral, they live for the moment, without any concern for larger issues, which are imponderables in the first place. Rather than vices, however, these traits are considered virtues. They allow postmodernists a flexible approach to life that enables them to pursue new modes of existence, free from all restraints or authority.

In the brave new world of postmodernism, the individual is no longer anchored in time or space. Both have been made obsolete in life as they have been in science. They are beyond normal human comprehension and are based on assumptions subject to doubt. Traditional definitions of time and space, moreover, were founded on hierarchies of thought that served the purposes of colonialism. However, the new "hyper-space" created by global communication makes it impossible to position oneself within customary boundaries.

Just as time and space have lost all meaning, so has history. The view of history as progressive was also tied to the established power centers of the capitalist system and used as a tool to oppress the Third World. Furthermore, its basic assumption is wrong. If linear logic is inherently invalid, there can be no linear history either. Since conventional knowledge and structures are questionable, nothing can be learned from history in the first place, and its "facts" are therefore of little interest.

Postmodernism makes no attempt to provide new answers to replace the old certitudes it destroys. It instead substitutes pluralism in the name of multicultural diversity. Pluralism leads inevitably to eclecticism in the arts, with which it is virtually interchangeable, since no one aesthetic is better than any other. Not only are the two functions of each other, they become ends in themselves.

By the same token, postmodernism does not try to make the world a better place. In its resolute antimodernism, it is socially and politically ambivalent at best, self-contradictory at worst. Its operating principle is anarchism. But although it is extremely liberal in its outlook—witness the rise of "political correctness" in the United States and Europe—to classical Marxists it is simply a decadent late phase of capitalism, while to conservatives it goes against traditional values. To the extent that it does offer an alternative, postmodernism embraces any new doctrine as superior to the one it seeks to displace. A large number of postmodernists can nevertheless be described as neo-Marxists, despite the fall of nearly all Communist regimes around the world. Radical politics is, in reality, a game played for its own sake. In the end, postmodernism remains essentially a form of cultural activism motivated by intellectual theory, not political causes. It is ill-suited to political action, because it lacks both a coherent agenda and practical plan.

Postmodernism has all the classic earmarks of an avant-garde, despite the fact that it vigorously—and disingenuously—denies such a connection. Its determined opposition to modernity makes it the latest foe of conventional authority, which it is dedicated to overthrowing. Like all avant-gardes, postmodernism is attacked as a "degenerate" movement that fosters an atmosphere of crisis in order to sustain and justify itself. In character it comes closest to Dada and Surrealism, but it lacks their high-pitched hysteria. Its anti-elitism is simply another means of attacking the cultural establishment, which it wishes to replace. The relativism and anarchism of postmodernism are openly subversive. Its nihilism reflects the prevailing skepticism of the late twentieth century, when very little was considered to have any significance or worth.

Postmodernism might well take its credo from Edgar Allan Poe:

All that we see or seem
Is but a dream within a dream.

Such a position has its problems. A sharp blow to the solar plexus immediately gives lie to the belief of a dualism between the mind and the body. As we examine it, we realize that the postmodernist rejection of reality is a philosophical assumption, just as its rejection of truth is a value judgment. Even if we grant that everything is ultimately unknowable, reality must nonetheless be capable of being understood in a functional sense; otherwise people could not survive. Postmodernism, then, is comparable to that higher understanding sought by mystics, for whom reason is insufficient.

Because it has so many meanings, postmodernism itself becomes a meaningless term, posing the kind of hopeless double-bind that it delights in. In fact, postmodernism as a whole is riddled with contradictions. But if nothing is valid, then the values it often espouses—feminism, pluralism, and the like—must be false as well. Seen in this light, postmodernism is a sterile philosophy that reflects the impotence of intellectuals to act.

In the end, however, postmodernism cannot escape the very laws of history it claims to deny. As a parody of modernity, it has its parallels—indeed, its origins—in the avant-garde of a hundred years ago. The same "decadence" and nihilism can be found toward the end of the nineteenth century in the Symbolist movement, with its apocalyptic vision of despair. Like pluralism, for example, Gauguin's quest for the spiritual assumed the superiority of "alternative" knowledge systems and asserted a belief in magic, which was widely shared by other Symbolists. Postmodernists espouse the same destructive values as the late nineteenth-century German philosopher Friedrich Nietzsche, who was one of the principal sources of the avant-garde. Although postmodernism offers nothing in exchange, people will undoubtedly devise a new system to replace the old one that it strives to overturn.

SEMIOTICS AND DECONSTRUCTION. The Information Age is obsessed with meaning and with the lack of it. Like the intellectual disciplines, nearly all branches of culture have come under the spell of semiotics—the study of signs—also known as semiology (though a distinction is sometimes made between the two). Semiotics is part of philosophy, linguistics, science, sociology, anthropology, communications, psychology, art, literature, cinema: any area of human activity that involves symbols. (There are other classes of signs that are the subject of semiotic inquiry as well.) Semiotics in turn has been undermined from within by deconstruction, which is undoubtedly the most powerful attack mounted to date by postmodernism. As the term suggests, deconstruction is destructive, not constructive. It tears a text apart by using the text against itself, until the text finally "deconstructs" itself. For those interested in exploring the issues further, we have supplied a brief overview in the Postscript at the end of this chapter. For our purposes it is not the theories that count, no matter how interesting they may be, but their effect on art.

POSTMODERN ART

We are, in a sense, the new Victorians. More than a century ago, Impressionism underwent a similar crisis, from which Post-Impressionism emerged as the direction for the next 20 years. Behind its complex rhetoric, postmodernism can be seen as a strategy for sorting through the past while making a decisive break with it that will allow new possibilities to emerge. Having received a rich heritage, artists are faced with a wide variety of alternatives. The principal feature of the new art is eclecticism. Another indication of the state of flux is the reemergence of many traditional European and regional American art centers.

Art since 1980 has been called Postmodern, but not all of it fits under this umbrella. We shall find that the participation of the visual arts in the postmodern adventure has varied greatly and taken some surprising turns. The traditional mediums of painting and sculpture have played a secondary role. They are closely identified with the modernist tradition and are therefore rejected as tools of the ruling class. Meanwhile, nontraditional forms, such as installations, performance and photography, have come to the forefront and have become highly politicized in the process.

Much of the basis for Postmodern art can be traced back to Conceptualism, which led the initial attack on modernism (see page 893). Indeed, it has been argued that the beginnings of Postmodernism can be dated to the rise of Conceptualism in the mid-1960s. The two, however, are products of two distinctly different generations. Furthermore, Conceptualism was itself derived from Dada, which has provided an "antimodern" alternative since early in the twentieth century. In the context of the 1960s, it was simply part of that ongoing dialogue, in which Pop Art also participated. That date, moreover, seems too early for the onset of what is fundamentally a late-twentieth-century phenomenon.

Installations and performance art have been around since the 1960s as well. What has changed is the content of these art forms as part of a larger shift in viewpoint. Focused as it was on matters of art, early Conceptualism seems almost innocent in hindsight. Postmodernists, in contrast, attack modern art as part of a larger offensive against contemporary society. They are far more issue-oriented than their predecessors, and their work cuts across a much wider range of concerns than ever before.

The principal manifestation of Postmodernism is appropriation, which looks back self-consciously to earlier art. It does so both by imitating previous styles and by taking over specific motifs or even entire images. Artists, of course, have always borrowed from tradition, but rarely so systematically as now. Such plundering is nearly always a sign of deepening cultural crisis, suggesting bankruptcy. (The same thing has been going on for some time in popular culture, with its endless "retro" revivals.) Since it is not tied to any system, Postmodernism is free to adopt earlier imagery and to alter its meaning radically by placing it in a new context. The traditional importance assigned to the artist and object is furthermore de-emphasized in this approach, which stresses content and process over aesthetics. The other chief characteristic of postmodernism is the merging of art forms. Thus there is no longer a clear difference between painting, sculpture, and photography, and we maintain the distinctions mostly as a matter of convenience.

Although it has an anti-intellectual side, Postmodernism is preoccupied with theory. As a result, art (and, along with it, art history) has become theory-bound. Despite a growing body of writing and criticism, however, it lags far behind literature and poetry in developing a postmodern approach. Compared to language, the visual arts are traditionally poor vehicles for theory. Perhaps they have become so word-oriented of late in an attempt to keep up with other disciplines.

Postmodernism has a fatal flaw. It has produced little art that is memorable—it is merely "symptomatic" of our age. But for that very reason it is worthy of our interest. Fittingly enough, the most devastating critique of postmodernism comes from that apostle of modernism, Charles Baudelaire:

Eclecticism has at all periods and places held itself superior to past doctrines because, coming last on to the scene, it finds the remotest horizons already open to it; but this impartiality only goes to prove the impotence of the eclectics. People who are so lavish with their time for reflection are not complete men: they lack the element of passion. No matter how clever he may be, an eclectic is but a feeble man; for he is a man without love. Therefore he has no ideal . . . ; neither star nor compass. Doubt has led certain artists to beg the aid of all the other arts. Experiment with contradictory means, the encroachment of one art upon another, the importation of poetry, wit, and sentiment into painting—all these modern miseries are vices peculiar to the eclectics.

ARCHITECTURE

We begin with architecture, which not only initiated the postmodern dialogue in the arts but also puts the issues literally in concrete form.

Postmodernism

Postmodernism in art was first coined to denote an eclectic mode of architecture that arose around 1980. Because it is a style, we shall capitalize it to distinguish it from the larger phenomenon of postmodernism, to which it is closely related. As the term implies, Postmodernism represents a broad rejection of mainstream twentieth-century architecture. Although it uses the same construction techniques, *Postmodernism* rejects not only the vocabulary of Gropius and his followers, but also the social and ethical ideals implicit in their lucid proportions. Looking at the Seagram Build-

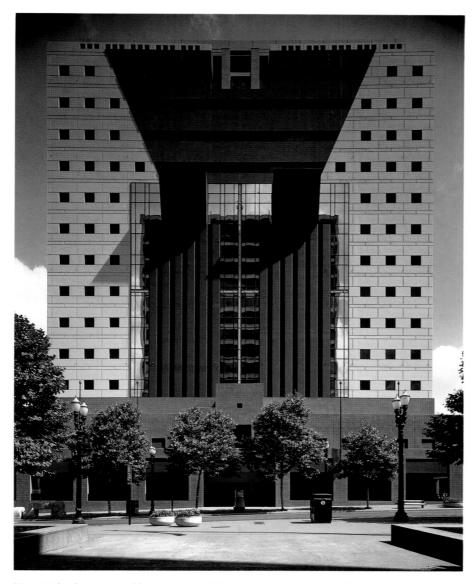

28-1. Michael Graves. Public Services Building, Portland, Oregon. 1980–82

ing (see fig. 26-28), we can well understand why. As a statement, it is so overwhelming in its authority that it prohibits deviation and is so cold that it lacks appeal. The Postmodernist critique was, then, essentially correct. In its search for universal ideals, the International Style failed to communicate with people, who neither understood nor liked it. Postmodernism is an attempt to reinvest architecture with the human meaning so clearly absent from High Modernism. It does so by returning to premodernist architecture.

The chief means of introducing greater expressiveness has been to appropriate elements from historical styles rich with association. All traditions are assumed to have equal validity, so that they can be combined at will. In the process, the compilation itself becomes a conscious parody characterized by ironic wit. This eclectic historicism is nevertheless highly selective in its sources. They are restricted mainly to various forms of classicism (notably Palladianism) and some of the more exotic strains of Art Deco, which, as we have seen (page 908), provided a genuine alternative to modernism during the 1920s and 1930s. Architects have repeatedly searched the past for fresh ideas. What counts is the originality of the final result.

VENTURI AND BROWN. The immediate antecedents of Postmodernism can be found in the work of Robert Venturi (b. 1925) and his wife, Denise Scott Brown (b. 1931). They realized that architecture in America had become filled with pictorial and commercial imagery. As a result, they advocated overturning the modernist credo of "form follows function" by divorcing the symbolic quality of a facade from the building's purpose and structure. To accomplish that end, they created an architecture of banality. Its triteness was proclaimed by ironic paraphrases of historical clichés from both the recent and distant past. Although few architects followed their lead in design, the theories of Venturi and Brown were important for opening the debate that led to Postmodernism.

MICHAEL GRAVES. The Public Services Building in Portland, Oregon (fig. 28-1), by Michael Graves (b. 1934) is a characteristic example of Postmodernism. [See Primary Sources, no. 103, pages 978–79.] Elevated on a pedestal, it mixes classical, Egyptian, and assorted other motifs in a whimsical building-block paraphrase of Art Deco, which shared an equal disregard for historical propriety.

In this way, Graves relieves the building of the monotony imposed by the tyranny of the cube that afflicts so much modern architecture. Although the lavish sculptural decoration was never added, the exterior has a surprising warmth that continues inside. At first glance, it is tempting to dismiss the Public Services Building as mere historicism. To do so, however, ignores the fact that no earlier structure looks at all like it. What holds this historical mix together is the architect's style. It is based on a mastery of abstraction that is as systematic and personal as Mondrian's. Indeed, Graves was a skilled Late Modernist who first earned recognition in 1969 at the same exhibition held by the Museum of Modern Art in New York that showcased Richard Meier (see page 916).

Today Postmodern buildings are found everywhere. They are instantly recognizable by their reliance on keyhole arches, round "Palladian" windows, and other relics from the architectural past. They are also marked by their luxuriance. Postmodernism may be characterized as architecture for the rich that has since been translated downward to the middle class. Its aura of wealth suggests the egocentricity and hedonism that spawned the "me" generation of the 1980s, one of the most prosperous and extravagant decades in recent history. Nevertheless, the retrospective eclecticism of Postmodernism soon became dated through the repetitious quotation of standard devices that were reduced to self-parodies lacking both wit and purpose. In a larger sense, however, this quick passage reflects the restless quest for novelty and, more important, a new modernism that has yet to emerge to replace the old.

SITE. In its playfulness and complexity Postmodernism has rightly been compared to Mannerist architecture, which added a note of decadence to the classical vocabulary inherited from the Renaissance. Both also share an element of self-conscious burlesque. Parody reaches a climax in the designs by SITE Inc. for Best Stores. One store in a Houston mall (fig. 28-2), for example, looks for all the world to be crumbling into ruins (compare fig. 14-22). This witty takeoff on standard commercial architecture is enhanced by the bleakness of the location itself.

The differences are equally profound, however. Postmodernism arises out of the general sense of disillusionment that afflicts our age and prevents the architect from seeing either the past or the present with innocent eyes. Such a claim might well be made of Mannerist architecture, of course. But because architects today must design for different "taste-cultures," the eclecticism of Postmodernism is intended as a reflection of our "social and metaphysical reality." Historicism, then, is part of the new pluralism, which can even include a caricature of modernism itself. Such parodies also change old meanings into new ones through "double-coding," which combines modernist techniques and traditional styles to communicate on a new plane with the public and architects alike. The result is a content that is entirely up-to-date, despite the apparent familiarity of its hybrid style.

JAMES STIRLING. Postmodernists criticize Late Modernism for its modernist commitment to the "tradition of the new" and its consequent lack of integrity in invention and usage. Moreover, they maintain, Late Modernism lacks both pluralism and a complex relation to the past, so that it fails to transform meaning. We may test this proposition for ourselves by comparing the Pompidou Center (see fig. 26-45) with the Neue Staatsgalerie in Stuttgart (fig. 28-3), which was immediately recognized as a classic example of Postmodernism. The latter has the grandiose scale befitting a "palace" of the arts, but instead of the monolithic cube of the Pompidou Center, English architect James Stirling

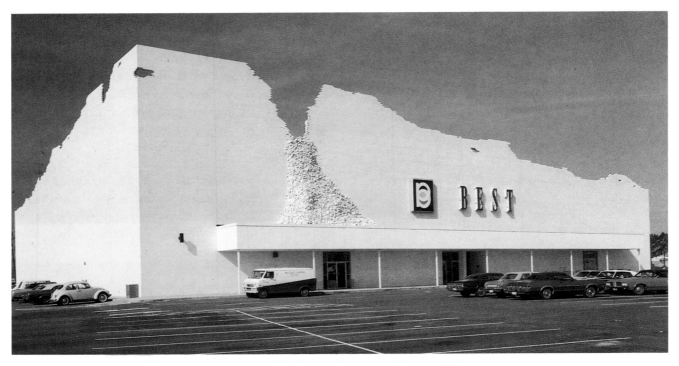

28-2. SITE Projects, Inc., with Maple-Jones Associates. Best Stores Showroom, Houston. 1975

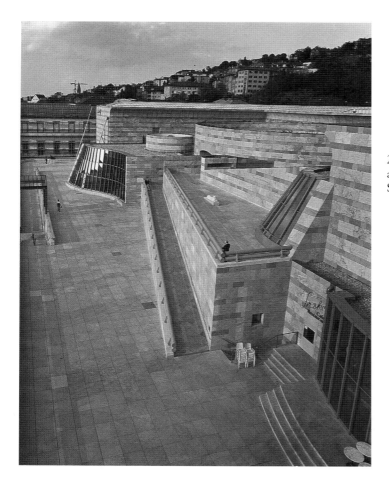

28-3. James Stirling, Michael Wilford and Associates. Neue Staatsgalerie, Stuttgart, Germany. Completed 1984

(1926–1992) incorporates a greater variety of shapes within more complex spatial relationships. There is also an openly decorative quality that will remind us, however indirectly, of Garnier's Paris Opéra (see fig. 21-77). The similarity does not stop there. Stirling has likewise resorted to a form of historicism through paraphrase that is far more subtle than Garnier's opulent revivalism, but no less self-conscious. The prim Neoclassical masonry facade, for example, is punctured by a narrow arched window recalling Italian Renaissance forms (compare fig. 12-28) and by a rusticated portal that has a distinctly Mannerist look. At the same time, there is an exaggerated quoting of modernism through the use of such "high-tech" materials as painted metal (compare fig. 26-11).

This eclecticism is more than a veneer—it lies at the heart of the building's success. The site, centering on a circular sculpture court, is designed along the lines of ancient temple complexes from Egypt through Rome, complete with a monumental entrance stairway. This plan enables Stirling to solve a wide range of practical problems with ingenuity and to provide a stream of changing views that fascinate and delight the visitor. The results have been compared to the Altes Museum of Karl Friedrich Schinkel (see fig. 21-66), among the most classical structures of the nineteenth century. Seen in this light, the Pompidou Center is actually a far more radical building!

Deconstructivism

Although it claims to deal with meaning, in the end Postmodernist historicism addresses mainly the decorative veneer of the International Style. Spurred by more revolutionary theories, Deconstructivism, another tendency that began to gather momentum about 1980, goes much further in challenging its substance. The term *Deconstructivism* combines *Constructivism* and *deconstruction*. Strictly speaking, there can be no architecture of deconstruction, because building puts things together instead of taking them apart. Deconstructivism nevertheless follows similar principles and is symptomatic of postmodernism as a whole. It dismembers modern architecture, then reassembles it again in new ways.

Like Postmodernism, it does so through appropriation. Deconstructivism returns to one of the earliest sources of modernism: the Russian avant-garde. The Russian experiment in architecture proved short-lived, and few of its ideas ever made it beyond the laboratory stage. However, recent architects have been inspired anew by the bold sculpture of the Constructivists and the graphic designs of the Suprematists. They seek to violate the integrity of modern architecture by subverting its internal logic, which the Russians themselves did little to undermine. Nevertheless, Deconstructivism does not abandon modern architecture and its principles altogether, and remains an architecture of the possible

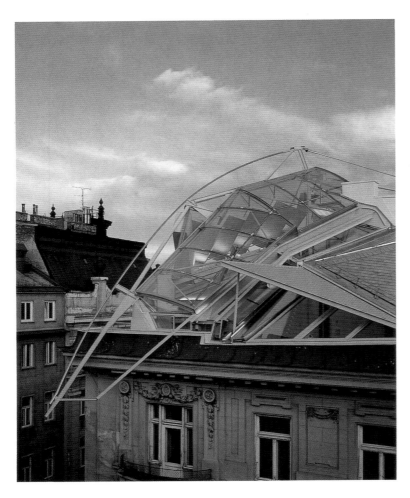

28-4. Coop Himmelblau. Roof Conversion Project, Vienna. 1983–88

based on structural engineering. Although it claims Michelangelo, Bernini, and Guarini as its ancestors, Deconstructivism goes far beyond anything that can be found in earlier architecture. We will find little common ground among its practitioners. The main devices they have in common are superimpositions of clashing systems or layers of space, and distortions from within that subvert the normal vocabulary and purposes of modern architecture.

COOP HIMMELBLAU. Although Deconstructivist designs have won major awards, their experimental approach and ambitious scale initially discouraged actual construction. The most advanced designs to get off the drawing board first were generally modest affairs, but no less exciting for that fact. The roof conversion for a Viennese lawyer's office by Coop Himmelblau (fig. 28-4) has been well described as "a writhing, disruptive animal breaking through the corner." The internal disturbances are incorporated into the structure itself, "as if some kind of parasite has infected the form and distorted it from the inside." This effect is closely related to how deconstruction uses language.

BEHNISCH AND PARTNER. An equally brilliant example is the Hysolar Research Institute at the University of Stuttgart (fig. 28-5) by the firm of Behnisch and Partner. The hall between the laboratory wings both reflects and parodies the scientific work being carried on. The materials suggest the high-tech purpose of the project, which is to investigate energy based on hydrogen

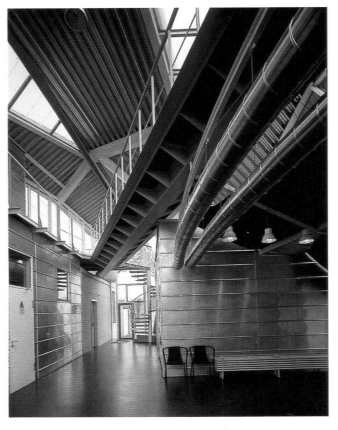

28-5. Behnisch and Partner. Hall between Laboratory Wings, Hysolar Research Institute, University of Stuttgart. 1987

produced by solar power. In turn, the free-flowing passage indicates the collaborative exchange of ideas. Yet the sensation produced by the collision of twisted forms is like careening down a roller coaster. Nothing, it seems, works the way it should in the orderly world of modern science!

BERNARD TSCHUMI. One of the first architects to be influenced by deconstruction was Bernard Tschumi (b. 1944). The most complete embodiment of his Deconstructivism is the Parc de La Villette in Paris, for which the founder of deconstruction, Jacques Derrida (b. 1930; see Postscript), later wrote an essay in the brochure explaining the project. The park had to incorporate a variety of functions (workshop, baths, gymnasium, playground, concert facilities), as well as other parks and buildings already on the site. Tschumi's design is directly based on this fact. It presents an intelligent solution to what could have been a hopelessly complex problem that would have overwhelmed any traditional approach.

To describe the Parc de La Villette, we must resort to the coded terminology of Deconstructivism itself. The architect began by laying out the grounds in a simple abstract grid to provide a strong, yet flexible conceptual framework for change, improvisation, and substitution. He then subverted it by superimposing two other grid systems on it, so as to prevent any dominant hierarchy or clear relation between the program and the solution. This multiple grid is deliberately antifunctional, anticontextual, and infinite. (In principle, it could be extended in any direction indefinitely.) Tschumi creates highly unorthodox relationships through decentralization, fragmentation, combination, and superimposition of elements, so that the architecture appears to serve no purpose. He further supplants form, function, and structure with contiguity, substitution, and permutation. To undermine the traditional rules of composition, hierarchy, and order, he uses crossprogramming (using space for a different purpose than intended), transprogramming (combining two incompatible programs and spaces), and disprogramming (combining two programs to create a new one from their contradictions). The functions are dispersed through a series of buildings *(folies)* whose components, appearance, and uses are interchangeable. The play between free and rigid form leads to ambiguity, disorder, impurity, imperfection. The result denies any inherent meaning to the forms, structure, or organization.

What does all this theory have to do with the actual experience? Surprisingly little. The ensemble is meant to induce a sense of disassociation, both within and between its elements. This disjointedness conveys an unstable programmatic madness *(folie)* through a form of cinematic montage inspired by the films of the Russian Sergei Eisenstein (1898–1948) and others. However, the visitor is hardly aware of this effect. On the contrary, the system creates an order and rhythm of its own, whether Tschumi intended it or not. We are left only with a feeling of enchantment, which suggests the more playful meaning of *folie,* not just madness.

The folies themselves resemble large-scale sculptures extended almost to the breaking point (fig. 28-6). Yet the tension between the reality of the built structures and their "impossibility" results in an architecture of rare vitality. It is especially fitting that two of the most captivating folies are for use by children. Although the architect insists that he was not expressing himself, this effect is perhaps the ultimate test of the park's success. Tschumi himself acknowledges the fact indirectly by speaking of affirmative deconstruction—a self-contradiction if ever there was one!

We may yet see one Deconstructivist deconstructing the work of another Deconstructivist. Peter Eisenman (b. 1932) has designed a second garden for the Parc de La Villette that poses what might be called "the battle of the grids": Tschumi's versus Eisenman's version of the Deconstructivist point grid, which the latter claims to have discovered first. Eisenman's garden was designed with Derrida's collaboration from the start. To pull it off, Eisenman added new layers of ever more complex rhetoric (called tropes in the current parlance) to justify what amounts to skillful one-upmanship. The question is whether the results justify the dense jargon.

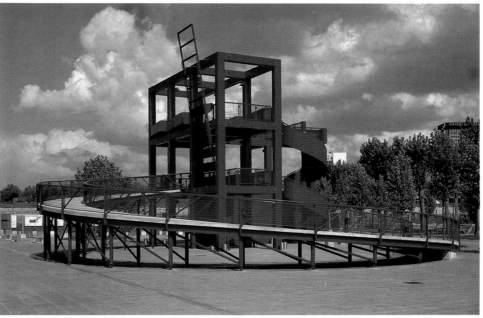

28-6. Bernard Tschumi Architects. Folie P6, Parc de La Villette, Paris. 1983

POSTMODERNISM VS. DECONSTRUCTIVISM. Try as their disciples might to deny it, Postmodernism and Deconstructivism are really two sides of the same postmodernist coin, which has pushed modern architecture to its limits. As a style, Postmodernism challenges it from the outside, while Deconstructivism as an approach corrupts it from within. It is a measure of how firmly postmodern thinking had taken hold of contemporary architecture that in 1988 Philip Johnson—who helped to design the interior of the Seagram Building (see fig. 26-28) and was himself the architect of one of the most controversial Postmodern buildings (the AT&T Building in New York)—declared modern architecture dead and mounted an exhibition of Tschumi, Eisenman, and other Deconstructivists. This sort of re-evaluation has gone on before. Postmodernism is a transition much like Art Nouveau at the turn of the century, which provided part of the foundation for modern architecture. It is a necessary part of the process that will redefine architecture as we have come to know it.

ARCHITECTURE AFTER POSTMODERNISM: WHAT'S NEXT

If Postmodernism is inherently a paradox, what are we to call the phase that follows it? We are tempted to name it The New Modernism, except that Neo-Modernism means the same thing, even if it implies something altogether different. Because this new trend is still unfolding, perhaps it is best not to confuse matters further by trying to pin a tag on it prematurely. The lack of a label does not mean, however, that a new direction cannot be discovered. On the contrary, there is a clear tendency toward convergence between Neo-Expressionism and Deconstructivism, despite the extraordinary variety that has characterized architecture around the world over the past decade or so. We may call it Sculptural Architecture. Such a merger is less strange than it may seem at first glance. After all, Neo-Expressionism is the most self-consciously sculptural of any school of architecture, while Deconstructivism takes as its point of departure Russian Constructivism, which, although primarily a sculptural movement, had a strong architectural bent (see fig. 25-7). Moreover, we may see this union as a way of bridging the gap between abstraction and expressionism that developed in modern architecture during the early 1920s.

Reconciliation does not imply compromise, however. It does suggest what the late-nineteenth-century art historian Alois Riegl (1848–1905) called "the will to form." It is as if contemporary architecture has been seized by an urge to create sculpture on a scale that surpasses even the grandiose dreams of environmental sculptors such as Mathias Goeritz (see page 879). Moreover, the architects who are pursuing this direction are a different breed from their predecessors. Not that they are youngsters. Most were born between 1943 and 1953; they are, in other words, baby boomers. But although they are very conscious of everything that has come before them, they think—and even talk—differently.

FRANK GEHRY. The oldest and most radical of these sculptural postmodernists is Frank Gehry (b. 1929), a Los Angeles architect who has always been a maverick in his sense of design and choice of materials. His earlier work was emphatically Deconstructivist, but the more recent buildings can only be described as assemblages of diverse parts. Undoubtedly his finest achievement is the Guggenheim Museum in Bilbao, Spain, which opened in 1997 (fig. 28-7). Situated strategically on a bend of the river that runs through the city, it is part cultural institution and part urban renewal project. (It replaces an abandoned lumber mill.) In accordance with the director's wishes, the galleries vary greatly in shape and size in order to provide different viewing experiences appropriate to various kinds of art. Once the main functional requirements had been determined, the building was conceived in a series of drawings. Often resembling abstract doodles, they were then translated into usable form by using the latest computer-aided design programs. Throughout the long development process, Gehry experimented with a number of shapes, many of which were incorporated into the final design.

The result is certainly as innovative and controversial as Frank Lloyd Wright's original Guggenheim Museum in New York (see figs. 26-39 and 26-40). The Bilbao Guggenheim is a structure of such dazzling complexity that no single photograph can begin to suggest its ever-changing views. As one critic observed, from head on it looks like a collision between two ships. Seen from above, the museum appears to unfold like a flower, but it also includes fish, snake, boot, and sail forms. In fact, the main body is clad in a skin of specially fabricated, ultra-thin titanium tiles suggesting the scales of a serpent or denizen of the deep. It has such organic vitality that it almost seems to take on a life of its own, especially when viewed from the side, as in our illustration. The building ends in a tower that is actually a piece of architectural sculpture rather than a functional piece of architecture. All told, the Bilbao Guggenheim is probably the most exciting building of the 1990s. It became an instant classic, defining the spirit of the decade much as Pompidou Center (see fig. 26-45) did for the 80s.

ERIC OWEN MOSS. Because of his experimental vision, Gehry is one of the most influential role models for younger architects wanting to explore new directions on both sides of the Atlantic. Among them is Eric Owen Moss (b. 1943), who is also based in Los Angeles. Even more than Gehry, with whom he once worked, Moss brings a new kind of elliptical intelligence, rather than linear logic, to architecture. He usually prefers the disjointed syntax of today's everyday speech to the measured tones of rational discourse. His concerns are equally new. Moss' work reflects not a desire to dissect the formal language of High Modernism but an acute awareness of the clash of forces in a chaotic world, which the architect does not so much resolve as join together.

A brilliant example of Moss' recent architecture is Samitaur (fig. 28-8), part of the rehabilitation of a decaying industrial section in Culver City near Los Angeles undertaken by the developer Frederick Smith. In his first designs for the site, Moss combined Deconstructivism with Postmodernism to create a hybrid style

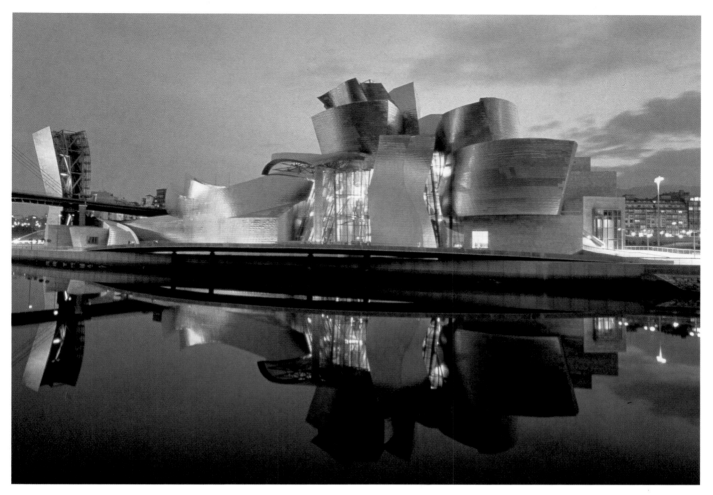

28-7. Frank Gehry. Guggenheim Museum, Bilbao, Spain. 1992–97

still seeking its own identity. Samitaur, by contrast, imposes a new building on top of old ones, so that it both deconstructs and historicizes. The whole structure is built over a roadway on braces placed at varying angles, with legs sunk into the existing warehouses. At several points the smooth regularity of the exterior is suddenly disrupted by a collision of sculptural forms that recall Mendelsohn's Einstein Tower (see fig. 26-22). The glance backward does not stop there. Such complex shapes cannot be made using standard hi-tech construction techniques. In fact, they rely heavily on handwork. In that regard, Samitaur is a throwback not simply to the Einstein Tower but to the Arts and Crafts Movement: its nearest counterpart is Antoní Gaudí's Casa Milá (see fig. 23-31). Yet the results can in no way be called retrospective.

What does such a building do? At the very least, it forces the user to reconsider the function of the structure itself. Moss conceives of the architect as a kind of high priest who imposes his ideas but in such a way they interact with those of the user, who becomes an active collaborator, to create something new and unexpected. This play back and forth accords with his view of life as a series of contradictions that seek a resolution, which in turn gives rise to a new set of questions. If the theory is obscure, the point of view is thoroughly postmodern, and it is expressed in compelling form.

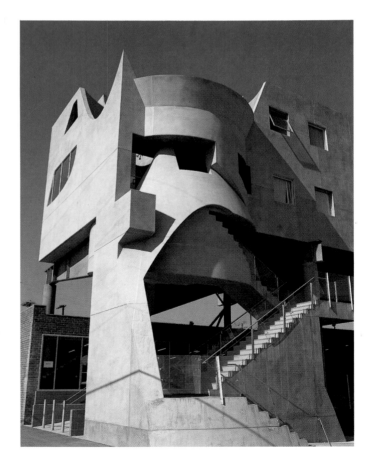

28-8. Eric Owen Moss. A building in the complex at Samitaur, Culver City, California. 1989–95

No matter how unconventional, Moss' buildings manage to fulfill their practical purpose remarkably well; otherwise the Culver City project would not have proved commercially viable. He is no less concerned with matters of structure and details of construction than he is with visual effects. The jury is still out as to whether this unique approach can be translated successfully into the mass construction techniques necessary for wide adoption. But there can be little doubt that Samitaur points to the future of architecture as space-defining sculpture, something that architects everywhere are working toward (see fig. 26-46).

SCULPTURE

LUCIANO FABRO. Traditional sculpture has been of little significance in postmodernism, because the emphasis on form in recent architecture has usurped its function. In fact, sculpture seems almost out of place when it does make an appearance. A rare example is *The Birth of Venus* (fig. 28-9) by Luciano Fabro (b. 1936), an original member of the *Arte Povera* movement (see page 864) who works in a wide variety of styles and techniques. The roughed-out "figure" is attached like a misshapen cocoon to the eroded capital atop the smooth column drums, each of contrasting color. What might she look like? Unlike Michelangelo's *Awakening Prisoner* (see fig. 13-16), Fabro's *Venus* remains imprisoned within the marble forever, with no more than the barest outlines to hint at her possible shape. Curiously enough, the column more closely resembles a statue, such as the Archaic Greek "Peplos" Kore in figure 5-15, than does this strange appendage. Although some would deny it, *The Birth of Venus* is clearly a Postmodern work. What makes it so is the improbable juxtaposition, which is a knowing misquotation of the past. Yet the ironic takeoff is accomplished with all the gravity of an artist for whom sculpture is both a living tradition and a dead language needing to be revived. It is a serious business that does not, however, rule out a certain irreverence for this vestigial relic. The real surprise is that the piece is so effective, for in its muteness it contains a spellbinding mystery.

AUDREY FLACK. In the introduction to Romantic sculpture (see page 718) and modern sculpture, we discussed Baudelaire's essay "Why Sculpture Is Boring" from his review of the Salon of 1846. It is time to revive the debate by asking, "Why is contemporary sculpture so boring?" Over the past 20 years, it has become bankrupt. It simply ran out of things to say using the vocabulary of abstraction that sustained it for most of the twentieth century, so that it is now an empty shell, as Fabro's sculpture suggests. At the same time, it has no place in Postmodernism, where it has been replaced by installations on the one hand (see page 954), and by architecture, which has recently usurped its form-giving function, on the other (see page 944). Through its exploitation of irony, Fabro's *The Birth of Venus* (see fig. 28-9) suggests the basic problem. Contemporary sculpture has lost its "idol" quality, in the full meaning of the term that Baudelaire intended: not simply its solid, space-filling reality but its role as fetish—an object to be worshiped for its demonic power, the symbol of something mysterious and profound—even if, according to the author, it prevents the artist from expressing his unique point of view. But how is it possible to

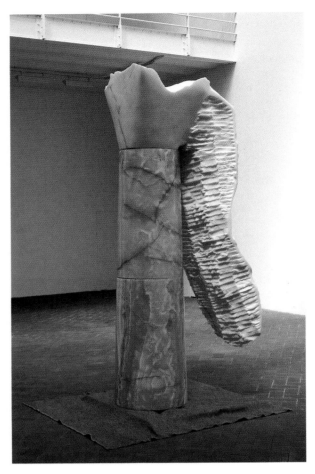

28-9. Luciano Fabro. *The Birth of Venus.* 1992. Onyx and marble, 8'7½" x 2'3½" x 3'10" (2.63 x 0.70 x 1.18 m). Courtesy of Galerie Durand-Dessert, Paris

endow sculpture with the status of a fetish in this post-modern age, with its pervasive belief in nothing except the failure of Western civilization? It can be done, but only by rediscovering the power of myth and using it to invest sculpture with new meaning.

One of the few artists who has succeeded in this difficult task is Audrey Flack. She gave up painting (see fig. 24-78) some 20 years ago after having achieved everything she wanted to in that medium. She reinvented herself as an artist by turning to sculpture, which she had to learn from the ground up. As a Photorealist, Flack naturally turned to traditional naturalism. It would be easy to dismiss her work as an obsolete throwback except for its undeniable power. An avowed feminist, she has transformed the art, history, and mythology of the past through personal alchemy to invent the new ideal woman of the twenty-first century: powerful but beautiful, filled with a magic force yet magnetic in its appeal. Flack has been condemned by a number of liberal critics for concentrating on classical white figures, instead of those of other races. However, she was criticized even more harshly for her statue of Princess Catherine of Braganza, Portugal, who later married Charles II of England (1630–1685). Instead of following contemporary portraits of Catherine, the artist gave her a multiracial face as an expression of the new ideal for the millennium, with its increasing ethnic mix. Flack has allied herself deliberately to the classical tradition because it is the basis for the Western tradition, even while she consciously violates its canon.

Yet she herself is the very antithesis of these classical figures. While she has used her own face in numerous photographs appropriated from other cultures, including Native American, no one would mistake her identity, any more than they will Cindy Sherman in even her more self-consciously disguised photos (see fig. 28-19).

A spectacular example of this new woman is Flack's *Head of Medusa* (fig. 28-10). We discuss this work at length here, making it a demonstration of what has been missing in late modern and Postmodern sculpture: imagery that compels our interest because of its profound content. The three Gorgons—Medusa, Stheno, and Euryale—were originally hideous goddesses of revenge. (Medusa has an even more ancient origin in Minoan art as the "Snake Goddess" and "The Mistress of the Animals"; see fig. 4-3 and fig. 4-8.) In traditional mythology, the snake-haired Medusa was so frightful that the sight of her face could turn a man (but not a woman) into stone (see figs. 5-3 and 5-17). Thus she was the ancestor of all sculptors. Unlike her sisters, Medusa was mortal. With the assistance of the goddess Athena, Perseus beheaded Medusa while she was asleep. In some versions of the story, her head was then attached to the shield of the goddess Athena to ward off evil. By the Hellenistic era, however, Medusa had become a beautiful woman who was a victim of tragic, unjust fate. Flack drew on these later myths that told of Medusa's rape by Poseidon in the Temple of Athena, and of the winged horse, Pegasus, born from their union. (Perseus later used Pegasus to help rescue Andromeda; see fig. 14-7.) In revenge, the goddess Athena punished the victim by turning her hair into snakes. According to Flack, however, the snakes were a gift to protect her from being raped again; moreover, she claims, Medusa hid herself in the underworld to protect others from being harmed by her.

The artist's quest for the "real" Medusa was set off by Benvenuto Cellini's famous statue in the Florence loggia, which incorporates both aspects of the myth: Perseus holds the Gorgon's beautiful head as he stands triumphantly over her sensual body. She is, then, both fearsome and alluring. Flack herself experimented with every kind of image, including a horrific, slightly less than lifesize bronze head that is indebted to a painting by Caravaggio, and a small pendant whose tragic expression is strikingly similar to the head in Cellini's sculpture. The definitive version, reproduced here, comes closest to the *Rondanini Medusa* (Staatliche Antikensammlungen und Glyptothek, Munich), a Roman copy of an original attributed to Androsthenes of Athens from around 200–170 B.C. Yet there was no single source for Flack's *Medusa*. She was also inspired by a wide range of Late Classical and Hellenistic examples. Thus she also partakes of Aphrodite, Athena, Diana, Eirene, and Klio. Comparison can also be made to Helios, Apollo, and Alexander the Great, especially for the snakelike hair (see figs. 5-83 and 5-84). The allusions are not a coincidence. Flack's new woman is muscular and supple, yet beautiful, like the Amazon of Classical Greek myths (compare fig. 5-66). Interestingly enough, late Greek sculpture of around the same time as the *Rondanini Medusa* shows a fascination with hermaphrodites (young men who look like beautiful women, with breasts but also male genitals).

Flack's Medusa is all of these and none, for she incorporates their characteristics into a mythological creature that adds up to

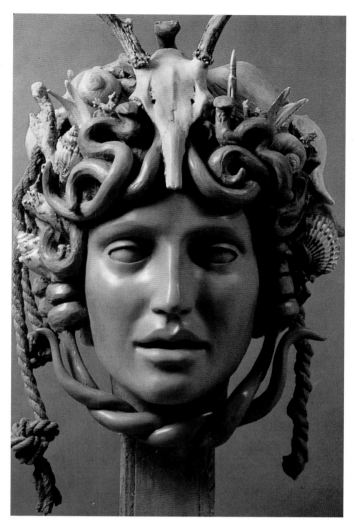

28-10. Audrey Flack. *Head of Medusa*. 1990. Polychromed terra-cotta-colored fiberglass, shells, bones, and bullet. Height 33" (83.8 cm) without base. Private collection

something entirely new. Her full significance emerges only in the context of the other mythological heads and figures Flack created in the mid-1990s. These include *Daphne, American Athena, Civitas, Medicine Woman, Sophia,* and *Islandia;* Medusa shares features with all of them and thus combines aspects of their different meanings. But the real import is found in *Amor Vincit Omnia (Love Conquers All),* which, too, is a severed head. This powerful work is an obvious self-portrait of the artist. On one side is a revolver, as if she had blown out her brains which have turned into snakelike ribbons of paint gushing from tubes. Tears of anguish stream from her closed eyes. The meaning is clear: life's pain can be resolved either by suicide or the creative act.

The piece proceeded from a series of canvases Flack painted in the early 1970s of Spanish statues of weeping Madonnas. She became interested in these sculptures through the work of Luisa Roldán (c. 1656–1704), one of the first important Spanish women artists, who had fallen into complete oblivion. Her father, Pedron Roldán (1624–1699), a leading sculptor in seventeenth-century Spain, was director of the Seville Academy from 1662 to 1672. Luisa had the unique distinction of being the only woman ever to hold the position of royal sculptor. Critics accepted Flack's

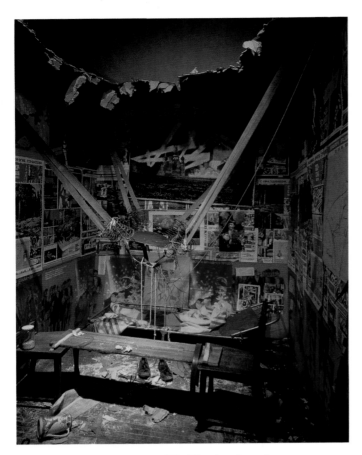

28-11. Ilya Kabakov. *The Man Who Flew into Space from His Apartment,* from "Ten Characters." 1981–88. Mixed-media installation at Ronald Feldman Fine Arts, New York, 1988

COURTESY RONALD FELDMAN FINE ARTS

weeping Madonnas so long as they could be seen as examples of Postmodern irony; but, in fact, the grief they express is very real.

Flack's life has been filled with tragedy, both personal and professional, from an early age. Although Medusa masks her pain behind her classical features, the artist's obsession with this mythological creature attests to a personal identification with her. To Flack, Medusa is a kind of personal talisman, so that she is, in effect, a fetish filled with magical powers. (The amulet of the Medusa head is meant to be worn around the neck as protection against evil.) Medusa thus becomes not merely a personal emblem but a worthy symbol of woman for the new age—strong, heroic, beautiful, yet tragic in being bound by what fate has decreed.

INSTALLATIONS. Installations have become the focal point of Postmodernism. They are the epitome of the deconstructionist idea of the world as "text." Because their intent can never be fully known even by their "authors," "readers" are free to interpret "texts" (including works of art) in light of their own experience (see Postscript). The installation artist creates a separate world that is a self-contained universe, at once alien and familiar. Left to their own devices to wander this microcosm, viewers bring their own understanding to bear on the experience in the form of memories that are evoked by the novel environment. In effect, then, they help to write the text. In themselves, installations are empty vessels. They may contain anything that the author and reader

wish to put into them. Hence they serve as a ready means for expressing social, political, or personal concerns—especially those that satisfy the postmodern agenda. The installation as text can become deliberately literal as well as literary: it is often linked to a written text that makes the program explicit.

ILYA KABAKOV. Russian artists have a special genius for installations. Cut off for decades from contemporary art in the West, they developed mostly provincial forms of painting and sculpture. Yet that very isolation allowed them to create a unique brand of Conceptual Art that in turn provided the foundation for their installations. The first to gain international acclaim was Ilya Kabakov (b. 1933), who now lives in New York. "Ten Characters" was a suite of rooms like those of a seedy communal apartment, each inhabited by an imaginary person with an "unusual idea, one all-absorbing passion belonging to him alone." The most spectacular cubicle was *The Man Who Flew into Space from His Apartment* (fig. 28-11). He achieved his dream of flying into space by being hurled from a catapult suspended by springs, while the ceiling and roof were blown off at the precise moment of launching. Like the other rooms, it was accompanied by a dark text worthy of Fyodor Dostoyevsky (1821–1881), which reflects the Russian talent for storytelling. The installation was more than an elaborate realization of this bizarre fantasy. The extravagant clutter was a bitter commentary on the bizarre dilemmas of life in the former Soviet Union—its tawdry reality, its broken dreams, the pervasive role of central authority.

ANN HAMILTON. Kabakov was inspired in part by the example of Joseph Beuys (see page 893), who was also an influence on the American installation artist Ann Hamilton (b. 1956). Her work is about loss, be it from personal tragedy or distortion of a natural relationship. Unlike Beuys, she seeks only to raise issues, not to resolve them, a matter that is left to the visitor, although she uses many of the same means. Her installations involve all of the senses through the use of unusual materials, often in disturbing ways, in order to present a paradox that lies at the center of each work. She exercises these choices through a train of free association until the idea crystallizes.

Hamilton's installations are labor-intensive—obsessively, even ritualistically, so. Thus *parallel lines* for the 1991 São Paulo Bienal (figs. 28-12 and 28-13) began with assistants coating the walls of one gallery with soot from burning candles, then attaching sequentially numbered copper tags to the floor. (This interest in seriality is also basic to Conceptual Art.) Finally, a huge bundle of candles was placed in the room so as to dominate it. A second room, covered entirely in the same copper tags, held nothing but two glass library cases containing turkey carcasses that were slowly devoured by beetles. This assault on the viewer's senses and values was intended to pose a number of questions. What is collected, why, and by whom? What is the moral difference between showing candles made by people from the fat of dead animals and exhibiting a dead bird with beetles carrying out their natural role as scavengers? Although death was treated matter-of-factly, there was a strangely mournful air to the entire installation, which invited viewers to think about these issues and to arrive at their own conclusions.

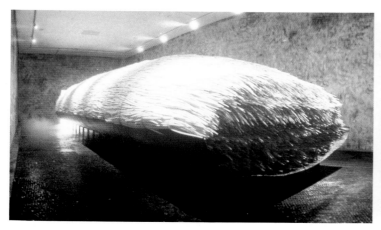 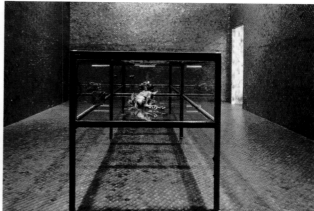

28-12 and 28-13. Ann Hamilton. *parallel lines.* Two parts of an installation in two rooms, São Paulo Bienal, September–December 1991. Mixed media

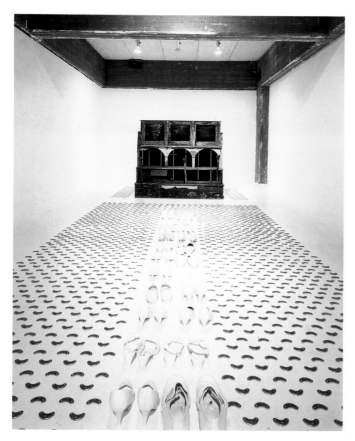

28-14. Mildred Howard. *Tap: Investigation of Memory.* 1989. Traveler shoe taps, an antique three-seat shoeshine stand, assorted painted shoes, and delayed playback of an ambient sound, 10' x 13'6" x 51'6" (3 x 4 x 15.5 m).

MILDRED HOWARD. Mildred Howard (b. 1945) uses many of the same principles as Hamilton, but constructs her installations as specifically African-American statements. She is a social activist who sometimes mounts her installations in storefronts and other locations within the black community. Howard draws chiefly on her own life to define the black experience. To her, memory is both individual and ethnic. Thus *Tap: Investigation of Memory* (fig. 28-14) has multiple layers of personal and cultural meaning. It celebrates the importance of this dance form to the artist's family during her childhood, as well as the special contribution African-Americans have made to it. The taps (labeled "Traveler," significantly enough) are lined up ritualistically in rows, with shoes leading in solemn procession down the center aisle to a beat-up shoeshine stand that becomes an altar. The spiritual references are intentional. Movement is closely identified in Howard's mind with African-American worship—especially as practiced in store-front churches, the subject of another of her installations— in contrast to the somber rituals traditional to Western churches. Yet *Tap* succeeds precisely because of its contemplative atmosphere, which evokes a broad range of associations.

PEPÓN OSORIO. Another artist who believes in taking his installations directly to the community is Pepón Osorio (b. 1955). A native of Puerto Rico who resides in New York City, he has used taxicabs literally as vehicles for mobile installations of urban Latino culture. *Badge of Honor* (fig. 28-15) was the result of a rare collaboration: it was placed first in downtown Newark, then at the Newark Museum, which originally commissioned it, in order to blur the traditional distinction between life and art. The installation addressed with dignity a serious social problem that affects many minority families. It consisted of two adjoining chambers, one a stark jail cell, the other a typical teenage boy's room whose garishness reflects the American Dream and the Baroque opulence that is part of the Latin heritage. These theatrically treated spaces formed the setting for a dialogue projected on opposite walls between a man in prison and his son. Although imaginary, the conversation drew on Osorio's experience as a social worker. Rather than seeming contrived, it managed to bridge the gap between father and son by expressing their feelings with convincing honesty. In the process, the stark contrast between the two rooms disappeared as well. Both emerged as empty because of the tear in the fabric of the family, yet rich because of the strong bond between the boy and his father. The impact on viewers was overwhelming, because Osorio's directness and artistry were unerring in their appeal to his audience.

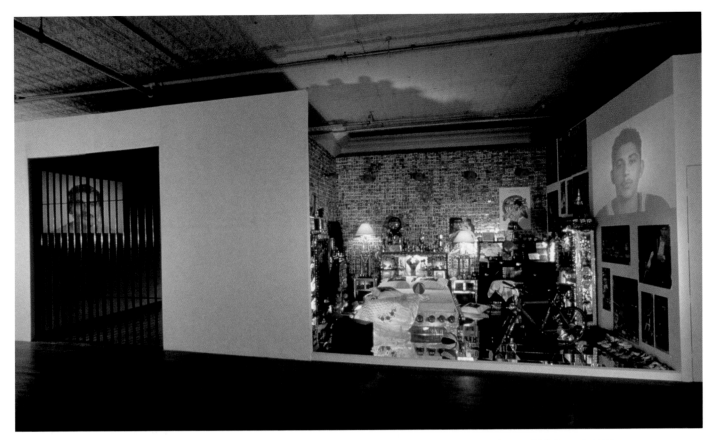

28-15. Pepón Osorio. *Badge of Honor.* 1995. Installation view at Ronald Feldman Fine Arts, New York, April 25–June 1, 1996, 12' x 26'10" x 12' (3.65 x 8.17 x 3.65 m)

PAINTING

Painting, like sculpture, is a traditional medium that does not lend itself well to Postmodernism. Indeed, most of what passes as Postmodern painting is really late modernism in disguise; in any event, there is no fixed boundary between the two. To the extent that it can be said to exist at all, however, postmodern painting is an outgrowth of Conceptualism, Pop Art, and Neo-Expressionism. However, it differs from them in a fundamental respect. Now painting acts like a deconstructed text gutted of all significance, except for whatever we choose to add through free association with our own experience.

How did painting come to be so barren? Traditional approaches such as allegory require a shared culture. However, this common bond is difficult, if not impossible, in the postmodern age, as the contrast between the sculptures of Fabro and Flack makes clear (see figs. 28-9 and 28-10). Our civilization is more fractured than ever, despite the widespread concept of the "global village." Deconstruction, moreover, proclaims both author and subject matter to be unnecessary remnants of humanism, thus rendering meaning null and void. It argues instead that representation in its broadest sense is both unnecessary and undesirable on the grounds that it strives to re-create a fraudulent reality, and therefore can never provide an authentic experience. Such an attitude is not confined to deconstruction, however. It is inherent in postmodernism as a whole.

A. R. PENCK. A group of Postmodern artists from the former German Democratic Republic have helped to make Germany the leading school of painting in the West today. One of the most interesting among them is A. R. Penck (b. 1939). Penck is the pseudonym adopted by Ralf Winkler from a famous geologist whose specialty was the Ice Age. Before emigrating to the West in 1980, the artist lived in East Germany during the political ice age that was the Cold War. The "primitive" and childish quality in *The Demon of Curiosity* (fig. 28-16), with its colorful directness, is deceptive. Although largely self-taught, Penck uses a fluid technique that is, in fact, very sophisticated.

But what are we to make of the picture's content? At first glance, it seems as bewildering as rock engravings in prehistoric caves (see fig 1-5). Upon closer inspection, we realize that the artist's "code" can be broken, at least enough for us to understand the basic meaning. The demon, as fierce as anything conjured up by Gauguin (compare fig. 23-14), is surmounted by a bird looking both ways (signifying inquisitiveness) to which the small crucified figure at the left has been sacrificed. The figures swim in a sea of hexlike signs, letters, and numbers, symbolizing knowledge, which fills up the man to the point where he seems literally "pregnant (or at least bloated) with meaning." The painting reflects Penck's fascination with cybernetics, the science of information systems. To him the artist is a kind of scientist, and he sees little difference between the two.

MARK TANSEY. If Penck follows in the footsteps of artists such as Paul Klee by inventing a personal form of pictographs, Mark Tansey (b. 1949) uses the Roman alphabet to accomplish the seem-

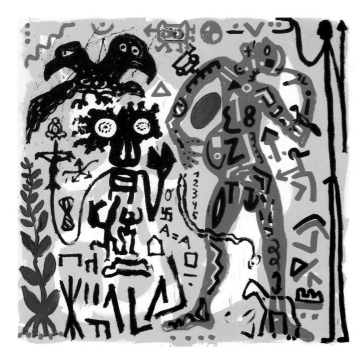

28-16. A. R. Penck. *The Demon of Curiosity*. 1982.
Acrylic on canvas, 9'2¼" x 9'2¼" (2.8 x 2.8 m).
The Rivendell Collection of Late-Twentieth-Century Art
on permanent loan to the Center for Curatorial Studies,
Bard College, Annandale-on-Hudson, New York

COURTESY MICHAEL WERNER GALLERY, NEW YORK AND COLOGNE

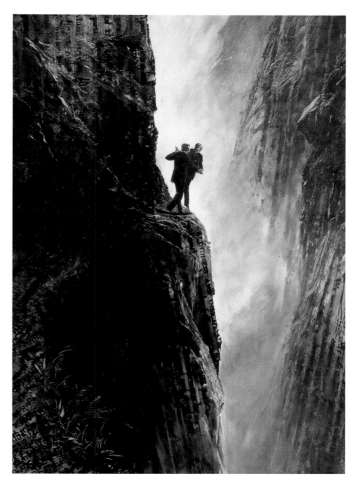

(ABOVE RIGHT) 28-17. Mark Tansey. *Derrida Queries De Man*. 1990.
Oil on canvas, 6'11" x 4'7" (2.13 x 1.4 m).
Collection Michael and Judy Ovitz, Los Angeles.

"The critical reading of Derrida's critical reading of Rousseau shows blindness to be the necessary correlative of the rhetorical nature of literary language," says [Paul] De Man. The critic is fated to be blind to what is before her eyes.

How on earth, if this is true, can people read texts? Or are texts but the permanent possibility of falling into error? The issue is raised in a summarizing work of 1990 that shows two figures wrestling on the edge of an abyss. The abyss is filled with rising vapor, and the sides of it fall steeply, sheerly away. The rocks seem to have the sort of geological texture we would expect in so bare and dramatic a location, but if we look closely, these marks are, in fact, letters: the abyss is a text we cannot make out (I can read the word "of" but nothing else). We know only that close reading will not decipher it for us. The painting of two figures wrestling with one another on a rock shelf, which makes one dizzy simply to look at it, is based on Sidney Paget's famous illustration of Sherlock Holmes and Doctor Moriarty in combat at Reichenbach

Falls. The title of the work is delicious: it is Derrida Queries De Man. *They are dressed in conservative business suits and are about to be deconstructed to smithereens. Or they would if the scene were real. But it is a picture only, and there they are locked in eternal combat over the meaning De Man gave to the meaning that Derrida gave to Rousseau. It is, to paraphrase a text of Kierkegaard's, a "Concluding Unliterary Masterpiece" whose subject is verbal but whose substance is pictorial.*

—Arthur C. Danto. *Mark Tansey: Visions and Revisions.*
New York: Harry N. Abrams, Inc., 1992, p. 29.

ARTHUR C. DANTO (b.1924) is an American philosopher who has taught at Columbia University since 1951. His contributions to art history have been in the area of aesthetics, where he has stimulated much debate and rethinking of the art world's "atmosphere of theory." The passage from Danto's monograph on painter Mark Tansey is a typically tantalizing commentary on deconstruction.

ingly impossible: he constructs representational images that are made up of texts following the principles of deconstruction. *Derrida Queries De Man* (fig. 28-17) shows the founder of deconstruction with his chief American disciple, Paul de Man (1919–1983). If we look closely, we see that the landscape is made up of typeset lines that merge to form the steep cliffs. Here the texture of the paint bridges the gap between text and illustration by embedding the idea within the image. In this sense, the painting functions as an illustration of a metaphor. But what is it saying? Certainly it makes a serious point about the relation between content, picture, and reality. Yet it does so with surprising wit, beginning with the very idea of building a painting out of words. And, in a gesture of supreme irony, Tansey has appropriated the image from a famous illustration showing the death of the fictional detective Sherlock Holmes at the hands of his archenemy, Professor Moriarty! We have seen such humor before, in the work of René Magritte (see fig. 24-42), who was an early inspiration for Tansey. By preventing a literal reading of the painting, the artist poses questions for the viewer that can never be fully resolved.

PHOTOGRAPHY

Photography, too, has taken up the theme of image as "text." Given the close association of words and photographs in Conceptual Art (see page 893), such a move was inevitable. It was aided, however, by the new importance attached to semiotics, which has opened up new avenues of investigation for the artist. How do signs acquire public meaning? What is the message? Who originates it? What (and whose) purpose does it serve? Who is the audience? What are the means of spreading the idea? Who controls the media?

Photographers, especially in the United States, raise these questions in order to challenge our assumptions about the world we live in and the social order it imposes. Unlike David Hockney or Joanne Leonard (see figs. 27-30 and 27-31), Postmodern photographers are "re-photographers," who for the most part do not take their own pictures but appropriate them from other mediums. To convey their message, these new Conceptualists often follow the formula established by John Baldessari of placing image and text side by side (compare fig. 25-43). Sometimes their pictures are intended as counterparts to paintings, and are enlarged on an unprecedented scale, using commercial processes developed for advertisements, which may also serve as sources. Here it is the choice of image that matters, since the act of singling it out and changing its location to a gallery wall (or even the side of a building) constitutes the comment. In both cases, however, we are asked to base our judgment solely on the message. The means of delivery deliberately shows so little individuality that it is often impossible to tell the work of one artist from another. In the process, the message often becomes equally forgettable.

BARBARA KRUGER. That is not a problem with Barbara Kruger (b. 1945): her pictures are instantly recognizable for their confrontational approach. Her work is like a sharp blow to the solar plexus: the message is direct, the response immediate, especially the first time around. The formula hardly varies, however. *You Are a Captive Audience* (fig. 28-18) illustrates her style. The image usually involves a tightly cropped close-up in black and white taken from a magazine or newspaper. It is blown up as crudely as possible to monumental proportions, so that the viewer cannot escape its presence or the message, which is stenciled in white letters against a red background. As in our example, the joining of unrelated text and image is clearly intended for radical ends. The statement is intended to create acute anxiety by playing on people's latent fears in our society of being controlled by nameless forces, especially such large, impersonal power centers as the government, the military, or corporations.

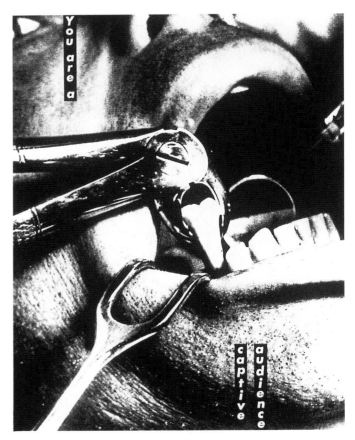

28-18. Barbara Kruger. *You Are a Captive Audience.* 1983. Gelatin-silver print, 48 x 37¾" (122 x 96 cm)

CINDY SHERMAN. Not all Postmodern photography is attached to words, nor is it taken from other sources. A curious in-between case is provided by Cindy Sherman (b. 1954). [See Primary Sources, no. 104, page 979.] Among her best works are the early photographs that were staged in imitation of old movie stills. They are so skillful that they look like the real thing. In them she fulfills the secret American dream of being star, caster, set designer, producer, and photographer all in one, except that she does so almost vicariously. As her own star, she can play any role she wants, and the choice is illuminating. Figure 28-19 shows her preference for 1940s and 1950s movies portraying beautiful women as vulnerable heroines. The picture is a perfect period piece, down to the last detail of costume, setting, and lighting. Only after we have looked at it for a while do we realize that the photograph raises intriguing questions about the image of women projected on the silver screen.

Whether the message is feminist has been the subject of considerable debate. Is Sherman's use of herself merely an exercise in narcissism and her reliance on stereotypes no more than an example of shallow consumerism? Or is there a feminist sense of irony in her choice of poses? However we choose to interpret it, the photograph is strangely affecting in its aura of nostalgia and the sense of mystery it communicates. Here the timeless image of the woman looking in the mirror is updated to one of its

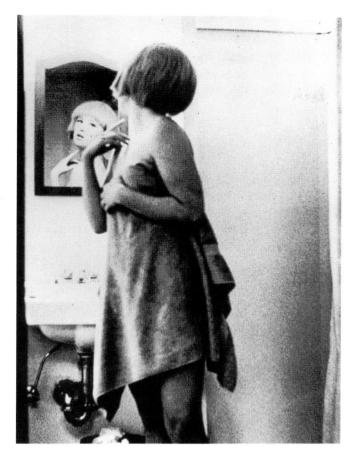

28-19. Cindy Sherman. *Untitled Film Still #2.* 1977.
Photograph, 18 x 10" (45.5 x 25.5 cm)

most daring—and puzzling—expressions ever. Sherman offers voyeurism at second hand, so to speak, a fantasy that forever precludes authentic experience. In that sense, it is a paradigm of postmodernism.

ANDREAS GURSKY. By the late 1960s, painters, sculptors, as well as conceptual, earth and performance artists, had stolen the avant-garde in photography from photographers. Unlike photographers, who traditionally made 8 x 10- or 11 x 14-inch prints, artists worked on a scale associated with good-size easel pictures. With the 1990s photographs of the German Andreas Gursky (b. 1955), photography now rivaled the scale of the largest Abstract Expressionist pictures. His prints regularly span six to nine feet in one direction, with some measuring $6\frac{1}{2}$ by $16\frac{1}{2}$ feet. His works also look like painting. A close-up shot of a crowd scene showing thousands of people has the overall look of a Jackson Pollock drip painting, while the 20-foot lobby of a Shanghai hotel looks like a Minimalist abstraction.

At first it appears Gursky has an extraordinary eye and has found these exceptional compositions in the real world. The truth is, in fact, that he has digitally manipulated his images through such means as sharpening lines, emphasizing certain colors, and heightening value contrasts, which allows him, in a sense, to color and draw like a painter. But through these sleights of hand, Gursky is doing more than just making photographs that conjure up the medium of painting. He is also intentionally capturing the spirit of our time, including the image barrage that invades daily life and the media manipulation that lies behind it.

Gursky has traveled the world for his imagery in order to capture the global sameness of contemporary life. Without a caption, it is impossible to tell if a hotel lobby, a stock exchange, an International Style high-rise, an industrial plant, or a rock concert is in New York, Brasilia, Shanghai, Athens, or Los Angeles. He portrays a high-tech, impersonal world that is both the present and future of civilization. What's special about all of Gursky's work is how unlike the actual place it is and, at the same time, how anywhere in the world it is. Thus *Paris, Montparnasse* (fig. 28-20) evokes nothing about this former working-class district on the Left Bank that was once the hub of the city's artistic life; it could just as well represent New York or London. In that respect, it is the exact opposite of Eugène Atget's haunting *Versailles* (fig. 27-2).

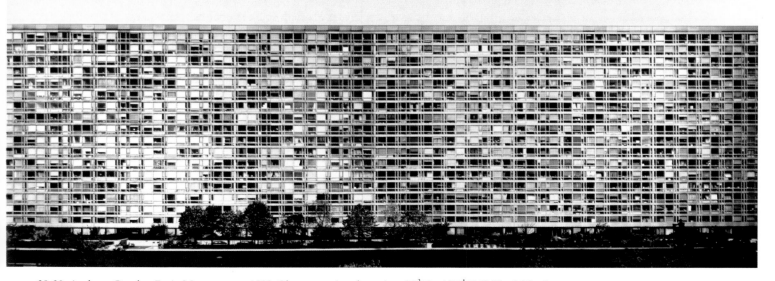

28-20. Andreas Gursky. *Paris, Montparnasse.* 1993. Chromogenic color print. 6'8¾" x 13'1¼" (2.05 x 3.99 m).

It is hardly possible to discuss postmodernism in music, which to date has not yielded significant results on matters of appropriation and deconstruction. The closest it has come is Minimalism. The composer Lukas Foss (b. 1922), who has been practicing a form of Minimalism since the late 1970s, describes his *Quintets for Orchestra* (1979) in terms very similar to deconstruction: "A five-note chord dominates the composition. It is endlessly repeated, varied, permutated, transposed, and inverted, invading the entire piece . . . like a wound." Theater, by contrast, is ideally suited to appropriation and deconstruction, especially the latter, since it readily permits viewers to participate actively in creating the text as they perceive it. The main tendency has been to reinterpret existing classics, as well as works of recent vintage, in extremely untraditional ways that challenge conventional ("received") ideas about their content and meaning. Such is the case with the Romanian director Andrei Serban (b. 1943), who was strongly affected by Peter Brook (b. 1925); Peter Sellars (b. 1957), former director of the American National Theater at the Kennedy Center in Washington, D.C.; Les Breuer (b. 1937), director of the Mabou Mines company, who was influenced by Beckett, Brecht, and Grotowski, among others; and Robert Wilson (b. 1942), who worked with Philip Glass (b. 1937) and the choreographers Andrew de Groat and Lucinda Childs on *Einstein on the Beach* (1976). Wilson's own works, stemming from his collaboration with the autistic teenager Christopher Knowles, juxtapose elements of different cultures and media in surreal fashion. Perhaps the most important contribution has been made by the Environmental Theater of Richard Schechner (b. 1934), who conceives of theater as a public event that can take place in any environment and who assigns an active role to the audience. Every element of theater becomes independent of text—indeed, there need not be any text at all. None of these ideas is new in itself. Rather, it is the combination that matters.

POSTSCRIPT: POSTMODERN THEORY

Postmodern theory is not for the faint of heart. It is dauntingly complex and obscure, intentionally contradictory and illogical. For those brave enough to take the plunge, however, postmodern theory opens up a fascinating view of contemporary life and thought.

SEMIOTICS. Semiotics (the study of signs) may be regarded ultimately as a branch of philosophy. Its foundations lie in ancient philosophy, as well as medieval theology, and its modern form is a direct outgrowth of Enlightenment rationalism. Moreover, the American school of semiotics was founded by a philosopher, Charles Sanders Peirce (1839–1914). Despite its seemingly endless diversity, semiotics retains some key features of all philosophical systems. It seeks a universal understanding, and its theoretical constructs frequently follow classical examples. It typically acts as a closed body of ideas, one that is concerned primarily with its own inner logic, rather than presenting a body of knowledge.

In essence, semiotics provides a stimulating approach to the age-old riddle, "What does the mind know, and how does it know it?" In an ultimate sense, the mind is elusive. To a Buddhist, for example, the mind cannot grasp itself, since it lacks physical substance and is ever-changing; hence it also has an almost endless capacity for self-delusion. Like most closed systems, semiotics generally assumes that the mind can know only itself through the concepts it builds. These act as filters through which all experience, internal as well as external, is interpreted. Semiotics is therefore little concerned with objective reality—if it exists at all—since it remains inherently unknowable and meaningless in itself. Some semiologists, however, postulate meaning stemming from God or some form of pure Idea.

Modern semiotics begins with the linguist Ferdinand de Saussure (1857–1913). Like many revolutionary intellectuals, he came late in life to rebel against the very ideas to which he had devoted much of his career—in his case, philology, the study of language. His contribution lay in the intuitive realization that language cannot be explained simply in terms of its development, because it always functions as a coherent system. For the dynamic (diachronic) paradigm of philology he substituted a static (synchronic) model. At the center of Saussure's system is his definition of a sign as consisting of a concept (signified) and its sound-image (signifier), which is a purely mental impression, not the sound itself. Identity is defined purely by difference, a philosophically suspect approach. Most identities are binary oppositions (for example, good and evil), built up into larger structures of increasing complexity. Meaning is determined by structure and the relationships it imposes rather than by traditional grammar. Thus context becomes critical to understanding. Saussure further distinguished between the everyday speech of the individual *(parole)* and language as a socially shared linguistic system *(langue)*. Because there are no concrete objects in language, external reality has no place in his analysis—it is simply assumed to lie parallel to, or else to be unknowable outside of, langue. The problem with Saussure's semiology is that it proves incapable of dealing with language as an evolving system, which requires a more organic model, and thus with time in general, both as past and as future.

Semiotics constitutes a form of system analysis that in principle can be applied to almost anything. Saussure's theories, for example, are comparable to those of Talcott Parsons (1902–1979) in sociology; both are indebted partly to the sociologist Émile Durkheim (1858–1917). What counts is the coherence of the theory itself, not its basis in reality, which, as we have seen, is considered of secondary importance at best. Data are merely the point of departure for constructing the conceptual model, thus raising the question whether it has any relevance to real life. This model suggests the main weakness of the structuralist approach to semiology: if the structure is undermined, then its related concepts are deprived of meaning, which is only an abstraction without independent existence. Logically the result must inevitably be chaos, an important point that we shall soon return to. We may nevertheless wonder whether this is necessarily so in actual fact.

In most cases, the relationship between sign and meaning is extremely complex. In human society it is arbitrary at face value and assigned only as a matter of convention. Otherwise most symbols could not possibly be understood and would remain entirely private. This fact points to a fundamental difficulty besetting semiotics. Like most bodies of theory, it is encumbered by a torturous thought process and tedious jargon. Even granting the inadequacy of normal language to express the formal rhetoric of intellectual disciplines, it functions as a needlessly complex code deliberately accessible only to "those in the know." The same critique may be taken to apply to the role of semiotics in contemporary art and art history.

DECONSTRUCTION. The assault on structuralist semiology that was begun in the late 1960s by the French philosopher Jacques Derrida soon blossomed into a wholesale war on traditional learning in all fields. Similar controversies have raged in philosophy before. The antecedents of deconstruction can be traced back to medieval Scholasticism, in the nominalism of thinkers like William of Ockham (1285–1347), which rejected universals, and in supposition theory, in which context determines meaning. In fact, virtually all of its lines of argumentation are to be found in the catalogue of Scholasticism's infamous errors in logic, which are familiar to every student of philosophy. More intriguing still is the relation to music of the fourteenth century, which featured tropes (added pieces of texts and music), as well as suspensions and ambiguities of rhythm, that exactly parallel Derrida's usage. Deconstruction nonetheless has a peculiar flavor that is specifically postmodern.

Derrida considered the structuralist approach inadequate to explain the human condition, which he investigated by exploring his own consciousness. As we have seen, Saussure's semiotics contains the seeds of its own destruction. To Derrida, language is a structure to be dismantled. Against the structuralists, he asserted the primacy of the written word over the spoken, which it at first supplements, then supplants. Since all cultural products are texts in the sense of documents, everything—history, life itself— becomes a text. However, texts never mean what they seem to say, because sign and meaning are entirely separate. This contradicts the fundamental assumption of all semiotics; yet it is a possibility that semiotics itself allows, because of the arbitrary relation between sign and meaning in the first place. In deconstruction theory, everything is intertextual; that is, it is dependent on everything else, to the point where no trait can be isolated and no order or causality can exist. Furthermore, any term *(supplement)* can be substituted for any other, so that it can pass for the original one, which it "infects" from inside. Because terms are free to recombine, no element can be a self-sufficient sign; rather, it must refer to another one that is not present. This gives the reader a new latitude to create his or her own meaning by mixing fragments of text and varying their context, regardless of the author's intent, which can never be truly determined anyway. Language thus

becomes "meaning-less," and truth a mere linguistic convention that implies an author and a subject, both of which deconstruction also rejects.

Deconstruction is adamantly against all forms of logocentrism (the belief that there are abstract truths that have a basis in reality), which is seen as an instrument of ethnocentrism (the belief that one's own culture is superior to others). It also rejects standard binary oppositions like good versus evil. To undermine such beliefs, it seeks out words that have multiple, even contradictory, meanings which are "undecidables," although these in turn sometimes become binary oppositions themselves!

Deconstruction relies on exceptions to disprove a principle. By focusing on weak points around the fringes where everything can be doubted and become unknowable, it creates an unending series of questions that cannot be answered. In addition to using obscure terms, a favorite technique of deconstruction is to invent new words (neologisms) that combine bits of old ones to create unusual, often illogical meanings. A case in point is *différance,* which compounds "to differ" and "to defer" to produce an "undecidable" by "suspending" between the two. *Différance* in this sense requires uniqueness of parts rather than coherence of whole. It ostensibly means the implicit reference to other "texts" which change or postpone indefinitely the meaning of the original one. This slippery concept of time exploits, we will recall, an intrinsic limitation of structuralism, which is turned against itself.

As this outline suggests, deconstruction is subversive in its methodology. By destabilizing time and, with it, meaning, suspending permits deconstructionists to change the rules at will to suit their purpose, which is ultimately to overturn the structure of language in order to subvert logical thought. Not only does it go against all the accepted laws of reason, it disallows all exceptions or criticisms. It furthermore utilizes (and openly advocates) the deliberate misuse of terms, inappropriate synonyms, willful misquotes, irrational positions, extreme interpretations, and even personal attacks against its opponents.

To a deconstructionist, texts, not facts, are what count. Reality is at best a mental construct whose apparent meaning is determined by context (as opposed to structure). As a result, everything becomes ultimately unknowable—including one's own feelings, even though the individual is left to arrive at a purely subjective understanding. Hence every understanding or interpretation is inherently false. Deconstruction denies the priority of any viewpoint, but implicitly holds its own above all others. It conveniently ignores the fact that despite its relativism, even deconstruction cannot fully escape the inherent authoritarianism of language, which creates its own logic structures. Moreover, it rarely, if ever, deconstructs its own texts, for it claims to be a "logic beyond all forms of reason."

Needless to say, deconstruction has provoked a storm of outrage from traditional intellectuals. It has been condemned as everything from irrational sophistry and contrived obscurantism to arid nihilism. Nevertheless deconstruction has had an extraordinary impact on contemporary thought, and remains a fascinating historical phenomenon. Of all the critiques mounted against deconstruction, perhaps the most telling is its predictability. Once its unwritten rules are understood, the game is simple to play and each step is easy to anticipate.

Primary Sources for Part Four

The following is a selection of excerpts from original texts by writers, critics, artists, architects, and photographers from the late eighteenth to the twentieth centuries. These readings supplement the main text and are keyed to it. Full citations are given in the Credits section at the end of the book.

62
JOHANN JOACHIM WINCKELMANN (1717–1768)
From *Thoughts on the Imitation of Greek Works in Painting and Sculpture*

Winckelmann's influential publications on classical antiquities, including Thoughts . . . *(1755) and the* History of Ancient Art *(1764), laid the foundation for modern scientific archaeology.*

To take the ancients for models is our only way to become great. . . . Their masterpieces reveal not only nature in its greatest beauty, but . . . certain ideal beauties of nature which . . . exist only in the intellect.

The most beautiful bodies found among us today might, perhaps not be more similar to the Greek bodies than Iphicles was to Hercules, his brother. . . . Take a young Spartan, bred, by a hero and heroine, never bound by swaddling clothes, who has slept on the bare ground from the age of seven and has been trained in wrestling and swimming from earliest infancy; put him beside a young Sybarite of our day and then decide which one the artist would choose as a model for a youthful Theseus. . . .

Through these exercises the bodies, free from superfluous fat, acquired the noble and manly contours that the Greek masters gave to their statues. . . . Everything that disfigured the body was carefully avoided; Alcibiades refused to play the flute in his youth because it might distort his face. . . . Furthermore, the clothing of the Greeks was so designed as not to interfere with the natural growth of the body, while today our tight and binding dress makes the natural beauty of our bodies suffer, especially at the neck, waist, and thighs. Even the fair sex of the Greeks refused any restricting fashions. . . .

The school of the artist was the gymnasium, where the youths, ordinarily clothed because of modesty, exercised quite naked. It was the gathering place of philosophers as well as artists: Socrates visited it to teach Charmides, Artolycus and Lysis; Phidias went there to enrich his art with these magnificent figures. There one learned the movement of muscles, and studied the contours of the body. . . . The most beautiful aspects of the nude revealed themselves here in many varied and noble poses unattainable by hired models such as are used in our academies. . . .

These frequent opportunities for observing nature caused the Greek artists to go even further: they began to form general concepts of beauty for the individual parts of the body as well as for its proportions: concepts that were meant to rise above nature, being taken from a spiritual realm that existed only in the mind.

In this way Raphael formed his Galathea. As he says in his letter to Count Balthasar Castiglione, "Since beauty is rare among women, I follow a certain idea formed in my imagination. . . ."

The imitation of natural beauty either focuses upon a single model or it collects data from many models and combines them. The first produces a faithful copy, a portrait; it leads to the shapes and figures of Dutch art. The second, however, leads to universal beauty and its ideal images, and this is the path taken by the Greeks.

63
DENIS DIDEROT (1713–1784)
From *Salon of 1763*, Greuze

Diderot's reviews of the biennial Salon exhibitions provided the cornerstone of art criticism in France for the next hundred years. The full title of the painting discussed below is The Paralytic Succoured by His Children, or the Fruit of a Good Education *(The Hermitage, St. Petersburg), which was subsequently acquired by Catherine II of Russia, with Diderot acting as intermediary.*

Now here is the man for my money, this Greuze fellow. Ignoring for the moment his smaller compositions . . . I come at once to his picture *Filial Piety,* which might better have been entitled *The Reward for Providing a Good Upbringing.*

To begin with, I like this genre: it is a painting with a moral. Come, now, you must agree! Don't you think the painter's brush has been employed long enough, and too long, in the portrayal of debauchery and vice? Ought we not to be glad to see it competing at last with dramatic poetry in moving us, instructing us, correcting us, and encouraging us to virtue? Courage, Greuze, my friend: you must go on painting pictures like this one!

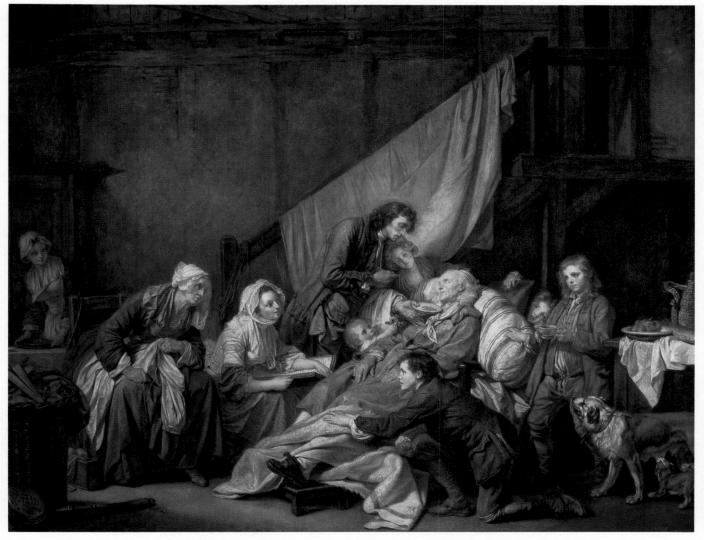

PS-63. Jean-Baptiste Greuze, *Le Paralytique,* 1763. Oil on canvas, 45½ x 57⅛" (114.4 x 146 cm). The Hermitage Museum, St. Petersburg, Russia

64

ÉTIENNE-LOUIS BOULLÉE (1728–1799)
From *Architecture, Essay on Art*

Boullée's philosophy was in the Romantic tradition of Jean-Jacques Rousseau. In this introduction to an undated manuscript, he set down his visionary ideas on architecture.

To Men Who Cultivate the Arts

Dominated by an excessive love for my profession, I have surrendered myself to it completely. But although I have yielded to this overweening passion, I have made it a rule that I shall work for the benefit of society and thus merit public esteem.

I should confess straightaway that I have refused to confine myself to the exclusive study of our ancient masters and have instead tried, through the study of Nature to broaden my ideas on my profession which, after much thought, I consider to be still in its infancy.

What little attention has been paid in the past to the poetry of architecture, which is a sure means of adding to man's enjoyment and of bestowing on artists the fame they deserve!

That is my belief. Our buildings—and our public buildings in particular—should be to some extent poems. The impression they make on us should arouse in us sensations that correspond to the function of the building in question. It seemed to me that if I was to incorporate in my Architecture all the poetry of which it was capable, then I should study the theory of volumes and analyse them, at the same time seeking to understand their properties, the power they have on our senses, their similarities to the human organism. I flattered myself that if I went back to the source of all the fine arts I should find new ideas and thus establish principles that would be all the more certain for having their source in nature.

You who are fascinated by the fine arts, surrender yourselves completely to all the pleasure that this sublime passion can procure! No other pleasure is so pure. It is this passion that makes us love to study, that transforms our pain into pleasure and, with its divine flame, forces genius to yield up its oracles. In short, it is this passion that summons us to immortality.

It is to you who cultivate the arts that I dedicate the fruits of my long vigils; to you who, with all your learning, are persuaded—and doubtless rightly so—that we must not presume that all we have left is to imitate the ancients!

65

JEAN-AUGUSTE-DOMINIQUE INGRES
(1780–1867)
From "The Doctrine of Ingres"

Maurice Denis, a member of the Nabis, compiled these aphorisms from Ingres' notebooks and from the reminiscences of his students.

Art should only depict beauty. . . .

And no matter what your genius, if you paint to the last stroke not according to nature, but your model, you will always be its slave; your manner of painting will smack of servitude. The proof of the contrary is seen in Raphael. He tamed the model to such a point and possessed it so thoroughly in his memory, that instead of the model giving him orders, one would say that the model obeyed him. . . .

To form yourself in beauty, . . . walk with your head raised to the sky instead of keeping it toward the earth like pigs searching in the mud. . . .

The figures of antiquity are only beautiful because they resemble the beauty of nature. . . . And nature will always be beautiful when it resembles the beauties of antiquity. . . .

I will write on the door of my studio: School of drawing, and I will make painters.

Drawing is the probity of art. . . .

Drawing is everything; it is all of art. The material processes of painting are very easy and may be learned in eight days. . . .

There is neither correct nor incorrect drawing; there is only beautiful or ugly drawing. That is all! . . .

In front of Rubens, put on blinders like those a horse wears.

The following were assembled by Henri Delaborde in 1870 from Ingres' correspondence and studio remarks supplied by Edouard Odier and Auguste Flandrin.

There are not two kinds of art, there is only one: it is the one which is based on timeless, natural Beauty. . . .

Love truth, for in it is beauty, if you can sense and discern it. . . .

The simpler your lines and forms, the more beauty and strength they will possess. . . .

Expression in painting calls for great knowledge of drawing, for expression cannot be good if it has not been formulated with absolute exactness. . . .

Color is an ornament of painting, but it is no more than a handmaiden to it, since it does no more than render more pleasing those things which are the true perfections of art. . . .

There exists no example of a great draftsman whose colors did not exactly suit the character of his design.

66

EUGÈNE DELACROIX (1798–1863)
From his *Journal*

Delacroix began his Journal *in 1822 and maintained it irregularly until his death in 1863. He wrote it, he said, "for myself alone" in the hope that it would "do me a lot of good." The first excerpt is from an entry of May 14, 1824.*

What torments my soul is its loneliness. The more it expands among friends and the daily habits or pleasures, the more, it seems to me, it flees me and retires into its fortress. The poet who lives in solitude, but who produces much, is the one who enjoys those treasures we bear in our bosom, but which forsake us when we give ourselves to others. When one yields completely to one's soul, it opens itself completely. . . .

Novelty is in the mind that creates, and not in nature, the thing painted.

This entry, dated October 20, 1853, was recorded at Champ Rosay.

What an adoration I have for painting! The mere memory of certain pictures, even when I don't see them, goes through me with a feeling which stirs my whole being. . . .

The type of emotion peculiar to painting is, so to speak, tangible; poetry and music cannot give it. You enjoy the actual representation of objects as if you really saw them, and at the same time the meaning which the images have for the mind warms you and transports you. These figures, these objects, which seem the thing itself to a certain part of your intelligent being are like a solid bridge on which imagination supports itself to penetrate to the mysterious and profound sensation for which the forms are, so to speak, the hieroglyph, but a hieroglyph far more eloquent than a cold representation, a thing equivalent to no more than a character in the printer's font of type. . . .

The arts are not algebra, in which the abbreviation of the figures contributes to the success of the problem; success in the arts is by no means a matter of abridging, but of amplifying, if possible, and prolonging the sensation by all possible means. What is the theater? One of the most certain witnesses to man's need for experiencing the largest possible number of emotions at one time. It gathers together all the arts so that each may make us feel their combined effect more strongly.

67

ROSA BONHEUR (1822–1899)
From *Reminiscences of Rosa Bonheur*

Bonheur's father, Raymond, was a landscape painter and a disciple of the utopian socialist Henri de Saint-Simon, who considered the artist the priest of his "new Christianity" and thought the Messiah of the future would be, as Bonheur states here, a woman. These reminiscences were published in 1910.

I have never counseled my sisters of the palette to wear men's clothes in the ordinary circumstances of life.

If, however, you see me dressed as I am, it is not in the least in order to make me into an original, but simply to facilitate my work. Consider that, at a certain period in my life, I spent whole days at the slaughterhouse. . . . I also had the passion for horses. Now where better to study these animals than in the fairs. . . . I was forced to recognize that the clothing of my sex was a constant bother. That is why I decided to solicit the authorization to wear men's clothing from the prefect of police.

But the suit I wear is my work attire, and nothing else. The epithets of imbeciles have never bothered me. . . .

Two years ago (October 8, 1896) on the occasion of the reception of the Russian royalty in Paris, the minister of the fine arts had the desire to introduce to them the leading figures of French art. . . . I wore my beautiful suit of black velvet and my little feathered bonnet. . . .

From the moment I arrived at the Louvre, I would have given I do not know what to have had on my head my gray felt hat. I was the only woman, in the middle of a crowd of men. . . . All the eyes turned toward me; I didn't know where to hide myself. This was a harsh test, and that day I really missed my masculine attire, I can assure you. . . .

In spite of my metamorphosis of costume, there is no daughter of Eve who appreciates more than I the nuances; my brusque and almost savage nature never prevented my heart from always remaining perfectly feminine. . . .

Why wouldn't I be proud of being a woman? My father, that enthusiastic apostle of humanity, repeated to me many times that woman's mission was to uplift the human race, that she was the Messiah of future centuries. I owe to his doctrines the great and proud ambition that I conceived for the sex to which I take glory in belonging and whose independence I will uphold until my last day. Moreover, I am persuaded that the future belongs to us.

68

JOHN CONSTABLE (1776–1837)
From a letter to John Fisher

Fisher, the archdeacon of Salisbury Cathedral, was a lifelong friend of the artist. This letter of October 23, 1821, reflects Constable's sensitivity to the beauties of the English landscape.

How much I wish I had been with you on your fishing excursion in the New Forest! What river can it be? But the sound of water escaping from mill-dams, etc., willows, old rotten planks, slimy posts, and brickwork, I love such things. Shakespeare could make everything poetical; he tells us of poor Tom's haunts among "sheep cotes and mills." As long as I do paint, I shall never cease to paint such places. They have always been my delight, and I should indeed have been delighted in seeing what you describe, and in your company, "in the company of a man to whom nature does not spread her volume in vain." Still I should paint my own places best; painting is with me but another word for feeling, and I associate "my careless boyhood" with all that lies on the banks of the Stour; those scenes made me a painter, and I am grateful; that is, I had often thought of pictures of them before I ever touched a pencil.

69

CHARLES BAUDELAIRE (1821–1867)
"The Modern Public and Photography," from Part 2 of *The Salon of 1859*

Baudelaire, now known for his controversial poems in The Flowers of Evil *(1857), was an important Parisian art critic at mid-century. The photographer Nadar was one of his close friends.*

In this country, the natural painter, like the natural poet, is almost a monster. Our exclusive taste for the true . . . oppresses and smothers the taste for the beautiful. Where only the beautiful should be looked for . . . our people look only for the true. They are not artistic, naturally artistic. . . .

In the domain of painting and statuary, the present-day credo of the worldly wise, especially in France . . . is this: I "believe in nature, and I believe only in nature. . . . I believe that art is, and can only be, the exact reproduction of nature. . . . Thus if an industrial process could give us a result identical to nature, that would be absolute art." An avenging God has heard the prayers of this multitude; Daguerre was his messiah. And then they said to themselves: "Since photography provides us with every desirable guarantee of exactitude . . . art is photography." From that moment onwards, our loathsome society rushed, like Narcissus, to contemplate its trivial image on the metallic plate. . . .

I am convinced that the badly applied advances of photography, like all purely material progress for that matter, have greatly contributed to the impoverishment of French artistic genius. . . . Poetry and progress are two ambitious men that hate each other, with an instinctive hatred, and when they meet along a pathway one or other must give way. If photography is allowed to deputize for art in some of art's activities, it will not be long before it has supplanted or corrupted art altogether, thanks to the stupidity of the masses, its natural ally. Photography must, therefore, return to its true duty, which is that of handmaid of the arts and sciences. . . . Let photography quickly enrich the traveller's album, and restore to his eyes the precision his memory may lack; let it adorn the library of the naturalist, magnify microscopic insects, even strengthen, with a few facts, the hypotheses of the astronomer; let it, in short, be the secretary and record-keeper of whomsoever needs absolute material accuracy for professional reasons. . . . But if once it be allowed to impinge on the sphere of the intangible and the imaginary, on anything that has value solely because man adds something to it from his soul, then woe betide us!

70
CHARLES BAUDELAIRE
"On the Heroism of Modern Life," from Part 18 of *The Salon of 1846*

Baudelaire thought that painters and sculptors should reject subjects drawn from history and choose those from contemporary life. His ideas influenced the work of a number of later painters, including his close friend Édouard Manet.

Before trying to distinguish the epic side of modern life, and before bringing examples to prove that our age is no less fertile in sublime themes than past ages, we may assert that since all centuries and all peoples have had their own form of beauty, so inevitably we have ours. That is in the order of things.

All forms of beauty, like all possible phenomena, contain an element of the eternal and an element of the transitory—of the absolute and of the particular. Absolute and eternal beauty does not exist, or rather it is only an abstraction skimmed from the general surface of different beauties. The particular element in each manifestation comes from the emotions: and just as we have our own particular emotions, so we have our own beauty.

. . . Is it not the necessary garb of our suffering age, which wears the symbol of a perpetual mourning even upon its thin black shoulders? Note, too, that the dress-coat and the frock-coat not only possess their political beauty, which is an expression of universal equality, but also their poetic beauty, which is an expression of the public soul—an immense cortège of undertaker's mutes. . . . We are each of us celebrating some funeral. . . .

The pageant of fashionable life and the thousands of floating existences—criminals and kept women—which drift about in the underworld of a great city . . . all prove to us that we have only to open our eyes to recognize our heroism. . . .

The life of our city is rich in poetic and marvellous subjects. We are enveloped and steeped as though in an atmosphere of the marvellous; but we do not notice it.

The *nude*—that darling of the artists, that necessary element of success—is just as frequent and necessary today as it was in the life of the ancients; in bed, for example, or in the bath, or in the anatomy theatre. The themes and resources of painting are equally abundant and varied; but there is a new element—modern beauty.

71
GUSTAVE COURBET (1819–1877)
From his letter to a group of students

A band of students who had withdrawn in protest from the state-run École des Beaux-Arts had invited Courbet to direct the alternative school they were hoping to open. In this letter dated December 25, 1861, he rejected their offer but did agree to give instruction and criticism for about a year in a rented studio, where the model was usually a peasant with a farm animal.

I do not have, and I can not have, students.

I who believe that every artist should be his own master. . . .

I can not teach my art . . . because I deny that art can be taught and because . . . I maintain that art is completely individual, and the talent of each artist is only the result of his own inspiration and his own study of tradition. . . .

Especially, art in painting can only consist of the representation of objects that are visible and tangible to the artist.

No age can be depicted except by its own artists. . . . I believe that the artists of one century are completely incompetent when it comes to depicting the objects of a preceding or future century. . . .

It is in this sense that I deny the term historical art as applied to the past. Historical art is, by its very essence, contemporary. Every age should have its artists, who will express it and depict it for the future. . . .

The true artists are those who take up their epoch at exactly the point to which it has been carried by preceding ages. To retreat is to do nothing. . . . This explains why all archaic schools have always ended by reducing themselves to the most useless compilations.

I also believe that painting is an essentially CONCRETE art and can only consist of the representation of REAL AND EXISTING objects. . . . Imagination in art consists in knowing how to find the most complete expression of an existing object, but never in imagining or in creating the object itself.

Beauty is in nature, and in reality is encountered under the most diverse forms. As soon as it is found, it belongs to art, or rather to the artist who is able to perceive it. . . . The beauty based on nature is superior to all artistic conventions.

72
LILLA CABOT PERRY (1848?–1933)
From "Reminiscences of Claude Monet from 1889 to 1909"

Perry was an American expatriate painter. Monet, a strict empiricist, had a horror of artistic theory and therefore refused to systematize his ideas on art. Perry's reminiscences, published in 1927, provide our best evidence of those ideas.

He never took any pupils, but he would have made a most inspiring master if he had been willing to teach. I remember his once saying to me:

"When you go out to paint, try to forget what objects you have before you—a tree, a house, a field, or whatever. Merely think, here is a little square of blue, here an oblong of pink, here a streak of yellow, and paint it just as it looks to you, the exact color and shape, until it gives your own naïve impression of the scene before you."

He said he wished he had been born blind and then had suddenly gained his sight so that he could have begun to paint in this way without knowing what the objects were that he saw before him. He held that the first real look at the motif was likely to be the truest and most unprejudiced one, and said that the first painting should cover as much of the canvas as possible, no matter how roughly, so as to determine at the outset the tonality of the whole. . . .

Monet's philosophy of painting was to paint what you really see, not what you think you ought to see; not the object isolated as in a test tube, but the object enveloped in sunlight and atmosphere, with the blue dome of Heaven reflected in the shadows.

73
JAMES ABBOTT MCNEILL WHISTLER (1834–1903)
From *The Gentle Art of Making Enemies*

Whistler's book, published in 1893, also contains his account of the famous libel suit he brought against the critic John Ruskin in 1878.

As music is the poetry of sound, so is painting the poetry of sight, and the subject-matter has nothing to do with harmony of sound or of colour.

The great musicians knew this. Beethoven and the rest wrote music—simply music; symphony in this key, concerto or sonata in that.

On F or G they constructed celestial harmonies . . . as combinations, evolved from the chords of F or G and their minor correlatives.

This is pure music as distinguished from airs—commonplace and vulgar in themselves, but interesting from their associations, as, for instance, "Yankee Doodle. . . ."

Art should be independent of all clap-trap—should stand alone, and appeal to the artistic sense of eye or ear, without confounding this with emotions entirely foreign to it, as devotion, pity, love, patriotism, and the like. All these have no kind of concern with it, and that is why I insist on calling my works "arrangements" and "harmonies."

Take the picture of my mother, exhibited at the Royal Academy as an "Arrangement in Grey and Black." Now that is what it is. To me it is interesting as a picture of my mother; but what can or ought the public to care about the identity of the portrait?

74
AUGUSTE RODIN (1840–1917)
From "Conversations" with Paul Gsell

The following remarks, recorded in 1911, reveal Rodin as an exponent of the unconventional idea that the beauty or ugliness of a work of art centers on its inherent "character" or "truth."

The vulgar readily imagine that what they consider ugly in existence is not fit subject for the artist. They would like to forbid us to represent what displeases and offends them in nature.

It is a great error on their part.

What is commonly called *ugliness* in nature can in art become full of great beauty.

In the domain of fact we call *ugly* whatever is deformed, whatever is unhealthy, whatever suggests the ideas of disease, of debility, or of suffering, whatever is contrary to regularity, which is the sign and condition of health and strength: a hunch-back is *ugly*, only who is bandy-legged is *ugly*, poverty in rags is *ugly*. . . .

But let a great artist or a great writer make use of one or the other of these uglinesses, instantly it is transfigured. . . .

To the great artist, everything in nature has *character*. . . . And that which is considered ugly in nature often presents more character than that which is termed beautiful, because in the contractions of a sickly countenance, in the lines of a vicious face, in all deformity, in all decay, the inner truth shines forth more clearly than in features that are regular and healthy.

And as it is solely the power of *character* which makes for beauty in art, it often happens that the uglier a being is in nature, the more beautiful it becomes in art.

There is nothing ugly in art except that which is without character, that is to say, that which offers no outer or inner truth.

Whatever is false, whatever is artificial, whatever seeks to be pretty rather than expressive, whatever is capricious and affected, whatever smiles without motive, bends or struts without cause, is mannered without reason; all that is without soul and without truth; all that is only a *parade* of beauty and grace; all, in short, that lies, is *ugliness* in art.

75

JORIS-KARL HUYSMANS (1848–1907)
From "Iron"

Huysmans, author of the radical antinaturalist novel Against the Grain *(1884), was also an important art critic in Paris at the end of the nineteenth century. The following is taken from a selection of his art criticism entitled* Certaines *(1889).*

In architecture, the situation is now this.

The architects build absurd monuments whose parts, borrowed from all ages, constitute in their ensemble the most servile parodies that one could see. . . .

One fact is certain: the age has produced no architect and is characterized by no style. . . . Another undoubted fact is that stone, considered until now the fundamental material of building, has foundered, drained by repetition. . . .

But our period may yet incarnate itself in buildings that symbolize its activity and its sadness, its cunning and its money, in works sullen and hard, in any case, new.

And the material is here named, it is iron.

Since the reign of Louis Philippe [1830–48], iron structure has been attempted many times, but . . . no new form has been discovered; the metal remains . . . linked to stone, a subordinate agent, incapable of creating by itself a monument that is not a railway station or a greenhouse, a monument that aesthetic criticism may cite. . . .

Iron's role is thus practical and limited, purely internal.

This was the state of architecture when the exposition of 1889 was resolved upon.

It is interesting to see if, in . . . the Eiffel Tower [see fig. 22-35], iron-making has come out of its gropings, and . . . has finally invented a new style. . . .

In a touching unanimity, . . . the entire press, flat on its stomach, exalts the genius of M. Eiffel.

And yet his tower resembles a factory chimney under construction, a carcass that waits to be filled with cut stone or bricks. One cannot imagine that [it] is finished, that this solitary suppository riddled with holes will remain as it is. . . .

The Eiffel Tower is truly of a disconcerting ugliness, and it is not even enormous! Seen from below, it does not seem to attain the height cited for it. . . .

From afar, from the center of Paris, from the depths of the suburbs, the effect is identical. The emptiness of this cage diminishes it; the lathing and the meshwork make of this trophy of iron a horrible bird cage. . . .

It is 300 meters tall and appears one hundred; it is finished and appears barely begun. . . .

Finally, one must ask oneself, what is the fundamental purpose for the existence of this tower?

76

PAUL CÉZANNE (1839–1906)
From a letter to Emile Bernard

Bernard had worked with Gauguin to formulate the style of the Pont-Aven school. He began a correspondence with Cézanne after meeting him at Aix-en-Provence in the spring of 1904, when this letter was written.

. . . May I repeat what I told you here: treat nature by the cylinder, the sphere, the cone, everything in proper perspective so that each side of an object or a plane is directed towards a central point. Lines parallel to the horizon give breadth, that is a section of nature or, if you prefer, of the spectacle that the Pater Omnipotens Aeterne Deus spreads out before our eyes. Lines perpendicular to this horizon give depth. But nature for us men is more depth than surface, whence the need of introducing into our light vibrations, represented by reds and yellows, a sufficient amount of blue to give the impression of air.

77

VINCENT VAN GOGH (1853–1890)
From a letter to his brother Theo

Theo, who worked for an art dealer in Paris, provided Vincent's chief emotional and economic support. This letter, dated April 30, 1885, was written from their father's house in Neunen.

I have tried to emphasize that those people, eating their potatoes in the lamplight, have dug the earth with those very hands they put in the dish, and so it speaks of manual labor, and how they have honestly earned their food [see fig. 23-10].

I have wanted to give the impression of a way of life quite different from that of us civilized people. Therefore I am not at all anxious for everyone to like it or to admire it at once. . . .

It would be wrong, I think, to give a peasant picture a certain conventional smoothness. If a peasant picture smells of bacon, smoke, potato steam—all right, that's not unhealthy; if a stable smells of dung—all right, that belongs to a stable; if the field has an odor of ripe corn or potatoes or of . . . manure—that's healthy, especially for city people.

78
VINCENT VAN GOGH
From an undated letter to Theo

I am returning to the ideas I had in the country before I knew the impressionists. And I should not be surprised if the impressionists soon find fault with my way of working, for it has been fertilized by Delacroix's ideas rather than by theirs. Because instead of trying to reproduce exactly what I see before my eyes, I use color more arbitrarily, in order to express myself forcibly. . . .

I should like to paint the portrait of an artist friend, a man who dreams great dreams, who works as the nightingale sings, because it is his nature. He'll be a blond man. I want to put my appreciation, the love I have for him, into the picture. So I paint him as he is, as faithfully as I can, to begin with.

But the picture is not yet finished. To finish it I am now going to be the arbitrary colorist. I exaggerate the fairness of the hair, I even get to orange tones, chromes and pale citron-yellow.

Behind the head, instead of painting the ordinary wall of the mean room, I paint infinity, a plain background of the richest, intensest blue that I can contrive, and by this simple combination of the bright head against the rich blue background, I get a mysterious effect, like a star in the depths of an azure sky.

79
PAUL GAUGUIN (1848–1903)
From a letter to J. F. Willumsen

The Danish painter J. F. Willumsen was a member of Gauguin's circle in Brittany. Gauguin wrote this letter in the autumn of 1890, before his departure for the South Seas.

As for me, my mind is made up. I am going soon to Tahiti, a small island in Oceania, where the material necessities of life can be had without money. I want to forget all the misfortunes of the past, I want to be free to paint without any glory whatsoever in the eyes of the others and I want to die there and to be forgotten there. . . . A terrible epoch is brewing in Europe for the coming generation: the kingdom of gold. Everything is putrefied, even men, even the arts. There, at least, under an eternally summer sky, on a marvellously fertile soil, the Tahitian has only to lift his hands to gather his food; and in addition he never works. When in Europe men and women survive only after unceasing labor during which they struggle in convulsions of cold and hunger, a prey to misery, the Tahitians, on the contrary, happy inhabitants of the unknown paradise of Oceania, know only sweetness of life. To live, for them, is to sing and to love. . . . Once my material life is well organized, I can there devote myself to great works of art, freed from all artistic jealousies and with no need whatsoever of lowly trade.

80
EDVARD MUNCH (1864–1944)
From notes on the *Frieze of Life*

Munch probably wrote his notes on the origin of the Frieze of Life *when it was exhibited in Oslo in 1918.*

One evening I was walking along a path—on the one side lay the city and below me the fjord.

I was tired and ill—I stopped and looked out across the fjord—the sun was setting—the clouds were dyed red like blood.

I felt a scream pass through nature; it seemed to me that I could hear the scream.

I painted this picture—painted the clouds as real blood.—The colors were screaming.—

This became the picture *The Scream* from the *Frieze of Life*.

81
LOUIS SULLIVAN (1856–1924)
From "The Tall Office Building Artistically Considered"

Sullivan had already completed several skyscrapers, including the Wainwright Building (see fig. 23-39) and the Guaranty Building, when he recorded these ideas in an essay of 1896.

The architects of this land and generation are now brought face to face with something new under the sun—namely, . . . a demand for the erection of tall office buildings. . . .

Offices are necessary for the transaction of business; the invention and perfection of the high-speed elevators make vertical travel, that was once tedious and painful, now easy and comfortable; development of steel manufacture has shown the way to safe, rigid, economical constructions rising to a great height; continued growth of population in the great cities, consequent congestion of centers and rise in value of ground, stimulate an increase in number of stories. . . . Thus has come about that form of lofty construction called the "modern office building. . . ."

Problem: How shall we impart to this sterile pile, . . . this stark, staring exclamation of eternal strife, the graciousness of those higher forms of sensibility and culture that rest on the lower and fiercer passions? . . .

What is the chief characteristic of the tall office building? . . . It is lofty. This loftiness is to the artist-nature its thrilling aspect. . . . It must be every inch a proud and soaring thing, rising in sheer exultation that from bottom to top it is a unit without a single dissenting line. . . .

Certain critics . . . have advanced the theory that the true prototype of the tall office building is the classical column, consisting of base, shaft and capital. . . .

Other theorizers, assuming a mystical symbolism as a guide, quote the many trinities in nature and art, and the beauty and conclusiveness of such trinity in unity. . . .

Others, seeking their examples and justification in the vegetable kingdom, urge that such a design shall above all things be organic. . . . They point to the pine-tree, its massy roots, its lithe, uninterrupted trunk, its tuft of green high in the air. Thus, they say, should be the design of the tall office building: again in three parts vertically.

Others still, more susceptible to the power of a unit than to the grace of a trinity, say that such a design should be struck out at a blow, as though by a blacksmith or by mighty Jove. . . .

I shall, with however much of regret, dissent from [these critics] as touching not at all upon . . . the quick of the entire matter, upon the true; the immovable philosophy of the architectural art. . . .

Unfailingly in nature [its] shapes express the inner life, the native quality, of the animal, tree, bird, fish, that they present to us; they are so characteristic, so recognizable, that we say, simply, it is "natural" it should be so. . . .

It is the pervading law of all things organic, and inorganic, . . . that form ever follows function. . . .

Shall we, then, daily violate this law in our art? . . .

Does this not . . . conclusively show that the lower one or two stories [of the tall office building] will take on a special character suited to the special needs, that the tiers of typical offices, having the same unchanging function, shall continue in the same unchanging form, and that as to the attic, . . . its function shall equally be so in force, in . . . outward expression? From this results, naturally, . . . a three-part division, not from any theory, symbol, or fancied logic.

82

GEORGIA O'KEEFFE (1887–1986)
From "Stieglitz: His Pictures Collected Him"

O'Keeffe met Alfred Stieglitz in 1908 and had her first show at his gallery in 1916. She married him in 1924. These remarks, published in 1949, were made after his death.

Stieglitz grew up during the period when photography was young, began working at it while studying mechanical engineering at the Berlin Polytechnic. . . . He soon decided to make himself an authority on photography and went about it by sending his photographs everywhere to exhibitions to get all the medals that were given in the world at that time. . . .

Although the photographs that he was making at this time were very much admired by painters and artists generally, the artists seemed to have the idea that photography could never be accepted as one of the arts. Stieglitz denied this. As he was naturally a fighter, he began to work for its recognition as one of the arts, not particularly for himself but for the idea of photography. . . . Painters would often say they wished they had painted what he had photographed. He always said he never regretted that he had not photographed what they were painting.

In 1890 Stieglitz returned to America from his European student period, twenty-six years old. Years of feverish activity with photography followed. He finally decided that for photography to be recognized as one of the arts, the work of a group could bring about this recognition better than the work of an individual. . . .

The Photo-Secession group was formed in 1902, . . . Stieglitz . . . was the leader. In 1905 they began having photographic exhibitions at the little gallery known as "291.". . . . Here the beginnings of modern art were also shown. . . .

I was sent, like all the other students, by the instructors of the Art Students League to see the first showing of Rodin drawings at "291." . . .

I very well remember the fantastic violence of Stieglitz's defense when the students with me began talking with him about the drawings.

83

HENRI MATISSE (1869–1954)
From "Notes of a Painter"

This 1908 article, Matisse's most complete statement on his art, reflects the transition from his early Fauve phase to his mature, post-Fauve period.

What I am after, above all, is expression. . . .

Expression, for me, does not reside in passions glowing in a human face or manifested by violent movement. The entire arrangement of my picture is expressive. . . . Composition is the art of arranging in a decorative manner the diverse elements at the painter's command to express his feelings. . . .

Both harmonies and dissonances of color can produce agreeable effects. Often when I settle down to work I begin by noting my immediate and superficial color sensations. Some years ago this first result was often enough for me—but today if I were satisfied with this, my picture would remain incomplete. I would have put down the passing sensations of a moment; they would not completely define my feelings and the next day I might not recognize what they meant. I want to reach that state of condensation of sensations which constitutes a picture. . . .

There are two ways of expressing things; one is to show them crudely, the other is to evoke them artistically. In abandoning the literal representation of movement it is possible to reach toward a higher ideal of beauty and grandeur.

Suppose I set out to paint an interior: I have before me a cupboard; it gives me a sensation of bright red—and I put down a red which satisfies me; immediately a relation is established between this red and the white of the canvas. If I put a green near the red, if I paint in a yellow floor, there must still be between this green, this yellow and the white of the canvas a relation that will be satisfactory to me. But these several tones mutually weaken one another. It is necessary, therefore, that the various elements that I use be so balanced that they do not destroy one another. To do this I must organize my ideas; the relation between tones must be so established that they will sustain one another. A new combination of colors will succeed the first one and will give more completely my interpretation. . . . I cannot copy nature in a servile way; I must interpret nature and submit it to the spirit of the picture. When I have found the relationship of all the tones the result must be a living harmony of tones, a harmony not unlike that of a musical composition. . . .

What I dream of is an art of balance, of purity and serenity devoid of troubling or depressing subject matter, an art which might be for every mental worker, be he businessman or writer, like an appeasing influence, like a mental soother, something like a good armchair in which to rest from physical fatigue.

84

WASSILY KANDINSKY (1866–1944)
Concerning the Spiritual in Art, from Chapter 5, "The Effect of Color"

Kandinsky hoped to inaugurate a new spiritual era for modern man through his art. These remarks first appeared in 1912.

If you let your eye stray over a palette of colors, you experience two things. In the first place you receive *a purely physical effect*, namely the eye itself is enchanted by the beauty and other qualities of color. You experience satisfaction and delight, like a gourmet savoring a delicacy. Or the eye is stimulated as the tongue is titillated by a spicy dish. But then it grows calm and cool, like a finger after touching ice. These are physical sensations, limited in duration. They are superficial, too, and leave no lasting impression behind if the soul remains closed. Just as we feel at the touch of ice a sensation of cold, forgotten as soon as the finger becomes warm again, so the physical action of color is forgotten as soon as the eye turns away. On the other hand, as the physical coldness of ice, upon penetrating more deeply, arouses more complex feelings, and indeed a whole chain of psychological experiences, so may also the superficial impression of color develop into an experience. . . .

And so we come to the second result of looking at colors: their psychological effect. They produce a correspondent spiritual vibration, and it is only as a step towards this spiritual vibration that the physical impression is of importance. . . .

Generally speaking, color directly influences the soul. Color is the keyboard, the eyes are the hammers, the soul is the piano with many strings. The artist is the hand that plays, touching one key or another purposively, to cause vibrations in the soul.

It is evident therefore that color harmony must rest ultimately on purposive playing upon the human soul.

85

FILIPPO TOMMASO MARINETTI (1876–1944)
From "The Foundation and Manifesto of Futurism"

After Marinetti's example of 1908, the manifesto became a popular device for innovative twentieth-century artists to publicize their views.

We declare our primary intentions to all living men of the earth:

1. We intend to glorify the love of danger, the custom of energy, the strength of daring. . . .

3. Literature having up to now glorified thoughtful immobility, ecstasy, and slumber, we wish to exalt the aggressive movement, the feverish insomnia, running, the perilous leap, the cuff, and the blow.

4. We declare that the splendor of the world has been enriched with a new form of beauty, the beauty of speed. A race-automobile adorned with great pipes like serpents with explosive breath . . . a race-automobile which seems to rush over exploding powder is more beautiful than the Victory of Samothrace. . . .

7. There is no more beauty except in struggle. No masterpiece without the stamp of aggressiveness. Poetry should be a violent assault against unknown forces to summon them to lie down at the feet of man. . . .

9. We will glorify war—the only true hygiene of the world—militarism, patriotism, the destructive gesture of anarchist, the beautiful Ideas which kill, and the scorn of woman.

10. We will destroy museums, libraries, and fight against moralism, feminism, and all utilitarian cowardice. . . .

It is in Italy that we hurl this overthrowing and inflammatory declaration, with which today we found Futurism, for we will free Italy from her numberless museums which cover her with countless cemeteries.

Museums, cemeteries! . . . Identical truly. . . .

To admire an old picture is to pour our sentiment into a funeral urn instead of hurling it forth in violent gushes of action and productiveness. . . .

The oldest among us are thirty; we have thus at least ten years in which to accomplish our task. When we are forty, let others—younger and more daring men—throw us into the wastepaper basket like useless manuscripts!

86

GIORGIO DE CHIRICO (1888–1978)
From "Mystery and Creation"

Though written in Paris before his return to Italy in 1915 at the onset of World War I, this manifesto of De Chirico's Metaphysical Painting was not published until 1928 by André Breton.

It is important that we should rid art of all that it has contained of *recognizable material* to date, all familiar subject matter, all traditional ideas, all popular symbols must be banished forthwith. More important still, we must hold enormous faith in ourselves: it is essential that the revelation we receive, the conception of an image which embraces a certain thing, which has no sense in itself, which has no subject, which means *absolutely nothing* from the logical point of view, I repeat, it is essential that such a revelation or conception should speak so strongly in us, evoke such agony or joy, that we feel compelled to paint, compelled by an impulse even more urgent than the hungry desperation which drives a man to tearing at a piece of bread like a savage beast.

I remember one vivid winter's day at Versailles. Silence and calm reigned supreme. Everything gazed at me with mysterious, questioning eyes. And then I realized that every corner of the palace, every column, every window possessed a spirit, an impenetrable soul. I looked around at the marble heroes, motionless in the lucid air, beneath the frozen rays of that winter sun which pours down on us *without love,* like a perfect song. A bird was warbling in a window cage. At that moment I grew aware of the mystery which urges men to create certain strange forms. And the creation appeared more extraordinary than the creators.

Perhaps the most amazing sensation passed on to us by prehistoric man is that of presentiment. It will always continue. We might consider it as an eternal proof of the irrationality of the universe. Original man must have wandered through a world full of uncanny signs. He must have trembled at each step.

87

PIET MONDRIAN (1872–1944)
From "Natural Reality and Abstract Reality"

This early essay, which appeared in the first issue of De Stijl *in 1919, already contains the germ of his mature art.*

We find that in nature all relations are dominated by a single primordial relation, which is defined by the opposition of two extremes. Abstract plasticism represents this primordial relation in a precise manner by means of the two positions which form the right angle. This positional relationship is the most balanced of all, since it expresses in a perfect harmony the relation between two extremes, and contains all other relations.

If we conceive these two extremes as manifestations of interiority and exteriority, we will find that in the new plasticism the tie uniting mind and life is not broken. . . .

If unity is contemplated in a precise and definite way, attention will [be] directed solely towards the universal, and as a consequence, the particular will disappear from art—as painting has already shown.

This, however, cannot appear before its proper time. For it is the spirit of the times that determines artistic expression. . . . But at the present moment, that form of art alone is truly alive which expresses our present—or future—consciousness.

Composition allows the artist the greatest possible freedom, so that his subjectivity can express itself, to a certain degree, for as long as needed.

The rhythm of relations of color and size makes the absolute appear in the relativity of time and space.

88

PIET MONDRIAN
From "Plastic Art and Pure Plastic Art"

This essay, published in 1937, is the culmination of Mondrian's attempts to work out his aesthetic theories in written form.

Art makes us realize that there are *fixed laws which govern and point to the use of the constructive elements of the composition and of the inherent inter-relationships between them.* These laws may be regarded as subsidiary law to the *fundamental* law of equivalence which creates *dynamic equilibrium and reveals the true content of reality.*

In spite of world disorder, instinct and intuition are carrying humanity to a real equilibrium. . . . Art certainly shows this clearly. But art shows also that in the course of progress, intuition becomes more and more conscious and instinct more and more purified.

Non-figurative art brings to an end the ancient culture of art; at present, therefore, one can review and judge more surely *the whole culture of art.* We are not at the turning-point of this culture; *the culture of particular form is approaching its end. The culture of determined relations has begun.*

In pure plastic art the significance of different forms and lines is very important; it is precisely this fact which makes it pure. . . .

Non-figurative art is created by establishing *a dynamic rhythm of determinate mutual relations* which *excludes the formation of any particular form.* . . .

In removing completely from the work all objects, 'the world is not separated from the spirit', but is on the contrary, *put into a balanced opposition* with the spirit, since the one and the other are purified.

89
RICHARD HUELSENBECK (1892–1974)
From "First German Dada Manifesto"

*In 1917 Huelsenbeck returned to Germany from Zurich,
where he participated in the Dada movement. The "First
Dada Manifesto" was written the following year.*

... The best and most extraordinary artists will be those who every
hour snatch the tatters of their bodies out of the frenzied cataract
of life, who, with bleeding hands and hearts, hold fast to the intelligence of their time. Has expressionism fulfilled our expectations
of such an art, which should be an expression of our most vital concerns?

No! No! No!

Have the expressionists fulfilled our expectations of an art that
burns the essence of life into our flesh?

No! No! No!

Under the pretext of turning inward, the expressionists in literature and painting have banded together into a generation
which is already looking forward to honorable mention in the histories of literature and art and aspiring to the most respectable
civic distinctions. . . . That sentimental resistance to the times,
which are neither better nor worse, neither more reactionary nor
more revolutionary than other times…is the quality of a youth
which never knew how to be young. Expressionism…has nothing
in common with the efforts of active men. The signers of this manifesto have, under the battle cry:

Dada!!!!

gathered together to put forward a new art. . . .

The word Dada symbolizes the most primitive relation to the
reality of the environment; with Dadaism a new reality comes into
its own. Life appears as a simultaneous muddle of noises, colors
and spiritual rhythms, which is taken unmodified into Dadaist
art, with all the sensational screams and fevers of its reckless everyday psyche and with all its brutal reality. . . . Dadaism for the first
time has ceased to take an aesthetic attitude toward life . . . by tearing all the slogans of ethics, culture and inwardness . . . into their
components.

90
ANDRÉ BRETON (1896–1966)
From "What Is Surrealism?"

*The first Surrealist manifesto appeared in 1924, the sec-
ond in 1930, and this one, considered the third, in 1934.
Although the Surrealist movement was dedicated to the
freedom of the individual, its founder, Breton, was both
moralistic and highly authoritarian. Because he sometimes excommunicated members of the group, he became
known as "the Pope of Surrealism."*

We still live under the reign of logic, but the methods of logic are
applied nowadays only to the resolution of problems of secondary interest. The absolute rationalism which is still the fashion does not permit consideration of any facts but those strictly
relevant to our experience. Logical ends, on the other hand,
escape us. Needless to say that even experience has had limits
assigned to it. It revolves in a cage from which it be comes more
and more difficult to release it. Even experience is dependent on
immediate utility, and common sense is its keeper. Under color
of civilization, under the pretext of progress, all that rightly or
wrongly may be regarded as fantasy or superstition has been
banished from the mind, all uncustomary searching after truth
has been proscribed. It is only by what must seem sheer luck that
there has recently been brought to light an aspect of mental life—
to my belief by far the most important—with which it was supposed that we no longer had any concern. All credit for these discoveries must go to Freud. Based on these discoveries a current
of opinion is forming that will enable the explorer of the human
mind to continue his investigations, justified as he will be in taking into account more than mere summary realities. The imagination is perhaps on the point of reclaiming its rights. If the
depths of our minds harbor strange forces capable of increasing
those on the surface, or of successfully contending with them,
then it is all in our interest to canalize them, to canalize them first
in order to submit them later, if necessary, to the control of the
reason. . . .

I am resolved to render powerless that *hatred of the marvelous*
which is so rampant. . . . Briefly: The marvelous is always beautiful, anything that is marvelous is beautiful; indeed, nothing but the
marvelous is beautiful.

The admirable thing about the fantastic is that it is no longer
fantastic: there is only the real.

91
MAX BECKMANN (1884–1950)
From "On My Painting"

*First given as a lecture in German in London in 1938 and
published in English in New York three years later, "On
My Painting" is the fullest statement of Beckmann's art.*

One of my problems is to find the self, which has only one form
and is immortal—to find it in animals and men, in the heaven and
in the hell which together form the world in which we live.

Space, and space again, is the infinite deity which surrounds us
and in which we are ourselves contained. . . .

Often, very often, I am alone. My studio . . . is again filled in
my imagination with figures from the old days and from the new,
like an ocean moved by storm and sun and always present in my
thoughts.

Then shapes become beings and seem comprehensible to me
in the great void and uncertainty of the space which I call God.

Sometimes I am helped by the constructive rhythm of the cabala, when my thoughts wander over Oannes Dagon to the last days of drowned continents. Of the same substance are streets of their men, women and children; great ladies and whores; servant girls and duchesses. I seem to meet them, like doubly significant dreams, in Samothrace and Piccadilly and Wall Street. They are Eros and the longing for oblivion.

92

JACKSON POLLOCK (1912–1956)
From "My Painting"

In 1947, when these remarks were recorded, Pollock rejected the usual easel format by placing his unstretched canvases directly on the floor. Using ordinary house paint, he claimed that he was not just throwing paint but delineating some real thing in the air above the canvas.

My painting does not come from the easel. I hardly ever stretch my canvas before painting. I prefer to tack the unstretched canvas to the hard wall or the floor. I need the resistance of a hard surface. On the floor I am more at ease. I feel nearer, more a part of the painting, since this way I can walk around it, work from the four sides and literally be in the painting. This is akin to the method of the Indian sand painters of the West.

I continue to get further away from the usual painter's tools such as easel, palette, brushes, etc. I prefer sticks, trowels, knives and dripping fluid paint or a heavy impasto with sand, broken glass and other foreign matter added.

When I am *in* my painting, I'm not aware of what I'm doing. It is only after a sort of "get acquainted" period that I see what I have been about. I have no fears about making changes, destroying the image, etc., because the painting has a life of its own. I try to let it come through. It is only when I lose contact with the painting that the result is a mess. Otherwise there is pure harmony, an easy give and take, and the painting comes out well.

The source of my painting is the unconscious. I approach painting the same way I approach drawing. That is direct—with no preliminary studies. The drawings I do are relative to my painting but not for it.

93

ROMARE BEARDEN (1911–1988)
From two interviews

In interviews conducted by Myron Schwartzman in 1983 and 1986, Bearden discussed the wide range of artistic influences on his working methods and ideas.

MYRON SCHWARTZMAN: So [collage] gets improvisational. . . .

ROMARE BEARDEN: Well, it's like jazz; you do this and then you improvise. You know Manet (I think) said, "A painting isn't

finished; sometimes you get on the surface." He meant, "Well, you've got it under control." Maybe sometimes a third of the way through [a painting], I'll say, "I know this is coming out." You get that feeling that the thing is going to be all right. And other things you just have to surrender. As my friend Carl Holty used to say, "Don't close your picture too quickly; keep it open until the very last, and that gives you room to maneuver." You reach a point when all the elements seem to focus, so that the colors and the forms will set. And at that point you can relinquish the painting. . . .

MS: What triggers [a] series, Romie?

RB: Well, the memories are just there; they're just really with me. It's strange, the memories are there. For instance, you see the Vermeer [reproduction of *The Concert*] up there on the wall? I'll say, "Well, I saw something like this; this used to be so-and-so." Because I guess art is made from other art. Yes, I've been in places like this; I've gone in with the same kind of stillness, and the light coming in from this source.

Those people [of Vermeer's time] moved on, and the people from Mecklenburg [North Carolina, Bearden's birthplace] have come in there; they stayed a while and now there is something else.

MS: Let's explore the theme of relationships. What does it mean to you in painting?

RB: In discussing relationships, we have to consider many disparate factors, or seemingly disparate factors, in the way a painting is put together, such as scale, space, line, and so forth. I think this is one of the most important things that Matisse talks about—the relationships, how one does things—and it changes. . . .

In the icons, and in African sculpture, they bring everything to a very beautiful shape. So long as you can get everything in a nice shape, the picture will be all right—you're just shaping it, not worrying so much about the anatomy. If you do that and it all moves in the right rhythms, you have a painting. We get deceived so much by appearances. You sometimes just have to forget about that, because you are working in another world here. And so you could easily take these [canvases] as being completely nonrepresentational.

Take Vermeer's drawings—you turn them upside down, and there's real, great abstraction. The wrinkles in the clothes, for instance; you turn the drawing upside down, and you see something else, the great relationships. This is the abstracting of things. People think abstraction means that you don't have figurative objects in a work. So a more accurate word is "nonrepresentational" rather than "abstract," because Poussin, Ingres are great abstractionists. . . .

The thing is that the artist confronts chaos. The whole thing of art is, how do you organize chaos? . . . Probably, if you take it symbolically, there is no greater chaos than in the inferno, down in hell. Dante, in his *Inferno*, meets Virgil. . . . He's lost and confused there, and Virgil says, "I'll guide you, . . . " to me he is like the artist. This is the help that he needs in understanding what is going on, . . . some kind of organization that he finds. And he's talking about sin, and the rest of these things. But he needs that guide.

So I think it's the same thing with the artist.

94

RICHARD HAMILTON (b. 1922)
From "For the Finest Art, Try Pop"

This excerpt first appeared in London in 1961.

A new generation of Dadaists has emerged today, as violent and ingenious as their forbears, but Son of Dada is accepted, lionized by public and dealers, certified by state museums—the act of mythmaking has been transferred from the subject-matter of the work to the artist himself as the content of his art.

Futurism has ebbed and has no successor. . . . The Pop-Fine-Art standpoint . . . is, like Futurism, fundamentally a statement of belief in the changing values of society. Pop-Fine-Art is a profession of approbation of mass culture, therefore also antiartistic. It is positive Dada, creative where Dada was destructive. Perhaps it is Mama—a cross-fertilization of Futurism and Dada which upholds a respect for the culture of the masses and a conviction that the artist in twentieth century urban life is inevitably a consumer of mass culture and potentially a contributor to it.

95

ROY LICHTENSTEIN (1923–1997)
From "What Is Pop Art?"

This interview with Gene R. Swenson appeared in 1963, the same year as Lichtenstein's Drowning Girl *(see fig. 24-76).*

ROY LICHTENSTEIN: I think my work is different from comic strips—but I wouldn't call it transformation. . . . What I do is form, whereas the comic strip is not formed in the sense I'm using the word; the comics have shapes but there has been no effort to make them intensely unified. The purpose is different, one intends to depict and I intend to unify. And my work is actually different from comic strips in that every mark is really in a different place, however slight the difference seems to some. The difference is often not great, but it is crucial. . . .

GENE R. SWENSON: A curator at the Modern Museum has called Pop Art fascistic and militaristic.

RL: The heroes depicted in comic books are fascist types, but I don't take them seriously in these paintings—maybe there is a point in not taking them seriously, a political point. I use them for purely formal reasons, and that's not what those heroes were invented for. . . .

The techniques I use are not commercial, they only appear to be commercial—and the ways of seeing and composing and unifying are different and have different ends.

96

MARCEL DUCHAMP (1898–1986)
From "Apropos of Readymade"

The following are excerpts from a lecture given at the Museum of Modern Art, New York, in October 1961.

IN 1913 I HAD THE HAPPY IDEA TO FASTEN A BICYCLE WHEEL TO A KITCHEN STOOL AND WATCH IT TURN.

IN NEW YORK IN 1915 I BOUGHT AT A HARDWARE STORE A SNOW SHOVEL ON WHICH I WROTE "IN ADVANCE OF THE BROKEN ARM."

IT WAS AROUND THAT TIME THAT THE WORD "READYMADE" CAME TO MIND TO DESIGNATE THIS FORM OF MANIFESTATION.

A POINT WHICH I WANT VERY MUCH TO ESTABLISH IS THAT THE CHOICE OF THESE "READYMADES" WAS NEVER DICTATED BY ESTHETIC DELECTATION.

THIS CHOICE WAS BASED ON A REACTION OF VISUAL INDIFFERENCE WITH AT THE SAME TIME A TOTAL ABSENCE OF GOOD OR BAD TASTE. . . .

ONE IMPORTANT CHARACTERISTIC WAS THE SHORT SENTENCE WHICH I OCCASIONALLY INSCRIBED ON THE "READYMADE."

THAT SENTENCE INSTEAD OF DESCRIBING THE OBJECT LIKE A TITLE WAS MEANT TO CARRY THE MIND OF THE SPECTATOR TOWARDS OTHER REGIONS MORE VERBAL.

ANOTHER ASPECT OF THE "READYMADE" IS ITS LACK OF UNIQUENESS. . . . THE REPLICA OF A "READYMADE" DELIVERING THE SAME MESSAGE; IN FACT NEARLY EVERY ONE OF THE "READYMADES" EXISTING TODAY IS NOT AN ORIGINAL IN THE CONVENTIONAL SENSE.

97

HENRY MOORE (1898–1986)
From "The Sculptor Speaks"

Moore's sculpture in the 1930s began to reveal the tension between solid and void. His interest in the human figure and in natural forms remained paramount, however, as is evident in these comments published in 1937.

Since the Gothic, European sculpture had become overgrown with moss, weeds—all sorts of surface excrescences which completely concealed shape. It has been Brancusi's special mission to get rid of this overgrowth, and to make us once more shape-conscious. To do this he has had to concentrate on very simple direct shapes, to keep his sculpture, as it were, one-cylindered, to refine and polish a single shape to a degree almost too precious. Brancusi's work, apart from its individual value, has been of historical importance in the development of contemporary sculpture. But it may now be no longer necessary to close down and restrict sculpture to the single (static) form unit. We can now begin to open out. To relate and combine together several forms of varied sizes, sections, and directions into one organic whole.

Although it is the human figure which interests me most deeply, I have always paid great attention to natural forms, such as bones, shells, and pebbles, etc. Sometimes for several years running I have been to the same part of the seashore—but each year a new shape of pebble has caught my eye, which the year before, though it was there in hundreds, I never saw. . . . A different thing happens if I sit down and examine a handful one by one. I may then extend my form-experience more, by giving my mind time to become conditioned to a new shape.

There are universal shapes to which everybody is subconsciously conditioned and to which they can respond if their conscious control does not shut them off.

Pebbles show nature's way of working stone.

98

EVA HESSE (1936–1970)
From an interview

An abbreviated version of this interview with Cindy Nemser was published in 1970, shortly before Hesse's death. Hesse resisted the impersonal formalism of 1960s art.

CINDY NEMSER: . . . Looking at your works they seem, to me, to be filled with sexual impulses or organic feeling. I feel there are anthropomorphic inferences.

EVA HESSE: It's not a simple question for me. First when I work it's only the abstract qualities that I'm really working with, which is to say the material, the form it's going to take, the size, the scale, the positioning. . . . However, I don't value the totality of the image on these abstract or esthetic points. For me it's a total image that has to do with me and life. It can't be divorced as an idea or composition or form. I don't believe art can be based on that. . . . I don't want to make that my problem. . . . Those problems are solvable, I solve them, can solve them *beautifully.* In fact, my idea now is to discount everything I've ever learned or been taught about those things and to find something else. So it is inevitable that it is my life, my feelings, my thoughts. And there I'm very complex. I'm not a simple person and the complexity . . . is the total absurdity of life. I guess that's where I relate, if I do, to certain artists who I feel very close to, and not so much through having studied their writings or works, but because, for me, there's this total *absurdity* in their work.

CN: Which artists are they?

EH: Duchamp, Yvonne Rainer, Ionesco, Carl Andre.

CN: Let's talk about some of your early sculptures.

EH: There was a piece I did for that show in the Graham Gallery . . . in 1965 or '66. It was called Hang-Up—a dumb name . . . but I can't change it. I think it was about the fifth piece I did and I think the most important statement I made. It's close to what I feel I achieve now in my best pieces. It was the first time where my idea of absurdity or extreme feeling came through.

99

LE CORBUSIER (1886–1965)
From *Towards a New Architecture*

First published in 1923, Towards a New Architecture *codified ideas that were being widely discussed among architects and in turn became the first manifesto of the International Style. The English translation appeared four years later in London. The following excerpts are from the opening Argument.*

The Engineer's Aesthetic, and Architecture, are two things that march together and follow one from the other. . . .

The Engineer, inspired by the law of Economy and governed by mathematical calculation, puts us in accord with universal law. He achieves harmony.

The Architect, by his arrangement of forms, realizes an order which is a pure creation of his spirit; by forms and shapes he affects our senses to an acute degree and provokes plastic emotions; by the relationships which he creates he wakes profound echoes in us, he gives us the measure of an order which we feel to be in accordance with that of our world, he determines the various movements of our heart and of our understanding; it is then that we experience the sense of beauty.

Primary forms are beautiful forms because they can be clearly appreciated.

The great problems of modern construction must have a geometrical solution.

Machinery contains in itself the factor of economy, which makes for selection.

The house is a machine for living in.

Standards are a matter of logic, analysis and minute study. . . .

Man looks at the creation of architecture with his eyes, which are 5 feet 6 inches from the ground.

Industry, overwhelming us like a flood which rolls on towards its destined ends, has furnished us with new tools adapted to this new epoch, animated by the new spirit.

The problem of the house is a problem of the epoch.

If we eliminate from our hearts and minds all dead concepts in regard to the house, and look at the question from a critical and objective point of view, we shall arrive at the "House-Machine," the mass-production house, healthy (and morally so too) and beautiful. . . .

100
WALTER GROPIUS (1883–1969)
From *Scope of Total Architecture*

*Gropius was interested in the social and aesthetic impli-
cations of housing and city planning, as these remarks of
1943 suggest.*

Every thinking contemporary searches his mind now trying to
figure out what may be the ultimate value of our stupendous scientific progress. We roar with new techniques and new inventions
for speedier means of transportation. But what do we do with all
the time saved? Do we use it for contemplation of our existence?
No, we plunge instead into an even more hectic current of activity, surrendering to that fallacious slogan: time is money. We
obviously need a clarification as to what exactly our spiritual and
intellectual aims are. . . .

I should like, therefore, to attempt to outline the potential
strategic aim of planning for my own profession, architecture,
within the cultural and political context of our industrial civilization. . . .

Our scientific age, by going to extremes of specialization, has
obviously prevented us from seeing our complicated life as an
entity. The average professional man, driven to distraction by the
multiplicity of problems spread out before him, seeks relief from
the pressure of general responsibilities by picking out one single,
rigidly circumscribed responsibility in a specialized field and
refuses to be answerable for anything that may happen outside this
field. A general dissolution of context has set in and naturally
resulted in shrinking and fragmentating life. As Albert Einstein
once put it: "Perfection of means and confusion of aims seem to be
characteristic of our age. . . ."

But there are indications that we are slowly moving away from
overspecialization and its perilous atomizing effect on the social
coherence of the community. . . . In the gigantic task of its reuni-
fication, the planner and architect will have to play a big role. He
must be well trained not ever to lose a total vision, in spite of the
infinite wealth of specialized knowledge which he has to absorb
and integrate. He must comprehend land, nature, man and his art,
as one great entity. In our mechanized society we should passionately emphasize that we are still a world of men, that man in his
natural environment must be the focus of all planning. We have
indulged our latest pets, the machines, to such an extent that we
have lost a genuine scale of values. Therefore, we need to investigate what makes up the really worthwhile relationships among
men, and between men and nature, instead of giving way to the
pressure of special interests or of shortsighted enthusiasts who
want to make mechanization an end in itself. . . .

There is no other way toward progress but to start coura-
geously and without prejudice new practical tests by building
model communities in one stroke and then systematically examining their living value. What a wealth of new information for the
sociologist, the economist, the scientist and the artist would be
forthcoming, if groups, formed of the most able planners and
architects available, should be commissioned to design and build
completely new model communities! Such information would
also offer most valuable preparatory data to solve the complicated
problem of rehabilitating our existing communities.

101
EDWARD WESTON (1886–1958)
From "Photographic Art"

*Weston insisted that the photographer should previsual-
ize the final print before making the exposure and not
crop or trim the print. This excerpt from an encyclopedia
entry published in 1942 attempts to synthesize some of the
reflections on photography that he kept in his* Daybooks.

The camera lens sees too clearly to be used successfully for recording the superficial aspects of a subject. . . .

But if the camera's innate honesty works any hardship on the
photographer by limiting his subject matter in one direction, the loss
is slight when weighed against the advantages it provides. For it
is that very quality that makes the camera expressly fitted for examining deeply into the meaning of things. The discriminating
photographer . . . can reveal the essence of what lies before his lens
with such clear insight that the beholder will find the re[-]created
image more real and comprehensible than the actual object.

The photograph isolates and perpetuates a moment of time: an
important and revealing moment, or an unimportant and meaningless one, depending upon the photographer's understanding of
his subject and mastery of his process. The lens does not reveal
a subject significantly of its own accord. On the contrary, its vision
is completely impartial and undiscriminating. It makes no distinction between important detail and meaningless detail. Selection,
emphasis, and meaning must be provided by the photographer in
his composition. . . . To compose a subject well means no more
than to see and present it in the strongest manner possible. . . . Its
capacity for rendering fine detail and tone makes photography
excel in recording form and texture. Its subtlety of gradation
makes it admirably suited to recording qualities of light or shadow. . . . The photographer cannot depend on rules deduced from
finished work in another medium. He must learn to see things
through his own eyes and his own camera; only then can he present his subject in a way that will transmit his feeling for it to
others.

An intuitive knowledge of composition in terms of the capac-
ities of his process enables the photographer to record his subject
at the moment of deepest perception; to capture the fleeting
instant when the light on a landscape, the form of a cloud, the gesture of a hand, or the expression of a face momentarily presents a
profound revelation of life.

The appeal to our emotions manifest in such a record is
largely due to the quality of authenticity in the photograph. The

spectator accepts its authority and, in viewing it, perforce believes that he would have seen that scene or object exactly so if he had been there. We know that the human eye is capable of no such feat, and furthermore that the photographer has not reproduced the scene exactly; quite possibly we would not even be able to identify the original scene from having seen the photograph. Yet it is this belief in the reality of the photograph that calls up a strong response in the spectator and enables him to participate directly in the artist's experience.

102

JERRY UELSMANN (b. 1934)
From "Some Humanistic Considerations of Photography"

Uelsmann's approach to photography—postvisualization—is the opposite of Edward Weston's previsualization. This excerpt is from a speech given by Uelsmann to the Royal Photographic Society of Great Britain in 1971.

As you may know the dominant aesthetic in photography has been called previsualization. This means that the image is essentially fully previsioned at the time the shutter is clicked. Now I propose that photographers keep themselves open to in-process discovery. . . .

It seems to me that all other areas of art allow for in-process discovery. The painter does not begin with a fully-conceived canvas, the sculptor with a fully-conceived piece. They allow for a dialogue to evolve, to develop, and as far as I'm concerned the darkroom is truly capable of being a visual research laboratory, a place for discovery, observation and meditation. . . .

Some of my photographs I don't understand. This disturbs some people. I would like to think that today we are sophisticated enough to realize that first of all there are systems of knowledge which are not necessarily verbal. There are levels of consciousness that we can engage ourselves in when we are encountering the world of photography that are not easy to talk about. . . . I think many times we are pressured into a verbalization of things that we don't fully understand but somehow the words are important. . . .

One recent photograph disturbs me a great deal. Literally I know what's happening: there is a wave and an organic form that was washed up on the beach after a hurricane. . . . But there is some strange thing happening, some strange statement within that I am in no way capable of articulating. I think the sooner that we as photographers become aware of this phenomenon that we can perhaps address each other visually at times, I think the happier we'll all be, because so many times I am pressed to have verbal responses to things that I can't defend verbally.

103

MICHAEL GRAVES (b. 1934)
From "What Is the Focus of Post-Modern Architecture?"

This 1981 interview with Michael McTwigan appeared while Graves was designing the Public Services Building (see fig. 28-1), which was dubbed the "Post-Modern building of the year."

MICHAEL McTWIGAN: It's interesting that you use the word "figural." By that, do you mean related to human scale . . . ?

MICHAEL GRAVES: Those things, as well as a range of architectonic ideas—elements like a door or a window, a configuration of space that is anthropomorphically related. For instance, if I make a Greek cross plan . . . there's no doubt where the primary space is for us in a room like that. If you look at De Stijl architecture, on the other hand, there is no clear identity of the human body within the plan. I can't locate the figure of myself within the work.

MM: That is presumably why so many people have felt alienated by modern architecture; it stands on its own and doesn't really have a relationship to the human being. . . .

Architect Robert Stern said not too long ago, "We're not in the business of educating and transforming human nature; we're in the business of responding to the human condition. We're not reformers or revolutionaries." That seems to be quite a statement, quite a change from the Bauhaus days. . . .

MG: . . . In part, what Robert is saying is that this is not a time of manifestos. I remember in the early '60s, when Peter Eisenman and I were working together, we wanted to write a manifesto. We wanted to be modern architects and say, "This is what ought to be, not what is. . . ."

We wanted to make clear our own ideas in a general sense, rather than in the peculiarities of site or client or whatever. It's not that one has softened today, but the manifesto is much more gentle now. I would not say we are not reformers, however. We are, in the best sense of the word, re-formers. We are trying to establish form as it relates to us more than to the machine. . . . We are reformers in the sense that we don't want to return to something, but, rather, to reestablish the language of architecture. That's where the manifesto comes.

Although literature can use the window as a metaphor, architecture possesses the window. It's the modern architect who wants to throw the window out. It's people like myself who want to say simply, "The window exists, and I will use the window." The window relates to the human body and it relates to the wall for very specific aesthetic, technical, and cultural reasons. It's not for nothing that the window existed for 2,000 years or more. That's a crucial issue.

So I would vary that rather dramatic statement of Robert's and say I'm interested in reestablishing the language of architecture. . . .

MM: So it's not just a matter of reeducating. It's a matter of teaching old skills as well. . . . It could be said that people almost forgot how to paint in the '60s, and the same could be said about architecture.

MG: Sure. There's an architect by the name of Leo Krier in London who says he won't build, because there's no craft tradition from which to build his buildings. His political standing is that we must dissolve the Industrial Revolution. So he does his drawings. He says, "Let's go back to the craft tradition."

104
CINDY SHERMAN (b. 1954)
From an interview

In these excerpts from a 1988 interview with Jeanne Siegel, Sherman discusses her photographic role-playing.

CINDY SHERMAN: I still wanted to make a filmic sort of image, but I wanted to work alone. I realized that I could make a picture of a character reacting to something outside the frame so that the viewer would assume another person.

Actually, the moment that I realized how to solve this problem was when Robert [Longo] and I visited David Salle, who had been working for some sleazy detective magazine. Bored as I was, waiting for Robert and David to get their "art talk" over with, I noticed all these 8 by 10 glossies from the magazine which triggered something in me. (I was never one to discuss issues—after all, at that time I was "the girlfriend.")

JEANNE SIEGEL: In the "Untitled Film Stills," what was the influence of real film stars? It seems that you had a fascination with European stars. You mentioned Jeanne Moreau, Brigitte Bardot and Sophia Loren in some of your statements. Why were you attracted to them?

CS: I guess because they weren't glamorized like American starlets. When I think of American actresses from the same peri-od, I think of bleached blonde, bejeweled and furred sex bombs. But, when I think of Jeanne Moreau and Sophia Loren, I think of more vulnerable, lower-class types of characters, more identifiable as working-class women.

At that time I was trying to emulate a lot of different types of characters. I didn't want to stick to just one. I'd seen a lot of the movies that these women had been in but it wasn't so much that I was inspired by the women as by the films themselves and the feelings in the films.

JS: And what is the relationship between your "Untitled Film Stills" and real film stills?

CS: In real publicity film stills from the 40s and 50s something usually sexy/cute is portrayed to get people to go see the movie. Or the woman could be shown screaming in terror to publicize a horror film.

My favorite film images (where obviously my work took its inspiration) didn't have that. They're closer to my own work for that reason, because both are about a sort of brooding character caught between the potential violence and sex. However, I've realized it is a mistake to make that kind of literal connection because my work loses in the comparison. I think my characters are not quite taken in by their roles so that they couldn't really exist in any of their so-called "films," which, next to a real still, looks unconvincing. They are too aware of the irony of their role and perhaps that's why many have puzzled expressions. My "stills" were about the fakeness of role-playing as well as contempt for the domineering "male" audience who would mistakenly read the images as sexy. . . .

JS: Another critical issue attached to the work was the notion that the stereotypical view was exclusively determined by the "male" gaze. Did you see it only in this light or did it include the woman seeing herself as well?

CS: Because I'm a woman I automatically assumed other women would have an immediate identification with the roles. And I hoped men would feel empathy for the characters as well as shedding light on their role-playing. What I didn't anticipate was that some people would assume that I was playing up to the male gaze. I can understand the criticism of feminists who therefore assumed I was reinforcing the stereotype of woman as victim or as sex object.

Timeline Four: 1800 to 2000

	1800–1820	1820–1840	1840–1850
HISTORY AND POLITICS	**1802** First child labor laws, in England **1803** United States purchases Louisiana from France for $15 million **1804** Napoleon crowned emperor of France, ending the republic established by the French Revolution; 1805–9, occupies Italy and Spain. He wins battles against allied England, Austria, Russia, and Sweden until he retreats from Moscow, 1812, losing the bulk of his army; 1814, successes of allies force him to abdicate; he is exiled to Elba **War of 1812** (European allies against Napoleon) draws United States into conflict with Britain; 1814, Washington, D.C., burned **1814** Allies at Congress of Vienna redivide Europe. Louis XVIII, Bourbon king of France (ruled 1814–24), establishes a constitutional monarchy; 1815, Napoleon returns; allies defeat him at Waterloo; he abdicates again and, 1821, dies a prisoner of war. Bourbon kings return to power until 1830 **1819–21** Spain sells Florida to United States	**1822** Simon Bolívar (1783–1830) leads revolution in Latin America: six countries gain independence from Spain **1823** Monroe Doctrine claims United States sphere of influence in the Western Hemisphere **1830** July Revolution in France; republican mobs riot against the monarchy; Louis Philippe, nominated as new king (r. 1830–48, the July Monarchy), continues conservative policies. This change of power mandated by popular acclaim spawns revolutionary movements across Europe **1833** Factory Act abolishes slavery in British colonies **Queen Victoria (r. 1837–1901)** rules Great Britain **1838** "Trail of Tears": Thousands of Cherokee and other Indians are moved by United States government on a forced march from the Southeast to Indian Territory (now Oklahoma); one in four dies	**1842** Oregon Trail opens western lands of North America for settlement **1846–48** War between United States and Mexico over territories of Texas and New Mexico **Revolution of 1848 in France;** 1848–52, Second Republic declared after abdication of Louis Philippe. Bloody insurrection leads to the election of Louis Napoleon, nephew of Napoleon I, as constitutional monarch; 1852, he overthrows republic and becomes Emperor Napoleon III (Second Empire, 1852–70); 1861–67, disastrous attempt by France to annex Mexico **1848** Revolutions throughout Europe; 1848–61, unification of Italy begins with a revolt led by Giuseppe Garibaldi against Austrian and French rule **1848** Discovery of gold in American West encourages westward expansion
RELIGION	**Pope Pius X (ruled 1803–14)** reforms church law, music, texts, and administration		

THÉODORE GÉRICAULT
The Raft of the "Medusa," 1818–19

JOHN CONSTABLE
Salisbury Cathedral from the Meadows, 1829–34

JOSEPH MALLORD WILLIAM TURNER
Rain, Steam and Speed—
The Great Western Railway, 1844

	1800–1820	1820–1840	1840–1850
MUSIC, LITERATURE, AND PHILOSOPHY	**1800s English Romantic poets:** Wordsworth, Byron, Shelley, Keats; novelists: Thackeray, Austen, Dickens, Trollope, the Brontës, Eliot, Kipling **1807** Georg Wilhelm Friedrich Hegel (1770–1831) writes *Phenomenology of Mind* **1819–37** Jacob and Wilhelm Grimm, brothers, collect authoritative versions of German folktales and myths	**Emily Dickinson (1830–86),** American poet **1833** Carl von Clausewitz, a general in the Napoleonic Wars, writes *On War,* a treatise on modern warfare **1840** Edgar Allan Poe publishes suspenseful and macabre short stories in United States	**1842** Honoré de Balzac completes *The Human Comedy,* a series of novels and stories **Modern economic theories:** 1848, Karl Marx and Friedrich Engels write *The Communist Manifesto* and John Stuart Mill publishes *Principles of Political Economy;* 1867, Marx's *Capital*
SCIENCE, TECHNOLOGY, AND EXPLORATION	**1800** Estimated world population nears one billion; that of Europe is 180 million; Alessandro Volta (1745–1827) constructs the first battery and demonstrates electric currents **1804–6** Lewis and Clark cross the American continent to the Pacific Ocean **1811** Invention of tin cans for food storage **1814** Steam locomotive, in England, used to power early railroad travel **1819** First steamship crossing of the Atlantic	**1825** Opening of the Erie Canal, allowing passage of ships from the Atlantic Ocean to the Great Lakes **1831** Invention of mechanical McCormick reaper; 1837, John Deere plow **c. 1837** Development of armaments: rifles, artillery, shrapnel, revolvers, and torpedoes by the 1880s **1839** First forms of photography: daguerreotype and negative-positive system	**1844** Samuel Morse's telegraph transforms communications by allowing transmission and reception of a coded signal through wires; 1866, transatlantic cable laid **1846** Sewing machine invented by Elias Howe; William Morton uses ether anesthesia in surgery **1847** First Law of Thermodynamics formulated by Julius von Mayer and James Joule; 1850, Second Law, by Rudolf Clausius

1853–55 Crimean War; England and France halt the advance of Russia into the Balkans

1854 Commodore Matthew Perry of the United States signs treaty opening Japan to foreign trade

1861 Russia abolishes serfdom

1861–65 Civil War in the United States, centering on the issue of slavery; 1863, Emancipation Proclamation frees slaves; 1865, assassination of President Abraham Lincoln

1864 First International Workingman's Association led by Karl Marx in England

1869 Susan B. Anthony organizes American movement for women's suffrage

1870 Franco-Prussian War; 1871, defeat of French brings collapse of the Second Empire government. Paris populace sets up Third Republic (1870–1914)—at first, ruling through the short-lived, radical Paris Commune—opposed to the monarchy. In German states, Prussian victory leads to a nationalist movement for unification (declared 1871) under Otto von Bismarck, Chancellor of Prussia (ruled 1862–90), and a conservative (antisocialist) government

1876 Battle of Little Bighorn, in Montana: troops of George Armstrong Custer (1839–76), United States general, defeated and killed by forces of Sitting Bull (Tatanka Iotake, c. 1831–90), Sioux leader

1876–1914 Peak of European colonialism worldwide

1848: NATIONALISM IN EUROPE The year 1848 may be said to mark the beginning of the modern political world. In France the collapse of the monarchy and the establishment of a republic in February of that year started a chain reaction across Europe. In the capitals of Germany, Spain, Italy, Hungary, Austria, and the Balkans, a general discontent with conservative politics found expression in public demonstrations by masses of students, peasants, and soldiers and in a general cry for the overthrow of monarchies. The anxieties of the working classes (the Industrial Revolution having created an urban bourgeoisie), incipient socialist ideas, and a popular desire for constitutional, representative government added fuel to these fires. In many countries, the revolutions of 1848 led to a permanent change in the form of government. Among the profound cultural effects of this rapid transition were a new sense of national identity, which encouraged the development of national styles in art, and a new sense of the value of freedom of expression.

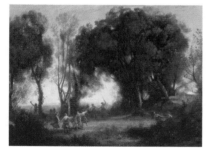

CAMILLE COROT
Morning: Dance of the Nymphs, 1850

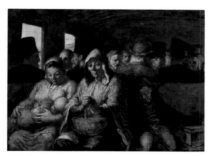

HONORÉ DAUMIER
The Third-Class Carriage, c. 1862

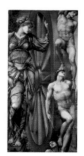

EDWARD BURNE-JONES
The Wheel of Fortune, 1877–83

Mid-1800s Russian literature: Gogol (1809–52), Turgenev (1818–83), Dostoyevsky (1821–81), Tolstoy (1828–1910), Chekhov (1860–1904)

1851 Melville's *Moby Dick;* Stowe's antislavery novel *Uncle Tom's Cabin;* 1853, Ruskin's *The Stones of Venice;* 1857, *Madame Bovary,* by Flaubert; *The Flowers of Evil,* by Baudelaire

Impressionist composers: Claude Debussy (1862–1918), Maurice Ravel (1875–1937); Romantics: Frédéric Chopin (1810–49), Robert Schumann (1810–56), Franz Liszt (1811–86), Johannes Brahms (1833–97). The Romantic work of Richard Wagner (1813–83) transforms opera

1862 Victor Hugo's novel *Les Misérables*

Carl G. Jung (1875–1961), Swiss psychologist, explores the concept of the collective unconscious

Thomas Mann (1875–1955), German novelist

1878–80 Friedrich Nietzsche, German philosopher, develops idea of an *Übermensch* (superman)

1855 First plastic material, celluloid, discovered by Alexander Parkes

c. 1856–63 Steel manufacturing processes invented; experimentation with alloys proliferates; 1890, first steel-frame skyscraper built, in Chicago

1859 Charles Darwin publishes *The Origin of Species,* formulating the theory of evolution

1863 First subways built, in London

1864 In France, Louis Pasteur's germ theory alters medical research and practice; 1865, antiseptic techniques introduced in surgery

1865 Genetic experiments of Gregor Mendel published in Austria

1866 Invention of dynamite by Alfred Nobel

1869 American transcontinental railroad completed; Suez Canal opens; periodic table of elements formulated by Dmitri Mendeleev

1872 Heinrich Schliemann excavates Troy

1876 Alexander Graham Bell patents the telephone

1876–85 In Germany, internal-combustion engine, running on gasoline fuel, developed

1877 Thomas Edison invents phonograph; 1879, incandescent bulb; 1894, motion pictures

1879 Ivan Pavlov explores the relationship between psychology and physiology

HISTORY AND POLITICS

RELIGION

MUSIC, LITERATURE, AND PHILOSOPHY

SCIENCE, TECHNOLOGY, AND EXPLORATION

| | 1880–1890 | 1890–1900 | 1900–1910 |

HISTORY AND POLITICS

1881–82 First pogroms against Jews in Russia
1886 Labor unrest in United States: Haymarket riot, Chicago, leads to the foundation of the American Federation of Labor, first national labor union; 1892, Carnegie steel strike, Pennsylvania
1886 Zionism, a doctrine calling for the establishment of a Jewish state in Palestine, appears in Europe; 1897, first Zionist Congress called by Theodor Hertzl in Basel, Switzerland

1890 Battle of Wounded Knee, between Sioux nation and United States Army, effectively ends Indian resistance
1893 World's Columbian Exposition, Chicago
1894–1906 Dreyfus Affair: a charge of treason brought fraudulently against a Jewish army officer stirs anti-Semitism and popular unrest in France
1895–98 Wars in Cuba and America weaken Spanish Kingdom and result in losses in territory and prestige
1899–1902 Boer War in South Africa; British defeat South Africans and annex territory

Edward VII of England (ruled 1901–10), whose government passes sweeping education reforms (1902)
1904–5 Russian-Japanese War over territory on the Pacific coast ends in humiliating defeat for the Russians and heightened unrest among the population; 1905, Bloody Sunday massacre of demonstrating workers in St. Petersburg leads to first Russian revolution; the Great General Strike gives birth to organized labor movement and the first soviets, or workers' councils

RELIGION

EARLY MODERNISM In Europe and America around the turn of the nineteenth century, just as visual artists were beginning to experiment with the concepts of collage and abstraction, and composers were testing unusual tonal systems and atonality in music, a number of writers were trying something parallel in prose and poetry: stream of consciousness, rhythmic language, fragmentation of form, and radical play with grammatical structures. Many were explicitly interested in the connections among art forms: the relationship between sound and color, for example, fascinated both the poet Charles Baudelaire and, later, the painter Wassily Kandinsky. Arthur Rimbaud shocked France in 1873 with the publication of the poem *A Season in Hell;* in 1896, Alfred Jarry's absurdist play *King Ubu* caused a riot in a Paris theater. In England in the 1880s Gerard Manley Hopkins invented "sprung rhythm" in poetry. The American Gertrude Stein, also in Paris, wrote *Three Lives* in 1908; Ezra Pound, in London, published the poems *Personae* in 1909. Thus, the pre–World War I radicalism of such artists as the painters Kandinsky, Pablo Picasso, and Kazimir Malevich and the architect Frank Lloyd Wright may be seen in the broader context of other revolutionary and visionary creative ideas.

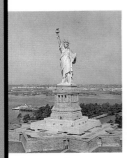

AUGUSTE BARTHOLDI
Statue of Liberty (Liberty Enlightening the World), 1875–84

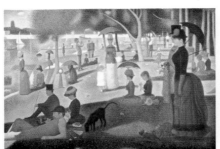

GEORGES SEURAT
A Sunday on La Grande Jatte, 1884–86

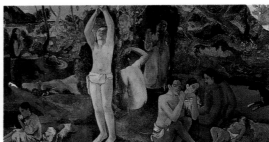

PAUL GAUGUIN
Where Do We Come From? What Are We? Where Are We Going? (detail), 1897

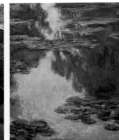

CLAUDE MONET
Water Lilies, Giverny, 1907

MUSIC, LITERATURE, AND PHILOSOPHY

French Symbolist poets: Stéphane Mallarmé (1842–98), Paul Verlaine (1844–96), Arthur Rimbaud (1854–91)
1881 *Portrait of a Lady,* by Henry James
1884 *The Adventures of Huckleberry Finn,* by Mark Twain; *Against the Grain,* by Joris-Karl Huysmans

1890–1903 Erik Satie composes *Three Small Pieces in the Form of a Pear*
1891 Oscar Wilde writes *The Picture of Dorian Gray*
1897 Bram Stoker publishes *Dracula*
Jorge Luis Borges (1899–1986), Argentine Surrealist author
1900 Joseph Conrad publishes *Lord Jim*

Pablo Neruda (1904–73), Chilean poet
1906 Upton Sinclair publishes *The Jungle,* an American documentary novel that exposes the injustices of the industrial system
1908 Filippo Tommaso Marinetti writes the *Futurist Manifesto;* the composer Arnold Schoenberg uses atonality in composition
Ferdinand de Saussure (1857–1913), French philologist, founds modern linguistics

SCIENCE, TECHNOLOGY, AND EXPLORATION

c. 1880 Barbed-wire fences of galvanized iron patented and used to fence in much of the open range in the American West
c. 1885 First automobiles invented, by Karl Benz and Gottlieb Daimler, in Germany

c. 1890 Reinforced concrete begins to be used as a primary building material
1892–95 Sigmund Freud, Austrian physician, formulates the theory and method of psychoanalysis
1895 X rays discovered by Wilhelm Röntgen; Guglielmo Marconi invents the wireless telegraph, a precursor of radio
1897 Joseph Thomson discovers the electron
1898 Marie Curie discovers radium

1903 First aircraft flight, made by Orville and Wilbur Wright, in North Carolina
1905 Albert Einstein (1879–1955), pioneering physicist, formulates the theory of relativity, radically changing modern views of space and time; 1953, Unified Field Theory
1909 American Robert Peary reaches North Pole; 1912, Robert Scott's American expedition reaches the South Pole (discovered by the Norwegian Roald Amundsen, 1911)

1911 Revolution in China: emperor deposed, Sun Yat-sen establishes a republic
1912 British ocean liner *Titanic* sinks
1914 Outbreak of World War I: assassination of Archduke Ferdinand of Austria in Sarajevo leads to war between Germany, Austro-Hungarian Empire, and allies on one side, and Serbia, Russia, France, England, and allies on the other; most of Europe and its colonies become involved; 1917, United States enters; 1918, defeat of Germany. Yugoslavia, Poland, Turkey, Czechoslovakia, Hungary, and Austria become independent nations; Syria, Iraq, and Palestine become mandates controlled by France and Britain
1916 Easter Rebellion in Ireland attempts to gain independence from Britain but fails
1917 Bolshevik Revolution in Russia, under Lenin, inaugurates first communist state
1919 Foundation of the League of Nations, an international congress to promote peace, forerunner of the modern United Nations

1920 Women enfranchised in the United States; 1928, in England; 1945, in France
1920 With the passage of the Home Rule Bill, the British concede autonomy to southern Ireland; Mohandas Gandhi initiates peaceful mass protests (*satyagraha,* or passive resistance) in India against British rule
1922 Fascists under Benito Mussolini seize power in Italy
1926–53 Joseph Stalin controls Soviet Union; his government is a rigid totalitarian state marked by purges, pogroms, and radical collectivization of farms and industries
1929 Stock market crash in United States inaugurates the Great Depression, worldwide economic crisis, during the 1930s

1931–41 Japanese wage undeclared war on China, annexing Manchuria
1933 In United States: the New Deal, a program of government spending to end the Depression; in Germany: Adolf Hitler's National Socialist (Nazi) Party seizes power
1934–35 Long March: 90,000 communist rebels led by Mao Tse-tung flee Chiang Kai-shek across China; less than half survive
1936–39 Spanish Civil War, won by Fascists
1938 Germany annexes Austria; 1939, occupies Czechoslovakia
1939–45 World War II: 1939, Germany invades Poland; 1940, Belgium and France; Italy enters war as ally of Germany. 1941, Germany attacks Russia; Japan, allied with Germany, bombs American fleet at Pearl Harbor; United States enters war. Holocaust in Europe: Nazis systematically exterminate more than six million Jews, communists, homosexuals, gypsies, and others; 1945, defeat of Germans and Japanese by Allies

HISTORY AND POLITICS

1917 British government, in control of much of the Middle East following World War I, promulgates the Balfour Declaration supporting the establishment of a Jewish state in Palestine

1923 Martin Buber, German Jewish theologian, writes *I and Thou*

1939–43 Rampant persecution of Orthodox church in Soviet Union

RELIGION

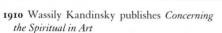

PABLO PICASSO
Still Life with Chair Caning, 1912

FRANZ MARC
Animal Destinies, 1913

PABLO PICASSO
Three Dancers, 1925

MERET OPPENHEIM
Object, 1936

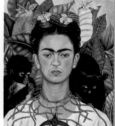

FRIDA KAHLO
Self-Portrait with Thorn Necklace, 1940

1910 Wassily Kandinsky publishes *Concerning the Spiritual in Art*
c. 1912–15 John Dewey (1859–1952) and Maria Montessori (1870–1952) pioneer new ideas about education
1913–28 Marcel Proust, French critic and novelist, writes *Remembrance of Things Past*
1919 *The Cabinet of Dr. Caligari,* innovative German Expressionist silent film

1920s American free verse and modernist poets: Robert Frost (1874–1963), Ezra Pound (1885–1972), T. S. Eliot (1888–1965)
1926 Franz Kafka's *The Castle;* Ernest Hemingway's *The Sun Also Rises;* 1927, Virginia Woolf's *To the Lighthouse;* Abel Gance makes the film *Napoléon;* 1928, D. H. Lawrence's *Lady Chatterley's Lover;* 1929, William Faulkner's *The Sound and the Fury*

Russian modernist composers: Rachmaninoff (1873–1943), Stravinsky (1882–1971), Prokoviev (1891–1953), Shostakovich (1906–1975)
1930s Gertrude Stein explores the forms and structure of language; 1939, James Joyce publishes *Finnegans Wake,* further experimenting with language
1932 Aldous Huxley's *Brave New World* describes a pseudo-utopian future

MUSIC, LITERATURE, AND PHILOSOPHY

1911 First model of atomic structure made, by Ernest Rutherford, in Britain
By 1913 Diesel engines replace steam locomotives on many railways
1914 Henry Ford's fully mechanized mass-production plant for the Model T car marks the beginning of American industrialization
1915 Birth-control movement, led by Margaret Sanger in the United States, advocates family planning

1920 Radio programs broadcast, Pittsburgh
1922 Howard Carter discovers the tomb of Tutankhamen in Egypt
1925–26 Werner Heisenberg and Erwin Schrödinger's theories of quantum mechanics
1926 Sound motion pictures and television demonstrated
1927 Charles Lindbergh flies an aircraft solo across the Atlantic
1929 Alexander Fleming discovers penicillin

1931 Radio waves from space detected by the American electrical engineer Karl Jansky: beginning of radio astronomy, using radio waves to trace objects; c. 1935–36, radar discovered by the Scottish physicist Robert Watson-Watt and others
1935 C. F. Richter, American, devises scale for measuring earthquakes

SCIENCE, TECHNOLOGY, AND EXPLORATION

	1940–1950	1950–1960	1960–1970
HISTORY AND POLITICS	**1945** United Nations founded as an international advisory and peacekeeping council; Yalta Conference: British prime minister Winston Churchill, American president Franklin D. Roosevelt, and Marshal Joseph Stalin of the Soviet Union plan division of Germany into zones of occupation and Europe into spheres of influence **1947** Marshall Plan, proposed to aid recovery of European states devastated by World War II, enacted by the United States. Division of Germany into East and West states **1948** Israel achieves nationhood with recognition by the United Nations; India gains independence from Britain **1949** Communist People's Republic of China founded under Mao Tse-tung	**1954** American civil rights movement begins: United States Supreme Court outlaws racial segregation in public schools; 1955, Montgomery, Alabama, bus boycott by African-Americans, led by Martin Luther King, Jr. **c. 1955–c. 1989** Cold War among Soviet Union, China, and United States: a period of mutual hostilities, espionage, arms escalation, and political maneuvering for influence in other countries by the three world powers; most other nations align themselves with one of the three. Conflicts center upon the opposition between communism and democracy; 1961, Berlin Wall built, isolating West Berlin within East Germany; 1962, Cuban Missile Crisis, Soviet Union attempts to install missiles in Cuba, threatening United States **1959** Fidel Castro establishes communist government in Cuba	**1963** Assassination of U.S. President John F. Kennedy **1965** America enters Vietnam War **1965–76** Cultural Revolution in China: hard-line Maoist Red Guards formed; educators, local governments, and other elements seen as "enemies of the Revolution" attacked; thousands are killed, millions sent to reeducation camps; many artworks and religious sites are destroyed **1967** Egypt and Israel at war; Egypt is defeated, Israel controls Sinai peninsula **1968** Prague Spring, an attempt by Czechoslovakia to win freedom from Soviet control, crushed by Soviet troops; in United States, presidential candidate Robert F. Kennedy and civil rights leader Martin Luther King, Jr., assassinated; mass protests in United States against Vietnam War
RELIGION	**1948** Thomas Merton, American Trappist monk, poet, and philosopher, writes *The Seven Story Mountain*	**1950s** In some Protestant and Jewish denominations, women become ministers. Chinese invade Tibet and destroy more than 6,000 ancient temples and monasteries; 1959, Dalai Lama, head of state and of Tibetan Buddhism, forced into exile in India	**1962** Pope John XXIII's Second Vatican Council institutes use of vernacular in church ritual and other reforms **1964** Pope Paul VI and Patriarch Athenagoras attempt to resolve differences between Eastern and Western Christian churches

ADOLPH GOTTLIEB
Descent into Darkness, 1947

MARK ROTHKO
White and Greens in Blue, 1957

ROY LICHTENSTEIN
Drowning Girl, 1963

ROMARE BEARDEN
The Prevalence of Ritual: Baptism, 1964

MUSIC, LITERATURE, AND PHILOSOPHY	**1941** Charlie Chaplin makes the film *The Great Dictator* **1942** Albert Camus publishes *The Stranger* **1943** Jean-Paul Sartre writes *Being and Nothingness,* a statement of Existentialism **1949** George Orwell's novel *1984* creates a futuristic totalitarian world **1949–50** Simone de Beauvoir authors the key feminist text *The Second Sex*	**1950s** Beat Generation: artists influenced by jazz whose works criticize American postwar materialism and complacency: 1952, John Cage composes *4'33";* 1956, Allen Ginsberg writes the narrative poem *Howl;* 1957, Jack Kerouac writes *On the Road*	**1960** Richard Wright writes *Native Son,* on the African-American experience **c. 1965** British invasion in popular music: the Beatles, the Rolling Stones, and other rock-and-roll groups sell millions of albums **1967** In Colombia, Gabriel García-Márquez writes *One Hundred Years of Solitude* **1969** Woodstock Festival in New York draws 500,000 fans of rock and roll
SCIENCE, TECHNOLOGY, AND EXPLORATION	**The Atomic Age:** 1942, in United States, first nuclear chain reaction; 1943, first nuclear fission bomb; 1945, United States drops atomic bombs on Japanese cities, killing more than 100,000 instantly; 1949, first Soviet nuclear bomb; 1956, first nuclear electrical generators built in England; by 1970s, nuclear power in widespread commercial use **1946** Radiocarbon dating **1947** Dead Sea Scrolls discovered in Israel	**c. 1950** Nuclear-powered submarines and ships in United States and Soviet Union **1953** In England, James Watson and Francis Crick publish a model of the structure of DNA and hypothesize the transmission of genetic codes **1954** Jonas Salk invents polio vaccine **Space Age begins:** 1957, Sputnik, first satellite, launched by Soviet Union; 1961, first human orbit of the earth by Yuri Gagarin	**1960** Laser technology developed **1963** Research in genetic engineering begins in United States; 1976, synthesis achieved **1967** First human heart transplant, by Dr. Christiaan Barnard, in South Africa **1969** United States' Apollo XI mission: Neil Armstrong and Edwin Aldrin walk on the moon; 1976, solar probe launched

1970–1980	1980–1990	1990–2000	
1973 Egypt and Syria attack Israel and are defeated. United States withdraws from Vietnam War, having failed militarily and in response to increasing public criticism. In Chile, Salvador Allende, a socialist, becomes president; he is murdered and a military dictatorship under Augusto Pinochet takes power until 1989. In Washington, D.C., Watergate scandal: President Richard Nixon is implicated in illegal activities; 1974, he resigns **1975** South Vietnam falls, ending the war; nation is unified under a communist regime **1978** Iranian revolution: Islamic fundamentalists rebel against the shah; the Ayatollah Khomeini takes power **1979** Afghan War: Soviet troops invade Afghanistan; they are forced to withdraw ten years later. Camp David Accords brokered by United States: Egypt formally recognizes Israel and regains Sinai territory **1979–81** Iran holds 52 Americans hostage	**1981** Assassination of President Anwar Sadat of Egypt, advocate for peace in the Middle East; 1982, Israel invades Lebanon, whose government falls, causing war among Lebanese and Palestinian factions **1985** Mikhail Gorbachev is premier of Soviet Union: policies of *glasnost* and *perestroika* permit economic, political, and cultural liberalization **1986** In United States, Iran-Contra scandal: secret, illegal sale of arms to Iran and diversion of funds to Nicaraguan rebels implicates high government officials **1989** Berlin Wall torn down; 1989–90, Soviet Union breaks up into independent states, with mostly noncommunist governments, along old ethnic and political boundaries; Yugoslavia and Czechoslovakia divide; student demonstrations (estimated over one million) in favor of democracy, in Tiananmen Square, Beijing, China, suppressed violently by Chinese military	**1990** Germany united **1991** Chechen president Dudayev declares independence from Russia and in 1993 dissolves the parliament; 1997, Chechnya is granted autonomy by Russia; 1999, fighting resumes following terrorist bombings on Russian soil **1991** In the USSR, a coup is launched against President Mikhail Gorbachev, and although the coup fails, Gorbachev resigns; Boris Yeltsin gains control of the government and the USSR is dissolved; Yeltsin becomes the first democratically elected president in the nation's history **1995** Yitzhak Rabin assassinated **1997** Death of Deng Xiaoping; Hong Kong reverts to China **1998** Irish Peace Talks **1999** Clinton impeachment hearings; Panama Canal ceded by U.S.; Macau reverts to China	**HISTORY AND POLITICS**
1977 End of Catholicism as state religion of Italy **1978** Pope John Paul II of Poland elected, first non-Italian pope in 455 years	**1980s** Rise of religious fundamentalism, especially among Muslims in the Middle East and central Asia, Hindus in India, Orthodox Jews in Israel, and some Christian sects in the United States	**Pope John Paul II** makes several important visits to places around the world, including Sarajevo (1997), Cuba (1998), Nigeria (1998), Croatia (1998), Mexico City (1999), and Poland (1999).	**RELIGION**

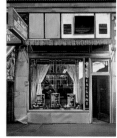

RICHARD ESTES
Food Shop, 1967

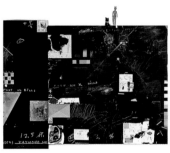

RAYMOND SAUNDERS
White Flower Black Flower, 1986

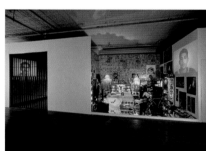

PEPÓN OSORIO
Badge of Honor, 1995

1970–1980	1980–1990	1990–2000	
1974 Aleksandr Solzhenitsyn (b. 1918), Russian writer whose novels describe life in a Soviet prison camp and criticize the government, is exiled to the United States	**1981** MTV (music television), introduced on cable television, brings the new medium of video music to a mass audience **1989** Anglo-Indian novelist Salman Rushdie's *Satanic Verses* outrages Islamic fundamentalists, who place him under a death threat and force him into hiding	**1990** Death of conductor and composer Leonard Bernstein **1993** Tony Kushner wins Pulitzer Prize for *Angels in America* **1997** Dario Fo wins Nobel Prize in Literature; John Updike publishes *Toward the End of Time*	**MUSIC, LITERATURE, AND PHILOSOPHY**
1973 Three babies born in England through in-vitro fertilization **c. 1978** Personal computers widely available **1979** Near meltdown of nuclear reactor at Three Mile Island electrical power plant in Pennsylvania; 1986, explosion of Chernobyl nuclear power plant in Ukraine devastates the area and causes severe radiation poisoning, as well as contamination of atmosphere over much of Europe	**1981** First space shuttle, a reusable manned rocket, launched by United States **1982** First artificial heart implanted **c. 1985** AIDS, identified as a new, incurable disease, spreads throughout the world and begins to claim thousands of lives; by 1995, HIV infection levels reach epidemic proportions **1989** *Voyager II* space probe passes Neptune and discovers a new moon	**1990** Hubble Space Telescope is launched by the crew of the space shuttle Discovery; Human Genome Project (HGP) is officially launched **1997** Cloning of sheep Dolly by scientists at Roslin Institute; NASA's Mars Pathfinder mission deploys its robotic rover called Sojourner on Mars	**SCIENCE, TECHNOLOGY, AND EXPLORATION**

Books for Further Reading

This list is intended to be as practical as possible. It is therefore limited to books of general interest that were printed over the past 20 years or have been generally available recently. However, certain indispensable volumes that have yet to be superseded are retained. This restriction means omitting numerous classics long out of print, as well as much specialized material of interest to the serious student. The reader is thus referred to the many specialized bibliographies noted below.

REFERENCE RESOURCES IN ART HISTORY

I. ANTHOLOGIES OF SOURCES AND DOCUMENTS

Documents of Modern Art. 14 vols. Wittenborn, New York, 1944–61. A series of specialized anthologies.

The Documents of Twentieth-Century Art. G. K. Hall, Boston. A new series of specialized anthologies, individually listed below.

Goldwater, R., and M. Treves, eds. *Artists on Art, from the Fourteenth to the Twentieth Century.* 3rd ed. Pantheon, New York, 1974.

Holt, E. G., ed. *A Documentary History of Art.* Vol. 1, The Middle Ages and the Renaissance. Vol. 2, Michelangelo and the Mannerists. The Baroque and the Eighteenth Century. Vol. 3, From the Classicists to the Impressionists. 2nd ed. Princeton University Press, Princeton, 1981.

Sources and Documents in the History of Art Series. General ed. H. W. Janson. Prentice Hall, Englewood Cliffs, N.J. Specialized anthologies, individually listed below.

2. BIBLIOGRAPHIES AND RESEARCH GUIDES

Arntzen, E., and R. Rainwater. *Guide to the Literature of Art History.* American Library Association, Chicago, 1980.

Barnet, S. *A Short Guide to Writing About Art.* 7th ed. Longman, New York, 2003.

Chiarmonte, P. *Women Artists in the United States: A Selective Bibliography and Resource Guide to the Fine and Decorative Arts, 1750–1986.* G. K. Hall, Boston, 1990.

Ehresmann, D. *Architecture: A Bibliographical Guide to Basic Reference Works, Histories, and Handbooks.* Libraries Unlimited, Littleton, Colo., 1984.

———. *Fine Arts: A Bibliographical Guide to Basic Reference Works, Histories, and Handbooks.* 3rd ed. Libraries Unlimited, Littleton, Colo., 1990.

Freitag, W. *Art Books: A Basic Bibliography of Monographs on Artists.* 2nd ed. Garland, New York, 1997.

Goldman, B. *Reading and Writing in the Arts: A Handbook.* Wayne State Press, Detroit, 1972.

Kleinbauer, W., and T. Slavens. *Research Guide to Western Art History.* American Library Association, Chicago, 1982.

Reference Publications in Art History. G. K. Hall, Boston. Specialized bibliographies, individually listed below.

3. DICTIONARIES AND ENCYCLOPEDIAS

Baigell, M. *Dictionary of American Art.* Harper & Row, New York, 1979.

Chilvers, I., H. Osborne, and D. Farr eds. *The Oxford Dictionary of Art.* 2nd ed. Oxford University Press, New York, 2001.

The Dictionary of Art. 34 vols. Grove's Dictionaries, New York, 1996.

Duchet-Suchaux, G., and M. Pastoureau. *The Bible and the Saints.* Flammarion Iconographic Guides. Flammarion, Paris and New York, 1994.

Encyclopedia of World Art. 14 vols., with index and supplements. McGraw-Hill, New York, 1959–68.

Fleming, J., and H. Honour. *A Dictionary of Architecture.* 4th ed. Penguin, Baltimore, 1991.

———. *The Penguin Dictionary of Decorative Arts.* New ed. Viking, London, 1989.

Hall, J. *Illustrated Dictionary of Symbols in Eastern and Western Art.* HarperCollins, New York, 1995.

———. *Subjects and Symbols in Art.* 2nd ed. Harper & Row, New York, 1979.

The Hutchinson Dictionary of the Arts. Helicon, London, 1994.

Lever, J., and J. Harris. *Illustrated Dictionary of Architecture, 800–1914.* Faber & Faber, Boston, 1993.

Mayer, R. *The Artist's Handbook of Materials and Techniques.* 5th ed. Viking, New York, 1991.

———. *The HarperCollins Dictionary of Art Terms & Techniques.* 2nd ed. HarperCollins, New York, 1995.

Murray, P. and L. *A Dictionary of Art and Artists.* 7th ed. Penguin, New York, 1998.

Osborne, H., ed. *Oxford Companion to Art.* Oxford, Clarendon Press, 1970.

Pierce, J. S. *From Abacus to Zeus: A Handbook of Art History.* 6th ed. Prentice Hall, Englewood Cliffs, N.J., 2000.

Reid, J. D., ed. *The Oxford Guide to Classical Mythology in the Arts 1300–1990.* 2 vols. Oxford University Press, New York, 1993.

Teague, E. *World Architecture Index: A Guide to Illustrations.* Greenwood Press, New York, 1991.

West, S., ed. *The Bulfinch Guide to Art History.* Little, Brown and Company, Boston, 1996.

The Worldwide Bibliography of Art Exhibition Catalogues, 1963–1987. 3 vols. Kraus, Millwood, N.Y., 1992.

Wright, C., comp. *The World's Master Paintings: From the Early Renaissance to the Present Day: A Comprehensive Listing of Works by 1,300 Painters and a Complete Guide to Their Locations Worldwide.* 2 vols. Routledge, New York, 1991.

4. INDEXES, PRINTED AND ELECTRONIC

ARTbibliographies Modern. 1969 to present. A semi-annual publication indexing and annotating more than 300 art periodicals, as well as books, exhibition catalogues, and dissertations. Data since 1984 also available electronically.

Art Index. 1929 to present. A standard quarterly index to more than 200 art periodicals. Data since 1984 also available electronically.

Avery Index to Architectural Periodicals. 1934 to present. 15 vols., with supplementary vols. G. K. Hall, Boston, 1973. Also available electronically.

BHA: Bibliography of the History of Art. 1991 to present. The merger of two standard indexes: RILA (Répertoire International de la Littérature de l'Art/International Repertory of the Literature of Art, vol. 1, 1975) and Répertoire d'Art et d'Archéologie (vol. 1, 1910).

5. WORLDWIDE WEBSITES

Visit the following Websites for reproductions and information regarding artists, periods, movements, and many more. Also refer to the Art and Architecture Websites directory in this book for museum Websites. Many art history departments and libraries of universities and colleges also maintain a Website where you can get reading lists and links to other Websites, such as museums, libraries, and periodicals.

http://aaln.org/ifla-idal International Directory of Art Libraries

http://www.aimco.org Art Museum Image Consortium

http://www.archaeological.org Archaeological Institute of America

http://archnet.asu.edu/archnet Virtual Library for Archaeology

http://www.artchive.com

http://art-history.concordia.ca/AHRC Art History Research Centre

http://www.arthistory.net Art History Network

http://classics.mit.edu The Internet Classics Archive

http://www.collegeart.org College Art Association

http://www.constable.net

http://www.cr.nps.gov/habshaer Historic American Buildings Survey

http://www.getty.edu Including museum, five institutes, and library

http://www.gold.ac.uk/aah Association of Art Historians

http://www.hart.bbk.ac.uk/VirtualLibrary.html Collection of resources maintained by the History of Art Department of Birkbeck College, University of London

http://www.icom.org International Council of Museums

http://www.icomos.org International Council on Monuments and Sites

http://www.ilpi.com/artsource

http://www.indiana.edu/~aah Association for Art History

http://www.siris.si.edu Smithsonian Institution Research Information System

http://www.umich.edu/~hartspc/histart/mother Mother of All Art History Links Pages, maintained by the Department of the History of Art at the University of Michigan

http://www.unesco.org/whc World Heritage Center

http://www.unites.uqam.ca/AHWA Art History Webmasters Association

http://vos.ucsb.edu Voice of the Shuttle: Art & Art History Page

http://witcombe.sbc.edu/ARTHLinks.html Art History Resources on the Web, maintained by Chris Whitcombe

http://wwar.com World Wide Arts Resources

6. GENERAL SOURCES ON ART HISTORY, METHOD, AND THEORY

Barasch, M. *Theories of Art 1: From Plato to Winckelmann.* Routledge, New York, 2000.

Baxandall, M. *Patterns of Intention: On the Historical Explanation of Pictures.* Yale University Press, New Haven, 1985.

Bois, Y.-A. *Painting as Model.* MIT Press, Cambridge, 1993.

Broude, N., and M. Garrard. *The Expanding Discourse: Feminism and Art History.* Harper & Row, New York, 1992.

———, eds. *Feminism and Art History: Questioning the Litany.* Harper & Row, New York, 1982.

Bryson, N. *Vision and Painting: The Logic of the Gaze.* Yale University Press, New Haven, 1983.

———, et al., eds. *Visual Theory: Painting and Interpretation.* Cambridge University Press, New York, 1991.

Cahn, W. *Masterpieces: Chapters on the History of an Idea.* Princeton University Press, Princeton, 1979.

Chadwick, W. *Women, Art, and Society.* 3rd ed. Thames & Hudson, New York, 2002.

Freedberg, D. *The Power of Images: Studies in the History and Theory of Response.* University of Chicago Press, Chicago, 1989.

Gage, J. *Color and Culture: Practice and Meaning from Antiquity to Abstraction.* University of California Press, Berkeley, 1999.

Gombrich, E. H. *Art and Illusion.* 6th ed. Phaidon, New York, 2002.

Harris, A. S., and L. Nochlin. *Women Artists, 1550–1950.* Random House, New York, 1999.

Kemal, S., and I. Gaskell. *The Language of Art History.* Cambridge Studies in Philosophy and the Arts. Cambridge University Press, New York, 1991.

Kleinbauer, W. E. *Modern Perspectives in Western Art History: An Anthology of Twentieth-Century Writings on the Visual Arts.* Reprint of 1971 ed., University of Toronto Press, Toronto, 1989.

Kostof, S. A. *History of Architecture: Settings and Rituals.* 2nd ed. Oxford University Press, New York, 1995.

Kris, E., and O. Kurz. *Legend, Myth, and Magic in the Image of the Artist: A Historical Experiment.* Yale University Press, New Haven, 1979.

Kruft, H-W. *A History of Architectural Theory from Vitruvius to the Present.* Princeton Architectural Press, Princeton, 1994.

Kultermann, U. *The History of Art History.* Abaris Books, New York, 1993.

Nochlin, L. *Women, Art, and Power, and Other Essays.* HarperCollins, New York, 1989.

Panofsky, E. *Meaning in the Visual Arts.* Reprint of 1955 ed., University of Chicago Press, Chicago, 1982.

———. *Tomb Sculpture: Four Lectures on Its Changing Aspects from Ancient Egypt to Bernini.* Introduction by M. Kemp. Harry N. Abrams, New York, 1992.

Parker, R., and G. Pollock. *Old Mistresses: Women, Art, and Ideology.* Pantheon, New York, 1981.

Penny, N. *The Materials of Sculpture.* Yale University Press, New Haven, 1993.

Pevsner, N. *A History of Building Types.* Princeton University Press, Princeton, 1976.

Podro, M. *The Critical Historians of Art.* Yale University Press, New Haven, 1982.

Pollock, G. *Vision and Difference: Femininity, Feminism, and the Histories of Art.* Routledge, New York, 1988.

Rees, A. L., and F. Borzello. *The New Art History.* Humanities Press International, Atlantic Highlands, N.J., 1986.

Roth, L. *Understanding Architecture: Its Elements, History, and Meaning.* Harper & Row, New York, 1993.

Sutton, I. *Western Architecture.* Thames & Hudson, New York, 1999.

Tagg, J. *Grounds of Dispute: Art History, Cultural Politics, and the Discursive Field.* University of Minnesota Press, Minneapolis, 1992.

Trachtenberg, M., and I. Hyman. *Architecture: From Prehistory to Post-Modernism.* 2nd ed. Harry N. Abrams, New York, 2002.

Watkin, D. *The Rise of Architectural History.* University of Chicago Press, Chicago, 1980.

Wittkower, R., and M. *Born Under Saturn: The Character and Conduct of Artists: A Documented History from Antiquity to the French Revolution.* Norton, New York, 1963.

Wolff, J. *The Social Production of Art.* 2nd ed. New York University Press, New York, 1993.

Wölfflin, H. *Principles of Art History: The Problem of the Development of Style in Later Art.* Dover, New York, 1932.

Wollheim, R. *Art and Its Objects.* 2nd ed. Cambridge University Press, New York, 1992.

PART THREE: THE RENAISSANCE THROUGH THE ROCOCO

GENERAL REFERENCES

Campbell, L. *Renaissance Portraits: European Portrait-Painting in the 14th, 15th, and 16th Centuries.* Yale University Press, New Haven, 1990.

De Winter, P. *European Decorative Arts, 1400–1600: An Annotated Bibliography.* G. K. Hall, Boston, 1988.

Hartt, F. and D. Wilkins. *Italian Renaissance Art.* 5th ed. Harry N. Abrams, New York, 2002.

Haskell, F., and N. Penny. *Taste and the Antique: The Lure of Classical Sculpture, 1500–1900.* Yale University Press, New Haven, 1981.

Held, J., and D. Posner. *Seventeenth and Eighteenth Century: Baroque Painting, Sculpture, Architecture.* Harry N. Abrams, New York, 1971.

Hind, A. *History of Engraving and Etching.* Reprint of 1923 3rd ed., Dover, New York, 1963.

———. *An Introduction to a History of Woodcut.* 2 vols. Reprint of 1935 ed., Dover, New York, 1963.

Ivins, W. M., Jr. *How Prints Look: Photographs with a Commentary.* Beacon Press, Boston, 1987.

Landau, D., and P. Parshall. *The Renaissance Print.* Yale University Press, New Haven, 1994.

Martin, J. R. *Baroque.* Penguin, Harmondsworth, England, 1989.

Norberg-Schultz, C. *Baroque Architecture.* Harry N. Abrams, New York, 1971.

———. *Late Baroque and Rococo Architecture.* Harry N. Abrams, New York, 1983.

Snyder, J. *Northern Renaissance Art: Painting, Sculpture, the Graphic Arts, from 1350–1575.* Harry N. Abrams, New York, 1985.

Wiebenson, D., ed. *Architectural Theory and Practice from Alberti to Ledoux.* 2nd ed. University of Chicago Press, Chicago, 1983.

Wittkower, R. *Architectural Principles in the Age of Humanism.* 5th ed. St. Martin's Press, New York, 1998.

CHAPTER 12. THE EARLY RENAISSANCE IN ITALY

Alberti, L. B. *On the Art of Building, in Ten Books.* Trans. J. Rykwert, et al. MIT Press, Cambridge, 1991.

———. *On Painting.* Trans. C. Grayson, introduction and notes M. Kemp. Penguin, New York, 1991.

Ames-Lewis, F. *Drawing in Early Renaissance Italy.* Yale University Press, New Haven, 1981.

Battisti, E. *Filippo Brunelleschi: The Complete Works.* Rizzoli, New York, 1981.

Baxandall, M. *Painting and Experience in Fifteenth-Century Italy: A Primer in the Social History of Pictorial Style.* 2nd ed. Oxford University Press, New York, 1988.

Blunt, A. *Artistic Theory in Italy, 1450–1600.* Reprint of 1940 ed., Oxford University Press, New York, 1983.

Bober, P., and R. Rubinstein. *Renaissance Artists and Antique Sculpture: A Handbook of Sources.* Oxford University Press, New York, 1986.

Borsook, E. *The Mural Painters of Tuscany: From Cimabue to Andrea del Sarto.* 2nd ed. Oxford University Press, New York, 1980.

Campbell, L. *Renaissance Portraits: European Portrait-Painting in the 14th, 15th, and 16th Centuries.* Yale University Press, New Haven, 1990.

Dunkelman, M. *Central Italian Painting, 1400–1465: An Annotated Bibliography.* G. K. Hall, Boston, 1986.

Gilbert, C. E. *Italian Art, 1400–1500: Sources and Documents.* Prentice Hall, Englewood Cliffs, N.J., 1980.

Goldthwaite, R. *Wealth and the Demand for Art in Italy, 1300–1600.* Johns Hopkins University Press, Baltimore, 1993.

Gombrich, E. H. *Norm and Form: Studies in the Art of the Renaissance.* 4th ed. Phaidon, London, 1985.

———. *Symbolic Images: Studies in the Art of the Renaissance.* 3rd ed. Phaidon, London, 1972.

Heydenreich, L., and W. Lotz. *Architecture in Italy, 1400–1500.* Pelican History of Art. Rev. ed. Yale University Press, New Haven, 1996.

Humfreys, P., and M. Kemp, eds. *The Altarpiece in the Renaissance.* Cambridge University Press, New York, 1990.

Huse, N., and W. Wolters. *The Art of Renaissance Venice: Architecture, Sculpture, and Painting, 1460–1590.* University of Chicago Press, Chicago, 1990.

Janson, H. W. *The Sculpture of Donatello.* 2 vols. Princeton University Press, Princeton, 1979.

Joannides, P. *Masaccio and Masolino: A Complete Catalogue.* Harry N. Abrams, New York, 1993.

Karpinsky, C. *Italian Printmaking, Fifteenth and Sixteenth Centuries: An Annotated Bibliography.* G. K. Hall, Boston, 1987.

Kempers, B. *Painting, Power, and Patronage: The Rise of the Professional Artist in the Italian Renaissance.* Penguin, New York, 1992.

Krautheimer, R., and T. Krautheimer-Hess. *Lorenzo Ghiberti.* 2nd ed. Princeton University Press, Princeton, 1970.

Lavin, M. A. *Piero della Francesca.* Harry N. Abrams, New York, 1992.

Murray, P. *The Architecture of the Italian Renaissance.* The World of Art. Rev. ed. Random House, New York, 1997.

Panofsky, E. *Perspective as Symbolic Form.* Zone Books, New York, 1997.

———. *Renaissance and Renascences in Western Art.* C. S. Wood, trans. Humanities Press, New York, 1970.

Paoletti, J. T., and G. M. Radke. *Art in Renaissance Italy.* 2nd ed. Harry N. Abrams, New York, 1997.

Pope-Hennessy, J. *Donatello.* Abbeville Press, New York, 1993.

———. *Italian Renaissance Sculpture.* 3rd ed. Oxford University Press, New York, 1986.

———. *The Portrait in the Renaissance.* Pantheon, New York, 1966.

Rosenberg, C. *Fifteenth-Century North Italian Painting and Drawing: An Annotated Bibliography.* G. K. Hall, Boston, 1986.

Seymour, C. *Sculpture in Italy, 1400–1500.* Pelican History of Art. Penguin, Harmondsworth, England, 1966.

Turner, A. R. *The Vision of Landscape in Renaissance Italy.* Princeton University Press, Princeton, 1974.

Vasari, G. *The Lives of the Painters, Sculptors, and Architects.* Trans. G. du C. De Vere. 2 vols. Everyman's Library. Knopf, New York, 1996.

Wackernagel, M. *The World of the Florentine Renaissance Artist: Projects and Patrons, Workshop and Art Market.* Princeton University Press, Princeton, 1981.

Wilk, S. *Fifteenth-Century Central Italian Sculpture: An Annotated Bibliography.* G. K. Hall, Boston, 1986.

CHAPTER 13. THE HIGH RENAISSANCE IN ITALY

Ackerman, J., and J. Newman. *The Architecture of Michelangelo.* 2nd ed. Penguin, Harmondsworth, England, 1986.

Boase, T. S. R. *Giorgio Vasari: The Man and the Book.* Princeton University Press, Princeton, 1979.

Brown, P. *Art and Life in Renaissance Venice.* Perspectives. Harry N. Abrams, New York, 1997.

———. *Venice and Antiquity: The Venetian Sense of the Past.* Yale University Press, New Haven, 1997.

Bruschi, A. *Bramante.* Thames & Hudson, New York, 1977.

Clark, K. *Leonardo da Vinci.* Revised and introduced by M. Kemp. Viking, New York, 1988.

Cole, A. *Virtue and Magnificence: Art of the Italian Renaissance Courts.* Perspectives. Harry N. Abrams, New York, 1995.

De Tolnay, C. *Michelangelo.* 4 vols. 2nd ed. Princeton University Press, Princeton, 1969–71.

Freedberg, S. *Painting of the High Renaissance in Rome and Florence.* 2 vols. Harvard University Press, Cambridge, 1961.

———. *Painting in Italy, 1500–1600.* Pelican History of Art. 3rd ed. Yale University Press, New Haven, 1993.

Hibbard, H. *Michelangelo.* 2nd ed. Harper & Row, New York, 1985.

Jones, R., and N. Penny. *Raphael.* Yale University Press, New Haven, 1983.

Kemp, M. *Leonardo da Vinci: The Marvellous Works of Nature and Man.* Harvard University Press, Cambridge, 1981.

———, ed. *Leonardo on Painting: An Anthology of Writings.* Yale University Press, New Haven, 1989.

Klein, R., and H. Zerner. *Italian Art, 1500–1600: Sources and Documents.* Reprint of 1966 ed., Northwestern University Press, Evanston, Ill., 1989.

Lightbown, R. *Mantegna: With a Complete Catalogue of the Paintings.* University of California Press, Berkeley, 1986.

———. *Sandro Botticelli.* 2 vols. University of California Press, Berkeley, 1978.

Panofsky, E. *Studies in Iconology: Humanist Themes in the Art of the Renaissance.* Harper & Row, New York, 1972.

Partridge, L. *The Art of Renaissance Rome.* Perspectives. Harry N. Abrams, New York, 1997.

Pietrangeli, C., et al. *The Sistine Chapel: A Glorious Restoration.* Harry N. Abrams, New York, 1992.

Pope-Hennessy, J. *Italian High Renaissance and Baroque Sculpture.* 3 vols. 3rd ed. Oxford University Press, New York, 1986.

Rosand, D. *Painting in Cinquecento Venice: Titian, Veronese, Tintoretto.* Yale University Press, New Haven, 1982.

Turner, A. R. *Renaissance Florence.* Perspectives. Harry N. Abrams, New York, 1997.

Wölfflin, H. *Classic Art: An Introduction to the High Renaissance.* Reprint of 1952 ed., Cornell University Press, Ithaca, 1980.

CHAPTER 14. THE LATE RENAISSANCE IN ITALY

Ackerman, J. *Palladio.* 2nd ed. Penguin, Harmondsworth, England, 1977.

Friedlaender, W. *Mannerism and Anti-Mannerism in Italian Painting.* Reprint of 1957 ed., Columbia University Press, New York, 1990.

Gould, C. H. M. *The Paintings of Correggio.* Cornell University Press, Ithaca, 1976.

Gruber, A., ed. *The History of Decorative Arts: The Renaissance and Mannerism in Europe.* Abbeville Press, New York, 1994.

Kaufmann, T. DaCosta. *Art and Architecture in Central Europe, 1550–1620: An Annotated Bibliography.* Reference Publications in Art History. G. K. Hall, Boston, 1988.

Mann, R. *El Greco and His Patrons: Three Major Projects.* Cambridge University Press, New York, 1986.

Rearick, W. R. *The Art of Paolo Veronese, 1528–1588.* Cambridge University Press, Cambridge, 1988.

Shearman, J. *Mannerism.* Penguin, Harmondsworth, England, 1967.

Smyth, C. H. *Mannerism and Maniera.* 2nd ed. IRSA, Vienna, 1992.

Tavernor, R. *Palladio and Palladianism.* The World of Art. Thames & Hudson, New York, 1991.

Tomlinson, J. *From El Greco to Goya: Painting in Spain 1561–1828.* Perspectives. Harry N. Abrams, New York, 1997.

Valcanover, F., and T. Pignatti. *Tintoretto.* Harry N. Abrams, New York, 1984.

CHAPTER 15. "LATE GOTHIC" PAINTING, SCULPTURE, AND THE GRAPHIC ARTS

Blum, S. *Early Netherlandish Triptychs: A Study in Patronage.* University of California Press, Berkeley, 1969.

De Vos, D. *Rogier van der Weyden: The Complete Works.* Harry N. Abrams, New York, 1999.

Dhanens, E. *Hubert and Jan van Eyck.* Alpine Fine Arts Collection, New York, 1980.

Friedländer, M. *Early Netherlandish Painting.* 14 vols. Praeger, New York, 1967–73.

———. *From Van Eyck to Bruegel: Early Netherlandish Painting.* 3rd ed. Cornell University Press, Ithaca, 1981.

Gibson, W. *Hieronymus Bosch.* Praeger, New York, 1973.

Mâle, E. *Religious Art in France, the Late Middle Ages: A Study of Medieval Iconography and Its Sources.* Princeton University Press, Princeton, 1986.

Muller, T. *Sculpture in the Netherlands, Germany, France, and Spain, 1400–1500.* Pelican History of Art. Penguin, Harmondsworth, England, 1966.

Panofsky, E. *Early Netherlandish Painting.* 2 vols. Harvard University Press, Cambridge, 1958.

CHAPTER 16. THE RENAISSANCE IN THE NORTH

Baxandall, M. *The Limewood Sculptors of Renaissance Germany.* Yale University Press, New Haven, 1980.

Chastel, A., et al. *The Renaissance: Essays in Interpretation.* Methuen, London, 1982.

Harbison, C. *The Mirror of the Artist: Northern Renaissance Art in Its Historical Context.* Perspectives. Harry N. Abrams, New York, 1995.

Hitchcock, H.-R. *German Renaissance Architecture.* Princeton University Press, Princeton, 1981.

Hutchison, J. C. *Albrecht Dürer: A Biography.* Princeton University Press, Princeton, 1990.

Koerner, J. *The Moment of Self-Portraiture in German Renaissance Art.* University of Chicago Press, Chicago, 1993.

Lane, B. *Flemish Painting Outside Bruges, 1400–1500: An Annotated Bibliography.* G. K. Hall, Boston, 1986.

Melion, W. *Shaping the Netherlandish Canon: Karel van Mander's Schilder-Boeck.* University of Chicago Press, Chicago, 1991.

Moxey, K. *Peasants, Warriors, and Wives: Popular Imagery in the Reformation.* University of Chicago Press, Chicago, 1989.

Mundy, E. *Painting in Bruges, 1470–1550: An Annotated Bibliography.* G. K. Hall, Boston, 1985.

Osten, G. von der, and H. Vey. *Painting and Sculpture in Germany and the Netherlands, 1500–1600.* Pelican History of Art. Penguin, Harmondsworth, England, 1969.

Panofsky, E. *The Life and Art of Albrecht Dürer.* 4th ed. Princeton University Press, Princeton, 1971.

Parshall, L. and P. *Art and the Reformation: An Annotated Bibliography.* G. K. Hall, Boston, 1986.

Stechow, W. *Northern Renaissance Art, 1400–1600: Sources and Documents.* Prentice Hall, Englewood Cliffs, N.J., 1966.

Van Mander, K. *Lives of the Illustrious Netherlandish and German Painters.* Ed. H. Miedema. 6 vols. Davaco, Doornspijk, Netherlands, 1993–1999.

Wood, C. *Albrecht Altdorfer and the Origins of Landscape.* University of Chicago Press, Chicago, 1993.

CHAPTER 17. THE BAROQUE IN ITALY AND SPAIN

Blunt, A. *Borromini.* Harvard University Press, Cambridge, 1979.

Brown, J. *Francisco de Zurbaran.* Harry N. Abrams, New York, 1991.

———. *Francisco de Zurbaran.* Yale University Press, New Haven, 1991.

———. *Velázquez: Painter and Courtier.* Yale University Press, New Haven, 1986.

Enggass, R., and J. Brown. *Italy and Spain, 1600–1750: Sources and Documents.* Reprint of 1970 ed., Northwestern University Press, Evanston, Ill., 1992.

Freedberg, S. *Circa 1600: A Revolution of Style in Italian Painting.* Harvard University Press, Cambridge, 1983.

Haskell, F. *Patrons and Painters: A Study in the Relations Between Italian Art and Society in the Age of the Baroque.* Rev. ed. Yale University Press, New Haven, 1980.

Hibbard, H. *Bernini.* Reprint of 1965 ed., Penguin, Baltimore, 1980.

———. *Caravaggio.* Harper & Row, New York, 1983.

Kubler, G., and M. Soria. *Art and Architecture in Spain and Portugal and Their American Dominions, 1500–1800.* Pelican History of Art. Penguin, Harmondsworth, England, 1959.

Montagu, J. *Roman Baroque Sculpture: The Industry of Art.* Yale University Press, New Haven, 1989.

Nicolson, B. *Caravaggism in Europe.* Ed. L. Vertova. 3 vols. 2nd ed., rev. and enl. Allemandi, Turin, 1989.

Posner, D. *Annibale Carracci.* 2 vols. Phaidon, London, 1971.

Smith, G. *Architectural Diplomacy: Rome and Paris in the Late Baroque.* MIT Press, Cambridge, 1993.

Spear, R. *Caravaggio and His Followers.* Harper & Row, New York, 1976.

Varriano, J. *Italian Baroque and Rococo Architecture.* Oxford University Press, New York, 1986.

Waterhouse, E. *Italian Baroque Painting.* 2nd ed. Phaidon, London, 1969.

Wittkower, R. *Art and Architecture in Italy, 1600–1750.* Pelican History of Art. 4th ed. Yale University Press, New Haven, 2000.

———. *Bernini: The Sculptor of the Roman Baroque.* 4th ed. Chronicle Books, San Francisco, 1997.

CHAPTER 18. THE BAROQUE IN FLANDERS AND HOLLAND

Alpers, S. *The Art of Describing: Dutch Art in the Seventeenth Century.* University of Chicago Press, Chicago, 1983.

Gerson, H., and E. ter Kuile. *Art and Architecture in Belgium, 1600–1800.* Pelican History of Art. Penguin, Baltimore, 1960.

Haak, B. *The Golden Age: Dutch Painters of the Seventeenth Century.* Harry N. Abrams, New York, 1984.

Rembrandt: The Master and His Workshop. Ed. S. Salvesen. 2 vols. Exh. cat. Yale University Press, New Haven, 1991.

Rosenberg, J. *Rembrandt: Life and Work.* Rev. ed. Cornell University Press, Ithaca, 1980.

———, S. Slive, and E. ter Kuile. *Dutch Art and Architecture, 1600–1800.* 3rd ed. Yale University Press, New Haven, 1997.

Schama, S. *The Embarrassment of Riches.* University of California Press, Berkeley, 1988.

Schwartz, G. *Rembrandt: His Life, His Paintings.* Viking, New York, 1985.

Slive, S. *Dutch Painting, 1600–1800.* Pelican History of Art. Yale University Press, New Haven, 1995.

———. *Frans Hals.* A. Wofsky Fine Arts, San Francisco, 1989.

Stechow, W. *Dutch Landscape Painting of the Seventeenth Century.* Reprint of 1966 ed., Cornell University Press, Ithaca, 1980.

Sutton, P. *The Age of Rubens.* Exh. cat. Museum of Fine Arts, Boston, 1993.

Walford, F. *Jacob van Ruisdael and the Perception of Landscape.* Yale University Press, New Haven, 1992.

Westermann, M. *A Worldly Art: The Dutch Republic 1585–1718.* Perspectives. Harry N. Abrams, New York, 1996.

Wheelock, A. K., ed. *Johannes Vermeer.* Exh. cat. Yale University Press, New Haven, 1995.

———, et al. *Anthony van Dyck.* Exh. cat. Harry N. Abrams, New York, 1990.

White, C. *Peter Paul Rubens.* Yale University Press, New Haven, 1987.

CHAPTER 19. THE BAROQUE IN FRANCE AND ENGLAND

Blunt, A. *Art and Architecture in France, 1500–1700.* Pelican History of Art. 5th ed. Yale University Press, New Haven, 1999.

———. *Nicolas Poussin.* 2 vols. Princeton University Press, Princeton, 1967.

Downes, K. *The Architecture of Wren.* Rev. ed. Redhedge, Reading, England, 1988.

Garreau, M. *Charles Le Brun: First Painter to King Louis XIV.* Harry N. Abrams, New York, 1992.

Liechtenstein, J. *The Eloquence of Color: Rhetoric and Painting in the French Classical Age.* University of California Press, Berkeley, 1993.

Mérot, A. *French Painting in the Seventeenth Century.* Yale University Press, New Haven, 1995.

———. *Nicolas Poussin.* Abbeville Press, New York, 1990.

Röthlisberger, M. *Claude Lorrain: The Paintings.* 2 vols. Yale University Press, New Haven, 1961.

Summerson, J. *Architecture in Britain, 1530–1830.* Pelican History of Art. 9th ed., rev. Yale University Press, New Haven, 1993.

Waterhouse, E. K. *Painting in Britain, 1530–1790.* Pelican History of Art. 5th ed. Yale University Press, New Haven, 1993.

———. *The Dictionary of Sixteenth and Seventeenth Century British Painters.* Antique Collectors' Club, Woodbridge, Suffolk, 1988.

CHAPTER 20. THE ROCOCO

Baillio, J. *Dictionary of Sixteenth and Seventeenth Century British Painters, 1755–1842.* Exh. cat. Kimbell Art Museum, Fort Worth, 1982.

Brunel, G. *Boucher.* Vendome, New York, 1986.

Brusatin, M., et al. *The Baroque in Central Europe: Places, Architecture, and Art.* Marsilio, Venice, 1992.

Conisbee, P. *Chardin.* Bucknell University Press, Lewisburg, Pa., 1985.

———. *Painting in Eighteenth-Century France.* Cornell University Press, Ithaca, 1981.

Cormack, M. *The Paintings of Thomas Gainsborough.* Cambridge University Press, New York, 1991.

Cuzin, J. P. *Jean-Honoré Fragonard: Life and Work: Complete Catalogue of the Oil Paintings.* Harry N. Abrams, New York, 1988.

Gaunt, W. *The Great Century of British Painting: Hogarth to Turner.* 2nd ed. Phaidon, London, 1978.

Levey, M. *Giambattista Tiepolo: His Life and Art.* Yale University Press, New Haven, 1986.

———. *Painting and Sculpture in France, 1700–1789.* Pelican History of Art. New ed. Yale University Press, New Haven, 1993.

———. *Rococo to Revolution: Major Trends in Eighteenth-Century Painting.* The World of Art. Reprint of 1966 ed., Thames & Hudson, New York, 1985.

Links, J. *Canaletto.* Oxford University Press, New York, 1982.

Paulson, R. *Hogarth: His Life, Art, and Times.* 2 vols. Yale University Press, New Haven, 1971.

Penny, N., ed. *Reynolds.* Exh. cat. Harry N. Abrams, New York, 1986.

Pointer, M. *Hanging the Head: Portraiture and Social Formation in Eighteenth-Century England.* Yale University Press, New Haven, 1993.

Posner, D. *Antoine Watteau.* Cornell University Press, Ithaca, 1984.

Von Kalnein, W. *Architecture in France in the Eighteenth Century.* History of Art. Yale University Press, New Haven, 1995.

PART FOUR: THE MODERN WORLD

GENERAL REFERENCES

Arnason, H. H., and M. F. Prather. *History of Modern Art.* 4th ed. Harry N. Abrams, New York, 1998.

Baigell, M. *A Concise History of American Painting and Sculpture.* Harper & Row, New York, 1984.

Barasch, M. *Modern Theories of Art.* Vol. 1, From Winckelmann to Baudelaire. New York University Press, New York, 1990.

Battcock, G., and R. Nickas, eds. *The Art of Performance: A Critical Anthology.* Dutton, New York, 1984.

Benevolo, L. *History of Modern Architecture.* MIT Press, Cambridge, 1971.

Boime, A. *A Social History of Modern Art.* 2 vols. University of Chicago Press, Chicago, 1987–90.

Brown, M., et al. *American Art: Painting, Sculpture, Architecture, Decorative Arts, Photography.* Prentice Hall, Englewood Cliffs, N.J., 1979.

Campbell, M., et al. *Harlem Renaissance: Art of Black America.* Harry N. Abrams, New York, 1987.

Castelman, R. *Prints of the Twentieth Century: A History.* Oxford University Press, New York, 1985.

Chipp, H., ed. *Theories of Modern Art: A Source Book by Artists and Critics.* University of California Press, Berkeley, 1968.

Crary, J. *Techniques of the Observer: On Vision and Modernity in the Nineteenth Century.* MIT Press, Cambridge, 1990.

Crook, J. *The Dilemma of Style: Architectural Ideas from the Picturesque to the Post Modern.* University of Chicago Press, Chicago, 1987.

Crow, T. *Modern Art in the Common Culture.* Yale University Press, New Haven, 1996.

The Documents of Twentieth-Century Art. G. K. Hall, Boston. Cited individually below.

Driskell, D. *Two Centuries of Black American Art.* Exh. cat. Knopf, New York, 1976.

Eitner, L. *An Outline of Nineteenth-Century European Painting: From David Through Cézanne.* 2 vols. Harper & Row, New York, 1986.

Frampton, K. *Modern Architecture: A Critical History.* 3rd ed. Thames & Hudson, New York, 1992.

———, and Y. Futagawa. *Modern Architecture, 1851–1945.* 2 vols. Rizzoli, New York, 1983.

Frascina, F., ed. *Modern Art and Modernism: A Critical Anthology.* Harper & Row, New York, 1982.

———. *Pollock and After: The Critical Debate.* 2nd ed. Routledge, New York, 2001.

———, and J. Harris, eds. *Art in Modern Culture: An Anthology of Critical Texts.* Harper & Row, New York, 1992.

Goddard, D. *American Painting.* Macmillan, New York, 1990.

Goldberg, R. *Performance Art: From Futurism to the Present.* Rev. and enl. ed. Harry N. Abrams, New York, 1988.

Goldwater, R. *Primitivism in Modern Art.* Enl. ed. Harvard University Press, Cambridge, 1986.

Harrison, C., and P. Wood, eds. *Art in Theory, 1900–1990: An Anthology of Changing Ideas.* Blackwell, Oxford, 1992.

Hertz, R., ed. *Theories of Contemporary Art.* Prentice Hall, Englewood Cliffs, N.J., 1985.

———, and N. Klein, eds. *Twentieth-Century Art Theory: Urbanism, Politics, and Mass Culture.* Prentice Hall, Englewood Cliffs, N.J., 1990.

Hitchcock, H. R. *Architecture: Nineteenth and Twentieth Centuries.* Pelican History of Art. 2nd ed. Penguin, Harmondsworth, England, 1971.

Hunter, S., and J. Jacobus. *Modern Art: Painting, Sculpture, Architecture.* 3rd. rev. ed. Harry N. Abrams, New York, 2000.

Janson, H. W. *Nineteenth-Century Sculpture.* Harry N. Abrams, New York, 1985.

———, and R. Rosenblum. *Nineteenth-Century Art.* Harry N. Abrams, New York, 1984.

Joachimides, C., et al. *American Art in the Twentieth Century: Painting and Sculpture, 1913–1933.* Exh. cat. Prestel, Munich, 1993.

Johnson, W. *Nineteenth-Century Photography: An Annotated Bibliography, 1839–1879.* G. K. Hall, Boston, 1990.

Marien, M. *Photography: A Cultural History.* Prentice Hall, Upper Saddle River, N.J., 2002.

McCoubrey, J. *American Art, 1700–1960: Sources and Documents.* Prentice Hall, Englewood Cliffs, N.J., 1965.

Newhall, B. *The History of Photography from 1830 to the Present Day.* 5th ed., rev. New York Graphic Society, Greenwich, 1982.

Nochlin, L. *The Politics of Vision: Essays on Nineteenth-Century Art and Society.* Harper & Row, New York, 1989.

Osborne, H., ed. *Oxford Companion to Twentieth-Century Art.* Reprint Ed. Oxford University Press, New York, 2000.

Phaidon Dictionary of Twentieth-Century Art. Phaidon, Oxford, 1973.

Pingeot, A., et al. *Sculpture: The Adventure of Modern Sculpture in the Nineteenth and Twentieth Centuries.* Rizzoli, New York, 1986.

Prown, J. D., and B. Rose. *American Painting: From the Colonial Period to the Present.* New ed. Rizzoli, New York, 1977.

Robins, C. *The Pluralist Era: American Art, 1968–1981.* Harper & Row, New York, 1984.

Rose, B. *American Art Since 1900.* Rev. ed. Praeger, New York, 1975.

Rosenblum, N. *A World History of Photography.* 3rd. ed. Abbeville Press, New York, 1997.

Sayre, H. *The Object of Performance: The American Avant-Garde Since 1970.* University of Chicago Press, Chicago, 1990.

Schapiro, M. *Modern Art: Nineteenth and Twentieth Centuries.* Braziller, New York, 1982.

Scharf, A. *Art and Photography.* Reprint ed. Penguin, Harmondsworth, England, 1995.

Stiles, K., and P. Selz. *Theories and Documents of Contemporary Art.* University of California Press, Berkeley, 1996.

Tafuri, M. *Modern Architecture.* 2 vols. Rizzoli, New York, 1986.

Taylor, J. *The Fine Arts in America*. University of Chicago Press, Chicago, 1979.

———, ed. *Nineteenth-Century Theories of Art*. University of California Press, Berkeley, 1991.

Tomkins, C. *Post to Neo: The Art World of the 1980s*. Holt, New York, 1988.

Walker, J. *Glossary of Art: Architecture and Design Since 1945*. 3rd ed. G. K. Hall, Boston, 1992.

Weaver, M. *The Art of Photography, 1839–1989*. Exh. cat. Yale University Press, New Haven, 1989.

Weintraub, L. *Art on the Edge and Over*. Art Insights, Litchfield, Conn.; dist. D.A.P., 1997.

Weiss, J. *The Popular Culture of Modern Art: Picasso, Duchamp and Avant Gardism*. Yale University Press, New Haven, 1994.

Wilmerding, J. *American Art*. Pelican History of Art. Penguin, Harmondsworth, England, 1976.

Witzling, M., ed. *Voicing Our Visions: Writings by Women Artists*. Universe, New York, 1991.

Wood, P., et al. *Modernism in Dispute: Art Since the Forties*. Yale University Press, New Haven, 1993.

CHAPTER 21. NEOCLASSICISM AND ROMANTICISM

Boime, A. *The Academy and French Painting in the Nineteenth Century*. New ed. Yale University Press, New Haven, 1986.

Braham, A. *The Architecture of the French Enlightenment*. University of California Press, Berkeley, 1980.

Bryson, N. *Tradition and Desire: From David to Delacroix*. Cambridge University Press, Cambridge, 1984.

———. *Word and Image: French Painting in the Ancient Régime*. Cambridge University Press, Cambridge, 1981.

Chiarmonte, P. *Women Artists in the United States: A Selective Bibliography and Resource Guide to the Fine and Decorative Arts, 1750–1986*. G. K. Hall, Boston, 1990.

Chu, P. *Nineteenth-Century European Art*. Prentice Hall, Upper Saddle River, N.J. 2002.

Crow, T. *Painters and Public Life in Eighteenth-Century Paris*. Yale University Press, New Haven, 1985.

Eitner, L. E. A. *Géricault: His Life and Work*. Cornell University Press, Ithaca, 1982.

———. *Neoclassicism and Romanticism, 1750–1850: Sources and Documents*. Reprint of 1970 ed., Harper & Row, New York, 1989.

Fried, M. *Absorption and Theatricality: Painting and Beholder in the Age of Diderot*. University of Chicago Press, Chicago, 1980.

Friedlaender, W. *From David to Delacroix*. Reprint of 1952 ed., Schocken Books, New York, 1968.

Goncourt, E. and J. de. French *Eighteenth-Century Painters*. Reprint of 1948 ed., Cornell University Press, Ithaca, 1981.

Goya and the Spirit of Enlightenment. Exh. cat. Little, Brown, Boston, 1989.

Herrmann, L. *British Landscape Painting of the Eighteenth Century*. Oxford University Press, New York, 1974.

Honour, H. *Neoclassicism*. Reprint of 1968 ed., Penguin, London, 1991.

———. *Romanticism*. Harper & Row, New York, 1979.

Johnson, E. *The Paintings of Eugène Delacroix: A Critical Catalogue, 1816–1831*. 4 vols. Clarendon Press, Oxford, 1981–86.

Koerner, J. *Caspar David Friedrich and the Subject of Landscape*. Yale University Press, New Haven, 1990.

Licht, F. *Canova*. Abbeville Press, New York, 1983.

———. *Goya: The Origins of the Modern Temper in Art*. Harper & Row, New York, 1983.

Mainardi, P. *Art and Politics of the Second Empire: The Universal Expositions of 1855 and 1867*. Yale University Press, New Haven, 1987.

———. *The End of the Salon: Art and the State in the Early Third Republic*. Cambridge University Press, Cambridge, 1993.

Middleton, R., and D. Watkin. *Neoclassical and Nineteenth-Century Architecture*. Rizzoli, New York, 1977.

Miles, E. G., ed. *The Portrait in Eighteenth-Century America*. University of Delaware Press, Newark, 1993.

Novotny, F. *Painting and Sculpture in Europe, 1780–1880*. Pelican History of Art. 3rd ed. Yale University Press, New Haven, 1992.

Rebora, C., P. Staiti et al. *John Singleton Copley in America*. Exh. cat. The Metropolitan Museum of Art, New York, 1995.

Reynolds, G. *Turner*. The World of Art. Thames & Hudson, New York, 1985.

Rosenblum, R. *Jean-Auguste-Dominique Ingres*. Harry N. Abrams, New York, 1990.

———. *Transformations in Late Eighteenth Century Art*. Princeton University Press, Princeton, 1967.

Saisselin, R. G. *The Enlightenment Against the Baroque: Economics and Aesthetics in the Eighteenth Century*. University of California Press, Berkeley, 1992.

Solkin, D. *Painting for Money: The Visual Arts and the Public Sphere in Eighteenth-Century England*. Yale University Press, New Haven, 1993.

Tomlinson, J. *Goya in the Twilight of Enlightenment*. Yale University Press, New Haven, 1992.

Vaughan, W. *German Romantic Painting*. Yale University Press, New Haven, 1980.

Watkin, D., and T. Mellinghoff. *German Architecture and the Classical Ideal*. MIT Press, Cambridge, 1987.

Wilton, A. J. M. W. *Turner: His Life and Art*. Rizzoli, New York, 1979.

CHAPTER 22. REALISM AND IMPRESSIONISM

Adler, K., and T. Garb. *Manet*. Phaidon, Oxford, 1986.

Broude, N. *Impressionism: A Feminist Reading*. Rizzoli, New York, 1991.

Cikovsky, N., and F. Kelly. *Winslow Homer*. Exh. cat. Yale University Press, New Haven, 1995.

Clark, T. J. *The Absolute Bourgeois: Artists and Politics in France, 1848–1851*. Princeton University Press, Princeton, 1982.

———. *The Painting of Modern Life: Paris in the Art of Manet and His Followers*. Princeton University Press, Princeton, 1984.

Denvir, B. *The Chronicle of Impressionism: A Timeline History of Impressionist Art*. Little, Brown, Boston, 1993.

———. *The Impressionists: A Documentary Study*. Thames & Hudson, New York, 1986.

———. *The Thames & Hudson Encyclopaedia of Impressionism*. Thames & Hudson, New York, 1990.

Fried, M. *Courbet's Realism*. University of Chicago Press, Chicago, 1990.

Gaunt, W. *Renoir*. Notes by K. Adler. Rev. and enl. ed. Phaidon, Oxford, 1982.

Goodrich, L. *Thomas Eakins*. 2 vols. Exh. cat. Harvard University Press, Cambridge, 1982.

Hamilton, G. H. *Manet and His Critics*. Reprint of 1954 ed., Yale University Press, New Haven, 1986.

Herbert, R. *Impressionism: Art, Leisure, and Parisian Society*. Yale University Press, New Haven, 1988.

Higonnet, A. *Berthe Morisot*. Harper & Row, New York, 1990.

Hilton, T. *The Pre-Raphaelites*. The World of Art. Reprint of 1970 ed., Thames & Hudson, London, 1985.

House, J. *Monet: Nature into Art*. Yale University Press, New Haven, 1986.

Jenkyns, R. *Dignity and Decadence: Victorian Art and the Classical Inheritance*. Harvard University Press, Cambridge, 1991.

Kendall, R., and G. Pollock, eds. *Dealing with Degas: Representations of Women and the Politics of Vision*. Universe, New York, 1992.

Lipton, E. *Looking into Degas*. University of California Press, Berkeley, 1986.

Miller, D., ed. *American Iconology: New Approaches to Nineteenth-Century Art and Literature*. Yale University Press, New Haven, 1993.

Mosby, D. *Henry Ossawa Tanner*. Exh. cat. Rizzoli, New York, 1991.

Needham, G. *Nineteenth-Century Realist Art*. Harper & Row, New York, 1988.

Nochlin, L. *Impressionism and Post-Impressionism, 1874–1904: Sources and Documents*. Prentice Hall, Englewood Cliffs, N.J., 1976.

———. *Realism and Tradition in Art, 1848–1900: Sources and Documents*. Prentice Hall, Englewood Cliffs, N.J., 1966.

Novak, B. *American Painting of the Nineteenth Century: Realism and the American Experience*. Harper & Row, New York, 1979.

———. *Nature and Culture: American Landscape Painting, 1825–1875*. Oxford University Press, New York, 1980.

Pollock, G. *Mary Cassatt*. Harper & Row, New York, 1980.

Reff, T. *Manet and Modern Paris*. Exh. cat. National Gallery of Art, Washington, D.C., 1982.

Rewald, J. *The History of Impressionism*. 4th ed., rev. New York Graphic Society, Greenwich, 1973.

Spate, V. *Claude Monet: Life and Work*. Rizzoli, New York, 1992.

Tucker, P. *Monet at Argenteuil*. Yale University Press, New Haven, 1981.

———. *Monet in the '90s: The Series Paintings*. Exh. cat. Yale University Press, New Haven, 1989.

Walther, I., ed. *Impressionist Art, 1860–1920*. 2 vols. Taschen, Cologne, 1996.

Weisberg, G. *Beyond Impressionism: The Naturalist Impulse*. Harry N. Abrams, New York, 1992.

Wilmerding, J. *Winslow Homer*. Praeger, New York, 1972.

Wood, C. *The Pre-Raphaelites*. Viking, New York, 1981.

CHAPTER 23. POST-IMPRESSIONISM, SYMBOLISM, AND ART NOUVEAU

Brettell, R., et al. *The Art of Paul Gauguin*. Exh. cat. Little, Brown, Boston, 1988.

Broude, N. *Georges Seurat*. Rizzoli, New York, 1992.

Cachin, F., I. Cahn, et al. *Cézanne*. Exh. cat. Harry N. Abrams, New York, 1995.

Denvir, B. *Post-Impressionism*. The World of Art. Thames & Hudson, New York, 1992.

Goldwater, R. *Paul Gauguin*. Concise ed. Harry N. Abrams, New York, 1983.

———. *Symbolism*. Harper & Row, New York, 1979.

Hamilton, G. H. *Painting and Sculpture in Europe, 1880–1940*. Pelican History of Art. 6th ed. Yale University Press, New Haven, 1993.

Hulsker, J. *The Complete Van Gogh*. Harry N. Abrams, New York, 1980.

Rewald, J. *Post-Impressionism: From Van Gogh to Gauguin*. 2nd ed. Museum of Modern Art, New York, 1962.

Schapiro, M. *Paul Cézanne*. Concise ed. Harry N. Abrams, New York, 1988.

———. *Van Gogh*. Rev. ed. Harry N. Abrams, New York, 1982.

Shiff, R. *Cézanne and the End of Impressionism: A Study of the Theory, Technique, and Critical Evaluation of Modern Art*. University of Chicago Press, Chicago, 1984.

Silverman, D. *Art Nouveau in Fin-de-Siècle France*. University of California Press, Berkeley, 1989.

Varnedoe, K. *Vienna 1900: Art, Architecture, and Design*. Exh. cat. Museum of Modern Art, New York, 1986.

CHAPTER 24. TWENTIETH-CENTURY PAINTING

Ades, D., et al., eds. *In the Mind's Eye: Dada and Surrealism*. Abbeville Press, New York, 1986.

Ashton, D. *American Art Since 1945*. Oxford University Press, New York, 1982.

Baker, K. *Minimalism*. Abbeville Press, New York, 1989.

Battcock, G., comp. *Idea Art: A Critical Anthology*. New ed. Dutton, New York, 1973.

Bearden, R., and H. Henderson. *A History of African-American Artists from 1972 to the Present*. Pantheon, New York, 1993.

Beardsley, J., and J. Livingston. *Hispanic Art in the United States: Thirty Contemporary Painters and Sculptors*. Exh. cat. Abbeville Press, New York, 1987.

Breton, A. *Manifestoes of Surrealism*. Trans. R. Seaver and H. R. Lane. University of Michigan Press, Ann Arbor, 1969.

Brown, M. *The Story of the Armory Show*. Rev. ed. Abbeville Press, New York, 1988.

Celant, G. *Unexpressionism: Art Beyond the Contemporary*. Rizzoli, New York, 1988.

Chadwick, W. *Women Artists and the Surrealist Movement*. Thames & Hudson, New York, 1991.

Crane, D. *The Transformation of the Avant-Garde: The New York Art World, 1940–1985*. University of Chicago Press, Chicago, 1987.

Crow, T. *The Rise of the Sixties: American and European Art in the Era of Dissent*. Perspectives. Harry N. Abrams, New York, 1996.

Duchamp, M. *Marcel Duchamp, Notes*. Trans. P. Matisse. The Documents of Twentieth-Century Art. G. K. Hall, Boston, 1983.

Fer, B., et al. *Realism, Rationalism, Surrealism: Art Between the Wars*. Modern Art-Practices and Debates. Yale University Press, New Haven, 1993.

Francis Bacon: A Retrospective. Harry N. Abrams, New York, 1999.

Gilbaut, S. *How New York Stole the Idea of Modern Art*. University of Chicago Press, Chicago, 1983.

———, ed. *Reconstructing Modernism: Art in New York, Paris, and Montreal, 1945–1964*. MIT Press, Cambridge, 1990.

Golding, J. *Cubism: A History and an Analysis, 1907–1914*. 3rd ed. Harvard University Press, Cambridge, 1988.

Goldwater, R. *Primitivism in Modern Art*. Enl. ed. Belknap Press, Cambridge, Mass., 1986.

Gordon, D. *Expressionism: Art and Idea*. Yale University Press, New Haven, 1987.

Gray, C. *The Russian Experiment in Art, 1863–1922*. rev. ed. The World of Art. Thames & Hudson, New York, 1986.

Green, C. *Cubism and Its Enemies*. Yale University Press, New Haven, 1987.

Greenberg, C. *Clement Greenberg, The Collected Essays and Criticism*. Ed. J. O'Brian. 4 vols. University of Chicago Press, Chicago, 1986–93.

Herbert, J. *Fauve Painting: The Making of Cultural Politics*. Yale University Press, New Haven, 1992.

Hoffman, K., ed. *Collage: Critical Views*. UMI Research Press, Ann Arbor, 1989.

Kallir, J. *Egon Schiele: The Complete Works*. Exp. ed. Harry N. Abrams, New York, 1998.

Kandinsky, W. *Kandinsky, Complete Writings on Art*. Eds. K. C. Lindsay and P. Vergo. The Documents of Twentieth-Century Art. 2 vols. G. K. Hall, Boston, 1982.

Krauss, R. *The Originality of the Avant-Garde and Other Modernist Myths*. MIT Press, Cambridge, 1986.

Kuspit, D. *The Cult of the Avant-Garde Artist*. Cambridge University Press, New York, 1993.

Langer, C. *Feminist Art Criticism: An Annotated Bibliography*. G. K. Hall, Boston, 1993.

Leggio, J., and S. Weiley, eds. *American Art of the 1960s*. Studies in Modern Art, 1. Museum of Modern Art, New York, 1991.

Leja, M. *Reframing Abstract Expressionism: Subjectivity and Painting in the 1940s*. Yale University Press, New Haven, 1993.

Lewis, H. *The Politics of Surrealism*. Paragon, New York, 1988.

Lewis, S. *African American Art and Artists*. University of California Press, Berkeley, 1990.

Lippard, L. R. *Overlay: Contemporary Art and the Art of Prehistory*. Pantheon, New York, 1983.

———, ed. *From the Center: Feminist Essays on Women's Art*. Dutton, New York, 1976.

———, et al. *Pop Art*. Praeger, New York, 1966.

Livingstone, M. *Pop Art: A Continuing History*. Thames & Hudson, New York, 2000.

Lodder, C. *Russian Constructivism*. Yale University Press, New Haven, 1983.

Lucie-Smith, E. *Art Today*. Phaidon, London, 1995.

Meisel, L. K. *Photorealism*. Harry N. Abrams, New York, 1980.

Miró, J. *Joan Miró: Selected Writings and Interviews*. Ed. M. Rowell. The Documents of Twentieth-Century Art. G. K. Hall, Boston, 1986.

Mitchell, W. J. T. *The Reconfigured Eye: Visual Truth in the Post-Photographic Era*. MIT Press, Cambridge, 1992.

Mondrian, P. *The New Art, the New Life: The Complete Writings*. Eds. and trans. H. Holtzmann and M. James. The Documents of Twentieth-Century Art. G. K. Hall, Boston, 1986.

Motherwell, R. *Collected Writings*. Ed. Stephanie Terenzio. Oxford University Press, New York, 1992.

———, ed. *The Dada Poets and Painters: An Anthology*. 2nd ed. Harvard University Press, Cambridge, 1989.

Nadeau, M. *History of Surrealism*. Harvard University Press, Cambridge, 1989.

Patton, S. F. *African-American Art*. Oxford University Press, New York, 1998.

Pincus-Witten, R. *Postminimalism into Maximalism: American Art, 1966–1986*. UMI Research Press, Ann Arbor, 1987.

Polcari, S. *Abstract Expressionism and the Modern Experience*. Cambridge University Press, New York, 1991.

Powell, R. J. *Black Art and Culture in the 20th Century*. Thames & Hudson, New York, 1997.

Rosen, R., and C. Brawer, eds. *Making Their Mark: Women Artists Move into the Mainstream, 1970–85*. Exh. cat. Abbeville Press, New York, 1989.

Rosenblum, R. *Cubism and Twentieth-Century Art*. Harry N. Abrams, New York, 2001.

Roskill, M. *Klee, Kandinsky, and the Thought of Their Time: A Critical Perspective*. University of Illinois Press, Urbana, 1992.

Ross, C. *Abstract Expressionism: Creators and Critics: An Anthology*. Harry N. Abrams, New York, 1990.

Rubin, W. S. *Dada and Surrealist Art*. Harry N. Abrams, New York, 1968.

———. *Picasso and Braque: Pioneering Cubism*. Exh. cat. Museum of Modern Art, New York, 1989.

Sandler, I. *The New York School: The Painters and Sculptors of the Fifties*. Harper & Row, New York, 1979.

———. *The Triumph of American Painting: A History of Abstract Expressionism*. Praeger, New York, 1970.

Seitz, W. *Abstract Expressionist Painting in America*. Harvard University Press, Cambridge, 1983.

Silver, K. E. *Esprit de Corps: The Art of the Parisian Avant-Garde and the First World War, 1914–1925*. Princeton University Press, Princeton, 1989.

Varnedoe, K., and A. Gopnik. *High and Low: Modern Art/Popular Culture*. Harry N. Abrams, New York, 1990.

Washton, R.-C., ed. *German Expressionism: Documents from the End of the Wilhelmine Empire to the Rise of National Socialism*. The Documents of Twentieth-Century Art. G. K. Hall, Boston, 1993.

CHAPTER 25. TWENTIETH-CENTURY SCULPTURE

Bach, F., T. Bach, and A. Temkin. *Constantin Brancusi*. Exh. cat. MIT Press, Cambridge, 1995.

Beardsley, J. *Earthworks and Beyond: Contemporary Art in the Landscape*. 3rd ed. Abbeville Press, New York, 1998.

Beaumont, M., et al. *Sculpture Today*. St. Martin's Press, New York, 1987.

Causey, A. *Sculpture Since 1945*. Oxford University Press, New York, 1998.

Elsen, A. *Origins of Modern Sculpture*. Braziller, New York, 1974.

Lucie-Smith, E. *Sculpture Since 1945*. Universe Books, New York, 1987.

Read, H. *Modern Sculpture: A Concise History*. The World of Art. Reprint of 1964 ed., Thames & Hudson, London, 1987.

Senie, H. *Public Sculpture: Tradition, Transformation, and Controversy*. Oxford University Press, New York, 1992.

Tucker, W. *The Language of Sculpture*. Reprint of 1974 ed., Thames & Hudson, New York, 1985.

Waldman, D. *Collage, Assemblage, and the Found Object*. Harry N. Abrams, New York, 1992.

CHAPTER 26. TWENTIETH-CENTURY ARCHITECTURE

Bayer, H., et al., eds. *Bauhaus, 1919–1928*. Reprint of 1938 ed., New York Graphic Society, Boston, 1986.

Curtis, W. *Modern Architecture Since 1900*. 3rd ed. Phaidon, New York, 1996.

Fitch, J. *American Building: The Historical Forces That Shaped It*. 2 vols. 2nd ed. Houghton Mifflin, Boston, 1966–72.

Frampton, K. *Modern Architecture*. 3rd ed. Thames & Hudson, New York, 1996.

Franciscono, M. *Walter Gropius and the Creation of the Bauhaus in Weimar*. University of Illinois Press, Urbana, 1971.

Gössel, P., and G. Leuthäuser. *Architecture in the Twentieth Century*. Taschen, Cologne, 1991.

Hitchcock, H. R., and P. Johnson. *The International Style*. 2nd ed. Norton, New York, 1966.

Johnson, P. *Mies van der Rohe*. 3rd ed., rev. The Museum of Modern Art, New York, 1978.

Kultermann, U. *Architecture in the Twentieth Century*. Van Nostrand Reinhold, New York, 1993.

Lane, B. *Architecture and Politics in Germany, 1918–1945*. New ed. Harvard University Press, Cambridge, 1985.

Le Corbusier. *Towards a New Architecture*. Dover, New York, 1986.

Ockman, J., ed. *Architecture Culture, 1943–1968: A Documentary Anthology*. Rizzoli, New York, 1993.

Pevsner, N. *The Sources of Modern Architecture and Design*. Oxford University Press, New York, 1977.

Steele, J. *Architecture Today*. Phaidon, New York, 2001.

Troy, N. J. *Modernism and the Decorative Arts in France: Art Nouveau to Le Corbusier*. Yale University Press, New Haven, 1991.

Wright, F. L. *Frank Lloyd Wright, Collected Writings*. 2 vols. Rizzoli, New York, 1992.

CHAPTER 27. TWENTIETH-CENTURY PHOTOGRAPHY

Ades, D. *Photomontage*. Pantheon, New York, 1976.

Ansel Adams: Images, 1923–1974. Foreword W. Stegner. New York Graphic Society, Boston, 1974.

August Sander: Photographs of an Epoch, 1904–1959. Aperture, Millerton, N.Y., 1980.

Burgin, V., ed. *Thinking Photography.* Communications and Culture. Macmillan Education, Houndsmills, England, 1990.

Coke, V. D. *The Painter and the Photograph: From Delacroix to Warhol.* Rev. ed. University of New Mexico Press, Albuquerque, 1972.

Dorothea Lange: Photographs of a Lifetime. Aperture, Millerton, N.Y., 1982.

Green, J. *American Photography: A Critical History, 1945 to the Present.* Harry N. Abrams, New York, 1984.

Greenough, S., and J. Hamilton. *Alfred Stieglitz, Photographs and Writings.* Little, Brown, New York, 1999.

Haus, A. *Moholy-Nagy: Photographs and Photograms.* Pantheon, New York, 1980.

Henri Cartier-Bresson. Photographer. Foreword E. Bonnefoy. New York Graphic Society, Boston, 1979.

Krauss, R. *L'Amour Fou: Photography and Surrealism.* Abbeville Press, New York, 1985.

Marzona, E., and R. Fricke. *Bauhaus Photography.* MIT Press, Cambridge, 1987.

Phillips, C., ed. *Photography in the Modern Era: European Documents and Critical Writings, 1913–1940.* The Metropolitan Museum of Art, New York, 1989.

Sontag, S. *On Photography.* Farrar, Straus & Giroux, New York, 1973.

Szarkowski, J., and M. Hambourg. *The Work of Atget.* 4 vols. The Museum of Modern Art, New York, 1981–84.

Walsh, G., et al. *Contemporary Photographers.* St. Martin's Press, New York, 1983.

CHAPTER 28. POSTSCRIPT: POSTMODERN THEORY

Barthes, R. *The Pleasure of the Text.* Blackwell, Oxford, 1990.

Brunette, P., and D. Wills, eds. *Deconstruction and the Visual Arts: Art, Media, Architecture.* Cambridge University Press, New York. 1993.

Derrida, J. *Writing and Difference.* University of Chicago Press, Chicago, 1978.

Eco, U. A *Theory of Semiotics.* Indiana University Press, Bloomington, 1976.

Foster, H., ed. *The Anti-Aesthetic: Essays on Postmodern Culture.* Bay Press, Seattle, 1983.

Ghirardo, D. *Architecture After Modernism.* Thames & Hudson, New York, 1996.

Jameson, F. *The Prison House of Language.* Princeton University Press, Princeton, 1972.

Jencks, C. *Architecture Today.* Rev. and enl. ed. Harry N. Abrams, New York, 1988.

———. *Post-Modernism: The New Classicism in Art and Architecture.* Rizzoli, New York, 1987.

———. *What Is Post-Modernism?* 3rd ed. St. Martin's Press, New York, 1989.

Norris, C., and A. Benjamin. *What Is Deconstruction?* St. Martin's Press, New York, 1988.

Papadakes, A., et al., eds. *Deconstruction: The Omnibus Volume.* Rizzoli, New York, 1989.

Portoghesi, P. *Postmodern: The Architecture of the Post-Industrial Society.* Rizzoli, New York, 1983.

Risatti, H., ed. *Postmodern Perspectives.* Prentice Hall, Englewood Cliffs, N.J., 1990.

Tafuri, M. *Contemporary Architecture.* Harry N. Abrams, New York, 1977.

Wallis, B., ed. *Art After Modernism: Rethinking Representation. Documentary Sources in Contemporary Art, 1.* Godine, Boston, 1984.

Selected Discography

¢ = Budget Recording
● = Period Instrument Recording
§ = Recording of Exceptional Merit
† = Monophonic Recording

EARLY MUSIC

- ● Music of Ancient Greece (Paniagua), Harmonia Mundi France
- ¢● Music from Ancient Rome (Synaulia), Amiata
- ¢● Chant I (Monks of Santo Domingo de Silos), EMI
- ¢● Ancient Music for a Modern Age (Sequentia), RCA
- ¢ Millenium, Music from the Middle Ages (Ensemble Gilles Binchois), Virgin
- ¢● Love Songs of the Middle Ages 1150–1450 (Sequentia), Deutsche Harmonia Mundi
- ¢● Early Music 1400–1500 (various groups), Deutsche Harmonia Mundi
- ¢●§ The Art of Courtly Love (Munrow), EMI
- ¢● A Medieval Banquet (Best), Nimbus
- ¢● French Chansons (The Scholars of London), Naxos
- ¢● Elizabethan Songs (Rose Consort of Viols), Naxos

COMPOSERS

- ¢● Bach: Brandenburg Concerti, *The Musical Offering* (Linde), EMI
- ● Bach: Mass in B-Minor (Koopman), Erato
- Bach: *St. Matthew Passion* (Corboz), Erato
- Bach: Sonatas for Cello (Maisky, Argerich), Deutsche Grammaphon
- Bach: Sonatas, Partitas for Solo Violin (Milstein), Deutsche Grammaphon
- Bach: Suites for Solo Cello (Ma), Sony
- Bach: Organ Toccatas (Biggs), Sony
- † Bach: *The Well-Tempered Clavier,* Book I (Landowksa), RCA
- Bach: *The Well-Tempered Clavier,* Book II (Koopman), Erato
- Barber: *Knoxville, Adagio,* Songs/Copland: Poems, *Quiet City* (Hendricks, Thomas), EMI
- ¢ Bartók: Concerto for Orchestra; Music for Strings, Percussion, and Celeste (Reiner), RCA
- Bartók: Concerti for Violin (Gotowsky, Gerhardt), Pyramid
- Bartók: Quartets #1–6 (Lindsay), ASV
- ¢§ Beethoven: Concerti for Piano #1 and #3, #2 and #4 (Fleischer, Szell), Sony
- § Beethoven: Concerto for Piano #5, Concerto for Violin (Immerseel, Beth, Weil), Sony
- § Beethoven: Quartets [Complete] (Emerson String Quartet), Deutsche Grammaphon
- ¢ Beethoven: Sonatas for Cello (DuPré, Barenboim), Deutsche Grammaphon
- ● Beethoven: Sonatas for Piano #11, #13, #14, #19, #20 (Tan), Virgin
- ¢●§ Beethoven: Sonatas for Piano #21, #23, #26 (Tan), Virgin

- Beethoven: Sonatas for Piano #30, #31, #32 (Ashkenazy), London
- Beethoven: Sonatas for Violin #5, #9 (Menuhin, Kempf), Deutsche Grammaphon
- § Beethoven: Symphonies [Complete] (Gardiner), Deutsche Grammaphon
- Berg: *Wozzeck, Lulu* (Boehm), Deutsche Grammaphon
- Berlioz: *Romeo and Juliet* (Dutoit), London
- Berlioz: *Symphonie Fantastique* (Abbado), Deutsche Grammaphon
- ¢ Brahms: Concerto for Piano #1/ R. Schumann: Introduction and Allegro/ Mendelssohn: *Capriccio Brilliant* (R. Serkin, Szell), Sony
- ¢§ Brahms: Concerto for Piano #2/ Beethoven: Sonata #23 (Richter, Leinsdorf), RCA
- ¢Brahms: Concerto for Violin/ Tchaikovsky: Concerto for Violin (Milstein, Steinberg, Fistoulari), EMI
- Brahms: Double Concerto, Piano Quartet #3 (Stern, Ma, Abbado), Sony
- ¢§ Brahms: Symphonies #1–3, Overtures (Jochum), EMI
- ¢ Brahms: Symphony #4 (Swarowsky), Infinity
- ¢ § Britten: Violin Concerto, Cello Symphony (Hirsch, Hughes, Yuasa), Naxos
- ¢ Britten: Quartets (Britten Quartet), Collins
- § Cage, Carter, Babbitt, Schuller: Orchestral Works (Levine), Deutsche Grammaphon
- ¢ Chopin: Concerti for Piano #1, #2 (Ax, Previn), RCA
- Chopin: Piano Music (Arrau), Philips
- § Copland: Orchestral Music (Bernstein), Sony
- ●§ Corelli: Opus 5 (Trio Sonnerie), Virgin
- ● Corelli: Opus 6 (Europa Galante), Opus 111
- § Crumb: *Ancient Voices of Children, Music for a Summer Evening* (Weisberg), Nonesuch
- Debussy: *La Mer,* Nocturnes (Previn), Philips
- Debussy: Quartet/Ravel: Quartet (Budapest String Quartet), Sony
- Donizetti: *Lucia di Lammermoor* (Bonynge), London
- ¢ ● Dowland: *Treasures from My Mind* (King), EMI
- ● § Dufay: Complete Secular Music (Medieval Ensemble of London), L'Oiseau Lyre
- ¢ Dvořák: Cello Concerto/Bloch: *Schelomo* (Fournier, Szell), Deutsche Grammaphon
- Dvořák: Quartet #12/Smetana: Quartet (Guarneri), Philips
- ¢ Dvořák: Symphonies #7, #8, #9 (Szell), Sony
- ¢ Elgar: Concerto for Cello, Serenade, Enigma Variations (Maisky, Chailly), Deutsche Grammaphon

- Foss: Complete Vocal Music (Foss), Koss
- Franck: Symphony in D (Monteux), RCA
- Gay: *The Beggar's Opera* (Barlow), Hyperion
- Geminiani: Opus 2 (Lamon), Sony
- Gesualdo: Madrigals (Rooley), L'Oiseau-Lyre
- Glass: Songs from the Trilogy (various artists), Sony
- ●§ Glück: *Orpheus & Eurydice* (Gardiner), Philips
- Handel: *Messiah* (Shaw), Telarc
- Handel: Opus 6 (Guildhall), RCA
- Haydn: *Lark, Rider* Quartets (Hagen), Deutsche Grammaphon
- ¢ Haydn: Symphonies #93–104 (Fischer), Nimbus
- Ives: *Three Places in New England,* Symphony #4 (Thomas, Ozawa), Deutsche Grammaphon
- Janáček : Sinfonietta, *Taras Bulba* (Mackerras), London
- ¢● Josquin: Motets and Chansons (Hilliard), EMI
- ¢● Lassus: Motets (Hilliard), Virgin
- Lutoslawski: Concerto for Orchestra, *Jeux Venitiens,* etc. (Lutoslawski), EMI
- ¢● Machaut: Messe de Nostre Dame (Parrot), EMI
- Mahler: Lieder (Baker, Barbirolli), EMI
- ¢ Mahler: Symphony #1 (Haitink), Philips
- § Mahler: Symphony #9 (Karajan), Deutsche Grammaphon
- ¢ Mendelssohn: Symphony #3, Overtures (Maag), London
- Messiaen: *Couleurs, Oiseaux,* etc. (Boulez), Montaigne
- ● Monteverdi: *Orfeo* (Harnoncourt), Deutsche Grammaphon Archiv
- ¢● Monteverdi: Soprano Duets (Rooley), IMP
- Moussorgsky: *Boris Godunov* (Semkow), EMI
- ¢ Mozart: Concerti for Piano [Complete] (Anda), Deutsche Grammaphon
- § Mozart: Concerti for Violin #4, #5 (Schumsky, Tortelier), Nimbus
- § Mozart: *Don Giovanni* (Giulini), EMI
- Mozart: *Marriage of Figaro* (Solti), London
- Mozart: "Haydn" Quartets (Guarneri), Philips
- ¢ Mozart: Requiem (Karajan), Deutsche Grammaphon
- Mozart: String Quintets K515, K516 (Melos), Deutsche Grammaphon
- ¢ Mozart: Symphonies #35–#41 (Karajan), Deutsche Grammaphon
- Offenbach: *La Belle Hélène* (Plasson), EMI
- Palestrina: *Missa Paper Marcelli*/Allegri: *Miserere*/Lotti: *Crucifixus* (Christophers), Collins
- § Piazzolla: *57 Minutos Con La Realidad* (Piazzolla), Intuition
- Prokoviev: Concerti for Violin (Perlman, Rozhdestvensky), EMI
- Prokoviev: *Romeo and Juliet* (Maazel), London

- § Puccini: *Tosca* (Karajan), London
- ● Purcell: *Dido and Aeneas* (Parrott), EMI
- ● Purcell: *Fairy Queen* (Christophers), Collins
- § Rachmaninov: Concerto for Piano #2, *Rhapsody on a Theme of Paganini* (Rubinstein), RCA
- ¢ Rachmaninov: Symphony #2 (Previn), RCA
- Rimsky-Korsakov: *Sheherazade* (Mackerras), Telarc
- Saint-Saëns: Symphony #3 (Ormandy), Telarc
- Schoenberg: *Survivor from Warsaw,* 5 Pieces, etc. (Craft), Koch
- Schoenberg: *Transfigured Night*/Wagner: *Siegried Idyll* (Ashkenazy), London
- Schubert: Impromptus (Perahia), Sony
- ¢ Schubert: Lieder (Ludwig), Deutsche Grammaphon
- Schubert: Octet (Academy of St. Martin's in the Fields), Philips
- Schubert: Quartets #13, #14, #15 (Chilingirian), Chandos
- ¢ Schubert: Piano Sonatas [Complete] (Kempf), Deutsche Grammaphon
- ¢ Schubert: *Trout* Quintet (Marlborough), Sony
- Schubert: Cello Quintet (Guarneri), Philips
- ¢● Schubert: Symphonies (Goodman), Nimbus
- Schubert: Trio #1 (Borodin), Chandos
- Schumann: Symphonies [Complete] (Haitink), Philips
- § Sessions: *When Lilacs Last in Dooryard Bloom'd* (Ozawa), New World
- ¢ Sibelius: Symphony #2, *Swan of Tuonela* (Barbirolli), EMI
- ¢ Sibelius: Symphonies #4, #5 (Karajan), EMI
- § Stravinsky: *The Firebird* (Stravinsky), Sony
- § Stravinsky: *Petrouchka, The Rite of Spring* (Stravinsky), Sony
- ¢ Tchaikovsky: Concerto for Piano #1 (Gilels, Mehta), Concerto for Violin (Zukerman), Sony
- Tchaikovsky: Symphonies #1–#3 (Haitink), Philips
- § Tchaikovsky: Symphonies #4–#6 (Mravinsky), Deutsche Grammaphon
- § Telemann: Double and Triple Concerti (Hogwood), Oiseau Lyre
- ● Telemann: *Tafelmusik* (Goebbel), Deutsche Grammaphon Archiv
- Vaughn-Williams: Symphony #8, Partita for Double String Orchestra (Thomas), Chandos
- † Verdi: *Aida* (Serafin), EMI
- Verdi: Requiem (Shaw), Telarc
- Vivaldi: *L'estro Armonico* (I Filarmonici), Tactus
- ¢ Vivaldi: *Four Seasons* (I Musici), Philips
- Wagner: Overtures (Tennstedt), EMI
- Wagner: *Tristan and Isolde* (Karajan), EMI
- Webern: Complete Music (Boulez), Sony
- Weill: *The Threepenny Opera* (Lemper, Mauceri), London

Glossary

A

ABACUS. A slab of stone at the top of a classical capital just beneath the ARCHITRAVE.

ABBEY. 1) A religious community headed by an abbot or abbess. 2) The buildings which house the community. An abbey church often has an especially large CHOIR to provide space for the monks or nuns.

ACADEMY. A place of study, the word coming from the Greek name of a garden near Athens where Plato and, later, Platonic philosophers held philosophical discussions from the 5th century B.C. to the 6th century A.D. The first academy of fine arts was the Academy of Drawing, founded 1563 in Florence by Giorgio Vasari. Later academies were the Royal Academy of Painting and Sculpture in Paris, founded 1648, and the Royal Academy of Arts in London, founded 1768. Their purpose was to foster the arts by teaching, by exhibitions, by discussion, and occasionally by financial aid.

ACANTHUS. 1) A Mediterranean plant having spiny or toothed leaves. 2) An architectural ornament resembling the leaves of this plant, used on MOLDINGS, FRIEZES, and Corinthian CAPITALS.

ACRYLIC. A plastic binder MEDIUM for pigments that is soluble in water. Developed about 1960 (fig. 24-65).

AERIAL PERSPECTIVE. See PERSPECTIVE.

AISLE. See SIDE AISLE.

ALLA PRIMA. A painting technique in which pigments are laid on in one application with little or no UNDERPAINTING.

ALTAR. 1) A mound or structure on which sacrifices or offerings are made in the worship of a deity. 2) In a Catholic church, a tablelike structure used in celebrating the Mass.

ALTARPIECE. A painted or carved work of art placed behind and above the ALTAR of a Christian church. It may be a single panel (fig. P-14) or a TRIPTYCH or a POLYPTYCH having hinged wings painted on both sides (figs. 15-1, 15-6). Also called a reredos or retable.

AMBULATORY. A covered walkway. 1) In a BASILICAN church, the semicircular passage around the APSE. 2) In a CENTRAL-PLAN church, the ring-shaped AISLE around the central space (fig. 17-21). 3) In a CLOISTER, the covered COLONNADED or ARCADED walk around the open courtyard.

ANNULAR. From the Latin word for "ring." Signifies a ring-shaped form, especially an annular barrel VAULT.

APOCALYPSE. The Book of Revelation, the last book of the New Testament. In it, St. John the Evangelist describes his visions, experienced on the island of Patmos, of Heaven, the future of humankind, and the Last Judgment.

APOSTLE. One of the 12 disciples chosen by Jesus to accompany him in his lifetime and to spread the GOSPEL after his death. The traditional list includes Andrew, Bartholomew, James the Greater (son of Zebedee), James the Lesser (son of Alphaeus), John, Judas Iscariot, Matthew, Peter, Philip, Simon the Canaanite, Thaddaeus (or Jude), and Thomas. In art, however, the same 12 are not always represented, since "apostle" was sometimes applied to other early Christians, such as St. Paul.

APSE. 1) A semicircular or polygonal niche terminating one or both ends of the NAVE in a Roman BASILICA. 2) In a Christian church, it is usually placed at the east end of the nave beyond the TRANSEPT or CHOIR (figs. 14-28, 19-22). It is also sometimes used at the end of transept arms.

AQUATINT. A print processed like an ETCHING, except that the ground or certain areas are covered with a solution of asphalt, resin, or salts which, when heated, produces a granular surface on the plate and rich gray tones in the final print (fig. 21-10). Etched lines are usually added to the plate after the aquatint ground is laid.

AQUEDUCT. Latin for "duct of water." 1) An artificial channel or conduit for transporting water from a distant source. 2) The overground structure which carries the conduit across valleys, rivers, etc.

ARCADE. A series of ARCHES supported by PIERS or COLUMNS (fig. 12-13). When attached to a wall, these form a blind arcade.

ARCH. A curved structure used to span an opening. Masonry arches are built of wedge-shaped blocks, called voussoirs, set with their narrow side toward the opening so that they lock together. The topmost voussoir is called the keystone. Arches may take different shapes, as in the pointed Gothic arch (fig. P-2) or the classical arch (fig. 21-72), but all require support from other arches or BUTTRESSES.

ARCHBISHOP. The chief BISHOP of an ecclesiastic district.

ARCHITRAVE. The lowermost member of a classical ENTABLATURE; i.e., a series of stone blocks that rest directly on the COLUMNS (figs. 14-26, 14-27, 21-20).

ARCHIVOLT. A molded band framing an ARCH, or a series of such bands framing a TYMPANUM, often decorated with sculpture (fig. 12-64).

ARRICCIO. See SINOPIA.

ATMOSPHERIC PERSPECTIVE. See PERSPECTIVE.

ATRIUM. 1) The central court of a Roman house or its open entrance court. 2) An open court, sometimes COLONNADED or ARCADED, in front of a church.

ATTIC. A low upper story placed above the main CORNICE or ENTABLATURE of a building and often decorated with windows and PILASTERS (fig. 13-27).

AUTOCHROME. A color photograph invented by Louis Lumière in 1903 using a glass plate covered with grains of starch dyed in three colors to act as filters and then a silver bromide emulsion (fig. 27-1).

B

BACCHANT (fem. **BACCHANTE**). A priest or priestess of the wine god, Bacchus (in Greek mythology, Dionysos) or one of his ecstatic female followers, who were sometimes called maenads (fig. 13-37).

BALUSTRADE. 1) A railing supported by short pillars called balusters (fig. 13-23). 2) Occasionally applied to any low parapet (fig. P-1).

BANQUET PIECE. A variant of the still life, the banquet piece depicts an after-meal scene. It focuses more on tableware than food and typically incorporates a VANITAS theme (fig. 18-24).

BAPTISTERY. A building or a part of a church, often round or octagonal, in which the sacrament of baptism is administered. It contains a baptismal font, a receptacle of stone or metal which holds the water for the rite.

BARREL VAULT. See VAULT.

BASE. 1) The lowermost portion of a COLUMN or PIER, beneath the SHAFT. 2) The lowest element of a wall, DOME, or building or occasionally of a statue or painting (see PREDELLA).

BASILICA. 1) In ancient Roman architecture, a large, oblong building used as a hall of justice and public meeting place, generally having a NAVE, SIDE AISLES, and one or more APSES. 2) In Christian architecture, a longitudinal church derived from the Roman basilica and having a nave, apse, two or four side aisles or side chapels, and sometimes a NARTHEX (fig. 12-21). 3) One of the seven main churches of Rome (St. Peter's, St. Paul Outside the Walls, St. John Lateran, etc.) or another church accorded the same religious privileges.

BATTLEMENT. A parapet consisting of alternating solid parts and open spaces designed originally for defense and later used for decoration (fig. 21-68).

BAY. A subdivision of the interior space of a building, usually in a series bounded by consecutive architectural supports.

BELVEDERE. A structure made for the purpose of viewing the surroundings, either atop the roof of a building or freestanding in a garden or other natural setting.

BISHOP. The spiritual overseer of a number of churches or a diocese. His throne, or cathedra, placed in the principal church of the diocese, designates it as a cathedral.

BLIND ARCADE. See ARCADE.

BLOCK BOOKS. Books, often religious, of the 15th century, containing WOODCUT prints in which picture and text were usually cut into the same block (compare fig. 15-22).

BOOK COVER. The stiff outer covers protecting the bound pages of a book. In the medieval period, frequently covered with precious metal and elaborately embellished with jewels, embossed decoration, etc.

BOOK OF HOURS. A private prayer book containing the devotions for the seven canonical hours of the Roman Catholic church (matins, vespers, etc.), liturgies for local saints, and sometimes a calendar (fig. P-13). They were often elaborately ILLUMINATED for persons of high rank, whose names are attached to certain extant examples.

BRACKET. A stone, wooden, or metal support projecting from a wall and having a flat top to bear the weight of a statue, CORNICE, beam, etc. The lower part may take the form of a SCROLL; it is then called a scroll bracket.

BROKEN PEDIMENT. See PEDIMENT.

BRUSH DRAWING. See DRAWING.

BURIN. See ENGRAVING.

BUTTRESS. 1) A projecting support built against an external wall, usually to counteract the lateral THRUST of a VAULT or ARCH within. 2) FLYING BUTTRESS. An arched bridge above the aisle roof that extends from the upper nave wall, where the lateral thrust of the main vault is greatest, down to a solid pier.

BYZANTIUM. City on the Sea of Marmara, founded by the ancient Greeks and renamed Constantinople in 330 A.D. Today called Istanbul.

C

CAESAR. The surname of the Roman dictator, Caius Julius Caesar, subsequently used as the title of an emperor; hence, the German Kaiser and the Russian czar (tsar).

CALLIGRAPHY. From the Greek word for "beautiful writing." 1) Decorative or formal handwriting executed with a quill or reed pen or with a brush. 2) A design derived from or resembling letters and used to form a pattern.

CALVARY. The hill outside Jerusalem where Jesus was crucified, the name being taken from the Latin word calvaris, meaning skull (Golgotha is the Greek transliteration of "skull" in Aramaic). The hill was thought to be the spot where Adam was buried and was thus traditionally known as "the place of the skull."

CAMEO. A LOW RELIEF carving made on agate, seashell, or other multi-layered material in which the subject, often in profile view, is rendered in one color while the background appears in another, darker color.

CAMERA OBSCURA. Latin for "dark room." A darkened enclosure or box with a small opening or lens on one wall through which light enters to form an inverted image on the opposite wall. The principle had long been known but was not used as an aid in picture making until the 16th century.

CAMPAGNA. Italian word for "countryside." When capitalized, it usually refers to the countryside near Rome.

CAMPANILE. From the Italian word campana, meaning "bell." A bell tower, either round or square, and sometimes freestanding (fig. 14-27).

CAMPOSANTO. Italian word for "holy field." A cemetery near a church, often enclosed.

CANOPY. In architecture, an ornamental, rooflike projection or cover above a statue or sacred object (fig. 17-16).

CAPITAL. The uppermost member of a COLUMN or PILLAR supporting the ARCHITRAVE.

CARDINAL. In the Roman Catholic church, a member of the Sacred College, the ecclesiastical body which elects the pope and constitutes his advisory council.

CARTOON. From the Italian word cartone, meaning "cardboard." 1) A full-scale DRAWING for a picture or design intended to be transferred to a wall, panel, tapestry, etc. 2) A drawing or print, usually humorous or satirical, calling attention to some action or person of popular interest (fig. 21-36).

CARVING. 1) The cutting of a figure or design out of a solid material such as stone or wood, as contrasted to the additive technique of MODELING. 2) A work executed in this technique (figs. 13-14, 13-15).

CASTING. A method of duplicating a work of sculpture by pouring a hardening substance such as plaster or molten metal into a mold. See CIRE-PERDU PROCESS.

CAST IRON. A hard, brittle iron produced commercially in blast furnaces by pouring it into molds where it cools and hardens. Extensively used as a building material in the early 19th century (figs. 22-33, 22-34), it was superseded by STEEL and FERROCONCRETE.

CATHEDRA, CATHEDRAL. See BISHOP.

CELLA. 1) The principal enclosed room of a temple, to house an image. Also called the naos. 2) The entire body of a temple as distinct from its external parts.

CENTERING. A wooden framework built to support an ARCH, VAULT, or DOME during its construction.

CENTRAL-PLAN CHURCH. 1) A church having four arms of equal length. The CROSSING is often covered with a DOME (figs. 12-35–12-37). Also called a Greek-cross church. 2) A church having a circular or polygonal plan (fig. 13-8).

CHANCEL. See CHOIR.

CHAPEL. 1) A private or subordinate place of worship (figs. 12-22–12-25). 2) A place of worship that is part of a church but separately dedicated (figs. 12-47, 13-17).

CHASING. 1) A technique of ornamenting a metal surface by the use of various tools. 2) The procedure used to finish a raw bronze cast.

CHÂTEAU (pl. **CHÂTEAUS** or **CHÂTEAUX**). French word for "castle," now used to designate a large country house as well (fig. 16-24).

CHIAROSCURO. Italian word for "light and dark." In painting, a method of modeling form primarily by the use of light and shade (figs. 13-1, 13-37, 17-2).

CHOIR. In church architecture, a square or rectangular area between the APSE and the NAVE or TRANSEPT. It is reserved for the clergy and the singing choir and is usually marked off by steps, a railing, or a CHOIR SCREEN. Also called the chancel. See PILGRIMAGE CHOIR.

CHOIR SCREEN. A screen, frequently ornamented with sculpture and sometimes called a rood screen, separating the CHOIR of a church from the NAVE or TRANSEPT. In Orthodox Christian churches it is decorated with ICONS and thus called an iconostasis.

CIRE-PERDU PROCESS. The lost-wax process of CASTING. A method in which an original is MODELED in wax or coated with wax then covered with clay. When the wax is melted out, the resulting mold is filled with molten metal (often bronze) or liquid plaster.

CITY-STATE. An autonomous political unit comprising a city and the surrounding countryside.

CLERESTORY. A row of windows in the upper part of a wall that rises above an adjoining roof; built to provide direct lighting, as in a BASILICA or church (fig. 12-20).

CLOISTER. 1) A place of religious seclusion such as a monastery or nunnery. 2) An open court attached to a church or monastery and surrounded by a covered ARCADED walk or AMBULATORY. Used for study, meditation, and exercise.

CODEX (pl. **CODICES**). A manuscript in book form made possible by the use of PARCHMENT instead of PAPYRUS. During the 1st to 4th centuries A.D., it gradually replaced the roll or SCROLL previously used for written documents.

COFFER. 1) A small chest or casket. 2) A recessed, geometrically shaped panel in a ceiling. A ceiling decorated with these panels is said to be coffered (figs. 17-20, 21-72).

COLLAGE. A composition made of cut and pasted scraps of materials, sometimes with lines or forms added by the artist (fig. 24-14).

COLONNADE. A series of regularly spaced COLUMNS supporting a LINTEL or ENTABLATURE (fig. 13-7).

COLOSSAL ORDER. COLUMNS, PIERS, or PILASTERS which extend through two or more stories (figs. 12-29, 13-26).

COLUMN. An approximately cylindrical, upright architectural support, usually consisting of a long, relatively slender SHAFT, a BASE, and a CAPITAL (fig. 12-13). When imbedded in a wall, it is called an engaged column (fig. 12-38). Columns decorated with wraparound RELIEFS were used occasionally as freestanding commemorative monuments.

COMPOUND PIER. See PIER.

CONCRETE. A mixture of sand or gravel with mortar and rubble, invented

in the ancient Near East and further developed by the Romans. Largely ignored during the Middle Ages, it was revived by Bramante in the early 16th century for St. Peter's.

CONTÉ CRAYON. A crayon made of graphite and clay used for DRAWING. Produces rich, velvety tones (fig. 23-6).

CONTRAPPOSTO. Italian word for "set against." A method developed by the Greeks to represent freedom of movement in a figure. The parts of the body are placed asymmetrically in opposition to each other around a central axis, and careful attention is paid to the distribution of the weight (fig. 12-6).

CORINTHIAN ORDER. See ORDER, ARCHITECTURAL.

CORNICE. 1) The projecting, framing members of a classical PEDIMENT, including the horizontal one beneath and the two sloping or "raking" ones above. 2) Any projecting, horizontal element surmounting a wall or other structure or dividing it horizontally for decorative purposes (fig. 12-27).

COUNTER REFORMATION. The movement of self-renewal and reform within the Roman Catholic church following the Protestant REFORMATION of the early 16th century and attempting to combat its influence. Also known as the Catholic Reform. Its principles were formulated and adopted at the Council of Trent, 1545–63.

CRENELATED. See BATTLEMENT.

CROSSHATCHING. See HATCHING.

CROSSING. The area in a church where the TRANSEPT crosses the NAVE, frequently emphasized by a DOME or crossing tower.

CROSS SECTION. See SECTION.

CRYPT. In a church, a VAULTED space beneath the CHOIR, causing the floor of the choir to be raised above the level of that of the NAVE.

D

DAGUERREOTYPE. Originally, a photograph on a silver-plated sheet of copper which had been treated with fumes of iodine to form silver iodide on its surface and, after exposure, was developed by fumes of mercury. The process, invented by L. J. M. Daguerre and made public in 1839 (fig. 21-80), was modified and accelerated as daguerreotypes gained popularity.

DEËSIS. From the Greek word for "entreaty." The representation of Christ enthroned between the Virgin Mary and St. John the Baptist, frequent in Byzantine MOSAICS and depictions of the Last Judgment (fig. 15-2); refers to the roles of the Virgin Mary and St. John as intercessors for humankind.

DIPTYCH. 1) Originally a hinged two-leaved tablet used for writing. 2) A pair of ivory CARVINGS or PANEL paintings, usually hinged together.

DISGUISED SYMBOLISM. "Hidden" meaning in the details of a painting that carry a symbolic message (fig. 15-1).

DOME. A true dome is a VAULTED roof of circular, polygonal, or elliptical plan, formed with hemispherical or ovoidal curvature (figs. 13-7, 17-20). May be supported by a circular wall or DRUM

and by PENDENTIVES or related constructions. Domical coverings of many other sorts have been devised (fig. 12-18, 17-26).

DONOR. The patron or client at whose order a work of art was executed; the donor may be depicted in the work (figs. 15-1, 15-16).

DORIC ORDER. See ORDER, ARCHITECTURAL.

DRAWING. 1) A work in pencil, pen and ink, charcoal, etc., often on paper (fig. 23-18). 2) A similar work in ink or WASH, etc., made with a brush and often called a brush drawing. 3) A work combining these or other techniques. A drawing may be large or small, a quick sketch or an elaborate work. Among its various forms are: a record of something seen; a study for another work (figs. 12-60, 21-32; see also OIL SKETCH; SINOPIA); an illustration associated with a text (fig. 13-5); and a technical aid.

DRESSED STONE. A masonry technique in which exposed stones are finished, or dessed, to produce a surface that is smooth and formal-looking (fig 14-31).

DRUM. 1) A section of the SHAFT of a COLUMN. 2) A wall supporting a DOME (fig. 13-27).

DRYPOINT. See ENGRAVING.

E

ELEVATION. 1) An architectural drawing presenting a building as if projected on a vertical plane parallel to one of its sides. 2) Term used in describing the vertical plane of a building.

ENAMEL. 1) Colored glassy substances, either opaque or translucent, applied in powder form to a metal surface and fused to it by firing. Two main techniques developed: champlevé (from the French for "raised field"), in which the areas to be treated are dug out of the metal surface; and cloisonné (from the French for "partitioned"), in which compartments or cloisons to be filled are made on the surface with thin metal strips. 2) A work executed in either technique (fig. 14-19).

EMBLEM BOOK. A reference book for paintings of Christian subjects that provides examples of objects and events associated with saints and other religious figures.

ENGAGED COLUMN. See COLUMN.

ENGRAVING. 1) A means of embellishing metal surfaces or gemstones by incising a design on the surface. 2) A PRINT made by cutting a design into a metal plate (usually copper) with a pointed steel tool known as a burin. The burr raised on either side of the incised line is removed; ink is then rubbed into the V-shaped grooves and wiped off the surface; the plate, covered with a damp sheet of paper, is run through a heavy press (fig. 15-23). The image on the paper is the reverse of that on the plate (figs. 20-11, 20-12). When a fine steel needle is used instead of a burin and the burr is retained, a drypoint engraving results, characterized by a softer line (fig. 15-24). 3) These techniques are called, respectively, engraving and drypoint.

ENTABLATURE. 1) In a classical order, the entire structure above the COLUMNS; this usually includes ARCHITRAVE, FRIEZE, and CORNICE. 2) The same structure in any building of a classical style (fig. 21-15).

ENTASIS. A swelling of the SHAFT of a COLUMN.

ETCHING. 1) A PRINT made by coating a copperplate with an acid-resistant resin and drawing through this ground, exposing the metal with a sharp instrument called a STYLUS. The plate is bathed in acid, which eats into the lines; it is then heated to remove the resin and finally inked and printed on paper (fig. 18-17). 2) The technique itself is also called etching.

EUCHARIST. 1) The sacrament of Holy Communion, the celebration in commemoration of the Last Supper (fig. 12-35). 2) The consecrated bread and wine used in the ceremony.

EVANGELISTS. Matthew, Mark, Luke, and John, traditionally thought to be the authors of the GOSPELS, the first four books of the New Testament, which recount the life and death of Christ. They are usually shown with their symbols, which are probably derived from the four beasts surrounding the throne of the Lamb in the Book of Revelation or from those in the vision of Ezekiel: a winged man or angel for Matthew (fig. 14-14), a winged lion for Mark, a winged ox for Luke, and an eagle for John. These symbols may also represent the evangelists.

F

FACADE. The principal face or the front of a building.

FERROCONCRETE. Reinforced CONCRETE, strengthened by STEEL rods and mesh placed in it before hardening. Introduced in France c. 1900 and widely used today (figs. 26-14, 26-18, 26-28, 26-34).

FIBULA. A clasp, buckle, or brooch, often ornamented.

FINIAL. A relatively small, decorative element terminating a GABLE, PINNACLE, or the like (fig. 19-21).

FLUTING. In architecture, the ornamental grooves channeled vertically into the SHAFT of a COLUMN or PILASTER (fig. 12-48). They may meet in a sharp edge, as in the Doric ORDER, or be separated by a narrow strip or fillet, as in the Ionic, Corinthian, and Composite orders.

FLYING BUTTRESS. See BUTTRESS.

FONT. See BAPTISTERY.

FORESHORTENING. A method of reducing or distorting the parts of a represented object which are not parallel to the PICTURE PLANE in order to convey the impression of three dimensions as perceived by the human eye (figs. 19-5, 21-31).

FRESCO. Italian word for "fresh." 1) True fresco is the technique of painting on moist plaster with pigments ground in water so that the paint is absorbed by the plaster and becomes part of the wall itself. Fresco secco is the technique of painting with the same colors on dry plaster. 2) A painting done in either of these techniques.

FRIEZE. 1) A continuous band of painted or sculptured decoration (fig. 22-39). 2) In a classical building, the part of the ENTABLATURE between the ARCHITRAVE and the CORNICE. A Doric frieze consists of alternating TRIGLYPHS and METOPES, the latter often sculptured.

An Ionic frieze is usually decorated with continuous RELIEF sculpture.

FROTTAGE. See RUBBING.

G

GABLE. 1) The triangular area framed by the CORNICE or eaves of a building and the sloping sides of a pitched roof. In classical architecture, it is called a PEDIMENT. 2) A decorative element of similar shape, such as the triangular structures above the PORTALS of a Gothic church and sometimes at the top of a Gothic picture frame.

GALLERY. A second story placed over the SIDE AISLES of a church and below the CLERESTORY or, in a church with a four-part ELEVATION, below the TRIFORIUM and above the NAVE ARCADE which supports it on its open side.

GENIUS (pl. **GENII**). A winged seminude figure, often purely decorative (fig. 12-48) but frequently representing the guardian spirit of a person or place or personifying an abstract concept (fig. 21-58).

GENRE. French word for "kind" or "sort." A work of art, usually a painting, showing a scene from everyday life represented for its own sake (fig. 20-8).

GESSO. A smooth mixture of ground chalk or plaster and glue used as the basis for TEMPERA PAINTING and for oil painting on PANEL.

GILDING. 1) A coat of gold or of a gold-colored substance that is applied mechanically or chemically to surfaces of a painting, sculpture, or architectural decoration (figs. 12-8, 20-20). 2) The process of applying same.

GISANT. Effigy sculpture depicting a nude corpse or corpses in a state of decay. Like VANITAS paintings, *gisants* are intended to remind the viewer of life's transience (fig. 16-30).

GLAZE. 1) A thin layer of translucent oil color applied to a painted surface or to parts of it in order to modify the tone. 2) A glassy coating applied to a piece of ceramic work before firing in the kiln as a protective seal and often as decoration.

GLORIOLE or **GLORY.** The circle of radiant light around the heads or figures of God, Christ, the Virgin Mary, or a saint. When it surrounds the head only, it is called a halo or nimbus (fig. P-11); when it surrounds the entire figure with a large oval, it is called a mandorla (the Italian word for "almond"). It indicates divinity or holiness, though originally it was placed around the heads of kings and gods as a mark of distinction.

GOLD LEAF, SILVER LEAF. 1) Gold beaten into very thin sheets or "leaves" and applied to ILLUMINATED MANUSCRIPTS and PANEL paintings (fig. P-11), to sculpture, or to the back of the glass TESSERAE used in MOSAICS. 2) Silver leaf is also used, though ultimately it tarnishes. Sometimes called gold foil, silver foil.

GOLGOTHA. See CALVARY.

GOSPEL. 1) The first four books of the New Testament. They tell the story of Christ's life and death and are ascribed to the evangelists Matthew, Mark, Luke, and John. 2) A copy of these, usually called a Gospel Book, often richly ILLUMINATED.

GREEK-CROSS CHURCH. See CENTRAL-PLAN CHURCH.

GRISAILLE. A monochrome drawing or painting using only values of black, gray, and white simulate the appearance of stone sculpture (fig. 15-4, at the top).

GROIN VAULT. See VAULT.

GROUND PLAN. An architectural drawing presenting a building as if cut horizontally at the floor level.

H

HALLENKIRCHE. German word for "hall church." A church in which the NAVE and the SIDE AISLES are of the same height. The type was developed in Romanesque architecture and occurs especially frequently in German Gothic churches.

HALO. See GLORIOLE.

HATCHING. A series of parallel lines used as shading in PRINTS and DRAWINGS (fig. 12-60). When two sets of crossing parallel lines are used, it is called crosshatching.

HIGH RELIEF. See RELIEF.

HÔTEL. French word for "hotel" but used also to designate an elegant town house (fig. 20-1).

I

ICON. From the Greek word for "image." A PANEL painting of one or more sacred personages, such as Christ, the Virgin, or a saint, particularly venerated in the Orthodox Catholic church (fig. P-4).

ICONOSTASIS. See CHOIR SCREEN.

ILLUMINATED MANUSCRIPT. A MANUSCRIPT decorated with drawings or with paintings in TEMPERA colors.

ILLUSIONISM. In artistic terms, the technique of manipulating pictorial or other means in order to cause the eye to perceive a particular reality. May be used in architecture (fig. 17-26) and sculpture (figs. 17-29, 17-30), as well as in painting (figs. 17-12, 17-13).

IMPASTO. From the Italian word meaning "in paste." Paint, usually oil paint, applied very thickly (figs. 17-35, 23-11).

IONIC ORDER. See ORDER, ARCHITECTURAL.

J

JAMBS. The vertical sides of an opening. In Romanesque and Gothic churches, the jambs of doors and windows are often cut on a slant outward, or "splayed," thus providing a broader surface for sculptural decoration.

JESUIT ORDER. The "Society of Jesus" was founded in 1534 by Ignatius of Loyola (1491–1556) and was especially devoted to the service of the pope. The order was a powerful influence in the struggle of the Catholic COUNTERREFORMATION with the Protestant REFORMATION, and also very important for its missionary work, disseminating Christianity in the Far East and the New World. The mother church in Rome, Il Gesù (figs. 14-29–14-31), conforms in design to the preaching aims of the new order.

K

KEYSTONE. See ARCH.

KITSCH. A German word for "trash," in English *kitsch* has come to describe a sensibility that is vulgar and/or sentimental, in contrast to the refinement of "high" art or fine art.

L

LABORS OF THE MONTHS. The various occupations suitable to the months of the year. Scenes or figures illustrating these were frequently represented in ILLUMINATED manuscripts (fig. P-13); sometimes with the symbols of the ZODIAC signs CARVED around the PORTALS of Romanesque and Gothic churches.

LANTERN. A relatively small structure crowning a DOME, roof, or tower, frequently open to admit light to an enclosed area below (fig. 13-27).

LIBERAL ARTS. Traditionally thought to go back to Plato, they comprised the intellectual disciplines considered suitable or necessary to a complete education, and included grammar, rhetoric, logic, arithmetic, music, geometry, and astronomy. During the Middle Ages and the Renaissance, they were often represented allegorically in paintings, engravings, and sculpture.

LINTEL. See POST AND LINTEL.

LITHOGRAPH. A PRINT made by drawing a design with an oily crayon or other greasy substance on a porous stone or, later, a metal plate; the design is then fixed, the entire surface is moistened, and the printing ink which is applied adheres only to the oily lines of the drawing. The design can then be transferred easily in a press to a piece of paper. The technique was invented c. 1796 by Aloys Senefelder and quickly became popular (figs. 21-36, 23-19). It is also widely used commercially, since many impressions can be taken from a single plate.

LOGGIA. A covered GALLERY or ARCADE open to the air on at least one side. It may stand alone or be part of a building (fig. 14-23).

LONGITUDINAL SECTION. See SECTION.

LOUVERS. A series of overlapping boards or slats which can be opened to admit air but are slanted so as to exclude sun and rain (fig. 26-29).

LOW RELIEF. See RELIEF.

LUNETTE. 1) A semicircular or pointed wall area, as under a VAULT or above a door or window. When it is above the PORTAL of a medieval church, it is called a TYMPANUM (fig. P-18). 2) A painting (fig. 17-7), relief sculpture (fig. 12-11), or window of the same shape (fig. 21-14).

M

MAESTÀ. Italian word for "majesty," applied in the 14th and 15th centuries to representations of the Madonna and Child enthroned and surrounded by her celestial court of saints and angels (fig. P-5).

MAGUS (pl. **MAGI**). 1) A member of the priestly caste of ancient Media and Persia. 2) In Christian literature, one of the three Wise Men or Kings who came from the East bearing gifts to the newborn Jesus (fig. P-14).

MANDORLA. See GLORIOLE.

MANUSCRIPT. From the Latin word

for "handwritten." 1) A document, scroll, or book written by hand, as distinguished from such a work in print (i.e., after c. 1450). 2) A book produced in the Middle Ages, frequently ILLUMINATED.

MAUSOLEUM. 1) The huge tomb erected at Halikarnassos in Asia Minor in the 4th century B.C. by King Mausolos and his wife Artemisia. 2) A generic term for any large funerary monument.

MEANDER. A decorative motif of intricate, rectilinear character applied to architecture and sculpture.

MEDIUM (pl. **MEDIUMS**). 1) The material or technique in which an artist works. 2) The vehicle in which pigments are carried in paint, pastel, etc.

METOPE. In a Doric FRIEZE, one of the panels, either decorated or plain, between the TRIGLYPHS. Originally it probably covered the empty spaces between the ends of the wooden ceiling beams.

MINIATURE. 1) A single illustration in an ILLUMINATED manuscript. 2) A very small painting, especially a portrait on ivory, glass, or metal (fig. 16-17).

MODEL. 1) The preliminary form of a sculpture, often finished in itself but preceding the final CASTING or CARVING (figs. 19-17, 19-18, 21-64). 2) Preliminary or reconstructed form of a building made to scale (fig. 19-24). 3) A person who poses for an artist.

MODELING. 1) In sculpture, the building up of a figure or design in a soft substance such as clay or wax (fig. 20-2). 2) In painting and drawing, producing a three-dimensional effect by changes in color, the use of light and shade, etc.

MOLDING. In architecture, any of various long, narrow, ornamental bands having a distinctive profile which project from the surface of the structure and give variety to the surface by means of their patterned contrasts of light and shade (figs. 12-48, 12-64, 21-19).

MOSAIC. Decorative work for walls, VAULTS, ceilings, or floors composed of small pieces of colored materials (called TESSERAE) set in plaster or concrete. The Romans, whose work was mostly for floors, used regularly shaped pieces of marble in its natural colors. The early Christians used pieces of glass whose brilliant hues, including gold, and slightly irregular surfaces produced an entirely different, glittering effect. See also GOLD LEAF.

MURAL. From the Latin word for wall, murus. A large painting or decoration either executed directly on a wall (FRESCO) or done separately and affixed to it (fig. 23-16).

MUSES. In Greek mythology, the nine goddesses who presided over various arts and sciences. They are led by Apollo as god of music and poetry and usually include Calliope, muse of epic poetry; Clio, muse of history; Erato, muse of love poetry; Euterpe, muse of music; Melpomene, muse of tragedy; Polyhymnia, muse of sacred music; Terpsichore, muse of dancing; Thalia, muse of comedy; and Urania, muse of astronomy.

N

NARTHEX. The transverse entrance hall of a church, sometimes enclosed but often open on one side to a preceding ATRIUM.

NAVE. 1) The central aisle of a Roman BASILICA, as distinguished from the SIDE AISLES. 2) The same section of a Christian basilican church extending from the entrance to the APSE or TRANSEPT (fig. 12-13).

NIKE. The ancient Greek goddess of victory, often identified with Athena and by the Romans with Victoria. She is usually represented as a winged woman with windblown draperies.

NIMBUS. See GLORIOLE.

O

OBELISK. A tall, tapering, four-sided stone shaft with a pyramidal top. First constructed as MEGALITHS in ancient Egypt; certain examples since exported to other countries (fig. 17-15).

ODALISQUE. Turkish word for "harem slave girl" or "concubine" (fig. 21-30).

OIL PAINTING. 1) A painting executed with pigments mixed with oil, first applied to a panel prepared with a coat of GESSO (as also in TEMPERA PAINTING), or later to a stretched canvas primed with a coat of white paint and glue. The latter method has predominated since the late 15th century. Oil painting also may be executed on paper, parchment, copper, etc. 2) The technique of executing such a painting.

OIL SKETCH. A work in oil painting of an informal character, sometimes preparatory to a finished work (fig. 18-2).

ORDER, ARCHITECTURAL. An architectural system based on the COLUMN and its ENTABLATURE, in which the form of the elements themselves (CAPITAL, SHAFT, BASE, etc.) and their relationships to each other are specifically defined. The five classical orders are the Doric, Ionic, Corinthian, Tuscan, and Composite. See also SUPERIMPOSED ORDER.

ORDER, MONASTIC. A religious society whose members live together under an established set of rules.

ORTHODOX. From the Greek word for "right in opinion." The Eastern Orthodox church, which broke with the Western Catholic church during the 5th century a.d. and transferred its allegiance from the pope in Rome to the Byzantine emperor in Constantinople and his appointed patriarch. Sometimes called the Byzantine church.

P

PALAZZO (pl. **PALAZZI**). Italian word for "palace" (in French, palais). Refers either to large official buildings (fig. 13-26) or to important private town houses (fig. 12-14).

PALETTE. 1) A thin, usually oval or oblong board with a thumbhole at one end, used by painters to hold and mix their colors. 2) The range of colors used by a particular painter. 3) In Egyptian art, a slate slab, usually decorated with sculpture in low RELIEF. The small ones with a recessed circular area on one side are thought to have been used for eye make-up. The larger ones were commemorative objects.

PANEL. 1) A wooden surface used for painting, usually in TEMPERA, and prepared beforehand with a layer of GESSO. Large ALTARPIECES require the joining together of two or more boards (fig. 15-19). 2) Recently, panels of Masonite or other composite materials have come into use (fig. 24-72).

PANTHEON. From pan, Greek for "all." A temple dedicated to all the gods, or housing tombs of the illustrious dead of a nation or memorials to them (fig. 21-16).

PARCHMENT. From Pergamon, the name of a Greek city in Asia Minor where parchment was invented in the 2nd century B.C. 1) A paperlike material made from bleached animal hides used extensively in the Middle Ages for MANUSCRIPTS. Vellum is a superior type of parchment, made from calfskin. 2) A document or miniature on this material.

PASSION. 1) In ecclesiastic terms, the events of Jesus' last week on earth. 2) The representation of these events in pictorial, literary, theatrical, or musical form (figs. 13-42, 15-10, 18-1).

PASTEL. 1) A soft, subdued shade of color. 2) A drawing stick made from pigments ground with chalk and mixed with gum water. 3) A drawing executed with these sticks (fig. 22-11).

PEDESTAL. An architectural support for a statue, vase, column, etc.

PEDIMENT. 1) In classical architecture, a low GABLE, typically triangular, framed by a horizontal CORNICE below and two raking cornices above; frequently filled with relief sculpture (fig. 21-16). 2) A similar architectural member, either round or triangular, used over a door, window, or niche (fig. 13-22). When pieces of the cornice are either turned at an angle or broken, it is called a broken pediment (fig. 13-23).

PENDENTIVE. One of the spherical triangles which achieves the transition from a square or polygonal opening to the round BASE of a DOME or the supporting DRUM (fig. 12-45).

PERIPTERAL. An adjective describing a building surrounded by a single row of COLUMNS or COLONNADE.

PERISTYLE. 1) In a Roman house or DOMUS, an open garden court surrounded by a COLONNADE. 2) A colonnade around a building or court (fig. 13-8).

PERSPECTIVE. A technique for representing spatial relationships and three-dimensional objects on a flat surface so as to produce an effect similar to that perceived by the human eye. In atmospheric or aerial perspective, this is accomplished by a gradual decrease in the intensity of local color and in the contrast of light and dark, so that everything in the far distance tends toward a light bluish-gray tone (fig. 15-2). In one-point linear perspective, developed in Italy in the 15th century, a mathematical system is used based on orthogonals (all lines receding at right angles to the picture plane) that converge on a single vanishing point on the horizon. Since this presupposes an absolutely stationary viewer and imposes rigid restrictions on the artist, it is seldom applied with complete consistency (figs. 12-5, 12-49).

PHOTOGRAM. A shadowlike photograph made without a camera by placing objects on light-sensitive paper and exposing them to a light source (fig. 27-21).

PHOTOGRAPH. The relatively permanent or "fixed" form of an image made by light that passes through the lens of a camera and acts upon light-sensitive substances. Often called a PRINT.

PHOTOMONTAGE. A photograph in which prints in whole or in part are combined to form a new image (fig. 27-20). A technique much practiced by the Dada group in the 1920s.

PIAZZA (pl. **PIAZZE**). Italian word for "public square" (in French, place; in German, Platz).

PICTURE PLANE. The flat surface on which a picture is painted.

PICTURESQUE. Visually interesting or pleasing, as if resembling a picture (fig. 21-15).

PIER. An upright architectural support, usually rectangular and sometimes with CAPITAL and BASE. When COLUMNS, PILASTERS, or SHAFTS are attached to it, as in many Romanesque and Gothic churches, it is called a compound pier.

PIETÀ. Italian word for both "pity" and "piety." A representation of the Virgin grieving over the dead Christ (fig. P-15). When used in a scene recording a specific moment after the Crucifixion, it is usually called a Lamentation (fig. P-7).

PILASTER. A flat, vertical element projecting from a wall surface and normally having a BASE, SHAFT, and CAPITAL. It has generally a decorative rather than a structural purpose (figs. 12-32, 12-35).

PILGRIMAGE CHOIR. The unit in a Romanesque church composed of the APSE, AMBULATORY, and RADIATING CHAPELS.

PILLAR. A general term for a vertical architectural support which includes COLUMNS, PIERS, and PILASTERS.

PINNACLE. A small, decorative structure capping a tower, PIER, BUTTRESS, or other architectural member and used especially in Gothic buildings.

PLAN. See GROUND PLAN.

PODIUM. 1) The tall base upon which rests an Etruscan or Roman temple. 2) The ground floor of a building made to resemble such a base (fig. 19-10).

POLYPTYCH. An ALTARPIECE or devotional work of art made of several panels joined together (fig. 15-3), often hinged.

PORCH. General term for an exterior appendage to a building which forms a covered approach to a doorway. See PORTICO for porches consisting of columns.

PORTA. Latin word for "door" or "gate."

PORTAL. A door or gate, usually a monumental one with elaborate sculptural decoration.

PORTICO. A columned porch supporting a roof or an ENTABLATURE and PEDIMENT, often approached by a number of steps (fig. 21-14). It provides a covered entrance to a building and a link with the space surrounding it.

POST AND LINTEL. A basic system of construction in which two or more uprights, the posts, support a horizontal member, the lintel. The lintel may be the topmost element or support a wall or roof (fig. 23-34).

PREDELLA. The base of an ALTAR-PIECE, often decorated with small scenes which are related in subject to that of the main panel or panels (fig. P-14).

PRINT. A picture or design reproduced, usually on paper and often in numerous copies, from a prepared wood block, metal plate, or stone slab or by photography. See AQUATINT, ENGRAVING, ETCHING, LITHOGRAPH, PHOTOGRAPH, WOODCUT.

PSALTER. 1) The book of Psalms in the Old Testament, thought to have been written in part by David, king of ancient Israel. 2) A copy of the Psalms, sometimes arranged for liturgical or devotional use, and often richly ILLUMINATED.

PULPIT. A raised platform in a church from which the clergy delivers a sermon or conducts the service. Its railing or enclosing wall may be elaborately decorated.

PUTTO (pl. **PUTTI**). A nude, male child, usually winged, often represented in classical and Renaissance art. Also called a cupid or amoretto when he carries a bow and arrow and personifies Love (fig. 13-33, 18-3).

PYLON. Greek word for "gateway." 1) The monumental entrance building to an Egyptian temple or forecourt consisting of either a massive wall with sloping sides pierced by a doorway or of two such walls flanking a central gateway. 2) A tall structure at either side of a gate, bridge, or avenue marking an approach or entrance.

Q

QUATREFOIL. An ornamental element composed of four lobes radiating from a common center.

R

RADIATING CHAPELS. Term for CHAPELS arranged around the AMBULATORY (and sometimes the TRANSEPT) of a medieval church.

READYMADE. An ordinary object which, when an artist gives it a new context and title, is transformed into an art object. Readymades were important features of the Dada and Surrealism movements of the early 20th century (fig. 25-11).

REFECTORY. 1) A room for refreshment. 2) The dining hall of a monastery, college, or other large institution.

REFORMATION. The religious movement in the early 16th century which had for its object the reform of the Catholic church and led to the establishment of Protestant churches. See also COUNTER-REFORMATION.

REINFORCED CONCRETE. See ferroconcrete.

RELIEF. 1) The projection of a figure or part of a design from the background or plane on which it is CARVED or MODELED. Sculpture done in this manner is described as "high relief" or "low relief" depending on the height of the projection. When it is very shallow, it is called schiacciato, the Italian word for "flattened out" (fig. 12-3). 2) The apparent projection of forms represented in a painting or drawing.

RESPOND. 1) A half-PIER, PILASTER, or similar element projecting from a wall

to support a LINTEL or an ARCH whose other side is supported by a freestanding COLUMN or pier, as at the end of an ARCADE. 2) One of several pilasters on a wall behind a COLONNADE (fig. 12-13) which echoes or "responds to" the columns but is largely decorative. 3) One of the slender shafts of a COMPOUND PIER in a medieval church which seems to carry the weight of the VAULT.

RIB. A slender, projecting, archlike member which supports a VAULT either transversely or at the GROINS, thus dividing the surface into sections. In Late Gothic architecture, its purpose is often primarily ornamental.

RIBBED VAULT. See VAULT.

ROOD SCREEN. See CHOIR SCREEN.

RUBBING. A reproduction of a relief surface made by covering it with paper and rubbing with pencil, chalk, etc. Also called frottage.

RUSTICATION. A masonry technique of laying rough-faced stones with sharply indented joints (figs. 12-27, 14-24).

S

SACRA CONVERSAZIONE. Italian for "holy conversation." A composition of the Madonna and Child with saints in which the figures all occupy the same spatial setting and appear to be conversing or communing with one another (figs. 12-63, 13-40).

SACRISTY. A room near the main altar of a church, or a small building attached to a church, where the vessels and vestments required for the service are kept. Also called a vestry.

SALON. 1) A large, elegant drawing or reception room in a palace or a private house. 2) Official government-sponsored exhibition of paintings and sculpture by living artists held at the Louvre in Paris, first biennially, then annually. 3) Any large public exhibition patterned after the Paris Salon.

SANCTUARY. 1) A sacred or holy place or building. 2) An especially holy place within a building, such as the CELLA of a temple or the part of a church around the altar.

SARCOPHAGUS (pl. **SARCOPHAGI**). A large stone coffin usually decorated with sculpture and/or inscriptions. The term is derived from two Greek words meaning "flesh" and "eating," which were applied to a kind of limestone in ancient Greece, since the stone was said to turn flesh to dust.

SATYR. One of a class of woodland gods thought to be the lascivious companions of Dionysos, the Greek god of wine (or of Bacchus, his Roman counterpart). They are represented as having the legs and tail of a goat, the body of a man, and a head with horns and pointed ears. A youthful satyr is also called a faun.

SCRIPTORIUM (pl. **SCRIPTORIA**). A workroom in a monastery reserved for copying and illustrating MANUSCRIPTS.

SCROLL. 1) An architectural ornament with the form of a partially unrolled spiral, as on the CAPITALS of the Ionic and Corinthian ORDERS. 2) A form of written text.

SCUOLA. Italian word for school. In Renaissance Venice it designated a frater-

nal organization or confraternity dedicated to good works, usually under ecclesiastic auspices.

SECTION. An architectural drawing presenting a building as if cut across the vertical plane at right angles to the horizontal plane. Cross section: a cut along the transverse axis. Longitudinal section: a cut along the longitudinal axis.

SEXPARTITE VAULT. See VAULT.

SFUMATO. Italian word meaning "gone up in smoke," used to describe very delicate gradations of light and shade in the MODELING of figures; applied especially to the work of Leonardo da Vinci (fig. 13-4).

SHAFT. In architecture, the part of a COLUMN between the BASE and the CAPITAL.

SIBYLS. In Greek and Roman mythology, any of numerous women who were thought to possess powers of divination and prophecy. They appear on Christian representations, notably in Michelangelo's Sistine ceiling, because they were believed to have foretold the coming of Christ.

SIDE AISLE. A passageway running parallel to the NAVE of a Roman BASILICA or Christian church, separated from it by an ARCADE or COLONNADE (fig. 17-21). There may be one on either side of the nave or two, an inner and outer.

SILENI. A class of minor woodland gods in the entourage of the wine god, Dionysos (or Bacchus). Like Silenus, the wine god's tutor and drinking companion, they are thick-lipped and snub-nosed and fond of wine. Similar to SATYRS, they are basically human in form except for having horses' tails and ears.

SILVER LEAF. See GOLD LEAF.

SILVER SALTS. Compounds of silver—bromide, chloride, and iodide—which are sensitive to light and are used in the preparation of photographic materials. This sensitivity was first observed by Johann Heinrich Schulze in 1725.

SINOPIA (pl. **SINOPIE**). Italian word taken from "Sinope," the ancient city in Asia Minor which was famous for its brick-red pigment. In FRESCO paintings, a full-sized, preliminary sketch done in this color on the first rough coat of plaster or arriccio.

SKETCH. See DRAWING; OIL SKETCH.

SPANDREL. The area between the exterior curves of two adjoining ARCHES, or, in the case of a single arch, the area around its outside curve from its springing to its keystone (fig. 13-38).

SPHINX. 1) In ancient Egypt, a creature having the head of a man, animal, or bird and the body of a lion; frequently sculpted in monumental form. 2) In Greek mythology, a creature usually represented as having the head and breasts of a woman, the body of a lion, and the wings of an eagle. It appears in classical, Renaissance, and Neoclassical art.

STANZA (pl. **STANZE**). Italian word for "room."

STEEL. Iron modified chemically to have qualities of great hardness, elasticity, and strength. For use in sculpture, see figs. 25-23, 25-31. For architectural use, see STRUCTURAL STEEL.

STELE. From the Greek word for "standing block." An upright stone slab or pillar with a CARVED commemorative design or inscription.

STEREOBATE. The substructure of a classical building, especially a Greek temple.

STEREOSCOPE. An optical instrument which enables the user to combine two pictures taken from points of view corresponding to those of the two eyes into a single image having the depth and solidity of ordinary binocular vision (fig. 21-85). First demonstrated by Sir Charles Wheatstone in 1838.

STILTS. Term for pillars or posts supporting a superstructure; in 20th-century architecture, these are usually of ferro-concrete (figs. 26-18, 26-29). Stilted, as in stilted arches, refers to tall supports beneath an architectural member.

STRUCTURAL STEEL. STEEL used as an architectural building material either invisibly (fig. 23-29) or exposed (fig. 26-7). See FERROCONCRETE.

STUCCO. 1) A concrete or cement used to coat the walls of a building. 2) A kind of plaster used for architectural decorations, such as CORNICES and MOLDINGS, or for sculptured RELIEFS (fig. 14-20).

STUDY. See DRAWING.

STYLOBATE. A platform or masonry floor above the STEREOBATE forming the foundation for the COLUMNS of a classical temple.

STYLUS. From the Latin word stilus, the writing instrument of the Romans. 1) A pointed instrument used in ancient times for writing on tablets of a soft material such as clay. 2) The needlelike instrument used in drypoint or etching. See ENGRAVING; ETCHING.

SUPERIMPOSED ORDERS. Two or more rows of COLUMNS, PIERS, or PILASTERS placed above each other on the wall of a building (fig. 14-23).

T

TABERNACLE. 1) A place or house of worship. 2) A CANOPIED niche or recess built for an image (fig. 12-2). 3) The portable shrine used by the ancient Jews to house the Ark of the Covenant.

TEMPERA PAINTING. 1) A painting made with pigments mixed with egg yolk and water. In the 14th and 15th centuries, it was applied to PANELS which had been prepared with a coating of GESSO; the application of GOLD LEAF and of underpainting in green or brown preceded the actual tempera painting (fig. P-8). 2) The technique of executing such a painting.

TERRA-COTTA. Italian word for "baked earth." 1) Earthenware, naturally reddish-brown but often GLAZED (fig. 12-11) in various colors and fired. Used for pottery, sculpture, or as a building material or decoration. 2) An object made of this material. 3) Color of the natural material.

TESSERA (pl. **TESSERAE**). A small piece of colored stone, marble, glass, or gold-backed glass used in a MOSAIC.

THEATINE ORDER. Founded in Rome in the 16th century by members of the recently dissolved Oratory of Divine

Love. Its aim was to reform the Catholic church, and its members were pledged to cultivate their spiritual lives and to perform charitable works.

THRUST. The lateral pressure exerted by an ARCH, VAULT, or DOME, which must be counteracted at its point of greatest concentration either by the thickness of the wall or by some form of BUTTRESS.

TRACERY. 1) Ornamental stonework in Gothic windows. In the earlier or plate tracery, the windows appear to have been cut through the solid stone. In bar tracery, the glass predominates, the slender pieces of stone having been added within the windows. 2) Similar ornamentation using various materials and applied to walls, shrines, facades, etc. (figs. P-8, 15-20).

TRANSEPT. A cross arm in a BASILI-CAN church placed at right angles to the NAVE and usually separating it from the CHOIR or APSE.

TREE OF KNOWLEDGE. The tree in the Garden of Eden from which Adam and Eve ate the forbidden fruit which destroyed their innocence.

TREE OF LIFE. A tree in the Garden of Eden whose fruit was reputed to give everlasting life; in medieval art it was frequently used as a symbol of Christ.

TRIFORIUM. The section of a NAVE wall above the ARCADE and below the CLERESTORY. It frequently consists of a BLIND ARCADE with three openings in each bay. When the GALLERY is also present, a four-story ELEVATION results, the triforium being between the gallery and clerestory. It may also occur in the TRANSEPT and the CHOIR walls.

TRIGLYPH. The element of a Doric FRIEZE separating two consecutive METOPES and being divided by channels (or glyphs) into three sections. Probably an imitation in stone of wooden ceiling beam ends.

TRIPTYCH. An ALTARPIECE or devotional picture, either CARVED or painted, with one central panel and two hinged wings (fig. 15-14)

TRIUMPHAL ARCH. 1) A monumental ARCH, sometimes a combination of three arches, erected by a Roman emperor in commemoration of his military exploits and usually decorated with scenes of these deeds in RELIEF sculpture. 2) The great transverse arch at the eastern end of a church which frames ALTAR and APSE and separates them from the main body of the church. It is frequently decorated with MOSAICS or MURAL paintings.

TROPHY. 1) In ancient Rome, arms or other spoils taken from a defeated enemy and publicly displayed on a tree, PILLAR, etc. 2) A representation of these objects, and others symbolic of victory, as a commemoration or decoration.

TRUSS. A triangular wooden or metal support for a roof which may be left exposed in the interior, or be covered by a ceiling.

TURRET. 1) A small tower, part of a larger structure. 2) A small tower at a corner of a building, often beginning some distance from the ground.

TYMPANUM. 1) In classical architecture, the recessed, usually triangular area, also called a PEDIMENT, often decorated with sculpture. 2) In medieval architecture, an arched area between an ARCH and the LINTEL of a door or window, frequently carved with RELIEF sculpture (fig. P-18).

U

UNDERPAINTING. See TEMPERA PAINTING.

V

VANITAS. The notion of life's brevity and the inevitability of death, the vanitas theme found expression especially in northern Baroque still life paintings.

VAULT. An arched roof or ceiling usu-ally made of stone, brick, or concrete. Several distinct varieties have been developed; all need BUTTRESSING at the point where the lateral THRUST is concentrated. 1) A barrel vault is a semicylindrical structure made up of successive ARCHES. It may be straight or ANNULAR in plan. 2) A groin vault is the result of the intersection of two barrel vaults of equal size which produces a BAY of four compartments with sharp edges, or groins, where the two meet. 3) A ribbed groin vault is one in which RIBS are added to the groins for structural strength and for decoration. When the diagonal ribs are constructed as half-circles, the resulting form is a domical ribbed vault. 4) A sexpartite vault is a ribbed groin vault in which each bay is divided into six compartments by the addition of a transverse rib across the center. 5) The normal Gothic vault is quadripartite with all the arches pointed to some degree. 6) A fan vault is an elaboration of a ribbed groin vault, with elements of TRACERY using conelike forms. It was developed by the English in the 15th century and was employed for decorative purposes.

VEDUTA (pl. **VEDUTE**). A view painting, generally a city landscape (fig. 20-26).

VELLUM. See PARCHMENT.

VESTRY. See SACRISTY.

VICES. Often represented allegorically in conjunction with the seven VIRTUES, they include Pride, Avarice, Wrath, Gluttony, Unchastity (Luxury), Folly, and Inconstancy, though others such as Injustice are sometimes substituted.

VILLA. Originally a large country house (fig. 14-26) but in modern usage also a detached house or suburban residence.

VIRTUES. The three theological virtues, Faith, Hope, and Charity, and the four cardinal ones, Prudence, Justice, Fortitude, and Temperance, were frequently represented allegorically, particularly in medieval manuscripts and sculpture.

VOLUTE. A spiraling architectural element found notably on Ionic and Composite CAPITALS, but also used decoratively on building FACADES and interiors (fig. 14-31).

VOUSSOIR. See ARCH.

W

WASH. A thin layer of translucent color or ink used in WATERCOLOR PAINTING and brush drawing and occasionally in OIL PAINTING.

WATERCOLOR PAINTING. Painting, usually on paper, in pigments suspended in water (figs. 16-5, 24-45).

WING. The side panel of an ALTARPIECE which is frequently decorated on both sides and is also hinged, so that it may be shown either open or closed (figs. 15-3, 15-6).

WOODCUT. A PRINT made by carving out a design on a wooden block cut along the grain, applying ink to the raised surfaces which remain, and printing from those (figs. 15-21, 16-6, 24-6).

WROUGHT IRON. A comparatively pure form of iron which is easily forged and does not harden quickly, so that it can be shaped or hammered by hand (fig. 25-16), in contrast to molded CAST IRON.

Z

ZODIAC. An imaginary belt circling the heavens, including the paths of the sun, moon, and major planets and containing 12 constellations and thus 12 divisions called signs, which have been associated with the months. The signs are: Aries, the ram; Taurus, the bull; Gemini, the twins; Cancer, the crab; Leo, the lion; Virgo, the virgin; Libra, the balance; Scorpio, the scorpion; Sagittarius, the archer; Capricorn, the goat; Aquarius, the water-bearer; and Pisces, the fish. They are frequently represented around the PORTALS of Romanesque and Gothic churches in conjunction with the LABORS OF THE MONTHS (fig. P-13).

Art and Architecture Websites

The directory below is made up mainly of the significant museums that provided illustrations for this book. A few additional art sites are also listed for your reference. All efforts have been made to gather up-to-date addresses, phone numbers, and Websites. Contact information is current as of the time of printing.

UNITED STATES

For additional information or to find out about museums not listed here, visit the following Websites:
http://www.amn.org
http://www.artcom.com
http://www.artmuseum.net
http://icom.museum/
http://www.museumstuff.com
http://www.world-arts-resources.com

ARIZONA

Center for Creative Photography
University of Arizona
1030 N. Olive Rd., Tucson 85719
(520) 621-7968
http://dizzy.library.arizona.edu/
branches/ccp

The Heard Museum
2301 N. Central Ave.
Phoenix 85004
(602) 252-8840
http://www.heard.org

Phoenix Art Museum
1625 N. Central Ave.
Phoenix 85004
(602) 257-1222
http://www.phxart.org

Tucson Museum of Art
140 N. Main Ave.
Tucson 85701
(520) 624-2333
http://www.tucsonarts.com

CALIFORNIA

Berkeley Art Museum and Pacific
Film Archive University of California
2626 Bancroft Way
Berkeley 94704
(510) 642-0808
http://www.bampfa.berkeley.edu

Crocker Museum of Art
216 O St., Sacramento 95814
(916) 264-5423
http://www.crockerartmuseum.org

The Fine Arts Museums of
San Francisco
California Palace of the Legion of Honor
Lincoln Park, near 34th Ave. and
Clement St.San Francisco 94122
(415) 863-3330

M. H. de Young Memorial Museum
75 Tea Garden Dr., Golden Gate Park
San Francisco 94118
(415) 863-3300
http://www.famsf.org

Huntington Library, Art Collections,
and Botanical Gardens
1151 Oxford Rd., San Marino 91108
(626) 405-2141
http://www.huntington.org

Iris and B. Gerald Cantor Center for
Visual Arts at Stanford University
Lomita Dr. at Museum Way
Stanford 94305
(650) 723-4177
http://www.huntington.org

The J. Paul Getty Museum
The Getty Center
1200 Getty Center Dr.
Los Angeles 90049
(310) 440-7300
http://www.getty.edu/museum

Los Angeles County Museum of Art
5905 Wilshire Blvd.
Los Angeles 90036
(213) 857-6111
http://www.lacma.org

The Museum of Contemporary Art,
Los Angeles
250 S. Grand Ave.
Los Angeles 90012
(213) 382-6222
http://www.MOCA-LA.org

Museum of Contemporary Art,
San Diego
1001 Kettner Blvd.
San Diego 92101
(619) 234-1001
http://www.mcasandiego.org

Norton Simon Museum
411 W. Colorado Blvd.
Pasadena 91105
(626) 449-6840
http://www.nortonsimon.org

San Diego Museum of Art
1450 El Prado, San Diego 92101
(619) 232-7931
http://www.sdmart.com

San Francisco Museum of Modern Art
151 3rd St., San Francisco 94103
(415) 357-4000
http://www.sfmoma.org

San Jose Museum of Art
110 S. Market St., San Jose 95113
(408) 294-2787
http://www.sjmusart.org

Santa Barbara Museum of Art
1130 State St., Santa Barbara 93101
(805) 963-4364
http://www.sbmuseart.org

COLORADO

Colorado Springs Fine Arts Center
30 W. Dale St.,
Colorado Springs 80903
(719) 634-5581
http://www.csfineartscenter.org

The Denver Art Museum
100 W. 14th Avenue Pkwy.
Denver 80204
(303) 640-2295
http://www.denverartmuseum.org

CONNECTICUT

Wadsworth Atheneum
600 Main St., Hartford 06103
(860) 278-2670
http://www.wadsworthatheneum.org

Yale Center for British Art
1080 Chapel St. , New Haven 06520
(203) 432-2800
http://www.yale.edu/ycba

Yale University Art Gallery
1111 Chapel St., New Haven 06520
(203) 432-0600
http://www.yale.edu/artgallery

DELAWARE

Delaware Art Museum
2301 Kentmere Pkwy
Wilmington 19806
(302) 571-9590
http://www.delart.org

DISTRICT OF COLUMBIA

The Corcoran Gallery of Art
500 17th St. NW, 20006
(202) 639-1700
http://www.corcoran.org

Freer Gallery of Art and
Arthur M. Sackler Gallery,
The National Museum of Asian
Art for the United States,
Smithsonian Institution
12th St. & Jefferson Dr. SW, 20560
(202) 357-4880
http://www.si.edu/asia

Hirshhorn Museum and Sculpture
Garden, Smithsonian Institution
Independence Ave. & 7th St. SW, 20560
(202) 357-1300
http://hirshhorn.si.edu

National Gallery of Art
600 Constitution Ave. NE, 20565
(202) 737-4215
http://www.nga.gov

National Museum of American Art,
Smithsonian Institution
8th & G St. NW, 20560
(202) 357-1300
Renwick Gallery
Pennsylvania Ave. at
17th St. NW, 20006
(202) 357-2700
http://www.nmaa.si.edu

National Museum of Women in the Arts
1250 New York Ave. NW, 20005
(202) 783-5000
http://www.nmwa.org

National Portrait Gallery,
Smithsonian Institution
910 F St. NW, 20560
(202) 357-1300
http://www.npg.si.edu

The Phillips Collection
1600 21st St. NW, 20009
(202) 387-2151
http://www.phillipscollection.org

FLORIDA

John and Mable Ringling Museum of Art
5401 Bay Shore Rd., Sarasota 34243
(941) 359-5700
http://www.ringling.org

Lowe Art Museum,
University of Miami
1301 Stanford Dr., Miami 33124
(305) 284-3535
http://www.lowemuseum.org

Saint Petersburg Museum of Fine Arts
255 Beach Dr. NE,
Saint Petersburg 33701
(727) 896-2667
http://www.fine-arts.org

GEORGIA

Georgia Museum of Art,
University of Georgia
Jackson St., North Campus
Athens 30602
(706) 542-GMOA
http://www.uga.edu/gamuseum

High Museum of Art
1280 Peachtree St. NE, Atlanta 30309
(404) 733-4400
http://www.high.org

Michael C. Carlos Museum,
Emory University, 571 S. Kilgo St.
Atlanta 30322
(404) 727-4282/0573
http://www.emory.edu/CARLOS

HAWAII

Honolulu Academy of Arts
900 S. Beretania St., Honolulu 96814
(808) 532-8700
http://www.honoluluacademy.org

ILLINOIS

The Art Institute of Chicago
111 S. Michigan Ave., Chicago 60603
(312) 443-3600
http://www.artic.edu

Krannert Art Museum,
University of Illinois
500 E. Peabody Dr., Champaign 61820
(217) 333-1860
http://www.art.uiuc.edu/galleries/kam/
index.html

Museum of Contemporary Art
220 E. Chicago Ave., Chicago 60611
(312) 280-2660
http://www.mcachicago.org

Oriental Institute Museum,
The University of Chicago
1155 E. 58th St., Chicago 60637
(773) 702-9521
http://www.oi.uchicago.edu

Terra Museum of American Art
666 N. Michigan Ave., Chicago 60611
(312) 664-3939
http://www.terramuseum.org

INDIANA
Indiana University Art Museum,
Indiana University
Bloomington 47405
(812) 855-5445
http://www.indiana.edu/~iuam

Indianapolis Museum of Art
1200 W. 38th St., Indianapolis 46208
(317) 923-1331
http://www.ima-art.org

The Snite Museum of Art,
University of Notre Dame
Notre Dame 46556
(219) 631-5466
http://www.nd.edu/~sniteart

IOWA
Cedar Rapids Museum of Art
410 Third Ave. SE, Cedar Rapids 52401
(319) 366-7503
http://www.crma.org

University of Iowa Museum of Art
150 N. Riverside Dr., Iowa City 52242
(319) 335-1727
http://www.uiowa.edu/~artmus

KANSAS
Spencer Museum of Art,
University of Kansas
1301 Mississippi St., Lawrence 66045
(785) 864-4710
http://www.ukans.edu/~sma

Wichita Art Museum
619 Stackman Dr., Wichita 67203
(316) 268-4921
http://www.wichitaartmuseum.org

KENTUCKY
J. B. Speed Art Museum
2035 S. 3rd St., Louisville 40208
(502) 634-2700
http://www.speedmuseum.org

University of Kentucky Art Museum
Singletary Center for the Arts
Rose St. and Euclid Ave.
Lexington 40506
(606) 257-5716
http://www.uky.edu/ArtMuseum

LOUISIANA
The Alexandria Museum of Art
933 Main Street, Alexandria 71309
(318) 443-3458
http://www.themuseum.org

The Contemporary Art Center
900 Camp St., New Orleans 70130
(504) 528-3800
http://www.cacno.org

New Orleans Museum of Art
1 Collins Diboll Circle, City Park
New Orleans 70124
(504) 488-2631
http://www.noma.org

MAINE
Bowdoin College Museum of Art
Walker Art Building, Brunswick 04011
(207) 725-3275
http://www.academic.bowdoin.edu/
    artmuseum

Portland Museum of Art
7 Congress Sq., Portland 04101
(207) 775-6148; (800) 639-4067
http://www.portlandmuseum.org

MARYLAND
The Baltimore Museum of Art
Art Museum Dr. at North Charles and
31st Sts., Baltimore 21218
(410) 396-7100
http://www.artbma.org

Walters Art Gallery
600 N. Charles St., Baltimore 21201
(410) 547-9000; 547-ARTS
http://www.thewalters.org

MASSACHUSETTS
Addison Gallery of American Art,
Phillips Academy
Andover 01810
(508) 749-4015
http://www.andover.edu/addison

Davis Museum and Cultural Center,
Wellesley College
106 Central St., Wellesley 02181
(617) 283-2051
http://www.wellesley.edu/Davis
    Museum/davismenu.html

Harvard University Art Museums
The Arthur M. Sackler Museum
485 Broadway
Cambridge 02138
(617) 495-9400
Busch-Reisinger Museum
32 Quincy St.
Fogg Art Museum
32 Quincy St.
http://www.artmuseums.harvard.edu

Isabella Stewart Gardner Museum
280 The Fenway, Boston 02115
(617) 566-1401
http://www.boston.com/gardner

Mead Art Museum, Amherst College
Amherst 01002
(413) 542-2335
http://www.amherst.edu/~mead

Mount Holyoke College Art Museum
South Hadley 01075
(413) 538-2245
http://www.mtholyoke.edu/offices/
    artmuseum

Museum of Fine Arts, Boston
465 Huntington Ave., Boston 02115
(617) 267-9300
http://www.mfa.org

Peabody Essex Museum
East India Square, Salem 01970
(508) 745-1876
http://www.pem.org

Rose Art Museum, Brandeis University
415 South St., Waltham 02254
(617) 736-3434
http://www.brandeis.edu/rose

Smith College Museum of Art
Elm St. at Bedford Terrace
Northampton 01063
(413) 585-2760
http://www.smith.edu/artmuseum

Sterling and Francine Clark
Art Institute
225 South St., Williamstown 01267
(413) 458-9545
http://www.clarkart.edu

Williams College Museum of Art
Main St., Williamstown 01267
(413) 597-2429
http://www.williams.edu/WCMA

Worcester Art Museum
55 Salisbury St., Worcester 01609
(508) 799-4406
http://www.worcesterart.org

MICHIGAN
The Detroit Institute of Arts
5200 Woodward Ave., Detroit 48202
(313) 833-7900
http://www.dia.org

Grand Rapids Art Museum
155 Division North
Grand Rapids 49503
(616) 459-4677
http://www.gramonline.org

The University of Michigan,
Museum of Art
525 S. State St., Ann Arbor 48109
(313) 764-0395
http://www.umich.edu/~umma

MINNESOTA
The Minneapolis Institute of Arts
2400 3rd Ave. S., Minneapolis 55404
(612) 870-3131; 870-3200
http://www.artsMIA.org

Walker Art Center
Vineland Pl., Minneapolis 55403
(612) 375-7622
http://www.walkerart.org

MISSOURI
The Nelson-Atkins Museum of Art
4525 Oak St., Kansas City 64111
(816) 561-4000
http://www.nelson-atkins.org

The Saint Louis Art Museum
1 Fine Arts Dr., Forest Park
St. Louis 63110
(314) 721-0072
http://www.slam.org

NEBRASKA
Joslyn Art Museum
2200 Dodge St., Omaha 68102
(402) 342-3300
http://www.joslyn.org

Sheldon Memorial Art Gallery and
Sculpture Garden, University of
Nebraska–Lincoln
12th and R Sts., Lincoln 68588
(402) 472-2461
http://sheldon.unl.edu

NEW HAMPSHIRE
Hood Museum of Art,
Dartmouth College
Wheelock St., Hanover 03755
(603) 646-2808
http://www.dartmouth.edu/~hood

NEW JERSEY
The Art Museum, Princeton University
Princeton 08544
(609) 258-3788
http://www.princetonartmuseum.org

Jane Voorhees Zimmerli Art Museum,
Rutgers–The State University of
New Jersey
Hamilton and George Sts.
New Brunswick 08903
(732) 932-7237
http://www.zimmerlimuseum.rutgers.
    edu

The Montclair Art Museum
3 S. Mountain Ave. at Bloomfield Ave.
Montclair 07042
(201) 746-5555
http://www.montclair-art.com

The Newark Museum
49 Washington St.
Newark 07101
(973) 596-6500; (800) 7MUSEUM
http://www.newarkmuseum.org

NEW MEXICO
Georgia O'Keeffe Museum
217 Johnson St. , Santa Fe 87501
(505) 995-0785
http://www.okeeffemuseum.org

Millicent Rogers Museum
1504 Millicent Rogers Rd., Taos 87571
(505) 758-2462
http://www.millicentrogers.com

NEW YORK
Albright-Knox Art Gallery
1285 Elmwood Ave.,
Buffalo 14222
(716) 882-8700
http://www.albrightknox.org

Museum of Contemporary
Arts and Design
[formerly American Craft Museum]
40 W. 53rd St., New York 10019
(212) 956-3535
http://www.americancraftmuseum.org

The Brooklyn Museum
200 Eastern Pkwy.,
Brooklyn 11238
(718) 638-5000
http://www.brooklynart.org

Cooper-Hewitt National Design
Museum, Smithsonian Institution
2 E. 91st St., New York 10128
(212) 860-6868
http://www.si.edu/ndm

Everson Museum of Art
401 Harrison St., Syracuse 13202
(315) 474-6064
http://www.everson.org

The Frick Collection
1 E. 70th St., New York 10021
(212) 288-0700
http://www.frick.org

George Eastman House, International
Museum of Photography and Film
900 East Ave., Rochester 14607
(716) 271-3361
http://www.eastman.org

The Grey Art Gallery,
New York University
100 Washington Sq. East
New York 10003
(212) 998-6780
http://www.nyu.edu/greyart

Herbert F. Johnson Museum of Art,
Cornell University
Ithaca 14853
(607) 255-6464
http://www.museum.cornell.edu

International Center of Photography
Midtown
1133 Avenue of the Americas
New York 10036
(212) 860-1783
Uptown
1130 5th Ave., New York 10028
(212) 860-1777
http://www.icp.org

The Jewish Museum
1109 5th Ave., New York 10128
(212) 423-3200
http://www.jewishmuseum.org

Memorial Art Gallery,
University of Rochester
500 University Ave., Rochester 14607
(716) 473-7720
http://mag.rochester.edu

The Metropolitan Museum of Art
1000 5th Ave. at 82nd St.
New York 10028
(212) 879-5500
The Cloisters
Fort Tryon Park, New York 10040
(212) 923-3700
http://www.metmuseum.org

Munson-Williams-Proctor Institute
Museum of Art
310 Genesee St., Utica 13502
(315) 797-0000
http://www.mwpi.edu

The Museum of Modern Art
11 W. 53rd St., New York 10019
(212) 708-9400
http://www.moma.org

Neuberger Museum of Art, State
University of New York at Purchase
735 Anderson Hill Rd., Purchase 10577
(914) 251-6133
http://www.neuberger.org

The New Museum of Contemporary Art
583 Broadway, New York 10012
(212) 219-1222
http://www.newmuseum.org

The Pierpont Morgan Library
29 E. 36th St., New York 10016
(212) 685-0008
http://www.morganlibrary.org

Solomon R. Guggenheim Museum
1071 5th Ave., New York 10128
(212) 423-3500
http://www.guggenheim.org

Storm King Art Center
Old Pleasant Hill Rd.
Mountainville 10953
(914) 534-3115
http://www.stormkingartcenter.org

The Studio Museum in Harlem
144 W. 125th St., New York 10027
(212) 864-4500
http://www.studiomuseuminharlem.org

Whitney Museum of American Art
945 Madison Ave., New York 10021
(212) 570-3676
http://www.whitney.org

NORTH CAROLINA
The Ackland Art Museum,
University of North Carolina,
Chapel Hill
Columbia and Franklin Sts.
Chapel Hill 27599
(919) 966-5736
http://www.ackland.org

Duke University Museum of Art
Buchanan Blvd. at Trinity
East Campus, Durham 27708
(919) 684-5135
http://www.duke.edu/duma

North Carolina Museum of Art
2110 Blue Ridge Rd., Raleigh 27607
(919) 833-1935
http://www.ncmoa.org

OHIO
Allen Memorial Art Museum,
Oberlin College
87 N. Main St., Oberlin 44074
(440) 775-8665
http://www.oberlin.edu/allenart

The Butler Institute of American Art
524 Wick Ave.
Youngstown 44502
(216) 743-1711
http://www.butlerart.com

Cincinnati Art Museum
Eden Park, Cincinnati 45202
(513) 721-5204
http://www.cincinnatiartmuseum.com

The Cleveland Museum of Art
11150 E. Blvd., Cleveland 44106
(216) 421-7340
http://www.clemusart.com

The Columbus Museum of Art
480 E. Broad St., Columbus 43215
(614) 221-6801
http://www.columbusmuseum.org

Dayton Art Institute
456 Belmonte Park N.,
Dayton 45405
(513) 223-5277
http://www.daytonartinstitute.org

The Taft Museum
316 Pike St., Cincinnati 45202
(513) 241-0343
http://www.taftmuseum.org

The Toledo Museum of Art
2445 Monroe St.,
Toledo 43620
(419) 255-8000; (800) 644-6862
http://www.toledomuseum.org

Wexner Center for the Arts,
The Ohio State University
North High St. at 15th Ave.
Columbus 43210
(614) 292-3535
http://www.wexarts.org

OKLAHOMA
Gilcrease Museum
1400 Gilcrease Museum Rd., Tulsa 74127
(918) 596-2700
http://www.gilcrease.org

The Philbrook Museum of Art
2727 S. Rockford Rd., Tulsa 74114
(918) 749-7941
http://www.philbrook.org

OREGON
Portland Art Museum
1219 SW Park Ave., Portland 97205
(503) 226-2811
http://www.pam.org

The University of Oregon,
Museum of Art
1223 University of Oregon, Eugene 97403
(541) 346-3027
http://uoma.uoregon.edu

PENNSYLVANIA
The Andy Warhol Museum
117 Sandusky St., Pittsburgh 15212
(412) 237-8300
http://www.warhol.org

Barnes Foundation
300 North Natch's Ln.
Merion Station 19066
(610) 667-0290
http://www.barnesfoundation.org

The Carnegie Museum of Art
4400 Forbes Ave.,
Pittsburgh 15213
(412) 622-3131
http://www.cmoa.org

Institute of Contemporary Art,
University of Pennsylvania
118 S. 36th St., Philadelphia 19104
(215) 898-7108
http://www.icaphila.org

Museum of American Art,
Pennsylvania Academy of the Fine Arts
118 N. Broad St., Philadelphia 19102
(215) 972-7600
http://www.pafa.org

Philadelphia Museum of Art
26th St. and Benjamin Franklin Pkwy.
Philadelphia 19130
(215) 763-8100
http://www.philamuseum.org

University of Pennsylvania Museum of
Archaeology and Anthropology
33rd and Spruce Sts.
Philadelphia 19104
(215) 895-4000
http://www.upenn.edu/museum

RHODE ISLAND
Museum of Art,
Rhode Island School of Design
224 Benefit St.
Providence 02903
(401) 454-6500
http://www.risd.edu/museum.cfm

SOUTH CAROLINA
The Columbia Museum of Art
Main and Hampton Sts., Columbia 29202
(803) 799-2810
http://www.colmusart.org

Greenville County Museum of Art
420 College St., Greenville 29601
(864) 271-7570
http://www.greenvillemuseum.org

TENNESSEE
Knoxville Museum of Art
410 10th Ave., World's Fair Park
Knoxville 37916
(615) 525-6101
http://www.knoxart.org

Memphis Brooks Museum of Art
Overton Park, 1934 Poplar Ave.
Memphis 38104
(901) 722-3500
http://www.brooksmuseum.org

TEXAS
Amon Carter Museum
3501 Camp Bowie Blvd. ,
Fort Worth 76107
(817) 738-1933
http://www.cartermuseum.org

Contemporary Arts Museum
5216 Montrose Blvd., Houston 77006
(713) 526-0773
http://www.camh.org

Dallas Museum of Art
1717 N. Harwood , Dallas 75201
(214) 922-1200
http://www.dm-art.org

Kimbell Art Museum
3333 Camp Bowie Blvd.
Fort Worth 76107
(817) 332-8451
http://www.kimbellart.org

Marion Koogler McNay Art Museum
6000 N. New Braunfels Ave.
San Antonio 78209
(210) 824-5368
http://www.mcnayart.org

The Menil Collection
1515 Sul Ross, Houston 77006
http://www.menil.org

Rothko Chapel
3900 Yupon at Sul Ross, Houston 77006
(713) 524-9839
http://www.menil.org/rothko.html

Modern Art Museum of Fort Worth
1309 Montgomery St. at Camp
Bowie Blvd.
Fort Worth 76107
(817) 738-9215
http://www.mamfw.org

The Museum of Fine Arts, Houston
1001 Bissonnet St.
Houston 77005
(713) 639-7300
http://www.mfah.org

San Antonio Museum of Art
200 W. Jones St.
San Antonio 78215
(210) 978-8100
http://www.samuseum.org

VIRGINIA
The Chrysler Museum
245 W. Olney Rd., Norfolk 23510
(804) 664-6200
http://www.chrysler.org

Hampton University Museum
Hampton 23668
(804) 727-5308
http://www.hamptonu.edu/museum

Monticello
Charlottesville 22902
(804) 984-9822
http://www.monticello.org

Virginia Museum of Fine Arts
2800 Grove Ave.
Richmond 23221
(804) 367-0844
http://www.vmfa.state.va.us

WASHINGTON
Seattle Art Museum
100 University St., Seattle 98101
(206) 625-8900; 654-3100
http://www.seattleartmuseum.org

Tacoma Art Museum
12th and Pacific Ave.,
Tacoma 98402
(206) 272-4258
http://www.tacomaartmuseum.org

WISCONSIN
Milwaukee Art Museum
750 N. Lincoln Memorial Dr.
Milwaukee 53202
(414) 224-3200
http://www.mam.org

OUTSIDE THE UNITED STATES

AUSTRIA
For more information, visit
http://info.wien.at

Graphische Sammlung Albertina
1, Makartgasse 3, 1010 Vienna
581 306021
http://www.albertina.at

Kunsthistoriches Museum
1., Maria-Theresien-Platz,
1010 Vienna
431 525240
http://www.khm.at

**Museum Moderner Kunst Stifflung
Ludwig**
Arsenalstr. 1, Vienna
431 7996900
http://www.mmkslw.or.at

Österreichische Galerie Belvedere
3, Prinz. Eugen. Str. 27, 1037 Vienna
79557134
http://www.belvedere.at

BELGIUM
For more information, visit
http://www.gotim.be/artexpo

Groeningemuseum, Stedelijke Musea
Dijver 12, 8000 Brugge
(05) 044.87.11

**Musées Royaux des Beaux-Arts
de Belgique**
Musée Royaux d'Art et d'Histoire
10 Parc du Cinquantenaire, 1040 Brussels
(02) 741.72.11
Musées d'Art Moderne
1–2, Place Royale, 1000 Brussels
(02) 508.32.11
Musée d'Art Ancien
3 rue de la Régence, 1000 Brussels
(02) 508.33.33

CANADA
Art Gallery of Ontario
317 Dundas St. W.
Toronto, Ontario M5S 2C6
(416) 977-6648
http://www.ago.on.ca

Glenbow
130 9th Ave., SE
Calgary, Alberta T2G 0P3
(403) 268-4100
http://www.glenbow.org

Montreal Museum of Fine Arts
1379–80 Sherbrook St. W.
Montréal, Quebec H36 2T9
(514) 285-1600; 285-2000
http://www.mmfa.qc.ca

National Gallery of Canada
380 Sussex Dr.
Ottawa, Ontario K1N 9N4
(613) 990-1985
http://national.gallery.ca

Royal Ontario Museum
100 Queen's Park
Toronto, Ontario M5S 2C6
(416) 586-5549
http://www.rom.on.ca

Vancouver Art Gallery
750 Hornby St.
Vancouver, British Columbia V6Z 2H7
(604) 662-4719
http://www.vanartgallery.bc.ca

DENMARK
Louisiana Museum of Modern Art
Gl. Strandvej 13, 3050 Humlebaek
(45) 49190719
http://www.louisiana.dk

Ny Carlsberg Glyptotek
Dantes Plads 7, 1556 Copenhagen
(45) 33418141
http://www.glyptoteket.dk

EGYPT
Egyptian Museum
Maydan El Tahrir, Cairo
(02) 57 42 681
http://www.egyptianmuseum.gov.eg

FRANCE
For more information, visit
http://www.tourisme.fr

Bibliothèque Nationale de France
25 rue de Richelieu, Paris 75002
01.47.03.81.26
http://www.bnf.fr

**Centre National d'Art et de
Culture Georges Pompidou**
Rue du Renard, Paris 75191
01.44.78.12.33
http://www.centrepompidou.fr

Château de Versailles
Versailles
01.30.84.74.00
http://www.chateauversailles.fr

Grand Palais
Ave. Winston Churchill, Paris
01.44.13.17.17

Musée de l'Orangerie
Jardin des Tuileries,
Palace de la Concorde, Paris
01.42.97.48.16

Musée des Antiquités Nationales
Château de Saint-Germain-en-Laye,
Saint-Germain-en-Laye 78103
01.34.51.53.65
http://www.musee-
antiquitesnationales.fr

Musée des Beaux-Arts, Lyon
Palais St. Pierre,
20 place des Terreaux,
Lyon 69001
04.72.10.17.40

Musée d'Orsay
1 rue de Bellechasse, Paris 75007
01.40.49.48.14
http://www.musee-orsay.fr

Musée du Louvre
Rue de Rivoli, Paris 75058
01.40.20.51.51
http://www.louvre.fr

Musée d'Unterlinden
1 rue des Unterlinden,
Colmar 68000
03.89.20.15.50
http://www.musee-unterlinden.com

Musée Picasso
Hôtel Salé, 5 rue de Torigny, Paris 75003
01.42.71.25.21

Musée Rodin
77 rue de Varenne, Paris 75007
01.44.18.61.10
http://www.musee-rodin.fr

GERMANY
Alte Pinakothek
Barer Str. 27, 80333 Munich
(089) 23805216
http://www.stmukwk.bayern.de/kunst/
museen/pinalt.html

Brücke-Museum Berlin
Bussardsteig 9, Berlin 14195
(030) 8312029
http://www.bruecke-museum.de

Hamburger Kunsthalle
Glockengiesserwall,
20095 Hamburg
(040) 24862612
http://www.hamburger-kunsthalle.de

Museum Ludwig
Bischofsgartenstr. 1,
50667 Cologne
(0221) 2212379
http://www.museenkoeln.de/ludwig

**Staatliche Antikensammlungen und
Glyptothek, Munich**
Konigspl 1–3, 80333 Munich
(089) 598359; 286100

**Staatliche Graphische Sammlung,
Munich**
Meierstr. 10, 80333 Munich
(089) 28927650

Staatliche Kunsthalle, Karlsruhe
Hans-Thoma-Str. 2–6,
76133 Karlsruhe
(0721) 9263355
http://www.kunsthalle-karlsruhe.de

Staatliche Museen zu Berlin
(17 museums in different locations)
http://www.smb.spk-berlin.de

Staatsgalerie Stuttgart
Konrad-Adenauer Str. 30–32,
70173 Stuttgart
(0711) 212 4050
http://www.staatsgalerie.de

**Städelsches Kunstinstitut und Städtische
Galerie, Frankfurt-am-Main**
Schaumainkai 63,
60596 Frankfurt-am-Main
(069) 6050980

GREAT BRITAIN
For more information, visit
http://www.artguide.org

**Apsley House,
The Wellington Museum**
149 Piccadilly, Hyde Park Corner,
London N1V 9FA
(0171) 4995676
http://www.vam.ac.uk/vastatic/
microsites/apsley

**Ashmolean Museum of Art and
Archaeology**
Beaumont St., Oxford 0X1 2PH
(01865) 278000
http://www.ashmol.ox.ac.uk

**Birmingham City Museum and
Art Gallery**
Chamberlain Sq.,
Birmingham B3 3DH
(0121) 3032834
http://www.birmingham.gov.uk/bmag

Blenheim Palace
Woodstock, Oxfordshire 0X20 1PX
(01993) 811091
http://www.blenheimpalace.com

British Library
Great Russell St.,
London WC1B 3DG
(0171) 3237595
http://portico.bl.uk

British Museum
Great Russell St.,
London WC1B 3DG
(0171) 6361555
http://www.british-museum.ac.uk

Courtauld Institute Galleries
Somerset House, Strand, London
WC2R 0RN
(0171) 8732526
http://www.courtauld.ac.uk

The National Gallery
Trafalgar Square,
London WC2N 5DN
(0171) 8393321
http://www.nationalgallery.org.uk

National Gallery of Scotland
The Mound, Edinburgh EH2 2EL
(0131) 5568921
http://www.natgalscot.ac.uk

Royal Academy of Arts
Burlington House, Piccadilly,
London W1V 0DS
(0171) 4397438
http://www.royalacademy.org.uk

Sir John Soane's Museum
13 Lincoln's Inn Fields,
London WC2A 3BP
(0171) 4052107
http://www.soane.org

Tate Gallery
Millbank, London SW1P 4RG
(0171) 8878000
http://www.tate.org.uk

Victoria and Albert Museum
Cromwell Rd., South Kensington,
London SW7 2R
(0171) 9388365
http://www.vam.ac.uk

GREECE
For more information, visit
http://www.culture.gr

Acropolis Museum
Athens
01 3214172
http://www.culture.gr/2/21/211/21101m/
e211am01.html

Corfu Archaeological Museum
Corfu 49100
0661 30680
Delphi Archaeological Museum
Delphi 33054
0265 82312

Eleusis Archaeological Museum
Eleusis
01 3463552

Heraklion Archaeological Museum
Xanthoudidou St. 1, Crete
081 226092

**National Archaeological Museum of
Athens**
Patission 44 St., Athens 10682
01 8217717
http://www.culture.gr/2/21/214/21405m/
e21405m1.html

IRELAND
For more information, visit
http://www.artguide.org

National Gallery of Ireland
Merrion Square W., Dublin 2
(01) 6615133
http://www.nationalgallery.ie

ITALY
Galleria Borghese
Piazzale Scipione Borghese 5,
Rome 00197
(06) 858577
http://www.galleriaborghese.it

Galleria degli Uffizi
Piazza degli Uffizi 6, Florence 50122
(055) 2388651
http://www.uffizi.firenze.it

Galleria dell'Academia, Florence
Via Ricasoli 58–60, Florence 50122
(055) 238809
http://www.sbas.firenze.it/accademia

Galleria dell'Academia, Venice
Campo della Carità, Venice 30121
(041) 22247

Galleria Nazionale d'Arte Antica
Via delle Quattro Fontane 13,
Rome 00184
(06) 4824184

Musei Capitolini
Piazza del Campidoglio, Rome 00186
(06) 67102475

Museo Archeologico Nazionale
Piazza Museo 19, Naples 80135
(081) 440166
http://www.cib.na.cnr.it/remuna/mann/
mann.html

**Museo Archeologico Nazionale
di Firenze**
Via della Colonna 38,
Florence 50121
(055) 23575

Museo Civico Archeologico
Via de' Musei, Bologna 840124
(051) 233849

**http://www.comune.bologna.it/bologna/
Musei/Archeologico**
Museo Civico Cristiana
Via Musei, 81, Brescia 25100
(030) 44327

**Museo e Gallerie Nazionale di
Capodimonte**
Palazzo di Capodimonte,
Naples 80136
(081) 7410801
http://www.cib.na.cnr.it/remuna/capod/
indice.html

Museo Nazionale del Bargello
Via del Proconsolo 4, Florence 5012
(055) 210801
http://www.thais.it/scultura/fmndb1.htm

Museo Nazionale di Villa Giulia
Piazza di Villa Giulia 9, Rome 00195
(06) 350719

Peggy Guggenheim Collection
Palazzo Venier dei Leoni,
701 Dorsoduro,
30123 Venice
(041) 2450 411
http://www.guggenheim-venice.it

Vatican Museums
Viale Vaticano 00165,
Città del Vaticano 00120
(06) 69884947
http://www.christusrex.org/www1/
vaticano/0-Musei.html

THE NETHERLANDS
For more information, visit
http://www.hollandmuseums.nl

Centraal Museum Utrecht
Agnietenst. 1
3500 Utrecht
(030) 2362362
http://www.centraalmuseum.nl

Frans Halsmuseum
Groot Heiligland 62,
2011 ES Haarlem
(020) 5115775
http://www.franshalsmuseum.nl

Kröller-Müller Museum
Houtkampweg 6,
6731 AW Otterlo
(0318) 591041
http://www.kmm.nl

Museum Boijmans Van Beuningen
Museumpark 18–20,
3015 CX Rotterdam
(010) 4419400
http://boijmans.kennisnet.nl

Rijksmuseum
Stadhouderskade 42,
1071 Amsterdam
(020) 6732121
http://www.rijksmuseum.nl

Rijksmuseum Vincent van Gogh
Paulus Potterstraat 7,
1071 CX Amsterdam
(020) 5705200
http://www.vangoghmuseum.nl

Stedelijk Museum of Modern Art
Paulus Potterstraat 13,
1070 AB Amsterdam
(020) 5732911
http://www.stedelijk.nl

NORWAY

Nasjonalgalleriet
Universitestsgaten 13,
Oslo 0033
22 20 04 04
http://www.museumsnett.no/
nasjonalgalleriet

PORTUGAL
Museu Calouste Gulbenkian
Av. de Berna 45 A (1)
1093 Lisboa
(01) 76 50 61
http://www.gulbenkian.pt

RUSSIA
Hermitage Museum
36 Dvortsovaya Naberezhnaya,
Saint Petersburg
(812) 110 96 25
http://www.hermitagemuseum.org

Pushkin Museum of Fine Arts
12 Volkhonka Str.
Moscow
(095) 203 74 12
http://www.museum.ru/gmii

SPAIN
Guggenheim Museum Bilbao
Abandoibarra Et. 2
48001 Bilbao
(94) 435 9080
http://www.guggenheim-bilbao.es

Museo Nacional del Prado
Paseo del Prado,
28014 Madrid
(91) 330 2800, 2900
http://museoprado.mcu.es

SWEDEN
Moderna Museet
Spårvagnshallarna,
Box 16382,
Stockholm 10327
(08) 6664250
http://www.modernamuseet.se

Nationalmuseum
S. Blasieholmshamnen,
Stockholm 10324
(08) 5195 4300
http://www.nationalmuseum.se

SWITZERLAND
For more information, visit
http://www.swissart.ch

Kunstmuseum Bern
Hodlerstrasse 12, 3000 Bern 7
313110944
http://www.kunstmuseumbern.ch

Musée d'Art et d'Histoire
2 rue Charles Gallard,
Geneva 1211
223114340
http://karaart.com/mah

**Öffentliche Kunstsammlung Basel,
Kunstmuseum**
St. Alban-Graben 16,
Basel CH-4010
612066262
http://www.kunstmuseumbasel.ch

Index

Credits and Copyrights

The author and publisher wish to thank the libraries, museums, galleries, and private collections for permitting the reproduction of works of art in their collections and for supplying the necessary photographs. Photographs from other sources are gratefully acknowledged below. With the exception of page and Primary Source numbers (indicated as p. xxx and PS-XX), all numbers refer to figure numbers.

PHOTOGRAPH CREDITS AND COPYRIGHTS

Harry N. Abrams Archives, New York: 7-32, 22-1; Albertina, Vienna: 17-21; ACL, Brussels: 10-31, 15-3, 15-4, 15-6, 15-22; Adros Studio, Rome: 10-36; AKG, London: 9-11, 9-12, 10-14, 11-3, 21-67; Stefan Brechsel/AKG, London: 11-30; Alison Frantz Collection, American School of Classical Studies, Athens: **5-34**, 8-40; Archivi Alinari, Florence: 6-5, 7-4, 7-10, 7-35, 7-36, 7-38, 7-40, 7-42, 8-52, 10-15, 10-29, 11-37, 11-59, 11-64, 12-2, **12-13, 12-18, 12-19, 12-20, 12-27, 12-28, 12-32, 12-37, 12-54, 12-59**, 13-1, 13-26, 14-23, 14-24, 14-31, **14-42**, 17-8, 17-17, 17-20, 17-23, 17-31; Ronald Sheridan's Ancient Art & Architecture Collection, Pinner, England: 4-13, **5-59**; Arcaid/David Churchill, Kingston upon Thames, U.K.: 21-68, 21-69; Andrea/Archivo White Star: 2-26; The Art Archive, London: 19-20; Artothek/Joachim Blauel, Peissenberg, Germany: 13-42, **16-7, 16-11, 16-13**, 16-18, 18-2, 18-15, 21-54; **Artothek/Ursula Edelmann. Peissenberg, Germany: Cover (Combined Edition); Alinari, Florence/Art Resource, New York; p. 19, 12-31, 12-52, 13-35;** Cameraphoto-Arte, Venice/Art Resource, New York: 11-40, **13-40, 14-13**, 14-25; Erich Lessing/Art Resource, New York: **p. 19, 5-13**, 8-50, **16-1**; Foto Marburg/Art Resource, New York: **5-39**, 9-8, 10-8, 10-13, 10-27, 11-8, 11-9, 11-13, 11-22, 11-47, 11-48, 11-52, 17-22, 19-9, **22-32, 22-33, 22-34**, 26-5, 26-6, 26-9; The Pierpont Morgan Library/Art Resource, New York: 9-19; **Museum of Modern Art, Mrs. Simon Guggenheim Fund/Art Resource, New York: p. 666;** Scala/Art Resource, New York: **5-36**, 7-44, 8-18, 10-25, 11-77, 11-78, 11-88, 11-98, **12-22, 12-48, 12-58**, 13-11, 13-31, 13-32, **13-38;** The Tate Gallery, London/Art Resource, New York: **22-17**, 23-2; James Austin, U.K.: 21-16; Bank of England, London: 21-73; Erika Barahona Ede, Bilbao: 28-7; Foto Barsotti, Florence: 11-61, 11-62; Herbert Bayer Studio, Montecito, California: 27-19; Bayerische Staatsbibliothek, Munich: 9-27, 9-28, 10-42; Benedittine di Priscilla, Roma: 7-10; Jean Bernard, Aix-en-Provence: 11-11, 11-15; Constantin Beyer, Weimar, Germany: 11-53; Bildarchiv Preussischer Kulturbesitz, Berlin: 2-27, 2-28, 3-11, 3-22, **5-74, 5-76**, 7-23, 9-29, 15-11, 15-16, 18-12, 21-51, 21-66; Black Star, New York: 27-26; Erwin Böhm, Mainz: 3-4; Lee Boltin Photo Library, Hastings-on-Hudson, New York: 2-29; Boyan & Sear, Glasgow: 23-33; W. Braunfels, *Mittelalterliche . . . Toskana*: 10-39; The Bridgeman Art Library, London: 19-14, PS-63; Brisighelli-Undine, Cividale, Italy: 9-7; The British Museum, London: **5-65, 5-28**; British National Tourist Office, New York: 21-70; Jutta Brüdern, Braunschweig: 9-24, 9-25, 10-32; Martin Bühler, Basel: 23-25, 25-9; Photographie Bulloz, Paris: 10-24, 16-28, 21-63; Bundesdenkmalsamt, Vienna: 21-58; Studio C.N.B. & C., Bologna, Italy: 2-30; Caisse Nationale des Monuments Historiques et des Sites/© Arch. Phot. Paris: 1-16, 10-4, 10-21, 10-23, 11-16, 11-21, 11-41, 11-55, 13-14, 13-15, 16-26, 21-64; Alain Longchampt/Caisse Nationale des Monuments Historiques et des Sites: 10-5; René Jacques/Caisse Nationale des Monuments Historiques et des Sites: 11-56; F. Camard, Ruhlmann, *Master of Art Deco:* 26-43; Canali Photobank, Capriolo: p. **35,** 316, 5-27, **5-28, 5-44**, 5-49, 6-1, 6-8, 6-9, 7-2, **7-18**, 7-21, 7-26, 7-31, 7-30, 7-47, 7-48, 7-49, 7-50, 7-51, 7-52, 7-53, 8-7, 8-10, 8-15, 8-16, 8-17, 8-19, **8-24, 8-27, 8-28, 8-29**, 8-37, 10-16, 10-18, 10-19, 10-37, 11-33, 11-57, 11-60, 11-63, 11-65, 11-73, 11-76, 11-79, 11-82, 11-83, 11-84, 11-85, 12-5, 12-9, **12-16, 12-29, 12-38, 12-35, 12-50, 12-56, 12-57**, 13-3, 13-7, 13-23, 13-27, 13-30, 13-33, **13-43,** 14-1, 14-2, 14-8, **14-14, 14-15**, 14-21, 14-22, 15-12, **16-16**, 16-23, 17-1, 17-2, 17-3, 17-5, 17-7, 17-10, 17-11, 17-12, 17-16, 17-18, 17-29, 17-32, 17-34, 21-45, 21-59; Canali Photobank/Bertoni, Capriolo: 7-25, 11-97, 12-3, 12-8, **12-14, 12-46,** 13-12; Canali Photobank/Codato: 8-44, 12-7, **12-17, 12-63**; Canali Photobank/ Rapuzzi, Capriolo: 5-6; **Centre des Monuments Nationaux, Paris: 20-1;** Chicago Historical Society: 21-86; Cinématèque Française, Paris: 23-50 a & b; Editions Citadelles & Mazenod, Paris: 2-18; Peter Clayton: 2-12, 2-15, 2-21; Colorphoto Hans Hinz, Alschwill-Basel: 1-3; K. J. Conant, *Carolingian and Romanesque Architecture,* 800–1200: 10-2, 10-10; Paula Cooper Gallery, New York: 24-83, 24-84; Costa and Lockhart, *Persia:* 3-31; The Conway Library/Courtauld Institute of Art, University of London: 9-14, 11-43, 21-11, **22-9**; Dennis Cowley, New York: 28-15; Culver Pictures, New York: 21-85; Dagli-Orti, Paris: 2-35, 8-51; D. James Dee, New York: 28-11; Deutsches Archäologisches Institut, Baghdad: 3-1, 3-3; Deutsches Archäologisches Institut, Rome: **7-16**, 7-29, 7-39, 7-46, 22-5; Jean Dieuzade [YAN], Toulouse: 10-1, 10-20; Dom- und Diözesanmuseum, Hildesheim: 9-26; M. Droste, *Bauhaus 1919–1933:* 26-25; E. Du Cerceau, *Les Plus Excellents Bâtissements . . . :* 16-25; Dumbarton Oaks Washington, D.C. © Byzantine Visual Resources: **8-40, 8-49**; Editoriale Museum/Pedicini, Rome: 7-15; **Egyptian Museum, Cairo/Preussischer Kulturbesitz: p.32;** Nikos Kontos Courtesy of Ekdotike Athenon, Athens: 8-39; English Heritage Photo Library, London: 21-8, 21-19; ESTO/© Peter Aaron, Mamaroneck, New York: 28-1; ESTO/© Peter Mauss, Mamaroneck, New York: 28-6; ESTO/© Ezra Stoller, Mamaroneck, New York: **25-32**, 26-33, 26-34, 26-35, 26-42; Fischbach Gallery, New York: 25-22; B. Fletcher, *A History of Architecture:* 5-29; **Foster and Partners/Nigel Young: 26-48;** Fotocielo, Rome: 17-15; Fototeca Unione, American Academy, Rome: **5-29**, 7-6, 7-8, 7-34; Peter Fowles, Glasgow: 23-34; © Klaus Frahm, Hamburg: 28-5; G. De Francovich, Rome: 10-30; H. Frankfort, *The Art and Architecture of the Ancient Orient*: 3-2; John R. Freeman, Limited, London: **12-60;** French National Tourist Board, Paris: 21-61; Gabinetto Fotografico Nazionale, Rome: 14-30, 17-6, 17-28, 19-17; Gabinetto Nazionale delle Stampe, Rome: 13-24, 13-25; Henry Gaud, Molsenay: 11-20; G.E.K.S., New York: 26-39, 26-40, 7-11, 7-37, 17-24, 26-20, 26-21, 26-29, 27-7; Philip Gendreau, New York: **22-35**; G. Gherardi/A. Fioretti, Rome: 26-36, 26-37; Photographie Giraudon, Paris: 10-26, 11-23, 11-42, 11-94, 13-6, 16-27, 20-3, 21-12, 21-75, 21-78, **22-36,** 23-9; P. Gössel and G. Leuthäuser, *Architecture in the Twentieth Century:* 26-44, 28-2; © Gianfranco Gorgoni, New York: **25-34;** Edward V. Gorn, New York: 8-45; Foto Grassi, Siena: 11-74, 11-58, PS-6; The Green Studio, Limited, Dublin: 9-4; Dr. Reha Günay, Istanbul: 8-56, 8-57; President and Fellows of Harvard College, Harvard University/Michael Nedzweski: 21-30; Hedrih-Blessing/Bill Engdahl, Chicago: 26-1; Hirmer Fotoarchiv, Munich: 1-7, 2-3, 4-14, **5-12, 5-17, 5-21, 5-23, 5-24, 5-33, 5-37, 5-40, 5-45, 5-46, 5-50, 5-52, 5-53, 5-54, 5-81, 5-82, 5-83, 5-84, 5-85**, 6-2, 6-4, 6-6, 7-33, 7-45, 8-11, 8-21, **8-35**, 12-1, 12-4, 13-13, 13-22, 15-23; H. R. Hitchcock, *Architecture: Nineteenth and Twentieth Centuries:* 21-76, 23-32; Foto Karl Hoffmann, Speyer: 10-14; © Angelo Hornak Library, London: 14-26; Christian Huelsen, *Il Libro di Giuliano da Sangallo:* **12-24;** Timothy Hursley: 28-3; Araldo de Luca/ IKONA, Rome: 7-41; Raffaello Bencini/IKONA, Rome: 11-38; Instituto di Etruscologia e Antichità Italiche, University of Rome: 1-5; *Jahrbuch des Deutschen Werkbundes (1915):* 23-35, 23-60, 26-7, 26-8; Anthony F. Janson: 21-18, **24-70**; H. W. Janson: 11-32, 12-23, 23-27, **24-72;** Bruno Jarret/ARS, New York/ADAGP, Paris: 22-30, 22-32; S. W. Kenyon, Wellington, U.K.: 1-9, 1-10; A. F. Kersting, London: 10-9, 11-28, 19-10; Jörg Klam, Berlin: 24-6; © Studio Kontos, Athens: 4-5, 4-6, 4-11, 4-12, 4-17, 4-18, 4-19, 4-21, 5-3, 5-11, 5-14, **5-16, 5-31, 5-35, 5-43, 5-47, 5-48, 5-51, 5-61, 5-70, 5-79**, PS-3; S. N. Kramer, *History Begins at Sumer:* 3-12; Studio Koppermann, Gauting, Germany: 5-5, **5-63, 5-75**; R. Krautheimer: *Early Christian and Byzantine Architecture:* 8-4; Kurt Lange, Oberstdorf, Allgäu, Germany: 2-1, 2-2; Ivan Lapper P., English Heritage Photo Library, London: 1-19; Lautman Photography, Washington, D.C.: 21-20; A.W. Lawrence, *Greek Architecture:* 5-32; William Lescaze, New York: **26-27;** Library of Congress, Washington, D.C.: 21-44; Ralph Liberman: 11-39; Lichtbildwerkstätte Alpenland, Vienna: 8-20, **8-23**, 10-6, **12-61**, 14-3, **14-11**, 14-19, **16-14**, 16-21, 16-22; Maya Lin, New York: **25-33** ; Jannes Linders, Rotterdam: 26-11, 26-13; The Louvre, Paris: 16-30; Magnum, New York: 27-17; Barbara Malterm, Rome: **5-73**; Marlborough Gallery, New York: **25-38**; Alexander Marshak, New York: 1-6; Arxiu MAS, Barcelona: **14-16**, 15-14, 17-35, 18-3, 21-23, 21-25, 21-36; Foto Maye, Vienna: 15-20; © Rollie McKenna, Stonington, Connecticut: **12-27**; Arlette and James Mellaart, London: 1-11, 1-12, 1-13; H. Millon, *Key Monuments in the History of Art:* 11-31, 13-28, 17-25; Ministry of Culture/Archaeological Receipts Fund (Service T.A.P.), Athens: **5-60**; Ministry of Public Buildings and Works, London: 1-17, 1-18, 21-14; Monumenti, Musei, e Gallerie Pontificie, Vatican City, Rome: **5-69**, 6-11, 7-28; © Museum of Modern Art, New York: 26-14, 26-15; Ann Münchow, Domkapitel Aachen: 9-9; National Buildings Record, London: 11-26, 11-27, 19-21, 19-23, 21-74; **National Gallery of Art, Washington DC: p. 402** Otto Nelson, New York: **24-69;** Richard Nickel, Chicago: 23-38, 23-39, 23-40, 23-41; Nippon Television Network Corporation, Tokyo: 13-17, 13-18, 13-19, 13-20, 13-21; © Takashi Okamura, Shizuoka City, Japan: 11-67, 11-98, **12-10, 12-11, 12-12, 12-25, 12-45, 13-36**; Bill Orcutt Studios, New York: 28-17; The Oriental Institute of the University of Chicago: 3-6, 3-21, 3-26, 3-28; Oroñoz, Madrid: 13-37, 16-19, 20-25, 23-31; Pace Wildenstein Gallery/Bill Jacobsen, New York: 25-24; Gustav Peichl, Vienna: 26-43; N. Pevsner, *Outline of European Architecture:* **12-26**; Erich Pollitzer, New York: 23-12; Winslow Pope/Michigan Consolidated Gas Company, Detroit, Michigan: **26-26**; Port Authority, New York: 21-65; Josephine Powell, Rome: **8-50**; © Museo del Prado: 15-10; Provinciebestuur van Antwerpen: 18-16; Pubbli Aer Foto, Milan: 7-3, **8-45**; Antonio Quattrone (Courtesy of Olivetti), Florence: **12-40, 12-41, 12-42, 12-43**; Mario Quattrone Fotostudio, Florence: 11-72, 11-80, **12-53**, 14-4, 14-7, PS-3; Studio Rémy, Dijon, France: 11-91; © Réunion des Musées Nationaux, Paris: 1-8, 2-16, 3-13, 3-14, 3-16, 3-23, 3-27, 5-4, 5-7, 5-8, 5-9, 5-13, **5-77**, 8-38, 8-53, 11-81, 11-92, 12-56, 13-2, 13-4, 13-29, **13-41**, 15-19, **16-15**, 17-9, 18-6, 18-23, 19-2, 19-3, 19-19, 20-4, 20-5, 20-7, 20-8, 21-1, 21-26, 21-28, 21-31, 21-32, 21-39, 21-42, 21-62, 22-2, 22-3, **22-4, 22-10, 22-11, 22-19, 22-20**, 23-16, 23-17, **24-30**, PS-2; © Réunion des Musées Nationaux, Paris/G. Blot/C. Lean: PS-60; © Réunion es Musées Nationaux, Paris/H. Lewndowski: 15-5, 21-33; Rheinisches Bildarchiv, Cologne: 9-20, 9-21, **24-77**, 25-35; **Rheinisches Landesmuseum, Bonn:p.222;** Ekkehard Ritter, Vienna: 10-40, 10-41; Photographie Roger-Viollet, Paris: 16-24, 21-77, 23-30, 26-23; Richard Ross: 28-12, 28-13; Jean Roubier, Paris: 7-9, 10-3, 11-5, 11-44, 11-45, 11-46, 11-49; Routhier/Studio Lourmel, Paris: **22-12**; The Royal Collection Enterprises, Windsor Castle: 13-5, **14-12**, 20-26; Sächsische Landesbibliothek, Deutsche Fotothek, Dresden: 11-51; Goro Sakamoto, Kyoto, Japan: 3-15; Armando Salas, Portugal: 25-21; Scala, Florence: 11-86, 11-97, **14-10**, 17-8, 21-24, 21-27, PS-55; Toni Schneiders, Lindau, Germany: 20-21, 20-23; Silvestris Photo-Service, Kastl, Germany: 20-19; Aaron Siskind: 27-24; Haldor Sochner, Munich: **14-17**; Société Archeologique et Historique, Avesnes-sur-Helpe: 10-38; Société Française de Photographie, Paris: 21-80; Holly Solomon Gallery, New York: 25-41; Soprintendenza Archaeologica, Ministero per i Beni Culturali Ambientali, Rome: 6-10; Soprintendenza Archaeologica all'Etruria Meridionale, Tarquinia: 6-3; Soprintendenza dei Monumenti, Pisa: 11-87; Spectrum Color Library, London: 16-32, **26-46, 26-47**; Sperone Westwater Gallery, New York: **24-81;** Stiftsbibliothek, St. Gallen, Switzerland: 9-13; Franz Stoedtner, Düsseldorf: 23-29; A. Stratton: *Life . . . : 19-22;* Adolph Studley, Pennsburg, Pennsylvania: 23-28; Wim Swaan: **p. 32,** 2-6, 2-8, 2-9, 2-13, 2-22 **(and Cover,Volume 1)**, 2-25, 2-32, 2-33, 3-17, 3-30, 10-7, 10-17, 11-1, 11-6, 11-7, 11-17, 11-24, 17-13, 17-26, 19-11, 19-12, 19-13, 20-17; © Jean Clothes, SYGMA, New York: 1-1; Kenneth Frampton, *Modern Architecture,* Thames & Hudson, 3rd rev. ed.: 26-30; J. W. Thomas, Oxford: 11-50; Richard Todd, Los Angeles: 28-8; Marvin Trachtenberg, New York: 5-39, **8-34, 8-43**, 11-35, **12-33,** 14-27, 19-15, 20-20, 26-18, 26-31, 26-32; University Library, Uppsala, Sweden: 16-20; © University Museum of National Antiquities, Oslo: **p. 224**, 9-2; Vatican Library, Rome: 8-5, 8-6; Jean Vertut, Issy-les-Moulineaux: 1-2; Robert Villani: 26-2, 26-12; John B. Vincent, Berkeley, California: 14-29; Wolfgang Volz © Christo: **25-35**; Leonard von Matt, Buochs, Switzerland: 9-16, 10-28; © Elke Walford, Hamburg: 11-96, 21-52, 21-53; Denise Walker, Baltimore: 21-71, 21-72; **Wallace Collection, London: p.404;** Clarence Ward: 11-4; © Lewis Watts, Anselmo, California: 28-14; Etienne Weil, Jerusalem: **p. 677,** 25-2, 26-45; Werner Forman Archive, London: **5-59**; Whitaker Studios, Richmond,Virginia: 21-13; Joachim Wilke, Stuttgart: 21-15; David Wilkins, Pittsburgh: 12-6; Ole Woldbye, Copenhagen: 21-60; © CORBIS/Roger Wood, Bellevue, Washington: 4-4; Woodfin Camp & Associates, New York: 11-10; (former) Yugoslav State Tourist Office, New York: 7-24; © Arq. Sergio Zepeda C., Guadalajara, Jalisco, Mexico: **24-52**; O. Zimmerman, Colmar, France: 16-1, 16-2 , 16-3; © Gerald Zugmann, Vienna: 28-4; Foto Zwicker-Berberich, Gerchsheim/Würzburg, Germany: 20-10.

ARTIST COPYRIGHTS

© 1997 by the Trustees of the Ansel Adams Publishing Rights Trust. All Rights Reserved: 27-9; © 1997 Richard Anuszkiewicz/Licensed by VAGA, New York: 24-73; © 1997 Artists Rights Society (ARS), New York/ADAGP, Paris: 23-26, 24-3, 24-4, **24-9, 24-15, 24-21, 24-22, 24-23, 24-32, 24-33, 24-39, 24-40, 24-44, 24-45, 24-46, 24-47, 24-58, 24-62**, 25-11, 25-13, 25-16, 25-17, 27-15, 27-21; © 1997 Artists Rights Society (ARS), New York/ADAGP, Paris/FLC: 26-19; © 1997 Artists Rights Society (ARS), New York/DACS, London: **24-38, 24-73**; © 1997 Artists Rights Society (ARS), New York/Beeldrecht, Amsterdam: 26-11, 26-13; © 1997 Artists Rights Society (ARS), New York/Pro Litteris, Zurich: **24-8**, 25-12; Artists Rights Society (ARS), New York/VBK, Vienna: 26-4; © 1997 Artists Rights Society (ARS), New York/V.G. Bild-Kunst, Bonn: **pp. 68-69, 22-14, 24-49, 24-50, 24-53, 24-71, 25-45**, 26-5, 26-16, 26-17, 26-28, 27-14, 27-19, 27-20, 27-22, **28-20**; © 1997 Demart Pro Arte ®, Geneva/Artists Rights Society (ARS), New York: **24-41**; © 1997 Romare Bearden Foundation/Licensed by VAGA, New York: **24-68**; © Black Star, New York: **25-46**; © Mrs. Noya Brandt, London: 27-28; © Gilberte Brassaü, Paris: 27-4; © Cartier-Bresson/Magnum, New York: 27-5; © 1997 Center for Creative Photography, Arizona Board of Regents, Tucson, Arizona: 27-8; © 1997 Foundacion Giorgio de Chirico/Licensed by VAGA, New York: **24-20**; © 1982 Christo, New York: **25-35;** © Condé Nast Publications, New York: 27-11; © 1997 Estate of James Ensor/Licensed by VAGA, New York: 23-20; © 1997 Richard Estes/Licensed by VAGA, New York/Marlborough Gallery, New York: **24-77**; © Anna Farovà, Prague: 27-16; © Helen Frankenthaler, New York: **24-65**; © 1997 Adolph and Esther Gottlieb Foundation/ Licensed by VAGA, New York: **24-57**; © 1997 Estate of George Grosz/Licensed by VAGA, New York: **24-48**; **Andreas Gursky,©2003 Artist Rights Society, New York/VG Bild-Kunst, Bonn: s28-20;** Hepworth Estate, © Alan Bowness, London: 25-20; © 1997 Charly Herscovici/Artists Rights Society (ARS), New York: **24-42**; © 1997 Estate of Eva Hesse: **25-39;** © David Hockney, Los Angeles: 27-30; © Instituto Nacional de Bellas Artes, Mexico City: **24-43**; © 1997 Jasper Johns/Licensed by VAGA, New York, New York: **24-74**; © Anselm Kiefer: **24-80**; Ernst Ludwig Kirchner, Dr. Wolfgang and Ingeborg Henze-Ketterer, Wichtrach,

Bern: 24-5, **24-31;** © 1997 Willem de Kooning Revocable Trust/Artists Rights Society (ARS), New York: **24-61;** © 1997 Joseph Kosuth/Artists Rights Society (ARS), New York: **25-43;** © Barbara Kruger: 28-18; © Roy Lichtenstein, New York: **24-75;** © 1997 Estate of Jacques Lipchitz/Licensed by VAGA, New York/Marlborough Gallery, New York: 25-10; © 1997 Succession H. Matisse, Paris/Artists Rights Society (ARS), New York: 24-1, 24-2, **24-30,** 25-1; © Wayne Miller/Magnum, New York: 27-12; © Mondrian Estate/Holtzman Trust: **24-36, 24-37;** © The Henry Moore Foundation, Much Hadham, Hertfordshire, U.K.: 25-18, 25-19; © 1997 The Munch Museum/The Munch-Ellingsen Group/Artists Rights Society (ARS), New York: 23-21; © 1997 Barnett Newman Foundation/Artists Rights Society (ARS), New York: **25-31;** © Stiftung Ada und Emil Nolde, Seebüll, Germany: 24-7; © 1997 The Georgia O'Keeffe Foundation/Artists Rights Society (ARS), New York: **24-53;** © 1997 Estate of Pablo Picasso, Paris/Artists Rights Society (ARS), New York: 23-23, **24-12, 24-13, 24-14, 24-25, 24-26, 24-27, 24-28, 24-29,** 25-14, 25-15; © 1997 The Pollock-Krasner Foundation/ Artists Rights Society (ARS), New York: **24-59, 24-60;** © 1997 Robert Rauschenberg/Licensed by VAGA, New York: **25-36;** © 1997 George Segal/ Licensed by VAGA, New York: **25-40;** © 1997 Estate of David Smith/ Licensed by VAGA, New York: 25-23; © The Estate of Edward Steichen, New York. Reprinted with permission of Joanna T. Steichen: 23-48; © 1997 Frank Stella/Artists Rights Society (ARS), New York: **24-67;** © 1997 Estate of Vladimir Tatlin/ Licensed by VAGA, New York: 25-7; © 1997 The Andy Warhol Foundation for the Visual Arts/Artists Rights Society (ARS), New York: **24-76;** © Margaret Bourke-White, LIFE Magazine © Time Inc., New York: 27-10; © The Minor White Archive, Princeton University, Princeton, New Jersey: 27-25.

TIMELINE PHOTO CREDITS

p. 200 (left to right): Naturhistorisches Museum; Vienna/Hirmer Fotoarchiv, Munich; Jean Vertut, Issy-les-Moulineaux; Iraq Museum, Baghdad; p. 201 (left to right): Peter Clayton; Goro Sakamoto, Kyoto, Japan; English Heritage Photo Library, London/Ministry of Public Buildings and Works, London; (top) Archaeological Museum, Heraklion, Crete; (bottom) Dagli-Orti, Paris; p. 202 (left to right): The British Museum, London; The British Museum, London; © Réunion des Musées Nationaux, Paris/Musée du Louvre, Paris; Harry N. Abrams Archives, New York; p. 203 (left to right): Archivi Alinari, Florence; Editoriale Museum/Pedicini, Rome; The Metropolitan Museum of Art, New York, Gift of Edward S. Harkness, 1918; p. 376: Nikos Kontos Courtesy of Ekdotike Athenon, Athens; p. 377 (left to right): National Museum of Ireland, Dublin; Trinity College Library, Dublin/ The Green Studio, Limited, Dublin; Dumbarton Oaks, Washington, D.C. © Byzantine Visual Resources, The Pierpont Morgan Library/Art Resource, New York p. 378 (left to right): Jutta Brüdern, Braunschweig; Musée du Louvre, Paris/© Réunion des Musées Nationaux, Paris; Dumbarton Oaks Washington, D.C./© Byzantine Visual Resources; p. 379 (left to right): AKG, London; Canali Photobank, Capriolo; p. 380 (left to right): Jean Bernard, Aix-en-Provence; Foto Marburg/Art Resource, New York; p. 381: The Metropolitan Museum of Art, The Cloisters Collection, Purchase, 1954; p. 626 (left to right): Museum of Fine Arts, Boston, William Francis Warden Fund. Seth K. Sweetser Fund. The Henry C. and Martha B. Angell Collection. Juliana Cheney Edwards Collection. Gift of Martin Brimmer and Mrs. Frederick Frothingham: by Exchange; Marvin Trachtenberg, New York; René Jacques/Caisse Nationale des Monuments Historiques et des Sites; Archivi Alinari, Florence; Galleria degli Uffizi, Florence/Scala/Art Resource, New York; p. 627 (left to right): The National Gallery, London, Reproduced by courtesy of the Trustees; © Takashi Okamura, Shizuoka City, Japan; Canali Photobank, Capriolo; Galleria degli Uffizi, Florence/Mario Quattrone Fotostudio, Florence; p. 628 (left to right): Canali Photobank/Bertoni, Capriolo; Museo del Prado, Madrid, Arxiu MAS, Barcelona; Canali Photobank, Capriolo; Artothek/Joachim Blauel, Peissenberg, Germany; p. 629 (left to right): The Detroit Institute of Arts, Gift of Leslie H. Green; The British Museum, London; p. 630 (left to right): Museo del Prado, Madrid/Arxiu MAS, Barcelona; Frans Halsmuseum, Haarlem, the Netherlands; The Metropolitan Museum of Art, New York, Rogers Fund, 1943; National Buildings Record, London; The Toledo Museum of Art, Toledo, Ohio, Purchased with Funds from the Library Endowment. Gift of Edward Drummond Libbey; p. 631 (left to right): The Royal Collection © 1993 Her Majesty Queen Elizabeth II; The Metropolitan Museum of Art, New York, Bequest of William K. Vanderbilt; Marvin Trachtenberg, New York; Foto Zwicker-Berberich, Gerchsheim/Würzburg, Germany; Freies Deutsches Hochstift-Frankfurter Goethe-Museum, Frankfurt; The Metropolitan Museum of Art, New York, gift of M. Knoedler & Co. 1918; p. 944 (left to right): Musée du Louvre, Paris; Private Collection on Loan to the National Gallery, London: reproduced by Courtesy of the Trustees; p. 945 (left to right): © Réunion des Musées Nationaux, Paris; The Metropolitan Museum of Art, Bequest of Mrs. H. O. Havemeyer, 1999.29. The H. O. Havemeyer Collection; © Réunion des Musées Nationaux, Paris; p. 946 (left to right): Port Authority, New York; The Art Institute of Chicago, Helen Birch Bartlett Memorial Collection; Museum of Fine Arts, Boston, Arthur Gordon Tompkins Residuary Fund; Kawamura Memorial Museum of Art, Sakura City, Chiba Preference, Japan; p. 947 (left to right): Musée Picasso, Paris, © 1997 Estate of Pablo Picasso, Paris/Artists Rights Society (ARS), New York; Öffentliche Kunstsammlung Basel, Kunstmuseum, Switzerland; The Tate Gallery, London/ © 1997 Estate of Pablo Picasso, Paris/Artists Rights Society (ARS), New York; The Museum of Modern Art, New York, Purchase; Art Collecion, Harry Ranson Research Center, University of Texas at Austin/ © Instituto Nacional de Bellas Artes, Mexico City; p. 948 (left to right): Smith College Museum of Art, Northampton, Massachusetts; © 1997 Adolph and Esther Gottlieb Foundation/Licensed by VAGA, New York; Collection of Mr. and Mrs. Paul Mellon, Virgina, Courtesy Estate of Paul Mellon, Artists Rights Society (ARS), New York; The Museum of Modern Art, New York/Philip Johnson Fund and the Gift of Mr. and Mrs. Bagley Wright; Hirshhorn Museum and Sculpture Garden, Smithsonian Institution, Washington, D.C./ © 1997 Romare Bearden Foundation/Licensed by VAGA, New York; p. 949 (left to right): Museum Ludwig, Cologne/ Rheinisches Bildarchiv, Cologne; Private Collection; Anthony F. Janson; Dennis Cowley, New York.

BOX PHOTO CREDITS

Harry N. Abrams Archives, New York: p. 610; The Art Archive, London: p. 189, p. 422, p. 691; A. C. Cooper Ltd. London: p. 656 ; AKG, London: p. 651; The Bridgeman Art Library, London: p. 588, p. 682; Christian Smith/Tropix Photographic Library, Meols, Wirral, England: p. 765; © The Cleveland Museum of Art, Ohio: p. 746; The Louvre, Paris/Erich Lessing : p. 442; © Museum of Fine Arts, Boston. All Rights Reserved: p. 732; Oronoz, Madrid: p. 279; Scala, Florence: p. 102, p. 228, p. 466, p. 720; Staatliches Museum, Schwein, H. Maetens: p. 125; Sumner Collection Fund, 1935.37. Wadsworth Atheneum, Hartford. The Ella Gallup Sumner and Mary Catlin: p. 785.

PRIMARY SOURCE TEXT CREDITS

PS-4: Vitruvius, from *On Architecture, Volumes 1 and 2,* translated by Frank Granger. Reprinted with the permission of Harvard University Press and the Loeb Classical Library. PS-6: Plato, excerpt from Book X from Allan Bloom (trans.), *The Republic of Plato.* Copyright © 1991 by Allan Bloom. Reprinted with the permission of Basic Books, a division of Perseus Books, LLC. PS-7: Aristotle, excerpt from Book VIII from *Aristotle: The Politics,* edited by Stephen Everson. Copyright © 1988. Reprinted with the permission of Cambridge University Press. PS-8: Virgil, excerpt from Book II from *The Aeneid,* translated by Allen Mandelbaum. Copyright © 1971 by Allen Mandelbaum. Reprinted with the permission of Bantam Books, a division of Random House, Inc. PS-9: Livy, excerpt from *Livy, Book I,* translated by B.O. Foster. Reprinted with the permission of Harvard University Press. PS-10: Polybius, excerpt from Book VI from *Polybius: The Histories, Volume 3,* translated by W. R. Paton. Reprinted with the permission of Harvard University Press PS-11: Josephus, excerpt from Book VII from *The Jewish War,* as found in J. J. Pollitt, *The Art of Rome* c. 753 B.C.–337 A.D. Copyright © 1966. Reprinted with the permission of Prentice-Hall, Inc., Upper Saddle River, NJ. PS-12: Plotinus, excerpt from "On Beauty" (Book I.6) from *Enneads,* translated by A.H. Armstrong. Copyright © 1988. Reprinted with the permission of Harvard University Press. PS-14: Pope Gregory I, excerpt from a letter to Serenus of Marseille. As found in Caecelia Davis-Weyer, *Early Medieval Art, 300–1150* (Toronto: University of Toronto Press, 1986). Reprinted with the permission of The Medieval Academy of America. PS-18: Nicholas Mesarites, excerpt from *Description of the Church of the Holy Apostles.* As found in Cyril Mango, *The Art of the Byzantine Empire 312–1453* (Toronto: University of Toronto Press, 1986). Reprinted with the permission of The Medieval Academy of America. PS-20: Hariulf, excerpt from *History of the Monastery of St.-Riquier.* Reprinted with the permission of The Medieval Academy of America. PS-22: St. Benedict of Nursia, excerpt from Anthony C. Meisel, *The Rule of St. Benedict.* Copyright © 1975 by Anthony C. Meisel and M. L. Del Mastro. Reprinted with the permission of Doubleday, a division of Random House, Inc. PS-23: William Melczer, excerpt from *The Pilgrim's Guide to Santiago de Compostela.* Copyright © 1993. Reprinted with the permission of Italica Press, Inc. PS-24: St. Bernard of Clairvaux, excerpt from "Apologia to Abbot William of St.-Thierry" from Conrad Rudolph, *The Things of Greater Importance: Bernard of Clairvaux's Apologia and the Medieval Attitude Toward Art.* Copyright © 1990 by the University of Pennsylvania Press. Reprinted with permission. PS-25: Suger of St.-Denis, excerpt from "On the Consecration of the Church of St.-Denis" from *Abbot Suger on the Abbey Church of St.-Denis and Its Art Treasures,* edited and translated by Erwin Panofsky (Princeton: Princeton University Press, 1946). Copyright © 1946 by Princeton University Press. Reprinted with permission. PS-27: Robert de Torigny, excerpt from *The Chronicle,* as found in *Chartres Cathedral,* edited by Robert Branner. Copyright © 1969 by Robert Branner. Reprinted with the permission of W. W. Norton & Company, Inc. PS-30: Dante Alighieri, excerpt from Canto XVII from *The Divine Comedy: Paradise,* translated by Mark Musa. Copyright © 1986 by Mark Musa. Reprinted with the permission of Indiana University Press. PS-31: Dante Alighieri, excerpt from Canto XI from *The Divine Comedy: Purgatory,* translated by Mark Musa. Copyright © 1986 by Mark Musa. Reprinted with the permission of Indiana University Press. PS-32, PS-33: Lorenzo Ghiberti, excerpts from Book 2 from *The Commentaries.* As found in *A Documentary History of Art, Volume 2,* edited by Elizabeth Gilmore Holt. Copyright © 1958, © renewed by Princeton University Press. Reprinted with the permission of Princeton University Press. PS-34: Theophilus Presbyter, excerpt from "Book II: The Art of the Worker in Glass" from On Divers Arts, translated by John Hawthone and Cyril Stanley Smith. Reprinted with the permission of Dover Publications, Inc. PS-35: Villard de Honnecourt, excerpt from *The Sketchbook of Villard de Honnecourt,* edited by Theodore Bowie (Bloomington: Indiana University Press, 1959). Copyright © 1959. Reprinted with the permission of the publisher. PS-36: Angolo di Tura del Grasso, excerpt from *History,* as found in Henk van Os, *Sienese Altarpieces, 1215–1460: Volume I: 1215–1344* (Groningen: Egbert Forsten, 1988). Reprinted with the permission of Egbert Forsten Publishing. PS-37: Anonymous, inscriptions on the frescoes in the Palazzo Publico, Siena from Randolph Starn and Loren Partridge, *Arts of Power: Three Halls of State in Italy: 1300–1600.* Copyright © 1992 by The Regents of the University of California. Reprinted with the permission of the University of California Press. PS-38: Giovanni Boccaccio, excerpt from "The First Day" from *Decameron: The John Payne Translation, Revised* and *Annotated,* translated and edited by Charles Singleton. Copyright © 1980, 1984 by the Regents of the University of California. Reprinted with the permission of the University of California Press. PS-39: Christine de Pizan, excerpt from *The Book of the City of Ladies,* translated by Earl Jeffrey Richards. Copyright © 1982, 1998 by Persea Books, Inc. Reprinted with the permission of Persea Books, Inc. (New York). PS-40: Leone Battista Alberti, excerpt from *On Painting and On Sculpture,* edited and translated by Cecil Grayson. Copyright © 1972. Reprinted with the permission of Phaidon Press. PS-42: Leonardo da Vinci, excerpt from undated manuscripts, from *The Literary Works of Leonardo da Vinci,* edited by Jean Paul Richter. Copyright © 1970. Reprinted with the permission of Phaidon Press. PS-47: Carel van Mander, excerpts from *Dutch and Flemish Painters.* Reprinted with the permission of Ayer Company Publishers. PS-52: Martin Luther, excerpt from *Against the Heavenly Prophets in the Matter of Images and Sacraments.* As found in *Luther's Works, Volume 40,* edited by Conrad Bergendorff Copyright © 1958 by Fortress Press. Reprinted with the permission of Augsberg Fortress. PS-54: Artemisia Gentileschi, excerpt from a letter to Don Antonio Ruffo from *Gentileschi's Letters.* Reprinted with the permission of Princeton University Press. PS-57: Nicolas Poussin, excerpt from an undated manuscript from Nicolas Poussin, translated by Fabia Claris. Copyright © 1990 by Thames & Hudson Ltd. Reprinted by permission. PS-58: Charles Perrault, excerpt from *Memoirs of My Life,* edited and translated by Jeanne Morgan Zarucchi. Copyright © 1989 by the Curators of the University of Missouri. Reprinted with the permission of the University of Missouri Press. PS-64: Étienne-Louis Boullée, excerpt from "Architecture, Essay on Art" from Helen Rosenau, Boullée and Visionary Architecture (New York: Harmony Books, 1976). Reprinted by permission. PS-66: Eugène Delacroix, excerpt from *The Journals of Eugène Delacroix,* translated by Peter Pach. Copyright © 1937 by Covici Friede, Inc. Copyright © 1948 by Crown Publishers. Reprinted with the permission of Crown Publishers, a division of Random House, Inc. PS-68: John Constable, excerpt from a letter to John Fisher (October 23, 1821), from C. R. Leslie, *Memoirs of the Life of John Constable,* edited by J. Mayne. Copyright © 1951. Reprinted with the permission of Phaidon Press. PS-69: Charles Baudelaire, "The Modern Public and Photography" and "On The Heroism of Modern Life" from Art in Paris, 1845–1862, translated by Jonathan Mayne. Copyright © 1965. Reprinted with the permission of Phaidon Press. PS-77, PS-78: Vincent van Gogh, excerpt from letter to his brother, Theo (April 30, 1885); and excerpt from an undated letter to his brother from *The Complete Letters of Vincent van Gogh.* Reprinted with the permission of C. CH. Mout and Thames & Hudson Ltd, London. PS-82: Georgia O'Keeffe, excerpt from "Steiglitz: His Pictures Collected Him" from *The New York Times Magazine* (December 11, 1949). Copyright © 1949 by The New York Times Company. Reprinted with permission. PS-83: Henri Matisse, excerpt from "Notes of a Painter" from Alfred H. Barr Jr., *Matisse: His Art and His Public* (New York: The Museum of Modern Art, 1951). Originally published in *La Grande Review* [Paris] (December 25, 1908). Copyright © 1994 by Artists Rights Society (ARS), NY/VG Bild-Kunst, Bonn. Reprinted with the permission of Artists Rights Society. PS-87: Piet Mondrian, excerpt from "Natural Reality and Abstract Reality" from *De Stijl* (1919). Excerpt from "Plastic Art and Pure Plastic Art." Reprinted with the permission of the Estate of Piet Mondrian/E.M. Holtzman Irrevocable Trust. PS-92: Jackson Pollock, excerpt from "My Painting" from Francis V. O'Connor, *Jackson Pollock* (New York: The Museum of Modern Art, 1967). Originally published in Possibilities, 1947–1948, edited by Robert Motherwell and Harold Rosenberg. Reprinted with permission. PS-93: Romare Bearden, excerpts from two interviews (1983 and 1986) from Myron Schwartman, *Romare Bearden: His Life and Art.* Copyright © 1990 by Myron Schwartman. Reprinted with the permission of the Estate of Romare Bearden. PS-95: Roy Lichtenstein, excerpt from "What is Pop Art?" from *Art News* (November 1963). Reprinted with the permission of the Estate of Roy Lichtenstein and Art News. PS-98: Eva Hesse, excerpt from an interview from Cindy Nemser, Art Talk: Conversations with 12 Women Artists. Copyright © 1975 by Cindy Nemser. Reprinted with the permission of Cindy Nemser. PS-99: Le Corbusier, excerpt from *Towards a New Architecture.* Reprinted with the permission of Dover Publications, Inc. PS-100: Walter Gropius, excerpt from *The Scope of Total Architecture, Volume 3.* Copyright © 1943, 1949, 1952, 1954, 1955 by Walter G. Gropius. Reprinted with the permission of HarperCollins Publishers, Inc. PS-102: Jerry Uelsmann, excerpt from "Some Humanistic Considerations of Photography" from *The Photographic Journal,* 111: 4 (April 1971). Reprinted with the permission of The Royal Photographic Society, The Octagon, Milsom Street, Bath BA1 1DN, Great Britain. PS-103: Michael Graves, excerpt from "What is the Focus of Post-Modern Architecture?" from *American Artist 45,* Issue 473 (December 1981). Copyright © 1981. Reprinted with the permission of American Artist. PS-104: Cindy Sherman, excerpt from an interview from Jeanne Siegel, *Artwords 2: The Early 80s* (New York: DaCapo Press, 1990). Reprinted with the permission of Jeanne Siegel.

SINGLE PC LICENSE AGREEMENT AND LIMITED WARRANTY

READ THIS LICENSE CAREFULLY BEFORE OPENING THIS PACKAGE. BY OPENING THIS PACKAGE, YOU ARE AGREEING TO THE TERMS AND CONDITIONS OF THIS LICENSE. IF YOU DO NOT AGREE, DO NOT OPEN THE PACKAGE. PROMPTLY RETURN THE UNOPENED PACKAGE AND ALL ACCOMPANYING ITEMS TO THE PLACE YOU OBTAINED THEM [[FOR A FULL REFUND OF ANY SUMS YOU HAVE PAID FOR THE SOFTWARE]]. THESE TERMS APPLY TO ALL LICENSED SOFTWARE ON THE DISK EXCEPT THAT THE TERMS FOR USE OF ANY SHAREWARE OR FREEWARE ON THE DISKETTES ARE AS SET FORTH IN THE ELECTRONIC LICENSE LOCATED ON THE DISK:

1. GRANT OF LICENSE and OWNERSHIP: The enclosed computer programs <<and data>> ("Software") are licensed, not sold, to you by Pearson Education, Inc. publishing as Prentice Hall ("We" or the "Company") and in consideration [[of your payment of the license fee, which is part of the price you paid]] [[of your purchase or adoption of the accompanying Company textbooks and/or other materials,]] and your agreement to these terms. We reserve any rights not granted to you. You own only the disk(s) but we and/or our licensors own the Software itself. This license allows you to use and display your copy of the Software on a single computer (i.e., with a single CPU) at a single location for academic use only, so long as you comply with the terms of this Agreement. You may make one copy for back up, or transfer your copy to another CPU, provided that the Software is usable on only one computer.

2. RESTRICTIONS: You may not transfer or distribute the Software or documentation to anyone else. Except for backup, you may not copy the documentation or the Software. You may not network the Software or otherwise use it on more than one computer or computer terminal at the same time. You may not reverse engineer, disassemble, decompile, modify, adapt, translate, or create derivative works based on the Software or the Documentation. You may be held legally responsible for any copying or copyright infringement that is caused by your failure to abide by the terms of these restrictions.

3. TERMINATION: This license is effective until terminated. This license will terminate automatically without notice from the Company if you fail to comply with any provisions or limitations of this license. Upon termination, you shall destroy the Documentation and all copies of the Software. All provisions of this Agreement as to limitation and disclaimer of warranties, limitation of liability, remedies or damages, and our ownership rights shall survive termination.

4. LIMITED WARRANTY AND DISCLAIMER OF WARRANTY: Company warrants that for a period of 60 days from the date you purchase this SOFTWARE (or purchase or adopt the accompanying textbook), the Software, when properly installed and used in accordance with the Documentation, will operate in substantial conformity with the description of the Software set forth in the Documentation, and that for a period of 30 days the disk(s) on which the Software is delivered shall be free from defects in materials and workmanship under normal use. The Company does not warrant that the Software will meet your requirements or that the operation of the Software will be uninterrupted or error-free. Your only remedy and the Company's only obligation under these limited warranties is, at the Company's option, return of the disk for a refund of any amounts paid for it by you or replacement of the disk. THIS LIMITED WARRANTY IS THE ONLY WARRANTY PROVIDED BY THE COMPANY AND ITS LICENSORS, AND THE COMPANY AND ITS LICENSORS DISCLAIM ALL OTHER WARRANTIES, EXPRESS OR IMPLIED, INCLUDING WITHOUT LIMITATION, THE IMPLIED WARRANTIES OF MER-CHANTABILITY AND FITNESS FOR A PARTICULAR PURPOSE. THE COMPANY DOES NOT WARRANT, GUARANTEE, OR MAKE ANY REPRESENTATION REGARDING THE ACCURACY, RELIABILITY, CURRENTNESS, USE, OR RESULTS OF USE, OF THE SOFTWARE.

5. LIMITATION OF REMEDIES AND DAMAGES: IN NO EVENT, SHALL THE COMPANY OR ITS EMPLOYEES, AGENTS, LICENSORS, OR CONTRACTORS BE LIABLE FOR ANY INCIDENTAL, INDIRECT, SPECIAL, OR CONSEQUENTIAL DAMAGES ARISING OUT OF OR IN CONNECTION WITH THIS LICENSE OR THE SOFTWARE, INCLUDING FOR LOSS OF USE, LOSS OF DATA, LOSS OF INCOME OR PROFIT, OR OTHER LOSSES, SUSTAINED AS A RESULT OF INJURY TO ANY PERSON, OR LOSS OF OR DAMAGE TO PROPERTY, OR CLAIMS OF THIRD PARTIES, EVEN IF THE COMPANY OR AN AUTHORIZED REPRESENTATIVE OF THE COMPANY HAS BEEN ADVISED OF THE POSSIBILITY OF SUCH DAMAGES. IN NO EVENT SHALL THE LIABILITY OF THE COMPANY FOR DAMAGES WITH RESPECT TO THE SOFTWARE EXCEED THE AMOUNTS ACTUALLY PAID BY YOU, IF ANY, FOR THE SOFTWARE OR THE ACCOMPANYING TEXTBOOK. BECAUSE SOME JURISDICTIONS DO NOT ALLOW THE LIMITATION OF LIABILITY IN CERTAIN CIRCUMSTANCES, THE ABOVE LIMITATIONS MAY NOT ALWAYS APPLY TO YOU.

6. GENERAL: THIS AGREEMENT SHALL BE CONSTRUED IN ACCORDANCE WITH THE LAWS OF THE UNITED STATES OF AMERICA AND THE STATE OF NEW YORK, APPLICABLE TO CONTRACTS MADE IN NEW YORK, AND SHALL BENEFIT THE COMPANY, ITS AFFILIATES AND ASSIGNEES. THIS AGREEMENT IS THE COMPLETE AND EXCLUSIVE STATEMENT OF THE AGREEMENT BETWEEN YOU AND THE COMPANY AND SUPERSEDES ALL PROPOSALS OR PRIOR AGREEMENTS, ORAL, OR WRITTEN, AND ANY OTHER COMMUNICATIONS BETWEEN YOU AND THE COMPANY OR ANY REPRESENTATIVE OF THE COMPANY RELATING TO THE SUBJECT MATTER OF THIS AGREEMENT. If you are a U.S. Government user, this Software is licensed with "restricted rights" as set forth in subparagraphs (a)-(d) of the Commercial Computer-Restricted Rights clause at FAR 52.227-19 or in subparagraphs (c)(1)(ii) of the Rights in Technical Data and Computer Software clause at DFARS 252.227-7013, and similar clauses, as applicable.

Should you have any questions concerning this agreement or if you wish to contact the Company for any reason, please contact in writing: Social Sciences Media Editor, Prentice Hall, One Lake Street, Upper Saddle River, NJ 07458.